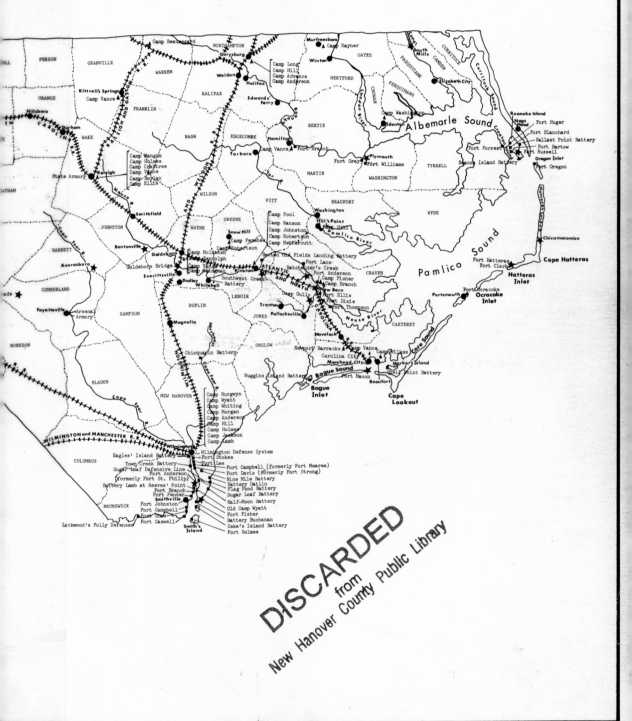

NORTH CAROLINA TROOPS

1861-1865

A ROSTER

TO ARMS!

"Those who would be Free, themselves must strike the blow!"

NOW IS THE TIME TO VOLUNTEER!

PRESIDENT DAVIS has called upon Governor Clarke for —

26,000 Regular Troops!

(NORTH-CAROLINA'S QUOTA,)

to fill the places of the twelve months volunteers, whose term of service will soon expire, and unless that number of volunteers are obtained a draft will be made from the militia. The undersigned is recruiting for the

Hon. Sion H. Rogers' Battalion!

To all recruits for the war a Bounty of $50 per man will be paid by the State, and $50 by the Confederate States, making a

BOUNTY OF $100!

We are to get the best Arms, Tents, Clothing, &c.

FREEMEN! do not wait to be drafted, but come forward at your Country's call!

D. A. WICKER, CAPT.

"Raleigh Register Steam Power Press." Print.

North Carolina Troops
1861-1865
A Roster

COMPILED BY
LOUIS H. MANARIN

VOL. III
INFANTRY

RALEIGH, NORTH CAROLINA

STATE DEPARTMENT OF ARCHIVES AND HISTORY

1971

PREFACE

This volume is the third in a projected series of volumes containing a roster of North Carolinians who served in the Confederate and Union forces in the Civil War. Begun in February, 1961, the project to compile such a roster is an outgrowth of the work of the North Carolina Confederate Centennial Commission, its chairman, the late Colonel Hugh Dortch, and its executive secretary, Mr. Norman C. Larson. Dr. Louis H. Manarin, the editor of the first two volumes, was first a member of the Confederate Centennial Commission staff. At the termination of that commission in June, 1965, the Roster Project was transferred to the State Department of Archives and History, and Dr. Manarin remained at the head of the project through January, 1970, when he resigned to become state archivist of Virginia. He consented to continue to act as editor of Volume III, which was well under way at the time of his departure from Raleigh.

Dr. Manarin has been ably assisted by Mr. Weymouth T. Jordan, Jr., who succeeded him in the post of editor of the North Carolina Roster Project. To both of these scholars and to Dr. H. G. Jones, director, Mr. C. F. W. Coker, archives and records administrator, and the staff of the State Department of Archives and History, I wish to express my appreciation for their efforts in making possible this memorial to those from our state who participated in that great conflict.

ROBERT W. SCOTT

June 1, 1971

Governor of North Carolina

CONTENTS

INTRODUCTION

When the war came in 1861, North Carolinians in large numbers answered the call to arms. Although the initial contingents from the state were volunteers, men were conscripted into service after the passage of the conscript act in April, 1862. The conscripts, and those who volunteered after that date, either joined or were assigned to established units or were organized into new units. In all, some eighty regiments, twenty battalions, and fifteen independent companies were organized from North Carolina and mustered into Confederate service.

The only military organization in the state when the war broke out was the Militia. This organization embraced all white males between the ages of 18 and 45. However, because of a long period of peace, the Militia was only organized on paper and had no practical existence.

When the Legislature assembled on May 1, 1861, it authorized Governor John W. Ellis to raise ten regiments of State Troops before the State Convention met. Under the act, an Adjutant General and other staff officers were provided for to carry out the organization. The regiments were numbered consecutively as they were mustered into state service regardless of branch of service; however, the cavalry and artillery regiments were also numbered consecutively according to their branch.

Under the pre-secession laws of the state, Colonel John F. Hoke was Adjutant General. It was through his office that the Volunteer regiments were organized independent of the ten regiments of State Troops authorized by the Legislature. By July 18, 1861, fourteen Volunteer regiments had been organized and transferred to the Confederate service. Colonel Hoke resigned his position as Adjutant General to assume command of one of the Volunteer regiments. General James G. Martin, who had been appointed Adjutant General under the act to organize ten regiments of State Troops, was ordered by the Governor to take charge of both offices, that of Adjutant General of State Troops and Adjutant General of Volunteers, until the Legislature met. That body elected General Martin Adjutant General of the state and thus consolidated the two previously independent offices.

When General Martin assumed his new office he found that there were ten regiments of State Troops designated 1st through 10th Regiment N.C. State Troops and fourteen regiments of Volunteers designated 1st through 14th Regiment N.C. Volunteers. The duplicate set of numbers created confusion in the field, at Richmond, and at Raleigh. The Confederate and state authorities decided that the State Troops should retain their designations of one through ten, while the Volunteer regiments should be redesignated starting with eleven. This was carried out on November 14, 1861, by Special Orders No. 222, Adjutant and

Inspector General's Office, Richmond. The Volunteer regiments were redesignated the 11th through the 24th Regiment N.C. Troops, but were also allowed to retain the Volunteer designation in parenthesis after the redesignated number. Thus, the 1st Regiment N.C. Volunteers was redesignated the 11th Regiment N.C. Troops (1st Regiment N.C. Volunteers). All regiments organized after the redesignation of the Volunteer regiments were numbered consecutively beginning with the 25th Regiment N.C. Troops.

This volume is the first in the series dealing specifically with infantry units. The first unit in this volume, 1st Regiment N.C. Infantry (6 months, 1861), was the first unit organized by the state and turned over to the Confederate authorities. It was also the first unit from the state to see action, and a member of the regiment was the first Confederate soldier killed in combat. Thus it deserves the honor of being the first unit in the infantry series. Many of the men later reenlisted in the 11th Regiment N.C. Troops (1st Regiment N.C. Volunteers). Following the 1st Regiment N.C. Infantry, the units are listed numerically with battalions preceding regiments of the same numerical designation. All units are entered under their final designation with reference to official and unofficial designations reported in the unit history.

Although the regiment was the principal organizational unit, battalions were organized under special authorization. A battalion could consist of from two to nine companies. A regiment usually contained ten companies lettered from A to K, there being no company designated as Company J. An infantry company usually contained from sixty-four to one hundred men when first organized. Some of the companies were smaller and some were larger; but, as the war progressed, they tended to be smaller. Although reference will be made to the specific locality in which each company was organized, the local character and nature of the company changed as conscripts were assigned.

Within the series of volumes provision has been made to devote a separate volume to the Militia and Home Guard units. Since there were only two battalions of Local Defense Troops and only one battalion of Sharpshooters, they have been included in this the first volume of infantry units. All infantry battalions will be included according to their line number designation.

The organization and reorganization of units during the war resulted in confusion over proper designations. The lack of clear lines of communication and authority added to the confusion at the time, and postwar writings tended to perpetuate the situation. One of the principle aims of this project is to help clarify the numerous reorganizations and redesignations so that a researcher might be able to determine a unit's status and designation at any given time in its career. All reorganizations and redesignations have been explained in the company and unit histories of those units affected. Since some units affected by the reorganization orders existed as distinct units prior to their consolidation or disbanding, separate rosters have been included.

The problems of organization are too complex to repeat here, and the reader is referred to the unit histories for the details. It should be noted that for clarity the editor has adopted a uniform method of designating the companies which served under one designation within a regiment. Reference is here made to the fact that two or three different companies served under one company designation, *e.g.*, 1st Company A, 2nd Company A, etc. Officially, when two companies served under one company designation they were referred to either as "old" and "new" or "1st" and "2nd." If three companies served under one company designation, then the numerals were used. The editor has standardized the form by using the numerical designations.

The material contained in the unit histories and rosters was obtained from many sources. The principal sources for the unit histories were: the Record of Events entries on the original muster rolls which contained information as to movements and battles; all references to the particular company, battalion, or regiment in R. N. Scott and others (eds.), *The War of the Rebellion: A Compilation of the Official Records of the Union and Confederate Armies* (Washington, D.C.: Government Printing Office, 70 volumes [127 books, atlases, and index], 1880-1901), herein cited *Official Records*; and Walter Clark (ed.), *Histories of the Several Regiments and Battalions from North Carolina in the Great War 1861-'65* (Raleigh and Goldsboro: State of North Carolina, 5 volumes, 1901), herein cited Clark's *Regiments*. In addition, printed company histories and diaries, as well as unpublished diaries and letters, were used. All official reports cited in the histories were quoted from the *Official Records*.

The principal source of information for the individual service record entries was the Compiled Military Service Records on file in Record Group 109 in the National Archives, Washington, D.C. This collection consists of individual envelopes on each man, in which are filed cards containing information extracted from original records. These envelopes are filed by unit, then alphabetically by name. The records from which the information was taken include Confederate muster rolls, payrolls, rosters, appointment books, hospital registers, prison registers and rolls, parole rolls, inspection reports, and other records containing service information. Some envelopes contain original documents such as enlistment and discharge papers, vouchers, and requisitions which relate to a man's service. In addition to the above, the Roll of Honor, compiled by the state Adjutant General during the war, was loaned to the War Department and cards were made on all entries and filed accordingly. It is important to note that several men herein listed in the 1st Regiment N.C. State Troops are reported on the roster of that unit because they were so filed by the clerks when the Compiled Military

Service Record file was compiled. These men were paroled at Athens, Georgia, and reported as members of the "1st N.C. Regiment." It is doubtful the men actually served with the 1st Regiment N.C. State Troops, but the editor has been unable to find evidence to the contrary or to the exact designation of the unit to which they belonged. The doubt results from the fact that the men do not appear on any of the surviving muster rolls of the 1st Regiment N.C. State Troops and that the regiment never served in Georgia but was paroled at Appomattox Court House, Virginia, on April 9, 1865.

A second source in the National Archives was the Papers of and Relating to Military and Civilian Personnel, 1861-1865. This collection consists of all cards and manuscripts compiled and collected for the Compiled Military Service Records but not filed in regular envelopes and units for various reasons. Original muster rolls—perhaps the most important original record—were also used. Made out every two months, the regular muster roll contained a list of the men; where, when, and for how long they enlisted; and whether they were present or absent. Additional information sometimes was recorded under a remarks column. In some cases the original muster-in roll was found. In addition to the information found on the regular muster roll, the muster-in roll contained the place of birth and residence, age, and occupation.

The material obtained from the National Archives was supplemented by the information contained in the records in the North Carolina State Department of Archives and History. These include the records of the Adjutant General's Office, Register of Commissions, muster rolls for periods not covered by muster rolls on file at the National Archives, bounty rolls, numerous private collections, and state pension applications filed by Confederate veterans and their widows. All information relative to Confederate service was abstracted from membership applications and Cross of Honor and Cross of Military Service certificates kept by the North Carolina Division, United Daughters of the Confederacy. Information was also extracted from the Confederate Gravestone Records compiled by the same organization. These thirteen volumes of gravestone records pertain only to Confederate soldiers buried in North Carolina. Also used were the published registers of Hollywood Cemetery, Richmond, Virginia; Stonewall Cemetery, Winchester, Virginia; Gettysburg and Sharpsburg cemeteries and the unpublished registers of Northern cemeteries, compiled by the Office of the Quartermaster General, United States Army, in 1912 and 1914.

After completing a regimental or battalion file in the National Archives, the editor checked the names against the *Roster of North Carolina Troops in the War Between the States*, edited by John W. Moore, (Raleigh [State of North Carolina], 4 volumes, 1882), hereafter cited Moore's *Roster*. Discrepancies in spelling and factual information were noted, and cards were made on men listed in Moore but not found in other sources. Upon comparison of the records compiled for this roster with the rosters of the organizations in Moore's *Roster*, many errors were found in the latter work. The research for the new project reveals that other errors were made by Moore in recording unit designations and reorganizations and individual transfers. A brief paragraph at the end of each unit history in this volume will deal with any major discrepancies between Moore's or Clark's works and the official records. In justice to Major Moore and his roster, it should be noted that although he was allowed to use the captured Confederate muster rolls in the War Department, they were unarranged. Since then the records have been arranged and carded, and the editor has had at his disposal the findings of the War Department clerks who arranged and cataloged the captured records.

Because of the defects in Moore's *Roster*, local rosters compiled from Moore's were not used. However, all available published and unpublished local rosters not compiled from Moore's were utilized. The names and accompanying information on all men mentioned in Clark's *Regiments* were extracted for use in the present roster, as were names and accompanying information on those mentioned in other relevant published and unpublished histories, diaries, and letters. In some cases the only source of service information came from the history of the unit in Clark's *Regiments*. Rather than cite the entire work each time, reference was made to the fact that the individual was mentioned in the unit history. Therefore, any mention of the unit history within an individual service record automatically refers to the history in Clark's *Regiments*.

Material was also found in other manuscript repositories in North Carolina and several neighboring states; and voluminous correspondence from all over the country has been received from interested individuals who supplied information on Confederate soldiers from North Carolina. A final source, which has remained almost untouched due to lack of time and staff, is the contemporary newspapers published in the state.

Information taken from the above mentioned sources was arranged and consolidated under each individual member of a unit. The method adopted for listing the members of each unit was as follows:

Field and Staff: By rank and date of appointment, *e.g.*,
                Colonel, Lieutenant Colonel, Major,
                Adjutant, and Staff members.
Band: Alphabetically.
Companies: 1.   Officers:
                A.   Captains: Chronologically by date of appointment.
                B.   Lieutenants: Alphabetically

2. Enlisted men:
   All noncommissioned officers and privates are listed alphabetically, regardless of rank. The final rank is given after the name, and promotions and demotions are given in the service record.

In all cases, the spelling of names was retained as recorded by the company clerk except when a signature spelling or other primary family source was available. The index has been arranged to assist the researcher in locating the various corrupted spellings.

In compiling this roster the editor has adhered to the date and place of enlistment as recorded by the company clerk on the muster rolls. There were approximately four dates on which a man entered service: date of enrollment, enlistment or conscription, muster into state service, and muster into Confederate service. For the initial roll, which generally set the precedent for succeeding rolls, the company clerk either chose the date of enlistment or one of the muster-in dates. Conscripts were usually entered on the rolls as enlisting on the date they reported for duty either to their local officer or to the company. Frequently, conscripts were sent to camps of instruction and then attached to a unit. The company clerk would then give the place of enlistment as either the county in which the man was conscripted, the county or town in which he joined the unit, or the camp of instruction from which he was assigned. No standard procedure was developed; even a company clerk might change his procedure at times. If the conscripts reported as a group, then they were usually listed as follows: date of enlistment recorded as date reported for duty to local officer; place of enlistment, either camp of instruction or county in which he was conscripted. If a conscript reported individually, then the clerk usually gave the date and place of enlistment as the date and place he joined the company. It should be noted that as the war progressed, and particularly in 1864-1865, the latter method was generally used.

Within the entry for each individual the editor has adhered to the following rules: All references to counties are as of the 1861-1865 boundaries; all names of places are as of the 1861-1865 designation (*e.g.*, Smithville is used in place of modern Southport); all place names of North Carolina counties, cities, towns, etc., are not followed by a reference to the state except for clarity, but all names of counties, cities, towns, etc., in other states are followed by the name of the state the first time they are mentioned within a history or service record. Each man is treated as an individual. To avoid confusion and to insure clarity for the researcher, reference is made in each man's record when he transferred, even though the company as a whole was transferred. All references to units are presented in full each time for the same reason.

The term "present or accounted for" is used to indicate that a man was either present or absent but accounted for over a specific time period. To record every time a man was sent to the hospital or furloughed would have expanded the volume beyond reasonableness. However, if his absence became permanent or if his service was terminated while he was absent, then it is duly noted. The final date given in a service record refers to the last date the individual's name was reported. Subsequent research may reveal that a man served after the last date given herein, and any additional information will be noted in an addendum.

Although this volume appears as the product of the joint efforts of the Roster Project staff, acknowledgment is made to the following persons and organizations without whose aid the publication would not have been possible:

—Dr. James B. Rhoads, Dr. Mabel E. Deutrich, Dr. Dallas D. Irvine, Mr. Elmer O. Parker, Mrs. Sara D. Jackson, Mr. James D. Walker, Mr. Joseph B. Ross, Mr. Wendle Evans, and the many other staff members of the National Archives who assisted in the research.

—The United Daughters of the Confederacy who furnished copies of information in their files, and particularly to Mrs. G. A. Moore of Wilmington and Mrs. Alvin Seippel of Winston-Salem for their assistance in organizing the campaigns to extract pertinent information from the membership applications and the certificates of the Cross of Honor and the Cross of Military Service. To the many unnamed Daughters who labored to locate and register the graves of Confederate soldiers we are truly grateful.

—Mr. Norman C. Larson, from 1961 to 1965 executive secretary, North Carolina Confederate Centennial Commission, under whose direction the program was initiated.

—The Editorial Advisory Board for advice and guidance.

—State Senator Hector McLean of Lumberton for his efforts in organizing the campaign to continue the work and to those who had faith in the project.

—The late Dr. Christopher Crittenden, former director, and Dr. H. G. Jones, director, North Carolina State Department of Archives and History, for their guidance and encouragement.

—The staffs of the North Carolina State Department of Archives and History, Raleigh; Southern Historical Collection and North Carolina Collection, University of North Carolina Library, Chapel Hill; Manuscript Department and Rare Book Room, Duke University Library, Durham; Wake Forest University Library, Winston-Salem; Museum of the Confederacy, Richmond, Virginia; Georgia Department of Archives and History, Atlanta, Georgia; and Tennessee State Library and Archives, Nashville, Tennessee.

As editor I would like to acknowledge the assistance of my staff. It underwent numerous changes from 1961 to 1970, but a debt is owed to all who helped compile the records and produce this volume. To my wife, Jo Ann, who served as part-time typist and full-time editorial assistant from 1961 through 1968, I wish to express my debt. She assisted in all phases of the project and worked arduously to maintain the high standards desired. She was ably succeeded by Mr. Ersell Lyles who served as editorial assistant from January through December, 1969. For approximately two years, Mr. Fleming C. Fraker, Jr., served on the staff as research assistant. He did a thorough job of tracing down North Carolinians filed in the Papers of and Relating to Military and Civilian Personnel, 1861-1865, in the National Archives. To the part-time typists and stenographers, Mrs. Hazel Madsen (November, 1961-March, 1964), Mrs. Essel G. Parker (May, 1964-August, 1968), Mrs. Patsy W. Vogel (November, 1967-August, 1968), Mrs. Jean D. Thaggard (October, 1968-January, 1969), Mrs. Kathy Mitchell (March, 1969-January, 1970), and Miss Dianne G. Massey (June-September, 1969), a special word of thanks is due for their assistance.

To Mr. Weymouth T. Jordan, Jr., who assumed the editorship of the Roster Project, a special note of thanks is due. I am particularly appreciative of the diligence shown by Mr. Jordan and his staff, Mrs. Susan W. Gaskins and Miss Dianne G. Massey, and the assistance of Miss Marie Moore of the Publications Division in the production of this volume. Their thoroughness in proofreading, checking cross-references, and indexing the text will be evident to everyone who uses this volume. Acknowledgment is also made to Mr. C. F. W. Coker, archives and records administrator, for assistance and guidance provided Mr. Jordan on the project and in coordinating arrangements with the printer.

To all those who assisted by extracting and sending information, by relating the existence of source materials, and by words of encouragement and guidance, I acknowledge my indebtedness. It is only justice to say that this volume is the product of all our efforts.

Louis H. Manarin
Editor

June 1, 1971

NORTH CAROLINA TROOPS

1861-1865

A ROSTER

1st REGIMENT N. C. INFANTRY
(6 MONTHS, 1861)

The first regiment to be organized by the state was authorized in a letter from state Adjutant General J. F. Hoke to Colonel D. H. Hill, commanding the Camp of Instruction at the State Fair Grounds, Raleigh. This letter, dated April 29, 1861, called for the organization of the Orange Light Infantry, Warrenton Guards, Hornet Nest Rifles, Enfield Blues, Lumberton Guards, Duplin Rifles, Charlotte Grays, Thomasville Rifles, Granville Grays, and Columbus Guards into the 1st Regiment of North Carolina Volunteers and stated that the service of the regiment would not exceed six months. Election of field officers was ordered for May 3.

The regiment was not organized as ordered in the letter, and the May 3 elections did not take place. This was probably due to the confused times, unexpected problems of mobilization, and the fact that some of the companies were either improperly organized, understrength, or had not arrived at the Camp of Instruction. By General Orders No. 7, Adjutant General's Office, Raleigh, May 9, 1861 four of the original companies mentioned in the April 29 letter and six new companies were assigned to the regiment. The original companies were the Orange Light Infantry, Hornet Nest Rifles, Enfield Blues, and Charlotte Grays. The new companies were the Edgecombe Guards, Burke Rifles, Buncombe Rifles, Southern Stars, Randlesburg Rifles and the Lafayette Light Infantry. The order called for the election of field officers on May 11. The election was held, and Colonel D. H. Hill was elected Colonel; Charles C. Lee, Lieutenant Colonel; and James H. Lane, Major. The regiment was ordered mustered into state service at 4:00 P.M. on May 13, 1861. At the time of muster-in it was found that the Randlesburg Rifles was understrength, so the company was not mustered in. On May 16 the Fayetteville Independent Light Infantry was assigned to the regiment to fill the vacancy caused by the rejection of the Randlesburg Rifles. As mustered in, the companies were given alphabetical designations within the regiment as follows: Edgecombe Guards—Company A; Hornet Nest Rifles—Company B; Charlotte Grays—Company C; Orange Light Infantry—Company D; Buncombe Rifles—Company E; Lafayette Light Infantry—Company F; Burke Rifles—Company G; Fayetteville Independent Light Infantry—Company H; Enfield Blues—Company I; Southern Stars—Company K.

On May 17, 1861, Governor John W. Ellis telegraphed Leroy Pope Walker, Confederate Secretary of War, requesting him to accept four regiments of twelve-months men. Walker replied that he would take the four regiments and directed they be ordered to Richmond, Virginia. Three companies of his regiment, F, H, and K, had been ordered on May 16 to move to Richmond on May 18, while the balance of the regiment was ordered to do so on May 20-21. The three companies left Raleigh on the morning of May 18 and arrived in Richmond that night at 11:00 P.M. They went into camp at Howard's Grove just outside of the city limits. The balance of the regiment left Raleigh on May 21 and arrived in Richmond on the same day. They joined the other three companies at Howard's Grove, and on May 24 the entire regiment moved to Yorktown, where it arrived on the same day.

At Yorktown the regiment went into camp and began drilling and entrenching. On May 30 Company K was ordered toward Newport News by Colonel John B. Magruder. After proceeding three miles, it was ordered back to camp. The next day, May 31, Company F marched four miles in the direction of Hampton before it was ordered back to camp. On Thursday, June 6, the entire regiment broke camp and moved to Bethel Church. Arriving there about dark, the regiment bivouacked for the night. The next day the men began entrenching. Detachments from Companies E and F were sent out against Federal scouting parties and succeeded in driving them back. At 3:00 A.M. on June 10 the regiment prepared to advance toward Hampton. After marching about three and one-half miles, word was received that a Federal column was advancing toward Bethel. The regiment was ordered back to the entrenchments at Bethel to await the advance of the Federal column. About 9:00 A.M. on the morning of June 10, the Federal column came into view. Shortly after that hour the battle of Big Bethel began with the firing of one of the Confederate artillery pieces. The Federal troops maneuvered into position and advanced against the Confederate lines in unsuccessful, disjointed attacks. By 2:00 P.M. the Federal troops began retiring from the field.

Confederate reinforcements arrived on the field just after the Federal troops retired. Later that evening the 1st Regiment N. C. Volunteers was relieved and marched back to Yorktown. On June 11 the work on the fortifications at Yorktown was resumed and continued through the month.

On June 20, 1861, the Bertie Volunteers and the Dixie Rebels were assigned to the regiment as Companies L an M. They did not join the regiment, however, until August. Company M arrived while the regiment was at Yorktown during the second week in August. On August 22 the regiment was moved from Yorktown to Ship Point, eight miles southeast of Yorktown, on the Poquosin River. Here it began fortifying the point, and it was here that Company L joined the regiment.

At Ship Point, on August 31, the regiment was mustered into Confederate service for six months service from May 13, 1861, the date it was mustered into state service. This act of muster-in carried out a resolution of the Confederate Congress approved July 30, 1861, which called for the president to receive and muster into service the regiment "for the term of six months, from the time they were sworn in and mustered into the service of North Carolina, and to discharge them after the expiration of that period." Actually, Secretary of War Leroy P. Walker had accepted the regiment into Confederate service on May 17, 1861, and the act of the resolution and muster-in completed the necessary details.

On September 6 the regiment left Ship Point and marched to Cocklestown on the Yorktown—Bethel Church road. Here it went into camp some six miles from Yorktown and nine miles from Bethel. The regimental camp was named Camp Fayetteville in honor the ladies of Fayetteville, who had made a regimental flag inscribed with the word "Bethel" and presented it to the regiment on September 9. Because of the part played by this regiment in the Battle of Big Bethel on June 10, 1861, the North Carolina Convention authorized the regiment to inscribe the word "Bethel" on its regimental flag, and the regiment became known as the "Bethel Regiment."

On September 28, 1861, the Adjutant General of North Carolina issued an order redesignating the regiment the 19th Regiment of N. C. Volunteers. A protest over the redesignation was voiced in a regimental meeting, which resulted in a request that the order be rescinded. The Adjutant General complied, and the regimental designation was not changed.

On October 7-8 the regiment was marched to Bay Tree, a distance of eight miles. After arriving there it was marched back to Camp Fayetteville and down the road to Bethel some three or four miles to Camp Rains. It moved to Bethel on October 20 and back to Yorktown on October 24, only to return to Bethel on October 25. Returning to Yorktown on November 1, detachments of four companies each left Yorktown for Richmond on November 8, 9, and 11. There the regiment was mustered out of Confederate service on November 12. It returned to Raleigh on the next day and was mustered out of state service.

By Special Orders No. 222, Adjutant and Inspector General's Office, Richmond, dated November 14, 1861, the Volunteer regiments from North Carolina were redesignated numerically from 1 through 14 to 11 through 24. This was to avoid confusion with the State Troops regiments which had been designated 1 through 10. This regiment, being the 1st Regiment N. C. Volunteers, was to be redesignated the 11th Regiment N. C. Troops (1st Regiment N. C. Volunteers). It differed from the other Volunteer regiments, however, because it had been mustered in for six months and not for twelve months. Thus, when the order to redesignate was carried out, the 1st Regiment N. C. Volunteers had been mustered out of service, and there was no 11th Regiment N. C. Troops (1st Regiment N. C. Volunteers) until one was organized in 1862. This new regiment was recognized as the successor of the 1st Regiment N. C. Volunteers, known as the Bethel Regiment, and was to be composed of men who had served in the original 1st Regiment N. C. Volunteers. Actually, many of the men had enlisted in

other companies, and two companies had joined other units. Many of the members of Company E went into the 60th Regiment N. C. Troops and Company F reenlisted and served as 2nd Company B, 36th Regiment N. C. Troops (2nd Regiment N. C. Artillery) which later became Company B, 13th Battalion N. C. Light Artillery. Even though the newly organized regiment did not contain a major portion of the men who served in the six-months regiment, it assumed the position vacated by the muster out of the six-months regiment and also adopted the title of Bethel Regiment. This accounts for the confusion in later writings about the two regiments.

In the Roll of Honor, compiled in the Adjutant General's Office, the six-months regiment was placed after the successor regiment. In his *Roster*, Major Moore followed the Roll of Honor order. Actually, the six months regiment was the first regiment organized and should have been recorded as the first regiment, as it was in Clark's *Regiments*. To avoid confusion, the 1st Regiment N. C. Volunteers was later officially referred to as the 1st Regiment N. C. Infantry (6 months, 1861).

FIELD AND STAFF

COLONELS

HILL, DANIEL HARVEY

Born in York District, South Carolina, and resided in Mecklenburg County as superintendent of the North Carolina Military Institute when the war started. He was assigned to command the camp of instruction for Volunteer forces at the State Fair Grounds, Raleigh, April 24, 1861, having tendered his services and the services of the corps of cadets of the North Carolina Military Institute as drillmasters. On May 11, 1861, he was elected Colonel of this regiment and served with the regiment until promoted to Brigadier General on July 10, 1861.

LEE, CHARLES COCHRANE

Born in South Carolina and resided in Mecklenburg County as an instructor at the North Carolina Military Institute when the war started. Accompanied the corps of cadets to Raleigh and was elected Lieutenant Colonel of this regiment on May 11, 1861. Elected Colonel on September 1, 1861, and appointed to rank from that date. Present or accounted for until mustered out on November 12-13, 1861. Later appointed Colonel of the 37th Regiment N. C. Troops.

LIEUTENANT COLONELS

LANE, JAMES HENRY

Born in Mathews County, Virginia, and resided in Mecklenburg County as an instructor at the North Carolina Military Institute when the war started. He accompanied the corps of cadets to Raleigh and was elected Major of this regiment on May 11, 1861. On September 3, 1861, he was elected Lieutenant Colonel and appointed to rank from that date. Present or accounted for until transferred to the 28th Regiment N. C. Troops upon appointment as Colonel on September 21, 1861.

STARR, JOSEPH BLAKE

Transferred from Company F of this regiment upon appointment as Lieutenant Colonel on September 28, 1861. Present or accounted for until mustered out on November 12-13, 1861. Later appointed Captain of 2nd Company B, 36th Regiment N. C. Troops (2nd Regiment N. C. Artillery).

MAJOR

HOKE, ROBERT FREDERICK

Transferred from Company K of this regiment upon election and appointment to Major to rank from September 1, 1861. Present or accounted for until mustered out November 12-13, 1861. Appointed Major in the 33rd Regiment N. C. Troops to rank from November 13, 1861.

ADJUTANT

POTEAT, JOHN M.

Enlisted in Wake County, April 28, 1861, for six months. Appointed Adjutant with the rank of 1st Lieutenant on May 13, 1861. Present or accounted for until transferred to the Field and Staff of the 19th Regiment N. C. Troops (2nd Regiment N. C. Cavalry) September 21, 1861, upon appointment as Adjutant of that regiment.

ASSISTANT QUARTERMASTER

BOONE, J. B. F.

Enlisted in Wake County at age 33, April 17-18, 1861, for six months. Appointed Captain, Assistant Quartermaster, May 13, 1861. Promoted to Major, Quartermaster, September 30, 1861, and assigned to Brigadier General D. H. Hill's Brigade.

ASSISTANT COMMISSARY OF SUBSISTENCE

WAYT, JOHN HENRY

Transferred from Company B of this regiment upon appointment as Captain, Assistant Commissary of Subsistence, on April 24, 1861. Present or accounted for until mustered out on November 12-13, 1861.

CHAPLAIN

YATES, EDWIN A.

Appointed Chaplain by Governor Ellis on May 21, 1861, being a minister in the Methodist Church. Present or accounted for until mustered out on November 12-13, 1861.

SURGEON

HINES, PETER E.

Born in Warren County and resided as a physician in Craven County when he was appointed Surgeon by Governor Ellis to rank from May 16, 1861. Detached as Chief Surgeon in hospital at Yorktown, Virginia, where he remained until

ordered to take charge of the North Carolina Hospital at Petersburg, Virginia, on October 14, 1861. The assignment transferred him from the regiment to the State Medical Department, of which he later became Medical Director.

ASSISTANT SURGEONS

BAKER, JOSEPH H.

Born in Edgecombe County where he resided when he was appointed Assistant Surgeon by Governor Ellis to rank from May 16, 1861. Present or accounted for until mustered out on November 12-13, 1861.

HARDY, JOHN GEDDINGS

Transferred from Company E of this regiment upon appointment as Assistant Surgeon to rank from May 16, 1861. Present or accounted for until mustered out on November 12-13, 1861. Later appointed Acting Surgeon of the 64th Regiment N. C. Troops.

SERGEANT MAJOR

KIBLER, GEORGE B.

Transferred from Company G of this regiment upon appointment as Sergeant Major to rank from June 1, 1861. Present or accounted for until mustered out on November 12-13, 1861. Later enlisted in Company B, 54th Regiment N. C. Troops.

QUARTERMASTER SERGEANTS

HAHR, FRANZ JOSEPH

Transferred from Company F of this regiment upon appointment as Quartermaster Sergeant on May 20, 1861. Present or accounted for until mustered out on November 12-13, 1861. Later appointed 1st Lieutenant, Drillmaster, and assigned to the Conscript Bureau, Raleigh.

PEARCE, BENJAMIN F.

Detailed from Company F of this regiment as Quartermaster Sergeant for the period August 13-31, 1861.

COMMISSARY SERGEANT

SUMMEY, JOHN S. E.

Detailed from Company E of this regiment as Commissary Sergeant and reported on the company muster rolls as detailed until mustered out on November 12-13, 1861.

ORDNANCE SERGEANT

MARTINE, THEODORE

Transferred from Company F of this regiment upon appointment as Ordnance Sergeant on May 22, 1861. Present or accounted for until mustered out on November 12-13, 1861.

HOSPITAL STEWARD

BOYD, T. B.

Transferred from Company C of this regiment

upon appointment as Hospital Steward on August 28, 1861. Present or accounted for until mustered out on November 12-13, 1861.

COMPANY A

This company, known as the "Edgecombe Guards," was organized in Edgecombe County. It received marching orders on April 17, 1861, and reported at Fort Macon on April 19. The next day it was ordered to the Camp of Instruction at Raleigh and was mustered into state service on May 13, 1861, as Company A of this regiment. After that date the company functioned as a part of the regiment, and its history for the war period is recorded as a part of the regimental history.

The information contained in the following roster of the company was compiled principally from company muster rolls which included the muster-in roll dated August 31, 1861, covering the period May 13-August 31, 1861, and muster rolls for the periods of April 18-May 12, 1861, and July-August, 1861. No muster rolls were found for the period after August 31, 1861. In addition to the company muster rolls, Roll of Honor records, receipt rolls, hospital records, prisoner of war records, and other primary records, supplemented by state pension applications, United Daughters of the Confederacy records, and postwar rosters and histories, all provided useful information.

OFFICERS

CAPTAINS

BRIDGERS, JOHN L.
Resided in Edgecombe County where he enlisted at the age of 41, April 18, 1861, for six months. Transferred to the Field and Staff, 10th Regiment N. C. State Troops (1st Regiment N. C. Artillery) upon appointment as Lieutenant Colonel to rank from August 16, 1861.

LLOYD, WHITNEL P.
Resided in Edgecombe County where he enlisted at age 25, April 18, 1861, for six months. Appointed 1st Lieutenant to rank from date of enlistment. Promoted to Captain to rank from September 7, 1861. Present or accounted for until mustered out November 12-13, 1861. Later appointed Captain of 1st Company G, 40th Regiment N. C. Troops (3rd Regiment N. C. Artillery).

LIEUTENANTS

LEWIS, WILLIAM GASTON, 1st Lieutenant
Born in Edgecombe County where he resided and enlisted at age 25, April 18, 1861, for six months. Appointed 3rd Lieutenant to rank from date of enlistment. Promoted to 1st Lieutenant to rank from September 7, 1861. Present or accounted for until mustered out November 12-13, 1861. Later appointed Major on the Field and Staff of the 33rd Regiment N. C. Troops.

LONG, WILLIAM S., 2nd Lieutenant
Enlisted in Edgecombe County at age 38, April 18, 1861, for six months. Appointed 2nd Lieutenant to rank from date of enlistment. Present or accounted for until mustered out November 12-13, 1861.

THIGPEN, KENNETH, 3rd Lieutenant
Resided in Edgecombe County where he enlisted at age 42, April 18, 1861, for six months. Mustered in as 1st Sergeant and appointed 3rd Lieutenant to rank from September 7, 1861. Present or accounted for until mustered out November 12-13, 1861. Later appointed 1st Lieutenant of 1st Company G, 40th Regiment N. C. Troops (3rd Regiment N. C. Artillery).

NONCOMMISSIONED OFFICERS AND PRIVATES

ALEXANDER, LEVI L., Private
Enlisted at Yorktown, Virginia, at age 22, July 16, 1861, for six months. Present or accounted for until mustered out November 12-13, 1861.

ALLEN, THOMAS F., Private
Enlisted in Edgecombe County at age 25, April 18, 1861, for six months. Present or accounted for until mustered out November 12-13, 1861.

ANDERSON, JAMES, Private
Enlisted in Edgecombe County at age 20, April 18, 1861, for six months. Present or accounted for until mustered out November 12-13, 1861.

ARMSTRONG, EDWARD H., Private
Enlisted at Yorktown, Virginia, at age 20, August 1, 1861, for six months. Present or accounted for until mustered out November 12-13, 1861.

BANKS, HARRISON, Private
Enlisted in Edgecombe County at age 28, April 18, 1861, for six months. Present or accounted for until mustered out November 12-13, 1861.

BARKER, BENJAMIN K., Private
Resided in Edgecombe County where he enlisted at age 32, April 18, 1861, for six months. Present or accounted for until discharged November 2, 1861. Later appointed Captain of Company F, 1st Battalion Virginia Local Defense Troops.

BASS, ISAAC W., Private
Enlisted in Edgecombe County at age 19, June 22, 1861, for six months. Present or accounted for until mustered out November 12-13, 1861.

BASSETT, RICHARD B., Private
Enlisted in Edgecombe County at age 30, April 18, 1861, for six months. Present or accounted for until mustered out November 12-13, 1861.

BATTS, BENJAMIN C., Private
Enlisted in Edgecombe County at age 18, June 22, 1861, for six months. Died near Yorktown, Virginia, after joining the regiment on July 2, 1861. Date of death not known.

BELCHER, HARRY, Private
Enlisted in Edgecombe County at age 40, April 18, 1861, for six months. Died at Yorktown, Virginia, July 5, 1861.

BELCHER, JOHN B., Private
Enlisted in Edgecombe County at age 24, April 18, 1861, for six months. Present or accounted for until mustered out November 12-13, 1861.

BELL, MARCUS B., Private
Enlisted in Edgecombe County at age 22, April 18, 1861, for six months. Present or accounted for until mustered out on November 12-13, 1861.

BEST, THOMAS, Private
Enlisted in Edgecombe County at age 23, April 18, 1861, for six months. Present or accounted for until mustered out November 12-13, 1861.

BRADLEY, ROBERT H., Private
Enlisted in Edgecombe County at age 23, April 18, 1861, for six months. Present or accounted for until mustered out November 12-13, 1861.

BRYAN, WILLIAM T., Private
Resided in Edgecombe County where he enlisted at age 22, April 18, 1861, for six months. Present or accounted for until mustered out November 12-13, 1861. Later enlisted in 1st Company G, 40th Regiment N. C. Troops (3rd Regiment N. C. Artillery).

CARTER, THOMAS M., Private
Enlisted in Edgecombe County at age 29, April 18, 1861, for six months. Present or accounted for until mustered out November 12-13, 1861.

CHERRY, HENRY RHODES, Private
Enlisted in Edgecombe County at age 37, April 18, 1861, for six months. Present or accounted for until mustered out November 12-13, 1861.

CHERRY, THOMAS F., Corporal
Enlisted in Edgecombe County at age 30, April 18, 1861, for six months. Mustered in as Corporal. Present or accounted for until mustered out November 12-13, 1861.

COBB, AMARIAH B., Private
Enlisted in Edgecombe County at age 32, April 18, 1861, for six months. Died at Yorktown, Virginia, July 11, 1861.

COBB, WILLIE J., Private
Enlisted in Edgecombe County at age 28, April 18, 1861, for six months. Present or accounted for until mustered out November 12-13, 1861.

COTTEN, GEORGE A. Private
Enlisted in Edgecombe County at age 20, April 18, 1861, for six months. Present or accounted for until mustered out November 12-13, 1861. Later enlisted in Company E, 17th Regiment N. C. Troops (2nd Organization).

COTTEN, M. AUGUSTUS, Private
Enlisted in Edgecombe County at age 20, April 18, 1861, for six months. Present or accounted for until mustered out November 12-13, 1861. Later enlisted in Company E, 17th Regiment N. C. Troops (2nd Organization).

CUTCHIN, JOHN M., Private
Enlisted in Edgecombe County at age 21, April 18, 1861, for six months. Present or accounted for until mustered out November 12-13, 1861.

DUNN, BURRELL, Private
Enlisted in Edgecombe County at age 21, April 18,

1861, for six months. Present or accounted for until mustered out November 12-13, 1861.

DUNN, RICHARD, Private
Enlisted in Edgecombe County at age 34, June 22, 1861, for six months. Present or accounted for until mustered out November 12-13, 1861.

DUNN, THEODORE, Private
Enlisted in Edgecombe County at age 26, April 18, 1861, for six months. Present or accounted for until mustered out November 12-13, 1861.

DUNN, WILLIE, Private
Enlisted in Edgecombe County at age 23, April 18, 1861, for six months. Present or accounted for until mustered out November 12-13, 1861.

EDMONDSON, HENDERSON, Private
Enlisted in Edgecombe County at age 20, April 18, 1861, for six months. Present or accounted for until mustered out November 12-13, 1861.

EDWARDS, JOSEPH M., Private
Enlisted in Edgecombe County at age 30, April 18, 1861, for six months. Present or accounted for until mustered out November 12-13, 1861.

FALLON, THOMAS, Private
Enlisted in Edgecombe County at age 25, April 18, 1861, for six months. Present or accounted for until mustered out November 12-13, 1861.

GARNETT, PHILLIP H., Private
Enlisted in Edgecombe County at age 27, April 18, 1861, for six months. Present or accounted for until mustered out November 12-13, 1861.

GORHAM, HENRY W., Private
Enlisted in Edgecombe County at age 23, April 18, 1861, for six months. Present or accounted for until mustered out November 12-13, 1861.

HARDAWAY, BENJAMIN M., Private
Enlisted in Edgecombe County, April 18, 1861, for six months. Present or accounted for until mustered out November 12-13, 1861.

HARPER, ALLEN, Private
Enlisted in Edgecombe County at age 22, April 18, 1861, for six months. Present or accounted for until mustered out November 12-13, 1861.

HARPER, JAMES M., Private
Enlisted in Edgecombe County at age 31, April 18, 1861, for six months. Present or accounted for until mustered out November 12-13, 1861.

HARPER, R. M., Private
Enlisted in Edgecombe County at age 23, June 22, 1861, for six months. Present or accounted for until mustered out November 12-13, 1861.

HARRISS, TIMOTHY, Private
Enlisted in Edgecombe County at age 20, April 18, 1861, for six months. Present or accounted for until mustered out November 12-13, 1861.

HOLLAND, BERRY L., Private
Enlisted in Edgecombe County at age 20, April 18, 1861, for six months. Present or accounted for until mustered out November 12-13, 1861.

HOWELL, ELI, Private
Enlisted in Edgecombe County at age 24, June 22, 1861, for six months. Present or accounted for

until mustered out November 12-13, 1861.

HUNTER. ARCHIBALD A., Private
Enlisted in Edgecombe County at age 19, April 18, 1861, for six months. Present or accounted for until mustered out November 12-13, 1861.

HUNTER, THEODORE, Private
Enlisted in Edgecombe County at age 20, April 18, 1861, for six months. Died at Yorktown, Virginia, of "typhoid or brain fever," August 21, 1861.

JOHNSON, JOSEPH A., Private
Enlisted in Edgecombe County at age 26, April 18, 1861, for six months. Died at Yorktown, Virginia, July 23, 1861.

KING, CHARLES R., Private
Enlisted in Edgecombe County at age 23, April 18, 1861, for six months. Present or accounted for until mustered out November 12-13, 1861.

KING, WILLIAM COFIELD, Private
Enlisted in Edgecombe County at age 21, April 18, 1861, for six months. Present or accounted for until mustered out November 12-13, 1861. Later enlisted in Company B, 44th Regiment N. C. Troops.

KNIGHT, ELISHA CROMWELL, Private
Enlisted in Edgecombe County at age 19, April 18, 1861, for six months. Present or accounted for until mustered out November 12-13, 1861. Later enlisted in Company B, 44th Regiment N. C. Troops.

KNIGHT, JESSE D., Private
Enlisted in Edgecombe County at age 24, April 18, 1861, for six months. Died at Yorktown, Virginia, September 20, 1861.

KNIGHT, NATHANIEL M., Private
Enlisted in Edgecombe County at age 25, April 18, 1861, for six months. Present or accounted for until mustered out November 12-13, 1861.

KNIGHT, ROBERT A., Private
Enlisted in Edgecombe County at age 22, April 18, 1861, for six months. Present or accounted for until mustered out November 12-13, 1861.

KNIGHT, WILLIS B., Private
Enlisted in Edgecombe County at age 21, April 18, 1861, for six months. Present or accounted for until mustered out November 12-13, 1861.

LAWRENCE, JOHN J., Private
Enlisted in Edgecombe County at age 22, April 18, 1861, for six months. Present or accounted for until mustered out November 12-13, 1861.

LEGGETT DAVID ADOLPHUS. Private
Enlisted in Edgecombe County at age 26, April 18, 1861, for six months. Present or accounted for until mustered out November 12-13, 1861.

LIPSCOMB, GEORGE B., Private
Enlisted in Edgecombe County at age 31, April 18, 1861, for six months. Present or accounted for until mustered out November 12-13, 1861.

LITTLEPAGE, HARMON, Private
Enlisted in Edgecombe County at age 22, April 18, 1861, for six months. Present or accounted for until mustered out November 12-13, 1861.

LONG, WILLIAM R., Private
Enlisted in Edgecombe County at age 21, April 18, 1861, for six months. Present or accounted for until mustered out November 12-13, 1861.

LYON, HARRISON P., Corporal
Enlisted in Edgecombe County at age 21, April 18, 1861, for six months. Mustered in as Corporal. Present or accounted for until mustered out November 12-13, 1861.

MABREY, BYTHAL, Private
Enlisted in Edgecombe County at age 27, April 18, 1861, for six months. Present or accounted for until mustered out November 12-13, 1861.

MABREY, CHARLES D., Private
Enlisted in Edgecombe County at age 20, June 22, 1861, for six months. Present or accounted for until mustered out November 12-13, 1861.

McDOWELL, WILLIAM, Private
Enlisted in Edgecombe County at age 30, April 18, 1861, for six months. Present or accounted for until mustered out November 12-13, 1861.

McMARKS, W. T., Private
Enlisted in Edgecombe County at age 24, April 18, 1861, for six months. Present or accounted for until mustered out November 12-13, 1861. Later enlisted in 1st Company G, 40th Regiment N. C. Troops (3rd Regiment N. C. Artillery).

MARRINER, WILLIAM W., Private
Enlisted in Edgecombe County at age 23, April 18, 1861, for six months. Present or accounted for until mustered out November 12-13, 1861.

MATHEWS, THOMAS, Private
Enlisted in Edgecombe County at age 28, April 18, 1861, for six months. Present or accounted for until mustered out November 12-13, 1861.

MATHEWSON, NATHAN, Private
Enlisted in Edgecombe County at age 43, April 18, 1861, for six months. Present or accounted for until mustered out November 12-13, 1861.

MAYO, HUGH B., Private
Enlisted in Edgecombe County at age 20, April 18, 1861, for six months. Died at Yorktown, Virginia, August 17, 1861.

MEEKS, JOSHUA, Private
Enlisted in Edgecombe County at age 35, April 18, 1861, for six months. Present or accounted for until mustered out November 12-13, 1861.

MEHEGAN, WALTER, Private
Enlisted in Edgecombe County at age 21, April 18, 1861, for six months. Present or accounted for until mustered out November 12-13, 1861.

MOORE, JOHN J., Private
Enlisted in Edgecombe County at age 26, April 18, 1861, for six months. Present or accounted for until mustered out November 12-13, 1861.

NEWSOM, DAVID A., Private
Enlisted in Edgecombe County at age 25, April 18, 1861, for six months. Present or accounted for until mustered out November 12-13, 1861.

OWEN, JAMES, Private
Enlisted in Edgecombe County at age 21, April 18,

1861, for six months. Present or accounted for until mustered out November 12-13, 1861. Later enlisted in Company K, 10th Regiment N. C. State Troops (1st Regiment N. C. Artillery).

PALAMOUNTAIN, I. B., Private
Enlisted in Edgecombe County at age 35, April 18, 1861, for six months. Present or accounted for until mustered out November 12-13, 1861.

PARKER, JOSEPH H., Private
Enlisted in Edgecombe County at age 30, April 18, 1861, for six months. Present or accounted for until mustered out November 12-13, 1861.

PARKER, JOSEPH J., Private
Enlisted in Edgecombe County at age 31, April 18, 1861, for six months. Present or accounted for until mustered out November 12-13, 1861.

PARKER, WEEKS B., Private
Enlisted in Edgecombe County at age 18, April 18, 1861, for six months. Present or accounted for until mustered out November 12-13, 1861.

PAYNE, JOSEPH H., Sergeant
Enlisted in Edgecombe County at age 30, April 18, 1861, for six months. Mustered in as Sergeant. Present or accounted for until mustered out November 12-13, 1861.

PIPPEN, CULLEN A., Private
Enlisted in Edgecombe County at age 20, April 18, 1861, for six months. Present or accounted for until mustered out November 12-13, 1861.

PIPPEN, NATHAN K., Private
Enlisted in Edgecombe County at age 18, June 22, 1861, for six months. Present or accounted for until mustered out November 12-13, 1861.

PITT, JOHN D., Private
Enlisted in Edgecombe County at age 26, April 18, 1861, for six months. Present or accounted for until mustered out November 12-13, 1861.

PITT, THEOPHILUS, Private
Enlisted in Edgecombe County at age 24, April 18, 1861, for six months. Present or accounted for until mustered out November 12-13, 1861.

PITT, TURNER, Private
Enlisted in Edgecombe County at age 28, April 18, 1861, for six months. Present or accounted for until mustered out November 12-13, 1861.

PITTMAN, JOSEPH W., Private
Enlisted in Edgecombe County at age 27, April 18, 1861, for six months. Present or accounted for until mustered out November 12-13, 1861.

POWELL, ROBERT J., Private
Enlisted in Edgecombe County at age 19, April 18, 1861, for six months. Present or accounted for until mustered out November 12-13, 1861.

PRICE, JOEL, Private
Enlisted in Edgecombe County at age 33, April 18, 1861, for six months. Present or accounted for until mustered out November 12-13, 1861.

REASONS, LEVI W., Private
Enlisted in Edgecombe County at age 25, April 18, 1861, for six months. Present or accounted for until mustered out November 12-13, 1861.

RICKS, ROBERT H., Private
Enlisted in Edgecombe County at age 23, April 18, 1861, for six months. Present or accounted for until mustered out November 12-13, 1861.

ROBERSON, JESSE B., Private
Enlisted in Edgecombe County at age 19, April 18, 1861, for six months. Died at Yorktown, Virginia, of "typhoid fever," June 22, 1861.

RODGERS, BUCKNER, Private
Enlisted in Edgecombe County at age 34, April 18, 1861, for six months. Present or accounted for until mustered out November 12-13, 1861.

RODGERS, COUNCIL, Private
Enlisted in Edgecombe County at age 32, April 18, 1861, for six months. Company muster roll for April 17-June 30, 1861, states that he was "wounded in battle of Bethel, June 16, 1861." Discharged July 11, 1861.

SAVAGE, JAMES M., Private
Enlisted in Edgecombe County at age 27, April 18, 1861, for six months. Present or accounted for until mustered out November 12-13, 1861.

SAVAGE. JESSE, Private
Enlisted in Edgecombe County at age 30, April 18, 1861, for six months. Present or accounted for until mustered out November 12-13, 1861.

SAVAGE, WILLIAM R., Private
Enlisted in Edgecombe County at age 22, April 18, 1861, for six months. Present or accounted for until mustered out November 12-13, 1861.

SLADE, HENRY, Private
Enlisted at Yorktown, Virginia, at age 18, July 14, 1861, for six months. Present or accounted for until mustered out November 12-13, 1861.

SMITH, JAMES M., Private
Enlisted in Edgecombe County at age 26, April 16, 1861, for six months. Present or accounted for until mustered out November 12-13, 1861.

SMITH, WILLIAM B., Sergeant
Enlisted in Edgecombe County at age 27, April 18, 1861, for six months. Mustered in as Sergeant. Present or accounted for until mustered out November 12-13, 1861.

SORG, HENRY. Private
Enlisted in Edgecombe County at age 19, June 22, 1861, for six months. Present or accounted for until mustered out November 12-13, 1861.

STAMPER, JOSEPH J., Private
Enlisted in Edgecombe County at age 24, April 18, 1861, for six months. Present or accounted for until mustered out November 12, 1861.

STATON, JOSEPH S., Sergeant
Enlisted in Edgecombe County at age 25, April 18, 1861, for six months. Mustered in as Sergeant. Present or accounted for until mustered out November 12-13, 1861.

STEWART, THOMAS J., Sergeant
Enlisted in Edgecombe County at age 37, April 18, 1861, for six months. Mustered in as Sergeant. Present or accounted for until mustered out November 12-13, 1861.

STRICKLAND, GEORGE W., Private
Enlisted in Edgecombe County at age 30, June 22, 1861, for six months. Present or accounted for until mustered out November 12-13, 1861.

TAYLOR, LEWIS, Private
Enlisted in Edgecombe County at age 24, June 22, 1861, for six months. Present or accounted for until mustered out November 12-13, 1861. Later enlisted in 1st Company G, 40th Regiment N. C. Troops (3rd Regiment N. C. Artillery).

TAYLOR, THOMAS M., Private
Enlisted in Edgecombe County at age 30, April 18. 1861, for six months. Present or accounted for until mustered out November 12-13, 1861.

THIGPEN, ALFRED MARION, Private
Enlisted in Edgecombe County at age 21, June 22, 1861, for six months. Present or accounted for until mustered out November 12-13, 1861.

THIGPEN, THOMAS D., Private
Enlisted in Edgecombe County at age 23, June 22, 1861, for six months. Present or accounted for until mustered out November 12-13, 1861.

THORPE, JOHN H., Corporal
Enlisted in Edgecombe County at age 22, April 18, 1861, for six months. Mustered in as Corporal. Present or accounted for until mustered out November 12-13, 1861. Later enlisted in Company A, 47th Regiment N. C. Troops.

WALSTON, JOHN, Private
Enlisted in Edgecombe County at age 25, April 18, 1861, for six months. Present or accounted for until mustered out November 12-13, 1861.

WEATHERSBEE, WILLIAM THOMAS, Private
Enlisted in Edgecombe County at age 30, April 18, 1861, for six months. Present or accounted for until mustered out November 12-13, 1861.

WEBB, JOSEPH, Private
Enlisted in Edgecombe County at age 33, April 18, 1861, for six months. Present or accounted for until mustered out November 12-13, 1861.

WELLS, MARK B., Private
Enlisted in Edgecombe County at age 18, April 18, 1861, for six months. Present or accounted for until mustered out November 12-13, 1861.

WILLIAMS, CHARLES, Private
Enlisted in Edgecombe County at age 24, April 18, 1861, for six months. Wounded in battle at Bethel, Virginia, June 10, 1861. Present or accounted for until mustered out November 12-13, 1861.

WILLIAMS, GEORGE T., Corporal
Enlisted in Edgecombe County at age 28, April 18, 1861, for six months. Mustered in as Corporal. Present or accounted for until mustered out November 12-13, 1861.

WOMBLE, BENJAMIN F., Private
Enlisted in Edgecombe County at age 20, April 18, 1861, for six months. Present or accounted for until mustered out November 12-13. 1861.

WYATT, HENRY LAWSON, Private
Born in Richmond, Virginia, and resided in Edgecombe County where he enlisted at age 19,
April 18, 1861, for six months. Killed in action at Bethel, Virginia, June 10, 1861.

ZOELLER, CHARLES A. L., Private
Enlisted in Edgecombe County at age 20, April 18, 1861, for six months. Present or accounted for until mustered out November 12-13, 1861.

ZOELLER, EDWARD, Private
Enlisted in Edgecombe County at age 31, June 22, 1861, for six months. Present or accounted for until mustered out November 12-13, 1861.

COMPANY B

This company, known as the "Hornet Nest Rifles," enlisted at Charlotte, Mecklenburg County, on April 17, 1861. It was ordered to Raleigh, April 23, 1861, where it was mustered into state service on May 13, 1861, as Company B of this regiment. After that date the company functioned as a part of the regiment, and its history for the war period is recorded as a part of the regimental history.

The information contained in the following roster of the company was compiled principally from company muster rolls which included the muster-in roll dated August 31, 1861, covering the period May 13-August 31, 1861, and muster rolls for the periods of April 18-May 13, 1861; May 13-June 30, 1861; and June 30-August 31, 1861. No muster rolls were found for the period after August 31, 1861. In addition to the company rolls, Roll of Honor records, receipt rolls, hospital records, prisoner of war records, and other primary records, supplemented by state pension applications, United Daughters of the Confederacy records, and postwar rosters and histories, all provided useful information.

OFFICERS

CAPTAINS

WILLIAMS, LEWIS S.
Resided in Mecklenburg County where he enlisted at age 35, April 16, 1861, for six months. Appointed Captain to rank from date of enlistment. Resigned September 28, 1861, by reason of being "appointed by the Secretary of the Treasury, Produce Loan Agent for North Carolina."

OWENS, WILLIAM A.
Resided in Mecklenburg County where he enlisted at age 27, April 16, 1861, for six months. Appointed 1st Lieutenant to rank from date of enlistment. Promoted to Captain to rank from September 28, 1861. Present or accounted for until mustered out November 12-13, 1861. Later appointed Major and assigned to the Field and Staff of the 34th Regiment N. C. Troops.

LIEUTENANTS

BRYCE, ROBERT S., 1st Lieutenant
Resided in Mecklenburg County where he enlisted at age 21, April 16, 1861, for six months. Mustered in as Sergeant and appointed 1st Lieutenant to rank from September 28, 1861. Present or accounted for until mustered out November

12-13, 1861. Later appointed 1st Lieutenant of Company E, 59th Regiment N. C. Troops (4th Regiment N. C. Cavalry).

GILLESPIE, THOMAS D., 3rd Lieutenant
Resided in Mecklenburg County where he enlisted at age 33, April 16, 1861, for six months. Appointed 3rd Lieutenant to rank from date of enlistment. Present or accounted for until mustered out November 12-13, 1861.

HILL, WILLIAM P., 2nd Lieutenant
Resided in Mecklenburg County where he enlisted at age 28, April 16, 1861, for six months. Appointed 2nd Lieutenant to rank from date of enlistment. Present or accounted for until mustered out November 12-13, 1861. Later appointed Captain, A. C. S., on the Field and Staff of the 53rd Regiment N. C. Troops.

NONCOMMISSIONED OFFICERS AND PRIVATES

ALDERSON, JOHN P., Private
Enlisted in Mecklenburg County, June 30, 1861, for six months. Present or accounted for until mustered out November 12-13, 1861.

ALEXANDER, C. C., Private
Enlisted at Yorktown, Virginia, June 30, 1861, for six months. Died at Yorktown on October 5, 1861, of disease.

ALEXANDER, DAVIDSON, Private
Enlisted at Yorktown, Virginia, July 8, 1861, for six months. Present or accounted for until mustered out November 12-13, 1861.

ALEXANDER, FRANCIS R., Private
Enlisted at Yorktown, Virginia, June 30, 1861, for six months. Present or accounted for until mustered out November 12-13, 1861.

ALEXANDER, JAMES L., Private
Enlisted in Mecklenburg County at age 21, April 16, 1861, for six months. Present or accounted for until mustered out November 12-13, 1861.

ALEXANDER, JOHN M., Private
Enlisted in Wake County, May 20, 1861, for six months. Present or accounted for until mustered out November 12-13, 1861.

ALEXANDER, JULIUS J., Private
Enlisted in Mecklenburg County at age 28, April 16, 1861, for six months. Present or accounted for until mustered out November 12-13, 1861.

ALEXANDER, MARSHAL E., Private
Born in Mecklenburg County where he resided as a trader prior to enlisting in Wake County at age 22, May 20, 1861, for six months. Present or accounted for until mustered out November 12-13, 1861. Later enlisted in Company B, 53rd Regiment N. C. Troops.

ALEXANDER, THOMAS F., Private
Enlisted at Richmond, Virginia, May 22, 1861, for six months. Present or accounted for until mustered out November 12-13, 1861.

ANDERSON, C. J., Private
Enlisted in Mecklenburg County at age 28, April

16, 1861, for six months. Present or accounted for until mustered out November 12-13, 1861.

BAKER, J. F., Private
Enlisted in Mecklenburg County, June 24, 1861, for six months. Present or accounted for until mustered out November 12-13, 1861.

BARNETT, ROBERT C., Private
Enlisted in Mecklenburg County, June 24, 1861, for six months. Present or accounted for until mustered out November 12-13, 1861.

BARNETT, WILLIAM A., Private
Enlisted in Mecklenburg County, June 24, 1861, for six months. Present or accounted for until mustered out November 12-13, 1861.

BARNETT, WILLIAM P., Private
Enlisted in Mecklenburg County at age 23, April 27, 1861, for six months. Present or accounted for until mustered out November 12-13, 1861.

BIGGERT, WILLIAM S., Private
Enlisted in Mecklenburg County at age 22, April 16, 1861, for six months. Present or accounted for until mustered out November 12-13, 1861.

BLACK, JOSEPH, Private
Enlisted in Mecklenburg County at age 20, April 18, 1861, for six months. Died at Yorktown, Virginia, September 24, 1861. Cause of death not known.

BLAIR, J. R., Private
Enlisted in Mecklenburg County, July 24, 1861, for six months. Present or accounted for until mustered out November 12-13, 1861.

BOND, NEWTON, Private
Enlisted in Wake County at age 25, May 17, 1861, for six months. Present or accounted for until mustered out November 12-13, 1861.

BORDEAUX, A. J., Private
Enlisted in Mecklenburg County at age 21, April 26, 1861, for six months. Present or accounted for until mustered out November 12-13, 1861.

BURWELL, ROBERT T., Private
Enlisted in Mecklenburg County, June 24, 1861, for six months. Present or accounted for until mustered out November 12-13, 1861.

CALDWELL, J. E., Private
Enlisted in Mecklenburg County, May 16, 1861, for six months. Present or accounted for until mustered out November 12-13, 1861.

CALDWELL, J. E., Private
Enlisted in Mecklenburg County, June 24, 1861, for six months. Present or accounted for until mustered out November 12-13, 1861.

CALDWELL, R. B., Private
Enlisted in Mecklenburg County at age 23, May 16, 1861, for six months. Present or accounted for until mustered out November 12-13, 1861.

CANNADY, ROBERT K., Private
Enlisted in Mecklenburg County, May 16, 1861, for six months. Present or accounted for until mustered out November 12-13, 1861.

CANNON, F. J., Private
Enlisted in Mecklenburg County, June 23, 1861,

for six months. Present or accounted for until mustered out November 12-13, 1861.

CRAWFORD, ROBERT R., Private
Enlisted in Mecklenburg County at age 21, April 16, 1861, for six months. Present or accounted for until mustered out November 12-13, 1861. Later enlisted in Company D, 42nd Regiment N. C. Troops.

CROWELL, E. M., Private
Enlisted in Mecklenburg County at age 22, April 16, 1861, for six months. Present or accounted for until mustered out November 12-13, 1861.

DAVIDSON, JAMES F., Private
Enlisted in Mecklenburg County at age 23, April 16, 1861, for six months. Present or accounted for until mustered out November 12-13, 1861. Later enlisted in Company F, 60th Regiment N. C. Troops.

DAVIDSON, ROBERT A., Private
Enlisted in Mecklenburg County, June 24, 1861, for six months. Present or accounted for until mustered out November 12-13, 1861.

DAVIS, J. T. A., Private
Enlisted in Mecklenburg County, April 16, 1861, for six months. Reported as "discharged" on company muster roll dated August 31, 1861.

DAVIS, JAMES T., Private
Enlisted in Mecklenburg County, June 24, 1861, for six months. Present or accounted for until mustered out November 12-13, 1861.

DAVIS, R. A. G., Private
Enlisted in Mecklenburg County at age 19, May 1, 1861, for six months. Present or accounted for until mustered out November 12-13, 1861.

DAVIS, R. B., Corporal
Enlisted in Mecklenburg County at age 26, April 16, 1861, for six months. Mustered in as Corporal. Present or accounted for until mustered out November 12-13, 1861.

DEWESE, F. F., Private
Enlisted in Mecklenburg County, June 24, 1861, for six months. Present or accounted for until mustered out November 12-13, 1861.

DORSET, JAMES F., Private
Enlisted in Mecklenburg County at age 19, April 16, 1861, for six months. Present or accounted for until mustered out November 12-13, 1861.

DUGAN, JAMES F., Private
Enlisted in Mecklenburg County, June 15, 1861, for six months. Reported as "absent without leave" on muster roll dated August 31, 1861.

DYER, WILLIAM J., Private
Enlisted in Mecklenburg County at age 23, April 16, 1861, for six months. Present or accounted for until mustered out November 12-13, 1861.

EAGLE, ALEXANDER, Private
Enlisted in Mecklenburg County at age 32, May 3, 1861, for six months. Present or accounted for until mustered out November 12-13, 1861.

EAGLE, JOHN, Private
Enlisted in Mecklenburg County at age 24, May 3, 1861, for six months. Present or accounted for

until mustered out November 12-13, 1861.

EARNHARDT, SOLOMON, Private
Enlisted at Yorktown, Virginia, June 30, 1861, for six months. Present or accounted for until mustered out November 12-13, 1861.

FINGER, JOHN, Private
Enlisted in Mecklenburg County at age 27, April 16, 1861, for six months. Present or accounted for until mustered out November 12-13, 1861.

FRAZIER, MARSHALL, Musician
Enlisted in Mecklenburg County at age 23, April 16, 1861, for six months. Mustered in as Musician. Present or accounted for until mustered out November 12-13, 1861.

FRENCH, JAMES B., Sergeant
Enlisted in Mecklenburg County at age 23, April 16, 1861, for six months. Mustered in as Sergeant. Present or accounted for until mustered out November 12-13, 1861.

FULLENWIDER, HENRY, Private
Enlisted in Mecklenburg County at age 26, May 1, 1861, for six months. Present or accounted for until mustered out November 12-13, 1861.

GILLETTO, J. H., Private
Enlisted at age 25, April 18, 1861, for six months.

GRAHAM, JOHN R., Private
Enlisted in Mecklenburg County at age 24, April 16, 1861, for six months. Present or accounted for until mustered out November 12-13, 1861.

GRAY, A. N., Private
Enlisted in Mecklenburg County at age 22, April 16, 1861, for six months. Present or accounted for until mustered out November 12-13, 1861.

GRAY, R. T., Private
Enlisted in Mecklenburg County at age 21, April 16, 1861, for six months. Died at Yorktown, Virginia, September 20, 1861, of disease.

GRIER, SAMUEL ANDREW, Private
Resided in Mecklenburg County where he enlisted at age 19, April 16, 1861, for six months. Present or accounted for until mustered out November 12-13, 1861. Later enlisted in Company F, 63rd Regiment N. C. Troops (5th Regiment N. C. Cavalry).

GRIFFITH, J. H., Private
Enlisted in Mecklenburg County, May 1, 1861, for six months. Present or accounted for until mustered out November 12-13, 1861.

GRIFFITH, JAMES L., Private
Enlisted in Mecklenburg County, June 24, 1861, for six months. Present or accounted for until mustered out November 12-13, 1861.

GRIFFITH, WILLIAM F., Private
Enlisted in Mecklenburg County, June 24, 1861, for six months. Present or accounted for until mustered out November 12-13, 1861.

HARGETT, A. J., Private
Enlisted in Mecklenburg County, June 24, 1861, for six months. Present or accounted for until mustered out November 12-13, 1861.

HARTIS, WILSON L., Private
Enlisted in Mecklenburg County at age 27, April

18, 1861, for six months. Present or accounted for until mustered out November 12-13, 1861.

HENDERSON, JAMES M., Private
Enlisted in Mecklenburg County, June 24, 1861, for six months. Present or accounted for until mustered out November 12-13, 1861.

HENDERSON, W. M. F., Private
Enlisted in Mecklenburg County at age 23, May 1, 1861, for six months. Present or accounted for until mustered out November 12-13, 1861.

HILTON, J. H., Private
Enlisted in Mecklenburg County, June 24, 1861, for six months. Present or accounted for until mustered out November 12-13, 1861.

HOLLINGSWORTH, BRYAN, Private
Enlisted in Mecklenburg County at age 20, April 16, 1861, for six months. Present or accounted for until mustered out November 12-13, 1861.

HOWEL, A., Private
Enlisted in Mecklenburg County, May 1, 1861, for six months. Died July 10, 1861.

HOWELL, EDMUND, Private
Enlisted in Mecklenburg County, May 19, 1861, for six months. Died of disease. Date of death reported as July 4, July 10, and September 3, 1861.

HOWELL, JAMES A., Private
Enlisted in Mecklenburg County at age 24, April 16, 1861, for six months. Present or accounted for until mustered out November 12-13, 1861.

HUNTER, J. H., Private
Enlisted in Mecklenburg County, May 16, 1861, for six months. Present or accounted for until mustered out November 12-13, 1861.

HUNTER, W. S., Private
Enlisted in Mecklenburg County, June 24, 1861, for six months. Present or accounted for until mustered out November 12-13, 1861.

JACOBS, G. W., Private
Enlisted in Mecklenburg County at age 32, April 16, 1861, for six months. Present or accounted for until mustered out November 12-13, 1861.

JOHNSON, S. R., Private
Enlisted in Mecklenburg County at age 22, April 16, 1861, for six months. Present or accounted for until mustered out November 12-13, 1861.

JONES, MILTON, Private
Enlisted in Mecklenburg County at age 24, April 16, 1861, for six months. Present or accounted for until mustered out November 12-13, 1861.

KEENAN, D. G., Private
Enlisted in Mecklenburg County, June 24, 1861, for six months. Present or accounted for until mustered out November 12-13, 1861.

KERR, WILLIAM J., Private
Enlisted in Mecklenburg County at age 30, April 16, 1861, for six months. Present or accounted for until mustered out November 12-13, 1861.

KEZIAH, WILLIAM, Private
Enlisted in Mecklenburg County at age 25, April 16, 1861, for six months. Present or accounted for until mustered out November 12-13, 1861.

KIRKPATRICK, H. Y., Private
Enlisted in Mecklenburg County, June 24, 1861, for six months. Present or accounted for until mustered out November 12-13, 1861.

KIRKPATRICK, THOMAS ALFRED, Private
Enlisted in Mecklenburg County at age 35, June 24, 1861, for six months. Present or accounted for until mustered out November 12-13, 1861. Later enlisted in Company B, 53rd Regiment N. C. Troops.

LACY, DRURY, Jr., Private
Enlisted in Mecklenburg County, June 24, 1861, for six months. Present or accounted for until mustered out November 12-13, 1861. Later enlisted in Company B, 43rd Regiment N. C. Troops.

LEE, JUNIUS M., Private
Enlisted in Mecklenburg County, May 4, 1861, for six months. Present or accounted for until mustered out November 12-13, 1861.

LOURIE, JAMES B., Private
Enlisted in Mecklenburg County, June 24, 1861, for six months. Present or accounted for until mustered out November 12-13, 1861.

MABRY, J. H., Private
Enlisted in Mecklenburg County, June 24, 1861, for six months. Reported as "absent without leave" on muster roll dated August 31, 1861.

McDONALD, ALLEN, Private
Enlisted in Mecklenburg County at age 24, April 16, 1861, for six months. Died in hospital of disease August 17, 1861.

McGINNIS, ROBERT CHARLES, Private
Enlisted in Mecklenburg County at age 28, May 16, 1861, for six months. Present or accounted for until mustered out November 12-13, 1861. Later enlisted in Company B, 43rd Regiment N. C. Troops.

McLELLAND, WILLIAM, Private
Enlisted in Mecklenburg County, June 24, 1861, for six months. Present or accounted for until mustered out November 12-13, 1861.

McORKLE, ROBERT B., Private
Enlisted in Mecklenburg County at age 21, May 1, 1861, for six months. Present or accounted for until mustered out November 12-13, 1861.

MARES, J. L., Private
Enlisted in Mecklenburg County, June 24, 1861, for six months. Present or accounted for until mustered out November 12-13, 1861.

MATHEWS, WILLIAM M., Corporal
Enlisted in Mecklenburg County at age 20, April 16, 1861, for six months. Mustered in as Corporal. Present or accounted for until mustered out November 12-13, 1861.

MEANS, WILLIAM N. M., Private
Enlisted in Mecklenburg County at age 22, May 1, 1861, for six months. Present or accounted for until mustered out November 12-13, 1861.

MEHRTONS, JOHN, Private
Enlisted in Mecklenburg County at age 18, April 16, 1861, for six months. Present or accounted for until mustered out November 12-13, 1861.

MOORE, THOMAS J., Private
Enlisted in Mecklenburg County, July 1, 1861, for six months. Present or accounted for until mustered out November 12-13, 1861. Later served as volunteer aide-de-camp and 1st Lieutenant and Ordnance Officer on the staff of General D. H. Hill, and as Adjutant with the rank of 1st Lieutenant on the Field and Staff of the 33rd Regiment N. C. Troops.

MOSELY, J. M., Private
Enlisted in Mecklenburg County at age 20, April 16, 1861, for six months. Present or accounted for until mustered out November 12-13, 1861.

MURRAY, J. W., Private
Enlisted in Mecklenburg County at age 22, April 16, 1861, for six months. Present or accounted for until mustered out November 12-13, 1861.

NICHOLS, JAMES S., Private
Enlisted in Mecklenburg County, April 16, 1861, for six months. Present or accounted for until mustered out November 12-13, 1861.

NORMENT, ALFRED A., Private
Enlisted in Mecklenburg County at age 42, April 16, 1861, for six months. Present or accounted for until mustered out November 12-13, 1861.

OATES, JAMES C., Private
Enlisted in Mecklenburg County, June 24, 1861, for six months. Present or accounted for until discharged on July 9, 1861.

OATES, JAMES H., Private
Enlisted in Mecklenburg County at age 35, April 16, 1861, for six months. Present or accounted for until mustered out November 12-13, 1861.

ORDERS, COONEY, Private
Enlisted in Mecklenburg County at age 24, April 16, 1861, for six months. Present or accounted for until mustered out November 12-13, 1861.

ORR, THOMAS J., Private
Enlisted in Mecklenburg County at age 22, April 16, 1861, for six months. Present or accounted for until mustered out November 12-13, 1861.

PARADOE, L. H., Private
Enlisted in Mecklenburg County at age 28, April 16, 1861, for six months. Present or accounted for until mustered out November 12-13, 1861.

PHELPS, HENRY M., 1st Sergeant
Enlisted in Mecklenburg County, April 16, 1861, for six months. Mustered in as 1st Sergeant. Present or accounted for until mustered out November 12-13, 1861.

PHIFER, ROBERT, Private
Enlisted in Mecklenburg County at age 20, April 27, 1861, for six months. Present or accounted for until mustered out November 12-13, 1861.

PHILLIPS, JUNIUS A., Private
Enlisted in Mecklenburg County at age 24, April 16, 1861, for six months. Present or accounted for until mustered out November 12-13, 1861.

POTTS, JAMES H., Private
Enlisted in Mecklenburg County at age 23, April 27, 1861, for six months. Present or accounted for until mustered out November 12-13, 1861.

PRATHER, S. F., Private
Enlisted in Mecklenburg County, June 24, 1861, for six months. Present or accounted for until mustered out November 12-13, 1861.

PRICE, WILLIAM J., Private
Enlisted in Mecklenburg County, June 24, 1861, for six months. Present or accounted for until mustered out November 12-13, 1861.

PRIM, JOSEPH T., Private
Enlisted in Mecklenburg County, April 16, 1861, for six months. Present or accounted for until mustered out November 12-13, 1861.

QUERY, R. W., Private
Enlisted in Mecklenburg County at age 24, April 16, 1861, for six months. Present or accounted for until mustered out November 12-13, 1861.

REA, WILLIAM P., Private
Enlisted in Mecklenburg County at age 22, April 16, 1861, for six months. Present or accounted for until mustered out November 12-13, 1861.

REID, H. C., Private
Enlisted in Mecklenburg County, June 24, 1861, for six months. Present or accounted for until mustered out November 12-13, 1861.

REID, H. K., Private
Enlisted in Mecklenburg County, June 24, 1861, for six months. Present or accounted for until mustered out November 12-13, 1861.

REID, J. L., Private
Enlisted in Mecklenburg County, June 24, 1861, for six months. Present or accounted for until mustered out November 12-13, 1861.

RHYNE, ADAM M., Corporal
Resided in Mecklenburg County where he enlisted at age 21, April 16, 1861, for six months. Mustered in as Corporal. Present or accounted for until mustered out November 12-13, 1861. Later enlisted in Company K, 42nd Regiment N. C. Troops.

RIGLER, GEORGE H., Private
Enlisted in Mecklenburg County at age 21, April 16, 1861, for six months. Present or accounted for until mustered out November 12-13, 1861.

RITCH, J. L., Private
Enlisted in Mecklenburg County, June 24, 1861, for six months. Present or accounted for until mustered out November 12-13, 1861.

ROSS, WILLIAM C., Private
Enlisted in Mecklenburg County at age 20, April 16, 1861, for six months. Present or accounted for until mustered out November 12-13, 1861.

ROZZELL, J. T., Private
Enlisted in Mecklenburg County, June 23, 1861, for six months. Present or accounted for until mustered out November 12-13, 1861.

ROZZELL, W. F., Private
Enlisted in Mecklenburg County at age 21, April 16, 1861, for six months. Present or accounted for until mustered out November 12-13, 1861.

SADLER, JULIUS, Private
Enlisted in Mecklenburg County at age 21, April

16, 1861, for six months. Died May 26, 1861, from injury received when he "fell from the platform of the cars on the way from Richmond to Yorktown, Virginia, May 24, 1861."

SADLER, O. M., Private
Born in York District, South Carolina, and was by occupation an apothecary when he enlisted in Mecklenburg County at age 19, April 16, 1861, for six months. Detailed as "dispensing apothecary" at Yorktown, Virginia, from June 20 through September 29, 1861. Discharged October 30, 1861.

SECRIST, WILLIAM A., Private
Enlisted in Mecklenburg County, June 24, 1861, for six months. Present or accounted for until mustered out November 12-13, 1861.

SHARP, ROBERT A., Private
Enlisted in Mecklenburg County, April 16, 1861, for six months. Present or accounted for until mustered out November 12-13, 1861.

SHAW, LOCK W. A., Private
Enlisted in Mecklenburg County at age 17, April 16, 1861, for six months. Present or accounted for until mustered out November 12-13, 1861. Later enlisted in Company F, 49th Regiment N. C. Troops.

SHEPHERD, JAMES W., Private
Resided in Mecklenburg County where he enlisted at age 20, May 1, 1861, for six months. Present or accounted for until mustered out November 12-13, 1861. Later enlisted in Company K, 56th Regiment N. C. Troops.

SLOAN, D. F. A., Private
Enlisted in Mecklenburg County, June 24, 1861, for six months. Present or accounted for until mustered out November 12-13, 1861.

SLOAN, W. E., Private
Enlisted in Mecklenburg County, June 24, 1861, for six months. Present or accounted for until mustered out November 12-13, 1861.

SMITH, J. P., Private
Enlisted in Mecklenburg County at age 22, April 27, 1861, for six months. Present or accounted for until mustered out November 12-13, 1861.

SMITH, THOMAS McG., Private
Enlisted in Mecklenburg County, July 15, 1861, for six months. Present or accounted for until mustered out November 12-13, 1861.

SPRINKLE, WILLIAM J., Private
Enlisted in Mecklenburg County, June 24, 1861, for six months. Present or accounted for until mustered out November 12-13, 1861.

SQUIERS, M. D., Private
Enlisted in Mecklenburg County, June 24, 1861, for six months. Present or accounted for until mustered out November 12-13, 1861.

SQUIRES, JOHN B., Private
Enlisted in Mecklenburg County at age 22, April 16, 1861, for six months. Present or accounted for until mustered out November 12-13, 1861.

STANFORD, CHARLES L., Private
Enlisted in Mecklenburg County, June 24, 1861, for six months. Present or accounted for until mustered out November 12-13, 1861.

STEELE, MANLINS D., Private
Enlisted in Mecklenburg County at age 27, May 1, 1861, for six months. Present or accounted for until mustered out November 12-13, 1861.

STITT, WILLIAM E., Private
Enlisted in Mecklenburg County, June 24, 1861, for six months. Present or accounted for until mustered out November 12-13, 1861.

STOWE, JOHN, Private
Enlisted in Mecklenburg County at age 29, May 1, 1861, for six months. Present or accounted for until mustered out November 12-13, 1861.

TATE, ABNER H., Private
Enlisted in Mecklenburg County at age 19, April 16, 1861, for six months. Present or accounted for until mustered out November 12-13, 1861.

TATE, H. H., Private
Enlisted at Yorktown, Virginia, June 24, 1861, for six months. Present or accounted for until mustered out November 12-13, 1861.

TATE, THOMAS A., Private
Born in Guilford County and enlisted at Yorktown, Virginia, at age 18, June 24, 1861, for six months. Present or accounted for until discharged on September 24, 1861, by reason of "inability on account of ill health."

TAYLOR, D. B., Private
Enlisted in Mecklenburg County May 1, 1861, for six months. Present or accounted for until mustered out November 12-13, 1861.

TAYLOR, J. W., Private
Enlisted in Mecklenburg County at age 22, May 1, 1861, for six months. Present or accounted for until mustered out November 12-13, 1861.

THOMPSON, ROBERT, Private
Enlisted in Mecklenburg County at age 33, May 1, 1861, for six months. Present or accounted for until mustered out November 12-13, 1861.

TIDDY, J. F., Private
Enlisted in Mecklenburg County at age 22, April 16, 1861, for six months. Present or accounted for until mustered out November 12-13, 1861. Later enlisted in Company A, 33rd Regiment N. C. Troops.

TIDDY, R. N., Private
Enlisted in Mecklenburg County at age 26, April 16, 1861, for six months. Present or accounted for until mustered out November 12-13, 1861.

TORRANCE, WILLIAM, Private
Enlisted in Mecklenburg County at age 20, May 1, 1861, for six months. Present or accounted for until mustered out November 12-13, 1861.

TORRENCE, GEORGE, Private
Enlisted in Mecklenburg County at age 18, May 1, 1861, for six months. Present or accounted for until mustered out November 12-13, 1861.

TREDEWICK, JOHN R., Private
Enlisted in Mecklenburg County at age 24, May 1, 1861, for six months. Present or accounted for until mustered out November 12-13, 1861.

TREDEWICK, W. S., Private
Enlisted in Mecklenburg County, June 24, 1861, for six months. Present or accounted for until mustered out November 12-13, 1861.

WAGNER, J. W., Private
Enlisted in Mecklenburg County, April 17, 1861, for six months. Present or accounted for until mustered out November 12-13, 1861.

WALKER, E. M., Private
Enlisted in Mecklenburg County, June 24, 1861, for six months. Present or accounted for until mustered out November 12-13, 1861.

WARWICK, JAMES M., Private
Enlisted in Mecklenburg County, June 24, 1861, for six months. Present or accounted for until mustered out November 12-13, 1861. Later enlisted in Company F, 49th Regiment N. C. Troops.

WAYT, JOHN HENRY, Private
Enlisted in Wake County at age 29, April 17, 1861, for six months. Transferred to the Field and Staff of this regiment upon appointment as Captain, A. C. S., April 24, 1861.

WICKS, J. L., Private
Enlisted in Mecklenburg County, June 24, 1861, for six months. Present or accounted for until mustered out November 12-13, 1861.

WILEY, W. J., Private
Enlisted in Mecklenburg County at age 23, April 17, 1861, for six months. Present or accounted for until mustered out November 12-13, 1861.

WILLIAMS, W. S., Private
Enlisted in Mecklenburg County at age 24, April 16, 1861, for six months. Present or accounted for until mustered out November 12-13, 1861.

WILLIAMSON, J. W., Private
Enlisted in Mecklenburg County, June 24, 1861, for six months. Present or accounted for until mustered out November 12-13, 1861.

WILSON, B. FRANKLIN, Private
Enlisted in Mecklenburg County, June 24, 1861, for six months. Present or accounted for until mustered out November 12-13, 1861. Later enlisted in Company K, 42nd Regiment N. C. Troops.

WINDLE, M. F., Sergeant
Enlisted in Mecklenburg County at age 26, April 16, 1861, for six months. Mustered in as Sergeant. Present or accounted for until mustered out November 12-13, 1861.

YOUNG, J. W., Private
Enlisted in Mecklenburg County, June 24, 1861, for six months. Present or accounted for until mustered out November 12-13, 1861.

COMPANY C

This company, known as the "Charlotte Grays," enrolled for active service at Charlotte, Mecklenburg County, on April 20, 1861. It was ordered to Raleigh and was assigned to the regiment on April 29. On May 13, 1861, it was mustered into state service as Company C of this regiment. After that date the company functioned as a part of the regiment, and its history for the war period is recorded as a part of the regimental history.

The information contained in the following roster of the company was compiled principally from company muster rolls which included the muster-in roll dated August 31, 1861, covering the period May 13-August 31, 1861, and muster rolls for the periods of April 20-May 13, 1861; May 13-June 30, 1861; and July-August, 1861. No muster rolls were found for the period after August, 1861. In addition to the company muster rolls, Roll of Honor records, receipt rolls, hospital records, prisoner of war records, and other primary records, supplemented by state pension applications, United Daughters of the Confederacy records, and postwar rosters and histories, all provided useful information.

OFFICERS
CAPTAIN

ROSS, EGBERT A.
Resided in Mecklenburg County where he enlisted at age 19, April 25, 1861, for six months. Appointed Captain to rank from February 1, 1861. Present or accounted for until mustered out November 12-13, 1861. Later appointed Major and assigned to the Field and Staff, 11th Regiment N. C. Troops (1st Regiment N. C. Volunteers).

LIEUTENANTS

ALEXANDER, CHARLES W., 3rd Lieutenant
Resided in Mecklenburg County where he enlisted at age 23, April 25, 1861, for six months. Appointed 3rd Lieutenant to rank from February 1, 1861. Present or accounted for until mustered out November 12-13, 1861. Later enlisted in Company A, 11th Regiment N. C. Troops (1st Regiment N. C. Volunteers).

COHEN, EDWARD B., 1st Lieutenant
Resided in Mecklenburg County where he enlisted at age 20, April 25, 1861, for six months. Appointed 1st Lieutenant to rank from February 1, 1861. Present or accounted for until mustered out November 12-13, 1861.

TROTTER, THOMAS B., 2nd Lieutenant
Resided in Mecklenburg County where he enlisted at age 21, April 25, 1861, for six months. Appointed 2nd Lieutenant to rank from February 1, 1861. Present or accounted for until mustered out November 12-13, 1861.

NONCOMMISSIONED OFFICERS AND PRIVATES

ADAMS, LINSEY, Private
Enlisted in Mecklenburg County at age 19, April 20, 1861, for six months. Present or accounted for until mustered out November 12-13, 1861.

ALEXANDER, F. E., Private
Enlisted at Yorktown, Virginia, at age 22, April 25,

1861, for six months. Present or accounted for until mustered out November 12-13, 1861.

ALEXANDER, J. G., Private
Enlisted at Yorktown, Virginia, at age 20, July 25, 1861, for six months. Present or accounted for until mustered out November 12-13, 1861.

ALEXANDER, M. R., Private
Enlisted in Mecklenburg County at age 23, April 20, 1861, for six months. Present or accounted for until mustered out November 12-13, 1861. Later enlisted in Company A, 11th Regiment N. C. Troops (1st Regiment N. C. Volunteers).

ALEXANDER, THOMAS A., Private
Enlisted at Yorktown, Virginia, at age 18, June 24, 1861, for six months. Present or accounted for until mustered out November 12-13, 1861.

ALEXANDER, W. R., Private
Enlisted in Mecklenburg County at age 23, April 25, 1861, for six months. Present or accounted for until mustered out November 12-13, 1861. Later enlisted in Company I, 60th Regiment N. C. Troops.

ARDREY, J. P., Private
Enlisted at Yorktown, Virginia, at age 23, July 1, 1861, for six months. Present or accounted for until mustered out November 12-13, 1861.

ARDREY, WILLIAM ERSKINE, Private
Enlisted at Yorktown, Virginia, at age 21, June 24, 1861, for six months. Present or accounted for until mustered out November 12-13, 1861. Later enlisted in Company K, 30th Regiment N. C. Troops.

BEHRENDS, L., Private
Enlisted at Yorktown, Virginia, at age 20, June 24, 1861, for six months. Present or accounted for until mustered out November 12-13, 1861.

BERRYHILL, W. G., Sergeant
Enlisted in Mecklenburg County at age 19, April 25, 1861, for six months. Mustered in as Sergeant. Present or accounted for until mustered out November 12-13, 1861.

BOYD, T. B., Private
Enlisted in Mecklenburg County at age 23, April 20, 1861, for six months. Present or accounted for until transferred to the Field and Staff of this regiment upon appointment as Hospital Steward August 28, 1861.

BRINGLE, D. L., Sergeant
Enlisted in Mecklenburg County at age 22, April 25, 1861, for six months. Mustered in as Sergeant. Present or accounted for until mustered out November 12-13, 1861.

BRITTON, E. F., Private
Enlisted in Mecklenburg County at age 17, April 20, 1861, for six months. Present or accounted for until mustered out November 12-13, 1861.

BROWN, A. H., Private
Enlisted in Mecklenburg County at age 18, April 20, 1861, for six months. Died at Yorktown, Virginia, October 22, 1861.

BROWN, W. H., Private
Enlisted at Yorktown, Virginia, at age 23, June 24, 1861, for six months. Present or accounted for until mustered out November 12-13, 1861.

BROWN, W. J., Private
Enlisted in Mecklenburg County at age 18, April 20, 1861, for six months. Present or accounted for until mustered out November 12-13, 1861.

CALDER, WILLIAM, Private
Enlisted in Mecklenburg County at age 17, April 20, 1861, for six months. Present or accounted for until mustered out November 12-13, 1861.

CALDWELL, J. S. P., Private
Enlisted at Yorktown, Virginia, at age 24, June 24, 1861, for six months. Present or accounted for until mustered out November 12-13, 1861.

CAMPBELL, T. J., Private
Enlisted at Yorktown, Virginia, at age 19, June 24, 1861, for six months. Present or accounted for until mustered out November 12-13, 1861.

CATHEY, WILLIAM, Private
Enlisted at Yorktown, Virginia, at age 21, June 24, 1861, for six months. Present or accounted for until mustered out November 12-13, 1861.

CLENDENEN, JOSEPH W., Private
Enlisted at Yorktown, Virginia, at age 17, June 24, 1861, for six months. Died at Yorktown, July 17, 19, 1861.

COLLINS, J. F., Private
Enlisted at Yorktown, Virginia, at age 22, July 8, 1861, for six months. Present or accounted for until mustered out November 12-13, 1861.

COWAN, T. B., Private
Enlisted at Yorktown, Virginia, at age 23, June 24, 1861, for six months. Died September 5, 10, 1861.

CROWSON, J. C., Private
Enlisted at Yorktown, Virginia, at age 21, June 24, 1861, for six months. Present or accounted for until mustered out November 12-13, 1861.

DAVIDSON, J. P. A., Private
Enlisted in Mecklenburg County at age 18, April 20, 1861, for six months. Present or accounted for until he was discharged September 17, 1861.

DAVIS, T. G., Private
Enlisted in Mecklenburg County at age 23, April 20, 1861, for six months. Present or accounted for until mustered out November 12-13, 1861.

DOWNS, J. T., Private
Enlisted in Mecklenburg County at age 20, April 20, 1861, for six months. Present or accounted for until mustered out November 12-13, 1861. Later enlisted in Company F, 63rd Regiment N. C. Troops (5th Regiment N. C. Cavalry).

DOWNS, L. M., Private
Enlisted at Yorktown, Virginia, at age 22, June 24, 1861, for six months. Present or accounted for until mustered out November 12-13, 1861.

DUNN, J. R., Private
Enlisted at Yorktown, Virginia, at age 28, July 1, 1861, for six months. Present or accounted for

until mustered out November 12-13, 1861.

EARNHEARDT, J. M., Private
Enlisted in Mecklenburg County at age 19, April 20, 1861, for six months. Present or accounted for until mustered out November 12-13, 1861.

ELLIOTT, J. A., Private
Enlisted at Yorktown, Virginia, at age 18, June 24, 1861, for six months. Present or accounted for until mustered out November 12-13, 1861.

ELLIOTT, S. H., Private
Enlisted at Yorktown, Virginia, at age 17, June 24, 1861, for six months. Present or accounted for until mustered out November 12-13, 1861. Later enlisted in Company I, 37th Regiment N. C. Troops.

ELMS, JOHN P., Sergeant
Enlisted in Mecklenburg County at age 23, April 20, 1861, for six months. Mustered in as Sergeant. Present or accounted for until mustered out November 12-13, 1861. Later enlisted in Company I, 37th Regiment N. C. Troops.

ELMS, WILLIAM D., Corporal
Enlisted in Mecklenburg County at age 20, April 20, 1861, for six months. Mustered in as Corporal. Present or accounted for until mustered out November 12-13, 1861. Later enlisted in Company I, 37th Regiment N. C. Troops.

ENGLE, JONAS, Private
Enlisted in Mecklenburg County at age 20, April 20, 1861, for six months. Present or accounted for until mustered out November 12-13, 1861.

EZZEL, J. A., Private
Enlisted at Yorktown, Virginia, at age 17, June 24, 1861, for six months. Present or accounted for until mustered out November 12-13, 1861.

EZZEL, M. F., Private
Enlisted at Yorktown, Virginia, at age 17, June 24, 1861, for six months. Present or accounted for until mustered out November 12-13, 1861.

FLOW, I. H., Private
Enlisted at Richmond, Virginia, at age 21, May 20, 1861, for six months. Present or accounted for until mustered out November 12-13, 1861.

FORE, JAMES, Private
Enlisted at age 28, April 20, 1861, for six months.

FRAZIER, ISAAC, Private
Enlisted at Yorktown, Virginia, at age 19, June 24, 1861, for six months. Present or accounted for until mustered out November 12-13, 1861.

GALLOWAY, J. S., Private
Enlisted at Yorktown, Virginia, at age 24, July 25, 1861, for six months. Present or accounted for until mustered out November 12-13, 1861.

GIBSON, J. A., Private
Enlisted in Mecklenburg County at age 17, April 25, 1861, for six months. Present or accounted for until mustered out November 12-13, 1861.

GILLESPIE, R. L., Private
Enlisted at Yorktown, Virginia, at age 26, July 8, 1861, for six months. Present or accounted for until discharged September 27, 1861.

GLENN, D. P., Private
Enlisted in Mecklenburg County at age 20, April 25, 1861, for six months. Present or accounted for until mustered out November 12-13, 1861.

GRAY, A. N., Private
Enlisted at Yorktown, Virginia, at age 18, June 12, 1861, for six months. Present or accounted for until mustered out November 12-13, 1861.

GRIBBLE, J. R., Private
Enlisted at Yorktown, Virginia, at age 21, June 24, 1861, for six months. Present or accounted for until mustered out November 12-13, 1861.

GRIER, J. C., Private
Enlisted at Yorktown, Virginia, at age 22, June 24, 1861, for six months. Present or accounted for until mustered out November 12-13, 1861.

GRIER, J. M., Private
Enlisted at Yorktown, Virginia, at age 17, June 24, 1861, for six months. Present or accounted for until mustered out November 12-13, 1861.

GRIER, R. H., Private
Enlisted in Mecklenburg County at age 19, April 20, 1861, for six months. Present or accounted for until mustered out November 12-13, 1861.

HALL, D. N., Private
Enlisted at Yorktown, Virginia, at age 22, June 24, 1861, for six months. Present or accounted for until mustered out November 12-13, 1861.

HAND, R. H., Private
Enlisted in Mecklenburg County at age 21, April 20, 1861, for six months. Present or accounted for until mustered out November 12-13, 1861. Later enlisted in Company A, 11th Regiment N. C. Troops (1st Regiment N. C. Volunteers).

HARKEY, J. C., Private
Enlisted at Yorktown, Virginia, at age 23, July 8, 1861, for six months. Present or accounted for until mustered out November 12-13, 1861.

HARKEY, T. M., Private
Enlisted in Mecklenburg County at age 21, April 20, 1861, for six months. Present or accounted for until mustered out November 12-13, 1861.

HARRIS, W. C., Private
Enlisted at Yorktown, Virginia, at age 25, July 25, 1861, for six months. Present or accounted for until discharged September 27, 1861.

HARRIS, W. O., Private
Enlisted at Yorktown, Virginia, at age 23, July 25, 1861, for six months. Present or accounted for until mustered out November 12-13, 1861.

HASKELL, J. T., Private
Enlisted in Mecklenburg County at age 20, April 20, 1861, for six months. Present or accounted for until mustered out November 12-13, 1861.

HENDERSON, L. P., Private
Enlisted at Yorktown, Virginia, at age 21, July 8, 1861, for six months. Died at Yorktown on August 16, 1861.

HERRING, G. T., Private
Enlisted in Mecklenburg County at age 18, April 20, 1861, for six months. Present or accounted for until mustered out November 12-13, 1861. Later

enlisted in Company A, 11th Regiment N. C. Troops (1st Regiment N. C. Volunteers).

HILL, H. H., Private
Enlisted at Yorktown, Virginia, at age 20, June 24, 1861, for six months. Present or accounted for until mustered out November 12-13, 1861.

HILL, J. C., Private
Enlisted in Mecklenburg County at age 25, April 20, 1861, for six months. Present or accounted for until mustered out November 12-13, 1861.

HILL, WILLIAM JAMES, Private
Resided in Cabarrus County and enlisted in Mecklenburg County at age 20, April 20, 1861, for six months. Present or accounted for until mustered out November 12-13, 1861.

HOLMES, T. L., Private
Enlisted in Mecklenburg County at age 21, April 20, 1861, for six months. Present or accounted for until mustered out November 12-13, 1861.

HOLTON, T. F., Private
Enlisted in Mecklenburg County at age 22, April 20, 1861, for six months. Present or accounted for until mustered out November 12-13, 1861.

HOUSTON, H. C., Private
Enlisted in Mecklenburg County at age 20, April 20, 1861, for six months. Present or accounted for until mustered out November 12-13, 1861.

HOWARD, THOMAS, Private
Enlisted at Yorktown, Virginia, at age 25, June 24, 1861, for six months. Present or accounted for until mustered out November 12-13, 1861.

HOWARD, W. D., Private
Enlisted at Yorktown, Virginia, at age 21, June 24, 1861, for six months. Present or accounted for until mustered out November 12-13, 1861.

HOWEY, G. W., Private
Enlisted at Yorktown, Virginia, at age 22, July 1, 1861, for six months. Present or accounted for until mustered out November 12-13, 1861.

HOWSER, W. T., Private
Enlisted in Mecklenburg County at age 18, April 20, 1861, for six months. Present or accounted for until mustered out November 12-13, 1861.

HUTCHINSON, C. N., Private
Enlisted at Yorktown, Virginia, at age 16, June 24, 1861, for six months. Present or accounted for until mustered out November 12-13, 1861.

HUTCHINSON, J. M., Private
Enlisted in Mecklenburg County at age 18, April 20, 1861, for six months. Present or accounted for until mustered out November 12-13, 1861.

HYMANS, S., Private
Enlisted in Mecklenburg County at age 20, April 20, 1861, for six months. Present or accounted for until mustered out November 12-13, 1861.

ICEHOWER, W. S., Private
Enlisted at Yorktown, Virginia, at age 18, June 12, 1861, for six months. Present or accounted for until mustered out November 12-13, 1861.

INGOLD, E. P., Private
Enlisted in Mecklenburg County at age 19, April

20, 1861, for six months. Present or accounted for until mustered out November 12-13, 1861.

ISRAEL, JOHN R., Private
Enlisted in Mecklenburg County at age 24, April 20, 1861, for six months. Present or accounted for until mustered out November 12-13, 1861.

JOHNSON, J. W., Private
Enlisted in Mecklenburg County at age 18, April 20, 1861, for six months. Present or accounted for until mustered out November 12-13, 1861.

JOHNSON, T. N., Private
Enlisted at Yorktown, Virginia, at age 20, July 25, 1861, for six months. Present or accounted for until mustered out November 12-13, 1861.

KATZ, J., Private
Enlisted in Mecklenburg County at age 20, April 20, 1861, for six months. Present or accounted for until mustered out November 12-13, 1861.

KENAN, ROBERT, Private
Enlisted at Yorktown, Virginia, at age 25, July 8, 1861, for six months. Present or accounted for until mustered out November 12-13, 1861.

KENNEDY, WILLIAM, Private
Enlisted at Yorktown, Virginia, at age 20, July 25, 1861, for six months. Present or accounted for until mustered out November 12-13, 1861.

KINSEY, J. A., Private
Enlisted in Mecklenburg County at age 21, April 20, 1861, for six months. Present or accounted for until mustered out November 12-13, 1861.

KISTLER, W. H., Private
Enlisted in Mecklenburg County at age 18, April 20, 1861, for six months. Present or accounted for until mustered out November 12-13, 1861.

KNOX, J. H., Private
Enlisted at Yorktown, Virginia, at age 22, June 24, 1861, for six months. Present or accounted for until mustered out November 12-13, 1861.

KNOX, JAMES, Private
Enlisted at Yorktown, Virginia, August 10, 1861, for six months. Present or accounted for until mustered out November 12-13, 1861.

LEON, LEWIS, Private
Enlisted in Mecklenburg County at age 19, April 20, 1861, for six months. Present or accounted for until mustered out November 12-13, 1861. Later enlisted in Company B, 53rd Regiment N. C. Troops.

LEOPOLD, J., Private
Enlisted at Yorktown, Virginia, at age 18, June 12, 1861, for six months. Present or accounted for until mustered out November 12-13, 1861.

LEVI, I. C., Private
Enlisted in Mecklenburg County at age 20, April 20, 1861, for six months. Present or accounted for until mustered out November 12-13, 1861.

McCORKLE, J. G., Sergeant
Enlisted in Mecklenburg County at age 21, April 20, 1861, for six months. Mustered in as Sergeant. Present or accounted for until mustered out November 12-13, 1861. Later enlisted in Company

E, 11th Regiment N. C. Troops (1st Regiment N. C. Volunteers).

McDONALD, DAVID W., Private
Resided in Mecklenburg County where he enlisted at age 19, April 20, 1861, for six months. Present or accounted for until mustered out November 12-13, 1861. Later enlisted in Company B, 11th Regiment N. C. Troops (1st Regiment N. C. Volunteers).

McDONALD, JOHN H., Private
Enlisted at Yorktown, Virginia, at age 17, June 24, 1861, for six months. Present or accounted for until mustered out November 12-13, 1861. Later enlisted in Company E, 11th Regiment N. C. Troops (1st Regiment N. C. Volunteers).

McELROY, S. J., Private
Enlisted at Yorktown, Virginia, at age 21, July 8, 1861, for six months. Present or accounted for until mustered out November 12-13, 1861.

McGINN, T. F., Private
Enlisted in Mecklenburg County at age 21, April 20, 1861, for six months. Present or accounted for until mustered out November 12-13, 1861.

McKEEVER, WILLIAM, Private
Enlisted in Mecklenburg County at age 24, April 20, 1861, for six months. Present or accounted for until mustered out November 12-13, 1861.

McKINLEY, JOHN, Private
Enlisted in Mecklenburg County at age 22, April 25, 1861, for six months. Present or accounted for until mustered out November 12-13, 1861.

MONTEITH, M. O., Private
Enlisted at Yorktown, Virginia, at age 27, June 24, 1861, for six months. Present or accounted for until mustered out November 12-13, 1861.

MONTEITH, R. J., Private
Enlisted at Yorktown, Virginia, at age 24, June 24, 1861, for six months. Present or accounted for until mustered out November 12-13, 1861.

MONTGOMERY, J. P. C., Private
Enlisted at Yorktown, Virginia, August 3, 1861, for six months. Present or accounted for until mustered out November 12-13, 1861.

MOYLE, H., Private
Enlisted in Mecklenburg County at age 16, April 20, 1861, for six months. Present or accounted for until mustered out November 12-13, 1861.

NEAL, P. A., Private
Enlisted at Yorktown, Virginia, at age 22, June 24, 1861, for six months. Present or accounted for until mustered out November 12-13, 1861.

NEIL, L. M., Private
Enlisted at Yorktown, Virginia, at age 18, June 24, 1861, for six months. Present or accounted for until mustered out November 12-13, 1861.

NEIL, S. R., Private
Enlisted at Yorktown, Virginia, at age 19, June 24, 1861, for six months. Present or accounted for until mustered out November 12-13, 1861.

NEIL, W. B., Private
Enlisted at Yorktown, Virginia, at age 27, June

24, 1861, for six months. Present or accounted for until mustered out November 12-13, 1861.

NEILY, T. W., Private
Enlisted at Yorktown, Virginia, at age 18, June 24, 1861, for six months. Present or accounted for until mustered out November 12-13, 1861.

NORMENT, ISAAC, Private
Enlisted at Yorktown, Virginia, at age 22, June 24, 1861, for six months. Present or accounted for until mustered out November 12-13, 1861.

NORMENT, JOHN, Private
Enlisted at Yorktown, Virginia, at age 19, June 24, 1861, for six months. Present or accounted for until mustered out November 12-13, 1861.

OPPENHEIM, S., Private
Enlisted in Mecklenburg County at age 21, April 20, 1861, for six months. Present or accounted for until mustered out November 12-13, 1861.

ORMAN, J. D., Private
Enlisted in Mecklenburg County at age 20, April 20, 1861, for six months. Died at Yorktown, Virginia. Date of death reported as July 22 and August 3, 1861.

ORR, J. F., Private
Enlisted in Mecklenburg County at age 28, April 20, 1861, for six months. Present or accounted for until mustered out November 12-13, 1861.

ORR, N. C. H., Private
Enlisted at Yorktown, Virginia, at age 18, July 25, 1861, for six months. Present or accounted for until mustered out November 12-13, 1861.

OSBORNE, J. L., Private
Enlisted in Mecklenburg County at age 20, April 20, 1861, for six months. Present or accounted for until mustered out November 12-13, 1861.

PETTIS, M., Private
Enlisted in Mecklenburg County at age 23, April 20, 1861, for six months. Present or accounted for until mustered out November 12-13, 1861.

PHILLIPS, S. A., Private
Enlisted in Mecklenburg County at age 21, April 20, 1861, for six months. Present or accounted for until mustered out November 12-13, 1861.

PORTER, R. A., Private
Enlisted at Yorktown, Virginia, at age 20, June 24, 1861, for six months. Present or accounted for until mustered out November 12-13, 1861.

PORTER, W. R., Private
Enlisted in Mecklenburg County at age 17, April 20, 1861, for six months. Present or accounted for until mustered out November 12-13, 1861.

POTTS, J. G., Private
Enlisted at Yorktown, Virginia, at age 18, June 24, 1861, for six months. Present or accounted for until mustered out November 12-13, 1861.

POTTS, L. A., Private
Enlisted at Yorktown, Virginia, at age 19, July 8, 1861, for six months. Present or accounted for until mustered out November 12-13, 1861. Later enlisted in Company C, 37th Regiment N. C. Troops.

POTTS, WILLIAM MARCELLUS, Private
Enlisted at Yorktown, Virginia, at age 16, June 24, 1861, for six months. Present or accounted for until mustered out November 12-13, 1861. Later enlisted in Company F, 9th Regiment N. C. State Troops (1st Regiment N. C. Cavalry).

QUERY, C. M., Private
Enlisted in Mecklenburg County at age 20, April 20, 1861, for six months. Present or accounted for until mustered out November 12-13, 1861.

RAY, D. B., Private
Enlisted at Yorktown, Virginia, at age 26, July 25, 1861, for six months. Present or accounted for until mustered out November 12-13, 1861.

REA, J. K., Private
Enlisted at Yorktown, Virginia, at age 28, June 24, 1861, for six months. Died at Yorktown, September 20, 1861.

RUDDOCK, T. C., Private
Enlisted at Yorktown, Virginia, at age 20, June 24, 1861, for six months. Present or accounted for until mustered out November 12-13, 1861.

SAMPLE, D. I., Private
Enlisted at Yorktown, Virginia, at age 23, July 8, 1861, for six months. Present or accounted for until mustered out November 12-13, 1861.

SAMPLE, I. W., Private
Enlisted at Yorktown, Virginia, at age 22, July 8, 1861, for six months. Present or accounted for until mustered out November 12-13, 1861.

SAMPLE, JOHN W., Private
Enlisted at Yorktown, Virginia, at age 21, July 8, 1861, for six months. Present or accounted for until he was discharged September 24, 1861. Later enlisted in Company B, 53rd Regiment N. C. Troops.

SAVILL, J. M., Private
Enlisted at Yorktown, Virginia, at age 21, June 24, 1861, for six months. Present or accounted for until mustered out November 12-13, 1861. Later enlisted in Company H, 11th Regiment N. C. Troops (1st Regiment N. C. Volunteers).

SAVILL, W. H., Private
Enlisted at Yorktown, Virginia, at age 22, June 24, 1861, for six months. Present or accounted for until mustered out November 12-13, 1861.

SIMPSON, ROBERT F., Private
Enlisted at Yorktown, Virginia, at age 29, June 24, 1861, for six months. Present or accounted for until mustered out November 12-13, 1861.

SIMS, JAMES MONROE, Private
Resided in Cabarrus County and enlisted in Mecklenburg County at age 20, April 20, 1861, for six months. Present or accounted for until mustered out November 12-13, 1861. Later enlisted in Company A, 11th Regiment N.C. Troops (1st Regiment N. C. Volunteers).

SIZER, W. E., Private
Enlisted in Mecklenburg County at age 20, April 20, 1861, for six months. Present or accounted for until mustered out November 12-13, 1861.

SMITH, C. E., Private
Enlisted in Mecklenburg County at age 20, April 20, 1861, for six months. Present or accounted for until mustered out November 12-13, 1861.

SMITH, MOSES H., Private
Enlisted at Yorktown, Virginia, at age 19, June 24, 1861, for six months. Present or accounted for until mustered out November 12-13, 1861.

SMITH, S. D., Private
Enlisted at Yorktown, Virginia, at age 32, June 24, 1861, for six months. Present or accounted for until mustered out November 12-13, 1861.

SMITH, WILLIAM J. B., Private
Enlisted at Yorktown, Virginia, at age 24, June 24, 1861, for six months. Present or accounted for until mustered out November 12-13, 1861.

SPRINGS, R. A., Private
Enlisted in Mecklenburg County at age 17, April 20, 1861, for six months. Present or accounted for until mustered out November 12-13, 1861.

STALEY, C. R., 1st Sergeant
Enlisted in Mecklenburg County at age 20, April 20, 1861, for six months. Mustered in as 1st Sergeant. Present or accounted for until mustered out November 12-13, 1861.

STEELE, WILLIAM, Private
Enlisted in Mecklenburg County at age 20, April 20, 1861, for six months. Present or accounted for until mustered out November 12-13, 1861.

STONE, W. D., Private
Enlisted in Mecklenburg County at age 25, April 20, 1861, for six months. Present or accounted for until mustered out November 12-13, 1861.

STOWE, J. M., Private
Enlisted in Mecklenburg County at age 18, April 20, 1861, for six months. Present or accounted for until mustered out November 12-13, 1861.

TATE, H. A., Private
Enlisted in Mecklenburg County at age 20, April 20, 1861, for six months. Present or accounted for until mustered out November 12-13, 1861. Later enlisted in Company D, 11th Regiment N. C. Troops (1st Regiment N. C. Volunteers).

TAYLOR, W. B., Corporal
Enlisted in Mecklenburg County at age 21, April 20, 1861, for six months. Mustered in as Corporal. Present or accounted for until mustered out November 12-13, 1861. Later enlisted in Company A, 11th Regiment N. C. Troops (1st Regiment N. C. Volunteers).

TERRIS, H., Corporal
Enlisted in Mecklenburg County at age 18, April 20, 1861, for six months. Mustered in as Corporal. Present or accounted for until mustered out November 12-13, 1861.

TODD, S. E., Private
Enlisted in Mecklenburg County at age 19, April 20, 1861, for six months. Present or accounted for until mustered out November 12-13, 1861.

TODD, WILLIAM, Private
Enlisted in Mecklenburg County at age 19, April

20, 1861, for six months. Present or accounted for until mustered out November 12-13, 1861.

TRELOAR, J. W., Private
Enlisted in Mecklenburg County at age 16, April 20, 1861, for six months. Present or accounted for until mustered out November 12-13, 1861.

WATT, B. F., Private
Enlisted at Yorktown, Virginia, at age 19, June 24, 1861, for six months. Present or accounted for until mustered out November 12-13, 1861.

WATT, C. B., Private
Enlisted in Mecklenburg County at age 17, April 20, 1861, for six months. Present or accounted for until mustered out November 12-13, 1861. Later enlisted in Company B, 4th Regiment South Carolina Cavalry.

WILEY, J., Private
Enlisted at Yorktown, Virginia, at age 18, June 24, 1861, for six months. Present or accounted for until mustered out November 12-13, 1861.

WINGATE, C. C., Private
Enlisted at Yorktown, Virginia, at age 19, June 24, 1861, for six months. Present or accounted for until mustered out November 12-13, 1861.

WOLFE, T. D., Private
Enlisted at Yorktown, Virginia, at age 19, June 24, 1861, for six months. Present or accounted for until mustered out November 12-13, 1861.

WOLFE, T. J., Private
Enlisted at Yorktown, Virginia, at age 17, June 24, 1861, for six months. Discharged September 15, 1861.

WOLFFE, GEORGE, Corporal
Enlisted in Mecklenburg County at age 20, April 20, 1861, for six months. Mustered in as Corporal. Present or accounted for until mustered out November 12-13, 1861.

COMPANY D

This company, known as the "Orange Light Infantry," began organizing on April 6, 1861, and enrolled for active service at Chapel Hill, Orange County, on April 22, 1861. The next day it was ordered to Raleigh, where it arrived on April 27 and was mustered into state service on May 13, 1861, as Company D of this regiment. After that date the company functioned as a part of the regiment, and its history for the war period is recorded as a part of the regimental history.

The information contained in the following roster of the company was compiled principally from company muster rolls which included the muster-in roll dated August 31, 1861, covering the period May 13-August 31, 1861, and muster rolls for the periods of April 6-May 13, 1861; May 13-June 30, 1861; and July-August, 1861. No muster rolls were found for the period after August, 1861. In addition to the company muster rolls, Roll of Honor records, receipt rolls, hospital records, prisoner of war records, and other primary records, supplemented by state pension applications, United Daughters of the Confederacy records, and postwar rosters and histories, all provided useful information.

OFFICERS
CAPTAIN
ASHE, RICHARD J.
Resided in Orange County where he enlisted at age 39, April 6, 1861, for six months. Appointed Captain to rank from date of enlistment. Present or accounted for until mustered out November 12-13, 1861.

LIEUTENANTS
JENNINGS, JAMES R., 1st Lieutenant
Enlisted in Orange County at age 33, April 22, 1861, for six months. Appointed 1st Lieutenant to rank from April 29, 1861. Present or accounted for until mustered out November 12-13, 1861. Later enlisted in Company G, 11th Regiment N. C. Troops (1st Regiment N. C. Volunteers).

MALLETT, RICHARDSON, Jr., 3rd Lieutenant
Enlisted in Orange County at age 21, April 22, 1861, for six months. Appointed 3rd Lieutenant to rank from April 29, 1861. Present or accounted for until mustered out November 12-13, 1861. Later appointed Adjutant and attached to the Field and Staff of the 46th Regiment N. C. Troops.

SAUNDERS, RICHARD B., 2nd Lieutenant
Enlisted in Orange County at age 27, April 22, 1861, for six months. Appointed 2nd Lieutenant to rank from date of enlistment. Present or accounted for until mustered out November 12-13, 1861. Later served in the Quartermaster Department.

NONCOMMISSIONED OFFICERS AND PRIVATES
ANDREWS, JOHN, Private
Enlisted in Orange County at age 16, April 22, 1861, for six months. Present or accounted for until mustered out November 12-13, 1861.

ATWATER, EDMOND W., Private
Enlisted in Orange County at age 19, April 16, 1861, for six months. Present or accounted for until mustered out November 12-13, 1861.

ATWATER, JOHN, Private
Enlisted in Orange County, April 22, 1861, for six months. Present or accounted for until mustered out November 12-13, 1861.

ATWATER, JOHN W., Private
Enlisted in Orange County at age 20, April 6, 1861, for six months. Present or accounted for until mustered out November 12-13, 1861.

ATWATER, SIDNEY B., Private
Enlisted in Orange County, June 28, 1861, for six months. Died in hospital October 19, 1861.

BALDWIN, LUCIAN F., Private
Enlisted in Orange County, June 28, 1861, for six months. Present or accounted for until mustered out November 12-13, 1861.

BALDWIN, WILLIAM, Private
Enlisted in Orange County at age 25, April 6, 1861.

for six months. Died in hospital at Yorktown, Virginia, August 7, 1861, of "brain fever."

BARBEE, JOHN, Private
Enlisted in Orange County at age 24, April 6, 1861, for six months. Present or accounted for until mustered out November 12-13, 1861.

BENNETT, JEHU, Private
Enlisted in Orange County at age 26, April 6, 1861, for six months. Present or accounted for until mustered out November 12-13, 1861.

BLACKWOOD, JOHN, Private
Enlisted in Orange County at age 18, April 6, 1861, for six months. Present or accounted for until mustered out November 12-13, 1861.

BLACKWOOD, PHILO, Private
Enlisted in Orange County at age 19, April 6, 1861, for six months. Present or accounted for until mustered out November 12-13, 1861.

BLAKE, JAMES S., Private
Enlisted in Orange County at age 24, April 6, 1861, for six months. Present or accounted for until mustered out November 12-13, 1861.

BREWER, STEPHEN, Private
Enlisted in Orange County at age 23, April 6, 1861, for six months. Present or accounted for until mustered out November 12-13, 1861.

BROCKWELL, JOHN, Private
Enlisted in Orange County at age 22, April 6, 1861, for six months. Present or accounted for until mustered out November 12-13, 1861.

CAMPBELL, ROBERT, Private
Enlisted in Orange County, April 6, 1861, for six months. Present or accounted for until mustered out November 12-13, 1861.

CAUDLE, GEORGE W., Private
Enlisted in Orange County, June 28, 1861, for six months. Present or accounted for until mustered out November 12-13, 1861.

CHISENHALL, JAMES R., Private
Enlisted in Orange County at age 21, April 6, 1861, for six months. Company muster roll dated June 30, 1861, states that he was "thrown from the train on his way from North Carolina and so badly crippled that he has not been able either to join the company or to return home." Company muster roll dated August 31, 1861, states that he was "absent by leave. Disabled by railroad accident on 22 May, 1861." Mustered out November 12-13, 1861.

CHISENHALL, SAMUEL, Private
Enlisted in Orange County, June 28, 1861, for six months. Present or accounted for until mustered out November 12-13, 1861.

CHISENHALL, WILLIAM, Private
Enlisted in Orange County at age 19, April 6, 1861, for six months. Died at Yorktown, Virginia, August 16, 1861.

CLAYTON, HARVEY, Private
Enlisted in Orange County at age 25, April 6, 1861, for six months. Present or accounted for until mustered out November 12-13, 1861.

CLAYTON, PATRICK HENRY, Private
Enlisted in Orange County at age 23, April 6, 1861, for six months. Present or accounted for until mustered out November 12-13, 1861.

CLAYTOR, HENRY, Private
Enlisted in Orange County, April 22, 1861, for six months. Present or accounted for until mustered out November 12-13, 1861.

CLAYTOR, SAMUEL B., Private
Enlisted in Orange County at age 27, April 6, 1861, for six months. Present or accounted for until mustered out November 12-13, 1861.

CLEMENTS, JAMES H., Private
Enlisted in Orange County at age 20, April 6, 1861, for six months. Present or accounted for until mustered out November 12-13, 1861.

CLEMENTS, JOHN R., Private
Resided in Orange County where he enlisted at age 24, June 28, 1861, for six months. Present or accounted for until mustered out November 12-13, 1861. Later enlisted in Company G, 11th Regiment N. C. Troops (1st Regiment N. C. Volunteers).

COLE, GEORGE O., Private
Enlisted in Orange County, June 28, 1861, for six months. Present or accounted for until mustered out November 12-13, 1861.

COLE, GEORGE W., Private
Enlisted in Orange County, June 28, 1861, for six months. Present or accounted for until mustered out November 12-13, 1861.

COUCH, WILLIAM H., Private
Enlisted in Orange County, April 6, 1861, for six months. Present or accounted for until mustered out November 12-13, 1861.

CRAWFORD, HENRY C., Private
Enlisted in Orange County, June 28, 1861, for six months. Present or accounted for until mustered out November 12-13, 1861.

DAVIS, THOMAS CORWIN, 1st Sergeant
Enlisted in Orange County at age 20, April 6, 1861, for six months. Enlisted as a Private and mustered in as a Corporal on May 13, 1861. Reported as 1st Sergeant on muster roll dated August 31, 1861. Exact date of promotion not given. Present or accounted for until mustered out November 12-13, 1861.

DURHAM, ROBERT A., Private
Enlisted in Orange County at age 18, April 6, 1861, for six months. Present or accounted for until mustered out November 12-13, 1861.

DURHAM, WILLIAM S., Private
Resided in Orange County where he enlisted at age 23, April 6, 1861, for six months. Present or accounted for until mustered out November 12-13, 1861. Later enlisted in Company G, 11th Regiment N. C. Troops (1st Regiment N. C. Volunteers).

EXUM, JAMES H., Private
Enlisted in Orange County at age 20, April 6, 1861, for six months. Present or accounted for until mustered out November 12-13, 1861.

FERRINGTON, JOHN E., Private

Enlisted in Orange County at age 19, April 6, 1861, for six months. Present or accounted for until mustered out November 12-13, 1861.

FETTER, FREDERICK AUGUSTUS, Private
Enlisted in Orange County at age 22, April 6, 1861, for six months. Present or accounted for until mustered out November 12-13, 1861. Later served in Mallett's Battalion N. C. Troops (Camp Holmes Guard).

FETTER, WILLIAM M., Private
Enlisted in Orange County at age 20, April 6, 1861, for six months. Present or accounted for until mustered out November 12-13, 1861.

FOWLER, JAMES W., Private
Enlisted in Orange County, June 28, 1861, for six months. Present or accounted for until mustered out November 12-13, 1861.

FOWLER, WILLIAM, Private
Enlisted in Orange County at age 21, April 6, 1861, for six months. Present or accounted for until mustered out November 12-13, 1861.

FREELAND, JOHN F., Sergeant
Enlisted in Orange County at age 21, April 6, 1861, for six months. Mustered in as Sergeant. Present or accounted for until mustered out November 12-13, 1861. Later enlisted in Company G, 11th Regiment N. C. Troops (1st Regiment N. C. Volunteers).

GATTIS, WILLIAM A., Corporal
Enlisted in Orange County at age 26, April 6, 1861, for six months. Mustered in as Corporal. Present or accounted for until mustered out November 12-13, 1861.

GIBBON, RALPH H., Private
Enlisted in Wake County, July 2, 1861, for six months. Present or accounted for until mustered out November 12-13, 1861.

GREEN, JAMES H., Private
Enlisted in Orange County at age 21, April 6, 1861, for six months. Present or accounted for until mustered out November 12-13, 1861.

HARWOOD, WESLEY J., Private
Enlisted in Orange County at age 20, April 6, 1861, for six months. Present or accounted for until mustered out November 12-13, 1861.

HAYMAN, SAMUEL L., Private
Enlisted in Wake County, July 2, 1861, for six months. Discharged on Surgeon's Certificate on May 30, 1861.

HESTER, JOHN, Private
Enlisted in Orange County at age 23, April 6, 1861, for six months. Present or accounted for until mustered out November 12-13, 1861.

HOGAN, JOHN R., Private
Enlisted in Orange County, April 22, 1861, for six months. Present or accounted for until mustered out November 12-13, 1861.

HUSKEY, WILLIAM, Private
Enlisted in Orange County, June 28, 1861, for six months. Present or accounted for until mustered out November 12-13, 1861.

IREDELL, CADWALLADER JONES, Private
Resided in Wake County where he enlisted, May 20, 1861, for six months. Transferred to Company E, 9th Regiment N. C. State Troops (1st Regiment N. C. Cavalry) upon appointment as 3rd Lieutenant to rank from October 4, 1861.

JOHNSTON, GEORGE BURGWYN, Private
Enlisted in Orange County, July 3, 1861, for six months. Present or accounted for until mustered out November 12-13, 1861. Later enlisted in Company G, 28th Regiment N. C. Troops.

JONES, AURELIUS C., Private
Enlisted in Orange County at age 19, April 6, 1861, for six months. Present or accounted for until mustered out November 12-13, 1861.

JONES, JOHN T., Private
Enlisted in Orange County at age 20, April 6, 1861, for six months. Transferred to Company I, 26th Regiment N.C. Troops upon appointment as 2nd Lieutenant to rank from July 26, 1861.

JONES, JOHN W., Private
Enlisted in Orange County at age 19, April 22, 1861, for six months. Present or accounted for until mustered out November 12-13, 1861.

KING, BAXTER, Private
Enlisted in Orange County at age 19, April 6, 1861, for six months. Present or accounted for until mustered out November 12-13, 1861.

KING, TURNER, Private
Enlisted in Orange County, June 28, 1861, for six months. Present or accounted for until mustered out November 12-13, 1861.

LLOYD, CALVIN WHIT, Private
Enlisted in Orange County at age 22, April 6, 1861, for six months. Present or accounted for until mustered out November 12-13, 1861.

LONG, JAMES H., Private
Enlisted in Orange County, April 6, 1861, for six months. Present or accounted for until mustered out November 12-13, 1861.

McCAULEY, DAVID, Private
Enlisted in Orange County at age 28, April 6, 1861, for six months. Present or accounted for until mustered out November 12-13, 1861.

McCOLLUM, JOSEPH, Private
Enlisted in Orange County, June 28, 1861, for six months. Muster roll for July-August, 1861, states that he "died at Chapel Hill, October 14, 1861."

McDADE, ALPHONSO J., Private
Enlisted in Orange County at age 27, April 6, 1861, for six months. Present or accounted for until mustered out November 12-13, 1861.

McDADE, JOHN H., Private
Enlisted in Orange County, April 6, 1861, for six months. Present or accounted for until mustered out November 12-13, 1861. Later enlisted in Company G, 11th Regiment N. C. Troops (1st Regiment N. C. Volunteers).

McDADE, JOSEPH A., Corporal
Enlisted in Orange County at age 20, April 6, 1861, for six months. Mustered in as Corporal.

Present or accounted for until mustered out November 12-13, 1861.

McDADE, JUDSON C., Private
Enlisted in Orange County, April 6, 1861, for six months. Present or accounted for until mustered out November 12-13, 1861.

McDADE, W. H., Private
Enlisted in Orange County at age 25, April 6, 1861, for six months. Present or accounted for until mustered out November 12-13, 1861.

McKEE, JAMES, Private
Enlisted in Wake County, June 28, 1861, for six months. Present or accounted for until mustered out November 12-13, 1861. Later enlisted in Company C, 7th Regiment N. C. State Troops.

MALLETT, CECIL, Private
Enlisted in Orange County at age 19, April 6, 1861, for six months. Present or accounted for until mustered out November 12-13, 1861.

MALLETT, JOHN W., Private
Enlisted in Orange County at age 19, April 6, 1861, for six months. Present or accounted for until mustered out November 12-13, 1861.

MARKHAM, CHARLES GREEN, Private
Resided in Orange County where he enlisted at age 39, April 6, 1861, for six months. Present or accounted for until mustered out November 12-13, 1861.

MAVERICK, LOUIS, Private
Enlisted in Orange County at age 22, April 6, 1861, for six months. Present or accounted for through August, 1861. Appointed Captain of company in the 32nd Regiment Texas Cavalry.

MEACHUM, JOHN, Private
Enlisted in Orange County, June 28, 1861, for six months. Present or accounted for until mustered out November 12-13, 1861.

MICKLE, WILLIAM N., Private
Enlisted in Orange County at age 18, April 6, 1861, for six months. Present or accounted for until mustered out November 12-13, 1861. Later enlisted in Company I, 41st Regiment N. C. Troops (3rd Regiment N. C. Cavalry).

MOORE, ANDREW, Private
Enlisted in Orange County at age 20, April 6, 1861, for six months. Present or accounted for until mustered out November 12-13, 1861.

MOORE, DUNCAN, Private
Enlisted at Yorktown, Virginia, July 10, 1861, for six months. Present or accounted for until mustered out November 12-13, 1861.

MOORE, JAMES B., Private
Enlisted in Orange County at age 22, April 6, 1861, for six months. Died at Yorktown, Virginia, September 22, 1861.

MORROW, RICHARD A., Private
Enlisted in Orange County, July 3, 1861, for six months. Present or accounted for until mustered out November 12-13, 1861.

MOWATT, JOHN, Corporal
Enlisted in Orange County at age 34, April 6,

1861, for six months. Mustered in as Corporal. Present or accounted for until mustered out November 12-13, 1861.

NUNN, WILLIAM H., Private
Enlisted in Orange County at age 19, April 6, 1861, for six months. Appointed Corporal when the company organized but was mustered in as a Private. Present or accounted for until mustered out November 12-13, 1861.

O'BRIEN, HUGH, Private
Enlisted in Wake County, June 25, 1861, for six months. Present or accounted for until mustered out November 12-13, 1861.

OLDHAM, ALVIS L., Private
Enlisted in Orange County at age 20, April 6, 1861, for six months. Present or accounted for until mustered out November 12-13, 1861.

OLDHAM, THOMAS J., Private
Enlisted in Orange County, June 28, 1861, for six months. Present or accounted for until mustered out November 12-13, 1861.

OLDHAM, THOMAS S., Private
Enlisted in Orange County, June 28, 1861, for six months. Discharged September 17, 1861.

PARKER, JOHN D., Private
Enlisted at Yorktown, Virginia, July 4, 1861, for six months. Present or accounted for until mustered out November 12-13, 1861.

PATTERSON, SAMUEL, Private
Enlisted in Orange County at age 28, April 6, 1861, for six months. Slightly wounded in battle at Bethel, Virginia, June 10, 1861. Present or accounted for until mustered out November 12-13, 1861.

PENDERGRASS, ALVIS, Private
Enlisted in Orange County at age 21, April 6, 1861, for six months. Present or accounted for until mustered out November 12-13, 1861.

PETTY, JOHN W., Private
Enlisted in Orange County, June 28, 1861, for six months. Reported on muster roll dated August 31, 1861, with the remark: "sick in hospital and ought to be discharged from service."

PILAND, PHILLIP A., Private
Enlisted in Orange County at age 30, April 6, 1861, for six months. Present or accounted for until mustered out November 12-13, 1861.

POE, NORFLEET, Private
Enlisted in Orange County at age 23, April 6, 1861, for six months. Present or accounted for until mustered out November 12-13, 1861.

POE, REUBEN F., Private
Enlisted in Orange County at age 25, April 6, 1861, for six months. Present or accounted for until mustered out November 12-13, 1861.

POWELL, THOMAS, Private
Enlisted in Wake County, July 2, 1861, for six months. Present or accounted for until mustered out November 12-13, 1861.

ROBERTSON, ROBERT, Private
Enlisted in Orange County at age 25, April 6,

1861, for six months. Present or accounted for until mustered out November 12-13, 1861.

ROBSON, WILLIAM, Private

Enlisted in Orange County at age 20, April 6, 1861, for six months. Present or accounted for until mustered out November 12-13, 1861.

SAUNDERS, JOSEPH H., Private

Enlisted in Orange County at age 21, April 6, 1861, for six months. Present or accounted for until mustered out November 12-13, 1861. Later enlisted in Company A, 33rd Regiment N. C. Troops.

SKINNER, THOMAS GREGORY, Private

Enlisted in Orange County at age 19, April 6, 1861, for six months. Present or accounted for until mustered out November 12-13, 1861. Later enlisted in Company B, 4th Battalion Virginia Light Artillery.

SNIPES, THOMAS B., Private

Enlisted in Orange County at age 20, April 6, 1861, for six months. Present or accounted for until mustered out November 12-13, 1861.

SNIPES, THOMAS E., Private

Enlisted in Orange County, June 28, 1861, for six months. Present or accounted for until mustered out November 12-13, 1861.

SPARROW, GEORGE, Private

Enlisted in Orange County at age 20, April 6, 1861, for six months. Present or accounted for until mustered out November 12-13, 1861.

STROUD, WILLIAM F., Private

Enlisted in Orange County at age 28, April 6, 1861, for six months. Present or accounted for until mustered out November 12-13, 1861.

SUGG, WILLIAM M., Private

Enlisted in Orange County at age 17, April 6, 1861, for six months. Present or accounted for until mustered out November 12-13, 1861. Later enlisted in Company G, 11th Regiment N. C. Troops (1st Regiment N. C. Volunteers).

TENNEY, WILLIAM C., Private

Enlisted in Orange County at age 18, April 6, 1861, for six months. Present or accounted for until mustered out November 12-13, 1861.

THRIFT, PINKNEY, Private

Enlisted in Orange County, June 28, 1861, for six months. Present or accounted for until mustered out November 12-13, 1861.

UTLEY, JOHN A., Private

Enlisted in Orange County, April 6, 1861, for six months. Present or accounted for until mustered out November 12-13, 1861.

VANN, LEMUEL D., Private

Enlisted in Orange County at age 20, April 6, 1861, for six months. Present or accounted for until mustered out November 12-13, 1861.

WATSON, ALEXANDER, Private

Enlisted in Orange County, April 6, 1861, for six months. Present or accounted for until mustered out November 12-13, 1861.

WATSON, JONES M., Sergeant

Enlisted in Orange County at age 20, April 6, 1861, for six months. Mustered in as Sergeant. Present or accounted for until mustered out November 12-13, 1861. Later enlisted in Company G, 11th Regiment N. C. Troops (1st Regiment N. C. Volunteers).

WATSON, WILLIE, Private

Enlisted in Orange County, April 22, 1861, for six months. Present or accounted for until mustered out November 12-13, 1861.

WHITAKER, DAVID, Private

Resided in Wake County where he enlisted at age 20, July 19, 1861, for six months. Present or accounted for until mustered out November 12-13, 1861. Later enlisted in Company C, 47th Regiment N. C. Troops.

WHITAKER, RUFFIN, Private

Enlisted in Orange County, April 6, 1861, for six months. Present or accounted for until mustered out November 12-13, 1861.

WHITAKER, SPIER, Jr., Private

Enlisted in Orange County, April 6, 1861, for six months. Present or accounted for until mustered out November 12-13, 1861. Later appointed Adjutant and attached to the Field and Staff, 33rd Regiment N. C. Troops.

WHITING, GEORGE W., Private

Enlisted in Wake County, July 2, 1861, for six months. Present or accounted for until mustered out November 12-13, 1861.

WHITTED, WILLIAM G., Private

Enlisted in Orange County at age 22, April 6, 1861, for six months. Present or accounted for until mustered out November 12-13, 1861.

WILLIAMS, JAMES W., Sergeant

Enlisted in Orange County at age 22, April 6, 1861, for six months. Mustered in as Sergeant. Present or accounted for until mustered out November 12-13, 1861. Later enlisted in Company G, 11th Regiment N. C. Troops (1st Regiment N. C. Volunteers).

WINSTON, WILLIAM A., Private

Enlisted in Orange County, April 6, 1861, for six months. Present or accounted for until mustered out November 12-13, 1861.

WITTICH, EARNEST L., Private

Enlisted in Orange County at age 18, April 6, 1861, for six months. Present or accounted for until mustered out November 12-13, 1861.

COMPANY E

This company was organized at Asheville, Buncombe County, as a volunteer company on December 20, 1859, following the John Brown raid on Harpers Ferry. It was originally known as the "Buncombe Riflemen," but in 1861 it was also referred to as the "Buncombe Rifles." The company commander received orders to proceed to Raleigh on April 16. On April 18 the company left Asheville and marched for three days to reach the end of the railroad a few miles east of Morganton. Two days later the company was in Raleigh, where it was mustered into state service on May 13, 1861, as Company E of this regiment. After that date the company functioned as a part of the regiment, and its history for the war period is recorded as a part of the regimental history.

The information contained in the following roster of the company was compiled principally from company muster rolls which included the muster-in roll dated August 31, 1861, covering the period May 13-August 31, 1861, and muster rolls for the period July-August, 1861. No muster rolls were found for May 13-June 30, 1861, or for the period after August, 1861. In addition to the company muster rolls, Roll of Honor records, receipt rolls, hospital records, prisoner of war records, and other primary records, supplemented by state pension applications, United Daughters of the Confederacy records, and postwar rosters and histories, all provided useful information.

OFFICERS
CAPTAIN

McDOWELL, WILLIAM WALLIS
Resided in Buncombe County where he enlisted at age 38, April 24, 1861, for six months. Appointed Captain to rank from April 27, 1861. Present or accounted for until mustered out November 12-13, 1861. Later appointed Major and assigned to the Field and Staff of the 60th Regiment N. C. Troops.

LIEUTENANTS

GREGORY, GEORGE HENRY, 2nd Lieutenant
Resided in Buncombe County where he enlisted at age 25, April 24, 1861, for six months. Appointed 2nd Lieutenant to rank from April 27, 1861. Present or accounted for until mustered out November 12-13, 1861

HARDY, WASHINGTON MORRIS, 1st Lieutenant
Resided in Buncombe County where he enlisted at age 26, April 24, 1861, for six months. Appointed 1st Lieutenant to rank from April 27, 1861. Present or accounted for until mustered out November 12-13, 1861. Later enlisted in Company A, 60th Regiment N. C. Troops.

PATTON, JAMES ALFRED, 3rd Lieutenant
Resided in Buncombe County where he enlisted at age 30, April 24, 1861, for six months. Appointed 3rd Lieutenant to rank from April 27, 1861. Present or accounted for until mustered out November 12-13, 1861.

NONCOMMISSIONED OFFICERS AND PRIVATES

ADAMS, G. H. A., Private
Enlisted in Buncombe County at age 29, April 24, 1861, for six months. Present or accounted for until mustered out November 12-13, 1861. Later enlisted in Company E, 11th Regiment N. C. Troops (1st Regiment N. C. Volunteers).

ALEXANDER, ALBURTES N., Private
Enlisted in Buncombe County at age 25, July 20, 1861, for six months. Present or accounted for until mustered out November 12-13, 1861.

ALEXANDER, GEORGE N., Private
Enlisted in Buncombe County at age 27, July 20, 1861, for six months. Present or accounted for until mustered out November 12-13, 1861.

ALEXANDER, J. B., Private
Enlisted in Buncombe County at age 33, July 20, 1861, for six months. Present or accounted for until mustered out November 12-13, 1861. Later enlisted in Company K, 42nd Regiment N. C. Troops.

ALEXANDER, WILLIAM R., Private
Enlisted in Buncombe County at age 21, April 24, 1861, for six months. Present or accounted for until mustered out November 12-13, 1861. Later enlisted in Company A, 11th Regiment N. C. Troops (1st Regiment N. C. Volunteers).

ALEXANDER, WILLIAM S., Private
Enlisted in Buncombe County at age 22, April 24, 1861, for six months. Present or accounted for until mustered out November 12-13, 1861. Later enlisted in Company A, 11th Regiment N. C. Troops (1st Regiment N. C. Volunteers).

ALLISON, J. E., Private
Enlisted in Buncombe County at age 23, July 1, 1861, for six months. Present or accounted for until mustered out November 12-13, 1861.

ALLISON, THOMAS J., Private
Enlisted in Buncombe County at age 25, April 24, 1861, for six months. Present or accounted for until mustered out November 12-13, 1861.

ANDERSON, WILLIAM W., Private
Resided in Buncombe County where he enlisted at age 21, April 24, 1861, for six months. Present or accounted for until mustered out November 12-13, 1861. Later enlisted in Company K, 11th Regiment N. C. Troops (1st Regiment N. C. Volunteers).

ATKIN, GEORGE T., Private
Enlisted in Buncombe County at age 18, April 24, 1861, for six months. Present or accounted for until mustered out November 12-13, 1861.

ATKIN, WILLIAM, Private
Enlisted in Buncombe County at age 14, July 1, 1861, for six months. Present or accounted for until mustered out November 12-13, 1861.

BAILEY, FRANCIS M., Private
Enlisted in Buncombe County at age 26, April 23, 1861, for six months. Present or accounted for until mustered out November 12-13, 1861.

BAILEY, WILLIAM H., Private
Enlisted in Buncombe County at age 30, April 24, 1861, for six months. Present or accounted for until mustered out November 12-13, 1861.

BAIRD, ALFRED HUNTER, Ensign
Enlisted in Buncombe County at age 18, April 24, 1861, for six months. Mustered in as Ensign. Present or accounted for until mustered out November 12-13, 1861. Later enlisted in Company A, 5th Battalion N.C. Cavalry.

BAIRD, WILLIAM B., Private
Enlisted in Buncombe County at age 33, April 24, 1861, for six months. Present or accounted for

until mustered out November 12-13, 1861.

BAIRDEN, HUGH M., Private

Enlisted in Buncombe County at age 18, April 24, 1861, for six months. Present or accounted for until mustered out November 12-13, 1861.

BALLEW, GEORGE M., Private

Enlisted in Buncombe County at age 25, May 23, 1861, for six months. Present or accounted for until mustered out November 12-13, 1861.

BARTLETT, JACOB·S., Private

Resided in Buncombe County where he enlisted at age 18, July 20, 1861, for six months. Present or accounted for until mustered out November 12-13, 1861. Later enlisted in Company K, 11th Regiment N. C. Troops (1st Regiment N. C. Volunteers).

BENSON, DAVID, Private

Enlisted in Buncombe County at age 26, July 10, 1861, for six months. Present or accounted for until mustered out November 12-13, 1861.

BLAIN, WILLIAM M., Private

Enlisted in Buncombe County at age 33, April 24, 1861, for six months. Present or accounted for until mustered out November 12-13, 1861.

BRIGHT, H. M., Private

Enlisted in Buncombe County, July 1, 1861, for six months. Present or accounted for until mustered out November 12-13, 1861.

BURGIN, B. J., Private

Enlisted in Buncombe County at age 20, July 1, 1861, for six months. Present or accounted for until mustered out November 12-13, 1861.

BURGIN, JOHN A., Private

Resided in Buncombe County where he enlisted at age 22, April 24, 1861, for six months. Present or accounted for until mustered out November 12-13, 1861. Later enlisted in Company K, 11th Regiment N. C. Troops (1st Regiment N. C. Volunteers).

BURGIN, JOHN D., Private

Enlisted in Buncombe County at age 28, April 24, 1861, for six months. Present or accounted for until mustered out November 12-13, 1861.

BURGIN, JOHN W., Private

Resided in Buncombe County where he enlisted at age 22, April 24, 1861, for six months. Present or accounted for until mustered out November 12-13, 1861. Later enlisted in Company K, 11th Regiment N. C. Troops (1st Regiment N. C. Volunteers).

BURNETT, DANIEL, Private

Enlisted in Buncombe County at age 29, April 24, 1861, for six months. Present or accounted for until mustered out November 12-13, 1861.

BURNETT, JESSE, Private

Enlisted at Yorktown, Virginia, at age 17, August 1, 1861, for six months. Present or accounted for until mustered out November 12-13, 1861.

BURNETT, JOHN, Private

Enlisted in Buncombe County at age 28, April 24, 1861, for six months. Died at Yorktown, Virginia. Date of death reported as July 30 and August 2, 1861

BURNETT, THOMAS H., Private

Enlisted in Buncombe County, July 20, 1861, for six months. Present or accounted for until mustered out November 12-13, 1861.

CLAYTON, EDWIN M., Sergeant

Resided in Buncombe County where he enlisted at age 23, April 24, 1861, for six months. Mustered in as Sergeant. Present or accounted for until mustered out November 12-13, 1861. Later enlisted in Company K, 60th Regiment N. C. Troops.

CLAYTON, JOHN B., Private

Enlisted in Buncombe County at age 21, April 24, 1861, for six months. Present or accounted for until mustered out November 12-13, 1861.

CLAYTON, ROBERT M., Private

Resided in Buncombe County where he enlisted at age 16, April 24, 1861, for six months. Present or accounted for until mustered out November 12-13, 1861. Later enlisted in Company B, 60th Regiment N. C. Troops.

COCHE, JOHN W., Private

Enlisted in Buncombe County at age 19, April 24, 1861, for six months. Present or accounted for until mustered out November 12-13, 1861.

COGGINS, CASWELL, Private

Enlisted in Buncombe County, July 20, 1861, for six months. Present or accounted for until mustered out November 12-13, 1861.

COGGINS, JOHN W., Private

Enlisted in Buncombe County at age 28, April 24, 1861, for six months. Present or accounted for until mustered out November 12-13, 1861.

COLEMAN, ROBERT L., Private

Enlisted in Buncombe County at age 25, April 24, 1861, for six months. Present or accounted for until mustered out November 12-13, 1861. Later appointed Captain, A. C. S., and assigned to the Field and Staff of the 60th Regiment N. C. Troops.

CORDELL, JOHN H., Private

Enlisted in Buncombe County at age 30, April 24, 1861, for six months. Present or accounted for until mustered out November 12-13, 1861. Later enlisted in Company B, 11th Regiment N. C. Troops (1st Regiment N. C. Volunteers).

DARNELL, JAMES C., Private

Enlisted in Buncombe County at age 17, July 20, 1861, for six months. Present or accounted for until mustered out November 12-13, 1861.

DAVIDSON, JOHN LYTLE, Private

Enlisted in Buncombe County at age 20, April 24, 1861, for six months. Died at Yorktown, Virginia, September 14, 1861.

DAVIDSON, SAMUEL W., Private

Enlisted in Buncombe County at age 20, April 24, 1861, for six months. Present or accounted for until mustered out November 12-13, 1861. Later enlisted in Company C, 60th Regiment N. C. Troops.

DAVIDSON, WILLIAM F., Private

Enlisted in Buncombe County at age 25, July 20, 1861, for six months. Present or accounted for until mustered out November 12-13, 1861.

DICKERSON, WILLIAM T., Private
Resided in Buncombe County where he enlisted at age 36, April 24, 1861, for six months. Present or accounted for until mustered out November 12-13, 1861. Later enlisted in Company K, 11th Regiment N. C. Troops (1st Regiment N. C. Volunteers).

DINGLER, JOHN J., Corporal
Enlisted in Buncombe County at age 34, April 24, 1861, for six months. Mustered in as Corporal. Present or accounted for until mustered out November 12-13, 1861.

EDNEY, HENRY C., Private
Enlisted in Buncombe County at age 18, April 24, 1861, for six months. Present or accounted for until mustered out November 12-13, 1861. Later enlisted in Company A, 5th Battalion N. C. Cavalry.

EDNEY, JOHN B., Private
Enlisted in Buncombe County at age 22, April 24, 1861, for six months. Present or accounted for until mustered out November 12-13, 1861.

EMBERS, WILLIAM A., Private
Enlisted in Buncombe County at age 22, April 24, 1861, for six months. Present or accounted for until mustered out November 12-13, 1861.

FLEMMING, JOHN A., Private
Enlisted in Buncombe County, April 24, 1861, for six months. Present or accounted for until mustered out November 12-13, 1861.

FRANKS, CORNELIUS, Private
Enlisted in Buncombe County at age 25, July 1, 1861, for six months. Present or accounted for until mustered out November 12-13, 1861.

GARRETT, WILLIAM N., Private
Enlisted in Buncombe County at age 23, April 24, 1861, for six months. Present or accounted for until mustered out November 12-13, 1861.

GUDGER, ROBERT V., Private
Enlisted in Buncombe County at age 34, April 24, 1861, for six months. Present or accounted for until mustered out November 12-13, 1861.

HAMBY, M., Private
Enlisted in Buncombe County at age 18, June 10, 1861, for six months. Present or accounted for until mustered out November 12-13, 1861.

HARDY, JOHN GEDDINGS, 1st Sergeant
Enlisted in Buncombe County at age 31, April 24, 1861, for six months. Served as 1st Sergeant to the company until transferred to the Field and Staff upon appointment as Assistant Surgeon to rank from May 16, 1861.

HAYES, JAMES M., Private
Enlisted in Buncombe County at age 23, April 24, 1861, for six months. Present or accounted for until mustered out November 12-13, 1861.

HEMPHILL, MILTON B., Private
Born in Guilford County and was by occupation a blacksmith when he enlisted in Buncombe County at age 24, July 1, 1861, for six months. Present or accounted for until mustered out November 12-13, 1861. Later enlisted in Company K, 45th Regiment N. C. Troops.

HEMPHILL, WILLIAM P., Private
Enlisted in Buncombe County at age 17, April 24, 1861, for six months. Died at Yorktown, Virginia, July 25, 1861.

HENDERSON, EZEKIEL, Private
Enlisted in Buncombe County at age 26, July 20, 1861, for six months. Present or accounted for until mustered out November 12-13, 1861.

HILL, WILLIAM A., Private
Enlisted in Buncombe County at age 24, July 1, 1861, for six months. Present or accounted for until mustered out November 12-13, 1861.

HOWARD, A. Z., Private
Enlisted in Buncombe County at age 26, April 24, 1861, for six months. Present or accounted for until mustered out November 12-13, 1861.

JARRETT, J. A., Private
Enlisted in Buncombe County at age 20, April 24, 1861, for six months. Present or accounted for until mustered out November 12-13, 1861.

JARRETT, ROBERT H., Private
Enlisted in Buncombe County at age 25, April 24, 1861, for six months. Present or accounted for until mustered out November 12-13, 1861.

JENKINS, B. F., Private
Enlisted in Buncombe County at age 18, April 24, 1861, for six months. Present or accounted for until mustered out November 12-13, 1861.

JONES, THEODORE, Private
Enlisted in Buncombe County at age 20, May 24, 1861, for six months. Present or accounted for until mustered out November 12-13, 1861.

KILLIAN, DANIEL A., Private
Enlisted in Buncombe County at age 21, July 20, 1861, for six months. Present or accounted for until mustered out November 12-13, 1861.

LANGE, JOHN H., Private
Enlisted in Buncombe County at age 27, April 24, 1861, for six months. Present or accounted for until mustered out November 12-13, 1861.

LANNING, JAMES R., Private
Enlisted in Buncombe County at age 23, April 24, 1861, for six months. Present or accounted for until mustered out November 12-13, 1861.

LEE, HENRY B., Corporal
Enlisted in Buncombe County at age 20, April 24, 1861, for six months. Mustered in as Corporal. Present or accounted for until mustered out November 12-13, 1861.

LEE, STEVEN, Jr., Private
Enlisted in Buncombe County at age 17, April 24, 1861, for six months. Present or accounted for until mustered out November 12-13, 1861.

LINDSAY, ANDREW JACKSON, Private
Enlisted in Buncombe County at age 30, July 20, 1861, for six months. Present or accounted for until mustered out November 12-13, 1861.

LOWINCE, HENRY C., Private
Enlisted in Buncombe County at age 17, April 24, 1861, for six months. Present or accounted for until mustered out November 12-13, 1861. Later

enlisted in Company D, 60th Regiment N. C. Troops.

LUSK, JOHN R., Private
Enlisted in Buncombe County at age 21, April 24, 1861, for six months. Present or accounted for until mustered out November 12-13, 1861.

LYTLE, THOMAS Y., Private
Enlisted in Buncombe County at age 17, April 24, 1861, for six months. Present or accounted for until mustered out November 12-13, 1861.

McDONALD, H. A., Private
Enlisted in Buncombe County at age 21, April 24, 1861, for six months. Present or accounted for until mustered out November 12-13, 1861. Later enlisted in Company K, 38th Regiment N. C. Troops.

McFALLS, DANIEL, Private
Enlisted in Buncombe County at age 18, April 24, 1861, for six months. Present or accounted for until mustered out November 12-13, 1861.

MELTON, JOHN W., Private
Enlisted in Buncombe County at age 16, July 20, 1861, for six months. Present or accounted for until mustered out November 12-13, 1861.

MERRIMAN, JAMES H., Private
Enlisted in Buncombe County at age 18, June 12, 1861, for six months. Present or accounted for until mustered out November 12-13, 1861.

MOONEY, J. R., Private
Enlisted in Buncombe County at age 22, July 1, 1861, for six months. Present or accounted for until mustered out November 12-13, 1861.

MORRISON, JOHN A., Private
Enlisted in Buncombe County at age 25, August 1, 1861, for six months. Present or accounted for until mustered out November 12-13, 1861.

MORRISON, WASHINGTON, Private
Enlisted in Buncombe County at age 24, April 24, 1861, for six months. Present or accounted for until mustered out November 12-13, 1861.

MURDOCH, FRANCIS JOHNSTONE, Private
Enlisted in Buncombe County at age 16, April 24, 1861, for six months. Discharged June 5, 1861.

MURDOCK, WILLIAM H., Private
Enlisted in Buncombe County at age 23, April 24, 1861, for six months. Present or accounted for until mustered out November 12-13, 1861.

O'KELLEY, C. W., Private
Enlisted in Buncombe County at age 18, April 24, 1861, for six months. Present or accounted for until mustered out November 12-13, 1861.

OWENBEY, SIMS, Jr., Private
Enlisted in Buncombe County at age 21, April 24, 1861, for six months. Present or accounted for until mustered out November 12-13, 1861.

OWENS, W. J., Private
Enlisted in Orange County at age 18, July 1, 1861, for six months. Present or accounted for until mustered out November 12-13, 1861.

PATTON, BENJAMIN FRANKLIN, 1st Sergeant
Resided in Buncombe County where he enlisted at age 18, April 24, 1861, for six months. Mustered in as 1st Sergeant. Present or accounted for until mustered out November 12-13, 1861. Later enlisted in Company B, 60th Regiment N. C. Troops.

PATTON, ROBERT H., Private
Enlisted in Buncombe County at age 16, April 24, 1861, for six months. Present or accounted for until mustered out November 12-13, 1861.

PATTON, THOMAS W., Corporal
Enlisted in Buncombe County at age 20, April 24, 1861, for six months. Mustered in as Corporal. Present or accounted for until mustered out November 12-13, 1861. Later enlisted in Company C, 60th Regiment N. C. Troops.

PLEMONS, JOSEPH J., Private
Enlisted in Buncombe County at age 25, June 10, 1861, for six months. Discharged July 10, 1861.

PORTER, WILLIAM Y., Corporal
Enlisted in Buncombe County at age 30, April 24, 1861, for six months. Mustered in as Corporal. Present or accounted for until mustered out November 12-13, 1861.

POUNDERS, JOSEPH W., Private
Enlisted in Buncombe County at age 18, April 24, 1861, for six months. Present or accounted for until mustered out November 12-13, 1861.

POUNDERS, W. E., Private
Resided in Buncombe County where he enlisted at age 15, July 20, 1861, for six months. Present or accounted for until mustered out November 12-13, 1861. Later enlisted in Company A, 60th Regiment N. C. Troops.

POWERS, WILLIAM, Private
Enlisted in Buncombe County at 37, April 24, 1861, for six months. Present or accounted for until mustered out November 12-13, 1861.

RAMSEY, JERRY, Private
Enlisted in Buncombe County at age 22, April 24, 1861, for six months. Present or accounted for until mustered out November 12-13, 1861.

RAMSEY, JOHN, Private
Resided in Lincoln County and enlisted at Yorktown, Virginia, at age 28, May 28, 1861, for six months. Present or accounted for until mustered out November 12-13, 1861.

RANDALL, JOHN, Musician
Enlisted in Buncombe County at age 57, April 24, 1861, for six months. Mustered in as Musician. Present or accounted for until mustered out November 12-13, 1861.

RHODES, A. H., Private
Enlisted in Buncombe County at age 21, April 24, 1861, for six months. Died at Yorktown, Virginia, August 22, 1861.

RICE, JOHN M., Private
Enlisted in Buncombe County at age 18, July 20, 1861, for six months. Present or accounted for until mustered out November 12-13, 1861.

ROBERTS, MARTIN P., Private
Enlisted in Buncombe County at age 17, April 24, 1861, for six months. Present or accounted for until mustered out November 12-13, 1861.

SALES, JOHN T., Private
Enlisted in Buncombe County at age 24, April 24, 1861, for six months. Present or accounted for until mustered out November 12-13, 1861. Later enlisted in Company K, 60th Regiment N. C. Troops.

SALES, JOSEPH B., Private
Enlisted in Buncombe County at age 22, July 20, 1861, for six months. Present or accounted for until mustered out November 12-13, 1861. Later enlisted in Company K, 60th Regiment N. C. Troops.

SAWYER, THOMAS T., Private
Enlisted in Buncombe County at age 33, April 24, 1861, for six months. Present or accounted for until mustered out November 12-13, 1861.

SHIPMAN, THOMAS J., Private
Enlisted in Buncombe County at age 20, April 24, 1861, for six months. Present or accounted for until mustered out November 12-13, 1861.

SMITH, ALFRED B., Private
Enlisted in Buncombe County at age 21, April 24, 1861, for six months. Present or accounted for until mustered out November 12-13, 1861.

SMITH, CHARLES L., Private
Enlisted in Buncombe County at age 20, July 20, 1861, for six months. Present or accounted for until mustered out November 12-13, 1861.

SMITH, JAMES C., Private
Enlisted in Buncombe County at age 16, April 24, 1861, for six months. Present or accounted for until mustered out November 12-13, 1861.

SMITH, JOHN B., Private
Enlisted in Buncombe County at age 22, April 24, 1861, for six months. Present or accounted for until mustered out November 12-13, 1861.

SMITH, LUCIUS H., Corporal
Enlisted in Buncombe County at age 20, April 24, 1861, for six months. Mustered in as Corporal. Present or accounted for until mustered out November 12-13, 1861.

SMITH, ROBERT H., Private
Enlisted in Buncombe County at age 17, April 24, 1861, for six months. Present or accounted for until mustered out November 12-13, 1861.

SMITH, THOMAS, Private
Enlisted in Buncombe County at age 17, April 24, 1861, for six months. Present or accounted for until mustered out November 12-13, 1861.

SMITH, WILLIAM E., Private
Enlisted in Buncombe County at age 26, April 24, 1861, for six months. Present or accounted for until mustered out November 12-13, 1861.

SNIDER, HENRY J., Private
Enlisted in Buncombe County at age 17, April 24, 1861, for six months. Present or accounted for until mustered out November 12-13, 1861.

SNIDER, JOHN W., Private
Enlisted in Buncombe County at age 45, April 24, 1861, for six months. Discharged June 26, 1861.

STRADLEY, JAMES M., Private
Enlisted in Buncombe County at age 29, April 24, 1861, for six months. Present or accounted for until mustered out November 12-13, 1861.

SULLIVAN, A. L., Private
Enlisted in Buncombe County at age 22, April 24, 1861, for six months. Present or accounted for until mustered out November 12-13, 1861.

SUMMEY, JOHN S. E., Commissary Sergeant
Enlisted in Buncombe County at age 43, April 24, 1861, for six months. Mustered in as Commissary Sergeant. Detailed to the Field and Staff. Present or accounted for until mustered out November 12-13, 1861.

TATE, WILLIAM L., Private
Enlisted in Buncombe County at age 32, April 24, 1861, for six months. Present or accounted for until mustered out November 12-13, 1861.

THOMAS, JOHN H., Private
Enlisted in Buncombe County at age 20, April 24, 1861, for six months. Present or accounted for until mustered out November 12-13, 1861.

TOMS, MARION C., Private
Enlisted in Buncombe County at age 18, July 20, 1861, for six months. Present or accounted for until mustered out November 12-13, 1861.

TOWNSEND, NOAH, Private
Enlisted in Buncombe County at age 18, July 1, 1861, for six months. Present or accounted for until mustered out November 12-13, 1861.

TRIPLETT, JAMES H., Private
Enlisted in Buncombe County at age 18, April 24, 1861, for six months. Present or accounted for until mustered out November 12-13, 1861. Later enlisted in Company B, 11th Regiment N. C. Troops (1st Regiment N. C. Volunteers).

WELLS, MARCUS B., Private
Enlisted in Buncombe County at age 17, May 24, 1861, for six months. Present or accounted for until mustered out November 12-13, 1861.

WEST, NOAH, 1st Sergeant
Enlisted in Buncombe County at age 29, April 24, 1861, for six months. Mustered in as 1st Sergeant. Present or accounted for until mustered out November 12-13, 1861.

WEST, WILLIAM R., Private
Enlisted in Buncombe County at age 21, April 24, 1861, for six months. Present or accounted for until mustered out November 12-13, 1861.

WILLIAMS, JOSEPH R., Private
Enlisted in Buncombe County at age 26, April 24, 1861, for six months. Present or accounted for until mustered out November 12-13, 1861.

WILLIAMS, RICHARD M., Private
Enlisted in Buncombe County at age 19, April 24, 1861, for six months. Present or accounted for until mustered out November 12-13, 1861.

WILSON, JOHN W., Private
Enlisted in Buncombe County at age 39, July 20, 1861, for six months. Present or accounted for until mustered out November 12-13, 1861.

WILSON, THOMAS H., Private
Enlisted in Buncombe County at age 31, April 24, 1861, for six months. Present or accounted for

until mustered out November 12-13, 1861.

WOLFE, JOSHUA E., Private
Enlisted in Buncombe County at age 20, July 20, 1861, for six months. Present or accounted for until mustered out November 12-13, 1861.

WOODS, J. MEREDITH, Private
Enlisted in Buncombe County at age 37, April 24, 1861, for six months. Present or accounted for until mustered out November 12-13, 1861.

WORLEY, GEORGE WILLIAM, Private
Resided in Buncombe County where he enlisted at age 19, April 24, 1861, for six months. Present or accounted for until mustered out November 12-13, 1861. Later enlisted in Company K, 11th Regiment N. C. Troops (1st Regiment N. C. Volunteers).

WRIGHT, A. WAYNE, Private
Enlisted in Buncombe County at age 19, April 24, 1861, for six months. Present or accounted for until mustered out November 12-13, 1861.

WRIGHT, ALBERT, Private
Enlisted in Buncombe County at age 22, April 24, 1861, for six months. Present or accounted for until mustered out November 12-13, 1861.

WRIGHT, JOHN C., Private
Enlisted in Buncombe County at age 20, April 24, 1861, for six months. Present or accounted for until mustered out November 12-13, 1861.

YOUNG, JAMES M., Sergeant
Enlisted in Buncombe County at age 25, April 24, 1861, for six months. Mustered in as Sergeant. Present or accounted for until mustered out November 12-13, 1861. Later enlisted in Company K, 11th Regiment N. C. Troops (1st Regiment N. C. Volunteers).

YOUNG, THOMAS J., Private
Enlisted in Buncombe County at age 20, April 24, 1861, for six months. Present or accounted for until mustered out November 12-13, 1861.

COMPANY F

This company, known as the "Lafayette Light Infantry," enrolled for active service at Fayetteville, Cumberland County, on April 17, 1861. On April 22 the company was ordered to occupy the arsenal at Fayetteville. There it remained until ordered to Raleigh on May 1. It arrived in Raleigh on May 2 and was mustered into state service on May 13, 1861, as Company F of this regiment. After that date the company functioned as a part of the regiment, and its history for the war period is recorded as a part of the regimental history.

The information contained in the following roster of the company was compiled principally from company muster rolls which included the muster-in roll dated August 31, 1861, covering the period May 13-August 31, 1861, and muster rolls for April 27-May 17, 1861; May 13-June 30, 1861; and July-August, 1861. No muster rolls were found for the period after August, 1861. In addition to the company muster rolls, Roll of Honor records, receipt rolls, hospital records, prisoner of war records, and

other primary records, supplemented by state pension applications, United Daughters of the Confederacy records, and postwar rosters and histories, all provided useful information.

OFFICERS

CAPTAINS

STARR, JOSEPH BLAKE
Born in Cumberland County where he resided as a merchant and enlisted at age 31, April 17, 1861, for six months. Appointed Captain to rank from date of enlistment. Promoted to Lieutenant Colonel and transferred to the Field and Staff of this regiment September 28, 1861.

ROBERTS, FRANK N.
Resided in Cumberland County where he enlisted at age 32, April 17, 1861, for six months. Appointed 1st Lieutenant to rank from date of enlistment and promoted to Captain to rank from September 30, 1861. Present or accounted for until mustered out November 12-13, 1861. Later enlisted in 2nd Company B, 36th Regiment N. C. Troops (2nd Regiment N. C. Artillery).

LIEUTENANTS

PEMBERTON, JOHN A., 1st Lieutenant
Resided in Cumberland County where he enlisted at age 33, April 17, 1861, for six months. Appointed 2nd Lieutenant to rank from date of enlistment and promoted to 1st Lieutenant to rank from September 30, 1861. Present or accounted for until mustered out November 12-13, 1861.

RUSH, BENJAMIN, Jr., 2nd Lieutenant
Resided in Cumberland County where he enlisted at age 24, April 17, 1861, for six months. Mustered in as 1st Sergeant and appointed 2nd Lieutenant to rank from September 30, 1861. Present or accounted for until mustered out November 12-13, 1861. Later enlisted in 2nd Company B, 36th Regiment N. C. Troops (2nd Regiment N. C. Artillery).

SLOAN, GEORGE, 3rd Lieutenant
Resided in Cumberland County where he enlisted at age 26, April 17, 1861, for six months. Appointed 3rd Lieutenant to rank from April 29, 1861. Present or accounted for until mustered out November 12-13, 1861. Later enlisted in 2nd Company B, 36th Regiment N. C. Troops (2nd Regiment N. C. Artillery).

NONCOMMISSIONED OFFICERS AND PRIVATES

ALDERMAN, DANIEL, Private
Enlisted in Cumberland County at age 19, April 17, 1861, for six months. Present or accounted for until mustered out November 12-13, 1861.

AREY, CHARLES R., Private
Enlisted in Cumberland County at age 23, April 17, 1861, for six months. Present or accounted for until mustered out November 12-13, 1861. Later enlisted in 2nd Company B, 36th Regiment N. C. Troops (2nd Regiment N. C. Artillery).

AREY, JOSEPH G., Musician
Enlisted in Cumberland County at age 32, April 17, 1861, for six months. Mustered in as Musician. Muster roll dated August 31, 1861, states that he was "detached telegraph office." Present or accounted for until mustered out November 12-13, 1861.

ATKINS, GEORGE BALDWIN, Corporal
Enlisted in Cumberland County at age 22, April 17, 1861, for six months. Mustered in as Corporal. Present or accounted for until mustered out November 12-13, 1861. Later enlisted in 2nd Company B, 36th Regiment N. C. Troops (2nd Regiment N. C. Artillery).

BAKER, GEORGE B., Private
Enlisted in Cumberland County at age 24, April 17, 1861, for six months. Present or accounted for until mustered out November 12-13, 1861. Later enlisted in 2nd Company B, 36th Regiment N. C. Troops (2nd Regiment N. C. Artillery).

BAKER, THOMAS W., Private
Enlisted in Cumberland County at age 21, April 17, 1861, for six months. Present or accounted for until mustered out November 12-13, 1861. Later enlisted in Company D, 43rd Regiment N. C. Troops.

BANKS, CHARLES R., Musician
Enlisted in Cumberland County at age 23, April 17, 1861, for six months. Mustered in as Musician. Present or accounted for until mustered out November 12-13, 1861.

BARNES, S. A., Private
Enlisted in Cumberland County at age 25, June 24, 1861, for six months. Present or accounted for until mustered out November 12-13, 1861.

BEASLEY, GEORGE C., Private
Enlisted in Cumberland County at age 21, April 17, 1861, for six months. Present or accounted for until mustered out November 12-13, 1861. Later enlisted in 2nd Company B, 36th Regiment N. C. Troops (2nd Regiment N. C. Artillery).

BENTON, HENRY E., Private
Enlisted in Cumberland County at age 22, April 17, 1861, for six months. Present or accounted for until mustered out November 12-13, 1861.

BRADDY, KINCHEN J., Private
Enlisted in Cumberland County at age 22, April 17, 1861, for six months. Present or accounted for until mustered out November 12-13, 1861. Later enlisted in Company C, 36th Regiment N. C. Troops (2nd Regiment N. C. Artillery).

BRANDT, GEORGE, Private
Enlisted in Cumberland County at age 36, April 17, 1861, for six months. Present or accounted for until mustered out November 12-13, 1861.

BROOKS, THOMAS J., Private
Enlisted in Cumberland County at age 21, April 17, 1861, for six months. Present or accounted for until mustered out November 12-13, 1861. Later enlisted in Company D, 41st Regiment N. C. Troops (3rd Regiment N.C. Cavalry).

BROWN, ARCHEY S., Private
Enlisted at Yorktown, Virginia, July 20, 1861, for six months. Present or accounted for until mustered out November 12-13, 1861.

BROWN, JAMES A., Private
Enlisted in Cumberland County, April 17, 1861, for six months. Muster roll for July-August, 1861, states that he was "never sworn, sick, went off on furlough about 10 days." Muster roll for August 31, 1861, states that he was "never mustered in." Later enlisted in 2nd Company B, 36th Regiment N. C. Troops (2nd Regiment N. C. Artillery).

CAGLE, MATHEW, Private
Born in Moore County and resided as a merchant in Cumberland County where he enlisted at age 25, April 17, 1861, for six months. Present or accounted for until mustered out November 12-13, 1861. Later enlisted in Company B, 56th Regiment N. C. Troops.

CAMERON, HUGH D., Private
Enlisted in Cumberland County at age 25, April 17, 1861, for six months. Present or accounted for until mustered out November 12-13, 1861.

CARVER, ALEXANDER R., Private
Resided in Cumberland County where he enlisted at age 23, April 17, 1861, for six months. Present or accounted for until mustered out November 12-13, 1861. Later enlisted in Company B, 56th Regiment N. C. Troops.

CARVER, WARREN, Private
Enlisted in Cumberland County at age 18, April 17, 1861, for six months. Discharged September 18, 1861.

CLARK, JAMES M., Private
Resided in Cumberland County where he enlisted at age 25, June 24, 1861, for six months. Present or accounted for until mustered out November 12-13, 1861. Later enlisted in 2nd Company B, 36th Regiment N. C. Troops (2nd Regiment N. C. Artillery).

CLARK, JOHN B., Private
Enlisted in Cumberland County at age 21, April 17, 1861, for six months. Present or accounted for until mustered out November 12-13, 1861.

CLARK, MALCOM D., Private
Enlisted in Cumberland County at age 23, April 17, 1861, for six months. Present or accounted for until mustered out November 12-13, 1861.

CROSSLAND, SABASTIAN T., Private
Enlisted in Cumberland County at age 19, June 24, 1861, for six months. Present or accounted for until mustered out November 12-13, 1861.

CULBRETH, DANIEL A., Private
Enlisted in Cumberland County at age 23, April 17, 1861, for six months. Present or accounted for until mustered out November 12-13, 1861. Later enlisted in Company C, 44th Regiment N. C. Troops.

CURRIE, A. McCOLLUM, Private
Enlisted in Cumberland County at age 30, June 24, 1861, for six months. Present or accounted for until mustered out November 12-13, 1861.

CURRIE, JOHN HENRY, Private
Enlisted in Cumberland County at age 21, June 24, 1861, for six months. Present or accounted for

until mustered out November 12-13, 1861. Later enlisted in Company A, 63rd Regiment N. C. Troops (5th Regiment N. C. Cavalry).

DAILEY, EDWARD O., Private
Enlisted in Cumberland County at age 21, April 17, 1861, for six months. Present or accounted for until mustered out November 12-13, 1861.

DODD, ISAAC C., Private
Enlisted in Cumberland County at age 17, April 17, 1861, for six months. Present or accounted for until mustered out November 12-13, 1861. Later enlisted in 2nd Company B, 36th Regiment N. C. Troops (2nd Regiment N. C. Artillery).

DODD, WILLIAM MURPHY, Private
Enlisted in Cumberland County at age 19, April 17, 1861, for six months. Present or accounted for until mustered out November 12-13, 1861.

DRAUGHON, GEORGE T., Private
Enlisted in Cumberland County at age 29, April 17, 1861, for six months. Present or accounted for until mustered out November 12-13, 1861.

DYE, M. EVANDER, Private
Enlisted in Cumberland County at age 28, April 17, 1861, for six months. Present or accounted for until mustered out November 12-13, 1861.

ELLIOTT, ALEXANDER, Private
Enlisted in Cumberland County at age 25, April 17, 1861, for six months. Present or accounted for until mustered out November 12-13, 1861.

ERAMBERT, JOHN M., Private
Enlisted in Cumberland County at age 24, April 17, 1861, for six months. Present or accounted for until mustered out November 12-13, 1861. Later enlisted in 2nd Company B, 36th Regiment N. C. Troops (2nd Regiment N. C. Artillery).

EVANS, JAMES, Private
Resided in Cumberland County where he enlisted at age 21, June 24, 1861, for six months. Present or accounted for until mustered out November 12-13, 1861. Later enlisted in 2nd Company B, 36th Regiment N. C. Troops (2nd Regiment N. C. Artillery).

EVANS, WILLIAM STEVENS, Private
Enlisted in Cumberland County at age 17, June 24, 1861, for six months. Present or accounted for until mustered out November 12-13, 1861. Later enlisted in 2nd Company B, 36th Regiment N. C. Troops (2nd Regiment N. C. Artillery).

FAULK, MALCOLM, Private
Enlisted in Cumberland County at age 33, April 17, 1861, for six months. Present or accounted for until mustered out November 12-13, 1861.

FULLER, JESSE W., Private
Enlisted in Cumberland County at age 21, April 17, 1861, for six months. Present or accounted for until mustered out November 12-13, 1861. Later enlisted in 2nd Company B, 36th Regiment N. C. Troops (2nd Regiment N. C. Artillery).

FULLER, THOMAS C., Private
Enlisted in Cumberland County at age 29, April 17, 1861, for six months. Present or accounted for until mustered out November 12-13, 1861. Later enlisted in 2nd Company B, 36th Regiment N.C.

Troops (2nd Regiment N. C. Artillery).

FURGUSON, HENRY B., Private
Enlisted in Cumberland County at age 33, April 17, 1861, for six months. Present or accounted for until mustered out November 12-13, 1861. Later enlisted in 2nd Company B, 36th Regiment N.C. Troops (2nd Regiment N. C. Artillery).

GILCHRIST, JOHN A., Private
Enlisted at Yorktown, Virginia, at age 23, August 3, 1861, for six months. Present or accounted for until mustered out November 12-13, 1861.

GILLIS, DUNCAN B., Private
Enlisted in Cumberland County at age 24, April 17, 1861, for six months. Present or accounted for until mustered out November 12-13, 1861.

GOLDSTON, CHARLES CARROLL, Private
Enlisted in Cumberland County at age 24, April 17, 1861, for six months. Present or accounted for until mustered out November 12-13, 1861. Later enlisted in Company H, 46th Regiment N. C. Troops.

GUY, CHARLES T., Private
Enlisted in Cumberland County at age 23, June 24, 1861, for six months. Present or accounted for until mustered out November 12-13, 1861.

HAHR, FRANZ JOSEPH, Corporal
Resided in Cumberland County where he enlisted at age 36, April 17, 1861, for six months. Mustered in as Corporal. Transferred to the Field and Staff of this regiment upon appointment as Quartermaster Sergeant on May 20, 1861.

HALL, WILBUR G., Private
Resided in Cumberland County where he enlisted at age 19, April 17, 1861, for six months. Present or accounted for until mustered out November 12-13, 1861. Later enlisted in 2nd Company B, 36th Regiment N. C. Troops (2nd Regiment N. C. Artillery).

HARRELL, DAVID J., Private
Resided in Cumberland County where he enlisted at age 21, June 24, 1861, for six months. Present or accounted for until mustered out November 12-13, 1861. Later enlisted in 2nd Company B, 36th Regiment N. C. Troops (2nd Regiment N. C. Artillery).

HARRIS, JAMES, Private
Enlisted in Cumberland County at age 29, April 17, 1861, for six months. Present or accounted for until mustered out November 12-13, 1861.

HENRY, WILLIAM, Private
Enlisted in Cumberland County at age 22, April 17, 1861, for six months. Present or accounted for until mustered out November 12-13, 1861.

HURST, LEONIDAS H., Private
Born in Orange County and resided as a carpenter in Cumberland County where he enlisted at age 22, June 24, 1861, for six months. Present or accounted for until mustered out November 12-13, 1861. Later enlisted in Company B, 56th Regiment N. C. Troops.

JENNINGS, WILLIAM L., Private
Enlisted in Cumberland County at age 19, April 17, 1861, for six months. Present or accounted for

until mustered out November 12-13, 1861.

JESSUP, ISAAC, Private
Resided in Cumberland County where he enlisted at age 18, April 17, 1861, for six months. Present or accounted for until mustered out November 12-13, 1861. Later enlisted in 2nd Company B, 36th Regiment N. C. Troops (2nd Regiment N. C. Artillery).

JOHNSON, JOHN ALEX, Private
Enlisted in Cumberland County at age 21, April 17, 1861, for six months. Present or accounted for until mustered out November 12-13, 1861.

JONES, JOHN V., Private
Enlisted in Cumberland County at age 36, June 24, 1861, for six months. Present or accounted for until mustered out November 12-13, 1861.

JORDAN, THOMAS J., Private
Enlisted in Cumberland County at age 25, April 17, 1861, for six months. Present or accounted for until mustered out November 12-13, 1861.

KETCHUM, DAVID W., Private
Born in New Hanover County where he resided as a merchant and enlisted at age 22, July 7, 1861, for six months. Present or accounted for until mustered out November 12-13, 1861. Later enlisted in Company G, 51st Regiment N. C. Troops.

KING, JAMES A., Private
Born in Cumberland County where he resided as a farmer and enlisted at age 22, April 17, 1861, for six months. Present or accounted for until mustered out November 12-13, 1861. Later enlisted in Company B, 56th Regiment N. C. Troops.

KING, NATHAN J., Private
Enlisted in Cumberland County at age 23, April 17, 1861, for six months. Present or accounted for until mustered out November 12-13, 1861.

KIRKPATRICK, JAMES, Private
Resided in Cumberland County where he enlisted at age 29, April 17, 1861, for six months. Present or accounted for until mustered out November 12-13, 1861. Later enlisted in Company A, 63rd Regiment N. C. Troops (5th Regiment N. C. Cavalry).

LEE, ALEXANDER, Private
Enlisted in Cumberland County at age 17, April 17, 1861, for six months. Present or accounted for until mustered out November 12-13, 1861.

LINEBERRY, ALFRED D., Private
Resided in Cumberland County where he enlisted at age 30, April 17, 1861, for six months. Present or accounted for until mustered out November 12-13, 1861. Later enlisted in 2nd Company B, 36th Regiment N. C. Troops (2nd Regiment N. C. Artillery).

McARTHUR, NEILL A., Private
Enlisted in Cumberland County at age 28, April 17, 1861, for six months. Present or accounted for until mustered out November 12-13, 1861.

McDANIEL, WILLIAM C., Private
Born in Cumberland County where he resided as a farmer and enlisted at age 18, June 24, 1861, for six months. Present or accounted for until mustered out November 12-13, 1861. Later enlisted in

Company C, 54th Regiment N. C. Troops.

McDONALD, DANIEL M., Corporal
Born in Bladen County and was by occupation a clerk in Cumberland County where he enlisted at age 24, April 17, 1861, for six months. Mustered in as Corporal. Present or accounted for until mustered out November 12-13, 1861. Later enlisted in Company B, 56th Regiment N. C. Troops.

McDONALD, JAMES R., Private
Born in Cumberland County where he resided as a merchant and enlisted at age 35, April 17, 1861, for six months. Present or accounted for until mustered out November 12-13, 1861. Later enlisted in Company D, 51st Regiment N. C. Troops.

McDONALD, KENETH A., Private
Enlisted in Cumberland County at age 28, April 17, 1861, for six months. Present or accounted for until mustered out November 12-13, 1861.

McDONALD, WILLIAM J., Private
Enlisted in Cumberland County at age 18, April 17, 1861, for six months. Present or accounted for until mustered out November 12-13, 1861. Later enlisted in 2nd Company B, 36th Regiment N. C. Troops (2nd Regiment N. C. Artillery).

McDUFFIE, JOHN W., Private
Enlisted in Cumberland County at age 23, April 17, 1861, for six months. Present or accounted for until mustered out November 12-13, 1861.

McDUFFIE, MALCOM J., Private
Enlisted in Cumberland County at age 32, April 17, 1861, for six months. Present or accounted for until mustered out November 12-13, 1861.

McDUFFIE, ROBERT H., Private
Enlisted in Cumberland County at age 25, April 17, 1861, for six months. Present or accounted for until mustered out November 12-13, 1861.

McEACHEN, ROBERT J., Private
Enlisted at Yorktown, Virginia, at age 25, July 9, 1861, for six months. Present or accounted for until mustered out November 12-13, 1861. Later enlisted in Company D, 51st Regiment N. C. Troops.

McKAY, HENRY ARCHIBALD, Private
Resided in Cumberland County where he enlisted at age 22, April 17, 1861, for six months. Present or accounted for until mustered out November 12-13, 1861. Later enlisted in Company A, 63rd Regiment N. C. Troops (5th Regiment N. C. Cavalry).

McLEAN, DUNCAN N., Private
Enlisted in Cumberland County at age 20, June 24, 1861, for six months. Present or accounted for until mustered out November 12-13, 1861.

McMILLAN, HAMILTON, Private
Resided in Cumberland County where he enlisted at age 23, April 17, 1861, for six months. Present or accounted for until mustered out November 12-13, 1861. Later enlisted in Company G, 6th Regiment N. C. State Troops.

McNAIR, JOHN W., Private
Enlisted at Yorktown, Virginia, at age 30, July 9, 1861, for six months. Present or accounted for through August, 1861.

McRAE, JOHN, Corporal
Enlisted in Cumberland County at age 36, April 17, 1861, for six months. Mustered in as Corporal. Present or accounted for until mustered out November 12-13, 1861. Later enlisted in 2nd Company B, 36th Regiment N. C. Troops (2nd Regiment N. C. Artillery).

McRIMMON, ARCHIBALD, Private
Enlisted in Cumberland County at age 26, April 17, 1861, for six months. Present or accounted for until mustered out November 12-13, 1861.

MARTINE, THEODORE, Sergeant
Enlisted in Cumberland County at age 28, April 17, 1861, for six months. Mustered in as Sergeant. Transferred to the Field and Staff of this regiment upon appointment as Ordnance Sergeant on May 22, 1861.

MATTHEWS, WILLIAM McINTYRE, Private
Enlisted in Cumberland County at age 17, June 24, 1861, for six months. Present or accounted for until mustered out November 12-13, 1861. Later enlisted in 2nd Company B, 36th Regiment N. C. Troops (2nd Regiment N. C. Artillery).

MONROE, DANIEL A., Private
Resided in Cumberland County where he enlisted at age 30, April 17, 1861, for six months. Present or accounted for until mustered out November 12-13, 1861. Later enlisted in Company K, 38th Regiment N. C. Troops.

MONROE, HENRY N., Private
Resided in Cumberland County where he enlisted at age 36, April 17, 1861, for six months. Present or accounted for until mustered out November 12-13, 1861.

MOORE, JOHN, Private
Resided in Cumberland County where he enlisted at age 25, April 17, 1861, for six months. Present or accounted for until mustered out November 12-13, 1861. Later enlisted in 2nd Company B, 36th Regiment N. C. Troops (2nd Regiment N. C. Artillery).

MURPHY, CHARLES B., Private
Born in Sampson County and resided as a farmer when he enlisted in Cumberland County at age 24, April 17, 1861, for six months. Present or accounted for until mustered out November 12-13, 1861. Later enlisted in Company A, 63rd Regiment N. C. Troops (5th Regiment N. C. Cavalry).

MURPHY, JOHN, Private
Resided in Cumberland County where he enlisted at age 27, April 17, 1861, for six months. Present or accounted for until mustered out November 12-13, 1861. Later enlisted in 2nd Company B, 36th Regiment N. C. Troops (2nd Regiment N. C. Artillery).

MYROVER, JAMES H., Private
Resided in Cumberland County where he enlisted at age 18, June 6, 1861, for six months. Present or accounted for until mustered out November 12-13, 1861. Later enlisted in 2nd Company B, 36th Regiment N. C. Troops (2nd Regiment N. C. Artillery).

NEWELL, JOHN G., Private
Enlisted in Cumberland County at age 24, April 17, 1861, for six months. Present or accounted for until mustered out November 12-13, 1861.

NOTT, JAMES D., Private
Resided in Cumberland County where he enlisted at age 28, April 17, 1861, for six months. Present or accounted for until mustered out November 12-13, 1861. Later enlisted in Company A, 63rd Regiment N. C. Troops (5th Regiment N. C. Cavalry).

O'HANLON, DUNCAN McRAE, Sergeant
Resided in Cumberland County where he enlisted at age 24, April 17, 1861, for six months. Mustered in as Sergeant. Present or accounted for until mustered out November 12-13, 1861.

ORRELL, ROBERT M., Private
Enlisted in Cumberland County at age 39, April 17, 1861, for six months. Present or accounted for until mustered out November 12-13, 1861.

PALMER, ROBERT D., Private
Enlisted in Cumberland County at age 32, April 17, 1861, for six months. Present or accounted for until mustered out November 12-13, 1861.

PARKER, WILLIAM M., Corporal
Enlisted in Cumberland County at age 32, April 17, 1861, for six months. Mustered in as Private and appointed Corporal June 30, 1861. Present or accounted for until mustered out November 12-13, 1861.

PEARCE, BENJAMIN F., Private
Enlisted in Cumberland County at age 33, April 17, 1861, for six months. Detailed as Quartermaster Sergeant August 13-31, 1861. Present or accounted for until mustered out November 12-13, 1861. Later enlisted in 2nd Company B, 36th Regiment N. C. Troops (2nd Regiment N. C. Artillery).

PHILLIPS, JOHN W., Private
Enlisted in Cumberland County at age 17, June 24, 1861, for six months. Present or accounted for until mustered out November 12-13, 1861.

POWERS, WILLIAM B., Private
Enlisted in Cumberland County at age 29, April 17, 1861, for six months. Present or accounted for until mustered out November 12-13, 1861.

PRIOR, JOHN N., Private
Enlisted in Cumberland County at age 23, April 17, 1861, for six months. Present or accounted for until mustered out November 12-13, 1861. Later served in the Adjutant and Inspector General's Department.

REGISTER, HERMAN H., Private
Enlisted in Cumberland County at age 24, May 15, 1861, for six months. Present or accounted for until mustered out November 12-13, 1861.

ROBERTS, CHARLES E., Private
Enlisted in Cumberland County at age 25, April 17, 1861, for six months. Present or accounted for until mustered out November 12-13, 1861.

ROSE, JAMES T., Sergeant
Enlisted in Cumberland County at age 26, April

17, 1861, for six months. Mustered in as Sergeant. Present or accounted for until mustered out November 12-13, 1861. Later enlisted in Company A, 63rd Regiment N. C. Troops (5th Regiment N. C. Cavalry).

ROSE, WALTER L., Private

Enlisted in Cumberland County at age 26, April 17, 1861, for six months. Present or accounted for until mustered out November 12-13, 1861. Later enlisted in Company A, 63rd Regiment N. C. Troops (5th Regiment N. C. Cavalry).

ROSE, WILLIAM A., Private

Enlisted in Cumberland County at age 38, April 17, 1861, for six months. Present or accounted for until mustered out November 12-13, 1861.

SHAW, ANGUS, Private

Enlisted in Cumberland County at age 35, April 17, 1861, for six months. Present or accounted for until mustered out November 12-13, 1861. Later enlisted in Company K, 38th Regiment N. C. Troops.

SHEMWELL, POINDEXTER, Private

Enlisted in Cumberland County at age 35, April 17, 1861, for six months. Present or accounted for until mustered out November 12-13, 1861.

SHEPHERD, WILLIAM W., Private

Enlisted in Cumberland County at age 29, April 17, 1861, for six months. Present or accounted for until mustered out November 12-13, 1861.

SMITH, JAMES B., Private

Enlisted in Cumberland County at age 22, April 17, 1861, for six months. Present or accounted for until mustered out November 12-13, 1861. Later enlisted in 2nd Company B, 36th Regiment N. C. Troops (2nd Regiment N. C. Artillery).

STEDMAN, ROBERT WINSHIP, Private

Resided in Cumberland County where he enlisted at age 24, April 17, 1861, for six months. Present or accounted for until mustered out November 12-13, 1861. Later enlisted in 2nd Company B, 36th Regiment N. C. Troops (2nd Regiment N. C. Artillery).

STERN, ISRAEL, Private

Enlisted in Cumberland County at age 24, April 17, 1861, for six months. Present or accounted for until mustered out November 12-13, 1861.

SUDDERTH, JOHN R., Private

Enlisted at Yorktown, Virginia, at age 33, July 3, 1861, for six months. Present or accounted for until mustered out November 12-13, 1861.

SURLES, SAMUEL R., Private

Enlisted in Cumberland County at age 28, April 17, 1861, for six months. Present or accounted for until mustered out November 12-13, 1861.

TAYLOR, JAMES H., Private

Enlisted in Cumberland County at age 22, April 17, 1861, for six months. Present or accounted for until mustered out November 12-13, 1861. Later enlisted in 2nd Company B, 36th Regiment N. C. Troops (2nd Regiment N. C. Artillery).

TAYLOR, WILLIAM T., Private

Enlisted in Cumberland County at age 20, April

17, 1861, for six months. Present or accounted for until mustered out November 12-13, 1861.

THORNTON, BENJAMIN W., Private

Enlisted in Cumberland County at age 21, April 17, 1861, for six months. Present or accounted for until mustered out November 12-13, 1861. Later enlisted in Company B, 56th Regiment N. C. Troops.

THORNTON, RICHARD W., Private

Enlisted in Cumberland County at age 22, April 17, 1861, for six months. Present or accounted for until mustered out November 12-13, 1861. Later enlisted in Company B, 56th Regiment N. C. Troops.

VALENTINE, BENJAMIN S., Private

Enlisted in Cumberland County at age 18, April 17, 1861, for six months. Present or accounted for until mustered out November 12-13, 1861.

WARDELL, THEO R., Private

Enlisted in Cumberland County at age 24, April 17, 1861, for six months. Present or accounted for until mustered out November 12-13, 1861.

WEIR, ANDREW, Private

Enlisted in Cumberland County at age 33, April 17, 1861, for six months. Present or accounted for until mustered out November 12-13, 1861. Later enlisted in Company E, 8th Regiment N. C. State Troops.

WEMYSS, JOHN, Private

Enlisted in Cumberland County at age 23, April 17, 1861, for six months. Present or accounted for until mustered out November 12-13, 1861. Later enlisted in 2nd Company B, 36th Regiment N. C. Troops (2nd Regiment N. C. Artillery).

WHITLOCK, JOHN G., Private

Resided in Cumberland County where he enlisted at age 27, April 17, 1861, for six months. Present or accounted for until mustered out November 12-13, 1861. Later enlisted in 2nd Company B, 36th Regiment N. C. Troops (2nd Regiment N. C. Artillery).

WHITMORE, JOHN, Private

Enlisted in Cumberland County at age 32, April 17, 1861, for six months. Present or accounted for until mustered out November 12-13, 1861. Later enlisted in 2nd Company B, 36th Regiment N. C. Troops (2nd Regiment N. C. Artillery).

WILLIAMS, CHARLES J., Private

Resided in Cumberland County where he enlisted at age 24, April 17, 1861, for six months. Present or accounted for until mustered out November 12-13, 1861. Later enlisted in 2nd Company C, 36th Regiment N. C. Troops (2nd Regiment N. C. Artillery).

COMPANY G

This company, known as the "Burke Rifles," was enrolled for active service at Morganton, Burke County, on April 18, 1861. It arrived in Raleigh on April 25 and was mustered into state service on May

13, 1861, as Company G of this regiment. After that date the company functioned as a part of the regiment, and its history for the war period is recorded as a part of the regimental history.

The information contained in the following roster of the company was compiled principally from company muster rolls which included the muster-in roll dated August 31, 1861, covering the period May 13-August 31, 1861, and muster rolls for the periods of April 25-May 13, 1861; May 13-June 30, 1861; and July-August, 1861. In addition to the company muster rolls, Roll of Honor records, receipt rolls, hospital records, prisoner of war records, and other primary records, supplemented by state pension applications, United Daughters of the Confederacy records, and postwar rosters and histories, all provided useful information.

OFFICERS

CAPTAIN

AVERY, CLARK MOULTON

Resided in Burke County where he enlisted at age 41, April 25, 1861, for six months. Appointed Captain to rank from date of enlistment. Present or accounted for until mustered out November 12-13, 1861. Later appointed Major on the Field and Staff of the 33rd Regiment N. C. Troops.

LIEUTENANTS

ARMFIELD, MARK D., 2nd Lieutenant

Resided in Burke County where he enlisted at age 54, April 25, 1861, for six months. Mustered in as Corporal and appointed 2nd Lieutenant to rank from October 24, 1861. Present or accounted for until mustered out November 12-13, 1861. Later enlisted in Company B, 11th Regiment N. C. Troops (1st Regiment N. C. Volunteers).

BROWN, CALVIN S., 1st Lieutenant

Resided in Burke County where he enlisted at age 33, April 25, 1861, for six months. Appointed 1st Lieutenant to rank from date of enlistment. Present or accounted for until mustered out November 12-13, 1861. Later enlisted in Company D, 11th Regiment N. C. Troops (1st Regiment N. C. Volunteers).

DICKSON, JOHN A., 2nd Lieutenant

Resided in Burke County where he enlisted at age 33, April 25, 1861, for six months. Appointed 2nd Lieutenant to rank from date of enlistment. Died of "pneumonia" October 24, 1861.

McDOWELL, JAMES CHARLES SHEFFIELD, 3rd Lieutenant

Resided in Burke County where he enlisted at age 30, April 25, 1861, for six months. Appointed 3rd Lieutenant to rank from date of enlistment. Present or accounted for until mustered out November 12-13, 1861. Later appointed Major on the Field and Staff of the 54th Regiment N. C. Troops.

NONCOMMISSIONED OFFICERS AND PRIVATES

ALLMAN, JOSEPH, Private

Enlisted at Yorktown, Virginia, at age 18, July 3, 1861, for six months. Present or accounted for until mustered out November 12-13, 1861.

ANTHONY, G. W., Private

Enlisted in Burke County at age 38, April 25, 1861, for six months. Present or accounted for until mustered out November 12-13, 1861.

ANTHONY, P. B., Private

Enlisted at Yorktown, Virginia, at age 22, August 8, 1861, for six months. Present or accounted for until mustered out November 12-13, 1861.

AVERY, H. H., Private

Enlisted in Burke County at age 21, April 25, 1861, for six months. Died at Yorktown, Virginia, August 7, 1861.

BENFIELD, JULIUS M., Private

Enlisted in Burke County at age 24, April 25, 1861, for six months. Present or accounted for until mustered out November 12-13, 1861.

BENFIELD, T. W., Private

Enlisted at Yorktown, Virginia, at age 21, July 3, 1861, for six months. Present or accounted for until mustered out November 12-13, 1861.

BLACK, S. J., Private

Enlisted in Burke County at age 43, April 25, 1861, for six months. Present or accounted for until mustered out November 12-13, 1861.

BRANCH, DAVID W., Private

Enlisted in Burke County at age 21, April 25, 1861, for six months. Died at Yorktown, Virginia, October 13, 1861.

BRANCH, REUBEN, Private

Enlisted at Yorktown, Virginia, at age 24, July 3, 1861, for six months. Present or accounted for until mustered out November 12-13, 1861.

BRISTOE, E. B., Private

Enlisted in Burke County at age 18, April 25, 1861, for six months. Present or accounted for until mustered out November 12-13, 1861.

BRITTAIN, O. J., Private

Enlisted in Burke County at age 23, April 25, 1861, for six months. Present or accounted for until mustered out November 12-13, 1861. Later enlisted in Company D, 11th Regiment N. C. Troops (1st Regiment N. C. Volunteers).

CARLTON, J. C., Private

Enlisted in Burke County at age 32, April 25, 1861, for six months. Present or accounted for until mustered out November 12-13, 1861.

CARLTON, R. W., Private

Enlisted in Burke County at age 30, April 25, 1861, for six months. Present or accounted for until mustered out November 12-13, 1861.

CARPENING, W. G., Private

Enlisted at Yorktown, Virginia, at age 16, July 3, 1861, for six months. Present or accounted for until mustered out November 12-13, 1861.

CAUSLEY, J. N., Private
Enlisted in Burke County at age 18, April 25, 1861, for six months. Present or accounted for until mustered out November 12-13, 1861.

CLAY, JOSEPH, Private
Enlisted at Yorktown, Virginia, at age 18, July 3, 1861, for six months. Present or accounted for until mustered out November 12-13, 1861.

CONLEY, AVERY W., Private
Enlisted in Burke County at age 21, April 25, 1861, for six months. Present or accounted for until mustered out November 12-13, 1861. Later enlisted in Company I, 39th Regiment N. C. Troops.

CONLEY, JAMES W., Private
Enlisted in Burke County at age 30, April 25, 1861, for six months. Present or accounted for until mustered out November 12-13, 1861.

CONLEY, JASON, Private
Enlisted in Burke County at age 29, April 25, 1861, for six months. Present or accounted for until mustered out November 12-13, 1861.

CONLEY, JOSEPH, Private
Enlisted in Burke County at age 23, April 25, 1861, for six months. Present or accounted for until mustered out November 12-13, 1861.

CONLEY, R. H., Private
Enlisted in Burke County at age 23, April 25, 1861, for six months. Died October 9. 1861.

CONLEY, S. E., Private
Enlisted at Yorktown, Virginia, at age 39, July 3, 1861, for six months. Present or accounted for until mustered out November 12-13, 1861.

COON, W. P., Private
Enlisted in Burke County at age 20, April 25, 1861, for six months. Present or accounted for until mustered out November 12-13, 1861.

CROUTCH, PATON, Private
Enlisted in Burke County at age 23, April 25, 1861, for six months. Present or accounted for until mustered out November 12-13, 1861.

CROWELL, J. H., Private
Enlisted in Burke County at age 27, April 25, 1861, for six months. Mustered in as Corporal and reduced to ranks July 13, 1861. Present or accounted for until mustered out November 12-13, 1861.

DENNIS, J. F., Private
Enlisted in Burke County at age 27, April 25, 1861, for six months. Present or accounted for until mustered out November 12-13, 1861.

DORSEY, J. N., Private
Enlisted in Burke County at age 21, April 25, 1861, for six months. Present or accounted for until mustered out November 12-13, 1861.

DORSEY, T. A., Private
Enlisted at Yorktown, Virginia, at age 18, August 8, 1861, for six months. Present or accounted for until mustered out November 12-13, 1861.

DUCKWORTH, GEORGE, Private
Enlisted in Burke County at age 23, April 25, 1861, for six months. Present or accounted for until mustered out November 12-13, 1861.

DUCKWORTH, J. L., Private
Enlisted in Burke County at age 18, April 25, 1861, for six months. Present or accounted for until mustered out November 12-13, 1861.

DUCKWORTH, J. W., Private
Enlisted in Burke County at age 23, April 25, 1861, for six months. Muster roll dated August 31, 1861, states that he "deserted May, 1861."

DUVAL, JOHN M., Private
Enlisted in Burke County at age 18, April 25, 1861, for six months. Present or accounted for until mustered out November 12, 1861.

FLEMING, J. L., Sergeant
Enlisted in Burke County at age 18, April 25, 1861, for six months. Mustered in as Sergeant. Present or accounted for until mustered out November 12-13, 1861.

FORNEY, WILLIAM, Private
Enlisted in Burke County at age 21, April 25, 1861, for six months. Present or accounted for until mustered out November 12-13, 1861.

FOX, J. A., Private
Enlisted at Yorktown, Virginia, at age 23, July 3, 1861, for six months. Present or accounted for until mustered out November 12-13, 1861.

FOX, LEONARD, Private
Enlisted in Burke County at age 19, April 25, 1861, for six months. Present or accounted for until mustered out November 12-13, 1861.

FULWOOD, J. M., Private
Enlisted in Burke County at age 20, April 25, 1861, for six months. Present or accounted for until mustered out November 12-13, 1861.

GALLOWAY, H. H., Private
Enlisted at Yorktown, Virginia, at age 21, July 3, 1861, for six months. Present or accounted for until mustered out November 12-13, 1861.

GALLOWAY, T. N., Private
Enlisted in Burke County at age 22, April 25, 1861, for six months. Present or accounted for until mustered out November 12-13, 1861.

GARRISON, WILLIAM, Private
Enlisted in Burke County at age 23, April 25, 1861, for six months. Present or accounted for until mustered out November 12-13, 1861.

GIBSON, WILLIAM, Private
Enlisted at Yorktown, Virginia, at age 16, July 3, 1861, for six months. Died at Yorktown, September 14, 1861.

GILES, CARLTON, Private
Enlisted at Yorktown, Virginia, at age 23, July 3, 1861, for six months. Present or accounted for until mustered out November 12-13, 1861.

GLASS, DAVID P., Private
Enlisted in Burke County at age 28, April 25, 1861, for six months. Present or accounted for until mustered out November 12-13, 1861. Later enlisted in Company K, 35th Regiment N. C. Troops.

GOOD, GEORGE, Private
Enlisted in Burke County at age 35, April 25, 1861, for six months. Present or accounted for until mustered out November 12-13, 1861.

GOOD, JOHN, Private
Enlisted in Burke County at age 27, April 25, 1861, for six months. Present or accounted for until mustered out November 12-13, 1861.

GREENLEE, G. E., Private
Enlisted in Burke County at age 23, April 25, 1861, for six months. Present or accounted for until mustered out November 12-13, 1861.

HENNESSEE, M. S., Private
Enlisted in Burke County at age 23, April 25, 1861, for six months. Present or accounted for until mustered out November 12-13, 1861.

HENNESSEE, R. J., Private
Enlisted at Yorktown, Virginia, at age 21, July 3, 1861, for six months. Present or accounted for until mustered out November 12-13, 1861.

HENNESSEE, THOMAS A., Private
Enlisted in Burke County at age 21, April 25, 1861, for six months. Present or accounted for until mustered out November 12-13, 1861.

HICKS, DANIEL M., Private
Enlisted in Burke County at age 49, April 25, 1861, for six months. Discharged on "Surgeon's Certificate" on June 27, 1861. Later enlisted in Company B, 54th Regiment N. C. Troops.

HICKS, JOSEPH S., Private
Enlisted in Burke County at age 20, April 25, 1861, for six months. Present or accounted for until mustered out November 12-13, 1861.

HICKS, RUFUS D., Private
Enlisted in Burke County at age 22, April 25, 1861, for six months. Present or accounted for until mustered out November 12-13, 1861.

HOWARD, J. EDWARD, Private
Enlisted in Burke County at age 18, April 25, 1861, for six months. Present or accounted for until mustered out November 12-13, 1861.

HOWARD, W. F., Corporal
Enlisted in Burke County at age 23, April 25, 1861, for six months. Mustered in as Corporal. Present or accounted for until mustered out November 12-13, 1861.

HUFFMAN, JOSEPH, Private
Enlisted in Burke County at age 27, April 25, 1861, for six months. Present or accounted for until mustered out November 12-13, 1861.

JOHNSON, PHILIP JEFFERSON, Private
Resided in Burke County where he enlisted at age 20, April 25, 1861, for six months. Present or accounted for until mustered out November 12-13, 1861. Later enlisted in Company K, 35th Regiment N. C. Troops.

KERLEY, R., Private
Enlisted in Burke County at age 20, April 25, 1861, for six months. Present or accounted for until mustered out November 12-13, 1861. Later enlisted in Company B, 54th Regiment N. C. Troops.

KIBLER, GEORGE B., Sergeant
Born in Burke County where he resided as a farmer and enlisted at age 26, April 25, 1861, for six months. Mustered in as Sergeant. Transferred to the Field and Staff upon appointment as Sergeant Major to rank from June 1, 1861.

KIBLER, S. M., Corporal
Enlisted in Burke County at age 28, April 25, 1861, for six months. Mustered in as Private and appointed Corporal July 13, 1861. Present or accounted for until mustered out November 12-13, 1861.

KINCAID, J. S., Private
Enlisted in Burke County at age 27, April 25, 1861, for six months. Discharged September 21, 1861.

KINCAID, W. J., 1st Sergeant
Enlisted in Burke County at age 20, April 25, 1861, for six months. Mustered in as 1st Sergeant. Present or accounted for until mustered out November 12-13, 1861. Later enlisted in Company D, 11th Regiment N. C. Troops (1st Regiment N. C. Volunteers).

LAFEVERS, A. M., Private
Enlisted in Burke County at age 27, April 25, 1861, for six months. Present or accounted for until mustered out November 12-13, 1861.

LANE, E. M., Private
Enlisted in Burke County at age 29, April 25, 1861, for six months. Present or accounted for until mustered out November 12-13, 1861.

LANE, J. E., Private
Enlisted in Burke County at age 22, April 25, 1861, for six months. Present or accounted for until mustered out November 12-13, 1861.

LAXTON, J. L., Private
Enlisted in Burke County at age 22, April 25, 1861, for six months. Present or accounted for until mustered out November 12-13, 1861.

LONDON, GEORGE M., Private
Enlisted in Burke County at age 20, April 25, 1861, for six months. Present or accounted for until mustered out November 12-13, 1861.

LONDON, JAMES WILBURN, Private
Enlisted in Burke County at age 21, April 25, 1861, for six months. Present or accounted for until mustered out November 12-13, 1861. Later enlisted in Company B, 11th Regiment N. C. Troops (1st Regiment N. C. Volunteers).

LOUDERMILK, W. B., Private
Enlisted at Yorktown, Virginia, at age 40, August 8, 1861, for six months. Present or accounted for until mustered out November 12-13, 1861.

LOWRANCE, WILLIAM B. A., Private
Enlisted in Burke County at age 18, April 25, 1861, for six months. Present or accounted for until mustered out November 12-13, 1861. Later enlisted in Company B, 46th Regiment N. C. Troops.

MACE, J. P., Private
Enlisted in Burke County at age 18, April 25,

1861, for six months. Present or accounted for until mustered out November 12-13, 1861.

MACE, JOHN, Private

Born in Yancey County and was by occupation a farmer when he enlisted in Burke County at age 22, April 25, 1861, for six months. Discharged October 2, 1861, by reason of "chronic diarrhoea."

MACE, W. H., Private

Enlisted at Yorktown, Virginia, at age 23, August 8, 1861, for six months. Present or accounted for until mustered out November 12-13, 1861.

McELRATH, J. J., Private

Enlisted at Yorktown, Virginia, at age 22, August 8, 1861, for six months. Present or accounted for until mustered out November 12-13, 1861.

McGIMSEY, CHARLES A., Private

Enlisted in Burke County at age 23, April 25, 1861, for six months. Present or accounted for until mustered out November 12-13, 1861. Later enlisted in Company F, 41st Regiment N. C. Troops (3rd Regiment N. C. Cavalry).

McGINSEY, W. W., Private

Enlisted in Burke County at age 19, April 25, 1861, for six months. Present or accounted for until mustered out November 12-13, 1861.

McKESSON, J. C., Private

Enlisted in Burke County at age 26, April 25, 1861, for six months. Present or accounted for until mustered out November 12-13, 1861.

MARLER, MARTIN S., Private

Enlisted in Burke County at age 25, April 25, 1861, for six months. Present or accounted for until mustered out November 12-13, 1861. Later enlisted in Company B, 54th Regiment N. C. Troops.

MELTON, E. A., Private

Enlisted in Burke County at age 16, April 25, 1861, for six months. Present or accounted for until mustered out November 12-13, 1861. Later enlisted in Company D, 11th Regiment N. C. Troops (1st Regiment N. C. Volunteers).

MILLER, J. M., Private

Enlisted in Burke County at age 24, April 25, 1861, for six months. Present or accounted for until mustered out November 12-13, 1861.

MISHAUX, JOHN P., Private

Enlisted in Burke County at age 18, April 25, 1861, for six months. Present or accounted for until mustered out November 12-13, 1861. Later enlisted in Company B, 11th Regiment N. C. Troops (1st Regiment N. C. Volunteers).

MOORE, J. B., Private

Enlisted in Burke County at age 27, April 25, 1861, for six months. Present or accounted for until mustered out November 12-13, 1861.

MOORE, J. R., Private

Enlisted in Burke County at age 18, April 25, 1861, for six months. Present or accounted for until mustered out November 12-13, 1861.

MOORE, THOMAS B., Private

Enlisted in Burke County at age 18, April 25, 1861, for six months. Present or accounted for

until mustered out November 12-13, 1861.

OMARK, J. H., Sergeant

Enlisted in Burke County at age 29, April 25, 1861, for six months. Mustered in as Sergeant. Present or accounted for until mustered out November 12-13, 1861.

OSBORNE, A. W., Private

Enlisted in Burke County at age 23, April 25, 1861, for six months. Present or accounted for until mustered out November 12-13, 1861.

PARKS, HARRISON, Private

Enlisted in Burke County at age 20, April 25, 1861, for six months. Present or accounted for until mustered out November 12-13, 1861.

PARKS, THOMAS, Sergeant

Enlisted in Burke County at age 42, April 25, 1861, for six months. Mustered in as Sergeant. Present or accounted for until mustered out November 12-13, 1861. Later enlisted in Company B, 11th Regiment N. C. Troops (1st Regiment N. C. Volunteers).

PEARSON, J. A., Private

Enlisted in Burke County at age 24, April 25, 1861, for six months. Present or accounted for until mustered out November 12-13, 1861.

PEARSON, JOHN, Private

Enlisted in Burke County at age 22, April 25, 1861, for six months. Present or accounted for until mustered out November 12-13, 1861.

PEARSON, MICHAEL L., Private

Enlisted in Burke County at age 42, April 25, 1861, for six months. Present or accounted for until mustered out November 12-13, 1861.

PEARSON, MICHAEL W., Private

Enlisted in Burke County at age 20, April 25, 1861, for six months. Present or accounted for until mustered out November 12-13, 1861.

PEARSON, THOMAS, Private

Enlisted in Burke County at age 24, April 25, 1861, for six months. Present or accounted for until mustered out November 12-13, 1861.

POTEAT, PETER, Private

Enlisted in Burke County at age 40, April 25, 1861, for six months. Present or accounted for until mustered out November 12-13, 1861.

POWELL, THOMAS S., Private

Enlisted in Burke County at age 21, April 25, 1861, for six months. Present or accounted for until mustered out November 12-13, 1861.

POWELL, WILLIAM, Private

Enlisted in Burke County at age 22, April 25, 1861, for six months. Present or accounted for until mustered out November 12-13, 1861.

PUCKETT, JOHN W., Private

Enlisted in Burke County at age 22, April 25, 1861, for six months. Present or accounted for until mustered out November 12-13, 1861.

RAY, D. B., Private

Enlisted at Yorktown, Virginia, July 25, 1861, for six months. Present or accounted for until mustered out November 12-13, 1861.

SIMPSON, JOHN E., Private
Enlisted in Burke County at age 22, April 25, 1861, for six months. Present or accounted for until mustered out November 12-13, 1861.

SINGLETON, MARCUS, Private
Enlisted in Burke County at age 22, April 25, 1861, for six months. Present or accounted for until mustered out November 12-13, 1861.

SMITH, GEORGE W., Private
Enlisted at Yorktown, Virginia, at age 53, July 3, 1861, for six months. Present or accounted for until mustered out November 12-13, 1861.

SOLOMON, JAMES, Private
Enlisted at Yorktown, Virginia, at age 19, July 3, 1861, for six months. Present or accounted for until mustered out November 12-13, 1861.

SOLOMON, JOHN M., Private
Enlisted at Yorktown, Virginia, at age 21, August 3, 1861, for six months. Present or accounted for until mustered out November 12-13, 1861.

STACY, GEORGE L., Private
Enlisted at Yorktown, Virginia, at age 17, August 8, 1861, for six months. Present or accounted for until mustered out November 12-13, 1861.

TATE, S. C. W., Private
Enlisted in Burke County at age 35, April 25, 1861, for six months. Present or accounted for until mustered out November 12-13, 1861.

TEEM, PETER A., Private
Enlisted at Yorktown, Virginia, at age 21, August 8, 1861, for six months. Present or accounted for until mustered out November 12-13, 1861.

TERRY, C. F., Private
Enlisted at Yorktown, Virginia, at age 16, July 3, 1861, for six months. Present or accounted for until mustered out November 12-13, 1861.

TIMBERLAKE, J. S., Private
Enlisted in Burke County at age 18, April 25, 1861, for six months. Present or accounted for until mustered out November 12-13, 1861.

TURNER, T. A., Private
Enlisted August 8, 1861, for six months. Present or accounted for until mustered out November 12-13, 1861.

WAKEFIELD, S. D., Private
Enlisted in Burke County at age 18, April 25, 1861, for six months. Present or accounted for until mustered out November 12-13, 1861.

WALTON, J. T., Private
Enlisted in Burke County at age 28, July 3, 1861, for six months. Present or accounted for until mustered out November 12-13, 1861.

WALTON, JOHN M., Private
Enlisted in Burke County at age 16, July 3, 1861, for six months. Present or accounted for until mustered out November 12-13, 1861. Later served in Company F, 41st Regiment N. C. Troops (3rd Regiment N. C. Cavalry).

WAMACK, W. T., Private
Enlisted in Burke County at age 30, April 25, 1861, for six months. Present or accounted for until mustered out November 12-13, 1861.

WARLICK, J. L., Corporal
Enlisted in Burke County at age 27, April 25, 1861, for six months. Mustered in as Corporal. Present or accounted for until mustered out November 12-13, 1861. Later enlisted in Company B, 11th Regiment N. C. Troops (1st Regiment N. C. Volunteers).

WARLICK, PORTLAND A., Private
Enlisted in Burke County at age 21, April 25, 1861, for six months. Present or accounted for until mustered out November 12-13, 1861. Later enlisted in Company B, 11th Regiment N. C. Troops (1st Regiment N. C. Volunteers).

WILLIAMS, COLUMBUS C., Private
Enlisted in Burke County at age 26, April 25, 1861, for six months. Present or accounted for until mustered out November 12-13, 1861.

WILLIAMS, HOUSTON E., Private
Enlisted in Burke County at age 22, April 25, 1861, for six months. Present or accounted for until mustered out November 12-13, 1861.

WILLIAMS, JOSEPH A., Private
Enlisted in Burke County at age 21, April 25, 1861, for six months. Present or accounted for until mustered out November 12-13, 1861.

WILLIAMS, MOULTON, Private
Enlisted in Burke County at age 19, April 25, 1861, for six months. Present or accounted for until mustered out November 12-13, 1861.

WILLIAMS, WILLIAM H., Private
Enlisted in Burke County at age 20, April 25, 1861, for six months. Present or accounted for until mustered out November 12-13, 1861.

WINTERS, ALFRED, Private
Enlisted at Yorktown, Virginia, at age 20, July 3, 1861, for six months. Present or accounted for until mustered out November 12-13, 1861.

WINTERS, MOULTON, Private
Enlisted in Burke County at age 21, April 25, 1861, for six months. Present or accounted for until mustered out November 12-13, 1861.

COMPANY H

This company, known as the "Fayetteville Independent Light Infantry," had been in continuous existence since its organization on August 23, 1793. It was enrolled at Fayetteville, Cumberland County, on April 17, 1861, and ordered to occupy the arsenal at that place on April 22. There it remained until it moved to Raleigh on May 9, 1861. On May 16, 1861, the company was ordered assigned to the regiment because the original company assigned, the "Randlesburg Rifles," was understrength. Accordingly, the company was mustered in retroactive to May 13 as Company H of this regiment. After that date the company functioned as a part of the regiment, and its history for the war period is recorded as a part of the regimental history.

The information contained in the following roster of the company was compiled principally from company muster rolls which included the muster-in roll dated August 31, 1861, covering the period May 13-August 31, 1861, and muster rolls for the periods of April 17-May 17, 1861; May 13-June 30, 1861; and July-August, 1861. No muster rolls were found for the period after August, 1861. In addition to the company muster rolls, Roll of Honor records, receipt rolls, hospital records, prisoner of war records, and other primary records, supplemented by state pension applications, United Daughters of the Confederacy records, and postwar rosters and histories, all provided useful information.

OFFICERS
CAPTAIN

HUSKE, WRIGHT
Resided in Cumberland County where he enlisted at age 29, April 17, 1861, for six months. Appointed Captain to rank from May 21, 1861. Present or accounted for until mustered out November 12-13, 1861. Later commissioned in the Conscript Bureau.

LIEUTENANTS

COOK, CHARLES BETTS, 2nd Lieutenant
Resided in Cumberland County where he enlisted at age 26, April 17, 1861, for six months. Appointed 2nd Lieutenant to rank from May 21, 1861. Present or accounted for until mustered out November 12-13, 1861. Later enlisted in Company A, 63rd Regiment N. C. Troops (5th Regiment N. C. Cavalry).

HUSKE, BENJAMIN ROBINSON, 1st Lieutenant
Resided in Cumberland County where he enlisted at age 31, April 17, 1861, for six months. Appointed 1st Lieutenant to rank from May 21, 1861. Present or accounted for until mustered out November 12-13, 1861. Later appointed Major on the Field and Staff of the 48th Regiment N. C. Troops.

McKETHAN, HECTOR, 3rd Lieutenant
Resided in Cumberland County where he enlisted at age 26, April 17, 1861, for six months. Appointed 3rd Lieutenant to rank from May 21, 1861. Present or accounted for until mustered out November 12-13, 1861. Later enlisted in Company I, 51st Regiment N. C. Troops.

NONCOMMISSIONED OFFICERS AND PRIVATES

ANDERSON, JOHN H., Corporal
Enlisted in Cumberland County at age 22, April 17, 1861, for six months. Mustered in as Corporal. Present or accounted for until mustered out November 12-13, 1861. Later enlisted in Company D, 48th Regiment N. C. Troops.

ARNETT, ALEXANDER, Private
Enlisted in Cumberland County at age 23, April 17, 1861, for six months. Present or accounted for

until mustered out November 12-13, 1861.

ATKINSON, WILLIAM J., Private
Enlisted in Cumberland County at age 19, April 17, 1861, for six months. Present or accounted for until mustered out November 12-13, 1861.

BARRINGER, WILLIAM R., Private
Enlisted in Cumberland County at age 27, April 17, 1861, for six months. Discharged on July 13, 1861, to report to Major Gurgas, Chief of Ordnance Bureau, at Fayetteville. Later served in Company E, 2nd Battalion N. C. Local Defense Troops.

BATTLEY, WILLIAM T., Sergeant
Enlisted in Cumberland County at age 26, April 17, 1861, for six months. Present or accounted for until mustered out November 12-13, 1861. Later served in Company E, 2nd Battalion N.C. Local Defense Troops.

BERNARD, WILLIAM H., Private
Enlisted in Cumberland County at age 24, April 17, 1861, for six months. Discharged September 17, 1861.

BLAKE, JOHN HALL, Private
Enlisted in Cumberland County at age 22, April 17, 1861, for six months. Present or accounted for until mustered out November 12-13, 1861. Later enlisted in 2nd Company B, 36th Regiment N. C. Troops (2nd Regiment N. C. Artillery).

BOON, WILLIAM R., Private
Enlisted in Cumberland County at age 19, April 17, 1861, for six months. Present or accounted for until mustered out November 12-13, 1861. Later enlisted in Company B, 51st Regiment N. C. Troops.

BROADFOOT, CHARLES WHITMORE, Private
Resided in Cumberland County where he enlisted at age 18, June 24, 1861, for six months. Present or accounted for until mustered out November 12-13, 1861. Later enlisted in Company D, 43rd Regiment N. C. Troops.

BUHMANN, GUSTAVUS W., Private
Enlisted in Cumberland County at age 27, April 17, 1861, for six months. Present or accounted for until mustered out November 12-13, 1861. Later enlisted in Company D, 41st Regiment N. C. Troops (3rd Regiment N. C. Cavalry).

BYRD, HENRY R., Private
Enlisted in Cumberland County at age 20, April 17, 1861, for six months. Present or accounted for until mustered out November 12-13, 1861.

CAMPBELL, THOMAS J., Private
Enlisted in Cumberland County at age 22, April 17, 1861, for six months. Present or accounted for until mustered out November 12-13, 1861.

CAMPBELL, WILLIAM F., Private
Enlisted in Cumberland County at age 17, April 17, 1861, for six months. Present or accounted for until mustered out November 12-13, 1861.

CARMON, SAMUEL, Private
Enlisted in Cumberland County at age 20, April 17, 1861, for six months. Present or accounted for until mustered out November 12-13, 1861.

CARROLL, JOHN W., Private
Enlisted in Cumberland County at age 21, April 17, 1861, for six months. Present or accounted for until mustered out November 12-13, 1861.

CLARK, ISAAC N., Private
Enlisted in Cumberland County at age 22, April 17, 1861, for six months. Present or accounted for until mustered out November 12-13, 1861.

CLARK, WILLIAM J., Private
Enlisted in Cumberland County at age 24, April 17, 1861, for six months. Present or accounted for until mustered out November 12-13, 1861.

COOK, WILLIAM, Private
Enlisted in Cumberland County at age 17, June 24, 1861, for six months. Present or accounted for until mustered out November 12-13, 1861.

DAVIS, ICABOD B., Private
Enlisted in Cumberland County at age 22, June 24, 1861, for six months. Present or accounted for until mustered out November 12-13, 1861.

DAVIS, JOHN M., Private
Enlisted in Cumberland County at age 19, April 17, 1861, for six months. Present or accounted for until mustered out November 12-13, 1861.

DOBBIN, JOHN H., Private
Enlisted in Cumberland County at age 20, April 17, 1861, for six months. Present or accounted for until mustered out November 12-13, 1861.

EVANS, DAVID, Private
Enlisted in Cumberland County at age 21, April 17, 1861, for six months. Present or accounted for until mustered out November 12-13, 1861.

FRIZELL, HENRY S., Corporal
Enlisted in Cumberland County at age 20, April 17, 1861, for six months. Mustered in as Corporal. Present or accounted for until mustered out November 12-13, 1861. Later enlisted in 2nd Company B, 36th Regiment N.C. Troops (2nd Regiment N.C. Artillery).

FURMAGE, ROBERT, Private
Enlisted in Cumberland County at age 24, April 17, 1861, for six months. Present or accounted for until mustered out November 12-13, 1861.

GAINEY, JAMES C., Private
Enlisted in Cumberland County at age 17, April 17, 1861, for six months. Present or accounted for until mustered out November 12-13, 1861.

GEE, GEORGE W., Private
Enlisted in Cumberland County at age 28, April 17, 1861, for six months. Present or accounted for until mustered out November 12-13, 1861.

GRAHAM, DANIEL McL., Private
Resided in Cumberland County where he enlisted at age 27, April 17, 1861, for six months. Present or accounted for until mustered out November 12-13, 1861. Later appointed Assistant Surgeon and assigned to the Field and Staff of the 37th Regiment N. C. Troops.

HAIGH, CHARLES, Private
Resided in Cumberland County where he enlisted at age 20, April 17, 1861, for six months. Present or accounted for until mustered out November 12-13, 1861. Later appointed Sergeant Major on the Field and Staff of the 63rd Regiment N. C. Troops (5th Regiment N. C. Cavalry).

HAIGH, GEORGE H., Private
Enlisted in Cumberland County at age 28, April 17, 1861, for six months. Present or accounted for until mustered out November 12-13, 1861. Later served in the Conscript Bureau.

HALE, PETER M., Private
Enlisted in Cumberland County at age 31, April 17, 1861, for six months. Present or accounted for until mustered out November 12-13, 1861.

HALL, JEPTHA, Private
Enlisted in Cumberland County at age 26, April 17, 1861, for six months. Present or accounted for until mustered out November 12-13, 1861.

HIEDE, RODOLPH E., Private
Enlisted in Cumberland County at age 28, April 17, 1861, for six months. Present or accounted for until mustered out November 12-13, 1861.

HORNE, HENRY RUFFIN, Private
Resided in Cumberland County where he enlisted at age 21, April 17, 1861, for six months. Present or accounted for until mustered out November 12-13, 1861. Later enlisted in Company D, 12th Battalion Virginia Light Artillery.

HUSKE, HENRY D., Private
Enlisted in Cumberland County at age 24, April 17, 1861, for six months. Present or accounted for until mustered out November 12-13, 1861.

HUSKE, JAMES W., Private
Enlisted in Cumberland County at age 19, April 17, 1861, for six months. Present or accounted for until mustered out November 12-13, 1861. Later enlisted in Company B, 52nd Regiment N. C. Troops.

HUSKE, JOHN D., Private
Enlisted in Cumberland County at age 20, April 17, 1861, for six months. Died at Yorktown, Virginia, October 21, 1861.

JAMES, ROBERT, Private
Enlisted in Cumberland County at age 18, April 17, 1861, for six months. Present or accounted for until mustered out November 12-13, 1861.

JAMES, WILLIAM DAVID, Corporal
Enlisted in Cumberland County at age 23, April 17, 1861, for six months. Mustered in as Corporal. Present or accounted for until mustered out November 12-13, 1861.

JENKINS, JOHN, Private
Enlisted in Cumberland County at age 22, June 29, 1861, for six months. Present or accounted for until mustered out November 12-13, 1861.

JONES, JAMES H., Private
Enlisted in Cumberland County at age 19, April 17, 1861, for six months. Present or accounted for until mustered out November 12-13, 1861.

JONES, JAMES L., Private
Enlisted in Cumberland County at age 18, April 17, 1861, for six months. Present or accounted for until mustered out November 12-13, 1861.

JONES, WILLIAM T., Private
Enlisted in Cumberland County at age 19, April

17, 1861, for six months. Present or accounted for until mustered out November 12-13, 1861.

KENDRICK, JAMES, Private
Enlisted in Cumberland County at age 19, April 17, 1861, for six months. Present or accounted for until mustered out November 12-13, 1861.

KENNEDY, CHARLES, Sergeant
Enlisted in Cumberland County at age 26, April 17, 1861, for six months. Mustered in as Sergeant. Present or accounted for until mustered out November 12-13, 1861.

KYLE, JESSE KNEEDER, Private
Enlisted in Cumberland County at age 25, April 17, 1861, for six months. Present or accounted for until mustered out November 12-13, 1861. Later enlisted in Company B, 52nd Regiment N. C. Troops.

KYLE, WILLIAM E., Private
Resided in Cumberland County where he enlisted at age 18, April 17, 1861, for six months. Present or accounted for until mustered out November 12-13, 1861. Later enlisted in Company B, 52nd Regiment N. C. Troops.

LUMSDEN, HAYWOOD A., Private
Enlisted in Cumberland County at age 19, April 17, 1861, for six months. Present or accounted for until mustered out November 12-13, 1861.

LUTTERLOH, JARVIS B., Private
Enlisted in Cumberland County at age 19, April 17, 1861, for six months. Present or accounted for until mustered out November 12-13, 1861. Later enlisted in Company E, 56th Regiment N. C. Troops.

McARTHUR, JOHN T., Private
Enlisted in Cumberland County at age 19, June 24, 1861, for six months. Present or accounted for until mustered out November 12-13, 1861.

McARTHUR, JOSEPH A., Private
Enlisted in Cumberland County at age 31, June 24, 1861, for six months. Present or accounted for until mustered out November 12-13, 1861. Later enlisted in Company I, 51st Regiment N. C. Troops.

McDONALD, HUGH A., Private
Enlisted in Cumberland County at age 24, April 17, 1861, for six months. Present or accounted for until mustered out November 12-13, 1861.

McDONALD, JOHN H., Private
Enlisted in Cumberland County at age 25, June 24, 1861, for six months. Present or accounted for until mustered out November 12-13, 1861. Later enlisted in 3rd Company B, 36th Regiment N. C. Troops (2nd Regiment N. C. Artillery).

McDONALD, KENETH, Private
Enlisted in Cumberland County at age 21, June 24, 1861, for six months. Present or accounted for until mustered out November 12-13, 1861.

McKAY, JOHN A., Private
Enlisted in Cumberland County at age 35, April 17, 1861, for six months. Present or accounted for until mustered out November 12-13, 1861.

McKELLAR, JOHN, Private
Enlisted in Cumberland County at age 36, June 24, 1861, for six months. Present or accounted for until mustered out November 12-13, 1861. Later enlisted in Company A, 63rd Regiment N. C. Troops (5th Regiment N.C. Cavalry).

McKETHAN, WILLIAM R., Private
Enlisted in Cumberland County at age 21, April 17, 1861, for six months. Died September 23, 1861.

McLAUGHLIN, ARCHIBALD N., Private
Enlisted in Cumberland County at age 18, April 17, 1861, for six months. Present or accounted for until mustered out November 12-13, 1861.

McLEAN, JOHN A., Private
Enlisted in Cumberland County at age 22, April 17, 1861, for six months. Present or accounted for until mustered out November 12-13, 1861.

McLEAN, JOHN P., Private
Enlisted in Cumberland County at age 38, April 17, 1861, for six months. Present or accounted for until mustered out November 12-13, 1861. Later enlisted in Company H, 50th Regiment N. C. Troops.

McLEAN, THOMAS H., Private
Enlisted in Cumberland County at age 20, April 17, 1861, for six months. Present or accounted for until mustered out November 12-13, 1861.

McNEIL, ALEXANDER D., Private
Enlisted in Cumberland County at age 19, April 17, 1861, for six months. Present or accounted for until mustered out November 12-13, 1861.

McNEILL, JAMES M., Private
Enlisted in Cumberland County at age 20, April 17, 1861, for six months. Present or accounted for until mustered out November 12-13, 1861. Later enlisted in Company D, 41st Regiment N. C Troops (3rd Regiment N. C. Cavalry).

McNEILL, NEILL, Private
Enlisted in Cumberland County at age 19, April 17, 1861, for six months. Present or accounted for until mustered out November 12-13, 1861.

McPHAIL, EVANDER N., Private
Resided in Cumberland County where he enlisted at age 19, April 17, 1861, for six months. Present or accounted for until mustered out November 12-13, 1861. Later enlisted in 2nd Company B, 36th Regiment N. C. Troops (2nd Regiment N. C. Artillery).

McPHERSON, WILLIAM D., Private
Enlisted in Cumberland County at age 21, June 24, 1861, for six months. Present or accounted for until mustered out November 12-13, 1861.

McRAE, JAMES CAMERON, Private
Resided in Cumberland County where he enlisted at age 22, April 17, 1861, for six months. Transferred to Company D, 5th Regiment N. C. State Troops upon appointment as 2nd Lieutenant August 1, 1861, to rank from May 16, 1861.

McRAE, NEILL, Private
Enlisted in Cumberland County at age 19, April 17, 1861, for six months. Present or accounted for until mustered out November 12-13, 1861.

MATTHEWS, JOHN W., Private
Enlisted in Cumberland County at age 42, April 17, 1861, for six months. Present or accounted for until mustered out November 12-13, 1861.

MORTON, EBEN, Private
Enlisted in Cumberland County at age 30, April 17, 1861, for six months. Present or accounted for until mustered out November 12-13, 1861.

MURPHY, DOUGALD, Corporal
Enlisted in Cumberland County at age 22, April 17, 1861, for six months. Mustered in as Corporal. Present or accounted for until mustered out November 12-13, 1861.

NANCE, JAMES H., Private
Enlisted in Cumberland County at age 22, April 17, 1861, for six months. Present or accounted for until mustered out November 12-13, 1861.

PEARCE, OLIVER W., Private
Enlisted in Cumberland County at age 21, April 17, 1861, for six months. Present or accounted for until mustered out November 12-13, 1861.

POWERS, EDWARD P., Private
Resided in Cumberland County where he enlisted at age 17, April 17, 1861, for six months. Present or accounted for until mustered out November 12-13, 1861. Later served in Company C of the 2nd Battalion N.C. Local Defense Troops.

POWERS, THOMAS J., Private
Enlisted in Cumberland County at age 18, April 17, 1861, for six months. Present or accounted for until mustered out November 12-13, 1861.

RAY, ALEXANDER, Private
Enlisted in Cumberland County at age 29, April 17, 1861, for six months. Present or accounted for until mustered out November 12-13, 1861. Later enlisted in Company D, 53rd Regiment N. C. Troops.

RAY, DAVID H., Private
Resided in Cumberland County where he enlisted at age 21, April 17, 1861, for six months. Present or accounted for until mustered out November 12-13, 1861. Later enlisted in Company A, 5th Regiment N. C. State Troops.

ROBINSON, CHARLES E., Private
Enlisted in Cumberland County at age 25, April 17, 1861, for six months. Present or accounted for until mustered out November 12-13, 1861.

ROBINSON, JOHN H., Sergeant
Resided in Cumberland County where he enlisted at age 26, April 17, 1861, for six months. Mustered in as Sergeant. Present or accounted for until mustered out November 12-13, 1861. Later appointed Adjutant with the rank of 1st Lieutenant and assigned to the Field and Staff of the 52nd Regiment N. C. Troops.

RODES, KING J., Private
Enlisted in Cumberland County at age 22, April 17, 1861, for six months. Present or accounted for until mustered out November 12-13, 1861. Later enlisted in Company E, 56th Regiment N. C. Troops.

RUSSELL, ARCHIBALD B., Private
Enlisted in Cumberland County at age 18, April

17, 1861, for six months. Present or accounted for until mustered out November 12-13, 1861.

RUSSELL, BENJAMIN R., Private
Enlisted in Cumberland County at age 24, April 17, 1861, for six months. Present or accounted for until mustered out November 12-13, 1861.

RUSSELL, STEPHEN, Private
Enlisted in Cumberland County at age 21, April 17, 1861, for six months. Present or accounted for until mustered out November 12-13, 1861.

SANDFORD, ROBERT H., Private
Resided in Cumberland County where he enlisted at age 29, April 17, 1861, for six months. Present or accounted for until mustered out November 12-13, 1861. Later enlisted in 2nd Company B, 36th Regiment N. C. Troops (2nd Regiment N. C. Artillery).

SCOTT, DAVID, Private
Enlisted in Cumberland County at age 23, April 17, 1861, for six months. Present or accounted for until mustered out November 12-13, 1861. Later enlisted in Company D, 53rd Regiment N. C. Troops.

SEDBERRY, BOND E., Private
Enlisted in Cumberland County at age 20, April 17, 1861, for six months. Present or accounted for until mustered out November 12-13, 1861.

SEDBERRY, HENRY O., Private
Resided in Cumberland County where he enlisted at age 18, April 17, 1861, for six months. Present or accounted for until mustered out November 12-13, 1861. Later enlisted in 2nd Company B, 36th Regiment N. C. Troops (2nd Regiment N. C. Artillery).

SHERWOOD, WATERS, Private
Enlisted in Cumberland County at age 25, April 17, 1861, for six months. Present or accounted for until mustered out November 12-13, 1861.

SIKES, ENOCH P., Private
Enlisted in Cumberland County at age 25, April 17, 1861, for six months. Present or accounted for until mustered out November 12-13, 1861.

SIKES, JOHN A., Private
Enlisted in Cumberland County at age 22, April 17, 1861, for six months. Present or accounted for until mustered out November 12-13, 1861.

SMITH, FARQUARD R., Private
Enlisted in Cumberland County at age 22, April 17, 1861, for six months. Present or accounted for until mustered out November 12-13, 1861.

SMITH, HENRY E., Private
Enlisted in Cumberland County at age 20, April 17, 1861, for six months. Discharged July 3, 1861, on Surgeon's Certificate.

SMITH, HENRY H., Private
Enlisted in Cumberland County at age 22, April 17, 1861, for six months. Present or accounted for until mustered out November 12-13, 1861. Later enlisted in Company D, 41st Regiment N. C. Troops (3rd Regiment N. C. Cavalry).

SMITH, JAMES, Private
Enlisted in Cumberland County at age 21, June

24, 1861, for six months. Present or accounted for until mustered out November 12-13, 1861.

SMITH, JOSEPH, Private
Enlisted in Cumberland County at age 19, April 17, 1861, for six months. Present or accounted for until mustered out November 12-13, 1861.

SMITH, WALTER J., Private
Resided in Cumberland County where he enlisted at age 21, April 17, 1861, for six months. Present or accounted for until mustered out November 12-13, 1861. Later enlisted in Company D, 41st Regiment N. C. Troops (3rd Regiment N. C. Cavalry).

STANTON, WILLIAM B., Private
Enlisted in Cumberland County at age 17, April 17, 1861, for six months. Present or accounted for until mustered out November 12-13, 1861.

STEDMAN, CHARLES M., Private
Resided in Cumberland County where he enlisted at age 20, April 17, 1861, for six months. Present or accounted for until mustered out November 12-13, 1861. Later served on the Field and Staff of the 44th Regiment N. C. Troops.

STRANGE, FRENCH, Private
Resided in Cumberland County where he enlisted at age 22, April 17, 1861, for six months. Transferred to the Field and Staff of the 5th Regiment N. C. State Troops upon appointment as Adjutant with the rank of 1st Lieutenant and discharged from this company May 24, 1861.

SUNDY, JOHN, Private
Enlisted in Cumberland County at age 28, April 17, 1861, for six months. Present or accounted for until mustered out November 12-13, 1861.

THOMPSON, EMANUEL C., Private
Enlisted in Cumberland County at age 26, April 17, 1861, for six months. Present or accounted for until mustered out November 12-13, 1861.

THOMPSON, JOHN A., Private
Enlisted in Cumberland County at age 23, April 17, 1861, for six months. Present or accounted for until mustered out November 12-13, 1861.

THOMSON, GEORGE A., Private
Resided in Cumberland County where he enlisted at age 18, April 17, 1861, for six months. Present or accounted for until mustered out November 12-13, 1861. Later enlisted in Company A, 63rd Regiment N. C. Troops (5th Regiment N. C. Cavalry).

WATERBERRY, WILLIAM M., Private
Enlisted in Cumberland County at age 25, April 17, 1861, for six months. Present or accounted for until mustered out November 12-13, 1861.

WEMYSS, JAMES, Private
Enlisted in Cumberland County at age 17, April 17, 1861, for six months. Died September 8, 1861.

WEMYSS, WILLIAM P., 1st Sergeant
Enlisted in Cumberland County at age 27, April 17, 1861, for six months. Mustered in as 1st Sergeant. Present or accounted for until mustered out November 12-13, 1861.

WHITEHEAD, WILLIAMSON, Private
Enlisted in Cumberland County at age 32, April 17, 1861, for six months. Present or accounted for until mustered out November 12-13, 1861.

WIDDERFIELD, WILLIAM, Private
Enlisted in Cumberland County at age 24, April 17, 1861, for six months. Present or accounted for until mustered out November 12-13, 1861.

WILLIAMS, EDMUND J., Private
Enlisted in Cumberland County at age 20, April 17, 1861, for six months. Present or accounted for until mustered out November 12-13, 1861. Later enlisted in Company I, 31st Regiment N. C. Troops.

WILLIAMS, JOHN MARSHALL, Private
Enlisted in Cumberland County at age 22, April 17, 1861, for six months. Present or accounted for until mustered out November 12-13, 1861. Later enlisted in Company C, 54th Regiment N. C. Troops.

WILLIAMSON, ISAAC T., Private
Enlisted in Cumberland County at age 34, April 17, 1861, for six months. Present or accounted for until mustered out November 12-13, 1861.

WILLIAMSON, NATHAN, Private
Enlisted in Cumberland County at age 20, April 17, 1861, for six months. Present or accounted for until mustered out November 12-13, 1861.

WOODWARD, WILLIAM J., Private
Enlisted in Cumberland County at age 18, April 17, 1861, for six months. Present or accounted for until mustered out November 12-13, 1861.

WOOTEN, JOHN W., Private
Enlisted in Cumberland County at age 16, June 24, 1861, for six months. Present or accounted for until mustered out November 12-13, 1861.

WORTH, ALBERT H., Private
Resided in Cumberland County where he enlisted at age 20, April 17, 1861, for six months. Present or accounted for until mustered out November 12-13, 1861. Later enlisted in Company I, 22nd Regiment N.C. Troops (12th Regiment N.C. Volunteers).

COMPANY I

This company, known as the "Enfield Blues," was organized at Enfield, Halifax County, soon after the John Brown raid on Harpers Ferry in the fall of 1859. It was enrolled for active service at Enfield on April 17, 1861, and was ordered to Raleigh on April 23, 1861. Arriving on April 27, the company was stationed at the Camp of Instruction, where it was mustered into state service on May 13, 1861, as Company I of this regiment. After that date the company functioned as a part of the regiment, and its history for the war period is recorded as a part of the regimental history.

The information contained in the following roster of the company was compiled principally from company muster rolls which included the muster-in roll dated August 31, 1861, covering the period May 13-August 31, 1861, and muster rolls for the periods of April 19-May 13, 1861; May 13-June 30, 1861; and July-August, 1861. No muster rolls were found for the period after August, 1861. In addition to the company muster rolls, Roll of Honor records, receipt rolls, hospital records, prisoner of war records, and other primary records, supplemented by state pension applications, United Daughters of the Confederacy records, and postwar rosters and histories, all provided useful information.

OFFICERS

CAPTAINS

BELL, DAVID BARNES
Resided in Halifax County where he enlisted at age 34, April 19, 1861, for six months. Appointed Captain to rank from date of enlistment. Resigned August 31, 1861, by reason of ill health.

PARKER, FRANCIS MARION
Enlisted in Halifax County at age 30, April 19, 1861, for six months. Appointed 2nd Lieutenant to rank from date of enlistment. Promoted to Captain to rank from September 1, 1861. Resigned October 8, 1861, upon election as Colonel of the 30th Regiment N. C. Troops. Transferred to the Field and Staff of that regiment.

WHITAKER, MONTGOMERY T.
Enlisted in Halifax County at age 35, April 19, 1861, for six months. Appointed 1st Lieutenant to rank from date of enlistment and promoted to Captain to rank from October 22, 1861. Present or accounted for until mustered out November 12-13, 1861.

LIEUTENANTS

CORBETT, CARR B., 3rd Lieutenant
Enlisted in Halifax County at age 31, April 19, 1861, for six months. Mustered in as 1st Sergeant. Appointed 3rd Lieutenant to rank from August 31, 1861. Present or accounted for until mustered out November 12-13, 1861.

WHITAKER, CARY W., 1st Lieutenant
Enlisted in Halifax County at age 29, April 19, 1861, for six months. Appointed 3rd Lieutenant to rank from date of enlistment. Promoted to 1st Lieutenant to rank from October 22, 1861. Present or accounted for until mustered out November 12-13, 1861. Later enlisted in Company D, 43rd Regiment N. C. Troops.

WHITAKER, THEODORE LUCIAN,
2nd Lieutenant
Enlisted in Halifax County at age 28, April 19, 1861, for six months. Mustered in as Sergeant. Appointed 2nd Lieutenant to rank from October 22, 1861. Present or accounted for until mustered out November 12-13, 1861. Later enlisted in Company D, 24th Regiment N. C. Troops (14th Regiment N. C. Volunteers).

NONCOMMISSIONED OFFICERS AND PRIVATES

ADKINS, JOSEPH B., Private
Resided in Halifax County and enlisted at Yorktown, Virginia, at age 32, June 6, 1861, for six months. Present or accounted for until mustered out November 12-13, 1861. Later enlisted in Company D, 43rd Regiment N. C. Troops.

ALLSBROOK, CLEMENT, Private
Enlisted at Yorktown, Virginia, at age 24, June 11, 1861, for six months. Present or accounted for until mustered out November 12-13, 1861.

ALLSBROOK, MARCUS, Private
Enlisted at Yorktown, Virginia, at age 25, June 11, 1861, for six months. Died at Yorktown, July 25, 1861.

APPLEWHITE, JOHN THOMAS, Private
Enlisted at Yorktown, Virginia, at age 19, June 11, 1861, for six months. Present or accounted for until mustered out November 12-13, 1861. Later enlisted in Company G, 41st Regiment N. C. Troops (3rd Regiment N. C. Cavalry).

ARRINGTON, JOSEPH C., Private
Enlisted in Wake County at age 18, May 13, 1861, for six months. Present or accounted for until mustered out November 12-13, 1861. Later enlisted in Company G, 41st Regiment N. C. Troops (3rd Regiment N. C. Cavalry).

ARRINGTON, SAMUEL F., Private
Enlisted at Yorktown, Virginia, at age 28, June 29, 1861, for six months. Died at Yorktown, July 26, 1861.

BARNES, JAMES H., Corporal
Enlisted in Wake County at age 27, May 13, 1861, for six months. Mustered in as Corporal. Present or accounted for until mustered out November 12-13, 1861.

BARNHILL, JOHN J., Private
Enlisted in Halifax County at age 23, April 19, 1861, for six months. Present or accounted for until mustered out November 12-13, 1861.

BATCHELOR, JAMES H., Private
Enlisted in Halifax County at age 21, April 19, 1861, for six months. Present or accounted for until mustered out November 12-13, 1861.

BEAVANS, JOHN, Private
Enlisted in Halifax County at age 18, April 19, 1861, for six months. Present or accounted for until mustered out November 12-13, 1861. Later enlisted in Company D, 43rd Regiment N. C. Troops.

BEAVANS, WILLIAM, Private
Enlisted in Halifax County at age 21, April 19, 1861, for six months. Present or accounted for until mustered out November 12-13, 1861. Later enlisted in Company D, 43rd Regiment N. C. Troops.

BELLAMY, W. E., Private
Discharged May 8, 1861, by order of the Adjutant General of North Carolina.

BOND, MARMADUKE N., Private
Enlisted in Halifax County at age 27, April 19, 1861, for six months. ·Present or accounted for until mustered out November 12-13, 1861.

BOONE, JOSEPH, Private
Born in Halifax County where he resided as a farmer prior to enlisting at Yorktown, Virginia, at age 28, June 11, 1861, for six months. Discharged October 2, 1861, by reason of "attack of pneumonia."

BRADLEY, JAMES D., Private
Enlisted in Halifax County at age 31, April 19, 1861, for six months. Present or accounted for until mustered out November 12-13, 1861.

BRANCH, ALPHEUS, Private
Enlisted in Halifax County at age 18, July 11, 1861, for six months. Present or accounted for until mustered out November 12-13, 1861. Later enlisted in Company G, 41st Regiment N. C. Troops (3rd Regiment N. C. Cavalry).

BRANCH, JOHN R., Private
Enlisted in Halifax County at age 22, April 19, 1861, for six months. Mustered in as Corporal and reduced to ranks June 14, 1861. Present or accounted for until mustered out November 12-13, 1861.

BRANTOM, TIMOTHY, Private
Enlisted in Halifax County at age 28, April 19, 1861, for six months. Present or accounted for until mustered out November 12-13, 1861.

BRASWELL, CHARLES J., Private
Enlisted in Halifax County at age 21, April 19, 1861, for six months. Present or accounted for until mustered out November 12-13, 1861.

BRITT, BENJAMIN F., Private
Enlisted in Halifax County at age 20, April 19, 1861, for six months. Died at Yorktown, Virginia, June 13-14, 1861.

BRITT, GEORGE W., Private
Enlisted in Halifax County at age 31, April 19, 1861, for six months. Present or accounted for until mustered out November 12-13, 1861.

BRITT, JAMES H., Private
Enlisted in Cumberland County at age 23, April 19, 1861, for six months. Present or accounted for until mustered out November 12-13, 1861.

BRITT, LAWRENCE, Private
Enlisted in Halifax County at age 19, April 19, 1861, for six months. Present or accounted for until mustered out November 12-13, 1861.

BRITT, MATHEW C., Private
Enlisted in Halifax County at age 17, April 19, 1861, for six months. Present or accounted for until mustered out November 12-13, 1861.

BRYAN, GEORGE, Private
Enlisted at Yorktown, Virginia, at age 23, June 29, 1861, for six months. Present or accounted for until mustered out November 12-13, 1861.

BRYAN, JAMES C., Private
Enlisted at Yorktown, Virginia, at age 33, June 29, 1861, for six months. Present or accounted for until mustered out November 12-13, 1861.

BUMPASS, GEORGE W., Private
Enlisted in Halifax County at age 24, April 19, 1861, for six months. Present or accounted for until mustered out November 12-13, 1861.

BURNETT, WILLIAM, Sergeant
Enlisted in Halifax County at age 35, April 19, 1861, for six months. Mustered in as Private and appointed Sergeant June 14, 1861. Present or accounted for until mustered out November 12-13, 1861.

BURT, ALPHEUS J., Private
Enlisted at Yorktown, Virginia, at age 19, June 29, 1861, for six months. Present or accounted for until mustered out November 12-13, 1861.

BURT, JOHN A., Private
Enlisted at Yorktown, Virginia, at age 21, June 29, 1861, for six months. Present or accounted for until mustered out November 12-13, 1861.

BURT, JOHN J., Private
Enlisted in Halifax County at age 22, April 19, 1861, for six months. Present or accounted for until mustered out November 12-13, 1861.

BURT, ROBERT T., Private
Enlisted at Yorktown, Virginia, at age 24, June 29, 1861, for six months. Present or accounted for until mustered out November 12-13, 1861.

BUSTIN, BENJAMIN C., Sergeant
Enlisted in Halifax County at age 28, April 19, 1861, for six months. Mustered in as Sergeant. Present or accounted for until mustered out November 12-13, 1861.

BUSTIN, WILLIAM, Private
Enlisted at Yorktown, Virginia, at age 23, June 6, 1861, for six months. Discharged August 31, 1861.

CHERRY, JOHN K., Private
Enlisted in Halifax County at age 20, April 19, 1861, for six months. Reported on muster roll for the period May 13-June 30, 1861, with the remark: "accidentally June 14 and absent by furlough since July 4, 1861." July-August, 1861, muster roll reports him as "absent, sick at home."

COHEN, JONAS, Private
Enlisted in Halifax County at age 30, April 9, 1861, for six months. Mustered in as Sergeant and reduced to ranks June 14, 1861. Present or accounted for until mustered out November 12-13, 1861.

COKER, JOHN J., Private
Enlisted at Yorktown, Virginia, at age 24, June 11, 1861, for six months. Died at Yorktown, June 26, 1861.

COLLINS, T. BENJAMIN, Private
Enlisted in Halifax County at age 34, April 19, 1861, for six months. Present or accounted for until mustered out November 12-13, 1861.

COOK, THOMAS C., Private
Enlisted in Halifax County at age 21, April 19, 1861, for six months. Present or accounted for until mustered out November 12-13, 1861.

CRAWLEY, JOHN W., Private
Enlisted in Halifax County at age 18, April 19,

1861, for six months. Present or accounted for until mustered out November 12-13, 1861. Later enlisted in Company F, 36th Regiment N. C. Troops (2nd Regiment N. C. Artillery).

CUMMINGS, JAMES M., Private
Enlisted in Halifax County at age 26, April 19, 1861, for six months. Present or accounted for until mustered out November 12-13, 1861.

CUTCHIN, GREEN, Private
Enlisted in Halifax County at age 20, April 19, 1861, for six months. Present or accounted for until mustered out November 12-13, 1861.

CUTCHIN, JOHN A., Private
Enlisted at Yorktown, Virginia, at age 18, June 11, 1861, for six months. Present or accounted for until mustered out November 12-13, 1861.

DENTON, THOMAS H., Private
Enlisted in Halifax County at age 28, April 19, 1861, for six months. Present or accounted for until mustered out November 12-13, 1861.

DICKENS, JOSEPH J., Private
Enlisted in Halifax County at age 25, April 19, 1861, for six months. Present or accounted for until mustered out November 12-13, 1861.

DICKENS, SAMUEL, Private
Enlisted at Yorktown, Virginia, at age 25, June 29, 1861, for six months. Present or accounted for until mustered out November 12-13, 1861.

DRURY, WILLIAM H., Private
Enlisted in Halifax County at age 26, April 19, 1861, for six months. Present or accounted for until mustered out November 12-13, 1861.

DUNN, JAMES LEONIDAS, Private
Enlisted in Halifax County at age 23, April 19, 1861, for six months. Present or accounted for until mustered out November 12-13, 1861.

EDMONDS, LUTHER R., Private
Enlisted in Halifax County at age 21, May 1, 1861, for six months. Present or accounted for until mustered out November 12-13, 1861.

ETHERIDGE, JAMES D., Private
Enlisted in Halifax County at age 19, April 19, 1861, for six months. Present or accounted for until mustered out November 12-13, 1861.

ETHERIDGE, WILLIAM J., Private
Enlisted in Halifax County at age 26, April 19, 1861, for six months. Present or accounted for until mustered out November 12-13, 1861.

EVANS, MARCUS, Private
Enlisted at Yorktown, Virginia, at age 19, June 19, 1861, for six months. Present or accounted for until mustered out November 12-13, 1861.

FLEMING, JESSE, Private
Enlisted in Halifax County at age 44, April 19, 1861, for six months. Present or accounted for until mustered out November 12-13, 1861.

GAY, GILBERT G., Private
Enlisted at Yorktown, Virginia, at age 22, June 11, 1861, for six months. Present or accounted for until mustered out November 12-13, 1861.

GAY, JOHN C., Private
Enlisted in Cumberland County at age 34, April

19, 1861, for six months. Present or accounted for until mustered out November 12-13, 1861.

GLASGOW, THOMAS, Private
Enlisted in Halifax County at age 34, April 19, 1861, for six months. Present or accounted for until mustered out November 12-13, 1861.

GLOVER, WILLIAM, Private
Enlisted in Halifax County at age 22, April 19, 1861, for six months. Present or accounted for until mustered out November 12-13, 1861.

GREGORY, CHARLES G., Private
Resided in Halifax County where he enlisted at age 25, April 19, 1861, for six months. Detailed as "Assistant Surgeon" to the regiment on August 25, 1861. Present or accounted for until mustered out November 12-13, 1861. Later assigned to the Field and Staff of the 30th Regiment N. C. Troops.

GREGORY, SAMUEL, Private
Enlisted in Halifax County at age 18, April 19, 1861, for six months. Company muster roll dated August 31, 1861, carries the remark: "Certificate of Discharge." Muster roll for April 19-May 13, 1861, carries the remark: "died in the fall of 1861."

HAMELL, JOHN, Private
Enlisted at Yorktown, Virginia, at age 22, June 29, 1861, for six months. Present or accounted for until mustered out November 12-13, 1861. Later enlisted in Company D, 24th Regiment N. C. Troops (14th Regiment N. C. Volunteers).

HARPER, GEORGE W., Private
Enlisted at Yorktown, Virginia, at age 21, June 29, 1861, for six months. Present or accounted for until mustered out November 12-13, 1861.

HARRELL, JOHN H., Private
Enlisted at Yorktown, Virginia, at age 19, June 11, 1861, for six months. Present or accounted for until mustered out November 12-13, 1861. Later enlisted in Company D, 24th Regiment N. C. Troops (14th Regiment N. C. Volunteers).

HEARN, WILLIAM A., Private
Enlisted at Yorktown, Virginia, at age 34, June 11, 1861, for six months. Present or accounted for until mustered out November 12-13, 1861.

HEPTINSTALL, PHILMA B., Private
Enlisted at Yorktown, Virginia, at age 21, June 19, 1861, for six months. Present or accounted for until mustered out November 12-13, 1861.

HUNTER, RICHARD T., Private
Enlisted at Yorktown, Virginia, at age 19, June 29, 1861, for six months. Present or accounted for until mustered out November 12-13, 1861.

JOHNSON, THOMAS C., Private
Enlisted in Halifax County at age 17, April 19, 1861, for six months. Present or accounted for until mustered out November 12-13, 1861.

JONES, CALVIN C., Private
Enlisted at Yorktown, Virginia, at age 25, June 29, 1861, for six months. Present or accounted for until mustered out November 12-13, 1861.

JONES, JOSEPH J., Private
Enlisted at Yorktown, Virginia, at age 18, June

29, 1861, for six months. Present or accounted for until mustered out November 12-13, 1861.

JONES, WILLIAM H., Private
Enlisted at Yorktown, Virginia, at age 20, June 29, 1861, for six months. Present or accounted for until mustered out November 12-13, 1861.

KING, EMELUS, Private
Enlisted in Halifax County at age 20, April 19, 1861, for six months. Present or accounted for until mustered out November 12-13, 1861.

LAUGHTER, JOHN E., Private
Born in Halifax County where he resided as a farmer prior to enlisting at Yorktown, Virginia, at age 19, June 29, 1861, for six months. Present or accounted for until mustered out October 2, 1861, by reason of "chronic diarrhoea from which he has been suffering for two months." Later enlisted in the 43rd Regiment N. C. Troops.

LAUGHTER, PETER, Private
Enlisted at Yorktown, Virginia, at age 18, June 29, 1861, for six months. Present or accounted for until mustered out November 12-13, 1861.

LOCK, BENNETT R., Private
Enlisted at Yorktown, Virginia, at age 18, June 29, 1861, for six months. Present or accounted for until mustered out November 12-13, 1861.

LOCK, WILLIAM, Private
Enlisted at Yorktown, Virginia, at age 28, June 29, 1861, for six months. Present or accounted for until mustered out November 12-13, 1861.

LUCAS, JAMES, Private
Enlisted in Halifax County at age 25, April 19, 1861, for six months. Died at Yorktown, Virginia, August 20, 1861.

McDOWELL, ELISHA C., Private
Enlisted in Halifax County at age 25, April 19, 1861, for six months. Present or accounted for until mustered out November 12-13, 1861.

MANNING, JOHN, Private
Resided in Chowan County and enlisted at Yorktown, Virginia, at age 20, June 29, 1861, for six months. Present or accounted for until mustered out November 12-13, 1861.

MASON, JOHN R., Private
Enlisted in Halifax County at age 34, April 19, 1861, for six months. Mustered in as Corporal and reduced to ranks June 14, 1861. Present or accounted for until mustered out November 12-13, 1861.

MATHEWS, THOMAS H., Private
Enlisted in Halifax County at age 32, April 19, 1861, for six months. Present or accounted for until mustered out November 12-13, 1861.

MOORE, HENRY A., Private
Enlisted in Cumberland County at age 24, April 19, 1861, for six months. Present or accounted for until discharged August 23, 1861.

MORGAN, ABRAHAM, Private
Enlisted at Yorktown, Virginia, at age 20, June 29, 1861, for six months. Present or accounted for until mustered out November 12-13, 1861.

MORRIS, JAMES H., Private
Enlisted in Halifax County at age 19, April 19,

1861, for six months. Present or accounted for until mustered out November 12-13, 1861. Later enlisted in Company F, 43rd Regiment N. C. Troops.

OVERTON, JOHN B., Private
Enlisted at Yorktown, Virginia, at age 27, June 11, 1861, for six months. Present or accounted for until mustered out November 12-13, 1861.

PAGE, JESSE H., Private
Enlisted in Halifax County at age 30, April 19, 1861, for six months. Present or accounted for until mustered out November 12-13, 1861. Later appointed to the Field and Staff of the 17th Regiment N. C. Troops (2nd Organization).

PARTIN, JOSEPH J., Private
Enlisted in Halifax County at age 18, April 19, 1861, for six months. Present or accounted for until mustered out November 12-13, 1861.

PEEL, JESSE, Private
Enlisted in Halifax County at age 35, April 19, 1861, for six months. Present or accounted for until mustered out November 12-13, 1861.

PIERCE, JAMES M., Private
Enlisted at Yorktown, Virginia, at age 19, July 9, 1861, for six months. Present or accounted for until mustered out November 12-13, 1861.

PITT, FRANK B., Private
Enlisted in Halifax County at age 26, April 19, 1861, for six months. Present or accounted for until mustered out November 12-13, 1861.

PITTMAN, FLAVIUS CICERO, Private
Enlisted in Halifax County at age 15, April 19, 1861, for six months. Present or accounted for until mustered out November 12-13, 1861.

PITTMAN, JAMES C., Private
Enlisted at Yorktown, Virginia, at age 25, June 11, 1861, for six months. Present or accounted for until mustered out November 12-13, 1861.

PITTMAN, OLIVER P., Private
Enlisted in Halifax County at age 28, April 19, 1861, for six months. Present or accounted for until mustered out November 12-13, 1861. Later enlisted in Company B, 63rd Regiment N. C. Troops (5th Regiment N. C. Cavalry).

PITTMAN, RUFFIN A., Corporal
Enlisted in Halifax County at age 32, April 19, 1861, for six months. Mustered in as Private and appointed Corporal June 14, 1861. Present or accounted for until mustered out November 12-13, 1861. Later enlisted in Company F, 36th Regiment N. C. Troops (2nd Regiment N. C. Artillery).

PITTMAN, WILLIAM K., Private
Enlisted in Halifax County at age 19, April 19, 1861, for six months. Present or accounted for until mustered out November 12-13, 1861.

POPE, CARTER, Private
Enlisted at Yorktown, Virginia, at age 18, June 11, 1861, for six months. Present or accounted for until mustered out November 12-13, 1861.

POPE, JAMES A., Private
Enlisted in Halifax County at age 35, April 19, 1861, for six months. Present or accounted for

until mustered out November 12-13, 1861.

POPE, WILLIAM A., Private
Enlisted at Yorktown, Virginia, at age 18, June 29, 1861, for six months. Present or accounted for until mustered out November 12-13, 1861.

PULLEN, TILLMAN, Private
Enlisted at Yorktown, Virginia, at age 25, June 29, 1861, for six months. Present or accounted for until mustered out November 12-13, 1861.

RANDOLPH, JOHN CARY, Private
Resided in Halifax County where he enlisted at age 22, April 19, 1861, for six months. Present or accounted for until mustered out November 12-13, 1861. Later enlisted in Company I, 11th Regiment N. C. Troops (1st Regiment N. C. Volunteers).

RASBERRY, ALLEN, Private
Enlisted in Halifax County at age 27, April 19, 1861, for six months. Present or accounted for until mustered out November 12-13, 1861.

RASBERRY, HENRY H., Private
Enlisted at Yorktown, Virginia, May 20, 1861, for six months. Present or accounted for until mustered out November 12-13, 1861.

RAWLINGS, WILLIAM, Private
Enlisted at Yorktown, Virginia, at age 21, July 9, 1861, for six months. Present or accounted for until mustered out November 12-13, 1861.

REID, JESSE J., Private
Enlisted at Yorktown, Virginia, at age 21, June 6, 1861, for six months. Discharged August 30, 1861, by reason of disability.

SAVAGE, WILLIAM H., Private
Enlisted at Yorktown, Virginia, at age 22, June 11, 1861, for six months. Present or accounted for until mustered out November 12-13, 1861.

SHERMAN, SPOTSWOOD, Private
Enlisted in Halifax County at age 48, April 19, 1861, for six months. Present or accounted for until mustered out November 12-13, 1861.

SHIELDS, WILLIAM T., Private
Enlisted in Halifax County at age 22, April 19, 1861, for six months. Present or accounted for until mustered out November 12-13, 1861.

SLEDGE, LAWRENCE H., Private
Enlisted at Yorktown, Virginia, at age 22, June 29, 1861, for six months. Present or accounted for until mustered out November 12-13, 1861. Later enlisted in Company D, 24th Regiment N. C. Troops (14th Regiment N. C. Volunteers).

SLEDGE, WILLIAM P., Private
Enlisted in Halifax County at age 19, April 19, 1861, for six months. Present or accounted for until mustered out November 12-13, 1861.

SMITH, PETER P., Private
Enlisted in Halifax County at age 30, April 19, 1861, for six months. Present or accounted for until mustered out November 12-13, 1861.

SMITH, PEYTON HARVEY, Private
Enlisted at Yorktown, Virginia, at age 22, June 29, 1861, for six months. Present or accounted for

until mustered out November 12-13, 1861. Later enlisted in Company G, 41st Regiment N. C. Troops (3rd Regiment N. C. Cavalry).

SMITH, THOMAS, Private
Enlisted in Halifax County at age 23, April 19, 1861, for six months. Present or accounted for until mustered out November 12-13, 1861.

SMITH, WILLIAM H., Private
Enlisted in Halifax County at age 18, April 19, 1861, for six months. Company muster roll dated August 31, 1861, carries the remark: "certificate of discharge."

STATON, EMERIAH R., Private
Born in Halifax County where he resided as a farmer prior to enlisting at Yorktown, Virginia, at age 21, June 6, 1861, for six months. Discharged October 2, 1861, by reason of "disability from pneumonia."

TALBERT, WILLIAM T., Private
Enlisted at Yorktown, Virginia, at age 35, June 11, 1861, for six months. Present or accounted for until mustered out November 12-13, 1861.

TAYLOR, BENJAMIN ROBINSON, Private
Enlisted in Halifax County at age 21, April 19, 1861, for six months. Present or accounted for until mustered out November 12-13, 1861.

TAYLOR, JAMES, Private
Enlisted in Halifax County at age 24, April 19, 1861, for six months. Present or accounted for until mustered out November 12-13, 1861. Later enlisted in Company D, 43rd Regiment N. C. Troops.

TURNER, LEWIS, Private
Enlisted at Yorktown, Virginia, at age 25, June 11, 1861, for six months. Present or accounted for until mustered out November 12-13, 1861.

WALLICE, JAMES H., Private
Enlisted at Yorktown, Virginia, at age 21, June 29, 1861, for six months. Present or accounted for until mustered out November 12-13, 1861.

WATSON, JAMES, Private
Enlisted at Yorktown, Virginia, at age 21, June 11, 1861, for six months. Present or accounted for until mustered out November 12-13, 1861.

WESTRY, GEORGE W., Private
Enlisted in Halifax County at age 24, April 19, 1861, for six months. Present or accounted for until mustered out November 12-13, 1861. Later enlisted in Company A, 47th Regiment N. C. Troops.

WHITAKER, JOHN SIMMONS, Corporal
Enlisted in Halifax County at age 31, April 19, 1861, for six months. Mustered in as Private and appointed Corporal June 14, 1861. Present or accounted for until mustered out November 12-13, 1861. Later enlisted in Company D, 43rd Regiment N. C. Troops.

WHITAKER, WILLIAM, Private
Enlisted at Yorktown, Virginia, at age 23, June 29, 1861, for six months. Died at Yorktown, July 29, 1861.

WHITAKER, WILSON H., Private
Enlisted in Halifax County at age 41, April 19, 1861, for six months. Mustered in as Sergeant and reduced to ranks June 14, 1861. Present or accounted for until mustered out November 12-13, 1861.

WHITEHEAD, HARDIMAN A., Private
Enlisted at Yorktown, Virginia, at age 23, June 29, 1861, for six months. Present or accounted for until mustered out November 12-13, 1861.

WHITEHEAD, JAMES A., Private
Enlisted at Yorktown, Virginia, at age 19, June 6, 1861, for six months. Died at Yorktown, August 9, 1861.

WHITEHEAD, JAMES F., Private
Enlisted in Halifax County at age 17, April 19, 1861, for six months. Present or accounted for until mustered out November 12-13, 1861.

WHITEHEAD, WILLIS S., Private
Enlisted at Yorktown, Virginia, at age 24, June 11, 1861, for six months. Discharged September 20, 1861, by reason of Surgeon's Certificate of Disability. Later enlisted in Company D, 43rd Regiment N. C. Troops.

WHITLEY, JAMES, Private
Enlisted at Yorktown, Virginia, at age 23, June 11, 1861, for six months. Present or accounted for until mustered out November 12-13, 1861.

WILKINS, MIKE C., Private
Enlisted at Yorktown, Virginia, at age 21, June 29, 1861, for six months. Present or accounted for until mustered out November 12-13, 1861.

WILLIAMS, JOHN R., Private
Enlisted in Halifax County at age 19, April 19, 1861, for six months. Present or accounted for until mustered out November 12-13, 1861.

WILLS, GEORGE WHITAKER, Corporal
Enlisted in Halifax County at age 18, April 19, 1861, for six months. Mustered in as Private and appointed Corporal June 14, 1861. Present or accounted for until mustered out November 12-13, 1861. Later enlisted in Company D, 43rd Regiment N.C. Troops.

WRIGHT, NATHANIEL M., Private
Enlisted at Yorktown, Virginia, at age 24, June 29, 1861, for six months. Present or accounted for until mustered out November 12-13, 1861.

COMPANY K

This company, originally known as the "Lincoln Guards," enrolled for active service at Lincolnton, Lincoln County, on April 25, 1861. After organizing, the company left for Raleigh and arrived there on May 1, 1861. In an order to detail men for guard duty on May 2, the company was referred to as "Lincoln Guards." On May 3, in an order to report to the Camp of Instruction for a parade, the company was referred to as the "Star Guard." When

mustered into state service on May 13, 1861, the company was referred to as the "Southern Stars" and became Company K of this regiment. After that date the company functioned as a part of the regiment, and its history for the war period is recorded as a part of the regimental history.

The information contained in the following roster of the company was compiled principally from company muster rolls which included the muster-in roll dated August 31, 1861, covering the period May 13-August 31, 1861, and muster rolls for the periods of April 25-May 14, 1861; May 14-June 30, 1861; and July-August, 1861. No muster rolls were found for the period after August, 1861. In addition to the company muster rolls, Roll of Honor records, receipt rolls, hospital records, prisoner of war records, and other primary records, supplemented by state pension applications, United Daughters of the Confederacy records, and postwar rosters and histories, all provided useful information.

OFFICERS

CAPTAIN

HOKE, WILLIAM J.
Resided in Lincoln County where he enlisted at age 35, April 25, 1861, for six months. Appointed Captain to rank from date of enlistment. Present or accounted for until mustered out November 12-13, 1861. Later appointed Colonel of the 38th Regiment N. C. Troops.

LIEUTENANTS

EDWARDS, WILLIAM R., 2nd Lieutenant
Resided in Lincoln County where he enlisted at age 43, April 25, 1861, for six months. Mustered in as 1st Sergeant and appointed 3rd Lieutenant on June 1, 1861, to rank from April 25, 1861. Promoted to 2nd Lieutenant on August 14, 1861. Present or accounted for until mustered out November 12-13, 1861. Later appointed Captain, A. Q. M., and assigned to the Field and Staff of the 38th Regiment N.C. Troops.

HAYNES, ALBERT SIDNEY, 3rd Lieutenant
Resided in Lincoln County where he enlisted at age 24, April 25, 1861, for six months. Mustered in as Sergeant and promoted to 1st Sergeant on June 1, 1861. Appointed 3rd Lieutenant to rank from September 7, 1861. Present or accounted for until mustered out November 12-13, 1861. Later enlisted in Company I, 11th Regiment N. C. Troops (1st Regiment N. C. Volunteers).

HOKE, ROBERT FREDERICK, 2nd Lieutenant
Born in Lincoln County where he resided as a manufacturer and enlisted at age 24, April 25, 1861, for six months. Appointed 2nd Lieutenant to rank from April 25, 1861. Transferred to the Field and Staff of this regiment upon appointment as Major on September 1, 1861.

REINHARDT, WALLACE M., 1st Lieutenant
Resided in Lincoln County where he enlisted at age 42, April 25, 1861, for six months. Appointed 1st Lieutenant to rank from April 25, 1861.

Present or accounted for until mustered out November 12-13, 1861.

SUMNER, EDWARD E., 3rd Lieutenant

Resided in Lincoln County where he enlisted at age 25, April 25, 1861, for six months. Appointed 3rd Lieutenant to rank from April 25, 1861. Transferred to Company D, 1st Regiment N. C. State Troops upon appointment as 1st Lieutenant on June 1, 1861.

NONCOMMISSIONED OFFICERS AND PRIVATES

ABERNATHY, JAMES M., Private

Enlisted in Lincoln County at age 28, April 25, 1861, for six months. Muster roll dated August 31, 1861, states that he was "detailed as physician for Company K and L." Present or accounted for until mustered out November 12-13, 1861. Later appointed Assistant Surgeon and assigned to the Medical Department.

ABERNATHY, WILLIAM A., Private

Resided in Lincoln County where he enlisted at age 19, June 25, 1861, for six months. Present or accounted for until mustered out November 12-13, 1861. Later enlisted in Company I, 11th Regiment N. C. Troops (1st Regiment N. C. Volunteers).

ADAMS, WILLIAM C., Private

Resided in Lincoln County where he enlisted at age 23, April 25, 1861, for six months. Present or accounted for until mustered out November 12-13, 1861. Later appointed Captain in the Home Guard.

ALEXANDER, JAMES L., Private

Resided in Lincoln County where he enlisted at age 24, April 25, 1861, for six months. Discharged September 25, 1861, on Surgeon's Certificate of Disability. Later enlisted in Company A, 42nd Regiment N. C. Troops.

ARENT, GEORGE A., Private

Resided in Lincoln County where he enlisted at age 26, April 25, 1861, for six months. Died at Yorktown, Virginia, October 16, 1861.

BALLARD, JAMES, Private

Resided in Lincoln County where he enlisted at age 26, April 25, 1861, for six months. Present or accounted for until mustered out November 12-13, 1861.

BALLARD, THOMAS J., Private

Resided in Lincoln County where he enlisted at age 22, April 25, 1861, for six months. Present or accounted for until mustered out November 12-13, 1861. Later enlisted in Company I, 11th Regiment N. C. Troops (1st Regiment N. C. Volunteers).

BERRYHILL, JAMES S., Private

Resided in Lincoln County where he enlisted at age 32, April 25, 1861, for six months. Present or accounted for until mustered out November 12-13, 1861.

BLAND, ALBERTO M., Private

Resided in Lincoln County where he enlisted at age 19, April 25, 1861, for six months. Present or accounted for until mustered out November 12-13, 1861. Later enlisted in a South Carolina artillery unit.

BOYD, PERRY L., Private

Resided in Lincoln County where he enlisted at age 24, April 25, 1861, for six months. Present or accounted for until mustered out November 12-13, 1861. Later enlisted in Company C, 9th Regiment N. C. State Troops (1st Regiment N. C. Cavalry).

BROWN, ROBERT F., Private

Resided in Lincoln County where he enlisted at age 30,, April 25, 1861, for six months. Present or accounted for until mustered out November 12-13, 1861.

BRUMEAD, JOHN J., Private

Resided in Lincoln County where he enlisted at age 32, April 25, 1861, for six months. Present or accounted for until mustered out November 12-13, 1861. Later served in the Home Guard.

CANSLER, THOMAS J., Corporal

Resided in Lincoln County where he enlisted at age 18, April 25, 1861, for six months. Mustered in as Corporal. Present or accounted for until mustered out November 12-13, 1861. Later enlisted in Company G, 57th Regiment N. C. Troops.

CAUBLE, EPHRAIM H., Private

Resided in Lincoln County where he enlisted at age 25, June 18, 1861, for six months. Present or accounted for until mustered out November 12-13, 1861.

CAUBLE, PETER VARDRY, Private

Resided in Lincoln County where he enlisted at age 32, April 25, 1861, for six months. Present or accounted for until mustered out November 12-13, 1861. Later enlisted in Company B, 23rd Regiment N. C. Troops (13th Regiment N. C. Volunteers).

CLOSE, JOHN E., Private

Resided in Guilford County and enlisted in Lincoln County at age 21, April 25, 1861, for six months. Present or accounted for until mustered out November 12-13, 1861. Later enlisted in the C. S. Navy.

CODY, JAMES, Private

Resided in Lincoln County where he enlisted at age 17, April 25, 1861, for six months. Present or accounted for until mustered out November 12-13, 1861. Later enlisted in Company I, 11th Regiment N. C. Troops (1st Regiment N. C. Volunteers).

CODY, JESSE, Private

Resided in Lincoln County where he enlisted at age 23, April 25, 1861, for six months. Present or accounted for until mustered out November 12-13, 1861. Later enlisted in Company B, 23rd Regiment N. C. Troops (13th Regiment N. C. Volunteers).

CONLEY, JAMES C., Private

Resided in Lincoln County where he enlisted at age 23, April 25, 1861, for six months. Present or accounted for until discharged August 15, 1861, by reason of Surgeon's Certificate of Disability. Later enlisted in Company B, 58th Regiment N. C. Troops.

COON, DAVID A., Sergeant

Resided in Lincoln County where he enlisted at age 26, April 25, 1861, for six months. Mustered in as Private and promoted to Sergeant on July 10, 1861. Present or accounted for until mustered out November 12-13, 1861. Later enlisted in Company K, 11th Regiment N. C. Troops (1st Regiment N. C. Volunteers).

DELLINGER, JACOB, Private

Resided in Lincoln County where he enlisted at age 18, April 25, 1861, for six months. Present or accounted for until mustered out November 12-13, 1861. Later enlisted in Company H, 34th Regiment N. C. Troops.

DELLINGER, JOHN CALVIN, Private

Resided in Lincoln County where he enlisted at age 20, June 25, 1861, for six months. Present or accounted for until mustered out November 12-13, 1861. Later enlisted in Company H, 52nd Regiment N. C. Troops.

DELLINGER, LAWSON A., Sergeant

Resided in Lincoln County where he enlisted at age 30, April 25, 1861, for six months. Mustered in as Corporal. Promoted to Sergeant on July 25, 1861. Present or accounted for until mustered out November 12-13, 1861. Later enlisted in Company A, 52nd Regiment N. C. Troops.

DELLINGER, PETER, Private

Resided in Lincoln County where he enlisted at age 21, April 25, 1861, for six months. Died at Yorktown, Virginia, October 19, 1861.

DELLINGER, SAMUEL W., Private

Resided in Lincoln County where he enlisted at age 21, June 25, 1861, for six months. Present or accounted for until mustered out November 12-13, 1861. Later enlisted in Company H, 52nd Regiment N.C. Troops.

EARNEY, LAFAYETTE, Private

Resided in Lincoln County where he enlisted at age 26, April 25, 1861, for six months. Present or accounted for until mustered out November 12-13, 1861. Later enlisted in Company H, 52nd Regiment N. C. Troops.

ELMER, CHARLES E., Private

Resided in Lincoln County where he enlisted at age 24, June 25, 1861, for six months. Present or accounted for until mustered out November 12-13, 1861. Later enlisted in Company G, 57th Regiment N. C. Troops.

ERSON, ERIC, Corporal

Resided in Lincoln County where he enlisted at age 21, April 25, 1861, for six months. Mustered in as Private and appointed Corporal on July 25, 1861. Present or accounted for until mustered out November 12-13, 1861. Later enlisted in Company H, 52nd Regiment N. C. Troops.

GALVIN, MAURICE, Private

Resided in Lincoln County where he enlisted at age 27, April 25, 1861, for six months. Present or accounted for until mustered out November 12-

13, 1861. Later enlisted in a South Carolina artillery unit.

GARRISON, EPHRAIM, Private

Resided in Lincoln County where he enlisted at age 21, April 25, 1861, for six months. Present or accounted for until mustered out November 12-13, 1861. Later enlisted in Company H, 52nd Regiment N. C. Troops.

GATENS, JOHN, Private

Resided in Lincoln County where he enlisted at age 25, April 25, 1861, for six months. Present or accounted for until mustered out November 12-13, 1861. Later enlisted in Company G, 52nd Regiment N. C. Troops.

GOODSON, HENRY M., Private

Resided in Lincoln County where he enlisted at age 22, April 25, 1861, for six months. Present or accounted for until mustered out November 12-13, 1861. Later enlisted in Company C, 9th Regiment N. C. State Troops (1st Regiment N. C. Cavalry).

GORDON, LEWIS B., Private

Resided in Lincoln County where he enlisted at age 30, June 18, 1861, for six months. Present or accounted for until discharged September 20, 1861, by reason of "chronic diarrhoea."

GRIGG, BENJAMIN F., Private

Resided in Lincoln County where he enlisted at age 23, April 25, 1861, for six months. Present or accounted for until mustered out November 12-13, 1861. Later enlisted in Company F, 56th Regiment N. C. Troops.

HAND, ANDREW J., Private

Resided in Lincoln County where he enlisted at age 31, April 25, 1861, for six months. Present or accounted for until mustered out November 12-13, 1861.

HARGROVE, ROBERT M., Private

Resided in Lincoln County where he enlisted at age 25, April 25, 1861, for six months. Present or accounted for until mustered out November 12-13, 1861.

HAWKINS, JAMES A., Private

Resided in Gaston County and enlisted in Lincoln County at age 29, April 25, 1861, for six months. Present or accounted for until mustered out November 12-13, 1861. Later enlisted in Company C, 10th Regiment N. C. State Troops (1st Regiment N. C. Artillery).

HAWKINS, JOSEPH P., Private

Resided in Gaston County and enlisted in Lincoln County at age 22, April 25, 1861, for six months. Present or accounted for until mustered out November 12-13, 1861. Later enlisted in Company C, 10th Regiment N. C. State Troops (1st Regiment N. C. Artillery).

HAYNES, JOHN C., Private

Resided in Lincoln County where he enlisted at age 24, April 25, 1861, for six months. Present or accounted for until mustered out November 12-13, 1861. Later enlisted in Company H, 52nd Regiment N. C. Troops.

HAYNES, JOHN F., Private
Resided in Lincoln County where he enlisted at age 19, April 25, 1861, for six months. Present or accounted for until mustered out November 12-13, 1861. Later enlisted in Company I, 11th Regiment N. C. Troops (1st Regiment N. C. Volunteers).

HELDERMAN, RUFUS M., Private
Resided in Lincoln County where he enlisted at age 28, June 25, 1861, for six months. Present or accounted for until mustered out November 12-13, 1861. Later enlisted in Company H, 52nd Regiment N. C. Troops.

HENRY, MARCUS H., Private
Resided in Lincoln County where he enlisted at age 21, April 25, 1861, for six months. Present or accounted for until mustered out November 12-13, 1861. Later enlisted in Company B, 23rd Regiment N. C. Troops (13th Regiment N. C. Volunteers).

HINES, HENRY L., Private
Resided in Gaston County and enlisted in Lincoln County at age 22, April 25, 1861, for six months. Present or accounted for until mustered out November 12-13, 1861. Later enlisted in Company D, 1st Regiment N. C. State Troops.

HINES, MOSES M., Private
Resided in Gaston County and enlisted in Lincoln County at age 20, April 25, 1861, for six months. Present or accounted for until mustered out November 12-13, 1861. Later enlisted in Company B, 23rd Regiment N. C. Troops (13th Regiment N. C. Volunteers).

HOKE, GEORGE M., Private
Resided in Lincoln County where he enlisted at age 18, April 25, 1861, for six months. Present or accounted for until mustered out November 12-13, 1861. Later appointed Adjutant with the rank of 1st Lieutenant and assigned to the Field and Staff of the 33rd Regiment N. C. Troops.

HOKE, J. ELI, Private
Resided in Lincoln County where he enlisted at age 20, April 25, 1861, for six months. Present or accounted for until mustered out November 12-13, 1861.

HOLBROOKS, ALLISON, Private
Resided in Lincoln County where he enlisted at age 22, April 25, 1861, for six months. Present or accounted for until mustered out November 12-13, 1861. Later enlisted in Company C, 9th Regiment N. C. State Troops (1st Regiment N. C. Cavalry).

HOPE, THOMAS L., Private
Resided in Lincoln County where he enlisted at age 22, April 25, 1861, for six months. Present or accounted for until mustered out November 12-13, 1861. Later enlisted in Company B, 23rd Regiment N. C. Troops (13th Regiment N. C. Volunteers).

HOUSER, A. MONROE, Private
Resided in Lincoln County where he enlisted at age 23, April 25, 1861, for six months. Present or accounted for until mustered out November 12-

13, 1861. Later enlisted in the 2nd Regiment South Carolina Cavalry.

HOUSER, ABSALOM JOSEPHUS, Private
Resided in Lincoln County where he enlisted at age 21, April 25, 1861, for six months. Present or accounted for until mustered out November 12-13, 1861. Later enlisted in Company D, 1st Regiment N. C. State Troops.

HOUSER, J. WORKMAN, Private
Resided in Lincoln County where he enlisted at age 18, April 25, 1861, for six months. Present or accounted for until mustered out November 12-13, 1861. Later enlisted in the 2nd Regiment South Carolina Cavalry.

HOVIS, LABAN L., Private
Resided in Lincoln County where he enlisted at age 22, June 25, 1861, for six months. Present or accounted for until mustered out November 12-13, 1861. Later enlisted in Company I, 11th Regiment N. C. Troops (1st Regiment N. C. Volunteers).

HOYLE, LEMUEL J., Sergeant
Resided in Lincoln County where he enlisted at age 21, April 25, 1861, for six months. Mustered in as Sergeant. Reported on July-August, 1861, muster roll as having "resigned July 25, 1861." Later enlisted in Company I, 11th Regiment N. C. Troops (1st Regiment N. C. Volunteers).

JACKSON, CURTIS L., Private
Resided as a house carpenter in Lincoln County where he enlisted at age 23, August 25, 1861, for six months. Present or accounted for until discharged September 25, 1861, by reason of "valvular disease of heart." Later enlisted in Company G, 57th Regiment N.C. Troops.

JETTON, WILLIAM H., Private
Resided in Lincoln County where he enlisted at age 21, April 25, 1861, for six months. Present or accounted for until mustered out November 12-13, 1861. Later enlisted in Company I, 11th Regiment N. C. Troops (1st Regiment N. C. Volunteers).

JOHNSON, CHARLES P., Musician
Resided as a student in Lincoln County where he enlisted at age 20, June 25, 1861, for six months. Mustered in as Musician. Discharged October 1, 1861, by reason of "debility consequent on intermittent fever and chronic rheumatism." Later served as a clerk in the hospital at Charlotte.

KILLIAN, JACOB B., Private
Resided in Lincoln County where he enlisted at age 29, April 25, 1861, for six months. Present or accounted for until mustered out November 12-13, 1861.

LANDER, SAMUEL, Private
Born in Lincoln County where he resided as a student and enlisted at age 20, April 25, 1861, for six months. Discharged July 1, 1861, by reason of his having "received the appointment of 1st Lieutenant State Troops of North Carolina." Commission never issued. Later enlisted in Company A, 33rd Regiment N.C. Troops.

LAURANCE, COLUMBUS J., Private
Resided in Lincoln County where he enlisted at age 20, June 25, 1861, for six months. Died at Yorktown, Virginia, August 10, 1861.

LENHARDT, CAMERON L., Private
Resided in Lincoln County where he enlisted at age 18, April 25, 1861, for six months. Present or accounted for until mustered out November 12-13, 1861. Later enlisted in Company I, 11th Regiment N. C. Troops (1st Regiment N. C. Volunteers).

LINES, CHARLES L., Private
Resided in Lincoln County where he enlisted at age 28, April 25, 1861, for six months. Present or accounted for until mustered out November 12-13, 1861. Later enlisted in Company B, 14th Regiment N. C. Troops (4th Regiment N. C. Volunteers).

LYONS, JOHN, Private
Resided in Lincoln County where he enlisted at age 29, April 25, 1861, for six months. Present or accounted for until mustered out November 12-13, 1861. Later enlisted in a South Carolina artillery unit.

MARTIN, WILLIAM, Musician
Resided in Lincoln County where he enlisted at age 21, April 25, 1861, for six months. Mustered in as Musician. Present or accounted for until mustered out November 12-13, 1861. Later enlisted in Company I, 11th Regiment N. C. Troops (1st Regiment N. C. Volunteers).

MILLSAPS, JAMES F., Private
Resided in Lincoln County where he enlisted at age 28, April 25, 1861, for six months. Present or accounted for until mustered out November 12-13, 1861. Later enlisted in Company A, 33rd Regiment N. C. Troops.

MOONEY, ANDREW J., Private
Resided in Lincoln County where he enlisted at age 42, April 25, 1861, for six months. Present or accounted for until discharged September 6, 1861.

MORTON, HENRY W., Private
Resided in Lincoln County where he enlisted at age 24, April 25, 1861, for six months. Present or accounted for until mustered out November 12-13, 1861. Later enlisted in Captain Graham's Battery, Virginia Light Artillery.

MOSTELLER, JACOB, Private
Resided in Lincoln County where he enlisted at age 21, June 25, 1861, for six months. Died at Petersburg, Virginia, in November, 1861.

MOTZ, GEORGE, Private
Resided in Lincoln County where he enlisted at age 20, June 25, 1861, for six months. Present or accounted for until mustered out November 12-13, 1861. Later enlisted in Company I, 11th Regiment N. C. Troops (1st Regiment N. C. Volunteers).

MULL, PETER M., Private
Resided in Catawba County and enlisted in Lincoln County at age 28, April 25, 1861, for six

months. Present or accounted for until mustered out November 12-13, 1861. Later enlisted in Company F, 55th Regiment N. C. Troops.

NICKLE, JAMES N., Private
Resided in Mississippi and enlisted in Lincoln County at age 20, April 25, 1861, for six months. Died at Bigler's Mills, Virginia, September 25, 1861.

PARDUE, LEANDER J., Private
Resided in Lincoln County where he enlisted at age 43, April 25, 1861, for six months. Present or accounted for until mustered out November 12-13, 1861.

PETTUS, JOHN W., Private
Resided in Lincoln County where he enlisted at age 25, April 25, 1861, for six months. Present or accounted for until mustered out November 12-13, 1861. Later enlisted in Company C, 37th Regiment N. C. Troops.

PRENDERGAST, JOHN, Private
Born in Ireland and resided as a stone mason in Gaston County prior to enlisting in Lincoln County at age 35, April 25, 1861, for six months. Discharged September 20, 1861, by reason of "chronic rheumatism."

RAGLAND, WILLIAM RUFUS, Private
Resided in Lincoln County where he enlisted at age 28, April 25, 1861, for six months. Present or accounted for until discharged September 18, 1861.

RAMSEUR, ALFRED A., Private
Resided in Lincoln County where he enlisted at age 33, April 25, 1861, for six months. Present or accounted for until mustered out November 12-13, 1861. Later enlisted in Company A, 33rd Regiment N. C. Troops.

RAMSEUR, HENRY E., Private
Resided in Lincoln County where he enlisted at age 29, June 25, 1861, for six months. Present or accounted for until mustered out November 12-13, 1861.

RAMSEUR, OLIVER A., Private
Resided in Lincoln County where he enlisted at age 27, April 25, 1861, for six months. Present or accounted for until mustered out November 12-13, 1861. Later enlisted in Company I, 11th Regiment N. C. Troops (1st Regiment N. C. Volunteers).

RAMSEUR, THEODORE J., Private
Resided in Lincoln County where he enlisted at age 29, April 25, 1861, for six months. Present or accounted for until mustered out November 12-13, 1861. Later enlisted in Company I, 11th Regiment N. C. Troops (1st Regiment N. C. Volunteers).

RAMSEUR, WALTER G., Private
Resided in Lincoln County where he enlisted at age 25, April 25, 1861, for six months. Present or accounted for until mustered out November 12-13, 1861. Later enlisted in Company I, 11th Regiment N. C. Troops (1st Regiment N. C. Volunteers).

RAMSEY, JOHN, Private
Resided in Lincoln County where he enlisted at age 22, June 25, 1861, for six months. Present or accounted for until mustered out November 12-13, 1861.

RAMSEY, WILLIAM W., Private
Resided in Lincoln County where he enlisted at age 20, June 25, 1861, for six months. Present or accounted for until mustered out November 12-13, 1861. Later enlisted in Company G, 57th Regiment N. C. Troops.

REINHARDT, JAMES W., Private
Resided in Lincoln County where he enlisted at age 19, April 25, 1861, for six months. Died at Yorktown, Virginia, July 14, 1861.

REINHARDT, JOHN FRANKLIN, Private
Resided in Lincoln County where he enlisted at age 16, April 25, 1861, for six months. Present or accounted for until mustered out November 12-13, 1861. Later enlisted in Company C, 9th Regiment N. C. State Troops (1st Regiment N. C. Cavalry).

RODGERS, WOOD M., Private
Enlisted in Lincoln County at age 21, April 25, 1861, for six months. Present or accounted for until mustered out November 12-13, 1861. Later enlisted in Company F, 9th Regiment N. C. State Troops (1st Regiment N. C. Cavalry).

RONEY, JOHN A., Private
Resided in Lincoln County where he enlisted at age 30, April 25, 1861, for six months. Present or accounted for until mustered out November 12-13, 1861. Later enlisted in Company K, 23rd Regiment N. C. Troops (13th Regiment N. C. Volunteers).

RUDISILL, JONAS G., Corporal
Resided in Lincoln County where he enlisted at age 24, April 25, 1861, for six months. Mustered in as Private and appointed Corporal on July 10, 1861. Died near Yorktown, Virginia, October 16, 1861.

RUSH, WILLIAM S., Private
Resided as a machinist in Lincoln County where he enlisted at age 21, April 25, 1861, for six months. Present or accounted for until mustered out November 12-13, 1861.

SHERRILL, G. POWELL, Private
Resided in Catawba County and enlisted in Lincoln County at age 17, June 25, 1861, for six months. Present or accounted for until mustered out November 12-13, 1861. Later enlisted in Company K, 49th Regiment N. C. Troops.

SHERRILL, NELSON M., Private
Resided in Lincoln County where he enlisted at age 19, April 25, 1861, for six months. Present or accounted for until mustered out November 12-13, 1861. Later enlisted in Company B, 23rd Regiment N. C. Troops (13th Regiment N. C. Volunteers).

SHERRILL, WILLIAM A., Private
Resided in Lincoln County where he enlisted at age 19, April 25, 1861, for six months. Present or accounted for until mustered out November 12-13, 1861. Later enlisted in Company I, 11th Regiment N. C. Troops (1st Regiment N. C. Volunteers).

SHUFORD, GEORGE W., Private
Resided in Lincoln County where he enlisted at age 22, April 25, 1861, for six months. Present or accounted for until mustered out November 12-13, 1861. Later enlisted in a Florida regiment.

SHUFORD, WILLIAM H., Private
Resided in Gaston County and enlisted in Lincoln County at age 20, April 25, 1861, for six months. Present or accounted for until mustered out November 12-13, 1861. Later enlisted in Company A, 33rd Regiment N.C. Troops.

SMITH, JULIUS L., Private
Resided in Rowan County and enlisted in Lincoln County at age 21, April 25, 1861, for six months. Present or accounted for until mustered out November 12-13, 1861. Later enlisted in Company B, 42nd Regiment N. C. Troops.

SMITH, MARK H., Private
Enlisted in Lincoln County at age 23, April 25, 1861, for six months. Present or accounted for until mustered out November 12-13, 1861. Later enlisted in Company G, 9th Regiment N. C. State Troops (1st Regiment N. C. Cavalry).

SMITH, WINSLOW A., Private
Resided as an iron contractor in Lincoln County where he enlisted at age 20, April 25, 1861, for six months. Present or accounted for until mustered out November 12-13, 1861.

SPECK, JOHN FRANKLIN, Sergeant
Resided in Lincoln County where he enlisted at age 20, April 25, 1861, for six months. Mustered in as Sergeant. Present or accounted for until mustered out November 12-13, 1861. Later enlisted in Company G, 57th Regiment N. C. Troops.

STAMEY, JOHN A, Private
Resided in Lincoln County where he enlisted at age 23, April 25, 1861, for six months. Present or accounted for until mustered out November 12-13, 1861. Later enlisted in Company D, 1st Regiment N. C. State Troops.

STOWE, ALLEN R., Private
Resided in Lincoln County where he enlisted at age 23, May 1, 1861, for six months. Mustered in as Sergeant. Present or accounted for until mustered out November 12-13, 1861. Later enlisted in Company D, 59th Regiment N.C. Troops (4th Regiment N.C. Cavalry).

STROUP, ROBERT, Private
Resided in Lincoln County where he enlisted at age 21, April 25, 1861, for six months. Discharged September 20-21, 1861, by reason of injury received "with a pick on the embankment at Yorktown" and "before it was cured he was taken with a severe cough, then with measles, then the chills and fever, and the surgeon says he has chronic diarrhoea."

STUBBS, ELBRIDGE W., Sergeant

Resided in Lincoln County where he enlisted at age 26, April 25, 1861, for six months. Mustered in as Sergeant. Present or accounted for until mustered out November 12-13, 1861.

STUBBS, FRANKLIN, Private

Resided in Lincoln County where he enlisted at age 17, June 25, 1861, for six months. Present or accounted for until mustered out November 12-13, 1861.

SULLIVAN, JAMES O., Private

Resided in Lincoln County where he enlisted at age 38, April 25, 1861, for six months. Present or accounted for until mustered out November 12-13, 1861. Later enlisted in a South Carolina artillery unit.

SUMMEROW, WILLIAM A., Corporal

Resided in Lincoln County where he enlisted at age 24, April 25, 1861, for six months. Mustered in as Corporal. Present or accounted for until mustered out November 12-13, 1861. Later enlisted in Company H, 52nd Regiment N. C. Troops.

SUMNER, JULIAN E., Private

Resided in Lincoln County where he enlisted at age 28, April 25, 1861, for six months. Present or accounted for until mustered out November 12-13, 1861.

WACASTER, ADOLPHUS, Private

Resided in Lincoln County where he enlisted at age 19, April 25, 1861, for six months. Present or accounted for until mustered out November 12-13, 1861. Later enlisted in Company I, 11th Regiment N. C. Troops (1st Regiment N. C. Volunteers).

WARLICK, RUFUS M., Private

Resided in Lincoln County where he enlisted at age 20, April 25, 1861, for six months. Present or accounted for until mustered out November 12-13, 1861. Later enlisted in Company K, 49th Regiment N. C. Troops.

WELLS, JAMES DANIEL, Musician

Resided in Lincoln County where he enlisted at age 21, April 25, 1861, for six months. Mustered in as Musician. Present or accounted for until mustered out November 12-13, 1861. Later enlisted in Company G, 52nd Regiment N. C. Troops.

WELLS, OLIVER, Private

Resided in Lincoln County where he enlisted at age 16, June 25, 1861, for six months. Present or accounted for until mustered out November 12-13, 1861. Later enlisted in Company I, 11th Regiment N. C. Troops (1st Regiment N. C. Volunteers).

WHITE, WILLIAM, Private

Resided in Lincoln County where he enlisted at age 20, April 25, 1861, for six months. Wounded at Bethel, Virginia, June 10, 1861. Present or accounted for until mustered out November 12-13, 1861.

WILLIAMS, WESTLY A., Private

Resided in Lincoln County where he enlisted at age 23, April 25, 1861, for six months. Present or accounted for until mustered out November 12-13, 1861. Later enlisted in Company F, 55th Regiment N. C. Troops.

WINGATE, ANGUS, Private

Resided in Lincoln County where he enlisted at age 22, April 25, 1861, for six months. Present or accounted for until mustered out November 12-13, 1861. Later enlisted in Company A, 11th Regiment N. C. Troops (1st Regiment N. C. Volunteers).

WINGATE, MURCHISON, Private

Resided in Lincoln County where he enlisted at age 21, April 25, 1861, for six months. Present or accounted for until mustered out November 12-13, 1861. Later enlisted in Company A, 11th Regiment N. C. Troops (1st Regiment N. C. Volunteers).

COMPANY L

This company, known as the "Bertie Volunteers," was enrolled for active service at Windsor, Bertie County, May 1, 1861. From Windsor the company moved to Garysburg, where it arrived on May 22, 1861. The company was mustered into Confederate service for twelve months' service on June 6, 1861, at Garysburg. On June 20 it was assigned to this regiment as Company L and ordered from Garysburg to Yorktown, Virginia. It was ordered to leave by rail for Richmond, Virginia, on June 22, and from there to proceed to Yorktown and join the regiment. The company did not join the regiment until the end of August. On the muster-in roll, dated August 31, 1861, the mustering officer noted that "this company only mustered with the regiment today for the first time, as previously it was on detached service." The nature of the detached service was not reported. After joining the regiment the company functioned as a part of the regiment, and its history for the war period is recorded as a part of the regimental history.

The information contained in the following roster of the company was compiled principally from company muster rolls, which included the muster-in roll dated August 31, 1861, covering the period June 6-August 31, 1861, and muster rolls for the periods of May 1-June 6, 1861; June 6-30, 1861; and July-August, 1861. No muster rolls were found for the period after August, 1861. In addition to the company muster rolls, Roll of Honor records, receipt rolls, hospital records, prisoner of war records, and other primary records, supplemented by state pension applications, United Daughters of the Confederacy records, and postwar rosters and histories, all provided useful information.

OFFICERS

CAPTAIN

JACOCKS, JESSE C.

Resided in Bertie County where he enlisted at

age 27, May 1, 1861, for six months. Appointed Captain to rank from May 1, 1861. Present or accounted for until mustered out November 12-13, 1861.

LIEUTENANTS

BIRD, FRANCIS W., 2nd Lieutenant
Resided in Bertie County where he enlisted on May 1, 1861, for six months. Appointed 2nd Lieutenant to rank from date of enlistment. Present or accounted for until mustered out November 12-13, 1861. Later enlisted in Company C, 11th Regiment N. C. Troops (1st Regiment N. C. Volunteers).

SPELLER, JAMES J., 3rd Lieutenant
Resided in Bertie County where he enlisted at age 25, May 1, 1861, for six months. Appointed 3rd Lieutenant to rank from date of enlistment. Present or accounted for until mustered out November 12-13, 1861. Later served in the Conscript Bureau.

SUTTON, STARK ARMISTEAD, 1st Lieutenant
Resided in Bertie County where he enlisted at age 24, May 1, 1861, for six months. Appointed 1st Lieutenant to rank from date of enlistment. Present or accounted for until mustered out November 12-13, 1861. Later appointed Adjutant with rank of 1st Lieutenant and assigned to the Field and Staff of the 44th Regiment N.C. Troops.

NONCOMMISSIONED OFFICERS AND PRIVATES

ASKEW, AARON O., Private
Resided in Bertie County where he enlisted at age 16, May 1, 1861, for six months. Present or accounted for until mustered out November 12-13, 1861.

ASKEW, BENJAMIN F., Private
Enlisted in Bertie County at age 20, May 1, 1861, for six months. Died at Garysburg, Northampton County, June 17, 1861.

ASKEW, WILLIAM L., Private
Resided in Bertie County where he enlisted at age 25, May 1, 1861, for six months. Present or accounted for until mustered out November 12-13, 1861.

ASKEW, WILLIAM W., Private
Enlisted in Bertie County at age 18, May 1, 1861, for six months. Present or accounted for until mustered out November 12-13, 1861.

BEST, JAMES J., Private
Enlisted in Bertie County at age 29, May 1, 1861, for six months. Present or accounted for until mustered out November 12-13, 1861.

BURDEN, JAMES M., Private
Resided in Bertie County where he enlisted at age 16, May 1, 1861, for six months. Present or accounted for until mustered out November 12-13, 1861. Later enlisted in Company C, 11th Regiment N. C. Troops (1st Regiment N. C. Volunteers).

BUTLER, GEORGE W., Private
Enlisted in Bertie County at age 22, May 1, 1861, for six months. Present or accounted for until mustered out November 12-13, 1861.

BUTLER, LEVIN E., Private
Resided in Bertie County where he enlisted at age 19, May 1, 1861, for six months. Present or accounted for until mustered out November 12-13, 1861. Later enlisted in Company C, 11th Regiment N. C. Troops (1st Regiment N. C. Volunteers).

BUTLER, WILLIAM H., Private
Resided in Bertie County where he enlisted at age 24, May 1, 1861, for six months. Present or accounted for until mustered out November 12-13, 1861. Later enlisted in Company C, 11th Regiment N. C. Troops (1st Regiment N. C. Volunteers).

CAPEHEART, JAMES W., Private
Enlisted in Bertie County at age 18, May 1, 1861, for six months. Present or accounted for until mustered out November 12-13, 1861.

CARTER, JOSEPH B., Private
Resided in Bertie County where he enlisted at age 19, May 1, 1861, for six months. Present or accounted for until mustered out November 12-13, 1861. Later enlisted in Company C, 11th Regiment N. C. Troops (1st Regiment N. C. Volunteers).

CARTER, ROBERT E., Corporal
Resided in Bertie County where he enlisted at age 22, May 1, 1861, for six months. Mustered in as Corporal. Present or accounted for until mustered out November 12-13, 1861.

CONNER, JAMES R., Private
Enlisted in Bertie County at age 19, May 1, 1861, for six months. Present or accounted for until mustered out November 12-13, 1861.

COOPER, THOMAS W., Corporal
Resided in Bertie County where he enlisted at age 20, May 1, 1861, for six months. Mustered in as Corporal. Present or accounted for until mustered out November 12-13, 1861. Later enlisted in Company C, 11th Regiment N. C. Troops (1st Regiment N. C. Volunteers).

CRAIGE, CLINGMAN, Private
Enlisted in Bertie County at age 20, May 1, 1861, for six months. Present or accounted for until mustered out November 12-13, 1861. Later enlisted in Company C, 11th Regiment N. C. Troops (1st Regiment N. C. Volunteers).

CRICHLOW, JOHN, Private
Enlisted in Bertie County at age 30, May 1, 1861, for six months. Present or accounted for until mustered out November 12-13, 1861.

DeBOW, JAMES N., Private
Enlisted in Bertie County at age 27, May 1, 1861, for six months. Discharged June 17, 1861, "to work in cap factory, Richmond, Virginia."

DUDLEY, JOHN T., Private
Enlisted in Bertie County at age 21, May 1, 1861, for six months. Present or accounted for until mustered out November 12-13, 1861.

ELLYSON, THOMAS J., Private
Resided in Bertie County where he enlisted at age 18, May 1, 1861, for six months. Present or accounted for until mustered out November 12-13, 1861.

FARMER, JOSEPH J., Private
Enlisted in Bertie County at age 20, May 1, 1861, for six months. Present or accounted for until mustered out November 12-13, 1861.

GASKINS, WILLIAM T., Private
Enlisted in Bertie County at age 23, May 1, 1861, for six months. Present or accounted for until mustered out November 12-13, 1861.

GILLIAM, JOHN H., Private
Resided in Bertie County where he enlisted at age 53, May 1, 1861, for six months. Present or accounted for until mustered out November 12-13, 1861.

GILLIAM, WILLIAM H., Private
Enlisted in Bertie County at age 19, May 1, 1861, for six months. Present or accounted for until mustered out November 12-13, 1861.

GRAY, WILLIAM L., Private
Enlisted in Bertie County at age 20, May 1, 1861, for six months. Present or accounted for until mustered out November 12-13, 1861.

GREEN, JOHN W., Private
Enlisted in Bertie County at age 22, May 1, 1861, for six months. Present or accounted for until mustered out November 12-13, 1861.

HARDY, JOHN H., Private
Resided in Bertie County where he enlisted at age 22, May 1, 1861, for six months. Present or accounted for until mustered out November 12-13, 1861.

HARMON, ENOCH, Private
Enlisted in Bertie County at age 32, May 1, 1861, for six months. Present or accounted for until mustered out November 12-13, 1861.

HARRELL, ASA T., Private
Enlisted in Bertie County at age 20, May 1, 1861, for six months. Present or accounted for until mustered out November 12-13, 1861.

HARRELL, GEORGE B., Private
Resided in Bertie County where he enlisted at age 21, May 1, 1861, for six months. Present or accounted for until mustered out November 12-13, 1861. Later enlisted in Company C, 11th Regiment N. C. Troops (1st Regiment N. C. Volunteers).

HARRELL, HIRAM P., Private
Born in Bertie County where he resided as a farmer and enlisted at age 24, May 1, 1861, for six months. Present or accounted for until discharged September 27, 1861, by reason of "intermittent fevers and general debility."

HAWKINS, WILLIAM H., Private
Enlisted in Bertie County at age 21, May 1, 1861, for six months. Present or accounted for until mustered out November 12-13, 1861.

HOGGARD, THOMAS W., Private
Enlisted in Bertie County at age 34, May 1, 1861, for six months. Present or accounted for until mustered out November 12-13, 1861.

JOHNSON, HENRY L., Private
Enlisted in Bertie County at age 24, May 1, 1861, for six months. Present or accounted for until mustered out November 12-13, 1861.

JORDAN, JESSE N., Private
Enlisted in Bertie County at age 32, May 1, 1861, for six months. Present or accounted for until mustered out November 12-13, 1861.

JORDON, JAMES B., Sergeant
Resided in Bertie County and enlisted May 1, 1861, for six months.

McGLAUGHAN, JOHN R., Private
Enlisted in Bertie County at age 33, May 1, 1861, for six months. Present or accounted for until mustered out November 12-13, 1861.

MARDRE, WILLIAM B., Private
Resided in Bertie County where he enlisted at age 31, May 1, 1861, for six months. Present or accounted for until mustered out November 12-13, 1861. Later enlisted in Company C, 11th Regiment N. C. Troops (1st Regiment N. C. Volunteers).

MILLER, ROBERT B., Private
Enlisted in Bertie County at age 23, May 1, 1861, for six months. Present or accounted for until mustered out November 12-13, 1861.

MILLER, WILLIAM C., Private
Enlisted in Bertie County at age 29, May 1, 1861, for six months. Present or accounted for until mustered out November 12-13, 1861.

MITCHELL, FRANKLIN V., Private
Enlisted in Bertie County at age 21, May 1, 1861, for six months. Present or accounted for until mustered out November 12-13, 1861.

MITCHELL, JEREMIAH P., Private
Resided in Bertie County where he enlisted at age 18, May 1, 1861, for six months. Present or accounted for until mustered out November 12-13, 1861. Later enlisted in Company C, 11th Regiment N. C. Troops (1st Regiment N. C. Volunteers).

MITCHELL, JOHN H., Private
Enlisted in Bertie County at age 20, May 1, 1861, for six months. Present or accounted for until mustered out November 12-13, 1861.

MITCHELL, JOSEPH S., Private
Enlisted in Bertie County at age 24, May 1, 1861, for six months. Present or accounted for until mustered out November 12-13, 1861.

MITCHELL, THOMAS H., Private
Enlisted in Bertie County at age 17, May 1, 1861, for six months. Present or accounted for until mustered out November 12-13, 1861.

MITCHELL, THOMAS J., Private
Enlisted in Bertie County at age 24, May 1, 1861, for six months. Present or accounted for until mustered out November 12-13, 1861.

MITCHELL, WILLIAM J., Private
Enlisted in Bertie County at age 19, May 1, 1861, for six months. Present or accounted for until

mustered out November 12-13, 1861.

MORRIS, CALVIN J., Private
Resided in Bertie County where he enlisted at age 22, May 1, 1861, for six months. Present or accounted for until mustered out November 12-13, 1861. Later enlisted in Company F, 59th Regiment N. C. Troops (4th Regiment N. C. Cavalry).

MORRIS, FREDERICK, Private
Enlisted in Bertie County at age 29, May 1, 1861, for six months. Died at Yorktown, Virginia, July 3, 1861.

MORRIS, JAMES D., Private
Enlisted in Bertie County at age 22, May 1, 1861, for six months. Present or accounted for until mustered out November 12-13, 1861.

MYERS, NATHAN, Private
Resided in Bertie County where he enlisted at age 22, May 1, 1861, for six months. Present or accounted for until mustered out November 12-13, 1861. Later enlisted in Company C, 11th Regiment N. C. Troops (1st Regiment N. C. Volunteers).

MYERS, SAMUEL L., Private
Enlisted in Bertie County at age 21, May 1, 1861, for six months. Present or accounted for until mustered out November 12-13, 1861.

MYERS, THOMAS L., Private
Resided in Bertie County where he enlisted at age 24, May 1, 1861, for six months. Present or accounted for until mustered out November 12-13, 1861. Later enlisted in Company C, 11th Regiment N. C. Troops (1st Regiment N. C. Volunteers).

NIXON, JOHN E., Private
Enlisted in Bertie County at age 22, May 1, 1861, for six months. Present or accounted for until mustered out November 12-13, 1861.

OUTLAW, DAVID C., Private
Resided in Bertie County where he enlisted at age 16, May 1, 1861, for six months. Present or accounted for until mustered out November 12-13, 1861. Later enlisted in Company F, 59th Regiment N. C. Troops (4th Regiment N. C. Cavalry).

OUTLAW, EDWARD R., Corporal
Resided in Bertie County where he enlisted at age 20, May 1, 1861, for six months. Mustered in as Corporal. Present or accounted for until mustered out November 12-13, 1861. Later enlisted in Company C, 11th Regiment N. C. Troops (1st Regiment N. C. Volunteers).

OUTLAW, JOSEPH S., Private
Resided in Bertie County where he enlisted at age 22, May 1, 1861, for six months. Present or accounted for until discharged September 27, 1861.

OWENS, RICHARD, Private
Enlisted in Bertie County at age 19, May 1, 1861, for six months. Present or accounted for until mustered out November 12-13, 1861. Later enlisted in Company C, 11th Regiment N. C. Troops (1st Regiment N.C. Volunteers).

PARKER, THOMAS H., Private
Enlisted in Bertie County at age 20, May 1, 1861, for six months. Present or accounted for until mustered out November 12-13, 1861. Later enlisted in Company C, 11th Regiment N. C. Troops (1st Regiment N. C. Volunteers).

PEELE, THOMAS H., Private
Resided in Bertie County where he enlisted at age 19, May 1, 1861, for six months. Present or accounted for until mustered out November 12-13, 1861. Later enlisted in Company C, 11th Regiment N. C. Troops (1st Regiment N. C. Volunteers).

PEELE, WILLIAM E., Private
Resided in Bertie County where he enlisted at age 25, May 1, 1861, for six months. Present or accounted for until mustered out November 12-13, 1861. Later enlisted in Company B, 3rd Battalion N. C. Light Artillery.

PHELPS, WILLIAM T., Private
Born in Bertie County where he resided as a farmer and enlisted at age 20, May 1, 1861, for six months. Present or accounted for until discharged September 29, 1861, by reason of "debility succeeding measles from which he has never recovered."

POWELL, WILLIAM W., Private
Resided in Bertie County where he enlisted at age 18, May 1, 1861, for six months. Present or accounted for until mustered out November 12-13, 1861. Later enlisted in Company C, 11th Regiment N. C. Troops (1st Regiment N. C. Volunteers).

RASCOE, PETER, Private
Enlisted in Bertie County at age 22, May 1, 1861, for six months. Present or accounted for until mustered out November 12-13, 1861.

RAWLS, JAMES R., Private
Resided in Bertie County where he enlisted at age 24, May 1, 1861, for six months. Present or accounted for until mustered out November 12-13, 1861. Later enlisted in Company C, 11th Regiment N. C. Troops (1st Regiment N. C. Volunteers).

RAYNER, JAMES T., Private
Enlisted in Bertie County at age 17, May 1, 1861, for six months. Present or accounted for until mustered out November 12-13, 1861.

RICE, NAPOLEON B., Private
Resided in Bertie County where he enlisted at age 19, May 1, 1861, for six months. Present or accounted for until mustered out November 12-13, 1861. Later enlisted in Company C, 11th Regiment N. C. Troops (1st Regiment N. C. Volunteers).

ROBBINS, HENRY T., Private
Enlisted in Bertie County at age 22, May 1, 1861, for six months. Present or accounted for until mustered out November 12-13, 1861.

ROUNTREE, JACKSON, Sergeant
Enlisted in Bertie County at age 32, May 1, 1861, for six months. Mustered in as Sergeant. Present

or accounted for until mustered out November 12-13, 1861.

RUFFIN, THOMAS, Sergeant
Resided in Bertie County where he enlisted at age 23, May 1, 1861, for six months. Mustered in as Sergeant. Present or accounted for until mustered out November 12-13, 1861. Later enlisted in Company D, 59th Regiment N.C. Troops (4th Regiment N.C. Cavalry).

SKILES, HENRY, Private
Resided in Bertie County where he enlisted at age 27, May 1, 1861, for six months. Present or accounted for until mustered out November 12-13, 1861. Later enlisted in Company C, 11th Regiment N. C. Troops (1st Regiment N. C. Volunteers).

SKIRVEN, GEORGE F., 1st Sergeant
Resided in Bertie County where he enlisted at age 31, May 1, 1861, for six months. Mustered in as 1st Sergeant. Present or accounted for until mustered out November 12-13, 1861. Later served in Mallett's Battalion N. C. Troops (Camp Holmes' Guard).

SPELLER, HUGH H., Private
Enlisted in Bertie County at age 20, May 1, 1861. for six months. Present or accounted for until mustered out November 12-13, 1861.

SUTTON, JOHN M., Private
Enlisted in Bertie County at age 18, May 1, 1861, for six months. Present or accounted for until mustered out November 12-13, 1861.

SUTTON, LEWIS B., Private
Enlisted in Bertie County at age 20, May 1, 1861, for six months. Present or accounted for until mustered out November 12-13, 1861.

SWAIN, WHITMELL W., Corporal
Enlisted in Bertie County at age 23, May 1, 1861, for six months. Mustered in as Corporal. Present or accounted for until mustered out November 12-13, 1861.

TAYLOE, FRANCIS M., Private
Enlisted in Bertie County at age 24, May 1, 1861, for six months. Present or accounted for until mustered out November 12-13, 1861.

THOMAS, JOHN, Private
Enlisted in Bertie County at age 21, May 1, 1861, for six months. Died near Yorktown, Virginia, September 19, 1861.

THOMAS, JOSEPH T., Private
Enlisted in Bertie County at age 19, May 1, 1861, for six months. Present or accounted for until mustered out November 12-13, 1861.

THOMPSON, DAVID, Private
Enlisted in Bertie County at age 24, May 1, 1861, for six months. Present or accounted for until mustered out November 12-13, 1861. Later enlisted in Company C, 11th Regiment N. C. Troops (1st Regiment N. C. Volunteers).

THOMPSON, THOMAS W., Private
Enlisted in Bertie County at age 27, May 1, 1861, for six months. Present or accounted for until mustered out November 12-13, 1861.

TODD, WILLIAM H., Private
Enlisted in Bertie County at age 21, May 1, 1861, for six months. Present or accounted for until mustered out November 12-13, 1861. Later enlisted in Company C, 11th Regiment N. C. Troops (1st Regiment N. C. Volunteers).

WATFORD, DAVID A., Private
Enlisted in Bertie County at age 20, May 1, 1861, for six months. Present or accounted for until mustered out November 12-13, 1861.

WATFORD, JOSEPH J., Private
Enlisted in Bertie County at age 23, May 1, 1861, for six months. Present or accounted for until mustered out November 12-13, 1861.

WHITE, JOHN H., Private
Enlisted in Bertie County at age 19, May 1, 1861, for six months. Present or accounted for until mustered out November 12-13, 1861.

WHITE, RENSELLAR C., Private
Enlisted in Bertie County at age 20, May 1, 1861, for six months. Present or accounted for until mustered out November 12-13, 1861.

WHYTE, SOLOMON H., Private
Enlisted in Bertie County at age 22, May 1, 1861, for six months. Present or accounted for until mustered out November 12-13, 1861.

WILKINS, WALTER W., Sergeant
Resided in Bertie County where he enlisted at age 21, May 1, 1861, for six months. Mustered in as Sergeant. Present or accounted for until mustered out November 12-13, 1861.

WILLIAMS, JAMES MARSHALL, Private
Enlisted in Bertie County at age 21, May 1, 1861, for six months. Present or accounted for until mustered out November 12-13, 1861. Later appointed 1st Lieutenant in the Adjutant and Inspector General's Department.

WILLIFORD, JOSEPH A., Private
Enlisted in Bertie County at age 20, May 1, 1861, for six months. Present or accounted for until mustered out November 12-13, 1861. Later enlisted in Company D, 17th Regiment N. C. Troops (2nd Organization).

WILLIFORD, RICHARD H., Private
Enlisted in Bertie County at age 21, May 1, 1861, for six months. Present or accounted for until mustered out November 12-13, 1861. Later enlisted in Company D, 17th Regiment N. C. Troops (2nd Organization).

WOODBURN, LUCIUS L., Private
Enlisted in Bertie County at age 30, May 1, 1861, for six months. Present or accounted for until mustered out November 12-13, 1861.

WOODMAN, ARTHUR, Private
Enlisted in Bertie County at age 23, May 1, 1861, for six months. Present or accounted for until mustered out November 12-13, 1861.

COMPANY M

This company, known as the "Chowan Dixie

Boys" and the "Dixie Rebels," was enrolled for active service at Edenton, Chowan County, on April 29, 1861. On May 26, 1861, the company was mustered into state service for twelve months' service. From Edenton the company moved to Garysburg, where it arrived on June 15, 1861. Five days later, June 20, it was assigned to this regiment as Company M. It was ordered to move from Garysburg to Richmond, Virginia, on June 22. From Richmond, the company was to proceed to Yorktown to join the regiment. The company joined the regiment during the first week in August, 1861. From that time the company functioned as a part of the regiment, and its history for the war period is recorded as a part of the regimental history.

The information contained in the following roster of the company was compiled principally from company muster rolls which included the muster-in roll dated August 31, 1861, covering the period May 26-August 31, 1861, and muster rolls for the periods April 29-May 26, 1861; May 26-June 30, 1861; and July-August, 1861. No muster rolls were found for the period after August, 1861. In addition to the company muster rolls, Roll of Honor records, receipt rolls, hospital records, prisoner of war records, and other primary records, supplemented by state pension applications, United Daughters of the Confederacy records, and postwar rosters and histories, all provided useful information.

OFFICERS

CAPTAIN

MARSHALL, JAMES K.
  Resided in Chowan County where he enlisted at age 22, April 29, 1861, for six months. Appointed Captain to rank from May 24, 1861. Present or accounted for until mustered out November 12-13, 1861. Later appointed Colonel of the 52nd Regiment N. C. Troops.

LIEUTENANTS

CAPEHART, THOMAS, 3rd Lieutenant
  Resided in Chowan County where he enlisted at age 21, April 29, 1861, for six months. Mustered in as Corporal and appointed 3rd Lieutenant to rank from June 29, 1861. Present or accounted for until mustered out November 12-13, 1861. Later enlisted in Company C, 3rd Battalion N. C. Light Artillery.

SMALL, EDWARD A., 2nd Lieutenant
  Resided in Chowan County where he enlisted at age 26, April 29, 1861, for six months. Appointed 2nd Lieutenant to rank from May 24, 1861. Present or accounted for until mustered out November 12-13, 1861. Later enlisted in Company F, 11th Regiment N. C. Troops (1st Regiment N. C. Volunteers).

WARREN, LEWELLYN P., 1st Lieutenant
  Resided in Chowan County where he enlisted at age 23, April 29, 1861, for six months. Appointed 1st Lieutenant to rank from May 24, 1861. Present or accounted for until mustered out No-

vember 12-13, 1861. Later appointed Adjutant with the rank of 1st Lieutenant and assigned to the Field and Staff of the 52nd Regiment N. C. Troops.

NONCOMMISSIONED OFFICERS AND PRIVATES

ANSLEY, BENJAMIN B., Private
  Enlisted in Washington County at age 21, May 26, 1861, for six months. Present or accounted for until mustered out November 12-13, 1861.

ANSLEY, SETH, Private
  Enlisted in Washington County at age 21, May 26, 1861, for six months. Present or accounted for until mustered out November 12-13, 1861.

BOYCE, MARTIN, Private
  Enlisted in Chowan County at age 24, April 29, 1861, for six months. Present or accounted for until mustered out November 12-13, 1861.

BRITT, THOMAS W., Sergeant
  Enlisted in Chowan County at age 25, April 29, 1861, for six months. Mustered in as Sergeant. Present or accounted for until mustered out November 12-13, 1861.

BRITT, WILLIAM G., Sergeant
  Resided in Chowan County where he enlisted at age 21, April 29, 1861, for six months. Mustered in as Sergeant. Present or accounted for until mustered out November 12-13, 1861.

BUNCH, JAMES W., Private
  Enlisted in Chowan County at age 28, April 29, 1861, for six months. Present or accounted for until mustered out November 12-13, 1861.

BUNCH, JOHN, Private
  Enlisted in Chowan County at age 26, April 29, 1861, for six months. Present or accounted for until mustered out November 12-13, 1861.

BUSH, PORTER, Private
  Enlisted in Chowan County at age 22, April 29, 1861, for six months. Present or accounted for until mustered out November 12-13, 1861.

BYRUM, ISAAC, Private
  Enlisted in Chowan County at age 21, June 13, 1861, for six months. Present or accounted for until mustered out November 12-13, 1861.

CAHOON, JESSE, Private
  Enlisted in Chowan County at age 23, May 26, 1861, for six months. Present or accounted for until mustered out November 12-13, 1861.

COLLINS, ARTHUR, Private
  Enlisted in Chowan County at age 18, May 26, 1861, for six months. Present or accounted for until mustered out November 12-13, 1861.

DAVENPORT, CHARLES, Private
  Enlisted in Chowan County at age 25, April 29, 1861, for six months. Present or accounted for until he was reported as having died. Date of death given as August 18 and September 18, 1861.

ELLIOTT, CHARLES, Private
  Enlisted in Hertford County at age 22, May 10, 1861, for six months. Present or accounted for

until "discharged in consequence of ill health" in August, 1861.

FULLERTON, THOMAS, Private
Enlisted in Chowan County at age 29, June 8, 1861, for six months. Present or accounted for until mustered out November 12-13, 1861.

GILLIAM, GEORGE, Private
Enlisted in Chowan County, June 25, 1861, for six months. Present or accounted for until mustered out November 12-13, 1861.

GILLIAM, JULIEN, Private
Enlisted in Chowan County at age 23, April 29, 1861, for six months. Present or accounted for until mustered out November 12-13, 1861.

GOODWIN, JACOB, Private
Enlisted in Chowan County at age 20, April 29, 1861, for six months. Present or accounted for until mustered out November 12-13, 1861.

GOODWIN, JOHN, Private
Enlisted in Chowan County at age 18, April 29, 1861, for six months. Present or accounted for until mustered out November 12-13, 1861.

GREGORY, HENRY, Corporal
Resided in Chowan County where he enlisted at age 19, April 29, 1861, for six months. Mustered in as Corporal. Present or accounted for until mustered out November 12-13, 1861.

HANCOCK, WILLIAM G., Private
Enlisted in Chowan County at age 36, April 29, 1861, for six months. Detailed for hospital duty June 26, 1861. Relieved from detail October 25, 1861. Present or accounted for until mustered out November 12-13, 1861.

HARRELL, JOHN, Private
Enlisted in Chowan County at age 18, June 8, 1861, for six months. Present or accounted for until mustered out November 12-13, 1861.

HARRIS, IRVIN, Private
Enlisted in Chowan County at age 26, April 29, 1861, for six months. Present or accounted for until mustered out November 12-13, 1861.

HARRIS, JOHN, Private
Enlisted in Chowan County at age 29, April 29, 1861, for six months. Present or accounted for until mustered out November 12-13, 1861.

HINES, ELIAS C., Corporal
Enlisted in Chowan County at age 34, May 10, 1861, for six months. Mustered in as Private and appointed Corporal on June 22, 1861. Present or accounted for until mustered out November 12-13, 1861.

HODDER, JAMES O., Private
Enlisted in Chowan County at age 25, June 1, 1861, for six months. Present or accounted for until mustered out November 12-13, 1861.

HOUGHTON, WILLIAM R., Corporal
Resided in Chowan County where he enlisted at age 22, April 29, 1861, for six months. Mustered in as Corporal. Present or accounted for until mustered out November 12-13, 1861.

JACKSON, JAMES S., Private
Enlisted in Chowan County at age 34, April

29, 1861, for six months. Present or accounted for until mustered out November 12-13, 1861.

JONES, JOHN M., Jr., 1st Sergeant
Resided in Chowan County where he enlisted at age 22, April 29, 1861, for six months. Mustered in as 1st Sergeant. Present or accounted for until mustered out November 12-13, 1861. Later enlisted in Company B, 3rd Battalion N. C. Light Artillery.

JONES, THEOPHILUS, Private
Enlisted in Chowan County at age 25, May 15, 1861, for six months. Present or accounted for until mustered out November 12-13, 1861.

KNAPP, JUDSON, Private
Enlisted in Chowan County at age 26, April 29, 1861, for six months. Present or accounted for until mustered out November 12-13, 1861.

LASSITER, WILLIAM, Private
Enlisted in Chowan County at age 23, April 29, 1861, for six months. Present or accounted for until mustered out November 12-13, 1861.

LEARY, WILLIAM H., Private
Enlisted at Yorktown, Virginia, at age 19, June 30, 1861, for six months. Present or accounted for until mustered out November 12-13, 1861.

McDONOUGH, JOHN, Private
Enlisted in Chowan County at age 28, April 29, 1861, for six months. Present or accounted for until mustered out November 12-13, 1861.

MANNING, JAMES H., Sergeant
Enlisted in Chowan County, April 29, 1861, for six months. Mustered in as Sergeant. Present or accounted for until mustered out November 12-13, 1861.

MARDRE, NATHANIEL, Private
Enlisted in Chowan County at age 19, April 29, 1861, for six months. Present or accounted for until mustered out November 12-13, 1861.

MODLIN, ELISHA, Private
Enlisted in Chowan County at age 20, April 29, 1861, for six months. Present or accounted for until mustered out November 12-13, 1861.

MONROE, THOMAS, Private
Enlisted in Chowan County at age 19, April 29, 1861, for six months. Present or accounted for until mustered out November 12-13, 1861.

MORGAN, JOHN E., Private
Enlisted in Hertford County at age 22, April 29, 1861, for six months. Present or accounted for until mustered out November 12-13, 1861.

MYERS, DAVID, Private
Enlisted in Chowan County at age 25, April 29, 1861, for six months. Present or accounted for until mustered out November 12-13, 1861.

NEWBY, CHARLES, Private
Enlisted in Chowan County at age 16, April 29, 1861, for six months. Present or accounted for until discharged September 13, 1861, by reason of Surgeon's Certificate of Disability.

PARRISH, JOHN DUNCAN, Private
Resided in Chowan County where he enlisted at age 21, April 29, 1861, for six months. Present or

accounted for until mustered out November 12-13, 1861.

PARRISH, JOSEPH, Private

Enlisted in Chowan County at age 19, April 29, 1861, for six months. Present or accounted for until mustered out November 12-13, 1861.

PARRISH, STEPHEN, Private

Enlisted in Chowan County at age 38, April 29, 1861, for six months. Present or accounted for until mustered out November 12-13, 1861.

PERRY, JOHN, Private

Enlisted in Chowan County at age 34, April 29, 1861, for six months. Present or accounted for until mustered out November 12-13, 1861.

QUINTON, JOHN T., Private

Enlisted in Chowan County at age 25, April 29, 1861, for six months. Present or accounted for until mustered out November 12-13, 1861.

REA, WILLIAM D., Private

Resided in Chowan County where he enlisted at age 19, April 29, 1861, for six months. Present or accounted for until mustered out November 12-13, 1861. Later enlisted in Company F, 11th Regiment N. C. Troops (1st Regiment N. C. Volunteers).

RIDDICK, JOHN, Private

Enlisted in Chowan County at age 21, April 29, 1861, for six months. Present or accounted for until mustered out November 12-13, 1861.

ROBERTS, STEPHEN W., Private

Resided in Chowan County where he enlisted at age 26, April 29, 1861, for six months. Present or accounted for until mustered out November 12-13, 1861. Later enlisted in Company F, 11th Regiment N. C. Troops (1st Regiment N. C. Volunteers).

ROBINSON, CHARLES, Corporal

Resided in Chowan County where he enlisted at age 33, April 29, 1861, for six months. Mustered in as Private and appointed Corporal June 22, 1861. Present or accounted for until mustered out November 12-13, 1861.

ROBINSON, WILLIAM H., Private

Enlisted in Chowan County at age 26, April 29, 1861, for six months. Present or accounted for until mustered out November 12-13, 1861.

RYLEY, JOHN, Private

Enlisted in Chowan County at age 19, April 29, 1861, for six months. Present or accounted for until mustered out November 12-13, 1861.

SAVAGE, DAVID, Private

Enlisted in Chowan County at age 18, April 29, 1861, for six months. Present or accounted for until mustered out November 12-13, 1861.

SIMPSON, SAMUEL, Private

Enlisted in Chowan County at age 19, April 29, 1861, for six months. Present or accounted for until mustered out November 12-13, 1861.

SKINNER, JOSEPH D., Private

Enlisted in Chowan County at age 18, April 29, 1861, for six months. Present or accounted for until mustered out November 12-13, 1861.

THOMPSON, CHARLES, Private

Enlisted in Chowan County at age 23, April 29, 1861, for six months. Present or accounted for until mustered out November 12-13, 1861.

TILLITT, ISAAC, Private

Enlisted in Chowan County at age 26, April 29, 1861, for six months. Present or accounted for until mustered out November 12-13, 1861.

WALKER, JAMES A., Private

Resided in Chowan County where he enlisted at age 18, April 29, 1861, for six months. Present or accounted for until mustered out November 12-13, 1861. Later enlisted in Company A, 1st Regiment N. C. State Troops.

WARD, AARON, Private

Resided in Chowan County where he enlisted at age 33, June 8, 1861, for six months. Present or accounted for until mustered out November 12-13, 1861. Later enlisted in Company F, 11th Regiment N. C. Troops (1st Regiment N. C. Volunteers).

WARD, AUGUSTUS, Private

Enlisted in Chowan County at age 16, April 29, 1861, for six months. Present or accounted for until mustered out November 12-13, 1861.

WATTS, JOHN H., Private

Enlisted in Chowan County at age 22, April 29, 1861, for six months. Present or accounted for until mustered out November 12-13, 1861.

WAUGH, EDWARD, Private

Enlisted in Chowan County at age 25, April 29, 1861, for six months. Present or accounted for until mustered out November 12-13, 1861.

WELCH, WILLIAM D., Private

Enlisted in Chowan County at age 26, April 29, 1861, for six months. Present or accounted for until mustered out November 12-13, 1861.

WHITE, ROBERT, Private

Resided in Chowan County where he enlisted at age 18, April 29, 1861, for six months. Present or accounted for until mustered out November 12-13, 1861. Later enlisted in Company F, 11th Regiment N. C. Troops (1st Regiment N. C. Volunteers).

WILLIAMS, JAMES W., Private

Enlisted in Chowan County at age 24, May 1, 1861, for six months. Present or accounted for until mustered out November 12-13, 1861.

WINSLOW, REUBEN, Private

Enlisted in Chowan County at age 30, April 29, 1861, for six months. Present or accounted for until discharged September 20, 1861, by reason of Surgeon's Certificate of Disability.

1st BATTALION N. C. INFANTRY

This battalion was organized by Special Orders No. 246, Paragraph 19, Adjutant and Inspector General's Office, Richmond, November 29, 1861, from the six surviving companies of the 32nd Regiment N. C. Troops. The 32nd Regiment N. C. Troops had been organized in September, 1861, when six companies at Norfolk, Virginia, and four companies at Hatteras, North Carolina, were combined to form the regiment. The four companies at Hatteras had been captured on August 29, 1861, and were disbanded after their exchange. Therefore, they never joined the regiment. On November 29, 1861, the Confederate authorities designated the six companies at Norfolk as the 1st Battalion N. C. Infantry. They served as such until March 17, 1862, when another attempt was made to organize the 32nd Regiment N. C. Troops. The companies of the 1st Battalion N. C. Infantry were assigned to the regiment and the battalion organization ceased to exist. In May, 1862, another company was added, and in June, 1862, three additional companies were assigned to bring the regiment up to ten companies.

The rosters of the companies of the 1st Battalion N. C. Infantry, together with histories of the companies, will be recorded in a subsequent volume under the 32nd Regiment N.C. Troops. Since their service as the 1st Battalion N.C. Infantry was temporary, no attempt will be made to report them separately.

1st BATTALION N. C. SHARPSHOOTERS

This battalion, also known as the 9th Battalion N. C. Sharpshooters, was organized when two companies of the 21st Regiment N. C. Troops (11th Regiment N. C. Volunteers) were transferred out of the regiment to form the battalion in April, 1862. Companies B and E of the regiment were transferred out and became Companies A and B, respectively, of the battalion. On April 26, 1862, the election of company and field officers was held, and on April 28, 1862, the companies reorganized under the Conscript Act for the war. Thus, by April 28, 1862, the battalion was organized.

At the time of organization, the 21st Regiment N. C. Troops (11th Regiment N. C. Volunteers) was in Brigadier General Isaac R. Trimble's Brigade, Major General Richard S. Ewell's Division, Army of Northern Virginia. This brigade consisted of the 15th Regiment Alabama Infantry, 21st Regiment Georgia Infantry, 16th Regiment Mississippi Infantry, and the 21st Regiment N. C. Troops (11th Regiment N. C. Volunteers). The organization of the battalion occurred while the division was halted near Gordonsville, Virginia, prior to moving into the Shenandoah Valley to join General Thomas J. Jackson. Even though organized as a separate unit at that time, the two companies remained with the regiment until after the battle at Winchester on May 25, 1862. Ewell's Division moved from Gordonsville and joined Jackson at Swift Run Gap. Here the division remained while Jackson moved and confronted Federal troops at McDowell on May 8. Rejoining Ewell, Jackson moved his entire force down the valley and defeated a Federal force at Front Royal on May 23. Moving against Winchester, Jackson attacked the Federal defenses there on May 25. It was here that the battalion, still attached to the regiment, received its baptism of fire. Attached to the regiment, the battalion took an active part in the battle and pursued the enemy to Martinsburg.

After the battle at Winchester, the two companies were detached from the 21st Regiment N. C. Troops (11th Regiment N. C. Volunteers) and became a separate command. The troops remained in Martinsburg some five or six days and rejoined the brigade at Winchester as Jackson began moving back up the valley to confront columns under Generals Fremont and Shields. The battalion was heavily engaged at Cross Keys on June 8, when Fremont's advance was driven in. Leaving Trimble's Brigade to watch Fremont, Jackson turned on Shields at Port Republic and defeated him on June 9. General Trimble moved to reinforce Jackson but arrived after the battle was won. After these two engagements the battalion went into camp on the Shenandoah River, near Weir's Cave, where it remained about two weeks.

From the valley, Jackson moved his men east to join with General Lee in driving McClellan from in front of Richmond. During the Seven Days' Battles around Richmond, the battalion was heavily engaged at Gaines' Mill (June 27, 1862) and was subjected to heavy artillery fire but was not engaged at Malvern Hill (July 1, 1862).

Following the battles around Richmond, Trimble's Brigade was moved back to Gordonsville. From there the brigade rejoined Jackson and took part in the battles at Cedar Mountain (August 9, 1862) and Second Manassas (August 29-30, 1862). As part of Jackson's Corps, the battalion advanced into Maryland and took part in the capture of Harpers Ferry (September 15, 1862) and in the battle at Sharpsburg (September 17, 1862). General Ewell had been wounded at Second Manassas and the division command passed to General Alexander R. Lawton. During the heavy fighting on the Confederate left at Sharpsburg, Lawton was wounded and General Jubal Early assumed command of the division. During the battle at Sharpsburg, the battalion was attached to the 21st Regiment N. C. Troops (11th Regiment N.C. Volunteers). Trimble had also been wounded at Second Manassas, and the brigade was commanded by Colonel James A. Walker of the 13th Regiment Virginia Infantry.

General Lee recrossed the Potomac River on the night of September 18 and waited for the Federal commander to move. When Burnside assumed command he began moving the Federal army toward Fredericksburg. General Lee moved his army to check any attempted advance at Fredericksburg. Before the battle at Fredericksburg, December 13, 1862, Colonel Robert F. Hoke of the 21st Regiment N. C. Troops (1st Regiment N. C. Volunteers) was assigned to command Trimble's Brigade. The activities of the battalion in that battle are described by the company clerk on the Company A muster roll for November-December, 1862, as follows:

On the 12 Dec. 1862 this Co., left its camp 15 miles below Fredericksburg a little before sundown and marched in the direction of that place. About midnight the troops were halted 2 miles from Hamiltons Crossing where they remained until after sunrise next morning when they again resumed the march & proceeded to the crossing & were formed into line of battle 350 yards west of the rail road. At this point the company remained an hour & half & during a part of the time was under a very heavy artillery fire. It then moved by the left flank about 300 & then to the front in line of battle through the woods until it met the enemy who had driven back Gen. Archers Brigade & gained the crest of the hill. As soon as the enemy was discovered the whole Brigade charged them, drove them back in great confusion & pursued them 250 yards beyond the rail road. After dark the Brigade fell back to the crest of the hill at the edge of the woods where it remained in line of battle until the morning of the 15 when it was relieved by troops of Gen. D. H. Hills Division. A number of the men went into the battle barefooted. The only loss sustained by the company was one man wounded. In this action the enemy left on the field in front of this Trimbles Brigade 200 dead including Gen. Jackson, 100 so badly wounded they could not get away. The brigade also captured 300 prisoners beside the wounded. This company had about 40 men in the fight who did their full share of what was performed by the brigade.

On December 16 the brigade marched 14 miles down the river and encamped near Port Royal. Here the brigade went into winter quarters. In late January, 1863, the brigade organization was in effect disbanded and a new brigade organized. It was composed of the 6th Regiment N. C. State Troops, 21st Regiment N. C. Troops (11th Regiment N. C. Volunteers), 54th Regiment N. C. Troops, 57th Regiment N. C. Troops, and the 1st Battalion N. C. Sharpshooters. The new brigade, commanded by Brigadier General Robert F. Hoke, was known as Hoke's Brigade and was assigned to Major General Jubal Early's Division, Lieutenant General Thomas J. Jackson's Corps.

On April 28 word came that the enemy was advancing up the Rappahannock River to get behind the Confederate position at Fredericksburg. Orders came to move to Fredericksburg where Early's Division was ordered to hold that line with two other brigades and a portion of the reserve artillery. While Lee moved with the rest of the army westward to meet the Federals under Hooker at Chancellorsville, Early deployed his troops. Hoke's Brigade was placed in line at Deep Run on the right of Early's line. On May 3, while Lee was engaging Hooker at Chancellorsville, the Federals penetrated the left of Early's line at Marye's Heights and drove the defenders back. Hoke's Brigade was only slightly engaged before it was ordered to retire. As the Federals advanced toward Salem Church, in Lee's rear, Early regrouped his troops on the Federal left. At Salem Church the Federal force ran into stiff opposition. Early's troops moved against their left and rear to cut them off from Fredericksburg. Combined pressure by the Confederates forced the Federal commander to retire after heavy fighting on May 4. He did so during the night of May 4-5, and Early's troops returned to the Fredericksburg line. General Hoke was wounded during the action on May 4 and Colonel Isaac E. Avery, 6th Regiment N. C. State Troops, succeeded to temporary command of the brigade.

Following the defeat of the Federals at Chancellorsville and Salem Church, the Army of Northern Virginia returned to the Fredericksburg line. There it was reorganized into three corps, following Jackson's death, and Hoke's Brigade (under Colonel Avery) remained in Early's Division, which was assigned to Lieutenant General Richard S. Ewell's Corps. On the march into Pennsylvania, which followed in June and culminated in the battle of Gettysburg, July 1-3, 1863, the battalion was detached from the brigade and attached to Ewell's headquarters. When Ewell's Corps reached Carlisle, Pennsylvania, the battalion commander, Major R. W. Wharton, served as Military Governor of that place. When Ewell's Corps was ordered to concentrate at Gettysburg, on July 1, the battalion remained behind under orders to bring up the rear. While en route to Gettysburg the battalion was ordered to Cashtown to protect the corps wagon train. On July 2 the train was moved to the right just behind Longstreet's Corps. Here it remained throughout the remainder of the battle. On July 4 General Ewell ordered the battalion to escort the train back to Williamsport, Maryland, on the Potomac River. During this march the train was under threatened attack from Federal cavalry, and at one point the battalion was called on to dislodge a Federal force at Jack's Mountain. After this skirmish the battalion continued to escort the train to Williamsport and crossed the Potomac with the army on July 13-14, 1863. A few weeks after the return of the army to Virginia the battalion was sent back to its old brigade.

Lee moved his army east of the Blue Ridge Mountains when the Federal army crossed into Virginia. By August 4 the Army of Northern Virginia occupied the Rapidan River line and the Federal army the Rappahannock River line.

In October Lee attempted to move around the Federal right flank in the Bristoe campaign of October 9-November 9, 1863. The activities of the battalion are not known, but it appears to have remained with the brigade and did not see any action. The next major action was the Mine Run campaign (November 26-December 1, 1863) launched by General Meade in order to maneuver Lee out of position. After crossing the Rapidan, Meade found Lee's army strongly entrenched at Mine Run. Deciding against attack, Meade withdrew back to Culpeper Court House. The activities of the battalion during this campaign and for the balance of 1863 were reported on the muster roll of Company B for November-December, 1863, as follows:

Since last muster there has been no general engagement which this company has been in. On the night of the 26th of November we marched from Rackcoon Ford on Rapidan River to Mine Run on old Orange & Fredericksburg turnpike, a distance of 10 ten miles at which place we arrived at before day on the morning of 27th & bivouaced in woods until after sunrise at which time we advanced beyond Mine Run a distance of one mile & met with the enemies advanced pickets. We were there thrown forward as skirmishers & on the 28th after falling back on Mine Run lost one man killed by the explosion of shells, & moved back to Rackcoon Ford on 2d December & took up our old camp and are at this time pleasantly situated heving completed our winter quarters. We can now set back in our cabbins & bed the cold whistling winds Defiance.

General Hoke returned to the command of his brigade in December, 1863, and in January, 1864, was ordered with his brigade to Kinston, North Carolina, to take part in General George E. Pickett's attack on New Bern. The activities of the battalion are best described by the entry on the January-February, 1864, muster roll of Company A:

On the 21st of Jan 1864 this company & Battalion left winter quarters in Orange County, Va., & marched to Gordonsville. From there we come to Kinston, N.C., via Richmond, Weldon & Goldsboro. Arrived at Kinston, N.C. on the 28 Jany 1864. Marched across Neuse river & camped five miles from Kinston on the evening of the 28. Bright and early on the 29 this company was on the march towards New Berne, N.C. On the morning of the 1 Feby 1864 this Battalion was sent on in advance about 4½ oclock. This first post (pickett Yankee) was captured, the 2d ditto, also 3rd. At the 4 post at Bachelors Creek Bridge the enemy being strongly entrenched did not give way at first. The battalion charged the Bridge (in the night) found a portion of it torn up and could not cross. Our loss was (2) killed & 7 wounded. After day light trees were cut across the creek below the bridge & the enemy flanked & driven away. The company & Batt since the return from New Berne have been doing Provo Guard duty in Kinston, N C

R.E. Wilson
Comdg Battn.

On April 21, 1864, the battalion took part in the capture of Plymouth under General Hoke. When Hoke's Brigade was recalled to the Army of Northern Virginia in May, the battalion appears to have been detached and left at Kinston on provost guard duty. The company muster rolls for March-June, 1864, report the station as Kinston, and the return of troops in the Department of North Carolina and Southern Virginia, dated September 1, 1864, reports the battalion as in the 2nd Military District at Kinston. The activities of the battalion during this period are not reported on the muster rolls, and no official report of its activities was found.

The activities of the companies and the battalion for the balance of 1864 were reported on the company muster rolls as follows:

Company A: Muster Roll for August 31-December 31, 1864.

Sept 6 orders received from Gen Baker Comg 2 Dis N.C. & S. Va., to report to Col Guillard at Weldon, N.C. He directed the company to be posted at the different Fords on the Roanoke River West of Weldon to Clarksville, Va., by detachments for the apprehension of deserters from A.N. Va. Oct 1 ordered to Greensboro, N.C., to rejoin the Battn on the way to join the A.V.D. Arrived at Army Hd Qrs Oct 23 near New Market, Va., and were assigned to Gen R. D. Johnson's Brigade temporarily. Remained in camp until the 10" November when we took up our line of march toward Winchester. Camped for the night at Woodstock, Va. Moved at daylight next morning & at 3 oclock P.M. was in line of battle two

miles beyond Middletown. Some skirmishing on the left, on the 12 moving from there at 9 oclock p.m. camped at Strawsburg. Returned to camp at New Market Nov 17, moved camp to Laceys Spring. In camp here until Dec 6. Started to Waynesboro thence by Rail Road via Richmond to Petersburg, Va. Camped on Hatchers Creek the right of Gen Lee's Army.

Company B: Muster Roll for September 1-December 31, 1864.

At the date of our last muster this company was at Kinston, N. Carolina, forming part of the Provost Guard of that Post, at which place they remained until the 11th Oct 1864, when the Battalion was ordered to rejoin its Brigade (Godwin's) then in the Valley of Virginia. It arrived at New Market, Va., where Gen. Early's Army was camping on the 22d Oct but instead of rejoining there old command it with the rest of the Battalion were ordered to report to Gen. Johnston to whose Brigade it was assigned. On the 10th Nov., we took our line of march down the Valley of Va., & found the enemy in force near Newtown, Va. Demonstration was made upon their front by our Sharp Shooters, & we were then returned to our old camp near New Market, having marched Eighty-six miles & been absent five days. On the 17th Nov we moved camp to near Lacy Springs, Va., eleven miles, where we remained until the 6th Dec 1864 when we took up our line of march to Waynesboro where we arrived on the 7th having marched forty miles. At Waynesboro we got aboard a train of cars on the 10th & the next day arrived near our present camp. We are at present comfortably quartered in good tight cabins on the right of the infantry lines in front of Petersburg.

The battalion arrived after the battle of Cedar Creek, October 19, 1864, and thus did not take part in any of the major engagements. It was assigned to Brigadier General Robert D. Johnston's Brigade, Early's Division, and remained with that brigade for the balance of the war. In addition to this battalion, Johnston's Brigade consisted of the 5th Regiment N. C. State Troops, 12th Regiment N. C. Troops (2nd Regiment N. C. Volunteers), 20th Regiment N. C. Troops (10th Regiment N. C. Volunteers), and the 23rd Regiment N. C. Troops (13th Regiment N. C. Volunteers).

In early 1865 portions of the brigade were detached to crossings on the Staunton and Roanoke rivers to arrest deserters. Those who remained in the line at Petersburg took part in the engagement on Hatcher's Run, February 5-7. In March the detachments from the brigade were ordered back to Petersburg, and on March 25 took part in the assault on Fort Stedman. The exact movements of the battalion during this period were not reported, and it can only be assumed that it took part in the brigade activities. When Petersburg was evacuated the battalion joined in the retreat, and the remnants under Lieutenant R. W. Woodruff were surrendered and paroled at Appomattox Court House, Virginia, April 9, 1865.

FIELD AND STAFF

MAJOR

WHARTON, RUFUS WATSON

Transferred from Company E, 21st Regiment N. C. Troops (11th Regiment N. C. Volunteers) and appointed Major to rank from April 26, 1862. Captured on the Rappahannock River near Port Royal, Virginia, January 11, 1863, and confined at Old Capitol Prison, Washington, D. C., until paroled and exchanged at City Point, Virginia, April 6, 1863. Reported as absent in North Carolina after September, 1863. Submitted his resignation March 16, 1864, by reason of his having been appointed Lieutenant Colonel in the 67th Regiment N. C. Troops to rank from January 18, 1864. Resignation accepted on March 29, 1864.

ASSISTANT QUARTERMASTER AND COMMISSARY OF SUBSISTENCE

COOPER, JOHN A.

Detailed from Company B of this battalion soon after the battalion was organized. He was never commissioned Assistant Quartermaster and Commissary of Subsistence but performed the duties until January 30, 1863, when he returned to Company B upon promotion to Captain of that company.

ACTING ASSISTANT QUARTERMASTER

WOODRUFF, RICHARD W.

Detailed from Company A of this battalion in January, 1863, and performed the duties of Acting Assistant Quartermaster until transferred back to his company in August, 1864.

ASSISTANT SURGEONS

HOKE, GEORGE M.

Resided in Lincoln County and appointed Assistant Surgeon to rank from February 1, 1863. Present until reported as "on detached service in North Carolina" after September, 1863. Reported as such through December, 1863. No further records.

GREENLEE, EDGAR G.

Transferred from the Field and Staff of the 54th Regiment N. C. Troops and assigned to this battalion in March, 1864. Present or accounted for through October, 1864.

SERGEANT MAJOR

ANDERSON, A. A.

Transferred from Company A of this battalion upon appointment as Sergeant Major on or about April 28, 1862. In addition to the duties of Sergeant Major, he was assigned the duties of Ordnance Sergeant. On May 8, 1864, a request was made that he be detailed as Ordnance Sergeant at Salisbury, N. C., and the endorsements on the request indicate that the battalion was not large enough to have an Ordnance Sergeant. As a result of this decision, he was transferred back to Company A in August, 1864, as a Private. Soon after the transfer he was detailed as "acting Sergeant Major" and in February, 1865, he was reported as "acting Ordnance Sergeant and Sergeant Major." Paroled at Appomattox Court House, Virginia, April 9, 1865.

QUARTERMASTER SERGEANT

BUTNER, AUGUSTUS B.

Transferred from Company B of this battalion upon appointment as Quartermaster Sergeant on May 1, 1862. Transferred back to Company B as Sergeant, July-August, 1864, and detailed as Quartermaster and Commissary Sergeant for the battalion.

BAND

The following men were detailed from Company B of this battalion and served in the band. Since the nature of the detail was temporary, their entire service record appears in the company roster.

CARMICHAEL, WILLIAM F., Chief Musician
BRENDLE, JOHN P., Musician
BRIETZ, SAMUEL, Musician
BUTNER, LEWIS E., Musician
CARMICHAEL, L. F., Musician
EBERHARDT, L. D., Musician
HALL, SAMUEL G., Musician
HILL, WILLIAM C., Musician
KEESLER, SAMUEL G., Musician
MURCHISON, DAVID B., Musician
PARKES, ROBERT T., Musician
REICH, JAMES A., Musician
SIEWERS, NATHANIEL S., Musician
WINKLER, CRIST, Musician

COMPANY A

This company was formerly Company B, 21st Regiment N. C. Troops (11th Regiment N. C. Volunteers). It was transferred to this battalion when the battalion was organized April 26-28, 1862. Its activities prior to transfer are recorded in the history of Company B, 21st Regiment N. C. Troops (11th Regiment N. C. Volunteers) and in the history of that regiment. After joining this battalion the company functioned as a part of the battalion, and its history is recorded as a part of the battalion history.

The following roster of the company covers the period from the date of transfer to the end of the war. For the period before April 26, 1862, consult the roster of Company B, 21st Regiment N.C. Troops (11th Regiment N.C. Volunteers). The information contained in the following roster of the company was compiled principally from company muster rolls for November, 1862, through April, 1863; September, 1863, through December, 1864; and one undated muster roll. No muster rolls were found for the period prior to November, 1862, or for the periods May-August, 1863, or after December, 1864. Although there are no Roll of Honor records for this company, useful information was obtained from receipt rolls, hospital records, prisoner of war records, and other primary records, supplemented by state pension applications, United Daughters of the Confederacy records, and postwar rosters and histories.

OFFICERS

CAPTAINS

HUNT, NATHAN G.

Transferred from Company B, 21st Regiment N. C. Troops (11th Regiment N. C. Volunteers) April 26, 1862. Appointed Captain to rank from April 26, 1862. Resigned June 27, 1862.

WILSON, REUBEN E.

Transferred from Company B, 21st Regiment N. C. Troops (11th Regiment N. C. Volunteers) April 26, 1862. Appointed 1st Lieutenant to rank from date of transfer. Promoted to Captain June 27, 1862. Wounded in the leg at Hazel River, Virginia, August 22, 1862. Absent wounded through December, 1863. Present or accounted for on company muster rolls through December, 1864. Paroled at Manchester, Virginia, April 29, 1865.

LIEUTENANTS

MASTEN, WILLIAM L., 3rd Lieutenant

Previously served in Company D, 21st Regiment N. C. Troops (11th Regiment N. C. Volunteers). Appointed 3rd Lieutenant in this company to rank from June 26, 1862. Captured August 9, 1862, and paroled and exchanged September 21, 1862. Place of capture not reported. Present or accounted for on company muster rolls through December, 1864. Reported as captured in Washington Street Hospital, Petersburg, Virginia, May 25, 1865, and transferred to the General Hospital on April 9, 1865. Federal hospital records do not give final disposition but the regimental history states that he was "killed in battle near Petersburg, Virginia in 1865."

OSBORNE, DAVID D., 2nd Lieutenant

Transferred from Company B, 21st Regiment N. C. Troops (11th Regiment N. C. Volunteers) April 26, 1862. Appointed 3rd Lieutenant to rank from date of transfer and promoted to 2nd Lieutenant June 27, 1862. Present or accounted for on company muster rolls through December, 1864. Paroled at Appomattox Court House, Virginia, April 9, 1865.

WOODRUFF, RICHARD W., 1st Lieutenant

Transferred from Company B, 21st Regiment N. C. Troops (11th Regiment N. C. Volunteers) April 26, 1862, as 2nd Lieutenant. Promoted to 1st Lieutenant June 27, 1862. Detailed as Acting Assistant Quartermaster for the battalion from January, 1863, through August, 1864. Present or accounted for on company muster rolls through December, 1864. Paroled at Appomattox Court

House, Virginia, April 9, 1865.

NONCOMMISSIONED OFFICERS AND PRIVATES

ADAMS, MARTIN, Private

Enlisted in Wake County, September 4, 1862, for the war. Present or accounted for on company muster rolls through December, 1864. Muster roll for August 31-December 31, 1864, states that he was "assigned to light duty at Richmond, Virginia." Records of the Medical Director's Office, Richmond, indicate that he was stationed at the C. S. Barracks until admitted to Howard's Grove Hospital, Richmond, March 26, 1865, with "variola." Final disposition not reported.

ALLEN, WILLIAM G., Private

Resided as a farmer in Alamance County prior to enlisting in Wake County, September 4, 1862, for the war. Wounded at Mine Run, Virginia, in November, 1863. Present or accounted for on company muster rolls through December, 1864. Captured at Hatcher's Run, near Petersburg, Virginia, February 6, 1865, and confined at Point Lookout, Maryland, until released after taking the Oath of Allegiance, May 13, 1865.

ANDERSON, A. A., Private

Transferred from Company B, 21st Regiment N. C. Troops (11th Regiment N. C. Volunteers) April 26, 1862, with rank of Sergeant. Transferred to the Field and Staff of this battalion upon appointment as Sergeant Major about April 28, 1862. Transferred back to the company in August, 1864, with the rank of Private and detailed as Acting Sergeant Major. Present or accounted for on muster rolls through December, 1864. Paroled at Appomattox Court House, Virginia, April 9, 1865.

ARNOLD, JACOB, Private

Enlisted "at camp in Virginia," November 1, 1863, for the war. Present or accounted for through December, 1864.

BALL, WILLIAM, Private

Transferred from Company B, 21st Regiment N. C. Troops (11th Regiment N. C. Volunteers) April 26, 1862. Wounded at Battle of Second Manassas, Virginia, August 28, 1862. Detailed for light duty December 29, 1863, and retired to the Invalid Corps July 8, 1864.

BENGE, U. D., Private

Transferred from Company B, 21st Regiment N. C. Troops (11th Regiment N. C. Volunteers) April 26, 1862. Wounded at Battle of Second Manassas, Virginia, August 28, 1862. Discharged August 24, 1864, by reason of "epilepsy of weekly occurrence from childhood."

BLUM, JAMES A., Private

Enlisted in Lenoir County, June 10, 1864, for the war. Present or accounted for on company muster rolls through December, 1864.

BRANN, JOHN H., Private

Transferred from Company B, 21st Regiment N. C. Troops (11th Regiment N. C. Volunteers)

April 26, 1862. Detailed as teamster for the battalion from time of transfer through December, 1864. Paroled at Appomattox Court House, Virginia, April 9, 1865.

BRANN, WILLIAM D., Private
Transferred from Company B, 21st Regiment N. C. Troops (11th Regiment N. C. Volunteers) April 26, 1862. Present or accounted for on company muster rolls through December, 1864.

BROOKS, JOHN, Corporal
Transferred from Company B, 21st Regiment N. C. Troops (11th Regiment N. C. Volunteers) April 26, 1862, as Corporal. Wounded near Fredericksburg, Virginia, May 4, 1863. Present or accounted for on company muster rolls through December, 1864. Admitted to hospital at Petersburg, Virginia, January 8, 1865, with a wound and returned to duty February 22, 1865. Paroled at Appomattox Court House, Virginia, April 9, 1865.

BROOKS, S. D., Private
Transferred from Company B, 21st Regiment N. C. Troops (11th Regiment N. C. Volunteers) April 26, 1862. Present or accounted for on company muster rolls through August, 1864. Reported as "absent without leave" on August 31-December 31, 1864, muster roll.

BROOKS, S. J., Private
Enlisted "at camp in Virginia," June 15, 1863, for the war. Present or accounted for on company muster rolls through December, 1864. Paroled at Appomattox Court House, Virginia, April 9, 1865.

BROWN, G. W., Private
Enlisted in Lenoir County, July 21, 1864, for the war. Present or accounted for on company muster rolls through December, 1864.

BROWN, THOMAS, Private
Enlisted in Lenoir County, April 20, 1864, for the war. Present or accounted for on company muster rolls through December, 1864.

CARTER, THOMAS J., Private
Enlisted "at camp in Virginia," November 1, 1863, for the war. Deserted December 26, 1863, and reported as a deserter until dropped from the rolls August 31, 1864.

CARTER, WILSON, Private
Paroled at Appomattox Court House, Virginia, April 9, 1865.

CAUDLE, ISAAC, Private
Enlisted in Wake County, September 4, 1862, for the war. Present or accounted for on company muster rolls through December, 1864.

CAUDLE, M. A., Private
Enlisted in Wake County, September 4, 1862, for the war. Discharged April 19, 1863.

CAUDLE, S. J., Private
Enlisted "at camp in Virginia," October 15, 1863, for the war. Present or accounted for on company muster rolls through December, 1864. Captured at Farmville, Virginia, April 6, 1865, and confined at Newport News, Virginia, April 15, 1865. Date of release not reported.

CHAMBERLAIN, WILLIAM, Private
Enlisted in Wake County, September 4, 1862, for the war. Present or accounted for until reported as "deserted from Greensboro, N. C., October 5, 1864." Dropped from the rolls, February 28, 1865.

CHILDRESS, HIRAM, Private
Enlisted in Lenoir County, April 20, 1864, for the war. Present or accounted for on company muster rolls through December, 1864. Paroled at Appomattox Court House, Virginia, April 9, 1865.

COCHRAN, DANIEL, Private
Enlisted "at camp in Virginia," January 20, 1864, for the war. Company muster roll for February 28-June 30, 1864, states that he was "wounded and died in enemies lines."

COLLINS, WILLIAM H., Private
Enlisted in Wake County, September 4, 1862, for the war. Present or accounted for on company muster rolls through February, 1864, when he was reported as "absent wounded in General Hospital, Goldsboro, N. C."

COOK, ISAM C., Private
Enlisted in Wake County, September 4, 1862, for the war. Wounded near Fredericksburg, Virginia, May 4, 1863, and reported as absent wounded through June, 1864. Present or accounted for on company muster rolls through December, 1864. Paroled at Appomattox Court House, Virginia, April 9, 1865.

CORNELIUS, H. W. L., Private
Enlisted "at camp in Virginia," November 1, 1863, for the war. Present or accounted for until he "deserted at Bachelor's Creek, N.C., February 1, 1864."

CORNELIUS, W. D., Private
Transferred from Company B, 21st Regiment N. C. Troops (11th Regiment N. C. Volunteers) April 26, 1862. Reported as "absent wounded in General Hospital, Goldsboro, N. C.," on January-February, 1864, muster roll. Present or accounted for on company muster roll through December, 1864.

COX, JAMES, Private
Enlisted "at camp in Virginia," November 1, 1863, for the war. Deserted December 26, 1863, and returned from desertion September 25, 1864. Reported as "absent, in Pioneer Corps" on August 31-December 31, 1864, muster roll.

CREWS, A. H., Private
Enlisted in Wake County, September 4, 1862, for the war. Wounded at Mine Run, Virginia, November 29, 1863. Present or accounted for on company muster rolls through December, 1864.

CREWS, E. W., Private
Enlisted "at camp in Virginia," January 7, 1864, for the war. Present or accounted for on company muster rolls through December, 1864. Paroled at Appomattox Court House, Virginia, April 9, 1865.

CREWS, M. J., Private
Transferred from Company B, 21st Regiment N. C. Troops (11th Regiment N. C. Volunteers) April 26, 1862. Present or accounted for on company muster rolls through December, 1864, when

he was reported as "absent without leave."

CREWS, MONFORD S., Private
Transferred from Company G, 21st Regiment N. C. Troops (11th Regiment N. C. Volunteers) September 9, 1863. Present or accounted for on company muster rolls through December, 1864.

CREWS, W. A., Private
Transferred from Company B, 21st Regiment N. C. Troops (11th Regiment N. C. Volunteers) April 26, 1862. Present or accounted for on company muster rolls through December, 1864.

DAVIS, MARTIN, Private
Enlisted in Lenoir County, July 21, 1864, for the war. Present or accounted for on company muster rolls through December, 1864. Paroled at Appomattox Court House, Virginia, April 9, 1865.

DENNY, EMMIT, Sergeant
Transferred from Company B, 21st Regiment N. C. Troops (11th Regiment N. C. Volunteers) April 26, 1862, as Corporal. Promoted to Sergeant in May, 1863. Wounded near Fredericksburg, Virginia, May 4, 1863. Present or accounted for on company muster rolls through December, 1864.

DENNY, JAMES, Private
Enlisted February 15, 1864, for the war. Present or accounted for on company muster rolls through December, 1864.

DINGLER, W. F., Private
Enlisted in Wake County, September 4, 1862, for the war. Deserted February 14, 1863.

DIXON, GILES, Private
Enlisted "at camp in Virginia," November 1, 1863, for the war. Present or accounted for until he "deserted March 1, 1864," and "joined from desertion 20 September and deserted again October 11, 1864." Dropped from the rolls February 28, 1865.

DOBBINS, L. B., Private
Transferred from Company B, 21st Regiment N. C. Troops (11th Regiment N. C. Volunteers) April 26, 1862. Reported as missing in action at Battle of Second Manassas, Virginia, August 28, 1862, and declared exchanged at Richmond, Virginia, September 19, 1862. Present or accounted for on company muster rolls through December, 1864.

DULL, G. E., Private
Transferred from Company B, 21st Regiment N. C. Troops (11th Regiment N. C. Volunteers) April 26, 1862. Deserted August 17, 1862.

FARRINGTON, WILLIAM S., Private
Enlisted in Wake County, September 4, 1862, for the war. Present or accounted for on company muster rolls through December, 1864.

FARRIS, ARCH, Private
Paroled at Appomattox Court House, Virginia, April 9, 1865.

GLOVER, HENRY, Private
Enlisted in Wake County, September 4, 1862, for the war. Present or accounted for until he "deserted from Greensboro, N. C., October 5, 1864." Dropped from the rolls February 28, 1865.

GROSS, J. A., Private
Enlisted in Wake County, September 4, 1862, for

the war. Reported as "absent wounded and in hospital" on November-December, 1863, muster roll. Present or accounted for on company muster rolls through December, 1864. An undated company muster roll states that he "deserted February 24, 1865, to the enemy" and was "dropped from the rolls February 28, 1865." Federal Provost Marshal records indicate that he was a "deserter from the enemy" who was received by the Provost Marshal, 5th Army Corps, February 23, 1865, and forwarded to Washington, D.C., February 26, 1865. Released after taking the Oath of Allegiance and was provided transportation to Indianapolis, Indiana, February 27, 1865.

HAMMONDS, J. M., Private
Transferred from Company B, 21st Regiment N. C. Troops (11th Regiment N. C. Volunteers) April 26, 1862, as Corporal. Reduced to ranks May, 1863. Present or accounted for on Company Muster Rolls through December, 1864.

HARRINGTON, WILLIAM D., Corporal
Transferred from Company I, 41st Regiment N. C. Troops (3rd Regiment N. C. Cavalry) November 28, 1864, as Private. Present or accounted for on company muster rolls through December, 1864, as Private. Reported as Corporal on undated muster roll which reports him as "prisoner of war, captured 5 February, 1865." Appears on a register of prisoners received and disposed of by the Provost Marshal General, Army of the Potomac, which states that he was received February 6, 1865, and transferred to Washington, D. C., February 10, 1865, having taken the Oath of Allegiance at City Point, Virginia, February 9, 1865. Received at Washington, D. C., February 13, 1865, and furnished transportation to Madison, Wisconsin.

HAUSER, JOHN HENRY, Private
Resided in Yadkin County and enlisted in Forsyth County, September 1, 1864, for the war. Present or accounted for on company muster rolls through December, 1864.

HAYNES, THOMAS L., Private
Transferred from Company B, 21st Regiment N. C. Troops (11th Regiment N. C. Volunteers) April 26, 1862. Present or accounted for on company muster rolls through December, 1864.

HEMRICK, JOHN F., Private
Born in Iredell County where he resided as a farmer prior to enlisting "at camp in Virginia," at age 19, October 15, 1863, for the war. Present or accounted for on company muster rolls through December, 1864. Paroled at Appomattox Court House, Virginia, April 9, 1865.

HENDRIX, S. E., Private
Transferred from Company B, 21st Regiment N. C. Troops (11th Regiment N. C. Volunteers) April 26, 1862. Deserted June 2, 1862.

HOBSON, J. D., Corporal
Enlisted in Wake County, September 4, 1862, for the war. Mustered in as Private. Present or accounted for on company muster rolls through December, 1864, as Private. Appointed Corporal January-February, 1865. Wounded at Petersburg,

Virginia, April 2, 1865, and admitted to General Hospital, Danville, Virginia, April 5, 1865. Final disposition not reported.

HOBSON, JOHN W., Sergeant

Transferred from Company B, 21st Regiment N. C. Troops (11th Regiment N. C. Volunteers) April 26, 1862, as Sergeant. Present or accounted for on company muster rolls through December, 1864. Paroled at Appomattox Court House, Virginia, April 9, 1865.

HOBSON, T. C., Private

Transferred from Company B, 21st Regiment N. C. Troops (11th Regiment N. C. Volunteers) April 26, 1862. Present or accounted for on company muster rolls through December, 1864. Paroled at Appomattox Court House, Virginia, April 9, 1865.

HOLDEN, WILLIAM S., Private

Enlisted in Wake County, September 4, 1862, for the war. Present or accounted for until he "deserted April, 1864." Dropped from the rolls on February 28, 1865.

HUTCHENS, B. F., Private

Enlisted March 15, 1864, for the war. Present or accounted for on company muster rolls through December, 1864.

HUTCHENS, DANIEL V., Private

Resided in Yadkin County where he enlisted June 1, 1862, for the war. Reported as present on company muster rolls until January-February, 1864, when he was reported as "absent wounded in General Hospital, Goldsboro, N.C." Reported as absent on furlough through June, 1864, and as present on July-August, 1864, muster roll. Deserted at Greensboro, N.C., October 5, 1864, and dropped from the rolls February 28, 1865. Captured at Five Forks, Virginia, April 1, 1865, and confined at Hart's Island, New York Harbor, April 7, 1865. Released after taking the Oath of Allegiance June 17, 1865.

HUTCHENS, HENRY R., Private

Transferred from Company B, 21st Regiment N. C. Troops (11th Regiment N. C. Volunteers) April 26, 1862. Present or accounted for on company muster rolls until reported as "absent without leave, furlough expired" on January-February, 1864, muster roll. Reported as such until July-August, 1864, muster roll when he was reported with the remark: "absent without leave. Dropped from rolls August 31, 1864."

HUTCHENS, JOHN C., Private

Transferred from Company B, 21st Regiment N. C. Troops (11th Regiment N. C. Volunteers) April 26, 1862. Present or accounted for until he "deserted from Greensboro, N. C., October 5, 1864." Dropped from the rolls February 28, 1865.

HUTCHENS, JOHN F., Private

Transferred from Company B, 21st Regiment N. C. Troops (11th Regiment N. C. Volunteers) April 26, 1862. Died at General Hospital, Danville, Virginia, September 23, 1862, of "chronic diarrhoea."

HUTCHENS, WILLIAM, Private

Enlisted in Yadkin County, June 1, 1862, for the war. Present or accounted for on company muster rolls through December, 1864.

JOHNSON, J. T., Private

Enlisted in Wake County, September 4, 1862, for the war. Died at Guinea Station, Virginia, February 16, 1863.

JOHNSON, WILEY F., Private

Transferred from Company B, 21st Regiment N. C. Troops (11th Regiment N. C. Volunteers) April 26, 1862. Present or accounted for on company muster rolls through December, 1864.

JONES, JAMES BENJAMIN, Private

Enlisted April 1, 1864, for the war. Present or accounted for on company muster rolls through December, 1864. Paroled at Appomattox Court House, Virginia, April 9, 1865.

JONES, OMEGA C., Private

Enlisted in Lenoir County, July 1, 1864, for the war. Present or accounted for on company muster rolls through December, 1864. Paroled at Appomattox Court House, Virginia, April 9, 1865.

JORDAN, J. A., Private

Enlisted in Lenoir County, April 20, 1864, for the war. Present or accounted for on company muster rolls through December, 1864.

LAWRENCE, LEE, Private

Transferred from Company B, 21st Regiment N. C. Troops (11th Regiment N. C. Volunteers) April 26, 1862. Present or accounted for on company muster rolls through December, 1864. Paroled at Appomattox Court House, Virginia, April 9, 1865.

McBRIDE, J. L., Corporal

Transferred from Company B, 21st Regiment N. C. Troops (11th Regiment N. C. Volunteers) April 26, 1862, as Corporal. Died at Staunton, Virginia, October 14, 1862, of "febris typhoides."

MAY, H. D., Private

Enlisted "at camp in Virginia," March 17, 1864, for the war. Present or accounted for through December, 1864.

MAY, J. M., Private

Enlisted in Wake County, September 4, 1862, for the war. Present or accounted for on company muster rolls through December, 1864.

MAY, JAMES, Private

Enlisted "at camp in Virginia," March 15, 1864, for the war. Present or accounted for on company muster rolls through December, 1864.

MAY, MONROE, Sergeant

Transferred from Company B, 21st Regiment N. C. Troops (11th Regiment N. C. Volunteers) April 26, 1862, as Sergeant. Present or accounted for on company muster rolls through December, 1864. Wounded and captured at Hatcher's Run, Virginia, February 6, 1865, and confined at U.S. Army General Hospital, West's Buildings, Baltimore, Maryland, until transferred to Fort McHenry, Maryland, May 9, 1865. Released after taking the Oath of Allegiance June 10, 1865.

MAYNARD, WILLIAM, Private

Enlisted "at camp in Virginia," November 1, 1863, for the war. Died January 13, 1864, "at winter quarters in Virginia."

MONDAY, FRANK, Private
Enlisted "at camp in Virginia," November 1, 1863, for the war. Deserted in Orange County, Virginia, December 26, 1863, and joined from desertion September 21, 1864. Deserted a second time on October 11, 1864, and was dropped from the rolls February 28, 1865, as a deserter.

MONTGOMERY, N. GREEN, Private
Paroled at Appomattox Court House, Virginia, April 9, 1865.

MOXLEY, DANIEL, Private
Enlisted "at camp in Virginia," November 1, 1863, for the war. Captured at New Bern, N. C., February 3, 1864, and confined at Point Lookout, Maryland, February 27, 1864. Released after taking the Oath of Allegiance at Point Lookout, Maryland, June 12, 1865.

NORTH, WILLIAM S., Private
Enlisted "at camp in Virginia," November 1, 1863, for the war. Deserted February 1, 1864, at Bachelor's Creek, N. C., and voluntarily gave himself up to the Federal forces. Provided transportation to Indianapolis, Indiana, February 24, 1864.

PATTERSON, A. C., Private
Enlisted "at camp in Virginia," November 1, 1863, for the war. Present or accounted for until he "deserted March 1, 1864." Dropped from the rolls for desertion on August 31, 1864.

PENDRY, A. L., Private
Enlisted "at camp in Virginia," November 1, 1863, for the war. Present or accounted for until he "deserted from Lynchburg, Virginia, October 15, 1864." Dropped from the rolls for desertion on February 28, 1865.

PENDRY, J. C., Private
Transferred from Company B, 21st Regiment N. C. Troops (11th Regiment N. C. Volunteers) April 26, 1862. Wounded near Fredericksburg, Virginia, May 4, 1863. Present or accounted for on company muster rolls through December, 1864.

PENDRY, W. A., Private
Transferred from Company B, 21st Regiment N. C. Troops (11th Regiment N. C. Volunteers) April 26, 1862. Present or accounted for on company muster rolls through December, 1864.

PHILLIPS, SAMUEL J., Private
Enlisted at New Market, Virginia, November 1, 1864, for the war. Present or accounted for on company muster rolls through February, 1865. Admitted to General Hospital No. 3, Greensboro, N. C., in April, 1865.

REAVIS, ABRAHAM H., Private
Resided in Yadkin County and enlisted in Wake County, September 4, 1862, for the war. Present or accounted for until reported 'in Military Prison, Salisbury, N. C., under sentence of Court Martial," on February 28-June 30, 1864, muster roll. Reported with same remark through December, 1864. Captured at Farmville, Virginia, on April 6, 1865, and confined at Newport News, Virginia, April 13, 1865. Released after taking the Oath of Allegiance on June 16, 1865.

REAVIS, GILES, Private
Enlisted in Wake County, September 4, 1862, for the war. Present or accounted for until he deserted on March 1, 1864. Dropped from the rolls for desertion on August 31, 1864. Reported as present in arrest on August 31-December 31, 1864, muster roll. Sentenced by Court Martial January 17, 1865, and reported as being confined in Castle Thunder, Richmond, Virginia, as late as March 15, 1865. Paroled at Appomattox Court House, Virginia, April 9, 1865.

REAVIS, J. F., Private
Transferred from Company B, 21st Regiment N. C. Troops (11th Regiment N. C. Volunteers) April 26, 1862. Present or accounted for on company muster rolls through December, 1864.

REAVIS, J. GRANVILLE, 1st Sergeant
Transferred from Company B, 21st Regiment N. C. Troops (11th Regiment N. C. Volunteers) April 26, 1862, as 1st Sergeant. Present or accounted for on company muster rolls through December, 1864. Paroled at Appomattox Court House, Virginia, April 9, 1865.

REAVIS, J. P. H., Private
Enlisted in Wake County, September 4, 1862, for the war. Present or accounted for on company muster rolls through December, 1864.

REAVIS, JAMES M., Private
Transferred from Company B, 21st Regiment N. C. Troops (11th Regiment N. C. Volunteers) April 26, 1862. Present or accounted for on company muster rolls through December, 1864.

REECE, W. D., Private
Enlisted "at camp in Virginia," June 9-10, 1864, for the war. Present or accounted for on company muster rolls through December, 1864. Paroled at Appomattox Court House, Virginia, April 9, 1865.

REED, WILLIAM F., Private
Transferred from Company B, 21st Regiment N. C. Troops (11th Regiment N. C. Volunteers) April 26, 1862. Wounded at Winchester, Virginia, September 15, 1862. Retired to the Invalid Corps on July 12, 1864.

ROYAL, ISAAC, Private
Enlisted in Lenoir County, September 20, 1864, for the war. Deserted at Greensboro on October 11, 1864, and dropped from the rolls for desertion February 28, 1865.

ROYAL, JOHN C., Sergeant
Transferred from Company B, 21st Regiment N. C. Troops (11th Regiment N. C. Volunteers) April 26, 1862, as Sergeant. Wounded in battle at Sharpsburg, Maryland, September 17, 1862, and captured. Paroled September 27, 1862, and discharged December 26-27, 1862, by reason of "gun shot wound of face, probability of loss of sight."

SAWYER, A. F., Private
Transferred from Company B, 21st Regiment N. C. Troops (11th Regiment N. C. Volunteers) April 26, 1862. Present or accounted for on company muster rolls through December, 1864.

SEAT, NED T., Private
Transferred from Company B, 21st Regiment

N. C. Troops (11th Regiment N. C. Volunteers) April 26, 1862. Present or accounted for on company muster rolls through December, 1864.

SHEEK, ASBERRY, Private
Enlisted "at camp in Virginia," January 20, 1864, for the war. Present or accounted for on company muster rolls through December, 1864.

SHEEK, MILES C., Corporal
Enlisted in Wake County, September 4, 1862, for the war. Mustered in as Private. Appointed Corporal April 1, 1864. Present or accounted for on company muster rolls through December, 1864. Paroled at Appomattox Court House, Virginia, April 9, 1865.

SHERMER, P. A., Private
Enlisted "at camp in Virginia," November 1, 1863, for the war. Present or accounted for until he "deserted February 23, 1864, Kinston, N. C." Reported on August 31-December 31, 1864, muster roll as absent with the remark: "In Military Prison, Salisbury, N. C., under sentence of Court Martial."

SHERMER, PERRY, Private
Enlisted "at camp in Virginia," November 1, 1863, for the war. Present or accounted for until he "deserted February 23, 1864, Kinston, N. C." Muster roll for August 31-December 31, 1864, carries him as absent with the remark: "In Military Prison, Salisbury, N. C., under sentence of Court Martial." Paroled at Appomattox Court House, Virginia, April 9, 1865.

SHORES, A. D., Private
Killed in battle at Second Manassas, Virginia, August 28, 1862.

SHUGART, E. JONES, Private
Enlisted "at camp in Virginia," June 15, 1863, for the war. Present or accounted for on company muster rolls through December, 1864. Wounded at Hatcher's Run, Virginia, February 6, 1865.

SHUGART, ISAAC L., Corporal
Transferred from Company B, 21st Regiment N. C. Troops (11th Regiment N. C. Volunteers) April 26, 1862, as Corporal. Wounded at Hazel River, Virginia, August 22, 1862. Present or accounted for until transferred to the C. S. Navy, April 19, 1864.

SHUGART, J. A., Private
Enlisted in Wake County, September 4, 1862, for the war. Present or accounted for on company muster rolls through December, 1864. Admitted to Jackson Hospital, Richmond, Virginia, February 10, 1865, with a gunshot wound of the left arm. Arm amputated and he was furloughed for 60 days March 12, 1865. Paroled at Appomattox Court House, Virginia, April 9, 1865.

SMITH, JAMES T., Corporal
Transferred from Company B, 21st Regiment N. C. Troops (11th Regiment N. C. Volunteers) April 26, 1862, as Private. Promoted to Corporal May-August, 1863. Present or accounted for on company muster rolls through December, 1864.

SMITH, REUBEN, Private
Enlisted in Lenoir County, April 1, 1864, for the

war. Present or accounted for on company muster rolls through December, 1864.

SNOW, HENRY, Private
Enlisted at New Market, Virginia, November 1, 1864, for the war. Present or accounted for on company muster rolls through December, 1864.

SNOW, J. C., Private
Transferred from Company B, 21st Regiment N. C. Troops (11th Regiment N. C. Volunteers) April 26, 1862. Present or accounted for on company muster rolls through December, 1864. Wounded at Hatcher's Run, Virginia, February 6, 1865, and confined in General Hospital, Richmond, Virginia, until furloughed February 23, 1865.

SPARKS, ALLEN, Private
Enlisted in Lenoir County, April 20, 1864, for the war. Deserted at Greensboro on October 11, 1864, and dropped from the rolls for desertion February 28, 1865.

SPARKS, WILLIAM, Private
Enlisted in Lenoir County, September 10, 1864, for the war. Deserted at Greensboro on October 11, 1864, and was dropped from the rolls for desertion February 28, 1865.

SPEER, SAMUEL H., Private
Enlisted "at camp in Virginia," November 1, 1863, for the war. Present or accounted for on company muster rolls through December, 1864.

SPILLMAN, THOMAS E., Private
Enlisted "at camp in Virginia," November 1, 1863, for the war. Died in Orange County, Virginia, January 14, 1864.

STOUT, W. F., Private
Transferred from Company B, 21st Regiment N. C. Troops (11th Regiment N. C. Volunteers) April 26, 1862. Deserted September 2, 1862.

TANNER, THOMAS, Private
Enlisted in Lenoir County, July 21, 1864, for the war. Present or accounted for on company muster rolls through December, 1864. Paroled at Appomattox Court House, Virginia, April 9, 1865.

TRANSON, E. L., Musician
Transferred from Company B, 21st Regiment N. C. Troops (11th Regiment N. C. Volunteers) April 26, 1862, as Musician. Present or accounted for on company muster rolls through December, 1864.

VESTAL, D. A., Corporal
Transferred from Company B, 21st Regiment N. C. Troops (11th Regiment N. C. Volunteers) April 26, 1862, as Private. Promoted to Corporal May-August, 1863. Present or accounted for on company muster rolls through December, 1864.

VESTAL, J. W., Private
Resided in Yadkin County and enlisted "at camp in Virginia," November 1, 1863, for the war. Present or accounted for on company muster rolls through December, 1864. Took the Oath of Allegiance at Hart's Island, New York Harbor, June 17, 1865. Date and place of capture not reported.

VESTAL, WILLIAM, Private
Enlisted January 20, 1864, for the war. Present or

accounted for on company muster rolls through December, 1864.

VESTAL, WILLIAM P. D., Private
Transferred from Company B, 21st Regiment N. C. Troops (11th Regiment N. C. Volunteers) April 26, 1862. Present or accounted for until he "deserted from Lynchburg, Virginia, October 15, 1864." Dropped from the rolls for desertion on February 28, 1865.

WAGONER, HENRY, Private
Enlisted "at camp in Virginia," January 20, 1864, for the war. Present or accounted for on company muster rolls through December, 1864.

WAGONER, WILLIAM, Private
Transferred from Company B, 21st Regiment N. C. Troops (11th Regiment N. C. Volunteers) April 26, 1862. Present or accounted for on company muster rolls through December, 1864.

WALDEN, GEORGE W., Private
Enlisted "at camp in Virginia," June 15, 1863, for the war. Present or accounted for on company muster rolls through December, 1864.

WHITAKER, HENRY M., Private
Transferred from Company B, 21st Regiment N. C. Troops (11th Regiment N. C. Volunteers) April 26, 1862. Wounded at Hazel River, Virginia, August 22, 1862. Died in hospital at Staunton, Virginia, November 23, 1862, of wounds.

WHITAKER, JAMES, Private
Enlisted in Lenoir County, September 20, 1864, for the war. Deserted at Greensboro on October 11, 1864, and dropped from the rolls on February 28, 1865.

WHITAKER, L. D., Sergeant
Transferred from Company B, 21st Regiment N. C. Troops (11th Regiment N. C. Volunteers) April 26, 1862, as Sergeant. Wounded in battle at Second Manassas, Virginia, August 28, 1862. Present or accounted for on company muster rolls through December, 1864.

WHITAKER, R. S., Private
Enlisted "at camp in Virginia," June 15, 1863, for the war. Present or accounted for until he "deserted March 1, 1864." Rejoined the regiment from desertion on September 20, 1864, and deserted again on October 11, 1864. Dropped from the rolls for desertion on February 28, 1865.

WHITAKER, W. A., Sergeant
Reported on undated company muster roll which states that he enlisted May 12, 1861, at Yadkinville for twelve months.

WHITAKER, W. A., Private
Enlisted "at camp in Virginia," March 10, 1863, for the war. Mustered in as Musician and reported as such through June, 1864. Reported as Private after June, 1864. Present or accounted for on company muster rolls through December, 1864.

WHITEHEAD, WILLIAM, Private
Transferred from Company B, 21st Regiment N. C. Troops (11th Regiment N. C. Volunteers) April 26, 1862. Present or accounted for on company muster rolls through December, 1864. Pa-

roled at Appomattox Court House, Virginia, April 9, 1865.

WHITLOCK, A. H., Private
Transferred from Company B, 21st Regiment N. C. Troops (11th Regiment N. C. Volunteers) April 26, 1862. Wounded in battle at Second Manassas, Virginia, August 28, 1862, and wounded a second time at Mine Run, Virginia, November 29, 1863. Reported as absent sick after being wounded at Mine Run, Virginia, until he was detailed for light duty February 6, 1865.

WILKINS, MARTIN, Private
Enlisted in Wake County, September 4, 1862, for the war. Reported as "wounded in General Hospital, Goldsboro, N. C." on January-February, 1864, muster roll. Reported as present in arrest on February 28-June 30, 1864, muster roll and as present on August 31-December 31, 1864, muster roll. Died in General Hospital, Petersburg, Virginia, January 19, 1865, of "pneumonia ty."

WILLIAMS, R. H., Private
Enlisted in Wake County, September 4, 1862, for the war. Wounded near Fredericksburg, Virginia, May 4, 1863. Present or accounted for until reported on February 28-June 30, 1864, muster roll with the remark: "died in General Hospital, November, 1863, but death not reported."

WILLIAMSON, BENJAMIN, Private
Paroled at Appomattox Court House, Virginia, April 9, 1865.

WOOD, H. R., Private
Transferred from Company B, 21st Regiment N. C. Troops (11th Regiment N. C. Volunteers) April 26, 1862. Wounded in battle at Second Manassas, Virginia, August 28, 1862. Detailed as courier for General Hoke, March-April, 1863, and remained on detail through December, 1864. Present or accounted for on company muster rolls through December, 1864.

WOODHOUSE, M. S., Private
Resided as a farmer in Yadkin County prior to enlisting "at camp in Virginia," at age 19, November 1, 1863, for the war. Present or accounted for on company muster rolls through December, 1864. Paroled at Appomattox Court House, Virginia, April 9, 1865.

WOODRUFF, VINCENT, Private
Transferred from Company B, 21st Regiment N. C. Troops (11th Regiment N. C. Volunteers) April 26, 1862. Detailed to General Hospital, Liberty, Virginia, as a nurse on May 3, 1862. Reported as absent on detail until he was reported with the remark on the March-April, 1863, muster roll that he "died April 19, 1863."

WOOTEN, F. N., Private
Admitted to Receiving and Wayside Hospital, Richmond, Virginia, February 15, 1865, and transferred to Winder Hospital, February 16, 1865. Hospital register carried the remark "P. P."

WOOTEN, JO G., Private
Enlisted in Wake County, September 4, 1862, for the war. Present or accounted for until he died at Richmond, Virginia, on June 25, 1863.

COMPANY B

This company was formerly Company E, 21st Regiment N.C. Troops (11th Regiment N.C. Volunteers). It was transferred to this battalion when the battalion was organized April 26-28, 1862. Its record prior to transfer is recorded in the history of Company E, 21st Regiment N.C. Troops (11th Regiment N. C. Volunteers) and in the history of that regiment. After joining this battalion the company functioned as a part of the battalion, and its history is recorded as a part of the battalion history.

The following roster of the company covers from the date of transfer to the end of the war. For the period before April 26, 1862, consult the roster of Company E, 21st Regiment N. C. Troops (11th Regiment N. C. Volunteers). The information contained in the following roster of the company was compiled principally from company muster rolls which covered April, 1862; November, 1862, through April, 1863; September, 1863, through December, 1864; and one undated muster roll. No muster rolls were found for the period May-October, 1862; May-August, 1863; or after December, 1864. Although there are no Roll of Honor records for this company, useful information was obtained from receipt rolls, hospital records, prisoner of war records, and other primary records, supplemented by state pension applications, United Daughters of the Confederacy records, and postwar rosters and histories.

OFFICERS

CAPTAINS

HEADLEY, PHILIP D.
Transferred from Company E, 21st Regiment N. C. Troops (11th Regiment N. C. Volunteers) April 26, 1862, and commissioned Captain to rank from that date. Submitted his resignation December 27, 1862, by reason of "chronic internal hemorrhoids," and it was accepted January 30, 1863.

COOPER, JOHN A.
Transferred from Company E, 21st Regiment N. C. Troops (11th Regiment N. C. Volunteers) April 26, 1862, and commissioned 1st Lieutenant to rank from that date. Detailed as "Quartermaster and Commissary" for the battalion until promoted to Captain to rank from January 30, 1863. Present or accounted for until detailed as Acting Assistant Adjutant General on General Robert F. Hoke's staff in January, 1864. Reported as absent on detail for the balance of the war and paroled at Greensboro on May 1, 1865, as Captain, Aide-de-Camp.

LIEUTENANTS

AMISTED, W., 2nd Lieutenant
Appears on an undated battalion roster of officers.

OWEN, WILLIAM L., 3rd Lieutenant
Transferred from Company E, 21st Regiment N. C. Troops (11th Regiment N. C. Volunteers) April 26, 1862, and commissioned 3rd Lieutenant

to rank from that date. Killed in Battle of Second Manassas, Virginia, August 28, 1862.

SAPP, NEWELL W., 3rd Lieutenant
Transferred from Company E, 21st Regiment N. C. Troops (11th Regiment N. C. Volunteers) April 26, 1862, and commissioned 2nd Lieutenant Lieutenant to rank from January 30, 1863. Present or accounted for through January, 1865. Paroled at Appomattox Court House, Virginia, April 9, 1865.

SHULTZ, CORNELIUS A., 1st Lieutenant
Transferred from Company E, 21st Regiment N. C. Troops (11th Regiment N. C. Volunteers) April 26, 1862, and commissioned 2nd Lieutenant to rank from that date. Promoted to 1st Lieutenant to rank from January 30, 1863. Wounded near Fredericksburg, Virginia, May 4, 1863. Present or accounted for through December, 1864. Lost an arm in battle near Petersburg, Virginia, in 1865.

WILLIAMSON, SWIFT, 2nd Lieutenant
Transferred from Company E, 21st Regiment N. C. Troops (11th Regiment N. C. Volunteers) April 26, 1862, as Private. Appointed Sergeant on May 1, 1862, and appointed 3rd Lieutenant to rank from August 28, 1862. Promoted to 2nd Lieutenant to rank from January 30, 1863. Present or accounted for through December, 1864.

NONCOMMISSIONED OFFICERS AND PRIVATES

ALDRIDGE, WILLIAM J., Private
Transferred from Company E, 21st Regiment N. C. Troops (11th Regiment N. C. Volunteers) April 26, 1862. Present or accounted for until reported as "captured by the enemy February 1, 1864 near New Bern, N. C."

BAHNSON, HENRY THEODORE, Private
Transferred from the Field and Staff, 2nd Battalion N. C. Infantry on November 5, 1864. Present or accounted for until paroled at Farmville, Virginia, April 11-21, 1865.

BALL, C. N., Private
Enlisted April 15, 1863, for the war. Detailed.

BARNES, N., Private
Enlisted in Lenoir County, September 1, 1864, for the war. Present or accounted for through December, 1864.

BARNEYCASTLE, EPHRAIM, Private
Transferred from Company E, 21st Regiment N. C. Troops (11th Regiment N. C. Volunteers) April 26, 1862. Wounded at Winchester, Virginia, May 25, 1862. Present or accounted for until paroled at Appomattox Court House, Virginia, April 9, 1865.

BARNEYCASTLE, H. L., Private
Enlisted in Lenoir County, June 22, 1864, for the war. Present or accounted for until paroled at Appomattox Court House, Virginia, April 9, 1865.

BARNEYCASTLE, JOHN, Private
Enlisted in Lenoir County, February 1, 1864, for

the war. Present or accounted for until paroled at Appomattox Court House, Virginia, April 9, 1865.

BAXTER, HARRY, Private

Enlisted in Spotsylvania County, Virginia, April 22, 1863, for the war. Wounded near Fredericksburg, Virginia, May 4, 1863, and reported as absent wounded through February, 1864. Wounded a second time on May 4, 1864, and "dropped from the rolls as dead" on August 31, 1864.

BELO, CHARLES, Private

Resided in Forsyth County and enlisted in Lenoir County, September 15, 1864, for the war. Present or accounted for until captured at Petersburg, Virginia, April 3, 1865. Confined at Hart's Island, New York Harbor, until released after taking the Oath of Allegiance June 17, 1865.

BRENDLE, EDWARD, Private

Enlisted in Greene County, Virginia, October 1, 1863, for the war. Present or accounted for until paroled at Appomattox Court House, Virginia, April 9, 1865.

BRENDLE, JOHN P., Private

Transferred from Company E, 21st Regiment N. C. Troops (11th Regiment N. C. Volunteers) April 26, 1862. Reported as being detailed as "musician in regimental band" through December, 1864.

BRENDLE, LIEUGENE G., Private

Transferred from Company E, 21st Regiment N. C. Troops (11th Regiment N. C. Volunteers) April 26, 1862, while absent sick. Discharged September 12, 1862, by reason of "disease of the heart, with dropsy."

BRIETZ, SAMUEL, Private

Enlisted in Orange County, Virginia, November 1, 1863, for the war. Detailed "as musician in band" from date of enlistment through December, 1864.

BUTNER, AUGUSTUS B., Sergeant

Transferred from Company E, 21st Regiment N. C. Troops (11th Regiment N. C. Volunteers) April 26, 1862, as Corporal. Transferred to the Field and Staff of this battalion upon appointment as Commissary Sergeant on May 1, 1862. Transferred back to the company as Sergeant, July-August, 1864, and detailed as Quartermaster and Commissary Sergeant for the battalion. Present or accounted for until paroled at Appomattox Court House, Virginia, April 9, 1865.

BUTNER, LEWIS E., Private

Enlisted in Spotsylvania County, Virginia, January 1, 1863, for the war. Reported as detailed as "musician in regimental band" from date of enlistment through December, 1864.

CARMICHAEL, L. F., Private

Transferred from Company E, 21st Regiment N. C. Troops (11th Regiment N. C. Volunteers) April 26, 1862, and detailed "as musician in regimental band." Reported as such until paroled at Greensboro, May 25, 1865.

CARMICHAEL, WILLIAM F., Private

Transferred from Company E, 21st Regiment N. C. Troops (11th Regiment N. C. Volunteers) April 26, 1862, and detailed "as Chief Musician in regimental band." Reported as such through December, 1864.

CHITTY, REUBEN, Private

Transferred from Company E, 21st Regiment N. C. Troops (11th Regiment N. C. Volunteers) April 26, 1862. Wounded near Fredericksburg, Virginia, May 3, 1863. Present or accounted for until wounded a second time at Raccoon Ford, Virginia, November 25, 1863. Absent wounded through June, 1864. Present or accounted for until furloughed on February 25, 1865.

CLEWELL, AUG., Private

Enlisted in Lenoir County, April 1, 1864, for the war. Present or accounted for through December, 1864.

CLEWELL, AUGUSTUS A., Private

Transferred from Company E, 21st Regiment N. C. Troops (11th Regiment N. C. Volunteers) April 26, 1862. Reported as present on March-April, 1862, muster roll and on receipt rolls for clothing issued during the third and fourth quarters of 1864.

CLOSE, THOMAS D., Sergeant

Transferred from Company E, 21st Regiment N. C. Troops (11th Regiment N. C. Volunteers) April 26, 1862, as Private. Appointed Sergeant on May 1, 1862. Wounded near Fredericksburg, Virginia, May 4, 1863. Present or accounted for until paroled at Appomattox Court House, Virginia, April 9, 1865.

COOPER, W. J., Private

Enlisted in Lenoir County, June 15, 1864, for the war. Present or accounted for until paroled at Appomattox Court House, Virginia, April 9, 1865.

CROWDER, NATHANIEL, Private

Transferred from Company E, 21st Regiment N. C. Troops (11th Regiment N. C. Volunteers) April 26, 1862. Present or accounted for until paroled at Appomattox Court House, Virginia, April 9, 1865.

DEAN, GEORGE, Private

Enlisted in Wake County, September 11, 1862, for the war. Present or accounted for until he "deserted April 1863."

DENNY, WASH, Private

Paroled at Appomattox Court House, Virginia, April 9, 1865.

DOUTHIT, THOMAS BYRON, Private

Transferred from Company E, 21st Regiment N. C. Troops (11th Regiment N. C. Volunteers) April 26, 1862. Present or accounted for until paroled at Appomattox Court House, Virginia, April 9, 1865.

EBERHARDT, L. D., Private

Transferred from Company E, 21st Regiment N. C. Troops (11th Regiment N. C. Volunteers) April 26, 1862, and detailed as "musician in regimental band." Reported as such through December, 1864.

ESSIC, THEOPHILUS, Private

Transferred from Company E, 21st Regiment N. C. Troops (11th Regiment N. C. Volunteers) April 26, 1862, and detailed as a blacksmith for the brigade. Admitted to hospital at Richmond, Virginia, July 18, 1863, with a gunshot wound of the left heel and transferred to Raleigh on July 24, 1863. Returned to company by September-October, 1863. Reported as absent detailed as blacksmith through December, 1864. Paroled at Appomattox Court House, Virginia, April 9, 1865.

FANT, J. E. P., Private

Enlisted in Spotsylvania County, Virginia, January 1, 1863, for the war. Present or accounted for through December, 1864.

FISHER, C. E., Private

Transferred from Company E, 21st Regiment N. C. Troops (11th Regiment N. C. Volunteers) April 26, 1862, and detailed as teamster. Present or accounted for as such until paroled at Appomattox Court House, Virginia, April 9, 1865.

FOGLE, SAMUEL, Private

Enlisted in Iredell County, September 1, 1862, for the war. Wounded near Fredericksburg, Virginia, May 4, 1863, and thumb amputated. Detailed as Assistant Hospital Steward at Kinston between March 1 and June 30, 1864, and reported as absent on detail through December, 1864.

FOOTE, JOHN W., Private

Enlisted in Iredell County, September 4, 1862, for the war. Present or accounted for until he "died at Kinston, N. C., February, 1864."

FRAZER, SMITH, Private

Enlisted in Rockingham County, Virginia, November 1, 1864, for the war. Detailed for light duty in hospital at Richmond, Virginia, December 27, 1864, and reported as such through February, 1865.

FULLER, WILLIAM L., Private

Transferred from Company E, 21st Regiment N. C. Troops (11th Regiment N. C. Volunteers) April 26, 1862. Wounded near Fredericksburg, Virginia, May 4, 1863. Present or accounted for until paroled at Appomattox Court House, Virginia, April 9, 1865.

GILLIAM, ANDREW H., Private

Transferred from Company E, 21st Regiment N. C. Troops (11th Regiment N. C. Volunteers) April 26, 1862. Present or accounted for through January, 1865.

GRIFFIN, JOHN A., Private

Transferred from Company E, 21st Regiment N. C. Troops (11th Regiment N. C. Volunteers) April 26, 1862. Present or accounted for until captured at Farmville, Virginia, April 6, 1865, and confined at Newport News, Virginia. Released after taking the Oath of Allegiance on June 27, 1865.

HALL, SAMUEL G., Private

Transferred from Company E, 21st Regiment N. C. Troops (11th Regiment N. C. Volunteers)

April 26, 1862, while absent detailed "as musician in regimental band." Reported as such through December, 1864.

HANES, JAMES, Private

Enlisted in Iredell County, September 11, 1862, for the war. Present or accounted for on company muster rolls through February, 1864.

HANES, S. C., Private

Enlisted in Greene County, Virginia, October 1, 1863, for the war. Died in hospital at Lynchburg, Virginia, December 10, 1863.

HANES, W. J., Private

Enlisted in Greene County, Virginia, October 1, 1863, for the war. Died at Brandy Station, Virginia, November 1, 1863.

HARNEY, LAWRENCE, Private

Enlisted in Spotsylvania County, Virginia, April 22, 1863, for the war. Killed in action at Bachelor's Creek, N. C., February 1, 1864.

HAUSER, CALVIN E., Private

Transferred from Company E, 21st Regiment N. C. Troops (11th Regiment N. C. Volunteers) April 26, 1862, while absent on detail as a teamster. Absent detailed until returned to company March-April, 1863. Present or accounted for until paroled at Appomattox Court House, Virginia, April 9, 1865.

HAUSER, WILLIAM H., Private

Transferred from Company E, 21st Regiment N. C. Troops (11th Regiment N. C. Volunteers) April 26, 1862. Wounded in the thigh near Fredericksburg, Virginia, May 4, 1863, and reported as absent wounded until returned to duty on August 15, 1863. Present or accounted for with the company until detailed as teamster at Kinston on October 1, 1864. Absent on detail through February, 1865. Paroled at Appomattox Court House, Virginia, April 9, 1865.

HAYNES, JAMES, Private

Enlisted in Iredell County, September 22, 1862, for the war. Present or accounted for through December, 1864.

HEGE, AMOS, Private

Enlisted in Greene County, Virginia, October 1, 1863, for the war. Present or accounted for until paroled at Appomattox Court House, Virginia, April 9, 1865.

HEGE, CHARLES, Private

Enlisted in Lenoir County, March 14, 1863, for the war. Present or accounted for until he "deserted October 14, 1864."

HENDRIX, JOHN, Private

Transferred from Company E, 21st Regiment N. C. Troops (11th Regiment N. C. Volunteers) April 26, 1862. Killed in action at Battle of Second Manassas, Virginia, August 28, 1862.

HENDRIX, LEE, Private

Resided as a miller in Forsyth County and enlisted in Wake County, July 8, 1862, for the war. Wounded "slightly in the stomach" near Fredericksburg, Virginia, May 4, 1863. Present or accounted for through December, 1864.

HENSDALE, DAVID, Private
Transferred from Company E, 21st Regiment
N. C. Troops (11th Regiment N. C. Volunteers)
April 26, 1862. Present or accounted for until
"killed at Greensboro by the cars February 1864."

HENSHAW, WILLIAM T., Private
Transferred from Company E, 21st Regiment
N. C. Troops (11th Regiment N. C. Volunteers)
April 26, 1862. Detailed as a teamster on June 1,
1862, and reported as such until paroled at Appo-
mattox Court House, Virginia, April 9, 1865.

HESTER, J. H., Private
Enlisted in Lenoir County, April 1, 1864, for the
war. Present or accounted for through December,
1864.

HILL, WILLIAM C., Private
Enlisted in Spotsylvania County, Virginia, June 1,
1863, for the war and detailed "as musician in
band." Reported as such through December, 1864.

HOOTS, W. A., Private
Enlisted in Greene County, Virginia, October 1,
1863, for the war. Present or accounted for
through December, 1864.

HUNT, NATHAN E., Private
Transferred from Company E, 21st Regiment
N. C. Troops (11th Regiment N. C. Volunteers)
April 26, 1862, while absent "in General Hospital."
No further records.

IDOL, A. M., Private
Enlisted in Lenoir County, August 1, 1864, for the
war. Present or accounted for until paroled at
Appomattox Court House, Virginia, April 9, 1865.

IDOL, HERBERT N., Private
Transferred from Company E, 21st Regiment
N. C. Troops (11th Regiment N. C. Volunteers)
April 26, 1862. Present or accounted for through
December, 1864.

IDOL, JOHN, Private
Transferred from Company E, 21st Regiment
N. C. Troops (11th Regiment N. C. Volunteers)
April 26, 1862. Present or accounted for until
paroled at Appomattox Court House, Virginia,
April 9, 1865.

INGRAM, ELI S., Private
Transferred from Company E, 21st Regiment
N. C. Troops (11th Regiment N. C. Volunteers)
April 26, 1862. Wounded slightly in the arm near
Fredericksburg, Virginia, May 4, 1863. Present or,
accounted for until he "deserted November 1864."
Took the Oath of Allegiance at Louisville,
Kentucky, January 31, 1865.

INGRAM, JAMES D. C., Private
Transferred from Company E, 21st Regiment
N. C. Troops (11th Regiment N. C. Volunteers)
April 26, 1862. Wounded in battle near Fred-
ericksburg, Virginia, December 13, 1862. Present
or accounted for until he "deserted November
1864." Took the Oath of Allegiance at Louisville,
Kentucky, January 31, 1865.

JARVIS, JOHN C., Private
Transferred from Company E, 21st Regiment
N. C. Troops (11th Regiment N. C. Volunteers)
April 26, 1862. Killed in the Battle of Second

Manassas, Virginia, August 28, 1862.

JOHNSON, JERRY C., Private
Enlisted in Iredell County, September 11, 1862,
for the war. Present or accounted for through
December, 1864.

JOHNSON, S. C., Private
Enlisted in Iredell County, September 9, 1862, for
the war. Present or accounted for through
December, 1862.

JOHNSON, W. T., Private
Enlisted in Iredell County, September 10, 1862,
for the war. Died in hospital October 27, 1862.

KEEHLN, FRANCIS E., Corporal
Transferred from Company E, 21st Regiment
N. C. Troops (11th Regiment N. C. Volunteers)
April 26, 1862, as a Private. Appointed Corporal
on March 1, 1864. Present or accounted for
through December, 1864.

KEESLER, SAMUEL G., Private
Transferred from Company H, 12th Regiment
S.C. Infantry on January 4, 1863, and detailed
"as musician in regimental band." Reported as
such until paroled at Appomattox Court House,
Virginia, April 9, 1865.

KIGER, JOHN A., Private
Transferred from Company E, 21st Regiment
N. C. Troops (11th Regiment N. C. Volunteers)
April 26, 1862. Present or accounted for until
paroled at Appomattox Court House, Virginia,
April 9, 1865.

KIGER, TANDY T., Private
Transferred from Company E, 21st Regiment
N. C. Troops (11th Regiment N. C. Volunteers)
April 26, 1862. Present or accounted for until
reported on the March-April, 1863, muster roll
as "absent sick in General Hospital."

KING, THOMAS, Private
Enlisted in Lenoir County, April 1, 1864, for the
war. No further records.

KINNAMON, GEORGE, Private
Transferred from Company E, 21st Regiment
N. C. Troops (11th Regiment N. C. Volunteers)
April 26, 1862. Reported on a list of prisoners of
war captured between June 26 and July 1, 1862,
and forwarded to Fort Columbus, New York,
July 3, 1862. No further records.

LEWIS, JACOB T., Private
Transferred from Company E, 21st Regiment
N. C. Troops (11th Regiment N. C. Volunteers)
April 26, 1862. Present or accounted for until
paroled at Appomattox Court House, Virginia,
April 9, 1865.

LEWIS, JOSEPH H., Private
Transferred from Company E, 21st Regiment
N. C. Troops (11th Regiment N. C. Volunteers)
April 26, 1862. Present or accounted for until
paroled at Appomattox Court House, Virginia,
April 9, 1865.

LOMAN, WILLIAM, Private
Enlisted in Lenoir County, April 1, 1864, for the
war. Deserted October 14, 1864, but returned after
February, 1865, and was paroled at Appomattox
Court House, Virginia, April 9, 1865.

LONG, ALFRED, Private
Enlisted in Iredell County, September 11, 1862, for the war. Present or accounted for until paroled at Farmville, Virginia, April 11-21, 1865.

MICKEY, F. W., Private
Resided in Forsyth County and enlisted in Rockingham County, Virginia, November 1, 1864, for the war. Present or accounted for until paroled at Greensboro on May 13, 1865.

MOCK, CRIST L., Private
Transferred from Company E, 21st Regiment N. C. Troops (11th Regiment N. C. Volunteers) April 26, 1862. Present or accounted for until paroled at Appomattox Court House, Virginia, April 9, 1865.

MOCK, EDWARD, Private
Resided in Forsyth County and enlisted in Orange County, Virginia, November 1, 1863, for the war. Captured at New Bern on February 6, 1864, and confined at Elmira, New York, until released after taking the Oath of Allegiance May 12, 1865.

MOORE, JAMES, Private
Transferred to the company in December, 1863, and detailed as Quartermaster Sergeant on General Robert F. Hoke's staff. Reported as such through December, 1864, and paroled at Greensboro on May 1, 1865, as "clerk to Major Hughes."

MOSER, JOHN HENRY, Private
Transferred from Company E, 21st Regiment N. C. Troops (11th Regiment N. C. Volunteers) April 26, 1862. Present or accounted for until transferred to Company G, 2nd Battalion N. C. Infantry on November 5, 1864.

MURCHISON, DAVID B., Private
Transferred from Company E, 21st Regiment N. C. Troops (11th Regiment N. C. Volunteers) April 26, 1862, while detailed "as musician in regimental band." Reported as such through December, 1864.

MURPHY, ROBERT, Private
Enlisted in Berkeley County, Virginia, July 17, 1863, for the war. Present or accounted for until paroled at Appomattox Court House, Virginia, April 9, 1865.

NEWSOM, GREEN, Private
Transferred from Company E, 21st Regiment N. C. Troops (11th Regiment N. C. Volunteers) April 26, 1862. Wounded in left hip at Battle of Second Manassas, Virginia, August 28, 1862, and reported as absent wounded through December, 1864, when he was reported as "on retired list."

NEWSOM, JOHN, Private
Enlisted in Orange County, Virginia, November 1, 1863, for the war. Present or accounted for until paroled at Appomattox Court House, Virginia, April 9, 1865.

NICHOLSON, J. A., Private
Enlisted in Rockingham County, Virginia, November 1, 1864, for the war. Died in hospital at Petersburg, Virginia, January 25, 1865, of "pneumonia."

NISSEN, GEORGE ELIAS, Corporal
Transferred from Company E, 21st Regiment N. C. Troops (11th Regiment N. C. Volunteers) April 26, 1862, as Private. Appointed Corporal on November 1, 1862. Present or accounted for until paroled at Appomattox Court House, Virginia, April 9, 1865.

PACK, CALVIN, Private
Enlisted in Lenoir County, May 1, 1864, for the war. Present or accounted for until he "died from disease November 1864."

PARKES, ROBERT T., Private
Transferred from Company E, 21st Regiment N. C. Troops (11th Regiment N. C. Volunteers) April 26, 1862, while detailed "as musician in regimental band." Reported as such through December, 1864.

PATTERSON, CYRUS, Private
Resided in Forsyth County and enlisted in Orange County, Virginia, November 1, 1863, for the war. Present or accounted for through December, 1864, and took the Oath of Allegiance at Nashville, Tennessee, May 5, 1865.

PHILLIPS, C. T., Sergeant
Transferred from Company E, 21st Regiment N. C. Troops (11th Regiment N. C. Volunteers) April 26, 1862, as Corporal. Promoted to Sergeant between May 1 and December 31, 1862. Wounded slightly in the hand near Fredericksburg, Virginia, May 3, 1863. Present or accounted for until paroled at Appomattox Court House, Virginia, April 9, 1865.

PORTER, FRANCIS M., Private
Transferred from Company E, 21st Regiment N. C. Troops (11th Regiment N. C. Volunteers) April 26, 1862. Present or accounted for through December, 1864.

PORTER, GEORGE W., Private
Transferred from Company E, 21st Regiment N. C. Troops (11th Regiment N. C. Volunteers) April 26, 1862. Present or accounted for through December, 1864.

PORTER, JOHN H., Private
Transferred from Company E, 21st Regiment N. C. Troops (11th Regiment N. C. Volunteers) April 26, 1862. Confined as a prisoner of war at Fort Monroe, Virginia, August 15, 1862, and paroled and exchanged on September 21, 1862. Place and date of capture not reported. Present or accounted for through December, 1864.

REICH, J. H., Private
Enlisted in Rockingham County, Virginia, November 1, 1864, for the war. Reported as a "rebel deserter" on Federal Provost Marshal records which show that he took the Oath of Allegiance at Washington, D.C., February 27, 1865, and was provided transportation to Hope, Indiana.

REICH, JAMES A., Private
Transferred from Company E, 21st Regiment N. C. Troops (11th Regiment N. C. Volunteers) April 26, 1862, while on detail as "musician in regimental band." Reported as such through December, 1864.

REID, JAMES L., Corporal
Transferred from Company E, 21st Regiment

N. C. Troops (11th Regiment N. C. Volunteers) April 26, 1862, as Private. Appointed Corporal on February 1, 1863. Present or accounted for through December, 1864.

RING, THOMAS, Private

Enlisted in Lenoir County, April 1, 1864, for the war. Present or accounted for through December, 1864.

ROTHROCK, JOHN M., Private

Transferred from Company E, 21st Regiment N. C. Troops (11th Regiment N. C. Volunteers) April 26, 1862. Present or accounted for through December, 1864.

ROYAL, H. A., Private

Enlisted in Iredell County, September 11, 1862, for the war. Present or accounted for until "killed in action November 28, 1863, near Rapidan River known as Mine Run."

ROYAL, JOHN, Private

Enlisted in Orange County, Virginia, October 1, 1863, for the war. Present or accounted for until he "deserted October 14, 1864." Reported as such through February, 1865.

SAPP, HART B., Private

Transferred from Company E, 21st Regiment N. C. Troops (11th Regiment N. C. Volunteers) April 26, 1862. Wounded in action at Winchester, Virginia, May 25, 1862. Present or accounted for through December, 1864.

SAPP, HENRY, Private

Enlisted in Orange County, Virginia, November 1, 1863, for the war. Present or accounted for through December, 1864.

SAPP, JESSE W., Private

Previously served in Company K, 45th Regiment N.C. Troops. Enlisted in this company and battalion in Rockingham County, Virginia, November 1, 1864, for the war. Present or accounted for until discharged at Charlottesville, Virginia, December 21, 1864, by reason of "paralysis of lower extremities."

SAPP, JOHN, Private

Transferred from Company E, 21st Regiment N.C. Troops (11th Regiment N.C. Volunteers) April 26, 1862. Present or accounted for until captured at Petersburg, Virginia, April 3, 1865. Confined at Hart's Island, New York Harbor, until released after taking the Oath of Allegiance on June 17, 1865.

SAPP, NEWELL, Sergeant

Transferred from Company E, 21st Regiment N.C. Troops (11th Regiment N.C. Volunteers) April 26, 1862, as Corporal. Promoted to Sergeant on February 1, 1863. Present or accounted for until captured at Petersburg, Virginia, April 3, 1865. Confined at Hart's Island, New York Harbor, until released after taking the Oath of Allegiance June 17, 1865.

SAPP, WILLIAM, Private

Enlisted in Orange County, Virginia, November 1, 1863, for the war. Present or accounted for through December, 1864.

SHEPPERD, WILLIAM HENRY, Sergeant

Transferred from Company E, 21st Regiment N.C.

Troops (11th Regiment N.C. Volunteers) April 26, 1862, as Sergeant. Wounded in action at Battle of Second Manassas, Virginia, August 28, 1862. Detailed as courier to General Robert F. Hoke in March-April, 1863, and reported as absent on detail through December, 1864. Paroled at Greensboro on May 1, 1865, with the remark: "Courier."

SHORE, HENRY LEWIS, Private

Transferred from Company E, 21st Regiment N.C. Troops (11th Regiment N.C. Volunteers) April 26, 1862. Captured at Frederick, Maryland, September 12, 1862, and paroled and exchanged at Aiken's Landing, Virginia, October 6, 1862. Detailed as an ambulance driver prior to December, 1862, and reported as absent on detail through December, 1864, when he was reported as present. Paroled at Appomattox Court House, Virginia, on April 9, 1865.

SHOUSE, CHARLES AUGUSTUS, Private

Enlisted in Culpeper County, Virginia, June 1, 1863, for the war. Present or accounted for through December, 1864.

SHOUSE, ELI A., Private

Transferred from Company E, 21st Regiment N.C. Troops (11th Regiment N.C. Volunteers) April 26, 1862. Present or accounted for until paroled at Appomattox Court House, Virginia, April 9, 1865.

SHOUSE, WILEY, Private

Transferred from Company E, 21st Regiment N.C. Troops (11th Regiment N.C. Volunteers) April 26, 1862, as Corporal. Reduced to ranks on January 1, 1863. Wounded in the head near Fredericksburg, Virginia, May 4, 1863. Wounded a second time in action at Bachelor Creek on February 1, 1864, and foot amputated. Retired to the Invalid Corps on August 25, 1864.

SIEWERS, NATHANIEL S., Private

Enlisted in Orange County, Virginia, November 1, 1863, for the war and detailed as "musician in regimental band." Reported as such through December, 1864.

SMITH, JOHN, Private

Transferred from Company E, 21st Regiment N.C. Troops (11th Regiment N.C. Volunteers) April 26, 1862. Present or accounted for until discharged at Lynchburg, Virginia, January 23, 1863, by reason of "organic diseased heart."

SNIDER, WILLIAM P., Private

Transferred from Company E, 21st Regiment N.C. Troops (11th Regiment N.C. Volunteers) April 26, 1862. Wounded in action near Fredericksburg, Virginia, December 13, 1862. Wounded a second time in battle near Fredericksburg on May 4, 1863. Detailed as teamster at General Hospital, Montgomery Springs, Virginia, while recuperating from wound and remained on detail until reported as "deserted" on March 1-June 30, 1864, muster roll. Reported to the Provost Marshal General, Washington, D. C., April 13, 1865, and was provided transportation to Baltimore, Maryland.

SPAUGH, W. E., Private

Enlisted in Rockingham County, Virginia, November 1, 1864, for the war. Present or accounted for through December, 1864. Federal Provost Marshal records show that he took the Oath of Allegiance at Washington, D. C., February 27, 1865, and was provided transportation to Hope, Indiana.

STAFFORD, ZADOC, Private
Transferred from Company E, 21st Regiment N.C. Troops (11th Regiment N.C. Volunteers) April 26, 1862. Present or accounted for on company muster rolls through April, 1863.

STANDIFORD, FUEL, Private
Enlisted in Orange County, Virginia, November 1, 1863, for the war. Wounded in action near Mine Run, Virginia, November 29, 1863. Present or accounted for until paroled at Appomattox Court House, Virginia, April 9, 1865.

STEWART, SAMUEL L., Private
Transferred from Company E, 21st Regiment N.C. Troops (11th Regiment N.C. Volunteers) April 26, 1862. Present or accounted for until discharged at Lynchburg, Virginia, July 10, 1863, by reason of "phthisis with breaking down of tuberele apex of both lungs."

SWAIM, COLUMBUS F., Corporal
Transferred from Company E, 21st Regiment N.C. Troops (11th Regiment N.C. Volunteers) April 26, 1862, as Private. Appointed Corporal on February 1, 1863. Present or accounted for until transferred to Company G, 2nd Battalion N.C. Infantry upon appointment as 2nd Lieutenant to rank from June 30, 1863.

SWAIM, ELI, Private
Transferred from Company E, 21st Regiment N.C. Troops (11th Regiment N. C. Volunteers) April 26, 1862. Wounded in action at Winchester, Virginia, May 25, 1862. Present or accounted for until killed in action at Bachelor Creek on February 1, 1864.

THOMAS, W. F., Private
Born in Forsth County and was by occupation a farmer when he enlisted in Orange County, Virginia, at age 19, November 1, 1863, for the war. Present or accounted for through December, 1864. Died in hospital at Richmond, Virginia, February 7, 1865, of "intermittent fever."

WAUGH, LUTHER, Private
Resided as a farmer in Surry County and enlisted in Lenoir County, July 1, 1864, for the war. Present or accounted for until captured in front of Petersburg, Virginia, February 6, 1865. Confined at Point Lookout, Maryland, until released after taking the Oath of Allegiance on May 14, 1865.

WAUGH, SAMUEL A., Private
Transferred from Company E, 21st Regiment N.C. Troops (11th Regiment N.C. Volunteers) April 26, 1862. Wounded in action at Battle of Second Manassas, Virginia, August 28, 1862. Present

until detailed as Hospital Steward January-February, 1864. Reported as absent on detail through December, 1864. Paroled at Appomattox Court House, Virginia, April 9, 1865.

WEATHERMAN, GEORGE, Private
Enlisted in Iredell County, September 9, 1862, for the war. Present or accounted for until he died in hospital at Lynchburg, Virginia, December 30, 1863, of "variola."

WEATHERMAN, WILLIAM ·R., Private
Enlisted in Iredell County, September 11, 1862, for the war. Wounded in left hip near Fredericksburg, Virginia, May 4, 1863. Present or accounted for through December, 1864.

WELCH, ALPHIUS L., Private
Transferred from Company E, 21st Regiment N.C. Troops (11th Regiment N.C. Volunteers) April 26, 1862, and detailed as a teamster for the division. Reported as such until paroled at Appomattox Court House, Virginia, April 9, 1865.

WELCH, HENRY N., Corporal
Transferred from Company E, 21st Regiment N.C. Troops (11th Regiment N.C. Volunteers) April 26, 1862, as Private. Appointed Corporal on August 31, 1863. Killed in action at Bachelor Creek on February 1, 1864.

WELCH, JACOB J., 1st Sergeant
Transferred from Company E, 21st Regiment N.C. Troops (11th Regiment N.C. Volunteers) April 26, 1862, as Sergeant. Promoted to 1st Sergeant on February 1, 1863. Present or accounted for until paroled at Appomattox Court House, Virginia, April 9, 1865.

WILLIAMSON, JAMES A., Private
Enlisted in Spotsylvania County, Virginia, February 16, 1863, for the war. Present or accounted for until paroled at Appomattox Court House, Virginia, April 9, 1865.

WILLIAMSON, L., Private
Hospitalized on April 10, 1865, at Richmond, Virginia, where he died May 15, 1865.

WILSON, JOSEPH H., Corporal
Transferred from Company E, 21st Regiment N.C. Troops (11th Regiment N.C. Volunteers) April 26, 1862, as Private. Appointed Corporal prior to December 31, 1862. Wounded slightly in the thigh near Fredericksburg, Virginia, May 4, 1863. Present or accounted for until paroled at Appomattox Court House, Virginia, April 9, 1865.

WINKLER, CRIST, Private
Enlisted in Orange County, Virginia, November 1, 1863, for the war and detailed as musician in band. Reported as such through December, 1864.

WRIGHT, LORENZO D., Private
Transferred from Company E, 21st Regiment N.C. Troops (11th Regiment N.C. Volunteers) April 26, 1862. Killed in action at Battle of Second Manassas, Virginia, August 28, 1862.

1st BATTALION N. C. LOCAL DEFENSE TROOPS
(WHITFORD'S BATTALION N. C. PARTISAN RANGERS)

This battalion was organized when Captain John D. Whitford's Company, 1st Company I, 10th Regiment N. C. State Troops (1st Regiment N. C. Artillery), was transferred out of that regiment and divided into two companies. These two companies became the nucleus of the battalion. The actual division of the original company began with the election of officers for the two new companies on March 28, 1863, and was completed when the men were divided and assigned to the companies on April 16, 1863. Additional companies were assigned to the battalion, and by the end of 1863 ten companies were in the battalion. On January 18, 1864, the battalion was redesignated the 67th Regiment N. C. Troops. It should be noted that some of the companies reported the parent unit as the 67th Regiment N. C. Troops on the November-December, 1863, muster roll, and some reported it as Whitford's Battalion on muster rolls for the same period. Even though it appears that the 67th Regiment N. C. Troops designation was used prior to the official order, January 18, 1864, the unit did not officially become the 67th Regiment N.C. Troops until the order was issued.

Although this battalion served with Confederate troops, it remained in state service and was never mustered into Confederate service. Since it remained in state service, it was frequently referred to as a State Troop organization, but it was not organized under the State Troops Act of 1861. The reference to it as a State Troops unit simply meant it was in state service and not Confederate service. Because it was in state service, it was officially designated the 1st Battalion N. C. Local Defense Troops. However, it was more frequently reported as Whitford's Battalion N.C. Troops or Whitford's Battalion N.C. Partisan Rangers in official correspondence and strength returns.

1st Company I, 10th Regiment N. C. State Troops (1st Regiment N. C. Artillery) was serving at Swift Creek, below Kinston, when the battalion was organized. Three additional companies were added in April and May, 1863. On May 9 it was reported that Major Whitford's Battalion was at Swift Creek Village with "scouts in every direction below Swift Creek." On May 27 General D. H. Hill reported the battalion at Coward's Bridge with about 400 men. The companies of the battalion served mainly on outpost duty to observe the Federal movements from New Bern. When General Edward E. Potter undertook his expedition from New Bern to Tarboro and back, July 19-22, he captured 15 men of one company on outpost duty 12 miles below Greenville and reported two companies at "Scupperton" on July 21.

In July, 1863, at least three additional companies were added to the battalion to bring it up to eight companies. Two additional companies, one a mounted company, were added in August and September. Thus the battalion had reached regimental size but remained a battalion. This was probably due to the

nature of its service. The companies were still scattered on outpost duty. On November 25, 1863, Companies E and I were surprised and routed at Haddock's Cross Roads, below Greenville. They lost over fifty men prisoners and all their equipment. At least one was reported killed and four wounded. Two days later the strength of the battalion was reported as 688 aggregate present and 812 aggregate present and absent. On December 31, 1863, the battalion was reported near Kinston with an effective total present of 512, aggregate present of 627, and aggregate present and absent of 847.

On January 18, 1864, by Special Orders No. 8, paragraph 2, Executive Department, Adjutant General's Office, Raleigh, the battalion was redesignated the 67th Regiment N. C. Troops with no change in company letters. The following roster of the battalion covers through the date of redesignation. A roster of the 67th Regiment N.C. Troops, beginning with the date of transfer, will appear in a future volume.

This battalion is not reported in Major Moore's *Roster*, and its history is recorded in Clark's *Regiments* as the 11th Battalion (Whitford's Battalion). Although Clark makes reference to the fact that the battalion history is reported with the 67th Regiment N. C. Troops, the author of the regimental history joined the regiment after the battalion became the 67th Regiment N.C. Troops and did not record the battalion's history.

FIELD AND STAFF

LIEUTENANT COLONEL

WHITFORD, JOHN N.

Transferred from 1st Company I, 10th Regiment N. C. State Troops (1st Regiment N. C. Artillery) April 16, 1863, and appointed Major on May 14, 1863, to rank from January 1, 1863. Promoted to Lieutenant Colonel on October 16, 1863, to rank from July 21, 1863. Present or accounted for through January 18, 1864, when the battalion was redesignated the 67th Regiment N.C. Troops and he was promoted to Colonel of the regiment to rank from that date.

MAJOR

WHITFORD, EDWARD

Transferred from Company A of this battalion on January 18, 1864, the date the battalion was redesignated the 67th Regiment N.C. Troops, and appointed Major to rank from that date.

ADJUTANT

SCHENCK, SAMUEL F.

Transferred from Company D of this battalion upon appointment as Adjutant, with the rank of

1st Lieutenant, on November 30, 1863, to rank from June 15, 1863. Present or accounted for through January 18, 1864, when the battalion was redesignated the 67th Regiment N. C. Troops and he was retained as Adjutant of the new unit.

QUARTERMASTERS AND COMMISSARIES OF SUBSISTENCE

WHITFORD, DAVID P.

Appointed Captain, Quartermaster and Commissary of Subsistence, May 14, 1863, to rank from May 13, 1863. Transferred to Company F of this battalion upon appointment as Captain on July 22, 1863, to rank from July 20, 1863.

O'NEIL, JOHN W.

Transferred from Company G, 10th Regiment N. C. State Troops (1st Regiment N. C. Artillery) upon appointment as Captain, Quartermaster and Commissary of Subsistence on September 15, 1863, to rank from August 1, 1863. Resigned September 20, 1863.

ROBINSON, THOMAS M.

Appointed Captain, Quartermaster and Commissary of Subsistence on September 22, 1863, to rank from September 20, 1863. Present or accounted for until transferred to the Field and Staff of the 67th Regiment N. C. Troops on January 18, 1864.

SURGEON

PRIMROSE, ROBERT S.

Appointed Surgeon to rank from May 13, 1863. Resigned.

ASSISTANT SURGEON

MORROW, WILLIAM H.

Appointed Assistant Surgeon to rank from January 22, 1863. Present or accounted for until transferred to the Field and Staff of the 67th Regiment N. C. Troops on January 18, 1864.

SERGEANT MAJOR

GUION, JOHN

Transferred from Company A of this battalion upon appointment as Sergeant Major in July-August, 1863. Present or accounted for until transferred to the Field and Staff of the 67th Regiment N. C. Troops on January 18, 1864.

ORDNANCE SERGEANT

LANCASTER, GEORGE F.

Detailed as Ordnance Sergeant from Company A of this battalion in April, 1863. Remained on detail through January 18, 1864, when the battalion was redesignated the 67th Regiment N.C. Troops. Officially transferred to the Field and Staff on that date.

COMPANY A

This company was organized when 1st Company I, 10th Regiment N. C. State Troops (1st Regiment

N. C. Artillery) was divided on April 16, 1863. The old company ceased to exist on that date, and the new company became one of the original companies of this battalion. The history of the original company is reported in the history of 1st Company I, 10th Regiment N. C. State Troops (1st Regiment N. C. Artillery) and in that regiment's regimental history. Since this company was one of the original companies of the battalion, its history is recorded as a part of the battalion history. By Special Orders No. 8, paragraph 2, Adjutant General's Office, Raleigh, January 18, 1864, the battalion was redesignated the 67th Regiment N.C. Troops and this company became Company A of the regiment.

The following roster of the company covers the period from the date of organization, April 16, 1863, through the date of redesignation, January 18, 1864. All events after that date are recorded in the roster of Company A, 67th Regiment N. C. Troops. The information contained in the following roster was compiled from company muster rolls which covered the period from November 1, 1863, through January 18, 1864, the date of redesignation. Information from muster rolls of 1st Company I, 10th Regiment N.C. State Troops (1st Regiment N.C. Artillery) was also used. No muster rolls were found for the period from April 16 through October 31, 1863. Although there are no Roll of Honor records for this company, useful information was obtained from receipt rolls, hospital records, prisoner of war records, and other primary records, supplemented by state pension applications, United Daughters of the Confederacy records, and postwar rosters and histories.

OFFICERS
CAPTAIN

WHITFORD, EDWARD

Transferred from 1st Company I, 10th Regiment N. C. State Troops (1st Regiment N. C. Artillery) and appointed Captain to rank from March 28, 1863. Present or accounted for through January 18, 1864, the date the battalion was redesignated the 67th Regiment N. C. Troops. Appointed Major of the 67th Regiment N. C. Troops to rank from January 18, 1864.

LIEUTENANTS

HIGGINS, WILEY F., 3rd Lieutenant

Transferred from Company K, 2nd Regiment N.C. State Troops upon appointment as 3rd Lieutenant to rank from March 28, 1863. Present or accounted for until transferred to Company A, 67th Regiment N.C. Troops on January 18, 1864.

TOLSON, JAMES H., 1st Lieutenant

Transferred from 1st Company I, 10th Regiment N.C. State Troops (1st Regiment N.C. Artillery) and appointed 1st Lieutenant to rank from March 28, 1863. Present or accounted for until transferred to Company A, 67th Regiment N.C. Troops on January 18, 1864, and promoted to Captain of the company to rank from that date.

WHITFORD, HARDY, 2nd Lieutenant

Transferred from 1st Company I, 10th Regiment

N.C. State Troops (1st Regiment N.C. Artillery) and appointed 2nd Lieutenant to rank from March 28, 1863. Present or accounted for until transferred to Company A, 67th Regiment N.C. Troops on January 18, 1864.

NONCOMMISSIONED OFFICERS AND PRIVATES

ADKINSON, WILLIAM, Private

Transferred from 1st Company I, 10th Regiment N.C. State Troops (1st Regiment N.C. Artillery) April 16, 1863. Captured at Tarboro on July 21, 1863, and paroled at Fort Monroe, Virginia, August 4, 1863. Present or accounted for until transferred to Company A, 67th Regiment N.C. Troops on January 18, 1864.

ANDERSON, NOAH, Private

Transferred from 1st Company I, 10th Regiment N.C. State Troops (1st Regiment N.C. Artillery) April 16, 1863. Present or accounted for until transferred to Company A, 67th Regiment N.C. Troops on January 18, 1864.

ASKINS, THOMAS T., Private

Transferred from 1st Company I, 10th Regiment N.C. State Troops (1st Regiment N.C. Artillery) April 16, 1863. Present or accounted for until transferred to Company A, 67th Regiment N. C. Troops on January 18, 1864.

BALL, JOHN, Private

Enlisted in Craven County, October 1, 1863, for the war. Deserted on November 27, 1863.

BARNETT, STEPHEN C., Musician

Transferred from 1st Company I, 10th Regiment N.C. State Troops (1st Regiment N.C. Artillery) April 16, 1863, as Musician. Present or accounted for until transferred to Company A, 67th Regiment N.C. Troops on January 18, 1864.

BARRINGTON, FURNIFOLD O., Private

Transferred from 1st Company I, 10th Regiment N.C. State Troops (1st Regiment N.C. Artillery) April 16, 1863. Present or accounted for until transferred to Company A, 67th Regiment N.C. Troops on January 18, 1864.

BENTLEY, BENJAMIN, Private

Transferred from 1st Company I, 10th Regiment N.C. State Troops (1st Regiment N.C. Artillery) April 16, 1863. Present or accounted for until transferred to Company A, 67th Regiment N.C. Troops on January 18, 1864.

BEXLEY, JAMES, Private

Transferred from 1st Company I, 10th Regiment N.C. State Troops (1st Regiment N.C. Artillery) April 16, 1863. Present or accounted for through December, 1863.

BEXLEY, NATHANIEL, Private

Transferred from 1st Company I, 10th Regiment N.C. State Troops (1st Regiment N.C. Artillery) April 16, 1863. Present or accounted for until transferred to Company A, 67th Regiment N.C.

Troops on January 18, 1864.

BOYD, ABNER, Private

Enlisted in Craven County, August 1, 1863, for the war. Present or accounted for until transferred to Company A, 67th Regiment N.C. Troops on January 18, 1864.

BREWER, RICHARD, Private

Enlisted in Craven County, August 1, 1863, for the war. Present or accounted for until transferred to Company A, 67th Regiment N.C. Troops on January 18, 1864.

BRIGHT, FRANKLIN, Private

Transferred from 1st Company I, 10th Regiment N.C. State Troops (1st Regiment N.C. Artillery) April 16, 1863. Present or accounted for until transferred to Company A, 67th Regiment N.C. Troops on January 18, 1864.

BRIGHT, GEORGE, Private

Transferred from 1st Company I, 10th Regiment N.C. State Troops (1st Regiment N.C. Artillery) April 16, 1863. Present or accounted for until transferred to Company A, 67th Regiment N.C. Troops on January 18, 1864.

BRYAN, LEWIS A., Private

Enlisted in Craven County, May 9, 1863, for the war. Present or accounted for until transferred to Company A, 67th Regiment N.C. Troops on January 18, 1864.

CALLAWAY, JESSE R., Private

Transferred from 1st Company I, 10th Regiment N.C. State Troops (1st Regiment N.C. Artillery) April 16, 1863. Present or accounted for until transferred to Company B, 40th Regiment N.C. Troops (3rd Regiment N.C. Artillery) July 1, 1863.

CARAWAN, HENRY J., Private

Transferred from 1st Company I, 10th Regiment N.C. State Troops (1st Regiment N.C. Artillery) April 16, 1863. Present or accounted for until transferred to Company A, 67th Regiment N. C. Troops on January 18, 1864.

CARAWAN, JOHN A., Private

Transferred from 1st Company I, 10th Regiment N. C. State Troops (1st Regiment N.C. Artillery) April 16, 1863. Present or accounted for until transferred to Company A, 67th Regiment N.C. Troops on January 18, 1864.

CARAWAN, WILLIAM G., Private

Transferred from 1st Company I, 10th Regiment N.C. State Troops (1st Regiment N. C. Artillery) April 16, 1863. Present or accounted for until transferred to Company A, 67th Regiment N. C. Troops on January 18, 1864.

CATON, ARTHUR, Private

Enlisted in Craven County, July 21, 1863, for the war. Present or accounted for until transferred to Company A, 67th Regiment N. C. Troops on January 18, 1864.

CATON, DAVID B., Sergeant

Transferred from 1st Company I, 10th Regiment N. C. State Troops (1st Regiment N. C. Artillery)

April 16, 1863, as Sergeant. Present or accounted for until transferred to Company A, 67th Regiment N.C. Troops on January 18, 1864.

CATON, JOHN, Private

Transferred from 1st Company I, 10th Regiment N. C. State Troops (1st Regiment N. C. Artillery) April 16, 1863. Present or accounted for until transferred to Company A, 67th Regiment N.C. Troops on January 18, 1864.

CLARK, HARVEY, Private

Transferred from 1st Company I, 10th Regiment N.C. State Troops (1st Regiment N.C. Artillery) April 16, 1863. Present or accounted for until transferred to Company A, 67th Regiment N.C. Troops on January 18, 1864.

CLARK, JOHN A., Private

Transferred from 1st Company I, 10th Regiment N. C. State Troops (1st Regiment N. C. Artillery) April 16, 1863. Present or accounted for until transferred to Company A, 67th Regiment N. C. Troops on January 18, 1864.

COOK, SAMUEL, Private

Enlisted in Craven County, January 2, 1864, for the war. Present or accounted for until transferred to Company A, 67th Regiment N.C. Troops on January 18, 1864.

COX, BENJAMIN C., Private

Transferred from 1st Company I, 10th Regiment N.C. State Troops (1st Regiment N.C. Artillery) April 16, 1863. Present or accounted for until transferred to Company A, 67th Regiment N.C. Troops on January 18, 1864.

DAUGHETY, CHARLES W., Private

Transferred from 1st Company I, 10th Regiment N.C. State Troops (1st Regiment N.C. Artillery) April 16, 1863. Present or accounted for until transferred to Company A, 67th Regiment N. C. Troops on January 18, 1864.

DAUGHETY, DURANT, Private

Transferred from 1st Company I, 10th Regiment N.C. State Troops (1st Regiment N.C. Artillery) April 16, 1863. Present or accounted for until transferred to Company A, 67th Regiment N. C. Troops on January 18, 1864.

DAUGHETY, EMANUEL, Corporal

Transferred from 1st Company I. 10th Regiment N.C. State Troops (1st Regiment N.C. Artillery) April 16, 1863, as Private. Appointed Corporal prior to December, 1863. Present or accounted for until transferred to Company A, 67th Regiment N.C. Troops on January 18, 1864.

DAUGHETY, FRANCIS L., Private

Transferred from 1st Company I, 10th Regiment N.C. State Troops (1st Regiment N.C. Artillery) April 16, 1863. Reported on October 31-December 31, 1863, muster roll as "deserted since December."

DAUGHETY, R. T., Corporal

Transferred from 1st Company I, 10th Regiment N.C. State Troops (1st Regiment N.C. Artillery) April 16, 1863, as Private. Appointed Corporal

prior to December, 1863. Present or accounted for until transferred to Company A, 67th Regiment N.C. Troops on January 18, 1864.

DEAL, JOHN, Private

Transferred from 1st Company I, 10th Regiment N.C. State Troops (1st Regiment N.C. Artillery) April 16, 1863. Present or accounted for until transferred to Company A, 67th Regiment N.C. Troops on January 18, 1864.

DESTRALL, DENNIS, Private

Transferred from 1st Company I, 10th Regiment N.C. State Troops (1st Regiment N.C. Artillery) April 16, 1863. Captured at Tarboro, July 21, 1863, and paroled at Fort Monroe, Virginia, August 4, 1863. Present or accounted for until transferred to Company A, 67th Regiment N. C. Troops on January 18, 1864.

DIXON, LEWIS S., Private

Transferred from 1st Company I, 10th Regiment N.C. State Troops (1st Regiment N.C. Artillery) April 16, 1863. Present or accounted for until transferred to Company A, 67th Regiment N.C. Troops on January 18, 1864.

DIXON, SYLVESTER, Private

Transferred from 1st Company I, 10th Regiment N.C. State Troops (1st Regiment N.C. Artillery) April 16, 1863. Reported on October 31-December 31, 1863, muster roll as "deserted since December."

DIXON, WILLIAM, Private

Enlisted in Craven County, December 25, 1863, for the war. Present or accounted for until transferred to Company A, 67th Regiment N.C. Troops on January 18, 1864.

DONALDSON, ANDREW J., Private

Transferred from 1st Company I, 10th Regiment N.C. State Troops (1st Regiment N.C. Artillery) April 16, 1863. Captured at Tarboro on July 21, 1863, and paroled at Fort Monroe, Virginia, August 4, 1863. Present or accounted for until transferred to Company A, 67th Regiment N.C. Troops on January 18, 1864.

DOWDY, WILLIAM R., Private

Transferred from 1st Company I, 10th Regiment N.C. State Troops (1st Regiment N.C. Artillery) April 16, 1863. Present or accounted for until transferred to Company A, 67th Regiment N.C. Troops on January 18, 1864.

DUDLEY, ARCHIBALD, Private

Enlisted in Craven County, April 14, 1863, for the war. Present or accounted for until transferred to Company A, 67th Regiment N.C. Troops on January 18, 1864.

DUDLEY, WILLIAM H., Private

Transferred from 1st Company I, 10th Regiment N.C. State Troops (1st Regiment N.C. Artillery) April 16, 1863. Captured at Tarboro on July 21, 1863, and paroled at Fort Monroe, Virginia, August 4, 1863. Present or accounted for until transferred to Company A, 67th Regiment N.C. Troops on January 18, 1864.

EDWARDS, JOSEPHUS, Private

Transferred from 1st Company I, 10th Regiment

N.C. State Troops (1st Regiment N.C. Artillery) April 16, 1863.

ERNUL, JOHN B., Private

Transferred from 1st Company I, 10th Regiment N.C. State Troops (1st Regiment N.C. Artillery) April 16, 1863. Present or accounted for until transferred to Company A, 67th Regiment N.C. Troops on January 18, 1864.

EWELL, WILEY A., Sergeant

Transferred from 1st Company I, 10th Regiment N.C. State Troops (1st Regiment N.C. Artillery) April 16, 1863, as Private. Appointed Sergeant prior to December, 1863. Present or accounted for until transferred to Company A, 67th Regiment N.C. Troops on January 18, 1864.

FIELDS, HENRY, Private

Enlisted in Craven County, July 21, 1863, for the war. Present or accounted for until transferred to Company A, 67th Regiment N.C. Troops on January 18, 1864.

FORNES, JESSE, Private

Transferred from 1st Company I, 10th Regiment N.C. State Troops (1st Regiment N.C. Artillery) April 16, 1863. Present or accounted for until transferred to Company A, 67th Regiment N.C. Troops on January 18, 1864.

FRANKS, WILLIAM, Private

Transferred from 1st Company I, 10th Regiment N.C. State Troops (1st Regiment N.C. Artillery) April 16, 1863. Present or accounted for until transferred to Company A, 67th Regiment N.C. Troops on January 18, 1864.

FULCHER, JOSEPH A., Private

Transferred from 1st Company I, 10th Regiment N.C. State Troops (1st Regiment N.C. Artillery) April 16, 1863. Present or accounted for until transferred to Company A, 67th Regiment N.C. Troops on January 18, 1864.

GASKINS, HENRY A., Private

Transferred from 1st Company I, 10th Regiment N.C. State Troops (1st Regiment N.C. Artillery) April 16, 1863. Present or accounted for until transferred to Company A, 67th Regiment N.C. Troops on January 18, 1864.

GASKINS, LEVIN, Private

Transferred from 1st Company I, 10th Regiment N.C. State Troops (1st Regiment N.C. Artillery) April 16, 1863. Present or accounted for until transferred to Company A, 67th Regiment N.C. Troops on January 18, 1864.

GASKINS, MAJOR, Private

Transferred from 1st Company I, 10th Regiment N.C. State Troops (1st Regiment N.C. Artillery) April 16, 1863. Present or accounted for until transferred to Company A, 67th Regiment N.C. Troops on January 18, 1864.

GASKINS, THOMAS J., Private

Transferred from 1st Company I, 10th Regiment N.C. State Troops (1st Regiment N.C. Artillery) April 16, 1863. Present or accounted for until transferred to Company A, 67th Regiment N.C.

Troops on January 18, 1864.

GASKINS, WEEKS, Private

Transferred from 1st Company I, 10th Regiment N.C. State Troops (1st Regiment N.C. Artillery) April 16, 1863. Present or accounted for until transferred to Company A, 67th Regiment N.C. Troops on January 18, 1864.

GIBSON, JOHN W., Private

Transferred from Company B, 40th Regiment N.C. Troops (3rd Regiment N.C. Artillery) July 1, 1863. Present or accounted for until transferred to Company A, 67th Regiment N.C. Troops on January 18, 1864.

GILBERT, JOHN, Private

Transferred from 1st Company I, 10th Regiment N.C. State Troops (1st Regiment N.C. Artillery) April 16, 1863. Present or accounted for until transferred to Company A, 67th Regiment N.C. Troops on January 18, 1864.

GODLEY, JOSEPH U., Private

Transferred from 1st Company I, 10th Regiment N.C. State Troops (1st Regiment N.C. Artillery) April 16, 1863. Present or accounted for until transferred to Company A, 67th Regiment N.C. Troops on January 18, 1864.

GODLEY, N. H., Private

Enlisted in Craven County, April 7, 1863, for the war. Reported on October 31-December 31, 1863, muster roll as "deserted since December."

GUION, JOHN, Private

Transferred from the Field and Staff, 31st Regiment N.C. Troops, July 25, 1863. Transferred to the Field and Staff of this battalion upon appointment as Sergeant Major soon after he joined the company.

GWALTNEY, WILLIAM D., Private

Transferred from 1st Company I, 10th Regiment N.C. State Troops (1st Regiment N.C. Artillery) April 16, 1863. Present or accounted for until transferred to Company A, 67th Regiment N.C. Troops on January 18, 1864.

HARDISON, C. W., Private

Enlisted in Craven County, January 8, 1864, for the war. Present or accounted for until transferred to Company A, 67th Regiment N.C. Troops on January 18, 1864.

HEATH, A. L., Private

Captured at Tarboro on July 21, 1863, and paroled at Fort Monroe, Virginia, August 4, 1863.

HEATH, JOSEPH R., Private

Transferred from 1st Company I, 10th Regiment N.C. State Troops (1st Regiment N.C. Artillery) April 16, 1863. Present or accounted for until transferred to Company A, 67th Regiment N.C. Troops on January 18, 1864.

HILL, ALONZO, Musician

Transferred from 1st Company I, 10th Regiment N.C. State Troops (1st Regiment N.C. Artillery) April 16, 1863, as Private. Present or accounted for until transferred to Company A, 67th Regiment N.C. Troops on January 18, 1864.

HILL, AMARIAH E., Corporal

Transferred from 1st Company I, 10th Regiment N.C. State Troops (1st Regiment N.C. Artillery) April 16, 1863, as Private. Appointed Corporal prior to December, 1863. Present or accounted for until transferred to Company A, 67th Regiment N.C. Troops on January 18, 1864.

HILL, GEORGE, Private

Transferred from 1st Company I, 10th Regiment N.C. State Troops (1st Regiment N.C. Artillery) April 16, 1863. Present or accounted for until transferred to Company A, 67th Regiment N.C. Troops on January 18, 1864.

HILL, GEORGE W., Private

Transferred from 1st Company I, 10th Regiment N.C. State Troops (1st Regiment N.C. Artillery) April 16, 1863. Present or accounted for until transferred to Company A, 67th Regiment N.C. Troops on January 18, 1864.

HILL, HARVEY G., Private

Enlisted in Craven County, April 1, 1863, for the war. Present or accounted for until transferred to Company A, 67th Regiment N.C. Troops on January 18, 1864.

HILL, HILLIARD H., Private

Enlisted in Craven County, April 1, 1863, for the war. Present or accounted for until transferred to Company A, 67th Regiment N.C. Troops on January 18, 1864.

HILL, THOMAS, Private

Enlisted in Craven County, April 1, 1863, for the war. Captured at Washington on December 27-28, 1863, and confined at Point Lookout, Maryland. Absent in confinement when company became Company A, 67th Regiment N.C. Troops on January 18, 1864.

HILL, WILLIAM H., Private

Transferred from 1st Company I, 10th Regiment N.C. State Troops (1st Regiment N.C. Artillery) April 16, 1863. Captured at Tarboro on July 21, 1863, and paroled at Fort Monroe, Virginia, August 4, 1863. Present or accounted for until transferred to Company A, 67th Regiment N.C. Troops on January 18, 1864.

HOELL, FRANKLIN, Private

Enlisted in Craven County, April 1, 1863, for the war. Present or accounted for until transferred to Company A, 67th Regiment N.C. Troops on January 18, 1864.

IPOCK, FREDERICK G., Private

Transferred from 1st Company I, 10th Regiment N.C. State Troops (1st Regiment N.C. Artillery) April 16, 1863. Present or accounted for until transferred to Company A, 67th Regiment N.C. Troops on January 18, 1864.

IPOCK, JAMES, Private

Transferred from 1st Company I, 10th Regiment N.C. State Troops (1st Regiment N.C. Artillery) April 16, 1863.

IVES, WILLIAM HENRY, Corporal

Transferred from 1st Company I, 10th Regiment

N.C. State Troops (1st Regiment N.C. Artillery) April 16, 1863, as Private. Appointed Corporal prior to December 31, 1863. Present or accounted for until transferred to Company A, 67th Regiment N.C. Troops on January 18, 1864.

JACKSON, FURNEY, Private

Transferred from 1st Company I, 10th Regiment N.C. State Troops (1st Regiment N.C. Artillery) April 16, 1863.

JONES, CHARLES C., Private

Enlisted in Craven County, July 1, 1863, for the war. Present or accounted for until transferred to Company A, 67th Regiment N.C. Troops on January 18, 1864.

JONES, DAVID, Private

Transferred from 1st Company I, 10th Regiment N.C. State Troops (1st Regiment N.C. Artillery) April 16, 1863.

JONES, HENDERSON, Private

Enlisted in Craven County, February 1, 1863, for the war. Present or accounted for until transferred to Company A, 67th Regiment N.C. Troops on January 18, 1864.

JONES, LUTHER A., Private

Transferred from 1st Company I, 10th Regiment N.C. State Troops (1st Regiment N.C. Artillery) April 16, 1863.

JONES, WILLIAM H., Private

Transferred from 1st Company I, 10th Regiment N.C. State Troops (1st Regiment N.C. Artillery) April 16, 1863. Present or accounted for until transferred to Company A, 67th Regiment N.C. Troops on January 18, 1864.

JONES, WILLIAM P., Private

Transferred from 1st Company I, 10th Regiment N.C. State Troops (1st Regiment N.C. Artillery) April 16, 1863.

KINSALL, JOHN, Private

Transferred from 1st Company I, 10th Regiment N.C. State Troops (1st Regiment N.C. Artillery) April 16, 1863. Present or accounted for until transferred to Company A, 67th Regiment N.C. Troops on January 18, 1864.

KIRKMAN, LAFAYETTE, Private

Transferred from Company D of this battalion in December, 1863. Present or accounted for until transferred to Company A, 67th Regiment N.C. Troops on January 18, 1864.

LANCASTER, GEORGE F., Private

Transferred from 1st Company I, 10th Regiment N.C. State Troops (1st Regiment N.C. Artillery) April 16, 1863, as Private. Detailed as Ordnance Sergeant on the Field and Staff of this battalion soon after transfer. Absent on detail when the battalion was redesignated and served on the Field and Staff of the 67th Regiment N.C. Troops after January 18, 1864.

LANCASTER, JESSE, Private

Transferred from 1st Company I, 10th Regiment N.C. State Troops (1st Regiment N.C. Artillery) April 16, 1863. Present or accounted for until

transferred to Company A, 67th Regiment N.C. Troops on January 18, 1864.

LANCASTER, ROSCOE, Private

Transferred from 1st Company I, 10th Regiment N.C. State Troops (1st Regiment N.C. Artillery) April 16, 1863. Present or accounted for until transferred to Company A, 67th Regiment N.C. Troops on January 18, 1864.

LATHINGHOUSE, JOHN, Private

Transferred from 1st Company I, 10th Regiment N.C. State Troops (1st Regiment N.C. Artillery) April 16, 1863. Present or accounted for until transferred to Company A, 67th Regiment N.C. Troops on January 18, 1864.

LEWIS, JAMES T., Private

Transferred from 1st Company I, 10th Regiment N.C. State Troops (1st Regiment N.C. Artillery) April 16, 1863. Present or accounted for until transferred to Company A, 67th Regiment N.C. Troops on January 18, 1864.

LONG, BENJAMIN F., Private

Transferred from 1st Company I, 10th Regiment N.C. State Troops (1st Regiment N.C. Artillery) April 16, 1863. Detailed as orderly to Colonel Whitford soon after transfer. Absent on detail when the battalion was redesignated and remained on detail after the battalion became the 67th Regiment N.C. Troops on January 18, 1864.

McROY, ASA, Private

Transferred from 1st Company I, 10th Regiment N.C. State Troops (1st Regiment N.C. Artillery) April 16, 1863. Present or accounted for until transferred to Company A, 67th Regiment N.C. Troops on January 18, 1864.

MAY, TURNER J., Private

Transferred from 1st Company I, 10th Regiment N.C. State Troops (1st Regiment N.C. Artillery) April 16, 1863. Present or accounted for until transferred to Company A, 67th Regiment N.C. Troops on January 18, 1864.

MOORE, DANIEL P., Private

Transferred from 1st Company I, 10th Regiment N.C. State Troops (1st Regiment N.C. Artillery) April 16, 1863. Present or accounted for until transferred to Company A, 67th Regiment N.C. Troops on January 18, 1864.

MOORE, SAMUEL, Private

Transferred from 1st Company I, 10th Regiment N.C. State Troops (1st Regiment N.C. Artillery) April 16, 1863. Present or accounted for until transferred to Company A, 67th Regiment N.C. Troops on January 18, 1864.

MORRIS, HENRY J., Private

Transferred from 1st Company I, 10th Regiment N.C. State Troops (1st Regiment N.C. Artillery) April 16, 1863. Present or accounted for until transferred to Company A, 67th Regiment N.C. Troops on January 18, 1864.

MORRIS, RANSON, Private

Transferred from 1st Company I, 10th Regiment N.C. State Troops (1st Regiment N.C. Artillery)

April 16, 1863.

NELSON, ABNER, Private

Enlisted in Craven County, April 14, 1863, for the war. Present or accounted for until transferred to Company A, 67th Regiment N.C. Troops on January 18, 1864.

NORMAN, W. H. H., Private

Transferred from 1st Company I, 10th Regiment N.C. State Troops (1st Regiment N.C. Artillery) April 16, 1863.

OGLESBY, GEORGE T., Private

Transferred from 1st Company I, 10 Regiment N.C. State Troops (1st Regiment N.C. Artillery) April 16, 1863. Present or accounted for until transferred to Company A, 67th Regiment N.C. Troops on January 18, 1864.

PATE, WILLIAM A., Private

Transferred from 1st Company I, 10th Regiment N.C. State Troops (1st Regiment N.C. Artillery) April 16, 1863.

PATE, WILLIAM NORWOOD, Private

Enlisted in Craven County, June 7, 1863, for the war. Present or accounted for until transferred to Company A, 67th Regiment N.C Troops on January 18, 1864.

PITTMAN, JOSEPH C., Private

Enlisted in Craven County, November 1, 1863, for the war. Present or accounted for until transferred to Company A, 67th Regiment N.C. Troops on January 18, 1864.

POWELL, FURNIFOLD, Private

Transferred from 1st Company I, 10th Regiment N.C. State Troops (1st Regiment N.C. Artillery) April 16, 1863. Captured at Swift Creek, Craven County, July 18, 1863, and confined at Point Lookout, Maryland. Absent in confinement when transferred to Company A, 67th Regiment N.C. Troops on January 18, 1864.

POWERS, JAMES R., Private

Transferred from 1st Company I, 10th Regiment N.C. State Troops (1st Regiment N.C. Artillery) April 16, 1863. Reported on October 31-December 31, 1863, muster roll as "deserted since December."

PRITCHETT, ALEXANDER, Private

Transferred from 1st Company I, 10th Regiment N.C. State Troops (1st Regiment N.C. Artillery) April 16, 1863. Present or accounted for until transferred to Company A, 67th Regiment N.C. Troops on January 18, 1864.

ROACH, WILLIAM S., Private

Transferred from 1st Company I, 10th Regiment N.C. State Troops (1st Regiment N.C. Artillery) April 16, 1863. Present or accounted for until transferred to Company A, 67th Regiment N.C. Troops on January 18, 1864.

ROUSE, ALEXANDER, Sergeant

Transferred from 1st Company I, 10th Regiment N.C. State Troops (1st Regiment N.C. Artillery) April 16, 1863, as Private. Appointed Sergeant prior to December, 1863. Present or accounted for until transferred to Company A, 67th Regiment N.C. Troops on January 18, 1864.

SALTER, WILLIAM, Private

Enlisted in Craven County, January 1, 1864, for the war. Present or accounted for until transferred to Company A, 67th Regiment N.C. Troops on January 18, 1864.

STEVENSON, CHARLES, Private

Enlisted in Craven County, January 1, 1864, for the war. Present or accounted for until transferred to Company A, 67th Regiment N.C. Troops on January 18, 1864.

STILLY, MARSHALL, Private

Enlisted in Craven County, April 14, 1863, for the war. Present or accounted for until transferred to Company A, 67th Regiment N.C. Troops on January 18, 1864.

SWINDLE, JAMES, Private

Transferred from 1st Company I, 10th Regiment N.C. State Troops (1st Regiment N.C. Artillery) April 16, 1863.

TAYLOR, JAMES E., Private

Transferred from 1st Company I, 10th Regiment N.C. State Troops (1st Regiment N.C. Artillery) April 16, 1863. Reported on muster rolls as "prisoner of war, captured June 25, 1863." No further records.

TAYLOR, ROBERT, Private

Enlisted in Craven County, March 10, 1863, for the war. Present or accounted for until transferred to Company A, 67th Regiment N.C. Troops on January 18, 1864.

TINGLE, JAMES, Private

Transferred from 1st Company I, 10th Regiment N.C. State Troops (1st Regiment N.C. Artillery) April 16, 1863. Present or accounted for until transferred to Company A, 67th Regiment N.C. Troops on January 18, 1864.

TISDALE, GEORGE F., Private

Enlisted in Craven County, September 25, 1863, for the war. Present or accounted for until transferred to Company A, 67th Regiment N.C. Troops on January 18, 1864.

WARD, FRANKLIN J., Private

Transferred from 1st Company I, 10th Regiment N.C. State Troops (1st Regiment N.C. Artillery) April 16, 1863. Present or accounted for until transferred to Company A, 67th Regiment N.C. Troops on January 18, 1864.

WARD, JOHN, Private

Transferred from 1st Company I, 10th Regiment N.C. State Troops (1st Regiment N.C. Artillery) April 16, 1863. Present or accounted for until transferred to Company A, 67th Regiment N.C. Troops on January 18, 1864.

WARREN, ROBERSON R., Private

Transferred from 1st Company I, 10th Regiment N.C. State Troops (1st Regiment N.C. Artillery) April 16, 1863. Present or accounted for until transferred to Company A, 67th Regiment N.C.

Troops on January 18, 1864.

WAYNE, BRYANT C., Private

Transferred from 1st Company I, 10th Regiment N.C. State Troops (1st Regiment N.C. Artillery) April 16, 1863. Detailed as a teamster in the Quartermaster Department, Kinston, August 1, 1863. Absent on detail when transferred to Company A, 67th Regiment N.C. Troops on January 18, 1864.

WETHERINGTON, RUEL E., Private

Transferred from 1st Company I, 10th Regiment N.C. State Troops (1st Regiment N.C. Artillery) April 16, 1863. Present or accounted for until transferred to Company A, 67th Regiment N.C. Troops on January 18, 1864.

WETHERINGTON, SPICER E., Private

Transferred from 1st Company I, 10th Regiment N.C. State Troops (1st Regiment N.C. Artillery) April 16, 1863. Present or accounted for until transferred to Company A, 67th Regiment N.C. Troops on January 18, 1864.

WHITE, EDWARD F., Private

Transferred from 1st Company I, 10th Regiment N.C. State Troops (1st Regiment N.C. Artillery) April 16, 1863. Transferred to Company I of this battalion upon appointment as 2nd Lieutenant to rank from August 1, 1863.

WHITE, GEORGE W., Private

Transferred from 1st Company I, 10th Regiment N.C. State Troops (1st Regiment N.C. Artillery) April 16, 1863. Transferred to Company I of this battalion upon appointment as 2nd Lieutenant to rank from September 22, 1863.

WHITE, LEWIS H., Private

Transferred from 1st Company I, 10th Regiment N.C. State Troops (1st Regiment N.C. Artillery) April 16, 1863. Transferred to Company E of this battalion upon appointment as 1st Sergeant in May, 1863.

WHITFORD, ADDISON P., Sergeant

Transferred from 1st Company I, 10th Regiment N.C. State Troops (1st Regiment N.C. Artillery) April 16, 1863, as Musician. Appointed Sergeant prior to December, 1863. Present or accounted for until transferred to Company A, 67th Regiment N.C. Troops on January 18, 1864.

WHITFORD, STEPHEN E., Private

Previously served in 1st Company H, 40th Regiment N.C. Troops (3rd Regiment N.C. Artillery). Enlisted in this company in Craven County in 1863 and reported as present on the October 31-December 31, 1863, muster roll. Present or accounted for until transferred to Company A, 67th Regiment N.C. Troops on January 18, 1864.

WIGGINS, EDWARD, Private

Enlisted in Craven County, May 1, 1863, for the war. Detailed as a Musician through December, 1863, and appointed Musician in January, 1864. Present or accounted for until transferred to Company A, 67th Regiment N.C. Troops on January 18, 1864.

WIGGINS, JOSEPH, Private

Transferred from 1st Company I, 10th Regiment N.C. State Troops (1st Regiment N.C. Artillery) April 16, 1863. Present or accounted for until transferred to Company A, 67th Regiment N.C. Troops on January 18, 1864.

WILLIAMS, GEORGE H., Private

Transferred from 1st Company I, 10th Regiment N.C. State Troops (1st Regiment N.C. Artillery) April 16, 1863.

WILLIS, PETER, 1st Sergeant

Transferred from 1st Company I, 10th Regiment N.C. State Troops (1st Regiment N.C. Artillery) April 16, 1863, as Private. Appointed 1st Sergeant prior to December, 1863. Present or accounted for until transferred to Company A, 67th Regiment N.C. Troops on January 18, 1864.

WITHERINGTON, WILLIS, Private

Transferred from 1st Company I, 10th Regiment N.C. State Troops (1st Regiment N.C. Artillery) April 16, 1863. Present or accounted for until transferred to Company A, 67th Regiment N.C. Troops on January 18, 1864.

WOOD, CASPER W., Private

Enlisted in Craven County, January 8, 1864, for the war. Present or accounted for until transferred to Company A, 67th Regiment N.C. Troops on January 18, 1864.

WOODARD, TILMAN F., Private

Transferred from 1st Company I, 10th Regiment N.C. State Troops (1st Regiment N.C. Artillery) April 16, 1863. Present or accounted for until transferred to Company A, 67th Regiment N.C. Troops on January 18, 1864.

YEATES, GALE, Private

Transferred from 1st Company I, 10th Regiment N.C. State Troops (1st Regiment N.C. Artillery) April 16, 1863. Present or accounted for until transferred to Company A, 67th Regiment N.C. Troops on January 18, 1864.

COMPANY B

This company was organized when 1st Company I, 10th Regiment N.C. State Troops (1st Regiment N.C. Artillery) was divided on April 16, 1863. The old company ceased to exist on that date, and the new company became one of the original companies of this battalion. The history of the original company is reported in the history of 1st Company I, 10th Regiment N.C. State Troops (1st Regiment N.C. Artillery) and in that regiment's regimental history. Since this company was one of the original companies of the battalion, its history is recorded as a part of the battalion history. By Special Orders No. 8, paragraph 2, Adjutant General's Office, Raleigh, January 18, 1864, the battalion was redesignated the 67th Regiment N.C. Troops, and this company became Company B of the regiment.

The following roster of the company covers from the date of organization, April 16, 1863, through the date of redesignation, January 18, 1864. All events after that date are recorded in the roster of Company B, 67th Regiment N.C. Troops. The information contained in the following roster was compiled from company muster rolls for April, 1863, and January 1-18, 1864. Information from muster rolls of 1st Company I, 10th Regiment N.C. State Troops (1st Regiment N.C. Artillery) was also used. No muster rolls were found for the period May through December, 1863. Although there are no Roll of Honor records for this company, useful information was obtained from receipt rolls, hospital records, prisoner of war records, and other primary records, supplemented by state pension applications, United Daughters of the Confederacy records, and postwar rosters and histories.

OFFICERS

CAPTAIN

BARRINGTON, STEPHEN G.

Transferred from 1st Company I, 10th Regiment N.C. State Troops (1st Regiment N.C. Artillery) and appointed Captain to rank from March 28, 1863. Present or accounted for until transferred to Company B, 67th Regiment N.C. Troops on January 18, 1864.

LIEUTENANTS

ALDRIDGE, JOHN W., 3rd Lieutenant

Transferred from 1st Company I, 10th Regiment N.C. State Troops (1st Regiment N.C. Artillery) April 16, 1863, as Sergeant and promoted to 1st Sergeant on the same day. Appointed 3rd Lieutenant to rank from November 28, 1863. Present or accounted for until transferred to Company B, 67th Regiment N.C. Troops on January 18, 1864.

GASKINS, THOMAS H., 1st Lieutenant

Previously served in Company K, 31st Regiment N.C. Troops. Enlisted in Craven County, December 1, 1862, for the war. Appointed 1st Lieutenant to rank from March 28, 1863. Present or accounted for until transferred to Company B, 67th Regiment N.C. Troops on January 18, 1864.

HOOKER, NATHAN, 2nd Lieutenant

Transferred from 1st Company I, 10th Regiment N.C. State Troops (1st Regiment N.C. Artillery) and appointed 2nd Lieutenant to rank from March 28, 1863. Present or accounted for until transferred to Company B, 67th Regiment N.C. Troops on January 18, 1864.

MYERS, JOSEPH D., 2nd Lieutenant

Transferred from 1st Company I, 10th Regiment N.C. State Troops (1st Regiment N.C. Artillery) and appointed 2nd Lieutenant to rank from March 28, 1863. Transferred to Company K of this battalion upon appointment as Captain to rank from August 1, 1863.

NONCOMMISSIONED OFFICERS AND PRIVATES

ALEXANDER, SOLOMON M., Private

Transferred from 1st Company I, 10th Regiment N.C. State Troops (1st Regiment N.C. Artillery) April 16, 1863. Captured in Craven County on August 10, 1863, and confined at Point Lookout, Maryland. Absent in confinement when transferred to Company B, 67th Regiment N.C. Troops on January 18, 1864.

ANDREWS, LEVI J., Private

Transferred from 1st Company I, 10th Regiment N.C. State Troops (1st Regiment N.C. Artillery) April 16, 1863. Present or accounted for until transferred to Company B, 67th Regiment N.C. Troops on January 18, 1864.

ARNOLD, WILLIAM W., Private

Transferred from 1st Company I, 10th Regiment N.C. State Troops (1st Regiment N.C. Artillery) April 16, 1863. Present or accounted for until transferred to Company B, 67th Regiment N.C. Troops on January 18, 1864.

BARRINGTON, WILLIAM R., Private

Transferred from 1st Company I, 10th Regiment N.C. State Troops (1st Regiment N.C. Artillery) April 16, 1863. Present or accounted for through April, 1863.

BEACHAM, J. H., Private

Enlisted in Craven County, September 20, 1863, for the war. Present or accounted for until transferred to Company B, 67th Regiment N.C. Troops on January 18, 1864.

BRINSON, DAVID H., Private

Enlisted in Craven County, April 25, 1863, for the war. Present or accounted for until transferred to Company B, 67th Regiment N.C. Troops on January 18, 1864.

BRINSON, NATHANIEL G., Private

Transferred from Company D, 40th Regiment N.C. Troops (3rd Regiment N.C. Artillery) June 1, 1863. Present or accounted for until transferred to Company B, 67th Regiment N.C. Troops on January 18, 1864.

BRINSON, WILLIAM H., Private

Transferred from 1st Company I, 10th Regiment N.C. State Troops (1st Regiment N.C. Artillery) April 16, 1863. Present or accounted for until transferred to Company B, 67th Regiment N.C. Troops on January 18, 1864.

BURCH, HARDY K., Private

Transferred from 1st Company I, 10th Regiment N.C. State Troops (1st Regiment N.C. Artillery) April 16, 1863. Present or accounted for until transferred to Company B, 67th Regiment N.C. Troops on January 18, 1864.

CAHOON, NATHAN, Private

Transferred from 1st Company I, 10th Regiment N.C. State Troops (1st Regiment N.C. Artillery)

April 16, 1863. Present or accounted for until transferred to Company D, 40th Regiment N.C. Troops (3rd Regiment N.C. Artillery) November 17, 1863.

CARMADAY, JAMES M., Private

Transferred from 1st Company I, 10th Regiment N.C. State Troops (1st Regiment N.C. Artillery) April 16, 1863. Died of "typhoid pneumonia" on January 18, 1864.

CARRAWAY, WILLIAM W., Private

Enlisted in Pitt County, November 1, 1863, for the war. Transferred to Company K of this battalion prior to December 31, 1863.

CHARLOTTE, WILLIAM, Private

Enlisted in Craven County, September, 1863, for the war. Present or accounted for until transferred to Company B, 67th Regiment N.C. Troops on January 18, 1864.

CHARLOTTE, WILLIAM E., Sergeant

Transferred from 1st Company I, 10th Regiment N.C. State Troops (1st Regiment N.C. Artillery) April 16, 1863, and appointed Sergeant. Present or accounted for until transferred to Company B, 67th Regiment N.C. Troops on January 18, 1864.

CLEAVES, WILLIAM, Private

Enlisted in Craven County, May 10, 1863, for the war. Present or accounted for until transferred to Company B, 67th Regiment N.C. Troops on January 18, 1864.

COLE, CHARLES, Private

Transferred from 1st Company I, 10th Regiment N.C. State Troops (1st Regiment N.C. Artillery) April 16, 1863. Present or accounted for until transferred to Company B, 67th Regiment N.C. Troops on January 18, 1864.

CUTHRELL, BENJAMIN F., Private

Transferred from 1st Company I, 10th Regiment N.C. State Troops (1st Regiment N.C. Artillery) April 16, 1863. Present or accounted for until transferred to Company B, 67th Regiment N.C. Troops on January 18, 1864.

DAUGHETY, JOSEPH D., Private

Transferred from 1st Company I, 10th Regiment N.C. State Troops (1st Regiment N.C. Artillery) April 16, 1863. Present or accounted for until transferred to Company B, 67th Regiment N.C. Troops on January 18, 1864.

DIXON, CHARLES S., Sergeant

Transferred from 1st Company I, 10th Regiment N.C. State Troops (1st Regiment N.C. Artillery) April 16, 1863, as Sergeant. Present or accounted for until transferred to Company B, 67th Regiment N.C. Troops on January 18, 1864.

DIXON, HASTEN, Private

Transferred from 1st Company I, 10th Regiment N.C. State Troops (1st Regiment N.C. Artillery) April 16, 1863. Present or accounted for until transferred to Company B, 67th Regiment N.C. Troops on January 18, 1864.

DIXON, LEWIS, Sergeant

Transferred from 1st Company I, 10th Regiment N.C. State Troops (1st Regiment N.C. Artillery) April 16, 1863, and appointed Sergeant. Present or accounted for until transferred to Company B, 67th Regiment N.C. Troops on January 18, 1864.

EDWARDS, BENJAMIN F., Private

Transferred from 1st Company I, 10th Regiment N.C. State Troops (1st Regiment N.C. Artillery) April 16, 1863. Present or accounted for until transferred to Company B, 67th Regiment N.C. Troops on January 18, 1864.

EDWARDS, WILLIAM T., Private

Transferred from 1st Company I, 10th Regiment N.C. State Troops (1st Regiment N.C. Artillery) April 16, 1863. Present or accounted for through April, 1863.

GASKILL, TILGHMAN, Private

Enlisted in Craven County, September 1, 1863, for the war. Present or accounted for until transferred to Company B, 67th Regiment N.C. Troops on January 18, 1864.

GOODING, JACOB, Jr., Private

Enlisted in Craven County, May 27, 1863, for the war. Present or accounted for until transferred to Company B, 67th Regiment N.C. Troops on January 18, 1864.

GRIFFIN, JOSIAH, Private

Transferred from 1st Company I, 10th Regiment N.C. State Troops (1st Regiment N.C. Artillery) April 16, 1863. Present or accounted for until transferred to Company B, 67th Regiment N.C. Troops on January 18, 1864.

HAWKINS, FURNIFOLD, Private

Transferred from 1st Company I, 10th Regiment N.C. State Troops (1st Regiment N.C. Artillery) April 16, 1863. Present or accounted for through April, 1863.

HAWKINS, GEORGE O., Private

Transferred from 1st Company I, 10th Regiment N.C. State Troops (1st Regiment N.C. Artillery) April 16, 1863. Deserted on January 12, 1864, and was absent when transferred to Company B, 67th Regiment N.C. Troops on January 18, 1864.

HODGES, MAJOR J., Private

Enlisted in Craven County, April 10, 1863, for the war. Present or accounted for through April, 1863.

HOWARD, FRANKLIN, Private

Transferred from 1st Company I, 10th Regiment N.C. State Troops (1st Regiment N.C. Artillery) April 16, 1863. Present or accounted for until transferred to Company B, 67th Regiment N.C. Troops on January 18, 1864.

HUMPHREY, JOHN, Private

Transferred from 1st Company I, 10th Regiment N.C. State Troops (1st Regiment N.C. Artillery) April 16, 1863. Present or accounted for until transferred to Company B, 67th Regiment N.C. Troops on January 18, 1864.

IPOCK, WILLIAM, Private

Enlisted in Craven County, September 22, 1863, for the war. Present or accounted for until transferred to Company B, 67th Regiment N.C. Troops on January 18, 1864.

JONES, JOSIAH, Private

Transferred from 1st Company I, 10th Regiment N.C. State Troops (1st Regiment N.C. Artillery) April 16, 1863. Present or accounted for until transferred to Company B, 67th Regiment N.C. Troops on January 18, 1864.

JONES, SAMUEL, Private

Transferred from 1st Company I, 10th Regiment N.C. State Troops (1st Regiment N.C. Artillery) April 16, 1863. Present or accounted for until transferred to Company B, 67th Regiment N.C. Troops on January 18, 1864.

KEEL, BENJAMIN H., Private

Enlisted in Craven County, April 25, 1863, for the war. Present or accounted for until transferred to Company B, 67th Regiment N.C. Troops on January 18, 1864.

KEEL, GEORGE W., Private

Enlisted in Craven County, April 25, 1863, for the war. Present or accounted for until transferred to Company B, 67th Regiment N.C. Troops on January 18, 1864.

KILPATRICK, EDWARD A., Corporal

Transferred from 1st Company I, 10th Regiment N.C. State Troops (1st Regiment N.C. Artillery) April 16, 1863, as Corporal. Present or accounted for until transferred to Company B, 67th Regiment N.C. Troops on January 18, 1864.

KILPATRICK, JAMES C., Private

Transferred from 1st Company I, 10th Regiment N.C. State Troops (1st Regiment N.C. Artillery) April 16, 1863. Present or accounted for until transferred to Company B, 67th Regiment N.C. Troops on January 18, 1864.

KINEON, RICHARD M., Private

Enlisted in Craven County, May 1, 1863, for the war. Present or accounted for until transferred to Company B, 67th Regiment N.C. Troops on January 18, 1864.

LEWIS, BRYAN W., Private

Transferred from 1st Company I, 10th Regiment N.C. State Troops (1st Regiment N.C. Artillery) April 16, 1863. Present or accounted for until transferred to Company B, 67th Regiment N.C. Troops on January 18, 1864.

LEWIS, ELIAS H., Private

Enlisted in Craven County, February 1, 1863, for the war. Present or accounted for until transferred to Company B, 67th Regiment N.C. Troops on January 18, 1864.

McCOTTER, JOSEPH, Private

Transferred from 1st Company I, 10th Regiment N.C. State Troops (1st Regiment N.C. Artillery) April 16, 1863. Present or accounted for until

transferred to Company B, 67th Regiment N.C. Troops on January 18, 1864.

McINTOSH, FIRNEY, Private

Transferred from 1st Company I, 10th Regiment N.C. State Troops (1st Regiment N.C. Artillery) April 16, 1863. Present or accounted for until transferred to Company B, 67th Regiment N.C. Troops on January 18, 1864.

McINTOSH, HENRY, Private

Transferred from 1st Company I, 10th Regiment N.C. State Troops (1st Regiment N.C. Artillery) April 16, 1863. Present or accounted for until transferred to Company B, 67th Regiment N.C. Troops on January 18, 1864.

MALLISON, BENJAMIN K., Corporal

Transferred from 1st Company I, 10th Regiment N.C. State Troops (1st Regiment N.C. Artillery) April 16, 1863 as Corporal. Present or accounted for until transferred to Company B, 67th Regiment N.C. Troops on January 18, 1864.

MARTIN, JAMES, Private

Enlisted in Craven County, June 29, 1863, for the war. Present or accounted for until transferred to Company B, 67th Regiment N.C. Troops on January 18, 1864.

MARTIN, JAMES W., Private

Transferred from 1st Company I, 10th Regiment N.C. State Troops (1st Regiment N.C. Artillery) April 16, 1863. Present or accounted for until transferred to Company B, 67th Regiment N.C. Troops on January 18, 1864.

MARTIN, SAMUEL, Private

Transferred from 1st Company I, 10th Regiment N.C. State Troops (1st Regiment N.C. Artillery) April 16, 1863. Present or accounted for until transferred to Company B, 67th Regiment N.C. Troops on January 18, 1864.

MAY, THOMAS D., Private

Enlisted in Craven County, January 16, 1863, for the war. Transferred to Company K of this battalion on December 1, 1863.

MAYO, CYRUS J., Private

Transferred from 1st Company I, 10th Regiment N.C. State Troops (1st Regiment N.C. Artillery) April 16, 1863. Present or accounted for until transferred to Company B, 67th Regiment N.C. Troops on January 18, 1864.

MILLER, JAMES A., Private

Transferred from 1st Company I, 10th Regiment N.C. State Troops (1st Regiment N.C. Artillery) April 16, 1863. Present or accounted for until transferred to Company B, 67th Regiment N.C. Troops on January 18, 1864.

MILLER, JAPHET D., Private

Transferred from 1st Company I, 10th Regiment N.C. State Troops (1st Regiment N.C. Artillery) April 16, 1863. Present or accounted for until transferred to Company B, 67th Regiment N.C. Troops on January 18, 1864.

MILLER, JOHN R., Private

Transferred from Company D, 40th Regiment N.C. Troops (3rd Regiment N.C. Artillery) June 1, 1863. Present or accounted for until transferred to Company B, 67th Regiment N.C. Troops on January 18, 1864.

MILLS, WILLIAM H., Private

Transferred from 1st Company I, 10th Regiment N.C. State Troops (1st Regiment N.C. Artillery) April 16, 1863. Present or accounted for until transferred to Company B, 67th Regiment N.C. Troops on January 18, 1864.

MORRIS, BENJAMIN W., Private

Enlisted in Craven County, September 22, 1863, for the war. Present or accounted for until transferred to Company B, 67th Regiment N.C. Troops on January 18, 1864.

MORRIS, SAMUEL D., Private

Transferred from 1st Company I, 10th Regiment N.C. State Troops (1st Regiment N.C. Artillery) April 16, 1863. Present or accounted for until transferred to Company B, 67th Regiment N.C. Troops on January 18, 1864.

MORRIS, WILLIAM C., Private

Transferred from 1st Company I, 10th Regiment N.C. State Troops (1st Regiment N.C. Artillery) April 16, 1863. Present or accounted for until transferred to Company E, 4th Regiment N.C. State Troops on December 9, 1863.

MUMFORD, JAMES, Private

Enlisted in Craven County, June 29, 1863, for the war. Present or accounted for until transferred to Company B, 67th Regiment N.C. Troops on January 18, 1864.

MUSE, JAMES, Private

Transferred from 1st Company I, 10th Regiment N.C. State Troops (1st Regiment N.C. Artillery) April 16, 1863. Present or accounted for until transferred to Company D, 40th Regiment N.C. Troops (3rd Regiment N.C. Artillery) September-October, 1863.

OWENS, JAMES, Private

Transferred from 1st Company I, 10th Regiment N.C. State Troops (1st Regiment N.C. Artillery) April 16, 1863. Present or accounted for until transferred to Company B, 67th Regiment N.C. Troops on January 18, 1864.

OXLEY, AUGUSTUS W., Private

Transferred from 1st Company I, 10th Regiment N.C. State Troops (1st Regiment N.C. Artillery) April 16, 1863. Present or accounted for until transferred to Company B, 67th Regiment N.C. Troops on January 18, 1864.

OXLEY, C. C., Private

Enlisted in Craven County, June 1, 1863, for the war. Present or accounted for until transferred to Company B, 67th Regiment N.C. Troops on January 18, 1864.

OXLEY, C. McKINEY, Private

Enlisted in Craven County, June 1, 1863, for the

war. Present or accounted for until transferred to Company B, 67th Regiment N.C. Troops on January 18, 1864.

PAUL, EDGAR H., Private

Enlisted in Craven County, May 1, 1863, for the war. Present or accounted for until transferred to Company B, 67th Regiment N.C. Troops on January 18, 1864.

PAUL, STEPHEN, Private

Transferred from 1st Company I, 10th Regiment N.C. State Troops (1st Regiment N.C. Artillery) April 16, 1863. Present or accounted for until transferred to Company B, 67th Regiment N.C. Troops on January 18, 1864.

PEARCE, WILLIAM B., Private

Enlisted in Craven County, May 1, 1863, for the war. Present or accounted for until transferred to Company B, 67th Regiment N.C. Troops on January 18, 1864.

PIPKIN, L. G., Private

Enlisted in Craven County, June 1, 1863, for the war. Present or accounted for until transferred to Company B, 67th Regiment N.C. Troops on January 18, 1864.

PITTMAN, ALONZO J., Private

Transferred from 1st Company I, 10th Regiment N.C. State Troops (1st Regiment N.C. Artillery) April 16, 1863. Present or accounted for until transferred to Company B, 67th Regiment N.C. Troops on January 18, 1864.

POTTER, WILLIAM, Corporal

Transferred from 1st Company I, 10th Regiment N.C. State Troops (1st Regiment N.C. Artillery) April 16, 1863, and appointed Corporal. Present or accounted for until transferred to Company B, 67th Regiment N.C. Troops on January 18, 1864.

POWELL, GEORGE W., Private

Transferred from 1st Company I, 10th Regiment N.C. State Troops (1st Regiment N.C. Artillery) April 16, 1863. Present or accounted for until transferred to Company B, 67th Regiment N.C. Troops on January 18, 1864.

POWELL, HARDY, Private

Transferred from 1st Company I, 10th Regiment N.C. State Troops (1st Regiment N.C. Artillery) April 16, 1863. Present or accounted for until transferred to Company D, 40th Regiment N.C. Troops (3rd Regiment N.C. Artillery) June 1, 1863.

POWELL, HENRY D., Private

Transferred from 1st Company I, 10th Regiment N.C. State Troops (1st Regiment N.C. Artillery) April 16, 1863. Present or accounted for until transferred to Company D, 40th Regiment N.C. Troops (3rd Regiment N.C. Artillery) June 1, 1863.

POWERS, JOHN H., Corporal

Transferred from 1st Company I, 10th Regiment N.C. State Troops (1st Regiment N.C. Artillery) April 16, 1863, as Corporal. Present or accounted for until transferred to Company B, 67th Regiment N.C. Troops on January 18, 1864.

RHEM, JOHN W., Private

Transferred from 1st Company I, 10th Regiment N.C. State Troops (1st Regiment N.C. Artillery) April 16, 1863. Transferred to Company I of this battalion and appointed Corporal prior to December 31, 1863.

RICE, GIDEON B., 1st Sergeant

Transferred from 1st Company I, 10th Regiment N.C. State Troops (1st Regiment N.C. Artillery) April 16, 1863, as Private. Appointed 1st Sergeant prior to December 31, 1863. Present or accounted for until transferred to Company B, 67th Regiment N.C. Troops on January 18, 1864.

RICHARDSON, WILLIAM, Private

Enlisted in Pitt County, December 1, 1863, for the war. Transferred to Company K of this battalion prior to December 31, 1863.

RIGGS, JOHN D., Private

Transferred from 1st Company I, 10th Regiment N.C. State Troops (1st Regiment N.C. Artillery) April 16, 1863. Present or accounted for until transferred to Company B, 67th Regiment N.C. Troops on January 18, 1864.

ROUSE, JOHN W., Private

Transferred from 1st Company I, 10th Regiment N.C. State Troops (1st Regiment N.C. Artillery) April 16, 1863. Present or accounted for until transferred to Company B, 67th Regiment N.C. Troops on January 18, 1864.

ROWE, WILEY A., Private

Transferred from 1st Company I, 10th Regiment N.C. State Troops (1st Regiment N.C. Artillery) April 16, 1863. Reported as "taken prisoner June, 1863" and "not paroled."

SAWYER, JOHN, Private

Transferred from 1st Company I, 10th Regiment N.C. State Troops (1st Regiment N.C. Artillery) April 16, 1863. Present or accounted for until transferred to Company B, 67th Regiment N.C. Troops on January 18, 1864.

SMITH, DAVID C., Private

Transferred from 1st Company I, 10th Regiment N.C. State Troops (1st Regiment N.C. Artillery) April 16, 1863. Present or accounted for until transferred to Company B, 67th Regiment N.C. Troops on January 18, 1864.

SMITH, NOAH, Private

Transferred from 1st Company I, 10th Regiment N.C. State Troops (1st Regiment N.C. Artillery) April 16, 1863. Present or accounted for until transferred to Company B, 67th Regiment N.C. Troops on January 18, 1864.

SPAIN, REDMOND, Private

Enlisted in Craven County, January 16, 1863, for the war. Present or accounted for until transferred to Company K of this battalion in December, 1863.

SQUIRES, JOHN F., Private

Transferred from 1st Company I, 10th Regiment N.C. State Troops (1st Regiment N.C. Artillery) April 16, 1863. Present or accounted for until

transferred to Company D, 40th Regiment N.C. Troops (3rd Regiment N.C. Artillery) September-October, 1863.

STILLEY, ALEXANDER H., Private

Enlisted in Pitt County, November 1, 1863, for the war. Transferred to Company K of this battalion in December, 1863.

STILLEY, HENRY D., Private

Previously served in Company E, 4th Regiment N. C. State Troops. Transferred to this Company December 9, 1863. Present or accounted for until transferred to Company B, 67th Regiment N.C. Troops on January 18, 1864.

STILLEY, ROBERT F., Private

Transferred from 1st Company I, 10th Regiment N.C. State Troops (1st Regiment N.C. Artillery) April 16, 1863. Present or accounted for until transferred to Company B, 67th Regiment N.C. Troops on January 18, 1864.

STILLEY, STEPHEN W., Private

Enlisted in Craven County, May 4, 1863, for the war. Present or accounted for until transferred to Company B, 67th Regiment N.C. Troops on January 18, 1864.

STOCKS, B. F., Private

Enlisted in Craven County, June 8, 1863, for the war. Present or accounted for until transferred to Company B, 67th Regiment N.C. Troops on January 18, 1864.

SWINDLE, DAVID, Private

Enlisted in Craven County, April 20, 1863, for the war. Present or accounted for until transferred to Company B, 67th Regiment N.C. Troops on January 18, 1864.

TEER, WILLIAM, Private

Transferred from 1st Company I, 10th Regiment N.C. State Troops (1st Regiment N.C. Artillery) April 16, 1863. Present or accounted for through April, 1863.

THOMPSON, JAMES, Private

Enlisted in Craven County, September 15, 1863, for the war. Present or accounted for until transferred to Company B, 67th Regiment N.C. Troops on January 18, 1864.

TINGLE, ANDREW J., Private

Transferred from 1st Company I, 10th Regiment N.C. State Troops (1st Regiment N.C. Artillery) April 16, 1863. Present or accounted for until transferred to Company B, 67th Regiment N.C. Troops on January 18, 1864.

WEEKS, SAMUEL R., Private

Enlisted in Craven County, April 6, 1863, for the war. Present or accounted for until transferred to Company B, 67th Regiment N.C. Troops on January 18, 1864.

WEST, ANSON C., Private

Transferred from 1st Company I, 10th Regiment N.C. State Troops (1st Regiment N.C. Artillery) April 16, 1863. Present or accounted for until transferred to Company B, 67th Regiment N.C. Troops on January 18, 1864.

WEST, TURRENCE L., Sergeant

Transferred from 1st Company I, 10th Regiment N.C. State Troops (1st Regiment N.C. Artillery) April 16, 1863, and appointed Sergeant. Present or accounted for until transferred to Company B, 67th Regiment N.C. Troops on January 18, 1864.

WETHERINGTON, RUEL, Private

Enlisted in Craven County, April 1, 1863, for the war. Present or accounted for until he "deserted to the enemy January 12, 1864." Absent when transferred to Company B, 67th Regiment N.C. Troops on January 18, 1864.

WHITE, EDWARD J., Private

Transferred from 1st Company I, 10th Regiment N.C. State Troops (1st Regiment N.C. Artillery) April 16, 1863. Present or accounted for until transferred to Company B, 67th Regiment N.C. Troops on January 18, 1864.

WHITEHURST, HENRY C., Private

Transferred from 1st Company I, 10th Regiment N.C. State Troops (1st Regiment N.C. Artillery) April 16, 1863. Present or accounted for until transferred to Company B, 67th Regiment N.C. Troops on January 18, 1864.

WILLIAMS, CHARLES, Private

Enlisted in Craven County, April 1, 1863, for the war. Present or accounted for until transferred to Company B, 67th Regiment N.C. Troops on January 18, 1864.

WINN, STARKEY, Private

Transferred from 1st Company I, 10th Regiment N.C. State Troops (1st Regiment N.C. Artillery) April 16, 1863. Present or accounted for until transferred to Company B, 67th Regiment N.C. Troops on January 18, 1864.

WISE, SMITH J., Private

Transferred from 1st Company I, 10th Regiment N.C. State Troops (1st Regiment N.C. Artillery) April 16, 1863. Present or accounted for until transferred to Company B, 67th Regiment N.C. Troops on January 18, 1864.

WOLFENDEN, JOHN J., Sergeant

Enlisted in Craven County, April 1, 1863, for the war. Appointed Sergeant on April 16, 1863. Present or accounted for until transferred to Company K of this battalion on November 1, 1863.

COMPANY C

This company was organized by the enlistment of men in Greene and Lenoir counties, beginning on October 6, 1862. The company officers were commissioned as of January 6, 1863, and the company was accepted into state service after that date. The exact date the company was attached to the battalion is not known, but it appears to have been in April-May, 1863. Nothing was found relative to the company's service prior to joining the battalion. It can only be assumed that the company served on outpost and scouting duty. After joining the battalion the company functioned as a part of the battalion, and its history is recorded as a part of the battalion history. By Special Orders No. 8, paragraph 2, Adjutant General's Office, Raleigh, January 18, 1864, the battalion was redesignated the 67th Regiment N.C. Troops, and this company became Company C of the regiment.

The following roster of the company covers from the date of enlistment through the date of redesignation. All events after that date are recorded in the roster of Company C, 67th Regiment N.C. Troops. The information contained in the following roster was compiled principally from company muster rolls which covered from November 1, 1863, through the date of redesignation, January 18, 1864. No muster rolls were found for the period prior to November 1, 1863. Although there are no Roll of Honor records for this company, useful information was obtained from receipt rolls, hospital records, prisoner of war records, and other primary records, supplemented by state pension applications, United Daughters of the Confederacy records, and postwar rosters and histories.

OFFICERS

CAPTAIN

EDWARDS, DANIEL W.

Appointed Captain to rank from January 6, 1863. Reported as "absent without leave" on October 31-December 31, 1863, muster roll. Transferred to Company C, 67th Regiment N.C. Troops on January 18, 1864.

LIEUTENANTS

EDWARDS, THEOPHILUS, 1st Lieutenant

Appointed 1st Lieutenant to rank from January 6, 1863. Present or accounted for until transferred to Company C, 67th Regiment N.C. Troops on January 18, 1864.

PATE, OWEN J., 3rd Lieutenant

Transferred from Company A, 3rd Regiment N.C. State Troops upon appointment as 3rd Lieutenant to rank from January 6, 1863. Present or accounted for until transferred to Company C, 67th Regiment N.C. Troops on January 18, 1864.

PATRICK, JOHN, 2nd Lieutenant

Transferred from Company A, 3rd Regiment N.C. State Troops upon appointment as 2nd Lieutenant to rank from January 6, 1863. Present or accounted for until transferred to Company C, 67th Regiment N.C. Troops on January 18, 1864.

NONCOMMISSIONED OFFICERS AND PRIVATES

BARFIELD, MILLS T., Private

Enlisted in Greene County, December 20, 1862. for the war. Present or accounted for until transferred to Company C, 67th Regiment N.C. Troops on January 18, 1864.

BARTLET, JESSE, Private

Enlisted in Greene County, November 2, 1862, for the war. Present or accounted for until transferred to Company C, 67th Regiment N.C. Troops on January 18, 1864.

BOWDEN, B. B., Private

Enlisted in Pitt County, May 15, 1863, for the war. Captured at Tarboro on July 21, 1863, and paroled at Fort Monroe, Virginia, August 4, 1863. Present or accounted for until transferred to Company C, 67th Regiment N.C. Troops on January 18, 1864.

BOWINS, CHARLES B., Private

Enlisted in Greene County, December 20, 1862, for the war. Present or accounted for until transferred to Company C, 67th Regiment N.C. Troops on January 18, 1864.

BRAND, NATHAN, Private

Enlisted in Greene County, August 10, 1863, for the war. Present or accounted for until transferred to Company C, 67th Regiment N.C. Troops on January 18, 1864.

BRAXTON, J., Private

Enlisted in Greene County, June 17, 1863, for the war. Present or accounted for until transferred to Company C, 67th Regiment N.C. Troops on January 18, 1864.

BRITT, JOHN G., Private

Enlisted in Greene County, May 15, 1863, for the war. Present or accounted for until transferred to Company C, 67th Regiment N.C. Troops on January 18, 1864.

BRUTON, SIMON, Private

Enlisted in Greene County, June 12, 1863, for the war. Present or accounted for until transferred to Company C, 67th Regiment N.C. Troops on January 18, 1864.

BUTTS, HAYWOOD H., Private

Enlisted in Greene County, January 26, 1863, for the war. Present or accounted for until transferred to Company C, 67th Regiment N.C. Troops on January 18, 1864.

BUTTS, JOSEPH J., Private

Enlisted in Greene County, December 20, 1863, for the war. Present or accounted for until transferred to Company C, 67th Regiment N.C. Troops on January 18, 1864.

CARR, JAMES S., 1st Sergeant

Enlisted in Lenoir County, December 20, 1862, for the war. Present or accounted for until transferred to Company C, 67th Regiment N.C. Troops on January 18, 1864.

CARTER, JOHN H., Private

Enlisted in Greene County, June 12, 1863, for the war. Present or accounted for until transferred to Company C, 67th Regiment N.C. Troops on January 18, 1864.

COWARD, EDWARD R., Private

Enlisted in Pitt County, November 1, 1863, for the war. Transferred to Company K of this battalion prior to December, 1863.

DAIL, ELBERT, Private

Enlisted in Greene County, August 15, 1863, for the war. Present or accounted for until transferred to Company C, 67th Regiment N.C. Troops on January 18, 1864.

DAIL, T. T., Private

Enlisted in Greene County, July 23, 1863, for the war. Present or accounted for until transferred to Company C, 67th Regiment N.C. Troops on January 18, 1864.

DIXON, JOSIAH, Sergeant

Enlisted in Greene County, December 20, 1862, for the war. Appointed Sergeant when the company was organized. Present or accounted for until transferred to Company C, 67th Regiment N.C. Troops on January 18, 1864.

EDWARDS, JOHN, Private

Enlisted in Greene County, January 16, 1863, for the war. Present or accounted for until transferred to Company C, 67th Regiment N.C. Troops on January 18, 1864.

EDWARDS, WILLIAM F., Private

Enlisted in Greene County, August 15, 1863, for the war. Present or accounted for until transferred to Company C, 67th Regiment N.C. Troops on January 18, 1864.

FAULKNER, REDDING, Private

Enlisted in Lenoir County, October 10, 1862, for the war. Present or accounted for until transferred to Company C, 67th Regiment N.C. Troops on January 18, 1864.

FIELDS, WILLIAM A., Private

Enlisted in the company prior to May 13, 1863, for the war. Discharged on May 13, 1863, when he provided Arthur Rodgers as his substitute.

FORREST, LEMUEL, Private

Enlisted in Greene County, October 10, 1862, for the war. Present or accounted for until transferred to Company C, 67th Regiment N.C. Troops on January 18, 1864.

GOFF, BENJAMIN, Private

Enlisted in Greene County, December 20, 1862, for the war. Present or accounted for until transferred to Company C, 67th Regiment N.C. Troops on January 18, 1864.

GRANT, LEWIS, Private

Enlisted in Greene County, January 15, 1863, for the war. Present or accounted for until transferred to Company C, 67th Regiment N.C. Troops on January 18, 1864.

GRIMSLEY, JOHN E., Private

Enlisted in Greene County, January 16, 1863, for the war. Present or accounted for until transferred to Company C, 67th Regiment N.C. Troops on January 18, 1864.

GRIZZARD, JOHN, Private

Enlisted in Greene County, January 29, 1863, for the war. Present or accounted for until transferred to Company C, 67th Regiment N.C. Troops on

January 18, 1864.

HARDY, ALLEN M., Corporal

Enlisted in Greene County, December 20, 1862, for the war. Appointed Corporal soon after the company was organized. Present or accounted for until transferred to Company C, 67th Regiment N.C. Troops on January 18, 1864.

HARDY, EDWIN, Sergeant

Enlisted in Greene County, July 1, 1863, for the war. Appointed Sergeant prior to December, 1863. Present or accounted for until transferred to Company C, 67th Regiment N.C. Troops on January 18, 1864.

HARDY, FRANCIS M., Private

Enlisted in Greene County, November 1, 1863, for the war. Present or accounted for until transferred to Company C, 67th Regiment N.C. Troops on January 18, 1864.

HARDY, WHITMILL, Private

Enlisted in Greene County, January 16, 1863, for the war. Present or accounted for until transferred to Company C, 67th Regiment N.C. Troops on January 18, 1864.

HARREL, N., Sergeant

Enlisted in Greene County, December 20, 1862, for the war. Appointed Sergeant soon after the company was organized. Present or accounted for through December, 1863.

HART, BARRAM, Corporal

Enlisted in Greene County, December 20, 1862, for the war. Appointed Corporal after the company was organized. Present or accounted for through December, 1863, when he was reported as "absent with leave wounded." Transferred to Company C, 67th Regiment N.C. Troops on January 18, 1864.

HART, J., Private

Enlisted in Greene County, August 15, 1863, for the war. Present or accounted for until transferred to Company C, 67th Regiment N.C. Troops on January 18, 1864.

HEATH, RICHARD R., Private

Enlisted in Greene County, October 5, 1862, for the war. Present or accounted for until transferred to Company C, 67th Regiment N.C. Troops on January 18, 1864.

HEATH, WILLIAM R., Private

Enlisted in Greene County, August 1, 1863, for the war. Present or accounted for until transferred to Company C, 67th Regiment N.C. Troops on January 18, 1864.

HINSON, JAMES, Private

Enlisted in Greene County, December 15, 1863, for the war. Present or accounted for until transferred to Company C, 67th Regiment N.C. Troops on January 18, 1864.

HOOKER, W. B., Private

Transferred from Company K of this battalion on January 1, 1864. Present or accounted for until transferred to Company C, 67th Regiment N.C.

Troops on January 18, 1864.

HOWELL, JAMES, Private

Enlisted in Greene County, January 15, 1863, for the war. Present or accounted for until transferred to Company C, 67th Regiment N.C. Troops on January 18, 1864.

JONES, BECTON B., Private

Enlisted in Lenoir County, November 15, 1862, for the war. Present or accounted for until transferred to Company C, 67th Regiment N.C. Troops on January 18, 1864.

JONES, ISHAM, Private

Enlisted in Lenoir County, December 10, 1862, for the war. Present or accounted for until transferred to Company C, 67th Regiment N.C. Troops on January 18, 1864.

JONES, JAMES K., Private

Enlisted in Pitt County, December 1, 1863, for the war. Transferred to Company K of this battalion prior to December 31, 1863.

JONES, WILEY, Private

Enlisted in Greene County, July 22, 1863, for the war. Present or accounted for until transferred to Company C, 67th Regiment N.C. Troops on January 18, 1864.

LANE, JOHN, Private

Enlisted in Greene County, January 15, 1863, for the war. Present or accounted for until transferred to Company C, 67th Regiment N.C. Troops on January 18, 1864.

LASSITTER, L. G., Private

Enlisted in Greene County, January 1, 1864, for the war. Present or accounted for until transferred to Company C, 67th Regiment N.C. Troops on January 18, 1864.

LASSITTER, WILLIAM A., Private

Enlisted in Lenoir County, January 17, 1863, for the war. Present or accounted for until transferred to Company C, 67th Regiment N.C. Troops on January 18, 1864.

LASSITTER, WILLIAM B., Private

Enlisted in Greene County, November 15, 1862, for the war. Present or accounted for until transferred to Company C, 67th Regiment N.C. Troops on January 18, 1864.

LEGGET, JOSEPH, Private

Enlisted in Greene County, December 15, 1862, for the war. Present or accounted for until transferred to Company C, 67th Regiment N.C. Troops on January 18, 1864.

LETCHWORTH, R., Private

Enlisted in Greene County, December 20, 1862, for the war. Present or accounted for until transferred to Company C, 67th Regiment N.C. Troops on January 18, 1864.

LYONS, WILLIAM E., Private

Enlisted in Greene County, January 1, 1864, for the war. Present or accounted for until transferred to Company C, 67th Regiment N.C. Troops on January 18, 1864.

MOORE, BENJAMIN, Private

Enlisted in Greene County, April 30, 1863, for the war. Present or accounted for until transferred to Company C, 67th Regiment N.C. Troops on January 18, 1864.

MURPHY, J. L., Private

Enlisted in Greene County, June 11, 1863, for the war. Present or accounted for until transferred to Company C, 67th Regiment N.C. Troops on January 18, 1864.

NELSON, JESSE, Private

Enlisted in Greene County, August 10, 1863, for the war. Present or accounted for until transferred to Company C, 67th Regiment N.C. Troops on January 18, 1864.

ORMAND, J. J., Private

Enlisted in Greene County, July 23, 1863, for the war. Present or accounted for through December, 1863.

ORMAND, JOHN J., Private

Enlisted in Greene County, June 12, 1863, for the war. Present or accounted for until transferred to Company C, 67th Regiment N.C. Troops on January 18, 1864.

PARKER, ALFRED F., Private

Enlisted in Greene County, March 1, 1863, for the war. Present or accounted for until transferred to Company C, 67th Regiment N.C. Troops on January 18, 1864.

PARKERSON, CHARLES E., Private

Enlisted in Greene County, January 16, 1863, for the war. Present or accounted for until transferred to Company C, 67th Regiment N.C. Troops on January 18, 1864.

PATE, ROBERT A., Private

Enlisted in Greene County, January, 1863, for the war. Present or accounted for until transferred to Company K of this battalion on December 1, 1863.

PHILLIPS, THOMAS, Private

Enlisted in Lenoir County, October 10, 1862, for the war. Present or accounted for until transferred to Company C, 67th Regiment N.C. Troops on January 18, 1864.

POTTER, NEWET S., Private

Enlisted in Greene County, June 12, 1863, for the war. Captured at Tarboro on July 21, 1863, and paroled at Fort Monroe, Virginia, August 4, 1863. Present or accounted for until transferred to Company C, 67th Regiment N.C. Troops on January 18, 1864.

PRICE, WILLIAM I., Private

Enlisted in Greene County, February 1, 1863, for the war. Captured at Tarboro on July 21, 1863, and paroled at Fort Monroe, Virginia, August 4, 1863. Present or accounted for until transferred to Company C, 67th Regiment N.C. Troops on January 18, 1864.

PRIDGEN, GEORGE W., Private

Enlisted in Duplin County, March 25, 1863, for the war. Present or accounted for until transferred to Company C, 67th Regiment N.C. Troops on January 18, 1864.

PRIDGEN, JESSE C., Sergeant

Enlisted in Greene County, December 20, 1862, for the war. Appointed Sergeant after the company was organized. Present or accounted for until transferred to Company C, 67th Regiment N.C. Troops on January 18, 1864.

PRIDGEN, LEONIDAS H., Private

Enlisted in Duplin County, February 15, 1863, for the war. Present or accounted for until transferred to Company C, 67th Regiment N.C. Troops on January 18, 1864.

RODGERS, ARTHUR, Private

Enlisted on May 13, 1863, for the war as a substitute for William A. Fields. Ordered discharged on July 17, 1863, by reason of an order forbidding the acceptance of substitutes into Partisan Ranger organizations.

RODGERS, H. B., Private

Enlisted in Greene County, December 15, 1862, for the war. Present or accounted for until transferred to Company C, 67th Regiment N.C. Troops on January 18, 1864.

ROSEBERRY, JAMES, Private

Enlisted in Greene County, June 17, 1863, for the war. Present or accounted for until transferred to Company C, 67th Regiment N.C. Troops on January 18, 1864.

SAWLS, HENRY, Private

Enlisted in Greene County, July 20, 1863, for the war. Present or accounted for until transferred to Company C, 67th Regiment N.C. Troops on January 18, 1864.

SHIRLEY, HENRY, Private

Enlisted in Greene County, November 15, 1862, for the war. Captured at Tarboro on July 21, 1863, and paroled at Fort Monroe, Virginia, August 4, 1863. Present or accounted for until transferred to Company C, 67th Regiment N.C. Troops on January 18, 1864.

SMITH, JAMES S., Private

Enlisted in Greene County, June 12, 1863, for the war. Present or accounted for until transferred to Company C, 67th Regiment N.C. Troops on January 18, 1864.

SPEIGHT, HENRY G., Private

Enlisted in Greene County, December 20, 1862, for the war. Present or accounted for until transferred to Company C, 67th Regiment N.C. Troops on January 18, 1864.

SPEIGHT, PELL B., Private

Enlisted in Greene County, June 12, 1863, for the war. Present or accounted for until transferred to Company C, 67th Regiment N.C. Troops on January 18, 1864.

STEPP, J., Private

Enlisted in Greene County, February 15, 1863, for the war. Reported as "deserted" on the October 31-December 31, 1863, muster roll.

STILLEY, HIRAM E., Private

Enlisted in Beaufort County, April 5, 1863, for the war. Present or accounted for until transferred to Company C, 67th Regiment N.C. Troops on January 18, 1864.

SUGGS, PATRICK, Private

Resided in Greene County where he enlisted June 12, 1863, for the war. Present or accounted for until transferred to Company C, 67th Regiment N.C. Troops on January 18, 1864.

TAYLOR, F., Private

Enlisted in Beaufort County, August 1, 1863, for the war. Reported as "deserted" on the October 31-December 31, 1863, muster roll.

THORN, THOMAS, Corporal

Enlisted in Greene County, December 15, 1862, for the war. Appointed Corporal after the company was organized. Captured at Tarboro on July 21, 1863, and paroled at Fort Monroe, Virginia, August 4, 1863. Present or accounted for until transferred to Company C, 67th Regiment N.C. Troops on January 18, 1864.

TYSON, WILLIAM, Private

Enlisted in Greene County, May 5, 1863, for the war. Present or accounted for until transferred to Company C, 67th Regiment N.C. Troops on January 18, 1864.

WALL, ROBERT D., Private

Enlisted in Beaufort County, August 1, 1863, for the war. Present or accounted for until transferred to Company C, 67th Regiment N.C. Troops on January 18, 1864.

WALSTON, LEVI, Private

Enlisted in Greene County, December 20, 1862, for the war. Present or accounted for until transferred to Company C, 67th Regiment N.C. Troops on January 18, 1864.

WALSTON, PHILLIP, Private

Enlisted in Greene County, June 5, 1863, for the war. Present or accounted for until transferred to Company C, 67th Regiment N.C. Troops on January 18, 1864.

WHITLEY, WILLIAM, Private

Enlisted in Greene County, June 12, 1863, for the war. Present or accounted for until transferred to Company C, 67th Regiment N.C. Troops on January 18, 1864.

WILLIAMS, WILLIAM F., Corporal

Enlisted in Greene County, October 4, 1862, for the war. Appointed Corporal after the company was organized. Present or accounted for until transferred to Company C, 67th Regiment N.C. Troops on January 18, 1864.

WOOTEN, JAMES G., Musician

Enlisted in Greene County, December 15, 1862, for the war. Appointed Musician after the company was organized. Present or accounted for until transferred to Company C, 67th Regiment N.C. Troops on January 18, 1864.

COMPANY D

This company began organizing in Wayne County in January, 1863. In February, 1863, recruits were added from Pitt and Lenoir counties, and the company commander was appointed to rank from February 21, 1863. After that date the company was accepted into state service. The exact date the company was attached to the battalion is not known but appears to have been in April-May, 1863. No records were found relative to the company's service prior to joining the battalion. It can only be assumed that the company served on outpost and scouting duty. After joining the battalion the company functioned as a part of the battalion, and its history is recorded as a part of the battalion history. By Special Orders No. 8, paragraph 2, Adjutant General's Office, Raleigh, January 18, 1864, the battalion was redesignated the 67th Regiment N. C. Troops, and this company became Company D of the regiment.

The following roster of the company covers from the date of enlistment through the date of redesignation. All events after that date are recorded in the roster of Company D, 67th Regiment N.C. Troops. The information contained in the following roster was compiled principally from company muster rolls which covered from November 1, 1863, through the date of redesignation, January 18, 1864. No muster rolls were found for the period prior to November 1, 1863. Although there are no Roll of Honor records for this company, useful information was obtained from receipt rolls, hospital records, prisoner of war records, and other primary records, supplemented by state pension applications, United Daughters of the Confederacy records, and postwar rosters and histories.

OFFICERS

CAPTAIN

COGDELL, DANIEL A.

Appointed Captain on February 21, 1863, to rank from February 25, 1863. Present or accounted for until transferred to Company D, 67th Regiment N. C. Troops on January 18, 1864.

LIEUTENANTS

BROTHERS, JOSEPH WARREN, 1st Lieutenant

Transferred from 1st Company I, 10th Regiment N. C. State Troops (1st Regiment N. C. Artillery) upon appointment as 1st Lieutenant to rank from February 21, 1863. Present or accounted for until transferred to Company D, 67th Regiment N. C. Troops on January 18, 1864.

COGDELL, DAVID, 3rd Lieutenant

Appointed 3rd Lieutenant to rank from December 15, 1863. Present or accounted for until transferred to Company D, 67th Regiment N. C. Troops on January 18, 1864.

LANE, WILLIAM P., 2nd Lieutenant

Appointed 2nd Lieutenant on March 10, 1863, to rank from February 21, 1863. Present or accounted for until transferred to Company D, 67th Regiment N. C. Troops on January 18, 1864.

SCHENCK, SAMUEL F., 3rd Lieutenant

Transferred from Company G, 10th Regiment N. C. State Troops (1st Regiment N. C. Artillery) upon appointment as 3rd Lieutenant to rank from February 21, 1863. Present or accounted for until transferred to the Field and Staff of this battalion upon appointment as Adjutant, November 30, 1863, to rank from June 15, 1863.

NONCOMMISSIONED OFFICERS AND PRIVATES

ABBOTT, R. M., Private

Enlisted at Coward's Bridge, Lenoir-Pitt counties, September 9, 1863, for the war. Present or accounted for until transferred to Company D, 67th Regiment N. C. Troops on January 18, 1864.

ADAMS, LEWIS, Musician

Enlisted in Pitt County, February 1, 1863, for the war. Present or accounted for until transferred to Company D, 67th Regiment N. C. troops on January 18, 1864.

ALDRIDGE, T. M., Private

Enlisted in Lenoir County, January 20, 1863, for the war. Present or accounted for until transferred to Company D, 67th Regiment N. C. Troops on January 18, 1864.

ALLEN, ICHABOD, Private

Enlisted in Pitt County, August 9, 1863, for the war. Present or accounted for until transferred to Company D, 67th Regiment N. C. Troops on January 18, 1864.

ALLEN, J. R., Private

Enlisted in Pitt County, January 15, 1863, for the war. Present or accounted for until transferred to Company D, 67th Regiment N. C. Troops on January 18, 1864.

ALLEN, ZACHARIAH, Private

Enlisted in Pitt County, January 15, 1863, for the war. Present or accounted for until transferred to Company D, 67th Regiment N. C. Troops on January 18, 1864.

AYCOCK, ELIAS, Private

Resided in Wayne County and enlisted in Wake County, July 15, 1862, for the war. Present or accounted for until transferred to Company D, 67th Regiment N. C. Troops on January 18, 1864.

BARFIELD, BRYAN, Private

Enlisted in Wayne County, February 3, 1863, for the war. Present or accounted for until transferred to Company D, 67th Regiment N. C. Troops on January 18, 1864.

BARFIELD, MICHAEL, Private

Enlisted in Wayne County, February 3, 1863, for

the war. Present or accounted for until transferred to Company D, 67th Regiment N. C. Troops on January 18, 1864.

BARWICK, ISAAC, Private

Enlisted in Lenoir County, January 20, 1863, for the war. Present or accounted for until transferred to Company D, 67th Regiment N. C. Troops on January 18, 1864.

BASS, AUGUSTUS, Private

Resided in Wayne County where he enlisted, September 24, 1862, for the war. Present or accounted for until transferred to Company D, 67th Regiment N. C. Troops on January 18, 1864.

BASS, JOHN, Private

Enlisted prior to August 31, 1863, for the war. Transferred to Company A, 66th Regiment N.C. Troops on September 11, 1863.

BELL, GEORGE, Corporal

Enlisted in Lenoir County, June 9, 1863, for the war. Appointed Corporal prior to December 31, 1863. Present or accounted for until transferred to Company D, 67th Regiment N. C. Troops on January 18, 1864.

BELL, JOSIAH, Private

Enlisted at Coward's Bridge, Lenoir-Pitt counties, June 18, 1863, for the war. Present or accounted for until transferred to Company D, 67th Regiment N. C. Troops on January 18, 1864.

BLOW, G. W., Private

Enlisted in Wayne County, October 2, 1862, for the war. Present or accounted for until transferred to Company D, 67th Regiment N.C. Troops on January 18, 1864.

BLOW, RICHARD, Private

Enlisted in Lenoir County, January 4, 1864, for the war. Present or accounted for until transferred to Company D, 67th Regiment N. C. Troops on January 18, 1864.

BOWDEN, JAMES B., Private

Enlisted in Wayne County, September 27, 1862, for the war. Present or accounted for until transferred to Company D, 67th Regiment N. C. Troops on January 18, 1864.

BRADSHAW, JEFFERSON, Private

Enlisted in Wayne County, September 22, 1862, for the war. Present or accounted for until transferred to Company D, 67th Regiment N. C. Troops on January 18, 1864.

BRADSHAW, WILLIAM, Private

Enlisted in Pitt County, September 12, 1863, for the war. Present or accounted for until transferred to Company D, 67th Regiment N.C. Troops on January 18, 1864.

BRITT, JAMES, Private

Enlisted in Wayne County, October 24, 1862, for the war. Present or accounted for until transferred to Company D, 67th Regiment N. C. Troops on January 18, 1864.

BROOKS, WILLIAM F., Private

Enlisted in Pitt County, July 18, 1863, for the war.

Present or accounted for until transferred to Company D, 67th Regiment N. C. Troops on January 18, 1864.

BROWN, G. W., Private

Enlisted in Wayne County, June 20, 1863, for the war. Present or accounted for until transferred to Company D, 67th Regiment N. C. Troops on January 18, 1864.

BUNN, J. H., Private

Enlisted in Lenoir County, February 21, 1863, for the war. Present or accounted for until transferred to Company D, 67th Regiment N. C. Troops on January 18, 1864.

CANNON, THOMAS, Private

Enlisted in Pitt County, January 15, 1863, for the war. Present or accounted for until transferred to Company D, 67th Regiment N. C. Troops on January 18, 1864.

CARLILSE, BENJAMIN, Private

Enlisted in Wayne County, October 6, 1862, for the war. Present or accounted for until transferred to Company D, 67th Regiment N. C. Troops on January 18, 1864.

CHASE, J. H., Private

Enlisted at Coward's Bridge, Lenoir-Pitt counties, June 21, 1863, for the war. Present or accounted for until transferred to Company D, 67th Regiment N. C. Troops on January 18, 1864.

CHASE, STARLIN, Private

Enlisted at Coward's Bridge, Lenoir-Pitt counties, July 18, 1863, for the war. Present or accounted for until transferred to Company D, 67th Regiment N. C. Troops on January 18, 1864.

COLE, W. H., Private

Enlisted in Wayne County, October 30, 1863, for the war. Present or accounted for until transferred to Company D, 67th Regiment N. C. Troops on January 18, 1864.

COLLIER, ISAIAH, Private

Enlisted in Wayne County, September 23, 1862, for the war. Present or accounted for until transferred to Company D, 67th Regiment N. C. Troops on January 18, 1864.

CORBITT, GEORGE W., Private

Enlisted in Wayne County, September 10, 1862, for the war. Present or accounted for until transferred to Company D, 67th Regiment N. C. Troops on January 18, 1864.

DAIL, J. E., Corporal

Enlisted in Wayne County, February 11, 1863, for the war. Appointed Corporal prior to December 31, 1863. Present or accounted for until transferred to Company D, 67th Regiment N. C. Troops on January 18, 1864.

DAWSON, COUNCIL, Private

Enlisted in Pitt County, June 20, 1863, for the war. Transferred to Company K of this battalion on December 1, 1863.

DAWSON, J. T., Private

Enlisted in Lenoir County, January 2, 1864, for

the war. Present or accounted for until transferred to Company D, 67th Regiment N. C. Troops on January 18, 1864.

DENNING, WILLIAM H., Private

Enlisted in Wayne County, February 9, 1863, for the war. Present or accounted for until transferred to Company D, 67th Regiment N. C. Troops on January 18, 1864.

EDMUNDSON, BRYAN, Private

Enlisted in Wayne County, September 22, 1862, for the war. Present or accounted for until transferred to Company D, 67th Regiment N. C. Troops on January 18, 1864.

EDMUNDSON, RILEY, Private

Enlisted in Pitt County, June 27, 1863, for the war. Present or accounted for until transferred to Company D, 67th Regiment N. C. Troops on January 18, 1864.

EDWARDS, J. M., Private

Enlisted in Pitt County, June 15, 1863, for the war. Present or accounted for until transferred to Company D, 67th Regiment N. C. Troops on January 18, 1864.

ELLIS, BENAJAH, Private

Enlisted at Coward's Bridge, Lenoir-Pitt counties, July 12, 1863, for the war. Present or accounted for until transferred to Company D, 67th Regiment N. C. Troops on January 18, 1864.

FIELDS, JESSE, Private

Enlisted at Coward's Bridge, Lenoir-Pitt counties, June 4, 1863, for the war. Transferred to Company K of this battalion on December 1, 1863.

FORBES, JAMES H., Private

Enlisted in Pitt County, August 18, 1863, for the war. Transferred to Company E of this battalion in December, 1863.

FULLER, WILLIAM W., Sergeant

Enlisted in Lenoir County, January 20, 1863, for the war. Appointed Sergeant prior to December, 1863. Present or accounted for until transferred to Company D, 67th Regiment N. C. Troops on January 18, 1864.

GRADY, JAMES, Private

Enlisted in Greene County, January 13, 1863, for the war. Present or accounted for until transferred to Company D, 67th Regiment N. C. Troops on January 18, 1864.

HARRIS, STEPHEN, Private

Enlisted in Pitt County, July 18, 1863, for the war. Present or accounted for until transferred to Company D, 67th Regiment N. C. Troops on January 18, 1864.

HART, JESSE, Private

Enlisted in Pitt County, January 15, 1863, for the war. Present or accounted for until transferred to Company D, 67th Regiment N. C. Troops on January 18, 1864.

HERRING, B. F., Sergeant

Enlisted in Lenoir County, January 20, 1863, for the war. Appointed Sergeant prior to December 31,

1863. Present or accounted for until transferred to Company D, 67th Regiment N. C. Troops on January 18, 1864.

HILL, ANANIAS, Private

Enlisted in Johnston County, December 17, 1862, for the war. Present or accounted for until transferred to Company D, 67th Regiment N. C. Troops on January 18, 1864.

HILL, RICHARD, Private

Enlisted in Lenoir County, January 20, 1863, for the war. Present or accounted for until transferred to Company D, 67th Regiment N. C. Troops on January 18, 1864.

HOLLAND, C. G., Private

Enlisted in Lenoir County, January 12, 1864, for the war. Present or accounted for until transferred to Company D, 67th Regiment N. C. Troops on January 18, 1864.

HOLLAND, W. D., Sergeant

Enlisted in Wayne County, September 22, 1862, for the war. Appointed Sergeant prior to December 31, 1863. Present or accounted for until transferred to Company D, 67th Regiment N. C. Troops on January 18, 1864.

HOWELL, WILLIAM, Private

Enlisted in Wayne County, September 26, 1863, for the war. Present or accounted for until transferred to Company D, 67th Regiment N. C. Troops on January 18, 1864.

HUMPHREY, ISAAC, Private

Enlisted in Pitt County, September 28, 1863, for the war. Present or accounted for until transferred to Company D, 67th Regiment N. C. Troops on January 18, 1864.

JENKINS, IRVIN, Private

Enlisted in Pitt County, August 3, 1863, for the war. Present or accounted for until transferred to Company D, 67th Regiment N. C. Troops on January 18, 1864.

JINNETT, B. W., Private

Enlisted in Wayne County, February 3, 1863, for the war. Present or accounted for until transferred to Company D, 67th Regiment N. C. Troops on January 18, 1864.

JINNETT, DAVID G., Private

Enlisted in Wayne County, February 3, 1863, for the war. Present or accounted for until transferred to Company D, 67th Regiment N. C. Troops on January 18, 1864.

JINNETT, J. S., Private

Enlisted in Wayne County, December 30, 1862, for the war. Present or accounted for until transferred to Company D, 67th Regiment N. C. Troops on January 18, 1864.

JONES, B. B., Private

Enlisted in Wayne County, September 20, 1862, for the war. Present or accounted for until transferred to Company D, 67th Regiment N. C. Troops on January 18, 1864.

JONES, B. L., Quartermaster Sergeant

Enlisted in Pitt County, August 26, 1863, for the war. Appointed Quartermaster Sergeant prior to December 31, 1863. Present or accounted for until transferred to Company D, 67th Regiment N. C. Troops on January 18, 1864.

JONES, JOHN, Private

Enlisted in Pitt County, August 18, 1863, for the war. Present or accounted for until transferred to Company D, 67th Regiment N. C. Troops on January 18, 1864.

JOYNER, HENRY, Private

Enlisted in Pitt County, January 15, 1863, for the war. Present or accounted for until transferred to Company D, 67th Regiment N.C. Troops on January 18, 1864.

KENNEDY, JOHN, Private

Enlisted in Wayne County, July 24, 1863, for the war. Present or accounted for until transferred to Company D, 67th Regiment N.C. Troops on January 18, 1864.

KIRKMAN, LAFAYETTE, Private

Transferred from Company E, 66th Regiment N.C. Troops on September 11, 1863. Present or accounted for until transferred to Company A of this battalion in December, 1863.

KNOX, ASHLEY, Private

Enlisted in Pitt County, August 18, 1863, for the war. Present or accounted for until transferred to Company D, 67th Regiment N.C. Troops on January 18, 1864.

LANGLEY, JOSEPH H., Private

Enlisted in Pitt County, January 15, 1863, for the war. Present or accounted for until transferred to Company D, 67th Regiment N.C. Troops on January 18, 1864.

LAWRENCE, J. R., Private

Enlisted in Pitt County, August 18, 1863, for the war. Present or accounted for until transferred to Company D, 67th Regiment N.C. Troops on January 18, 1864.

LEE, HENRY S., Commissary of Subsistence Sergeant

Transferred from Company B, 10th Regiment N.C. State Troops (1st Regiment N.C. Artillery) prior to December 31, 1863, and appointed Commissary of Subsistence Sergeant. Present or accounted for until transferred to Company D, 67th Regiment N. C. Troops on January 18, 1864.

McARTHUR, WILLIAM, Private

Enlisted in Pitt County, August 20, 1863, for the war. Present or accounted for until transferred to Company D, 67th Regiment N. C. Troops on January 18, 1864.

McKEEL, WILLIAM HENRY, Private

Enlisted at Coward's Bridge, Lenoir-Pitt counties, June 4, 1863, for the war. Present or accounted for until transferred to Company D, 67th Regiment N.C. Troops on January 18, 1864.

McKINDLER, JAMES, Private

Enlisted in Wayne County, October 3, 1862, for the war. Present or accounted for until transferred to Company D, 67th Regiment N.C. Troops on January 18, 1864.

MAY, DAVID, Private

Enlisted in Pitt County, January 15, 1863, for the war. Present or accounted for until transferred to Company D, 67th Regiment N.C. Troops on January 18, 1864.

MILLER, EDWARD H., Private

Resided in Wayne County where he enlisted February 15, 1863, for the war. Present or accounted for until transferred to Company D, 67th Regiment N.C. Troops on January 18, 1864.

MOORE, P. W., Private

Enlisted in Pitt County, June 15, 1863, for the war. Present or accounted for until transferred to Company D, 67th Regiment N.C. Troops on January 18, 1864.

MORING, JOHN R., Private

Enlisted in Wayne County, September 22, 1862, for the war. Present or accounted for until transferred to Company D, 67th Regiment N.C. Troops on January 18, 1864.

MUMFORD, JESSE, Private

Enlisted in Wayne County, September 22, 1862, for the war. Present or accounted for until transferred to Company D, 67th Regiment N.C. Troops on January 18, 1864.

MUMFORD, WILLIAM, Private

Enlisted in Lenior County, December 23, 1863, for the war. Present or accounted for until transferred to Company D, 67th Regiment N.C. Troops on January 18, 1864.

MUSGRAVE, WILLIAM C., Private

Enlisted in Wayne County, February 3, 1863, for the war. Present or accounted for until transferred to Company D, 67th Regiment N.C. Troops on January 18, 1864.

NELSON, JOSEPH, Private

Enlisted in Wayne County, September 19, 1862, for the war. Detailed in the Ordnance Department at Goldsboro on March 6, 1863. Absent on detail when transferred to Company D, 67th Regiment N.C. Troops on January 18, 1864.

PARKER, AMOS D., Private

Enlisted at Coward's Bridge, Lenior-Pitt counties, June 18, 1863, for the war. Present or accounted for until transferred to Company D, 67th Regiment N.C. Troops on January 18, 1864.

PARKER, W. F., Private

Resided in Wayne County and enlisted in Lenior County, January 8, 1864, for the war. Present or accounted for until transferred to Company D, 67th Regiment N.C. Troops on January 18, 1864.

PARKER, W. T., Private

Enlisted in Duplin County, February 15, 1863, for the war. Present or accounted for until transferred to Company D, 67th Regiment N.C. Troops on January 18, 1864.

PARRISH, JOHN B., Private
Enlisted in Wayne County, September 22, 1862, for the war. Present or accounted for until transferred to Company D, 67th Regiment N.C. Troops on January 18, 1864.

PARRISH, SAMUEL, Private
Enlisted in Wayne County, September 22, 1862, for the war. "Deserted October 20, 1863."

PATE, WILLIAM H., Private
Enlisted in Wayne County, September 22, 1862, for the war. Present or accounted for until transferred to Company D, 67th Regiment N.C. Troops on January 18, 1864.

POLLARD, J. O., Private
Enlisted in Pitt County, June 15, 1863, for the war. Present or accounted for until transferred to Company D, 67th Regiment N.C. Troops on January 18, 1864.

POPE, JOHN T., Private
Enlisted in Wayne County, September 27, 1862, for the war. Present or accounted for until transferred to Company D, 67th Regiment N.C. Troops on January 18, 1864.

POTTER, ROBERT, Private
Enlisted in Lenoir County, January 4, 1864, for the war. Present or accounted for until transferred to Company D, 67th Regiment N.C. Troops on January 18, 1864.

PUGH, WILLIAM NICHOLAS, Private
Previously served in Company F, 10th Regiment N.C. State Troops (1st Regiment N.C. Artillery). Enlisted in this company prior to December, 1863, and transferred to Company K of this battalion in December, 1863.

RAMSEY, W. J., Private
Enlisted in Wayne County, October 24, 1862, for the war. Present or accounted for until transferred to Company D, 67th Regiment N.C. Troops on January 18, 1864.

RAYNER, W. D., Private
Enlisted in Sampson County, December 15, 1862, for the war. Present or accounted for until transferred to Company D, 67th Regiment N.C. Troops on January 18, 1864.

ROBINSON, GEORGE L., Private
Enlisted in Pitt County, August 16, 1863, for the war. Present or accounted for until transferred to Company D, 67th Regiment N.C. Troops on January 18, 1864.

ROUSE, J. L., Corporal
Enlisted in Lenoir County, February 11, 1863, for the war. Appointed Corporal prior to December 31, 1863. Present or accounted for until transferred to Company D, 67th Regiment N. C. Troops on January 18, 1864.

ROUSE, JAMES, Private
Enlisted in Lenoir County, January 20, 1863, for the war. Present or accounted for until transferred to Company D, 67th Regiment N. C. Troops on January 18, 1864.

ROUSE, MARCELLUS, Private
Enlisted in Pitt County, October 22, 1863, for the

war. Transferred to Company K of this battalion December 1, 1863.

SATTERTHWAITE, JAMES H., Corporal
Enlisted in Pitt County, January 15, 1863, for the war. Mustered in as Private. Captured at Tarboro on July 21, 1863, and paroled at Fort Monroe, Virginia, August 4, 1863. Appointed Corporal prior to December 31, 1863. Present or accounted for until transferred to Company D, 67th Regiment N. C. Troops on January 18, 1864.

SIMPSON, PETER, Private
Enlisted in Wayne County, December 20, 1862, for the war. Present or accounted for until transferred to Company D, 67th Regiment N. C. Troops on January 18, 1864.

SMITH, GEORGE W., Private
Enlisted in Pitt County, September 19, 1863, for the war. Transferred to Company K of this battalion on October 1, 1863.

SMITH, J. T., Sergeant
Enlisted in Wayne County, September 26, 1862, for the war. Appointed Sergeant prior to December 31, 1863. Present or accounted for until transferred to Company D, 67th Regiment N. C. Troops on January 18, 1864.

STAFFORD, GASTON, Private
Resided in Wayne County where he enlisted September 20, 1862, for the war. Present or accounted for until transferred to Company D, 67th Regiment N. C. Troops on January 18, 1864.

STRICKLAND, JERRY, Private
Resided in Wayne County where he enlisted September 20, 1862, for the war. Present or accounted for until transferred to Company D, 67th Regiment N. C. Troops on January 18, 1864.

STUARD, PATRICK, Private
Enlisted in Duplin County, January 23, 1863, for the war. Present or accounted for until transferred to Company D, 67th Regiment N. C. Troops on January 18, 1864.

SUTTON, JAMES, Private
Enlisted in Pitt County, August 9, 1863, for the war. Present or accounted for until transferred to Company D, 67th Regiment N. C. Troops on January 18, 1864.

SUTTON, THOMAS, Private
Enlisted in Lenoir County, June 9, 1863, for the war. Present or accounted for until transferred to Company D, 67th Regiment N. C. Troops on January 18, 1864.

TAYLOR, JAMES, Private
Enlisted in Lenoir County, January 20, 1863, for the war. Present or accounted for until transferred to Company D, 67th Regiment N. C. Troops on January 18, 1864.

TUCKER, W. D., Private
Enlisted at Coward's Bridge, Lenoir-Pitt counties, June 1, 1863, for the war. Present or accounted for until transferred to Company D, 67th Regiment N. C. Troops on January 18, 1864.

VINSON, JOHN, Private
Enlisted in Pitt County, August 9, 1863, for the war. Present or accounted for until transferred to

Company D, 67th Regiment N. C. Troops on January 18, 1864.

WARD, B. F., Private
Enlisted in Lenoir County, January 20, 1863, for the war. Present or accounted for until transferred to Company D, 67th Regiment N. C. Troops on January 18, 1864.

WARTERS, ASA T., 1st Sergeant
Enlisted in Lenoir County, January 20, 1863, for the war. Appointed 1st Sergeant prior to December 31, 1863. Present or accounted for until transferred to Company D, 67th Regiment N. C. Troops on January 18, 1864.

WARTERS, TOBIAS, Private
Enlisted in Lenoir County, January 4, 1864, for the war. Present or accounted for until transferred to Company D, 67th Regiment N. C. Troops on January 18, 1864.

WEAVER, W. H., Private
Enlisted in Johnston County, February 25, 1863, for the war. Present or accounted for until transferred to Company D, 67th Regiment N. C. Troops on January 18, 1864.

WEST, JOHN B., Private
Enlisted in Wayne County, October 2, 1862, for the war. Present or accounted for until transferred to Company D, 67th Regiment N. C. Troops on January 18, 1864.

WHITE, SHERWOOD, Private
Enlisted in Pitt County, August 20, 1863, for the war. Discharged in November-December, 1863.

WIGGINS, BRYAN, Private
Enlisted in Pitt County, August 14, 1863, for the war. Present or accounted for until transferred to Company D, 67th Regiment N. C. Troops on January 18, 1864.

WIGGINS, WILLIAM, Private
Enlisted in Lenoir County, January 9, 1864, for the war. Present or accounted for until transferred to Company D, 67th Regiment N. C. Troops on January 18, 1864.

WILLIAMS, ISAIAH, Private
Enlisted in Wayne County, July 23, 1863, for the war. Present or accounted for until transferred to Company D, 67th Regiment N. C. Troops on January 18, 1864.

WILLIAMS, JACKSON, Private
Enlisted in Pitt County, January 20, 1863, for the war. Present or accounted for until transferred to Company D, 67th Regiment N. C. Troops on January 18, 1864.

WILLIAMS, LEONIDAS, Private
Enlisted in Wayne County, September 6, 1862, for the war. Present or accounted for until transferred to Company D, 67th Regiment N. C. Troops on January 18, 1864.

WOODARD, B. T., Private
Enlisted in Wayne County, September 9, 1862, for the war. Present or accounted for until transferred to Company D, 67th Regiment N. C. Troops on January 18, 1864.

WOODARD, W. G., Private
Enlisted in Wayne County, October 18, 1862, for the war. Present or accounted for until transferred to Company D, 67th Regiment N. C. Troops on January 18, 1864.

COMPANY E

This company was organized at Camp Burney, near Greenville, Pitt County, in January-February, 1863, and the company commander was commissioned to rank from February 10, 1863. The company was accepted into state service after that date. The exact date the company was attached to the battalion is not known but appears to have been in April-May, 1863. Nothing was found relative to the company's service prior to joining the battalion. It can only be assumed that the company served on outpost and scouting duty. After joining the battalion the company functioned as a part of the battalion, and its history is recorded as a part of the battalion history. By Special Orders No. 8, paragraph 2, Adjutant General's Office, Raleigh, January 18, 1864, the battalion was redesignated the 67th Regiment N.C. Troops, and this company became Company E of the regiment.

The following roster of the company covers from the date of enlistment through the date of redesignation. All events after that date are recorded in the roster of Company E, 67th Regiment N.C. Troops. The information contained in the following roster was compiled principally from company muster rolls which covered from November 1, 1863, through the date of redesignation, January 18, 1864. No muster rolls were found for the period prior to November 1, 1863. Although there are no Roll of Honor records for this company, useful information was obtained from receipt rolls, hospital records, prisoner of war records, and other primary records, supplemented by state pension applications, United Daughters of the Confederacy records, and postwar rosters and histories.

OFFICERS
CAPTAIN
WHITE, CHARLES A.
Transferred from 1st Company I, 10th Regiment N. C. State Troops (1st Regiment N. C. Artillery) upon appointment as Captain to rank from February 10, 1863. Present or accounted for until transferred to Company E, 67th Regiment N. C. Troops on January 18, 1864.

LIEUTENANTS
CLARK, WEEKS H., 2nd Lieutenant
Appointed 2nd Lieutenant on February 10, 1863, to rank from date of appointment. Present or accounted for until transferred to Company E, 67th Regiment N. C. Troops on January 18, 1864.

JONES, ASA WARREN, 1st Lieutenant

Appointed 1st Lieutenant on February 10, 1863, to rank from date of appointment. Present or accounted for until transferred to Company G of this battalion upon appointment as Captain to rank from June 30, 1863.

WHITE, JOSEPH M., 1st Lieutenant

Appointed 2nd Lieutenant on February 10, 1863, to rank from date of appointment. Promoted to 1st Lieutenant on August 19, 1863, to rank from July 1, 1863. Present or accounted for until transferred to Company E, 67th Regiment N. C. Troops on January 18, 1864.

NONCOMMISSIONED OFFICERS AND PRIVATES

ADAMS, BLUNT, Private

Enlisted in Pitt County, January 15, 1863, for the war. Present or accounted for until transferred to Company E, 67th Regiment N. C. Troops on January 18, 1864.

ARNOLD, JOSEPH, Private

Enlisted in Pitt County, January 15, 1863, for the war. Present or accounted for until transferred to Company E, 67th Regiment N. C. Troops on January 18, 1864.

BARNES, ASA, Sergeant

Enlisted in Pitt County, February 1, 1863, for the war. Appointed Sergeant after the company was organized. Present or accounted for until transferred to Company E, 67th Regiment N. C. Troops on January 18, 1864.

BARRINGTON, W. H., Private

Enlisted in Pitt County, April 1, 1863, for the war. Present or accounted for until transferred to Company I of this battalion in September, 1863.

BEDDARD, WILLIAM, Private

Enlisted in Pitt County, June 15, 1863, for the war. Present or accounted for until transferred to Company E, 67th Regiment N.C. Troops on January 18, 1864.

BUCK, NOAH A., Private

Enlisted in Pitt County, February 8, 1863, for the war. Present or accounted for until transferred to Company E, 67th Regiment N. C. Troops on January 18, 1864.

BURNEY, JOHN H., Corporal

Enlisted in Pitt County, January 15, 1863, for the war. Appointed Corporal after the company organized. Captured near Haddock's Cross Roads, Pitt County, November 25, 1863, and confined at Point Lookout, Maryland. Absent in confinement when transferred to Company E, 67th Regiment N. C. Troops on January 18, 1864.

CANNON, DAVID, Private

Enlisted in Pitt County, July 21, 1863, for the war. Present or accounted for until transferred to Company E, 67th Regiment N. C. Troops on January 18, 1864.

CANNON, THOMAS, Private

Enlisted in Pitt County, July 1, 1863, for the war. Present or accounted for until transferred to Company E, 67th Regiment N. C. Troops on January 18, 1864.

CORBIT, ALLEN, Private

Enlisted in Pitt County, February 1, 1863, for the war. Present or accounted for until transferred to Company I, 67th Regiment N. C. Troops on January 18, 1864.

CORBIT, JAMES, Private

Enlisted in Pitt County, January 15, 1864, for the war. Transferred to Company E, 67th Regiment N. C. Troops on January 18, 1864.

CORBIT, JOHN I., Private

Enlisted in Pitt County, January 15, 1864, for the war. Transferred to Company E, 67th Regiment N. C. Troops on January 18, 1864.

COREY, JAMES A., Private

Enlisted in Pitt County, February 15, 1863, for the war. Present or accounted for until transferred to Company I of this battalion in September, 1863.

COWARD, ALLEN, Private

Enlisted in Pitt County, January 20, 1863, for the war. Captured near Haddock's Cross Roads, Pitt County, November 25, 1863, and confined at Point Lookout, Maryland. Absent in confinement when transferred to Company E, 67th Regiment N. C. Troops on January 18, 1864.

COX, ABRAM, Private

Enlisted in Pitt County, September 1, 1863, for the war. Captured near Haddock's Cross Roads, Pitt County, November 25, 1863, and confined at Point Lookout, Maryland, December 29, 1863. Absent in confinement when transferred to Company E, 67th Regiment N. C. Troops on January 18, 1864.

COX, ARCHIBALD, Private

Enlisted in Pitt County, June 15, 1863, for the war. Present or accounted for until transferred to Company E, 67th Regiment N. C. Troops on January 18, 1864.

COX, GUILFORD, Private

Enlisted in Pitt County, January 15, 1863, for the war. Present or accounted for until transferred to Company E, 67th Regiment N. C. Troops on January 18, 1864.

COX, JESSE A., Private

Enlisted in Pitt County, January 10, 1863, for the war. Present or accounted for until transferred to Company E, 67th Regiment N. C. Troops on January 18, 1864.

COX, THOMAS, Private

Transferred from Company I of this battalion after October 31, 1863. Present or accounted for until transferred to Company E, 67th Regiment N. C. Troops on January 18, 1864.

DAUGHETY, ALFRED, Private

Enlisted in Pitt County, January 17, 1863, for the war. Transferred to Company I of this battalion in July, 1863.

DAUGHETY, RICHARD, Private
Enlisted in Pitt County, January 1, 1863, for the war. Transferred to Company I of this battalion in July, 1863.

DEAL, THEOPHILUS, Private
Enlisted in Pitt County, January 15, 1863, for the war. Present or accounted for until transferred to Company E, 67th Regiment N. C. Troops on January 18, 1864.

DIXON, E. O., Private
Enlisted in Pitt County, January 8, 1863, for the war. Present or accounted for until transferred to Company E, 67th Regiment N. C. Troops on January 18, 1864.

EDWARDS, JOHN A., Private
Enlisted in Pitt County, June 25, 1863, for the war. Captured near Haddock's Cross Roads, Pitt County, November 25, 1863, and confined at Point Lookout, Maryland, December 29, 1863. Absent in confinement when transferred to Company E, 67th Regiment N. C. Troops on January 18, 1864.

EDWARDS, THOMAS M., Private
Enlisted in Pitt County, January 15, 1863, for the war. Present or accounted for until he "deserted from camp near Haddock's Cross Roads, January 1, 1864."

ELKS, CHARLES A., Sergeant
Enlisted in Pitt County, April 12, 1863, for the war. Present or accounted for until transferred to Company I of this battalion in September, 1863.

EMERY, WILLIAM, Private
Enlisted in Pitt County, January 19, 1863, for the war. Captured at Haddock's Cross Roads, Pitt County, November 25, 1863, and confined at Point Lookout, Maryland, December 29, 1863. Absent in confinement when transferred to Company E, 67th Regiment N. C. Troops on January 18, 1864.

EVANS, EPHRIAM, Private
Enlisted in Pitt County, January 17, 1863, for the war. Present or accounted for until transferred to Company I of this battalion in July, 1863.

EVANS, IVY, Private
Enlisted in Pitt County, July 1, 1863, for the war. Captured near Haddock's Cross Roads, Pitt County, November 25, 1863, and confined at Point Lookout, Maryland, December 29, 1863. Transferred to Company I of this battalion while absent in confinement.

EWELL, JAMES J., Private
Enlisted in Pitt County, January 15, 1863, for the war. Captured near Haddock's Cross Roads, Pitt County, November 25, 1863, and confined at Point Lookout, Maryland, December 29, 1863. Absent in confinement when transferred to Company E, 67th Regiment N.C. Troops on January 18, 1864.

FILES, BAZEL, Private
Enlisted in Pitt County, February 1, 1863, for the war. Captured near Haddock's Cross Roads, Pitt County, November 25, 1863, and confined at

Point Lookout, Maryland, December 29, 1863. Absent in confinement when transferred to Company E, 67th Regiment N. C. Troops on January 18, 1864.

FORBES, JAMES H., Private
Transferred from Company D of this battalion in December, 1863. Present or accounted for until transferred to Company E, 67th Regiment N. C. Troops on January 18, 1864.

FOREST, SYLVESTER B., Private
Enlisted in Pitt County, January 15, 1863, for the war. Captured near Haddock's Cross Roads, Pitt County, November 25, 1863, and confined at Point Lookout, Maryland, December 29, 1863. Absent in confinement when transferred to Company E, 67th Regiment N. C. Troops on January 18, 1864.

FRIZZLE, MARVIN T., Private
Enlisted in Pitt County, January 1, 1863, for the war. Present or accounted for until transferred to Company E, 67th Regiment N. C. Troops on January 18, 1864.

GARDNER, WYATT, Private
Transferred from Company I of this battalion in November-December, 1863. Transferred to Company E, 67th Regiment N. C. Troops on January 18, 1864.

GASKINS, R. T., Private
Enlisted in Pitt County, January 1, 1863, for the war. Present or accounted for until transferred to Company E, 67th Regiment N. C. Troops on January 18, 1864.

GODLEY, JOHN, Private
Enlisted in Pitt County, April 1, 1863, for the war. Transferred to Company I of this battalion prior to October 31, 1863, and transferred back to this company in January, 1864. Transferred to Company E, 67th Regiment N. C. Troops on January 18, 1864.

GODLEY, JOSEPH, Private
Enlisted in Pitt County, December 8, 1863, for the war. Present or accounted for until transferred to Company E, 67th Regiment N. C. Troops on January 18, 1864.

GRAY, ALEXANDER, Private
Enlisted in Pitt County, January 15, 1863, for the war. Captured at Haddock's Cross Roads, Pitt County, November 25, 1863, and confined at Point Lookout, Maryland, December 29, 1863. Absent in confinement when transferred to Company E, 67th Regiment N. C. Troops on January 18, 1864.

GRAY, JAMES H., Private
Enlisted in Pitt County, January 15, 1863, for the war. Present or accounted for until transferred to Company E, 67th Regiment N. C. Troops on January 18, 1864.

GRIFFIN, C. M., Private
Enlisted in Pitt County, January 19, 1863, for the war. Present or accounted for until transferred to Company E, 67th Regiment N. C. Troops on January 18, 1864.

HADDOCK, ARNASBY, Private
Enlisted in Pitt County, June 15, 1863, for the war. Captured near Haddock's Cross Roads, Pitt County, November 25, 1863, and confined at Point Lookout, Maryland, December 29, 1863. Absent in confinement when transferred to Company E, 67th Regiment N. C. Troops on January 18, 1864.

HADDOCK, JESSE, Private
Enlisted in Pitt County, June 10, 1863, for the war. Captured near Haddock's Cross Roads, Pitt County, November 25, 1863, and confined at Point Lookout, Maryland, December 29, 1863. Absent in confinement when transferred to Company E, 67th Regiment N. C. Troops on January 18, 1864.

HARRINGTON, JOAB, Private
Enlisted in Pitt County, January 15, 1863, for the war. "Deserted January 1, 1864, near Haddock's Cross Roads."

HARRIS, A., Private
Enlisted in Pitt County, January 1, 1863, for the war. Present or accounted for until transferred to Company I of this battalion July 1-October 31, 1863.

HARRIS, JAMES F., Private
Enlisted in Pitt County, November 20, 1863, for the war. Present or accounted for until transferred to Company E, 67th Regiment N. C. Troops on January 18, 1864.

HATHAWAY, NATHANIEL H., Sergeant
Enlisted in Pitt County, January 1, 1863, for the war. Appointed Sergeant when company organized. Captured near Haddock's Cross Roads, Pitt County, November 25, 1863, and confined at Point Lookout, Maryland, December 29, 1863. Absent in confinement when transferred to Company E, 67th Regiment N. C. Troops on January 18, 1864.

HODGE, MATHEW, Private
Enlisted in Pitt County, January 15, 1863, for the war. Present or accounted for until transferred to Company E, 67th Regiment N. C. Troops on January 18, 1864.

HUDSON, H. H., Private
Enlisted in Pitt County, February 8, 1863, for the war. "Deserted January 1, 1864, near Haddock's Cross Roads."

HUMPHREY, JOSEPH H., Sergeant
Enlisted in Pitt County, January 1, 1863, for the war. Appointed Sergeant after the company organized. Present or accounted for until transferred to Company E, 67th Regiment N. C. Troops on January 18, 1864.

JACKSON, JAMES S., Private
Enlisted in Pitt County, February 1, 1863, for the war as a substitute for William A. Stocks. Captured near Haddock's Cross Roads, Pitt County, November 25, 1863, and confined at Point Lookout, Maryland, December 29, 1863. Absent in confinement when transferred to Company E, 67th Regiment N. C. Troops on January 18, 1864.

JACKSON, JOHN, Private
Enlisted in Pitt County, January 15, 1863, for the war. Present or accounted for until transferred to Company E, 67th Regiment N. C. Troops on January 18, 1864.

JACKSON, MAJOR, Private
Enlisted in Pitt County, January 15, 1863, for the war. Captured near Haddock's Cross Roads, Pitt County, November 25, 1863, and confined at Point Lookout, Maryland, December 29, 1863. Absent in confinement when transferred to Company E, 67th Regiment N. C. Troops on January 18, 1864.

JONES, FRED, Private
Enlisted in Pitt County, January 12, 1863, for the war. Transferred to Company I of this battalion in July, 1863, and appointed Corporal.

JONES, JAMES, Private
Enlisted in Pitt County, January 15, 1863, for the war. Reported as "deserter" on the November-December, 1863, muster roll.

LATHINGHOUSE, FURNEY, Private
Enlisted in Pitt County, January 1, 1863, for the war. Present or accounted for until transferred to Company E, 67th Regiment N. C. Troops on January 18, 1864.

McCOTTER, ROBERT B., Private
Enlisted in Pitt County, May 1, 1863, for the war. Transferred to Company G of this battalion September-October, 1863.

McLAWHORN, B. F., Private
Enlisted in Pitt County, January 15, 1863, for the war. Present or accounted for until transferred to Company E, 67th Regiment N. C. Troops on on January 18, 1864.

McLAWHORN, JONATHAN, Private
Enlisted in Pitt County, February 1, 1863, for the war. Present or accounted for until transferred to Company I of this battalion in January, 1864.

MANNING, GREEN, Private
Enlisted in Pitt County, May 1, 1863, for the war. Captured near Haddock's Cross Roads, Pitt County, November 25, 1863, and confined at Point Lookout, Maryland, December 29, 1863. Absent in confinement when transferred to Company E, 67th Regiment N. C. Troops on January 18, 1864.

MEWBORN, WILLIAM P., Private
Enlisted in Pitt County, January 1, 1863, for the war. Present or accounted for until transferred to Company E, 67th Regiment N.C. Troops on January 18, 1864.

MILLS, JESSE B., Private
Enlisted in Pitt County, April 1, 1863, for the war. Present or accounted for until transferred to Company E, 67th Regiment N.C. Troops on January 18, 1864.

MOORE, FRANKLIN, Private
Enlisted in Pitt County, January 15, 1863, for the war. Present or accounted for until transferred to Company E, 67th Regiment N.C. Troops on January 18, 1864.

MOYE, JAMES C., Private

Enlisted in Pitt County, November 20, 1863, for the war. Present or accounted for until transferred to Company E, 67th Regiment N.C. Troops on January 18, 1864.

NOBLE, EVAN E., Corporal

Enlisted in Pitt County, January 15, 1863, for the war. Appointed Corporal when the company organized. Present or accounted for until transferred to Company E, 67th Regiment N.C. Troops on January 18, 1864.

OXLEY, C. C., Private

Enlisted in Pitt County, January 15, 1863, for the war. Present or accounted for through December, 1863.

PAGE, BARTHOLOMEW, Private

Enlisted in Pitt County, June 15, 1863, for the war. Present or accounted for until transferred to Company E, 67th Regiment N.C. Troops on January 18, 1864.

PARRAMO, WILLIAM B., Private

Enlisted in Pitt County, April 15, 1863, for the war. Captured near Haddock's Cross Roads, Pitt County, November 25, 1863, and confined at Point Lookout, Maryland, December 29, 1863. Absent in confinement when transferred to Company E, 67th Regiment N.C. Troops on January 18, 1864.

PAUL, ALEXANDER W., Musician

Enlisted in Pitt County, January 1, 1863, for the war. Appointed Musician after the company organized. Present or accounted for until transferred to Company E, 67th Regiment N.C. Troops on January 18, 1864.

PEATON, OLIVER, Private

Enlisted in Pitt County, January 15, 1863, for the war. Present or accounted for until transferred to Company E, 67th Regiment N.C. Troops on January 18, 1864.

PHILLIPS, THOMAS, Private

Transferred from Company K of this battalion in December, 1863. Present or accounted for until transferred to Company E, 67th Regiment N.C. Troops on January 18, 1864.

PUSSER, JOSHUA, Private

Enlisted in Pitt County, April 15, 1863, for the war. Present or accounted for until transferred to Company E, 67th Regiment N.C. Troops on January 18, 1864.

QUINN, BRYAN, Private

Enlisted in Pitt County, May 11, 1863, for the war. Transferred to Company F, 13th Battalion N.C. Light Artillery, November-December, 1863.

QUINN, GEORGE W., Private

Enlisted in Pitt County, January 20, 1863, for the war. Present or accounted for until transferred to Company E, 67th Regiment N.C. Troops on January 18, 1864.

RINGOLD, JAMES, Corporal

Enlisted in Pitt County, February 1, 1863, for the

war. Appointed Corporal when the company organized. Present or accounted for until transferred to Company I of this battalion in January, 1864.

SIMMONS, JOHN A., Private

Resided in Pitt County where he enlisted, January 15, 1863, for the war. Captured near Haddock's Cross Roads, Pitt County, November 25, 1863, and confined at Point Lookout, Maryland, December 29, 1863. Absent in confinement when transferred to Company E, 67th Regiment N.C. Troops on January 18, 1864.

SKEANS, JESSE S., Private

Enlisted in Pitt County, January 29, 1863, for the war. Captured near Haddock's Cross Roads, Pitt County, November 25, 1863, and confined at Point Lookout, Maryland, December 29, 1863. Absent in confinement when transferred to Company E, 67th Regiment N.C. Troops on January 18, 1864.

SLOAN, JAMES R., Private

Enlisted in Pitt County, January 28, 1863, for the war. Detailed as a teamster at Kinston around August 1, 1863. Absent on detail when transferred to Company E, 67th Regiment N.C. Troops on January 18, 1864.

SMITH, ABNER, Private

Enlisted in Pitt County, January 1, 1863, for the war. Present or accounted for until transferred to Company E, 67th Regiment N.C. Troops on January 18, 1864.

SMITH, ALFRED, Private

Enlisted in Pitt County, January 1, 1863, for the war. Present or accounted for until transferred to Company E, 67th Regiment N.C. Troops on January 18, 1864.

SMITH, DENIS C., Private

Enlisted in Pitt County, January 1, 1863, for the war. Captured near Haddock's Cross Roads, Pitt County, November 25, 1863, and confined at Point Lookout, Maryland, December 29, 1863. Absent in confinement when transferred to Company E, 67th Regiment N.C. Troops on January 18, 1864.

SMITH, LEWIS W., Private

Enlisted in Pitt County, February 1, 1863, for the war. Present or accounted for until transferred to Company E, 67th Regiment N.C. Troops on January 18, 1864.

SMITH, ROBERT, Private

Enlisted in Pitt County, February 1, 1863, for the war. Present or accounted for until transferred to Company E, 67th Regiment N.C. Troops on January 18, 1864.

STANTON, ROBERT B., Sergeant

Enlisted in Pitt County, January 15, 1863, for the war. Appointed Sergeant when the company organized. Present or accounted for until transferred to Company E, 67th Regiment N.C. Troops on January 18, 1864.

STOCKS, J. A., Private

Enlisted in Pitt County, January 1, 1864, for the

war. Transferred to Company E, 67th Regiment N.C. Troops on January 18, 1864.

STOCKS, SAMUEL, Private

Enlisted in Pitt County, January 24, 1863, for the war. Present or accounted for until transferred to Company I of this battalion in January, 1864.

STOCKS, WILLIAM A., Private

Enlisted in Pitt County, April 15, 1863, for the war. Discharged when he provided James S. Jackson as his substitute.

STOKES, EDMOND, Private

Transferred from Captain Guilford W. Cox's Company, N.C. Local Defense Troops on November 1, 1863. Present or accounted for until transferred to Company E, 67th Regiment N.C. Troops on January 18, 1864.

STOKES, THOMAS W., Private

Enlisted in Pitt County, September 4, 1863, for the war. Present or accounted for until transferred to Company E, 67th Regiment N.C. Troops on January 18, 1864.

SUTTON, JAMES R., Private

Enlisted in Pitt County, April 14, 1863, for the war. Captured near Haddock's Cross Roads, Pitt County, November 25, 1863, and confined at Point Lookout, Maryland, December 29, 1863. Absent in confinement when transferred to Company E, 67th Regiment N.C. Troops on January 18, 1864.

TRIPP, THOMAS, Private

Enlisted in Pitt County, January 15, 1863, for the war. Present or accounted for until transferred to Company E, 67th Regiment N.C. Troops on January 18, 1864.

TYSON, JOSEPH, Private

Enlisted in Pitt County, October 31, 1863, for the war. Present or accounted for until transferred to Company E, 67th Regiment N.C. Troops on January 18, 1864.

WATSON, FRANK L., Private

Enlisted in Pitt County, January 1, 1863, for the war. Transferred to Company I of this battalion in July, 1863.

WATSON, LEVI J., Private

Enlisted in Pitt County, January 1, 1863, for the war. Transferred to Company I of this battalion in July, 1863.

WATSON, NATHAN, Private

Enlisted in Pitt County, June 30, 1863, for the war. Transferred to Company I of this battalion in July, 1863.

WEST, ALEX W., Sergeant

Enlisted in Pitt County, January 15, 1863, for the war. Reported as Sergeant on November-December, 1863, muster roll. Present or accounted for until transferred to Company E, 67th Regiment N.C. Troops on January 18, 1864.

WETHERINGTON, ALFRED, Private

Enlisted in Pitt County, June 1, 1863, for the war. Present or accounted for until transferred to Company E, 67th Regiment N.C. Troops on January 18, 1864.

WHITE, LEWIS H., 1st Sergeant

Transferred from Company A of this battalion in May, 1863, and appointed 1st Sergeant. Present or accounted for until transferred to Company E, 67th Regiment N.C. Troops on January 18, 1864.

WILLIAMS, JOEL, Private

Enlisted in Pitt County, April 1, 1863, for the war. Present or accounted for until transferred to Company E, 67th Regiment N.C. Troops on January 18, 1864.

WILLIAMS, THOMAS G., Private

Enlisted in Pitt County, January 1, 1863, for the war. Present or accounted for until transferred to Company K of this battalion in December, 1863.

WILSON, JAMES, Private

Enlisted in Pitt County, January 1, 1863, for the war. Present or accounted for until transferred to Company E, 67th Regiment N.C. Troops on January 18, 1864.

WILSON, JOSEPH, Private

Enlisted in Pitt County, January 1, 1863, for the war. Present or accounted for until transferred to Company E, 67th Regiment N.C. Troops on January 18, 1864.

WILSON, ROBERT W., Private

Enlisted in Pitt County, February 4, 1863, for the war. Present or accounted for until transferred to Company E, 67th Regiment N.C. Troops on January 18, 1864.

WINGATE, HENRY, Private

Enlisted in Pitt County, January 1, 1863, for the war. Present or accounted for until transferred to Company E, 67th Regiment N.C. Troops on January 18, 1864.

COMPANY F

This company began organizing in Craven County in April, 1863. In June, 1863, recruits were added from Jones County, and the company commander was commissioned to rank from July 20, 1863. The company was accepted into state service after that date and was attached to this battalion in July-August, 1863. After joining the battalion the company functioned as a part of the battalion, and its history is recorded as a part of the battalion history. By Special Orders No. 8, paragraph 2, Adjutant General's Office, Raleigh, January 18, 1864, the battalion was redesignated the 67th Regiment N.C. Troops, and this company became Company F of the regiment.

The following roster of the company covers from the date of enlistment through the date of redesignation. All events after that date are recorded in the roster of Company F, 67th Regiment N.C. Troops. The information contained in the following roster was compiled principally from company muster rolls which covered from November 1, 1863, through the date of redesignation, January 18, 1864. No muster rolls were found for the period prior to November 1, 1863. Although there are no Roll of Honor records for this company, useful information was obtained from receipt rolls, hospital records, prisoner of war records, and other primary records, supplemented by state pension applications, United Daughters of the Confederacy records, and postwar rosters and histories.

OFFICERS

CAPTAIN

WHITFORD, DAVID P.
Appointed Captain on July 22, 1863, to rank from July 20, 1863. Present or accounted for until transferred to Company F, 67th Regiment N.C. Troops on January 18, 1864.

LIEUTENANTS

BROWN, JOHN ISAAC, 1st Lieutenant
Transferred from Company C, 2nd Regiment N.C. State Troops upon appointment as 1st Lieutenant on July 22, 1863, to rank from July 20, 1863. Present or accounted for until transferred to Company F, 67th Regiment N.C. Troops on January 18, 1864.

HEATH, JAMES FRANK, 2nd Lieutenant
Transferred from 1st Company I, 10th Regiment N.C. State Troops (1st Regiment N.C. Artillery) and appointed 2nd Lieutenant on July 22, 1863, to rank from July 20, 1863. Present or accounted for until transferred to Company F, 67th Regiment N.C. Troops on January 18, 1864.

MARSHALL, JAMES H., 2nd Lieutenant
Appointed 2nd Lieutenant on July 22, 1863, to rank from July 20, 1863. Present or accounted for until transferred to Company F, 67th Regiment N.C. Troops on January 18, 1864.

NONCOMMISSIONED OFFICERS AND PRIVATES

ANDREWS, JAMES M., Private
Enlisted in Jones County, June 1, 1863, for the war. Present or accounted for until transferred to Company F, 67th Regiment N.C. Troops on January 18, 1864.

ANDREWS, JOHN B., Private
Enlisted in Craven County, April 1, 1863, for the war. Present or accounted for until transferred to Company F, 67th Regiment N.C. Troops on January 18, 1864.

BARROW, BENJAMIN, Private
Enlisted in Craven County, June 13, 1863, for the war. Present or accounted for until transferred to Company F, 67th Regiment N.C. Troops on January 18, 1864.

BOWEN, CHARLES C., Private
Enlisted in Craven County, May 26, 1863, for the war. Present or accounted for until transferred to

Company F, 67th Regiment N.C. Troops on January 18, 1864.

BRIGHT, JOHN, Private
Enlisted in Craven County, April 1, 1863, for the war. Present or accounted for until transferred to Company F, 67th Regiment N.C. Troops on January 18, 1864.

BRIGHT, JOHN B., Private
Enlisted in Craven County, May 25, 1863, for the war. Present or accounted for until transferred to Company F, 67th Regiment N.C. Troops on January 18, 1864.

BROWN, A., Private
Enlisted in Craven County for the war. Reported on November 1-December 31, 1863, muster roll with the remark: "Died January 6, 1864."

BUCK, SPENSER, Private
Enlisted in Craven County, June 13, 1863, for the war. Reported on November 1-December 31, 1863, muster roll as "absent without leave since September, 1863." Absent without leave when transferred to Company F, 67th Regiment N.C. Troops on January 18, 1864.

CASPER, F. A., Private
Enlisted in Craven County, April 1, 1863, for the war. Present or accounted for until transferred to Company F, 67th Regiment N.C. Troops on January 18, 1864.

CATON, NOAH G., Private
Enlisted in Craven County, March 11, 1863, for the war. Present or accounted for until transferred to Company F, 67th Regiment N.C. Troops on January 18, 1864.

CLARK, EDWARD E., Private
Enlisted in Craven County, August 20, 1863, for the war. Present or accounted for until transferred to Company F, 67th Regiment N.C. Troops on January 18, 1864.

COOMS, JOHN, Private
Enlisted in Jones County, June 1, 1863, for the war. Present or accounted for until transferred to Company F, 67th Regiment N.C. Troops on January 18, 1864.

COSEWAY, WILEY A., Private
Enlisted in Craven County, May 26, 1863, for the war. Present or accounted for until transferred to Company F, 67th Regiment N.C. Troops on January 18, 1864.

COX, GABRIEL P., Private
Enlisted in Jones County, June 1, 1863, for the war. Present or accounted for until transferred to Company F, 67th Regiment N.C. Troops on January 18, 1864.

DAIL, A. B., Private
Enlisted in Craven County for the war. "Deserted to yankees December, 1863."

DANIELS, WILSON, Private
Enlisted in Craven County, January 1, 1864, for the war. Present or accounted for until transferred to Company F, 67th Regiment N.C. Troops on January 18, 1864.

DAVIS, GEORGE W., Private

Enlisted in Craven County, June 12, 1863, for the war. Reported on November 1-December 31, 1863, muster roll as "absent without leave since December, 1863." Absent without leave when transferred to Company F, 67th Regiment N.C. Troops on January 18, 1864.

DUDLY, CHRISTOPHER J., Private

Enlisted in Craven County, July 1, 1863, for the war. Present or accounted for until transferred to Company F, 67th Regiment N.C. Troops on January 18, 1864.

EDWARDS, WILLIAM, Private

Enlisted in Craven County, May 25, 1863, for the war. Reported on November 1-December 21, 1863, muster roll as "absent without leave." Absent without leave when transferred to Company F, 67th Regiment N.C. Troops on January 18, 1864.

EUBANKS, BENJAMIN, Private

Enlisted in Jones County, June 1, 1863, for the war. Present or accounted for until transferred to Company F, 67th Regiment N.C. Troops on January 18, 1864.

EVANS, EDWARD, Private

Enlisted in Craven County, April 1, 1863, for the war. Reported as "absent without leave" on the November 1-December 31, 1863, muster roll. Absent without leave when transferred to Company F, 67th Regiment N.C. Troops on January 18, 1864.

FARNELL, BENJAMIN N., Private

Enlisted in Onslow County, October 14, 1863, for the war. Present or accounted for until transferred to Company F, 67th Regiment N.C. Troops on January 18, 1864.

FOY, THOMAS, Private

Enlisted in Craven County, May 14, 1863, for the war. Present or accounted for until transferred to Company F, 67th Regiment N.C. Troops on January 18, 1864.

FRAZIER, JACKSON, Private

Enlisted in Onslow County, October 14, 1863, for the war. Present or accounted for until transferred to Company F, 67th Regiment N.C. Troops on January 18, 1864.

FULSHIRE, BARNEY, Private

Enlisted in Craven County, May 25, 1863, for the war. Present or accounted for until transferred to Company F, 67th Regiment N.C. Troops on January 18, 1864.

FULSHIRE, ENOCH, Private

Enlisted in Craven County, May 25, 1863, for the war. Present or accounted for until transferred to Company F, 67th Regiment N.C. Troops on January 18, 1864.

FULSHIRE, FURNEY, Private

Enlisted in Craven County, May 25, 1863, for the war. Present or accounted for until transferred to Company F, 67th Regiment N.C. Troops on January 18, 1864.

GASKINS, ALFRED, Corporal

Enlisted in Craven County, May 14, 1863, for the war. Appointed Corporal when the company was organized. Present or accounted for until transferred to Company F, 67th Regiment N.C. Troops on January 18, 1864.

GASKINS, C. P., 1st Sergeant

Enlisted in Craven County, May 1, 1863, for the war. Appointed 1st Sergeant when the company organized. Present or accounted for until transferred to Company F, 67th Regiment N.C. Troops on January 18, 1864.

GASKINS, EDMON, Private

Enlisted in Craven County, January 15, 1864, for the war. Transferred to Company F, 67th Regiment N.C. Troops on January 18, 1864.

GASKINS, ELISHA A., Private

Enlisted in Craven County, May 20, 1863, for the war. Present or accounted for until transferred to Company F, 67th Regiment N.C. Troops on January 18, 1864.

GASKINS, FRED P., Corporal

Enlisted in Craven County, May 26, 1863, for the war. Appointed Corporal when the company organized. Present or accounted for until transferred to Company F, 67th Regiment N.C. Troops on January 18, 1864.

GASKINS, NATHANIEL, Private

Enlisted in Craven County, May 23, 1863, for the war. Present or accounted for until transferred to Company F, 67th Regiment N.C. Troops on January 18, 1864.

GASKINS, NOAH B., Private

Enlisted in Craven County, June 1, 1863, for the war. Present or accounted for until transferred to Company F, 67th Regiment N.C. Troops on January 18, 1864.

GATLIN, JOHN, Private

Enlisted in Craven County, May 26, 1863, for the war. Present or accounted for until transferred to Company F, 67th Regiment N.C. Troops on January 18, 1864.

GOODING, ISAAC, Private

Enlisted in Craven County, April 1, 1863, for the war. Present or accounted for until transferred to Company F, 67th Regiment N.C. Troops on January 18, 1864.

GREEN, J. F., Private

Enlisted in Craven County for the war. Transferred to Company H of this battalion on December 15, 1863.

GREEN, W. M., Private

Enlisted in Craven County for the war. Transferred to Company H of this battalion on December 15, 1863.

GURGANUS, THOMAS, Private

Enlisted in Craven County, April 1, 1863, for the war. Present or accounted for until transferred to Company F, 67th Regiment N.C. Troops on January 18, 1864.

HARGET, JAMES R., Corporal

Enlisted in Craven County, April 1, 1863, for the war. Appointed Corporal when the company was organized. Present or accounted for until transferred to Company F, 67th Regiment N.C. Troops on January 18, 1864.

HARTLY, JESSE A., Private
Enlisted in Craven County, May 10, 1863, for the war. Present or accounted for until transferred to Company F, 67th Regiment N.C. Troops on January 18, 1864.

HASKINS, CALHOUN, Sergeant
Enlisted in Craven County, April 1, 1863, for the war. Appointed Sergeant when the company organized. Present or accounted for until transferred to Company F, 67th Regiment N.C. Troops on January 18, 1864.

HASKINS, ELIJAH, Sergeant
Enlisted in Jones County, June 1, 1863, for the war. Appointed Sergeant when the company organized. Present or accounted for until transferred to Company F, 67th Regiment N.C. Troops on January 18, 1864.

HAWKINS, JOHN, Private
Enlisted in Craven County for the war. Present or accounted for until transferred to Company F, 67th Regiment N.C. Troops on January 18, 1864.

HAWKINS, LAMBS, Private
Enlisted in Jones County, June 1, 1863, for the war. Present or accounted for until transferred to Company F, 67th Regiment N.C. Troops on January 18, 1864.

HEATH, ALFRED L., Musician
Enlisted in Craven County, March 11, 1863, for the war. Appointed Musician when the company organized. Present or accounted for until transferred to Company F, 67th Regiment N.C. Troops on January 18, 1864.

HEATH, CURTIS, Corporal
Enlisted in Jones County, June 1, 1863, for the war. Appointed Corporal when the company organized. Present or accounted for until transferred to Company F, 67th Regiment N.C. Troops on January 18, 1864.

HEATH, JOHN A. B., Private
Enlisted in Craven County, June 1, 1863, for the war. Present or accounted for until transferred to Company F, 67th Regiment N.C. Troops on January 18, 1864.

HILL, MARSHAL, Private
Enlisted in Craven County, May 3, 1863, for the war. Present or accounted for until transferred to Company F, 67th Regiment N.C. Troops on January 18, 1864.

HUGGINS, S. B., Private
Enlisted in Craven County for the war. Reported on November 1-December 31, 1863, muster roll, but date of enlistment not recorded. Transferred to Company F, 67th Regiment N.C. Troops on January 18, 1864.

IPOCH, EDWARD, Private
Transferred from 1st Company I, 10th Regiment N.C. State Troops (1st Regiment N.C. Artillery) April 16, 1863, and assigned to this company. Present or accounted for until transferred to Company F, 67th Regiment N.C. Troops on January 18, 1864.

IPOCH, LEWIS, Private
Enlisted in Craven County, March 11, 1863, for the war. Present or accounted for until transferred to Company F, 67th Regiment N.C. Troops on January 18, 1864.

JENKINS, JAMES O., Private
Enlisted in Jones County, June 1, 1863, for the war. Present or accounted for until transferred to Company F, 67th Regiment N.C. Troops on January 18, 1864.

JONES, FRANK W., Private
Enlisted in Jones County, June 1, 1863, for the war. Present or accounted for until transferred to Company F, 67th Regiment N.C. Troops on January 18, 1864.

KILPATRICK, FRANCIS, Private
Transferred from Company H of this battalion on December 15, 1863. Present or accounted for until transferred to Company F, 67th Regiment N.C. Troops on January 18, 1864.

KING, JOHN, Private
Enlisted in Jones County, June 1, 1863, for the war. Present or accounted for until transferred to Company F, 67th Regiment N.C. Troops on January 18, 1864.

LANE, JAMES, Private
Enlisted in Craven County, June 12, 1863, for the war. Present or accounted for until transferred to Company F, 67th Regiment N.C. Troops on January 18, 1864.

LEE, ABRAM, Private
Enlisted in Craven County, May 26, 1863, for the war. Present or accounted for until transferred to Company F, 67th Regiment N.C. Troops on January 18, 1864.

LEE, JOHN, Private
Enlisted in Jones County, June 1, 1863, for the war. Present or accounted for until transferred to Company F, 67th Regiment N.C. Troops on January 18, 1864.

LOCKEY, JOHN, Private
Enlisted in Jones County, October 1, 1863, for the war. Present or accounted for until transferred to Company F, 67th Regiment N.C. Troops on January 18, 1864.

MARSHAL, BRICE, Private
Enlisted in Onslow County, June 1, 1863, for the war. Present or accounted for until transferred to Company F, 67th Regiment N.C. Troops on January 18, 1864.

MILLER, JOHN S., Private
Enlisted in Craven County, May 21, 1863, for the war. Present or accounted for until transferred to Company F, 67th Regiment N.C. Troops on January 18, 1864.

MORRIS, RANSOM, Private
Enlisted in Craven County, July 23, 1863, for the war. Reported as "absent without leave since November, 1863," on the November 1-December 31, 1863, muster roll. Absent without leave when transferred to Company F, 67th Regiment N.C. Troops on January 18, 1864.

MORRIS, WILLIAM A., Private
Enlisted in Craven County, May 19, 1863, for the war. Present or accounted for until transferred to Company F, 67th Regiment N.C. Troops on January 18, 1864.

MURPHY, JOSEPH, Private
Enlisted in Craven County, January 1, 1864, for the war. Transferred to Company F, 67th Regiment N.C. Troops on January 18, 1864.

NORRIS, JAMES, Private
Enlisted in Craven County, January 7, 1864, for the war. Transferred to Company F, 67th Regiment N.C. Troops on January 18, 1864.

PATRICK, F. A., Private
Transferred from Company H of this battalion December 15, 1863. Present or accounted for until transferred to Company F, 67th Regiment N.C. Troops on January 18, 1864.

PAUL, MITCHEL, Private
Enlisted in Craven County, May 21, 1863, for the war. Present or accounted for until transferred to Company F, 67th Regiment N.C. Troops on January 18, 1864.

POTTER, HIRAM B., Private
Enlisted in Craven County, May 24, 1863, for the war. Present or accounted for until transferred to Company F, 67th Regiment N.C. Troops on January 18, 1864.

PRICE, JAMES J., Private
Enlisted in Craven County, May 21, 1863, for the war. Present or accounted for until transferred to Company F, 67th Regiment N.C. Troops on January 18, 1864.

REEL, JOHN B., Private
Enlisted in Craven County, May 17, 1863, for the war. Present or accounted for until transferred to Company F, 67th Regiment N.C. Troops on January 18, 1864.

REEL, McDUFFIE, Private
Enlisted in Craven County, May 17; 1863, for the war. Present or accounted for until transferred to Company F, 67th Regiment N.C. Troops on January 18, 1864.

ROE, HENRY W., Private
Enlisted in Craven County, June 12, 1863, for the war. Reported as "absent without leave since December, 1863," on the November 1-December 31, 1863, muster roll. Absent without leave when transferred to Company F, 67th Regiment N.C. Troops on January 18, 1864.

ROE, JOHN T., Private
Enlisted in Craven County, June 12, 1863, for the war. Reported as "absent without leave since December, 1863," on the November 1-December 31, 1863, muster roll. Absent without leave when transferred to Company F, 67th Regiment N.C. Troops on January 18, 1864.

SEVARTS, W. R., Private
Enlisted in Craven County, June 12, 1863, for the war. Reported as "absent without leave" on the November 1-December 31, 1863, muster roll.

SIMPKINS, MELVIN, Private
Enlisted in Craven County, March 11, 1863, for

the war. Present or accounted for until transferred to Company F, 67th Regiment N.C. Troops on January 18, 1864.

SMITH, JOHN, Private
Enlisted in Jones County, June 1, 1863, for the war. Present or accounted for until transferred to Company F, 67th Regiment N.C. Troops on January 18, 1864.

SMITH. WILLIAM T., Private
Enlisted in Craven County, March 1, 1863, for the war. Present or accounted for until transferred to Company F, 67th Regiment N.C. Troops on January 18, 1864.

SPENSER, JESSE N., Private
Enlisted in Craven County, June 12, 1863, for the war. Present or accounted for until transferred to Company F, 67th Regiment N.C. Troops on January 18, 1864.

SPIER, LEWIS B., Private
Enlisted in Craven County, August 1, 1863, for the war. Present or accounted for until transferred to Company F, 67th Regiment N.C. Troops on January 18, 1864.

SPIER, WILLIAM H., Private
Enlisted in Craven County, May 20, 1863, for the war. Present or accounted for until transferred to Company F, 67th Regiment N.C. Troops on January 18, 1864.

STANLY, ABNER, Private
Enlisted in Jones County, June 1, 1863, for the war. Present or accounted for until transferred to Company F, 67th Regiment N.C. Troops on January 18, 1864.

SULLIVAN, B. H., Private
Enlisted in Jones County, June 1, 1863, for the war. Present or accounted for until transferred to Company F, 67th Regiment N.C. Troops on January 18, 1864.

TAYLOR, CORNELIUS, Private
Enlisted in Jones County, June 1, 1863, for the war. Present or accounted for until transferred to Company F, 67th Regiment N.C. Troops on January 18, 1864.

TAYLOR, JESSE G., Private
Enlisted in Jones County, June 1, 1863, for the war. Present or accounted for until transferred to Company F, 67th Regiment N.C. Troops on January 18, 1864.

THOMSON, JOHN, Private
Enlisted in Craven County, October 1, 1863, for the war. Present or accounted for until transferred to Company F, 67th Regiment N.C. Troops on January 18, 1864.

TILGHMAN, ALEX, Private
Enlisted in Jones County, June 1, 1863, for the war. Present or accounted for until transferred to Company F, 67th Regiment N.C. Troops on January 18, 1864.

WESTON, JOHN W., Sergeant
Enlisted in Craven County, June 12, 1863, for the war. Appointed Sergeant when the company organized. Present or accounted for until transferred to Company F, 67th Regiment N.C. Troops on

January 18, 1864.

WHITFORD, WILLIAM D., Private
Enlisted in Craven County, October 1, 1863, for the war. Present or accounted for until transferred to Company F, 67th Regiment N.C. Troops on January 18, 1864.

WILCOX, STEPHEN, Private
Enlisted in Craven County for the war. Reported on the November 1-December 31, 1863, muster roll, but the date of enlistment was not recorded. Transferred to Company F, 67th Regiment N.C. Troops on January 18, 1864.

WILLIAMS, GEORGE W., Private
Enlisted in Craven County for the war. Reported on the November 1-December 31, 1863, muster roll with the remark: "Deserted to Yankees December, 1863."

WILLIS, HARDY B., Private
Enlisted in Craven County, August 13, 1863, for the war. Present or accounted for until transferred to Company F, 67th Regiment N.C. Troops on January 18, 1864.

COMPANY G

This company was organized at Camp Burney, near Greenville, Pitt County, in June, 1863, and the company commander was appointed to rank from June 30, 1863. The company was accepted into state service soon after that date and attached to this battalion in July-August, 1863. After joining the battalion the company functioned as a part of the battalion, and its history is recorded as a part of the battalion history. By Special Orders No. 8, paragraph 2, Adjutant General's Office, Raleigh, January 18, 1864, the battalion was redesignated the 67th Regiment N.C. Troops, and this company became Company G of the regiment.

The following roster of the company covers from the date of enlistment through the date of redesignation. All events after that date are recorded in the roster of Company G, 67th Regiment N.C. Troops. The information contained in the following roster was compiled principally from company muster rolls which covered from November 1, 1863, through the date of redesignation, January 18, 1864. No muster rolls were found for the period prior to November 1, 1863. Although there are no Roll of Honor records for this company, useful information was obtained from receipt rolls, hospital records, prisoner of war records, and other primary records, supplemented by state pension applications, United Daughters of the Confederacy records, and postwar rosters and histories.

OFFICERS

CAPTAIN

JONES, ASA WARREN
Transferred from Company E of this battalion upon appointment as Captain to rank from June 30, 1863. Present or accounted for until transferred to Company G, 67th Regiment N.C. Troops on January 18, 1864.

LIEUTENANTS

HOOD, DAVID W., 1st Lieutenant
Transferred from Company D, 66th Regiment N.C. Troops on October 4, 1863, upon appointment as 1st Lieutenant to rank from September 17, 1863. Present or accounted for until transferred to Company G, 67th Regiment N.C. Troops on January 18, 1864.

McCOTTER, GEORGE B., 2nd Lieutenant
Transferred from Company A, 27th Regiment N.C. Troops upon appointment as 2nd Lieutenant to rank from August 31, 1863. Present or accounted for until transferred to Company G, 67th Regiment N.C. Troops on January 18, 1864.

PITTMAN, PHILETUS N., 3rd Lieutenant
Appointed 3rd Lieutenant to rank from January 2, 1864. Present or accounted for until transferred to Company G, 67th Regiment N.C. Troops on January 18, 1864.

NONCOMMISSIONED OFFICERS AND PRIVATES

BEARDSLEY, L. P., Private
Enlisted in Pitt County, December 1, 1863, for the war. Present or accounted for until transferred to Company G, 67th Regiment N.C. Troops on January 18, 1864.

BEDARD, OLIVER, Corporal
Enlisted in Pitt County, July 1, 1863, for the war. Appointed Corporal when the company organized. Present or accounted for until transferred to Company G, 67th Regiment N.C. Troops on January 18, 1864.

BENSON, WILLIAM, Private
Enlisted in Pitt County, June 15, 1863, for the war. Present or accounted for until transferred to Company G, 67th Regiment N.C. Troops on January 18, 1864.

BROWN, HENRY, Private
Enlisted in Pitt County, August 20, 1863, for the war. Present or accounted for until transferred to Company G, 67th Regiment N.C. Troops on January 18, 1864.

BUNDY, W. J., Private
Enlisted in Pitt County, June 15, 1863, for the war. Present or accounted for until transferred to Company G, 67th Regiment N.C. Troops on January 18, 1864.

CANNON, HENRY, Private
Enlisted in Pitt County, January 15, 1863, for the war. Present or accounted for until transferred to Company G, 67th Regiment N.C. Troops on January 18, 1864.

CANNON, JOHN, Private
Enlisted in Pitt County, June 6, 1863, for the war. Present or accounted for until transferred to Company G, 67th Regiment N.C. Troops on January 18, 1864.

CHESTNUT, LEMUEL, Private
Enlisted in Pitt County, June 15, 1863, for the war. Present or accounted for until transferred to Company G, 67th Regiment N.C. Troops on January 18, 1864.

DAUGHETY, JAMES F., Private
Enlisted in Pitt County, July 21, 1863, for the war. Present or accounted for until transferred to Company G, 67th Regiment N.C. Troops on January 18, 1864.

DAUGHETY, RICHARD, Private
Transferred from Company I of this battalion November-December, 1863. Present or accounted for until transferred to Company G, 67th Regiment N.C. Troops on January 18, 1864.

DUNN, JOHN, Private
Enlisted in Pitt County, June 14, 1863, for the war. Deserted December 21, 1863, and was absent without leave when transferred to Company G, 67th Regiment N.C. Troops on January 18, 1864.

DURHAM, RICHARD, Private
Enlisted in Pitt County, September 19, 1863, for the war. Present or accounted for until transferred to Company G, 67th Regiment N.C. Troops on January 18, 1864.

EDWARDS, ALFRED, Private
Enlisted in Pitt County, June 25, 1863, for the war. Transferred to Company I of this battalion September-October, 1863.

EDWARDS, E. P., 1st Sergeant
Enlisted in Pitt County, June 9, 1863, for the war. Appointed 1st Sergeant when the company was organized. Present or accounted for until transferred to Company G, 67th Regiment N.C. Troops on January 18, 1864.

ELKS, DAVID, Private
Enlisted in Pitt County, December 1, 1863, for the war. Present or accounted for until transferred to Company G, 67th Regiment N.C. Troops on January 18, 1864.

EVANS, I. J., Private
Enlisted in Pitt County, June 6, 1863, for the war. Present or accounted for until transferred to Company G, 67th Regiment N.C. Troops on January 18, 1864.

FAULKNER, LEANDER, Private
Transferred from Company B, 63rd Regiment N.C. Troops (5th Regiment N.C. Cavalry) October 3, 1863. Present or accounted for until transferred to Company G, 67th Regiment N.C. Troops on January 18, 1864.

FAULKNER, SIMON, Private
Enlisted in Pitt County, December 1, 1863, for the war. Present or accounted for until transferred to Company G, 67th Regiment N.C. Troops on January 18, 1864.

FAULKNER, W. E., Private
Enlisted in Pitt County, July 21, 1863, for the war. Present or accounted for until transferred to Company G, 67th Regiment N.C. Troops on January 18, 1864.

FERRELL, E., Private
Enlisted in Pitt County, July 20, 1863, for the war. Present or accounted for until transferred to Company G, 67th Regiment N.C. Troops on January 18, 1864.

FULFORD, JAMES, Private
Enlisted in Pitt County, June 1, 1863, for the war. Present or accounted for until transferred to Company G, 67th Regiment N.C. Troops on January 18, 1864.

GRAY, ALEXANDER, Private
Enlisted in Pitt County, January 19, 1863, for the war. Present or accounted for until transferred to Company G, 67th Regiment N.C. Troops on January 18, 1864.

GRAY, GEORGE, Private
Enlisted in Pitt County, September 10, 1863, for the war. Present or accounted for until transferred to Company G, 67th Regiment N.C. Troops on January 18, 1864.

HARRIS, A., Private
Transferred from Company I of this battalion November-December, 1863. Present or accounted for until transferred to Company G, 67th Regiment N.C. Troops on January 18, 1864.

HARRIS, JACKSON, Private
Enlisted in Pitt County, February 1, 1863, for the war. Present or accounted for until transferred to Company G, 67th Regiment N.C. Troops on January 18, 1864.

HARRIS, R. F., Private
Enlisted in Pitt County, January 1, 1863, for the war. Present or accounted for until transferred to Company G, 67th Regiment N.C. Troops on January 18, 1864.

HARTSFIELD, THOMAS L., Private
Enlisted in Pitt County, December 19, 1863, for the war. Present or accounted for until transferred to Company G, 67th Regiment N.C. Troops on January 18, 1864.

HARTSFIELD, WILLIAM B., Sergeant
Enlisted in Pitt County, June 9, 1863, for the war. Appointed Sergeant when the company organized. Present or accounted for until transferred to Company G, 67th Regiment N.C. Troops on January 18, 1864.

HARVEY, MATHIAS, Sergeant
Enlisted in Pitt County, June 9, 1863, for the war. Appointed Sergeant when the company organized. Present or accounted for until transferred to Company G, 67th Regiment N.C. Troops on January 18, 1864.

HATCH, J. R., Private
Enlisted in Pitt County, April 1, 1863, for the war. Present or accounted for until transferred to Company G, 67th Regiment N.C. Troops on January 18, 1864.

HERRINGTON, BIGGS, Private
Enlisted in Pitt County, June 10, 1863, for the war. Present or accounted for until transferred to Company G, 67th Regiment N.C. Troops on January 18, 1864.

HILL, HARDY, Private
Enlisted in Pitt County, June 6, 1863, for the war. Present or accounted for until transferred to Com-

pany G, 67th Regiment N.C. Troops on January 18, 1864.

JACKSON, FRANCIS, Private
Enlisted in Pitt County, December 1, 1863, for the war. Present or accounted for until transferred to Company G, 67th Regiment N.C. Troops on January 18, 1864.

JACKSON, S. S., Private
Enlisted in Pitt County, July 6, 1863, for the war. Present or accounted for until transferred to Company G, 67th Regiment N.C. Troops on January 18, 1864.

JACKSON, W. C., Private
Enlisted in Pitt County, June 6, 1863, for the war. Present or accounted for until transferred to Company G, 67th Regiment N.C. Troops on January 18, 1864.

JACKSON, WILLIAM J., Private
Enlisted in Pitt County, December 1, 1863, for the war. Present or accounted for until transferred to Company G, 67th Regiment N.C. Troops on January 18, 1864.

JOHNSON, G. M., Private
Enlisted in Pitt County, July 20, 1863, for the war. Present or accounted for until transferred to Company G, 67th Regiment N.C. Troops on January 18, 1864.

JOHNSON, WILLIAM T., Private
Enlisted in Pitt County, August 1, 1863, for the war. Present or accounted for until transferred to Company G, 67th Regiment N.C. Troops on January 18, 1864.

JONES, CALVIN, Private
Enlisted in Pitt County, October 1, 1863, for the war. Present or accounted for until transferred to Company G, 67th Regiment N.C. Troops on January 18, 1864.

KILPATRICK, J. L., Sergeant
Enlisted in Pitt County, September 1, 1863, for the war. Appointed Sergeant when the company organized. Present or accounted for until transferred to Company G, 67th Regiment N.C. Troops on January 18, 1864.

KNOX, THOMAS S., Private
Enlisted in Pitt County, July 1, 1863, for the war. Present or accounted for until transferred to Company G, 67th Regiment N.C. Troops on January 18, 1864.

LANG, JONATHAN, Private
Enlisted in Pitt County, June 21, 1863, for the war. Present or accounted for until transferred to Company G, 67th Regiment N.C. Troops on January 18, 1864.

LaROGUE, F. M., Private
Enlisted in Pitt County, July 1, 1863, for the war. Present or accounted for until transferred to Company G, 67th Regiment N.C. Troops on January 18, 1864.

LEE, AMOS, Private
Transferred from Company K of this battalion on November 1, 1863. Present or accounted for until transferred to Company G, 67th Regiment N.C.

Troops on January 18, 1864.

LITTLE, F. M., Private
Enlisted in Pitt County, November 1, 1863, for the war. Present or accounted for until transferred to Company G, 67th Regiment N.C. Troops on January 18, 1864.

McCOTTER, ROBERT B., Private
Transferred from Company E of this battalion September-October, 1863. Present or accounted for until transferred to Company G, 67th Regiment N.C. Troops on January 18, 1864.

McCOY, WILLIAM F., Private
Enlisted in Pitt County, July 18, 1863, for the war. Present or accounted for until transferred to Company G, 67th Regiment N.C. Troops on January 18, 1864.

McGLAWHON, AARON, Private
Enlisted in Pitt County, July 17, 1863, for the war. Present or accounted for until transferred to Company G, 67th Regiment N.C. Troops on January 18, 1864.

McGLAWHON, B. F., Private
Enlisted in Pitt County, June 6, 1863, for the war. Present or accounted for until transferred to Company G, 67th Regiment N.C. Troops on January 18, 1864.

McGLAWHON, HARVY, Private
Enlisted in Pitt County, July 17, 1863, for the war. Present or accounted for until transferred to Company G, 67th Regiment N.C. Troops on January 18, 1864.

McGLAWHON, JERRY, Private
Enlisted in Pitt County, June 15, 1863, for the war. Present or accounted for until transferred to Company G, 67th Regiment N.C. Troops on January 18, 1864.

MANNING, CHARLES, Private
Enlisted in Pitt County, June 15, 1863, for the war. Present or accounted for until transferred to Company G, 67th Regiment N.C. Troops on January 18, 1864.

MANNING, JAMES, Private
Enlisted in Pitt County, June 1, 1863, for the war. Present or accounted for until transferred to Company G, 67th Regiment N.C. Troops on January 18, 1864.

MOORE, STEPHEN, Private
Enlisted in Pitt County, July 21, 1863, for the war. Present or accounted for until transferred to Company G, 67th Regiment N.C. Troops on January 18, 1864.

MOSLEY, AUGUSTUS, Private
Enlisted in Pitt County, June 6, 1863, for the war. Present or accounted for until transferred to Company G, 67th Regiment N.C. Troops on January 18, 1864.

MOYE, WILLIAM B., Private
Enlisted in Pitt County, July 21, 1863, for the war. Transferred to Company I of this battalion September-October, 1863.

NORMAN, WILLIAM H., Private
Enlisted in Pitt County, June 17, 1863, for the war.

Present or accounted for until transferred to Company G, 67th Regiment N.C. Troops on January 18, 1864.

PARKER, R. B., Private
Enlisted in Pitt County, September 1, 1863, for the war. Present or accounted for until transferred to Company G, 67th Regiment N.C. Troops on January 18, 1864.

PATE, HUTCHING, Private
Enlisted in Pitt County, January 15, 1863, for the war. Present or accounted for until transferred to Company G, 67th Regiment N.C. Troops on January 18, 1864.

SLAUGHTER, WILLIAM JAMES, Private
Enlisted in Pitt County, September 10, 1863, for the war. Present or accounted for until transferred to Company G, 67th Regiment N.C. Troops on January 18, 1864.

SMITH, ABRAHAM, Private
Enlisted in Pitt County, November 1, 1863, for the war. Transferred to Company K of this battalion November-December, 1863.

SMITH, HARDY, Private
Enlisted in Pitt County, June 15, 1863, for the war. Present or accounted for until transferred to Company G, 67th Regiment N.C. Troops on January 18, 1864.

SMITH. R. L., Corporal
Enlisted in Pitt County, April 1, 1863, for the war. Appointed Corporal when the company organized. Present or accounted for until transferred to Company G, 67th Regiment N.C. Troops on January 18, 1864.

SMITH, THOMAS H., Private
Enlisted in Pitt County, April 1, 1863, for the war. Present or accounted for until transferred to Company G, 67th Regiment N.C. Troops on January 18, 1864.

SUGGS, REUBEN, Corporal
Resided in Greene County and enlisted in Pitt County, June 1, 1863, for the war. Appointed Corporal when the company organized. Present or accounted for until transferred to Company G, 67th Regiment N.C. Troops on January 18, 1864.

SUMERELL, SAMUEL, Private
Enlisted in Pitt County, November 1, 1863, for the war. Transferred to Company K of this battalion November-December, 1863.

SUMERELL, W S., Private
Enlisted in Pitt County, June 6, 1863, for the war. Present or accounted for until transferred to Company G, 67th Regiment N.C. Troops on January 18, 1864.

TAYLOR, FREDERICK G., Private
Transferred from Company K of this battalion in January, 1864. Present or accounted for until transferred to Company G, 67th Regiment N.C. Troops on January 18, 1864.

TAYLOR, R. B., Sergeant
Enlisted in Pitt County, July 21, 1863, for the war. Appointed Sergeant when the company organized. Present or accounted for until transferred to

Company G, 67th Regiment N.C. Troops on January 18, 1864.

TILGHMAN, J. J., Private
Enlisted in Pitt County, June 1, 1863, for the war. Present or accounted for until transferred to Company G, 67th Regiment N.C. Troops on January 18, 1864.

TULL, LEMUEL H., Private
Enlisted in Pitt County, August 1, 1863, for the war while still a member of Company I, 66th Regiment N.C. Troops. Returned to his original organization November-December, 1863.

TURNER, B. C., Corporal
Enlisted in Pitt County, June 9, 1863, for the war. Appointed Corporal when the company organized. Present or accounted for until transferred to Company G, 67th Regiment N.C. Troops on January 18. 1864.

TUTON, W. J., Musician
Enlisted in Pitt County, April 15, 1863, for the war. Appointed Musician when the company organized. Present or accounted for until transferred to Company G, 67th Regiment N.C. Troops on January 18, 1864.

TYSON, BENJAMIN F., Private
Resided in Wayne County and enlisted in Pitt County, June 1, 1863, for the war. Present or accounted for until transferred to Company G, 67th Regiment N.C. Troops on January 18, 1864.

WILSON, WILLIAM, Private
Enlisted in Pitt County, June 14, 1863, for the war. Present or accounted for until transferred to Company G, 67th Regiment N.C. Troops on January 18, 1864.

WINDLY, WILLIAM E., Private
Enlisted in Pitt County, June 15, 1863, for the war. Present or accounted for until transferred to Company G, 67th Regiment N.C. Troops on January 18, 1864.

YELVINGTON, ASA A., Private
Enlisted in Pitt County, September 19, 1863, for the war. Present or accounted for until transferred to Company G, 67th Regiment N.C. Troops on January 18, 1864.

YOUNG, B. F., Private
Enlisted in Pitt County, January 19, 1863, for the war. Present or accounted for until transferred to Company G, 67th Regiment N.C. Troops on January 18, 1864.

COMPANY H

This company, known as "Tecumseh Scouts," began organizing in July, 1863, with recruits from Craven, Lenoir, and Duplin counties. In August recruits were added from Jones and Onslow counties, and in September men enlisted from Sampson County. The company commander was appointed to rank from June 25, 1863, and the lieutenants were appointed to rank from August 12 and 20, 1863. Thus it appears the company organization was completed in August, and it was accepted into state service and attached to this battalion. After joining the battalion the company functioned as a part of the battalion, and its history is recorded as a part of the battalion history. By Special Orders No. 8, paragraph 2, Adjutant General's Office, Raleigh, January 18, 1864, the battalion was redesignated the 67th Regiment N.C. Troops, and this company became Company H of the regiment.

The following roster of the company covers from the date of enlistment through the date of redesignation. All events after that date are recorded in the roster of Company H, 67th Regiment N.C. Troops. The information contained in the following roster was compiled principally from company muster rolls which covered from the date of enlistment to September 2, 1863, and from November 1, 1863, to the date of redesignation, January 18, 1864. No muster rolls were found for the period September 3-October 31, 1863. Although there are no Roll of Honor records for this company, useful information was obtained from receipt rolls, hospital records, prisoner of war records, and other primary records, supplemented by state pension applications, United Daughters of the Confederacy records, and postwar rosters and histories.

OFFICERS

CAPTAIN

FOY, CHRISTOPHER D.
Previously served in Company A, 8th Battalion N.C. Partisan Rangers. Appointed Captain of this company to rank from June 25, 1863. Present or accounted for until transferred to Company H, 67th Regiment N.C. Troops on January 18, 1864.

LIEUTENANTS

HOUSTON, ALFRED, 2nd Lieutenant
Appointed 2nd Lieutenant of this company to rank from August 20, 1863. Present or accounted for until transferred to Company H, 67th Regiment N.C. Troops on January 18, 1864.

MATTOCKS, EDWARD WARD, 3rd Lieutenant
Appointed 3rd Lieutenant of this company to rank from August 26, 1863. Present or accounted for until transferred to Company H, 67th Regiment N.C. Troops on January 18, 1864.

WOOTEN, JOHN BARCLIFF, 1st Lieutenant
Appointed 1st Lieutenant of this company to rank from August 12, 1863. Present or accounted for until transferred to Company H, 67th Regiment N.C. Troops on January 18, 1864.

NONCOMMISSIONED OFFICERS AND PRIVATES

ALPHIN, JESSE, Private
Enlisted in Lenoir County, July 12, 1863, for the war. Present or accounted for until transferred to Company H, 67th Regiment N.C. Troops on January 18, 1864.

AMBROSE, D. R., 1st Sergeant
Enlisted in Onslow County, August 20, 1863, for the war. Appointed 1st Sergeant when the company organized. Present or accounted for until transferred to Company H, 67th Regiment N.C. Troops on January 18, 1864.

AMYETT. AMOS. Private
Enlisted in Jones County, August 20, 1863, for the war. Reported as present on muster roll dated September 2, 1863. No further records.

ARNOLD, BRYAN, Private
Enlisted in Craven County, July 13, 1863, for the war. "Deserted January 1, 1864." Absent without leave when transferred to Company H, 67th Regiment N.C. Troops on January 18, 1864.

ARNOLD, FREEMAN, Private
Enlisted in Craven County, July 12, 1863, for the war. Present or accounted for until transferred to Company H, 67th Regiment N.C. Troops on January 18, 1864.

AVERY, JOHN EDWARD, Private
Enlisted in Craven County, July 12, 1863, for the war. Present or accounted for until transferred to Company H, 67th Regiment N.C. Troops on January 18, 1864.

BAILEY, CLEMOND, Private
Enlisted in Craven County, July 12, 1863, for the war. "Deserted to the enemy October 15, 1863." Absent without leave when transferred to Company H, 67th Regiment N.C. Troops on January 18, 1864.

BAILEY, HENRY, Private
Enlisted in Craven County, July 12, 1863, for the war. "Deserted to the enemy October 15, 1863." Absent without leave when transferred to Company H, 67th Regiment N.C. Troops on January 18, 1864.

BAKER, WILLIAM J., Private
Enlisted in Craven County, July 12, 1863, for the war. Reported on the September 2, 1863, muster roll with the remark: "Captured by the enemy on the night of August 5, having been ordered to report on the 6th."

BALLARD, WILLIAM R., Private
Enlisted in Jones County, August 12, 1863, for the war. Present or accounted for until transferred to Company H, 67th Regiment N.C. Troops on January 18, 1864.

BASS, B. L., Private
Enlisted in Sampson County, September 29, 1863, for the war. Present or accounted for until transferred to Company H, 67th Regiment N.C. Troops on January 18, 1864.

BASS, HILLERY, Private
Enlisted in Sampson County, September 29, 1863, for the war. Present or accounted for until transferred to Company H, 67th Regiment N.C. Troops on January 18, 1864.

BELL, J. M., Private
Enlisted in Onslow County, November 9, 1863, for the war. Present or accounted for until transferred to Company H, 67th Regiment N.C. Troops on January 18, 1864.

BLACKWELL, THOMAS L., Sergeant
Enlisted in Lenoir County, August 19, 1863, for the war. Appointed Sergeant when the company organized. Transferred to Company H, 10th Regiment N.C. State Troops (1st Regiment N.C. Artillery) January 3, 1864.

BLAKE, JACOB, Private
Enlisted in Onslow County, August 20, 1863, for the war. Present or accounted for until transferred to Company H, 67th Regiment N.C. Troops on January 18, 1864.

BLIZZARD, ALEXANDER, Private
Enlisted in Duplin County, August 20, 1863, for the war. Present or accounted for until transferred to Company H, 67th Regiment N.C. Troops on January 18, 1864.

BLIZZARD, E. H., Private
Enlisted in Duplin County at age 36, August 20, 1863, for the war. Detailed as a teamster at Kinston on October 11, 1863. Absent on detail when transferred to Company H, 67th Regiment N.C. Troops on January 18, 1864.

BONEY, TIMOTHY W., Private
Enlisted in Duplin County, August 20, 1863, for the war. Present or accounted for until transferred to Company H, 67th Regiment N.C. Troops on January 18, 1864.

BOYETT, JOHN W., Private
Enlisted in Duplin County, July 21, 1863, for the war. Present or accounted for until transferred to Company H, 67th Regiment N.C. Troops on January 18, 1864.

BRINSON, D. J., Private
Enlisted "in camp" on December 1, 1863, for the war. Present or accounted for until transferred to Company H, 67th Regiment N.C. Troops on January 18, 1864.

BROCK, ROBERT M., Private
Enlisted in Craven County, July 12, 1863, for the war. "Deserted to the enemy January 1, 1864." Absent without leave when transferred to Company H, 67th Regiment N.C. Troops on January 18, 1864.

BROWN, G. W., Private
Enlisted "in camp" on January 7, 1864, for the war. Transferred to Company H, 67th Regiment N.C. Troops on January 18, 1864.

BROWN, NEEDHAM, Private
Enlisted "in camp" on December 1, 1863, for the war. Present or accounted for until transferred to Company H, 67th Regiment N.C. Troops on January 18, 1864.

BUTTS, SAMUEL J., Private
Enlisted in Duplin County, August 20, 1863, for the war. Present or accounted for until transferred to Company H, 67th Regiment N.C. Troops on January 18, 1864.

CANNON, CANNY, Private
Enlisted "in camp" on November 17, 1863, for the war. Present or accounted for until transferred to Company H, 67th Regiment N.C. Troops on January 18, 1864.

CARMAC, GEORGE W., Private
Enlisted in Craven County, August 20, 1863, for the war. Present or accounted for until transferred to Company H, 67th Regiment N.C. Troops on January 18, 1864.

CARR, J. D., Private
Enlisted in Duplin County, November 6, 1863, for the war. Present or accounted for until transferred to Company H, 67th Regiment N.C. Troops on January 18, 1864.

CARR, J. O., Sergeant
Enlisted in Duplin County, October 3, 1863, for the war. Appointed Sergeant when the company organized. Present or accounted for until transferred to Company H, 67th Regiment N.C. Troops on January 18, 1864.

CARR, JACOB W., Private
Enlisted in Duplin County, December 16, 1863, for the war. Present or accounted for until transferred to Company H, 67th Regiment N.C. Troops on January 18, 1864.

CARR, W. B., Corporal
Enlisted in Duplin County, October 3, 1863, for the war. Appointed Corporal when the company organized. Present or accounted for until transferred to Company H, 67th Regiment N.C. Troops on January 18, 1864.

CHAMBERS, JOHN W., Private
Enlisted in Duplin County, July 21, 1863, for the war. Present or accounted for until transferred to Company H, 67th Regiment N.C. Troops on January 18, 1864.

COLE, JOSEPH, Private
Enlisted in Duplin County, July 21, 1863, for the war. Present or accounted for until transferred to Company H, 67th Regiment N.C. Troops on January 18, 1864.

COSTON, JAMES, Private
Enlisted in Duplin County, August 7, 1863, for the war. Present or accounted for until transferred to Company H, 67th Regiment N.C. Troops on January 18, 1864.

COTTLE, McDONALD, Private
Enlisted in Duplin County, August 6, 1863, for the war. Present or accounted for until transferred to Company H, 67th Regiment N.C. Troops on January 18, 1864.

DEAL, JOHN, Private
Enlisted in Duplin County, July 21, 1863, for the war. Present or accounted for until transferred to Company H, 67th Regiment N.C. Troops on January 18, 1864.

DIXON, ROBERT L., Private
Enlisted in Duplin County, August 20, 1863, for the war. Present or accounted for until transferred to Company H, 67th Regiment N.C. Troops on January 18, 1864.

DOYETY, GEORGE W., Private
Enlisted in Craven County, July 12, 1863, for the war. Reported on the September 2, 1863, muster roll with the remark: "Captured by the enemy on the night of 5 August, having been ordered to report on the 6th."

DOYETY, HARDY, Private

Enlisted in Craven County, July 12, 1863, for the war. Reported on the September 2, 1863, muster roll with the remark: "Captured by the enemy on the night of 5 August, having been ordered to report on the 6th."

DUFF, RILEY, Private

Enlisted in Duplin County, October 19, 1863, for the war. Present or accounted for until transferred to Company H, 67th Regiment N.C. Troops on January 18, 1864.

DUNN, JOHN, Private

Enlisted in Craven County, July 12, 1863, for the war. Present or accounted for until transferred to Company H, 67th Regiment N.C. Troops on January 18, 1864.

FAISON, J. A., Private

Enlisted "in camp" on September 29, 1863, for the war. Present or accounted for until transferred to Company H, 67th Regiment N.C. Troops on January 18, 1864.

FARRIOR, E. W., Private

Enlisted "in camp" on November 25, 1863, for the war. Present or accounted for until transferred to Company H, 67th Regiment N.C. Troops on January 18, 1864.

FARRIOR, HUGH, Private

Enlisted "in camp" on November 25, 1863, for the war. Present or accounted for until transferred to Company H, 67th Regiment N.C. Troops on January 18, 1864.

FISHER, THOMAS, Private

Enlisted "in camp" on December 10, 1863, for the war. Present or accounted for until transferred to Company H, 67th Regiment N.C. Troops on January 18, 1864.

FOSCUE, J. N., Private

Enlisted "in camp" on September 23, 1863, for the war. Present or accounted for until transferred to Company H, 67th Regiment N.C. Troops on January 18, 1864.

FOUNTAIN, J. W., Private

Enlisted in Onslow County, August 20, 1863, for the war. Present or accounted for until transferred to Company H, 67th Regiment N.C. Troops on January 18, 1864.

FOY, E. W., Private

Enlisted in Onslow County, August 20, 1863, for the war. Present or accounted for until transferred to Company H, 67th Regiment N.C. Troops on January 18, 1864.

FREDERICK, N. F., Private

Enlisted in Duplin County, August 20, 1863, for the war. Accidentally wounded in camp and absent sick when transferred to Company H, 67th Regiment N.C. Troops on January 18, 1864.

FURLOW, D. W., Private

Enlisted "in camp" on November 17, 1863, for the war. Present or accounted for until transferred to Company H, 67th Regiment N.C. Troops on January 18, 1864.

FUSSELL, JOHN G., Corporal

Enlisted in Duplin County, August 20, 1863, for the war. Appointed Corporal when the company organized. Present or accounted for until transferred to Company H, 67th Regiment N.C. Troops on January 18, 1864.

FUSSELL, STEPHEN, Private

Enlisted in Duplin County, August 20, 1863, for the war. Present or accounted for until transferred to Company H, 67th Regiment N.C. Troops on January 18, 1864.

GAYLORD, CHARLES A. R., Private

Captured at Plymouth on December 19, 1863, and confined at Point Lookout, Maryland. Absent in confinement when transferred to Company H, 67th Regiment N.C. Troops on January 18, 1864.

GOODING, F. C. G., Private

Enlisted in Craven County, July 12, 1863, for the war. Present or accounted for until transferred to Company H, 67th Regiment N.C. Troops on January 18, 1864.

GOODING, STEPHEN, Private

Enlisted in Lenoir County, August 20, 1863, for the war. Present or accounted for until transferred to Company H, 67th Regiment N.C. Troops on January 18, 1864.

GOODSON, GEORGE W., Private

Enlisted in Duplin County, August 20, 1863, for the war. Present or accounted for until transferred to Company H, 67th Regiment N.C. Troops on January 18, 1864.

GRADY, ELISHA, Private

Enlisted in Duplin County, July 21, 1863, for the war. Present or accounted for until transferred to Company H, 67th Regiment N.C. Troops on January 18, 1864.

GRADY, J. K., Private

Enlisted "in camp" on December 5, 1863, for the war. Present or accounted for until transferred to Company H, 67th Regiment N.C. Troops on January 18, 1864.

GREEN, J. F., Private

Transferred from Company F of this battalion on December 15, 1863. No further records.

GREEN, W. M., Private

Transferred from Company F of this battalion on December 15, 1863. No further records.

HALL, JAMES, Private

Enlisted "in camp" on December 4, 1863, for the war. Present or accounted for until transferred to Company H, 67th Regiment N.C. Troops on January 18, 1864.

HALSO, WILSON W., Corporal

Enlisted in Duplin County, July 21, 1863, for the war. Appointed Corporal when the company organized. Present or accounted for until transferred to Company H, 67th Regiment N.C. Troops on January 18, 1864.

HARRISON, JAMES L., Private

Enlisted in Jones County, August 20, 1863, for the war. Present or accounted for until transferred to Company H, 67th Regiment N.C. Troops on January 18, 1864.

HASSELL, J. T., Private

Captured near Plymouth on December 17, 1863, and confined at Point Lookout, Maryland. Absent in confinement when transferred to Company H, 67th Regiment N.C. Troops on January 18, 1864.

HAWKINS, W. H., Private

Enlisted "in camp" on December 15, 1863, for the war. Present or accounted for until transferred to Company H, 67th Regiment N.C. Troops on January 18, 1864.

HAY, LORENZO, Private

Enlisted "in camp" on November 18, 1863, for the war. Present or accounted for until transferred to Company H, 67th Regiment N.C. Troops on January 18, 1864.

HEATH, JESSE, Private

Enlisted in Craven County, July 12, 1863, for the war. Reported on the September 2, 1863, muster roll with the remark: "Captured by the enemy on the night of 5 August, having been ordered to report on the 6th."

HEATH, WILLIAM, Private

Enlisted in Craven County, July 12, 1863, for the war. Reported on the September 2, 1863, muster roll with the remark: "Absent without leave."

HENDERSON, ELIZA, Private

Enlisted in Duplin County, July 21, 1863, for the war. Present or accounted for until transferred to Company H, 67th Regiment N.C. Troops on January 18, 1864.

HENDERSON, L. H., Private

Enlisted in Onslow County, August 15, 1863, for the war. Present or accounted for until transferred to Company H, 67th Regiment N.C. Troops on January 18, 1864.

HENDERSON, NIXON, Private

Enlisted in Duplin County, August 20, 1863, for the war. Present or accounted for until transferred to Company H, 67th Regiment N.C. Troops on January 18, 1864.

HENDERSON, THOMAS, Private

Enlisted in Duplin County, October 20, 1863, for the war. Present or accounted for until transferred to Company H, 67th Regiment N.C. Troops on January 18, 1864.

HOUSTON, EDWARD W., Sergeant

Enlisted in Duplin County, July 21, 1863, for the war. Appointed Sergeant when the company organized. Present or accounted for until transferred to Company H, 67th Regiment N.C. Troops on January 18, 1864.

HOUSTON, H. C., Corporal

Enlisted in Duplin County, August 6, 1863, for the war. Appointed Corporal when the company organized. Present or accounted for until transferred to Company H, 67th Regiment N.C. Troops on January 18, 1864.

HOUSTON, WILLIAM, Private

Enlisted in Duplin County, July 20, 1863, for the war. Present or accounted for until transferred to Company H, 67th Regiment N.C. Troops on January 18, 1864.

HOWARD, B. S., Private

Enlisted in Onslow County, November 9, 1863, for the war. Present or accounted for until transferred to Company H, 67th Regiment N.C. Troops on January 18, 1864.

HUGGINS, JAMES F., Private

Enlisted in Jones County, August 6, 1863, for the war. Present or accounted for until transferred to Company H, 67th Regiment N.C. Troops on January 18, 1864.

JONES, RILEY, Private

Enlisted in Duplin County, July 21, 1863, for the war. Present or accounted for until transferred to Company H, 67th Regiment N.C. Troops on January 18, 1864.

KENNEDY, HILLERY, Private

Enlisted in Onslow County, August 20, 1863, for the war. Present or accounted for until transferred to Company H, 67th Regiment N.C. Troops on January 18, 1864.

KENNEDY, JOHN W., Private

Enlisted in Duplin County at age 45, August 20, 1863, for the war. Detailed as a teamster at Kinston on October 11, 1863. Absent on detail when transferred to Company H, 67th Regiment N.C. Troops on January 18, 1864.

KILPATRICK, FRANCIS, Private

Enlisted in Craven County, July 12, 1863, for the war. Transferred to Company F of this battalion on December 15, 1863.

KIMMEY, JAMES, Private

Enlisted in Duplin County, August 6, 1863, for the war. Detailed as a teamster at Kinston on October 11, 1863. Absent on detail when transferred to Company H, 67th Regiment N.C. Troops on January 18, 1864.

KING, FREDERICK, Private

Enlisted "in camp" on December 20, 1863, for the war. Present or accounted for until transferred to Company H, 67th Regiment N.C. Troops on January 18, 1864.

KORNEGAY, DANIEL, Private

Enlisted in Duplin County, August 20, 1863, for the war. Present or accounted for until transferred to Company H, 67th Regiment N.C. Troops on January 18, 1864.

KORNEGAY, WILLIAM, Private

Enlisted "in camp" on December 1, 1863, for the war. Present or accounted for until transferred to Company H, 67th Regiment N.C. Troops on January 18, 1864.

LANIER, S. L., Private

Enlisted "in camp" on January 7, 1864, for the war. Present or accounted for until transferred to Company H, 67th Regiment N.C. Troops on January 18, 1864.

LANIER, W. W., Private

Enlisted in Duplin County, August 20, 1863, for the war. Present or accounted for until transferred to Company H, 67th Regiment N.C. Troops on January 18, 1864.

LOYD, THOMAS, Private
Enlisted in Onslow County, August 20, 1863, for the war. Present or accounted for until transferred to Company H, 67th Regiment N.C. Troops on January 18, 1864.

McCOY, ALEXANDER, Private
Enlisted in Craven County, July 12, 1863, for the war. "Deserted to the enemy January 1, 1864." Absent without leave when transferred to Company H, 67th Regiment N.C. Troops on January 18, 1864.

McCREARY, ROBERT A., Private
Enlisted in Davidson County at age 17, August 4, 1863, for the war. Present or accounted for until transferred to Company H, 67th Regiment N.C. Troops on January 18, 1864.

MAIDES, W. F., Private
Enlisted "in camp" on November 17, 1863, for the war. Present or accounted for until transferred to Company H, 67th Regiment N.C. Troops on January 18, 1864.

MALLARD, A. B., Private
Enlisted in Duplin County, July 21, 1863, for the war. Present or accounted for until transferred to Company H, 67th Regiment N.C. Troops on January 18, 1864.

MARSHALL, JOSEPH, Private
Enlisted in Onslow County, August 15, 1863, for the war. Present or accounted for until transferred to Company H, 67th Regiment N.C. Troops on January 18, 1864.

MARTIN, THOMAS, Private
Enlisted in Onslow County, November 20, 1863, for the war. Present or accounted for until transferred to Company H, 67th Regiment N.C. Troops on January 18, 1864.

MASHBURN, HALSO, Private
Enlisted in Duplin County, July 20, 1863, for the war. Present or accounted for until transferred to Company H, 67th Regiment N.C. Troops on January 18, 1864.

MASHBURN, JAMES M., Private
Enlisted in Duplin County, August 20, 1863, for the war. Present or accounted for until transferred to Company H, 67th Regiment N.C. Troops on January 18, 1864.

MELTON, FRANK, Private
Enlisted "in camp" on January 4, 1864, for the war. Present or accounted for until transferred to Company H, 67th Regiment N.C. Troops on January 18, 1864.

MEREADY, OBID, Private
Enlisted in Duplin County, August 20, 1863, for the war. Present or accounted for until transferred to Company H, 67th Regiment N.C. Troops on January 18, 1864.

MERRITT, J. T., Private
Enlisted in Duplin County, November 20, 1863, for the war. Present or accounted for until transferred to Company H, 67th Regiment N.C. Troops on January 18, 1864.

MERRITT, J. W., Private
Enlisted in Duplin County, October 3, 1863, for the war. Present or accounted for until transferred to Company H, 67th Regiment N.C. Troops on January 18, 1864.

MOORE, JAMES, Private
Enlisted in Duplin County, August 20, 1863, for the war. Present or accounted for until transferred to Company H, 67th Regiment N.C. Troops on January 18, 1864.

MOORE, W. R., Sergeant
Enlisted in Johnston County, October 17, 1863, for the war. Mustered in as Private and appointed Sergeant on December 1, 1863. Present or accounted for until transferred to Company H, 67th Regiment N.C. Troops on January 18, 1864.

MORTON, A. D., Private
Enlisted in Onslow County, August 20, 1863, for the war. Died at home on September 30, 1863.

MORTON, DAVID, Private
Enlisted in Craven County, July 12, 1863, for the war. "Deserted to the enemy January 1, 1864." Absent without leave when transferred to Company H, 67th Regiment N.C. Troops on January 18, 1864.

MURRAY, J. W., Private
Enlisted "in camp" on November 23, 1863, for the war. Present or accounted for until transferred to Company H, 67th Regiment N.C. Troops on January 18, 1864.

NEWBERN, HUNTER, Private
Captured near Plymouth on December 17, 1863, and confined at Point Lookout, Maryland. Absent in confinement when transferred to Company H, 67th Regiment N.C. Troops on January 18, 1864.

NEWCOM, JAMES, Private
Negro. Enlisted "in camp" on January 1, 1864, for the war and "transferred to Enrolling Officer of 3rd Congressional District."

NEWKIRK, J. L., Private
Enlisted "in camp" on January 2, 1864, for the war. Transferred to Company H, 67th Regiment N.C. Troops on January 18, 1864.

NOBLES, KINSEY, Private
Enlisted in Lenoir County, August 20, 1863, for the war. Present or accounted for until transferred to Company H, 67th Regiment N.C. Troops on January 18, 1864.

OGLESBY, F. V., Private
Enlisted in Lenoir County, July 12, 1863, for the war. Detailed as a carpenter at Kinston in August, 1863. Absent on detail when transferred to Company H, 67th Regiment N.C. Troops on January 18, 1864.

PARKER, RICHARD, Private
Enlisted in Onslow County, November 9, 1863, for the war. Present or accounted for until transferred to Company H, 67th Regiment N.C. Troops on January 18, 1864.

PATRICK, AUGUSTUS, Private
Enlisted in Pitt County, July 12, 1863, for the war. Present or accounted for until transferred to Company H, 67th Regiment N.C. Troops on January 18, 1864.

PATRICK, F. A., Private

Enlisted in Jones County, July 12, 1863, for the war. Transferred to Company F of this battalion on December 15, 1863.

PICKET, J. Q., Private

Enlisted in Onslow County, August 20, 1863, for the war. Present or accounted for until transferred to Company H, 67th Regiment N.C. Troops on January 18, 1864.

POWELL, A. M., Private

Enlisted in Duplin County, July 21, 1863, for the war. Reported on the September 2, 1863, muster roll as "retained by the Superintendent of the W & W Railroad." No further records.

POWELL, J. W., Private

Enlisted in Duplin County, July 21, 1863, for the war. Present or accounted for until transferred to Company H, 67th Regiment N.C. Troops on January 18, 1864.

RAYNER, JOHN J., Private

Enlisted in Duplin County, July 21, 1863, for the war. Present or accounted for until transferred to Company H, 67th Regiment N.C. Troops on January 18, 1864.

RAYNER, JOHN L., Private

Enlisted in Duplin County, July 21, 1863, for the war. Present or accounted for until transferred to Company H, 67th Regiment N.C. Troops on January 18, 1864.

RHODES, GEORGE C., Private

Enlisted in Duplin County, July 21, 1863, for the war. Present or accounted for until transferred to Company H, 67th Regiment N.C. Troops on January 18, 1864.

ROGERS, GILES, Private

Enlisted "in camp" on December 16, 1863, for the war. Present or accounted for until transferred to Company H, 67th Regiment N.C. Troops on January 18, 1864.

ROUSE, DAVID W., Private

Enlisted "in camp" on January 2, 1864, for the war. Present or accounted for until transferred to Company H, 67th Regiment N.C. Troops on January 18, 1864.

ROUSE, OWEN W., Private

Enlisted "in camp" on January 2, 1864, for the war. Present or accounted for until transferred to Company H, 67th Regiment N.C. Troops on January 18, 1864.

SEARS, ALEXANDER, Private

Enlisted in Lenoir County, August 20, 1863, for the war. Present or accounted for until transferred to Company H, 67th Regiment N.C. Troops on January 18, 1864.

SHOLAR, J. R., Private

Enlisted in Duplin County, November 2, 1863, for the war. Present or accounted for until transferred to Company H, 67th Regiment N.C. Troops on January 18, 1864.

SMITH, ELIAS, Private

Enlisted in Lenoir County, August 6, 1863, for the war. Present or accounted for until transferred to

Company H, 67th Regiment N.C. Troops on January 18, 1864.

SMITH, LEWIS, Sergeant

Enlisted in Craven County, July 12, 1863, for the war. Appointed Sergeant when the company organized. Present or accounted for until transferred to Company H, 67th Regiment N.C. Troops on January 18, 1864.

SNELL, S. H., Private

Captured near Plymouth on December 17, 1863, and confined at Point Lookout, Maryland. Absent in confinement when transferred to Company H, 67th Regiment N.C. Troops on January 18, 1864.

STANLY, BRYAN, Private

Enlisted in Onslow County, November 20, 1863, for the war. Present or accounted for until transferred to Company H, 67th Regiment N.C. Troops on January 18, 1864.

STINSON, ED F., Private

Enlisted in Davidson County at age 17, August 4, 1863, for the war. Present or accounted for until transferred to Company H, 67th Regiment N.C. Troops on January 18, 1864.

SWINSON, G. L., Private

Enlisted "in camp" on November 24, 1863, for the war. Present or accounted for until transferred to Company H, 67th Regiment N.C. Troops on January 18, 1864.

SWINSON, JACOB, Private

Enlisted in Onslow County, August 20, 1863, for the war. Present or accounted for until transferred to Company H, 67th Regiment N.C. Troops on January 18, 1864.

SWINSON, JOHN, Private

Enlisted in Onslow County, August 20, 1863, for the war. Present or accounted for until transferred to Company H, 67th Regiment N.C. Troops on January 18, 1864.

TAYLOR, J. A., Private

Enlisted "in camp" on November 17, 1863, for the war. Present or accounted for until transferred to Company H, 67th Regiment N.C. Troops on January 18, 1864.

TAYLOR, JOSEPH, Private

Enlisted in Craven County, July 12, 1863, for the war. Reported on September 2, 1863, muster roll as "absent without leave." No further records.

TEACHY, OWEN J., Private

Enlisted "in camp" on January 2, 1864, for the war. Present or accounted for until transferred to Company H, 67th Regiment N.C. Troops on January 18, 1864.

THOMPSON, DANIEL H., Private

Enlisted "in camp" on January 12, 1864, for the war. Transferred to Company H, 67th Regiment N.C. Troops on January 18, 1864.

VENTERS, W. G., Private

Enlisted "in camp" on January 5, 1864, for the war. Transferred to Company H, 67th Regiment N.C. Troops on January 18, 1864.

WALLER, HAYWOOD, Private

Enlisted "in camp" on December 2, 1863, for the

war. Present or accounted for until transferred to Company H, 67th Regiment N.C. Troops on January 18, 1864.

WATERS, HASKEL, Private

Enlisted "in camp" on December 17, 1863, for the war. Present or accounted for until transferred to Company H, 67th Regiment N.C. Troops on January 18, 1864.

WELLS, W. B., Private

Enlisted in Duplin County, October 3, 1863, for the war. Present or accounted for until transferred to Company H, 67th Regiment N.C. Troops on January 18, 1864.

WHITE, DORSEY, Private

Captured at Greenville on December 17, 1863, and confined at Point Lookout, Maryland. Absent in confinement when transferred to Company H, 67th Regiment N.C. Troops on January 18, 1864.

WHITE, ELI, Private

Enlisted in Craven County, August 12, 1863, for the war. Reported on September 2, 1863, muster roll as "captured by the enemy on the night of August 5, having been ordered to report on the 6th."

WHITE, RICHARD, Private

Enlisted in Craven County, July 12, 1863, for the war. Reported on September 2, 1863, muster roll as "captured by the enemy on the night of August 5, having been ordered to report on the 6th."

WHITE, ROBERT, Private

Enlisted in Craven County, July 12, 1863, for the war. Reported on September 2, 1863, muster roll as "captured by the enemy on the night of August 5, having been ordered to report on the 6th."

WHITE, VAN BUREN, Private

Captured near Greenville on December 17, 1863, and confined at Point Lookout, Maryland. Absent in confinement when transferred to Company H, 67th Regiment N.C. Troops on January 18, 1864.

WILKERSON, ELISHA, Private

Enlisted "in camp" on November 17, 1863, for the war. Present or accounted for until transferred to Company H, 67th Regiment N.C. Troops on January 18, 1864.

WILLIAMS, DURANT, Private

Enlisted "in camp" on December 22, 1863, for the war. Present or accounted for until transferred to Company H, 67th Regiment N.C. Troops on January 18, 1864.

WILLIAMS, EVANS, Private

Enlisted in Lenoir County, August 19, 1863, for the war. "Deserted to the enemy October 20, 1863." Absent without leave when transferred to Company H, 67th Regiment N.C. Troops on January 18, 1864.

WILLIAMS, HARPER, Private

Enlisted in Duplin County, July 21, 1863, for the war. Present or accounted for until transferred to Company H, 67th Regiment N.C. Troops on January 18, 1864.

WILLIAMS, JEREMIAH, Corporal

Enlisted in Craven County, July 12, 1863, for the war. Appointed Corporal when the company organized. "Deserted to the enemy November 15, 1863." Absent without leave when transferred to Company H, 67th Regiment N.C. Troops on January 18, 1864.

WILLIAMS, JOHN A., Private

Enlisted in Craven County, July 12, 1863, for the war. "Deserted to the enemy October 20, 1863." Absent without leave when transferred to Company H, 67th Regiment N.C. Troops on January 18, 1864.

WILLIAMS, JOHN W., Private

Enlisted in Onslow County, August 20, 1863, for the war. Present or accounted for until transferred to Company H, 67th Regiment N.C. Troops on January 18, 1864.

WILLIAMS, ROBERT J., Private

Enlisted in Duplin County, July 21, 1863, for the war. Present or accounted for until transferred to Company H, 67th Regiment N.C. Troops on January 18, 1864.

WILLIAMSON, ELISHA, Private

Enlisted in Onslow County, November 20, 1863, for the war. Present or accounted for until transferred to Company H, 67th Regiment N.C. Troops on January 18, 1864.

WILSON, Mc., Private

Enlisted in Onslow County, July 7, 1863, for the war. Present or accounted for until transferred to Company H, 67th Regiment N.C. Troops on January 18, 1864.

WILSON, WILLIAM, Private

Enlisted in Craven County, July 12, 1863, for the war. Present or accounted for until transferred to Company H, 67th Regiment N.C. Troops on January 18, 1864.

YEAMONS, EDEN, Private

Enlisted in Onslow County, November 20, 1863, for the war. Present or accounted for until transferred to Company H, 67th Regiment N.C. Troops on January 18, 1864.

COMPANY I

This company began organizing in Pitt County in July, 1863, and the commanding officer was commissioned to rank from September 22, 1863. After that date the company was accepted into state service and attached to this battalion in September-October, 1863. After joining the battalion the company functioned as a part of the battalion, and its history is recorded as a part of the battalion history. By Special Orders No. 8, paragraph 2, Adjutant General's Office, Raleigh, January 18, 1864, the battalion was redesignated the 67th Regiment N.C. Troops, and this company became Company I of the regiment.

The following roster of the company covers from the date of enlistment through the date of redesignation, January 18, 1864. All events after that date are recorded in the roster of Company I, 67th Regiment N.C. Troops. The information contained in the following roster was compiled principally from company muster rolls which covered from the date of enlistment through the date of redesignation. Although there are no Roll of Honor records for this company, useful information was obtained from receipt rolls, hospital records, prisoner of war records, and other primary records, supplemented by state pension applications, United Daughters of the Confederacy records, and postwar rosters and histories.

OFFICERS
CAPTAIN

WHITE, EDWARD F.
Transferred from Company A of this battalion upon appointment as 2nd Lieutenant to rank from August 1, 1863. Promoted to Captain on November 6, 1863, to rank from September 22, 1863. Present or accounted for until transferred to Company I, 67th Regiment N.C. Troops on January 18, 1864.

LIEUTENANTS

NEATHERY, JAMES K. P., 2nd Lieutenant
Transferred from Company C, 8th Regiment N.C. State Troops upon appointment as 2nd Lieutenant in this company to rank from November 20, 1863. Present or accounted for until transferred to Company I, 67th Regiment N.C. Troops on January 18, 1864.

TUCKER, WILLIAM W., 1st Lieutenant
Appointed 1st Lieutenant, November 6, 1863, to rank from September 22, 1863. Present or accounted for until transferred to Company I, 67th Regiment N.C. Troops on January 18, 1864.

WHITE, GEORGE W., 2nd Lieutenant
Transferred from Company A of this battalion upon appointment as 2nd Lieutenant to rank from September 22, 1863. Present or accounted for until transferred to Company I, 67th Regiment N.C. Troops on January 18, 1864.

NONCOMMISSIONED OFFICERS AND PRIVATES

ADAMS, JOHN A., Private
Transferred from Company K, 17th Regiment N.C. Troops (2nd Organization) November 1, 1863. Captured near Haddock's Cross Roads, Pitt County, November 25, 1863, and confined at Point Lookout, Maryland. Absent in confinement when transferred to Company I, 67th Regiment N.C. Troops on January 18, 1864.

BARRINGTON, W. H., Private
Transferred from Company E of this battalion in September, 1863. Present or accounted for until transferred to Company I, 67th Regiment N.C. Troops on January 18, 1864.

BELCHER, SHERWOOD, Private
Enlisted in Pitt County, September 15, 1863, for the war. Captured near Haddock's Cross Roads, Pitt County, November 25, 1863, and confined at Point Lookout, Maryland. Absent in confinement when transferred to Company I, 67th Regiment N.C. Troops on January 18, 1864.

BROADWAY, JESSE W., Private
Enlisted in Pitt County, July 3, 1863, for the war. Present or accounted for until transferred to Company I, 67th Regiment N.C. Troops on January 18, 1864.

CAMPBELL, ARCHIBALD E. Private
Enlisted in Pitt County, July 2, 1863, for the war. Captured near Haddock's Cross Roads, Pitt County, November 25, 1863, and confined at Point Lookout, Maryland. Absent in confinement when transferred to Company I, 67th Regiment N.C. Troops on January 18, 1864.

CARROL, JOHN. Private
Enlisted in Pitt County, October 15, 1863, for the war. Captured near Haddock's Cross Roads, Pitt County, November 25, 1863, and confined at Point Lookout, Maryland. Absent in confinement when transferred to Company I, 67th Regiment N.C. Troops on January 18, 1864.

CLARK, JOHN, Private
Enlisted in Pitt County, August 3, 1863, for the war. Captured near Haddock's Cross Roads, Pitt County, November 25, 1863, and confined at Point Lookout, Maryland. Absent in confinement when transferred to Company I, 67th Regiment N.C. Troops on January 18, 1864.

CLARK, WILLIAM H., Private
Enlisted in Pitt County, July 3, 1863, for the war. Captured near Haddock's Cross Roads, Pitt County, November 25, 1863, and confined at Point Lookout, Maryland. Absent in confinement when transferred to Company I, 67th Regiment N.C. Troops on January 18, 1864.

COBB, JAMES, Private
Enlisted in Pitt County, July 17, 1863, for the war. Present or accounted for until transferred to Company I, 67th Regiment N.C. Troops on January 18, 1864.

COBB. STEPHEN. Private
Enlisted in Pitt County, July 20, 1863, for the war. Captured near Haddock's Cross Roads, Pitt County, November 25, 1863, and confined at Point Lookout, Maryland. Absent in confinement when transferred to Company I, 67th Regiment N.C. Troops on January 18, 1864.

COBB, WILLIAM, Private
Enlisted in Pitt County, July 5, 1863, for the war. Captured near Haddock's Cross Roads, Pitt County, November 25, 1863, and confined at Point Lookout, Maryland. Absent in confinement when transferred to Company I, 67th Regiment N.C. Troops on January 18, 1864.

COLLINS, H. J., Private
Enlisted in Pitt County, November 10, 1863, for the war. Transferred to Company K of this battalion on January 1, 1864.

CORBITT, WILEY, Private
Enlisted in Pitt County, July 3, 1863, for the war. Present or accounted for until transferred to Company I, 67th Regiment N.C. Troops on January 18, 1864.

COREY, JAMES A., Sergeant
Transferred from Company E of this battalion in

September, 1863, and appointed Sergeant. Reported as "captured near Haddock's Cross Roads, November 25, 1863," and as "captured near Charles City Court House, December 13, 1863." Confined at Point Lookout, Maryland, December 29, 1863, and absent in confinement when transferred to Company I, 67th Regiment N.C. Troops on January 18, 1864.

COX, ABRAM, Private
Enlisted in Pitt County, July 2, 1863, for the war. Present or accounted for until transferred to Company I, 67th Regiment N.C. Troops on January 18, 1864.

COX, JOSEPH, Musician
Enlisted in Pitt County, September 9, 1863, for the war. Appointed Musician when the company organized. Present or accounted for until transferred to Company I, 67th Regiment N.C. Troops on January 18, 1864.

COX, JOSIAH, Private
Enlisted in Pitt County, July 10, 1863, for the war. Present or accounted for until transferred to Company I, 67th Regiment N.C. Troops on January 18, 1864.

COX, THOMAS, Private
Enlisted in Pitt County, July 1, 1863, for the war. Transferred to Company E of this battalion after October 31, 1863

DANIEL, JOHN L., Corporal
Enlisted in Pitt County, July 1, 1863, for the war. Mustered in as Private and appointed Corporal after October 31, 1863. Present or accounted for until transferred to Company I, 67th Regiment N.C. Troops on January 18, 1864.

DAUGHETY, ALFRED, Private
Transferred from Company E of this battalion in July, 1863. Present or accounted for until transferred to Company I, 67th Regiment N.C. Troops on January 18, 1864.

DAUGHETY, RICHARD, Private
Transferred from Company E of this battalion in July, 1863. Transferred to Company G of this battalion November-December, 1863.

DAVIS, WILLIAM J., Private
Enlisted in Pitt County, July 17, 1863, for the war. Captured near Haddock's Cross Roads, Pitt County, November 25, 1863, and confined at Point Lookout, Maryland. Absent in confinement when transferred to Company I, 67th Regiment N.C. Troops on January 18, 1864.

DEAL, MATTHEW, Private
Enlisted in Pitt County, August 14, 1863, for the war. Captured near Haddock's Cross Roads, Pitt County, November 25, 1863, and confined at Point Lookout, Maryland. Absent in confinement when transferred to Company I, 67th Regiment N.C. Troops on January 18, 1864.

DEAL, WILLIAM, Private
Enlisted in Pitt County, October 1, 1863, for the war. Captured near Haddock's Cross Roads, Pitt County, November 25, 1863, and confined at Point Lookout, Maryland. Absent in confinement when transferred to Company I, 67th Regiment N.C. Troops on January 18, 1864.

DIXON, ED S., Private
Enlisted in Pitt County, July 2, 1863, for the war. Present or accounted for through December, 1863, and reported as "absent without leave" when transferred to Company I, 67th Regiment N.C. Troops on January 18, 1864.

DIXON, SAMUEL J., Private
Enlisted in Pitt County, July 15, 1863, for the war. Captured near Haddock's Cross Roads, Pitt County, November 25, 1863, and confined at Point Lookout, Maryland. Absent in confinement when transferred to Company I, 67th Regiment N.C. Troops on January 18, 1864.

DOWNS, KENION, Private
Enlisted in Pitt County, July 1, 1863, for the war. Captured near Haddock's Cross Roads, Pitt County, November 25, 1863, and confined at Point Lookout, Maryland. Absent in confinement when transferred to Company I, 67th Regiment N.C. Troops on January 18, 1864.

EDWARDS, ALFRED, Private
Transferred from Company G of this battalion September-October, 1863. Captured near Haddock's Cross Roads, Pitt County, November 25, 1863, and confined at Point Lookout, Maryland. Absent in confinement when transferred to Company I, 67th Regiment N.C. Troops on January 18, 1864.

EDWARDS, WILLIAM H., Private
Enlisted in Pitt County, July 20, 1863, for the war. Present or accounted for until transferred to Company I, 67th Regiment N.C. Troops on January 18, 1864.

ELKS, CHARLES A., Private
Transferred from Company E of this battalion in September, 1863. Present or accounted for until transferred to Company I, 67th Regiment N.C. Troops on January 18, 1864.

ELKS, JACOB, Private
Enlisted in Pitt County, September 20, 1863, for the war. Captured near Haddock's Cross Roads, Pitt County, November 25, 1863, and confined at Point Lookout, Maryland. Absent in confinement when transferred to Company I, 67th Regiment N.C. Troops on January 18, 1864.

ELLIS, GEORGE B., Private
Enlisted in Pitt County, July 3, 1863, for the war. Present or accounted for until transferred to Company I, 67th Regiment N.C. Troops on January 18, 1864.

EVANS, ELIAS M., Private
Enlisted in Pitt County, July 1, 1863, for the war. Captured near Haddock's Cross Roads, Pitt County, November 25, 1863, and confined at Point Lookout, Maryland. Absent in confinement when transferred to Company I, 67th Regiment N.C. Troops on January 18, 1864.

EVANS, EPHRIAM, Private
Transferred from Company E of this battalion in July, 1863. Present or accounted for until transferred to Company I, 67th Regiment N.C. Troops on January 18, 1864.

EVANS, HENRY, Private
Enlisted in Pitt County, October 1, 1863, for the

war. Captured near Haddock's Cross Roads, Pitt County, November 25, 1863, and confined at Point Lookout, Maryland. Absent in confinement when transferred to Company I, 67th Regiment N.C. Troops on January 18, 1864.

EVANS, IVY, Private

Transferred from Company E of this battalion while absent in confinement at Point Lookout, Maryland, having been captured near Haddock's Cross Roads, Pitt County, November 25, 1863. Absent in confinement when transferred to Company I, 67th Regiment N.C. Troops on January 18, 1864.

FLEMMING, JAMES, Private

Enlisted in Pitt County, August 1, 1863, for the war. Captured near Haddock's Cross Roads, Pitt County, November 25, 1863, and confined at Point Lookout, Maryland. Absent in confinement when transferred to Company I, 67th Regiment N.C. Troops on January 18, 1864.

FORBES, JOHN, Private

Enlisted in Pitt County, September 22, 1863, for the war. Captured near Haddock's Cross Roads, Pitt County, November 25, 1863, and confined at Point Lookout, Maryland. Absent in confinement when transferred to Company I, 67th Regiment N.C. Troops on January 18, 1864.

GALLAWAY, JAMES, Private

Enlisted in Pitt County, July 1, 1863, for the war. Present or accounted for until transferred to Company I, 67th Regiment N.C. Troops on January 18, 1864.

GARDNER, WYATT, Private

Enlisted in Pitt County, July 17, 1863, for the war. Transferred to Company E of this battalion November-December, 1863.

GODLEY, JOHN, Private

Transferred from Company E of this battalion prior to October 31, 1863, and transferred back to Company E in January, 1864.

GRIZZARD, JESSE, Private

Enlisted in Pitt County, August 5, 1863, for the war. Captured near Haddock's Cross Roads, Pitt County, November 25, 1863, and confined at Point Lookout, Maryland. Absent in confinement when transferred to Company I, 67th Regiment N.C. Troops on January 18, 1864.

HADDOCK, WILLIAM H., Private

Enlisted in Pitt County, July 10, 1863, for the war. Present or accounted for until transferred to Company I, 67th Regiment N.C. Troops on January 18, 1864.

HARPER, FRANK, Private

Enlisted in Pitt County, July 10, 1863, for the war. Present or accounted for until transferred to Company I, 67th Regiment N.C. Troops on January 18, 1864.

HARRIS, A., Private

Transferred from Company E of this battalion July 1-October 31, 1863, and transferred to Company G of this battalion November-December, 1863.

HARRIS, HENRY, Private

Enlisted in Pitt County, October 28, 1863, for the war. Present or accounted for until transferred to Company I, 67th Regiment N.C. Troops on January 18, 1864.

HARRIS, THOMAS, Jr., Private

Enlisted in Pitt County, October 28, 1863, for the war. Reported on July 1-October 31, 1863, muster roll. No further records.

HARRIS, THOMAS, Sr., Private

Enlisted in Pitt County, July 17, 1863, for the war. Captured near Haddock's Cross Roads, Pitt County, November 25, 1863, and confined at Point Lookout, Maryland. Absent in confinement when transferred to Company I, 67th Regiment N.C. Troops on January 18, 1864.

HATHAWAY, FRANK, Private

Enlisted in Pitt County, July 17, 1863, for the war. Present or accounted for until transferred to Company I, 67th Regiment N.C. Troops on January 18, 1864.

JOHNSON, GREEN L., Musician

Enlisted in Pitt County, November 10, 1863, for the war. Appointed Musician when mustered in. Present or accounted for until transferred to Company I, 67th Regiment N.C. Troops on January 18, 1864.

JONES, FRED, Private

Transferred from Company E of this battalion in July, 1863, and appointed Corporal. Reduced to ranks after October 31, 1863. Present or accounted for until transferred to Company I, 67th Regiment N.C. Troops on January 18, 1864.

KEEL, SIMON J., Private

Enlisted in Pitt County, July 10, 1863, for the war. Present or accounted for until transferred to Company I, 67th Regiment N.C. Troops on January 18, 1864.

McLAWHORN, JONATHAN, Private

Transferred from Company E of this battalion in January, 1864. Transferred to Company I, 67th Regiment N.C. Troops on January 18, 1864.

MANNING, HENRY D., Private

Enlisted in Pitt County, August 1, 1863, for the war. Present or accounted for until transferred to Company I, 67th Regiment N.C. Troops on January 18, 1864.

MANNING, WILLIAM A., Private

Enlisted in Pitt County, November 1, 1863, for the war. Present or accounted for until transferred to Company I, 67th Regiment N.C. Troops on January 18, 1864.

MILLS, EDWARD, Private

Enlisted in Pitt County, October 1, 1863, for the war. Present or accounted for until transferred to Company I, 67th Regiment N.C. Troops on January 18, 1864.

MILLS, WILLIAM, Private

Enlisted in Pitt County, October 5, 1863, for the war. Present or accounted for until transferred to Company I, 67th Regiment N.C. Troops on January 18, 1864.

MOORE, GUILFORD, Sergeant
Enlisted in Pitt County, August 1, 1863, for the war. Appointed Sergeant when the company organized. Captured near Haddock's Cross Roads, Pitt County, November 25, 1863, and confined at Point Lookout, Maryland. Absent in confinement when transferred to Company I, 67th Regiment N.C. Troops on January 18, 1864.

MOSLEY, WILLIAM, Private
Enlisted in Pitt County, October 1, 1863, for the war. Present or accounted for until transferred to Company I, 67th Regiment N.C. Troops on January 18, 1864.

MOYE, WILLIAM B., Private
Transferred from Company G of this battalion September-October, 1863. Captured near Haddock's Cross Roads, Pitt County, November 25, 1863, and confined at Point Lookout, Maryland. Absent in confinement when transferred to Company I, 67th Regiment N.C. Troops on January 18, 1864.

PARKER, JOHN A., Private
Enlisted in Pitt County, December 1, 1863, for the war. Present or accounted for until transferred to Company I, 67th Regiment N.C. Troops on January 18, 1864.

PETERSON, CHARLES E., Private
Enlisted in Pitt County, July 10, 1863, for the war. Reported as 1st Sergeant on the July 1-October 31, 1863, muster roll and as Private on the October 31, 1863-February 29, 1864, muster roll. Transferred to Company I, 67th Regiment N.C. Troops on January 18, 1864.

POLLARD, REDDICK, Private
Enlisted in Pitt County, July 2, 1863, for the war. Captured near Haddock's Cross Roads, Pitt County, November 25, 1863, and confined at Point Lookout, Maryland. Absent in confinement when transferred to Company I, 67th Regiment N.C. Troops on January 18, 1864.

POLLARD, STANLY, Private
Enlisted in Pitt County, August 3, 1863, for the war. Captured near Haddock's Cross Roads, Pitt County, November 25, 1863, and confined at Point Lookout, Maryland. Absent in confinement when transferred to Company I, 67th Regiment N.C. Troops on January 18, 1864.

PORTER, ALLEN T., Corporal
Enlisted in Pitt County, July 1, 1863, for the war. Appointed Corporal when the company organized. Present or accounted for until transferred to Company I, 67th Regiment N.C. Troops on January 18, 1864.

RANDAL, ALEX, Private
Enlisted in Pitt County, November 20, 1863, for the war. Present or accounted for until transferred to Company I, 67th Regiment N.C. Troops on January 18, 1864.

RHEM, JOHN W., Sergeant
Transferred from Company B of this battalion prior to December 31, 1863, and appointed Corporal. Promoted to Sergeant soon after. Present or accounted for until transferred to Company I, 67th Regiment N.C. Troops on January 18, 1864.

RINGOLD, JAMES, Sergeant
Transferred from Company E of this battalion in January, 1864, as a Corporal and promoted to Sergeant soon after. Present or accounted for until transferred to Company I, 67th Regiment N.C. Troops on January 18, 1864.

SLAUGHTER, THEO, Private
Enlisted in Pitt County, August 8, 1863, for the war. Present or accounted for until transferred to Company I, 67th Regiment N.C. Troops on January 18, 1864.

SMITH, ABEL, Corporal
Enlisted in Pitt County, August 13, 1863, for the war. Appointed Corporal when the company organized. Captured near Haddock's Cross Roads, Pitt County, November 25, 1863, and confined at Point Lookout, Maryland. Absent in confinement when transferred to Company I, 67th Regiment N.C. Troops on January 18, 1864.

SMITH, JAMES, Private
Enlisted in Pitt County, November 20, 1863, for the war. Present or accounted for until transferred to Company I, 67th Regiment N.C. Troops on January 18, 1864.

SMITH, JOHN A., Private
Enlisted in Pitt County, August 15, 1863, for the war. Present or accounted for until transferred to Company I, 67th Regiment N.C. Troops on January 18, 1864.

SPAIN, FEATHERSTON, Private
Enlisted in Pitt County, July 20, 1863, for the war. Captured near Haddock's Cross Roads, Pitt County, November 25, 1863, and confined at Point Lookout, Maryland. Absent in confinement when transferred to Company I, 67th Regiment N.C. Troops on January 18, 1864.

STOCKS, HENRY, Private
Enlisted in Pitt County, July 2, 1863, for the war. Captured near Washington, North Carolina, October 11, 1863, and confined at Point Lookout, Maryland, where he died January 8, 1864.

STOCKS, RHODERICK, Private
Enlisted in Pitt County, July 2, 1863, for the war. Present or accounted for until transferred to Company I, 67th Regiment N.C. Troops on January 18, 1864.

STOCKS, SAMUEL, Private
Transferred from Company E of this battalion in January, 1864. Present or accounted for until transferred to Company I, 67th Regiment N.C. Troops on January 18, 1864.

TEEL, RICHARD, Private
Enlisted in Pitt County, July 20, 1863, for the war. Present or accounted for until transferred to Company I, 67th Regiment N.C. Troops on January 18, 1864.

TRIPP, CHARLES, Private
Enlisted in Pitt County, January 1, 1864, for the war. Transferred to Company I, 67th Regiment N.C. Troops on January 18, 1864.

accounted for until transferred to Company I, 67th Regiment N.C. Troops on January 18, 1864.

TRIPP, LEONARD, Private
Enlisted in Pitt County, October 15, 1863, for the war. Present or accounted for until transferred to Company I, 67th Regiment N.C. Troops on January 18, 1864.

VINSON, ANDREW, Private
Enlisted in Pitt County, July 30, 1863, for the war. Captured near Haddock's Cross Roads, Pitt County, November 25, 1863, and confined at Point Lookout, Maryland. Absent in confinement when transferred to Company I, 67th Regiment N.C. Troops on January 18, 1864.

WALTERS, HARDY, Private
Enlisted in Pitt County, November 20, 1863, for the war. Present or accounted for until transferred to Company I, 67th Regiment N.C. Troops on January 18, 1864.

WATSON, FRANK L., Private
Transferred from Company E of this battalion in July, 1863. Present or accounted for until transferred to Company I, 67th Regiment N.C. Troops on January 18, 1864.

WATSON, LEVI J., Private
Transferred from Company E of this battalion in July, 1863. Present or accounted for until transferred to Company I, 67th Regiment N.C. Troops on January 18, 1864.

WATSON, NATHAN, Corporal
Transferred from Company E of this battalion in July, 1863. Appointed Corporal when the company organized. Present or accounted for until transferred to Company I, 67th Regiment N.C. Troops on January 18, 1864.

WEBB, WILLIAM F., Private
Enlisted in Pitt County, September 30, 1863, for the war. Transferred to Company K, 17th Regiment N.C. Troops (2nd Organization) November 1, 1863.

WILLOUGHBY, JOHN F., Private
Enlisted in Pitt County, August 4, 1863, for the war. Present or accounted for until transferred to Company I, 67th Regiment N.C. Troops on January 18, 1864.

WILLOUGHBY, WILLIAM, Private
Enlisted in Pitt County, November 20, 1863, for the war. Died January 6, 1864.

WINDHAM, JOHN A., Private
Enlisted in Pitt County, July 2, 1863, for the war. Captured near Haddock's Cross Roads, Pitt County, November 25, 1863, and confined at Point Lookout, Maryland. Absent in confinement when transferred to Company I, 67th Regiment N.C. Troops on January 18, 1864.

WINFIELD, BENJAMIN P., 1st Sergeant
Enlisted in Pitt County, July 20, 1863, for the war. Mustered in as Sergeant and promoted to 1st Sergeant after October 31, 1863. Captured near Haddock's Cross Roads, Pitt County, November 25, 1863, and confined at Point Lookout, Maryland. Absent in confinement when transferred to Company I, 67th Regiment N.C. Troops on January 18, 1864.

YARBROUGH, JOHN, Private
Enlisted in Pitt County, November 20, 1863, for the war. Present or accounted for until transferred to Company I, 67th Regiment N.C Troops on January 18, 1864.

COMPANY K

This company of "Mounted Infantry" began organizing in Pitt County on August 1, 1863, and the commanding officer was appointed to rank from that date. Additional recruits were added in September, 1863, and the company was accepted into state service and attached to this battalion in September-October, 1863. After joining the battalion the company functioned as a part of the battalion, and its history is recorded as a part of the battalion history. By Special Orders No. 8, paragraph 2, Adjutant General's Office, Raleigh, January 18, 1864, the battalion was redesignated the 67th Regiment N.C. Troops, and this company became Company K of the regiment.

The following roster of the company covers from the date of enlistment through the date of redesignation, January 18, 1864. All events after that date are recorded in the roster of Company K, 67th Regiment N.C. Troops. The information contained in the following roster was compiled from company muster rolls which covered from September 15, 1863, through the date of redesignation, January 18, 1864. No muster rolls were found for the period prior to September 15, 1863. Although there are no Roll of Honor records for this company, useful information was obtained from receipt rolls, hospital records, prisoner of war records, and other primary records, supplemented by state pension applications, United Daughters of the Confederacy records, and postwar rosters and histories.

OFFICERS
CAPTAIN

MYERS, JOSEPH D.
Transferred from Company B of this battalion upon appointment as Captain of this company to rank from August 1, 1863. Present or accounted for until transferred to Company K, 67th Regiment N.C. Troops on January 18, 1864.

LIEUTENANT

TAYLOR, WILLIAM S., 1st Lieutenant
Resided in Greene County and enlisted on September 1, 1863, for the war. Appointed 1st Lieutenant on September 30, 1863, to rank from September 1, 1863. Present or accounted for until transferred to Company K, 67th Regiment N.C. Troops on January 18, 1864.

NONCOMMISSIONED OFFICERS AND PRIVATES

BAKER, IVEY R., Private
Enlisted in Pitt County, December 14, 1863, for

the war. Present or accounted for until transferred to Company K, 67th Regiment N.C. Troops on January 18, 1864.

BELL, OTTAWAY S., Private

Enlisted in Pitt County, September 15, 1863, for the war. Present or accounted for until transferred to Company K, 67th Regiment N.C. Troops on January 18, 1864.

BEXLEY, JAMES, Private

Enlisted in Pitt County, January 1, 1864, for the war. Present or accounted for until transferred to Company K, 67th Regiment N.C. Troops on January 18, 1864.

BLOW, HENRY A., Private

Enlisted in Pitt County, October 5, 1863, for the war. Present or accounted for until transferred to Company K, 67th Regiment N.C. Troops on January 18, 1864.

CARR, ROBERT A. L., Private

Enlisted in Pitt County, December 31, 1863, for the war. Present or accounted for until transferred to Company K, 67th Regiment N.C. Troops on January 18, 1864.

CARRAWAY, WILLIAM W., Private

Transferred from Company B of this battalion prior to December 31, 1863. Present or accounted for until transferred to Company K, 67th Regiment N.C. Troops on January 18, 1864.

COLLINS, H. J., Private

Transferred from Company I of this battalion on January 1, 1864. Present or accounted for until transferred to Company K, 67th Regiment N.C. Troops on January 18, 1864.

COWARD, EDWARD R., Private

Transferred from Company C of this battalion prior to December, 1863. Present or accounted for until transferred to Company K, 67th Regiment N.C. Troops on January 18, 1864.

CUMMINGS, WILLIAM A., Private

Enlisted in Pitt County, September 15, 1863, for the war. Present or accounted for until transferred to Company K, 67th Regiment N.C. Troops on January 18, 1864.

DAWSON, COUNCIL, Private

Transferred from Company D of this battalion on December 1, 1863. Present or accounted for until transferred to Company K, 67th Regiment N.C. Troops on January 18, 1864.

FIELDS, JESSE, Private

Transferred from Company D of this battalion on December 1, 1863. Present or accounted for until transferred to Company K, 67th Regiment N.C. Troops on January 18, 1864.

FORBES, BENJAMIN J., Private

Enlisted in Pitt County, January 1, 1864, for the war. Present or accounted for until transferred to Company K, 67th Regiment N.C. Troops on January 18, 1864.

FORBES, GUSTAVUS, Private

Enlisted in Pitt County, December 15, 1863, for the war. Present or accounted for until transferred

to Company K, 67th Regiment N.C. Troops on January 18, 1864.

GIBBS WILLIAM C., Private

Enlisted in Pitt County, September 17, 1863, for the war. Present or accounted for until transferred to Company K, 67th Regiment N.C. Troops on January 18, 1864.

HART, CHRISTOPHER C., Private

Enlisted in Pitt County, December 24, 1863, for the war. Present or accounted for until transferred to Company K, 67th Regiment N.C. Troops on January 18, 1864.

HAVENS, JONATHAN, Private

Enlisted in Pitt County, August 18, 1863, for the war. Present or accounted for until transferred to Company K, 67th Regiment N.C. Troops on January 18, 1864.

HAWKINS, DAVID T., Private

Enlisted in Pitt County, December 30, 1863, for the war. Present or accounted for until transferred to Company K, 67th Regiment N.C. Troops on January 18, 1864.

HEMBY, JOAB, Private

Enlisted in Pitt County, August 18, 1863, for the war. Present or accounted for until transferred to Company K, 67th Regiment N.C. Troops on January 18, 1864.

HOLMES, THOMAS J., Private

Enlisted in Pitt County, September 20, 1863, for the war. Present or accounted for until transferred to Company K, 67th Regiment N.C. Troops on January 18, 1864.

HOOKER, W. B., Private

Enlisted in Greene County, September 7, 1863, for the war. Present or accounted for until transferred to Company C of this battalion on January 1, 1864.

JONES, JAMES K., Private

Transferred from Company C of this battalion prior to December 31, 1863. Present or accounted for until transferred to Company K, 67th Regiment N.C. Troops on January 18, 1864.

JOYNER, FRANK, Corporal

Enlisted in Pitt County, August 18, 1863, for the war. Appointed Corporal when the company organized. Present or accounted for until transferred to Company K, 67th Regiment N.C. Troops on January 18, 1864.

LEE, AMOS, Private

Enlisted in Pitt County, September 20, 1863, for the war. Present or accounted for until transferred to Company G of this battalion on November 1, 1863.

McCOY, ASA, Private

Enlisted in Pitt County, January 1, 1864, for the war. Present or accounted for until transferred to Company K, 67th Regiment N.C. Troops on January 18, 1864.

MARLOW, WILLIAM, Private

Enlisted in Pitt County, December 1, 1863, for the war. Present or accounted for until transferred to Company K, 67th Regiment N.C. Troops on January 18, 1864.

MAY, THOMAS D., Private
Transferred from Company B of this battalion on December 31, 1863. Present or accounted for until transferred to Company K, 67th Regiment N.C. Troops on January 18, 1864.

MYERS, N. D., Corporal
Enlisted in Pitt County, September 16, 1863, for the war. Appointed Corporal when the company organized. Present or accounted for until transferred to Company K, 67th Regiment N.C. Troops on January 18, 1864.

NOBLES, W. R. W., Private
Enlisted in Pitt County, September 7, 1863, for the war. Present or accounted for until transferred to Company K, 67th Regiment N.C. Troops on January 18, 1864.

PATE, ROBERT A., Private
Transferred from Company C of this battalion on December 1, 1863. Present or accounted for until transferred to Company K, 67th Regiment N.C. Troops on January 18, 1864.

PATRICK, CHRISTOPHER, Private
Enlisted in Pitt County, December 11, 1863, for the war. Present or accounted for until transferred to Company K, 67th Regiment N.C. Troops on January 18, 1864.

PHILLIPS, THOMAS, Private
Enlisted in Pitt County, November 1, 1863, for the war. Present or accounted for until transferred to Company E of this battalion in December, 1863.

POLLARD, JOSEPH T., Private
Enlisted in Pitt County, December 30, 1863, for the war. Present or accounted for until transferred to Company K, 67th Regiment N.C. Troops on January 18, 1864.

PRIDGEN, J. A., Corporal
Enlisted in Pitt County, December 15, 1863, for the war. Appointed Corporal soon after he enlisted. Present or accounted for until transferred to Company K, 67th Regiment N.C. Troops on January 18, 1864.

PROCTOR, JAMES R., Private
Enlisted in Pitt County, August 18, 1863, for the war. Present or accounted for until transferred to Company K, 67th Regiment N.C. Troops on January 18, 1864.

PUGH, WILLIAM NICOLAS, Private
Transferred from Company D of this battalion in December, 1863. Present or accounted for until transferred to Company K, 67th Regiment N.C. Troops on January 18, 1864.

RASBERRY, S. S., 1st Sergeant
Enlisted in Pitt County, December 31, 1863, for the war. Appointed 1st Sergeant when the company organized. Present or accounted for until transferred to Company K, 67th Regiment N.C. Troops on January 18, 1864.

RICHARDSON, WILLIAM, Private
Transferred from Company B of this battalion prior to December 31, 1863. Present or accounted for until transferred to Company K, 67th Regiment N.C. Troops on January 18, 1864.

ROLLINGS, JAMES W., Private
Enlisted in Pitt County, August 18, 1863, for the war. Present or accounted for until transferred to Company K, 67th Regiment N.C. Troops on January 18, 1864.

ROUSE, MARCELLUS, Private
Transferred from Company D of this battalion on December 1, 1863. Present or accounted for until transferred to Company K, 67th Regiment N.C. Troops on January 18, 1864.

SMITH, ABRAHAM, Private
Transferred from Company G of this battalion November-December, 1863. Present or accounted for until transferred to Company K, 67th Regiment N.C. Troops on January 18, 1864.

SMITH, GEORGE W., Private
Transferred from Company D of this battalion on October 1, 1863. Deserted November 1, 1863, and absent without leave when transferred to Company K, 67th Regiment N.C. Troops on January 18, 1864.

SPAIN, REDMOND, Private
Transferred from Company B of this battalion in December, 1863. Present or accounted for until transferred to Company K, 67th Regiment N.C. Troops on January 18, 1864.

STILLEY, ALEXANDER H., Private
Transferred from Company B of this battalion in December, 1863, and reported as having "deserted December 1, 1863." Absent without leave when transferred to Company K, 67th Regiment N.C. Troops on January 18, 1864.

SUMERELL, SAMUEL, Private
Transferred from Company G of this battalion November-December, 1863. Present or accounted for until transferred to Comany K, 67th Regiment N.C. Troops on January 18, 1864.

SUTTON, HUGH A., Sergeant
Enlisted in Pitt County, August 18, 1863, for the war. Appointed Sergeant when the company organized. Present or accounted for until transferred to Company K, 67th Regiment N.C. Troops on January 18, 1864.

TAYLOR, FREDERICK G., Private
Enlisted in Pitt County, September 20, 1863, for the war. Present or accounted for until transferred to Company G of this battalion in January, 1864.

THOMPSON, H. M., Sergeant
Enlisted in Pitt County, September 7, 1863, for the war. Appointed Sergeant when the company organized. Present or accounted for until transferred to Company K, 67th Regiment N.C. Troops on January 18, 1864.

TURNAGE, ROBERT E., Private
Enlisted in Pitt County, August 18, 1863, for the war. Present or accounted for until transferred to Company K, 67th Regiment N.C. Troops on January 18, 1864.

TURNAGE, TRAVIS, Private
Enlisted in Pitt County, December 2, 1863, for the war. Present or accounted for until transferred to Company K., 67th Regiment N.C. Troops on January 18, 1864.

TYSON, JOSEPH, Private
Enlisted in Pitt County, December 23, 1863, for the war. Present or accounted for until transferred to Company K, 67th Regiment N.C. Troops on January 18, 1864.

TYSON, R. S., Quartermaster Sergeant
Enlisted in Pitt County, August 18, 1863, for the war. Appointed Quartermaster Sergeant when the company organized. Present or accounted for until transferred to Company K, 67th Regiment N.C. Troops on January 18, 1864.

VAUGHN, JAMES W., Private
Enlisted in Pitt County, September 20, 1863, for the war. Present or accounted for until transferred to Company K, 67th Regiment N.C. Troops on January 18, 1864.

VENTERS, GEORGE W., Private
Enlisted in Pitt County, January 1, 1864, for the war. Present or accounted for until transferred to Company K, 67th Regiment N.C. Troops on January 18, 1864.

WILLIAMS, THOMAS G., Private
Transferred from Company E of this battalion in December, 1863. Present or accounted for until transferred to Company K, 67th Regiment N.C.

Troops on January 18, 1864.

WILLOUGHBY, ROBERT T., Private
Enlisted in Pitt County, December 14, 1863, for the war. Present or accounted for until transferred to Company K, 67th Regiment N.C. Troops on January 18, 1864.

WILSON, SIMON B., Corporal
Enlisted in Pitt County, December 31, 1863, for the war. Present or accounted for until transferred to Company K, 67th Regiment N.C. Troops on January 18, 1864.

WOLFENDEN, JOHN J., Sergeant
Transferred from Company B of this battalion on November 1, 1863, as a Sergeant. Present or accounted for until transferred to Company K, 67th Regiment N.C. Troops on January 18, 1864.

MISCELLANEOUS

GODLEY, JOSEPH F., Private
Transferred from Company K, 41st Regiment N.C. Troops (3rd Regiment N.C. Cavalry) November 1, 1863. His name does not appear on any of the surviving muster rolls and there is no record that he ever reported. No further records.

1st REGIMENT N. C. STATE TROOPS

The 1st Regiment N.C. State Troops was organized at Warrenton, Warren County, June 3, 1861. On July 22, 1861, the regiment was ordered to Richmond, Virginia. Only eight companies proceeded to Richmond, however, since Companies D and I had not completed their organization. The eight companies remained in camp near Richmond until ordered to the Aquia District on August 15, 1861. Arriving there at 6:00 P.M. that day, the regiment went into camp at Camp Bee, Brooke's Station. On August 30, 1861, Companies D and I joined the regiment at Camp Bee. Company B was detached in September, 1861, and stationed at Game Point Battery. With the exception of two marches, the regiment remained in camp. From November 9 to 15 it marched to Mathias Point and returned, and from December 9 to 17 it marched to Chatterton and returned.

When the regiment was assigned to the Aquia District it was ordered to report to General Theophilus H. Holmes, commanding. As the number of troops increased they were brigaded, and this regiment was assigned to Brigadier General John G. Walker's Brigade. In addition to this regiment, the brigade consisted of the 2nd and 3rd Regiments N.C. State Troops, 30th Regiment Virginia Infantry, and the 1st Regiment Arkansas Infantry. During its stay in the Aquia District the regiment aided in the construction of batteries at Aquia Creek and Evansport. On January 27, 1862, Company A was ordered to duty at Game Point Battery.

When General A. E. Burnside's troops began advancing from New Bern, troops were sent to North Carolina from Virginia. The regiment received orders to move on March 22, 1862, and marched to Fredericksburg on March 23. There it took the train to Richmond on March 24. Arriving at Richmond on the same day, the regiment proceeded by rail to Petersburg. On March 25 the regiment moved by rail to Goldsboro and went into camp near that town on the Wilmington and Weldon Railroad for about ten days. It then moved to a point on the Atlantic and North Carolina Railroad about four miles from Goldsboro, where the entire brigade had encamped at Camp McIntosh. Here the brigade remained until ordered to Petersburg, Virginia, where it began arriving on May 27. From Petersburg a portion of the brigade moved to Drewry's Bluff, while this regiment was ordered to Richmond. It arrived on the battlefield of Seven Pines just after the battle of May 31. Here it was assigned to a new brigade commanded by Brigadier General Roswell S. Ripley, Major General D. H. Hill's Division. In addition to this regiment, Ripley's Brigade consisted of the 3rd Regiment N.C. State Troops and the 44th and 48th Regiments Georgia Infantry. On June 15, 1862, the regiment was engaged in a skirmish near Seven Pines.

On the morning of June 26, 1862, the brigade moved from its camp near the Williamsburg Road, about five miles from Richmond, to Chickahominy

Bridge on the Mechanicsville Turnpike. General Robert E. Lee was concentrating his troops to attack the Federal right at Mechanicsville. At 4:00 P.M., June 26, 1862, the brigade crossed the bridge to aid General A. P. Hill's troops engaged at Mechanicsville. This regiment and the 44th Regiment Georgia Infantry were ordered to move to assist Brigadier General William D. Pender's Brigade and moved against the Federal position at Ellerson's Mill. The attack was made against heavy artillery and infantry fire. Reaching the pond opposite the enemy, the two regiments halted and moved by the right flank into a skirt of woods. The unsuccessful attack cost the regiment 142 men killed and wounded. The 44th Regiment Georgia Infantry lost 335 men killed and wounded. During the night of June 26-27 the survivors of the regiment were gathered together. A portion of the regiment was detailed to guard the Chickahominy Bridge, while a battalion of the regiment, under Captain Hamilton A. Brown, rejoined the brigade. This battalion remained with the brigade throughout the Seven Days' Battles and was engaged on June 27 at Gaines' Mill, where it lost 4 killed and 16 wounded, and on July 1 at Malvern Hill, where it lost 9 killed, 60 wounded, and 6 missing. All totaled, the regiment lost 51 killed and 175 wounded in three of the five major battles of the Seven Days'.

Following the unsuccessful attack on Malvern Hill, the brigade remained in bivouac near that place until it returned to its camp near Richmond on July 9-10. Here it remained until marched to Malvern Hill on August 6, returning to Richmond on the night of August 7. D. H. Hill's Division was left in front of Richmond to watch McClellan's troops at Harrison's Landing while Jackson and then Longstreet moved to confront General John Pope in middle Virginia. On August 19 General Ripley's Brigade moved by rail to Orange Court House, arriving the next day. The balance of Hill's Division moved up and joined Ripley's Brigade and then proceeded to join the Army of Northern Virginia on August 28. The division reached the army on September 2 at Chantilly and crossed into Maryland on September 4-5. Upon reaching Frederick, the army halted, and General Lee determined to send Jackson to capture Harpers Ferry while Longstreet moved to Hagerstown. On September 10 D. H. Hill's Division moved out of Frederick as the rear guard of Longstreet's column. Mounting pressure from the advancing Federals, plus the necessity of protecting Jackson at Harpers Ferry, resulted in the deployment of Hill's Division on the South Mountain gaps below Boonsboro on September 13. This regiment, still in Ripley's Brigade, saw heavy action at Fox's Gap on September 14 and withdrew the next day to follow the army now concentrating at Sharpsburg. Arriving at Antietam Creek on September 15, the brigade went into position on the heights east of the creek. Here they bivouacked through the evening of the next day, when they were moved to the extreme left of General Hill's line and connected with the right of General Jackson's line.

On the morning of September 17 the Federals advanced against Jackson's line. During the seesaw battle, Ripley's Brigade was ordered to close to his left and advance. In the charge General Ripley was wounded, and Colonel George Doles assumed command of the brigade. The brigade advanced as far as the Miller cornfield, when the entire advance was forced to retire. The brigade withdrew and went into position west of the Hagerstown Road. The fighting then shifted to the Confederate center, and the troops on the left established a new line. The fighting continued on the center and right until the Federals discontinued efforts to drive the Confederates from the field. The following day the troops rested on the field and retired across the Potomac during the night of September 18. During the Maryland campaign the regiment lost 18 killed and 148 wounded.

The Army of Northern Virginia remained in the Shenandoah Valley until the Army of the Potomac crossed over east of the Blue Ridge. Using his cavalry, Lee sought to discover the enemy's intentions. On October 28, 1862, Longstreet's Corps moved east of the mountains to Culpeper Court House while Jackson's Corps moved closer to Winchester. D. H. Hill's Division was posted at the forks of the Shenandoah River to guard the mountain passes. On October 31 this regiment was at Upperville, just east of the mountains. On November 7, 1862, Colonel Doles was promoted to brigadier general and assumed command of the brigade.

When the enemy's intention was discerned, Lee moved Longstreet to Fredericksburg and ordered Jackson to prepare to move. Hill's Division was pulled back, and on November 21 the regiment left Strasburg in column of march for Gordonsville. From Gordonsville it moved to Fredericksburg. On December 3 Hill's Division was sent to Port Royal, below Fredericksburg, to prevent any crossing at or near that point. Here it stayed until ordered to Fredericksburg on December 12. The division arrived in the morning of December 13 and was placed in the third line of battle. During the Battle of Fredericksburg, December 13, 1862, the division was subjected to heavy artillery fire but saw little action. After the battle it was moved up to the second line. On the 15th it went into the first line where it remained through the 16th. While on the field, the regiment was never actually engaged but suffered 15 wounded from the artillery fire.

Following the Battle of Fredericksburg, the regiment went into winter quarters on the Rappahannock River near Skinker's Neck. There it spent the winter on picket duty. On January 19, 1863, the regiment was transferred to Brigadier General William B. Taliaferro's Brigade, Major General Isaac R. Trimble's Division, Jackson's Corps. General Taliaferro was transferred on February 20, 1863, and Brigadier General Raleigh E. Colston was assigned to command the brigade. In addition to this regiment, the brigade consisted of the 3rd Regiment N.C. State Troops and the 10th, 23rd, and 37th

Regiments Virginia Infantry. On April 29, 1863, the division received orders to march to Hamilton's Crossing, below Fredericksburg. General Hooker's Federal army had moved up the left bank of the Rappahannock to cross over behind the Confederates at Fredericksburg, and General Lee was moving to oppose it. The two armies would meet at Chancellorsville.

Jackson's Corps moved down the Orange and Fredericksburg Plank Road toward Chancellorsville on May 1. It reached the Confederate position that evening, and early the next day Jackson's men started the flank march which carried them to a point on the exposed right flank of Hooker's army about four miles west of Chancellorsville. General Colston was in command of the division, which was placed in the second of three lines preparatory to the advance. The brigade was commanded by the senior colonel and was on the right of the divisional line. Soon after the advance the second line began to catch up to the first line, and the two became one as they drove in Hooker's right flank. The advance continued until night, when strong resistance forced a halt.

During the night the lines were reformed, and the brigade was placed on the left side of the Plank Road in the second line. Early the next morning, May 3, the brigade was moved to the right and sent in to support the first line. As the battle raged, a threatened Federal flank attack was met and driven back. During this action the brigade lost four commanders, and Lieutenant Colonel Hamilton A. Brown of this regiment assumed command as ranking officer. The regiment was commanded at the end by Acting Adjutant 1st Lieutenant John A. Morgan. Under these repeated attacks, supported by heavy artillery fire and the pressure exerted on the Federal left and center by troops under Lee, the Federal army began to retire. Once over the strong Federal entrenchments, which had been the object of attack, the Confederates converged on Chancellorsville. From there, the remnants of the brigade were ordered to advance on the left of the United States Ford Road. Finding the enemy strongly posted, the troops were ordered to retire and went into position in the vicinity of the Chancellor house. The next morning the entire brigade was ordered to entrench on the right, perpendicular to the United States Ford Road. In this new line the regiment acted as infantry support to a battery. Here it remained for two days. Finding the Federal army had recrossed the Rappahannock River on May 6, Lee moved his army back to Fredericksburg.

Colston's Brigade was left at United States Ford, where the men supervised the movement of Federal ambulances sent over to care for the Federal wounded. Upon the completion of this task the brigade rejoined the division at Hamilton's Crossing, below Fredericksburg, on May 15. During the Chancellorsville campaign the regiment lost 32 killed, 140 wounded, and 27 missing.

Following the Chancellorsville campaign and the death of Jackson, the Army of Northern Virginia was divided into three corps. Colston's Brigade was assigned to Major General Edward Johnson's Division,

Lieutenant General Richard S. Ewell's 2nd Corps. On May 28 General Colston was relieved from duty, and Brigadier General George H. Steuart was assigned to command the brigade. Thus, for the coming campaign the regiment would be in Steuart's Brigade, Johnson's Division, Ewell's Corps. The division left camp near Hamilton's Crossing on June 5 and moved with the corps in the direction of Winchester, crossing the Blue Ridge at Chester Gap. At daylight on the morning of June 13 the division left camp at Cedarville and moved down the Winchester and Front Royal turnpike toward Winchester. General Ewell sent Major General Jubal Early's Division down the Valley turnpike to gain the heights west of Winchester. Johnson's Division proceeded to within four miles of Winchester, where they encountered the enemy. The division was deployed with the Stonewall Brigade and Steuart's Brigade on the right of the road and the other two brigades of the division on the left. The brigades on the right advanced under cover of woods to a position nearer town and halted. Here the two brigades remained until the morning of June 14, when they were moved farther to the right. Johnson's mission was to engage the enemy's attention on the right while Early moved in on the left to deliver the main attack.

After nightfall, Johnson received orders to proceed farther to the right and get behind the town to cut the Federal line of retreat. Steuart's Brigade was ordered to move together with another brigade and artillery supports. Moving by way of Jordan Springs, Johnson succeeded in getting his men into position at Stephenson's just as the retreating Federals charged. With the aid of the Stonewall Brigade, Johnson succeeded in routing the Federals and captured between 2,300 and 2,600 prisoners. The men of the regiment mounted some captured horses and attempted to overtake General Robert H. Milroy, the Federal commander, but failed to do so. In this action at Winchester and Stephenson's the regiment lost 5 killed and 12 wounded.

On June 18 the regiment, with the brigade, crossed the Potomac River at Shepherdstown and camped on the old battlefield at Sharpsburg. From this camp the division marched, via Hagerstown and Chambersburg, to within three miles of Carlisle, Pennsylvania. Steuart's Brigade had been ordered to McConnellsburg from Greencastle to collect horses, cattle, and other supplies. It rejoined the division near Carlisle. On June 29 the division moved to Greenville and then to Gettysburg, where it arrived too late to participate in the action on July 1. That evening the division moved through Gettysburg and formed a line of battle facing south. Late the next day, after a heavy artillery engagement, the division advanced over Rock Creek to assault the Federal positions on Culp's Hill. The brigade was on the extreme left of the advancing line. This regiment was held in reserve until ordered to support the 3rd Regiment N.C. State Troops on the right of the brigade line. After taking the first line of works, efforts to take the second line failed, but the Confederates successfully defended their position against repeated attacks. During the night

of July 2-3, four companies of this regiment were posted as pickets on the opposite side of Rock Creek. The remaining six companies were placed on the extreme left flank of the brigade. The next morning, July 3, a general assault failed to dislodge the Federal defenders. Later Steuart's Brigade was withdrawn to Rock Creek, where it remained the rest of the day.

Failure to break the Federal center by the Pickett-Pettigrew charge during the afternoon of July 3 necessitated withdrawal. Johnson's Division was withdrawn across Rock Creek and retired through the town to a position north and west of Gettysburg during the night of July 3-4. On July 5 the division began the retreat to Virginia by way of Waynesboro to Hagerstown. A line of battle was established at Hagerstown, but no general engagement occurred. On the night of July 13 the division recrossed the Potomac and marched to near Martinsburg. During the Gettysburg campaign the regiment lost 4 killed and 48 wounded.

From Martinsburg the division moved to Darkesville on July 15, then back to Martinsburg to destroy the Baltimore & Ohio Railroad and repel an enemy advance. When the Federal army began crossing the Potomac River east of the Blue Ridge, General Lee moved his army east of the mountains to interpose it between the enemy and Richmond. By August 1, 1863, the Army of Northern Virginia was encamped near Orange Court House, with the Army of the Potomac at Warrenton. By August 4 Lee withdrew his army to the Rapidan River line. In October Lee attempted to turn the flank of the Federal army. The movement maneuvered the Federal commander into falling back, and on October 14 the Federal rear guard was intercepted at Bristoe Station. Failure to coordinate the attack resulted in the escape of the Federal rear guard and in heavy casualties to A. P. Hill's troops. The regiment took part in the movement as part of the brigade and division, but Ewell's Corps was not engaged at Bristoe Station.

With the escape of the Federal army to Centreville, Lee retired to the upper Rappahannock River. The Federal army soon followed and overran Lee's positions at Rappahannock Bridge on November 7. Lee withdrew his army south across the upper Rapidan River, toward Orange Court House. On November 26 the Federal army crossed the lower Rapidan and turned west to face Lee's army. Lee thought the Federal army was heading south and moved to strike it on its flank. On November 27 the two armies met at Payne's Farm, where this regiment was heavily engaged, losing 5 men killed and 50 wounded. The action proved to Lee that the Federals were advancing westward, not southward. He therefore withdrew his army to Mine Run and entrenched to await attack. General Meade moved his army up and began entrenching opposite the Confederate line. Finding the Federal left flank exposed, Lee determined to strike it. However, General Meade discovered his flank was exposed and decided to withdraw. When Lee's men began to advance on the morning of December 2, they found that the entire Federal army had withdrawn across the Rapidan. Thus ended the Mine Run campaign. Both armies went into winter quarters. This regiment built winter quarters near Pisgah Church and did picket duty at Mitchell's and Morton's fords during the winter of 1863-1864.

The morning of May 4, 1864, dawned with Steuart's Brigade picketing along the upper Rapidan River, while the Federal army under General U. S. Grant was moving across the lower Rapidan. About noon the brigade was put in motion toward the Old Turnpike, along which Johnson's Division would advance as the lead element of Ewell's Corps. The night of May 4-5 was spent in bivouac some two and one-half miles east of Locust Grove. Contact was made with the enemy as the column moved forward on May 5, and Ewell began to deploy his troops. Before his deployment was completed, the enemy launched a surprise attack which routed one brigade and seriously threatened the destruction of another. General Steuart's Brigade moved in on the left of the threatened brigade, while General Ewell advanced fresh troops directly into the threatened area. The whole line moved forward to repulse the Federal advance. In the counterattack Steuart's Brigade captured the 146th Regiment New York Infantry and two guns. Efforts to storm a heavily entrenched Federal line failed, and Ewell's men retired and established their own line. This ended the fighting on this part of the long Confederate line.

It was quiet on the brigade front on May 6, and on May 7 it was discovered that the enemy had retired. Late in the evening of May 7 orders came to close up on the right. Throughout the night of May 7-8 the troops moved to the right. On May 8 the brigade marched to Spotsylvania Court House, where Lee had placed his army to confront Grant's advance. Late in the evening of May 8 the brigade was put into position on the right side of the salient and was firmly entrenched when dawn broke on the morning of May 9. Johnson's Division was placed in that portion of the Confederate line which resembled an inverted V and became known as the Mule Shoe. Steuart's Brigade was on the right side of the Mule Shoe, and on May 10, when the left side was attacked, Steuart's men faced to the rear and advanced to recapture the line.

The initial success of the Federal attack forced the Confederates to strengthen their lines on May 11. As the morning of May 12 began to dawn, a heavy fog lay close to the ground. It began to lift slightly about 4:30 A.M. The noise of activity during the night had led Generals Johnson and Steuart to expect an attack, and they had their men as ready as possible and anticipated the momentary return of the artillery which had been withdrawn the previous evening. However, before the artillery arrived, the Federals advanced in column formation, broke through the Confederate lines, and captured most of Johnson's Division. The Confederates succeeded in stopping the attackers and in driving them back, but the captured men had already been taken to the rear. Because so many of the men had been captured, including General Steuart, Steuart's Brigade ceased to exist as a unit. All but about 30 men of the 1st

Regiment N.C. State Troops were captured.

The survivors of the three Virginia regiments in Steuart's Brigade were consolidated into a brigade with the survivors from two other Virginia brigades. The two North Carolina regiments (1st and 3rd Regiments N.C. State Troops) were assigned to Brigadier General Stephen D. Ramseur's Brigade, Major General Robert E. Rodes' Division, Ewell's Corps. General Ramseur was promoted to major general and assigned to command a division, and Colonel William R. Cox, 2nd Regiment N.C. State Troops, was promoted to brigadier general and assigned to command Ramseur's old brigade. Thus, the 1st Regiment N.C. State Troops was brigaded with the 2nd, 3rd, 4th Regiments N.C. State Troops, 14th Regiment N.C. Troops (4th Regiment N.C. Volunteers), and the 30th Regiment N.C. Troops. The ranks of the regiment would increase as men returned or were assigned from conscript camps, but it would never reach regimental size again.

The survivors of Johnson's Division remained with the 2nd Corps following the action of May 12. General Grant made several attempts to break or turn the Confederate line and failed. As he began moving to the east, the 2nd Corps was ordered to reconnoiter and find out if Grant's army was on the move. Ewell's Corps, with Ramseur's Brigade leading, moved out of the entrenchments and engaged the rear elements of the Federal army on May 19. An attack was made but was repulsed, and with reinforcements coming up the Federals began to press Ewell's men. The Confederates held and took advantage of night to break off the engagement and retire. This move disclosed the enemy's movement, and Lee moved his army accordingly. On May 22 Ewell's Corps arrived at Hanover Junction with Longstreet's Corps. Hills Corps arrived on the morning of May 23. From here the Army of Northern Virginia moved to the North Anna, where they blocked the Federal army once again. At North Anna, May 24-25, Ewell's Corps, now commanded by General Early, was on the Confederate right and was not engaged. Grant withdrew during the night of May 26-27 and crossed the Pamunkey River, again sidestepping to the Confederate right. Early's Corps marched some 24 miles on May 27 and entrenched between Beaver Dam Creek and Pole Green Church. Longstreet's Corps came up on Early's right, and Hill's Corps extended along the left of Early's line. On May 30, under orders from General Lee, Early moved to attack the Federal left at Bethesda Church. The attack failed to turn the Federal left but did reveal that the enemy was moving to the Confederate right.

The two armies began to concentrate at Cold Harbor, and on June 1 a spirited engagement occurred. Again Lee moved to his right, and the new alignment left Early's Corps on the Confederate left. Early was ordered to move out on June 2 to strike the Federal right. The attack was led by Rodes' Division and met with partial success until Federal reinforcements arrived to drive them back. During the Battle of Cold Harbor, June 3, 1864, Early's Corps was under attack by General A. E. Burnside's IX Corps and a part of General G. K. Warren's V Corps. The men of Warren's Corps struck the line held by Rodes' Division and were repulsed. Following the battle, the armies remained in position observing and skirmishing until June 12, when Grant began moving his army to cross the James River. General Early's Corps was withdrawn from the line on June 11 and was ordered to Lynchburg on June 12 to defend that city against an anticipated attack by troops under General David Hunter. Early was directed to remain in the Shenandoah Valley after striking Hunter's force.

General Early's troops began arriving at Lynchburg on June 17, and the balance arrived the next day. Hunter retired, and after an unsuccessful attempt to overtake the retreating Federals, Early proceeded into the Shenandoah Valley. Still in Cox's Brigade, Rodes' Division, this regiment took part in Early's Valley campaign of 1864. On July 6, 1864, Early crossed into Maryland and advanced on Washington, D.C. At the battle of Monocacy River, July 9, 1864, Rodes' Division operated on the Baltimore road while the main fighting occurred on the Washington road to the division's right. Rodes' Division was in the van when the defenses of Washington came in sight on July 11. Finding the defenses heavily manned on the morning of July 12, Early called off a planned assault, and during the night of July 12 the army began to retire toward Virginia. Back in the Shenandoah Valley, Early's troops were engaged at Stephenson's Depot, July 20, and at Kernstown, July 24, before he moved to Martinsburg and gave his men a rest.

Early in August, 1864, the Federals began concentrating a large force under General Phil Sheridan at Harpers Ferry. On August 10 Early began a series of maneuvers to create the impression of a larger force than he had. His men were northeast of Winchester when Sheridan began to move. On September 19 contact was made, and Early concentrated to receive the attack. The Confederates were making a determined defense east of Winchester when the left came under heavy attack and the whole line began to retire. During the initial stages of the battle General Rodes was killed as he deployed his division between Gordon's and Ramseur's divisions. These three divisions held the main line against repeated assaults, and only when the left appeared to be turned did they begin to retire to a defensive line close to the town. Again the Federals assaulted the front and left of the line. Word of a Federal column turning the right caused Early to issue orders for a general withdrawal. Finding the troops moving on the right were his own men adjusting the alignment, Early tried to counter the order. It was too late. The troops continued to the rear through Winchester and rallied south of the town. From there they continued the retreat to Fisher's Hill, near Strasburg.

At Fisher's Hill, Major General Stephen D. Ramseur was placed in command of Rodes' Division. Sheridan struck Early's left and center at Fisher's Hill on September 22 and forced a general retreat. Early regrouped at Waynesboro on September 28. Here he received reinforcements and again began to move down the valley. On October 7 his troops occupied New Market. Moving to Fisher's Hill on

October 12-13, Early found the enemy on the north bank of Cedar Creek. On October 19, 1864, Early launched a surprise, three-pronged attack on the Federal camp. The attack was initially successful, and the Confederates succeeded in driving the Federals from two defensive lines. Early delayed the attack on the third line and assumed the defensive. Rallying his troops, Sheridan launched a devastating counterattack and routed Early's army. In this battle the three divisions of the 2nd Corps were commanded by General John B. Gordon. While attempting to rally the men, General Ramseur was mortally wounded and captured. Brigadier General Bryan Grimes, as senior brigadier, was assigned to command the division. Thus, when the 2nd Corps regrouped at New Market after the Cedar Creek disaster, the 1st Regiment N.C. State Troops was in Cox's Brigade, Grimes' Division. With the exception of minor skirmishing and a repulse of a Federal cavalry force on November 22, the army remained inactive.

On December 9 two divisions of the 2nd Corps moved under orders to return to Richmond. A few days later the Rodes-Ramseur Division, under Grimes, was ordered to return to the main army in the Richmond-Petersburg line. The company clerk of Company D recorded activities of the regiment for the month of December, 1864, on the November-December, 1864, muster roll as follows:

The Company broke up camp on the morning of the 14. December 1864 near New Market, and marched to Mount Crofford, a distance of twenty five miles. Next morning we started for Staunton, distance of eighteen miles, which place we reached 4 o'clock P.M. and took the cars to Richmond. After traveling all night we arrived at Richmond 2 o'clock P.M. We marched to the Petersburg Depot and took the cars for Dunlops Station which place we reached about dark. After disembarking we camped one mile and a half West of Dunlop Station. Next morning we were ordered to build winter quarters, and since that time we have been hard at work.

The brigade went into winter quarters at Swift Creek, about three miles north of Petersburg. Here it remained until ordered to the right of the Confederate line about February 20, 1865. Grimes' Division had been placed on alert to be ready to move at a moment's notice. On February 17 three brigades moved to Sutherland's Depot on the right of the line. Cox's Brigade covered the division front at Swift Creek until relieved and then joined the division at Sutherland's. In mid-March, 1865, the division was ordered into the trenches in front of Petersburg. There it remained until the night of March 24 when the 2nd Corps, still under General Gordon, was massed for an attack on Fort Stedman. The Sharpshooters who led the attacking force on the morning of March 25 were commanded by Colonel Hamilton A. Brown of this regiment. Although initially successful, the concentrated firepower and manpower of the Federal army forced the Confederates to retreat. Colonel Brown and many of his men were cut off and captured.

The remnants of the regiment returned to the trenches with the rest of the brigade and division. During the general assault on the morning of April 2, 1865, the Federals reached the divisional line near Fort Mahone. Grimes' Division attacked and reoccupied its trenches, only to have other portions of the line fall to the Federal assault. Retreat was necessary, and it began the night of April 2-3. Gordon's Corps acted as rear guard as the army moved to Amelia Court House. It camped five miles east of the town on April 4 while the army awaited the collection of supplies. The next day the retreat resumed and continued through the night of April 5-6. As the rear guard, Gordon's Division was subjected to attacks by Federal cavalry and infantry. At a crossing of Sayler's Creek, on April 6, Gordon's men made a stand and repulsed the assault on their front. To the south of Gordon's position, the Confederates under Generals Ewell and Anderson were severely defeated and captured. The Federals then moved on Gordon's right. The pressure forced the line to break in confusion, but Gordon rallied the survivors west of the creek and rejoined the army. At Farmville, on April 7, the men of Gordon's Corps went to the relief of General Mahone's Division. The Federals were held, and the army continued the retreat.

On the night of April 7-8, Gordon's Corps moved to the advance of the army. His lead elements reached Appomattox Court House in the late afternoon of April 8 and halted. Later that evening they found the Federal cavalry in their front. It was decided that an attack would be made the next morning to cut through the enemy. Gordon's men moved into position west of the town during the night. At 5:00 A.M. the advance began and drove the Federal cavalry from the crossroads. The Confederates then took up a defensive position and came under attack by Federal infantry and cavalry. Gordon held his line until word came of the truce. A cease-fire was arranged, and Gordon began to withdraw. Cox's Brigade had not received the cease-fire order, and as it moved back the men turned and fired on an advancing Federal cavalry force. After hearing the volley General Gordon sent word of the truce. The last shot had been fired. The Army of Northern Virginia was surrendered on that date, and on April 12, 1865, 72 members of the 1st Regiment N.C. State Troops were paroled.

FIELD AND STAFF
COLONELS

WINDER, JOHN H.
Appointed Colonel to rank from May 16, 1861, but declined the appointment.

STOKES, MUMFORD SIDNEY
Resided in Wilkes County and served as Captain of Company B of this regiment before he was appointed Colonel to rank from May 16, 1861. Wounded at Ellerson's Mill, Virginia, June 26, 1862, and died of wound on July 8, 1862.

McDOWELL, JOHN A.
Resided in Bladen County and appointed Major

at age 34 to rank from May 16, 1861. Promoted to Lieutenant Colonel to rank from April 21, 1862. Wounded at Ellerson's Mill, Virginia, June 26, 1862. Promoted to Colonel to rank from July 8, 1862. Present or accounted for until he resigned on December 14, 1863.

BROWN, HAMILTON A.
Transferred from Company B of this regiment upon appointment as Lieutenant Colonel to rank from July 8, 1862. Wounded at Payne's Farm, Virginia, November 27, 1863. Promoted to Colonel to rank from December 14, 1863. Present or accounted for until captured at Fort Stedman, Petersburg, Virginia, March 25, 1865. Confined at Fort Delaware, Delaware, until released after taking the Oath of Allegiance on June 24, 1865.

LIEUTENANT COLONELS

RANSOM, MATTHEW WHITAKER
Resided as a lawyer in Northampton County and appointed Lieutenant Colonel to rank from May 16, 1861. Present or accounted for until transferred to the Field and Staff, 35th Regiment N.C. Troops upon appointment as Colonel on April 21, 1862.

HARRELL, JARRETT NORFLEET
Transferred from Company F of this regiment upon appointment as Major to rank from July 29, 1863. Promoted to Lieutenant Colonel to rank from December 14, 1863. Present or accounted for until captured at Wilderness, Virginia, May 10, 1864. Confined at Fort Delaware, Delaware, until transferred to Hilton Head, South Carolina, June 26, 1864. Transferred back to Fort Delaware where he was released after taking the Oath of Allegiance on July 24, 1865.

MAJORS

SKINNER, TRISTRIM LOWTHER
Transferred from Company A of this regiment upon appointment as Major to rank from April 21, 1862. Killed at Ellerson's Mill, Virginia, June 26, 1862.

HINES, JAMES S.
Transferred from Company C of this regiment upon appointment as Major to rank from July 8, 1862. Present or accounted for until he resigned on July 29, 1863, by reason of "irritation of the spine and partial paralysis of both legs—also great nervous derangement."

LATHAM, LOUIS CHARLES
Transferred from Company G of this regiment upon appointment as Major to rank from December 14, 1863. Present or accounted for until admitted to hospital at Richmond, Virginia, May 7, 1864, with a gunshot wound of the left side. Detailed in North Carolina with a detachment of convalescents from the regiment from August through November, 1864. Reported as absent in December, 1864, and January, 1865, by reason of his being a member of the state legislature. Paroled at Appomattox Court House, Virginia, April 9, 1865.

ADJUTANTS

MILLER, JOHN S. R.

Resided in Caldwell County and appointed Adjutant with the rank of 1st Lieutenant at age 30 to rank from May 16, 1861. Present or accounted for until transferred to Company H of this regiment upon appointment to Captain to rank from October 22, 1862.

STRANGE, FRENCH

Transferred from Company A, 63rd Regiment N.C. Troops (5th Regiment N.C. Cavalry) upon appointment as Adjutant with the rank of 1st Lieutenant on March 16, 1863, to rank from December 30, 1862. Present until furloughed on sick leave on September 7, 1863. Detailed on enrolling duty in North Carolina on December 3, 1863, and reported as absent on detail through December, 1864. Paroled at Appomattox Court House, Virginia, April 9, 1865.

ASSISTANT QUARTERMASTERS

FLEMING, N. N.

Appointed 1st Lieutenant, Assistant Quartermaster, and paid as such for the period June 12 through August 20, 1861, the date he was dropped from the rolls.

DUDLEY, GUILFORD L.

Transferred from Company E of this regiment upon appointment as Captain, Assistant Quartermaster, to rank from November 1, 1861. Present or accounted for until "relieved from duty . . . and . . . assigned to duty with Major J. W. Cameron, Quartermaster, Wilmington" on August 11, 1864. Ordered to report to Raleigh to assist in railroad transportation on March 23, 1865. Paroled at Greensboro on May 2, 1865.

ASSISTANT COMMISSARIES OF SUBSISTENCE

HACKETT, JAMES W.

Resided in Wilkes County and appointed Captain, Assistant Commissary of Subsistence, to rank from May 16, 1861. Present or accounted for until he submitted his resignation on July 9, 1862, by reason of physical disability. Resignation officially accepted on July 23, 1862.

FENNELL, OWEN, Jr.

Transferred from Company C of this regiment upon appointment as Captain, Assistant Commissary of Subsistence, to rank from December 15, 1862. Position abolished by Act of Congress and name dropped from rolls July 31, 1863.

CHAPLAINS

SPAINHOUR, JAMES H.

Resided in Burke County and appointed Chaplain to rank from May 16, 1861. Died October 18, 1861, of disease.

KERR, DAVID

Appointed Chaplain to rank from October 29, 1861, and confirmed December 24, 1861.

HOWELL, JAMES K.

Resided in Granville County and appointed

Chaplain to rank from April 28, 1862. Submitted his resignation on December 7, 1862, by reason of ill health. Resignation officially accepted on December 28, 1862.

GWALTNEY, WILLIAM R.

Resided in Alexander County and appointed Chaplain on February 12, 1863, to rank from December 30, 1862. Present or accounted for until he submitted his resignation on December 30, 1864, by reason of ill health. Resignation officially accepted January 19, 1865.

SURGEONS

GEE, CHARLES J.

Resided in Halifax County and appointed Surgeon to rank from May 16, 1861. Resigned December 26-28, 1861.

MACON, HENRY J.

Resided in Halifax County and appointed Surgeon to rank from February 1, 1862. Resigned in February, 1863, by reason of ill health and assigned to hospital.

CROMWELL, BENJAMIN M.

Resided in Georgia and appointed Surgeon to rank from April 23, 1861, and assigned to this regiment in February, 1863. Present or accounted for through February, 1864.

HERNDON, DABNEY

Resided in Richmond, Virginia, and appointed Surgeon to rank from June 18, 1861. Assigned to this regiment in February, 1864. Relieved from duty with the regiment on February 2, 1865, by reason of ill health and ordered to report to Surgeon W. A. Carrington in Richmond for duty.

ASSISTANT SURGEONS

SCALES, NATHANIEL M.

Transferred from Company B of this regiment upon appointment as Assistant Surgeon in July, 1861, to rank from May 16, 1861. Submitted his resignation on July 10, 1862, by reason of physical disability. Resignation officially accepted on July 15, 1862.

COKE, LUCIUS C.

Transferred from Company G of this regiment upon appointment as Assistant Surgeon to rank from June 12, 1862. Present or accounted for through August, 1864, when he was "temporarily assigned to duty with the 30th Regiment N.C. Troops."

GREGORY, T. R.

Confined at Military Prison, Camp Hamilton, Virginia, January 26, 1865, from Washington, D.C., and forwarded "to point of exchange per Flag of Truce steamer" February 2, 1865.

ENSIGN

BROWN, ISAIAH MARSHALL

Transferred from Company B of this regiment upon appointment as Ensign with the rank of 1st Lieutenant on May 13, 1864, to rank from April 30, 1864. Wounded October 19, 1864. Submitted his resignation on November 22, 1864.

DRILLMASTERS

MARKS, A. J.
Reported on regimental return for August, 1861, as Drillmaster, 1st Class.

NEWLIN, WILLIAM E.
Paid for service as Drillmaster for the period July 20-August 20, 1861. Later enlisted in Company B of this regiment.

RICHARDSON, THOMAS
Reported on regimental return for August, 1861, as Drillmaster, 1st Class.

SHINNER, JOSHUA
Reported on regimental return for August, 1861, as Drillmaster, 2nd Class.

SERGEANTS MAJOR

NICHOLS, STEPHEN
Transferred from Company B of this regiment upon appointment as Sergeant Major on July 1, 1861. Discharged August 25, 1861. Later enlisted in Company K, 19th Regiment N.C. Troops (2nd Regiment N.C. Cavalry).

MOORE, AUGUSTUS M.
Transferred from Company A of this regiment upon appointment as Sergeant Major on August 18, 1861. Present or accounted for until transferred to Company B, 3rd Battalion N.C. Light Artillery upon appointment as 2nd Lieutenant on February 26, 1862.

McINTIRE, THOMAS HENRY WILLIAMS
Transferred from Company C of this regiment upon appointment as Sergeant Major to rank from March 1, 1862. Absent sick after May 12, 1862, and detailed as Hospital Steward on September 13, 1862. Transferred back to Company C on January 25, 1863, as a Private.

SCOTT, OBEDIAH R.
Transferred from Company C of this regiment early in November, 1862, upon appointment as Sergeant Major. Transferred back to Company C upon appointment as 2nd Lieutenant to rank from November 12, 1862.

CROWSON, JOHN C.
Transferred from Company B of this regiment upon appointment as Sergeant Major on February 11, 1863. Captured at Gettysburg, Pennsylvania, July 3, 1863, and confined at Fort Delaware, Delaware, until transferred to Point Lookout, Maryland, October 18, 1863. Paroled at Point Lookout on February 13, 1865, and sent to Cox's Landing, James River, Virginia, for exchange. Received in exchange February 14-15, 1865.

ALLEN, WILLIAM O.
Transferred from Company I of this regiment upon appointment as Sergeant Major to rank from July 15, 1863. Captured at Spotsylvania Court House, Virginia, May 12, 1864, and confined at Point Lookout, Maryland, until transferred to Elmira, New York, in August, 1864. Paroled at Elmira and sent to James River, Virginia, for exchange on March 10, 1865.

QUARTERMASTER SERGEANT

BOONE, JAMES D.
Transferred from Company F of this regiment upon appointment as Quartermaster Sergeant November-December, 1862. Present or accounted for until paroled at Appomattox Court House, Virginia, April 9, 1865.

COMMISSARY SERGEANT

SPAINHOUR, RUFUS A.
Transferred from Company B of this regiment upon appointment as Commissary Sergeant on June 18, 1862. Present or accounted for until paroled at Appomattox Court House, Virginia, April 9, 1865.

ORDNANCE SERGEANT

WILBAR, ALFRED W.
Transferred from Company B of this regiment upon appointment as Ordnance Sergeant to rank from September 17, 1862. Present or accounted for until paroled at Appomattox Court House, Virginia, April 9, 1865.

HOSPITAL STEWARD

WRIGHT, WILLIAM F.
Transferred from Company A of this regiment upon appointment as Hospital Steward on August 6, 1862. Present or accounted for until reduced to ranks on October 1, 1864, and returned to Company A.

BAND

COLLINS, SAMUEL N.
Transferred from Company B of this regiment upon appointment as Chief Musician July-August, 1861. Transferred back to Company B November-December, 1861, as Musician.

CRANOR, WALTER E.
Transferred from Company B of this regiment July-August, 1861. Transferred back to Company B on November 20, 1861.

CURTIS, LARKIN J.
Transferred from Company B of this regiment July-August, 1861. Transferred back to Company B on November 20, 1861.

FRAZIER, CHARLES
Transferred from Company B of this regiment July-August, 1861. Discharged on November 21, 1861.

LYLES, ELI W.
Transferred from Company B of this regiment in July, 1861. Discharged in November, 1861.

COMPANY A

This company, known as "Albemarle Guards," was raised in Chowan County and enlisted at Edenton on May 18, 1861. It tendered its service to the state and was ordered to Warrenton, Warren County, where it became Company A of this regiment on June 3, 1861. After that date the company functioned as a part of the regiment, and its history for the war period is recorded as a part of the regimental history.

The information contained in the following roster of the company was compiled principally from company muster rolls for July through August, 1861; November, 1861, through April, 1862; and June 30, 1862, through December, 1864. No company muster rolls were found for the period prior to July, 1861; for September through October, 1861; for May through June 29, 1862; or for the period after December, 1864. In addition to the company muster rolls, Roll of Honor records, receipt rolls, hospital records, prisoner of war records, and other primary records, supplemented by state pension applications, United Daughters of the Confederacy records, and postwar rosters and histories, all provided useful information.

OFFICERS

CAPTAINS

SKINNER, TRISTRIM LOWTHER
Resided in Chowan County and was appointed Captain to rank from May 16, 1861. Present or accounted for until transferred to the Field and Staff of this regiment upon appointment as Major on April 21, 1862.

BENBURY, JOHN AVERY
Resided in Chowan County and appointed 1st Lieutenant to rank from May 16, 1861. Promoted to Captain to rank from April 21, 1862. Wounded in action at Malvern Hill, Virginia, July 1, 1862, and died of wounds July 3, 1862.

BOND, FRANCIS WAYLAND
Resided in Chowan County where he enlisted at age 23, May 18, 1861, for the war. Mustered in as Corporal. Appointed 2nd Lieutenant to rank from December 1, 1861, and promoted to 1st Lieutenant to rank from July 6, 1862. Wounded in shoulder at Malvern Hill, Virginia, July 1, 1862. Absent wounded through October 27, 1862. Promoted to Captain to rank from November 6, 1862. Present or accounted for until he resigned on February 4, 1864, by reason of disability.

JOHNSTON, THOMAS L.
Resided in Chowan County where he enlisted at age 34, May 18, 1861, for the war. Mustered in as 1st Sergeant. Appointed 2nd Lieutenant to rank from October 8, 1862, and promoted to 1st Lieutenant January 17, 1863. Captured near Fredericksburg, Virginia, May 3, 1863, and confined at Old Capitol Prison, Washington, D.C., until paroled on May 18, 1863. Promoted to Captain to rank from February 4, 1864. Captured at Spotsylvania Court House, Virginia, May 10-12, 1864, and confined at Fort Delaware, Delaware, until transferred to Hilton Head, South Carolina, August 20, 1864. Sent to Fort Pulaski, Georgia, in October, 1864, and back to Hilton Head in December, 1864. Returned to Fort Delaware from Hilton Head on March 12, 1865. Released after taking the Oath of Allegiance on June 16, 1865.

LIEUTENANTS

BENBURY, LEMUEL CREECY, 1st Lieutenant
Resided in Chowan County and appointed 2nd

Lieutenant to rank from May 16, 1861. Promoted to 1st Lieutenant to rank from April 21, 1862. Submitted his resignation September 28, 1862, by reason of "having been elected to a seat in the Legislature from Chowan County." Resignation accepted November 6, 1862.

BRATTEN, JOHN L., 2nd Lieutenant
Resided in Chowan County where he enlisted at age 41, May 15, 1861, for the war. Appointed 2nd Lieutenant on June 3, 1861, to rank from May 16, 1861. Submitted his resignation November 17, 1861, and it was accepted on November 22, 1861.

GALLAGHER, D. H., 2nd Lieutenant
Captured and paroled at Athens, Georgia, May 8, 1865.

MORGAN. JOHN A., 1st Lieutenant
Resided in Perquimans County and enlisted in Chowan County at age 20, June 1, 1861, for the war. Mustered in as Private and appointed Corporal on December 1, 1861. Promoted to Sergeant on April 15, 1862. Wounded in action at Malvern Hill, Virginia, July 1, 1862, and promoted to 1st Sergeant on August 8, 1862. Appointed 2nd Lieutenant December 26, 1862. Promoted to 1st Lieutenant on February 4, 1864. Admitted to hospital at Richmond, Virginia, May 7, 1864, with a gunshot wound of the left leg. Furloughed June 10, 1864. Captured at Plymouth on October 31, 1864, and confined at Point Lookout, Maryland. Transferred from Point Lookout to Old Capitol Prison, Washington, D.C., January 3, 1865, and to Fort Delaware, Delaware, February 4, 1865. Released at Fort Delaware after taking the Oath of Allegiance on June 8, 1865.

PARKER, JOSEPH J., 1st Lieutenant
Resided in Chowan County where he enlisted at age 19, May 18, 1861, for the war. Mustered in as Private. Appointed 2nd Lieutenant to rank from August 18, 1862, and promoted to 1st Lieutenant to rank from November 6, 1862. Wounded in action at Sharpsburg, Maryland, September 17, 1862, and died in hospital at Winchester, Virginia, on January 17, 1863.

WILLIAMS, JAMES DANIEL, 3rd Lieutenant
Resided in Chowan County where he enlisted at age 33, May 18, 1861, for the war. Mustered in as Private and appointed Corporal on July 30, 1862. Promoted to Sergeant in November-December, 1862. Appointed 3rd Lieutenant to rank from January 24, 1863. Left the company on sick leave on May 2, 1863, and never rejoined the company. Dropped from the rolls as an officer on June 27, 1864.

NONCOMMISSIONED OFFICERS AND PRIVATES

ALLEN, DANIEL, Private
Enlisted in Guilford County, January 15, 1864, for the war. Company muster rolls cover through December, 1864, and report him as absent sick from May through December.

AMICK, JOHN, Private
Resided in Guilford County where he enlisted at

age 27, July 15, 1862, for the war. Died of disease August 25, 1862.

ANTHONY, HENRY, Private
Resided in Guilford County where he enlisted at age 27, July 15, 1862, for the war. Present or accounted for on company muster rolls through December, 1864.

APPLE, PETER, Private
Resided in Guilford County where he was conscripted at age 27, July 15, 1862, for the war. Discharged on August 11, 1862, after providing John Kelly as his substitute.

ASBILL, ELISHA, Private
Resided in Chowan County where he enlisted at age 25, May 18, 1861, for the war. Present or accounted for until he deserted to the enemy on March 27, 1863. Took the Oath of Allegiance at the office of the Provost Marshal General, Army of the Potomac, near Falmouth, Virginia, March 30, 1863.

BASS, ALPHEUS, Private
Resided in Chowan County where he enlisted at age 19, May 18, 1861, for the war. Wounded in action at Ellerson's Mill, Virginia, June 26, 1862. Permanently disabled by the wound and was reported as absent on company muster rolls through December, 1864.

BEST, BENJAMIN, Private
Captured at Goldsboro on March 24, 1865, and confined at Hart's Island, New York Harbor, until released on June 18, 1865.

BEVILL, ARCHER, Private
Born in Guilford County where he resided as a farmer and enlisted at age 28, July 15, 1862, for the war. Discharged at Danville, Virginia, February 17, 1863, by reason of "cystoplexia."

BEVILL, JESSE H., Private
Resided in Guilford County where he enlisted at age 33, July 15, 1862, for the war. Present or accounted for on company muster rolls through December, 1864. Paroled at Appomattox Court House, Virginia, April 9, 1865.

BOGUE, JOHN J., Private
Resided in Perquimans County and enlisted in Chowan County at age 21, May 18, 1861, for the war. Captured at South Mountain, Maryland, September 15, 1862, and paroled and exchanged at Aiken's Landing, Virginia, November 10, 1862. Captured at Spotsylvania Court House, Virginia, May 12, 1864, and confined at Elmira, New York, until released after taking the Oath of Allegiance on June 12, 1865.

BRATTEN, JAMES H., Private
Resided in Chowan County where he enlisted at age 18, May 18, 1861, for the war. Wounded in action at Sharpsburg, Maryland, September 17, 1862. Present or accounted for on company muster rolls through December, 1864.

BRATTEN, JOHN L., Jr., Private
Resided in Chowan County and enlisted at Skinker's Neck, Virginia, at age 17, February 28, 1863, for the war as a substitute for William M. Donnell. Wounded at Chancellorsville, Virginia,

May 3, 1863. Deserted to the enemy near Plymouth on March 15, 1864, and took the Oath of Amnesty at Fort Monroe, Virginia, June 2, 1864.

BROUGHTON, WILLIAM, Private
Born in Chowan County and resided as a farmer in Perquimans County prior to enlisting in Chowan County at age 19, August 18, 1861, for the war. Present or accounted for until captured at Gettysburg, Pennsylvania, July 3, 1863. Confined at Fort Delaware, Delaware, until transferred on October 18, 1863, to Point Lookout, Maryland, where he joined the United States service on February 11, 1864. Assigned to Company E, 1st Regiment U. S. Volunteer Infantry.

BRUER, JAMES D., Sergeant
Resided in Chowan County where he enlisted at age 30, May 15, 18, 1861, for the war. Mustered in as Sergeant. Present or accounted for until he was discharged on October 15, 1861.

BUDD, G. C., Private
Captured and paroled at Athens, Georgia, May 8, 1865.

BUNCH, EDWARD F., Private
Resided in Chowan County where he enlisted at age 18, May 18, 1861, for the war. Died at Richmond, Virginia, July 30, 1862, of disease.

BUNCH, POUNCEY J., Private
Resided in Guilford County where he enlisted at age 23, July 15, 1862, for the war. Present or accounted for on company muster rolls through December, 1864. Captured at Farmville, Virginia, April 6, 1865, and confined at Point Lookout, Maryland, until released after taking the Oath of Allegiance on June 1, 1865.

BUNCH, WILLIAM H., Private
Resided in Guilford County where he enlisted at age 25, July 15, 1862, for the war. Captured at Spotsylvania Court House, Virginia, May 12, 1864. Confined at Point Lookout, Maryland, until transferred to Elmira, New York, August 3, 1864. Released after taking the Oath of Allegiance at Elmira on June 12, 1865.

BURNS, JOHN, Private
Resided in Guilford County and enlisted at Skinker's Neck, Virginia, at age 36, February 28, 1863, for the war, as a substitute for John C. Love. Present or accounted for on company muster rolls through December, 1864.

BYRUM, BRINKLEY, Private
Resided in Chowan County where he enlisted at age 21, May 18, 1862, for the war. Present or accounted for until he deserted to the enemy on March 27, 1863. Confined at Old Capitol Prison, Washington, D. C., March 31, 1863.

BYRUM, JAMES W., Private
Resided in Chowan County where he enlisted at age 33, May 18, 1861, for the war. Present or accounted for on company muster rolls through December, 1864.

CALE, JOHN H., Private
Resided in Chowan County where he enlisted at age 18, May 18, 1861, for the war. Died at Camp

Bee, Virginia, December 1, 1861, with "congestion of the brain."

CALHOUN, WILLIAM H., Private
Resided in Guilford County where he enlisted at age 28, July 15, 1862, for the war. Died September 25, 1862, of disease.

CARMINE, JOSEPH, Private
Resided in Chowan County where he enlisted at age 20, May 18, 1861, for the war. Present or accounted for until he transferred to the C. S. Navy on February 1, 1862.

CARROLL, BEN, Private
Resided in Guilford County where he enlisted at age 27, July 15, 1862, for the war. Killed at Sharpsburg, Maryland, September 17, 1862.

CARTER, ROBERT W., Private
Resided in Guilford County where he enlisted at age 18, July 15, 1862, for the war. Wounded in the side on September 14, 1862, and admitted to hospital at Richmond, Virginia, October 4, 1862. Returned to duty on December 13, 1862. Wounded at Gettysburg, Pennsylvania, July 2, 1863, and reported on hospital rolls of General Hospital, Staunton, Virginia, through October, 1863. Present or accounted for on company muster rolls through December, 1864. Appears on a register of refugees and rebel deserters received by the Provost Marshal General, Washington, D. C., February 24, 1865, from the Army of the James. Took the Oath of Allegiance and was provided transportation to Greensboro, Indiana.

CHAMBERLAIN, CHARLES, Private
Transferred from Company G, 2nd Battalion N. C. Infantry on March 13, 1864. Captured at Spotsylvania Court House, Virginia, May 12, 1864, and confined at Elmira, New York, until released after taking the Oath of Allegiance on May 29, 1865.

CHRISTOPHER, JOHN F., Private
Resided in Guilford County where he enlisted at age 18, July 15, 1862, for the war. Present or accounted for on company muster rolls through December, 1864. Deserted and took the Oath of Allegiance at Headquarters, Army of the James, Bermuda Hundred, Virginia, March 16, 1865, and transportation furnished to Plymouth, Illinois.

COFFIELD, WILLIAM R., Private
Resided in Chowan County where he enlisted at age 21, May 18, 1861, for the war. Died in hospital at Richmond, Virginia, August 27, 1862, of "diarrhoea."

COLE, G. M., Sergeant
Captured at Winchester, Virginia, September 19, 1864, and sent to Point Lookout, Maryland, September 23, 1864.

COOPER, R. L., Sergeant
Captured at Winchester, Virginia, September 19, 1864, and sent to Point Lookout, Maryland, September 23, 1864.

CORNELIOUS, W. D., Private
Admitted to hospital at Farmville, Virginia, March 2, 1865, with "spinal irritation" and

returned to duty March 8, 1865. Paroled at Burkeville Junction, Virginia, April 14-17, 1865.

CORNELIUS, HENRY W. L., Private
Resided in Yadkin County. Appears on a register of rebel deserters and refugees received at Fort Monroe, Virginia, February 17, 1864, which states: "rebel deserter came into Federal lines, New Bern, North Carolina." Took the Oath of Allegiance at Fort Monroe on February 24, 1864, and was sent to Indianapolis, Indiana.

CUMMINGS, NEWTON J., Private
Resided in Guilford County where he enlisted at age 18, July 15, 1862, for the war. Present or accounted for on company muster rolls until captured at Spotsylvania Court House, Virginia, May 12, 1864. Confined at Point Lookout, Maryland, until transferred to Elmira, New York, August 6, 1864. Released after taking the Oath of Allegiance on June 12, 1865.

DAVENPORT, WILLIAM J., Private
Resided in Chowan County where he enlisted at age 24, February 1, 1862, for the war. Deserted September 15, 1862, and returned to company under arrest in January-February, 1863. Remained under arrest until released on June 4, 1863. Captured at Spotsylvania Court House, Virginia, May 12, 1864, and confined at Point Lookout, Maryland, until transferred to Elmira, New York, August 3, 1864. Paroled at Elmira and exchanged at Boulware's Wharf, James River, Virginia, March 18-21, 1865. Appears on a register of refugees and rebel deserters, Provost Marshal General, Washington, D. C., received April 20, 1865, from City Point, Virginia, with the remark that "transportation ordered to Baltimore, Maryland."

DAVIS, MICHAEL C., Private
Resided in Guilford County where he enlisted at age 22, July 15, 1862, for the war. Wounded at Gettysburg, Pennsylvania, July 2, 3, 1863. Absent wounded through February, 1864. Captured at Spotsylvania Court House, Virginia, May 12, 1864, and confined at Point Lookout, Maryland. Transferred August 6, 1864, to Elmira, New York, where he died December 20, 1864, of pneumonia.

DENNIS, SAMUEL R., Private
Resided in Chowan County where he enlisted at age 18, May 18, 1861, for the war. Died at Petersburg, Virginia, July 20, 1863, of wounds.

DICKSON, J., Private
Captured and paroled at Athens, Georgia, May 8, 1865.

DIXON, DUNCAN A., Private
Resided in Chowan County and enlisted at Orange Court House, Virginia, at age 16, August 20, 1862, for the war. Present or accounted for until he was discharged on June 28, 1863, upon receiving an appointment as Acting Midshipman, C. S. Navy.

DONNELL, D. J., Private
Resided in Guilford County where he enlisted at age 33, July 15, 1862, for the war. Wounded at Sharpsburg, Maryland, September 17, 1862, and

reported absent wounded until returned to duty May 12, 1863. Wounded at Gettysburg, Pennsylvania, July 2-3, 1863. Discharged on April 12, 1864, by reason of his being "incapable of performing the duties of a soldier because of phthisis pulmonalis."

DONNELL, WILLIAM M., Private
Resided in Guilford County where he enlisted at age 27, July 15, 1862, for the war. Present or accounted for until discharged on providing John L. Bratten, Jr., as his substitute on February 28, 1863.

ELLIOTT, AMBROSE, Corporal
Resided in Chowan County where he enlisted at age 20, May 15, 1861, for the war. Mustered in as Private and appointed Corporal on December 1, 1861. Wounded in the "thigh and hand" at Ellerson's Mill, Virginia, June 26, 1862. Discharged on January 21, 1863, by reason of disability.

ELLIOTT, GEORGE W., Private
Born in Pasquotank County where he resided prior to enlisting in Chowan County at age 30, May 18, 1861, for the war. Died at Fredericksburg, Virginia, October 30, 1861, of disease.

ELLIS, JAMES O., Sergeant
Resided in Chowan County where he enlisted at age 23, May 18, 1861, for the war. Mustered in as Private and promoted to Sergeant on April 15, 1862. Wounded at Sharpsburg, Maryland, September 17, 1862. Deserted to U.S. forces near Falmouth, Virginia, March 27, 1863, and took the Oath of Allegiance on March 30, 1863.

EVANS, ROBERT, Private
Enlisted in Guilford County, July 15, 1862, for the war. Captured at Gettysburg, Pennsylvania, July 3, 1863. Died at Point Lookout, Maryland, August 30, 1864.

EVANS, W. W., Private
Resided in Guilford County where he enlisted at age 26, July 15, 1862, for the war. Wounded at Chancellorsville, Virginia, May 3, 1863, and reported as absent wounded through October, 1863. Captured at Spotsylvania Court House, Virginia, May 12, 1864, and confined at Point Lookout, Maryland, until transferred to Elmira, New York, August 6, 1864. Transferred to Venus Point, Savannah River, Georgia, October 11, 1864, for exchange; however, he died en route and was buried at Point Lookout, Maryland, October 23, 1864.

EVELIN, WILLIAM J., Private
Captured at Gettysburg, Pennsylvania, July 5, 1863. Paroled at DeCamp General Hospital, Davids Island, New York Harbor, and delivered for exchange at City Point, Virginia, September 27, 1863.

FELLOWS, HENRY, Private
Resided in Guilford County where he enlisted at age 18, July 15, 1862, for the war. Captured at Spotsylvania Court House, Virginia, May 12, 1864, and confined at Point Lookout, Maryland, until transferred to Elmira, New York, August 6, 1864.

Died at Elmira on February 21, 1865, of pneumonia.

GALLOP, SAMUEL, Private
Born in Currituck County where he resided as a sailor prior to enlisting in Chowan County at age 28, June 1, 1861, for the war. Wounded at Sharpsburg, Maryland, September 17, 1862. Wounded at Gettysburg, Pennsylvania, July 3, 1863, and captured at Williamsport, Maryland, July 14, 1863. Confined at U. S. Army hospital until transferred to Point Lookout, Maryland, October 2, 1863. Took the Oath of Allegiance at Point Lookout and joined the U.S. service on February 16, 1864. Assigned to Company E, 1st Regiment U.S. Volunteer Infantry.

GARDENER, A. C., Private
Resided in Guilford County where he was conscripted at age 34, July 15, 1862, for the war. Wounded in hip at Sharpsburg, Maryland, September 17, 1862, and returned to duty December 9, 1862. Wounded at Chancellorsville, Virginia, May 3, 1863, and returned to duty on June 10, 1863. Captured at Gettysburg, Pennsylvania, July 3, 1863, and confined at Fort Delaware, Delaware, until transferred to Point Lookout, Maryland, October 18, 1863. Remained at Point Lookout until transferred to Aiken's Landing, Virginia, February 24, 1865, for exchange. Records indicate that he was not exchanged but was provided transportation from Point Lookout, Maryland, to Washington, D.C., May 12-14, 1865. Reported as a "refugee and rebel deserter."

GARENER, ANDREW, Private
Resided in Guilford County where he enlisted at age 33, July 15, 1862, for the war. Wounded in arm at Sharpsburg, Maryland, September 17, 1862, and returned to company in December, 1862. Wounded in the head at Chancellorsville, Virginia, May 3, 1863, and returned to company in September, 1863. Captured at Spotsylvania Court House, Virginia, May 12, 1864, and confined at Point Lookout, Maryland, until transferred to Elmira, New York, August 6, 1864. Remained at Elmira until released after taking the Oath of Allegiance on June 16, 1865.

GARENER, PETER, Private
Resided in Guilford County where he enlisted at age 26, July 15, 1862, for the war. Mortally wounded at Sharpsburg, Maryland, September 17, 1862, and died September 24, 1862.

GATES, R. W., Private
Resided in Guilford County where he enlisted at age 20, July 15, 1862, for the war. Died in hospital at Danville, Virginia, February 1, 1863, of "pneumonia."

GILBERT, ISAAC N., Private
Resided in Pasquotank County and enlisted in Chowan County at age 30, May 18, 1861, for the war. Mustered in as Corporal and reduced to ranks April 15, 1862. Killed in action at Malvern Hill, Virginia, July 1, 1862.

GOOD, S. B., Private
Captured and paroled at Athens, Georgia, May 8, 1865.

GREEN, WILLIAM, Private

Resided in Guilford County where he enlisted at age 26, July 15, 1862, for the war. Captured at Sharpsburg, Maryland, September 17, 1862, and paroled near Keedysville, Maryland, September 20, 1862. Present or accounted for until captured at Spotsylvania Court House, Virginia, May 12, 1864. Confined at Point Lookout, Maryland, until transferred to Elmira, New York, August 6, 1864. Remained at Elmira until released after taking the Oath of Allegiance on June 16, 1865.

HALL, E. M., Private

Captured and paroled at Athens, Georgia, May 8, 1865.

HALL, M. O., Private

Captured and paroled at Athens, Georgia, May 8, 1865.

HANKINS, JAMES M., Corporal

Resided in Chowan County where he enlisted at age 22, May 18, 1861, for the war. Mustered in as Private and appointed Corporal April 15, 1862. Killed in action at Ellerson's Mill, Virginia, June 26, 1862.

HARRELL, AMOS, Private

Resided in Chowan County where he enlisted at age 25, August 22, 1861, for the war. Died in hospital at Richmond, Virginia, between June 30 and October 31, 1862, of disease.

HARRELL, THOMAS, Private

Resided in Chowan County where he enlisted at age 19, May 18, 1861, for the war. Died at Camp Bee, Virginia, August 29, 1861, of disease.

HARRIS, FRANCIS A., Sergeant

Resided in Chowan County where he enlisted at age 36, February 1, 1862, for the war. Mustered in as Private and appointed Corporal October 15, 1862. Promoted to Sergeant on April 20, 1863. Captured at Gettysburg, Pennsylvania, July 3, 1863, and confined at Fort Delaware, Delaware, until transferred to Point Lookout, Maryland, October 18, 1863. Died at Point Lookout on December 21, 1863.

HARVEY, JOSHUA S., Private

Resided in Chowan County where he enlisted at age 21, May 18, 1861, for the war. Wounded in action at Malvern Hill, Virginia, July 1, 1862, and died of wounds on July 18, 1862.

HARVEY, THOMAS E., Sergeant

Resided in Chowan County where he enlisted at age 23, May 18, 1861, for the war. Mustered in as Private and appointed Sergeant on October 15, 1862. Present or accounted for until captured at Spotsylvania Court House, Virginia, May 12, 1864. Confined at Point Lookout, Maryland, until transferred to Elmira, New York, August 6, 1864. Remained at Elmira until released after taking the Oath of Allegiance on June 12, 1865.

HASTE, JOHN, Private

Resided in Chowan County where he enlisted at age 32, May 18, 1861, for the war. Killed in action at Sharpsburg, Maryland, September 17, 1862.

HAUGHTON, JOHN P., Drummer

Born in Chowan County where he resided as a mariner prior to enlisting at Camp Bee, Virginia, at age 30, August 26, 1861, for the war. Mustered in as a Drummer. Discharged at Camp Bee on December 1, 1861, by reason of "disability on account of disease of kidneys and bladder."

HEDRICK, RICHARD S., Sergeant

Resided in Chowan County where he enlisted at age 23, May 18, 1861, for the war. Mustered in as Private and appointed Corporal on October 15, 1862. Promoted to Sergeant March-April, 1863. Present or accounted for until captured at Spotsylvania Court House, Virginia, May 12, 1864, and confined at Point Lookout, Maryland. Transferred August 6, 1864, to Elmira, New York, where he remained until released after taking the Oath of Allegiance on June 12, 1865.

HILTON, JAMES M., Corporal

Resided in Guilford County where he enlisted at age 30, July 15, 1862, for the war. Mustered in as Private. Captured near Sharpsburg, Maryland, September 17, 1862, and paroled near Keedysville, Maryland, September 20, 1862. Appointed Corporal June 15, 1863. Present or accounted for until captured at Spotsylvania Court House, Virginia, May 12, 1864. Confined at Point Lookout, Maryland, until transferred to Elmira, New York, August 6, 1864. Remained at Elmira until released after taking the Oath of Allegiance on May 19, 1865.

HOGE, J. A., Private

Captured at Gettysburg, Pennsylvania, July 5, 1863, and confined at Fort Delaware, Delaware. Released at Fort Delaware on July 30, 1865.

HOPKINS, WILLIAM, Private

Appears on a roll of noncommissioned officers and privates employed as boatmen on extra duty at Smithville, North Carolina, during the months of May and June, 1864.

HORNEY, P. P., Private

Resided in Guilford County where he enlisted at age 28, July 15, 1862, for the war. Admitted to hospital at Charlottesville, Virginia, December 7, 1862, with "pneumonia" and died January 6, 1863, of "typhoid fever."

HOSKINS, BLAKE B., Sergeant

Born in Chowan County where he resided as a farmer prior to enlisting at age 22, May 18, 1861, for the war. Mustered in as Corporal and appointed Sergeant on December 1, 1861. Present or accounted for until transferred to Company F, 11th Regiment N.C. Troops (1st Regiment N.C. Volunteers) upon appointment as 3rd Lieutenant to rank from April 7, 1862.

HOSKINS, GEORGE O., Private

Resided in Guilford County where he enlisted at age 22, July 15, 1862, for the war. Wounded in action at Sharpsburg, Maryland, September 17, 1862, and reported as absent wounded through October, 1862. Present or accounted for until captured at Spotsylvania Court House, Virginia, May 12, 1864. Confined at Point Lookout, Maryland, until transferred to Elmira, New York, August 6, 1864. Remained at Elmira until released after taking the Oath of Allegiance on May 17, 1865.

JESSOP, THOMAS, Private

Resided in Guilford County where he enlisted at age 26, July 15, 1862, for the war. Present or accounted for until captured at Spotsylvania Court House, Virginia, May 12, 1864. Confined at Point Lookout, Maryland, until transferred to Elmira, New York, August 6, 1864. Remained at Elmira until released after taking the Oath of Allegiance on May 17, 1865.

JOHNSON, ROBERT, 1st Sergeant

Resided in Chowan County where he enlisted at age 34, May 18, 1861, for the war. Mustered in as Private and appointed Corporal July 30, 1862. Promoted to Sergeant October 18, 1862. Wounded at Fredericksburg, Virginia, December 13, 1862, and returned to duty January 26, 1863. Promoted to 1st Sergeant in 1863. Present or accounted for until wounded at Payne's Farm, Virginia, November 27, 1863. Reported as absent wounded through December, 1864.

JONES, JEREMIAH, Corporal

Resided in Chowan County where he enlisted at age 22, May 18, 1861, for the war. Mustered in as Private. Left sick at Frederick, Maryland, where he was captured and paroled on September 26, 1862. Appointed Corporal on June 15, 1863. Present or accounted for until captured at Spotsylvania Court House, Virginia, May 12, 1864. Confined at Point Lookout, Maryland, until transferred to Elmira, New York, August 3, 1864. Remained at Elmira until paroled on March 14, 1865, and sent to the James River, Virginia, for exchange.

JONES, WHITMEL, Private

Resided in Chowan County where he enlisted on August 22, 1861, for the war. Present or accounted for until captured at Spotsylvania Court House, Virginia, May 12, 1864, and confined at Point Lookout, Maryland. Transferred to Elmira, New York, August 6, 1864. Remained at Elmira until released after taking the Oath of Allegiance on June 19, 1865.

KELLOG, A. J., Private

Paroled at Talladega, Alabama, May 22, 1865.

KELLY, JAMES, Private

Enlisted at Richmond, Virginia, at age 36, August 10, 1862, for the war as a substitute. Deserted at Richmond on August 17, 1862.

KENNEDY, JAMES F., Private

Resided in Chowan County where he enlisted at age 30, May 18, 1861, for the war. Present or accounted for until discharged at Richmond, Virginia, September 3, 1862, by reason of "opthalmitis of two years standing which has resulted in the loss of the sight of the left eye."

KIRKMOND, CALVIN, Private

Resided in Guilford County where he enlisted at age 25, July 15, 1862, for the war. Killed in action at Sharpsburg, Maryland, September 17, 1862.

LANE, ELISHA, Private

Resided in Chowan County and enlisted in Warren County at age 33, June 28, 1861, for the war. Wounded and captured at Sharpsburg, Maryland, September 17, 1862. Paroled at Fort McHen-

ry, Maryland, April 3, 1863. The Roll of Honor states that he was "wounded and permanently disabled in battle at Ellerson's Mill, Virginia, June 26, 1862." Claim filed by his widow in 1887 states that he was "mortally wounded in Virginia, 1863 or 1864."

LANE, GEORGE D., Private

Resided in Guilford County where he enlisted at age 30, July 15, 1862, for the war. Wounded in the knee at Payne's Farm, Virginia, November 27, 1863, and retired to Invalid Corps on October 5, 1864. Stationed at Gordonsville, Virginia, December 1, 1864. Paroled at Greensboro on May 4, 1865.

LANE, HENRY, Private

Resided in Chowan County where he enlisted at age 25, May 18, 1861, for the war. Present or accounted for until captured at Spotsylvania Court House, Virginia, May 12, 1864. Confined at Point Lookout, Maryland, until transferred to Elmira, New York, August 6, 1864. Died at Elmira on February 12, 1865, of "variola."

LANE, SAMUEL, Private

Resided in Chowan County where he enlisted at age 23, May 18, 1861, for the war. Died at Charlottesville, Virginia, December 16, 1862, of "pneumonia."

LEARY, QUENTIN T., Private

Resided in Chowan County where he enlisted at age 18, June 1, 1861, for the war. Discharged on September 2, 1861, by reason of disability.

LEARY, THOMAS J., Private

Born in Chowan County where he resided as a preacher and enlisted at age 28, June 1, 1861, for the war. Mustered in as Sergeant and reduced to ranks on April 15, 1862. Discharged on February 1, 1863.

LEONARD, JOHN H., Private

Resided in Maryland and enlisted in Chowan County at age 25, May 18, 1861, for the war. Discharged on February 1, 1862, and transferred to the C. S. Navy.

LITCHFIELD, SPENCER, Private

Resided in Chowan County where he enlisted at age 22, May 18, 1861, for the war. Present or accounted for until discharged on February 1, 1862, and transferred to the C. S. Navy.

LLOYD, JOHN S., Private

Born in Guilford County where he resided as a farmer and enlisted at age 23, July 15, 1862, for the war. Wounded at Sharpsburg, Maryland, September 17, 1862. Admitted to hospital at Richmond, Virginia, December 14, 1862, with "varioloid" and transferred to hospital at Danville, Virginia, on May 4, 1863, with "rheumatism chronic." Discharged at Danville on September 14, 1863, by reason of "chronic rheumatism with hypertrophy, and dilitation of left ventrical of heart and disease of aortic valves."

LOVE, JOHN C., Private

Resided in Guilford County where he enlisted at age 25, July 15, 1862, for the war. Discharged on February 28, 1863, by reason of his having provided John Burns as his substitute.

LOYD, THOMAS, Private
Resided in Guilford County where he enlisted at age 21, July 15, 1862, for the war. Wounded at Sharpsburg, Maryland, September 17, 1862. Captured at Gettysburg, Pennsylvania, July 3, 1863, and confined at Fort Delaware, Delaware, where he died September 20, 1863, of "chronic diarrhoea."

McCLENNY, KADER, Private
Born in Bertie County and resided as a farmer in Chowan County where he enlisted at age 21, May 18, 1861, for the war. Discharged at hospital in Richmond, Virginia, September 6, 1862, by reason of "phthisis pulmonalis."

McNIDER, WILLIAM H., Private
Resided in Perquimans County and enlisted in Chowan County at age 19, May 18, 1861, for the war. Mustered in as Sergeant and reduced to ranks on April 15, 1862. Transferred to Company K, 61st Regiment Virginia Infantry.

MANSFIELD, HOSEA, Private
Resided in Chowan County where he enlisted at age 21, August 22, 1861, for the war. Present or accounted for until hospitalized on September 1, 1862, at Richmond, Virginia, where he died October 9, 1862, of "typhoid fever."

MARSHALL, J. L., Private
Captured at Hanover, Virginia, May 24, 1864, and confined at Point Lookout, Maryland, where he was released after joining the U.S. service on June 13, 1864.

MAXWELL, R. T., Private
Resided in Guilford County where he enlisted at age 18, July 15, 1862, for the war. Present or accounted for until he died in hospital at Richmond, Virginia, September 14-15, 1862, of "typhoid fever."

MILES, EDWARD, Private
Resided in Guilford County where he enlisted at age 22, July 15, 1862, for the war. Present or accounted for until he was wounded on October 19, 1864, and sent to hospital. Furloughed for 30 days November 12, 1864. Admitted to hospital at Richmond, Virginia, on March 6, 1865, with a gunshot wound of the right leg. Captured in hospital on April 3, 1865, and confined at Libby Prison, Richmond, until transferred to Newport News, Virginia, April 23, 1865. Took the Oath of Allegiance at Newport News on June 30, 1865.

MILLAWAY, E., Private
Resided in Guilford County where he enlisted at age 28, July 15, 1862, for the war. Died at Richmond, Virginia, August 25, 1862, of disease.

MILLER, AUGUSTUS, Private
Resided in Chowan County where he enlisted at age 30, May 18, 1861, for the war. Present or accounted for until captured at Spotsylvania Court House, Virginia, May 12, 1864. Confined at Point Lookout, Maryland, until transferred to Elmira, New York, August 6, 1864. Remained at Elmira until he was released after taking the Oath of Allegiance on June 14, 1865.

MILLER, JONATHAN, Private
Born in Chowan County where he resided and enlisted at age 38, May 18, 1861, for the war. Died

in hospital at Fredericksburg, Virginia, November 27, 1861, of disease.

MITCHELL, JEREMIAH, Private
Born in Chowan County where he resided as a laborer and enlisted at age 21, May 18, 1861, for the war. Present or accounted for until he was discharged on June 12, 1863, by reason of disability.

MONROE, PATRICK McC., Private
Resided in Chowan County where he enlisted at age 38, May 18, 1861, for the war. Mustered in as Private and appointed Sergeant on October 15, 1862. Reduced to ranks April 30, 1863, for prolonged absence. Reported as present or absent accounted for through December, 1862, and as absent without leave from January, 1863, until he was reported on the February 29-August 31, 1864, muster roll with the remark that he was "promoted to Lieutenancy in 68th N.C. Regiment August, 1863." However, he does not appear as an officer on the surviving records of that regiment.

MOODY, JAMES, Private
Resided in Chowan County where he enlisted at age 25, May 18, 1861, for the war. Present or accounted for until killed in action at Ellerson's Mill, Virginia, June 26, 1862.

MOONEY, J. M., Private
Born in Guilford County where he resided as a teacher and enlisted at age 22, July 15, 1862, for the war. Present or accounted for until discharged on January 31, 1864, by reason of "incipient phthisis pulmonalis."

MOORE, AUGUSTUS M., Private
Born in Chowan County where he resided as a farmer and enlisted at age 19, May 18, 1861, for the war. Mustered in as Sergeant. Reduced to ranks June 13, 1861, when he withdrew from the company. Rejoined the company on July 10, 1861, as a Private. Appointed Sergeant Major on August 18, 1861, and transferred to the Field and Staff of this regiment.

MOORE, ROBERT D., Private
Resided in Guilford County where he enlisted at age 22, July 15, 1862, for the war. Present or accounted for until he deserted to the enemy on March 27, 1863, and took the Oath of Allegiance near Falmouth, Virginia, March 30, 1863.

MOORE, THOMAS E., Private
Born in Guilford County where he resided as a farmer and enlisted at age 26, July 15, 1862, for the war. Wounded at Sharpsburg, Maryland, September 17, 1862. Returned to duty December 13, 1862. Admitted to hospital at Lynchburg, Virginia, April 10, 1863, and discharged on July 20, 1863, by reason of: "disease of spine resulting from mechanical injury to back."

MORAN, QUENTIN, Private
Born in Gates County and resided in Chowan County where he enlisted at age 23, May 18, 1861, for the war. Died at Camp Bee, Virginia, August 27, 1861, of disease.

NIXON, HARVEY, Private
Resided in Chowan County where he enlisted at

age 27, May 18, 1861, for the war. Present or accounted for until captured at Spotsylvania Court House, Virginia, May 12, 1864. Confined at Point Lookout, Maryland, until transferred to Elmira, New York, August 6, 1864. Died at Elmira on November 23, 1864, of "pneumonia."

NORCOM, JOHN H., Private
Resided in Perquimans County and enlisted in Chowan County at age 22, June 1, 1861, for the war. Discharged on January 1, 1862, by reason of disability and died soon after being discharged.

NORCOM, WILLIAM J., Private
Resided in Chowan County where he enlisted at age 19, June 1, 1861, for the war. Died at Fredericksburg, Virginia, November 15, 1861, of disease.

OLIVER, JOHN, Private
Resided in Chowan County where he enlisted at age 24, May 18, 1861, for the war. Present or accounted for until captured at Spotsylvania Court House, Virginia, May 12, 1864, and confined at Point Lookout, Maryland. Transferred to Elmira, New York, August 6, 1864. Remained at Elmira until released after taking the Oath of Allegiance on June 21, 1865.

OWEN, T. M. R. M., Private
Captured at Gettysburg, Pennsylvania, July 3, 1863, and confined at Fort Delaware, Delaware. Transferred to Point Lookout, Maryland, October 18, 1863.

PARRISH, JOHN L., Private
Resided in Chowan County where he enlisted at age 19, May 18, 1861, for the war. Wounded at Sharpsburg, Maryland, September 17, 1862. Present or accounted for until captured at Spotsylvania Court House, Virginia, May 12, 1864. Released after taking the Oath of Allegiance at Elmira, New York, June 27, 1865.

PATE, JESSE, Private
Resided in Cherokee County and took the Oath of Allegiance at Chattanooga, Tennessee, May 21, 1865.

PHIBBS, L. D., Private
Resided in Guilford County where he enlisted at age 27, July 15, 1862, for the war. Present or accounted for until he died at Charlottesville, Virginia, December 9, 1862, of "pneumonia."

PHIBBS, ROBERT J., Private
Resided in Guilford County where he enlisted at age 30, July 15, 1862, for the war. Present or accounted for until he was captured at Spotsylvania Court House, Virginia, May 12, 1864. Confined at Point Lookout, Maryland, until transferred to Elmira, New York, August 6, 1864. Died at Elmira on February 3, 1865, of "chronic diarrhoea."

PITCHFORD, JAMES, Private
Resided in Guilford County where he enlisted at age 34, July 15, 1862, for the war. Wounded at Sharpsburg, Maryland, September 17, 1862. Captured at Gettysburg, Pennsylvania, July 3, 1863, and confined at Fort Delaware, Delaware. Transferred October 18, 1863, to Point Lookout, Maryland, where he died February 5, 1864.

PITCHFORD, W. D., Private
Resided in Guilford County where he enlisted at age 23, July 15, 1862, for the war. Present or accounted for until he died July 1, 1863, of disease.

PRATT, WILLIAM H., Private
Resided in Chowan County where he enlisted at age 19, May 18, 1861, for the war. Wounded and captured at Sharpsburg, Maryland, September 17, 1862, and confined at Fort McHenry, Maryland, until paroled and sent to Fort Monroe, Virginia, for exchange on October 18, 1862. Declared exchanged on November 10, 1862. Admitted to hospital at Richmond, Virginia, October 23, 1862, with a wound of the left shoulder and transferred to Goldsboro on April 3, 1863. Admitted to hospital at Danville, Virginia, on October 12, 1864. Company muster rolls carry him as absent wounded through December, 1864. Paroled at Greensboro on May 10, 1865.

PREDDY, JOEL, Private
Resided in Guilford County where he enlisted at age 28, July 15, 1862, for the war. Present or accounted for until he deserted on March 27, 1863. Took the Oath of Allegiance near Falmouth, Virginia, March 30, 1863.

PRIVETT, JACOB R., Private
Resided in Chowan County where he enlisted at age 23, May 18, 1861, for the war. Present or accounted for on company muster rolls through December, 1864. Rolls indicate that he was absent sick from March, 1864, through December, 1864.

PRIVETT, THOMAS H., Private
Resided in Chowan County where he enlisted at age 19, May 18, 1861, for the war. Wounded at Winchester, Virginia, June 15, 1863. Captured near Edenton on August 16, 1863, and confined at Point Lookout, Maryland, until transferred to Elmira, New York, August 16, 1864. Paroled at Elmira and sent to James River, Virginia, March 14, 1865, for exchange.

PUGH, JAMES, Private
Resided in Currituck County and enlisted in Chowan County at age 27, June 1, 1861, for the war. Wounded at Gettysburg, Pennsylvania, July 3, 1863. Present or accounted for until transferred to the C.S. Navy on April 18, 1864.

PYEMAN, J. F., Private
Paroled at Greensboro on May 9, 1865.

RAYLE, E. A., Private
Resided in Guilford County where he enlisted at age 32, July 15, 1862, for the war. Wounded at Sharpsburg, Maryland, September 17, 1862, and captured. Died in U.S. Army Hospital at Hestonville, Pennsylvania, October 23, 1862, of "pneumonia typhoides."

RILEY, JOHN, Musician
Resided in Chowan County where he enlisted at age 16, January 13, 1862, for the war. Mustered in as Private but appointed Musician after March, 1862. Present or accounted for on company muster rolls through December, 1864.

ROBERTS, JOHN, Private

Resided in Chowan County where he enlisted at age 26, March 18, 1861, for the war. Discharged October 15, 1861.

ROGERSON, JEREMIAH, Private

Resided in Chowan County where he enlisted at age 20, May 18, 1861, for the war. Mustered in as Private and appointed Corporal April 15, 1862. Reduced to ranks prior to October 31, 1862. Present or accounted for until he died at Staunton, Virginia, December 17, 1862, of disease.

ROGERSON, JESSE W., Private

Born in Gates County and resided as a butcher in Chowan County where he enlisted at age 26, May 18, 1861, for the war. Present or accounted for until discharged on December 1, 1861, by reason of "disability on account of disease of kidneys and bladder."

SAWYER, LEMUEL, Private

Resided in Chowan County where he enlisted at age 27, May 18, 1861, for the war. Discharged on August 1, 1861.

SEXTON, ROBERT K., Private

Resided in Perquimans County and enlisted in Chowan County at age 30, May 18, 1861, for the war. Present or accounted for until he was killed in battle at Ellerson's Mill, Virginia, June 26, 1862.

SHERGILL, J. M., Private

Captured at Gettysburg, Pennsylvania, July 3, 1863, and confined at Point Lookout, Maryland, until paroled and sent to Boulware's and Cox's Wharf, James River, Virginia, for exchange on February 18, 1865.

SHORT, J. N., Corporal

Paroled at Greensboro on May 6, 1865.

SKINNER, BENJAMIN, Private

Resided in Chowan County where he enlisted at age 18, May 18, 1861, for the war. Captured at South Mountain, Maryland, September 15, 1862, and confined at Fort Delaware, Delaware. Exchanged at Aiken's Landing, Virginia, November 10, 1862. Wounded at Chancellorsville, Virginia, May 3, 1863. Present or accounted for until captured at Spotsylvania Court House, Virginia, May 12, 1864, and confined at Point Lookout, Maryland. Transferred on August 6, 1864, to Elmira, New York, where he died on September 23, 1864, of "chronic diarrhoea."

SKINNER, HENRY, Private

Resided in Chowan County where he enlisted at age 20, May 18, 1861, for the war. Died at home in Chowan County on January 8, 1862.

SKINNER, RICHARD QUINTON, Corporal

Born in Perquimans County and resided as a carpenter in Chowan County where he enlisted at age 19, May 18, 1861, for the war. Mustered in as Private and appointed Corporal on June 15, 1863. Present or accounted for until captured at Gettysburg, Pennsylvania, July 3, 1863. Confined at Fort Delaware, Delaware, until released after joining the U.S. service on October 4, 1863. Assigned to Company F, 1st Regiment Connecticut Cavalry.

SKINNER, THOMAS G., Private

Resided in Chowan County where he enlisted at age 35, May 18, 1861, for the war. Discharged September 12, 1861.

SMALL, DAVID A., Private

Resided in Chowan County where he enlisted at age 27, May 18, 1861, for the war. Mustered in as Private and appointed Sergeant March-April, 1862. Reduced to ranks September 18, 1862. Present or accounted for on company muster rolls through December, 1864, being reported as absent sick after October, 1863.

SMITH, DANIEL G., Private

Resided in Guilford County where he enlisted at age 20, July 15, 1862, for the war. Reported as missing in action at Sharpsburg, Maryland, on September 17, 1862, and reported as paroled at Keedysville, Maryland, September 20, 1862. Died at home on September 23, 1863.

SMITH, HENRY, Private

Resided in Bertie County and enlisted in Chowan County at age 21, May 18, 1862, for the war. Wounded at Sharpsburg, Maryland, September 17, 1862, and died in hospital at Richmond, Virginia, on December 1, 1862.

SMITH, JAMES, Private

Resided in Chowan County where he enlisted at age 22, May 18, 1861, for the war. Wounded at Ellerson's Mill, Virginia, June 26, 1862. Died in hospital at Richmond, Virginia, November 9, 1863, of "pneumonia."

SMITH, JAMES D., Private

Captured at Gettysburg, Pennsylvania, July 3, 1863, and confined at Fort Delaware, Delaware, until transferred to Point Lookout, Maryland, on October 18, 1863.

SMITH, LASSITER, Private

Resided in Chowan County where he enlisted at age 21, May 18, 1861, for the war. Wounded at Ellerson's Mill, Virginia, June 26, 1862. Captured at Spotsylvania Court House, Virginia, May 12, 1864, and confined at Point Lookout, Maryland, until transferred to Elmira, New York, August 6, 1864. Released at Elmira after taking the Oath of Allegiance on June 12, 1865.

SMITH, NORMAN, Private

Resided in Chowan County where he enlisted at age 20, May 18, 1861, for the war. Present or accounted for until captured at Spotsylvania Court House, Virginia, May 12, 1864. Confined at Point Lookout, Maryland, until transferred to Elmira, New York, August 6, 1864. Died at Elmira on March 2, 1865, of "chronic diarrhoea."

SPRUILL, GEORGE W., Sergeant

Resided in Chowan County where he enlisted at age 18, May 18, 1861, for the war. Mustered in as Private and appointed Corporal November-December, 1862. Reduced to ranks for prolonged absence due to illness on June 15, 1863. Promoted to Sergeant on May 1, 1864. Present or accounted for on company muster rolls through December, 1864. Appears on a register of rebel deserters who were received at the headquarters of the Provost

Marshal, Bermuda Hundred, Virginia, February 25, 1865. Transferred to Provost Marshal General, Washington, D.C., February 27, 1865. Took the Oath of Allegiance and was furnished transportation to New Bern.

SPRUILL, WILLIAM C., Private

Resided in Chowan County where he enlisted at age 32, May 18, 1861, for the war. Discharged on October 3, 1861.

STAMM, ABRAHAM, Sergeant

Resided in Perquimans County and enlisted in Chowan County at age 37, May 18, 1861, for the war. Mustered in as Corporal and appointed Sergeant April 1, 1862. Wounded at Ellerson's Mill, Virginia, June 26, 1862. Killed in action at Sharpsburg, Maryland, September 17, 1862.

SUMMERS, N. M., Private

Resided in Guilford County where he enlisted at age 28, July 15, 1862, for the war. Captured near Fredericksburg, Virginia, May 3, 1863. Exchanged at City Point, Virginia, May 10, 1863. Detached as a wagon driver from July, 1863, through December, 1864. Captured in hospital at Richmond, Virginia, April 3, 1865, and confined at Libby Prison, Richmond, until transferred to Newport News, Virginia, April 23-24, 1865. Released at Newport News after taking the Oath of Allegiance on June 30, 1865.

SWAIM, ASHLEY, Private

Resided in Guilford County where he enlisted at age 27, July 15, 1862, for the war. Wounded at Sharpsburg, Maryland, September 17, 1862. Furloughed from hospital at Richmond, Virginia, for 30 days on October 5, 1862. Admitted to hospital at Richmond, Virginia, May 2, 1863, with "debilitas" and transferred to Danville, Virginia, on June 15, 1863. Returned to duty July 3, 1863, but was readmitted to hospital in Danville on July 12, 1863. Returned to duty August 18, 1863. Detailed for light duty on February 5, 1864. Reported as absent on detail through December, 1864. Paroled at Appomattox Court House, Virginia, April 9, 1865.

SWAIN, PETER, Private

Resided in Perquimans County and enlisted in Chowan County on August 18, 1861, for the war. Present or accounted for until captured at Spotsylvania Court House, Virginia, May 12, 1864. Confined at Point Lookout, Maryland, until transferred to Elmira, New York, August 6, 1864. Released at Elmira after taking the Oath of Allegiance on June 12, 1865.

THOMAS, BENJAMIN, Private

Resided in Guilford County where he enlisted at age 31, July 15, 1862, for the war. Wounded at Sharpsburg, Maryland, September 17, 1862. Present or accounted for until captured at Wilderness, Virginia, May 5-12, 1864. Confined at Point Lookout, Maryland, where he died July 31, 1864.

THOMAS, JAMES, Private

Resided in Guilford County where he enlisted at age 28, July 15, 1862, for the war. Present or accounted for until captured at Spotsylvania Court House, Virginia, May 12, 1864, and confined at Point Lookout, Maryland. Transferred to Elmira, New York, August 3-6, 1864. Died at Elmira on March 8, 1865, of "pneumonia."

TODD. BRYANT, Private

Resided in Chowan County where he enlisted at age 25, June 1, 1861, for the war. Present or accounted for until captured at Spotsylvania Court House, Virginia, May 12, 1864. Confined at Point Lookout, Maryland, until transferred to Elmira, New York, August 6, 1864. Died at Elmira on April 7, 1865, of "chronic diarrhoea."

TROXLER, DANIEL, Private

Resided in Guilford County where he enlisted at age 31, July 15, 1862, for the war. Wounded at Chancellorsville, Virginia, May 3, 1863. Reported absent wounded through December, 1863. Present or accounted for until captured at Spotsylvania Court House, Virginia, May 12, 1864. Confined at Point Lookout, Maryland, until transferred to Elmira, New York, August 6, 1864. Died at Elmira on October 26, 1864, of "pneumonia."

VISTALL, J. W., Private

Captured at Petersburg, Virginia, April 3, 1865, and confined at Hart's Island, New York Harbor, until released June 17, 1865.

WALKER, JAMES A., Musician

Previously served in Company M, 1st Regiment N.C. Infantry (6 months, 1861). Enlisted in this company in Chowan County on June 13, 1862, for the war. Mustered in as Private and appointed Musician after March, 1862. Present or accounted for on company muster rolls through December, 1864. Paroled at Burkeville Junction, Virginia, April 14-17, 1865.

WALKER, JOSEPH M., Private

Resided in Chowan County where he enlisted at age 22, May 18, 1861, for the war. Mustered in as Private and appointed Corporal November-December, 1862. Reduced to ranks on June 15, 1863, by reason of "prolonged absence without leave." Reported as absent without leave on company muster rolls through December, 1864. Date of desertion given as February 7, 9, 14, 1863, and March 4, 1863.

WALTON, JAMES R., Private

Resided in Chowan County where he enlisted at age 18, May 18, 1861, for the war. Present or accounted for until he deserted on March 27, 1863, and took the Oath of Allegiance at Falmouth, Virginia, March 30, 1863. Sent to Washington, D.C.

WARREN, C. W., Private

Resided in Guilford County where he enlisted at age 29, July 15, 1862, for the war. Present or accounted for until captured at Gettysburg, Pennsylvania, July 3, 1863. Confined at Fort Delaware, Delaware, until transferred to Point Lookout, Maryland, October 15-18, 1863. Paroled at Point Lookout and sent to City Point, Virginia, for exchange on April 27, 1864. Admitted to hospital at Richmond, Virginia, May 1, 1864, with "diarrhoea chronic" and furloughed for 30 days May 12, 1864. Paroled at Greensboro on May 25, 1865.

WARREN, G. H., Private

Captured at Winchester, Virginia, September 19, 1864, and confined at West's Buildings, Baltimore, Maryland, October 13, 1864, with "bronchitis." Transferred to Point Lookout, Maryland, October 25-26, 1864. Exchanged at Point Lookout on October 20, 1864.

WARREN, THOMAS H., Private

Resided in Guilford County where he enlisted at age 26, July 15, 1862, for the war. Present or accounted for on company muster rolls until detailed as a nurse in hospital at Richmond, Virginia, on January 28, 1864. Captured at Winchester, Virginia, September 19, 1864, and confined at Point Lookout, Maryland, on October 22, 1864. Paroled and sent to Venus Point, Savannah River, Georgia, November 15, 1864. Admitted to hospital at Macon, Georgia, on November 15, 1864, with "diarrhoea chronic" and transferred on November 18, 1864.

WELCH, JAMES, Private

Resided in Guilford County where he enlisted at age 30, July 15, 1862, for the war. Killed in action at Gettysburg, Pennsylvania, July 3, 1863.

WELCH, MOSES, Private

Resided in Guilford County where he enlisted at age 24, July 15, 1862, for the war. Present or accounted for until transferred to Company G, 2nd Battalion N.C. Infantry on March 13, 1864.

WHITAKER, WILLIAM C. M., Private

Resided in Chowan County where he enlisted at age 30, May 18, 1861, for the war. Present or accounted for until discharged on February 1, 1862, and transferred to the C.S. Navy.

WHITE, MARTIN V., Private

Resided in Chowan County where he enlisted at age 17, August 22, 1861, for the war. Present or accounted for until captured at Spotsylvania Court House, Virginia, May 12, 1864. Confined at Point Lookout, Maryland, until transferred to Elmira, New York, August 6, 1863. Released at Elmira after taking the Oath of Allegiance on June 12, 1865.

WHITE, WILLIAM, Private

Born in Chowan County where he resided as a butcher and enlisted at age 24, May 18, 1861, for the war. Discharged on December 28, 1862, by reason of "disability on account of severe and frequent attacks of rheumatism."

WHITEMAN, LAFAYETTE, Private

Resided in Chowan County where he enlisted at age 20, May 18, 1861, for the war. Captured at South Mountain, Maryland, September 15, 1862, and confined at Fort Delaware, Delaware, until transferred to Aiken's Landing, Virginia, October 2, 1862. Declared exchanged on November 10, 1862. Present or accounted for until he deserted to the enemy on March 27, 1863. Took the Oath of Allegiance at Falmouth, Virginia, on March 30, 1863.

WIGGINS, JAMES M., Corporal

Resided in Bertie County and enlisted in Chowan County at age 24, May 18, 1861, for the war.

Mustered in as Corporal. Wounded in action at Malvern Hill, Virginia, July 1, 1862, and died on July 11, 1862.

WILSON, RICHARD, Private

Resided in Guilford County where he enlisted at age 30, July 15, 1862, for the war. Died at home in Guilford County on October 26, 1862, of disease.

WOODARD, STEPHEN M., Corporal

Resided in Chowan County where he enlisted at age 19, May 18, 1861, for the war. Mustered in as Private and appointed Corporal on June 15, 1863. Present or accounted for until captured at Spotsylvania Court House, Virginia, May 12, 1864. Confined at Point Lookout, Maryland, until transferred to Elmira, New York, August 6, 1864. Released at Elmira after taking the Oath of Allegiance on June 12, 1865.

WRIGHT, GEORGE, Private

Resided in Guilford County where he enlisted at age 26, July 15, 1862, for the war. Present or accounted for until captured at Spotsylvania Court House, Virginia, May 12, 1864. Confined at Point Lookout, Maryland, until transferred to Elmira, New York, August 6, 1864. Released after taking the Oath of Allegiance at Elmira on June 12, 1865.

WRIGHT, WILLIAM F., Private

Resided in Guilford County where he enlisted at age 28, July 15, 1862, for the war. Transferred to the Field and Staff of this regiment upon appointment as Hospital Steward on August 6, 1862. Reduced to ranks on October 1, 1864, and returned to company. November-December, 1864, muster roll carries him with the remark: "extra duty regimental hospital attendant."

WYRICK, ABSALOM, Private

Resided in Guilford County where he enlisted at age 30, July 15, 1862, for the war. Wounded at Sharpsburg, Maryland, September 17, 1862. Present or accounted for until wounded at Payne's Farm, Virginia, November 27, 1863. Reported as absent wounded until captured at Mechanicsville, Virginia, May 30, 1864. Confined at Point Lookout, Maryland, where he died on March 30, 1865, of "chronic diarrhoea."

WYRICK, ALFRED, Private

Resided in Guilford County where he enlisted at age 23, July 15, 1862, for the war. Wounded at Sharpsburg, Maryland, September 17, 1862. Died in hospital at Richmond, Virginia, December 5, 1862, of "pneumonia."

WYRICK, WILLIAM, Private

Resided in Guilford County where he enlisted at age 26, July 15, 1862, for the war. Wounded in action at Sharpsburg, Maryland, September 17, 1862. Present or accounted for on company muster rolls through December, 1864.

WYRICK, WILLIAM S., Private

Resided in Guilford County where he enlisted at age 32, July 15, 1862, for the war. Admitted to hospital at Richmond, Virginia, on September 6, 1862, with "rubeola." Transferred to hospital at Danville on November 3, 1862, and returned to duty on December 1, 1862. Killed in action at Fredericksburg, Virginia, December 13, 1862.

COMPANY B

This company, known as "Wilkes Volunteers," was raised in Wilkes County and ordered to Raleigh, where it enlisted on May 31, 1861. From Raleigh it was ordered to Warrenton, Warren County, where it became Company B of this regiment on June 3, 1861. After that date the company functioned as a part of the regiment, and its history for the war period is recorded as a part of the regimental history.

The information contained in the following roster of the company was compiled principally from company muster rolls for July 20, 1861, through August 31, 1861; November through December, 1861; March through April, 1862; and June 30, 1862, through December, 1864. No company muster rolls were found for the period prior to July 20, 1861; for September through October, 1861; for January through February, 1862; for May through June 29, 1862; or for the period after December, 1864. In addition to the company muster rolls, Roll of Honor records, receipt rolls, hospital records, prisoner of war records, and other primary records, supplemented by state pension applications, United Daughters of the Confederacy records, and postwar rosters and histories, all provided useful information.

OFFICERS

CAPTAINS

GORDON, JAMES B.
Resided in Wilkes County and served as Captain of this company until appointed Major of the 9th Regiment N.C. State Troops (1st Regiment N.C. Cavalry) to rank from May 16, 1861.

BROWN, HAMILTON A.
Resided in Wilkes County and served as 1st Lieutenant of this company from June 3 to July 25, 1861, when he was appointed Captain to rank from May 16, 1861. Present or accounted for until transferred to the Field and Staff of this regiment upon appointment as Lieutenant Colonel to rank from July 8, 1862.

BOUCHELLE, THOMAS S.
Resided in Wilkes County and appointed 2nd Lieutenant on June 4, 1861, to rank from May 16, 1861. Promoted to 1st Lieutenant on April 12, 1862, and to Captain on July 8, 1862. Wounded in action at Sharpsburg, Maryland, September 17, 1862, and detailed as Enrolling Officer, 9th Congressional District, North Carolina, with the rank of Captain on August 22, 1863. Retired to the Invalid Corps on February 24, 1865. Appears on a register of the Invalid Corps which states that

he was assigned to enrolling service on March 1, 1865.

LIEUTENANTS

CURTIS, LARKIN J., 1st Lieutenant
Resided in Wilkes County and enlisted in Wake County at age 26, May 31, 1861, for the war. Mustered in as Musician and transferred to the Field and Staff as a member of the regimental band. Transferred back to the company on November 20, 1861, as a Private. Appointed Sergeant on July 2, 1862, and promoted to 1st Sergeant on September 2, 1862. Promoted to 2nd Lieutenant on June 11, 1863, and to 1st Lieutenant on October 3, 1863. Killed in action at Spotsylvania Court House, Virginia, May 10, 1864.

HAMPTON, JOHN A., 1st Lieutenant
Resided in Wilkes County and enlisted at age 23, May 31, 1861, for the war. Mustered in as 1st Sergeant and appointed 3rd Lieutenant on August 23, 1861. Promoted to 1st Lieutenant July 8, 1862. Resigned September 5, 1863, by reason of ill health.

PARKS, MARCUS A., 1st Lieutenant
Resided in Wilkes County and appointed 1st Lieutenant on June 4, 1861, to rank from May 16, 1861. Age at time of appointment reported as 28. Present or accounted for until he resigned on April 12, 1862, upon appointment as Captain of Company F, 52nd Regiment N.C. Troops to rank from March 14, 1862.

PEDEN, JOSEPH W., 2nd Lieutenant
Resided in Wilkes County and enlisted in Wake County at age 19, May 31, 1861, for the war. Mustered in as Sergeant and appointed 1st Sergeant April 25, 1862. Appointed 2nd Lieutenant to rank from September 1, 1862. Captured near Richmond, Virginia, June 15, 1862, and confined at Fort Delaware, Delaware, June 21, 1862. Exchanged at Aiken's Landing, Virginia, August 5, 1862. Wounded in action at Sharpsburg, Maryland, September 17, 1862, and admitted to hospital at Richmond, Virginia, on October 4, 1862, with a "gun shot wound in the thigh." Furloughed for 60 days on October 19, 1862, and reported as absent wounded on company muster rolls through December, 1864. Inspection report dated February 25, 1865, carries the remark: "premanently disabled. Retiring papers sent up. Have not yet been heard from."

VANNOY, WILLIAM W., 2nd Lieutenant
Resided in Wilkes County and enlisted in Wake County at age 25, May 31, 1861, for the war. Mustered in as Sergeant and promoted to 1st Sergeant on August 23, 1861. Appointed 2nd Lieutenant on April 25, 1862. Captured near Richmond, Virginia, June 15, 1862, and confined at Fort Delaware, Delaware. Exchanged at Aiken's Landing, Virginia, August 5, 1862. Wounded in battle near Fredericksburg, Virginia, on December 13, 1862. Absent wounded until discharged on June 11, 1863, by reason of "the loss of one eye by a gun shot wound and the consequent impairment of sight in the other."

NONCOMMISSIONED OFFICERS AND PRIVATES

ALEXANDER, JESSE THOMPSON, Sergeant

Resided in Wilkes County and enlisted in Wake County at age 29, May 31, 1861, for the war. Mustered in as Private. Slightly wounded in battle at Malvern Hill, Virginia, July 1, 1862. Detailed as a teamster on January 1, 1862. Absent detailed through June, 1863. Appointed Corporal on July 3, 1863, and promoted to Sergeant on November 1, 1863. Captured at Spotsylvania Court House, Virginia, May 12, 1864, and confined at Elmira, New York. Paroled and sent to James River, Virginia, for exchange on March 10, 1865.

ATKINS, WILLIAM, Private

Reported on a register of General Hospital No. 7, Raleigh, showing receipt for clothing issued on January 4, 1864.

ATKINSON, WILLIAM V., Private

Resided in Wilkes County and enlisted at Richmond, Virginia, at age 16, July 15, 1862, for the war as a substitute. Mustered in as a Musician. Reported as absent sick from October 18, 1863, through December, 1863. Reduced to ranks on January 1, 1864. Captured at Spotsylvania Court House, Virginia, May 12, 1864, and confined at Point Lookout, Maryland, until transferred to Aiken's Landing, Virginia, September 18, 1864, for exchange. Reported as being at home on furlough on the November-December, 1864, muster roll.

AYRES, SAMUEL P., Private

Resided in Wilkes County and enlisted in Wake County at age 28, May 31, 1861, for the war. Detailed as a regimental teamster in November-December, 1862, and as an ambulance driver in March, 1863. Absent on detail as ambulance driver through December, 1864. Paroled at Appomattox Court House, Virginia, April 9, 1865.

BACHELOR, B. A., Private

Reported on a register of Medical Director's Office, Richmond, Virginia, showing that he was returned to duty on December 9, 1862.

BARNES, W. A., Private

Appears on an undated list of prisoners who took the Oath of Allegiance.

BARNETT, JOSIAH M., Private

Transferred from Company D of this regiment on November 1, 1861. Died April 4, 1862, of disease.

BATCHELOR, JAMES S., Private

Resided in Nash County and enlisted in Guilford County at age 27, July 15, 1862, for the war. Reported as absent sick from date of enlistment through April 1, 1863, when he was reported as a deserter. Rejoined from desertion January 13, 1864. Appears on a muster roll of Company B, Ward's Battalion C.S. Prisoners, released from Military Prison, Lynchburg, Virginia, dated July, 1864, with the remark: "sentence expired." Company muster roll for February 29-August 31,

1864, carries the remark: "absent. Released from prison by order of the President and absent without leave." Hospitalized on December 22, 1864, at Richmond, Virginia, where he was captured on April 3, 1865.

BATCHELOR, ROBERT H., Private

Resided in Nash County and enlisted in Guilford County at age 22, July 15, 1862, for the war. Present or accounted for until captured at Spotsylvania Court House, Virginia, May 12, 1864. Confined at Elmira, New York, until released after taking the Oath of Allegiance on June 27, 1865.

BATCHELOR, S. JONES, Private

Resided in Nash County and enlisted in Guilford County at age 34, July 15, 1862, for the war. Wounded in the left eye at Gettysburg, Pennsylvania, July 3, 1863, and reported as absent in hospital at Richmond, Virginia, through April, 1865.

BIVENS, STEPHEN, Private

Resided in Alamance County where he enlisted at age 19, July 15, 1862, for the war. Deserted to Maryland on September 17, 1862. Admitted to U.S. Army General Hospital No. 1, Frederick, Maryland, during the months of September-October, 1862, and transferred on October 22, 1862.

BLAYLOCK, JOHN R., Corporal

Resided in Wilkes County and enlisted in Wake County at age 22, May 31, 1861, for the war. Mustered in as Private. Wounded in action at Malvern Hill, Virginia, July 1, 1862. Promoted to Corporal on July 3, 1863. Captured at Spotsylvania Court House, Virginia, May 10, 1864, and confined at Elmira, New York, until released after taking the Oath of Allegiance on June 23, 1865.

BRACK, REAVES, Private

Resided in Wilkes County where he enlisted at age 42, February 28, 1862, for the war. Wounded in leg at Malvern Hill, Virginia, July 1, 1862. Failed to return from furlough and declared absent without leave after November 1, 1862. Appears on a register of General Hospital No. 13, Richmond, Virginia, dated October 29, 1863, with the remark that he was sent to Castle Thunder Prison on December 16, 1863. Discharged from the prison on March 18, 1864, to be returned to his company.

BRITET, JOHN, Private

Captured at Gettysburg, Pennsylvania, July 3, 1863, and confined at Fort Delaware, Delaware, until transferred to Point Lookout, Maryland, October 18, 1863. Joined the U.S. service on January 24, 1864.

BROWN, ELIAS W., Private

Resided in Wilkes County and enlisted in Wake County at age 33, May 31, 1861, for the war. Discharged at Richmond, Virginia, December 9, 1861.

BROWN, ISAIAH MARSHALL, Color Sergeant

Resided in Wilkes County and enlisted in Wake County at age 18, May 31, 1861, for the war. Mustered in as Private. Appointed Color Sergeant October 1, 1863. Present or accounted for until transferred to the Field and Staff upon appointment as Ensign and 1st Lieutenant, May 13, 1864, to rank from April 30, 1864.

BROWN, TIMOTHY W., Private
Resided in Wilkes County and enlisted in Wake County at age 31, May 31, 1861, for the war. Wounded in action at Chancellorsville, Virginia, May 3, 1863, and died of wounds at Richmond, Virginia, August 9, 1863.

BUNDLE, C. E., Private
Paroled at Burkeville Junction, Virginia, April 14-17, 1865.

CALL, PINKNEY CALDWELL, Sergeant
Resided in Wilkes County and enlisted in Wake County at age 26, May 31, 1861, for the war. Mustered in as Private and appointed Corporal on May 5, 1863. Promoted to Sergeant, July-August, 1863. Present or accounted for until paroled at Appomattox Court House, Virginia, April 9, 1865.

CALLOWAY, ABNER S., Sergeant
Resided in Wilkes County and enlisted in Wake County at age 22, May 31, 1861, for the war. Mustered in as Sergeant. Present or accounted for until transferred to Company B, 55th Regiment N.C. Troops upon appointment as Captain to rank from March 27, 1862.

CANTER, GEORGE W., Private
Resided in Wilkes County and enlisted in Wake County at age 21, May 31, 1861, for the war. Discharged July-August, 1862.

CARLTON, DANIEL M., 1st Sergeant
Resided in Watauga County and enlisted in Wake County at age 27, May 31, 1861, for the war. Mustered in as Private and appointed Sergeant in May, 1862. Wounded in action at Malvern Hill, Virginia, July 1, 1862. Wounded at Chancellorsville, Virginia, May 3, 1863. Promoted to 1st Sergeant June 11, 1863. Died May 15, 1864, of wounds received in battle at Spotsylvania Court House, Virginia, May 12, 1864.

CHAPPELL, GEORGE W., Private
Resided in Wilkes County where he enlisted at age 18, March 22, 1862, for the war. Deserted December 1, 1862.

CHATHAM, MARTIN, Private
Resided in Wilkes County and enlisted in Wake County at age 22, May 31, 1861, for the war. Captured at Gettysburg, Pennsylvania, July 5, 1863, and confined at Fort Delaware, Delaware, until paroled and exchanged at City Point, Virginia, August 1, 1863. Company muster rolls report him as absent sick from October 3, 1863, through December, 1864. Admitted to hospital at Charlottesville, Virginia, on December 20, 1864, with "hemorrhoids" and returned to duty on January 10, 1865.

CHATHAM, ROBERT, Private
Resided in Wilkes County and enlisted in Wayne County at age 18, April 10, 1862, for the war. Captured at Gettysburg, Pennsylvania, July 3, 1863, and confined at Fort Delaware, Delaware, until transferred to Point Lookout, Maryland,

October 18, 1863. Remained at Point Lookout until paroled and exchanged at Boulware's Wharf, James River, Virginia, February 20-21, 1865. Appears as present on a muster roll of a detachment of paroled and exchanged prisoners at Camp Lee, near Richmond, Virginia, dated February 23, 1865.

CHATHAM, WILLIAM H., Private
Born in Wilkes County where he resided as a farmer prior to enlisting in Wake County at age 21, May 31, 1861, for the war. Died of disease at Fredericksburg, Virginia, January 10, 1862.

CHEEK, HENRY, Private
Resided in Wilkes County and enlisted in Wake County at age 29, May 31, 1861, for the war. Died in hospital at Fredericksburg, Virginia, October 28, 1861. Date of death also reported as November 25, 1861.

CHEEK, NATHANIEL W., Private
Enlisted in Alamance County, March 13, 1864, for the war. Captured at Spotsylvania Court House, Virginia, May 12, 1864, and confined at Point Lookout, Maryland. Transferred to Elmira, New York, August 3, 1864, and died at Elmira on December 1, 1864, of "pleuro pneumonia."

CHEEK, ROBERT G., Private
Resided in Alamance County where he enlisted at age 19, July 15, 1862, for the war. Wounded in action at Gettysburg, Pennsylvania, July 3, 1863. Captured at Spotsylvania Court House, Virginia, May 12, 1864, and confined at Point Lookout, Maryland, until transferred to Elmira, New York, August 6, 1864. Remained at Elmira until released after taking the Oath of Allegiance on May 19, 1865.

CLARK, JEREMIAH D., Private
Resided in Buncombe County and enlisted in Wake County at age 22, May 31, 1861, for the war. Transferred to the Field and Staff of this regiment and assigned to the band soon after he enlisted. Transferred back to the company on November 20, 1861. Wounded in left hip at Chancellorsville, Virginia, May 3, 1863, and admitted to hospital at Richmond, Virginia. Furlough for 60 days on August 18, 1863, with the remark: "gun shot wound, left hip-hospital gangrene." November-December 1863, muster roll reports that he "died of wounds at Jonesboro, Tennessee, November 1, 1863."

COCKERHAM, DAVID, Private
Born in Wilkes County where he resided as a laborer prior to enlisting in Wake County at age 34, May 31, 1861, for the war. Wounded in action at Gaines' Mill, Virginia, June 29, 1862, and detailed to hospital duty on December 8, 1862. Company muster rolls indicate that he was absent on detail through December, 1864. Paroled at Burkeville Junction, Virginia, April 14-17, 1865.

COCKERHAM, HENDERSON, Private
Resided in Wilkes County and enlisted in Wake County at age 24, May 31, 1861, for the war. Killed in battle at Chancellorsville, Virginia, May 3, 1863.

COLDWELL, DAVID F., Private
Captured at Fort Anderson, February 19, 1865, and confined at Point Lookout, Maryland, February 28, 1865. Released after taking the Oath of Allegiance on June 26, 1865.

COLLINS, SAMUEL N., Musician
Born in Rockbridge County, Virginia, and resided in Orange County when he originally enlisted in Captain Pride Jones' Company at Hillsboro on April 20, 1861, for one year. Transferred from Captain Jones' company to this company at Raleigh on June 8, 1861, and appointed Musician. Transferred to the Field and Staff of this regiment upon promotion to Chief Musician July-August, 1861. Transferred back to this company November-December, 1861, as Musician, and reported as present or accounted for on company muster rolls through August, 1863. Transferred back to the Field and Staff of this regiment upon promotion to Chief Musician, September-October, 1863, to rank from February 1, 1863.

CRANOR, WALTER E., Private
Resided in Wilkes County and enlisted in Wake County at age 20, May 31, 1861, for the war. Mustered in as Musician and transferred to the Regimental Band July-August, 1861. Transferred back to the company November 20, 1861, as Private. Wounded in action at Mine Run, Virginia, November 27-December 5, 1863. Company muster rolls report him as absent sick from February 24, 1864, through December, 1864. Paroled at Appomattox Court House, Virginia, April 9, 1865.

CROWSON, JOHN C., Sergeant
Resided in Wilkes County and enlisted in Wake County at age 22, May 31, 1861, for the war. Mustered in as Private and appointed Sergeant on November 1, 1862. Transferred to the Field and Staff upon appointment as Sergeant Major on February 11, 1863.

CURTIS, ADONIVAN J., Private
Resided in Wilkes County and enlisted in Wake County at age 24, May 31, 1861, for the war. Wounded in arm at Gaines' Mill, Virginia, June 27, 1862, and reported as absent wounded until detailed in hospital at Richmond, Virginia, on April 8, 1863. Absent on detail until returned to company in September, 1864. Present or accounted for on muster rolls through December, 1864. Paroled at Appomattox Court House, Virginia, April 9, 1865.

CURTIS, FINLEY PATTERSON, Sr., Private
Born in Caldwell County and resided in Wilkes County prior to enlisting in Wake County at age 20, May 31, 1861, for the war. Mustered in as Private. Wounded in right shoulder and neck at Chancellorsville, Virginia, May 3, 1863. Appointed Corporal December 1, 1863. Reduced to ranks between May 1 and August 31, 1864. Captured at Burkeville, Virginia, April 6, 1865, and confined at Point Lookout, Maryland, until released after taking the Oath of Allegiance on June 24, 1865.

DOBBS, WILLIAM, Private
Captured at Ringgold, Georgia, November 26,

1863, and confined at Rock Island Barracks, Illinois. Joined the U.S. service October 17, 1864.

EDMONDS, F. M., Private
Captured at Fisher's Hill, Virginia, September 22, 1864, and confined at Point Lookout, Maryland. Paroled at Point Lookout on January 17, 1865, and transferred to the James River, Virginia, for exchange. Received at Boulware's Wharf, James River, January 21, 1865, and exchanged.

EDWARDS, SOWELL N., Private
Resided in Wilkes County and enlisted in Wake County at age 20, May 31, 1861, for the war. Died at Fredericksburg, Virginia, December 30, 1861, of typhoid fever.

ELLER, CLEVELAND, Private
Born in Wilkes County where he resided as a farmer prior to enlisting in Wake County at age 23, May 31, 1861, for the war. Wounded in action at Malvern Hill, Virginia, July 1, 1862. Discharged on March 1, 1863, by reason of his having provided a substitute.

ELLER, RUFUS F., Private
Resided in Wilkes County where he enlisted at age 18, March 1, 1862, for the war. Wounded at Gettysburg, Pennsylvania, July 1-3, 1863. Captured at Spotsylvania Court House, Virginia, May 12, 1864, and confined at Point Lookout, Maryland, until transferred to Elmira, New York. Released from Elmira after taking the Oath of Allegiance on June 27, 1865.

ELLER, THOMAS J., Private
Enlisted in Warren County at age 23, July 1, 1861, for the war. Killed in battle at Chancellorsville, Virginia, May 3, 1863.

ESTES, JOHN L. J., Private
Born in Knox County, Tennessee, and resided in Caldwell County as a farmer prior to enlisting in Warren County at age 20, 26, July 1, 1861, for the war. Wounded in action at Malvern Hill, Virginia, July 1, 1862. Wounded in right arm at Chancellorsville, Virginia, May 3, 1863, and arm amputated. Discharged at camp near Raccoon Ford, Virginia, December 12, 1863, by reason of wound.

FARD, A. J., Private
Clothing issued on September 4, 1864. Paroled at Appomattox Court House, Virginia, April 9, 1865.

FAW, ALEXANDER J., Sergeant
Resided in Wilkes County and enlisted in Wake County at age 18, May 31, 1861, for the war. Mustered in as Private. Wounded in action at Ellerson's Mill, Virginia, June 26, 1862, and at Malvern Hill, Virginia, July 1, 1862. Promoted to Corporal March-April, 1863, and to Sergeant on June 11, 1863. Present or accounted for on company muster rolls through December, 1864.

FOX, WILLIAM F., Private
Resided in Wilkes County and enlisted in Wake County at age 20, May 31, 1861, for the war. Discharged at Richmond, Virginia, December 9, 1861, by reason of "measles."

FRAZIER, CHARLES, Musician
Resided in Mecklenburg County and enlisted in Warren County at age 44, July 1, 1861, for the war. Transferred to the Field and Staff July-August, 1861, and assigned to the Regimental Band.

GILREATH, BURREL C., 1st Sergeant
Resided in Wilkes County and enlisted in Wake County at age 26, May 31, 1861, for the war. Mustered in as Sergeant and promoted to 1st Sergeant on August 11, 1861. Died in hospital at Fredericksburg, Virginia, December 5, 1861.

GILREATH, LEANDER, Corporal
Resided in Wilkes County and enlisted in Wake County at age 23, May 31, 1861, for the war. Mustered in as Private. Promoted to Corporal after April, 1862. Present or accounted for until transferred to Company B, 55th Regiment N. C. Troops on April 6, 1863, having been appointed 2nd Lieutenant to rank from March 27, 1863.

GINNINGS, JAMES A., Private
Resided in Yadkin County and enlisted in Wilkes County at age 25, January 16, 1862, for the war. Wounded in action at Ellerson's Mill, Virginia, June 26, 1862. Detailed as brigade butcher in September, 1862. Reported as absent on detail through February, 1864, and as absent sick from February through December, 1864.

GINNINGS, SAMUEL J., Private
Born in Wilkes County where he resided as a farmer prior to enlisting in Wake County at age 34, May 31, 1861, for the war. Rank reported on rolls of company as Private with the comments that he was Acting Commissary Sergeant and Sutler. Reported as such on rolls through December, 1864. Captured at Fair Oaks, Virginia, June 15, 1862, and confined at Fort Delaware, Delaware, until paroled and exchanged at Aiken's Landing, Virginia, August 5, 1862. Admitted to hospital at Raleigh, November 17, 1864, with a gunshot wound of the right leg and transferred to Kittrells on January 1, 1865. Retired to the Invalid Corps, March 21, 1865, and detailed to hospital in Richmond, Virginia, on March 31, 1865. Detail revoked and he was detailed as a farmer on April 1, 1865, with orders to report to the enrolling officer of his county.

GRAGG, WILLIAM, Private
Resided in Caldwell County and enlisted in Lenoir County at age 18, March 19, 1862, for the war. Deserted at Hamilton's Crossing, Virginia, May 27, 1862. Took the Oath of Allegiance at Knoxville, Tennessee, on January 21, 1864.

GRAY, ELI G., Sergeant
Resided in Wilkes County and enlisted in Wake County at age 25, May 31, 1861, for the war. Mustered in as Corporal and appointed Sergeant on September 5, 1861. Present or accounted for until transferred to Company G, 54th Regiment N. C. Troops upon appointment to 2nd Lieutenant to rank from April 5, 1862.

GRAY, TERRELL, Private
Resided in Wilkes County and enlisted in Wake County at age 36, May 31, 1861, for the war.

Detailed as regimental teamster in November-December, 1862. Absent on detail through December, 1864. Paroled at Appomattox Court House, Virginia, April 9, 1865.

HACKET, JAMES S., Private
Resided in Wilkes County and enlisted in Wake County at age 23, May 31, 1861, for the war. Killed in action at Sharpsburg, Maryland, September 17, 1862.

HAGENS, GEORGE, Private
Resided in Wilkes County and enlisted in Wake County at age 21, May 31, 1861, for the war. Captured at Boonsboro Gap, Maryland, in September, 1862, and paroled near Keedysville, Maryland, September 20, 1862. Present or accounted for until captured at Gettysburg, Pennsylvania, July 4, 1863. Confined at Fort Delaware, Delaware, until released after taking the Oath of Allegiance on May 11, 1865.

HALL, ROBERT A., Private
Resided in Wilkes County and enlisted in Wake County on November 26, 1863, for the war. Deserted to the enemy on January 17, 1864. Confined at Old Capitol Prison, Washington, D. C., January 20, 1864, with the remark that he was captured at Morton's Ford, Virginia, January 18, 1864. Released after taking the Oath of Allegiance and sent to Philadelphia, Pennsylvania, March 15, 1864.

HARLEY, THOMAS, Private
Resided in Caldwell County and enlisted in Wake County at age 36, May 31, 1861, for the war. Killed in action at Malvern Hill, Virginia, July 1, 1862.

HARRIS, R. W., Private
Captured at Chickamauga, Georgia, September 19, 1863, and confined at Camp Douglas, Illinois. Died February 13, 1864, of "consumption."

HARTIN, JEREMIAH S., Private
Resided in Wilkes County and enlisted at Skinker's Neck, Virginia, at age 18, March 16, 1863, for the war. Killed in action at Chancellorsville, Virginia, May 3, 1863.

HEMPHILL, ISRAEL LAFAYETTE, Private
Resided in Burke County and enlisted in Wayne County at age 25, May 16, 1862, for the war. Present or accounted for until killed in action at Spotsylvania Court House, Virginia, May 12, 1864.

HENDREN, JOHN E., Private
Resided in Wilkes County and enlisted in Wake County at age 22, May 31, 1861, for the war. Killed in action at Malvern Hill, Virginia, July 1, 1862.

HICKERSON, JOHN C., Corporal
Resided in Wilkes County and enlisted in Wake County at age 21, May 31, 1861, for the war. Mustered in as Private and appointed Corporal September 5, 1861. Present or accounted for until transferred to Company F, 37th Regiment N. C. Troops on December 4, 1861.

HINES, BENJAMIN, Private
Resided in Caldwell County where he enlisted at age 30, March 7, 1862, for the war. Detailed as a nurse in hospital at Richmond, Virginia, July

through December, 1862. Reported as absent sick from January through August, 1863. Detailed as a teamster on October 8, 1863. Absent on detail until paroled at Appomattox Court House, Virginia, April 9, 1865.

HOLLOWAY, DANIEL H., Private

Resided in Wilkes County and enlisted in Wake County on November 26, 1863, for the war. Deserted to the enemy on January 17, 1863, at Morton's Ford, Virginia, where he was reported as captured on January 18, 1864. Released and sent to Philadelphia, Pennsylvania, after taking the Oath of Amnesty on March 15, 1864.

HOWARD, J., Private

Admitted to hospital at Farmville, Virginia, April 14, 1865, with a gunshot wound. Died April 27, 1865.

INGRAM, E. S., Private

Confined at Knoxville, Tennessee, January 16, 1865, and released the next day after taking the Oath of Allegiance.

INGRAM, J. C., Private

Confined at Knoxville, Tennessee, January 16, 1865, and released the next day after taking the Oath of Allegiance.

ISARD, ZION J., Private

Resided in Alamance County where he enlisted at age 31, July 15, 1862, for the war. Wounded in the hand at Chancellorsville, Virginia, May 3, 1863. Reported as absent wounded until detached to hospital on February 23, 1864, and officially detailed on April 29, 1864. Reported as absent on detail through December, 1864.

JARVIS, JOHN, Private

Killed at Manassas, Virginia, August 28, 1862.

JARVIS, NELSON, Private

Resided in Wilkes County. Admitted to hospital at Richmond, Virginia, March 20, 1865, with "rubeola." Captured in hospital on April 3, 1865, and transferred to hospital at Point Lookout, Maryland. Released after taking the Oath of Allegiance on June 26, 1865.

JENNINGS, JAMES A., Private

Paroled at New Market, Virginia, April 19, 1865, as an employee of the Commissary Department.

JOHNSON, ELLIS H., Private

Enlisted in Wake County at age 22, May 31, 1861, for the war. Present or accounted for on company muster rolls until paroled at Appomattox Court House, Virginia, April 9, 1865.

JOHNSON, GEORGE P., Private

Transferred from Company D of this regiment on July 24, 1861. Wounded in the leg at Gaines' Mill, Virginia, June 27, 1862. Wounded in the arm at Chancellorsville, Virginia, May 3, 1863, and arm amputated. Reported as absent wounded on company muster rolls until September-October, 1864, roll carries him with the remark: "retired September 8, 1864."

JOHNSON, JOSHUA J., Private

Resided in Wilkes County and enlisted in Wake County at age 27, May 31, 1861, for the war. Wounded in battle at Malvern Hill, Virginia,

July 1, 1862, and at Fredericksburg, Virginia, December 13, 1862. Reported as absent on sick furlough through October 9, 1864, when he was reported as absent without leave. Reported as absent without leave through December, 1864.

JOHNSON, RANDOLPH L., Private

Resided in Wilkes County and enlisted in Wake County at age 21, May 31, 1861, for the war. Wounded in battle at Malvern Hill, Virginia, and died of wounds at Richmond, Virginia, on July 14, 17, 1862.

JOHNSON, SAMUEL W., Private

Resided in Mitchell County and enlisted in Warren County at age 30, July 1, 1861, for the war. Wounded in foot at Malvern Hill, Virginia, July 1, 1862, and reported as absent wounded until detailed for hospital duty in Richmond, Virginia, on June 8, 1863. Transferred to hospital duty at Bristol, Tennessee, prior to January, 1864. Died in hospital at Salisbury, North Carolina, December 17, 1864, of "phthisis."

JONES, JOHN, Private

Resided in Guilford County and enlisted May 1, 1861, for the war.

JONES, WILLIAM E., Private

Resided in Wilkes County and enlisted in Wake County at age 21, May 31, 1861, for the war. Died at Hanover Junction, Virginia, May 6, 1863, of "pneumonia."

JONES, WILLIAM RUFUS, Private

Resided in Wilkes County and enlisted in Wake County at age 22, May 31, 1861, for the war. Admitted to hospital at Charlottesville, Virginia, September 23, 1864, with a gunshot wound of the left hand. Date and place he was wounded was not reported. Present or accounted for until paroled at Appomattox Court House, Virginia, April 9, 1865.

LAND, THOMAS C., Corporal

Resided in Wilkes County and enlisted in Wake County at age 33, May 31, 1861, for the war. Mustered in as Corporal. Wounded in action at Malvern Hill, Virginia, July 1, 1862. Present or accounted for until transferred to Company K, 53rd Regiment N.C. Troops upon appointment as 2nd Lieutenant to rank from August 2, 1862.

LAWS, COFFEY, Private

Resided in Wilkes County and enlisted in Wake County at age 23, May 31, 1861, for the war. Wounded at Chancellorsville, Virginia, May 3, 1863. Present or accounted for until captured at Spotsylvania Court House, Virginia, May 12, 1864, and confined at Point Lookout, Maryland. Transferred to Elmira, New York, August 6, 1864. Paroled at Elmira and transferred to Point Lookout on October 11-14, 1864, for exchange. Declared exchanged on October 29, 1864. November-December, 1864, muster roll states that he was "exchanged and at home on furlough."

LAXTON, THOMAS W., Private

Resided in Wilkes County and enlisted in Wake County at age 19, May 31, 1861, for the war. Present or accounted for until captured at Spotsylvania Court House, Virginia, May 12, 1864. Confined at Point Lookout, Maryland, until transferred to Elmira, New York, August 6, 1864. Died at Elmira on March 8, 1865, of "chronic diarrhoea."

LEACH, CALVIN C., Private
Resided in Wilkes County and enlisted in Warren County at age 19, July 1, 1861, for the war. Present or accounted for until he was "killed May 30, 1864, in action."

LENDERMAN, L. JACK, Private
Resided in Wilkes County where he enlisted at age 20, April 16, 1862, for the war. Present or accounted for until he "deserted July 26, 1863." Confined at Knoxville, Tennessee, February 17, 1865, and released the next day on bond.

LOYD, THOMAS, Private
Resided in Wilkes County where he enlisted at age 25, February 28, 1862, for the war. Reported as missing in action at South Mountain, Maryland, September 14, 1862. Later muster rolls state that he deserted November 1, 1862, and report him as absent under sentence of court-martial from February 29-August 31, 1864, through December, 1864. Federal Cemetery Register states that he died at Fort Delaware, Delaware, September 20, 1863, and was buried in the National Cemetery, Finn's Point (Salem), New Jersey.

LYLES, ELI W., Musician
Resided in Mecklenburg County and enlisted in Warren County at age 32, July 1, 1861, for the war. Mustered in as Musician. Transferred to the Field and Staff and assigned to the Regimental Band in July, 1861.

McBRIDE, LEWIS WILLIAM, Private
Resided in Wilkes County where he enlisted at age 18, February 24, 1862, for the war. Present or accounted for until he died at Goldsboro on May 4, 1862.

McLEAN, DAVID, Private
Resided in Wilkes County where he enlisted at age 42, September 1, 1863, for the war. Wounded in action at Wilderness, Virginia, May 5, 1864, and retired to the Invalid Corps, December 3, 1864, by reason of disability. Assigned to temporary duty at Salisbury, North Carolina, as a member of the Invalid Corps.

MARTIN, ISAAC N., Sergeant
Resided in Wilkes County and enlisted in Wake County at age 23, May 31, 1861, for the war. Mustered in as Private and appointed Corporal on November 1, 1862. Promoted to Sergeant on February 1, 1863. Killed in action at Chancellorsville, Virginia, May 3, 1863.

MARTIN, JOHN B., Private
Resided in Wilkes County and enlisted in Wake County at age 21, May 31, 1861, for the war. Present or accounted for until he died in hospital in Lynchburg, Virginia, May 7, 1864, of "pneumonia."

MARTIN, NATHAN GREEN, Sergeant
Resided in Wilkes County and enlisted in Wake County at age 42, May 31, 1861, for the war. Mus-

tered in as Corporal and appointed Sergeant November-December, 1861. Wounded in action in Malvern Hill, Virginia, July 1, 1862, and reported as absent wounded through December, 1862. Captured at Fredericksburg, Virginia, May 3, 1863, and paroled and exchanged at City Point, Virginia, May 10, 1863. Wounded at Gettysburg, Pennsylvania, July 2, 1863, and died of wounds on July 4, 1863.

MICKLE, COLUMBUS F., Private
Resided in Wilkes County and enlisted in Wayne County at age 18, April 16, 1862, for the war. Present or accounted for until captured at Spotsylvania Court House, Virginia, May 12, 1864. Confined at Point Lookout, Maryland, until transferred to Elmira, New York, August 6, 1864. Paroled at Elmira and sent to Point Lookout, October 11, 1864. Exchanged October 29, 1864. Captured at Burkeville, Virginia, April 6, 1865, and confined at Point Lookout until released after taking the Oath of Allegiance on June 29, 1865.

MILLER, THOMAS C., Musician
Resided in Wilkes County and enlisted in Wake County at age 20, May 31, 1861, for the war. Mustered in as Musician for the company. Present or accounted for until transferred to Company K, 53rd Regiment N.C. Troops upon appointment as 2nd Lieutenant to rank from March 25, 1862.

MITCHELL, JAMES M., Private
Resided in Wilkes County and enlisted in Wake County at age 24, May 31, 1861, for the war. Wounded in action at Malvern Hill, Virginia, July 1, 1862, and at Gettysburg, Pennsylvania, July 3, 1863. Returned to company September-October, 1863, and reported as present until wounded at Payne's Farm, Virginia, November 27, 1863. Furloughed for 60 days from hospital at Richmond, Virginia, on January 5, 1864, by reason of "extensive gun shot flesh diagonally through left leg." Detailed on hospital duty on April 29, 1864. Returned to company September-October, 1864. Present or accounted for on company muster rolls through December, 1864. Admitted to hospital at Danville, Virginia, March 18, 1865, with "iritis rheumatica." Returned to duty on April 11, 1865.

MOONEY, WILLIAM, Musician
Resided in Wilkes County and enlisted in Wake County at age 30, May 31, 1861, for the war. Mustered in as Private. Appointed Musician March-April, 1862. Wounded in action at Malvern Hill, Virginia, July 1, 1862, and reported as absent wounded until retired to the Invalid Corps on November 26, 1864, by reason of wounds received at Malvern Hill.

MOORE, JAMES M., Private
Resided in Alamance County where he enlisted at age 20, July 15, 1862, for the war. Present or accounted for until wounded at Chancellorsville, Virginia, May 3, 1863. Returned to duty September 25, 1863. Died in hospital at Richmond, Virginia, December 10, 1863, of "pyaemia."

MOORE, WILLIAM CHESTLEY, Private

Resided in Alamance County where he enlisted at age 18, July 15, 1862, for the war. Wounded at Sharpsburg, Maryland, September 17, 1862. Captured at Gettysburg, Pennsylvania, July 5, 1863, and confined in hospital at Baltimore, Maryland, until transferred to City Point, Virginia, for exchange on November 12, 1863. Admitted to hospital at Richmond, Virginia, November 16, 1863, and reported as absent on company muster rolls through December, 1863. Captured at Spotsylvania Court House, Virginia, May 12, 1864, and confined at Point Lookout, Maryland. Transferred to Elmira, New York, August 3-6, 1864. Released at Elmira after taking the Oath of Allegiance on June 14, 1865.

MOSLEY, ALEXANDER, Private

Enlisted in Wake County, November 12, 1863, for the war. "Deserted November 25, 1863."

MYERS, THOMAS P., Private

Resided in Yadkin County and enlisted in Wilkes County at age 21, March 8, 1862, for the war. Wounded in action at Ellerson's Mill, Virginia, June 26, 1862. Reported as missing in action at Sharpsburg, Maryland, September 17, 1862, and dropped from the rolls as a deserter November 1, 1862.

NEWLIN, WILLIAM E., Private

Resided in Alamance County where he enlisted at age 18, July 15, 1862, for the war. Killed in action at Sharpsburg, Maryland, September 17, 1862.

NICHOLS, STEPHEN, Private

Born in Orange County where he resided as a laborer prior to enlisting in Warren County at age 35, July 1, 1861, for the war. Transferred to the Field and Staff of this regiment upon appointment as Sergeant Major on the date of enlistment.

OAKLEY, WILLIAM, Private

Born in Wilkes County where he resided as a farmer and enlisted at age 40, February 16, 1862, for the war. Died at Winchester, Virginia, September 26, 1862, of disease.

PARIS, NELSON, Private

Captured at Spotsylvania Court House, Virginia, May 12, 1864, and confined at Point Lookout, Maryland. Transferred to Elmira, New York, August 3, 1864.

PARKER, CYRUS, Private

Resided in Wilkes County where he enlisted at age 43, September 1, 1863, for the war. Wounded in action at Mine Run, Virginia, November 27-December 5, 1863. Present or accounted for until discharged on February 28, 1865, by reason of disability.

PARKER, ELIJAH, Private

Born in McDowell County and resided in Caldwell County as a laborer prior to enlisting in Warren County at age 24, July 1, 1861, for the war. Discharged August 27, 1861, by reason of disability.

PARKER, RICHARD H., Private

Resided in Wilkes County and enlisted at Brook's

Station, Virginia, December 2, 1862, for the war. Present or accounted for until paroled at Appomattox Court House, Virginia, April 9, 1865.

PARKER, W. H., Private

Enlisted at Camp Bee, Virginia, December 2, 1861, for the war. Present or accounted for through April, 1862, when he was reported as "absent sick."

PARKS, WILLIS, Private

Resided in Wilkes County and enlisted in Wake County at age 21, May 31, 1861, for the war. Present or accounted for until transferred to Company F, 37th Regiment N.C. Troops, April 15, 1862.

PARRIS, JOHNSTON, Private

Transferred from Company A of this regiment in April, 1863. Present or accounted for until captured at Spotsylvania Court House, Virginia, May 12, 1864. Confined at Point Lookout, Maryland, until transferred to Elmira, New York, August 6, 1864. Released at Elmira after taking the Oath of Allegiance on May 29, 1865.

PARSONS, GEORGE, Private

Resided in Wilkes County and enlisted at Skinker's Neck, Virginia, at age 50, March 1, 1863, for the war as a substitute. Wounded in action at Chancellorsville, Virginia, May 3, 1863. Died in hospital at Richmond, Virginia, May 27, 1863, of "febris intermittens."

PAYNE, JACOB D., Private

Resided in Caldwell County and enlisted in Warren County at age 20, July 1, 1861, for the war. Died in hospital at Fredericksburg, Virginia, December 21, 1861.

PENNEL, JOHN, Corporal

Resided in Wilkes County and enlisted in Wake County at age 18, May 31, 1861, for the war. Mustered in as Corporal. Present or accounted for until killed in action at Chancellorsville, Virginia, May 3, 1863.

PENNEL, SAMUEL, Private

Resided in Wilkes County and enlisted at Skinker's Neck, Virginia, at age 36, March 16, 1863, for the war. Killed in action at Chancellorsville, Virginia, May 3, 1863.

PERKINS, JOHN M., Private

Resided in Wilkes County where he enlisted at age 18, February 25, 1862, for the war. Captured near Richmond, Virginia, June 15, 1862, and confined at Fort Delaware, Delaware. Exchanged at Aiken's Landing, Virginia, August 5, 1862. Wounded at Chancellorsville, Virginia, May 3, 1863. Absent wounded through December, 1864.

PERKINS, WYATT L., Private

Resided in Wilkes County and enlisted at Skinker's Neck, Virginia, at age 32, March 16, 1863, for the war. Wounded in action at Chancellorsville, Virginia, May 3, 1863. Reported as absent wounded through February, 1864. Captured at Spotsylvania Court House, Virginia, May 12, 1864, and confined at Point Lookout, Maryland, until transferred to Elmira, New York, August 6, 1863. Died at Elmira March 28, 1865, of "pneumonia."

PERTEET, ALFRED, Private
Resided in Wilkes County where he enlisted at age 34, February 16, 1862, for the war. Present or accounted for until he died July 15, 1862, of disease.

PICKARD, ROBERT P., Private
Resided in Alamance County where he enlisted at age 25, July 15, 1862, for the war. Present or accounted for until captured at Spotsylvania Court House, Virginia, May 12, 1864, and confined at Point Lookout, Maryland. Transferred to Elmira, New York, August 3, 1864. Released at Elmira after taking the Oath of Allegiance on June 27, 1865.

PILKINTON, WILLIAM, Private
Resided in Wilkes County and enlisted in Wake County at age 19, May 31, 1861, for the war. Wounded in action at Chancellorsville, Virginia, May 3, 1863, and died of wounds on May 4, 1863.

PORTER, JOHN A., Private
Resided in Wilkes County where he enlisted at age 19, April 9, 1862, for the war. Wounded in July, 1862. Reported as absent wounded until reported as "deserted March 9, 1863." Federal prisoner of war records indicate that he was a "rebel deserter" who was captured in Wilkes County and confined in Military Prison, Louisville, Kentucky, where he took the Oath of Allegiance on September 25, 1864.

PORTER, WILLIAM F., Private
Resided in Wilkes County and enlisted in Wake County at age 20, May 31, 1861, for the war. Transferred to the Field and Staff and appointed Musician in July, 1861. Transferred back to the company in November, 1861, as a Private. Present or accounted for until he "deserted March 9, 1863."

PRICE, JOSEPH A., Private
Resided in Wilkes County and enlisted in Wake County at age 24, May 31, 1861, for the war. Captured at Frederick, Maryland, September 12, 1862, and confined at Fort Delaware, Delaware, until transferred to Aiken's Landing, Virginia, for exchange on October 2, 1862. Declared exchanged on November 10, 1862. Present or accounted for on company muster rolls through December, 1864, when he was reported as absent wounded. Hospital records for General Hospital, Danville, Virginia, indicate that he was admitted June 4, 1864, with a gunshot wound of the foot and furloughed on June 8, 1864. Captured at Petersburg, Virginia, April 3, 1865, and confined at Hart's Island, New York Harbor, April 7, 1865. Released after taking the Oath of Allegiance on June 17, 1865.

PROFFIT, WILLIAM H., Sergeant
Resided in Wilkes County and enlisted in Wake County at age 21, May 31, 1861, for the war. Mustered in as Musician. Reduced to Private after April, 1862. Appointed Corporal February 1, 1863, and promoted to Sergeant on May 3, 1863. Died in hospital at Gordonsville, Virginia, October 23, 1863, of "febris typhoides."

PURVIS, JAMES E., Corporal
Resided in Wilkes County and enlisted in Wake County at age 18, May 31, 1861, for the war. Mustered in as Private. Appointed Corporal February 2, 1863. Captured at Fredericksburg, Virginia, May 3, 1863, and paroled and exchanged at City Point, Virginia, May 13, 1863. Killed in action at Gettysburg, Pennsylvania, July 3, 1863.

ROACH, WILLIAM, Private
Paroled at Greensboro on May 11, 1865.

ROBERSON, JAMES H., Private
Resided in Alamance County where he enlisted at age 20, July 15, 1862, for the war. Killed in action at Sharpsburg, Maryland, September 17, 1862.

ROBERSON, JOHN, Private
Resided in Wilkes County where he enlisted at age 44, September 1, 1863, for the war. Wounded in action at Payne's Farm, Virginia, November 27, 1863. Reported as absent wounded through December 1, 1864, and as absent without leave through December, 1864. Present or accounted for on company muster rolls through December, 1864.

SCALES, NATHANIEL M., Private
Resided in Wilkes County and enlisted in Wake County at age 22, May 31, 1861, for the war. Present or accounted for until transferred to the Field and Staff of this regiment upon appointment as Assistant Surgeon in July, 1861, to rank from May 16, 1861.

SHAW, JAMES P., Private
Resided in Alamance County where he enlisted at age 23, July 15, 1862, for the war. Wounded in action at Winchester, Virginia, June 15, 1863. Wounded at Payne's Farm, Virginia, November 27, 1863. Present or accounted for until captured at Spotsylvania Court House, Virginia, May 12, 1864. Confined at Point Lookout, Maryland, until transferred to Elmira, New York, August 6, 1864. Paroled at Elmira and sent to Point Lookout, Maryland, for exchange. Exchanged on October 29, 1864. Reported on November-December, 1864, muster roll as absent prisoner.

SHAW, ROBERT, Private
Resided in Alamance County where he enlisted at age 34, July 15, 1862, for the war. Wounded and captured at Sharpsburg, Maryland, September 17, 1862. Confined at Fort McHenry, Maryland, until paroled and sent to Fort Monroe, Virginia, for exchange on October 18, 1862. Declared exchanged at Aiken's Landing, Virginia, November 10, 1862. Present or accounted for until captured at Spotsylvania Court House, Virginia, May 12, 1864. Confined at Point Lookout, Maryland, until transferred to Elmira, New York, August 6, 1864. Released at Elmira after taking the Oath of Allegiance on June 30, 1865.

SHEPHERD, DANIEL, Private
Resided in Alamance County where he enlisted at age 30, July 15, 1862, for the war. Present or accounted for until he was captured at Spotsylvania Court House, Virginia, May 12, 1864. Confined at Point Lookout, Maryland, until transferred to Elmira, New York, August 6, 1864. Re-

leased at Elmira after taking the Oath of Allegiance on June 27, 1865.

SHEPHERD, JACOB, Private
Resided in Alamance County where he enlisted at age 36, July 15, 1862, for the war. Present or accounted for until paroled at Appomattox Court House, Virginia, April 9, 1865.

SHEPHERD, SAMUEL, Private
Resided in Alamance County where he enlisted at age 28, July 15, 1862, for the war. Wounded in battle at Chancellorsville, Virginia, May 3, 1863, and died of wounds on May 24, 1863.

SHORES, JAMES C., Private
Born in Wilkes County where he resided as a blacksmith prior to enlisting in Wake County at age 33, May 31, 1861, for the war. Wounded in action at Malvern Hill, Virginia, July 1, 1862. Absent wounded through December, 1862. Detailed as regimental blacksmith March-April, 1863. Admitted to hospital at Charlottesville, Virginia, May 7, 1864, with gunshot wound. Captured at Winchester, Virginia, September 19, 1864, and confined at Point Lookout, Maryland. Released after he joined the U.S. service on October 12, 1864. Assigned to Company B, 4th Regiment U.S. Volunteer Infantry.

SPAINHOUR, JOHN C., Private
Resided in Burke County and enlisted in Wayne County at age 19, May 1, 1862, for the war. Died in camp near Richmond, Virginia, August 9, 1862, of "typhoid fever."

SPAINHOUR, RUFUS A., Private
Resided in Burke County and enlisted in Wake County at age 21, May 31, 1861, for the war. Mustered in as Private. Present or accounted for until transferred to the Field and Staff of this regiment upon appointment as Commissary Sergeant on June 18, 1862.

SPAINHOUR, WILLIAM ROBERT, Private
Born in Burke County where he resided as a farmer and enlisted at age 18, March 21, 1863, for the war. Wounded in the left hand at Chancellorsville, Virginia, May 3, 1863, and discharged at camp near Orange Court House, Virginia, September 10, 1863, by reason of wounds.

SPARKS, REUBEN, Private
Resided in Wilkes County and enlisted in Wake County at age 21, May 31, 1861, for the war. Captured at South Mountain, Maryland, September 15, 1862, and confined at Fort Delaware, Delaware. Transferred to Aiken's Landing, Virginia, October 2, 1862, and declared exchanged on November 10, 1862. Admitted to hospital at Richmond, Virginia, October 10-11, 1862, and transferred to Camp Lee, near Richmond, October 17, 1862. Never rejoined the company and reported on company muster rolls as absent without leave.

SPICER, GEORGE WASHINGTON, Corporal
Resided in Wilkes County and enlisted in Wake County at age 18, May 31, 1861, for the war. Mustered in as Private. Captured at Fredericksburg, Virginia, May 3, 1863, and paroled and exchanged at City Point, Virginia, May 10, 1863.

Appointed Corporal June 11, 1863. Present or accounted for until captured at Spotsylvania Court House, Virginia, May 12, 1864. Confined at Point Lookout, Maryland, until transferred to Elmira, New York, August 6, 1864. Paroled at Elmira and sent to Point Lookout for exchange. Declared exchanged on October 29, 1864. Admitted to hospital at Macon, Georgia, November 15, 1864, and transferred November 18, 1864. Issued clothing at Hood Hospital, Cuthburt, Georgia, November 23, 1864. Took the Oath of Allegiance at Knoxville, Tennessee, March 29, 1865. Oath of Allegiance states that he deserted at Cuthburt, Georgia, on November 23, 1864, and was "sent North."

SPICER, WILLIAM, Private
Resided in Wilkes County and enlisted in Wake County at age 20, May 31, 1861, for the war. Wounded in action at Chancellorsville, Virginia, May 3, 1863, and died of wounds June 3, 1863.

STOCKARD, JOSEPH S., Private
Resided in Alamance County where he enlisted at age 21, July 15, 1862, for the war. Present or accounted for until captured at Winchester, Virginia, September 19, 1864. Confined at Point Lookout, Maryland, until paroled and transferred to Aiken's Landing, Virginia, March 15, 1865, for exchange.

SUMMERS, GEORGE W., Private
Born in Alamance County where he resided as a farmer and enlisted at age 34, July 15, 1862, for the war. Discharged on November 3, 1863, by reason of "phthisis pulmonalis."

TAYLOR, JESSE H., Private
Resided in Wilkes County and enlisted in Warren County at age 19, July 1, 1861, for the war. Wounded in action at Malvern Hill, Virginia, July 1, 1862. Present or accounted for until captured at Mine Run, Virginia, November 27-28, 1863. Confined at Old Capitol Prison, Washington, D.C., until transferred to Fort Delaware, Delaware, June 15-17, 1864. Paroled at Fort Delaware and sent to City Point, Virginia, February 27, 1865. Admitted to hospital at Richmond, Virginia, on March 4, 1865, with "chronic diarrhoea." Left the hospital on April 18, 1865.

TAYLOR, JONATHAN F., Private
Resided in Ashe County and enlisted in Wayne County at age 31, May 8, 1862, for the war. Detailed in Pioneer Corps, November-December, 1862. Absent on detail through August, 1864. Present or accounted for on company muster rolls through December, 1864. Captured at Amelia Court House, Virginia, April 7, 1864, and confined at Point Lookout, Maryland, until released after taking the Oath of Allegiance on June 20, 1865.

THOMPSON, J. A., Private
Resided in Alamance County where he enlisted at age 25, July 15, 1862, for the war. Killed in battle at Chancellorsville, Virginia, May 3, 1863.

THOMPSON, J. F., Private
Born in Alamance County where he resided as a farmer, and enlisted at age 30, July 15, 1862, for

the war. Present or accounted for until discharged on September 3, 1862, by reason of "pulmonary phthisis."

THOMPSON, JAMES M., Private
Resided in Alamance County where he enlisted at age 28, July 15, 1862, for the war. Present or accounted for until captured at Spotsylvania Court House, Virginia, May 12, 1864. Confined at Point Lookout, Maryland, until transferred to Elmira, New York, August 6, 1864. Released from Elmira after taking the Oath of Allegiance on June 30, 1865.

THOMPSON, JAMES P., Private
Resided in Alamance County where he enlisted at age 19, July 15, 1862, for the war. Died December 10, 1862, of disease.

THOMPSON, JOHN H., Private
Resided in Alamance County where he enlisted at age 23, July 15, 1862, for the war. Mortally wounded at Sharpsburg, Maryland, September 17, 1862.

THOMPSON, LEVIN W., Private
Resided in Alamance County where he enlisted at age 26, July 15, 1862, for the war. Present or accounted for until he died in hospital at Staunton, Virginia, June 16-17, 1863, of "phthisis pulmonalis."

THOMPSON, MILTON M., Private
Resided in Alamance County where he enlisted at age 18, July 15, 1862, for the war. Present or accounted for until captured at Spotsylvania Court House, Virginia, May 12, 1864. Confined at Point Lookout, Maryland, until transferred to Elmira, New York, August 6, 1864. Released from Elmira after taking the Oath of Allegiance on June 30, 1865.

THOMPSON, OLIVER N., Private
Resided in Alamance County where he enlisted at age 22, July 15, 1862, for the war. Present or accounted for until captured at Gettysburg, Pennsylvania, July 3, 1863. Confined at Fort Delaware, Delaware, until transferred to Point Lookout, Maryland, October 15-18, 1863. Died at Point Lookout on January 26, 1864, of "chronic diarrhoea."

THOMPSON, S. C., Private
Born in Alamance County where he resided as a farmer and enlisted at age 19, July 15, 1862, for the war. Present or accounted for until he was discharged on October 27, 1862, at Farmville, Virginia. Died in hospital at Farmville on October 30, 1862, of "bronchitis."

THOMPSON, S. W., Private
Resided in Alamance County where he enlisted at age 28, July 15, 1862, for the war. Present or accounted for until he died in hospital at Richmond, Virginia, November 14, 1862, of "typhoid fever."

THOMPSON, WILLIAM P., Private
Resided in Alamance County where he enlisted at age 20, July 15, 1862, for the war. Present or accounted for until captured at Spotsylvania Court House, Virginia, May 12, 1864. Confined at

Point Lookout, Maryland, until transferred to Elmira, New York, August 3, 1864. Released at Elmira after taking the Oath of Allegiance on June 30, 1865.

TINNER, ASHLEY, Private
Paroled at Raleigh, April 22, 1865.

TINSLEY, DAVID H., Private
Resided in Wilkes County where he enlisted at age 19, February 15, 1862, for the war. Captured at Frederick, Maryland, September 12, 1862, and confined at Fort Delaware, Delaware. Transferred to Aiken's Landing, Virginia, October 2, 1862, for exchange. Declared exchanged on November 10, 1862. Reported as present on company muster rolls through February, 1863, and as absent sick on muster rolls through August 10, 1863. Reported as absent without leave after August 10, 1863.

TRUETT, HENRY J., Private
Enlisted in Wake County, November 12, 1863, for the war. "Deserted November 25, 1863."

VANNOY, ALEXANDER W., Private
Resided in Wilkes County and enlisted in Wake County at age 22, May 31, 1861, for the war. Died at Wilkesboro on June 21, 1862, of disease.

VANNOY, ANDERSON M., Private
Resided in Wilkes County where he enlisted at age 18, March 17, 1862, for the war. Wounded in the left hand at Chancellorsville, Virginia, May 3, 1863. Appointed Musician January 1, 1864, and reduced to Private when he was detailed to hospital duty on April 14, 1864. Assigned as a nurse in Jackson Hospital, Richmond, Virginia. Reported on hospital rolls of Jackson Hospital through February, 1865. Paroled at Appomattox Court House, Virginia, April 9, 1865.

VANNOY, HARVEY S., Private
Resided in Wilkes County and enlisted in Wake County at age 21, May 31, 1861, for the war. Present or accounted for until he "deserted from ordnance train June 20, 1863."

VICKERS, LINSEY, Private
Resided in Wilkes County and enlisted in Wake County at age 38, May 31, 1861, for the war. Died at Fredericksburg, Virginia, January 7, 1862, of disease.

WALKER, JAMES, Private
Resided in Wilkes County and enlisted in Wake County at age 22, May 31, 1861, for the war. Wounded in scalp at Ellerson's Mill, Virginia, June 26, 1862, and died of wounds July 21, 1862.

WALSH, ALFRED, Private
Born in Wilkes County where he resided as a farmer prior to enlisting at Wake County at age 20, May 31, 1861, for the war. Present or accounted for until killed in action at Malvern Hill, Virginia, July 1, 1862.

WALSH, WILLIAM, Private
Born in Wilkes County where he resided as a laborer prior to enlisting in Wake County at age 25, May 31, 1861, for the war. Present or accounted for until discharged on September 30, 1862, by reason of disease contracted in the malarious district of Aquia Creek, Virginia.

WATKINS, JESSE M., Private
Resided in Wilkes County and enlisted in Wake County at age 24, May 31, 1861, for the war. Died in hospital at Richmond, Virginia on January 16, 1863, of "pneumonia."

WEBB, JAMES C., Corporal
Born in Caldwell County where he resided prior to enlisting in Warren County at age 20, July 1, 1861, for the war. Mustered in as Private and appointed Corporal, December 1, 1861. Killed in battle at Ellerson's Mill, Virginia, June 26, 1862.

WELLBORN, LYNDON M., Corporal
Resided in Wilkes County and enlisted in Wake County at age 21, May 31, 1861, for the war. Mustered in as Private. Promoted to Corporal March-April, 1863. Wounded in left thigh at Chancellorsville, Virginia, May 3, 1863. Present or accounted for until killed in action at Payne's Farm, Virginia, November 27, 1863.

WHITESELL, GEORGE G., Private
Resided in Alamance County where he enlisted at age 20, July 15, 1862, for the war. Present or accounted for until transferred to Company E of this regiment on May 1, 1863.

WHITTINGTON, LORENZO D., Private
Resided in Wilkes County and enlisted in Wake County at age 21, May 31, 1861, for the war. Captured at Boonsboro Gap, Maryland, September 14, 1862, and paroled near Keedysville, Maryland, September 20, 1862. Wounded in battle at Chancellorsville, Virginia, May 3, 1863, and died of wounds in hospital at Richmond, Virginia, June 11, 1863.

WILBAR, ALFRED W., Private
Resided in Mitchell County and enlisted in Warren County at age 21, July 1, 1861, for the war. Present or accounted for until transferred to the Field and Staff on November 1, 1862, upon promotion to Ordnance Sergeant to rank from September 17, 1862. "Promoted to Ordnance Sergeant for gallant conduct in battle at Sharpsburg, Maryland."

WILKERSON, GEORGE, Private
Resided in Wilkes County and enlisted in Wake County at age 22, May 31, 1861, for the war. Present or accounted for until captured at Mine Run, Virginia, November 28, 1863. Confined at Old Capitol Prison, Washington, D.C., until transferred to Point Lookout, Maryland, February 3, 1864. Paroled at Point Lookout and sent to City Point, Virginia, for exchange March 3-6, 1864. Present or accounted for until he was admitted to hospital at Charlottesville, Virginia, on October 24, 1864, with a gunshot wound of the right thigh. Wounded at Cedar Creek, Virginia, October 19, 1864. Furloughed from hospital on December 25, 1864.

WILKERSON, SAMUEL, Private
Resided in Wilkes County and enlisted in Wake County at age 20, May 31, 1861, for the war. Present or accounted for until captured at Spotsylvania Court House, Virginia, May 12, 1864. Confined at Point Lookout, Maryland, until transferred to Elmira, New York, August 6, 1864. Died

at Elmira on June 30, 1865, of "chronic diarrhoea."

WILSON, T. M., Private
Captured in hospital at Raleigh on April 13, 1865.

WITHERSPOON, LUCIUS LeROY, Private
Transferred from Company H, 37th Regiment N.C. Troops on April 15, 1862. Wounded in action at Ellerson's Mill, Virginia, June 26, 1862, and at Malvern Hill, Virginia, July 1, 1862. Wounded at Chancellorsville, Virginia, May 3, 1863, and returned to company in August, 1863. Wounded in action at Payne's Farm, Virginia, November 27, 1863. Returned to company in January, 1864, and was captured at Spotsylvania Court House, Virginia, May 12, 1864. Confined at Point Lookout, Maryland, until transferred to Elmira, New York, August 6, 1864. Released at Elmira after taking the Oath of Allegiance on July 3, 1865.

WITHERSPOON, SIDNEY L., Private
Resided in Ashe County and enlisted in Wayne County at age 29, April 1, 1862, for the war. Wounded in action at Cold Harbor, Virginia, June 27, 1862. Present or accounted for until captured at Spotsylvania Court House, Virginia, May 12, 1864. Confined at Point Lookout, Maryland, until transferred to Elmira, New York, August 6, 1864. Paroled at Elmira and sent with a group of invalid prisoners to Point Lookout for exchange on October 11-14, 1864. Exchanged at Point Lookout on October 29, 1864, but company muster roll for November-December, 1864, states that he "died at Fortress Monroe, in November, 1864."

WITHERSPOON, WILLIAM H., Corporal
Resided in Wilkes County and enlisted in Wake County at age 19, May 31, 1861, for the war. Mustered in as Private and appointed Corporal on September 5, 1861. Wounded in action at Malvern Hill, Virginia, July 1, 1862. Reported as absent wounded until returned to the company on March 28, 1863. Reduced to ranks and detailed for hospital duty in March, 1863. Returned to company after August, 1863, and reappointed Corporal on November 1, 1863. Admitted to hospital at Richmond, Virginia, May 15, 1864, with a gunshot wound of the head and transferred on May 21, 1864. Date and place wounded and date returned to company not reported. Present or accounted for until paroled at Appomattox Court House, Virginia, April 9, 1865.

WOODRUFF, DAVID C., Sergeant
Resided in Wilkes County and enlisted in Wake County at age 24, May 31, 1861, for the war. Mustered in as Corporal and appointed Sergeant January-February, 1862. Wounded in action at Sharpsburg, Maryland, September 17, 1862, and again at Chancellorsville, Virginia, May 3, 1863. Wounded at Payne's Farm, Virginia, November 27, 1863. Present or accounted for until captured at Spotsylvania Court House, Virginia, May 12, 1864. Confined at Point Lookout, Maryland, until transferred to Elmira, New York, August 6, 1864. Released at Elmira after taking the Oath of Allegiance on June 21, 1865.

WOODY, JAMES, Private

Resided in Alamance County where he enlisted at age 22, July 15, 1862, for the war. Present or accounted for until reported on March-April, 1863, muster roll with the remark: "Discharged under act of Congress providing for the Society of Friends."

WOODY, MALAN, Private

Resided in Alamance County where he enlisted at age 19, July 15, 1862, tor the war. Present or accounted for until reported on March-April, 1863, muster roll with the remark: "Discharged under act of Congress providing for the Society of Friends."

WOODY, WILLIAM N., Private

Resided in Alamance County where he enlisted at age 23, July 15, 1862, for the war. Present or accounted for until he "deserted in Maryland, September 17, 1862."

YOUNG, JAMES, Private

Died at home on September 20, 1862.

COMPANY C

This company, known as "Lillington Rifle Guards," was raised in Harnett County and enlisted at Lillington on June 11, 1861. It tendered its service to the state and was ordered to Warrenton, Warren County, where it became Company C of this regiment. After joining the regiment the company functioned as a part of the regiment, and its history for the war period is recorded as a part of the regimental history.

The information contained in the following roster of the company was compiled principally from company muster rolls for July through August, 1861; November through December, 1861; March through April, 1862; and June 30, 1862, through December, 1864. No company muster rolls were found for the period prior to July, 1861; for September through October, 1861; January through February, 1862; May through June 29, 1862; or for the period after December, 1864. In addition to the company muster rolls, Roll of Honor records, receipt rolls, hospital records, prisoner of war records, and other primary records, supplemented by state pension applications, United Daughters of the Confederacy records, and postwar rosters and histories, all provided useful information.

OFFICERS

CAPTAINS

HINES, JAMES S.

Resided in New Hanover County and appointed Captain to rank from May 16, 1861. Present or accounted for until he transferred to the Field and Staff of this regiment upon appointment to Major to rank from July 8, 1862.

FENNELL, HARDY L.

Resided in New Hanover County and appointed 1st Lieutenant to rank from May 16, 1861.

Wounded severely in battle of Cold Harbor, Virginia, June 27, 1862, "by a minnie ball across both hips." Promoted to Captain to rank from July 8, 1862. Submitted his resignation November 1, 1862, by reason of wounds received June 27, 1862. Resignation excepted December 15, 1862.

THOMSON, WILLIAM HENRY

Resided in New Hanover County where he enlisted at age 31, June 11, 1861, for the war. Mustered in as 1st Sergeant. Promoted to 2nd Lieutenant to rank from October 1, 1861. Promoted to Captain to rank from December 15, 1862. Present or accounted for until wounded at Wilderness, Virginia, May 1-12, 1864. Returned to duty May 25, 1864. Present or accounted for until paroled at Appomattox Court House, Virginia, April 9, 1865.

LIEUTENANTS

CHARLES, MARSTELLER, 3rd Lieutenant

Resided in New Hanover County where he enlisted at age 24, June 11, 1861, for the war. Mustered in as Corporal and promoted to Sergeant on December 1, 1862. Appointed 3rd Lieutenant to rank from December 30, 1862. Present or accounted for until admitted to hospital at Danville, Virginia, on May 9, 1864, with a gunshot wound of the right arm. Date and place wounded not given. Furloughed for 30 days on May 15, 1864. Admitted to hospital at Charlottesville, Virginia, on September 26, 1864, with a gunshot wound of the face and transferred to Lynchburg, Virginia, September 28, 1864. Furloughed from hospital at Lynchburg on October 3, 1864. Submitted his resignation January 12, 1865, by reason of "the company to which I belong contains a less number of enlisted men than required by law." Resignation accepted effective January 12, 1865.

FENNELL, OWEN, Jr., 1st Lieutenant

Resided in New Hanover County and appointed 2nd Lieutenant to rank from May 16, 1861. Promoted to 1st Lieutenant July 8, 1862. Transferred to the Field and Staff of this regiment upon appointment as Captain, Assistant Commissary, December 15, 1862.

LARKINS, JOHN R., 3rd Lieutenant

Resided in New Hanover County and appointed 3rd Lieutenant to rank from May 16, 1861. Submitted his resignation September 25, 1861, and it was accepted October 2, 1861.

McMILLAN, JOHN J., 1st Lieutenant

Resided in New Hanover County where he enlisted at age 30, June 11, 1861, for the war. Mustered in as Sergeant. Promoted to 1st Sergeant November-December, 1861. Appointed 1st Lieutenant to rank from December 15, 1862. Wounded in action at Chancellorsville, Virginia, May 3, 1863. Present or accounted for until captured at Spotsylvania Court House, Virginia, May 12, 1864. Confined at Old Capitol Prison, Washington, D.C., until transferred to Fort Delaware, Delaware, June 17, 1864. Forwarded to Hilton Head, South Carolina, August 20, 1864, and from there to Fort Pulaski, Georgia, October 20, 1864. Transferred back to

Hilton Head on January 1, 1865, and from there to Fort Delaware on March 12, 1865. Released at Fort Delaware on taking the Oath of Allegiance on June 16, 1865.

SCOTT, OBEDIAH R., 2nd Lieutenant

Resided in New Hanover County where he enlisted at age 22, June 11, 1861, for the war. Mustered in as Corporal and promoted to Sergeant prior to December, 1861. Wounded in battle at Ellerson's Mill, Virginia, June 26, 1862. Present or accounted for until transferred to the Field and Staff of this regiment upon appointment as Sergeant Major early in November, 1862, and transferred back to this company upon appointment as 2nd Lieutenant to rank from November 12, 1862. Wounded and captured at Cedar Creek, Virginia, October 19, 1864, and confined at West's Buildings, U.S. Army General Hospital, Baltimore, Maryland, October 25, 1864. Transferred to Fort McHenry, Maryland, January 5, 1865, and to Point Lookout, Maryland, on February 20, 1865, for exchange.

NONCOMMISSIONED OFFICERS AND PRIVATES

ALLEN, GEORGE, Private

Name appears on a roll of noncommissioned officers and privates employed on extra duty "working road" at Brooke's Station, Virginia, December 1-10, 1861.

BAGGETT, R. A., Private

Admitted to hospital at Richmond, Virginia, December 23, 1864, and transferred December 24, 1864.

BAKER, CALVIN H., Private

Resided in Nash County and enlisted in Wake County at age 24, July 15, 1862, for the war. Admitted to hospital at Richmond, Virginia, November 14, 1862, with "intermittent fever" and returned to duty March 30, 1863. Wounded in action at Chancellorsville, Virginia, May 3, 1863. Reported on muster rolls as absent wounded at home through December, 1864.

BARNES, DOCTOR L., Private

Resided in Johnston County and enlisted in Wake County at age 20, July 15, 1862, for the war. Wounded in action at Sharpsburg, Maryland, September 17, 1862, and reported as absent wounded on furlough through April 15, 1864, when he was returned to duty. Captured at Spotsylvania Court House, Virginia, May 12, 1864, and confined at Elmira, New York, until transferred to James River, Virginia, for exchange March 14, 1865. Admitted to hospital at Richmond on March 21, 1865, and furloughed for 30 days on March 28, 1865. Paroled at Raleigh on May 2, 1865.

BARNHILL, GRIFFIN W., Private

Resided in New Hanover County where he enlisted at age 33 for the war. Date of enlistment reported as January 30, February 20, and February 29, 1862. Died at Goldsboro. Date of death

reported as March 5, March 30, and April 3, 1862.

BASS, GOODMAN, Private

Resided in Nash County and enlisted in Wake County at age 30, July 15, 1862, for the war. Wounded in action at Wilderness, Virginia, May 5, 1864. Reported as absent wounded through December, 1864.

BASS, JOSEPH J., Private

Resided in Nash County and enlisted in Wake County at age 24, July 15, 1862, for the war. Captured at Spotsylvania Court House, Virginia, May 12, 1864, and confined at Elmira, New York. Released after taking the Oath of Allegiance on June 27, 1865.

BATTEN, ABRAM, Corporal

Resided in Johnston County and enlisted in Wake County at age 26, July 15, 1862, for the war. Appointed Corporal soon after enlisting. Wounded in hip at Sharpsburg, Maryland, September 17, 1862, and furloughed for 40 days on November 12, 1862. Present or accounted for on company muster rolls from January, 1863, until captured at Spotsylvania Court House, Virginia, May 12, 1864. Confined at Elmira, New York. Released after taking the Oath of Allegiance on June 30, 1865.

BATTEN, JOHN, Private

Born in Johnston County where he resided as a farmer prior to enlisting in Wake County at age 28, July 15, 1862, for the war. Admitted to hospital at Richmond, Virginia, September 16, 1862, with "phthisis" and discharged from the service on December 1, 1862, by reason of "chronic bronchitis and general debility."

BATTEN, WILLIAM H., Private

Born in Johnston County where he resided as a farmer prior to enlisting in Wake County at age 24, July 15, 1862, for the war. Wounded in action at Sharpsburg, Maryland, September 17, 1862, and died of wounds on September 25, 1862.

BATTEN, WILLIAM W., Private

Resided in Johnston County and enlisted in Wake County at age 34, July 15, 1862, for the war. Wounded in hand at Chancellorsville, Virginia, May 3, 1863, and two fingers amputated. Furloughed from hospital at Richmond, Virginia, for 60 days on June 4, 1863. Retired to the Invalid Corps on December 12, 1864, by reason of permanent disability.

BEARD, J. T., Private

Born in Johnston County and resided as a farmer in Nash County prior to enlisting in Wake County at age 27, July 15, 1862, for the war. Discharged at camp near Pisgah Church, Virginia, February 15, 1864, by reason of "mental imbecility."

BIMKLEY, WILLIAM, Private

Paroled at Greensboro, May 9, 1865.

BIRTHRIGHT, ROBERT, Private

Born in Prince William County, Virginia, and resided in New Hanover County as a coach maker prior to enlisting in New Hanover County at age 31, July 11, 1861, for the war. Discharged September 5, 1861, at Camp Bee, Virginia, by reason of "physical disability."

BOURDEAUX, F. M., Corporal

Resided in New Hanover County where he enlisted at age 19, August 22, 1861, for the war. Mustered in as Private and appointed Corporal on December 1, 1862. Present or accounted for until captured at Spotsylvania Court House, Virginia, May 12, 1864. Confined at Point Lookout, Maryland, until transferred to Elmira, New York, August 6, 1864. Released June 19, 1865.

BOYLAN, DAVID L., Corporal

Resided in New Hanover County where he enlisted at age 23, June 11, 1861, for the war. Mustered in as Private and appointed Corporal April 1, 1862. Present or accounted for until paroled at Appomattox Court House, Virginia, April 9, 1865.

BRADSHAW, W. F., Private

Born in Sampson County where he resided and enlisted at age 19, January 29, 1862, for the war. Killed in action at Malvern Hill, Virginia, July 1, 1862.

BRIDGES, GEORGE D., Private

Resided in Johnston County and enlisted in Wake County at age 18, July 15, 1862, for the war. Wounded in action at Sharpsburg, Maryland, September 17, 1862, and reported as absent on furlough until detailed in hospital at Goldsboro, November-December, 1863. Discharged from hospital at Goldsboro and ordered to return to his company on June 14, 1864. Reported as absent from the company in hospital at Lynchburg, Virginia, from August 1, 1864, with the remark that he was detailed as a nurse by reason of disability. Reported on company muster rolls as absent on detail through December, 1864. Admitted to hospital at Greensboro, January 26, 1865, with a gunshot wound. Paroled at Greensboro, May 1, 1865.

BRIDGES, JOSEPH T., Private

Resided in Johnston County and enlisted in Wake County at age 20, July 15, 1862, for the war. Wounded in action at Sharpsburg, Maryland, September 17, 1862. Captured at Chancellorsville, Virginia, May 3, 1863, and paroled and exchanged at City Point, Virginia, May 10, 1863. Detailed as guard in hospital at Lynchburg, Virginia, November 18, 1863, by reason of disability. Reported as absent on detail through December, 1864. Detail continued by special order on March 15, 1865.

BRINSON, JOHN H., Private

Resided in New Hanover County where he enlisted at age 20, June 11, 1861, for the war. Wounded in action at Ellerson's Mill, Virginia, June 26, 1862, and at Chancellorsville, Virginia, May 3, 1863. Wounded in thigh at Payne's Farm, Virginia, November 27, 1863, and detailed as a nurse in hospital at Richmond, Virginia, May 29, 1864. Reported as absent on detail until he was paroled at Richmond on April 20, 1865.

BRINSON, JOSEPH C., Private

Resided in New Hanover County where he enlisted at age 18, June 11, 1861, for the war. Present or accounted for until he was killed in battle at Malvern Hill, Virginia, July 1, 1862.

BRINSON, WILLIAM R., Private

Resided in New Hanover County and enlisted at Richmond, Virginia, at age 26, August 3, 1861, for the war. Deserted May 23, 1863, and returned voluntarily August 1, 1863. Wounded in action at Payne's Farm, Virginia, November 27, 1863. Present or accounted for until captured at Spotsylvania Court House, Virginia, May 20, 1864. Confined at Point Lookout, Maryland, until transferred to Elmira, New York, July 3, 1864. Released from Elmira after taking the Oath of Allegiance on May 15, 1865.

BROWN, JOHN W., Private

Born in Johnston County where he resided prior to enlisting in Wake County at age 26, July 15, 1862, for the war. Captured at Spotsylvania Court House, Virginia, May 12, 1864, and confined at Point Lookout, Maryland, where he died June 2, 1864, of disease.

BROWN, RICHARD W., Private

Resided in New Hanover County where he enlisted at age 32, June 11, 1861, for the war. Admitted to hospital at Richmond, Virginia, August 19, 1862, and detailed as Wardmaster at Camp Winder Hospital, Richmond, Virginia, October 7, 1862. Absent on detail by reason of disability until retired to the Invalid Corps on July 12, 1864. Assigned to light duty at Wilmington. Admitted to hospital in Greensboro on March 5, 1865, with "diarrhoea acute."

BRYANT, H. W., Private

Resided in New Hanover County where he enlisted at age 18, February 21, 1862, for the war. Present or accounted for until captured at Spotsylvania Court House, Virginia, May 12, 1864. Confined at Point Lookout, Maryland, until transferred to Elmira, New York, August 3, 1864. Released at Elmira after taking the Oath of Allegiance on June 12, 1865.

BRYANT, MICHAEL W., Private

Transferred from Company C, 3rd Regiment Arkansas Infantry in April, 1862. Present or accounted for until captured at Spotsylvania Court House, Virginia, May 12, 1864. Confined at Point Lookout, Maryland, where he died June 11, 1865, of "diarrhoea chronic."

BURTON, JOHN W., Private

Resided in New Hanover County where he enlisted at age 44, February 28, 1862, for the war. Wounded in action at Ellerson's Mill, Virginia, June 26, 1862. Admitted to hospital at Charlottesville, Virginia, December 2, 1862, and deserted from hospital on July 17, 1863. Captured and sentenced by court-martial on December 26, 1863, to twelve months in prison for desertion. Released from Military Prison at Salisbury, December 1, 1864, and reported as present until paroled at Appomattox Court House, Virginia, April 9, 1865.

CARR, JOSEPH, Private
Resided in New Hanover County where he enlisted at age 22, June 11, 1861, for the war. Wounded in action at Ellerson's Mill, Virginia, June 26, 1862, and died of wounds July 1, 15, 1862.

CLARK, H., Private
Confined at Knoxville, Tennessee, April 15, 1865, as a "rebel deserter." Transferred to Chattanooga, Tennessee, on August 17, 1865.

CONE, JOHN TURNER, Private
Resided in Nash County and enlisted in Wake County at age 24, July 15, 1862, for the war. Captured at Spotsylvania Court House, Virginia, May 12, 1864, and confined at Point Lookout, Maryland. Transferred on August 6, 1864, to Elmira, New York, where he died June 4, 1865, of "chronic diarrhoea."

COWAN, WILLIAM E., Musician
Resided in New Hanover County where he enlisted at age 17, June 11, 1861, for the war. Mustered in as Drummer and reported as Musician after April, 1862. Present or accounted for until captured at Spotsylvania Court House, Virginia, June 10, 1864. Confined at Point Lookout, Maryland, until paroled and transferred to Aiken's Landing, Virginia, for exchange on March 17, 1865.

CREECH, J. J., Private
Resided in Johnston County and enlisted in Wake County at age 22, July 15, 1862, for the war. Captured at Boonsboro, Maryland, September 14, 1862, and confined on January 15, 1863, in U.S. Army Hospital, where he remained until transferred to Fort McHenry, Maryland, June 25, 1863. Sent to Fort Monroe, Virginia, for exchange on June 26, 1863. Absent on sick furlough from date of exchange until returned to duty June 18, 1864. Present or accounted for until he was paroled at Lynchburg, Virginia, April 15, 1865.

CRICKMAN, W. H., Private
Resided in Nash County and enlisted in Wake County at age 23, July 15, 1862, for the war. Admitted to hospital at Richmond, Virginia, on September 1, 1862, with "typhoid fever" and furloughed for 30 days on September 21, 1862. Present or accounted for until captured at Gettysburg, Pennsylvania, July 3, 1863. Confined at Fort Delaware, Delaware, until transferred to Point Lookout, Maryland, on October 22, 1863. Admitted to General Hospital at Point Lookout on date of transfer. Died at Point Lookout on November 23, 1863, of "scorbutus and parditis."

CROCKER, AVIRITT, Private
Resided in Johnston County and enlisted at age 30, July 15, 1862, for the war. Reported as missing in action in Maryland on September 14, 1862. Also reported to have died in September, 1862.

CROOM, JESSE, Private
Born in New Hanover County where he resided as a student and enlisted at age 18, June 11, 1861, for the war. Discharged at Camp Bee, Virginia, September 4, 1861, by reason of "physical inability to discharge the duties of a soldier."

CROOM, WILLIAM, Private
Resided in New Hanover County where he enlisted at age 27, June 11, 1861, for the war. Wounded in action at Winchester, Virginia, June 15, 1863. Reported as absent on furlough through December, 1863. Killed in action at Spotsylvania Court House, Virginia, May 10, 1864.

CROOM, WILLIAM J., Jr., Private
Born in New Hanover County where he resided as a farmer and enlisted at age 18, June 11, 1861, for the war. Discharged at Camp Bee, Virginia, September 4, 1861, by reason of "physical inability to discharge the duties of a soldier."

CUNNINGHAM, JAMES K., Private
Captured at Piedmont, Virginia, June 5, 1864, and confined at Camp Morton, Indiana, until forwarded to City Point, Virginia, for exchange on February 26, 1865.

DAVIS, ISAAC, Private
Resided in Nash County and enlisted in Wake County at age 20, July 15, 1862, for the war. Admitted to hospital at Richmond, Virginia, September 1, 1862, with "pain in breast" and returned to duty October 22, 1862. Sent home on sick furlough March-April, 1863. Died at home of disease. Date of death given as April, 1863, and June, 1863.

DeBOSE, CHARLES M., Private
Resided in New Hanover County where he enlisted at age 22, June 11, 1861, for the war. Present or accounted for until captured at Spotsylvania Court House, Virginia, May 12, 1864. Confined at Point Lookout, Maryland, until transferred to Elmira, New York, August 6, 1864. Released after taking the Oath of Allegiance at Elmira on June 12, 1865.

EURE, GILHAM, Private
Resided in Nash County and enlisted in Wake County at age 33, July 15, 1862, for the war. Wounded in left foot at Chancellorsville, Virginia, May 3, 1863. Admitted to hospital at Richmond, Virginia, May 10, 1863, and transferred to Wilson, N.C., July 5, 1863. Attached to hospital at Wilson as a nurse and a cook on October 29, 1863. Company muster rolls report him as absent on detail through December, 1864. Paroled at hospital at Greensboro on April 29, 1865.

FENNELL, JOHN G., Sergeant
Resided in New Hanover County where he enlisted at age 18, June 11, 1861, for the war. Mustered in as Sergeant. Discharged November 5, 1861.

FRACE, L., Private
Paroled at Goldsboro on May 4, 1865.

FRANKLIN, J. W., Private
Admitted to hospital at Richmond, Virginia, on March 11, 1865, and sent to Camp Lee, near Richmond, March 12, 1865. Records indicate that he was a paroled prisoner.

FRANKLIN, JACOB, Private
Paroled at Greensboro on May 6, 1865.

GARNER, MABRY, Private
Resided in Johnston County and enlisted in Wake County at age 31, July 15, 1862, for the war. Captured near Sharpsburg, Maryland, September 19, 1862, and paroled September 27, 1862. Reported as present or accounted for on muster rolls through February 29-August 31, 1864, muster roll, which reports him with the remark: "Absent at hospital wounded since May 19, 1864." Reported as absent on furlough through December, 1864.

GAY, CHARLES B., Private
Resided in Nash County and enlisted in Wake County at age 33, July 15, 1862, for the war. Present or accounted for until he was killed in action at Chancellorsville, Virginia, May 3, 1863.

GAY, GREEN, Private
Resided in Nash County and enlisted in Wake County at age 22, July 15, 1862, for the war. Admitted to hospital at Richmond, Virginia, May 8, 1863, with "febris intermittence" and furloughed for 40 days on July 23, 1863. Died in field hospital on May 6, 1864, of wounds received in battle on May 5, 1864, at Wilderness, Virginia.

GAY, WILLIAM, Private
Resided in Nash County and enlisted in Wake County at age 20, July 15, 1862, for the war. Wounded in battle at Chancellorsville, Virginia, May 3, 1863. Furloughed from hospital at Richmond, Virginia, for 60 days on June 2, 1863. Wound described as "gunshot neck and paralysis of left arm." Present or accounted for until captured at Spotsylvania Court House, Virginia, May 12, 1864. Confined at Point Lookout, Maryland, until transferred to Elmira, New York, where he was paroled and sent to James River, Virginia, for exchange. Received at Boulware's Wharf, James River, Virginia, March 18-21, 1865.

GRIBBS, H. H., Private
Paroled at Greensboro on May 15, 1865.

GRICE, ISAAC W., Private
Resided in New Hanover County where he enlisted at age 25, June 11, 1861, for the war. July-August, 1861, muster roll reports him as absent "from sickness." Roll of Honor states that he was "discharged July, 1861, at Warrenton, N.C."

HAINEY, F., Private
Captured at Gettysburg, Pennsylvania, July 3, 1863, and confined at Fort Delaware, Delaware, July 7, 1863.

HARPER, JOEL, Private
Enlisted in Orange County, Virginia, on March 21, 1864, for the war. Captured at Spotsylvania Court House, Virginia, May 12, 1864, and confined at Point Lookout, Maryland, where he died August 6-7, 1864, of "canacumoras."

HEATH, H. J., Private
Admitted to hospital at Charlottesville, Virginia, November 21, 1862, with "phthisis" and transferred to Lynchburg, Virginia.

HERRING, ARCHIBALD B., Private
Resided in New Hanover County where he en-

listed at age 20, June 11, 1861, for the war. Died in hospital at Fredericksburg, Virginia, November 2, 5, 1861.

HERRING, DAVID P., Private
Resided in New Hanover County where he enlisted at age 19, June 11, 1861, for the war. Killed in action at Sharpsburg, Maryland, September 17, 1862.

HERRING, MARQUIS D., Sergeant
Resided in New Hanover County where he enlisted at age 18, June 11, 1861, for the war. Mustered in as Private. Appointed Corporal December 1, 1862, and promoted to Sergeant January-February, 1863. Present or accounted for until captured at Fisher's Hill, Virginia, September 22, 1864. Confined at Point Lookout, Maryland, until paroled and transferred to Aiken's Landing, Virginia, for exchange on March 17, 1865.

HERRING, THOMAS E., Private
Resided in New Hanover County where he enlisted at age 18, June 11, 1861, for the war. Admitted to hospital at Richmond, Virginia, on July 1, 1862, with a gunshot wound in the foot and furloughed for 30 days on July 6, 1862. Admitted to hospital at Richmond on May 8, 1863, with gunshot wound of foot and returned to duty May 27, 1863. Present or accounted for until captured at Gettysburg, Pennsylvania, July 2, 1863. Confined at Fort McHenry, Maryland, until transferred to Fort Delaware, Delaware, July, 1863. Released at Fort Delaware after taking the Oath of Allegiance on June 19, 1865.

HERRING, WILLIAM J., 1st Sergeant
Resided in New Hanover County where he enlisted at age 26, June 11, 1861, for the war. Mustered in as Sergeant and promoted to 1st Sergeant on November 12, 1862. Wounded in action at Chancellorsville, Virginia, May 3, 1863, and reported as absent wounded through October, 1863. Returned to company November-December, 1863, and reported as present until wounded September 19, 1864, in battle at Winchester, Virginia. Hospital records at Lynchburg, Virginia, indicate that he was wounded in the left shoulder. Furloughed on November 11, 1864, and furlough extended for 30 day periods on January 6 and February 7, 1865.

HINNANT, JOHN, Private
Born in Johnston County where he resided prior to enlisting in Wake County at age 21, July 15, 1862, for the war. Captured at Boonsboro, Maryland, September 14, 1862, and confined at Fort Delaware, Delaware, until transferred to Aiken's Landing, Virginia, October 2, 1862. Declared exchanged on November 10, 1862. Reported as absent without leave from October 23, 1862, to November 11, 1863. Confined in the "brigade house" December 11, 1863. Killed in battle at Spotsylvania Court House, Virginia, May 10, 1864.

HINNANT, RANSOM J., Private
Born in Johnston County where he resided as a farmer prior to enlisting in Wake County at age 24, July 15, 1862, for the war. Wounded in action

at Sharpsburg, Maryland, September 17, 1862, and furloughed from hospital for 40 days on October 8, 1862. Admitted to hospital at Richmond, Virginia, May 8, 1863, with a gunshot wound in the thigh and returned to duty May 27, 1863. Captured at Gettysburg, Pennsylvania, July 3, 1863, and confined at Fort Delaware, Delaware, until transferred to Point Lookout, Maryland, October 15, 1863. Released after taking the Oath of Allegiance at Point Lookout and joined the U.S. service on January 26, 1864. Assigned to Company B, 1st Regiment U.S. Volunteer Infantry.

HINNANT, THEOPILUS, Private

Resided in Johnston County prior to enlisting in Wake County at age 18, July 15, 1862, for the war. Wounded at Winchester, Virginia, June 15, 1863. Reported as absent wounded through December, 1863, and as absent sick in hospital from May, 1864, through December, 1864. Union prisoner of war records indicate that he was captured at Spotsylvania, Virginia, June 10, 1864, and confined at Point Lookout, Maryland. Transferred to Elmira, New York, July 25-28, 1864. Released at Elmira after taking the Oath of Allegiance on June 14, 1865.

HINNARD, P., Private

Captured at Gettysburg, Pennsylvania, July 3, 1863, and confined at Fort Delaware, Delaware, until transferred to Point Lookout, Maryland, October 18, 1863.

HIRMAND, L., Private

Captured at South Mountain, Maryland, September 14, 1862, and confined at Fort Delaware, Delaware, until transferred to Aiken's Landing, Virginia, October 2, 1862. Declared exchanged on November 10, 1862.

HOLLAND, WILLIAM P., Private

Resided in New Hanover County where he enlisted at age 20, June 11, 1861, for the war. Mustered in as Private and appointed Corporal on December 1, 1862. Promoted to Sergeant in April, 1863. Reduced to ranks March 31, 1864. Admitted to hospital at Richmond, Virginia, June 1, 1864, with a gunshot wound and returned to duty July 8, 1864. Admitted to hospital at Charlottesville, Virginia, September 26, 1864, with a gunshot wound of the thigh and transferred to Lynchburg, Virginia, the next day.

HOLLIMAN, H. B., Private

Resided in Nash County and enlisted in Wake County at age 32, July 15, 1862, for the war. Captured at South Mountain, Maryland, September 15, 1862, and confined at Fort Delaware, Delaware, until paroled and sent to Aiken's Landing, Virginia, October 2, 1862, for exchange. Declared exchanged November 10, 1862. Deserted from Camp Lee, Richmond, Virginia, October 27, 1862. Reported as absent without leave on company muster rolls through December, 1864.

HOLLY, H., Private

Resided in New Hanover County where he enlisted at age 48, January 30, 1862, for the war. Captured at Falling Waters, Maryland, July 14, 1863. Confined at Old Capitol Prison, Washington, D.C., until transferred to Point Lookout, Maryland, August 9, 1863. Paroled and sent to Venus Point, Savannah River, Georigia, October 30, 1864, for exchange. Received at Venus Point on November 15, 1864, in exchange. Reported as "absent at home sick, lately exchanged" on November-December, 1864, muster roll.

HOLLY, WILLIAM D., Private

Born in New Hanover County where he resided as a farmer and enlisted at age 21, June 11, 1861, for the war. Wounded in the leg at Sharpsburg, Maryland, September 17, 1862, and captured. Confined at Fort McHenry, Maryland, until paroled and sent to Fort Monroe, Virginia, for exchange October 13, 1862. Admitted to hospital at Richmond, Virginia, October 23, 1862, and furloughed for 30 days November 5-10, 1862. Reported on company muster rolls through December, 1864, as absent sick. Certificate of disability for retiring an invalid soldier dated February 17, 1865, indicates that he was "permanently disabled." Certificate approved by the Surgeon General on February 25, 1865.

HOPKINS, JOSEPH, Private

Born in Nash County where he resided as a farmer prior to enlisting in Wake County at age 21, July 15, 1862, for the war. Admitted to hospital at Richmond, Virginia, September 1, 1862, with "rheumatism" and "typhoid fever." Discharged from the service on September 19, 1862, by reason of "permanent contraction of the left knee joint."

HOWELL, C. D., Private

Resided in Nash County and enlisted in Wake County at age 18, July 15, 1862, for the war. Captured at Boonsboro, Maryland, September 15, 1862, and confined at Fort Delaware, Delaware, until paroled and sent to Aiken's Landing, Virginia, October 2, 1862. Declared exchanged on November 10, 1862. Wounded in action at Chancellorsville, Virginia, May 3, 1863, and reported as absent wounded or absent sick on company muster rolls through December, 1864.

HUGGINS, ALFRED, Private

Born in New Hanover County where he resided and enlisted at age 25, June 11, 1861, for the war. Died at home in New Hanover County on May 2, 4, 1862, of disease.

JOHNSON, WILLIAM B., Private

Resided in Nash County and enlisted in Wake County at age 21, July 15, 1862, for the war. Wounded in action at Sharpsburg, Maryland, September 17, 1862. Reported as absent without leave from September through December, 1862. Reported as present after January, 1863. Captured at Chancellorsville, Virginia, May 3, 1863, and paroled and sent to City Point, Virginia, for exchange May 10, 1863. Present or accounted for until killed in a skirmish near Morton's Ford, Virginia, February 6, 1864.

JONES, JAMES C., Corporal

Resided in New Hanover County where he enlisted at age 18, June 11, 1861, for the war. Mustered in as Corporal. Wounded in action at

Malvern Hill, Virginia, July 1, 1862, and died of wounds on July 4, 1862.

JONES, JOHN, Private

Resided in Guilford County and enlisted in Wake County at age 18, May 31, 1861, for the war. Deserted April 1, 1863, and rejoined from desertion January 3, 1864. Sentenced to death for desertion but the sentence was commuted on March 3, 1864, and he was sentenced to hard labor until March 31, 1864. Returned to the company in April, 1864, and reported as absent wounded on February 29-August 31, 1864, muster roll. Detached to hospital at Danville, Virginia, November 28, 1864. Federal Provost Marshal records at Bermuda Hundred, Virginia, indicate that he deserted March 14, 1865, and was forwarded to City Point, Virginia.

JONES, RAMSEY, Private

Resided in Nash County and enlisted in Wake County at age 37, July 15, 1862, for the war. Company muster roll for June 3-October 31, 1862, states that he "died September, 1862." Roll of Honor states that he "died August 10, 1862, at Richmond, Virginia."

JOYNER, J. J., Private

Resided in Nash County and enlisted in Wake County at age 19, July 15, 1862, for the war. Captured and paroled at Warrenton, Virginia, September 29, 1862. Company muster rolls carry him as absent sick from August 31, 1862, until January 1, 1863, and as absent without leave after that date. January-February, 1864, muster roll carries the following remarks: "absent without leave from March 1, 1863, to November 11, 1863. Two months wages to be deducted by sentence of Court Martial." Company muster roll for February 29-August 31, 1864, states that he was "absent—prisoner of war since May 12, 1864." No prisoner of war records were found relative to his capture. Reported as absent prisoner on company muster rolls through December, 1864.

KEITH, FRANCIS M., Sergeant

Resided in New Hanover County where he enlisted at age 21, June 11, 1861, for the war. Mustered in as Private. Captured at South Mountain, Maryland, September 15, 1862, and confined at Fort Delaware, Delaware, until transferred to Aiken's Landing, Virginia, October 2, 1862, for exchange. Declared exchanged on November 10, 1862. Appointed Corporal January-February, 1863. Promoted to Sergeant April 1, 1864. Wounded in action at Wilderness, Virginia, May 5, 1864, and reported as absent wounded on company muster rolls through December, 1864. Certificate of disability for retiring an invalid soldier dated January 23, 1865, states that he was permanently disabled because of "gunshot wound causing necrosis of right tibia."

KEITH, HENRY S., Private

Resided in Wake County where he enlisted at age 22, January 30, 1862, for the war. Wounded in action at Ellerson's Mill, Virginia, June 26, 1862, and at Sharpsburg, Maryland, September 17, 1862. Wounded in the ankle at Chancellorsville, Virginia, May 3, 1863, and admitted to hospital at Richmond, Virginia, May 6, 1863. Transferred on June 17, 1863, to Danville, Virginia, where he was confined until returned to duty July 21, 1863. Wounded in action at Payne's Farm, Virginia, November 27, 1863. Admitted to hospital at Charlottesville, Virginia, January 16, 1864, with "syphilis prim." and returned to duty June 19, 1864. Captured at Rockville, Maryland, July 14, 1864, and confined at Old Capitol Prison, Washington, D.C., until transferred to hospital in Washington, July 21, 1864, with "intermittent fever." Returned to prison August 23, 1864, and transferred to Fort Delaware, Delaware, September 19, 1864. Released at Fort Delaware after taking the Oath of Allegiance on June 19, 1865.

KEITH, JAMES T., Private

Resided in New Hanover County where he enlisted at age 19, June 11, 1861, for the war. Discharged November 20, 1861. Later enlisted in Company G, 61st Regiment N.C. Troops.

KEITH, LEMUEL L., Private

Resided in New Hanover County where he enlisted at age 25, June 11, 1861, for the war. Present or accounted for until he transferred to Company G, 61st Regiment N.C. Troops upon appointment to 2nd Lieutenant to rank from March 20, 1862.

KELLY, FRANCIS, Private

Resided in New Hanover County where he enlisted at age 25, June 11, 1861, for the war. Present or accounted for until captured at Gettysburg, Pennsylvania, July 4-5, 1863. Confined at Fort McHenry, Maryland, until transferred to Fort Delaware, Delaware, in July, 1863. Released at Fort Delaware after taking the Oath of Allegiance on January 27, 1865.

KELLY, WILLIAM D., Private

Resided in New Hanover County where he enlisted at age 41, January 30, 1862, for the war. Present or accounted for on company muster rolls until he deserted on May 23, 1863. Returned to the company on November 20, 1863, and reported as present through December, 1864. Paroled near Appomattox Court House, Virginia, April 7, 1865.

KELLY, WILLIAM P., Private

Resided in New Hanover County and enlisted in Wayne County at age 16, April 15, 1862, for the war. Present or accounted for until captured at Spotsylvania Court House, Virginia, May 12, 1864. Confined at Point Lookout, Maryland, until transferred to Elmira, New York, August 6, 1864. Paroled at Elmira and sent to James River, Virginia, for exchange on March 14, 1865. Date of exchange not given but he was reported as remaining in U.S. Army Military Prison (Libby), Richmond, Virginia, April 10, 1865. Date of release not reported.

LEE, GEORGE R., Private

Born in Screven County, Georgia, and resided as a farmer in New Hanover County where he enlisted at age 17, June 11, 1861, for the war. Discharged September 4, 1861, by reason of "physical inability to discharge the duties of a soldier."

LEWIS, HOLDEN M., Private

Resided in New Hanover County where he enlisted at age 35, June 11, 1861, for the war. November-December, 1861, muster roll states that he was "absent sick at hospital at Petersburg, Virginia." Roll of Honor states that he was "discharged April, 1862."

LEWIS, JOHN H., Private

Resided in South Carolina and enlisted at Richmond, Virginia, at age 21, August 3, 1861, for the war. Captured at Boonsboro, Maryland, September 14, 1862, and exchanged in September, 1862. Admitted to hospital at Richmond, Virginia, October 14, 1862, and transferred to Camp Lee, near Richmond, two days later. Wounded in the left hand at Chancellorsville, Virginia, May 3, 1863, and admitted to hospital at Richmond, Virginia, May 6, 1863. Transferred to Lynchburg, Virginia, May 9, 1863. Reported as absent wounded on company muster rolls until September-October, 1863, when he appears as present. Present or accounted for until transferred to Company E, 1st Regiment South Carolina Volunteer Infantry on February 26, 1864.

LITTLE, JOHN M., Private

Paroled at Greensboro on May 16, 1865.

McALISTER, CHARLES A., Private

Resided in New Hanover County where he enlisted at age 21, June 11, 1861, for the war. Detailed in Pioneer Corps July, 1863, and reported as absent on detail through August, 1864. Present or accounted for on company muster rolls through December, 1864. Paroled at Richmond, Virginia, April 25, 1865.

McCAULEY, JAMES, Private

Resided in New Hanover County where he enlisted at age 33, January 30, 1862, for the war. Present or accounted for until captured at Gettysburg, Pennsylvania, July 3, 1863. Confined at Fort McHenry, Maryland, until transferred to Fort Delaware, Delaware, July 7-12, 1863. Federal Provost Marshal records indicate that he "allowed some other prisoner to take his name and place" when he was ordered transferred to Point Lookout, Maryland, on October 18, 1863, for exchange. Remained at Fort Delaware and took the Oath of Allegiance on February 27, 1865.

McINTIRE, FRANKLIN P., Sergeant

Resided in New Hanover County where he enlisted at age 18, June 11, 1861, for the war. Mustered in as Private. Wounded in action at Ellerson's Mill, Virginia, June 26, 1862. Promoted to Sergeant December 1, 1862. Wounded in the chin at Chancellorsville, Virginia, May 3, 1863, and admitted to hospital at Richmond, Virginia, May 6, 1863. Transferred to hospital at Wilmington, May 19, 1863, and furloughed on May 31, 1863. Returned to company on September 17, 1863. Captured at Spotsylvania Court House, Virginia, May 12, 1864, and confined at Point Lookout, Maryland, until transferred to Elmira, New York, August 6, 1864. Appears on a roll of invalid prisoners sent from Elmira to Point Lookout on October 25, 1864, for exchange. Exchanged

on October 29, 1864. Captured at Burkeville, Virginia, April 6, 1865, and confined at Point Lookout, Maryland, until released after taking the Oath of Allegiance on June 29, 1865.

McINTIRE, THOMAS HENRY WILLIAMS, Private

Resided in New Hanover County where he enlisted at age 23, August 22, 1861, for the war. Mustered in as Private and appointed Sergeant prior to December, 1861. Transferred to the Field and Staff of this regiment upon appointment as Sergeant Major to rank from March 1, 1862. Returned to this company January 25, 1863, as a Private. Transferred to Company F of this regiment upon appointment as 2nd Lieutenant to rank from January 1, 1864.

MAHN, OWEN, Private

Resided in New Hanover County where he enlisted at age 22, June 11, 1861, for the war. Present or accounted for until discharged in September, 1861.

MARBLE, JOSEPH B., Private

Born in Onslow County and resided as a farmer in New Hanover County where he enlisted at age 26, June 11, 1861, for the war. Present or accounted for until wounded at Winchester, Virginia, September 19, 1864. Admitted to hospital at Charlottesville, Virginia, September 25, 1864, with a gunshot wound of the left shoulder and transferred to Lynchburg, Virginia, the next day. Admitted to hospital at Wilmington on December 8, 1864, and transferred to Goldsboro on December 26, 1864. Admitted to Pettigrew General Hospital No. 13, Raleigh, on December 27, 1864, and transferred to Kittrell's on January 1, 1865. Retired to the Invalid Corps on February 17, 1865, and assigned to light duty.

MONROE, C. M., Private

Captured at Gettysburg, Pennsylvania, July 3, 1863, and confined at Fort Delaware, Delaware, where he died October 26, 1863, of "diarrhoea chronic."

MONTAGUE, JAMES, Corporal

Resided in New Hanover County where he enlisted at age 18, June 11, 1861, for the war. Mustered in as Private and appointed Corporal April 30, 1862. Died at Mechanicsville, Virginia, July 5, 1862, of disease.

MOORE, ANDREW J., Private

Born in New Hanover County where he resided as a farmer and enlisted at age 24, June 11, 1861, for the war. Present or accounted for until discharged on March 1, 1863, by reason of "phthisis pulmonalis."

MOORE, GEORGE W., Jr., Private

Born in New Hanover County where he resided and enlisted at age 30, June 11, 1861, for the war. Present or accounted for until captured at Gettysburg, Pennsylvania, July 3, 1863. Confined at Fort McHenry, Maryland, until paroled and sent to Fort Delaware, Delaware, July 12, 1863. Transferred October 18, 1863, to Point Lookout, Maryland, where he died on August 18, 1864.

MOORE, JOHN WILSON, Private
Resided in New Hanover County where he enlisted at age 21, June 11, 1861, for the war. Wounded in action at Ellerson's Mill, Virginia, June 26, 1862, and furloughed for 30 days from hospital at Richmond, Virginia, July 6, 1862. Absent sick with "variola" from November 4, 1862, until returned to duty March 5, 1863. Absent with "dyspepsia" from May 8 to August 13, 1863. Wounded in action at Wilderness, Virginia, May 5, 1864, and furloughed for 60 days on May 20, 1864. Admitted to hospital at Raleigh on September 12, 1864, with "debility from typhoid fever" and returned to duty October 2, 1864. Wounded in action at Cedar Creek, Virginia, October 19, 1864. Reported as absent wounded through December, 1864.

MOORE, JOSEPH W., Private
Resided in New Hanover County where he enlisted at age 28, June 11, 1861, for the war. Wounded in action at Cold Harbor, Virginia, June 27, 1862. Present or accounted for through August 31, 1864, when he was reported as "at home on wounded furlough since August 15, 1864." Reported as present on company muster rolls for September-October and November-December, 1864. Captured at Petersburg, Virginia, April 3, 1865, and confined at Hart's Island, New York Harbor, until released after taking the Oath of Allegiance on June 14, 1865.

MOORE, LEWIS, Private
Resided in Sampson County where he enlisted at age 19, February 26, 1862, for the war. Wounded in action at Wilderness, Virginia, May 5, 1864. Reported as absent wounded through December, 1864.

MOORE, MOSES JAMES, Private
Resided in Sampson County and enlisted in New Hanover County at age 15, March 31, 1862, for the war. Present or accounted for until captured at Spotsylvania Court House, Virginia, May 12, 1864. Confined at Point Lookout, Maryland, until transferred to Elmira, New York, August 6, 1864. Paroled at Elmira and sent to James River, Virginia, for exchange on February 15, 1865. Admitted to hospital at Richmond, Virginia, on February 20, 1865, and furloughed on February 25, 1865.

MORGAN, MARSHALL H., Private
Resided in New Hanover County where he enlisted at age 24, June 11, 1861, for the war. Mustered in as Private and appointed Corporal January, 1863. Wounded in right arm at Chancellorsville, Virginia, May 3, 1863, and arm amputated above the elbow. Admitted to hospital at Richmond, Virginia, May 11, 1863, and transferred to Wilson, North Carolina, June 11, 1863. Detailed as cook and nurse in hospital at Wilson on July 1, 1863. Reduced to ranks after February, 1864, while still absent on detail. Retired to the Invalid Corps on November 24, 1864.

MORRIS, SAMUEL A., Private
Resided in Nash County and enlisted in Wake County at age 19, July 15, 1862, for the war.

Wounded in action at Sharpsburg, Maryland, September 17, 1862. Reported as absent wounded through January 1, 1863, and as absent without leave from that date through February, 1864. Date of return to company not reported, but he was captured at Spotsylvania Court House, Virginia, May 12, 1864. Confined at Point Lookout, Maryland, until transferred to Elmira, New York, August 6, 1864. Died at Elmira on December 8, 1864, of "chronic diarrhoea."

MORSE, J. W., Private
Paroled at Appomattox Court House, Virginia, April 9, 1865.

NELSON, J. A., Private
Paroled at Goldsboro in May, 1865.

O'NEIL, O. W., Private
Resided in Nash County and enlisted in Wake County at age 34, July 15, 1862, for the war. Died in hospital at Gordonsville, Virginia, September 23, 1862, of "chronic diarrhoea."

O'NEILL, GASTON, Private
Resided in Nash County and enlisted in Wake County at age 19, July 15, 1862, for the war. Mortally wounded in action at Sharpsburg, Maryland, September 17, 1862.

O'QUINN, HENRY, Private
Resided in New Hanover County where he enlisted at age 33, June 11, 1861, for the war. Wounded in thigh at Chancellorsville, Virginia, May 3, 1863, and furloughed from hospital at Richmond, Virginia, for 60 days on August 26, 1863. Reported as absent wounded until he was retired to the Invalid Corps on November 17, 1864.

O'QUINN, JAMES, Private
Born in Sampson County and resided in New Hanover County where he enlisted at age 28, June 11, 1861, for the war. Present or accounted for until he was killed in battle at Ellerson's Mill, Virginia, June 26, 1862.

ORR, TULLEY W., Private
Born in New Hanover County where he resided as a cooper and enlisted at age 47, June 11, 1861, for the war. Present or accounted for until discharged on June 12, 1861.

PACE, LARRY, Private
Resided in Johnston County and enlisted in Wake County at age 25, July 15, 1862, for the war. Wounded in action at Sharpsburg, Maryland, September 17, 1862, and again at Chancellorsville, Virginia, May 3, 1863. Wound received at Chancellorsville was through the elbow joint and paralyzed the arm. Reported as absent wounded until retired to the Invalid Corps on December 12, 1864.

PADGETT, R. A., Private
Resided in New Hanover County where he enlisted at age 55, March 17, 1863, as a substitute. Reported as absent sick in hospital; absent without leave; and absent on sick furlough from May 17, 1863, through December, 1864.

PARKER, NEEDHAM, Private
Resided in Johnston County and enlisted in Wake County at age 19, July 15, 1862, for the war.

Wounded in the arm at Chancellorsville, Virginia, May 3, 1863. Reported as absent wounded until detailed for hospital duty on February 19, 1864. Reported as absent on detail until retired to the Invalid Corps on December 7, 1864.

PARNELL, JEREMIAH, Private

Born in Johnston County where he resided as a farmer prior to enlisting in Wake County at age 34, July 15, 1862, for the war. Present or accounted for until he died in hospital at Richmond, Virginia, December 23, 1862, of "febris typhoides."

PEDEN, WILLIAM N., Private

Resided in Johnston County and enlisted in Wake County at age 27, July 15, 1862, for the war. Present or accounted for until admitted to hospital at Richmond, Virginia, May 8, 1864, with a gunshot wound of the right hand. Transferred to Danville, Virginia, and furloughed on May 27, 1864. Captured at Plymouth, North Carolina, October 31, 1864, and confined at Military Prison, Camp Hamilton, Virginia, until transferred to Point Lookout, Maryland, November 24, 1864. Died at Point Lookout on February 11, 1865, of "pneumonia."

PENNY, MAJOR R., Private

Resided in New Hanover County where he enlisted at age 20, June 11, 1861, for the war. Present or accounted for until killed in action at Malvern Hill, Virginia, July 1, 1862.

PIERCE, C., Private

Admitted to hospital at Richmond, Virginia, on June 26, 1863, with "int. feb." Returned to duty August 6, 1863.

PILKINTON, JOHN, Private

Resided in Johnston County and enlisted in Wake County at age 18, July 15, 1862, for the war. Captured at Boonsboro, Maryland, September 14-15, 1862, and confined at Fort Delaware, Delaware, until sent to Aiken's Landing, Virginia, October 2, 1862, for exchange. Declared exchanged on November 10, 1862. Wounded in action at Chancellorsville, Virginia, May 3, 1863, and died of wounds on May 6, 1863.

PITTMAN, A. G., Private

Born in Johnston County where he resided prior to enlisting in Wake County at age 21, July 15, 1862, for the war. Killed in action at Sharpsburg, Maryland, September 15, 1862.

PITTMAN, B. F., Private

Resided in Johnston County and enlisted in Wake County at age 27, July 15, 1862, for the war. Wounded in the hip joint at Gettysburg, Pennsylvania, July 3, 1863, and captured at Gettysburg on July 4, 1863. Died at Camp Letterman U.S. Army General Hospital, Gettysburg, September 14, 1863.

PITTMAN, JOHN R., Private

Born in Johnston County where he resided as a farmer prior to enlisting in Wake County at age 25, July 15, 1862, for the war. Died in hospital at Richmond, Virginia, March 10, 1863, of "pneumonia."

POTTER, JOHN T., Private

Resided in New Hanover County where he en-

listed at age 21, June 11, 1861, for the war. Died at home of smallpox on April 3, 1863.

POTTER, WILLIAM K., Private

Born in South Carolina and resided as a farmer in New Hanover County· where he enlisted at age 22, June 11, 1861, for the war. Admitted to hospital in Richmond, Virginia, December 4, 1862, with "disease of the lungs, inertia." Discharged from the service on December 8, 1862, by reason of "being incapable of performing the duties of a soldier because of consolidation of the right lung, the chest being in consequence forced in. He has also paralysis of the right arm."

POWELL, JAMES B., Private

Resided in New Hanover County where he enlisted at age 35, January 15, 1862, for the war. Present or accounted for until captured at Spotsylvania Court House, Virginia, May 12, 1864. Confined at Point Lookout, Maryland, until transferred to Elmira, New York, August 6, 1864. Paroled at Elmira and sent to James River, Virginia, for exchange on March 2, 1865.

POWELL, JOSEPH T., Private

Resided in New Hanover County where he enlisted at age 29, January 30, 1862, for the war. Wounded at Ellerson's Mill, Virginia, June 26, 1862, and reported as absent wounded through February, 1863. Reported as present on March-April, 1863, muster roll and on May-June, 1863, muster roll with the remark: "Missing at Cove Mountain, Pennsylvania, June 25, 1863." Died near McConnellsburg, Pennsylvania, June 27, 1863.

REEVES, HENRY B., Private

Born in New Hanover County where he resided and enlisted at age 23, June 11, 1861, for the war. Wounded in action at Gettysburg, Pennsylvania, July 3, 1863. Wounded at Wilderness, Virginia, May 5, 1864, and died in hospital at Staunton, Virginia, May 25, 1864, of wounds.

REEVES, JAMES B., Private

Resided in Johnston County and enlisted in Wake County at age 34, July 15, 1862, for the war. Left in hospital at Richmond, Virginia, August 10, 1862, and furloughed for 20 days. Remained absent until brought back to the regiment under guard on December 11, 1863. Captured at Spotsylvania Court House, Virginia, May 12, 1864. Confined at Point Lookout, Maryland, until transferred to Elmira, New York, August 6, 1864. Released at Elmira after taking the Oath of Allegiance on June 27, 1865.

RIVENBARK, CHARLES W., Sergeant

Resided in New Hanover County where he enlisted at age 20, June 11, 1861, for the war. Mustered in as Private and appointed Sergeant April 1, 1862. Captured at Chancellorsville, Virginia, May 3, 1863, and paroled until exchanged at City Point, Virginia, May 10, 1863. Present or accounted for until captured at Gettysburg, Pennsylvania, July 3, 1863. Confined at Fort McHenry, Maryland, until transferred to Fort Delaware, Delaware, July 10, 1863. Federal Provost Marshal records indicate that he was released from Fort Delaware, May 28, 1865; however, he appears on a register of General Hospital No. 9, Richmond, Virginia, which indicates that he was admitted March 2, 1865, and transferred to Camp Lee, near Richmond, March 3, 1865. Reported on hospital register with the remark: "P. P."

RIVENBARK, JOHN W., Private

Born in New Hanover County where he resided as a mechanic and enlisted at age 27, June 11, 1861, for the war. Wounded in action at Malvern Hill, Virginia, July 1, 1862, and died of wounds on July 19, 1862.

ROBINSON, EVAN L., Corporal

Resided in New Hanover County where he enlisted at age 18, June 11, 1861, for the war. Mustered in as Private. Wounded in the forehead at Fredericksburg, Virginia, December 13, 1862. Appointed Corporal April 1, 1864. Captured at Spotsylvania Court House, Virginia, May 12, 1864. Confined at Point Lookout, Maryland, until paroled and sent to Boulware's Wharf, James River, Virginia, February 18, 1865. Reported as present on a muster roll of a detachment of paroled and exchanged prisoners at Camp Lee, near Richmond, Virginia, dated February 23, 1865.

ROBINSON, JAMES M., Private

Resided in New Hanover County where he enlisted at age 38, June 11, 1861, for the war. Wounded in action at Ellerson's Mill, Virginia, June 26, 1862. Furloughed from hospital at Richmond, Virginia, July 18, 1862, for 60 days. Reported as absent wounded through February, 1863. Present or accounted for on company muster rolls through December, 1864. Wounded and captured at Harper's Farm, Virginia, April 6, 1865. Confined at West's Buildings U.S. Army General Hospital, Baltimore, Maryland, until transferred to Fort McHenry, Maryland, May 9, 1865. Released after taking the Oath of Allegiance on June 10, 1865.

ROBITZSCH, JOHN E., Private

Born in New Hanover County where he resided as a farmer and enlisted at age 30, May 15, 1862, for the war. Wounded in action at Ellerson's Mill, Virginia, June 26, 1862. Furloughed from hospital at Richmond, Virginia, July 10, 1862, for 30 days. Reported as absent wounded until discharged from the service on February 7, 1863, by reason of "an obscure injury caused by a gunshot wound of the neck by which the functions of the right arm are impeded."

ROBITZSCH, RICHARD F., Sergeant

Resided in New Hanover County where he enlisted at age 22, June 11, 1861, for the war. Mustered in as Sergeant. Wounded in the left knee at Ellerson's Mill, Virginia, June 26, 1862, and died of wounds in hospital at Richmond, Virginia, July 12, 1862.

ROBITZSCH, ROBERT B., Private

Resided in New Hanover County where he enlisted at age 21, June 11, 1861, for the war. Killed in action at Cold Harbor, Virginia, June 27, 1862.

SAVAGE, GEORGE W., Private

Resided in New Hanover County where he en-

listed at age 25, June 11, 1861, for the war. Reported as absent on detail from November, 1861, through February, 1863, and present from March, 1863, until detailed on the Virginia Central Railroad on August 19, 1863. Reported on company muster rolls as absent on detail through December, 1864.

SELLERS, DAVID, Private

Born in Sampson County and resided as a farmer in New Hanover County prior to enlisting at Camp Bee, Virginia, at age 28, June 11, 1861, for the war. Discharged from the service August 31, 1861, on Surgeon's Certificate of Disability.

SIKES, CHATHAM D., Private

Born in New Hanover County where he resided as a farmer and enlisted at age 25, July 11, 1862, for the war. Discharged from the service December 28, 1861, by reason of "disability on account of stricture."

SIKES, COLUMBUS F., Private

Born in New Hanover County where he resided as a farmer and enlisted at age 18, June 11, 1861, for the war. Discharged from the service May 15, 1862, by reason of disability.

SMITH, ISAAC W., Private

Resided in Johnston County and enlisted in Wake County at age 23, July 15, 1862, for the war. Admitted to hospital at Richmond, Virginia, August 23, 1862, with "fever." Furloughed from the hospital in Richmond and died on the way home in hospital at Raleigh on October 1, 1862.

SMITH, JOHN, Private

Resided in New Hanover County where he enlisted at age 26, June 11, 1861, for the war. Present or accounted for until captured at Spotsylvania Court House, Virginia, May 12, 1864. Confined at Point Lookout, Maryland, until transferred to Aiken's Landing, Virginia, March 18, 1865, for exchange. Received in exchange March 15, 1865, and admitted to hospital at Richmond, Virginia. Transferred to Camp Lee, near Richmond, March 19, 1865.

SMITH, SPIVAS SHEARD, Private

Resided in Sampson County and enlisted in New Hanover County at age 19, June 11, 1861, for the war. Captured at Gettysburg, Pennsylvania, July 3, 1863. Confined at Fort Delaware, Delaware, until transferred to Point Lookout, Maryland, October 18, 1863. Paroled at Point Lookout and transferred to Boulware's Wharf, James River, Virginia, February 18, 1865. Reported as present on a muster roll of a detachment of paroled and exchanged prisoners at Camp Lee, near Richmond, Virginia, dated February 23, 1865.

SMITH, WILLIAM E., Private

Born in Cumberland County and resided as a farmer in New Hanover County where he enlisted at age 33, June 11, 1861, for the war. Discharged May 15, 1862, on Surgeon's Certificate of Disability.

SOMERS, WILLIAM D., Private

Resided in New Hanover County where he enlisted at age 29, June 11, 1861, for the war. Transferred to the Medical Department upon appointment as Assistant Surgeon, September 13, 1861.

STANLEY, SAMUEL J., Private
Born in New Hanover County where he resided as a painter and enlisted at age 24, June 11, 1861, for the war. Discharged December 21, 1861, on Surgeon's Certificate of Disability. Reenlisted in this company in New Hanover County on March 10, 1862, for the war. Wounded in action at Malvern Hill, Virginia, July 1, 1862. Captured at Gettysburg, Pennsylvania, July 3, 1863. Confined at Fort Delaware, Delaware, until transferred to Point Lookout, Maryland, October 18, 1863. Released from Point Lookout after taking the Oath of Allegiance January 21-31, 1864, and joining the U.S. service. Assigned to Company E, 1st Regiment U.S. Volunteer Infantry.

STARLING, ISAAC, Private
Resided in Sampson County where he enlisted at age 48, February 20, 1862, for the war. Present or accounted for on company muster rolls through December, 1864. Detailed for hospital duty February 16, 1865, and ordered to report to the commanding officer at Richmond, Virginia.

STARLING, JAMES A., Private
Born in Johnston County where he resided as a farmer and enlisted at age 18, July 15, 1862, for the war. Discharged September 3, 1862, by reason of "phthisis pulmonalis."

STUCKEY, J. C., Private
Resided in New Hanover County where he enlisted at age 23, February 14, 1862, for the war. Present or accounted for until captured at Spotsylvania Court House, Virginia, May 12, 1864. Confined at Point Lookout, Maryland, until transferred to Elmira, New York, August 6, 1864. Paroled at Elmira on October 11, 1864, and sent with a group of invalid prisoners to Point Lookout, Maryland, for exchange. Exchanged at Point Lookout on October 29, 1864. Company muster roll for November-December, 1864, states that he was "absent at home—lately exchanged." Captured at Petersburg, Virginia, April 2, 1865, and confined at Hart's Island, New York Harbor, until released after taking the Oath of Allegiance on June 17, 1865.

STUCKY, WILLIAM J., Private
Resided in New Hanover County where he enlisted at age 25, June 11, 1861, for the war. Died at Fredericksburg, Virginia, October 25, 1861, of disease.

TAYLOR, JOHN, Private
Resided in New Hanover County where he enlisted at age 22, June 11, 1861, for the war. Discharged November 21, 1861.

THOMPSON, D., Private
Captured at New Market, Virginia, September 24, 1864, and confined at Point Lookout, Maryland, until paroled and sent to Boulware's Wharf, James River, Virginia, February 18, 1865, for exchange. Received in exchange February 20-21, 1865.

THOMPSON, E. Y., Private
Resided in Johnston County and enlisted in Wake County at age 22, July 15, 1862, for the war. Killed in action at Sharpsburg, Maryland, September 17, 1862.

THOMPSON, F., Private
Paroled at Greensboro on May 3, 1865.

THOMPSON, J. R., Private
Resided in Johnston County and enlisted in Wake County at age 34, July 15, 1862, for the war. Wounded in action at Sharpsburg, Maryland, September 17, 1862, and reported as absent wounded through February 25, 1864. Reported as absent without leave after that date.

THOMPSON, J. W., Private
Resided in Johnston County and enlisted in Wake County at age 20, July 15, 1862, for the war. Captured at Boonsboro, Maryland, September 15, 1862, and confined at Fort Delaware, Delaware, until sent to Aiken's Landing, Virginia, for exchange on October 2, 1862. Declared exchanged on November 10, 1862. Present or accounted for until killed in action at Chancellorsville, Virginia, May 3, 1863.

WAGSTAFF, JOHN W., Private
Resided in New Hanover County where he enlisted at age 31, June 11, 1861, for the war. Present or accounted for until wounded in action at Payne's Farm, Virginia, November 27, 1863. Absent wounded until detailed to Wilmington and Weldon Railroad on April 16, 1864. Reported as absent on detail through October, 1864. Reported as present on November-December, 1864, muster roll. Paroled at Appomattox Court House, Virginia, April 9, 1865, and at Greensboro on May 2, 1865.

WALKER, EDWARD DeCOIN, Jr., Sergeant
Born in New Hanover County where he resided as a farmer and enlisted at age 33, June 11, 1861, for the war. Mustered in as Corporal and promoted to Sergeant on April 1, 1862. Present or accounted for until discharged on March 17, 1863, by reason of "furnishing R. A. Padgett as a substitute."

WALKER, JOHN W., Private
Resided in New Hanover County where he enlisted at age 23, June 11, 1861, for the war. Wounded in action at Malvern Hill, Virginia, July 1, 1862, and died of wounds July 25, 1862.

WALKER, JOSEPH M., Corporal
Resided in New Hanover County where he enlisted at age 25, June 11, 1861, for the war. Mustered in as Corporal. Killed in action at Cold Harbor, Virginia, June 27, 1862.

WALKER, SAMUEL J., Private
Born in New Hanover County where he resided as a farmer and enlisted in Prince William County, Virginia, at age 18, August 30, 1861, for the war. Discharged August 30, 1861, by reason of disability.

WALKER, WASHINGTON H., Private
Resided in New Hanover County where he enlisted at age 24, June 11, 1861, for the war. Killed in action at Sharpsburg, Maryland, September 17, 1862.

WALL, M. T., Private

Born in Johnston County where he resided as a farmer prior to enlisting in Wake County at age 31, July 15, 1862, for the war. Captured at Boonsboro, Maryland, September 16, 1862, and confined at Fort Delaware, Delaware, until sent to Aiken's Landing, Virginia, October 2, 1862, for exchange. Declared exchanged November 10, 1862. Present or accounted for until wounded in action at Wilderness, Virginia, May 5, 1864. Certificate of disability for retiring an invalid soldier was filed in his case February 18, 1865, stating that the wound caused contraction of the flexors of the right leg.

WHITE, JOHN W., Private

Resided in New Hanover County where he enlisted at age 18, June 11, 1861, for the war. Killed in action at Cold Harbor, Virginia, June 27, 1862.

WHITLEY, B. T., Private

Born in Johnston County where he resided as a farmer and enlisted at age 26, July 15, 1862, for the war. Discharged September 3, 1862, by reason of "pulmonary phthisis."

WHITLEY, H. H., Private

Resided in Johnston County and enlisted in Wake County at age 32, July 15, 1862, for the war. Wounded in action at Payne's Farm, Virginia, November 27, 1863. Present or accounted for until paroled at Appomattox Court House, Virginia, April 9, 1865.

WHITLEY, REUBEN W., Private

Resided in Johnston County and enlisted in Wake County at age 19, July 15, 1862, for the war. Wounded in action at Chancellorsville, Virginia, May 3, 1863. Wounded and captured at Strausburg, Virginia, October 19, 1864. Confined in hospital at Baltimore, Maryland, until transferred to Fort McHenry, Maryland, November 19, 1864. Transferred to Point Lookout, Maryland, January 1-2, 1865. Released at Point Lookout after taking the Oath of Allegiance on June 21, 1865.

WIGGS, WILEY P., Private

Resided in Johnston County and enlisted in Wake County at age 34, July 15, 1862, for the war. Killed in action at Chancellorsville, Virginia, May 3, 1863.

WILLIAMS, THOMAS H., Private

Resided in New Hanover County where he enlisted at age 18, June 11, 1861, for the war. Died in hospital at Lynchburg, Virginia, June 8, 1863, of "gastritis."

WILLIAMSON, S. A., Private

Born in Sampson County where he resided as a farmer and enlisted at age 25, February 1, 1862, for the war. Wounded in action in Malvern Hill, Virginia, July 1, 1862. Discharged February 23, 1863, by reason of "paralysis of the right arm caused by gunshot wound in the axilla."

WILSON, JOHN J., Private

Born in New Hanover County where he resided as a farmer and enlisted at age 31, June 11, 1861, for the war. Discharged October 28, 1861, by reason of Surgeon's Certificate of Disability.

WISTMAN, C. D., Private

Paroled at Greensboro on May 6, 1865.

WOOD, ALFRED J., Private

Resided in New Hanover County where he enlisted at age 22, June 11, 1861, for the war. Left sick at Rapidan Station, Virginia, August 28, 1862, and admitted to hospital at Richmond, Virginia, August 3, 1862, with "rheumatism." Furloughed November 1, 1862, for 60 days. Died at home while on furlough. Date of death reported on company muster roll for January-February, 1863, as January, 1863. Roll of Honor gives date of death as November, 1863.

COMPANY D

This company was composed of men from Lincoln and Orange counties. Those from Lincoln County enlisted at Lincolnton beginning June 18, 1861, and the men from Orange County began enlisting on July 2, 1861. By the end of July the two groups were at Warrenton, Warren County, where the regiment had been organized on June 3, 1861. There the company was mustered in as Company D of this regiment. The company remained behind when the regiment was ordered to Virginia on July 22, 1861, and after completing its organization was ordered to join the regiment. It did so at Camp Bee, Brooke's Station, Virginia, August 30, 1861. After that date the company functioned as a part of the regiment, and its history for the war period is recorded as a part of the regimental history.

The information contained in the following roster of the company was compiled principally from company muster rolls for June 30 through August 31, 1861; November through December, 1861; March through April, 1862; and June 30, 1862, through December, 1864. No company muster rolls were found for the period prior to June 30, 1861, for September through October, 1861; January through February, 1862; May through June 29, 1862; or for the period after December, 1864. In addition to the company muster rolls, Roll of Honor records, receipt rolls, hospital records, prisoner of war records, and other primary records, supplemented by state pension applications, United Daughters of the Confederacy records, and postwar rosters and histories, all provided useful information.

OFFICERS

CAPTAINS

SCOTT, EDWARD M.

Previously served in a volunteer company which later became Company G, 22nd Regiment N.C. Troops (12th Regiment N.C. Volunteers). Appointed Captain of this company at age 31 to rank from May 16, 1861. Present or accounted for as absent sick until discharged on June 11, 1863, by reason of disability. Died at Hillsboro in 1863.

WILLIAMSON, JOHN WILLIAM

Transferred from the Field and Staff of the 13th Regiment N.C. Troops (3rd Regiment N.C. Volunteers) upon appointment as 1st Lieutenant in this company to rank from April 30, 1863. Appointed Captain to rank from June 11, 1863. Admitted to hospital at Danville, Virginia, May 18, 1864, with a gunshot wound of the breast and returned to duty July 17, 1864. Present or accounted for on company muster ·rolls from date of transfer through December, 1864.

LIEUTENANTS

CHEEK, ADOLPHUS W., 2nd Lieutenant

Resided in Orange County and appointed 2nd Lieutenant to rank from May 16, 1861. Resigned October 31, 1861, on Surgeon's Certificate of Disability.

FORCE, CHARLES F., 1st Lieutenant

Appointed 2nd Lieutenant to rank from February 21, 1862, but he declined the appointment. Appointed 1st Lieutenant to rank from September 19, 1862, and declined the appointment.

GRADY, PATRICK HENRY, 3rd Lieutenant

Resided in Virginia and served as drillmaster of this company from May 25, 1861, to August 23, 1861, while a cadet at the Virginia Military Institute. Appointed 3rd Lieutenant to rank from August 23, 1861. Killed in action at Ellerson's Mill, Virginia, June 26, 1862.

HOUSER, ABSALOM JOSEPHUS, 2nd Lieutenant

Previously served in Company K, 1st Regiment N.C. Infantry (6 months, 1861). Enlisted in this company in Lincoln County at age 20, March 9, 1862, for the war. Mustered in as Sergeant and reduced to ranks October 1, 1862. Promoted to 1st Sergeant December 13, 1862. Wounded in the left hand at Chancellorsville, Virginia, May 3, 1863. Admitted to hospital at Richmond, Virginia, May 6, 1863, and returned to duty July 29, 1863. Promoted to 2nd Lieutenant to rank from October 5, 1863. Captured at Spotsylvania Court House, Virginia, May 10, 1864. Confined at Fort Delaware, Delaware, until transferred to Hilton Head, South Carolina, August 20, 1864. Transferred from Hilton Head to Fort Pulaski, Georgia; then back to Hilton Head; and then back to Fort Delaware on March 12, 1865. Released at Fort Delaware after taking the Oath of Allegiance on June 16, 1865.

HOWARD, WILLIAM M., 1st Lieutenant

Transferred from the Field and Staff of the 13th Regiment N.C. Troops (3rd Regiment N.C. Volunteers) upon appointment as 1st Lieutenant to rank from October 5, 1863. Killed in action at Wilderness, Virginia, May 5, 1864.

LACK, JOHN PIERRE, 3rd Lieutenant

Resided in Orange County where he enlisted at age 25, July 15, 1861, for the war. Mustered in as 1st Sergeant. Appointed 3rd Lieutenant to rank from September 24, 1862, for gallant conduct at the battle of Sharpsburg, Maryland, September 17, 1862. Mortally wounded at Chancellorsville, Virginia, May 3, 1863, and died of wounds May 10, 1863.

SCOTT, JAMES G., 2nd Lieutenant

Resided in Granville County and appointed 2nd Lieutenant to rank from September 19, 1862. Reported on all rolls as absent sick from date of commission until he resigned September 15, 1863. Letter of endorsement requesting the acceptance of Scott's resignation written by Lieutenant Colonel Brown of this regiment states that before Scott "was commissioned he was permanently disabled by a fall from a horse."

STOKES, DAVID E., 2nd Lieutenant

Transferred from Company K of this regiment upon appointment as 2nd Lieutenant to rank from March 18, 1862. Died on June 26, 1862, of wounds received in battle of Ellerson's Mill, Virginia, on that date.

SUMNER, EDWARD E., 1st Lieutenant

Transferred from Company K, 1st Regiment N.C. Infantry (6 months, 1861) upon appointment as 1st Lieutenant on June 1, 1861, to rank from May 16, 1861. Present or accounted for until he was discharged on August 2, 1862, by reason of "chronic ulceration of the throat; the extent to which it deprives him of the articulation of his voice."

NONCOMMISSIONED OFFICERS AND PRIVATES

ADAMS, THOMAS, Private

Resided in Orange County and enlisted in Guilford County at age 33, June 28, 1861, for the war. Detailed as Sergeant of the Brigade Guard November-December, 1861, through March-April, 1862. Killed in action at Ellerson's Mill, Virginia, June 26, 1862.

ANDERSON, N. F., Private

Issued clothing November 4, 1864.

ANTHONY, JOHN A., Private

Resided in Lincoln County where he enlisted on May 2, 1862, for the war. Captured at Spotsylvania Court House, Virginia, May 12, 1864. Confined at Elmira, New York, where he died October 26, 1864, of "typhoid fever."

BAKER, ———, Private

Resided in Franklin County and was conscripted at age 20, July 15, 1862, for the war. Died near Richmond, Virginia, August, 1862, of disease.

BAKER, VARDREY E., Corporal

Resided in Lincoln County where he enlisted at age 19, June 18, 1861, for the war. Mustered in as Private. Wounded in action at Sharpsburg, Maryland, September 17, 1862, and at Chancellorsville, Virginia, May 3, 1863. Appointed Corporal October 31, 1863. Captured at Spotsylvania Court House, Virginia, May 12, 1864. Confined at Elmira, New York, until released after taking the Oath of Allegiance on June 19, 1865.

BALDWIN, JOHN W., Private

Resided in Wake County where he enlisted at age 27, August 25, 1861, for the war. Reported as present on company muster rolls through December, 1861. Buried in Hollywood Cemetery, Richmond, Virginia, July 21, 1862.

BARNETT, JOSIAH M., Private

Resided in Wilkes County and enlisted in Warren County at age 18, July 24, 1861, for the war. Transferred to Company B of this regiment on November 1, 1861.

BARTON, WESLEY, Private

Resided in Orange County where he enlisted at age 32, August 1, 1861, for the war. Died in hospital at Fredericksburg, Virginia, in December, 1861.

BEAM, GEORGE W., Sergeant

Resided in Guilford County and enlisted in Lincoln County at age 23, July 8, 1861, for the war. Mustered in as Sergeant. Discharged November 25, 1861.

BLAKE, JAMES S., Private

Born in Orange County where he resided as a carpenter and enlisted at age 23, February 26, 1862, for the war. Present or accounted for until captured at Gettysburg, Pennsylvania, July 3, 1863. Confined at Fort Delaware, Delaware, where he joined the U.S. service and was enlisted into Company G, 1st Regiment Connecticut Cavalry on October 1, 1863.

BOGGS, LEWIS, Private

Resided in Orange County where he enlisted at age 20, July 2, 1861, for the war. Present or accounted for on company muster rolls through December, 1864.

BOGGS, STANFORD, Private

Enlisted in Orange County at age 50, March 3, 1862, for the war. Died at Richmond, Virginia, August 10, 1862, of disease.

BORLAND, ANDREW J., Private

Resided in Orange County where he enlisted at age 32, July 25, 1861, for the war. Died near Richmond, Virginia, July, 1862, of disease.

BOSWELL, JOHN A., Private

Transferred from Mallett's Battalion N.C. Troops (Camp Holmes Guard) June 12, 1864. Wounded at Winchester, Virginia, September 19, 1864, and captured at Harrisonburg, Virginia, September 25, 1864. Confined at Point Lookout, Maryland, until paroled and exchanged October 31, 1864. Present or accounted for until paroled at Appomattox Court House, Virginia, April 9, 1865.

BOYLES, MARCUS W., Private

Resided in Lincoln County where he enlisted at age 18, July 12, 1861, for the war. Detailed in hospital at Fredericksburg, Virginia, October 31, 1861. Reported as absent detailed as a nurse in hospitals at Fredericksburg and Richmond, Virginia, through October, 1863. Ordered back to his company October 17, 1863. Present or accounted for until captured at Farmville, Virginia, April 6, 1865. Confined at Point Lookout, Maryland, until released after taking the Oath of Allegiance on June 23, 1865.

BRAGG, J. S., Private

Captured at Gettysburg, Pennsylvania, July 3, 1863, and confined at Fort Delaware, Delaware, until transferred to Point Lookout, Maryland, October 18, 1863. Register at Point Lookout indi-

cates that he "joined U.S. service January 29, 1864." Unit to which he was assigned in the U.S. service not reported.

BREWER, STEPHEN W., Private

Resided in Orange County where he enlisted at age 22, February 25, 1862, for the war. Captured at South Mountain, Maryland, September 15, 1862, and confined at Fort Delaware, Delaware, until transferred to Aiken's Landing, Virginia, October 2, 1862. Declared exchanged November 10, 1862. Deserted from hospital in Richmond, Virginia, December 27, 1862, and reported as absent without leave on company muster rolls. Admitted to hospital at Charlottesville, Virginia, July 27, 1863, with "debilitas." Transferred to Lynchburg, Virginia, the next day. January-February, 1864, muster roll reports him as: "absent without leave since June 1, 1863. Arrested and sent to Raleigh, North Carolina." Reported as absent without leave on company muster rolls through December, 1864.

BRIMAR, WILLIAM, Private

Resided in Lincoln County where he enlisted at age 33, July 6, 1861, for the war. Present or accounted for until reported as "absent without leave since October 13, 1864" on November-December, 1864, muster roll.

BROWN, CHRISTOPHER J., Private

Resided in Lincoln County where he enlisted at age 26, July 6, 1861, for the war. Captured and paroled near Keedysville, Maryland, September 20, 1862. Paroled a second time at Winchester, Virginia, October 4, 1862. Present or accounted for until captured at Spotsylvania Court House, Virginia, May 12, 1864. Confined at Point Lookout, Maryland, May 18, 1864, and transferred to Elmira, New York, August 3, 1864. Released at Elmira after taking the Oath of Allegiance on June 30, 1865.

BROWN, DANIEL, Private

Resided in Orange County where he enlisted at age 46, February 25, 1862, for the war. Killed in action at Ellerson's Mill, Virginia, June 26, 1862.

BROWN, JAMES M., Private

Resided in Orange County where he enlisted on February 23, 1862, for the war. Captured at South Mountain, Maryland, September 15, 1862, and confined at Fort Delaware, Delaware, until transferred to Aiken's Landing, Virginia, October 2, 1862. Declared exchanged on November 10, 1862. Sent to hospital and deserted from hospital in May, 1863. Returned from desertion September 30, 1863. Wounded in action at Mine Run, Virginia, November 27-December 5, 1863. Admitted to hospital at Richmond, Virginia, with a gunshot wound of the hand on May 8, 1864. Date he was wounded not reported. Present or accounted for on company muster rolls through December, 1864.

BROWN, JOHN M., Private

Resided in Gaston County and enlisted in Lincoln County at age 16, March 15, 1862, for the war. Discharged at Richmond, Virginia, September 9, 1862, by reason of disability.

BROWN, ROBERT F., Private
Resided in Lincoln County where he enlisted at age 32, January 26, 1862, for the war. Present or accounted for until captured at Spotsylvania Court House, Virginia, May 12, 1864. Confined at Point Lookout, Maryland, May 18, 1864, and transferred to Elmira, New York, August 3, 1864. Paroled at Elmira on October 11, 1864, and exchanged at Venus Point, Savannah River, Georgia, November 15, 1864. Issued clothing November 18, 1864.

BUTLER, WILLIAM F., Private
Transferred from Mallett's Battalion N.C. Troops (Camp Holmes Guard) June 12, 1864. Present or accounted for until paroled at Appomattox Court House, Virginia, April 9, 1865.

CALHOUN, JAMES N., 1st Sergeant
Resided in Guilford County and enlisted in Warren County July 13, 1861, for the war. Mustered in as Corporal. Wounded in the head at Sharpsburg, Maryland, September 17, 1862. Promoted to Sergeant September 24, 1862. Wounded in the arm at Wilderness, Virginia, May 5, 1864. Absent wounded until retired to the Invalid Corps on January 5, 1865, and detailed in hospital at Danville, Virginia. Muster rolls report him as Sergeant through October, 1864, and as 1st Sergeant on November-December, 1864, muster roll.

CALHOUN, WILLIAM A., Private
Resided in Guilford County where he enlisted at age 22, July 6, 1861, for the war. Detailed as an ambulance driver on December 27, 1863. Reported as absent on detail until paroled at Greensboro on May 4, 1865.

CANADAY, A. L., Private
Transferred from Mallett's Battalion N.C. Troops (Camp Holmes Guard) June 12, 1864. Present or accounted for until paroled at Appomattox Court House, Virginia, April 9, 1865.

CARPENTER, ELIJAH, Private
Resided in Lincoln County and enlisted in Gaston County at age 22, June 11, 1861, for the war. Killed in action at Sharpsburg, Maryland, September 17, 1862.

CARPENTER, JONAS, Private
Resided in Gaston County and enlisted in Lincoln County at age 29, March 15, 1862, for the war. Captured at Middletown, Maryland, September 18, 1862, and confined at Fort Delaware, Delaware, until paroled and exchanged at Aiken's Landing, Virginia, November 10, 1862. Present or accounted for until captured at Spotsylvania Court House, Virginia, May 12, 1864. Confined at Elmira, New York, where he died October 18, 1864, of "typhoid fever."

CARPENTER, MONROE, Private
Enlisted in Gaston County at age 21, March 15, 1862, for the war. Captured at Gettysburg, Pennsylvania, July 3, 1863, and confined at Point Lookout, Maryland. Died at Point Lookout on February 21, 1865, of "chronic dysentery."

CARROLL, MOSES, Private
Born in Orange County where he resided as a farmer and enlisted at age 37, July 29, 1861, for the war. Discharged September 2, 1862, by reason of disability. Died in hospital at Hugenot Springs, Virginia, September 17, 1862, of "chronic diarrhoea."

CARROLL, S. F., Private
Admitted to hospital at Richmond, Virginia, July 22, 1863, and transferred. Admitted to hospital at Charlottesville, Virginia, March 13, 1864, with "amputated thigh" and furloughed April 17, 1864, for 60 days.

CARROLL, STEPHEN L., Private
Enlisted in Orange County on February 22, 1862, for the war. Killed in action at Ellerson's Mill, Virginia, June 26, 1862.

CARROLL, WILLIAM, Private
Resided in Orange County where he enlisted at age 29, July 25, 1861, for the war. Detailed as a nurse in Smallpox Hospital at Guinea Station, Virginia, March-April, 1863. Absent on detail through August, 1864. Present or accounted for on company muster rolls through December, 1864.

CATES, HENRY F., Private
Resided in Orange County where he enlisted at age 20, February 24, 1862, for the war. Wounded in action at Mine Run, Virginia, November 27, 1863. Captured at Spotsylvania Court House, Virginia, May 12, 1864. Confined at Point Lookout, Maryland, until transferred to Elmira, New York, August 6, 1864. Released at Elmira after taking the Oath of Allegiance on June 27, 1865.

CATES, JAMES W., Private
Resided in Orange County where he enlisted at age 18, July 3, 1861, for the war. Killed in action at Winchester, Virginia, June 15, 1863.

CATES, THOMAS E., Private
Resided in Orange County where he enlisted at age 46, February 24, 1862, for the war. Wounded at Chancellorsville, Virginia, May 3, 1863, and died of wounds in hospital at Richmond, Virginia, May 19, 1863.

CHEEK, BURRUS, Private
Resided in Orange County where he enlisted at age 50, March 3, 1862, for the war. Detailed as a nurse in hospital at Gordonsville, Virginia, July 17, 1862, and reported as absent on detail through January, 1865.

CHEEK, JAMES, Private
Born in Orange County where he resided as a farmer and enlisted at age 20, March 3, 1862, for the war. Discharged September 2, 1862, by reason of his being "incapable of performing the duties of a soldier because of pulmonary phthisis in an early stage."

CHRISTMAS, CHARLES R., Corporal
Resided in Orange County where he enlisted at age 31, July 2, 1861, for the war. Mustered in as Corporal. Captured at Boonsboro, Maryland, September 15, 1862, and confined at Fort Delaware, Delaware, until paroled and exchanged at Aiken's Landing, Virginia, November 10, 1862. Killed in action at Winchester, Virginia, June 15, 1863.

CHURCHMAN, W. H., Private
Captured at Gettysburg, Pennsylvania, July 3, 1863, and confined at Fort Delaware, Delaware, until transferred to Point Lookout, Maryland, October 20, 186?.

CLARK, JOHN, Private
Issued clothing at Guinea Station, Virginia, in May, 1863.

CLARK, JOHN O., Private
Resided in Orange County where he enlisted at age 37, July 18, 1861, for the war. Wounded at Winchester, Virginia, June 15, 1863, and "permanently disabled." Reported as absent wounded on company muster rolls through December, 1864.

COATS, HENRY F., Private
Captured at Boonsboro, Maryland, September 15, 1862, and confined at Fort Delaware, Delaware, until transferred to Aiken's Landing, Virginia, October 2, 1862. Declared exchanged November 10, 1862. Wounded in the hand at Payne's Farm, Virginia, November 27, 1863.

COLE, MARTIN, Private
Resided in Orange County where he enlisted at age 24, February 27, 1862, for the war. Killed in action at Ellerson's Mill, Virginia, June 26, 1862.

COLE, VOETUS, Private
Resided in Orange County where he enlisted at age 24, February 22, 1862, for the war. Present or accounted for until captured at Spotsylvania Court House, Virginia, May 12, 1864. Confined at Point Lookout, Maryland, until transferred to Elmira, New York, August 6, 1864. Paroled at Elmira on October 11, 1864, and sent to Venus Point, Savannah River, Georgia, for exchange. Exact date of exchange not reported but he was issued clothing on November 17, 1864.

COTHRAN, LESLIE D., Private
Born in Person County and resided as a farmer in Orange County where he enlisted at age 35, 42, February 28, 1862, for the war. Discharged February 27, 1863, by reason of "palsy."

COTTON, JOHN A., Private
Resided in Orange County where he enlisted at age 19, August 1, 1861, for the war. Present or accounted for on company muster rolls through December, 1864.

CRABTREE, ASA, Private
Resided in Orange County where he enlisted at age 21, August 1, 1861, for the war. Deserted August 17, 1863, and returned to the company on September 29, 1863. Sentenced by court-martial on November 4, 1863, for desertion. Reported as absent in arrest through December, 1864. Admitted to hospital at Salisbury, February 16, 1865, with "debilitias" and returned to duty March 15, 1865. Paroled at Raleigh on May 10, 1865.

CRABTREE, GASTON, Private
Resided in Orange County and enlisted in Wayne County at age 30, May 15, 1862, for the war. Absent without leave from August 12, 1862, until returned to the company February 1, 1864. Captured at Spotsylvania Court House, Virginia,

May 12, 1864. Confined at Point Lookout, Maryland, until transferred to Elmira, New York, August 6, 1864. Died at Elmira on November 1, 1864, of "chronic diarrhoea."

CRABTREE, JOHN, Private
Resided in Orange County where he enlisted at age 39, August 1, 1861, for the war. Wounded in action at Winchester, Virginia, June 15, 1863. Reported as "permanently disabled" on muster rolls through December, 1864.

CRABTREE, LEONARD, Private
Resided in Orange County where he enlisted at age 30, February 1, 24, 1862, for the war. Reported as present on March-April, 1862, muster roll. Roll of Honor states that he was "discharged." Date of discharge not reported.

CRABTREE, MONROE, Private
Resided in Orange County where he enlisted at age 44, March 4, 1862, for the war. Present or accounted for until he was killed in action at Winchester, Virginia, September 19, 1864.

CRABTREE, RICHARD, Private
Resided in Orange County where he enlisted at age 18, March 3, 1862, for the war. Present or accounted for until paroled at Appomattox Court House, Virginia, April 9, 1865.

CRABTREE, THOMAS, Private
Resided in Orange County where he enlisted at age 38, March 1, 1862, for the war. Captured at Spotsylvania Court House, Virginia, May 12, 1864, and confined at Point Lookout, Maryland, until transferred to Elmira, New York, August 6, 1864. Released from Elmira after taking the Oath of Allegiance on June 21, 1865.

CRABTREE, THOMAS H., Private
Resided in Orange County where he enlisted at age 24, June 27, 1861, for the war. Never mustered into the company and joined Company K, 19th Regiment N.C. Troops (2nd Regiment N.C. Cavalry).

CRABTREE, WILLIAM, Private
Resided in Orange County where he enlisted at age 27, February 20, 1862, for the war. Wounded in the hand at Fredericksburg, Virginia, December 13, 1862. Died in hospital at Richmond, Virginia, February 3, 1863, of "erysipelas."

CRABTREE, WILLIAM F., Private
Enlisted at Pisgah Church, Virginia, March 14, 1864, for the war. Captured at Spotsylvania Court House, Virginia, May 12, 1864, and confined at Point Lookout, Maryland, where he died August 16, 1864, of "acute dysentery."

DAVIS, A., Private
Transferred from hospital in Richmond, Virginia, to High Point, North Carolina, September 3, 1864.

DAVIS, ROBERT M., Private
Resided as a saddler in Gaston County prior to enlisting in Lincoln County at age 34, July 12, 1861, for the war. Deserted June 6, 1863, and returned to company October 26, 1863. Placed in confinement through December, 1863. Admitted to hospital at Danville, Virginia, June 17, 1864, with a gunshot wound of the left hand

and transferred on June 21, 1864. Deserted at Fisher's Hill, Virginia, September 25, 1864, and took the Oath of Allegiance at New Creek, West Virginia, in October, 1864.

DAVIS, WILEY, Private

Resided in Orange County where he enlisted at age 38, July 29, 1861, for the war. Deserted August 17, 1863, and returned to company October 24, 1863, and confined in guardhouse through December, 1863. Captured at Spotsylvania Court House, Virginia, May 12, 1864, and confined at Point Lookout, Maryland, until transferred to Elmira, New York, August 6, 1864. Released after taking the Oath of Allegiance at Elmira on June 30, 1865.

DORITY, SAMUEL, Private

Resided in Orange County where he enlisted at age 32, July 17, 1861, for the war. Muster roll for June 30-August 31, 1861, carries him as absent "sick at Camp Macon." Roll of Honor states that he was "discharged for disability." Date of discharge not reported.

DUNN, JARRETT T., Private

Resided in Orange County where he enlisted at age 29, July 4, 1861, for the war. Present or accounted for until he died in hospital at Mount Jackson, Virginia, September 24, 1864, of "gunshot wound of abdomen."

EDMONDS, JOHN J., Musician

Born in Warren County where he resided as a laborer and enlisted at age 17, August 12, 1861, for the war. Mustered in as Musician and detailed to the regimental band until discharged October 25, 1861, by reason of disability.

EDWARDS, LEMMON G., Private

Resided in Franklin County and enlisted in Nash County at age 27, July 15, 1862, for the war. Wounded in action at Sharpsburg, Maryland, September 17, 1862, and died of wounds December 19, 1862.

EVANS, HINTON, Private

Resided in Wake County where he enlisted at age 34, August 24, 1861, for the war. Present or accounted for until captured at Spotsylvania Court House, Virginia, May 12, 1864. Confined at Point Lookout, Maryland, until transferred to Elmira, New York, August 6, 1864. Released at Elmira after taking the Oath of Allegiance on June 16, 1865.

EVANS, JEFFERSON G., 1st Sergeant

Resided in Guilford County and enlisted in Warren County at age 22, July 19, 1861, for the war. Mustered in as Corporal and appointed Sergeant March-April, 1862. Wounded at Sharpsburg, Maryland, September 17, 1862, and at Gettysburg, Pennsylvania, July 3, 1863. Captured at South Mountain, Maryland, July 4, 1863, and admitted to hospital at Frederick, Maryland, with a "compound fracture of the right elbow joint." Transferred to Baltimore, Maryland, September 23, 1863, and sent to City Point, Virginia, for exchange November 12, 1863. Received at City Point on November 17, 1863. Reported as 1st Sergeant on September-October, 1863, muster

roll and reported as such through December, 1864. Muster rolls also report him as absent at home on furlough through December, 1864. Paroled at Greensboro on May 16, 1865.

EVANS, JOHN S., Private

Resided in Orange County where he enlisted at age 31, February 28, 1862, for the war as a substitute. Killed in action at Sharpsburg, Maryland, September 17, 1862.

FINCANNON, JAMES M., Private

Resided in Lenoir County where he enlisted at age 23, March 12, 1862, for the war. Wounded in battle at Sharpsburg, Maryland, September 17, 1862. Captured near Washington, D.C., July 12, 1864, and confined at Old Capitol Prison, Washington, D.C. Transferred to Elmira, New York, July 25, 1864. Released after taking the Oath of Allegiance at Elmira on May 29, 1865.

FORREST, WILLIAM, Private

Resided in Orange County where he enlisted at age 21, March 26, 1862, for the war. Died in hospital at Wilmington on February 22, 1863, of "februs typhoides."

GIBSON, JOHN L., Private

Transferred from Mallett's Battalion N.C. Troops (Camp Holmes Guard) June 12, 1864. Reported on November-December, 1864, muster roll as "missing in action at Winchester, September 19, 1864."

GILLIAM, S., Private

Resided in Franklin County where he enlisted at age 24, July 15, 1862, for the war. Died in hospital August, 1862, of disease.

GREEN, JOSEPH, Private

Resided in Watauga County and deserted at Bellefield, Virginia, March 1, 1865. Took the Oath of Allegiance to the United States in Knoxville, Tennessee, April 17, 1865, and paroled April 28, 1865, at Louisville, Kentucky, to remain north of the Ohio River. Admitted to hospital at Louisville, July 3, 1865, with "diarrhoea" and discharged July 6, 1865.

GUESS, WILLIAM, Private

Resided in Orange County where he enlisted February 24, 1862, for the war. Died near Richmond, Virginia, September 21, 1862, of "diarrhoea acute."

HALL, ROBERT J., Corporal

Resided in Orange County where he enlisted at age 18, July 13, 1861, for the war. Mustered in as Private and appointed Corporal March-April, 1863. May-June, 1863, muster roll carries him with the remark: "Deserted June 28, 1863, in Pennsylvania."

HANCOCK, JOHN R., Private

Resided in Orange County where he enlisted at age 36, July 20, 1861, for the war. Mustered in as Private and appointed Corporal October 31, 1863. Wounded in action at Wilderness, Virginia, May 5, 1864, and reduced to ranks because of prolonged absence prior to August 31, 1864. Absent wounded through December, 1864.

HEFNER, MARTIN, Private
Born in Lincoln County where he resided as a farmer and enlisted at age 34, March 15, 1862, for the war. Discharged November 5, 1862, by reason of "permanent dislocation of the hip joint, the effect of a severe fall."

HENNESSEE, P. W., Private
Captured at Greencastle, Pennsylvania, July 3, 1863, and paroled at Fort Delaware, Delaware, July 20, 1863.

HERK, B. C., Private
Paroled April 25, 1865.

HERNDON, CAMERON, Private
Resided in Orange County where he enlisted at age 24, August 1, 1861, for the war. Discharged in November, 1861, by reason of disability.

HERNDON, HAYWOOD, Private
Resided in Orange County and enlisted in Guilford County at age 21, June 29, 1861, for the war. Died in hospital at Fredericksburg, Virginia, December 25, 1861.

HILDEBRAND, MARCUS, Private
Resided in Lincoln County where he enlisted at age 27, March 18, 1862, for the war. Died near Richmond, Virginia, August 8, 1862, of disease.

HINES, HENRY L., Private
Previously served in Company K, 1st Regiment N.C. Infantry (6 months, 1861). Enlisted in this company in Lincoln County on March 15, 1862, for the war. Wounded in the shoulder at Payne's Farm, Virginia, November 27, 1863. Captured at Spotsylvania Court House, Virginia, May 12, 1864, and confined at Point Lookout, Maryland, where he died August 5, 1864.

HOGAN, G. W., Private
Captured at Gettysburg, Pennsylvania, July 3, 1863, and confined at Fort Delaware, Delaware, July 7-12, 1863. Register at Fort Delaware carries him with the remark: "Dead."

HOKE, FRANK, Private
Resided in Lincoln County where he enlisted at age 27, March 14, 1862, for the war. Deserted June 6, 1863, and returned to company August-September, 1863. Transferred to Company A, 38th Regiment N.C. Troops on August 11, 1864.

HOLMES, JOHN J., Private
Resided in Franklin County where he enlisted at age 26, July 15, 1862, for the war. Captured at Spotsylvania Court House, Virginia, May 12, 1864, and confined at Point Lookout, Maryland. The records of parole and exchange were not found but his name appears on a muster roll of a detachment of paroled and exchanged prisoners at Camp Lee, near Richmond, Virginia, dated February 23, 1865, which carries him as present.

HOOD, WILEY R., Private
Appears on a list of rebel deserters received at Headquarters, Provost Marshal, 23rd Army Corps, during the month of April, 1865, with the remark that he was received at Raleigh on April 25, 1865.

HOPE, JOSEPH A., Private
Resided in Orange County and enlisted in Gaston County at age 20, June 11, 1861, for the war. Died in Richmond, Virginia, August 8, 1862, of disease. Date of death also given as August 5 and 6, 1862.

HOUPE, J. F., Private
Paroled at Salisbury on May 29, 1865.

HOUSER, CHARLES T. J., Sergeant
Resided in Orange County and enlisted in Lincoln County at age 16, August 4, 1861, for the war. Mustered in as Private and appointed Sergeant March-April, 1863, "for good conduct in every battle." Captured at Spotsylvania Court House, Virginia, May 12, 1864. Confined at Point Lookout, Maryland, until transferred to Elmira, New York, August 6, 1864. Released after taking the Oath of Allegiance at Elmira on June 21, 1865.

HOWARD, THOMAS P., Private
Born in Orange County where he resided as a farmer and enlisted at age 22, July 9, 1861, for the war. Discharged October 31, 1861, by reason of Surgeon's Certificate of Disability.

HUCKERTY, JOHN, Private
Captured at Gettysburg, Pennsylvania, July 3, 1863, and confined at Fort Delaware, Delaware, until transferred to Point Lookout, Maryland, October 18, 1863. Exchanged November 1, 1864, at Point Lookout.

HULL, ELIAS, Sergeant
Resided in Lincoln County where he enlisted at age 28, July 9, 1861, for the war. Mustered in as Private and appointed Corporal November-December, 1861. Promoted to Sergeant September 24, 1862. Captured near Fredericksburg, Virginia, May 3, 1863, and paroled and exchanged at City Point, Virginia, May 10, 1863. Captured at Gettysburg, Pennsylvania, July 3, 1863, and confined at Fort Delaware, Delaware, until transferred to Point Lookout, Maryland, October 18, 1863. Paroled at Point Lookout and sent to James River, Virginia, February 18, 1865, for exchange. Appears on a muster roll of a detachment of paroled and exchanged prisoners at Camp Lee, near Richmond, Virginia, dated February 23, 1865, as present.

HULL, HENRY, Private
Resided in Lincoln County where he enlisted at age 18, August 5, 1861, for the war. Deserted June 6, 1863, and returned to company September 30, 1863. Admitted to hospital at Richmond, Virginia, May 8, 1864, with "amputated little finger right hand." Admitted to hospital at Danville, Virginia, May 18, 1864, with a gunshot wound of the hand and transferred May 23, 1864. Company muster rolls carry him as "absent without leave" through December, 1864.

HULL, MILES O., Private
Resided in Lincoln County where he enlisted at age 26, March 5, 1862, for the war. Captured at Gettysburg, Pennsylvania, July 3, 1863, and confined at Fort Delaware, Delaware, until transferred to Point Lookout, Maryland, October 18, 1863. Paroled at Point Lookout and sent to Venus Point, Savannah River, Georgia, for exchange on October 30, 1864. Received in exchange at Venus Point on November 15, 1864.

HUNT, EDWIN, Private
Enlisted in Orange County on March 3, 1862, for the war. Died near Richmond, Virginia, August 8, 1862, of disease.

HUSKEY, GEORGE W., Private
Enlisted in Orange County at age 28, June 27, 1861, for the war. Present or accounted for until he died in hospital at Richmond, Virginia, September 7, 1862, of "fever cont."

JACKSON, WILLIAM L., Private
Born in Orange County where he resided as a farmer prior to enlisting at age 24, August 1, 1861, for the war. Discharged October 21, 1861, by reason of disability.

JAMES, B. M. W., Private
Appears on a muster roll of a detachment of paroled and exchanged prisoners at Camp Lee, near Richmond, Virginia, dated January 26, 1865, as present.

JOHNSON, GEORGE P., Private
Resided in Orange County where he enlisted at age 34, July 1, 1861, for the war. Transferred to Company B of this regiment on July 24, 1861.

JOHNSON, JOHN WESLEY, Private
Resided in Orange County where he enlisted at age 24, June 24, 1861, for the war. Discharged in November, 1861.

JOHNSON, JOHN WILLIAM, Private
Resided in Orange County where he enlisted at age 19, July 24, 1861, for the war. Present or accounted for until paroled at Appomattox Court House, Virginia, April 9, 1865.

JONAS, ANDREW, Corporal
Resided in Lincoln County where he enlisted at age 18, March 17, 1862, for the war. Mustered in as Private and appointed Corporal March 10, 1864. Captured at Spotsylvania Court House, Virginia, May 12, 1864. Confined at Point Lookout, Maryland, until transferred to Elmira, New York, August 6, 1864. Released at Elmira after taking the Oath of Allegiance on June 19, 1865.

JONAS, DANIEL, Private
Resided in Lincoln County where he enlisted at age 40, March 24, 1862, for the war. Present or accounted for until captured at Spotsylvania Court House, Virginia, May 12, 1864. Confined at Point Lookout, Maryland, until transferred to Elmira, New York, August 6, 1864. Died at Elmira on January 17, 1865, of "pneumonia."

JOYNER, ELIJAH J., Private
Resided in Edgecombe County and enlisted in Nash County at age 33, July 15, 1862, for the war. Present or accounted for until captured at Spotsylvania Court House, Virginia, May 12, 1864. Confined at Point Lookout, Maryland, until transferred to Elmira, New York, August 6, 1864. Paroled at Elmira and sent to Point Lookout, October 11, 1864. Exchanged on October 29, 1864.

JOYNER, JOHN S., Private
Resided in Nash County where he enlisted at age 30, July 15, 1862, for the war. Present or accounted for until captured at Gettysburg, Penn-

sylvania, July 3, 1863. Confined at Fort Delaware, Delaware, until transferred to Point Lookout, Maryland, October 18, 1863. Died in hospital at Point Lookout on December 6, 1863, of smallpox.

JOYNER, RIX, Private
Resided in Nash County where he enlisted at age 28, July 15, 1862, for the war. Wounded in action at Sharpsburg, Maryland, September 17, 1862. Reported as absent wounded through August, 1864, and as present on November-December, 1864, muster roll.

KEEVER, WILLIAM, Private
Resided in Lincoln County where he enlisted at age 18, June 3, 1861, for the war. Present or accounted for until captured at Gettysburg, Pennsylvania, July 3, 1863. Confined at Fort Delaware, Delaware, until released after taking the Oath of Allegiance on June 19, 1865.

KENIPE, JOSEPH, Private
Born in Lincoln County where he resided as a farmer and enlisted at age 40, August 5, 1861, for the war. Discharged January 14, 1862, by reason of disability.

KENIPE, LEMUEL, Private
Resided in Lincoln County where he enlisted at age 35, August 5, 1861, for the war. Captured and paroled near Keedysville, Maryland, September 20, 1862. Deserted November 10, 1862, and returned to company March 9, 1863. Deserted a second time June 6, 1863, and returned to company September 30, 1863. Wounded in action at Mine Run, Virginia, November 27-December 5, 1863. Wounded in the finger at Wilderness, Virginia, May 5, 1864, and reported as absent without leave on company muster rolls through December, 1864. Paroled at Athens, Georgia, on May 8, 1865.

KERN, JACOB, Private
Captured at Salisbury on April 12, 1865, and confined in hospital at Nashville, Tennessee, where he died May 9, 1865, of "typhoid fever."

KING, BENJAMIN F., Private
Born in Orange County where he resided as a farmer prior to enlisting in Warren County at age 14, August 12, 1861, for the war. Mustered in as Musician. Discharged December 28, 1863, by reason of "his being a minor, his guardian having applied for his discharge."

KING, SIDNEY, Private
Resided in Lincoln County and enlisted July 25, 1861, for the war.

KING, THOMAS L., Private
Born in Orange County where he resided as a carriage maker and enlisted at age 51, May 12, 1862, for the war as a substitute. Discharged October 22, 1862, by reason of "chronic rheumatism and age."

KING, WILLIAM, Private
Resided in Lincoln County and enlisted at age 19, July 25, 1861, for the war.

LEDFORD, RUFUS F., Private
Resided in Lincoln County where he enlisted at age 21, August 3, 1861, for the war. Present or

accounted for until captured at Spotsylvania Court House, Virginia, May 12, 1864. Confined at Point Lookout, Maryland, until transferred to Elmira, New York, August 6, 1864. Released at Elmira after taking the Oath of Allegiance on June 27, 1865.

LESTER, ANDREW W., Private
Resided in Nash County where he enlisted at age 35, July 15, 1862, for the war. Captured at Gettysburg, Pennsylvania, July 3, 1863, and confined at Fort Delaware, Delaware, until transferred to Point Lookout, Maryland, October 18, 1863. Paroled at Point Lookout and transferred to City Point, Virginia, March 16, 1864, for exchange. Received at City Point on March 20, 1864. Admitted to hospital at Richmond, Virginia, March 25, 1864.

LEWIS, H. D., Private
Captured at Sharpsburg, Maryland, October 12, 1862, and confined at Fort McHenry, Maryland, until paroled and sent to Fort Monroe, Virginia, for exchange on December 8, 1862. Received at City Point, Virginia, for exchange on December 10, 1862.

LONG, HENRY, Private
Resided in Orange County and enlisted in Gaston County at age 30, March 8, 1862, for the war. Wounded in action at Sharpsburg, Maryland, September 17, 1862, and died in hospital at Staunton, Virginia, October 5, 1862, of "febris typhoides."

LONG, JAMES, Private
Resided in Orange County where he enlisted at age 26, February 24, 1862, for the war. Deserted September 14, 1862.

McCALL, JAMES M., Private
Resided in Caldwell County and enlisted in Lenoir County at age 26, May 15, 1862, for the war. Wounded in the shoulder at Payne's Farm, Virginia, November 27, 1863. Captured at Spotsylvania Court House, Virginia, May 12, 1864. Confined at Point Lookout, Maryland, until transferred to Elmira, New York, August 6, 1864. Released at Elmira after taking the Oath of Allegiance on June 14, 1865.

McCALL, ROBERT F., Private
Born in Caldwell County where he resided as a farmer prior to enlisting in Lenoir County at age 30, February 24, 1862, for the war. Discharged on April 7, 1863, by reason of his being incapable of performing the duties of a soldier because of "phthisis pulmonalis."

McCALL, SAMUEL A., Corporal
Resided in Caldwell County and enlisted in Lenoir County at age 24, February 24, 1862, for the war. Mustered in as Private and appointed Corporal October 31, 1863. Wounded in action at Payne's Farm, Virginia, November 27, 1863. Admitted to hospital at Richmond, Virginia, with a gunshot wound of the left thigh and furloughed for 60 days January 26, 1864. Admitted to hospital at Raleigh on August 3, 1864, for treatment of the same wound and transferred upon

detail as shoemaker August 25, 1864. Paroled at Greensboro April 29, 1865.

McCAULEY, GEORGE, Private
Enlisted in Orange County on February 25, 1862, for the war. Admitted to hospital at Farmville, Virginia, May 6, 1863, with "disease of kidney" and furloughed for 30 days June 5, 1863. Company muster rolls carry him as absent without leave through December, 1864. Paroled at Greensboro on May 17, 1865.

McCESSON, J. C., Private
Captured at Gettysburg, Pennsylvania, July 5, 1863, and paroled at Fort Delaware, Delaware, July 30, 1863.

McCOY, GEORGE, Private
Resided in Orange County and enlisted at age 40, February 6, 1862, for the war.

MAINARD, B., Private
Captured at Bentonville, March 22, 1865, and confined at Hart's Island, New York Harbor, April 10, 1865. Released after taking the Oath of Allegiance on June 18, 1865.

MANN, THOMAS L., Private
Resided in Granville County and enlisted in Nash County at age 35, July 15, 1862, for the war. Wounded in the left wrist at Chancellorsville, Virginia, May 3, 1863. Wounded at Payne's Farm, Virginia, November 27, 1863. Captured at Spotsylvania Court House, Virginia, May 12, 1864. Confined at Point Lookout, Maryland, until paroled and transferred to Aiken's Landing, Virginia, September 18, 1864, for exchange. Present or accounted for until paroled at Appomattox Court House, Virginia, April 9, 1865. 1865.

MAY, JOHN WILLIAM, Private
Resided in Franklin County where he enlisted at age 26, July 15, 1862, for the war. Wounded and captured at Gettysburg, Pennsylvania, July 3, 1863. Confined at Fort Delaware, Delaware, until transferred to Point Lookout, Maryland, October 18, 1863. Paroled at Point Lookout, May 3, 1864, and sent to Aiken's Landing, Virginia, for exchange. Admitted to hospital at Richmond, Virginia, May 8, 1864, with "diarrhoea chronic" and furloughed for 30 days May 21, 1864. Present or accounted for until paroled at Appomattox Court House, Virginia, April 9, 1865.

MEADOWS, DUDLEY, Private
Born in Warren County where he resided as a farmer and enlisted at age 22, August 2, 1861, for the war. Transferred to Company K, 8th Regiment N.C. State Troops on the same day of enlistment.

MINNIS, ASHBURN, Private
Resided in Orange County where he enlisted at age 42, July 30, 1861, for the war. Present or accounted for until killed in action at Ellerson's Mill, Virginia, June 26, 1862.

MINTON, JOHN A., Private
Enlisted in Lenoir County on February 15, 1862, for the war. Reported as present on March-April, 1862, muster roll.

MULLINS, THOMAS F., Private
Resided in Lincoln County where he enlisted at age 18, August 5, 1861, for the war. Killed in action at Sharpsburg, Maryland, September 17, 1862.

MURRAY, JAMES D., Private
Resided in Franklin County where he enlisted at age 28, July 15, 1862, for the war. Captured at Gettysburg, Pennsylvania, July 3, 1863. Confined at Fort Delaware, Delaware, where he died January 22, 1864, of "inflammation of lungs."

MURRAY, JOSEPH J., Private
Resided in Franklin County where he enlisted at age 26, July 15, 1862, for the war. Reported as absent sick on August, 1862, through October, 1864, muster rolls and as present on November-December, 1864, muster roll.

NANCE, JAMES L., Private
Resided in Orange County and reported on the Roll of Honor as "discharged August, 1861."

NEILL, ANDREW H., Private
Resided in Orange County where he enlisted at age 25, March 3, 1862, for the war. Wounded in action at Sharpsburg, Maryland, September 17, 1862. Company muster rolls report him as present or absent sick due to wound through February, 1864, the last roll on which his name appears. Hospital records indicate that he was in and out of hospitals during that period suffering from "dyspepsia," "hemorrhage of lungs," "bilious fever," "erysipelas," and "debility." Appears on a register of effects of deceased soldiers which states that the receipt was filed in 1864 but does not give date, place, or cause of death.

NEILL, ARCHIBALD M., Private
Resided in Orange County where he enlisted at age 25, August 1, 1861, for the war. Wounded in action at Fredericksburg, Virginia, December 13, 1862. Reported as absent sick through February, 1863, and as present "in Brigade guardhouse" on March-April, 1863, muster roll. "Deserted June 28, 1863." There are no records after June, 1863, until he appears as being admitted to hospital at Greensboro on March 7, 1865, with "catarrhus."

NEILL, JOHN R., Private
Resided in Orange County where he enlisted at age 32, August 1, 1861, for the war. Discharged in August, 1861, but reported as "sick in Richmond" on March-April, 1862, muster roll. Claim for balance of pay due filed by his father. Date and place of death not given.

OWENS, B. H., Private
Paroled at Leesburg, Virginia, October 2, 1862.

PARDUE, ROBERT H., Private
Resided in Nash County and enlisted in Lincoln County at age 30, February 18, 1862, for the war. Wounded in action at Ellerson's Mill, Virginia, June 26, 1862, and died of wounds in hospital at Richmond, Virginia, September 4, 1862.

PAUL, DAVID C., Sergeant
Born in Orange County where he resided as a wagon maker and enlisted at age 19, July 20, 1861, for the war. Mustered in as Sergeant. Dis-

charged on October 29, 1861, by reason of "disability."

PAUL, WILLIAM C., Private
Resided in Orange County where he enlisted at age 18, July 20, 1861, for the war. Wounded in the abdomen and captured at Gettysburg, Pennsylvania, July 3, 1863. Died in hospital at Gettysburg on July 12, 1863.

PEARSON, JOHN M., Private
Resided in Orange County where he enlisted at age 23, July 17, 1861, for the war. Captured at Gettysburg, Pennsylvania, July 3, 1863, and confined at Fort Delaware, Delaware, until transferred to Point Lookout, Maryland, October 18, 1863. Paroled at Point Lookout and transferred to Aiken's Landing, Virginia, March 17, 1865, for exchange. Admitted to hospital at Richmond, Virginia, March 19, 1865. Captured in hospital at Richmond on April 3, 1865, and took the Oath of Allegiance at Richmond on June 26, 1865.

PENDLETON, JOHN, Private
Resided in Lincoln County where he enlisted at age 28, March 15, 1862, for the war. Paroled at the Provost Marshal's Office, Army of the Potomac, May 4, 1863. Date and place of capture not reported. Present or accounted for until he deserted on June 6, 1863. Rejoined the company from desertion on December 11, 1863, and sentenced by court-martial to two years imprisonment at hard labor. Reported as absent in arrest on company muster rolls through December, 1864. Paroled at Athens, Georgia, May 8, 1865.

PERRY, JOHN, Private
Enlisted in Wake County on July 15, 1862, for the war. Present or accounted for on company muster rolls through December, 1864.

PERRY, SIMON, Private
Resided in Nash County and enlisted in Franklin County at age 26, July 15, 1862, for the war. Admitted to hospital at Richmond, Virginia, August 28, 1862, with "typhoid fever." Died in hospital at Richmond on September 7, 1862.

PHILLIPS, CORNELIUS, Private
Confined at Fort Delaware, Delaware, January, 1865, from Fort Fisher, New Hanover County.

PICKETT, JOHN, Private
Born in Orange County where he resided as a farmer and enlisted at age 20, February 25, 1862, for the war. Captured at Gettysburg, Pennsylvania, July 3, 1863, and confined at Point Lookout, Maryland. Released from Point Lookout after taking the Oath of Allegiance and joining the U. S. service on January 24, 1864. Assigned to Company B, 1st Regiment U. S. Volunteer Infantry.

PIERSON, J. H., Sergeant
Captured in hospital at Richmond, Virginia, April 3, 1865.

PLEASANTS, ALBERT B., Private
Resided in Orange County and enlisted in Guilford County at age 27, June 28, 1861, for the war. Died in hospital at Fredericksburg, Virginia,

November 27, 1861.

POVEE, A. C., Private
Paroled at Greensboro on May 13, 1865.

QUALLES, WILLIAM H., Private
Resided in Orange County where he enlisted at age 18, July 24, 1861, for the war. Died in hospital at Fredericksburg, Virginia, September 19, 1861.

REAGAN, FRANK, Private
Resided in Orange County where he enlisted at age 21, March 4, 1862, for the war. Reported as absent without leave from May, 1862, through December, 1864.

REDDICK, H. L., Private
Paroled at Greensboro on May 11, 1865.

REDMOND, DUNCAN, Private
Resided in Orange County where he enlisted at age 18, July 17, 1861, for the war. "Deserted June 28, 1863."

REED, W. C., Private
Captured at Winchester, Virginia, September 19, 1864, and sent to Point Lookout, Maryland, September 23, 1864.

REEVES, WILLIAM, Private
Resided in Lincoln County and enlisted on June 30, 1863, for the war.

REYNOLDS, CHRISTOPHER, Private
Born in Lincoln County where he resided as a farmer and enlisted at age 35, March 15, 1862, for the war. Discharged October 21, 1862, by reason of "deafness."

RILEY, JAMES, Private
Resided in Orange County where he enlisted at age 23, February 24, 1862, for the war. Reported as absent sick after June 30, 1862, and signed pay voucher at Richmond, Virginia, February 2, 1863. Reported on May-June, 1863, muster roll with the remark: "Died at home, time unknown."

RILEY, JAMES W., Private
Resided in Orange County where he enlisted at age 21, February 25, 1862, for the war. Reported as present through April, 1862. Roll of Honor carries the remark: "Died."

RILEY, WILLIAM, Private
Resided in Orange County where he enlisted at age 20, March 4, 1862, for the war. Killed in action at Ellerson's Mill, Virginia, June 26, 1862.

ROBBINS, ELBERT, Private
Resided in Nash County and enlisted in Wake County at age 24, July 15, 1862, for the war. Wounded in action at Sharpsburg, Maryland September 17, 1862, and reported as absent wounded through February 28, 1864. Reported as absent without leave after February 28, 1864.

ROPER, HARVEY A., Private
Resided in Orange County and enlisted in Lincoln County at age 27, August 12, 1861, for the war. Present or accounted for until reported as "absent without leave December 23, 1862." Reported as absent in arrest in the guardhouse January-February and March-April, 1863. Deserted a second time on June 28, 1863. Sentenced by court-martial on September 10, 1863.

SCOTT, HARRISON, Private
Born in Orange County where he resided as a farmer and enlisted at age 45, February 28, 1862, for the war. Discharged at hospital, Farmville, Virginia, February 10, 1863, by reason of his "being incapable of performing the duties of a soldier because of internal injury, result of contused wound."

SCOTT, WALTER, Private
Enlisted at age 23, July 17, 1861, for the war. "Discharged August, 1861, at Warrenton, North Carolina."

SHARP, MAURICE H., Private
Resided in Orange County where he enlisted at age 37, August 1, 1861, for the war. Died in hospital at Fredericksburg, Virginia, December 14, 1861.

SHERRILL, RODERICK M., Sergeant
Resided in Caldwell County and enlisted in Warren County at age 23, July 24, 1861, for the war. Mustered in as Corporal. Appointed Sergeant November-December, 1861. Admitted to hospital at Richmond, Virginia, August 11, 1862, with "dispepsia" and died September 8, 1862, of "typhoid fever."

SHIRES, AMOS, Private
Resided in Gaston County where he enlisted at age 23, February 1, 1862, for the war. Reported as absent without leave after April, 1862.

SHIRES, ELISHA L., Private
Resided in Gaston County where he enlisted at age 20, February 1, 1862, for the war. Wounded in the hand at Ellerson's Mill, Virginia, June 26, 1862. Furloughed from hospital at Richmond, Virginia, for 30 days on July 10, 1862. Reported as absent disabled from wounds through December, 1864.

SHYTLE, ANDREW, Private
Enlisted in Lincoln County at age 28, March 14, 1862, for the war. Present or accounted for until captured at Spotsylvania Court House, Virginia, May 12, 1864. Confined at Point Lookout, Maryland, until transferred to Elmira, New York, August 6, 1864. Died at Elmira on June 19, 1865, of "chronic diarrhoea."

SMITH, CHARLES C., Private
Born in Orange County where he resided as a farmer and enlisted in Wake County at age 23, August 1, 1861, for the war. Discharged October 21, 1861, by reason of disability.

STAMEY, JOHN A., Private
Previously served in Company K, 1st Regiment N.C. Infantry (6 months, 1861). Enlisted in this company in Lincoln County on March 18, 1862, for the war. Wounded in action at Winchester, Virginia, June 15, 1863. Present or accounted for on company muster rolls as absent wounded through December, 1863. Reported as present or accounted for on company muster rolls for 1864. Admitted to hospital at Richmond, Virginia, March 7, 1865, with "debilitas" and furloughed for 30 days on March 9, 1865.

STAMEY, JOSEPH A., Private
Resided in Lincoln County where he enlisted at

age 18, July 8, 1861, for the war. Wounded in action at Sharpsburg, Maryland, September 17, 1862. Captured at Spotsylvania Court House, Virginia, May 12, 1864. Confined at Point Lookout, Maryland, until transferred to Elmira, New York, August 3, 1864. Paroled at Elmira and sent to James River, Virginia, for exchange on March 2, 1865. Paroled at Appomattox Court House, Virginia, April 9, 1865.

STOWE, A., Private
Resided in Lincoln County and enlisted at age 30, March 29, 1862, for the war. Killed in action at Ellerson's Mill, Virginia, June 26, 1862.

SUMMERS, WILLIAM, Private
Resided in Caswell County. Captured at Farmville, Virginia, April 6, 1865, and confined at Point Lookout, Maryland, until released after taking the Oath of Allegiance on June 19, 1865.

SUMMIT, DANIEL F., Private
Enlisted in Lincoln County at age 35, August 3, 1861, for the war. Wounded in action at Payne's Farm, Virginia, November 27, 1863. Died in hospital at Richmond, Virginia, January 13, 1864, of wounds.

THOMAS, MOSES W., Private
Resided in Lincoln County where he enlisted at age 23, July 15, 1861, for the war. Wounded in the left foot at Winchester, Virginia, June 15, 1863. Captured at Spotsylvania Court House, Virginia, May 12, 1864. Confined at Point Lookout, Maryland, until transferred to Elmira, New York, August 3, 1864. Released at Elmira after taking the Oath of Allegiance on June 21, 1865.

TOMER, J. S., Private
Admitted to Hammond U. S. Army General Hospital, Point Lookout, Maryland, November 7, 1863, with "diarrhoea chronic" and sent to "G. H." December 5, 1863.

TURNER, ABEL T., Private
Resided in Warren County where he enlisted at age 23, June 19, 1861, for the war. Died at Fredericksburg, Virginia, in January, 1862.

TURRENTINE, JOSEPH S., Private
Resided in Orange County where he enlisted at age 20, August 21, 1861, for the war. Captured and paroled near Keedysville, Maryland, September 20, 1862. Present or accounted for until he "deserted June 28, 1863."

TYLER, NATHAN A., Sergeant
Born in Rockingham County and resided as a tobacco manufacturer in Guilford County prior to enlisting in Warren County at age 19, June 13, 1861, for the war. Mustered in as Sergeant. Discharged on April 6, 1862, by reason of "disability —hepatization of both lungs."

UNDERWOOD, DeWITT C., Private
Resided in Orange County where he enlisted at age 18, June 29, 1861, for the war. Killed in action at Sharpsburg, Maryland, September 17, 1862.

UNDERWOOD, JOHN, Private
Resided in Alamance County where he enlisted at age 45, February 28, 1862, for the war. Captured at Spotsylvania Court House, Virginia, May 12,

1864, and confined at Point Lookout, Maryland, until transferred to Elmira, New York, August 6, 1864. Transferred in July, 1865, to U.S. General Hospital, Elmira, where he was released after taking the Oath of Allegiance on August 7, 1865.

VAUGHAN, SIMPSON, Private
Resided in Orange County where he enlisted at age 19, July 25, 1861, for the war. Killed in action at Ellerson's Mill, Virginia, June 26, 1862.

WATSON, WESLEY F., Private
Previously served in Company G, 27th Regiment N.C. Troops. Enlisted in this company in Orange County at age 17, July 9, 1861, for the war. Mustered in as Sergeant. Reduced to ranks March-April, 1862. Reported as "deserted" on June 30-October 31, 1862, muster roll. Absent deserted until reported on January-February, 1863, muster roll as "present in arrest in guard tent. Returned from desertion." Reported as absent in guardhouse until he deserted a second time on August 17, 1863. Absent deserted until committed to Castle Thunder Prison, Richmond, Virginia, November 13, 1864. Reported on November-December, 1864, muster roll as "absent in military prison at Richmond. Joined from desertion."

WATSON, WILLIAM H., Private
Resided in Lincoln County and enlisted in Orange County at age 22, March 1, 1862, for the war. Died in hospital at Richmond, Virginia, July, 1862, of disease.

WHITE, CHARLES, Corporal
Born in Wake County where he resided as a schoolboy and enlisted at age 14-15, August 25, 1861, for the war. Captured in Maryland, September 18, 1862, and confined at Fort McHenry, Maryland, until paroled and exchanged at Aiken's Landing, Virginia, October 25, 1862. Declared exchanged November 10, 1862. Appointed Corporal March-April, 1863. Discharged May 19, 1863, by reason of disability.

WILLIAMS, GEORGE W., Private
Resided in Lincoln County where he enlisted at age 17, August 12, 1861, for the war. Present or accounted for until he was captured at Gettysburg, Pennsylvania, July 3, 1863, and confined at Fort Delaware, Delaware. Transferred on October 18, 1863, to Point Lookout, Maryland, where he died December 21, 1863.

WILLIAMS, JOHN W., Corporal
Resided in Lincoln County where he enlisted at age 19, August 12, 1861, for the war. Mustered in as Private. Promoted to Corporal July-August, 1863, "for gallant conduct in all battles." Captured at Spotsylvania Court House, Virginia, May 12, 1864. Confined at Point Lookout, Maryland, until transferred to Elmira, New York, August 6, 1864. Released at Elmira after taking the Oath of Allegiance on June 21, 1865.

WISE, WILLIAM F., Private
Resided in Lincoln County where he enlisted at age 29, May 22, 1862, for the war. Wounded in action at Ellerson's Mill, Virginia, June 26, 1862. Reported as absent wounded until detailed at Louisa Court House, Virginia, April 11, 1863, to

guard baggage. Absent detailed through 1863. Captured at Spotsylvania Court House, Virginia, May 12, 1864. Confined at Point Lookout, Maryland, until transferred to Elmira, New York, August 6, 1864. Released at Elmira after taking the Oath of Allegiance on June 21, 1865.

WOOD, CALEB, Private

Resided in Lincoln County where he enlisted at age 18, March 14, 1862, for the war. Present or accounted for until captured at Spotsylvania Court House, Virginia, May 12, 1864. Confined at Point Lookout, Maryland, until transferred to Elmira, New York, August 6, 1864. Released at Elmira after taking the Oath of Allegiance on June 30, 1865.

WORKMAN, ELBERT G., Sergeant

Born in Orange County and resided as a farmer in Chatham County where he enlisted at age 20, July 23, 1861, for the war. Mustered in as Private and appointed Corporal September 24, 1862. Captured at Gettysburg, Pennsylvania, July 3, 1863, and confined at Fort Delaware, Delaware. Promoted to Sergeant while a prisoner of war October 31, 1863. Released from Fort Delaware in October, 1863, after taking the Oath of Allegiance and joining the U. S. service. Assigned to Company G, 1st Regiment Connecticut Cavalry.

YODER, SIDNEY, Private

Resided in Lincoln County where he enlisted at age 23, July 4, 1861, for the war. Detailed as teamster September-October, 1863, and reported as absent on detail through December, 1864 Captured at Amelia Court House, Virginia, April 6, 1865, and confined at Point Lookout, Maryland, until released after taking the Oath of Allegiance on June 22, 1865.

COMPANY E

This company was composed of men from New Hanover County and enlisted at Wilmington on May 31, 1861. It tendered its service to the state and was ordered to Warrenton, Warren County, where it became Company E of this regiment. After joining the regiment the company functioned as a part of the regiment, and its history for the war period is recorded as a part of the regimental history.

The information contained in the following roster of the company was compiled principally from company muster rolls which covered from May 31 through August 31, 1861; November through December, 1861; March through April, 1862; and June 30, 1862, through December, 1864. No company muster rolls were found for September through October, 1861; January through February, 1862; May through June 29, 1862; or for the period after December, 1864. In addition to the company muster rolls, Roll of Honor records, receipt rolls, hospital records, prisoner of war records, and other primary records, supplemented by state pension applications, United Daughters of the Confederacy records, and postwar rosters and histories, all provided useful information.

OFFICERS

CAPTAINS

WRIGHT, JAMES A.

Resided in New Hanover County and appointed Captain to rank from May 16, 1861. Present or accounted for until killed in action at Ellerson's Mill, Virginia, June 26, 1862.

WOOSTER, JOHN L.

Resided in New Hanover County and appointed 1st Lieutenant to rank from May 16, 1861. Promoted to Captain to rank from June 26, 1862. Wounded in action at Malvern Hill, Virginia, July 1, 1862, and reported as absent wounded until he resigned June 29, 1863.

MOORE, FREDERICK S.

Resided in New Hanover County where he enlisted at age 25, May 31, 1861, for the war. Mustered in as 1st Sergeant. Appointed 2nd Lieutenant to rank from December 6, 1861. Wounded in action at Ellerson's Mill, Virginia, June 26, 1862. Promoted to 1st Lieutenant January 29, 1863. Wounded in action at Chancellorsville, Virginia, May 3, 1863, and reported as absent wounded until returned to the company in January, 1864. Promoted to Captain while absent wounded on June 29, 1863. Present or accounted for until he was paroled at Appomattox Court House, Virginia, April 9, 1865.

LIEUTENANTS

BISHOP, THOMAS N., 2nd Lieutenant

Resided in New Hanover County where he enlisted at age 26, May 31, 1861, for the war. Mustered in as Sergeant and appointed 2nd Lieutenant to rank from June 29, 1863. Present or accounted for until he was paroled at Appomattox Court House, Virginia, April 9, 1865.

DUDLEY, GUILFORD L., 2nd Lieutenant

Resided in New Hanover County and appointed 2nd Lieutenant to rank from May 16, 1861. Transferred to the Field and Staff of this regiment upon appointment as Captain, Assistant Quartermaster, November 1, 1861.

LANGDON, RICHARD F., 1st Lieutenant

Resided in New Hanover County and appointed 2nd Lieutenant to rank from May 16, 1861. Promoted to 1st Lieutenant to rank from June 26, 1862. Present or accounted for until he was transferred to the Field and Staff, 3rd Regiment N.C. State Troops, upon appointment as Captain, Assistant Quartermaster, January 29, 1863.

WRIGHT, JOSHUA G., Jr., 1st Lieutenant

Transferred from Company C, 59th Regiment N.C. Troops (4th Regiment N.C. Cavalry) upon appointment as 2nd Lieutenant to rank from August 1, 1862. Wounded in action at Chancellorsville, Virginia, May 3, 1863. Promoted to 1st Lieutenant while absent wounded to rank from June 29, 1863. Reported as absent wounded; as absent on detached service at Raleigh; and as Provost Marshal of Wilmington, from November-December, 1863, through January-February, 1864. Reported as absent sick through December, 1864, when he was reported as "present sick." Retired to the Invalid Corps February 24, 1865, and assigned to the Reserve Forces of North Carolina on March 1, 1865.

NONCOMMISSIONED OFFICERS AND PRIVATES

ALBERT, JAMES, Private
Enlisted in Wake County on July 15, 1862, for the war. Died in hospital near Richmond, Virginia, August 24, 1862.

ALBRIGHT, SAMUEL A., Private
Resided in Alamance County and enlisted in Wake County at age 32, July 15, 1862, for the war. Present or accounted for until transferred to Company F, 53rd Regiment N.C. Troops, upon appointment as 2nd Lieutenant to rank from September 20, 1862.

ALBRIGHT, SAUREN, Private
Resided in Alamance County and enlisted in Wake County at age 30, July 15, 1862, for the war. Wounded in action at Sharpsburg, Maryland, September 17, 1862. Present or accounted for until he was killed in action at Mine Run, Virginia, November 27, 1863.

ALLEN, FRANKLIN, Private
Born in Chatham County and resided in Alamance County as a farmer prior to enlisting in Wake County at age 34, July 15, 1862, for the war. Discharged October 7, 1862, by reason of "scrofula, necrosis of the tibia & white swelling resulting in anchylosis of the right ankle."

ALLEN, JOHN, Private
Resided in New Hanover County where he enlisted at age 19, July 15, 1861, for the war. Captured at Gettysburg, Pennsylvania, July 1, 1863, and confined at Fort Delaware, Delaware. Reported as a "rebel deserter from Beaufort, North Carolina" at Camp Distribution, July 23, 1864, with the remark that he was discharged July 24, 1864.

ATKINSON, EVAN, Private
Resided in New Hanover County where he enlisted at age 35, May 31, 1861, for the war. Present or accounted for until killed in action at Wilderness, Virginia, May 5, 1864.

ATKINSON, JOHN, Private
Resided in New Hanover County where he enlisted at age 34, June 7, 1861, for the war. Present or accounted for until killed in action at Ellerson's Mill, Virginia, June 26, 1862.

BALDWIN, ANDERSON, Private
Resided in Alamance County and enlisted in Wake County at age 22, July 15, 1862, for the war. Sent to the rear, sick, from Orange Court House, Virginia, August 21, 1862, and deserted from hospital at Lynchburg, Virginia, September 26, 1862.

BALLARD, J. D., Private
Admitted to hospital at Richmond, Virginia, on October 10, 1862.

BARNHEART, MILTON, Private
Resided in Alamance County and enlisted in

Wake County on July 15, 1862, for the war. Wounded in action on June 19, 1864. Captured at Chester Station, Virginia, April 3, 1865, and confined at Hart's Island, New York Harbor, until released after taking the Oath of Allegiance on June 19, 1865.

BARR, GEORGE A., 1st Sergeant
Resided in New Hanover County where he enlisted at age 31, June 14, 1861, for the war. Mustered in as Sergeant and appointed 1st Sergeant December, 1861. Died at Fredericksburg, Virginia, December 29, 1861, of disease.

BARRY, JOHN, Private
Resided in New Hanover County where he enlisted at age 33, June 6, 1861, for the war. Mustered in as Private and appointed Sergeant after May 31, 1861. Reduced to ranks August 3, 1862. Detached to the Pioneer Corps, October 1, 1862, and remained absent on detail until February 9, 1864, when he was detailed for duty in the Quartermaster Department and ordered to report to the Superintendent of the Wilmington and Weldon Railroad at Wilmington. Assigned to the Quartermaster Department as an engineer on February 9, 1864. Absent on detail through December, 1864.

BEATEN, THOMAS, Private
Paroled in Mocksville on June 7, 1865.

BELL, JAMES H., Private
Resided in New Hanover County where he enlisted at age 18, February 5, 1862, for the war. Wounded in action at Ellerson's Mill, Virginia, June 26, 1862. Present or accounted for on company muster rolls through December, 1864.

BELL, PETER, Private
Enlisted in New Hanover County on January 18, 1862, for the war. Died at Camp Bee, Virginia, March 17, 1862.

BELL, STEPHEN R., Private
Resided in New Hanover County where he enlisted at age 40, June 3, 1861, for the war. Wounded in action at Sharpsburg, Maryland, September 17, 1862, and never returned to the company.

BISHOP, JOHN S., Private
Resided in New Hanover County where he enlisted at age 18, June 18, 1861, for the war. Company muster rolls carry him as present until reported as absent sick after August 19, 1862. Reported as absent sick until reported as captured at Winchester, Virginia, July 15, 1863. No Federal Provost Marshal records relative to his capture or imprisonment were found.

BLANK, CHARLES, Private
Born in France and resided in New Hanover County where he enlisted at age 28, July 15, 1861, for the war. Captured near Richmond, Virginia, June 26-28, 1862, and confined at Fort Columbus, New York Harbor, until transferred to Aiken's Landing, Virginia, for exchange on August 5, 1862. Took the Oath of Allegiance to the United States at Fort Delaware, Delaware, August 10, 1862.

BOND, JAMES D., Private
Resided as a farmer in Wake County where he enlisted at age 18, April 23, 1862, for the war. Discharged July 1, 1863, by reason of "phthisis pulmonalis."

BOONE, DANIEL, Private
Resided in Alamance County and enlisted in Wake County at age 33, July 15, 1862, for the war. Present or accounted for on company muster rolls through December, 1864.

BRADY, JOHN W., Private
Resided in New Hanover County where he enlisted at age 33, June 14, 1861, for the war. Wounded in action at Malvern Hill, Virginia, July 1, 1862, and at Fredericksburg, Virginia, December 15, 1862. Admitted to hospital at Richmond, Virginia, where he died February 20, 1863, of "variola conft."

BRANTLEY, JOHN H., Private
Resided in New Hanover County where he enlisted on August 27, 1861, for the war. Mustered in as Private and appointed Corporal December 6, 1861. Reduced to ranks September 5, 1862. Died at Wilmington on October 9, 1862, of "yellow fever."

BRODERICK, PATRICK, Private
Resided in New Hanover County where he enlisted at age 21, June 18, 1861, for the war. Mustered in as Corporal and reduced to ranks July 18, 1861. Present or accounted for until wounded in the right leg and captured at Winchester, Virginia, September 19, 1864. Confined at Point Lookout, Maryland, until paroled October 29, 1864, and exchanged at Venus Point, Savannah River, Georgia, November 15, 1864.

BURNS, EDWARD, Private
Resided in New Hanover County where he enlisted at age 25, June 24, 1861, for the war. Mustered in as Corporal and reduced to ranks August 26, 1861. Present or accounted for until transferred to the C. S. Vavy on February 3, 1862.

CAMPBELL, THOMAS J., Corporal
Resided in New Hanover County where he enlisted at age 32, June 21, 1861, for the war. Mustered in as Corporal. Discharged September 10, 1861, by reason of "consumption."

CAPPS, CHARLES, Private
Resided in Alamance County and enlisted in Wake County at age 35, July 15, 1862, for the war. Captured at South Mountain, Maryland, September 14, 1862, and confined at Fort Delaware, Delaware. Paroled and exchanged at Aiken's Landing, Virginia, November 10, 1862. Wounded in action at Gettysburg, Pennsylvania, July 3, 1863. Captured at Spotsylvania Court House, Virginia, May 12, 1864, and confined at Elmira, New York, where he died June 30, 1865, of "pneumonia."

CAPPS, JOHN M., Private
Resided in Alamance County and enlisted in Wake County at age 30, July 15, 1862, for the war. Present or accounted for until captured at Spotsylvania Court House, Virginia, May 12, 1864. Confined at Elmira, New York, where he died January 1, 1865, of "pneumonia."

CAPPS, ROBERT, Private
Resided in Alamance County and enlisted in Wake County at age 32, July 15, 1862, for the war. Captured in Maryland after the battle of Sharpsburg, Maryland, September 17, 1862, and paroled and exchanged at Aiken's Landing, Virginia, November 10, 1862. Captured at Fredericksburg, Virginia, May 3, 1863, and paroled and exchanged on May 13, 1863. Admitted to hospital at Richmond, Virginia, June 7, 1863, and transferred to Danville, Virginia, July 20, 1863. Disease listed on hospital records as "diarrhoea acute," "scorbutis," and "vulnus sclopeticum in hip." Deserted from hospital at Danville on August 18, 1863.

CASTEEN, JOHN, Sergeant
Resided in New Hanover County where he enlisted at age 33, June 12, 1861, for the war. Mustered in as Sergeant. Present or accounted for until captured at Spotsylvania Court House, Virginia, May 12, 1864. Confined at Point Lookout, Maryland, until transferred to Elmira, New York, August 6, 1864. Released at Elmira after taking the Oath of Allegiance on June 12, 1865.

CLANNARD, F., Private
Paroled at Greensboro on May 12, 1865.

CLAPP, GEORGE, Private
Resided in Alamance County and enlisted in Wake County at age 18, July 15, 1862, for the war. Wounded in the hand at Payne's Farm, Virginia, November 27, 1863. Reported on company muster rolls as captured May 12, 1864.

CLAPP, JOHN, Private
Enlisted in Wake County on February 10, 1864, for the war. Captured at Spotsylvania Court House, Virginia, May 12, 1864. Confined at Point Lookout, Maryland, until transferred to Elmira, New York, August 6, 1864. Died at Elmira on December 5, 1864, of "pneumonia."

CLAPP, TUBAL A., Private
Resided in Alamance County and enlisted in Wake County at age 27, July 15, 1862, for the war. Died at Richmond, Virginia, August 25, 1862, of disease.

CLAPP, WESLEY, Private
Resided in Alamance County and enlisted in Wake County at age 34, July 15, 1862, for the war. Wounded in action at Winchester, Virginia, June 14-15, 1863. Captured at Spotsylvania Court House, Virginia, May 12, 1864. Confined at Point Lookout, Maryland, until transferred to Elmira, New York, August 6, 1864. Died at Elmira on March 20, 1865, of "diarrhoea."

CLARK, G. M., Private
Confined at Knoxville, Tennessee, April 15, 1865, as a "rebel deserter" and sent to Chattanooga on April 17, 1865.

CLARY, DANIEL, Private
Resided in New Hanover County where he enlisted at age 28, June 27, 1861, for the war. Deserted at Richmond, Virginia, August 1, 1861.

CLEVINI, JOSEPH, Private
Resided in New Hanover County where he enlisted at age 33, June 14, 1861, for the war. Discharged August 19, 1861.

COBLE, AUGUSTUS L., Private

Resided in Alamance County and enlisted in Wake County at age 20, July 15, 1862, for the war. Absent without leave from October 10, 1862, to January 1, 1863. Present or accounted for until captured at Spotsylvania Court House, Virginia, May 12, 1864. Confined at Point Lookout, Maryland, until transferred to Elmira, New York, August 3, 1864. Released at Elmira after taking the Oath of Allegiance on June 21, 1865.

COBLE, EMSLEY M., Private

Resided in Alamance County and enlisted in Wake County on February 26, 1864, for the war. Captured at Spotsylvania Court House, Virginia, May 12, 1864. Confined at Point Lookout, Maryland, until transferred to Elmira, New York, August 3, 1864. Released at Elmira after taking the Oath of Allegiance on June 30, 1865.

COBLE, HENRY M., Private

Born in Guilford County and resided as a farmer in Alamance County prior to enlisting in Wake County at age 18, July 15, 1862, for the war. Discharged May 13, 1863, at Chancellorsville, Virginia, by reason of his being "unable to perform military duty of any kind for the time specified on account of general debility."

DANIELLY, JOHN W., Private

Resided in Alamance County and enlisted in Wake County at age 34, July 15, 1862, for the war. Died in hospital at Lynchburg, Virginia, January 23, 1864.

DAVIS, GEORGE, Private

Resided in New Hanover County where he enlisted at age 33, June 7, 1861, for the war. Reported as absent without leave after May 9, 1862, and November-December, 1864, muster roll carries him with the remark: "Exact date of desertion cannot be given, having been repeatedly arrested and as often escaped the guards. Has not been with his command since December, 1862."

DAVIS, ROBERT, Corporal

Resided in New Hanover County where he enlisted at age 31, May 31, 1861, for the war. Mustered in as Private and appointed Corporal on July 1, 1862. Wounded in the neck at Chancellorsville, Virginia, May 3, 1863. Admitted to hospital at Richmond, Virginia, May 10, 1863, and furloughed for 40 days on June 14, 1863. Company muster roll for February 29-August 31, 1864, states that he returned to duty September 15, 1863, and was "sent to the hospital on account of same wound, November 15, 1863. Furloughed to January 27, 1864. Absent without leave since January 27, 1864."

DEEL, RODERICK, Private

Resided in New Hanover County where he enlisted at age 30, June 8, 1861, for the war. Killed in action at Malvern Hill, Virginia, July 1, 1862.

DICKSON, JOHN, Private

Resided in New Hanover County where he enlisted at age 24, June 12, 1861, for the war. Captured at South Mountain, Maryland, September 14, 1862, and confined at Fort Delaware, Delaware,

until sent to Aiken's Landing, Virginia, for exchange on October 2, 1862. Declared exchanged on November 10, 1862. Never returned to company.

DUDLEY, JOHN, Private

Resided in New Hanover County where he enlisted at age 23, June 14, 1861, for the war. Wounded in action at Malvern Hill, Virginia, July 1, 1862, and died of wounds in hospital at Richmond, Virginia, July 26, 1862.

DUNN, JACOB H., Private

Resided in New Hanover County where he enlisted at age 29, July 1, 1861, for the war. Discharged on December 4, 1861, by reason of disability.

DUNN, THOMAS, Private

Resided in New Hanover County where he enlisted at age 38, June 24, 1861, for the war. Wounded at Malvern Hill, Virginia, July 1, 1862. Reported as absent wounded and on hospital detail until retired to the Invalid Corps on April 18, 1864.

DUNN, WALTER, Private

Captured at Kinston on March 19, 1865, and confined at New Bern.

DURHAM, JOHN R. K., Private

Resided in Alamance County and enlisted in Wake County at age 19, July 15, 1862, for the war. Present or accounted for until captured at Spotsylvania Court House, Virginia, May 12, 1864. Confined at Point Lookout, Maryland, until paroled and sent to Aiken's Landing, Virginia, September 18, 1864, for exchange. Admitted to hospital at Richmond, Virginia, September 23, 1864, with the remark that he was "brought from the flag of truce boat dead." Date of death given as September 20, 1864.

EDWARDS, G. B., Private

Captured at Gettysburg, Pennsylvania, July 3, 1863, and confined at Fort McHenry, Maryland, until sent to Fort Delaware, Delaware, July, 1863.

FAUCETT, ROBERT J., Private

Resided in Alamance County and enlisted in Wake County at age 34, July 15, 1862, for the war. Present or accounted for until captured at Spotsylvania Court House, Virginia, May 12, 1864. Confined at Point Lookout, Maryland, until transferred to Elmira, New York, August 6, 1864. Died at Elmira on April 8, 1865, of "chronic diarrhoea."

FAUCETT, WILLIAM J., Private

Resided in Alamance County and enlisted in Wake County at age 26, July 15, 1862, for the war. Wounded in action at Sharpsburg, Maryland, September 17, 1862. Deserted from hospital at Richmond, Virginia, June 3, 1863, and reported as absent without leave on company muster rolls through December, 1863. Returned to company in January, 1864, and was captured at Spotsylvania Court House, Virginia, May 12, 1864. Confined at Point Lookout, Maryland, until transferred to Elmira, New York, August 6, 1864. Released after taking the Oath of Allegiance at Elmira on July 3, 1865.

FINN, HENRY, Private
Resided in New Hanover County where he enlisted at age 36, June 18, 1861, for the war. Present or accounted for until captured at Spotsylvania Court House, Virginia, May 12, 1864. Confined at Point Lookout, Maryland, until transferred to Elmira, New York, August 3, 1864. Released at Elmira after taking the Oath of Allegiance on June 27, 1865.

FOGLEMAN, PETER, Private
Resided in Alamance County and enlisted in Wake County at age 27, July 15, 1862, for the war. Present or accounted for until captured at Amelia Court House, Virginia, April 6, 1865. Confined at Point Lookout, Maryland, until released after taking the Oath of Allegiance on June 26, 1865.

FORTNER, JULIAN, Private
Resided in Alamance County and enlisted in Wake County at age 22, July 15, 1862, for the war. Wounded in action at Chancellorsville, Virginia, May 2, 1863. Present or accounted for until captured at Spotsylvania Court House, Virginia, May 12, 1864. Confined at Point Lookout, Maryland, until transferred to Elmira, New York, August 6, 1864. Released at Elmira after taking the Oath of Allegiance on June 14, 1865.

FOSHEE, GABRIEL, Private
Born in Guilford County and resided as a farmer in Alamance County prior to enlisting in Wake County at age 34, July 15, 1862, for the war. Discharged October 7, 12, 1862, by reason of "inguinal hernia (double)."

FOUST, PETER Z., Private
Resided in Alamance County and enlisted in Wake County at age 35, July 15, 1862, for the war. Wounded at Sharpsburg, Maryland, September 17, 1862, and killed in action at Chancellorsville, Virginia, May 3, 1863.

GARNER, ADDISON, Private
Resided in Alamance County and enlisted in Wake County at age 32, July 15, 1862, for the war. Present or accounted for until captured at Spotsylvania Court House, Virginia, May 12, 1862. Confined at Point Lookout, Maryland, until transferred to Elmira, New York, August 6, 1864. Died at Elmira on March 23, 1865, of "pneumonia."

GARRETT, GEORGE W., Private
Resided in Alamance County and enlisted in Wake County at age 20, July 15, 1862, for the war. Present or accounted for until captured at Spotsylvania Court House, Virginia, May 12, 1864. Confined at Point Lookout, Maryland, until transferred to Elmira, New York, August 6, 1864. Released at Elmira after taking the Oath of Allegiance on June 30, 1865.

GARRETT, HENRY W., Corporal
Resided in Alamance County and enlisted in Wake County at age 24, July 15, 1862, for the war. Mustered in as Private and appointed Corporal soon after enlistment. Present or accounted for until captured at Spotsylvania Court House, Virginia, May 12, 1864. Confined at Point Lookout, Maryland, until transferred to Elmira, New

York, August 6, 1864. Released at Elmira after taking the Oath of Allegiance on June 30, 1865.

GARRIS, ALEXANDER, Private
Resided in New Hanover County where he enlisted at age 22, June 11, 1861, for the war. Wounded in action at Malvern Hill, Virginia, July 1, 1862, and died of wounds in hospital at Richmond, Virginia, August 3, 1862.

GARRIS, PATRICK H., Private
Resided in New Hanover County where he enlisted at age 20, June 12, 1861, for the war. Killed in action at Malbern Hill, Virginia, July 1, 1862.

GRAHAM, JOHN, Private
Resided in New Hanover County and enlisted on June 4, 1861, for the war. Discharged in 1861.

GRAHAM, JOHN B., Private
Resided in New Hanover County where he enlisted on August 27, 1861, for the war. Deserted at Richmond, Virginia, August 29, 1861.

GREELY, JAMES, Private
Resided in New Hanover County where he enlisted at age 21, June 14, 1861, for the war. "Deserted" or "captured" at Sharpsburg, Maryland, September 17, 1862. Took the Oath of Allegiance on September 27, 1862, and was sent north.

GURGANUS, HOSEA, Private
Resided in New Hanover County and enlisted June 18, 1861, for the war. "Disabled and discharged."

GUTHRIE, GEORGE CLAYBORN, Sergeant
Resided in Alamance County and enlisted in Wake County at age 29, July 15, 1862, for the war. Mustered in as Private and appointed Sergeant September 1, 1862. Wounded in the thigh at Sharpsburg, Maryland, September 17, 1862, and reported as absent wounded on furlough through February, 1863. Wounded and captured at Chancellorsville, Virginia, May 3, 1863. Confined at Lincoln U.S. Army General Hospital, Washington, D.C., May 7, 1863, with a flesh wound of the left thigh. Transferred to Old Capitol Prison, Washington, D.C., May 27, 1863. Furoled and sent to City Point, Virginia, for exchange, June 10, 1863. Admitted to hospital at Williamsburg, Virginia, June 12, 1863, and furloughed July 6, 1863. Present or accounted for until captured at Spotsylvania Court House, Virginia, May 12, 1864. Confined at Point Lookout, Maryland, until transferred to Elmira, New York, August 6, 1864. Paroled at Elmira and sent to James River, Virginia, for exchange on March 2, 1865. Admitted to hospital at Richmond, Virginia, March 7, 1865, with "debilitas" and furloughed for 30 days on March 9, 1865.

HAMILTON, WILLIAM J., Private
Enlisted in Wake County on July 15, 1862, for the war. Wounded at Sharpsburg, Maryland, September 17, 1862, and "supposed to be dead."

HINES, EDWARD, Private
Resided in New Hanover County where he enlisted at age 19, May 31, 1861, for the war. Present or accounted for until captured at Spotsylvania Court House, Virginia, May 12, 1864. Con-

fined at Point Lookout, Maryland, until transferred to Elmira, New York, August 6, 1864. Released at Elmira after taking the Oath of Allegiance on June 14, 1865.

HOGAN, MARTIN, Private
Resided in New Hanover County where he enlisted at age 25, July 6, 1861, for the war. "Shot for desertion, near Richmond, Virginia," August 12, 1862.

HOLT, GEORGE W., Private
Born in Alamance County where he resided as a farmer and enlisted in Wake County at age 28, July 15, 1862, for the war. Discharged near Fredericksburg, Virginia, December 30, 1862, by reason of "phthisis pulmonalis."

HOUGHMAN, D., Private
Paroled at Appomattox Court House, Virginia, April 9, 1865.

HUFFMAN, DANIEL, Private
Resided in Alamance County and enlisted in Wake County at age 34, July 15, 1862, for the war. Wounded at Sharpsburg, Maryland, September 17, 1862, and reported as absent wounded until detailed to the Pioneer Corps on March 8, 1863. Absent on detail through August, 1864. Reported as present on November-December, 1864, muster roll.

HUFFMAN, GEORGE, Private
Resided in Alamance County and enlisted in Wake County at age 26, July 15, 1862, for the war. Detailed to the Pioneer Corps on February 3, 1863, and remained absent on detail through August, 1864. November-December, 1864, muster roll reported him as "absent sick in North Carolina." Paroled at Greensboro on May 10, 1865.

HUFFMAN, JOHN, Private
Resided in Alamance County and enlisted in Wake County at age 22, July 15, 1862, for the war. Wounded at Chancellorsville, Virginia, May 3, 1863, and admitted to hospital at Richmond, Virginia, where he died May 30, 1863.

HUNT, SYLVESTER, Private
Resided in New Hanover County where he enlisted at age 22, June 10, 1861, for the war. November-December, 1861, muster roll reports him as "absent sick in Fredericksburg." Roll of Honor states that he "died of disease." Date and place of death not given.

INGLE, JOHN C., Private
Resided in Alamance County and enlisted in Wake County at age 33, July 15, 1862, for the war. Present or accounted for until captured at Spotsylvania Court House, Virginia, May 12, 1864. Confined at Point Lookout, Maryland, until transferred to Elmira, New York, August 6, 1864. Released at Elmira after taking the Oath of Allegiance on June 19, 1865.

INGOLD, EDWARD, Private
Resided in Alamance County and enlisted in Wake County at age 35, July 15, 1862, for the war. Present or accounted for until captured at Spotsylvania Court House, Virginia, May 12, 1864. Confined at Point Lookout, Maryland, until trans-

ferred to Elmira, New York, August 6, 1864. Released at Elmira after taking the Oath of Allegiance on May 19, 1865.

ISLEY, AUSTIN, Private
Resided in Alamance County and enlisted in Wake County at age 35, July 15, 1862, for the war. Present or accounted for until captured at Spotsylvania Court House, Virginia, May 12, 1864. Confined at Point Lookout, Maryland, until transferred to Elmira, New York, August 3, 1864. Transferred from Elmira to James River, Virginia, February 9, 1865, and "transferred to West's Building Hospital, Baltimore, Maryland, en route February 15, 1865." Transferred from hospital to Fort McHenry, Maryland, May 9, 1865, and released after taking the Oath of Allegiance on June 10, 1865.

ISLEY, BENJAMIN, Private
Resided in Alamance County and enlisted in Wake County at age 33, July 15, 1862, for the war. Present or accounted for until killed in action at Cedar Creek, Virginia, October 19, 1864.

ISLEY, GEORGE, Private
Resided in Alamance County and enlisted in Wake County at age 22, July 15, 1862, for the war. Present or accounted for until captured at Spotsylvania Court House, Virginia, May 12, 1864. Confined at Point Lookout, Maryland, until transferred to Elmira, New York, August 3, 1864. Released at Elmira after taking the Oath of Allegiance on June 19, 1865.

JAMES, ALLEN B., Private
Resided in New Hanover County where he enlisted at age 47, February 4, 1862, for the war. Present or accounted for on company muster rolls as absent sick until January 28, 1864. Reported as absent without leave after that date. Federal Provost Marshal records indicate that he "came into Federal lines at Beaufort, North Carolina" and took the Oath of Allegiance at Fort Monroe, Virginia, March 14, 1864.

JARRELL, DAVID, Private
Resided in New Hanover County where he enlisted at age 22, June 10, 1861, for the war. Died at Camp Bee, Virginia, August 22, 1861.

JARRELL, JAMES, Private
Resided in New Hanover County where he enlisted at age 23, June 8, 1861, for the war. May 31-August 31, 1861, muster roll carries the remark: "Dead."

JENKINS, OSBORNE W., Private
Resided in New Hanover County where he enlisted at age 31, June 7, 1861, for the war. Died at Fredericksburg, Virginia, December 7, 1861, of disease.

JOHNSON, MATHEW, Private
Enlisted in Wake County April 22, 1862, for the war. Reported as present on March-April, 1862, muster roll.

JOHNSTON, JAMES E., Private
Enlisted in Wake County on July 15, 1862, for the war. Muster roll for May-June, 1863, states that he "died."

JONES, W. T., Private
Paroled at Mocksville on June 6, 1865.

KEEL, THOMAS, Private
Resided in Brunswick County and enlisted in New Hanover County on August 19, 1861, for the war. May 31-August 31, 1861, muster roll states that he was "discharged."

KEETER, WILLIAM, Private
Resided in Brunswick County and enlisted in New Hanover County at age 25, June 13, 1861, for the war. "Deserted in Wilmington, June 16, 1861."

LEE, HENRY, Private
Resided in New Hanover County where he enlisted at age 45, June 8, 1861, for the war. Present or accounted for until captured at Gettysburg, Pennsylvania, July 3, 1863. Confined at Fort Delaware, Delaware, until transferred to Point Lookout, Maryland, October 18, 1863. Paroled at Point Lookout and sent to Cox's Landing, James River, Virginia, for exchange on February 13, 1865. Appears on a muster roll of a detachment of paroled and exchanged prisoners at Camp Lee, near Richmond, Virginia, dated February 17, 1865.

LEHAY, JOHN, Private
Resided in New Hanover County where he enlisted at age 45, June 7, 1861, for the war. Left sick in Frederick, Maryland, September 11, 1862, and captured. Paroled September 27, 1862. Reported as absent without leave after December, 1862.

LEWIS, HENRY D., Private
Enlisted in Wake County July 15, 1862, for the war. Captured in Maryland in September, 1862, and died at Frederick, Maryland, on November 11, 1862.

LEWIS, WILLIAM HENRY, Private
Resided in New Hanover County where he enlisted at age 18, February 13, 1862, for the war. Wounded at Ellerson's Mill, Virginia, June 26, 1862, and reported as absent wounded until detailed as a nurse in hospitals at Richmond and Petersburg beginning April 28, 1864. Transferred to Goldsboro on January 20, 1865.

LEWIS, WOODSON, Private
Resided in Alamance County and enlisted in Wake County at age 31, July 15, 1862, for the war. Reported as absent sick from August 19, 1862, until he died in hospital at Richmond, Virginia, March 24, 1864.

LINDSAY, ARNOLD, Private
Resided in Alamance County and enlisted in Wake County at age 29, July 15, 1862, for the war. Died in hospital at Richmond, Virginia, November 25, 1862, of "variola."

LONG, GEORGE J., Private
Resided in Alamance County and enlisted in Wake County at age 30, July 15, 1862, for the war. Wounded in action at Chancellorsville, Virginia, May 3, 1863, and reported as absent wounded through November, 1863. Detailed in hospital at Wilmington on April 4, 1864. Retired to the Invalid Corps on January 16, 1865. Paroled at

Greensboro on May 9, 1865.

LONG, HENRY, Private
Resided in New Hanover County where he enlisted at age 40, June 20, 1861, for the war. Discharged on August 17, 1861, by reason of disability.

LONG, JACOB S., Private
Enlisted in Wake County on July 15, 1862, for the war. "Leg shot off" at Sharpsburg, Maryland, September 17, 1862, and "supposed to be dead."

LOY, MILTON, Private
Resided in Alamance County and enlisted in Wake County at age 30, July 15, 1862, for the war. Present or accounted for until wounded in action at Payne's Farm, Virginia, November 27, 1863. Captured at Spotsylvania Court House, Virginia, May 12, 1864, and confined at Point Lookout, Maryland. Transferred to Elmira, New York, August 6, 1864. Released at Elmira after taking the Oath of Allegiance on June 14, 1865.

LUMSDEN, GEORGE A., Corporal
Resided in New Hanover County where he enlisted at age 21, May 31, 1861, for the war. Mustered in as Private and appointed Corporal on September 5, 1862. Wounded in action at Gettysburg, Pennsylvania, July 3, 1863. Captured at Spotsylvania Court House, Virginia, May 12, 1864. Confined at Point Lookout, Maryland, until transferred to Elmira, New York, July 23, 1864. Released after taking the Oath of Allegiance at Elmira on May 13, 1865.

LUMSDEN, HENRY C., Private
Born in New Hanover County where he resided as a laborer and enlisted at age 18, June 6, 1861, for the war. Discharged at Skinker's Neck, Virginia, February 11, 1863, by reason of disability. Later conscripted at Pisgah Church, Virginia, February 14, 1864, for the war. Present or accounted for until transferred to the C.S. Navy on April 17, 1864.

McCORKLE, PETER, Private
Captured at Falling Waters, Maryland, July 14, 1863, and confined at Point Lookout, Maryland. Transferred for exchange on March 17, 1864.

McCORMICK, HUGH, Private
Resided in New Hanover County where he enlisted at age 33, June 18, 1861, for the war. Detailed as a nurse in Winder Hospital, Richmond, Virginia, September 22, 1862, and remained on detail at Winder Hospital until transferred to General Hospital No. 13, Richmond, on February 2, 1864, and detailed as a guard. Remained absent on detail through December, 1864. Disease listed as "chronic ulcer and varicose veins." Paroled at Appomattox Court House, Virginia, April 9, 1865.

McKEON, JOHN, Private
Resided in New Hanover County where he enlisted at age 40, June 18, 1861, for the war. "Deserted August 19, 1862."

McLAINE, JOHN, Private
Born in Boston, Massachusetts, and was by occupation a sailor. Captured at Gettysburg, Pennsyl-

vania, July 4, 1863, and confined at Fort Delaware, Delaware. Joined the U.S. service August 30,
1863, and was assigned to Company D, 3rd Regiment Maryland Cavalry.

MASSEY, LEGO, Private
Resided in Haywood County. Captured in Hay-
wood County and confined at Military Prison,
Louisville, Kentucky, where he took the Oath of
Allegiance on May 30, 1864, and was released on
the condition that he "remain North of the Ohio
River during the war."

MASSEY, PHILIP, Private
Captured in Haywood County in May, 1864. Took
the Oath of Allegiance at Military Prison, Louisville, Kentucky, June 4, 1864, and was released on
the condition that he "remain north of the Ohio
during the war."

MORTON, JOHN, Private
Resided in Alamance County and enlisted in
Wake County at age 31, July 15, 1862, for the war.
Deserted near Manassas, Virginia, September 1,
1862.

MOSLEY, DAVID W., Private
Resided in Nash County and enlisted in Wake
County at age 29, July 15, 1862, for the war. Present or accounted for until captured at Spotsylvania Court House, Virginia, May 12, 1864. Confined at Point Lookout, Maryland, until transferred to Elmira, New York, August 6, 1864. Released at Elmira after taking the Oath of Allegiance on June 27, 1865.

MULCAHY, PATRICK, Private
Resided in New Hanover County where he enlisted at age 38, June 18, 1861, for the war. "Deserted March 16, 1863."

OWENS, THOMAS S., Private
Resided in New Hanover County where he enlisted at age 18, June 7, 1861, for the war.
Wounded in action at Sharpsburg, Maryland,
September 17, 1862. Present or accounted for
until captured at Spotsylvania Court House,
Virginia, May 12, 1864. Confined at Point Lookout, Maryland, until transferred to Elmira, New
York, August 6, 1864. Paroled at Elmira and sent
to James River, Virginia, for exchange on March 2,
1865. Admitted to hospital on March 10, 1865, at
Richmond, Virginia, where he was captured April
3, 1865. Died in hospital on April 19, 1865, of
"typhoid fever."

PARKER, WILLIAM R., Private
Resided in New Hanover County where he en-
listed at age 18, June 15, 1861, for the war. Absent
without leave from this company when he en-
listed in Company A, 41st Regiment N.C. Troops
(3rd Regiment N.C. Cavalry) on October 1, 1861.
"Proved a deserter and returned to his company"
June 20, 1862. Reported in confinement at Castle
Godwin, Richmond, Virginia, August, 1862.
Escaped from Castle Godwin in September, 1862.
March-April, 1863, muster roll states that he was
in jail at Wilmington "for murder."

PASAY, JOSEPH, Private
Enlisted in New Hanover County on August 15,

1861, for the war. "Deserted August 18, 1861, in
Wilmington."

PATTERSON, JOSEPH C., Private
Resided in New Hanover County where he en-
listed on August 13, 1861, for the war. Died at
Wilmington on October 28, 1862, of "yellow fever."

PAYNE, JAMES M., Private
Resided in Alamance County and enlisted in
Wake County at age 35, July 15, 1862, for the
war. Present or accounted for until killed in
action at Wilderness, Virginia, May 5, 1864.

PEACOCK, WILLIAM W., Sergeant
Resided in New Hanover County where he en-
listed at age 18, June 7, 1861, for the war. Mus-
tered in as Private and appointed Corporal on
September 1, 1862. Promoted to Sergeant on
June 30, 1863. Mortally wounded near Harpers
Ferry, West Virginia, July 4, 1864, and died the
next day.

PETTIGREW, ROBERT, Private
Resided in Alamance County and enlisted in
Wake County at age 22, July 15, 1862, for the
war. Present or accounted for until killed in
action at Fisher's Hill, Virginia, September 19,
1864.

PICKETT, JOSEPH, Private
Resided in New Hanover County where he enlisted at age 31, May 31, 1861, for the war. Died at
Fredericksburg, Virginia, December 5, 1861, of
disease.

POTTER, THOMAS J., Musician
Resided in New Hanover County where he enlisted at age 18, June 19, 1861, for the war. Mustered in as Musician. Present or accounted for on
company muster rolls through December, 1864.
Captured at Bermuda Hundred, Virginia, April 3,
1865, and confined at Hart's Island, New York
Harbor, until released after taking the Oath of
Allegiance on June 19, 1865.

RAMSEY, HENRY, Private
Resided in New Hanover County where he enlisted at age 18, June 14, 1861, for the war. Present
or accounted for on company muster rolls until
reported on February 29-August 31, 1864, muster
roll with the remark: "Absent furloughed on
account of wounds, July 26, 1864, for 60 days."
Reported as absent on furlough through September 26, 1864, and as absent without leave after
that date.

RHODES, JOHN, Private
Resided in New Hanover County where he enlisted at age 23, May 31, 1861, for the war. Died
near Wilmington on August 3, 1862.

RICHARDSON, FREDERICK, Private
Enlisted in Wake County on April 22, 1862, for
the war. Died in hospital at Richmond, Virginia,
July 28, 1862.

ROBERTS, JAMES C., Private
Resided in Alamance County and enlisted in
Wake County at age 24, July 15, 1862, for the war.
Wounded in action at Gettysburg, Pennsylvania,
July 3, 1863, and captured at South Mountain,

Maryland, July 5, 1863. Admitted to U.S. Army General Hospital, Frederick, Maryland, July 6, 1863, and transferred to U.S. Army General Hospital, West's Buildings, Baltimore, Maryland, August 7, 1863. Paroled at Baltimore on August 23, 1863, and delivered at City Point, Virginia, August 24, 1863, for exchange. Exact date of exchange not given; however, muster roll for January-February, 1864, states that he was "absent, nurse at hospital, Raleigh, North Carolina, November 24, 1863." Date of return to company not reported. Captured at Spotsylvania Court House, Virginia, May 12, 1864, and confined at Point Lookout, Maryland, until transferred to Elmira, New York, August 6, 1864. Released at Elmira after taking the Oath of Allegiance on May 19, 1865.

ROBINSON, HENRY, Private
Resided in New Hanover County where he enlisted at age 22, June 3, 1861, for the war. Wounded in action at Malvern Hill, Virginia, July 1, 1862. Present or accounted for until captured at Chancellorsville, Virginia, May 3, 1863. Confined at Old Capitol Prison, Washington, D.C., until paroled on June 10, 1863. Present or accounted for until killed in action at Fisher's Hill, Virginia, September 19, 1864.

ROSS, HENRY, Private
Resided in New Hanover County where he enlisted at age 23, June 18, 1861, for the war. Present or accounted for until captured at Spotsylvania Court House, Virginia, May 12, 1864. Confined at Point Lookout, Maryland, where he died on September 16, 1864.

ROSS, JOSEPH G., Private
Resided in Alamance County and enlisted in Wake County at age 21, July 15, 1862, for the war. Present or accounted for until detailed in the Pioneer Corps on April 11, 1863. Reported as absent on detail through August 31, 1864. Present or accounted for on company muster rolls through December, 1864. Captured at Burkeville Junction, Virginia, April 6, 1865, and confined at Point Lookout, Maryland, until released after taking the Oath of Allegiance on June 17, 1865.

ROURK, JOHN, Private
Resided in New Hanover County where he enlisted at age 42, June 24, 1861, for the war. Present or accounted for until killed in action at Ellerson's Mill, Virginia, June 26, 1862.

RYAN, PATRICK, Private
Resided in New Hanover County where he enlisted at age 35, June 27, 1861, for the war. Wounded in action at Ellerson's Mill, Virginia, June 26, 1862, and admitted to hospital at Richmond, Virginia, June 27, 1862. Died in hospital on July 7, 1862, of "wound in hip."

SIMMONS, EDWARD, Private
Resided in New Hanover County where he enlisted at age 23, June 10, 1861, for the war. "Missing after the battle of Sharpsburg, Maryland, September 17, 1862."

SMITH, J., Private
Died in hospital at Lynchburg, Virginia, on July 2,

1863, of "febris contin."

SMITH, JAMES G., Private
Resided in New Hanover County where he enlisted at age 35, June 14, 1861, for the war. "Deserted July 14, 1861, at Wilmington."

SMITH, TAYLOR, Private
Resided in Bladen County and enlisted in New Hanover County at age 18, June 17, 1861, for the war. Died in hospital at Lynchburg, Virginia, July 2, 1863.

SOMMERSETT, BRIANT, Sergeant
Resided in New Hanover County where he enlisted at age 33, June 12, 1861, for the war. Mustered in as Corporal. Promoted to Sergeant prior to December, 1861. Present or accounted for until wounded in action at Payne's Farm, Virginia, November 27, 1863. Died in hospital at Richmond, Virginia, December 15, 1863, of "gunshot wound of head, fracture and depression."

SPOON, GEORGE M., Private
Enlisted in Wake County on July 15, 1862, for the war. Died in hospital at Farmville, Virginia, September 13, 1862, of "typhoid fever."

SPOON, HENRY M., Private
Resided in Guilford County and enlisted in Wake County on March 11, 1864, for the war. Captured at Spotsylvania Court House, Virginia, May 12, 1864, and confined at Point Lookout, Maryland, until transferred to Elmira, New York, August 6, 1864. Released at Elmira after taking the Oath of Allegiance on May 29, 1865.

SPOON, SAMUEL, Private
Resided in Guilford County and enlisted in Wake County at age 33, July 15, 1862, for the war. Present or accounted for until captured at Spotsylvania Court House, Virginia, May 12, 1864. Confined at Point Lookout, Maryland, until transferred to Elmira, New York, August 6, 1864. Released at Elmira after taking the Oath of Allegiance on June 21, 1865.

SPOON, WILLIAM L., Private
Resided in Alamance County and enlisted in Wake County at age 30, July 15, 1862, for the war. Present or accounted for until captured at Spotsylvania Court House, Virginia, May 12, 1864. Confined at Point Lookout, Maryland, until transferred to Elmira, New York, August 6, 1864. Released at Elmira after taking the Oath of Allegiance on May 15, 1865.

SULLIVAN, DANIEL, Private
Resided in New Hanover County where he enlisted at age 40, July 9, 1861, for the war. Died at Wilmington on October 15, 1862, of "yellow fever."

SULLIVAN, FREDERICK, Private
Resided in New Hanover County where he enlisted at age 45, June 19, 1861, for the war. Discharged on January 1, 1862, by reason of "disability."

SUTTON, FREELAND, Private
Resided in Alamance County and enlisted in Wake County at age 35, July 15, 1862, for the war. Wounded at Sharpsburg, Maryland, September 17, 1862, and reported as absent wounded through

December, 1862. Wounded in the right arm and mouth at Chancellorsville, Virginia, May 3, 1863, and right arm amputated. Reported as absent wounded on company muster rolls through December, 1864. Paroled at Greensboro on May 5, 1865.

SWING, KINGSLY, Private
Resided in Alamance County and enlisted in Wake County at age 22, July 15, 1862, for the war. Present or accounted for until captured at Spotsylvania Court House, Virginia, May 12, 1864. Confined at Point Lookout, Maryland, until transferred to Elmira, New York, August 6, 1864. Released at Elmira after taking the Oath of Allegiance on June 30, 1865.

TAYLOR, JACOB L., Private
Resided in New Hanover County where he enlisted at age 38, June 19, 1861, for the war. Present or accounted for until he died at Jordan's Springs Hospital, near Winchester, Virginia, June 24, 1863. Cause of death not reported.

TERRY, STEPHEN L., Private
Resided in New Hanover County where he enlisted at age 21, June 24, 1861, for the war. Present or accounted for until reported as absent wounded on May 14, 1864. Hospital records indicate that he was admitted to hospital at Richmond, Virginia, May 15, 1864, with a gunshot wound of the left hand. Furloughed from hospital and absent on furlough through November 4, 1864. Reported as present on November-December, 1864, muster roll.

THOMPSON, SAMUEL D., Private
Resided in Alamance County and enlisted in Wake County at age 18, July 15, 1862, for the war. Wounded in action at Sharpsburg, Maryland, September 17, 1862. Captured at Gettysburg, Pennsylvania, July 3, 1863, and confined at Fort Delaware, Delaware. Transferred to Point Lookout, Maryland, October 18, 1863. Paroled at Point Lookout on May 3, 1864, and sent to Aiken's Landing, Virginia, for exchange. Company muster rolls report him as absent prisoner through August 31, 1864. September-October, 1864, muster roll states that he was "captured September 22, 1864." Reported as absent prisoner through December, 1864. Appears as present on a muster roll of a detachment of paroled and exchanged prisoners at Camp Lee, near Richmond, Virginia, dated February 23, 1865. Paroled at Greensboro on May 18, 1865.

TUMBRETON, GEORGE A., Private
Captured at Spotsylvania Court House, Virginia, May 12, 1864, and reported on a roll of prisoners of war at Elmira, New York, "desirous of taking the Oath of Allegiance to the United States." Roll dated August, 1864, and carries the remark: "Was conscripted July 15, 1862. Wants to remain north."

TURNER, JOHN J., Private
Resided in New Hanover County where he enlisted at age 24, June 19, 1861, for the war. "Deserted in Wilmington, June 27, 1861."

WALTON, SETH, Private
Resided in New Hanover County where he enlisted at age 29. May 31, 1861, for the war. Left sick September 11, 1862, at Frederick, Maryland, where he was captured. Paroled on September 24, 1862. Captured at Fredericksburg, Virginia, May 3, 1863, and confined at Washington, D.C. Paroled and exchanged at City Point, Virginia, May 10, 1863. Present or accounted for until captured at Spotsylvania Court House, Virginia, May 12, 1864. Confined at Point Lookout, Maryland, until transferred to Elmira, New York, August 6, 1864. Released at Elmira after taking the Oath of Allegiance on June 30, 1865.

WEBSTER, CHARLES W., Private
Resided in Alamance County and enlisted in Wake County at age 34, July 15, 1862, for the war. Died in hospital at Richmond, Virginia, September 22, 1862, of "fever continued."

WHITESELL, DAVID R., Private
Resided in Alamance County and enlisted at Skinker's Neck, Virginia, April 23, 1863, for the war. Present or accounted for until captured at Spotsylvania Court House, Virginia, May 12, 1864. Confined at Point Lookout, Maryland, until transferred to Elmira, New York, August 6, 1864. Released at Elmira after taking the Oath of Allegiance on June 30, 1865.

WHITESELL, GEORGE G., Private
Transferred from Company B of this regiment on May 1, 1863. Present or accounted for until captured at Spotsylvania Court House, Virginia, May 12, 1864. Confined at Point Lookout, Maryland, until transferred to Elmira, New York, August 6, 1864. Paroled at Elmira and sent to Point Lookout for exchange on October 14, 1864. Exchanged on October 29, 1864. Captured at Savannah, Georgia, December 21, 1864, and confined at Fort Delaware, Delaware, until released after taking the Oath of Allegiance on June 7, 1865.

WHITLEDGE, STARKIE B., Private
Resided in New Hanover County where he enlisted at age 36, June 4, 1861, for the war. Mustered in as Private and appointed Corporal prior to December, 1861. Reduced to ranks on September 1, 1862. Wounded in action at Chancellorsville, Virginia, May 2-3, 1863. Reported as absent wounded until retired to the Invalid Corps on September 19, 1864, and assigned to the Quartermaster Department at Wilmington on October 20, 1864. Paroled at Goldsboro on May 4, 1865.

WILLIAMS, BENJAMIN FRANKLIN, Private
Resided in New Hanover County and enlisted in Wayne County at age 17, May 5, 1862, for the war. Present or accounted for until wounded in action at Payne's Farm, Virginia, November 27, 1863. Detailed for duty as hospital guard on April 9, 1864, by reason of his "being unfit for field service." Retired to the Invalid Corps on December 5, 1864. Admitted to hospital at Wilmington on December 29, 1864, with "rubeola" and furloughed on January 9, 1865.

WILLIAMS, BRYCE, Corporal
Resided in New Hanover County where he en-

listed at age 23, June 11, 1861, for the war. Mustered in as Private and appointed Corporal on June 30, 1863. Wounded in action at Payne's Farm, Virginia, November 27, 1863. Present or accounted for until captured at Spotsylvania Court House, Virginia, May 12, 1864. Confined at Point Lookout, Maryland, until transferred to Elmira, New York, August 6, 1864. Released at Elmira after taking the Oath of Allegiance on May 19, 1865.

WILLIAMS, GEORGE W., Private
Resided in New Hanover County where he enlisted at age 18, June 20, 1861, for the war. Reported as present on May 31-August 31, 1861, muster roll. Roll of Honor states that he "died of disease."

WILLIAMS, HENRY G., Private
Resided in New Hanover County where he enlisted at age 19, June 17, 1861, for the war. Present or accounted for until killed in action at Sharpsburg, Maryland, on September 17, 1862.

WILLIAMS, LEMUEL H., Private
Resided in New Hanover County where he enlisted at age 44, June 19, 1861, for the war. Discharged on October 31, 1861, by reason of disability.

WILLIAMS, WILLIAM HILL, 1st Sergeant
Resided in New Hanover County where he enlisted at age 21, June 7, 1861, for the war. Mustered in as Private and appointed Corporal on July 18, 1861. Promoted to Sergeant prior to February, 1862, and appointed 1st Sergeant on June 30, 1863. Wounded in action at Spotsylvania Court House, Virginia, May 12, 1864. Present or accounted for until paroled at Appomattox Court House, Virginia, April 9, 1865.

WILLIAMSON, ABRAHAM, Sergeant
Resided in New Hanover County where he enlisted at age 29, June 7, 1861, for the war. Mustered in as Private and appointed Corporal on August 26, 1861. Wounded in action at Sharpsburg, Maryland, September 17, 1862. Promoted to Sergeant January-February, 1864. Captured at Spotsylvania Court House, Virginia, May 12, 1864. Confined at Point Lookout, Maryland, until transferred to Elmira, New York, August 6, 1864. Released at Elmira after taking the Oath of Allegiance on June 19, 1865.

COMPANY F

This company, known as "Hertford Greys," from Hertford County, enlisted at Murfreesboro on July 5, 1861. It tendered its service to the state and was ordered to Warrenton, Warren County, where it became Company F of this regiment. After joining the regiment the company functioned as a part of the regiment, and its history for the war period is recorded as a part of the regimental history.

The information contained in the following roster of the company was compiled principally from company muster rolls which covered from June 15 through August 31, 1861; November through December

ber, 1861; March through April, 1862; and June 30, 1862. through December, 1864. No company muster rolls were found for September through October, 1861; January through February, 1862; May through June 29, 1862; or for the period after December, 1864. In addition to the company muster rolls, Roll of Honor records, receipt rolls, hospital records, prisoner of war records, and other primary records, supplemented by state pension applications, United Daughters of the Confederacy records, and postwar rosters and histories, all provided useful information.

OFFICERS
CAPTAINS

HARRELL, JARRETT NORFLEET
Resided in Hertford County and appointed Captain at age 37 to rank from May 16, 1861. Accepted appointment on June 3, 1861. Wounded in action at Chancellorsville, Virginia, May 3, 1863. Present or accounted for until transferred to the Field and Staff of this regiment upon appointment as Major on July 29, 1863.

BOONE, THOMAS D.
Resided in Hertford County where he enlisted at age 20, July 5, 1861, for the war. Mustered in as 1st Sergeant and appointed 2nd Lieutenant September 9, 1862. Promoted to 1st Lieutenant to rank from November 19, 1862, and to Captain on July 29, 1863. Admitted to hospital at Charlottesville, Virginia, September 25, 1864, with a gunshot wound of the chest. Date and place he received the wound was not reported. Present or accounted for until paroled at Appomattox Court House, Virginia, April 9, 1865.

LIEUTENANTS

ADKINS, JAMES F., 1st Lieutenant
Resided in Hertford County where he enlisted at age 18, July 5, 1861, for the war. Mustered in as Sergeant and appointed 2nd Lieutenant to rank from January 3, 1863. Promoted to 1st Lieutenant to rank from October 14, 1863. Present or accounted for until admitted to hospital at Richmond, Virginia, April 17, 1864, with "dysenteria acuta" and furloughed for 30 days on May 16, 1864. Reported as absent without leave after July 1, 1864; however, records indicate that he was absent on duty with a detachment at Plymouth, N.C. "without authority." Submitted his resignation on January 16, 1865, by reason of "phthisis pulmonalis." Resignation accepted on February 7, 1865.

JENKINS, JAMES P., 1st Lieutenant
Appointed 2nd Lieutenant at age 21 to rank from May 16, 1861. Promoted to 1st Lieutenant to rank from September 19, 1862. Present or accounted for until he died at Strasburg, Virginia, November 19, 1862, of disease.

LANDBERRY, W. S., 2nd Lieutenant
Paroled at Greensboro on May 5, 1865.

LAWRENCE, LEWIS C., 1st Lieutenant
Resided in Hertford County where he enlisted at age 21, July 5, 1861, for the war. Mustered in as

Sergeant and appointed 2nd Lieutenant to rank from September 23, 1862. Promoted to 1st Lieutenant on July 29, 1863. Present or accounted for until transferred to the Field and Staff of the 68th Regiment N.C. Troops upon appointment as Captain, Assistant Commissary of Subsistence, October 14, 1863.

LYON, CICERO F., 2nd Lieutenant
Resided in Hertford County and appointed 2nd Lieutenant at age 27 to rank from May 16, 1861. Accepted appointment on June 3, 1861. Wounded in action at Ellerson's Mill, Virginia, June 26, 1862. Died in hospital at Petersburg, Virginia, August 7, 1862, of wounds.

McINTIRE, THOMAS HENRY WILLIAMS, 2nd Lieutenant
Transferred from Company C of this regiment upon appointment as 2nd Lieutenant to rank from January 1, 1864. Wounded in the left leg on May 30, 1864, and reported absent wounded until returned to duty on October 17, 1864. Present or accounted for until paroled at Appomattox Court House, Virginia, April 9, 1865.

SHEPHERD, WILLIAM S., 1st Lieutenant
Resided in Hertford County and appointed 1st Lieutenant at age 23 to rank from May 16, 1861. Present or accounted for until killed in action at Sharpsburg, Maryland, September 17, 1862.

NONCOMMISSIONED OFFICERS AND PRIVATES

ASKEW, ROBERT J. R., Private
Resided in Northampton County and enlisted in Hertford County at age 18, July 8, 1861, for the war. Wounded in the hand and knee at Fredericksburg, Virginia, December 13, 1862. Returned to duty from hospital in Richmond, Virginia, on February 10, 1863. Present or accounted for on company muster rolls through December, 1864, being absent in hospital at Richmond from February, 1864, through December, 1864. Paroled at Appomattox Court House, Virginia, April 9, 1865.

ASKEW, ZEPHANIAH, Private
Resided in Hertford County where he enlisted at age 20, February 13, 1862, for the war. Wounded in the thigh at Ellerson's Mill, Virginia, June 26, 1862. Reported as absent on furlough through February, 1864, when he was detailed for duty to "collect tithes." Absent detailed through October, 1864. Reported as present on November-December, 1864, muster roll.

ATKINS, JOHN B., Private
Resided in Hertford County where he enlisted at age 18, July 5, 1861, for the war. Discharged at Richmond, Virginia, October 25, 1861, by reason of disability.

BAGGETT, JAMES T., Private
Resided in Northampton County where he enlisted at age 18, January 13, 1862, for the war. Wounded in action at Ellerson's Mill, Virginia, June 26, 1862. Reported as absent wounded through December, 1862. Present or accounted for

until captured at Spotsylvania Court House, Virginia, May 12, 1864. Confined at Elmira, New York, until released after taking the Oath of Allegiance on May 29, 1865.

BAILEY, J. G., Private
Resided in Hertford County where he enlisted at age 19, May 9, 1862, for the war. Present or accounted for until he died in hospital at Richmond, Virginia, February 18, 1863, of "variola conf."

BANTY, WILLIAM T., Private
Resided as a farmer in Northampton County where he enlisted at age 22, July 26, 1861, for the war. Died at Goldsboro on April 16, 1862.

BARBEE, H. T., Private
Born in Orange County where he resided as a farmer and enlisted at age 22, July 15, 1862, for the war. Discharged at Huguenot Springs, Virginia, July 18, 1862, by reason of "endocarditis."

BARBOUR, JOSEPH, Private
Admitted to hospital at Richmond, Virginia, September 22, 1862.

BARHAM, RANDOLPH, Private
Resided in Northampton County and enlisted at age 16, May 15, 1862, for the war as a substitute. Wounded in action at Sharpsburg, Maryland, September 17, 1862. Wound necessitated amputation of both legs. Never returned to duty.

BARING, H. M., Private
Captured at Hanover Junction, Virginia, May 24, 1864, and confined at Point Lookout, Maryland. Reported on a roll of "prisoners who arrived under assumed names, or who assumed one for purpose of being transferred, exchanged, or released."

BAUGHAM, TILMAN P., Corporal
Resided in Northampton County where he enlisted at age 18, July 26, 1861, for the war. Mustered in as Private. Wounded in action at Chancellorsville, Virginia, May 3, 1863. Promoted to Corporal on January 1, 1864. Present or accounted for on company muster rolls through December, 1864.

BEALE, GEORGE W., Private
Resided in Hertford County where he enlisted at age 22, July 5, 1861, for the war. Present or accounted for until captured at Spotsylvania Court House, Virginia, May 12, 1864. Confined at Elmira, New York, until transferred to James River, Virginia, for exchange on February 20, 1865. Admitted to hospital at Richmond, Virginia, March 4, 1865, and furloughed for 60 days March 17, 1865.

BEALE, JAMES H., Private
Born in Hertford County where he resided as a mechanic and enlisted at age 32, July 5, 1861, for the war. Present or accounted for until discharged on June 24, 1862. Later conscripted on August 20, 1863, and assigned to the conscript camp at Raleigh. Again discharged on February 10, 1864.

BEALE, WILLIAM E., Private
Resided in Hertford County where he enlisted at

age 20, July 10, 1861, for the war. Present or accounted for until he died on August 6, 1862, of disease.

BENTLEY, PAUL H., Private
Born in Northampton County where he resided as a farmer and enlisted at age 20, February 6, 1862, for the war. Present or accounted for until he died in hospital at Richmond, Virginia, August 27, 1862, of disease.

BLACKSTONE, WILLIAM R., Private
Resided in Bertie County and enlisted in Hertford County at age 21, July 8, 1861, for the war. Discharged at Camp Bee, Virginia, December 9, 1861, for disability.

BLALOCK, L. D. H., Private
Resided in Orange County where he enlisted at age 20, July 15, 1862, for the war. Discharged. Date of discharge not given.

BLANCHARD, JOSEPH E., Private
Reported as a "deserter" taken at Bernard's Mills, Virginia, January 6, 1865.

BLANCHARD, JOSEPH H., Sergeant
Resided in Northampton County where he enlisted at age 20, July 5, 6, 1861, for the war. Mustered in as Private and appointed Corporal on September 1, 1862. Promoted to Sergeant on January 3, 1863. Wounded at Winchester, Virginia, June 15, 1863, and reported as absent wounded through December, 1864.

BLEDSOE, J. J., Private
Born in Orange County where he resided as a farmer and enlisted at age 19, July 15, 1862, for the war. Discharged at Richmond, Virginia, September 10, 1862, by reason of "very feeble constitution with disease of the heart."

BOLTON, LEMUEL, Private
Resided in Northampton County where he enlisted at age 30, February 11, 1862, for the war. Reported on September-October, 1863, muster roll with the remark: "Deserted, having been absent more than twelve months without leave."

BOONE, JAMES D., Private
Resided in Northampton County and enlisted in Hertford County at age 23, July 11, 1861, for the war. Present or accounted for until transferred to the Field and Staff of this regiment upon appointment as Quartermaster Sergeant, November-December, 1862.

BOONE, JOHN W., Private
Resided in Northampton County and enlisted in Hertford County at age 18, July 11, 1861, for the war. Died at Fredericksburg, Virginia, December 18, 1861, of disease.

BOONE, SOLON G., Private
Resided in Halifax County and enlisted in Northampton County at age 34, April 16, 1862, for the war. Wounded in action at Ellerson's Mill, Virginia, June 26, 1862. Present or accounted for until he was reported as missing in action at Cedar Creek, Virginia, October 19, 1864.

BOONE, W. F., Private
Resided in Northampton County and enlisted in

Wayne County at age 25, May 1, 1862, for the war. Present or accounted for until paroled at Appomattox Court House, Virginia, April 9, 1865.

BOWDEN, JOHN, Private
Paroled at Greensboro on May 16, 1865.

BRACEY, WILLIAM, Private
Born in Hertford County and resided in Northampton County where he enlisted at age 40, January 30, 1862, for the war. Present or accounted for until he died on August 12, 1862, of disease.

BRANTLEY, GEORGE M., Private
Resided in Hertford County where he enlisted at age 40, July 11, 1861, for the war. Reported as absent without leave after June 1, 1862.

BRANTLEY, ROBERT E., Private
Resided in Hertford County where he enlisted at age 31, February 13, 1862, for the war. Discharged April 16, 1862, by reason of "physical inability."

BRANTLEY, SAMUEL J., Private
Resided in Hertford County where he enlisted at age 34, July 5, 1861, for the war. Present or accounted for until furloughed from hospital at Richmond, Virginia, December 12, 1862, for 40 days. Reported as absent without leave on company muster rolls until September-October, 1864, when he was reported as "absent on duty at Plymouth, North Carolina." Reported as present on November-December, 1864, muster roll. Paroled at Burkeville Junction, Virginia, April 14-17, 1865.

BRISTOW, JAMES A., Private
Resided in Northampton County where he enlisted at age 31, February 1, 1862, for the war. Present or accounted for until captured at Spotsylvania Court House, Virginia, May 12, 1864. Confined at Point Lookout, Maryland, until transferred to Elmira, New York, August 6, 1864. Died at Elmira on April 6, 1865, of "chronic diarrhoea."

BRISTOW, WILLIAM F., Private
Resided in Northampton County where he enlisted at age 33, January 13, 1862, for the war. Present or accounted for until reported as captured at Spotsylvania Court House, Virginia, Present or accounted for until reported on muster rolls as captured at Spotsylvania Court House, Virginia, May 12, 1864.

BRITT, JAMES E., Private
Resided in Hertford County where he enlisted at age 20, July 5, 1861, for the war. Wounded and captured at Sharpsburg, Maryland, September 17, 1862. Confined at Fort McHenry, Maryland, until paroled on October 13, 1862, and sent to Fort Monroe, Virginia, for exchange. Declared exchanged on November 10, 1862. Furloughed from hospital at Richmond, Virginia, November 12, 1862, for 40 days. Company muster rolls report him as absent wounded through December, 1864.

BRITTON, NOAH J., Private
Resided in Northampton County where he enlisted at age 30, February 1, 1862, for the war. Present or accounted for until captured at Spot-

sylvania Court House, Virginia, May 12, 1864. Confined at Point Lookout, Maryland, until transferred to Elmira, New York, August 6, 1864. Released at Elmira after taking the Oath of Allegiance on May 29, 1865.

BUTLER, J. F., Private
Resided as a farmer in Northampton County where he enlisted at age 31, February 10, 1862, for the war. Discharged at Goldsboro on April 16, 1862, by reason of "paralysis of the arm."

CHISENHALL, JAMES, Private
Resided in Orange County where he enlisted at age 20, July 15, 1862, for the war. Present or accounted for until captured at Winchester, Virginia, September 19, 1864. Confined at Point Lookout, Maryland, until paroled and exchanged at Boulware's Wharf, James River, Virginia, March 18, 1865.

COLE, THOMAS J., Private
Born in Amelia County, Virginia, and enlisted in Halifax County at age 43, August 20, 1861, for the war. Died in hospital at Petersburg, Virginia, March 26, 1862.

COPELAND, JOSHUA F., Private
Resided in Bertie County and enlisted in Hertford County at age 21, July 5, 1861, for the war. Wounded in action at Sharpsburg, Maryland, September 17, 1862, and admitted to hospital at Richmond, Virginia, September 22, 1862, with "contusion of shoulder with dislocation of left arm." Returned to duty October 20, 1862. Present or accounted for on company muster rolls through February, 1864, and reported as "absent, prisoner of war since May 12, 1864" on muster rolls for March-December, 1864. No Federal Provost Marshal records relative to his capture on May 12, 1864, were found.

COPLEY, J. A., Private
Resided in Orange County where he enlisted at age 23, July 15, 1862, for the war. Killed in action at Sharpsburg, Maryland, September 17, 1862.

COPLEY, WILLIAM, Private
Resided in Orange County where he enlisted at age 35, July 15, 1862, for the war. Present or accounted for on company muster rolls through December, 1864. Admitted to hospital at Charlottesville, Virginia, December 20, 1864, with "hernia" and returned to duty February 2, 1865. Detailed on February 16, 1865.

COUCH, WILLIAM, Private
Born in Orange County where he resided as a farmer and enlisted at age 23, July 15, 1862, for the war. Present or accounted for until captured at Gettysburg, Pennsylvania, July 3, 1863. Confined at Fort Delaware, Delaware, until transferred to Point Lookout, Maryland, October 15, 1863. Released after taking the Oath of Allegiance and joining the U.S. service at Point Lookout on January 24, 1864. Assigned to Company A, 1st Regiment U.S. Volunteer Infantry.

CRABN, J. M., Private
Paroled at Greensboro on May 13, 1865.

CRAIG, JOSEPH A., Private
Resided in Orange County where he enlisted at

age 23, July 15, 1862, for the war. Died in hospital at Richmond, Virginia, December 25, 1862, of "febris typh."

CUTRELL, WASHINGTON, Private
Resided in Northampton County and enlisted in Hertford County at age 26, July 6, 1861, for the war. Present or accounted for until killed in action at Chancellorsville, Virginia, May 3, 1863.

DARDEN, JAMES P., Private
Resided in Hertford County where he enlisted at age 18, July 5, 1861, for the war. Wounded and captured at Sharpsburg, Maryland, September 17, 1862, and paroled on September 27, 1862. Wounded in action at Gettysburg, Pennsylvania, July 2, 3, 1863. Present or accounted for on company muster rolls through December, 1864. Paroled at Appomattox Court House, Virginia, April 9, 1865.

DAVIS, DREWRY T., Private
Resided in Northampton County and enlisted in Wayne County at age 23, May 27, 1862, for the war. Present or accounted for until captured at Spotsylvania Court House, Virginia, May 12, 1864. Confined at Point Lookout, Maryland, until transferred to Elmira, New York, August 6, 1864. Died at Elmira on March 27, 1865, of "diarrhoea."

DAVIS, O'CONNELL, Private
Resided in Northampton County where he enlisted at age 30, January 30, 1862, for the war. Wounded at Sharpsburg, Maryland, September 17, 1862. Absent wounded until detailed for hospital duty March-April, 1863. Absent on detail in hospital until September-October, 1864, when he was detailed as a guard at "the President's house." Reported as detailed through December, 1864.

DAVIS, WINBORN C., Sergeant
Resided in Northampton County and enlisted at Camp Bee, Virginia, at age 20, August 18, 1861, for the war. Mustered in as Private. Wounded in action at Sharpsburg, Maryland, September 17, 1862. Promoted to Sergeant on June 1, 1863. Wounded at Gettysburg, Pennsylvania, July 1-3, 1863, and captured in hospital at Gettysburg, July 4-5, 1863. Undated roll of prisoners of war in hospitals at Gettysburg sent to the Provost Marshal on December 2, 1863, states that he was "transferred to Provost Marshal." Company muster roll for January-February, 1864, states: "Died from wounds received at Gettysburg, time unknown." Appears on a list of North Carolina Confederate troops buried after the battle of Gettysburg with the remark: "Buried under little apple tree."

DEAM, CHARLES T., Private
Resided in Northampton County and enlisted at age 24, May 10, 1862, for the war. Discharged on June 8, 1862, upon providing Wiley Hunter as his substitute.

DISERN, JOHN, Private
Resided in Orange County where he enlisted at age 19, July 15, 1862, for the war. Present or accounted for until captured at Spotsylvania Court House, Virginia, May 12, 1864. Confined at Point Lookout, Maryland, until transferred to Elmira,

New York, August 6, 1864. Transferred to James River, Virginia, for exchange on March 14, 1865, and exchanged at Boulware's Wharf, James River, Virginia, March 18-21, 1865.

DUNNING, JAMES W., Private
Resided in Bertie County and enlisted in Hertford County at age 30, July 11, 1861, for the war. Discharged on May 30, 31, 1862.

DUNNING, JOSEPH J., Private
Resided in Bertie County and enlisted in Hertford County at age 23, July 5, 1861, for the war. Wounded in action at Chancellorsville, Virginia, May 3, 1863, and captured in hospital at Winchester, Virginia, July 30, 1863, while on detail as nurse. Paroled and remained in hospital at Winchester through November, 1863, on detail. Captured at Spotsylvania Court House, Virginia, May 12, 1864. Confined at Point Lookout, Maryland, until transferred to Elmira, New York, August 6, 1864. Released after taking the Oath of Allegiance at Elmira on May 17, 1865.

DUNNING, WILLIAM J., Private
Resided in Bertie County and enlisted in Hertford County at age 21, July 5, 1861, for the war. Company muster rolls indicate that he was absent sick from November, 1862, through February, 1863, and absent detailed as nurse in hospital at Richmond, Virginia, from February, 1863, through December, 1864.

EARLY, JAMES H., Private
Born in Bertie County where he resided prior to enlisting in Hertford County at age 18, July 5, 1861, for the war. Died at Petersburg, Virginia, April 5, 1862, of disease.

EDWARDS, RICHARD T., Private
Resided in Northampton County where he enlisted at age 18, February 13, 1862, for the war. Present or accounted for until captured at Spotsylvania Court House, Virginia, May 12, 1864. Confined at Point Lookout, Maryland, until transferred to Elmira, New York, August 6, 1864. Released at Elmira after taking the Oath of Allegiance on June 16, 1865.

ELLIS, DURELL, Private
Resided in Orange County where he enlisted at age 34, July 15, 1862, for the war. Present or accounted for until captured at Spotsylvania Court House, Virginia, May 12, 1864. Confined at Point Lookout, Maryland, until transferred to Elmira, New York, August 6, 1864. Died at Elmira on October 10, 1864, of "pneumonia."

EURE, ELISHA F., Private
Resided in Hertford County where he enlisted at age 18, February 18, 1862, for the war. Present or accounted for until he died in camp near Port Royal, Virginia, March 14, 1863.

EVANS, WILLIAM, Private
Born in Hertford County where he resided and enlisted at age 39, January 28, 1862, for the war. Died "at home" February 28, 1863.

FERRELL, LEWIS F., Private
Resided in Orange County where he enlisted at age 26, July 15, 1862, for the war. Killed in action at Sharpsburg, Maryland, September 17, 1862.

FOSTER, LYMAN L., 1st Sergeant
Resided in Hertford County where he enlisted at age 20, July 5, 1861, for the war. Mustered in as Sergeant and promoted to 1st Sergeant after October, 1862. Wounded in action at Chancellorsville, Virginia, May 3, 1863. Present or accounted for through January-February, 1864, muster roll when he was reported with the remark: "Promoted to Master in the Navy, December 15, 1863." Transferred to the C.S. Navy on that date.

FOWLER, W. JEFFERSON, Private
Resided in Orange County where he enlisted at age 30, July 15, 1862, for the war. Present or accounted for until killed in action at Sharpsburg, Maryland, September 17, 1862.

GALLAHOEN, J. M., Private
Paroled at Greensboro on May 13, 1865.

GARDNER, JAMES HENRY, Private
Resided in Northampton County and enlisted in Hertford County at age 23, June 15, 1861, for the war. Wounded in action at Wilderness, Virginia, May 5, 1864. Reported as absent wounded through December, 1864. Captured at Sayler's Creek, Virginia, April 6, 1865, and confined at Point Lookout, Maryland. Released at Point Lookout after taking the Oath of Allegiance on June 27, 1865.

GARDNER, WILLIAM R., Private
Resided in Northampton County and enlisted in Hertford County at age 20, July 5, 1861, for the war. Mustered in as Musician and reported as Musician through December, 1861. Reported as Private after that date. Present or accounted for until captured at Spotsylvania Court House, Virginia, May 12, 1864. Confined at Point Lookout, Maryland, until transferred to Elmira, New York, August 6, 1864. Paroled at Elmira and sent for exchange on March 14, 1865. Received at Boulware's Wharf, James River, Virginia, March 18-21, 1865, in exchange. Admitted to hospital at Richmond, Virginia, March 19, 1865, with "scorbutis" and furloughed for 30 days on March 23, 1865.

GATLING, N. B., Private
Resided in Northampton County where he enlisted at age 24, May 1, 1862, for the war. Wounded in action at Payne's Farm, Virginia, November 27, 1863. Present or accounted for until paroled at Farmville, Virginia, April 11-21, 1865.

GEORGE, CHARLES, Private
Resided in Orange County where he enlisted at age 20, July 15, 1862, for the war. Wounded in action at Sharpsburg, Maryland, September 17, 1862. Killed in action at Chancellorsville, Virginia, May 3, 1863.

GEORGE, HENDERSON, Private
Resided in Orange County where he enlisted at age 28, July 15, 1862, for the war. Present or accounted for until paroled at Farmville, Virginia, April 11-21, 1865.

GRIFFIN, JAMES H., Private
Resided in Northampton County where he enlisted at age 23, February 1, 1862, for the war. Captured at Boonsboro, Maryland, September 15, 1862, and confined at Fort Delaware, Dela-

ware. Transferred to Aiken's Landing, Virginia, October 2, 1862, and exchanged on November 10, 1862. Present or accounted for until captured at Spotsylvania Court House, Virginia, May 12, 1864. Confined at Point Lookout, Maryland, until transferred to Elmira, New York, August 6, 1864. Released at Elmira after taking the Oath of Allegiance on May 29, 1865.

GRIFFIN, WILLIAM T., Private

Resided in Northampton County where he enlisted at age 21, July 6, 1861, for the war. Discharged at Richmond, Virginia, September 20, 1861, by reason of disability.

HAMPTON, J. W., Private

Resided in Orange County where he enlisted at age 18, July 15, 1862, for the war. Died at Richmond, Virginia, September 15, 1862, of "typhoid fever."

HARRELL, WILLIAM A., Sergeant

Resided in Hertford County where he enlisted at age 37, July 5, 1861, for the war. Mustered in as Private and appointed Corporal on December 1, 1862. Promoted to Sergeant on June 1, 1863. Present or accounted for until captured at Spotsylvania Court House, Virginia, May 12, 1864. Confined at Point Lookout, Maryland, until transferred to Elmira, New York, August 6, 1864. Released at Elmira after taking the Oath of Allegiance on May 29, 1865.

HARRIS, JAMES M., Private

Resided in Orange County where he enlisted at age 32, July 15, 1862, for the war. Admitted to hospital at Richmond, Virginia, September 27-28, 1862, with a gunshot wound and furloughed October 7-8, 1862. Returned to company January-February, 1863, and killed in action at Chancellorsville, Virginia, May 3, 1863.

HASTY, NORFLEET, Private

Resided in Northampton County and enlisted at Camp Bee, Virginia, at age 24, August 18, 1861, for the war. Wounded in action at Ellerson's Mill, Virginia, June 26, 1862. Present or accounted for until paroled at Appomattox Court House, Virginia, April 9, 1865.

HENDSON, C., Private

Paroled at Greensboro on May 15, 1865.

HERNDON, JAMES, Private

Resided in Orange County where he enlisted at age 21, July 15, 1862, for the war. Present or accounted for until captured at Spotsylvania Court House, Virginia, May 12, 1864. Confined at Point Lookout, Maryland, until transferred to Elmira, New York, August 6, 1864. Paroled at Elmira on October 11, 1864, and sent to Point Lookout. Declared exchanged at James River, Virginia, October 29, 1864. Reported as absent on November-December, 1864, muster roll.

HERNDON, WILLIAM, Private

Resided in Orange County where he enlisted at age 33, July 15, 1862, for the war. Present or accounted for until he "lost left arm at Wilderness, Virginia, May 5, 1864." Reported as absent "permanently disabled" through December, 1864.

HORN, SAMUEL J., Private

Resided in Orange County where he enlisted at age 30, July 15, 1862, for the war. Present or accounted for until he died in hospital at Richmond, Virginia, January 15, 1863, of disease.

HOWE, JOHN C., Private

Paroled at Greensboro on May 8, 1865.

HUNTER, WILEY, Private

Resided in Northampton County where he enlisted at age 42 on June 8, 1862, for the war as a substitute for Charles T. Beam. Killed in action at Ellerson's Mill, Virginia, June 26, 1862.

HUSON, JOHN C., Private

Resided in Hertford County where he enlisted at age 20, July 5, 1861, for the war. Present or accounted for until he was killed in action at Gettysburg, Pennsylvania, July 2, 1863.

JACKSON, EDGAR ALLAN, Sergeant

Born in Squan Village, New Jersey, and resided as a printer in Hertford County where he enlisted at age 18, July 5, 1861, for the war. Mustered in as Private and appointed Corporal after July 1, 1862. Promoted to Sergeant on September 23, 1862. Killed in action at Chancellorsville, Virginia, May 3, 1863.

JACOBS, JASON, Private

Enlisted in Hertford County at age 32, February 11, 1862, for the war. Present or accounted for until captured at Spotsylvania Court House, Virginia, May 12, 1864. Confined at Point Lookout, Maryland, until transferred to Elmira, New York, August 6, 1864. Died at Elmira on May 16, 1865, of "chronic diarrhoea."

JELKS, WILLIAM J., Private

Resided in Hertford County where he enlisted at age 18, July 5, 1861, for the war. Present or accounted for until killed in action at Chancellorsville, Virginia, May 3, 1863.

JENKINS, JOHN, Private

Resided in Northampton County and enlisted in Hertford County at age 18, July 11, 1861, for the war. Wounded in action at Ellerson's Mill, Virginia, June 26, 1862, and at Gettysburg, Pennsylvania, July 3, 1863. Present or accounted for until captured at Winchester, Virginia, September 19, 1864. Confined at Point Lookout, Maryland, until paroled and transferred to Aiken's Landing, Virginia, March 15, 1865, for exchange.

JENKINS, PATRICK H., Corporal

Resided in Northampton County and enlisted in Hertford County at age 20, July 5, 1861, for the war. Mustered in as Corporal. Killed in action at Ellerson's Mill, Virginia, June 26, 1862.

JENKINS, WILLIAM, Private

Born in Nansemond County, Virginia, and resided in Hertford County where he enlisted at age 49, July 11, 1861, for the war. Died at Fredericksburg, Virginia, May 2, 1862, of disease.

JEWELL, E. H., Private

Paroled at Greensboro on May 8, 1865.

JOHNSON, ANDREW W., Private

Resided in Northampton County where he enlisted at age 30, July 26, 1861, for the war. Wounded in action at Sharpsburg, Maryland, September 17, 1862. Present or accounted for until captured at Spotsylvania Court House, Virginia, May 12, 1864. Confined at Point Lookout, Maryland, until transferred to Elmira, New York, August 6, 1864. Paroled at Elmira on March 14, 1865, and sent to James River, Virginia, for exchange. Admitted to hospital at Richmond, Virginia, March 18, 1865, with "scorbutis." Furloughed for 30 days on March 23, 1865.

JOHNSON, EDWARD D., Corporal
Resided in Northampton County where he enlisted at age 26, July 26, 1861, for the war. Mustered in as Private. Wounded in action at Ellerson's Mill, Virginia, June 26, 1862, and again at Chancellorsville, Virginia, May 3, 1863, where he "received three wounds before leaving the field." Promoted to Corporal on January 1, 1864. Died May 13, 15, 1864, of wounds received at Spotsylvania Court House, Virginia, on May 10, 1864.

JOHNSON, WALKER, Private
Resided in Orange County where he enlisted at age 27, July 15, 1862, for the war. Wounded in action at Chancellorsville, Virginia, May 3, 1863, and "deserted May 10, 1863."

JOYNER, EDWARD, Private
Resided in Hertford County where he enlisted at age 27, July 5, 1861, for the war. Present or accounted for until captured at Gettysburg, Pennsylvania, July 2, 1863. Confined at Fort Delaware, Delaware, until released after taking the Oath of Allegiance on June 7, 1865.

JOYNER, H. H., Private
Resided in Northampton County where he enlisted at age 24, April 28, 1862, for the war. Present or accounted for until he was "shot to death by sentence of General Court Marshal, February 11, 1864."

JOYNER, JAMES H., Private
Resided in Northampton County and enlisted in Hertford County at age 23, July 10, 1861, for the war. Discharged at Camp Bee, Virginia, November 29, 1861, for disability.

JOYNER, JOHN E., Corporal
Resided in Northampton County and enlisted in Hertford County at age 28, July 6, 1861, for the war. Mustered in as Private and appointed Corporal on December 1, 1862. Killed in action at Chancellorsville, Virginia, May 3, 1863.

JULICK, FREDERICK, Private
Transferred from the Regimental Band on the Field and Staff on November 18, 1861. Wounded in action at Chancellorsville, Virginia, May 3, 1863. Captured at Jackson, N.C., while absent on furlough on July 27, 1863, and exchanged at Fort Monroe, Virginia, on August 4, 1863. Admitted to hospital at Petersburg, Virginia, August 5, 1863, and returned to duty on August 11, 1863. Present or accounted for through December, 1864.

KIFF, PATRICK P., Corporal
Resided in Hertford County where he enlisted at age 18, July 5, 1861, for the war. Mustered in as

Private and appointed Corporal on January 3, 1863. Killed in action at Chancellorsville, Virginia, May 3, 1863.

LANE, JAMES A., Private
Resided in Northampton County where he enlisted at age 19, February 13, 1862, for the war. Reported as present or accounted for through March 20, 1864, and as absent without leave after that date. Federal Provost Marchal records report him as a "rebel deserter" with the remark that he "came into Federal lines, Plymouth, North Carolina." Received at Fort Monroe, Virginia, April 23, 1864, and released after taking the Oath of Amnesty on April 25, 1864.

LASSITER, ANDREW A., Private
Resided in Northampton County and enlisted in Hertford County at age 21, July 5, 1861, for the war. Wounded in action at Ellerson's Mill, Virginia, June 26, 1862. Reported as absent wounded through March 10, 1863, and as absent without leave after that date through December, 1864.

LEE, WILLIAM A., Private
Resided in Hertford County where he enlisted at age 21, July 5, 1861, for the war. Present or accounted for until killed in action at Sharpsburg, Maryland, September 17, 1862.

McNAMEE, PETER F., Sergeant
Born in Ireland and resided as a tailor in Hertford County where he enlisted at age 26, July 5, 1861, for the war. Mustered in as Sergeant. Discharged at Richmond, Virginia, January 23, 1863, by reason of "heart disease." Detailed in Quartermaster Department at Richmond, Virginia, February 17, 1863, and reported as absent on detail through December, 1864. While on detail he was assigned to the 2nd Battalion Virginia Infantry (Local Defense)

MANNING, D. M., Private
Resided in Nash County where he enlisted at age 24, July 15, 1862, for the war. Killed in action at Payne's Farm, Virginia, November 27, 1863.

MANNING, N. N., Private
Resided in Nash County where he enlisted at age 19, July 15, 1862, for the war. Reported as absent sick from date of enlistment through March 1, 1864, and as absent without leave after that date through December, 1864.

MANNING, W. W., Private
Born in Nash County where he resided as a farmer and enlisted at age 30, July 15, 1862, for the war. Present or accounted for until discharged at Richmond, Virginia, September 29, 1862, by reason of "an old fracture of the scapula and the clavicle impeding the free use of the shoulder joint, rendering him unfit for military duty."

MARSHBORNE, JOHN R., Private
Resided in Nash County where he enlisted at age 19, July 15, 1862, for the war. Present or acounted for until killed in action at Wilderness, Virginia, May 5, 1864.

MELSON, J. T., Private
Born in Tyrrell County and resided as a farmer in Hertford County where he enlisted at age 37, May 5-7, 1862, for the war. Killed in action at

Ellerson's Mill, Virginia, June 26, 1862.

MILLER, T. C., Private
Discharged on March 25, 1862.

MILLER, THOMAS H., Corporal
Resided in Hertford County where he enlisted at age 19, July 5, 1861, for the war. Mustered in as Corporal. Discharged August 1, 1862, upon providing John White as his substitute.

MODLIN, JORDAN, Private
Resided in Hertford County where he enlisted at age 19, July 9, 1861, for the war. Died at Fredericksburg, Virginia, October 26, 1861, of disease.

MONTGOMERY, WILLIAM PRESTON, Private
Born in Hertford County where he resided as a farmer and enlisted at age 18, July 5, 1861, for the war. Wounded in action at Ellerson's Mill, Virginia, June 26, 1862. Discharged on July 20, 1862, by reason of wounds "causing amputation of the foot."

MORRIS, JOHN A., Private
Born in Hertford County and resided in Bertie County prior to enlisting in Hertford County at age 21, February 13, 1862, for the war. Killed in action at Sharpsburg, Maryland, September 17, 1862.

MULDER, FRANCIS S., Private
Resided in Northampton County where he enlisted at age 23, January 30, 1862, for the war. Wounded in action at Ellerson's Mill, Virginia, June 26, 1862. Reported as absent wounded and disabled through December, 1864.

NEWSOM, JOHN W., Private
Captured at Gettysburg, Pennsylvania, July 2, 1863, and confined at Point Lookout, Maryland, where he "joined U.S. service March 12, 1864."

ODOM, CORNELIUS J., Corporal
Resided in Northampton County where he enlisted at age 18, July 26, 1861, for the war. Mustered in as Private. Captured in September, 1862, and paroled September 24, 1862. Appointed Corporal in May, 1863. Killed in action at Winchester, Virginia, June 15, 1863.

OUTLAND, HENRY E., Private
Resided in Northampton County and enlisted in Hertford County at age 24, July 5, 1861, for the war. Present or accounted for on company muster rolls through December 1, 1862, and reported as absent without leave after that date.

PARKER, HENRY T., Private
Resided in Northampton County where he enlisted at age 19, July 26, 1861, for the war. Captured near Richmond, Virginia, June 15, 1862, and confined at Fort Delaware, Delaware, until paroled and exchanged at Aiken's Landing, Virginia, August 5, 1862. Present or accounted for on company muster rolls through December, 1864.

PARKER, JAMES B., Corporal
Born in Northampton County where he resided as a farmer and enlisted in Hertford County at age 18, July 5, 1861, for the war. Mustered in as Private. Promoted to Corporal June 1, 1863. Reported as present or accounted for on company muster rolls until July 14, 1864, when he was

reported as absent on wounded furlough. Reported as such through December, 1864.

PARKER, JOHN D. H., Sergeant
Resided in Hertford County where he enlisted at age 24, July 5, 1861, for the war. Mustered in as Corporal. Captured at Boonsboro, Maryland, September 15, 1862. Confined at Fort Delaware, Delaware, until transferred to Aiken's Landing, Virginia, October 2, 1862, for exchange. Declared exchanged on November 10, 1862. Promoted to Sergeant on December 1, 1862. Killed in action at Chancellorsville, Virginia, May 3, 1863.

PARKER, KING S., Private
Resided in Northampton County and enlisted in Hertford County at age 20, July 5, 1861, for the war. Surrendered at Mount Union, Pennsylvania, June 29, 1863, and confined at Fort Mifflin, Pennsylvania. Escaped from Fort Mifflin on February 6, 1864. Company muster rolls reported him as present or accounted for through June 27, 1863, and as absent without leave after that date.

PARRISH, W. C., Private
Resided in Orange County where he enlisted at age 33, July 15, 1862, for the war. Wounded and captured at Sharpsburg, Maryland, September 17, 1862. Paroled at Fort McHenry, Maryland, October 18, 1862, and declared exchanged at Aiken's Landing, Virginia, November 10, 1862. Admitted to hospital at Richmond, Virginia, October 23, 1862, and furloughed for 40 days on November 17, 1862. Reported on company muster rolls as absent wounded through December, 1864.

PICKETT, JAMES, Private
Born in Orange County where he resided as a farmer and enlisted at age 18, July 15, 1862, for the war. Discharged at Richmond, Virginia, September 3, 1862, by reason of "feeble constitution."

PICKETT, WILLIAM, Private
Resided in Orange County where he enlisted at age 30, July 15, 1862, for the war. Killed in action at Gettysburg, Pennsylvania, July 2, 1863.

POPE, GEORGE M., Private
Born in Cumberland County and resided as a farmer in Northampton County where he enlisted at age 19, July 26, 1861, for the war. Present or accounted for until captured at Spotsylvania Court House, Virginia, May 12, 1864. Confined at Point Lookout, Maryland, where he joined the U.S. service on May 28, 1864. Assigned to Company I, 1st Regiment U.S. Volunteer Infantry.

POWELL, JAMES R., Private
Resided in Bertie County and enlisted in Hertford County at age 19, July 5, 1861, for the war. Present or accounted for until paroled at Appomattox Court House, Virginia, April 9, 1865.

POWELL, SAMUEL RALSTON, Private
Appears on a list of prisoners who volunteered in the Winder Legion for the defense of Richmond against General Sheridan's raid and who were pardoned by President Jefferson Davis. List dated August 3, 1864.

QUINN, HUGH, 1st Sergeant
Resided in Hertford County where he enlisted at

age 33, July 5, 1861, for the war. Mustered in as Corporal. Detailed in hospital at Richmond, Virginia, from July, 1862, through June, 1863. Promoted to 1st Sergeant on January 1, 1864. Wounded in action at Spotsylvania Court House, Virginia, May 10, 1864. Present or accounted for until paroled at Appomattox Court House, Virginia, April 9, 1865.

REAMS, JOHN, Private

Resided in Northampton County where he enlisted at age 18, January 30, 1862, for the war. Present or accounted for until captured at Spotsylvania Court House, Virginia, May 12, 1864. Confined at Point Lookout, Maryland, until transferred to Elmira, New York, August 6, 1864. Released at Elmira after taking the Oath of Allegiance on May 19, 1865.

RHEW, JEFFERSON, Private

Resided in Orange County where he enlisted at age 29, July 15, 1862, for the war. Admitted to hospital at Richmond, Virginia, May 7, 1864, with a gunshot wound of the hand. Exact date returned to company not reported, but he was admitted to hospital in Richmond, December 23, 1864, with gunshot wound of the heel. Returned to duty January 24, 1865. Captured at Burkeville Junction, Virginia, April 6, 1865, and confined at Point Lookout, Maryland, until released after taking the Oath of Allegiance on June 17, 1865.

RICE, WILLIAM C., Private

Born in Tyrrell County and resided in Hertford County where he enlisted at age 18, July 5, 1861, for the war. Died in hospital at Richmond, Virginia, September 6, 1861.

RICKS, EDWIN, Private

Resided in Northampton County where he enlisted at age 20, June 15, 1861, for the war. Wounded in action at Malvern Hill, Virginia, July 1, 1862, and at Chancellorsville, Virginia, May 3, 1863. Admitted to hospital at Richmond, Virginia, May 29, 1863, with a gunshot wound of the thigh and furloughed for 40 days on July 26, 1863. Retired to the Invalid Corps on January 13, 1865, and assigned to light duty on January 19, 1865, at Richmond.

RICKS, JAMES S., Private

Born in Northampton County where he resided and enlisted at age 19, June 15, 1861, for the war. Killed in action at Ellerson's Mill, Virginia, June 26, 1862.

SAUNDERS, ASA, Private

Resided in Hertford County where he enlisted at age 18, January 28, 1862, for the war. Captured at Fredericksburg, Virginia, May 3, 1863, and confined at Washington, D.C., until paroled and exchanged at City Point, Virginia, May 10, 1863. Present or accounted for until captured at Spotsylvania Court House, Virginia, May 12, 1864. Confined at Point Lookout, Maryland, until transferred to Elmira, New York, August 6, 1864. Released at Elmira after taking the Oath of Allegiance on May 29, 1865.

SHERRELL, PHIDELIA E., Private

Captured at Jonesboro, Tennessee, October 12,

1863, and confined at Rock Island, Illinois, January 17, 1864. Transferred for exchange on February 15, 1865.

SLADE, WILLIAM T., Private

Resided in Northampton County where he enlisted at age 20, April 28, 1862, for the war. Captured near Fredericksburg, Virginia, May 3, 1863, and confined at Washington, D.C., until paroled and exchanged at City Point, Virginia, May 10, 1863. Present or accounted for until captured at Spotsylvania Court House, Virginia, May 12, 1864. Confined at Point Lookout, Maryland, until transferred to Elmira, New York, August 6, 1864. Released at Elmira after taking the Oath of Allegiance on May 15, 1865.

TAYLOE, JAMES, Private

Resided in Hertford County where he enlisted at age 22, July 11, 1861, for the war. Wounded in action at Ellerson's Mill, Virginia, June 26, 1862, and died of wounds on August 25, 1862.

TAYLOE, JOHN, Private

Resided in Hertford County where he enlisted at age 21, February 13, 1862, for the war. Present or accounted for until captured at Gettysburg, Pennsylvania, July 2, 1863. Confined at Fort Delaware, Delaware, in July, 1863. Later transferred to Point Lookout, Maryland, where he took the Oath of Allegiance on June 21, 1865.

TYLER, LUCIUS A., Private

Resided in Bertie County and enlisted in Hertford County at age 20, July 5, 1861, for the war. Discharged October 30, 1861, by reason of disability.

VANN, JOHN R., Private

Resided in Orange County where he enlisted at age 19, July 15, 1862, for the war. Wounded in action at Wilderness, Virginia, May 5, 1864. Died in hospital at Staunton, Virginia, May 10, 1864, of wounds.

VAUGHN, PIPKIN, Private

Resided in Hertford County where he enlisted at age 20, May 10, 1862, for the war. Killed in action at Ellerson's Mill, Virginia, June 26, 1862.

VICK, BRITTON C., Private

Resided in Northampton County and enlisted in Hertford County at age 22, July 5, 1861, for the war. Present or accounted for until captured at Payne's Farm, Virginia, November 27, 1863. Confined at Old Capitol Prison, Washington, D.C., until transferred to Point Lookout, Maryland, February 3, 1864. Paroled at Point Lookout, and transferred to Aiken's Landing, Virginia, February 24, 1865, for exchange. Admitted to hospital at Richmond, Virginia, February 26, 1865, and furloughed on March 8, 1865.

VICK, ELIAS R., Private

Resided in Northampton County where he enlisted at age 18, June 15, 1861, for the war. Wounded in action at Ellerson's Mill, Virginia, June 26, 1862. Present or accounted for until captured at Cedar Creek, Virginia, October 19, 1864. Confined at Point Lookout, Maryland, until released after taking the Oath of Allegiance on May 14, 1865.

VINCENT, PERRY, Private

Born in Northampton County where he resided as a farmer prior to enlisting in Hertford County at age 19, June 15, 1861, for the war. Wounded in action at Sharpsburg, Maryland, September 17, 1862, and died the next day.

VINSON, DREWRY D., Private

Resided in Northampton County and enlisted in Hertford County at age 33, July 27, 1861, for the war. Present or accounted for until captured and paroled at Fredericksburg, Virginia, May 4, 1863. Captured a second time at Spotsylvania Court House, Virginia, May 12, 1864. Confined at Point Lookout, Maryland, and died September 22, 1864, while en route for exchange at Aiken's Landing, Virginia.

VUNCANON, I. J. M., Private

Paroled at Greensboro on May 13, 1865.

WALL, HANSEL J., Private

Resided in Northampton County and enlisted in Hertford County at age 22, July 11, 1861, for the war. Present or accounted for until captured at Gettysburg, Pennsylvania, July 2-3, 1863. Confined at Fort Delaware, Delaware, until released after taking the Oath of Allegiance on June 19, 1865.

WARREN, THOMAS K., Private

Resided in Northampton County and enlisted at Hertford County at age 21, July 26, 1861, for the war. Present of accounted for until captured at Spotsylvania Court House, Virginia, May 12, 1864. Confined at Point Lookout, Maryland, until transferred to Elmira, New York, August 6, 1864. Released at Elmira after taking the Oath of Allegiance on June 12, 1865.

WELSH, JOHN, Private

Born in Ireland and resided in Iredell County prior to enlisting in Wake County at age 32, July 15, 1862, for the war. Captured at Williamsport, Maryland, June 23-27, 1863, and confined at Fort Delaware, Delaware. Released after joining the U.S. service on September 22, 1863. Assigned to Company C, 3rd Regiment Maryland Cavalry.

WHITAKER, T. J., Private

Resided in Orange County where he enlisted at age 19, July 15, 1862, for the war. Wounded and captured at Chancellorsville, Virginia, May 3, 1863, and confined in hospital at Washington, D.C., until transferred to Old Capitol Prison, Washington, June 25, 1863. Paroled and sent to City Point, Virginia, and declared exchanged June 30, 1863. Company muster rolls report him as absent wounded through February, 1864, and as absent without leave from February through December, 1864.

WHITE, J. N., Private

Captured at Gettysburg, Pennsylvania, July 5, 1863, and confined at Fort Delaware, Delaware, until paroled July 30, 1863.

WHITE, JOHN, Private

Resided in Maryland and enlisted at Richmond, Virginia, at age 40, August 1, 1862, for the war as a substitute for Thomas H. Miller. Deserted on August 2, 1862.

WHITLEY, BENJAMIN, Private

Born in Hertford County where he resided as a farmer and enlisted at age 18, July 10, 1861, for the war. Killed in action at Ellerson's Mill, Virginia, June 26, 1862.

WHITLEY, HENRY, Private

Resided in Hertford County where he enlisted at age 18, July 10, 1861, for the war. Captured near Richmond, Virginia, June 15, 1862, and confined at Fort Delaware, Delaware. Sent from Fort Delaware to Aiken's Landing, Virginia, and exchanged on August 5, 1862. Present or accounted for until wounded and captured at Gettysburg, Pennsylvania, July 3, 1863. Died in hospital at Hagerstown, Maryland. Date of death reported as July 17, 1863, and August 3, 1863.

WHITLEY, THOMAS J., Private

Resided in Hertford County where he enlisted at age 22, July 12, 1861, for the war. Died in hospital at Richmond, Virginia, December 25, 1862. Cause of death listed as "disease" and "gunshot wound of leg."

WILKINS, JAMES, Private

Born in Orange County where he resided as a farmer and enlisted at age 29, July 15, 1862, for the war. Died in hospital at Richmond, Virginia, October 19, 1862, of "typhoid fever."

WILKINS, WILLIAM, Private

Resided in Orange County where he enlisted at age 29, July 15, 1862, for the war. Wounded in action at Wilderness, Virginia, May 5, 1864, and died in hospital at Gordonsville, Virginia, May 13, 1864. Date of death also reported as May 15, 1864.

WILLIAMS, JAMES F., Corporal

Resided in Hertford County where he enlisted at age 23, July 9, 1861, for the war. Mustered in as Private and appointed Corporal June 1, 1863. Present or accounted for until captured at Spotsylvania Court House, Virginia, May 12, 1864. Confined at Point Lookout, Maryland, until transferred to Elmira, New York, August 6, 1864. Released at Elmira after taking the Oath of Allegiance on May 13, 1865.

WILLOUGHBY, JOSIAH, Drummer

Resided in Hertford County where he enlisted at age 18, February 14, 1862, for the war. Mustered in as Musician and reported as Drummer. Discharged June 13, 1862, by reason of disability.

WILLOUGHBY, LEMUEL, Musician

Resided in Hertford County where he enlisted at age 23, February 9, 1862, for the war. Mustered in as Musician. Deserted at Richmond, Virginia, between July and October, 1862.

WILSON, THOMAS H., Private

Resided in Hertford County where he enlisted at age 18, July 5, 1861, for the war. Present or accounted for until transferred to the C.S. Navy on April 18, 1864, to take effect from April 5, 1864.

WOODS, ELBERT A., Private

Resided in Orange County where he enlisted at age 20, July 15, 1862, for the war. Wounded in action at Sharpsburg, Maryland, September 17, 1862. Reported as absent wounded until detailed in hospital as a nurse on April 8, 1863. Reported as absent detailed through August, 1864. Muster rolls report him as present from August through December, 1864. Captured at Dinwiddie Court House, Virginia, April 6, 1865, and confined at Point Lookout, Maryland, until released after taking the Oath of Allegiance on June 21, 1865.

YOUNG, EDWARD, Private
Captured at Gettysburg, Pennsylvania, July 3, 1863, and confined at Fort Delaware, Delaware. Record of prisoners transferred to Point Lookout, Maryland, October 18, 1863, states that he was "left at Fort Delaware."

COMPANY G

This company, known as "Washington Volunteers," was raised in Washington County and enlisted at Plymouth on June 24, 1861. On July 3, 1861, the company was ordered to New Bern and from there to Raleigh and then to Warrenton, Warren County. Arriving at Warrenton about July 20, the company was assigned to this regiment as Company G. After joining the regiment the company functioned as a part of the regiment, and its history for the war period is recorded as a part of the regimental history.

The information contained in the following roster of the company was compiled principally from company muster rolls which covered from July through August, 1861; November through December, 1861; March through April, 1862; and June 30, 1862, through December, 1864. No company muster rolls were found for the period prior to July, 1861; for September through October, 1861; January through February, 1862; May through June 29, 1862; or for the period after December, 1864. In addition to the company muster rolls, Roll of Honor records, receipt rolls, hospital records, prisoner of war records, and other primary records, supplemented by state pension applications, United Daughters of the Confederacy records, and postwar rosters and histories, all provided useful information.

OFFICERS
CAPTAINS

LATHAM, LOUIS CHARLES
Resided in Washington County and appointed Captain at age 20 to rank from May 16, 1861. Wounded in action at Sharpsburg, Maryland, September 17, 1862. Present or accounted for until transferred to the Field and Staff of this regiment upon appointment as Major to rank from December 14, 1863.

WHITEHURST, NEHEMIAH J.
Resided in Washington County and appointed 1st Lieutenant at age 35 to rank from May 16, 1861. Promoted to Captain to rank from December 14, 1863. Captured at Spotsylvania Court House, Virginia, May 10-12, 1864. Confined at Fort Delaware, Delaware, until released after taking the Oath of Allegiance on June 16, 1865.

LIEUTENANTS

COKE, LUCIUS C., 3rd Lieutenant
Resided in Washington County where he enlisted

at age 24, July 23, 1861, for the war. Mustered in as 1st Sergeant and appointed 3rd Lieutenant to rank from September 19, 1861. Present or accounted for until transferred to the Field and Staff of this regiment upon appointment as Assistant Surgeon on June 12, 1862.

HARGETT, JOHN M., 2nd Lieutenant
Resided in Craven County and appointed 2nd Lieutenant at age 20 to rank from December 27, 1862. Present or accounted for until captured at Spotsylvania Court House, Virginia, May 10, 1864. Confined at Fort Delaware, Delaware, until transferred to Hilton Head, South Carolina, August 20, 1864. Transferred to Fort Pulaski, Georgia; back to Hilton Head; and then back to Fort Delaware on March 12, 1865. Released at Fort Delaware after taking the Oath of Allegiance on June 19, 1865.

HOLLIDAY, SAMUEL S., 3rd Lieutenant
Resided in Washington County and appointed 3rd Lieutenant at age 26 to rank from May 16, 1861. Resigned on July 31, 1861.

LATHAM, JULIAN A., 1st Lieutenant
Resided in Washington County and appointed 2nd Lieutenant at age 18 to rank from May 16, 1861. Wounded in action at Chancellorsville, Virginia, May 3, 1863. Promoted to 1st Lieutenant to to rank from December 14, 1863. Present or accounted for until captured at Spotsylvania Court House, Virginia, May 10, 1864. Confined at Fort Delaware, Delaware, until transferred to Hilton Head, South Carolina, August 24, 1864. Transferred to Fort Pulaski, Georgia, around October 20, 1864, and then back to Hilton Head on December 26, 1864. Transferred back to Fort Delaware on March 12, 1865. Released at Fort Delaware after taking the Oath of Allegiance on June 16, 1865.

MILLER, JOHN S. R., 3rd Lieutenant
Appointed 3rd Lieutenant to rank from August 23, 1861, but transferred to the Field and Staff of this regiment upon appointment as Adjutant, 1st Lieutenant, to rank from May 16, 1861.

NONCOMMISSIONED OFFICERS AND PRIVATES

ADAMS, DAVID C., Private
Resided in Wake County where he enlisted at age 26, July 15, 1862, for the war. Present or accounted for until transferred to Company D, 26th Regiment N.C. Troops in August, 1863.

AIRS, ROBERT E., Private
Resided in Washington County where he enlisted at age 28, June 24, 1861, for the war. Present or accounted for until discharged on February 3, 1862, upon transfer to the C.S. Navy.

ALLEN, GABRIEL, Private
Resided in Washington County where he enlisted at age 28, June 28, 1861, for the war. Present or accounted for until discharged on February 3, 1862, upon transfer to the C.S. Navy.

ANGLEY, JESSE B., Private
Resided in Washington County where he enlisted at age 24, June 24, 1861, for the war. Wounded in action at Ellerson's Mill, Virginia, June 26, 1862, and reported as absent until detailed as a nurse in hospital at Richmond, Virginia, on December 24, 1862. Reported as absent on detail as a nurse through December, 1864. Captured in hospital at Richmond on April 3, 1865, and confined at Point Lookout, Maryland, until released after taking the Oath of Allegiance on June 23, 1865.

ATKINSON, JORDAN C., Private
Enlisted in Washington County on August 13, 1861, for the war. Reported as present on company muster rolls through April, 1862. Roll of Honor states that he died at Wilson, N.C., in 1862.

BALLENTINE, DAVID GASTON, Private
Enlisted in Wake County at age 27, July 15, 1862, for the war. Present or accounted for until captured at Gettysburg, Pennsylvania, on July 3, 1863. Confined at Point Lookout, Maryland, until exchanged on February 13, 1865. Reported as present on a muster roll of a detachment of paroled and exchanged prisoners at Camp Lee, near Richmond, Virginia, dated February 17, 1865.

BARBEE, GEORGE LESLIE, Private
Resided in Wake County where he enlisted at age 25, July 15, 1862, for the war. Died in hospital at Richmond, Virginia, September 8, 1862, of "febris typhoides."

BARKER, L. G., Private
Enlisted in Wake County at age 24, July 15, 1862, for the war. Died in hospital at Richmond, Virginia, September 11, 1862, of "int. fever."

BARKER, QUINTON, Private
Resided in Wake County where he enlisted at age 24, July 15, 1862, for the war. Present or accounted for until captured at Spotsylvania Court House, Virginia, May 12, 1864. Confined at Elmira, New York, where he died February 16, 1865, of "chronic diarrhoea."

BARLEY, G. J., Private
Resided in Wake County where he enlisted on July 15, 1862, for the war. July-August, 1863, muster roll states: "Not heard from in twelve months. Supposed to be dead." Roll of Honor states that he "never reported to this command."

BARNES, JAMES J., Private
Resided in Washington County where he enlisted at age 33, June 24, 1861, for the war. Present or accounted for on company muster rolls through December, 1864.

BARNES, LEONARD, Private
Resided in Washington County where he enlisted at age 22, June 24, 1861, for the war. Present or accounted for until discharged on February 3, 1862, after being transferred to the C.S. Navy.

BARNES, REUBEN, Private
Born in Tyrrell County and was by occupation a farmer prior to enlisting in Washington County on January 28, 1862, for the war. Captured at Gettysburg, Pennsylvania, July 3, 1863, and con-

fined at Fort Delaware, Delaware, until he joined the U.S. service on July 27, 1863. Assigned to Captain Ahl's Independent Company, Delaware Heavy Artillery.

BARNES, THOMAS J., Private
Enlisted in Tyrrell County on January 28, 1862, for the war. Admitted to hospital at Farmville, Virginia, September 24, 1863, with a gunshot wound. Hospital records give age as 44 and occupation as cooper. Reported as absent without leave on company muster rolls in 1864.

BARNES, WILLIAM R., Private
Enlisted in Tyrrell County on January 28, 1862, for the war. Killed in action at Ellerson's Mill, Virginia, June 26, 1862.

BATEMAN, JOHN, Private
Resided in Washington County where he enlisted at age 45, June 24, 1861, for the war. Present or accounted for until he was discharged on May 14, 1862, by reason of disability.

BATEMAN, JOSEPH T., Corporal
Resided in Washington County and enlisted in Warren County at age 20, July 21, 1861, for the war. Mustered in as Private and appointed Corporal after October 31, 1862. Captured at Charles City Court House, Virginia, October 12, 1863-December 13, 1863, and confined at Point Lookout, Maryland, until transferred to Aiken's Landing, Virginia, February 24, 1865, for exchange.

BELL, THOMAS W., Corporal
Transferred from Company H, 17th Regiment N.C. Troops (1st Organization), October 18, 1861, and appointed Corporal. Present or accounted for until discharged April 30, 1862, upon transfer to the 3rd Regiment Alabama Infantry.

BEMBRIDGE, THOMAS, Private
Resided in Washington County where he enlisted at age 43, June 25, 1861, for the war. Company muster rolls carry him as present through February, 1863, and as absent without leave and absent sick from March, 1863, through December, 1864. Roll of Honor states that he "deserted to the enemy at Plymouth, North Carolina."

BOOTHE, MERRITT, Private
Resided in Wake County where he enlisted at age 28, July 15, 1862, for the war. Wounded in action at Sharpsburg, Maryland, September 17, 1862, and furloughed from hospital at Richmond, Virginia, October 17, 1862. Reported as absent sick or absent without leave on company muster rolls through December, 1864. Hospital records indicate that he was admitted to hospital at Raleigh on June 18, 1864, and furloughed for 60 days August 15, 1864. Admitted to hospital again at Raleigh on October 31, 1864, and returned to duty February 13, 1865. Admitted to hospital April 1, 1865, at Richmond, Virginia, where he was captured on April 3, 1865. Confined at Newport News, Virginia, until released after taking the Oath of Allegiance on June 30, 1865.

BRICKHOUSE, GEORGE W., Private
Enlisted in Tyrrell County on January 28, 1862, for the war. Wounded in action at Ellerson's

Mill, Virginia, June 26, 1862, and never returned to the ranks.

BRIGHT, CORNELIUS Q., Private

Resided in Wake County where he enlisted at age 30, July 15, 1862, for the war. Wounded in action at Mine Run, Virginia, November 27-December 5, 1863. Captured at Spotsylvania Court House, Virginia, May 12, 1864, and confined at Point Lookout, Maryland, until transferred to Elmira, New York, August 3, 1864. Released at Elmira after taking the Oath of Allegiance on June 12, 1865.

BROADWELL, JAMES, Private

Resided in Wake County where he enlisted at age 18, July 15, 1862, for the war. Present or accounted for on company muster rolls through December, 1864. Captured at Farmville, Virginia, April 6, 1865, and confined at Point Lookout, Maryland, until released after taking the Oath of Allegiance on June 23, 1865.

BROWER, ALLEN, Corporal

Resided in Washington County where he enlisted at age 30, June 24, 1861, for the war. Mustered in as Corporal. Present or accounted for until discharged on February 3, 1862, upon transfer to the C.S. Navy.

BUMGARTNER, W., Sergeant

Captured at Winchester, Virginia, September 19, 1864, and "sent to Point Lookout, Maryland, September 23, 1864." No other records relative to his service were found.

BURGESS, MACK, Private

Resided in Washington County where he enlisted at age 25, June 25, 1861, for the war. Died at Plymouth, N.C., in March, 1863.

BUTTERY, ELISHA, Private

Resided in Washington County where he enlisted at age 34, June 24, 1861, for the war. Present or accounted for until captured at Gettysburg, Pennsylvania, July 3, 1863. Confined at Point Lookout, Maryland, where he took the Oath of Allegiance and joined the U.S. service on January 23, 1864.

BUTTERY, JOHN, Private

Resided in Washington County where he enlisted at age 44, June 24, 1861, for the war. Present or accounted for until discharged at Richmond, Virginia, September 2, 1861, by reason of disability.

BUTTERY, JORDAN L., Private

Resided in Washington County where he enlisted at age 25, June 24, 1861, for the war. Died at Fredericksburg, Virginia, December 10, 1861.

BUTTERY, REUBEN, Private

Resided in Washington County where he enlisted at age 27, June 24, 1861, for the war. Present or accounted for until he died in Fredericksburg, Virginia, October 20, 1861.

CARPENTER, WILLIAM, Private

Resided in Wake County where he enlisted at age 30, July 15, 1862, for the war. Present or accounted for through December, 1864. Captured at Burkeville Junction, Virginia, April 6, 1865,

and confined at Point Lookout, Maryland, until paroled after taking the Oath of Allegiance on June 24, 1865.

CHESSON, WILLIAM B., Private

Resided in Washington County where he enlisted at age 25, June 26, 1861, for the war. Present or accounted for until he died at Fredericksburg, Virginia, November 7, 1861.

COLLINS, A. B., Private

Resided in Wake County where he enlisted at age 21, July 15, 1862, for the war. Present or accounted for until reported as "absent. Wounded and on furlough" on May-June, 1863, muster roll. Detailed for light duty in hospital at Richmond, Virginia, March 25, 1864. Detailed as a nurse and returned to company on September 8, 1864. Killed in action at Winchester, Virginia, September 19, 1864.

COLLINS, DALLAS P., Private

Resided in Wake County where he enlisted at age 18, July 15, 1862 for the war. Wounded in action at Payne's Farm, Virginia, November 27, 1863. Captured at Spotsylvania Court House, Virginia, May 12, 1864, and confined at Point Lookout, Maryland. Transferred on August 6, 1864, to Elmira, New York, where he died on January 20, 1865, of "pneumonia."

COLLINS, G. W., Private

Resided in Wake County where he enlisted at age 23, July 15, 1862, for the war. Present or accounted for until admitted to hospital at Richmond, Virginia, November 1, 1862. Died in hospital on January 18, 1863. Disease reported as "anasarca," "eresypelus," and "dropsey."

COLLINS, J. W., Private

Resided in Wake County where he enlisted at age 22, July 15, 1862, for the war. Wounded in action at Payne's Farm, Virginia, November 27, 1863, and died of wounds at Lynchburg, Virginia, February 24, 1864.

COLLINS, SAMUEL N., Musician

Transferred from the Field and Staff of this regiment September-October, 1861, and appointed Musician. Present or accounted for until transferred back to the Field and Staff on February 1, 1863, upon appointment as Chief Musician.

COLLINS, SIDNEY G., Private

Resided in Wake County where he enlisted at age 24, July 15, 1862, for the war. Captured at Frederick, Maryland, September 12, 1862, and confined at Fort Delaware, Delaware, until sent to Aiken's Landing, Virginia, October 2, 1862, for exchange. Declared exchanged on November 10, 1862. Admitted to hospital at Richmond, Virginia, October 8, 1862, and furloughed for 20 days October 26, 1862. Company muster rolls report him as "absent wounded" through December, 1862, and as present in January-February, 1863. Reported as absent sick and absent without leave after February, 1863.

COLLINS, WILLIAM F., Private

Resided in Wake County where he enlisted at age 25, July 15, 1862, for the war. Captured at

Frederick, Maryland, September 12, 1862, and confined at Fort Delaware, Delaware, until paroled and exchanged at Aiken's Landing, Virginia, October 2, 1862. Declared exchanged on November 10, 1862. Wounded in action May 19, 1864. Reported as absent wounded through October, 1864. Present or accounted for until paroled at Burkeville Junction, Virginia, April 14-17, 1865.

COLLINS, WILLIAM G., Private

Resided in Washington County where he enlisted at age 24, June 24, 1861, for the war. Mustered in as Sergeant and reported as Sergeant through December, 1861. Reported as Private after that date. Wounded in action at Sharpsburg, Maryland, September 17, 1862, and Federal Provost Marshal records indicate that he was captured and paroled on September 30, 1862. Admitted to hospital at Richmond, Virginia, October 7, 1862, and furloughed for 40 days on November 22, 1862. Reported as absent wounded on company muster rolls through December, 1864.

COOPER, WILLIAM S., Corporal

Resided in Washington County where he enlisted at age 20, June 30, 1861, for the war. Mustered in as Private and appointed Corporal March-April, 1862. Killed in action at Malvern Hill, Virginia, July 1, 1862.

COUNCIL, A. B., Private

Resided in Wake County where he enlisted at age 33, July 15, 1862, for the war. Discharged upon providing Henry Cowan as his substitute.

COWAN, HENRY, Private

Resided in Wake County where he enlisted at age 25, July 15, 1862, for the war as a substitute for A. B. Council. Roll of Honor states that he "deserted two days after he joined the company."

COWEY, ROBERT E., Private

Resided in Washington County where he enlisted at age 26, June 25, 1861, for the war. Present or accounted for until killed in action at Malvern Hill, Virginia, July 1, 1862.

CRADDOCK, LEVI, Private

Enlisted in Washington County on January 28, 1862, for the war. Wounded in action at Sharpsburg, Maryland, September 17, 1862. Reported as absent wounded or absent prisoner of war until May-June, 1863, when he was reported as "absent without leave." Reported as absent without leave through August 31, 1864, when he was reported as "absent without leave for nearly two years. Deserted."

CROWDER, RICHARD, Private

Resided in Washington County and enlisted in Warren County at age 37, July 17, 1861, for the war. Discharged at White Sulphur Springs, Virginia, October 8, 1862, by reason of his inability to perform the duties of a soldier because of "ascites."

CULLIFER, JOSEPH, Private

Resided in Washington County where he enlisted at age 26, June 24, 1861, for the war. Present or accounted for until discharged on February 3, 1862, upon transfer to the C.S. Navy.

CULLINGTON, JAMES, Private

Resided in Washington County where he enlisted at age 19, June 24, 1861, for the war. Mustered in as Corporal and reduced to ranks on November 15, 1861. Present or accounted for until discharged on February 3, 1862, upon transfer to the C.S. Navy.

DAVENPORT, BENJAMIN S., Corporal

Enlisted in Tyrrell County on January 28, 1862, for the war. Mustered in as Private. Wounded in action at Sharpsburg, Maryland, September 17, 1862, and at Fredericksburg, Virginia, December 13, 1862. Promoted to Corporal in December, 1862. Present or accounted for until captured at Gettysburg, Pennsylvania, July 3, 1863. Confined at Point Lookout, Maryland, until transferred to Elmira, New York, where he died on February 19, 1864.

DAVENPORT, HARVEY S., Sergeant

Resided in Washington County and enlisted in Warren County at age 25, July 21, 1861, for the war. Mustered in as Private and appointed Corporal, July-October, 1862. Captured at Gettysburg, Pennsylvania, July 3, 1863, and confined at Point Lookout, Maryland. Promoted to Sergeant, November-December, 1863, while a prisoner of war. Remained at Point Lookout until released after taking the Oath of Allegiance on May 13, 1865.

DAVENPORT, SNOWDEN B., Private

Enlisted in Tyrrell County on June 28, 1862, for the war. Present or accounted for until transferred to the C.S. Navy on December 30, 1863.

DAVIS, A., Private

Captured at Gettysburg, Pennsylvania, July 3, 1863, and confined at Fort Delaware, Delaware, July 7-12, 1863.

DIXON, GEORGE H., Private

Resided as a farmer in Washington County where he enlisted at age 19, June 30, 1861, for the war. Present or accounted for until discharged at Camp Bee, Virginia, October 22, 1861, by reason of "inability to perform the duties of a soldier."

DIXON, JOSEPH S., Private

Resided in Washington County where he enlisted at age 20, June 30, 1861, for the war. Died at Brook's Station, Virginia, October 17, 1861, of disease.

DOUGLAS, WILLIAM, Private

Resided in Washington County where he enlisted at age 25, June 24, 1861, for the war. Present or accounted for until discharged on February 3, 1862, upon transfer to the C.S. Navy.

DUPREE, JOHN HAILEY, Private

Resided in Wake County where he enlisted at age 31, July 15, 1862, for the war. Present or accounted for until captured at Spotsylvania Court House, Virginia, May 12, 1864. Confined at Point Lookout, Maryland, until transferred to Elmira, New York, August 6, 1864. Released at Elmira after taking the Oath of Allegiance on June 12, 1865.

ENNIS, JAMES, Corporal
Resided in Wake County where he enlisted at age 32, July 15, 1862, for the war. Mustered in as Private and appointed Corporal after December, 1862. Present or accounted for until captured at Spotsylvania Court House, Virginia, May 12, 1864. Confined at Point Lookout, Maryland, until transferred to Elmira, New York, August 6, 1864. Released at Elmira after taking the Oath of Allegiance on June 16, 1865.

FAGAN, MARCUS FRILEY, Sergeant
Resided in Washington County where he enlisted at age 31, June 24, 1861, for the war. Mustered in as Sergeant and reduced to ranks November-December, 1861. Reappointed to the rank of Sergeant in November-December, 1862. Killed in action at Spotsylvania Court House, Virginia, May 10, 1864.

FISH, J. Q., Private
Resided in Wake County where he enlisted at age 28, July 15, 1862, for the war. Present or accounted for until killed in action at Payne's Farm, Virginia, November 27, 1863.

FOLEY, THOMAS W., Sergeant
Resided in Washington County where he enlisted at age 24, June 24, 1861, for the war. Mustered in as Sergeant. Died in hospital at Richmond, Virginia, July 20, 1862.

FRAZIER, JAMES M., Private
Born in Washington County where he resided as ship carpenter and enlisted at age 44, June 24, 1861, for the war. Present or accounted for through March-April, 1863, when he was reported with the remark: "Transferred to hospital on Surgeon's Certificate of Disability for field duty." Detailed as a nurse on April 11, 1863, and remained on detail until discharged on April 20, 1864, by reason of "chronic diarrhoea of 18 months standing."

GARDNER, C. W., Corporal
Resided in Washington County where he enlisted at age 24, June 24, 1861, for the war. Mustered in as Corporal. Present or accounted for until he died at Brook's Station, Virginia, October 11, 1861.

GEORGE, WILLIAM, Private
Resided in Wake County where he enlisted at age 25, July 15, 1862, for the war. Wounded in action at Chancellorsville, Virginia, May 3, 1863. Detailed for light duty on February 19, 1864, and remained on detail through December, 1864. Paroled at Appomattox Court House, Virginia, April 9, 1865.

GILBERT, S. M., Private
Resided in Wake County where he enlisted at age 30, July 15, 1862, for the war. Wounded in action at Sharpsburg, Maryland, September 17, 1862. Present or accounted for until killed in action at Chancellorsville, Virginia, May 2, 1863.

GODWIN, BENNETT A., Private
Resided in Wake County where he enlisted at age 28, July 15, 1862, for the war. Wounded in

action at Payne's Farm, Virginia, November 27, 1863. Detailed for light duty as a nurse in hospital at Richmond, Virginia, March 25, 1864. Hospital records indicate that he remained on detail through February, 1865. Captured on April 3, 1865, in hospital at Richmond, where he died on April 6, 1865, of "acute dysentery."

GOWER, G. P., Private
Born in Wake County where he resided as a farmer and enlisted at age 25, July 15, 1862, for the war. Admitted to hospital at Richmond, Virginia, September 1, 1862, with "rubeola." Transferred to hospital in Danville, Virginia, November 2, 1862. Discharged at Danville on December 1, 1862, by reason of "general debility and anemia."

GRAY, WILLIAM, Private
Resided in Washington County where he enlisted at age 25, June 24, 1861, for the war. Wounded in action at Chancellorsville, Virginia, May 3, 1863. Reported as absent wounded on company muster rolls through October, 1864. Captured on the South Side Railroad on April 2, 1865, and confined at Hart's Island, New York Harbor, until released after taking the Oath of Allegiance on June 17, 1865.

GRIFFIS, Y. R., Private
Resided in Wake County where he enlisted at age 30, July 15, 1862, for the war. Present or accounted for until he died in hospital at Richmond, Virginia, September 2, 1862, of "febris typhoides."

GUNTER, G. P., Private
Enlisted July 15, 1862, for the war. Reported on November-December, 1862, muster roll with the remark that he "died at home."

GUNTER, JOSEPH M., Private
Resided in Wake County where he enlisted at age 31, July 15, 1862, for the war. Admitted to hospital at Richmond, Virginia, September 1, 1862, with "dysentery" and furloughed for 30 days on October 1, 1862. Furlough extended for 30 days on November 3, 1862. Admitted to hospital at Richmond on April 2, 1863, with "phthisis pulmonalis" and died April 9-10, 1863.

HAMILTON, F. F., Private
Enlisted at Orange Court House, Virginia, March 11, 1864, for the war. Died in hospital at Lynchburg, Virginia, May 7, 1864, of "pneumonia."

HARRAND, EDMUND, Private
Resided in Wake County where he enlisted at age 32, July 15, 1862, for the war. Present or accounted for until "killed in a private brawl" on March 22, 1863.

HARRISS, WILLIAM, Private
Resided in Washington County where he enlisted at age 22, June 25, 1861, for the war. Died in hospital at Richmond, Virginia, in 1861.

HASSELL, CALVIN, Private
Enlisted in Tyrrell County on January 28, 1862, for the war. Admitted to hospital at Richmond, Virginia, September 8, 1862, with measles and deserted from hospital October 28-30, 1862. Reported as absent without leave on company muster rolls after November-December, 1862.

HASTE, HENRY, Private

Resided in Washington County where he enlisted at age 19, June 26, 1861, for the war. Present or accounted for until discharged on February 3, 1862, upon transfer to the C.S. Navy.

HILLIARD, JOHN, Private

Resided in Wake County where he enlisted at age 20, July 15, 1862, for the war. Captured in Maryland in September, 1862, and paroled on September 24, 1862. Place and date of capture not reported. Present or accounted for until killed in action at Chancellorsville, Virginia, May 2, 1863.

HOARD, JAMES, Private

Resided in Washington County where he enlisted at age 26, June 25, 1861, for the war. Wounded in action at Ellerson's Mill, Virginia, June 26, 1862. Present or accounted for until captured at Spotsylvania Court House, Virginia, May 12, 1864. Confined at Point Lookout, Maryland, until transferred to Elmira, New York, August 6, 1864. Died at Elmira on March 28, 1865, of "pneumonia."

HODDER, HUMPHREY, Private

Resided in Washington County where he enlisted at age 22, June 24, 1861, for the war. Present or accounted for until discharged on February 3, 1862, upon transfer to the C.S. Navy.

HOLLAND, D. C., Private

Resided in Wake County where he enlisted at age 34, July 15, 1862, for the war. Roll of Honor states that he "never reported to this command." Muster roll for November-December, 1863, states that he "died."

HOLLAND, G. B., Private

Resided in Wake County where he enlisted at age 26, July 15, 1862, for the war. Died in camp near Richmond, Virginia, August 24, 1862.

HOLLAND, YOUNG M., Private

Resided in Wake County where he enlisted at age 27, July 15, 1862, for the war. Died in hospital at Richmond, Virginia, October 4, 1862, of "typhoid fever."

HOLLEMON, THOMAS, Private

Resided in Wake County where he enlisted at age 31, July 15, 1862, for the war. Reported on muster rolls from date of enlistment as absent sick or absent without leave until May-June, 1863, when he was reported with the remark: "Died at home." Roll of Honor states that he "died 1863, at home."

HOLLIS, ASA T., Private

Resided in Washington County where he enlisted at age 20, June 25, 1861, for the war. Wounded in action at Sharpsburg, Maryland, September 17, 1862. Reported as absent wounded through October, 1862, and as "absent, prisoner of war" through June, 1863. Reported as absent without leave from July, 1863, through August, 1864, when he was reported with the remark: "Absent without leave for nearly two years. Deserted." Roll of Honor states that he "deserted to the enemy at Plymouth, North Carolina."

HOLLIS, SAMUEL, Private

Resided in Washington County where he enlisted

at age 43, June 25, 1861, for the war. Reported as present through April, 1862, and as "prisoner" from April, 1862, through April, 1863, when he was reported with the remark: "Died March, 1863, Plymouth, North Carolina." Roll of Honor carries the remark that he "deserted to the enemy," but was "captured and died in prison at Salisbury, North Carolina."

HOLT, ALEXANDER, Private

Resided in Wake County where he enlisted at age 18, July 15, 1862, for the war. Present or accounted for until admitted to hospital at Richmond, Virginia, April 14, 1864, with a gunshot wound of the left thigh. Absent wounded until returned to duty on December 6, 1864. Federal Provost Marshal records indicate that he deserted and took the Oath of Allegiance on March 18-24, 1865, and was furnished transportation to New Bern.

HOLT, ELBERT F., Private

Transferred from Company D, 26th Regiment N.C. Troops in September-October, 1863. Present or accounted for until captured at Spotsylvania Court House, Virginia, May 12, 1864. Confined at Point Lookout, Maryland, until transferred to Elmira, New York, August 6, 1864. Released at Elmira after taking the Oath of Allegiance on June 30, 1862.

JAMES, BENONI, Private

Resided in Pitt County and enlisted in Warren County at age 24, July 21, 1861, for the war. Present or accounted for until captured at Gettysburg, Pennsylvania, July 3-5, 1863. Confined at Fort McHenry, Maryland, until transferred to Fort Delaware, Delaware, July 10, 1863. Transferred on October 18, 1863, to Point Lookout, Maryland, where he remained until paroled and sent to the James River, Virginia, for exchange on January 17, 1865.

JONES, W. H., Private

Resided in Wake County where he enlisted at age 19, July 15, 1862, for the war. Present or accounted for until captured at Spotsylvania Court House, Virginia, May 12, 1864. Confined at Point Lookout, Maryland, until transferred to Elmira, New York, August 6, 1864. Died at Elmira on March 28, 1865, of "diarrhoea."

LAMB, WILLIAM F., Private

Born in Tyrrell County and resided as a farmer in Washington County where he enlisted at age 28, July 1, 1861, for the war. Discharged October 16, 1861, by reason of his "inability to perform his duties."

LATHAM, EDGAR R., Private

Enlisted May 1, 1862, for the war. Wounded in action at Ellerson's Mill, Virginia, June 26, 1862, and reported as absent wounded until detailed in hospital for light duty on July 17, 1863. Absent on detail as a clerk and a nurse in hospital at Goldsboro through December, 1863. Returned to company and was captured at Spotsylvania Court House, Virginia, May 12, 1864. Confined at Point Lookout, Maryland, until transferred to Elmira,

New York, August 6, 1864. Paroled at Elmira on March 10, 1865, and sent to James River, Virginia, for exchange. Received at Boulware's Wharf, James River, March 15, 1865. Paroled in hospital at High Point on May 1, 1865.

LATHAM, THOMAS JOSEPH, Private

Transferred from Company H, 17th Regiment N.C. Troops (1st Organization), October 18, 1861, as a Sergeant. Present or accounted for on company muster rolls until June 30-October 31, 1862, roll when he appears with the remark: "Absent without leave." Reduced to ranks while absent without leave. While absent from this company he served in Company K, 41st Regiment N.C. Troops (3rd Regiment N.C. Cavalry) and was captured at Plymouth, North Carolina, on May 27, 1863. Confined at Fort Monroe, Virginia, until exchanged at City Point, Virginia, July 17, 1863. Returned to his original company after being exchanged. Present or accounted for on company muster rolls through December, 1864. Federal Provost Marshal records indicate that he deserted and took the Oath of Allegiance at Washington, D.C., February 21-24, 1865.

LAWRENCE, ALLEN, Private

Resided in Wake County where he enlisted at age 33, July 15, 1862, for the war. Present or accounted for until captured at Spotsylvania Court House, Virginia, May 12, 1864. Confined at Point Lookout, Maryland, until transferred to Elmira, New York, August 6, 1864. Died at Elmira on September 6, 1864, of "meningitis."

LAWRENCE, J. A., Private

Resided in Wake County where he enlisted at age 31, July 15, 1862, for the war. Wounded in action at Sharpsburg, Maryland, September 17, 1862. Present or accounted for on company muster rolls through December, 1864. Federal Provost Marshal records indicate that he deserted and took the Oath of Allegiance at the Headquarters of the Army of the James on March 19-24, 1865.

LAWRENCE, JOHN, Private

Resided in Wake County where he enlisted at age 28, July 15, 1862, for the war. Present or accounted for until wounded in the "ankle joint" in battle at Payne's Farm, Virginia, November 27, 1863. Reported as absent wounded through December, 1864. Hospital records indicate that his left leg was amputated and that he was retired to the Invalid Corps on November 9, 1864.

LAWRENCE, W. B., Private

Resided in Wake County where he enlisted at age 23, July 15, 1862, for the war. Present or accounted for until captured at Spotsylvania Court House, Virginia, May 12, 1864. Confined at Point Lookout, Maryland, until transferred to Elmira, New York, August 6, 1864. Died at Elmira on March 4, 1865, of "diarrhoea."

LEARY, ELIAS, Corporal

Resided in Tyrrell County and enlisted in Warren County at age 21, July 21, 1861, for the war. Mustered in as Private and appointed Corporal January-February, 1863. Present or accounted for until killed in action at Spotsylvania Court House, Virginia, May 10, 1864.

LEARY, EMANUEL, Private

Enlisted in Washington County on January 1, 1862, for the war. Muster roll for June 30-October 31, 1862, states that he "deserted May 10, 1862."

LEARY, HENRY S., Private

Resided in Washington County where he enlisted at age 18, October 1, 1861, for the war. Killed in action at Sharpsburg, Maryland, September 17, 1862.

LEE, NATHAN A., Private

Resided in Wake County where he enlisted at age 28, July 15, 1862, for the war. Wounded in action at Sharpsburg, Maryland, September 17, 1862. Present or accounted for until killed in action at Spotsylvania Court House, Virginia, May 10, 1864.

LEE, THOMAS J., Private

Resided in Washington County where he enlisted at age 21, July 3, 1861, for the war. Present or accounted for until discharged on February 3, 1862, upon transfer to the C.S. Navy.

LIVERMAN, FREDERICK, Private

Resided in Washington County where he enlisted at age 36, June 29, 1861, for the war. Died at Brook's Station, Virginia, October 20, 1861, of disease.

LOUIS, FRANCIS P., Private

Resided in Washington County and enlisted in Warren County at age 23, July 21-22, 1861, for the war. Died at Brook's Station, Virginia, October 12, 1861, of disease.

LUDFORD, SAMUEL, Sergeant

Resided in Washington County where he enlisted at age 23, June 24, 1861, for the war. Mustered in as Corporal. Wounded in action at Ellerson's Mill, Virginia, June 26, 1862. Promoted to Sergeant November-December, 1862. Wounded in action at Chancellorsville, Virginia, May 3, 1863. Present or accounted for until captured at Spotsylvania Court House, Virginia, May 10, 1864. Confined at Point Lookout, Maryland, until transferred to Elmira, New York, August 6, 1864. Released at Elmira after taking the Oath of Allegiance on June 12, 1865.

LUDFORD, THOMAS, Private

Enlisted in Washington County on January 28, 1862, for the war. Killed in action at Ellerson's Mill, Virginia, June 26, 1862.

LUTER, G. C., Private

Resided in Wake County where he enlisted at age 21, July 15, 1862, for the war. Died in camp near Richmond, Virginia, August 11, 1862.

LUTER, W., Private

Resided in Wake County where he enlisted at age 18, July 15, 1862, for the war. Wounded in action at Payne's Farm, Virginia, November 27, 1863. Reported as absent wounded on company muster rolls through December, 1864. Paroled in hospital at Greensboro on April 29, 1865, with the remark: "Attendant."

MARINER, DOCTRINE M., Private

Resided in Washington County where he enlisted at age 19, July 11, 1861, for the war. Discharged December 20, 1861, by reason of Surgeon's Certificate of Disability.

MARINER, JAMES, Private

Resided in Washington County where he enlisted at age 39, June 25, 1861, for the war. Wounded in action at Malvern Hill, Virginia, July 1, 1862. Furloughed from hospital in Richmond, Virginia, December 8, 1862, for 30 days. Federal Provost Marshal records indicate that he was paroled at Plymouth, N.C., on December 23, 1862, but do not give date of capture or exchange. Company muster rolls carry him as absent without leave through December, 1864, when he was reported with the remark that he "died of disease October 20, 1864, at home, Washington County."

MARINER, WILLIAM B., Private

Resided in Washington County where he enlisted at age 26, June 24, 1861, for the war. Present or accounted for until he "died August, 1862, at home."

MATHIAS, ELSY, Private

Resided in Washington County where he enlisted at age 33, June 26, 1861, for the war. Wounded in action at Payne's Farm, Virginia, November 27-28, 1863. Captured at Spotsylvania Court House, Virginia, May 12, 1864. Confined at Point Lookout, Maryland, until transferred to Elmira, New York, August 6, 1864. Died at Elmira on December 29, 1864, of "pneumonia."

MESSER, REUBEN, Private

Appears on a list of prisoners at Staunton, Virginia, June 8, 1864, with the endorsement: "Roll of prisoners of war captured by General Hunter's forces and sent to Wheeling, Virginia, July, 1864."

MILLS, BENJAMIN B., Private

Resided in Washington County where he enlisted at age 18, June 24, 1861, for the war. Present or accounted for until discharged on February 3, 1862, upon transfer to the C.S. Navy.

MOORE, WILLIAM, Private

Resided in Washington County where he enlisted at age 18, June 24, 1861, for the war. Wounded in action at Ellerson's Mill, Virginia, June 26, 1862. Admitted to hospital at Richmond, Virginia, June 27, 1862, and transferred to hospital at Petersburg, Virginia, where his right leg was amputated on January 13, 1863. Remained absent on sick furlough for the balance of the war. Captured in hospital at Richmond, Virginia, April 3, 1865, and confined at Libby Prison, Richmond, Virginia, until transferred to Newport News, Virginia, April 23, 1865.

MORRIS, WILLIAM, Private

Resided in Tyrrell County and enlisted in Washington County at age 25, June 24, 1861, for the war. Present or accounted for until discharged on February 3, 1862, upon transfer to the C.S. Navy.

MULLIGAN, JOHN, Private

Enlisted in Wake County at age 24, July 15, 1862, for the war as a substitute for John Williams. "Deserted the day after he joined the company."

MYATT, JOHN A., Private

Resided in Wake County where he enlisted on July 15, 1862, for the war. Captured at South Mountain, Maryland, in September, 1862, and paroled at Boonsboro, Maryland, October 3, 1862. Confined at Fort McHenry, Maryland, until sent to Fort Monroe, Virginia, for exchange on October 17, 1862. Present or accounted for until captured at Farmville, Virginia, April 6, 1865. Confined at Point Lookout, Maryland, until released after taking the Oath of Allegiance on June 29, 1865.

MYERS, JOSEPH H., Private

Resided in Washington County where he enlisted at age 19, June 24, 1861, for the war. Present or accounted for until discharged on February 20, 1862, upon transfer to the C.S. Navy.

NORCOM, BENJAMIN J., Private

Previously served in Company H, 17th Regiment N.C. Troops (1st Organization). Enlisted in this company in Washington County on May 1, 1862, for the war. Present or accounted for until captured at Spotsylvania Court House, Virginia, May 12, 1864. Confined at Point Lookout, Maryland, until paroled and sent to Venus Point, Savannah River, Georgia, for exchange on October 30, 1864. Received in exchange at Venus Point on November 30, 1864. Company muster rolls report him as absent prisoner of war through December, 1864. Federal Provost Marshal records indicate that he deserted and took the Oath of Allegiance at Bermuda Hundred, Virginia, March 19, 1865, and was sent on March 24, 1865, to the Provost Marshal General, Washington, D.C., where transportation was furnished to Plymouth, N.C.

NORMAN, ELSBERRY, Private

Enlisted in Washington County on January 1, 1862, for the war. Reported as absent sick through October, 1862, and as absent without leave from that date through August, 1864, when he was reported as: "Absent without leave for nearly two years—deserted."

NORTON, J. C., Private

Resided in Wake County where he enlisted at age 18, July 15, 1862, for the war. Killed in action at Chancellorsville, Virginia, May 2, 1863.

OLIVE, D. H., Private

Resided in Wake County where he enlisted at age 31, July 15, 1862, for the war. Present or accounted for until captured at Spotsylvania Court House, Virginia, May 12, 1864. Confined at Point Lookout, Maryland, until transferred to Elmira, New York, August 6, 1864. Released at Elmira after taking the Oath of Allegiance on June 21, 1865.

OLIVER, ALFRED, Private

Resided in Washington County where he enlisted at age 24, June 24, 1861, for the war. Died in hospital at Richmond, Virginia, August 18, 1861, of "pneumonia."

OLIVER, DAVID, Private

Resided in Washington County where he enlisted at age 20, June 24, 1861, for the war. Died in hospital at Lynchburg, Virginia, July 23, 1862, of disease. Place and date of death also reported as "in camp September 5, 1862."

OLIVER, JAMES, Private

Enlisted in Washington County on October 1, 1861, for the war. Died in camp on July 15, 1862.

OLIVER, JOSEPH, Private

Resided in Washington County where he enlisted at age 24, June 24, 1861, for the war. Wounded in action at Wilderness, Virginia, May 5, 1864, and admitted to hospital at Charlottesville, Virginia, May 12, 1864. Furloughed from hospital on May 28, 1864. Reported as absent wounded through October, 1864, and as present on November-December, 1864, muster roll.

OLIVER, JOSEPH L., Private

Resided in Washington County where he enlisted at age 20, June 24, 1861, for the war. Present or accounted for until discharged on February 20, 1862, upon transfer to the C.S. Navy.

OLIVER, ORMAND, Private

Resided in Washington County where he enlisted at age 18, June 25, 1861, for the war. Died at Fredericksburg, Virginia, November 15, 1861.

PATRICK, AARON, Private

Resided in Washington County where he enlisted at age 20, June 24, 1861, for the war. Died in hospital at Raleigh in 1862.

PHELPS, ISAAC, Private

Resided in Washington County where he enlisted at age 21, June 25, 1861, for the war. Wounded in action at Ellerson's Mill, Virginia, June 26, 1862, and died of wounds in hospital at Richmond, Virginia, September 8, 1862.

PLEDGER, BEDFORD B., Private

Enlisted in Washington County on January 18, 1862, for the war. Wounded in action at Malvern Hill, Virginia, July 1, 1862, and died in hospital at Richmond, Virginia, July 11, 1862.

POPE, WILLIAM, Private

Resided in Wake County where he enlisted at age 37, July 15, 1862, for the war as a substitute. Present or accounted for on company muster rolls from date of enlistment until furloughed from hospital at Gordonsville, Virginia, March 25, 1863, for 30 days by reason of "hydrothorax and plural pneumonia." Reported as absent without leave after his furlough expired until admitted to hospital at Raleigh on September 19, 1864, with "rheumatism and asthma." Returned to duty February 21, 1865.

POWERS, RICHARD, Private

Resided in Washington County where he enlisted at age 34, June 25, 1861, for the war. Died in August, 1862, at Richmond, Virginia.

PRITCHET, ADAM, Private

Resided in Washington County where he enlisted at age 25, June 24, 1861, for the war. Present or accounted for until discharged on February 3, 1862, upon transfer to the C.S. Navy.

RAGANS, WILLIAM J., Private

Resided in Wake County where he enlisted at age 27, July 15, 1862, for the war. Present or accounted for until captured at Spotsylvania Court

House, Virginia, May 12, 1864. Confined at Point Lookout, Maryland, until transferred to Aiken's Landing, Virginia, September 18, 1864, for exchange. Declared exchanged September 22, 1864. Present or accounted for through December, 1864. Captured at Farmville, Virginia, April 6, 1865, and confined at Point Lookout, Maryland, until released after taking the Oath of Allegiance on June 19, 1865.

REAL, J. L., Private

Captured at Gettysburg, Pennsylvania, July 3, 1863, and confined at Fort Delaware, Delaware.

RESPESS, GEORGE W., Private

Resided in Washington County where he enlisted at age 20, June 24, 1861, for the war. Wounded in action at Ellerson's Mill, Virginia, June 26, 1862, and reported as absent wounded until detailed for light duty on April 9, 1863, in hospital at Richmond, Virginia. Reported as absent detailed through October, 1864. Present or accounted for until paroled at Appomattox Court House, Virginia, April 9, 1865.

RIGBY, WILLIAM, Private

Resided in Wake County where he enlisted at age 20, July 15, 1862, for the war. Died at home in 1862.

RUNNELLS, JOHN, Private

Resided in Washington County where he enlisted at age 26, June 25, 1861, for the war. Present or accounted for until discharged on February 3, 1862, upon transfer to the C.S. Navy.

RUTLEDGE, F. E., Private

Captured and paroled at Burkeville Junction, Virginia, April 14-17, 1865.

SALLINGER, THOMAS, Private

Enlisted in Washington County on January 1, 1862, for the war. Admitted to hospital at Richmond, Virginia, September 2, 1862, with "typhoid fever" and furloughed for 20 days on October 5, 1862. Reported as absent without leave from the expiration of his furlough until August, 1864, when he was reported with the remark: "Absent without leave for nearly two years. Deserted."

SAWYER, LEWIS, Private

Enlisted in Tyrell County or Washington County on January 28, 1862, for the war. Killed in action at Ellerson's Mill, Virginia, June 26, 1862,

SCOTT, ALBERT H., Private

Resided in Wake County where he enlisted at age 30, July 15, 1862, for the war. Present or accounted for until captured at Spotsylvania Court House, Virginia, May 12, 1864. Confined at Point Lookout, Maryland, until transferred to Elmira, New York, August 6, 1864. Released at Elmira after taking the Oath of Allegiance on June 27, 1865.

SCOTT, J. H., Private

Resided in Wake County where he enlisted at age 19, July 15, 1862, for the war. Killed in action at Sharpsburg, Maryland, September 17, 1862.

SEAGRAVES, CALVIN, Private

Resided in Wake County where he enlisted at age 30, July 15, 1862, for the war. Wounded in action at Sharpsburg, Maryland, September 17, 1862. Reported as absent wounded on company muster rolls through December, 1864. Captured in hospital at Richmond, Virginia, April 3, 1865, and transferred to Newport News, Virginia, April 23, 1865. Released at Newport News after taking the Oath of Allegiance on June 30, 1865.

SEAGRAVES, JAMES, Private
Resided in Wake County where he enlisted at age 24, July 15, 1862, for the war. Paroled near Sharpsburg, Maryland, September 20, 1862. Date and place of capture not given. Muster roll for June 30-October 31, 1862, states that he was: "Absent wounded." Present or accounted for until captured at Spotsylvania Court House, Virginia, May 12, 1864. Confined at Point Lookout, Maryland, until transferred to Elmira, New York, August 6, 1864. Released at Elmira after taking the Oath of Allegiance on June 12, 1865.

SEAGRAVES, THOMAS, Private
Resided in Wake County where he enlisted at age 27, July 15, 1862, for the war. Wounded in action at Chancellorsville, Virginia, May 3, 1863, and reported as absent wounded through February, 1864. Reported as present after February, 1864. Admitted to hospital at Charlottesville, Virginia, September 23, 1864, with a gunshot wound of the left leg and transferred to Lynchburg, Virginia, September 26, 1864. Admitted to hospital at Richmond, Virginia, December 24, 1864, and returned to duty December 27, 1864. Hospital records give same wound. Date wounded not reported. Captured at Farmville, Virginia, April 6, 1865, and confined at Point Lookout, Maryland, until released after taking the Oath of Allegiance on June 19, 1865.

SEAGRAVES, WILLIAM H., Private
Resided in Wake County where he enlisted at age 22, July 15, 1862, for the war. Captured near Sharpsburg, Maryland, in September, 1862, and paroled on September 27, 1862. Exchanged at City Point, Virginia, December 4, 1862. Company muster rolls report him as absent sick after June, 1863, and July-August, 1863, muster roll carries the remark: "Dead."

SENNETT, ISHAM, Private
Enlisted in Washington County on May 1, 1862, for the war. Company muster rolls reported him as absent sick from November-December, 1862, until May-June, 1863, when he was reported with the remark: "Died at Raleigh, North Carolina."

SENNETT, RICHARD, Private
Appears on the Roll of Honor with the remark that he volunteered and "died, 1862."

SERTAIN, SIDNEY, Private
Resided in Wake County where he enlisted at age 21, July 15, 1862, for the war. Died September 10, 1862.

SEXTON, SAMUEL, Private
Enlisted in Tyrrell or Washington County on January 28, 1862, for the war. Killed in action at Ellerson's Mill, Virginia, June 26, 1862.

SHUGARS, CHARLES H., Private
Resided in Washington County where he enlisted

at age 19, July 3, 1861, for the war. Present or accounted for until discharged on February 3, 1862, upon transfer to the C.S. Navy.

SIMMONS, WILLIAM A., Private
Resided in Washington County where he enlisted at age 33, June 24, 1861, for the war. Discharged in May, 1862, at Goldsboro.

SIVELS, WILLIAM, Private
Resided in Washington County where he enlisted at age 18, June 24, 1861, for the war. Reported as present or absent accounted for on company muster rolls until reported on February 29-August 31, 1864, muster roll with the remark that he was absent wounded. Admitted to hospital at Raleigh, December 27, 1864, with a gunshot wound of the left leg, and transferred to Kittrell's, N.C., January 1, 1865. Captured at Sayler's Creek, Virginia, April 6, 1865, and confined at Point Lookout, Maryland. Released at Point Lookout after taking the Oath of Allegiance on June 20, 1865.

SKITTLETHARP, HARDY, Private
Resided in Washington County where he enlisted at age 29, June 24, 1861, for the war. Present or accounted for until wounded in action at Fisher's Hill, Virginia, September 19, 1864. Returned to duty from hospital at Richmond, Virginia, on December 27, 1864. Federal Provost Marshal records indicate that he deserted at Bermuda Hundred, Virginia, March 10, 1865, and took the Oath of Allegiance at Washington, D.C., March 13, 1865.

SKITTLETHARP, S., Private
Resided in Washington County where he enlisted at age 31, June 24, 1861, for the war. Killed in action at Malvern Hill, Virginia, July 1, 1862.

SMITH, JOHN, Private
Resided in Washington County where he enlisted at age 18, June 24, 1861, for the war. Present or accounted for until captured at Gettysburg, Pennsylvania, July 3, 1863. Confined at Fort McHenry, Maryland, July 6, 1863, and transferred to Fort Delaware, Delaware, July 7-12, 1863. Transferred October 18, 1863, to Point Lookout, Maryland, where he joined the U.S. service on February 12, 1864.

SMITH, RICHARD P., Private
Resided in Wake County where he enlisted at age 18, July 15, 1862, for the war. Wounded in action at Chancellorsville, Virginia, May 3, 1863. Present or accounted for until captured at Spotsylvania Court House, Virginia, May 12, 1864. Confined at Point Lookout, Maryland, until transferred to Elmira, New York, August 6, 1864. Released at Elmira after taking the Oath of Allegiance on June 12, 1865.

SNELL, SWAIN S., Private
Resided in Washington County where he enlisted at age 28, June 25, 1861, for the war. Present or accounted for until captured at Spotsylvania Court House, Virginia, May 12, 1864. Confined at Point Lookout, Maryland, until transferred to Elmira, New York, August 6, 1864. Died at Elmira on April 4, 1865, of "chronic diarrhoea."

SPRUILL, WOODSON, Private
Enlisted in Tyrrell County on January 28, 1862, for the war. Died at Richmond, Virginia, in 1862.

STEPHENSON, J. D., Private
Resided in Wake County where he enlisted at age 25, July 15, 1862, for the war. Died in hospital at Mount Jackson, Virginia, November 1, 1862, of "diarrhoea chronic."

SWINSON, JEREMIAH, Private
Resided in Washington County where he enlisted at age 38, June 24, 1861, for the war. Present or accounted for until discharged on May 24, 1862. Took the Oath of Allegiance at Goldsboro on May 19, 1865.

TWIDDY, JOSEPH, Private
Born in Tyrrell County and resided as a laborer in Washington County where he enlisted at age 19, June 25, 1861, for the war. Discharged at Brook's Station, Virginia, September 5, 1861, by reason of "general debility following rubeola."

UPCHURCH, A. B., Private
Resided in Wake County where he enlisted at age 18, July 15, 1862, for the war. Present or accounted for on company muster rolls through December, 1864. Captured at Farmville, Virginia, April 2, 1865, and confined at Point Lookout, Maryland, until released after taking the Oath of Allegiance on June 21, 1865.

UPCHURCH, B. J., Private
Resided in Wake County where he enlisted at age 21, July 15, 1862, for the war. Admitted to hospital at Richmond, Virginia, October 2, 1862, with "shock of arm from explosion of shell." Transferred to hospital at Danville, Virginia, January 8, 1863. Wound described on transfer as "contusion shoulder." Returned to duty February 27, 1863. Present or accounted for until wounded in the hand at Payne's Farm, Virginia, November 27, 1863. Reported as absent wounded through December, 1863. Captured at Spotsylvania Court House, Virginia, May 12, 1864, and confined at Point Lookout, Maryland. Transferred to Elmira, New York, August 6, 1864. Paroled at Elmira on March 14, 1865, and sent to James River, Virginia, for exchange. Received at Boulware's Wharf, James River, March 18-21, 1865, in exchange. Admitted to hospital at Richmond, Virginia, March 21, 1865, and furloughed for 30 days on March 28, 1865.

UPCHURCH, LINDAMAN, Private
Resided in Wake County where he enlisted at age 28, July 15, 1862, for the war. Present or accounted for until captured at Spotsylvania Court House, Virginia, May 12, 1864. Confined at Point Lookout, Maryland, until transferred to Elmira New York, August 6, 1864. Paroled at Elmira on March 14, 1865, and sent to James River, Virginia, for exchange. Received at Boulware's Wharf, James River, March 18-21, 1865. Admitted to hospital at Richmond, Virginia, March 21, 1865, with "debilitas" and furloughed for 30 days on March 28, 1865.

WAMBLE, PARINGTON, Private
Resided in Wake County where he enlisted at age 27, July 15, 1862, for the war. Died at home in 1863.

WARD, ASSADANA, Sergeant
Resided in Washington County where he enlisted at age 22, June 24, 1861, for the war. Mustered in as Sergeant. Deserted from the hospital on July 1, 1862, and "joined the enemy in Plymouth."

WARD, JOHN, Private
Resided in Wake County where he enlisted at age 30, July 15, 1862, for the war as a substitute. Hospital records indicate that he was in and out of hospitals from November, 1862, through February, 1864, when he was furloughed for 40 days. Appears on a muster roll for Company G, 2nd Battalion N.C. Local Defense Troops for November-December, 1864, as present.

WELCH, MURPHY SAUNDERS, Private
Resided in Wake County where he enlisted at age 27, July 15, 1862, for the war. Present or accounted for until captured at Spotsylvania Court House, Virginia, May 12, 1864. Confined at Point Lookout, Maryland, until transferred to Elmira, New York, August 6, 1864. Died at Elmira on January 26, 1865, of "pneumonia."

WHITAKER, A. B., Private
Resided in Washington County where he enlisted at age 43, June 24, 1861, for the war. Died at Camp Bee, Virginia, December 7, 1861.

WHITE, FRILEY, Sergeant
Enlisted in Tyrell County on January 28, 1862, for the war. Mustered in as Private and appointed Sergeant, November-December, 1862. Wounded in action at Chancellorsville, Virginia, May 3, 1863. Present or accounted for until captured at Spotsylvania Court House, Virginia, May 12, 1864. Confined at Point Lookout, Maryland, until transferred to Elmira, New York, August 6, 1864. Released at Elmira after taking the Oath of Allegiance on June 12, 1865.

WILLIAMS, AMOS, Private
Resided in Wake County where he enlisted at age 27, July 15, 1862, for the war. Wounded in action at Sharpsburg, Maryland, September 17, 1862. Died in hospital at Gordonsville, Virginia, May 15, 1864, of "pneumonia."

WILLIAMS, HENRY JOSEPH, 1st Sergeant
Resided in Washington County where he enlisted at age 22, June 25, 1861, for the war. Mustered in as Private and appointed Corporal on November 15, 1861. Wounded in action at Ellerson's Mill, Virginia, June 26, 1862, and at Sharpsburg, Maryland, September 17, 1862. Promoted to 1st Sergeant in November-December, 1862. Present or accounted for until captured at Spotsylvania Court House, Virginia, May 12, 1864. Confined at Point Lookout, Maryland, until transferred to Elmira, New York, August 6, 1864. Released at Elmira after taking the Oath of Allegiance on June 12, 1865.

WILLIAMS, JOHN, Private
Resided in Wake County where he enlisted at age 31, July 15, 1862, for the war. Discharged soon after enlistment upon providing John Mulligan as his substitute.

WILLIAMS, JOHN M., Private
Resided in Washington County where he enlisted at age 27, June 26, 1861, for the war. Killed in action at Sharpsburg, Maryland, September 17, 1862.

WILLIS, ALGERNON D., Sergeant
Paroled April 25, 1865, and May 10, 1865.

YATES, SIMEON, Private
Resided in Wake County where he enlisted at age 40, July 15, 1862, for the war. Died at home in Wake County in March, 1863.

YOUNG, EZEKIEL, Private
Resided in Wake County where he enlisted at age 20, July 15, 1862, for the war. Wounded in action at Payne's Farm, Virginia, November 27, 1863. Captured at Spotsylvania Court House, Virginia, May 12, 1864. Confined at Point Lookout, Maryland, until transferred to Elmira, New York, August 6, 1864. Released at Elmira after taking the Oath of Allegiance on June 12, 1865.

COMPANY H

This company was composed of men from Martin County and enlisted at Williamston on June 24, 1861. It tendered its service to the state and was ordered to Warrenton, Warren County, where it was assigned to this regiment as Company H. After joining the regiment the company functioned as a part of the regiment, and its history for the war period is recorded as a part of the regimental history.

The information contained in the following roster of the company was compiled principally from company muster rolls which covered from July through August, 1861; November through December, 1861; March through April, 1862; and June 30, 1862, through December, 1864. No company muster rolls were found for the period prior to July, 1861; September through October, 1861; January through February, 1862; May through June 29, 1862; or for the period after December, 1864. In addition to the company muster rolls, Roll of Honor records, receipt rolls, hospital records, prisoner of war records, and other primary records, supplemented by state pension applications, United Daughters of the Confederacy records, and postwar rosters and histories, all provided useful information.

OFFICERS
CAPTAINS

RIVES, RICHARD W.
Resided in Martin County and appointed Captain to rank from May 16, 1861. Present or accounted for until mortally wounded in action at Ellerson's Mill, Virginia, June 26, 1862. Died of wounds on June 28, 1862.

MILLER, JOHN S. R.
Transferred from the Field and Staff of this regiment where he was serving as Adjutant, 1st Lieutenant, upon promotion to Captain of this

company to rank from October 22, 1862. Present or accounted for until killed in action at Winchester, Virginia, June 15, 1863.

MIZELL, ALFRED
Resided in Martin County where he enlisted at age 26, May 1, 1862, for the war. Mustered in as Corporal and appointed 2nd Lieutenant to rank from January 3, 1863. Promoted to 1st Lieutenant on May 22, 1863, and to Captain to rank from June 15, 1863. Admitted to hospital in Richmond, Virginia, on May 15, 1864, with a gunshot wound in the hand. Date and place he received wound not reported. Present or accounted for until paroled at Appomattox Court House, Virginia, April 9, 1865.

LIEUTENANTS

BURRAS, EUGENE, 2nd Lieutenant
Resided in Martin County and appointed 2nd Lieutenant to rank from May 16, 1861. Resigned on August 15, 1861.

COFFIELD, JOSEPH BRYANT, 2nd Lieutenant
Transferred from the Field and Staff of the 15th Regiment N.C. Troops (5th Regiment N.C. Volunteers) upon appointment as 2nd Lieutenant to rank from February 9, 1864. Captured at Spotsylvania Court House, Virginia, May 10, 1864. Confined at Fort Delaware, Delaware, until transferred to Hilton Head, South Carolina, August 20, 1864. Transferred to Fort Pulaski, Georgia, after October 20, 1864, and then back to Hilton Head. Returned to Fort Delaware by May 12, 1865. Released at Fort Delaware after taking the Oath of Allegiance on June 7, 1865.

FAGAN, NAPOLEON B., 1st Lieutenant
Resided in Martin County and appointed 1st Lieutenant to rank from May 16, 1861. Dropped from the rolls on October 27, 1862, by reason of "prolonged absence without leave." Submitted his resignation November 8, 1862, by reason of "my health and the condition of my family." Resignation not acted upon since he had been officially dropped on October 27, 1862.

GUYTHER, JOHN M., 1st Lieutenant
Transferred from Company H, 17th Regiment N.C. Troops (2nd Organization) May 27, 1862, as a Private. Wounded in action at Sharpsburg, Maryland, September 17, 1862. Appointed 2nd Lieutenant to rank from January 3, 1863, and promoted to 1st Lieutenant to rank from June 15, 1863. Present or accounted for until captured at Spotsylvania Court House, Virginia, May 12, 1864. Confined at Old Capitol Prison, Washington, D.C., and transferred to Fort Delaware, Delaware, June 15-17, 1864. Sent to Hilton Head, South Carolina, August 20, 1864, and to Fort Pulaski, Georgia, October 20, 1864. Returned to Fort Delaware on March 12, 1865. Released at Fort Delaware after taking the Oath of Allegiance on June 16, 1865.

KERR, JOHN E., 3rd Lieutenant
Previously served as a Drillmaster and appointed 3rd Lieutenant in this company to rank from August 23, 1861. Wounded in action at Ellerson's

Mill, Virginia, June 26, 1862. Died of disease on August 6, 1862.

MIZELL, JOHN R., 1st Lieutenant
Resided in Martin County and appointed 3rd Lieutenant to rank from May 16, 1861. Promoted to 2nd Lieutenant in August, 1861, and to 1st Lieutenant on July 1, 1862. Resigned May 22, 1863, by reason of "dyspepsia and chronic diarrhoea."

MOORE, JAMES E., 2nd Lieutenant
Commissioned 2nd Lieutenant to rank from July 31, 1863, but "resigned."

NONCOMMISSIONED OFFICERS AND PRIVATES

ALBRIGHT, JACOB, Private
Enlisted at Orange Court House, Virginia, March 1, 1864, for the war. Captured at Spotsylvania Court House, Virginia, May 12, 1864, and confined at Elmira, New York, where he died October 1, 1864, of "chronic diarrhoea."

ANDERSON, WILLIAM DANIEL, Private
Resided in Martin County where he enlisted at age 19, June 24, 1861, for the war. Detailed for extra duty in the Pioneer Corps from November-December, 1862, through August, 1864. Absent on furlough after December 14, 1864, and appears on a register of refugees and rebel deserters received at the Provost Marshal's Office, Washington, D.C., April 10, 1865, from City Point, Virginia, with the remark that he had taken the Oath of Allegiance and was provided transportation to Plymouth, N.C.

ANDREW, RUFUS A., Private
Resided in Guilford County where he enlisted at age 18, July 8, 1862, for the war. Present or accounted for until captured at Spotsylvania Court House, Virginia, May 12, 1864. Confined at Elmira, New York, until released after taking the Oath of Allegiance on June 12, 1865.

APPLE, L. L., Private
Paroled at Greensboro on May 10, 1865.

ASBY, NOAH, Private
Born in Beaufort County and resided as a farmer in Martin County where he enlisted at age 30, June 24, 1861, for the war. Wounded in both thighs at Chancellorsville, Virginia, May 2-3, 1863. Reported as absent wounded on company muster rolls through December, 1864. Certificate of Disability dated March 2, 1865, states that he was "permanently disabled because of gunshot wound through both thighs, resulting in paralysis, and atrophy of left limb." Certificate filed requesting retirement to the Invalid Corps.

ASKEW, ALLEN, Private
Resided in Martin County where he enlisted at age 20, June 24, 1861, for the war. Wounded in action at Cold Harbor, Virginia, June 27, 1862. Present or accounted for until he "gave himself up" at Martinsburg, Virginia, August 13, 1864. Took the Oath of Allegiance on August 18, 1864, and was provided transportation to Philadelphia, Pennsylvania.

ASKEW, THOMAS, Private
Resided in Martin County and enlisted at Richmond, Virginia, at age 18, September 11, 1862, for the war. Present or accounted for until captured at Spotsylvania Court House, Virginia, May 12, 1864. Confined at Elmira, New York, where he died December 13, 1864, of "pneumonia."

AUSBON, ALLEN, Private
Resided in Martin County where he enlisted at age 20, June 24, 1861, for the war. Present or accounted for through December, 1864. Appears on a Federal Provost Marshal record of refugees and rebel deserters received at Washington, D.C., March 24, 1865, with the remark that he took the Oath of Allegiance and was provided transportation to Raysville, Indiana.

AUSBON, JOHN H., Private
Resided in Washington County and enlisted in Martin County at age 18, February 1, 1862, for the war. Killed in action at Ellerson's Mill, Virginia, June 26, 1862.

AUSBORN, JOHN, Private
Resided in Martin County where he enlisted at age 18, May 1, 1862, for the war. Present or accounted for until captured at Spotsylvania Court House, Virginia, May 12, 1864. Confined at Elmira, New York, until released after taking the Oath of Allegiance on June 21, 1865.

AYRES, TILMAN, Private
Born in Martin County where he resided as a farmer and enlisted at age 37, June 24, 1861, for the war. Present or accounted for until captured at Spotsylvania Court House, Virginia, May 12, 1864. Confined at Point Lookout, Maryland, until released after joining the U.S. service on June 4, 1864. Assigned to Company G, 1st Regiment U.S. Volunteer Infantry.

AYRES, WILLIAM BRYANT, Private
Resided in Martin County where he enlisted at age 33, February 1, 1862, for the war. Killed in action at Sharpsburg, Maryland, September 17, 1862.

BAILEY, WILLIAM E., Private
Resided in Martin County where he enlisted at age 34, June 24, 1861, for the war. Company muster rolls and hospital records indicate that he was present through 1861 and absent sick or on furlough in 1862. Detailed as a nurse in the Smallpox Hospital at Richmond, Virginia, from January 1, 1863, until transferred to Danville, Virginia, on January 14, 1865.

BARBER, HENRY, Private
Resided in Martin County where he enlisted at age 28, June 24, 1861, for the war. Present or accounted for until he died in hospital at Lynchburg, Virginia, January 25, 1863, of "pneumonia."

BARRETT, JAMES A., Private
Resided in Rowan County. Captured at Salisbury on April 12, 1865, and confined at Camp Chase, Ohio, until released after taking the Oath of Allegiance on June 13, 1865.

BATEMAN, WILLIAM, Private
Born in Martin County where he resided as a

farmer and enlisted at age 20, June 24, 1861, for the war. Captured in Bertie County August 18, 1863, and confined at Point Lookout, Maryland, until released after joining the U.S. service on January 23, 1864. Date of capture also given as September 8, 1863. Assigned to Company G, 1st Regiment U.S. Volunteer Infantry.

BEACH, JESSE, Private
Resided in Martin County where he enlisted at age 29, June 24, 1861, for the war. Mortally wounded at Chancellorsville, Virginia, May 2, 1863, and died of wounds in May, 1863.

BELANGER, WILLIAM, Private
Resided in Martin County where he enlisted at age 26, June 24, 1861, for the war. Present or accounted for until discharged at Richmond, Virginia, February 3, 1862, upon transfer to the C.S. Navy.

BEST, WILLIAM, Corporal
Resided in Martin County where he enlisted at age 18, June 24, 1861, for the war. Mustered in as Private. Present or accounted for until captured at Spotsylvania Court House, Virginia, May 12, 1864. Confined at Elmira, New York, until paroled for exchange on October 29, 1864. Promoted to Corporal February-September, 1864. Died at Port Royal, South Carolina, November 12, 1864.

BIGGS, EASON, Private
Resided in Martin County where he enlisted at age 18, May 1, 1862, for the war. Present or accounted for on company muster rolls through March-April, 1862, when he was reported with the remark: "Discharged March 20, 1862, by order of General Lee." Register of payments to discharged soldiers gives date of discharge as May 1, 1862.

BOONE, ALSAN, Private
Resided in Guilford County where he enlisted at age 18, July 8, 1862, for the war. Captured in Maryland in September, 1862, and paroled on September 24, 1862. Present or accounted for until captured at Spotsylvania Court House, Virginia, May 12, 1864. Confined at Point Lookout, Maryland, until paroled and exchanged on November 1, 1864. Present or accounted for until paroled at Appomattox Court House, Virginia, April 9, 1865.

BOSTON, JOHN, Private
Resided in Rowan County. Captured at Salisbury on April 12, 1865, and confined at Camp Chase, Ohio, until released after taking the Oath of Allegiance on June 13, 1865.

BOWEN, LAWRENCE, Private
Resided in Martin County where he enlisted at age 42, February 1, 1862, for the war. Wounded in action at Payne's Farm, Virginia, November 27, 1863. Present or accounted for until captured at Spotsylvania Court House, Virginia, May 12, 1864. Confined at Point Lookout, Maryland, until transferred to Elmira, New York, August 6, 1864. Died at Elmira on September 21, 1864, of "chronic diarrhoea."

BOWIE, J. H., Private
Enlisted in Cumberland County on November 1,

1863, for the war. January-February, 1864, muster roll states that he "deserted to the enemy January 17, 1864."

BROWN, ASA, Private
Resided in Lincoln County and enlisted in Martin County at age 44, June 24, 1861, for the war. Present or accounted for on company muster rolls through December, 1864. Roll of Honor states that he "never has been in battle, being on detached service as hospital cook." Deserted on March 18, 1865, and took the Oath of Allegiance at Bermuda Hundred, Virginia, March 19, 1865. Furnished transportation to Plymouth, N.C., from Washington, D.C., on March 24, 1865.

BROWN, JOHN C., Private
Resided in Rowan County. Captured at Salisbury on April 12, 1865, and confined at Camp Chase, Ohio, until released after taking the Oath of Allegiance on June 11, 1865.

BROWN, WILLIAM R., Private
Resided in Martin County where he enlisted at age 18, May 1, 1862, for the war. Present or accounted for until captured at Spotsylvania Court House, Virginia, May 12, 1864. Confined at Point Lookout, Maryland, until transferred to Elmira, New York, August 6, 1864. Paroled at Elmira and sent to James River, Virginia, March 2, 1865, for exchange. Admitted to hospital at Richmond, Virginia, March 2, 1865, with "debilitas" and furloughed for 30 days on March 8, 1865.

CARAWAY, DAVID E., Private
Resided in Martin County where he enlisted at age 27, February 1, 1862, for the war. Died April 4, 1862, at Goldsboro of disease.

CLAPP, G. N., Private
Resided in Guilford County. Captured at Salisbury on April 12, 1865, and confined at Camp Chase, Ohio, until released after taking the Oath of Allegiance on June 13, 1865.

CLAPP, GEORGE M., Private
Resided in Guilford County. Captured at Salisbury on April 12, 1865, and confined at Camp Chase, Ohio, until released after taking the Oath of Allegiance on June 13, 1865.

CLAPP, JAMES F. R., Corporal
Resided in Guilford County where he enlisted at age 24, July 8, 1862, for the war. Mustered in as Private. Wounded in action at Sharpsburg, Maryland, September 17, 1862. Promoted to Corporal on May 3, 1863. Present or accounted for until captured at Spotsylvania Court House, Virginia, May 12, 1864. Confined at Point Lookout, Maryland, until transferred to Elmira, New York, August 6, 1864. Released at Elmira after taking the Oath of Allegiance on June 12, 1865.

CLAPP, P. W., Private
Enlisted at Orange Court House, Virginia, April 15, 1864, for the war. Wounded and sent to hospital on May 30, 1864. Furloughed from hospital on June 13, 1864, for 60 days. Reported as absent without leave after November 1, 1864.

CLAPP, WILLIAM M., Private
Resided in Guilford County where he enlisted at

age 34, July 8, 1862, for the war. Present or accounted for until admitted to hospital at Farmville, Virginia, June 10, 1863, with "chronic rheumatism." Returned to duty and detailed as shoemaker at Richmond, Virginia, December 4, 1863. Absent detailed as shoemaker until assigned as guard at Jackson Hospital, Richmond, February 21, 1864. Reported as present on hospital muster rolls until admitted to hospital October 17, 1864, with "acute diarrhoea." Furloughed for 60 days on December 22, 1864. Hospital muster roll dated February 28, 1865, carries him as "absent without leave."

CLARK, JAMES M., Private
Resided in Guilford County where he enlisted at age 24, July 8, 1862, for the war. Wounded in action at Chancellorsville, Virginia, May 2-3, 1863, and died of wounds.

COBB, PETER, Private
Resided in Guilford County where he enlisted at age 32, July 8, 1862, for the war. Present or accounted for until captured at Winchester, Virginia, September 19, 1864. Confined at Point Lookout, Maryland, until transferred for exchange on March 15, 1865. Received at Boulware's Wharf, James River, Virginia, March 18, 1865, in exchange. Paroled at Greensboro on May 16, 1865.

COBBLE, GEORGE, Private
Captured at Salisbury on April 12, 1865, and confined at Camp Chase, Ohio, where he died on June 5, 1865, of "typhoid fever."

COBURN, ADOLPHUS, Private
Born in Martin County where he resided as a farmer prior to enlisting in Warren County at age 18, June 24, 1861, for the war. Discharged on September 6, 1861, by reason of disability.

COLETRAIN, JAMES W., Private
Resided in Martin County where he enlisted at age 22, June 24, 1861, for the war. Present or accounted for until captured at Spotsylvania Court House, Virginia, May 12, 1864. Confined at Point Lookout, Maryland, until transferred to Elmira, New York, August 6, 1864. Released at Elmira after taking the Oath of Allegiance on June 11-12, 1865.

COLLINS, DANIEL, Private
Resided in Guilford County where he enlisted at age 29, July 8, 1862, for the war. Mortally wounded in action at Chancellorsville, Virginia, May 2-3, 1863.

COLTRAIN, JOHN D., Private
Resided in Martin County where he enlisted at age 30, February 1, 1862, for the war. Captured at Gettysburg, Pennsylvania, July 5, 1863, and confined at Fort McHenry, Maryland, until transferred to Fort Delaware, Delware, July 7-12, 1863. Paroled at Fort Delaware and sent to James River, Virginia, for exchange on July 31, 1863. Admitted to hospital at Petersburg, Virginia, August 1, 1863, with "diarrhoea chronic" and furloughed for 30 days on September 18, 1863. Wounded in action at Cedar Creek, Virginia, October 19, 1864. Reported as absent wounded on

company muster rolls through December, 1864.

COWAN, JOHN, Private
Resided in Martin County where he enlisted at age 20, June 24 1861, for the war. Present or accounted for until captured at Spotsylvania Court House, Virginia, May 12, 1864. Confined at Point Lookout, Maryland, until transferred to Elmira, New York, August 6, 1864. Paroled at Elmira and sent to James River, Virginia, where he was exchanged on March 18-21, 1865.

CRADDOCK, BAILEY, Private
Resided in Martin County where he enlisted at age 21, June 24, 1861, for the war. Wounded in action at Ellerson's Mill, Virginia, June 26, 1862, and admitted to hospital at Richmond, Virginia, the next day. Died in hospital on August 1, 1862, of gunshot wound and "erysiphilis."

CRADDOCK, FRANCIS M., Private
Resided in Martin County where he enlisted at age 21, June 24, 1861, for the war. Wounded in the head at Gettysburg, Pennsylvania, July 2-3, 1863, and reported as absent wounded until detailed in hospital at Richmond, Virginia, January 19, 1865. Captured in hospital at Richmond on April 3, 1865, and paroled on April 20, 1865.

CUNNINGHAM, E., Private
Appears on a report of persons employed in the Quartermaster Department dated June 14, 1864. Report gives his age as 33 and occupation as helper to blacksmith. Ordered to rejoin his command July 13, 1864.

DAVIS, JAMES R., Private
Resided in Rowan County. Captured at Salisbury on April 12, 1865, and confined at Camp Chase, Ohio, until released after taking the Oath of Allegiance on June 13, 1865.

DENNIS, J. O., Private
Reported on a register of prisoners of war at Knoxville, Tennessee, captured December 9, 1863. Died in hospital January 5, 1864.

DICKSON, T. M., Private
Resided in Cleveland County. Captured at Salisbury on April 12, 1865, and confined at Camp Chase, Ohio, until released after taking the Oath Oath of Allegiance on June 13, 1865.

FETNER, JOHN, Private
Resided in Richland District, South Carolina. Captured at Salisbury on April 12, 1865, and confined at Camp Chase, Ohio, until released after taking the Oath of Allegiance on June 13, 1865.

FIELDS, PETER LINDSEY, Private
Resided in Guilford County where he enlisted at age 18, July 8, 1862, for the war. Present or accounted for until captured at Spotsylvania Court House, Virginia, May 12, 1864. Confined at Point Lookout, Maryland, until transferred to Elmira, New York, July 28, 1864. Released at Elmira after taking the Oath of Allegiance on May 21, 1865.

FITZSIMMONS, CHARLES B., Private
Resided in Charleston District, South Carolina. Captured at Salisbury on April 12, 1865, and confined at Camp Chase, Ohio, until released after taking the Oath of Allegiance on June 13, 1865.

FOWLER, W. S., Private
Resided in Randolph County. Captured at Salisbury on April 12, 1865, and confined at Camp Chase, Ohio, until released after taking the Oath of Allegiance on June 13, 1865.

FREEMAN, GEORGE W., Private
Resided in Martin County where he enlisted at age 30, February 1, 1862, for the war. Wounded in action at Malvern Hill, Virginia, July 1, 1862. Present or accounted for until captured at Spotsylvania Court House, Virginia, May 12, 1864. Confined at Point Lookout, Maryland, until transferred to Elmira, New York, August 6, 1864. Died at Elmira on September 20, 1864, of "chronic diarrhoea."

FRIDDLE, LEWIS, Private
Resided in Guilford County where he enlisted at age 34, July 8, 1862, for the war. Wounded and captured at Gettysburg, Pennsylvania, July 3, 1863. Admitted to Field Hospital at Gettysburg and transferred to General Hospital, Davids Island, New York Harbor, July 20, 1863. Paroled at Davids Island and sent to City Point, Virginia, for exchange on August 24, 1863. Present or accounted for until captured at Spotsylvania Court House, Virginia, May 12, 1864. Confined at Point Lookout, Maryland, until transferred to Elmira, New York, August 6, 1864. Paroled at Elmira and sent to Venus Point, Savannah River, Georgia, for exchange. Received at Venus Point on November 15, 1864. Paroled at Greensboro on May 24, 1865.

FRIDDLE, WILLIAM G., Private
Resided in Guilford County where he enlisted at age 30, July 8, 1862, for the war. Present or accounted for until captured at Spotsylvania Court House, Virginia, May 12, 1864. Confined at Point Lookout, Maryland, until transferred to Elmira, New York, August 6, 1864. Died at Elmira on August 20, 1864, of "typhoid fever."

GARDNER, SPENCER, Corporal
Resided in Martin County where he enlisted at age 39, June 24, 1861, for the war. Mustered in as Private and appointed Corporal after December, 1861. Killed in action at Ellerson's Mill, Virginia, June 26, 1862.

GEORGE, W., Sergeant
Captured at Winchester, Virginia, September 19, 1864, and sent to Point Lookout, Maryland, September 23, 1864.

GERINGER, JOHN H., Private
Resided in Guilford County where he enlisted at age 33, July 8, 1862, for the war. Wounded and captured at Gettysburg, Pennsylvania, July 1-4, 1863. Admitted to Field Hospital at Gettysburg where his left leg was amputated. Died at General Hospital, Gettysburg on July 28, 1863.

GLADSON, JOHN M., Private
Captured at Salisbury on April 12, 1865, and confined at Camp Chase, Ohio, where he died June 21, 1865.

GREESON, GEORGE C., Private
Resided in Guilford County where he enlisted at age 22, July 8, 1862, for the war. Wounded in

action at Fredericksburg, Virginia, December 13, 1862. Absent wounded until detailed as a nurse in hospital at Goldsboro on March 7, 1864. Reported as absent on detail for the balance of the war.

GURGANIS, HOSEA, Private
Resided in New Hanover County where he enlisted at age 48, June 18, 1861, for the war. Discharged in hospital at Richmond, Virginia, November 8, 1861.

GURGANUS, ELI, Sergeant
Resided in Martin County where he enlisted at age 21, June 24, 1861, for the war. Mustered in as Private and appointed Corporal, November-December, 1861. Promoted to Sergeant in May, 1864. Missing in action after the battle of Winchester on September 19, 1864.

GURGANUS, JAMES R., Private
Resided in Martin County where he enlisted at age 43, June 24, 1861, for the war. Wounded in action at Chancellorsville, Virginia, May 2, 1863. Absent wounded through December, 1863. Captured at Spotsylvania Court House, Virginia, May 12, 1864. Confined at Point Lookout, Maryland, until transferred to Elmira, New York, August 6, 1864. Died at Elmira on September 17, 1864, of "chronic diarrhoea."

GURGANUS, NOAH T., Private
Resided in Martin County where he enlisted at age 18, June 24, 1861, for the war. Reported on company muster rolls through December, 1861. Roll of Honor states that he was "discharged, 1861."

GURKIN, HENRY A., 1st Sergeant
Born in Washington County and resided as a farmer in Martin County where he enlisted at age 22, June 24, 1861, for the war. Mustered in as 1st Sergeant. Discharged at Camp Bee, Virginia, September 5, 1861, by reason of "physical inability to discharge the duties of a soldier."

GURKINS, CHARLES, Private
Enlisted in Martin County on May 1, 1862, for the war. Reported as absent without leave until "dropped" on January-February, 1863, muster roll.

GUTHIEM, ISAAC, Private
Resided in Martin County where he enlisted at age 37, June 24, 1861, for the war. Wounded in action at Chancellorsville, Virginia, May 2, 1863, and died of wounds on August 3, 1863.

HALLECH, R. A., Private
Resided in Rowan County. Captured at Salisbury on April 12, 1865, and confined at Camp Chase, Ohio, until released after taking the Oath of Allegiance on June 13, 1865.

HAMILTON, JAMES, Private
Resided in Martin County where he enlisted at age 31, February 1, 1862, for the war. Died in hospital at Richmond, Virginia, October 27, 1862, of "double pneumonia."

HAMILTON, RICHARD, Private
Resided in Martin County where he enlisted at age 26, June 24, 1861, for the war. Present or accounted for until captured at Spotsylvania Court

House, Virginia, May 12, 1864. Confined at Point Lookout, Maryland, until transferred to Elmira, New York, August 6, 1864. Released at Elmira after taking the Oath of Allegiance on June 19, 1865.

HANNER, SOLOMON SHANNON, Private
Resided in Guilford County where he enlisted at age 34, July 8, 1862, for the war. Reported as absent without leave after September 1, 1862.

HARDISON, ASA, Private
Born in Martin County where he resided as a farmer and enlisted at age 43, June 24, 1861, for the war. Present or accounted for until discharged on April 9, 1862, by reason of disability.

HARDISON, JOSEPH R., Private
Resided in Martin County where he enlisted at age 31, May 1, 1862, for the war. Captured near Plymouth, N.C., February 24, 1864, and confined at Fort Monroe, Virginia, until transferred to Point Lookout, Maryland, March 14-15, 1864. Died at Point Lookout on January 20, 1865.

HARDISON, WILLIAM H., Private
Resided in Martin County where he enlisted at age 19, June 24, 1861, for the war. Present or accounted for until captured at Spotsylvania Court House, Virginia, May 12, 1864. Confined at Elmira, New York, until released after taking the Oath of Allegiance on June 30, 1865.

HARLICK, RICHARD A., Private
Captured at Salisbury on April 12, 1865, and confined at Military Prison, Louisville, Kentucky, until transferred to Camp Chase, Ohio, May 4, 1865.

HARMON, JULIUS S., Private
Resided in Forsyth County. Captured at Salisbury on April 12, 1865, and confined at Camp Chase, Ohio, until released after taking the Oath of Allegiance on June 13, 1865.

HARRISON, EDMUND, Private
Resided in Martin County where he enlisted at age 25, June 24, 1861, for the war. Wounded in action at Payne's Farm, Virginia, November 27, 1863. Died in hospital at Richmond, Virginia, December 28, 1863, of wounds.

HARRISON, LOVICK B., Sergeant
Resided in Martin County where he enlisted at age 26, June 24, 1861, for the war. Mustered in as Corporal. Wounded in action at Malvern Hill, Virginia, July 1, 1862. Promoted to Sergeant on May 3, 1863. Present or accounted for until captured at Spotsylvania Court House, Virginia, May 12, 1864. Confined at Point Lookout, Maryland, until transferred to Elmira, New York, August 6, 1864. Died at Elmira on December 6, 1864, of "pleuro pneumonia."

HARTISON, W. H., Private
Captured at Spotsylvania Court House, Virginia, May 12, 1864, and confined at Point Lookout, Maryland, until transferred to Elmira, New York, August 6, 1864. Released at Elmira after taking the Oath of Allegiance on June 30, 1865.

HOLLIDAY, HENRY W., 1st Sergeant
Resided in Martin County where he enlisted at

age 22, June 24, 1861, for the war. Mustered in as Corporal and appointed 1st Sergeant on September 6, 1861. Wounded in action at Malvern Hill, Virginia, July 1, 1862. Present or accounted for until captured at Winchester, Virginia, September 19, 1864. Confined at Point Lookout, Maryland, until paroled and exchanged on September 30, 1864. Present or accounted for until paroled at Appomattox Court House, Virginia, April 9, 1865.

HOLLIDAY, JOHN D., Private
Enlisted at Orange Court House, Virginia, March 15, 1864, for the war. Captured at Spotsylvania Court House, Virginia, May 12, 1864. Confined at Point Lookout, Maryland, until transferred to Elmira, New York, August 6, 1864. Died at Elmira on September 16, 1864, of "typhoid fever."

HOPE, H., Private
Captured at Spotsylvania Court House, Virginia, May 12, 1864. Confined at Point Lookout, Maryland, until exchanged on September 18, 1864.

HOPKINS, LUKE, Private
Resided in Martin County where he enlisted at age 28, June 24, 1861, for the war. Present or accounted for until captured at Spotsylvania Court House, Virginia, May 12, 1864. Confined at Point Lookout, Maryland, until transferred to Elmira, New York, August 6, 1864. Died at Elmira on February 20, 1865, of "variola."

HOWELL, STEPHEN M., Private
Resided in "Mecklenburg County, Tennessee." Captured at Salisbury on April 12, 1865, and confined at Camp Chase, Ohio, until released after taking the Oath of Allegiance on June 10, 1865.

JACKSON, WILLIAM, Private
Resided in Guilford County where he enlisted at age 18, July 8, 1862, for the war. Wounded in action at Sharpsburg, Maryland, September 17, 1862. Reported as absent wounded or absent sick until returned to the company on January 16, 1864. Sent to hospital on May 12, 1864, and died in hospital at Richmond, Virginia, May 28, 1864, of "typhoid fever."

JOB, JAMES M., Private
Resided in Guilford County where he enlisted at age 33, July 8, 1862, for the war. Deserted August 23, 1863, and returned to company under sentence of court-martial, December 26, 1863. Sentenced to one year hard labor and confined at Castle Thunder, Richmond, Virginia, and at Salisbury Prison, Salisbury, until released December 1, 1864. Sent to hospital sick on December 18, 1864, and admitted to hospital at Richmond, Virginia, on December 19, 1864.

JOB, JESSE R., Private
Enlisted at Orange Court House, Virginia, March 1, 1864, for the war. Captured at Spotsylvania Court House, Virginia, May 12, 1864. Confined at Point Lookout, Maryland, until transferred to Elmira, New York, August 6, 1864. Died at Elmira on January 13, 1865, of "pneumonia."

JOB, JONATHAN F., Private
Resided in Guilford County where he enlisted at

age 21, July 8, 1862, for the war. Wounded in action at Payne's Farm, Virginia, November 27, 1863. Captured at Spotsylvania Court House, Virginia, May 12, 1864. Confined at Point Lookout, Maryland, until transferred to Elmira, New York, August 6, 1864. Died at Elmira on April 8, 1865, of "chronic diarrhoea."

JOLLEY, MILFORD, Private
Resided in Martin County where he enlisted at age 18, June 24, 1861, for the war. Present or accounted for on company muster rolls through December, 1864.

JOLLEY, WILLIAM, Jr., Private
Resided in Martin County where he enlisted at age 27, June 24, 1861, for the war. Wounded in action at Payne's Farm, Virginia, November 27, 1863. Present or accounted for until wounded at Winchester on September 19, 1864. Reported absent wounded through December, 1864. Deserted and took the Oath of Allegiance at Bermuda Hundred, Virginia, March 16, 1865. Sent to Washington, D.C., where transportation was furnished to Plymouth, N.C.

JOLLEY, WILLIAM, Sr., Private
Resided in Martin County where he enlisted at age 37, June 24, 1861, for the war. Died of disease at Fredericksburg, Virginia, March, 1862.

KEEL, JAMES F., Private
Resided in Martin County where he enlisted at age 27, June 24, 1861, for the war. Wounded in action at Sharpsburg, Maryland, September 17, 1862, and captured at Antietam, Maryland, September 30, 1862. Confined at Fort McHenry, Maryland, until paroled and sent to Fort Monroe, Virginia, for exchange. Exact date of exchange not given but he was admitted to hospital at Richmond, Virginia, on October 24, 1862. Furloughed for 40 days on November 12, 1862. Present or accounted for on company muster rolls through December, 1864, and retired to the Invalid Corps on January 10, 1865.

KEEL, JAMES L., Private
Born in Martin County where he resided as a farmer and enlisted at age 18, June 24, 1861, for the war. Present or accounted for until captured at Gettysburg, Pennsylvania, July 3-4, 1863. Confined at Fort Delaware, Delaware, until released after joining the U.S. service on July 27, 1863. Assigned to Ahl's Independent Company, Delaware Heavy Artillery.

KELLY, DAVID JOHN, Private
Resided in Martin County where he enlisted at age 23, June 24, 1861, for the war. Mustered in as Private and appointed Musician, July-October, 1862. Served as Musician until reduced to ranks on December 24, 1864. Present or accounted for through December, 1864. Deserted and took the Oath of Allegiance at Bermuda Hundred, Virginia, on February 24, 1865.

KERN, OBADIAH, Private
Captured at Salisbury on April 12, 1865, and confined at Military Prison, Louisville, Kentucky, until transferred to Camp Chase, Ohio, May 2-4, 1865.

KERSEY, JERSEY, Private
Resided in Guilford County where he enlisted at age 22, July 8, 1862, for the war. Died of disease at home in Guilford County on November 5, 1862.

KESTER, WILLIAM H., Private
Resided in Rowan County. Captured at Salisbury on April 12, 1865, and confined at Camp Chase, Ohio, until released after taking the Oath of Allegiance on June 13, 1865.

KIRKMAN, ROBERT, Private
Resided in Guilford County where he enlisted at age 34, July 8, 1862, for the war. Present or accounted for until transferred to Company B, 45th Regiment N.C. Troops on June 2, 1863.

LATHAM, CLEOPAS BRYAN, Corporal
Resided in Washington County and enlisted in Martin County at age 19, February 1, 1862, for the war. Mustered in as Private and appointed Corporal on January 1, 1863. Present or accounted for until captured at Gettysburg, Pennsylvania, July 3, 1863. Confined at Fort McHenry, Maryland, until transferred to Fort Delaware, Delaware, July 7, 1863. Transferred on October 15, 1863, to Point Lookout, Maryland, where he was paroled and sent to Cox's Landing, James River, Virginia, for exchange on February 13, 1865. Reported as present on a muster roll of a detachment of paroled and exchanged prisoners at Camp Lee, near Richmond, Virginia, dated February 18, 1865.

LEARY, JASPER, Private
Resided in Martin County where he enlisted at age 28, June 24, 1861, for the war. Wounded in action at Ellerson's Mill, Virginia, June 26, 1862. Died in hospital at Wilson, N.C., February 23, 1863, of "erysipelas."

LEGGETT, JAMES B., Private
Resided in Martin County where he enlisted at age 27, June 24, 1861, for the war. Wounded in action at Malvern Hill, Virginia, July 1, 1862, and died of wounds on July 15, 1862.

LERRY, REUBEN, Private
Resided in Washington County and enlisted in Martin County at age 20, February 1, 1862, for the war. Killed in action at Ellerson's Mill, Virginia, June 26, 1862.

LITTLE, GREEN B., Private
Transferred from Company B, 45th Regiment N.C. Troops on June 2, 1863. Captured at Gettysburg, Pennsylvania, July 3, 1863, and confined at Fort Delaware, Delaware. Paroled at Fort Delaware on July 30, 1863. Admitted to hospital at Petersburg, Virginia, August 1, 1863, with "debilitas" and returned to duty on August 19, 1863. Admitted to hospital at Danville, Virginia, June 21, 1864, with gunshot wound of the foot. Date and place he was wounded and date he was returned to company not reported. Wounded in action at Cedar Creek, Virginia, October 19, 1864, and died in hospital at Mount Jackson, Virginia, November 16, 1864.

LITTLE, RICHARD, Private
Resided in Guilford County where he enlisted at

age 23, July 8, 1862, for the war. Present or accounted for until captured at Gettysburg, Pennsylvania, July 3, 1863. Confined at Fort Delaware, Delaware, where he died on October 30, 1863, of "typhoid fever."

LOMERS, A., Private
Paroled at Greensboro on May 12, 1865.

McGEE, JAMES, Private
Resided in Guilford County where he enlisted at age 20, July 8, 1862, for the war. Wounded and captured at Sharpsburg, Maryland, September 17, 1862. Died of wounds at Frederick, Maryland, October 4, 1862.

MARTIN, EDMUND, Private
Born in Martin County where he resided as a farmer and enlisted at age 38, June 24, 1861, for the war. Discharged on August 10, 1861, by reason of "hernia."

MAY, E. RILEY, Private
Resided in Guilford County where he enlisted at age 22, July 8, 1862, for the war. Died in hospital at Richmond, Virginia, September 15, 1862, of "typhoid fever."

MAY, PETER W., Private
Resided in Guilford County where he enlisted at age 30, July 8, 1862, for the war. Wounded in action at Sharpsburg, Maryland, September 17, 1862, and died in hospital at Richmond, Virginia, October 19, 1862, of "typhoid fever."

MAY, WILLIAM R., Private
Resided in Guilford County where he enlisted at age 23, July 8, 1862, for the war. Captured at Gettysburg, Pennsylvania, July 3-4, 1863, and confined at Fort Delaware, Delaware, where he died October 7, 1863.

MIZELL, JAMES H., Private
Resided in Martin County where he enlisted at age 23, May 1, 1862, for the war. Company muster rolls report him as absent sick after October, 1862, until May-June, 1863, when he was reported with the remark: "Died of disease, Lynchburg Hospital, Virginia."

MIZELL, RANDEL, Private
Born in Martin County where he resided as a farmer and enlisted at age 18, June 24, 1861, for the war. Discharged September 6, 1861, on Surgeon's Certificate of Disability. Later enlisted in Company K, 41st Regiment N.C. Troops (3rd Regiment N.C. Cavalry).

MIZELL, WILLIAM R., Private
Resided in Martin County where he enlisted at age 18, June 24, 1861, for the war.

MIZELL, WILLIAM W., Private
Resided in Martin County where he enlisted at age 18, June 24, 1861, for the war. Wounded in action at Gettysburg, Pennsylvania, July 1-3, 1863. Present or accounted for until captured at Spotsylvania Court House, Virginia, May 12, 1864. Confined at Point Lookout, Maryland, until transferred to Elmira, New York, August 6, 1864. Released at Elmira after taking the Oath of Allegiance on June 27, 1865.

MOBLEY, JOHN L., Sergeant
Resided in Martin County where he enlisted at age 20, June 24, 1861, for the war. Mustered in as Private and appointed Corporal on May 3, 1863. Wounded in action at Payne's Farm, Virginia, November 27, 1863. Promoted to Sergeant March-April, 1864. Captured at Spotsylvania Court House, Virginia, May 12, 1864, and confined at Point Lookout, Maryland, until transferred to Elmira, New York, August 6, 1864. Paroled at Elmira and sent to Point Lookout on October 11, 1864. Exchanged on October 29, 1864. November-December, 1864, muster roll states that he was "home on parole."

MODLIN, ASHLEY, Private
Resided in Martin County where he enlisted at age 27, June 24, 1861, for the war. Admitted to hospital in Richmond, Virginia, November 12, 1862, with a gunshot wound of the ankle and furloughed on November 27, 1862. Date and place he was wounded not reported. Reported as absent sick until detailed in hospital at Orange Court House, Virginia, on January 15, 1864. Deserted March 1, 1864.

MODLIN, JAMES A., Private
Resided in Martin County where he enlisted at age 21, June 24, 1861, for the war. Wounded in action at Chancellorsville, Virginia, May 2-3, 1863. Present or accounted for until captured at Spotsylvania Court House, Virginia, May 12, 1864. Confined at Point Lookout, Maryland, until transferred to Elmira, New York, August 6, 1864. Released at Elmira after taking the Oath of Allegiance on June 27, 1865.

MODLIN, WILLIAM S., Corporal
Resided in Martin County where he enlisted at age 22, May 1, 1862, for the war. Mustered in as Private and appointed Corporal on January 2, 1863. Killed in action at Chancellorsville, Virginia, May 3, 1863.

MOORE, WILLIAM W., Musician
Resided in Martin County where he enlisted at age 18, February 1, 1862, for the war. Mustered in as Musician. Present or accounted for until paroled at Burkeville Junction, Virginia, April 14-17, 1865.

MORRISON, W. T., Private
Captured at Greencastle, Pennsylvania, July 5, 1863, and confined at Fort Delaware, Delaware, until paroled on July 30, 1863, and sent to City Point, Virginia, for exchange.

MURRAY, LUCIEN H., Private
Resided in Guilford County where he enlisted at age 19, July 8, 1862, for the war. Wounded in action at Payne's Farm, Virginia, November 27, 1863. Present or accounted for on company muster rolls through December, 1864. Admitted to hospital at Richmond, Virginia, March 2, 1865, with "diarrhoea chronic" and transferred to Farmville, Virginia, April 1, 1865. Paroled at Greensboro on May 5, 1865.

NEESE, ELIAS, Private
Resided in Guilford County where he enlisted at

age 34, July 8, 1862, for the war. Present or accounted for until captured at Gettysburg, Pennsylvania, July 3, 1863. Confined at Fort Delaware, Delaware, where he died on October 14, 1863.

O'DONOHUE, PATRICK, 1st Sergeant
Captured at Salisbury on April 12, 1865, and confined at Camp Chase, Ohio, May 2, 1865. Released after taking the Oath of Allegiance on June 13, 1865. Residence given on Oath as Georgetown, D. C.

OTWELL, JESSE R., Private
Resided in Guilford County where he enlisted at age 26, July 8, 1862, for the war. Present or accounted for until captured at Spotsylvania Court House, Virginia, May 12, 1864. Confined at Point Lookout, Maryland, until transferred to Elmira, New York, August 6, 1864. Died at Elmira on October 4, 1864, of "intermittent fever."

PAYNE, PATTERSON, Private
Resided in Alamance County. Captured at Salisbury on April 12, 1865, and confined at Camp Chase, Ohio, until released after taking the Oath of Allegiance on June 13, 1865.

PEAL, ASA A., Corporal
Resided in Martin County where he enlisted at age 18, June 24, 1861, for the war. Mustered in as Corporal. Died in Richmond, Virginia, on August 25, 1861, of disease.

PERRY, WILEY K., Private
Confined at Fort Delaware, Delaware, from Gettysburg, Pennsylvania, in July, 1863.

POLLARD, THOMAS, Sergeant
Born in Louisiana and resided as a student in Martin County where he enlisted at age 18, June 24, 1861, for the war. Mustered in as Sergeant. Present or accounted for until captured at Payne's Farm, Virginia, November 28, 1863. Confined at Old Capitol Prison, Washington, D. C., until transferred to Point Lookout, Maryland, February 3, 1864. Released from Point Lookout after joining the U. S. service on February 16, 1864, and assigned to Company E, 1st Regiment U. S. Volunteer Infantry.

PRICE, ASA, Private
Enlisted in Martin County on June 24, 1861, for the war. Died at Fredericksburg, Virginia, November 16, 1861, of disease.

PRICE, DENNIS, Private
Resided in Martin County where he enlisted at age 43, June 24, 1861, for the war. Died at Fredericksburg, Virginia, November 15-16, 1861, of disease.

REASON, COTTON, Private
Resided in Martin County where he enlisted at age 24, June 24, 1861, for the war. Present or accounted for until captured at Spotsylvania Court House, Virginia, May 12, 1864. Confined at Point Lookout, Maryland, until transferred to Elmira, New York, August 6, 1864. Released at Elmira after taking the Oath of Allegiance on June 12, 1865.

REAVES, JAMES S., Private
Federal Provost Marshal records report him as a "rebel deserter" and state that he was captured at Tobacco Ford, Virginia, January 17, 1864, and was confined at Old Capitol Prison, Washington, D.C., until released after taking the Oath of Amnesty on March 15, 1864. Sent to Philadelphia, Pennsylvania. Residence given on Oath as "Soumberton County, North Carolina."

RICHARDS, ALBERT, Private
Resided in Martin County where he enlisted at age 21, June 24, 1861, for the war. Died in April, 1862, of disease.

ROBERSON, AMOS, Private
Resided in Martin County where he enlisted at age 24, February 1, 1862, for the war. Discharged at Goldsboro on March 31, 1863, by reason of "phthisis pulmonalis."

ROBERSON, WILLIAM H., Private
Enlisted in Martin County on July 24, 1861, for the war. Admitted to hospital at Richmond, Virginia, June 27, 1862, with a gunshot wound and died July 3, 1862.

ROBERTSON, CHARLES, Private
Resided in Martin County where he enlisted at age 37, February 1, 1862, for the war. Died in hospital at Montgomery White Sulphur Springs, Virginia, January 13, 1863, of "variola."

ROBERTSON, NOAH P., Private
Resided in Martin County where he enlisted at age 34, June 24, 1861, for the war. Wounded in action at Ellerson's Mill, Virginia, June 26, 1862. Present or accounted for until captured at Spotsylvania Court House, Virginia, May 12, 1864. Confined at Point Lookout, Maryland, until transferred to Elmira, New York, July 12, 1864. Released at Elmira after taking the Oath of Allegiance on June 27, 1865.

ROBISON, JOSEPH A., Private
Enlisted at Orange Court House, Virginia, April 1, 1864, for the war. Captured at Spotsylvania Court House, Virginia, May 12, 1864, and confined at Point Lookout, Maryland, until transferred to Elmira, New York, August 6, 1864. Paroled at Elmira on March 14, 1865, and sent James River, Virginia, for exchange. Received at Boulware's Wharf, James River, March 18-21, 1865, in exchange.

RODGERS, N. J., Private
Died at Fort Delaware, Delaware, September 8, 1863, of "typhoid fever."

ROEBUCK, H. L., Private
Resided in Martin County where he enlisted at age 20, May 1, 1862, for the war. Killed in action at Chancellorsville, Virginia, May 2, 1863.

ROEBUCK, SAMUEL H., Corporal
Resided in Martin County where he enlisted at age 34, May 1, 1862, for the war. Mustered in as Private. Wounded in action at Malvern Hill, Virginia, July 1, 1862. Appointed Corporal in October, 1862. Died in hospital at Lynchburg, Virginia, December 9, 1862, of "pneumonia."

ROGERSON, ARDEN, Private
Resided in Martin County where he enlisted at age 18, June 24, 1861, for the war. Died in hospital

at Richmond, Virginia, December 4, 1862, of "typhoid fever."

ROGERSON, THOMAS, Private

Resided in Martin County where he enlisted at age 21, June 24, 1861, for the war. Wounded in action at Winchester, Virginia, June 15, 1863. Present or accounted for until captured at Spotsylvania Court House, Virginia, May 12, 1864. Confined at Point Lookout, Maryland, until transferred to Elmira, New York, August 6, 1864. Released at Elmira after taking the Oath of Allegiance on June 12, 1865.

RUSS, WILLIAM CHARLES, Private

Resided in Martin County where he enlisted at age 18, June 24, 1861, for the war. Present or accounted for until captured at Spotsyvania Court House, Virginia, May 12, 1864. Confined at Point Lookout, Maryland, until transferred to Elmira, New York, August 6, 1864. Released at Elmira after taking the Oath of Allegiance on June 14, 1865.

SALINGER, WILLIAM HENRY, Private

Born in Martin County where he resided as a farmer and enlisted at age 20, February 1, 1862, for the war. Company muster rolls report him as present or accounted for through March-April, 1863, when he was first reported as absent sick. Reported as absent sick through January 1, 1864, when he was first reported as absent without leave. February 29-August 31, 1864, muster roll states that he "deserted to enemy in 1863." Federal Provost Marshal records indicate that he was captured at Plymouth, N. C., February 6, 1864, and confined at Point Lookout, Maryland. Released at Point Lookout after joining the U. S. service on March 9, 1864. Assigned to Company E, 1st Regiment U. S. Volunteer Infantry.

SALLENGER, DAVID P., Sergeant

Born in Martin County where he resided as a farmer and enlisted at age 24, June 24, 1861, for the war. Mustered in as Private and appointed Sergeant prior to December 31, 1861. Wounded in action at Chancellorsville, Virginia, May 2-3, 1863. Present or accounted for until captured at Gettysburg, Pennsylvania, July 3-4, 1863. Confined at Fort McHenry, Maryland, until sent to Fort Delaware, Delaware, July 12, 1863. Transferred on October 18, 1863, to Point Lookout, Maryland, where he was released on January 23, 1864, on joining the U.S. service. Assigned to Company G, 1st Regiment U.S. Volunteer Infantry.

SALLINGER, JAMES, Private

Resided in Martin County and enlisted at Camp Bee, Virginia, on January 1, 1862, for the war. Died at Ashland, Virginia, in 1862, of disease.

SETTLE, G. B., Private

Captured at Gettysburg, Pennsylvania, July 3, 1863, and confined at Fort Delaware, Delaware, July 7-12, 1863.

SEXTON, WILLIAM H., Private

Resided in Martin County where he enlisted at age 19, June 24, 1861, for the war. Died in hospital at Richmond, Virginia, July 6, 1862, of "typhoid fever" and "pneumonia."

SHARP, OSCAR D., Private

Resided in Guilford County where he enlisted at age 29, July 8, 1862, for the war. Wounded and captured at Sharpsburg, Maryland, September 17, 1862. Died in hospital at Frederick, Maryland, November 21, 1862.

SHEPHERD, JAMES M., Private

Resided in Guilford County where he enlisted at age 22, July 8, 1862, for the war. Present or accounted for on company muster rolls through December, 1864. Federal Provost Marshal records report him as a "rebel deserter" received at Washington, D.C., on March 18, 1865, from the Army of the James. Took the Oath of Allegiance on March 24, 1865, and was furnished transportation to Goshen, Orange County, New York.

SHEPHERD, JOSHUA, Private

Enlisted at New Market, Virginia, October 19, 1864, for the war. Present or accounted for on company muster rolls through December, 1864, and detailed on February 4, 1865. Federal Provost Marshal records report him as "rebel deserter" received from the Army of the James at Washington, D.C., on March 19, 1865. Took the Oath of Allegiance on March 24, 1865, and was furnished transportation to Indianapolis, Indiana.

SHEPHERD, SIMEON, Private

Resided in Guilford County where he enlisted at age 21, July 8, 1862, for the war. Present or accounted for until captured at Spotsylvania Court House, Virginia, May 12, 1864. Confined at Point Lookout, Maryland, until transferred to Elmira, New York, August 6, 1864. Paroled at Elmira and sent to James River, Virginia, for exchange on February 20, 1865. Admitted to hospital at Richmond, Virginia, March 2, 1865, and furloughed for 30 days on March 11, 1865.

SHEPPERD, SOLOMON, Private

Resided in Guilford County where he enlisted at age 29, July 8, 1862, for the war. Present or accounted for until captured at Spotsylvania Court House, Virginia, May 12, 1864. Confined at Point Lookout, Maryland, until transferred to Elmira, New York, August 6, 1864. Released at Elmira after taking the Oath of Allegiance on June 12, 1865.

SIMPSON, FRANKLIN, Private

Born in Martin County where he resided as a merchant and enlisted at age 20, June 24, 1861, for the war. Detailed in Medical Department on December 21, 1861. Reported as absent detailed until discharged at Richmond, Virginia, September 8, 1862, by reason of "malformation of fingers and toes."

SIMPSON, JAMES A., Private

Resided in Martin County where he enlisted at age 21, June 24, 1861, for the war. Present or accounted for until captured at Spotsylvania Court House, Virginia, May 12, 1864. Confined at Point Lookout, Maryland, until transferred to Elmira, New York, August 6, 1864. Paroled at Elmira on October 11, 1864, and sent to Point Lookout to be exchanged. Exchanged on October 29, 1864. November-December, 1864, muster roll reports him as "home paroled since December 1, 1864." Took the Oath of Allegiance at Bermuda Hundred, Virginia, March 16, 1865, and was sent to Washington, D.C.

SIMPSON, WILLIAM, Private
Resided in Martin County where he enlisted at age 36, June 24, 1861, for the war. Wounded in action at Ellerson's Mill, Virginia, June 26, 1862, and died of wounds on July 24, 1862.

SLOUGH, DAVID, Private
Resided in Cabarrus County. Captured at Salisbury on April 12, 1865, and confined at Camp Chase, Ohio, until released after taking the Oath of Allegiance on June 13, 1865.

SMITH, RICHARD, Private
Resided in Guilford County where he enlisted at age 30, July 8, 1862, for the war. Wounded in action at Sharpsburg, Maryland, September 17, 1862. Reported as absent wounded or absent sick until detailed in hospital at Richmond, Virginia, March 26, 1864. Reported as absent detailed until November-December, 1864, muster roll reports him as present. Detailed again on February 4, 1865. Federal Provost Marshal records report him as a "rebel deserter" with the remark that he took the Oath of Allegiance at Bermuda Hundred, Virginia, March 16, 1865, and was sent to Washington, D.C., where he was furnished transportation to Raysville, Indiana, on March 24, 1865.

SMITHWICK, ASA, Private
Resided in Martin County where he enlisted at age 26, June 24, 1861, for the war. Present or accounted for until captured at Gettysburg, Pennsylvania, July 3, 1863. Confined at Fort McHenry, Maryland, until transferred to Fort Delaware, Delaware, July 7-12, 1863. Transferred on October 15, 1863, to Point Lookout, Maryland, where he remained until paroled and sent to City Point, Virginia, for exchange on March 17, 1864. Reported as present on muster rolls through December, 1864, after exchange. Federal Provost Marshal records indicate that he took the Oath of Allegiance at Bermuda Hundred, Virginia, March 16, 1865, and was sent to Washington, D.C., where he was provided transportation to Raysville, Indiana, on March 24, 1865.

SOURS, JACOB, Private
Resided in Rowan County. Captured at Salisbury on April 12, 1865, and confined at Camp Chase, Ohio, until released after taking the Oath of Allegiance on June 13, 1865.

STAFFORD, LEWIS, Private
Captured at Salisbury on April 12, 1865, and confined at Camp Chase, Ohio, where he died May 18, 1865, of "typhoid fever."

SUMMERS, MARTIN, Private
Resided in Guilford County where he enlisted at age 25, July 8, 1862, for the war. Died in hospital at Richmond, Virginia, September 19, 1862, of "typhoid fever."

TAYLOR, HENRY D., Private
Resided in Martin County where he enlisted at age 18, June 24, 1861, for the war. Died in hospital at Richmond, Virginia, on October 20, 1862, of "pneumonia."

TAYLOR, JAMES B., Private
Born in Martin County where he resided as a farmer and enlisted at age 32, June 24, 1861, for the war. Discharged on April 10, 1862, by reason of disability.

TAYLOR, JOHN, Sergeant
Resided in Pitt County and enlisted in Martin County at age 24, June 24, 1861, for the war. Mustered in as Sergeant. Discharged at Camp Bee, Virginia, November 20, 25, 1861, and died shortly thereafter.

TAYLOR, JOSEPH D., Sergeant
Resided in Pitt County and enlisted in Martin County at age 28, June 24, 1861, for the war. Mustered in as Sergeant. Wounded in action at Ellerson's Mill, Virginia, June 26, 1862. Present or accounted for on company muster rolls until captured at Spotsylvania Court House, Virginia, May 12, 1864. Confined at Point Lookout, Maryland, until transferred to Elmira, New York, August 6, 1864. Died at Elmira on March 24, 1865, of "variola."

TAYLOR, McGILBERT, Private
Resided in Martin County where he enlisted at age 23, June 24, 1861, for the war. Present or accounted for until captured at Spotsylvania Court House, Virginia, May 12, 1864. Confined at Point Lookout, Maryland, where he died August 10, 1864.

TAYLOR, WILEY F., Private
Born in Martin County where he resided as a farmer and enlisted at age 23, June 24, 1861, for the war. Mustered in as Corporal and reduced to ranks by December, 1861. Present or accounted for until captured at Spotsylvania Court House, Virginia, May 12, 1864. Confined at Point Lookout, Maryland, where he was released after joining the U.S. service on June 4, 1864. Assigned to Company K, 1st Regiment U.S. Volunteer Infantry.

TETTERTON, WILLIAM R., Private
Enlisted in Washington County on July 29, 1861, for the war. Present or accounted for until discharged on February 3, 1862, upon transfer to the C.S. Navy.

THOMAS, JAMES K. P., Private
Captured at Petersburg, Virginia, April 3, 1865, and confined at Point Lookout, Maryland, until released after taking the Oath of Allegiance on June 21, 1865.

TOGHMAN, HENRY, Private
Paroled at Greensboro on May 31, 1865.

TRIBBLE, W. G., Private
Captured at Spotsylvania Court House, Virginia, May 12, 1864, and confined at Point Lookout, Maryland, until transferred to Elmira, New York, August 6, 1864. Died at Elmira on August 29, 1864, of "typhoid fever."

TRICKER, RICHARD, Corporal
Resided in Martin County where he enlisted at age 34, June 24, 1861, for the war. Mustered in as

Corporal. Killed in action at Ellerson's Mill, Virginia, June 26, 1862.

TWEEDY, HENRY H., Private

Resided in Martin County where he enlisted at age 21, June 24, 1861, for the war. Wounded in action at Malvern Hill, Virginia, July 1, 1862, and killed in action at Sharpsburg, Maryland, September 17, 1862.

TWEEDY, JAMES G., Sergeant

Resided in Martin County where he enlisted at age 26, June 24, 1861, for the war. Mustered in as Sergeant. Killed in action at Chancellorsville, Virginia, May 2-3, 1863.

TWEEDY, WILLIAM W., Private

Resided in Martin County where he enlisted at age 22, June 24, 1861, for the war. Killed in action at Sharpsburg, Maryland, September 17, 1862.

UTZMAN, ROBERT M., Private

Captured at Salisbury on April 12, 1865, and confined at Camp Chase, Ohio, May 2, 1865.

VANHORN, JOSEPH, Private

Resided in Martin County where he enlisted at age 24, June 24, 1861, for the war. Killed in action at Chancellorsville, Virginia, May 3, 1863.

VANHORN, SAMUEL, Private

Resided in Martin County where he enlisted at age 19, June 24, 1861, for the war. Killed in action at Sharpsburg, Maryland, September 17, 1862.

WAGONER, DAVID, Private

Resided in Guilford County where he enlisted at age 24, July 8, 1862, for the war. Present or accounted for until detailed as teamster January-February, 1863. Reported as absent on detail as teamster through December, 1864. Captured at High Bridge, Virginia, April 6, 1865, and confined at Point Lookout, Maryland, until released after taking the Oath of Allegiance on June 22, 1865.

WAGONER, REUBEN, Private

Resided in Guilford County where he enlisted at age 20, July 8, 1862, for the war. Wounded in action at Sharpsburg, Maryland, September 17, 1862, and died of wounds at Staunton, Virginia, November 2, 1862.

WEAR, GEORGE W., Private

Resided in Iredell County. Captured at Salisbury on April 12, 1865, and confined at Camp Chase, Ohio, until released after taking the Oath of Allegiance on June 13, 1865.

WEBB, JOSEPH D., Private

Resided in Martin County where he enlisted at age 18, June 24, 1861, for the war. Wounded in action at Chancellorsville, Virginia, May 3, 1863. Present or accounted for until captured at Spotsylvania Court House, Virginia, May 12, 1864. Confined at Point Lookout, Maryland, until transferred to Elmira, New York, August 6, 1864. Died at Elmira on November 6, 1864, of "erysipelas."

WHITAKER, JOHN S., Private

Resided in Martin County where he enlisted at age 34, June 24, 1861, for the war. Discharged on May 14, 1862.

WHITE, CLINTON, Private

Resided in Guilford County where he enlisted at age 19, July 8, 1862, for the war. Wounded and captured at Gettysburg, Pennsylvania, July 3-4, 1863. Admitted to Field Hospital at Gettysburg on July 4, 1863, with the remark that his right leg had been amputated the previous day. Died in hospital at Gettysburg on July 26, 1863.

WHITE, JOHN, Private

Resided in Guilford County where he enlisted at age 30, July 8, 1862, for the war. Died in hospital at Richmond, Virginia, September 11, 1862, of "typhoid fever."

WILLIAMS, SETH, Private

Resided in Martin County where he enlisted at age 34, June 24, 1861, for the war. Wounded in action at Sharpsburg, Maryland, September 17, 1862. Died in hospital at Richmond, Virginia, April 1, 1863, of "phthisis."

WILSON, CHAMBERLAIN W., Private

Captured at Salisbury on April 12, 1865, and confined at Camp Chase, Ohio, May 2-4, 1865.

WOOLDRIDGE, C. W., Private

Resided in Powhatan County, Virginia. Captured at Salisbury on April 12, 1865, and confined at Camp Chase, Ohio, until released after taking the Oath of Allegiance on June 13, 1865.

WYNN, JAMES B., Private

Resided in Martin County where he enlisted at age 27, June 24, 1861, for the war. Discharged on January 13, 1862, by reason of disability.

WYNN, McGILBERT, Private

Resided as a farmer in Martin County where he enlisted at age 18, June 24, 1861, for the war. Present or accounted for until captured at Strasburg, Virginia, October 19, 1864. Confined at Point Lookout, Maryland, until released after taking the Oath of Allegiance on May 14, 1865.

WYNN, THOMAS D., Private

Resided in Martin County where he enlisted at age 22, June 24, 1861, for the war. Present or accounted for until captured at Spotsylvania Court House, Virginia, May 12, 1864. Confined at Point Lookout, Maryland until transferred to Elmira, New York, August 6, 1864. Died at Elmira on April 7, 1865, of "pneumonia."

YATES, DANIEL F., Private

Resided in Guilford County where he enlisted at age 18, July 8, 1862, for the war. Present or accounted for until captured at Spotsylvania Court House, Virginia, May 12, 1864. Confined at Point Lookout, Maryland, until transferred to Elmira, New York, August 6, 1864. Died at Elmira on April 3, 1865, of "variola."

COMPANY I

This company, known as "Wake Light Infantry," was organized in Wake County and enlisted at Forestville on July 16, 1861. It tendered its services to the state and was ordered to Warrenton, Warren County, where it was assigned to this regiment as Company I. When the regiment was ordered to Virginia on July 22, the company remained behind to complete its organization. It rejoined the regiment at Camp Bee, Brooke's Station, Virginia, on August 30, 1861. After joining the regiment the company functioned as a part of the regiment, and its history for the war period is recorded as a part of the regimental history.

The information contained in the following roster of the company was compiled principally from company muster rolls which covered from July through August, 1861; November through December, 1861; March through April, 1862; and June 30, 1862, through December, 1864. No company muster rolls were found for September through October, 1861; January through February, 1862; May through June 29, 1862; or for the period after December, 1864. In addition to the company muster rolls, Roll of Honor records, receipt rolls, hospital records, prisoner of war records, and other primary records, supplemented by state pension applications, United Daughters of the Confederacy records, and postwar rosters and histories, all provided useful information.

OFFICERS
CAPTAINS

FOOTE, JAMES HENRY
Resided in Wake County as a professor at Wake Forest College when he was appointed Captain, at age 33, to rank from May 16, 1861. Submitted his resignation December 19, 1862, stating that "he had vacated his seat as professor with the proviso that he return within a year and that now after 19 months he is being urged to return." Resignation accepted on January 6, 1863, and he was appointed Assistant Adjutant General, State of North Carolina, with the rank of Major and assigned to the Roll of Honor.

FOWLER, HARDIMAN D.
Resided in Wake County and appointed 2nd Lieutenant at age 28 to rank from May 16, 1861. Promoted to 1st Lieutenant to rank from September 20, 1862, and to Captain to rank from January 6, 1863. Present or accounted for until captured at Spotsylvania Court House, Virginia, May 10-12, 1864. Confined at Fort Delaware, Delaware, until transferred to Hilton Head, South Carolina, August 20, 1864. Transferred to Fort Pulaski, Georgia, October 20, 1864, and returned to Hilton Head on November 19, 1864. Sent to Fort Delaware, Delaware, on March 12, 1865, where he was released after taking the Oath of Allegiance on June 16, 1865.

LIEUTENANTS

CARVER, ELIAS A., 2nd Lieutenant
Resided in Wake County where he enlisted at age 17, July 16, 1861, for the war. Mustered in as Private and appointed Sergeant, November-December, 1862. Elected 2nd Lieutenant on February 20, 1863, and appointed to rank from date of election. Present or accounted for until captured at Spotsylvania Court House, Virginia, May 10, 1864. Confined at Fort Delaware, Dela-

ware, until transferred to Hilton Head, South Carolina, on August 20, 1864. Transferred to Fort Pulaski, Georgia, October 20, 1864, and then back to Hilton Head on January 1, 1865. Transferred on March 12, 1865, to Fort Delaware, where he was released after taking the Oath of Allegiance on June 16, 1865.

HEARTSFIELD, JACOB A., 1st Lieutenant
Resided in Wake County where he enlisted at age 22, July 16, 1861, for the war. Mustered in as Private and appointed Sergeant June 26, 1862. Promoted to 2nd Lieutenant to rank from October 25, 1862, and to 1st Lieutenant to rank from January 6, 1863. Present or accounted for until captured at Spotsylvania Court House, Virginia, May 12, 1864. Confined at Old Capitol Prison, Washington, D.C., until transferred to Fort Delaware, Delaware, June 17, 1864. Transferred from Fort Delaware to Hilton Head, South Carolina on August 20, 1864, and from there to Fort Pulaski, Georgia, October, 1864. Returned to Fort Delaware by way of Hilton Head on March 12, 1865. Released after taking the Oath of Allegiance at Fort Delaware on June 16, 1865.

PATTERSON, HENRY HOUSTON,
2nd Lieutenant
Resided in Wake County where he enlisted at age 17, August 8, 1861, for the war. Mustered in as Sergeant and appointed 1st Sergeant November-December, 1862. Elected 2nd Lieutenant January 9, 1863, and appointed to rank from date of election. Wounded in action at Spotsylvania Court House, Virginia, May 10, 1864, and reported as absent wounded until returned to duty on December 29, 1864. Furloughed on January 4, 1865. Paroled at Appomattox Court House, Virginia, April 9, 1865.

SCARBOROUGH, WILLIAM D., 1st Lieutenant
Resided in Wake County and appointed 1st Lieutenant at age 28 to rank from May 16, 1861. Wounded and captured at Sharpsburg, Maryland, September 17, 1862. Died of wounds in hospital at Frederick, Maryland, on September 20, 1862.

TERRELL, JAMES J., 3rd Lieutenant
Resided in Wake County and appointed 3rd Lieutenant, at age 26, to rank from May 16, 1861. Wounded in action at Malvern Hill, Virginia, July 1, 1862, and leg amputated. Resigned January 31, 1863.

NONCOMMISSIONED OFFICERS AND PRIVATES

ALFORD, JOSIAH, Private
Resided in Wake County where he enlisted at age 20, January 27, 1862, for the war. Wounded in action at Chancellorsville, Virginia, May 2-3, 1863. Present or accounted for until captured at Spotsylvania Court House, Virginia, May 12, 1864. Confined at Elmira, New York, where he died October 24, 1864, of "chronic diarrhoea."

ALLEN, G. D., Private
Paroled at Salisbury on May 11, 1865.

ALLEN, JOHN D., Corporal
Resided in Wake County where he enlisted at

age 21, July 16, 1861, for the war. Mustered in as Private. Detailed as a cook, March-April, 1862. Detailed as a nurse in hospital at Richmond, Virginia, January-April, 1863. Promoted to Corporal after January, 1864. Present or accounted for until captured at Spotsylvania Court House, Virginia, May 12, 1864. Confined at Elmira, New York, until released after taking the Oath of Allegiance on June 12, 1865.

ALLEN, WILLIAM O., Private

Resided in Wake County where he enlisted at age 19, July 16, 1861, for the war. Mustered in as Private and appointed Corporal after June 30, 1862. Reduced to ranks October 31, 1862, after being absent sick for five months. Present or accounted for until transferred to the Field and Staff of this regiment upon appointment as Sergeant Major to rank from July 15, 1863.

ALLGOOD, JOHN G. W., Private

Resided in Wake County where he enlisted at age 20, July 16, 1861, for the war. Admitted to hospital at Richmond, Virginia, July 7, 1862, with "typhoid fever" and transferred to Danville, Virginia, July 22, 1862. Returned to duty August 20, 1862. November-December, 1862, muster roll states that he was: "Discharged in hospital. No official information." Roll of Honor states that he was "discharged 1862 on Surgeon's Certificate of Disability at hospital at Lynchburg, Virginia."

ANDREWS, J. A., Private

Paroled at Greensboro on May 19, 1865.

ATKINSON, RICHARD H. C., Private

Resided in Wake County where he enlisted at age 21, July 16, 1861, for the war. Mustered in as Sergeant and reduced to ranks November-December, 1862, by reason of his being absent sick for five months. Killed in action at Chancellorsville, Virginia, May 3, 1863.

BAILEY, GEORGE W., Private

Resided in Wake County where he enlisted at age 18, August 12, 1861, for the war. Rejected when the company was mustered in. Reenlisted in Wayne County on May 12, 1862, for the war. Present or accounted for until wounded in action at Payne's Farm, Virginia, November 27, 1863. Died of wounds November 28, 1863.

BAILEY, WILLIAM A., Private

Resided in Wake County where he enlisted at age 19, July 16, 1861, for the war. Wounded in action at Chancellorsville, Virginia, May 2, 1863. Present or accounted for until captured at Spotsylvania Court House, Virginia, May 12, 1864. Confined at Elmira, New York, until transferred to James River, Virginia, for exchange on February 20, 1865. Admitted to hospital at Richmond, Virginia, March 1, 1865, and furloughed for 30 days on March 6, 1865.

BARHAM, GEORGE S., Private

Resided in Franklin County and enlisted in Wake County at age 34, June 18, 1863, for the war. Present or accounted for until captured at Spotsylvania Court House, Virginia, May 12, 1864. Confined at Elmira, New York, until trans-

ferred to James River, Virginia, for exchange on February 20, 1865.

BARKER, J., Private

Appears on a register of enlisted men, rebel deserters, and refugees detained at Camp Distribution, Virginia. Register states that he was received from Annapolis, Maryland, May 22, 1864, and was forwarded to New Bern on May 26, 1864.

BASSCLOUD, J., Private

Captured at Gettysburg, Pennsylvania, July 3, 1863, and confined at Fort Delaware, Delaware, where he died October 18, 1863, of "diptheria."

BELVIN, ELIJAH W., Private

Resided in Wake County where he enlisted at age 19, August 15, 1861, for the war. Wounded in action at Ellerson's Mill, Virginia, June 26, 1862. Reported as absent sick until detailed as a nurse on May 29, 1863. Assigned to General Hospital at Staunton, Virginia. Retired to the Invalid Corps on November 11, 1864. Paroled at Farmville, Virginia, April 11-21, 1865.

BELVIN, JAMES, Private

Resided in Wake County and enlisted in Wayne County at age 24, May 9, 1862, for the war. Killed in action at Chancellorsville, Virginia, May 3, 1863.

BLACKBURN, THOMAS M., Private

Resided in Wake County where he enlisted at age 27, August 19, 1861, for the war. Wounded in the leg at Sharpsburg, Maryland, September 17, 1862, and returned to duty December 8, 1862. Present or accounted for until captured at Gettysburg, Pennsylvania, July 3, 1863. Confined at Point Lookout, Maryland, until paroled for exchange on February 13, 1865. Reported as present on a roll of a detachment of paroled and exchanged prisoners at Camp Lee, near Richmond, Virginia, dated February 17, 1865.

BRINKLEY, THOMAS H., Private

Resided in Wake County where he enlisted at age 28, July 1, 1863, for the war. Present or accounted for until captured at Spotsylvania Court House, Virginia, May 12, 1864. Confined at Point Lookout, Maryland, until transferred to Elmira, New York, August 6, 1864. Released at Elmira after taking the Oath of Allegiance on June 12, 1865.

BROGDEN, JAMES I., Private

Resided in Wake County where he enlisted at age 21, August 13, 1861, for the war. Present or accounted for until killed in action at Wilderness, Virginia, May 5, 1864.

BROWNING, LOUIS R., Private

Resided in Wake County where he enlisted at age 23, July 16, 1861, for the war. Wounded in action at Ellerson's Mill, Virginia, June 26, 1862, and at Sharpsburg, Maryland, September 17, 1862. Present or accounted for until captured at Spotsylvania Court House, Virginia, May 12, 1864. Confined at Point Lookout, Maryland, until transferred to Elmira, New York, August 6, 1864. Released after taking the Oath of Allegiance at Elmira on June 12, 1865.

BUFFALOE, DAVID, Private
Resided in Wake County where he enlisted at age 19, March 4, 1862, for the war. Present or accounted for until captured at Spotsylvania Court House, Virginia, May 12, 1864. Confined at Point Lookout, Maryland, until transferred to Elmira, New York, August 6, 1864. Paroled at Elmira on February 9, 1865, and transferred for exchange. Paroled and exchanged at Boulware's and Cox's Wharf, James River, Virginia, February 20-21, 1865. Reported as present on a muster roll of a detachment of paroled and exchanged prisoners at Camp Lee, near Richmond, Virginia, dated February 3, 1865.

BUFFALOE, W. CALVIN, Private
Resided in Wake County where he enlisted at age 18, March 3, 1862, for the war. Wounded in action at Chancellorsville, Virginia, May 3, 1863. Present or accounted for until captured at Spotsylvania Court House, Virginia, May 12, 1864. Confined at Point Lookout, Maryland, until transferred to Elmira, New York, August 6, 1864. Released at Elmira after taking the Oath of Allegiance on June 12, 1865.

BUFFALOE, WILLIAM H., Private
Resided in Wake County and enlisted in Wayne County at age 22, May 12, 1862, for the war. Wounded in action at Ellerson's Mill, Virginia, June 26, 1862. Present or accounted for until captured at Spotsylvania Court House, Virginia, May 12, 1864. Confined at Point Lookout, Maryland, until transferred to Elmira, New York, August 6, 1864. Paroled at Elmira and sent to James River, Virginia, for exchange on February 13, 1865. Received in exchange at Boulware's and Cox's Wharf, James River, Virginia, February 20-21, 1865. Admitted to hospital at Richmond, Virginia, February 21, 1865, and furloughed to Raleigh on February 25, 1865.

BURKE, WILLIAM, Private
Resided in Franklin County and enlisted in Wake County at age 25, July 15, 1862, for the war. Present or accounted for until he deserted and surrendered at Mercersburg, Pennsylvania, June 23, 1863. Confined at Fort Mifflin, Pennsylvania, until released after taking the Oath of Allegiance on January 1, 1864.

CANBURRY, M. A., Sergeant
Captured at Winchester, Virginia, September 19, 1864, and sent to Point Lookout, Maryland, September 23, 1864.

CARTER, GEORGE W., Private
Resided in Wake County where he enlisted at age 23, August 23, 1861, for the war. Present or accounted for until discharged at Camp Bee, Virginia, November 17, 1861, by reason of disability.

CLIFTON, YOUNG B., Private
Resided in Wake County where he enlisted at age 16, March 1, 1862, for the war. Wounded in action at Malvern Hill, Virginia, July 1, 1862, and reported as absent until returned to company on February 5, 1863. Wounded at Gettysburg, Pennsylvania, July 2, 1863, and his leg was amputated. Captured in hospital at Gettysburg on July 5,

1863, and confined at U.S. General Hospital, Chester, Pennsylvania until transferred to City Point, Virginia, August 17, 1863, for exchange. Received in exchange on September 23, 1863. Retired to the Invalid Corps on November 4, 1864.

COPPAGE, WILLIAM, Private
Born in Franklin County where he resided as a farmer prior to enlisting at age 33, July 15, 1862, for the war. Discharged at Richmond, Virginia, September 12, 1862, by reason of "chronic rheumatism."

CURLLE, WILLIAM, Private
Paroled at Salisbury on May 11, 1865.

DAVIS, GEORGE W., Corporal
Resided in Wake County where he enlisted at age 18, July 18, 1861, for the war. Mustered in as Private and appointed Corporal, November-December, 1862. Wounded in action at Winchester, Virginia, June 15, 1863. Present or accounted for until paroled at Appomattox Court House, Virginia, April 9, 1865.

DEAN, WILLIAM, Private
Name appears as signature to a roll of prisoners of war paroled at Point Lookout, Maryland, and sent to City Point, Virginia, April 27, 1864, for exchange. Admitted to hospital at Richmond, Virginia, May 1, 1864, with "diarrhoea chronic" and furloughed for 30 days on May 6, 1864.

DENT, ROBERT J., Private
Resided in Franklin County and enlisted in Wake County at age 26, August 12, 1861, for the war. Discharged October 18, 1861. Reenlisted in Wake County on February 27, 1862, or March 27, 1862, for the war. Wounded in action at Chancellorsville, Virginia, May 3, 1863, and died of wounds on May 8, 1863.

DENTON, JAMES, Private
Resided in Wake County and enlisted in Wayne County at age 29, May 12, 1862, for the war. Wounded in action at Payne's Farm, Virginia, November 27, 1863, and died in hospital at Orange Court House, Virginia, December 20-30, 1863.

DICKERSON, WILLIAM, Private
Resided in Granville County and enlisted in Wake County at age 38, July 15, 1862. Died in hospital at Richmond, Virginia, October 23, 1862, of "pneumonia."

DUNN, CHARLES E., Private
Resided in Wake County where he enlisted at age 19, July 16, 1861, for the war. Discharged October 12, 1861, by reason of disability.

EDDENS, SAMUEL P., Private
Resided in Wake County where he enlisted at age 30, March 4, 1862, for the war. Died in Wake County on sick furlough on June 25, 1862.

EDWARDS, J. N., Private
Resided in Nash County and enlisted in Wake County on July 15, 1862, for the war. Admitted to hospital at Richmond, Virginia, September 1, 1862, with "dysentery acute" and died September 5, 1862.

EDWARDS, JOSEPH, Private
Born in Wake County where he enlisted at age 22, May 12, 1862, for the war. Died June 14, 1862.

ELLIS, JACKSON J., Private
Resided in Wake County where he enlisted at age 35, March 8, 1862, for the war. Captured at Boonsboro. Maryland. September 15, 1862, and confined at Fort Delaware, Delaware, until sent to Aiken's Landing, Virginia, October 2, 1862, for exchange. Declared exchanged on November 10 1862. Deserted near Hamilton's Crossing, near Fredericksburg, Virginia, June 5, 1863.

FAISON, CALVIN, Private
Resided in Wake County where he enlisted at age 22, July 16, 1861, for the war. Died September 17, 1861, of disease.

FAISON, WILLIAM PERRY, Private
Resided in Wake County and enlisted in Wayne County at age 32, May 16, 1862, for the war. Captured at Sharpsburg, Maryland, September 17, 1862, and confined at Fort Delaware, Delaware, until paroled and exchanged at Aiken's Landing, Virginia, November 10, 1862. Admitted to hospital at Richmond, Virginia, December 4, 1862, with "diarrhoea and fever" and returned to duty January 12, 1863. Wounded and captured at Gettysburg, Pennsylvania, July 3-5, 1863. Confined at U.S. Army General Hospital, Chester, Pennsylvania, until sent to City Point, Virginia, for exchange on August 17, 1863. Received at City Point on August 20, 1863. Company muster rolls indicate that he did not return to duty and report him as absent "unfit for duty." Admitted to hospital at Raleigh on June 19, 1864, with a gunshot wound and returned to duty March 6, 1865. Captured in hospital at Raleigh on April 13, 1865, and paroled.

FAW, G. P., Private
Wounded and captured at Gettysburg, Pennsylvania, July 1-3, 1863, and transferred to the Provost Marshal on July 15, 1863.

FOWLER, WILLIAM B., Private
Resided in Wake County where he enlisted at age 36, July 16, 1861, for the war. Present or accounted for until discharged on September 9, 1862, by reason of his providing a substitute.

FRAZIER, JACOB, Private
Resided in Wake County where he enlisted at age 17, March 8, 1862, for the war. Present or accounted for until captured at Spotsylvania Court House, Virginia, May 12, 1864. Confined at Point Lookout, Maryland, until transferred to Elmira, New York, August 6, 1864. Released at Elmira after taking the Oath of Allegiance on June 12, 1865.

FREEMAN, JAMES, Private
Provided Robert Freeman as his substitute.

FREEMAN, ROBERT, Private
Resided in Wake County and enlisted in Wayne County at age 17, May 16, 1862, for the war as a substitute for James Freeman. Wounded in action at Chancellorsville, Virginia, May 2-3, 1863. Wounded in action at Wilderness, Virginia, May

5, 1864. Present or accounted for until captured at Farmville, Virginia, April 6, 1865. Confined at Point Lookout, Maryland, until released after taking the Oath of Allegiance on June 26, 1865.

GILL, J. T., Private
Resided in Franklin County and enlisted in Wake County at age 24, July 15, 1862, for the war. Discharged October 2, 1862, by reason of disability.

GRADY, JAMES H., Private
Resided in Wake County where he enlisted at age 27, February 27, 1862, for the war. Wounded in action at Ellerson's Mill, Virginia, June 26, 1862. Reported as absent wounded until returned to company in September-October, 1863. Captured at Spotsylvania Court House, Virginia, May 12, 1864. Confined at Point Lookout, Maryland, until transferred to Elmira, New York, August 6, 1864. Released from Elmira after taking the Oath of Allegiance on June 12, 1865.

GREEN, JAMES, Private
Resided in Wake County where he enlisted on May 11, 1862, for the war. Discharged August 18, 1862, on providing Samuel Hunt as his substitute.

GREEN, JOHN, Private
Furloughed from hospital at Richmond, Virginia, on October 11, 1862.

GREEN, RUFFIN, Private
Resided in Johnston County and enlisted in Wake County at age 18, July 15, 1862, for the war. Admitted to hospital at Richmond, Virginia, September 5, 1862, with "inter fever" and furloughed for 35 days on October 10, 1862. January-February, 1863, muster roll carries the remark: "Conscript, left at Richmond last August. Not heard from since. Dropped."

GRIFFIN, JOHN Y., Private
Resided in Wake County where he enlisted at age 25, July 16, 1861, for the war. Died in hospital at Lynchburg, Virginia, March 24, 1863, of "pneumonia."

GRIFFIN, KEARNEY, Private
Resided in Wake County where he enlisted at age 35, July 16, 1861, for the war. Deserted near Hamilton's Crossing, near Fredericksburg, Virginia, June 5, 1863, and arrested and delivered to Camp Holmes, Raleigh, December 24, 1863.

HALL, SUMNER T., Private
Resided in Wake County where he enlisted at age 16, July 16, 1862, for the war. Wounded in action at Chancellorsville, Virginia, May 3, 1863. Present or accounted for until admitted to hospital at Charlottesville, Virginia, September 23, 1864, with a gunshot wound of the forearm. Transferred to Lynchburg, Virginia, September 26, 1864. Date and place he received wound not reported. Captured at Farmville, Virginia, April 6, 1865, and confined at Point Lookout, Maryland, until released after taking the Oath of Allegiance on June 13, 1865.

HARLIN, HAZEL M., Private
Captured at Spotsylvania Court House, Virginia, May 12, 1864, and confined at Old Capitol Prison, Washington, D.C., until transferred to Elmira,

New York, on October 24, 1864.

HARPER, JOHN, Private

Resided in Franklin County and enlisted in Wake County at age 26, July 15, 1862, for the war. March-April, 1863, muster roll states that he was: "Dropped. Supposed to have died in Winchester Hospital in October last."

HARRIS, AARON L., Private

Resided in Wake County where he enlisted at age 21, February 21, 1862, for the war. Wounded in action at Winchester, Virginia, September 19, 1864. Present or accounted for on company muster rolls through December, 1864. Appears on a list of prisoners confined in Military Prison at Wheeling, West Virginia, which states that he was arrested April 2, 1865, and was administered the Oath at Clarksburg, West Virginia. List dated April 3, 1865.

HARRIS, J. WILLIS, Private

Resided in Wake County where he enlisted at age 27, March 1, 1862, for the war. Admitted to hospital at Richmond, Virginia, September 2, 1862, with "gunshot wound left thumb" and returned to duty October 18, 1862. Present or accounted for until captured at Spotsylvania Court House, Virginia, May 12, 1864. Confined at Point Lookout, Maryland, until transferred to Elmira, New York, August 6, 1864. Died at Elmira on June 24, 1865, of "chronic diarrhoea."

HARRIS, PINKNEY, Private

Resided in Franklin County and enlisted in Wake County at age 20, July 15, 1862, for the war. Died in hospital at Richmond, Virginia, November 16, 1862, of "bronchitis."

HARRISON, JAMES ROBERT, Private

Born in Franklin County where he resided as a carpenter prior to enlisting in Wake County at age 35, July 15, 1862, for the war. Discharged at Richmond, Virginia, September 15, 1862, by reason of "phthisis pulmonalis of several years standing—much reduced now by chronic diarrhoea."

HARRISON, JOHN H., Private

Resided in Wake County where he enlisted at age 27, July 16, 1861, for the war. Died in hospital at Petersburg, Virginia, March 31, 1862, of disease.

HAYES, GEORGE, Private

Born in Franklin County where he resided as a watchmaker prior to enlisting in Wake County at age 32, July 15, 1862, for the war. Discharged at Richmond, Virginia, September 15, 1862, by reason of his having a "very delicate constitution with hereditary scrofulous tendency—with ankle injury."

HEARTSFIELD, JOHN W., 1st Sergeant

Resided in Wake County where he enlisted at age 23, July 16, 1861, for the war. Mustered in as 1st Sergeant. Killed in action at Ellerson's Mill, Virginia, June 26, 1862.

HENDRICK, BADGER, Private

Resided in Wake County where he enlisted at age 19, March 4, 1862, for the war. Deserted in Wake County on April 30-May 1, 1862.

HICKS, AUGUSTUS, Private

Resided in Wake County where he enlisted at age 21, August 5, 1861, for the war. Present or accounted for until captured at Spotsylvania Court House, Virginia, May 12, 1864. Confined at Point Lookout, Maryland, where he died August 21, 1864.

HICKS, PEYTON, Private

Resided in Wake County and enlisted in Wayne County on May 12, 1862, for the war. Deserted near Hamilton's Crossing, near Fredericksburg, Virginia, June 5, 1863. Reported as a deserter on company muster rolls through July-August, 1863, when his name appears to have been dropped. He is not reported on muster rolls after that date. Federal Provost Marshal records indicate that he was captured at Cold Harbor, Virginia, May 30, 1864. Confined at Point Lookout, Maryland, until transferred to Elmira, New York, July 9-12, 1864. Died at Elmira on September 30, 1864, of "typhoid pneumonia."

HODGE, CURTIS, Private

Resided in Wake County where he enlisted at age 40, August 6, 1861, for the war. Detailed as regimental teamster from November-December, 1862, through February, 1864. Reported as absent sick from March through December, 1864.

HODGE, HENRY, Private

Born in Johnston County and resided in Wake County as a farmer prior to enlisting in Wayne County at age 16, May 6, 1862, for the war as a substitute for H. C. Lyon. Discharged September 11, 1862, by reason of "anemia and feeble physical development and also not yet 17 years of age."

HODGE, HENRY C., Private

Resided in Wake County where he enlisted at age 17, July 16, 1861, for the war. Died in regimental hospital near Richmond, Virginia, July 20, 1862, "from exhaustion in battles around Richmond."

HOLDEN, WILLIS, Private

Resided in Wake County prior to enlisting in Wayne County at age 34, May 15, 1862, for the war. Present or accounted for until captured at Spotsylvania Court House, Virginia, May 12, 1864. Confined at Point Lookout, Maryland, until transferred to Elmira, New York, August 6, 1864. Paroled at Elmira and sent to James River, Virginia, for exchange on February 9, 1865. Admitted to hospital at Richmond, Virginia, February 21, 1865, and furloughed on February 25, 1865.

HOLDER, M., Private

Resided in Bertie County and enlisted in Wake County at age 16, July 15, 1862, for the war as a substitute. Admitted to hospital at Richmond, Virginia, September 2, 1862, with "R. fever" and died September 10, 1862, of "pneumonia."

HOLLINGSWORTH, W. H., Private

Resided in Franklin County and enlisted in Wake County at age 26, July 15, 1862, for the war. Wounded in action at Sharpsburg, Maryland, September 17, 1862. Admitted to hospital at Richmond, Virginia, November 26, 1862, and transferred to Danville, Virginia, January 8, 1863. Died in hospital at Danville on January 15, 1863, of "scrofula external" and "debility from typhoid fever."

HOLLOWAY, JOHN, Private

Resided in Wake County where he enlisted at age 28, February 6, 1862, for the war. Admitted to hospital at Richmond, Virginia, January 21, 1863, with "variolloid" and furloughed for 40 days on March 31, 1863. Died at home on April 15, 1864.

HOPKINS, WILLIAM P., Private

Resided in Wake County where he enlisted at age 18, July 1, 1863, for the war. Present or accounted for until captured at Spotsylvania Court House, Virginia, May 12, 1864. Confined at Point Lookout, Maryland, until transferred to Elmira, New York, August 6, 1864. Died at Elmira on October 5, 1864, of "chronic diarrhoea."

HUBBARD, JOSIAH, Private

Resided in Wake County where he enlisted at age 25, July 20, 1861, for the war. Died in hospital at Fredericksburg, Virginia, September 19, 1861.

HUNT, SAMUEL, Private

Resided in Wake County and enlisted at Richmond, Virginia, at age 50, August 19, 1862, for the war as a substitute for James Green. Present or accounted for until captured at Spotsylvania Court House, Virginia, May 12, 1864. Confined at Point Lookout, Maryland, where he died September 9, 1864.

JONES, ATLAS G., Sergeant

Resided in Wake County where he enlisted at age 22, July 16, 1861, for the war. Mustered in as Private and appointed Corporal, July-October, 1862. Wounded in action at Boonsboro, Maryland, September 15, 1862. Promoted to Sergeant on January 9, 1863. Wounded in action at Chancellorsville, Virginia, May 3, 1863. Killed in action at Wilderness, Virginia, May 5, 1864.

JONES, ATLAS H., Private

Resided in Wake County where he enlisted at age 21, January 21, 1862, for the war. Wounded in action at Ellerson's Mill, Virginia, June 26, 1862. Present or accounted for until captured at Spotsylvania Court House, Virginia, May 12, 1864. Confined at Point Lookout, Maryland, until transferred to Elmira, New York, August 6, 1863. Died at Elmira on January 23, 1865, of "chronic diarrhoea."

JONES, H. K., Private

Enlisted in Wake County on March 10, 1864, for the war. Captured at Spotsylvania Court House, Virginia, May 12, 1864. Confined at Point Lookout, Maryland, until transferred to Elmira, New York, August 6, 1864. Paroled at Elmira on October 11, 1864, and sent to Venus Point, Savannah River, Georgia, for exchange.

JONES, H. STANLEY, Private

Born in Wake County where he resided as a student prior to enlisting in Wayne County at age 18, May 12, 1862, for the war. Killed in action at Sharpsburg, Maryland, September 17, 1862.

JONES, JAMES A., Private

Resided in Wake County where he enlisted at age 22, August 13, 1861, for the war. Died in hospital at Richmond, Virginia, July 11, 1862.

JONES, WESLEY, Private

Resided in Wake County where he enlisted at age 19, February 21, 1862, for the war. Present or accounted for until captured at Spotsylvania Court House, Virginia, May 12, 1864. Confined at Point Lookout, Maryland, until transferred to Elmira, New York, August 6, 1864. Died at Elmira on November 17, 1864, of "chronic diarrhoea."

JONES, WILLIAM A., 1st Sergeant

Resided in Wake County where he enlisted at age 23, August 13, 1861, for the war. Mustered in as Private. Promoted to Corporal, July-October, 1862, and to Sergeant in January, 1863. Promoted to 1st Sergeant in February, 1864. Wounded in action on September 22, 1864, at Fisher's Hill, Virginia. Present or accounted for until paroled at Appomattox Court House, Virginia, April 9, 1865.

JORDAN, LEWIS G., Private

Resided in Wake County where he enlisted at age 22, August 13, 1861, for the war. Wounded in action at Payne's Farm, Virginia, November 27, 1863. Captured at Spotsylvania Court House, Virginia, May 12, 1864. Confined at Point Lookout, Maryland, until transferred to Elmira, New York, August 6, 1864. Released at Elmira after taking the Oath of Allegiance on June 19, 1865.

KING, GEORGE W., Private

Resided in Wake County where he enlisted at age 16, April 21, 1862, for the war. Killed in action at Malvern Hill, Virginia, July 1, 1862.

KING, H. SMITH, Private

Resided in Wake County where he enlisted at age 26, January 21, 1862, for the war. Wounded in action at Gettysburg, Pennsylvania, July 1-3, 1863, and at Payne's Farm, Virginia, November 27, 1863. Killed in action at Wilderness, Virginia, May 5, 1864.

KING, J. R., Sergeant

Furloughed from hospital at Richmond, Virginia, November 5, 1862, for 30 days.

KING, JAMES W., Private

Born in Wake County where he resided as a farmer and enlisted at age 34, July 16, 1861, for the war. Died February 13, 1863.

KING, JOSEPH R., Private

Resided in Wake County where he enlisted at age 33, July 26, 1861, for the war. Killed in action at Sharpsburg, Maryland, September 17, 1862.

KING, N. S., Corporal

Wounded in action at Payne's Farm, Virginia, November 27, 1863.

KING, RICHARD, Private

Resided in Wake County where he enlisted at age 23, July 16, 1861, for the war. Present or accounted for until captured at Spotsylvania Court House, Virginia, May 12, 1864. Confined at Point Lookout, Maryland, until transferred to Elmira, New York, August 6, 1864. Released at Elmira after taking the Oath of Allegiance on June 27, 1865.

KING, SIDNEY S., Private
Resided in Wake County where he enlisted at age 32, January 21, 1862, for the war. Present or accounted for until killed in action at Wilderness, Virginia, May 5, 1864.

KING, WILLIAM P., Private
Resided in Wake County where he enlisted at age 27, July 16, 1861, for the war. Mustered in as Private and promoted to Corporal on January 15, 1863. Reduced to ranks March-April, 1863, when he was detailed in the Quartermaster Department. Absent on detail until paroled at Appomattox Court House, Virginia, on April 9, 1865.

LEE, WILLIAM H., Private
Transferred from Company H, 31st Regiment N.C. Troops on March 10, 1862. Present or accounted for until killed in action at Wilderness, Virginia, May 5, 1864.

LILES, AUGUSTUS, Private
Resided in Wake County where he enlisted at age 18, January 21, 1862, for the war. Died in hospital at Goldsboro on September 5, 1863, of disease.

LOYD, JAMES W., Private
Resided in Wake County where he enlisted at age 19, January 21, 1862, for the war. Present or accounted for until captured at Spotsylvania Court House, Virginia, May 12, 1864. Confined at Point Lookout, Maryland, until transferred to Elmira, New York, August 6, 1864. Died at Elmira on December 30, 1864, of "pneumonia."

LOYD, PERRY, Private
Resided in Wake County where he enlisted at age 17, January 21, 1862, for the war. Wounded in action at Ellerson's Mill, Virginia, June 26, 1862. Captured in Maryland on June 20, 1863, and confined at Fort McHenry, Maryland, until sent to Fort Delaware, Delaware, July 12, 1863. Transferred on October 15-18, 1863, to Point Lookout, Maryland, where he was released after taking the Oath of Allegiance and joining the U.S. service. Unit to which he was assigned not reported.

LYON, H. C., Private
Provided Henry Hodge as his substitute.

MASSINGALE, WILLIAM T., Private
Born in Wake County where he resided as a farmer and enlisted at age 17, August 6, 1861, for the war. Wounded in action at Ellerson's Mill, Virginia, June 26, 1862. Died in hospital at Richmond, Virginia, August 6, 1862, of wounds.

MEDLIN, HAWKINS, Private
Resided in Wake County where he enlisted at age 26, March 5, 1862, for the war. Captured at Boonsboro, Maryland, September 15, 1862, and confined at Fort Delaware, Delaware, until paroled and sent to Aiken's Landing, Virginia, for exchange on October 2, 1862. Declared exchanged on November 10, 1862. Deserted June 5, 1863, and records do not indicate that he returned to the company; however, he was captured at Cold Harbor, Virginia, May 30, 1864. Confined at Point Lookout, Maryland, until transferred to Elmira, New York, July 9, 1864. Died at Elmira on May 23, 1865, of "pneumonia."

MERCER, G. A., Private
Captured at Gettysburg, Pennsylvania, July 3, 1863, and confined at Fort Delaware, Delaware, where he died September 25, 1863.

MITCHELL, BENJAMIN, Private
Resided in Wake County where he enlisted at age 22, January 27, 1862, for the war. Wounded in action at Chancellorsville, Virginia, May 3, 1863. Captured at Gettysburg, Pennsylvania, July 3, 1863, and confined at Fort Delaware, Delaware, until transferred to U. S. Army General Hospital, Chester, Pennsylvania, August 10, 1863. Paroled at hospital and sent to City Point, Virginia, for exchange and received in exchange on September 23, 1863. Captured at Spotsylvania Court House, Virginia, May 12, 1864. Confined at Point Lookout, Maryland, until transferred to Elmira, New York, August 6, 1864. Died at Elmira on March 14, 1865, of "diarrhoea."

MITCHELL, ISHAM W., Private
Resided in Wake County where he enlisted at age 18, January 21, 1862, for the war. Killed in action at Ellerson's Mill, Virginia, June 26, 1862.

MITCHELL, JOHN C., Private
Resided in Wake County and enlisted in Wayne County at age 34, May 4, 1862, for the war. Present or accounted for until captured at Spotsylvania Court House, Virginia, May 12, 1864. Confined at Point Lookout, Maryland, where he died June 24, 1864.

MITCHELL, JOHN W., Musician
Born in Wake County where he resided as a laborer and enlisted at age 14, July 21, 1861, for the war. Mustered in as Musician. Present or accounted for until paroled at Appomattox Court House, Virginia, April 9, 1865.

MITCHELL, OSCAR L., Private
Resided in Wake County where he enlisted at age 17, July 16, 1861, for the war. Killed in action at Ellerson's Mill, Virginia, June 26, 1862.

MITCHELL, RICHARD S., Private
Resided in Wake County where he enlisted at age 18, June 18, 1863, for the war. Present or accounted for until captured at Spotsylvania Court House, Virginia, May 12, 1864. Confined at Point Lookout, Maryland, until transferred to Elmira, New York, August 6, 1864. Released at Elmira after taking the Oath of Allegiance on June 27, 1865.

MOODY, RICHARD, Private
Born in Franklin County and resided as a farmer in Wake County where he enlisted at age 20, January 27, 1862, for the war. Wounded in action at Fredericksburg, Virginia, December 13, 1862. Discharged May 25, 1863, by reason of disability caused by wounds.

MORSE, GEORGE, Private
Resided in Stanly County. Captured at Burkeville Junction, Virginia, April 3, 1865, and confined at Point Lookout, Maryland, until released after taking the Oath of Allegiance on June 29, 1865.

PACE, ELIAS R., Sergeant
Resided in Wake County and enlisted in Wayne County at age 32, May 6, 1862, for the war. Mustered in as Private. Present or accounted for on company muster rolls through December, 1864, as Private. Paroled at Appomattox Court House, Virginia, April 9, 1865, as Sergeant.

PACE, HENRY V., Private
Resided in Wake County where he enlisted at age 23, January 21, 1862, for the war. Wounded in action at Chancellorsville, Virginia, May 2-3, 1863. Present or accounted for until captured at Spotsylvania Court House, Virginia, May 12, 1864. Confined at Point Lookout, Maryland, until transferred to Elmira, New York, August 6, 1864. Released at Elmira after taking the Oath of Allegiance on June 12, 1865.

PACE, WILLIAM H., Private
Resided in Wake County where he enlisted at age 17, July 16, 1861, for the war. Wounded in action at Ellerson's Mill, Virginia, June 26, 1862. Reported as absent wounded through December, 1862; as absent on detail as a nurse from January, 1863, through April, 1863; and as absent on detail as an enrolling officer from April, 1863, through December, 1864. Paroled at Appomattox Court House, Virginia, April 9, 1865.

PATRICK, S., Private
Died in hospital at Richmond, Virginia, November 7, 1863, of a gunshot wound.

PEARCE, ARCHIBALD, Private
Resided in Wake County where he enlisted at age 20, January 21, 1862, for the war. Wounded in action at Ellerson's Mill, Virginia, June 26, 1862. Present or accounted for until captured at Gettysburg, Pennsylvania, July 4, 1863. Confined at Fort Delaware, Delaware, until released after taking the Oath of Allegiance on June 19, 1865.

PEARCE, CALVIN, Private
Resided in Wake County where he enlisted at age 22, January 27, 1862, for the war. Wounded in action at Ellerson's Mill, Virginia, June 26, 1862. Present or accounted for until captured at Winchester, Virginia, September 19, 1864. Confined at Point Lookout, Maryland, until paroled and sent to Aiken's Landing, Virginia, March 15, 1865, for exchange.

PEARCE, MARCELLUS E., Private
Resided in Wake County where he enlisted at age 24, August 1, 1861, for the war. Present or accounted for until captured at Spotsylvania Court House, Virginia, May 12, 1864. Confined at Point Lookout, Maryland, until transferred to Elmira, New York, August 6, 1864. Released at Elmira after taking the Oath of Allegiance on June 27, 1865.

PEARCE, SIDNEY, Private
Resided in Wake County where he enlisted at age 18, January 21, 1862, for the war. Wounded in action at Ellerson's Mill, Virginia, June 26, 1862. Present or accounted for until captured at Spotsylvania Court House, Virginia, May 12, 1864. Confined at Point Lookout, Maryland, until paroled and sent to Aiken's Landing, Vir-

ginia, for exchange on September 18, 1864. Admitted to hospital at Raleigh on January 25, 1865, with "anasarca." Captured in hospital at Raleigh on April 13, 1865, and paroled.

PERRY, CALVIN, Private
Resided in Wake County where he enlisted at age 18, July 1, 1863, for the war. Present or accounted for until killed in action at Payne's Farm, Virginia, November 27, 1863.

PERRY, GIDEON, Private
Born in Wake County where he resided as a laborer and enlisted at age 32, July 22, 1861, for the war. Discharged on October 18, 1861, by reason of disability.

PERRY, HENRY, Private
Born in Wake County where he resided as a farmer prior to enlisting in Wayne County on May 12, 1862, for the war. Wounded in action at Ellerson's Mill, Virginia, June 26, 1862. Arm amputated. Discharged December 20, 1863.

PERRY, JOHN W., Private
Resided in Wake County where he enlisted at age 20, July 16, 1861, for the war. Present or accounted for until paroled at Appomattox Court House, Virginia, April 9, 1865.

PIERSON, JOHN P., Private
Captured at Gettysburg, Pennsylvania, July 4, 1863, and confined at U. S. Army General Hospital, Chester, Pennsylvania, July 17, 1863. Transferred to City Point, Virginia, September 17, 1863, for exchange.

PIPER, FRANCIS D., Private
Resided in Wake County where he enlisted at age 22, March 1, 1862, for the war. Died in hospital at Richmond, Virginia, September 2, 1862, of "typhoid fever."

PITMAN, A. G., Private
Born in Johnston County where he resided and enlisted in Wake County at age 21, July 15, 1862, for the war. Killed in action at Sharpsburg, Maryland, September 17, 1862.

POWELL, JAMES, Private
Resided in Wake County and enlisted in Wayne County at age 22, May 1, 1862, for the war. Wounded in action at Ellerson's Mill, Virginia, June 26, 1862. Absent wounded until detailed for hospital duty on September 11, 1863. Detailed in hospitals for the balance of the war. Captured in hospital at Raleigh on April 13, 1865, and paroled.

POWELL, THOMAS F., Private
Born in McDowell County and was a farmer by occupation prior to enlisting. Date, place, and period of enlistment not reported. Captured at Gettysburg, Pennsylvania, July 4, 1863, and confined at Fort Delaware, Delaware. Released after joining the U. S. service on September 18, 1863, and assigned to Company E, 3rd Regiment Maryland Cavalry.

PRICE, CINCINNATTI, Private
Resided in Ashe County and enlisted in Wake County at age 22, July 15, 1862, for the war. Died in hospital at Richmond, Virginia, June 12, 1863, of "febris typhoides." Buried in Hollywood

Cemetery, Richmond, Virginia.

PRIVETT, RILEY, Corporal

Resided in Wake County where he enlisted at age 27, July 16, 1861, for the war. Mustered in as Corporal. Present or accounted for until he was discharged on May 1, 1862, by reason of Surgeon's Certificate of Disability.

PRIVETT, SIDNEY, Private

Born in Wake County where he resided as a farmer and enlisted at age 22, July 16, 1861, for the war. Discharged at Fredericksburg, Virginia, November 17, 1861, by reason of disability. Died at home on November 25, 1861.

PRIVETT, WILLIAM ALPHEUS, Private

Resided in Wake County where he enlisted at age 24, August 15, 1861, for the war. Captured at Boonsboro, Maryland, September 15, 1862, and confined at Fort Delaware, Delaware. Sent to Aiken's Landing, Virginia, October 2, 1862, for exchange and declared exchanged on November 10, 1862. Present or accounted for until he was captured at Gettysburg, Pennsylvania, July 3, 1863. Confined at Fort Delaware, Delaware, until released after taking the Oath of Allegiance on June 19, 1865.

PULLEY, JOHN A., Private

Resided in Wake County where he enlisted at age 17, August 2, 1861, for the war. Wounded in action at Ellerson's Mill, Virginia, June 26, 1862. Deserted and surrendered to Federal forces at Mercersburg, Pennsylvania, June 23, 1863, and confined at Fort Mifflin, Pennsylvania. Released after taking the Oath of Allegiance on December 2, 1863, and joined the U. S. Marine Corps.

PUREFOY, JOHN K., Private

Resided in Wake County where he enlisted at age 24, July 16, 1861, for the war. Mustered in as Sergeant. Reduced to ranks on April 16, 1862. Discharged July 15, 1862, at Richmond, Virginia, by reason of disability.

RAINS, JOHN W., Private

Resided in Wake County where he enlisted at age 23, July 20, 1861, for the war. Discharged on December 31, 1861, "having shot his own hand intentionally to avoid service."

RAYBORN, HENRY, Private

Resided in Wake County where he enlisted at age 28, July 16, 1861, for the war. Present or accounted for until captured at Spotsylvania Court House, Virginia, May 12, 1864. Confined at Point Lookout, Maryland, until transferred to Elmira, New York, August 6, 1864. Released at Elmira after taking the Oath of Allegiance on June 12, 1865.

RAYBORN, WILLIAM, Private

Resided in Wake County where he enlisted at age 35, August 5, 1861, for the war. Discharged by reason of disability. Date of discharge reported as November 5, 1861, and December 1, 1861.

REDFORD, WILLIAM E., Private

Resided in Wake County where he enlisted at age 18, August 12, 1861, for the war. Captured at Boonsboro, Maryland, September 15, 1862. Confined at Fort Delaware, Delaware, until trans-

ferred to Aiken's Landing, Virginia, October 2, 1862, for exchange. Declared exchanged on November 10, 1862. Wounded in action at Wilderness, Virginia, May 5, 1864, and reported as absent wounded on company muster rolls through December, 1864. Paroled at Appomattox Court House, Virginia, April 9, 1865.

RICHARDSON, C., Private

Resided in Alleghany County. Paroled at Salisbury on May 2, 1865.

RIGGAN, MATTHEW H., Private

Resided in Warren County where he enlisted at age 39, August 26, 1861, for the war. Died in hospital at Fredericksburg, Virginia, October 11, 1861.

RIGGAN, RICHARD, Private

Resided in Warren County where he enlisted at age 36, August 28, 1861, for the war. Detailed as regimental teamster March-April, 1862, through May-June, 1863. Detailed in Pioneer Corps in 1864. Present or accounted for on company muster rolls through December, 1864. Paroled at Appomattox Court House, Virginia, April 9, 1865.

ROBERTSON, JOHN T., Private

Transferred from Company H, 31st Regiment N. C. Troops on March 11, 1862. Died in hospital at Richmond, Virginia, May 9, 1863, of "typhoid pneumonia."

ROGERS, G. B., Private

Enlisted at Richmond, Virginia, May 1, 1864, for the war. Company muster rolls report that he was captured on September 22, 1864, and carry him as absent prisoner through December, 1864. No Federal Provost Marshal records were found relative to his capture.

ROGERS, WILLIAM WASHINGTON, Private

Resided in Wake County where he enlisted at age 26, July 29, 1861, for the war. Present or accounted for until captured at Spotsylvania Court House, Virginia, May 12, 1864. Confined at Point Lookout, Maryland, until transferred to Elmira, New York, August 6, 1864. Released at Elmira after taking the Oath of Allegiance on June 27, 1865.

ROWLAND, HINTON, Private

Resided in Wake County where he enlisted at age 18, July 1, 1863, for the war. Present or accounted for until captured at Spotsylvania Court House, Virginia, May 12, 1864. Confined at Point Lookout, Maryland, until transferred to Elmira, New York, August 6, 1864. Died at Elmira on March 19, 1865, of "pneumonia."

ROWLAND, JOSEPH N., Private

Resided in Wake County where he enlisted at age 24, August 5, 1861, for the war. Wounded in action at Ellerson's Mill, Virginia, June 26, 1862. Present or accounted for until captured at Sharpsburg, Maryland, September 17, 1862, and confined at Fort McHenry, Maryland, until transferred to Fort Monroe, Virginia, for exchange on October 17, 1862. Declared exchanged at Aiken's Landing, Virginia, November 10, 1862. Present or accounted for until captured at Cedar Creek, Virginia, October 19, 1864. Confined at West's

Buildings U.S. Army Hospital, Baltimore, Maryland, with "gunshot wound" and died November 9, 1864.

RYALS, JOSEPH, Private

Captured at Spotsylvania Court House, Virginia, June 16, 1864, and confined at Elmira, New York, where he died September 18, 1864, of "chronic diarrhoea."

SANDERFORD, NATHANIEL GREEN, Private

Resided in Wake County where he enlisted at age 26, July 26, 1861, for the war. Present or accounted for until captured at Spotsylvania Court House, Virginia, May 12, 1864. Confined at Point Lookout, Maryland, until transferred to Elmira, New York, August 6, 1864. Paroled at Elmira and sent to James River, Virginia, for exchange on February 20, 1865. Admitted to hospital at Richmond, Virginia, February 28, 1865, and transferred to General Hospital, Howard's Grove, Richmond, the next day.

SCARBOROUGH, JOHN C., Sergeant

Transferred from Company K, 14th Regiment N.C. Troops (4th Regiment N.C. Volunteers), December 31, 1862, as Corporal. Promoted to Sergeant, November-December, 1863. Wounded in action at Cedar Creek, Virginia, October 19, 1864. Paroled at Appomattox Court House, Virginia, April 9, 1865.

SCARBOROUGH, MALCOM F., 1st Sergeant

Resided in Wake County where he enlisted at age 22, July 22, 1861, for the war. Mustered in as Corporal. Wounded in action at Ellerson's Mill, Virginia, June 26, 1862. Promoted to Sergeant July-October, 1862. Promoted to 1st Sergeant on January 9, 1863. Wounded in action at Winchester, Virginia, June 15, 1863. Discharged upon appointment as 2nd Lieutenant and Enrolling Officer for Wake County on September 25, 1863.

SCARBOROUGH, W. T., Private

Resided in Wake County and enlisted in Wayne County on May 12, 1862, for the war. Deserted near Hamilton's Crossing, near Fredericksburg, Virginia, June 5, 1863. Captured and confined at Military Prison at Lynchburg, Virginia, until released in July, 1864. Captured at Winchester, Virginia, September 19, 1864, and confined at Point Lookout, Maryland, until paroled and transferred to Aiken's Landing, Virginia, March 15, 1865, for exchange. Exhanged at Boulware's Wharf, James River, Virginia, March 18, 1865.

SMITH, GASTON R., Private

Born in Wake County where he resided as a farmer and enlisted at age 16, April 21, 1862, for the war. Discharged at Richmond, Virginia, September 4, 1862, by reason of "permanent contraction of flexor muscles of the leg, the result of chronic rheumatism."

SMITH, JOHN B., Private

Resided in Ashe County and enlisted in Wake County at age 30, July 15, 1861, for the war. Discharged at Richmond, Virginia, August 5, 1862. Died in hospital at Richmond on September 2, 1862.

SMITH, JOHN S., Private

Resided in Wake County where he enlisted at age 18, July 26, 1861, for the war. Killed in action at Ellerson's Mill, Virginia, June 26, 1862.

SOWERS, WILLIAM C., Private

Paroled at Salisbury on May 15, 1865.

THROWER, WESLEY P., Private

Resided in Wake County where he enlisted at age 23, August 6, 1861, for the war. Present or accounted for until captured. at Gettysburg, Pennsylvania, July 3, 1863. Confined at Fort Delaware, Delaware, until transferred to Point Lookout, Maryland, on October 18, 1863. Died in hospital at Point Lookout, on November 17, 1863, of "diarrhoea chronic."

TIPPET, L. M., Private

Resided in Wake County where he enlisted at age 17, September 9, 1862, for the war as a substitute for William B. Fowler. Died in camp at Upperville, Virginia, November 2, 1862.

TRAWICK, JAMES M., Corporal

Born in Wake County where he resided as a farmer and enlisted at age 27, July 22, 1861, for the war. Mustered in as Corporal. "Died August 9, 1862, in camp near Richmond, Virginia, from exhaustion in the Seven Days' battles around the city."

UPCHURCH, CALVIN W., Corporal

Resided in Wake County where he enlisted at age 23, July 16, 1861, for the war. Mustered in as Corporal. Present or accounted for until wounded in action at Payne's Farm, Virginia, November 27, 1863. Detailed in Captain Samuel B. Water's Company, Provost Guard, Raleigh, March 10, 1864. Absent on detail through December, 1864. Admitted to hospital at Richmond, Virginia, March 1, 1865.

UPCHURCH, DALLAS H., Private

Transferred from Company H, 31st Regiment N.C. Troops on March 10, 1862. Discharged on August 5, 1862, by reason of disability.

UPCHURCH, JAMES W., Sergeant

Resided in Wake County where he enlisted at age 22, July 16, 1861, for the war. Mustered in as Sergeant. Present or accounted for until captured at Spotsylvania Court House, Virginia, May 12, 1864. Confined at Point Lookout, Maryland, until transferred to Elmira, New York, August 6, 1864. Paroled at Elmira and sent to James River, Virginia, for exchange on February 20, 1865. Admitted to hospital at Richmond, Virginia, February 27, 1865, and furloughed for 30 days on March 7, 1865.

VENEBLE, ISAAC, Private

Surrendered to Federal authorities at Bridgeport, Alabama, May 8, 1864.

WALKER, JESSE J., Private

Resided in Ashe County and enlisted in Wake County at age 28, July 15, 1862, for the war. Present or accounted for until sent home sick May-June, 1863. Reported as absent sick until September 6, 1863, when he was reported as absent without leave. Reported as absent without leave on company muster rolls through December,

1864. Roll of Honor states that he "went home on sick furlough and deserted to the enemy about March 1, 1864." Federal Provost Marshal records indicate that he "came into Federal lines Plymouth, North Carolina" and took the Oath of Allegiance at Fort Monroe, Virginia, March 14, 1864.

WALL, JAMES, Private
Resided in Wake County where he listed at age 30, July 18, 1861, for the war. Present or accounted for until wounded in action at Payne's Farm, Virginia, November 27, 1863. Died in hospital at Richmond, Virginia, December 10, 1863, of gunshot wound.

WALT, GEORGE F., Private
Paroled at Greensboro on May 22, 1865.

WATKINS, CLINTON, Private
Resided in Wake County where he enlisted at age 23, July 18, 1861, for the war. Wounded in action at Sharpsburg, Maryland, September 17, 1862, and captured and paroled near Keedysville, Maryland, September 20, 1862. Present or accounted for until captured at Spotsylvania Court House, Virginia, May 12, 1864. Confined at Point Lookout, Maryland, until transferred to Elmira, New York, August 6, 1864. Released at Elmira after taking the Oath of Allegiance on June 27, 1865.

WATKINS, GASTON, Private
Resided in Wake County where he enlisted at age 19, July 18, 1861, for the war. Died at Fredericksburg, Virginia, September 30, 1861.

WATKINS, JAMES H., Private
Resided in Wake County and enlisted in Wayne County on May 3, 1862, for the war. Present or accounted for until transferred to Company K, 14th Regiment N.C. Troops (4th Regiment N.C. Volunteers), December 31, 1862.

WATKINS, KINCHEN B., Private
Resided in Wake County where he enlisted at age 22, July 18, 1861, for the war. "Deserted July 25, 1863, in Wake County."

WEATHERS, J. D., Private
Resided in Wake County where he enlisted on November 7, 1863, for the war. Present or accounted for until reported on February 29-August 31, 1864, muster roll with the remark that he was "absent prisoner of war since May 12, 1864." Reported as absent prisoner through December, 1864. Roll of Honor states that he "died in prison at Elmira, New York." No Federal Provost Marshal records were found relative to his capture or confinement and death.

WHITFIELD, J. R., Private
Resided as a farmer in Ashe County prior to enlisting in Wake County at age 30, July 15, 1862, for the war. Discharged at Richmond, Virginia, September 3, 1862, by reason of "hernia and spinal irritation."

WHITFIELD, R. C., Private
Resided in Ashe County as a farmer prior to enlisting in Wake County at age 30, July 15, 1862, for the war. Discharged on September 3, 1862, by reason of "hernia."

WILLIAMS, ANDERSON, Private
Resided in Wake County where he enlisted at age 18, July 16, 1861, for the war. Present or accounted for on company muster rolls until captured at Spotsylvania Court House, Virginia, May 12, 1864. Confined at Point Lookout, Maryland, until transferred to Elmira, New York, August 6, 1864. Released at Elmira after taking the Oath of Allegiance on June 12, 1865.

WILLIAMS, JAMES M., Private
Resided in Franklin County and enlisted in Wake County at age 21, August 12, 1861, for the war. Died in hospital at Fredericksburg, Virginia, January 3, 1862.

WILLIAMS, MATHEW T., Private
Resided in Franklin County and enlisted at age 24, August 24, 1861, for the war. Roll of Honor States that he was "discharged August 24, 1861. Rejected on examination on account of disability."

WILLIAMS, WILLIAM, Private
Born in Wake County where he resided as a farmer prior to enlisting in Wayne County on May 12, 1862, for the war. Discharged at Richmond, Virginia, September 28, 1862, by reason of "permanent deafness."

WITHERS, A., Private
Captured at Spotsylvania Court House, Virginia, May 12, 1864, and confined at Point Lookout, Maryland, until transferred to Elmira, New York, August 3, 1864.

WITHERS, JAMES D., Private
Captured at Spotsylvania Court House, Virginia, May 12, 1864, and confined at Point Lookout, Maryland, until transferred to Elmira, New York, August 6, 1864. Died at Elmira on September 26, 1864, of "typhoid fever."

WOODARD, JOHN P., Private
Resided in Wake County and enlisted in Wayne County at age 17, May 1, 1862, for the war as a substitute for William Bobbit. Wounded in action at Chancellorsville, Virginia, May 2-3, 1863. Killed in action at Wilderness, Virginia, May 5, 1864.

WOODWARD, GEORGE O., Private
Resided in Wake County where he enlisted at age 18, July 16, 1861, for the war. Present or accounted for on company muster rolls until he was reported as captured at Gettysburg, Pennsylvania, July 2-3, 1863. No Federal Provost Marshal records were found relative to his capture.

YOUNG, F. M., Private
Resided in Franklin County and enlisted in Wake County at age 26, July 15, 1862, for the war. Present or accounted for until captured at Gettysburg, Pennsylvania, July 3, 1863. Confined at Fort Delaware, Delaware, where he died October 6, 1863, and was buried in the National Cemetery at Finn's Point (Salem), New Jersey.

YOUNG, JAMES, Corporal
Resided in Wake County where he enlisted at age 22, January 10, 1862, for the war. Mustered in as Private and appointed Corporal, March-April, 1863. Present or accounted for until wounded in action at Payne's Farm, Virginia, November 27, 1863. Captured at Spotsylvania Court House,

Virginia, May 12, 1864, and confined at Point Lookout, Maryland, where he died July 7, 1864.

YOUNG, JOHN C., Private
Born in Wake County where he resided as a laborer and enlisted at age 24, August 23, 1861, for the war. Discharged on October 25, 1861, by reason of "epilepsy."

YOUNG, JOSEPH, Private
Resided in Franklin County and enlisted in Wake County at age 26, July 15, 1862, for the war. Present or accounted for until captured at Spotsylvania Court House, Virginia, May 12, 1864. Confined at Point Lookout, Maryland, until transferred to Elmira, New York, August 6, 1864. Paroled at Elmira and sent to Point Lookout, Maryland, for exchange on October 11, 1864. Reported exchanged at James River, Virginia, October 29, 1864.

YOUNG, THOMAS J., Private
Resided in Wake County and enlisted in Wayne County at age 20, May 9, 1862, for the war. Present or accounted for until captured at Spotsylvania Court House, Virginia, May 12, 1864. Confined at Point Lookout, Maryland, until paroled and transferred to Aiken's Landing, Virginia, for exchange on September 18, 1864. Admitted to hospital at Richmond, Virginia, September 22, 1864, with "chronic diarrhœa." Died in hospital at Richmond on September 24, 1864.

YOUNG, WESLEY M., Private
Resided in Wake County and enlisted in Wayne County at age 21, May 9, 1862, for the war. Wounded in action at Ellerson's Mill, Virginia, June 26, 1862, and at Chancellorsville, Virginia, May 2-3, 1863. Present or accounted for until captured at Spotsylvania Court House, Virginia, May 12, 1864. Confined at Point Lookout, Maryland, until transferred to Elmira, New York, August 6, 1864. Released at Elmira after taking the Oath of Allegiance on June 12, 1865.

COMPANY K

This company was organized in Halifax County and enlisted at Weldon on July 4, 1861. It tendered its service to the state and was ordered to Warrenton, Warren County, where it was assigned to this regiment as Company K. After joining the regiment the company functioned as a part of the regiment, and its history for the war period is recorded as a part of the regimental history.

The information contained in the following roster of the company was compiled principally from company muster rolls which covered from July through August, 1861; November through December, 1861; March through April, 1862; and June 30, 1862, through December, 1864. No company muster rolls were found for September through October, 1861; January through February, 1862; May through June 29, 1862; or for the period after December, 1864. In addition to the company muster rolls, Roll of Honor records, receipt rolls, hospital records, prisoner of war records, and other primary records, supplemented by state pension applications, United

Daughters of the Confederacy records, and postwar rosters and histories, all provided useful information.

OFFICERS

CAPTAINS

GEE, STERLING H.
Resided in Halifax County and appointed Captain to rank from May 16, 1861. Wounded in action at Chancellorsville, Virginia, May 2-3, 1863. Present or accounted for until transferred to the staff of Brigadier General Ransom upon appointment as Captain, Assistant Adjutant General, to rank from November 11, 1863.

DAY, WILLIAM H.
Resided in Halifax County and appointed 2nd Lieutenant to rank from April 20, 1862. Promoted to 1st Lieutenant to rank from January 3, 1863, and to Captain to rank from November 11, 1863. Present or accounted for until captured at Spotsylvania Court House, Virginia, May 12, 1864. Confined at Point Lookout, Maryland, until transferred to Fort Delaware, Delaware, June 23, 1863. Transferred to Hilton Head, South Carolina, November 12, 1864, and returned to Fort Delaware on March 12, 1865. Released at Fort Delaware after taking the Oath of Allegiance on June 16, 1865.

LIEUTENANTS

BRANCH, CORNELIUS E., 2nd Lieutenant
Resided in Halifax County where he enlisted at age 24, July 4, 1861, for the war. Mustered in as Sergeant and elected 2nd Lieutenant on March 20, 1863. Appointed 2nd Lieutenant to rank from date of election. Killed in action at Wilderness, Virginia, May 5, 1864.

DAY, ROBERT J., 2nd Lieutenant
Resided in Halifax County and appointed 2nd Lieutenant to rank from May 5, 1864. Present or accounted for until paroled at Appomattox Court House, Virginia, April 9, 1865.

PIERCE, ALBERT L., 1st Lieutenant
Resided in Halifax County and appointed 1st Lieutenant to rank from May 16, 1861. Resigned on January 3, 1863, by reason of "ill health."

STOKES, WILLIAM B., 3rd Lieutenant
Resided in Virginia and appointed 3rd Lieutenant to rank from August 23, 1861. Roll of Honor states that he was "dropped for absence without leave April 20, 1862." Name dropped from the rolls by Special Order No. 251, Paragraph 3, October 27, 1862, for prolonged absence without leave.

WILLIAMS, WILLIAM R., 2nd Lieutenant
Resided in Halifax County and appointed 2nd Lieutenant to rank from May 16, 1861. Captured at Middletown, Maryland, September 13, 1862, and confined at Fort Delaware, Delaware, until paroled and exchanged at Aiken's Landing, Virginia, October 2, 1862. Declared exchanged November 10, 1862. Resigned his commission on November 6, 1862.

WYNN, JOHN, 1st Lieutenant
Resided in Halifax County where he enlisted at age 36, July 8, 1861, for the war. Mustered in as 1st Sergeant. Wounded in action at Ellerson's Mill, Virginia, June 26, 1862. Appointed 2nd Lieutenant to rank from November 1, 1862, and promoted to 1st Lieutenant to rank from November 11, 1863. Wounded in action at Payne's Farm, Virginia, November 27, 1863. Present or accounted for until wounded a second time at Cedar Run, Virginia, October 19, 1864. Admitted to hospital at Charlottesville, Virginia, Octobeı 22, 1864, and furloughed on November 29, 1864. Reported as absent wounded through December, 1864.

NONCOMMISSIONED OFFICERS AND PRIVATES

ADKINS, ELISHA, Private
Resided in Halifax County and enlisted in Wake County at age 18, July 15, 1862, for the war. Wounded in action at Chancellorsville, Virginia, May 3, 1863, and reported as absent wounded on company muster rolls through December, 1864.

ALSBROOK, JESSE, Private
Resided in Halifax County and enlisted at age 21, July 15, 1862, for the war. Present or accounted for on company muster rolls through December, 1864. Muster rolls report him as being absent sick, absent without leave, and absent detailed at hospital at Wilson, N.C.

ALSBROOK, JOHNSON, Private
Born in Halifax County where he resided as a shoemaker prior to enlisting in Wake County at age 25, July 15, 1862, for the war. Discharged at Morton's Ford, Virginia, December 19, 1863, by reason of "an obscure disease of the heart thought to be organic. The patient has been under treatment in the hospital for nearly a year, judging from his present appearance, without benefit."

ATKINS, WILEY, Private
Resided in Halifax County and enlisted in Wake County at age 20, July 15, 1862, for the war. Detailed as nurse in hospital at Richmond, Virginia, September 1, 1862, and remained absent on detail through December, 1863. Returned to company in January, 1864. Captured at Spotsylvania Court House, Virginia, May 12, 1864. Confined at Elmira, New York, where he died January 6, 1865, of "variola."

BAKER, BLAKE, Private
Resided in Halifax County and enlisted in Wake County at age 25, July 15, 1862, for the war. Killed in action at Chancellorsville, Virginia, May 3, 1863.

BARBER, WILLIAM L., Private
Resided in Georgia and enlisted in Halifax County at age 21, January 30, 1862, for the war. Present or accounted for until transferred to Company K, 3rd Regiment Georgia Infantry on March 5, 1863.

BASS, GIDEON, Private
Resided in Halifax County and enlisted in Warren County at age 17, July 19, 1861, for the war. July-August, 1861, muster roll states that he "deserted July 28, 1861."

BEARD, JOSEPH, Private
Resided in Halifax County where he enlisted at age 21, July 5, 1861, for the war. Died in November, 1861, at Brook's Station, Virginia.

BEDFORD, BERRY, Private
Captured at Farmville, Virginia, April 6, 1865, and confined at Point Lookout, Maryland, April 14, 1865. Date of release not reported.

BELL, B. W., Private
Resided in Halifax County and enlisted in Wake County at age 30, July 15, 1862, for the war. Wounded and captured at Sharpsburg, Maryland, September 17, 1862. Died in hospital at Frederick, Maryland, on November 2, 1862, of gunshot wounds.

BELL, MARCUS L., Private
Born in Halifax County where he resided as a farmer prior to enlisting in Wake County at age 25, July 15, 1862, for the war. Captured at South Mountain, Maryland, September 17, 1862, and confined at Fort Delaware, Delaware, until transferred to Aiken's Landing, Virginia, October 2, 1862. Declared exchange on November 10, 1862, at Aiken's Landing. Present or accounted for until reported on February-August, 1864, muster roll that he was absent wounded. Retired from military service on March 21, 1865, and assigned to light duty with Surgeon Hancock, Jackson Hospital, Richmond, Virginia. Captured in hospital at Richmond, April 3, 1865, and paroled on April 22, 1865.

BELLAMY, W. E., Private
Born in Edgecombe County and resided as a farmer in Halifax County prior to enlisting in Wake County at age 26, July 15, 1862, for the war. Discharged at Richmond, Virginia, September 3, 1862, by reason of "pulmonary phthisis."

BILLIPS, JAMES, Private
Resided in Halifax County and enlisted in Wake County at age 23, July 15, 1862, for the war. Captured at Sharpsburg, Maryland, September 17, 1862, and confined at Fort Delaware, Delaware, until paroled and exchanged at Aiken's Landing, Virginia, November 10, 1862. Present or accounted for on company muster rolls through December, 1864. Paroled at Appomattox Court House, Virginia, April 9, 1865.

BIRDSONG, GEORGE W., Private
Resided in Northampton County and enlisted in Halifax County at age 18, June 10, 1861, for the war. Died in hospital at Lynchburg, Virginia, November 10, 1862, of "dysenteria chronic."

BOLAN, PETER, Private
Name reported on monthly report of enlisted men paroled at the Provost Marshal's Office, Houston, Texas, for the month of August, 1865. Residence reported on report as New Bern.

BRANCH, WILLIAM R., Private
Resided in Halifax County where he enlisted at age 18, September 16, 1863, for the war. Mustered in as Musician and reduced to Private on December 24, 1864. Present or accounted for on com-

pany muster rolls through December, 1864. Paroled at Appomattox Court House, Virginia, April 9, 1865.

BROWN, JOHN J., Private

Resided in Halifax County where he enlisted at age 18, July 5, 1861, for the war. Wounded in action at Chancellorsville, Virginia, May 2-3, 1863. Wounded a second time at Wilderness, Virginia, May, 1864. Reported as absent wounded after May, 1864, until November-December, 1864, muster roll reports him as "absent without leave July, 1864."

BROWN, PRESLEY, Private

Resided in Halifax County where he enlisted at age 30, January 24, 1862, for the war. Killed in action at Chancellorsville, Virginia, May 3, 1863.

BROWN, THOMAS, Private

Resided in Halifax County where he enlisted at age 30, January 14, 1862, for the war. Wounded in action at Malvern Hill, Virginia, July 1, 1862. Reported as absent wounded or absent sick until reported as "detailed as hospital attendant" on February 29-August 31, 1864, muster roll. Admitted to hospital at Richmond, Virginia, July 21, 1864, and furloughed on August 31, 1864. Present or accounted for on company muster rolls through December, 1864.

BRYANT, STEPHEN N., Private

Resided in Halifax County and enlisted in Wake County at age 30, July 15, 1862, for the war. Captured at Fredericksburg, Virginia, May 3, 1863, and paroled and exchanged at City Point, Virginia, May 13, 1863. Wounded and captured at Gettysburg, Pennsylvania, July 3, 1863. Died in hospital at Gettysburg on July 17, 1863.

BUTTS, JESSE, Private

Resided in Halifax County and enlisted in Wake County at age 21, July 15, 1862, for the war. Admitted to hospital at Richmond, Virginia, September 2, 1862, and furloughed September 5, 1862. November-December, 1862, muster roll states that he "died in Halifax County, North Carolina, September 8, 1862."

BUTTS, MATHEW W., Private

Resided in Halifax County and enlisted in Wake County at age 35, July 15, 1862, for the war. Present or accounted for on company muster rolls until captured at Spotsylvania Court House, Virginia, May 12, 1864. Confined at Elmira, New York, where he died November 11, 1864, of "chronic diarrhoea."

CALLUM, GEORGE, Private

Resided in Halifax County and enlisted at age 22, July 15, 1862, for the war.

CARPENTER, RICHARD, Sergeant

Resided in Halifax County where he enlisted at age 19, June 10, 1861, for the war. Mustered in as Corporal and promoted to Sergeant, November-December, 1862. Present or accounted for until paroled at Appomattox Court House, Virginia, April 9, 1865.

CARTER, J., Private

Resided in Halifax County and enlisted at age 21,

July 4, 1862, for the war. Discharged October 20, 1862.

CHAMBLISS, STITH O., Private

Resided in Halifax County and enlisted in Northampton County at age 30, July 17, 1861, for the war. Died in hospital at Richmond, Virginia, April 3, 1863, of "typhoid fever."

CLARKE, GEORGE W., Private

Resided in Halifax County where he enlisted at age 25, January 14, 1862, for the war. Present or accounted for until he died of wounds received in battle of Spotsylvania Court House, Virginia, May 8, 1864.

COLLINS, WILLIAM H., Private

Resided in Halifax County where he enlisted at age 22, July 22, 1861, for the war. Killed in action at Malvern Hill, Virginia, July 1, 1862.

CONWELL, GEORGE, Private

Resided in Halifax County where he enlisted at age 24, June 10, 1861, for the war. Wounded in action at Winchester, Virginia, June 15, 1863. Detailed in hospital at Richmond, Virginia, October 31, 1863. Absent on detail until returned to company September-October, 1864. Present or accounted for on company muster rolls through December, 1864. Took the Oath of Allegiance on March 19, 1865.

COOKE, JOHN, Private

Resided in Halifax County where he enlisted at age 31, July 22, 1861, for the war. Discharged at Richmond, Virginia, August 31, 1861.

CULLUM, JAMES R., Private

Enlisted in Wake County on July 15, 1862, for the war. Present or accounted for until captured at Spotsylvania Court House, Virginia, May 12, 1864. Confined at Point Lookout, Maryland, until transferred to Elmira, New York, August 3, 1864. Paroled at Elmira and transferred to James River, Virginia, where he was exchanged on March 15, 1865. Admitted to hospital at Richmond, Virginia, on March 15, 1865.

CUNNINGHAM, G. E., Private

Captured at Abingdon, Virginia, June 1, 1864, and confined at Point Lookout, Maryland, until transferred to Elmira, New York. Released at Elmira after taking the Oath of Allegiance on June 3, 1865. Residence given on Oath as Greeneville, Tennessee.

DAY, NORMAN D., Private

Resided in Halifax County and enlisted in Wayne County at age 19, April 28, 1862, for the war. Roll of Honor states that he "died November, 1862, at Petersburg, Virginia."

DAY, WILLIAM, Private

Resided in Halifax County where he enlisted at age 22, July 1, 1861, for the war. Admitted to hospital at Richmond, Virginia, September 8, 1862, with "debility, diarrhoea chronic." Died in hospital on October 18, 1862.

DICKENS, ASBURY, Private

Resided in Halifax County where he enlisted at age 18, July 5, 1861, for the war. Killed in action at Chancellorsville, Virginia, May 3, 1863.

DICKENS, CHARLES AUGUSTUS, Sergeant
Resided in Halifax County where he enlisted at age 20, July 5, 1861, for the war. Mustered in as Private and appointed Corporal on March 20, 1862. Promoted to Sergeant on October 1, 1862. Present or accounted for until captured at Spotsylvania Court House, Virginia, May 12, 1864. Confined at Point Lookout, Maryland, until transferred to Elmira, New York, August 6, 1864. Remained at Elmira until released after taking the Oath of Allegiance on June 12, 1865.

DICKENS, HARDY D., Private
Resided in Halifax County where he enlisted at age 35, January 14, 1862, for the war. Present or accounted for until captured at South Mountain, Maryland, September 15, 1862. Confined at Fort Delaware, Delaware, until paroled and sent to Aiken's Landing, Virginia, October 2, 1862, for exchange. Declared exchanged on November 10, 1862. Present or accounted for until captured at Spotsylvania Court House, Virginia, May 12, 1864. Confined at Point Lookout, Maryland, until transferred to Elmira, New York, August 6, 1864. Released at Elmira after taking the Oath of Allegiance on June 12, 1865.

DICKENS, HAYWOOD, Private
Resided in Halifax County where he enlisted at age 18, January 24, 1862, for the war. Wounded in action at Ellerson's Mill, Virginia, June 26, 1862, and died of wounds in hospital at Richmond, Virginia, July 12, 1862.

DICKENS, HENRY K., Private
Resided in Halifax County where he enlisted at age 23, March 1, 1862, for the war. Wounded in action at Fredericksburg, Virginia, December 13, 1862. Died in hospital at Richmond, Virginia, September 18, 1863, of "diphtheria."

DICKENS, HIDER C., Private
Resided in Halifax County where he enlisted at age 24, February 11, 1862, for the war. Wounded in action at Payne's Farm, Virginia, November 27, 1863. Captured at Spotsylvania Court House, Virginia, May 12, 1864, and confined at Point Lookout, Maryland, until transferred to Elmira, New York, August 6, 1864. Transferred from Elmira to the James River, Virginia, for exchange on February 20, 1865. Admitted to U.S. Army Post Hospital, Bermuda Hundred, Virginia, March 2, 1865, and "transferred to charge of General Mulford, March 23, 1865." Admitted to U.S. Army Smallpox Hospital, Richmond, Virginia, April 19, 1865. Sent to the Provost Marshal on May 17, 1865, and paroled on the same day.

DICKENS, ISAAC F., Sergeant
Resided in Halifax County where he enlisted at age 25, May 10, 1862, for the war. Mustered in as Private and appointed Corporal on August 1, 1862. Promoted to Sergeant on March 20, 1863. Killed in action at Winchester, Virginia, June 13-15, 1863.

DICKENS, OSCAR, Private
Resided in Halifax County and enlisted at age 34, on May 10, 1861, for the war. Roll of Honor states that he was "discharged May 23, 1862."

DICKENS, REDDIN ANDERSON, Private
Resided in Halifax County where he enlisted at age 25, May 10, 1862, for the war. Wounded in action at Malvern Hill, Virginia, July 2, 1862. Detailed in hospital at Richmond, Virginia, sometime late in 1862 or early 1863 as a nurse and guard. Returned to duty September, 1863. Detailed as a guard in hospital at Gordonsville, Virginia, November 5, 1863. Reported as absent on detail on company muster rolls through August, 1864. Reported as present on company muster rolls from September through December, 1864. Paroled at Burkeville Junction, Virginia, April 14-17, 1865.

DICKENS, WILLIAM B., Private
Resided in Halifax County and enlisted in Wake County at age 30, July 15, 1862, for the war. Wounded in the left thigh at Chancellorsville, Virginia, May 3, 1863. Reported as absent wounded through December, 1863. Captured at Spotsylvania Court House, Virginia, May 12, 1864. Confined at Point Lookout, Maryland, until transferred to Elmira, New York, August 6, 1864. Died at Elmira on March 23, 1865, of "diarrhoea."

DREW, BENJAMIN W., Private
Resided in Halifax County and enlisted in Wake County at age 21, July 15, 1862, for the war. Present or accounted for until he died at Orange Court House, Virginia, March 17-20, 1864, of "pneumonia."

DREW, LAWRENCE, Private
Resided in Halifax County and enlisted in Wake County at age 25, July 15, 1862, for the war. Reported as absent sick or absent without leave from date of enlistment through November-December, 1863, muster roll when he was reported with the remark: "Died October 1, 1862, hospital Culpepper Court House."

DUPREE, PETER C., Sergeant
Resided in Wake County and enlisted in Halifax County on July 22, 1861, for the war. Mustered in as Private. Captured at South Mountain, Maryland, September 15, 1862, and confined at Fort Delaware, Delaware, until transferred to Aiken's Landing, Virginia, October 2, 1862, for exchange. Declared exchanged on November 10, 1862. Appointed Corporal January-February, 1863. Promoted to Sergeant on June 15, 1863. Wounded in action at Payne's Farm, Virginia, November 27, 1863. Captured at Spotsylvania Court House, Virginia, May 12, 1864. Confined at Point Lookout, Maryland, until transferred to Elmira, New York, August 6, 1864. Released at Elmira after taking the Oath of Allegiance on June 12, 1865.

ENROUGHTY, J., Private
Resided in Halifax County and enlisted at age 56, on June 10, 1861, for the war. Roll of Honor states that he was "discharged July 10, 1861."

EVERETT, JOHN H., Private
Resided in Halifax County and enlisted in Northampton County on July 17, 1861, for the war. Mustered in as Sergeant. Reduced to ranks prior to June 30, 1862. Captured at Frederick,

Maryland, September 12, 1862, and confined at Fort Delaware, Delaware, until transferred to Aiken's Landing, Virginia, where he was paroled and exchanged on November 10, 1862. Admitted to hospital at Richmond, Virginia, April 10, 1863, with "pneumonia" and transferred to Lynchburg, Virginia, May 15, 1863. Detailed in hospital at Lynchburg for the balance of 1863 and returned to company after being relieved from hospital duty on March 8, 1864. Captured at Spotsylvania Court House, Virginia, May 12, 1864, and confined at Point Lookout, Maryland, until released after taking the Oath of Allegiance on May 12, 1865.

EVERITT, EPPIMETUS GUION, Private
Born in Warren County and resided as a farmer in Halifax County where he enlisted at age 28, January 16, 186-, for the war. Wounded in right thigh at Gettysburg, Pennsylvania, July 3, 1863, and captured in hospital at Gettysburg, July 4-5, 1863. Transferred to U.S. Army General Hospital, West's Buildings, Baltimore, Maryland, November 10, 1863, and transferred to Hammond U.S. Army General Hospital, Point Lookout, Maryland, January 12, 1864. Paroled at Point Lookout and sent to City Point, Virginia, for exchange on March 17, 1864. Declared exchanged on March 20, 1864. Admitted to hospital at Richmond, Virginia, on date of exchange and furloughed for 60 days on March 29, 1864. Retired to the Invalid Corps on February 4, 1865, by reason of being "permanently disabled for duty in any branch of service because of gunshot wound."

FLOYD, WILLIAM, Corporal
Resided in Halifax County where he enlisted at age 24, July 5, 1861, for the war. Mustered in as Private. Wounded in action at Fredericksburg, Virginia, December 13, 1862. Promoted to Corporal, January-February, 1863. Captured at Gettysburg, Pennsylvania, July 3-4, 1863. Confined at Fort Delaware, Delaware, until released after taking the Oath of Allegiance on June 19, 1865.

FRANCIS, ALEXANDER, Private
Resided in Halifax County where he enlisted at age 20, June 27, 1861, for the war. Wounded in action at Ellerson's Mill, Virginia, June 26, 1862. Died in hospital at Richmond, Virginia, on November 23, 1862, of "double pneumonia" and "of wounds received at Richmond."

FRANCIS, SAMUEL, Private
Resided in Halifax County where he enlisted at age 24, June 27, 1861, for the war. Present or accounted for until captured at Spotsylvania Court House, Virginia, May 12, 1864. Confined at Point Lookout, Maryland, until transferred to Elmira, New York, August 6, 1864. Released at Elmira after taking the Oath of Allegiance on June 12, 1865.

GREEN, AMBROSE G., Sergeant
Resided in Halifax County where he enlisted at age 18, June 10, 1861, for the war. Mustered in as Corporal and promoted to Sergeant on March 20, 1862. Present or accounted for on company muster rolls until captured at Spotsylvania

Court House, Virginia, May 12, 1864. Confined at Point Lookout, Maryland, until transferred to Elmira, New York, August 6, 1864. Paroled at Elmira and sent to James River, Virginia, for exchange on March 14, 1865. Received at Boulware's Wharf, James River, March 18-21, 1865, in exchange.

GRIFFIS, CHARLES, Private
Resided in Halifax County where he enlisted at age 43, June 10, 1861, for the war. Killed in action at Chancellorsville, Virginia, May 3, 1863.

GRIFFIS, JOHN, Private
Resided in Halifax County and enlisted at Camp Bee, Virginia, at age 50, February 20, 1862, for the war. Wounded in action at Chancellorsville, Virginia, May 3, 1863. Killed in action at Wilderness, Virginia, May 4-5, 1864.

GRIFFIS, REUBEN, Private
Resided in Halifax County and enlisted at Camp Bee, Virginia, at age 33, January 18, 1862, for the war. Present or accounted for on company muster rolls until he was "killed in action, battle before Richmond, June 5, 1864."

HACKNEY, THOMAS, Private
Resided in Halifax County where he enlisted at age 29, June 21, 1861, for the war. Admitted to hospital at Richmond, Virginia, on December 15, 1862, with "varioloid" and returned to duty April 3, 1863. Wounded and captured at Spotsylvania Court House, Virginia, May 12, 1864. Confined at Lincoln U.S. Army General Hospital, Washington, D.C., until transferred to Old Capitol Prison, Washington, September 7, 1864. Transferred on September 19-20, 1864, to Fort Delaware, Delaware, where he remained until released after taking the Oath of Allegiance on June 19, 1865.

HALE, BENJAMIN, Private
Resided in Halifax County where he enlisted at age 18, January 20, 1862, for the war. Present or accounted for until captured at Spotsylvania Court House, Virginia, May 12, 1864. Confined at Point Lookout, Maryland, until transferred to Elmira, New York, August 6, 1864. Released at Elmira after taking the Oath of Allegiance on June 30, 1865.

HALE, GEORGE, Private
Resided in Halifax County where he enlisted at age 50, February 10, 1862, for the war. Killed in action at Cold Harbor, Virginia, June 27, 1862.

HARRISON, THOMAS, Private
Resided in Halifax County where he enlisted at age 49, February 18, 1862, for the war. Died in Halifax County on April 18, 1862.

HOCKADAY, THOMAS J. E., Corporal
Resided in Halifax County and enlisted in Northampton County at age 22, July 17, 1861, for the war. Mustered in as Private. Promoted to Corporal November-December, 1862. Captured at Gettysburg, Pennsylvania, July 3-4, 1863, and confined at Fort McHenry, Maryland, until transferred to Fort Delaware, Delaware, July 10, 1863. Transferred to Point Lookout, Maryland. Date of transfer not reported. Sent from Point Lookout, to Venus Point, Savannah River, Georgia, for

exchange and declared exchanged on November 15, 1864.

HOCKADAY, WARRICK, Corporal

Resided in Halifax County and enlisted in Wayne County at age 33, May 14, 1862, for the war. Mustered in as Private and appointed Corporal on March 20, 1863. Present or accounted for on company muster rolls until he was reported as "killed in action battle Spotsylvania Court House, Virginia, May 8, 1864."

HOWELL, ABNER, Private

Resided in Halifax County where he enlisted at age 24, June 10, 1861, for the war. Captured near Fredericksburg, Virginia, May 3, 1863, and paroled and exchanged at City Point, Virginia, May 10, 1863. Captured a second time at Gettysburg, Pennsylvania, July 3, 1863, and confined at Fort Delaware, Delaware. Transferred on August 6, 1864, to Elmira, New York, where he died December 30, 1864, of pneumonia.

HUBBARD, WYATT, Private

Resided in Northampton County and enlisted in Halifax County at age 23, June 10, 1861, for the war. Died in Northampton County on August 28, 1862.

HUDSON, BURTON, Private

Resided in Halifax County where he enlisted at age 30, January 20, 1862, for the war. Company muster rolls report him as present through August, 1862, and as absent sick from September, 1862, through December, 1863. Detailed in hospital at Lynchburg, Virginia, April 13, 1864, and transferred to Weldon, July 14, 1864. Company muster rolls report him as absent detailed on light duty through December, 1864.

HUDSON, JAMES L., Private

Resided in Halifax County where he enlisted at age 20, June 11, 1861, for the war. Admitted to hospital at Richmond, Virginia, July 2, 1862, with a gunshot wound, but hospital records and company muster rolls do not give date or place he was wounded. Absent through December, 1862. Present or accounted for from January, 1863, until captured at Spotsylvania Court House, Virginia, May 12, 1864. Confined at Point Lookout, Maryland, until transferred to Elmira, New York, August 6, 1864. Released at Elmira after taking the Oath of Allegiance on June 30, 1865.

HUDSON, LAFAYETTE, Private

Resided in Halifax County where he enlisted at age 20, January 20, 1862, for the war. Reported as present or accounted for until reported as absent without leave beginning October 23, 1862. Reported as absent without leave through December, 1862. January-February, 1863, muster roll reports him as present, and records indicate that he was present until admitted to hospital at Richmond, Virginia, May 15, 1863, with "intermittent fever." Returned to duty on December 26, 1863. Reported as present until admitted to hospital at Richmond, Virginia, May 18, 1864, with a gunshot wound. Returned to duty July 8, 1864. Present or accounted for on company muster rolls until reported as "wounded and sent

hospital on 19 September 1864." Reported as such through December, 1864.

HUX ELDRIDGE, Private

Resided in Halifax County where he enlisted at age 23, June 12, 1861, for the war. Present or accounted for until captured at Spotsylvania Court House, Virginia, May 12, 1864. Confined at Point Lookout, Maryland, until trasnferred to Elmira, New York, August 6, 1864. Died at Elmira on March 3, 1865, of "diarrhoea."

HUX, HARVEY P., Private

Resided in Halifax County where he enlisted at age 34, January 24, 1862, for the war. Died in Halitax County on April 21, 1862.

JACKSON, JOHN, Private

Resided in Halifax County and enlisted in Warren County at age 18, July 19, 1861, for the war. Present or accounted for until captured at Spotsylvania Court House, Virginia, May 12, 1864. Confined at Point Lookout, Maryland, until transferred to Elmira, New York, August 3, 1864. Died at Elmira on February 27, 1865, of "chronic diarrhoea."

JACKSON, WILLIAM, Private

Resided in Halifax County and enlisted in Warren County at age 22, July 23, 1861, for the war. Wounded in action at Fredericksburg, Virginia, December 13, 1862. Present or accounted for until captured at Mine Run, Virginia, November, 30, 1863. Confined at Old Capitol Prison, Washington, D.C., until released after taking the Oath of Amnesty on March 19, 1864.

JOHNSON, MADISON, Private

Resided in Halifax County where he enlisted at age 30, January 15, 1862, for the war. Present or accounted for until captured at Spotsylvania Court House, Virginia, May 12, 1864. Confined at Point Lookout, Maryland, until paroled and sent to Aiken's Landing, Virginia, March 15, 1865, for exchange.

JOHNSON, MILTON, 1st Sergeant

Resided in Halifax County and enlisted in Northampton County at age 23, July 17, 1861, for the war. Mustered in as Sergeant and promoted to 1st Sergeant, November-December, 1862. Present or accounted for on company muster rolls from date of enlistment until February 29-August 31, 1864, muster roll which reported him with the remark: "Prisoner of war since May 12, 1864." Reported with same remark on company muster rolls through December, 1864. No Federal Provost Marshal records were found relative to his capture.

JONES, HENRY, Private

Resided in Halifax County where he enlisted at age 23, July 5, 1861, for the war. Present or accounted for on company muster rolls until captured at Spotsylvania Court House, Virginia, May 12, 1864. Confined at Point Lookout, Maryland, until transferred to Elmira, New York, August 6, 1864. Died at Elmira on July 15, 1865.

JONES, THADDEUS BAKER, Private

Resided in Halifax County where he enlisted at age 23, June 12, 1861, for the war. Killed in action at Ellerson's Mill, Virginia, June 26, 1862.

JONES, WILLIAM R., Private
Resided in Halifax County where he enlisted at age 22, June 10, 1861, for the war. Present or accounted for until admitted to hospital at Richmond, Virginia, January 9, 1864, with a gunshot wound. Date and place he was wounded not reported. Furloughed for 18 days on January 10, 1864. Present or accounted for until captured at Fisher's Hill, Virginia, September 22, 1864. Confined at Point Lookout, Maryland, until paroled and sent to James River, Virginia, for exchange on March 17, 1865.

JONNER, J. C., Private
Name appears on a roll of rebel prisoners of war sent from Harrisburg, Pennsylvania, to Philadelphia, Pennsylvania, July 22, 1863.

JOYNER, J. R., Private
Captured at Spotsylvania Court House, Virginia, May 12, 1864, and confined at Point Lookout, Maryland. Transferred on August 3, 1864, to Elmira, New York, where he died May 7, 1865, of "chronic diarrhoea."

KEETER, HENRY M., Private
Resided in Halifax County and enlisted at Camp Bee, Virginia, at age 17, January 31, 1862, for the war. Company muster rolls report him as absent sick from June 30-October 31, 1862, until he was discharged on January 26, 1864, by reason of his "being a minor and having enlisted without the consent of the Mother and having also been pronounced unfit for field service by Medical Examining Board."

KEETER, WILLIAM M., Private
Resided in Halifax County where he enlisted at age 34, January 28, 1862, for the war. Reported as absent sick on company muster rolls from November-December, 1862, until February 29-August 31, 1864, muster roll when he was reported with the remark: "Wounded and sent to hospital." Balance of muster rolls for 1864 state that he was wounded May 12, 1864, and report him as absent wounded through December, 1864. Federal Provost Marshal records indicate that he was captured at Harrisonburg, Virginia, September 25, 1864, and confined at Fort McHenry, Maryland, December 9, 1864. Transferred on January 1, 1865, to Point Lookout, Maryland, where he was paroled and transferred to Aiken's Landing, Virginia, March 17, 1865, for exchange.

KELLY, JAMES, Private
Resided in Halifax County and enlisted in Northampton County at age 19, June 14, 1861, for the war. Died at Goldsboro on April 1, 1862.

KING, HENRY C., Private
Resided in Halifax County and enlisted in Wake County at age 26, July 15, 1862, for the war. Died in hospital at Danville, Virginia, January 27, 1863, of "scarlatina."

KING, JOHN, Private
Enlisted in Warren County, July 15-25, 1861, for the war. Wounded in action at Fredericksburg, Virginia, December 15, 1862, and died of wound in hospital at Richmond, Virginia, March 3, 1863.

KING, WILLIAM, Private
Resided in Halifax County where he enlisted at age 25, June 10, 1861, for the war. Present or accounted for until captured at Spotsylvania Court House, Virginia, May 12, 1864. Confined at Point Lookout, Maryland, until transferred to Elmira, New York, August 6, 1864. Released at Elmira after taking the Oath of Allegiance on June 27, 1865.

KING, WILLIAM E. F. X. Y., Private
Born in Halifax County where he resided as a farmer and enlisted at age 60, July 26, 1861, for the war. Discharged on October 4, 1862, by reason of "old age, he being 60 years of age, and some contraction of muscles of left leg, together with varicose veins."

LEWIS, JAMES H., Private
Resided in Halifax County and enlisted at Camp Bee, Virginia, at age 19, January 7, 1862, for the war. Mustered in as Fifer. Reported on company muster rolls as a Musician until reduced to ranks November-December, 1863. Present or accounted for as absent sick on muster rolls from date of enlistment until captured at Spotsylvania Court House, Virginia, May 12, 1864. Confined at Point Lookout, Maryland, until transferred to Elmira, New York, August 6, 1864. Released at Elmira after taking the Oath of Allegiance on July 11, 1865.

LEWIS, JOSEPH, Private
Resided in Halifax County and enlisted in Wake County at age 21, July 15, 1862, for the war. Died at Richmond, Virginia, August 2, 1862, of disease.

LEWIS, McD., Private
Resided in Halifax County and enlisted in Wake County at age 25, July 15, 1862, for the war. Died in hospital at Richmond, Virginia, October 24, 1862, of "febris typhoid."

LEWIS, ROBERT, Private
Resided in Halifax County where he enlisted at age 22, July 8, 1861, for the war. Discharged at Richmond, Virginia, September 2, 1861, by reason of disability.

LEWIS, THOMAS M., Private
Born in Halifax County where he resided as a farmer and enlisted at age 16, 18, June 12, 1861, for the war. Discharged at Richmond, Virginia, August 23, 1862, by reason of "wound received in the leg at battle of Seven Pines, Virginia," and because he was "under the age to perform military duty and has a feeble constitution."

LYLES, PRESTON, Private
Resided in Halifax County where he enlisted at age 24, July 9, 1861, for the war. Present or accounted for on company muster rolls until captured at Spotsylvania Court House, Virginia, May 12, 1864. Confined at Point Lookout, Maryland, until transferred to Elmira, New York, August 6, 1864. Died at Elmira on February 24, 1865, of "chronic diarrhoea."

LYNCH, ELIJAH, Private
Resided in Halifax County where he enlisted at age 29, July 2, 1861, for the war. Present or accounted for until captured at Spotsylvania Court

House, Virginia, May 12, 1864. Confined at Point Lookout, Maryland, until transferred to Elmira, New York, August 3, 1864. Died at Elmira on September 11, 1864, of "epilepsy."

LYNN, MARCUS D., Private

Born in Sussex County, Virginia, and resided as a shoemaker in Halifax County where he enlisted at age 23, July 1, 1861, for the war. Discharged on April 11, 1863, by reason of "disease of liver and general debility."

MATHEWS, THOMAS H., Private

Resided in Nash County and enlisted in Wake County at age 30, July 15, 1862, for the war. Present or accounted for until captured at Fredericksburg, Virginia, May 3, 1863. Paroled and exchanged at City Point, Virginia, May 10, 1863. Present or accounted for until captured a second time at Spotsylvania Court House, Virginia, May 12, 1864. Confined at Point Lookout, Maryland, until transferred to Elmira, New York, August 6, 1864. Released at Elmira after taking the Oath of Allegiance on June 27, 1865.

MATTHEWS, WILLIAM, Private

Resided in Halifax County where he enlisted at age 19, July 4, 1861, for the war. Wounded in action at Fredericksburg, Virginia, December 13, 1862. Wounded a second time after he returned to the company in January-February, 1863, when the May-June, 1863, muster roll reports him as "absent wounded, North Carolina." Date and place he was wounded the second time was not reported. Present or accounted for until captured at Spotsylvania Court House, Virginia, May 12, 1864. Confined at Point Lookout, Maryland, until transferred to Elmira, New York, August 6, 1864. Released at Elmira after taking the Oath of Allegiance on June 27, 1865.

MEDFORD, BERRY, Private

Resided in Halifax County where he enlisted at age 35, June 12, 1861, for the war. Wounded in action at Winchester, Virginia, June 15, 1863. Present or accounted for on company muster rolls through December, 1864. Captured at Farmville, Virginia, April 6, 1865, and confined at Point Lookout, Maryland, until released after taking the Oath of Allegiance on June 15, 1865.

MERRITT, HENRY, Private

Resided in Halifax County and enlisted in Wake County at age 20, July 15, 1862, for the war. Reported as absent sick from date of enlistment through April, 1863, and from July, 1863, through August 19, 1864, when he was reported as absent without leave. Hospital records indicate that he was hospitalized many times during his enlistment period and the last hospital record on file states that he was furloughed for 60 days from General Hospital, Farmville, Virginia, June 7, 1864. Paroled at Farmville, April 11-21, 1865.

MILLIKIN, R. B., Private

Enlisted in Wake County, July 15, 1862, for the war. Died in hospital at Richmond, Virginia, September 15, 1862, of "typhoid fever."

MOODY, JOSEPH, Private

Resided in Halifax County and enlisted at

Camp Bee, Virginia, at age 45, February 4, 1862, for the war. Died in hospital at Fredericksburg, Virginia, March 15, 1862, of disease.

MORECOCK, ROBERT E., Private

Resided in Halifax County where he enlisted at age 19, July 4, 1861, for the war. Mustered in as Sergeant and reduced to ranks November-December, 1861, when he was "discharged by substitute."

MORRIS, WILLIAM, Private

Born in Halifax County where he resided as a farmer and enlisted at age 23, July 1, 1861, for the war. Discharged on September 8, 1861, by reason of "general debility."

MUMFORD, H. T., Private

Paroled at Greensboro on April 28, 1865.

NEVILLE, JAMES H., Private

Resided in Halifax County and enlisted in Wake County at age 30, July 15, 1862, for the war. Present or accounted for until captured at Spotsylvania Court House, Virginia, May 12, 1864. Confined at Point Lookout, Maryland, until transferred to Elmira, New York, August 6, 1864. Died at Elmira on April 24, 1865, of "variola."

PITTARD, DOCK, Private

Resided in Halifax County where he enlisted at age 23, July 8, 1861, for the war. Died in hospital at Fredericksburg, Virginia, November 17, 1861.

POPE, WILLIAM A., Private

Resided in Halifax County and enlisted in Wake County at age 20, July 15, 1862, for the war. Captured at Frederick, Maryland, September 12, 1862, and confined at Fort Delaware, Delaware, until transferred to Aiken's Landing, Virginia, October 2, 1862, for exchange. Declared exchanged on November 10, 1862. Wounded in action at Chancellorsville, Virginia, May 2-3, 1863. Reported as absent wounded through December, 1863. Returned to company in 1864 and captured at Spotsylvania Court House, Virginia, May 12, 1864. Confined at Point Lookout, Maryland, until transferred to Elmira, New York, August 6, 1864. Died at Elmira on January 22, 1865, of "chronic diarrhoea."

POWELL, WILLIAM Z., Private

Resided in Halifax County where he enlisted at age 46, January 20, 1862, for the war. Killed in action at Gettysburg, Pennsylvania, July 1-3, 1863.

PULLEY, HENRY J., Private

Resided in Halifax County where he enlisted at age 20, January 1, 1862, for the war. Present or accounted for on company muster rolls from date of enlistment until February 29-August 31, 1864, muster roll when he was reported as absent sick in hospital at Richmond, Virginia. Reported as absent through November-December, 1864, when he was reported with the remark: "Absent without leave since July, 1864."

PULLEY, JOHN, Private

Resided in Halifax County where he enlisted at age 35, July 8, 1861, for the war. Killed in action at Wilderness, Virginia, May 5, 1864.

RATLEY, WILLIAM, Private

Born in Nash County where he resided as a shoemaker prior to enlisting in Wake County at age 21, July 15, 1862, for the war. Admitted to hospital at Richmond, Virginia, on August 20, 1862, with "debility" and transferred to Huguenot Springs, Virginia, September 4, 1862. Attached to hospital at Huguenot Springs on September 5, 1862. Detailed for light duty as a nurse at Jackson Hospital, Richmond, Virginia, February 18, 1864, and served as such until detailed as a guard at the same hospital on June 8, 1864. Remained at hospital until returned to duty in February, 1865.

ROGERS, FRANK, Private
Resided in Halifax County and enlisted in Wake County at age 20, July 15, 1862, for the war. Admitted to hospital at Richmond, Virginia, March 28, 1863, with "bronchitis" and "pneumonia." Transferred to Weldon, April 29, 1863. May-June, 1863, muster roll reports that he "died of disease May 18, 1863, in North Carolina."

ROGERS, LEWIS L., Private
Resided in Halifax County and enlisted in Wake County at age 25, July 15, 1862, for the war. Present or accounted for until captured at Spotsylvania Court House, Virginia, May 12, 1864. Confined at Point Lookout, Maryland, until transferred to Elmira, New York, August 6, 1864. Died at Elmira on May 17, 1865, of "chronic diarrhoea."

SAVAGE, WILLIAM M., Private
Resided in Halifax County and enlisted in Wake County at age 25, July 15, 1862, for the war. Captured at Fredericksburg, Virginia, May 3, 1863, and paroled and exchanged at City Point, Virginia, May 10, 1863. Wounded in the left leg at Gettysburg, Pennsylvania, July 2-3, 1863, and admitted to hospital at Richmond, Virginia, July 19, 1863. Furloughed from hospital for 40 days on August 3, 1863. Company muster rolls cover through December, 1864, and report him as absent wounded. Hospital records indicate that he was again admitted to hospital at Richmond, Virginia, on December 15, 1864, with a gunshot wound of the leg. Records do not indicate if this was new or old wound. Captured in hospital at Richmond on April 3, 1865, and confined at Libby Prison, Richmond, until transferred to Newport News, Virginia, April 23, 1865. Released at Newport News after taking the Oath of Allegiance on June 30, 1865.

SCHISANO, STEPHEN P., Sergeant
Resided in Virginia and enlisted at Camp Bee, Virginia, at age 25, October 6, 1861, for the war. Mustered in as Sergeant. Present or accounted for until discharged on October 27, 1862, by reason of his "having been appointed an officer of the C.S. Navy."

SCREWS, JAMES, Private
Resided in Halifax County where he enlisted at age 23, June 12, 1861, for the war. Detailed as a nurse in hospital at Richmond, Virginia, September 5, 1861. Company muster rolls report him as absent without leave from June 20-October 31, 1862, muster roll, through January-February, 1863, muster roll when he was reported as absent sick. Date returned from detail as nurse not reported. Reported on company muster rolls from January-

February, 1863, through November-December, 1864, as absent sick.

SHAW, ALBERT, Private
Born in Halifax County where he resided as a mechanic and enlisted at age 35, January 15, 1862, for the war. Discharged at Danville, Virginia, April 4, 1863, by reason of "chronic rheumatism, chronic diarrhoea, and valvular disease of the heart." Roll of Honor states that he was "discharged on account of wounds received in battle at Ellerson's Mill," but hospital records do not indicate that he was wounded.

SHAW, ELLIOTT, Private
Resided in Halifax County and enlisted at Camp Bee, Virginia, at age 20, January 1, 1862, for the war. Died at Richmond, Virginia, October 13, 1862, of disease.

SHAW, JOHN D., Corporal
Born in Halifax County where he resided as a farmer prior to enlisting in Northampton County at age 25, July 17, 1861, for the war. Mustered in as Corporal. Wounded in action at Ellerson's Mill, Virginia, June 26, 1862, and discharged on November 20, 1862, by reason of "anchylosis of the left elbow joint, wrist, and hand caused by wound from fragments of shell."

SHAW, ROBERT, Private
Resided in Halifax County where he enlisted at age 18, June 10, 1861, for the war. Present or accounted for on company muster rolls until captured at Spotsylvania Court House, Virginia, May 12, 1864. Confined at Point Lookout, Maryland, until transferred to Elmira, New York, August 6, 1864. Paroled at Elmira and sent to James River, Virginia, for exchange on February 20, 1865; however, Provost Marshal records indicate that he was admitted to U.S. Army General Hospital, West's Buildings, Baltimore, Maryland, February 22, 1865, "convalescent from typhoid fever." Transferred from hospital to Post Hospital, Fort McHenry, Maryland, May 9, 1865. Released at Fort McHenry after taking the Oath of Allegiance on June 9, 1865.

SHAW, THOMAS, Private
Resided in Halifax County where he enlisted at age 45, February 15, 1862, for the war. Present or accounted for on company muster rolls until May-June, 1863, muster roll reports him as "absent wounded." Date and place he was wounded was not reported. Reported as present on July-August, 1863, muster roll. Present or accounted for until captured at Spotsylvania Court House, Virginia, May 12, 1864. Confined at Point Lookout, Maryland, until transferred to Elmira, New York, August 6, 1864. Released at Elmira after taking the Oath of Allegiance on June 12, 1865.

SHAW, WILLIAM D., Private
Resided in Halifax County and enlisted in Wayne County at age 23, April 13, 1862, for the war. Wounded in action at Payne's Farm, Virginia, November 27, 1863. Present or accounted for on company muster rolls through December, 1864. Paroled at Appomattox Court House, Virginia, April 9, 1865.

SHEARIN, THOMAS W., Private

Resided in Halifax County and enlisted in Warren County at age 30, July 22, 1861, for the war. Admitted to hospital at Richmond, Virginia, October 18, 1862, with "contused wound" and returned to duty November 17, 1862. Date and place he was wounded not reported. Present or accounted for on company muster rolls until captured at Spotsylvania Court House, Virginia, May 12, 1864. Confined at Point Lookout, Maryland, where he remained until paroled and sent to James River, Virginia, for exchange on February 13, 1865.

SHORT, BENJAMIN, Private

Resided in Halifax County and enlisted in Wake County at age 25, July 15, 1862, for the war. Present or accounted for until captured at Spotsylvania Court House, Virginia, May 12, 1864. Confined at Point Lookout, Maryland, until transferred to Elmira, New York, August 6, 1864. Transferred from Elmira with a group of invalid prisoners to be exchanged and exchanged on October 29, 1864. Paroled at Appomattox Court House, Virginia, April 9, 1865.

SHORT, JOHN, Private

Resided in Halifax County and enlisted at age 25, January 10, 1862, for the war. Roll of Honor states that he "died February 22, 1862, at Brook's Station, Virginia."

SMITH, WILLIAM T., Private

Resided in Northampton County and enlisted in Halifax County at age 24, June 10, 1861, for the war. Present or accounted for on company muster rolls from date of enlistment through December, 1864. Federal Provost Marshal records report him as a rebel deserter received by the Provost Marshal General, Washington, D.C., March 24, 1865, from the Provost Marshal at Bermuda Hundred, Virginia. Provost Marshal records indicate that he took the Oath of Allegiance and was furnished transportation to "Goshen, Orange County, N.Y."

SNIPES, ROBERT, Private

Resided in Halifax County where he enlisted at age 17, June 12, 1861, for the war. Company muster rolls report him as absent without leave or absent sick from June, 1862, until March-April, 1863, muster roll reports him as having "died from disease, time not known." Hospital register for Receiving and Wayside Hospital, Richmond, Virginia, states that he died August 22, 1862, of "gunshot wound in right hip." Roll of Honor carries the remark that he he was "killed June 26, 1862, in battle at Ellerson's Mill."

SPEARS, HENRY, Private

Resided in Halifax County where he enlisted at age 20, July 7, 1861, for the war. Discharged November 14, 1861.

SPEARS, WILLIAM W., Musician

Resided in Halifax County where he enlisted at age 18, June 10, 1861, for the war. Mustered in as Musician. Present or accounted for on company muster rolls from date of enlistment through December, 1864. Federal Provost Marshal records report him as a rebel deserter received by the

Provost Marshal General, Washington, D.C., March 24, 1865, from the Provost Marshal at Bermuda Hundred, Virginia. Records indicate that he took the Oath of Allegiance and was furnished transportation to "Goshen, Orange County, N.Y."

STAMPER, JAMES, Private

Resided in Halifax County and enlisted in Wake County at age 20, July 18, 1862, for the war. Present or accounted for until admitted to hospital at Richmond, Virginia, August 29, 1862, with "feb. intermitt." Furloughed for 30 days on October 18, 1862. Roll of Honor states that he "died November 10, 1862."

STANSBERRY, ALBERT, Private

Resided in Halifax County and enlisted in Warren County at age 30, July 22, 1861, for the war. Captured at Fredericksburg, Virginia, May 3, 1863, and paroled and exchanged at City Point, Virginia, May 10, 1863. Present or accounted for until captured at Spotsylvania Court House, Virginia, May 12, 1864. Confined at Point Lookout, Maryland, until transferred to Elmira, New York, August 6, 1864. Transferred from Elmira to James River, Virginia, for exchange on March 2, 1865. Admitted to hospital at Richmond, Virginia, March 7, 1865, with "debilitas" and furloughed for 30 days on March 9, 1865.

STANSBERRY, ROBERT, Private

Resided in Halifax County where he enlisted at age 37, June 10, 1861, for the war. Died at Fredericksburg, Virginia, November 18-22, 1861.

STOKES, DAVID E., Sergeant

Resided in Virginia and enlisted at Camp Bee, Virginia, at age 21, 24, September 13, 1861, for the war. Mustered in as Sergeant. Present or accounted for until transferred to Company D of this regiment upon appointment as 2nd Lieutenant on March 18, 1862.

STOLL, BENJAMIN, Private

Born in Germany and resided in Halifax County prior to enlisting in Wayne County at age 26, May 11, 1862, for the war. Present or accounted for on company muster rolls from date of enlistment until May-June, 1863, muster roll when he was reported with the remark: "Absent wounded." Reported as absent wounded or absent without leave until detailed as shoemaker in Richmond, Virginia, on April 13, 1864. Absent on detail through December, 1864.

STRICKLAND, THOMAS, Private

Resided in Halifax County where he enlisted at age 21, July 1, 1861, for the war. Present or accounted for on company muster rolls through December, 1864. Paroled at Appomattox Court House, Virginia, April 9, 1865.

THOMPSON, JAMES, Private

Resided in Halifax County and enlisted at Camp Bee, Virginia, at age 21, February 25, 1862, for the war. Present or accounted for until admitted to hospital at Farmville, Virginia, June 4, 1863, with "int. fever." Hospital records indicate that he was returned to duty on July 1, 1863, and was admitted to hospital at Richmond, Virginia,

July 2, 1863, with "diarrhoea acute." Discharged from hospital and returned to duty on July 23, 1863; however, company muster rolls indicate that he did not return to the company and report him as absent sick or absent without leave through December, 1864.

THOMPSON, JOHN, Private

Resided in Halifax County where he enlisted at age 25, June 10, 1861, for the war. Killed in action at Chancellorsville, Virginia, May 3, 1863.

THOMPSON, RICHARD, Private

Resided in Halifax County where he enlisted at age 21, July 5, 1861, for the war. Present or accounted for on company muster rolls until captured at Spotsylvania Court House, Virginia, May 12, 1864. Confined at Point Lookout, Maryland, until transferred to Elmira, New York, August 6, 1864. Paroled at Elmira and sent to Point Lookout with a group of invalid prisoners on October 14, 1864, for exchange. Declared exchanged on October 29, 1864, at James River, Virginia. November-December, 1864, muster roll reports him as "absent prisoner."

THOMPSON, SAMUEL P., Corporal

Resided in Halifax County and enlisted in Warren County at age 25, July 23, 1861, for the war. Mustered in as Corporal. Died in hospital at Richmond, Virginia, July 10, 1862, of disease.

THROWER, WILLIAM, Private

Resided in Halifax County and enlisted in Wake County at age 23, July 15, 1862, for the war. Wounded in action at Fredericksburg, Virginia, December 13, 1862. Admitted to hospital at Richmond, Virginia, December 15, 1862, with a gunshot wound in the left hand and transferred to Farmville, Virginia, December 31, 1862. Returned to duty on April 25, 1863. Admitted to hospital at Richmond, Virginia, with a gunshot wound of the hand—"finger amputated"—May 7, 1863. Furloughed for 30 days on June 11, 1863. Company muster rolls report him as absent wounded, absent sick, or absent in North Carolina from May-June, 1863, through December, 1864; however, Federal Provost Marshal records indicate that he was captured at Spotsylvania Court House, Virginia, May 12, 1864. Confined at Point Lookout, Maryland, until transferred to Elmira, New York, August 6, 1864. Paroled at Elmira and returned to Point Lookout on October 11-14, 1864, with a group of invalid prisoners, for exchange. Exchanged on October 29, 1864, at James River, Virginia.

TURNER, JOHN C., Private

Resided in Halifax County where he enlisted at age 21, July 5, 1861, for the war. Present or accounted of on company muster rolls until reported as "absent without leave" on July-August, 1863, muster roll. Subsequent muster rolls state that he was captured at Gettysburg, Pennsylvania, July 3, 1863. Federal Provost Marshal records indicate that he was arrested in the 16th District of Pennsylvania and confined at Harrisburg, Pennsylvania, July 22, 1863. Transferred to Fort Delaware, Delaware, July 23, 1863. Prisoner of war records also give place of capture as Williamsport, Maryland, on June 27, 1863. Transferred from Fort Delaware to Point Lookout, Maryland, October 18, 1863. Released at Point Lookout after taking the Oath of Allegiance and joining the U.S. service on January 23, 1864. Unit to which he was assigned not reported.

WALSTON, JARRETT, Private

Resided in Halifax County and enlisted in Wake County at age 22, July 15, 1862, for the war. Present or accounted for until captured at Spotsylvania Court House, Virginia, May 12, 1864. Confined at Point Lookout, Maryland, until transferred to Elmira, New York, August 6, 1864. Died at Elmira on March 15, 1865, of "pneumonia."

WAMMOCK, K. T., Private

Resided in Halifax County where he enlisted at age 22, July 1, 1861, for the war. Wounded in action at Chancellorsville, Virginia, May 2-3, 1863. Present or accounted for until captured at Spotsylvania Court House, Virginia, May 12, 1864. Confined at Point Lookout, Maryland, until transferred to Elmira, New York, August 6, 1864. Released at Elmira after taking the Oath of Allegiance on June 12, 1865.

WAMMOCK, RICHARD, Private

Resided in Halifax County and enlisted in Wake County at age 21, July 15, 1862, for the war. Company muster rolls report him as absent sick from date of enlistment through December, 1862, and as absent without leave for the entire year of 1863. Reported as absent sick on January-February, 1864, muster roll, and February 29-October 31, 1864, muster roll carries him as "wounded and sent to hospital." Reported as such on November-December, 1864, muster roll. Date and place he was wounded not reported.

WEBB, THADDEUS, Private

Resided in Halifax County where he enlisted at age 18, January 21-25, 1862, for the war. Died in hospital at Staunton, Virginia, May 11, 1863, of disease.

WEBB, WILLIAM E., Private

Born in Halifax County where he resided as a farmer and enlisted at age 38, July 5, 1861, for the war. Present or accounted for until discharged on August 12, 1862, by reason of "chronic rheumatism and ulcers."

WHITE, SHANON M., Private

Resided in Halifax County where he enlisted at age 24, July 1, 1861, for the war. Wounded in action at Fredericksburg, Virginia, December 13, 1862, and died of wounds in hospital at Richmond, Virginia, December 25, 1862.

WILLIAMS, J. A., Private

Federal Provost Marshal records indicate that he was captured at Middletown, Maryland, September 13, 1862, and declared exchanged at Aiken's Landing, Virginia, November 10, 1862.

WINTERS, JOHN, Private

Resided in Halifax County where he enlisted at age 36, February 4, 1862, for the war. Present or accounted for on company muster rolls through

May-June, 1863, when he was reported as "absent wounded Staunton." Date and place he was wounded not reported. Carried as absent sick or absent wounded through December, 1863. Reported as present on January-February, 1864, muster roll. February 29-August 31, 1864, muster roll carries him as "absent wounded and sent to hospital." Admitted to Receiving and Wayside Hospital, Richmond, Virginia, May 16, 1864, and transferred to Winder Hospital, Richmond, the next day. Hospital records do not indicate when he was discharged from the hospital, but the November-December, 1864, muster roll carries him as "absent without leave since June, 1864." Appears on a Register of C. S. Hospital, Petersburg, Virginia, being admitted March 17, 1865. Returned to duty March 28, 1865. Paroled at Appomattox Court House, Virginia, April 9, 1865.

WINTERS, ROBERT W., Corporal
Resided in Halifax County where he enlisted at age 23, June 25, 1861, for the war. Mustered in as Private and appointed Corporal on July 1, 1863. Wounded in action at Payne's Farm, Virginia, November 27, 1863. Returned to duty from hospital June 21, 1864. Killed in action at Cedar Creek, Virginia, October 19, 1864.

WOOD, BRITTON, Private
Resided in Halifax County and enlisted in Wake County at age 23, July 15, 1862, for the war. Present or accounted for until captured at Spotsylvania Court House, Virginia, May 13-18, 1864. Confined at Point Lookout, Maryland, until transferred to Elmira, New York, July 3-6, 1864. Paroled at Elmira on March 14, 1865, and sent to James River, Virginia, for exchange. Admitted to hospital at Richmond, Virginia, March 19, 1865, with "scorbutis" and furloughed for 30 days on March 23, 1865.

MISCELLANEOUS

The following list of men was compiled from primary records which record the unit as the 1st Regiment N.C. State Troops but do not indicate the company to which they belonged. The names do not appear on the surviving muster rolls of any company in the regiment, but they have been checked for possible misspelling or incorrect unit designation. Some names appear on records created in areas where the regiment did not serve. It is possible the individual either gave an assumed name or purposely gave an incorrect unit designation. This is particularly true with prisoner of war records. Since it is not possible to identify these men with a company, they are listed separately.

ASHMAN, L., ——————
Name appears on a register of prisoners received by the Provost Marshal General, Army of the Potomac, March 29, 1863, and forwarded to Washington, D. C., April 1, 1863. Rank not reported but register states that he was arrested at Headquarters, Cavalry Corps.

BRYANT, J. W., Private
Released at Elmira, New York, after taking the

Oath of Allegiance on July 3, 1865. Residence given on Oath as Augusta, Georgia.

CAMANADE, J. C., Private
Captured near Richmond, Virginia, June 15, 1862, and confined at Fort Wool, Virginia, where he died July 4, 1862. Federal Provost Marshal records indicate that he was born in North Carolina and report his age as 22.

DOZIER, A. W., Lieutenant
Reported on a list of persons forwarded to point of exchange on Flag of Truce steamer on February 2, 1865.

EHGENS, G. N., Private
Name reported on a copy of an undated parole forwarded with a letter of transmittal dated Winchester, Virginia, October 4, 1862.

ELLIOTT, JOSEPH, Private
Appears on a register of oaths taken by rebel deserters, Headquarters, Provost Marshal, Bermuda Hundred, Virginia, with the remark that he took the Oath on March 19, 1865, and was turned over to the Provost Marshal at City Point, Virginia.

GILBERT, MACK, Private
Federal Provost Marshal records indicate that he was captured at Warrenton, Virginia, after October 1, 1862, and paroled by the Provost Marshal General, Army of the Potomac, near Warrenton, November 9, 1862. Delivered in exchange at City Point, Virginia, November 18, 1862.

GRAY, A. F., Private
Paroled at Greensboro on May 9, 1865.

GRAY, JOHN F., Private
Captured at Raleigh on April 17, 1865.

GROW, JACOB, Private
Appears on a parole of prisoners of war dated Office of the Provost Marshal General, Army of the Potomac, May 5, 1863. Forwarded from Old Capitol Prison, Washington, D. C., to Fort Delaware, Delaware, May 7, 1863. Pay voucher on file indicates that he was paid on June 23, 1863, for the period February 28-April 30, 1863, and carries the remark: "Exchanged prisoner."

GUILE, WILLIAM, Private
Released at Elmira, New York, after taking the Oath of Allegiance on June 12, 1865. Residence given on Oath as Walhalla, South Carolina.

HANSFIELD, J. R., Lieutenant
Federal Provost Marshal records indicate that he was captured at Spotsylvania Court House, Virginia, May 12, 1864, and confined at Old Capitol Prison, Washington, D. C., May 17, 1864. Transferred to Fort Delaware, Delaware, June 15, 1864.

HAYS, ROBERT B., ——————
Federal Provost Marshal records report him on a register of enlisted men, rebel deserters, and refugees detained at Camp Distribution awaiting orders. Register dated March 20, 1864, with the remark that he was sent to Beaufort. Rank not reported.

HICKS, S., Private
Captured and paroled at Athens, Georgia, on May 8, 1865.

HOOKS, J. Z., Private
Captured and paroled at Athens, Georgia, on May 8, 1865.

JERNIGAN, JOSEPH, Private
Paroled at Office of the Provost Marshal General, Army of the Potomac, September 26, 1862.

JONES, J. W., Private
Resided in New Hanover County and captured at Smithfield, N.C., March 19, 1865. Took the Oath of Allegiance at Newport News, Virginia, June 30, 1865.

KING, J., Private
Captured at Raleigh on March 14, 1865.

KING, N., Private
Released at Elmira, New York, after taking the Oath of Allegiance on June 27, 1865. Residence given on Oath as Gaston, N.C.

MILLER, E. F., Private
Released at Elmira, New York, after taking the Oath of Allegiance on June 14, 1865. Residence given on Oath as Suffolk, Virginia.

MILLER, JORDAN, ————
Name reported on a register of enlisted men, rebel deserters, and refugees detained at Camp Distribution awaiting orders, which states that he was received from Alexandria, Virginia, and sent to New Bern, September 21, 1864. Rank not reported.

MOCK, E. G., Private
Captured near New Bern on February 3, 1864, and confined at Point Lookout, Maryland, until transferred to Elmira, New York, July 23, 1864.

MOODIN, JOHN, Private
Paroled at Leesburg, Virginia, October 2, 1862.

MORGAN, THOMAS, Private
Confined at Camp Hamilton, Virginia, December 26, 1864, as a prisoner of war. Released December 27, 1864.

MORSE, J. R., Private
Captured at Raleigh on April 15, 1865.

MURPHY, JOHN, Private
Captured at Rapidan River, Virginia, December 9, 1863, and confined at Old Capitol Prison, Washington, D.C., until released on oath and sent to Philadelphia, Pennsylvania, March 15, 1865.

NEWTON, JAMES B., Conscript
Federal Provost Marshal records indicate that he died at Camp Chase, Ohio, June 3, 1865, of "scurvy."

NORTH, WILLIAM S., Private
Federal Provost Marshal records indicate that he took the Oath of Allegiance at Fort Monroe, Virginia, March 3, 1864, and report him with the remark: "A rebel deserter—came into Federal lines at New Bern, North Carolina." Oath of Allegiance records his county of residence as Yadkin and carries the endorsement that he was sent to Indianapolis, Indiana.

OLIVER, J., Private
Federal Provost Marshal records indicate that he took the Oath of Allegiance at Headquarters, Army of the James, in March, 1865, and was sent to the Provost Marshal General at Washington, D.C., where transportation was furnished to Plymouth, N.C.

PHELPS, BALEY, ————
Appears on a register of enlisted men, refugees, and rebel deserters detained at Camp Distribution, Camp Hamilton, Virginia, which states that he was received from Bermuda Hundred, Virginia, March 12, 1865, and forwarded to the Provost Marshal at Norfolk, Virginia, March 13, 1865. Rank not reported on record.

PICKERING, R., Private
Name appears as signature to a parole dated Office of the Provost Marshal General, Army of the Potomac, May 4, 1863.

PINKINS, HENRY, ————
Name appears on a register of enlisted men, rebel deserters, and refugees detained at Camp Distribution awaiting orders. Register dated September 20, 1864, and indicates that he was received from Alexanderia, Virginia, and sent to New Bern, September 21, 1864.

REDDY, JOEL, Private
Confined at Old Capitol Prison, Washington, D.C., March 31, 1863, with the remark that he was a "deserter."

RILEY, J. H. F., Sergeant
Name appears on a record of paroled prisoners, Provost Marshal's Office, Middle Military Department, which states that he deserted in North Carolina on January 22, 186?, and took the Oath at Goldsboro on July 14, 186?. Records indicate that he was sent to Baltimore, Maryland, but do not give the year.

SHERMAN, JOHN, Private
Name appears on a register of prisoners of war at Old Capitol Prison, Washington, D.C., with the remark that he was captured at Mine Run, Virginia, November 28, 1863, and confined at the prison on December 5, 1863. Register carries the following remark: "Sent to Colonel Ingraham's office March 28, 1864. Transferred to 95th New York from which he proved to be a deserter."

SUMMERSET, D. T., Private
Captured near Fredericksburg, Virginia, May 3, 1863, and paroled at Headquarters, Army of the Potomac, May 4, 1863. Sent to Washington, D.C., and then to City Point, Virginia, for exchange. Declared exchanged May 10, 1863.

SWAIN, C., Private
Released at Elmira, New York, after taking the Oath of Allegiance on June 12, 1865. Residence given on Oath as Suffolk, Virginia.

TAYLOR, CHARLES, Private
Name appears on a register of enlisted men, rebel deserters, and refugees, detained at Camp Distribution awaiting orders. Register dated September 23, 1864, and indicates that he was sent to New Bern, September 27, 1864.

TAYLOR, W. P., Private
Name appears on a register of rebel deserters forwarded from Fort Monroe, Virginia, to Provost Marshal General, Washington, D.C., April 8, 1865. Register carries the remark that he took the Oath and was provided transportation to Philadelphia, Pennsylvania.

THOMPSON, E. W., Private
Captured at Fredericksburg, Virginia, May 3, 1863, and paroled at Headquarters, Army of the Potomac, May 4, 1863. Forwarded to Washington, D.C., and sent to City Point Virginia, for exchange. Declared exchanged on May 10, 1863.

TYSINGER, ROBERT, Private
Captured at Salisbury on April 12, 1865, and confined at Camp Chase, Ohio, until released after taking the Oath of Allegiance on June 13, 1865. Oath of Allegiance reports his age as 29 and his county of residence as Davidson.

WARD, HENRY, Private
Captured at Culpeper Court House, Virginia, December 4, 1863, and confined at Old Capitol Prison, Washington, D.C., December 5, 1863. Transferred to Kalorama Hospital, Washington, January 28, 1864.

WHITE, D., Private
Captured and paroled at Athens, Georgia, May 8, 1865.

WHITE, GEORGE F., Private
Appears on a register of Medical Director's Office, Richmond, Virginia, which states that he was transferred from General Hospital No. 25, Richmond, to Camp Lee, near Richmond, November 11, 1862. Captured at Culpeper Court House, Virginia, December 4, 1863, and confined at Old Capitol Prison, Washington, D.C., until released after taking the Oath of Allegiance on January 4, 1864.

WINDCUFF, M., Private
Captured at Fredericksburg, Virginia, May 3, 1863, and paroled at Headquarters, Army of the Potomac. Forwarded to Washington, D.C., May 4, 1863, and sent to City Point, Virginia, for exchange. Declared exchanged May 10, 1863.

ZOELLE, F., Private
Captured at Richmond, Virginia, April 3, 1865. Took the Oath of Allegiance at Richmond on April 8, 1865, and was provided transportation to New York.

2nd BATTALION N. C. INFANTRY

This battalion was organized at Richmond, Virginia, November 1, 1861. Originally, Wharton J. Green was authorized to raise a regiment for General Henry A. Wise's Legion to be known as Colonel Green's Independent Regiment, Wise Legion. The regimental organization was never completed, however, and the companies recruited for the regiment were organized into a battalion on or about November 15, 1861, and designated the 2nd Battalion N.C. Infantry. The battalion never comprised more than eight companies, A to H, three of which were not North Carolina companies. In addition to some Virginians who enlisted in the North Carolina companies, there was one complete company of Virginians and two companies of Georgians.

When the battalion was authorized on November 1, 1861, it consisted of five companies. Although recruited as a part of General Wise's Legion, the battalion remained at Richmond during the Kanawha Valley-Sewell Mountain campaigns in which the legion participated. During this organizational period the companies frequently changed company letters, but these were stabilized when the battalion completed its organization with the addition of three companies in January, 1862.

The battalion remained at Camp Lee, near Richmond, until ordered to Wilmington on December 9, 1861. Leaving Richmond on December 10, it arrived at Wilmington on the next day. There it went into camp at Camp Belvedere. From there it moved to Camp Patterson where three new companies were mustered in and the battalion organization was completed. On February 1, 1862, the battalion was ordered to proceed to Roanoke Island to join General Wise's command at that place. Proceeding by way of Norfolk, Virginia, the battalion arrived on Roanoke Island on the morning of February 8, 1862, the day after the Federals under General A. E. Burnside had landed. As the men disembarked they could hear the fighting at Fort Russell. Before they reached that position word came that the battle was lost. Colonel Green attempted to form a line but could not do so. After a brief skirmish, the battalion, along with all the other troops on the island, was surrendered. On February 21, 1862, the prisoners of war were paroled at Elizabeth City and released to return to their homes until properly exchanged. The battalion existed on paper from February 21 until August 18, 1862, when the men were declared exchanged and ordered to re-form their companies.

Soon after their exchange the officers and men were ordered to rendezvous at Drewry's Bluff, near Richmond, Virginia. Here on September 25, 1862, the battalion was reorganized for the war and assigned to Brigadier General Junius Daniel's Brigade. In addition to the battalion, the brigade was composed of the 32nd, 43rd, 45th, and 53rd Regiments N.C. Troops. The battalion remained encamped near Drewry's Bluff for the balance of 1862. In November, 1862, Company C transferred out of the battalion and became Company G, 59th

Regiment Virginia Infantry by Special Orders No. 268, Adjutant and Inspector General's Office, Richmond, November 15, 1862.

Early in January, 1863, the battalion and a portion of the brigade was ordered to Goldsboro. There it joined the rest of the brigade which had been ordered to Goldsboro the previous month. It remained in camp near Goldsboro until early in February, 1863, when the brigade was ordered to Kinston. In February, 1863, Major General Daniel H. Hill was placed in command of the troops and formulated plans for an attack on New Bern and Washington, North Carolina. Daniel's Brigade moved on New Bern by the upper Trent road while two other attacking columns moved on the town. General Daniel's Brigade drove in the enemy at Deep Gully about 8 miles from New Bern on March 13. The next day the Federals were repulsed in their effort to recapture their former position. The failure of the other two attacking columns to carry out their part of the plan forced General Hill to withdraw his forces from New Bern. He then turned to move on Washington, and by the end of March, 1863, the Confederates had the town under siege. When the Federals ran the Confederate blockade and reinforced and resupplied the town, Hill was forced to abandon his efforts. He did so on April 15, 1863. By the end of April, 1863, the battalion was in camp near Hookerton. The clerk of Company F reported the movements of the battalion during this campaign on the March-April, 1863, muster roll as follows:

> Left camp near Kinston, N.C., and marched in the direction of Washington, N.C., March 25, 1863. Left camp near Washington, April 14, 1863, and arrived at camp near Greenville, N.C., April 18. Left Greenville April 29, and arrived at Hookerton the same evening.

In May, 1863, Daniel's Brigade was ordered to join the Army of Northern Virginia at Fredericksburg. There it was assigned to Major General Robert E. Rodes' Division, Lieutenant General Richard S. Ewell's Corps. This corps, known as the 2nd Corps, would lead the advance into Pennsylvania. Rodes' Division left camp on June 4 and reached just beyond Culpeper Court House on June 7. From there the division moved to Brandy Station to assist the cavalry on June 9 but arrived after the battle had ended. It then resumed its march toward the Shenandoah Valley. Rodes' Division received orders on June 12 to proceed to Cedarville by way of Chester Gap in advance of the other two divisions of the corps. At Cedarville, Rodes received orders to move on Berryville and Martinsburg and into Maryland while the other two divisions of the corps moved on Winchester. Berryville was occupied on June 13 after its defenders made good their escape. Rodes then proceeded to Martinsburg. On the march to Martinsburg, Daniel's Brigade was assigned to guard the division train and remained on that duty until the division reached Williamsport on June 15.

On June 14 Rodes' Division deployed before the defenses in front of Martinsburg. Fearing the defenders might escape, Rodes ordered a charge. The enemy was driven from the town on the run. However, the infantry escaped by taking the Shepherdstown road while the Confederates concentrated on the Federal cavalry and artillery on the Williamsport road. On June 15 Rodes heard of the victory at Winchester and moved his men to Williamsport. There he ordered three brigades to cross to the other side of the Potomac River while Daniel's Brigade and the rest of the division occupied Williamsport. The brigade was moved over the river on June 17.

The division was put in motion for Hagerstown on June 19 and arrived there that evening. Here it remained two days. Resuming the march on June 22, the division crossed into Pennsylvania and bivouacked at Greencastle. The next day it moved toward Chambersburg and passed through that town on June 24. At midnight on June 24 General Daniel received orders to move his brigade to Shippensburg to assist the cavalry. Starting at 1:00 A.M., it reached that town about 5:00 A.M. On June 26 the remainder of the division joined the force at Shippensburg, and on June 27 the entire division marched to Carlisle.

On the night of June 30 Rodes' Division was at Heidlersburg, where General Ewell received orders to proceed to Cashtown or Gettysburg, as circumstances might dictate. Rodes' Division moved on the morning of July 1 for Cashtown. While en route, word came that A. P. Hill's Corps was moving on Gettysburg, and General Ewell directed Rodes to proceed toward Gettysburg. When Rodes' Division arrived on the field, A. P. Hill's men were already engaged. Rodes moved his division into position on Hill's left, placing Daniel's Brigade on the right of his line. During the coming battle the battalion would lose its commander and two thirds of its men killed and wounded.

As the line moved forward, the brigade on Daniel's left became engaged and General Daniel had to shift some of his regiments to his left to support that brigade. This shift put this battalion on the right of center position with the 45th Regiment N.C. Troops on its right. The battle became general, with A. P. Hill's men on Rodes' right lying down in line of battle while Rodes' Division began to advance. Rodes expected Early's Division to come in on his left, but it had not arrived as yet. General Daniel reported the activities of his brigade just after the line became engaged as follows (O.R., S. I., Vol. 27, pt. 2, pp. 566-567):

I immediately moved the Second Battalion and the Forty-fifth Regiment forward, and engaged the enemy, very strongly posted along a railroad cut, and in the edge of the woods in rear of the cut, their line of battle being nearly at right angles with General Iverson's line, and supported by two batteries of artillery posted near a stone barn on the right of the railroad cut, and another on the hill to the left of the

railroad. This line of the enemy brought a very strong fire both of artillery and musketry upon my own and a portion of the right of General Iverson's line. Seeing that the enemy was strong, and other troops coming up to their support, I ordered the Forty-third and Fifty-third Regiments from my center and right to the left, to support General Iverson and my left. The Forty-fifth Regiment and Second Battalion, under command of Lieutenant-Colonels [S. H.] Boyd and [H. L.] Andrews, moved forward under a murderous line of artillery in the most gallant manner to a fence, under cover of a slight eminence, and engaged the enemy at short range, and by their steady and well-directed fire soon forced them to fall back.

After seeing the Forty-third and Fifty-third Regiments (which had been moved from the right) in position, I ordered the Second Battalion and Forty-fifth Regiment, supported on the left by the Forty-third and Fifty-third Regiments, to charge the enemy, at the same time ordering the Thirty-second Regiment, Colonel [E. C.] Brabble commanding, to move forward on the right, and get a position where he could reach the flank of the enemy, posted about the barn and in the woods in the rear of the barn.

The Forty-Fifth Regiment and Second Battalion, gallantly led by their commanders and supported by the rest of the line, advanced at a charge, driving the enemy from the cut in confusion, killing and wounding many and taking some prisoners; also compelling their artillery to retire from the barn.

At the railroad cut, which had been partially concealed by the long grass growing around it, and which, in consequence of the abruptness of its sides, was impassable, the advance was stopped. Seeing that it was impossible to advance this part of the line, and the ground affording no cover, I ordered the Forty-fifth Regiment and Second Battalion to fall back some 40 paces, to the crest of a hill, which afforded some shelter. From this position I kept up a heavy fire on the columns of the enemy that came down to the relief of the lines that had been broken, and in the meantime examined the cut from which the enemy had been driven. This I found could only be carried by moving a force across the cut to support the line advancing on the left of the cut, and that it could only be crossed by moving a regiment by the flank in rear and on the right of my position, and in front of some troops of General A. P. Hill's Corps who were lying down in line of battle, and to whom I had sent an officer with a request that they would act in conjunction with me in my previous advance, and with which request they had for some cause failed to comply.

Seeing that the enemy was strengthening himself on my right, and was occupying the cut and the hill to the right and left of it in great force, that General Iverson's left had been broken, and that one of the enemy's flags had almost gotten in his rear, I saw the necessity of carrying the hill at all hazards, and ordered Colonel Brabble to advance across the cut, keeping his left on the cut and his line perpendicular to it, and to carry the battery at the barn, and drive in the line of infantry between the barn and the hill. This advance of Colonel Brabble took the enemy in flank. At the same time, I ordered Captain Hammond to proceed to the left, and order all my troops to advance with the center, of which portion I had the immediate command, and also to endeavor to get all the troops on my left to advance with me, as I intended to carry the hill.

About this time a body of troops, which I afterward learned belonged to Major-General Pender's division, commenced a most spirited advance on my right, leaving, however, an interval of some hundreds of yards between themselves and my right. My own troops advanced in fine order, under a heavy fire, the Twelfth North Carolina Regiment, of Iverson's Brigade, keeping abreast with my left. After severe fighting, I succeeded in taking the hill, with a very heavy loss. Here a very large number of prisoners were captured, and in the advance my troops passed over several stand of colors that had been abandoned by the enemy. The Forty-fifth Regiment captured a stand of colors of the enemy, and recaptured the colors of the Twentieth North Carolina Regiment. My command continued to move forward until it reached the outskirts of the town, where, agreeably to instructions received through Major [H. A.] Whiting, I halted. Subsequently, having received orders from the major-general commanding to hold the railroad, I rested here during the night, under cover of an embankment.

On July 1, 1863, the battalion lost 29 killed and approximately 124 wounded.

The brigade moved to the right of the railroad embankment on the morning of July 2. Here it was subjected to artillery shelling during the afternoon. That evening it was moved up to support a proposed assault on the enemy lines. The assault was called off and the brigade moved into the town. Around midnight General Daniel received orders to move through the town to the left and report to General Edward Johnson, whose troops were engaged on Culp's Hill. Arriving at 4:00 A.M., the brigade was sent into the line where it remained until moved to the left of the line. In conjunction with General George H. Steuart's Brigade, the brigade attacked the Federal right. This attack failed, but the troops continued to fight from the positions they had attained. During the afternoon the entire line was pulled back to Rock Creek where a skirmish line was established. Late in the evening of July 3, before midnight, General Daniel received word to move his brigade back into town to join the division. On the morning of July 4 the brigade took up its assigned position on the left of the division. During the actions of July 2 and 3, the battalion lost 3 men wounded.

On the night of July 4-5 the division began to move toward Hagerstown by way of Fairfield. On the morning of July 6 the division became the rear guard of the army and was engaged in several brief skirmishes on that date. Daniel's Brigade brought up the rear of the division and was in regular contact with the enemy until contact was broken. On July 7 the division reached Hagerstown. Here a line of battle was established, but no general engagement occurred. On the night of July 14 the division recrossed the Potomac and marched to near Darkesville.

When the Federal army began crossing the Potomac River east of the Blue Ridge, General Lee had to move his army east of the mountains to interpose his army between the enemy and Richmond. By August 1, 1863, the Army of Northern Virginia was encamped near Orange Court House and the Army of the Potomac was at Warrenton. By August 4 Lee withdrew his army to the Rapidan River line. In October Lee attempted to turn the flank of the Federal army. The movement maneuvered the Federal commander into falling back, and on October 14 the Federal rear guard was intercepted at Bristoe Station. Failure to coordinate the attack resulted in heavy casualties to troops of A. P. Hill's Corps and the escape of the Federal rear guard. The battalion took part in the movement as part of the brigade and division, but Ewell's Corps was not engaged at Bristoe Station.

With the escape of the Federal army to Centreville, Lee retired to the upper Rappahannock River. Rodes' Division was positioned opposite Kelly's Ford. The Federal army followed the Confederates and launched an attack at Kelly's Ford on November 7. The brigade was in line of battle, but the enemy did not advance beyond the ford.

Lee withdrew his army south across the upper Rapidan River, toward Orange Court House. Here the army went into camp. Daniel's Brigade encamped near Morton's Ford, and companies from the battalion went on picket duty at various fords on the river. On November 26 the Federal army crossed the lower Rapidan and turned west to face Lee's army. Lee thought the Federal army was heading south and moved to strike it on its flank. The activities of Daniel's Brigade in the move and the resulting Mine Run campaign were described in Daniel's report as follows (*O.R.*, S.I., Vol. XXIX, pt. 1, p. 879):

My brigade (consisting of the Thirty-second North Carolina Troops, Colonel Brabble; Forty-third North Carolina Troops, Lieutenant-Colonel [W. G.] Lewis; Fifty-third North Carolina Troops, Colonel [W. A.] Owens; Forty-fifth North Carolina Troops, Major [M. T.] Smith; and the Second North Carolina Battalion, Capt. Edward Smith) moved with the division about 1 o'clock on the morning of November 27, 1863, from its breastworks at Morton's Ford to Zoar Church, and there took a position in the road, the right resting at the church.

About 8 a.m. the same day the division moved toward Locust Grove, this brigade being in advance. On reaching the hill near Locust Grove, my skirmishers came in contact with the enemy, who appeared in very strong force upon the Germanna road. I was ordered by the major-general commanding to form my line across the road. Before this order was executed I received further orders from the same source to hold the enemy in check with my line of skirmishers and occupy with my brigade a position about 1,000 yards in rear, upon a wooded hill, and hold it until the remainder of the division came up and could be placed in position. During the execution of this order the enemy, greatly outnumbering our troops, pressed my line of skirmishers, but were gallantly held in check by them, under the command of Captain Foster, until the main body of the division came up and threw out skirmishers on his right and left, driving his sharpshooters beyond the crest of the hill.

We occupied this position until about 2 a.m. of the next day, the enemy occasionally feeling our position, but making no direct attack. From here I moved with the division to Mine Run, and occupied the west bank of that stream, my right resting on the turnpike. This position we fortified strongly, and held until the morning of December 2. During this time my skirmishers were frequently engaged with those of the enemy....

On the morning of December 2, I moved, agreeably to instructions, by the right, and crossed the turnpike and occupied the position previously held by Anderson's division, my right resting at a small stream near a furnace. As soon as it was light I discovered that the enemy had retired from my front and pushed my skirmishers well forward to find his whereabouts.

A short time after sunrise I received orders to move to the turnpike and follow the division in pursuit of the enemy on the Germanna road. After marching some 5 or 6 miles on this road, I was ordered to countermarch, and bivouacked for the night near Locust Grove. The next morning I returned with the division to Morton's Ford.

Thus ended the Mine Run campaign, during which the battalion lost 1 man killed and 3 wounded. Both armies went into winter quarters. This battalion went into winter quarters near Orange Court House and did picket duty at Morton's and Raccoon fords during the winter of 1863-1864. On April 11, 1864, Companies D and E of the battalion, being Georgia companies, were transferred out of the battalion and assigned to Georgia regiments. Company D became 2nd Company E, 21st Regiment Georgia Infantry, and Company E became Company A, 60th Regiment Georgia Infantry. For the balance of the war the 2nd Battalion N.C. Infantry consisted of 5 companies.

On the morning of May 4, 1864, while the Federal army under General U. S. Grant was moving across the lower Rapidan, Rodes' Division was picketing the upper Rapidan. About noon of that day General Ewell's Corps began to move down the old turnpike to find the enemy. Rodes' Division was second in line of march. The corps marched to within 2 miles of Locust Grove and halted for the evening. The next morning the march resumed, and contact was made about 11:00 A.M. General Ewell then deployed his front brigades in line of battle. The enemy attacked these troops and drove them back. Daniel's Brigade came up and was sent in on the right of the hard-pressed front line and, with Gordon's Brigade on the left, regained the lost ground. The enemy continued to launch local attacks throughout the day. That night General Stephen D. Ramseur's Brigade was put into position on Daniel's right. During May 6-7 there was no heavy fighting reported on Daniel's front.

Late in the evening of May 7 the orders came to close up on the right. Throughout the night of May 7-8 the troops moved to the right. On May 8 the division arrived on the field at Spotsylvania Court House and formed on the right of the forces entrenched at that place. The division arrived in time to drive the enemy back from the right flank. In doing so, the division drove the enemy for half a mile to his entrenchments. Returning to the original position, the division was placed on the right of the original position and to the left of the famous Mule Shoe. On May 10, 1864, the enemy assaulted and broke through the line held by the brigade on Daniel's right. This forced Daniel to pull back his right. As reinforcements came in to close up the gap, the right of Daniel's Brigade, together with the reinforcements, struck the enemy in flank and forced him to retire from the line he had captured. Rain on May 11 prevented any offensive movements on either side.

When the Federal assault broke through the angle of the Mule Shoe on the morning of May 12, Daniel's Brigade was moved from its works on the left of the Mule Shoe and ordered to advance against the right of the Federal attacking column. Ramseur's Brigade moved in on Daniel's right and, together with Gordon's Division, drove the enemy back to the original line. During the attack and counterattack General Daniel was killed. Desperate hand to hand fighting occurred for the rest of the day and part of the next. Early on the morning of May 13 the men were withdrawn to a new line in their rear. Colonel Bryan Grimes of the 4th Regiment N.C. State Troops was promoted Brigadier General to rank from May 19, 1864, and assigned to command Daniel's old brigade. The brigade remained in line until moved out on May 19.

General Grant made several attempts to break or turn the Confederate line and failed. As Grant's army began moving to the east, the 2nd Corps was ordered to reconnoiter in front of the Confederate line. Ewell's Corps, with Ramseur's Brigade leading, moved out of the entrenchments and engaged the rear elements of the Federal army on May 19. An unsuccessful attack was made, and the Federals, being reinforced, began to press Ewell's men. The Confederates held and took advantage of night to break off the engagement and retire.

This move disclosed the enemy's movement and Lee moved his army accordingly. On May 22 Ewell's Corps arrived at Hanover Junction with Longstreet's Corps. Hill's Corps arrived on the morning of May 23. From here the Army of Northern Virginia moved to the North Anna where they blocked the Federal army once again. At North Anna, May 24-25, Ewell's Corps, now commanded by General Jubal Early, was on the Confederate right and was not engaged. Grant withdrew during the night of May 26-27 and crossed the Pamunkey River, again sidestepping to the Confederate right. Early's Corps marched some 24 miles on May 27 and entrenched between Beaver Dam Creek and Pole Green Church. Longstreet's Corps came up on Early's right, and Hill's Corps extended along the left of Early's line. On May 30, under orders from General Lee, Early moved to attack the Federal left at Bethesda Church. The attack failed to turn the Federal left but did reveal that the enemy was moving to the Confederate right.

The two armies began to concentrate at Cold Harbor, and on June 1 a spirited engagement occurred. Again Lee moved to his right, and the new alignment left Early's Corps on the Confederate left. Early was ordered to move out on June 2 to strike the Federal right. The attack was led by Rodes' Division and met with partial success until Federal reinforcements arrived to drive it back. During the battle of Cold Harbor, June 3, 1864, Early's Corps was under attack by General A. E. Burnside's IX Corps and a part of General G. K. Warren's V Corps. The men of Warren's Corps struck the line held by Rodes' Division and were repulsed. Following the battle, the armies remained in position, observing and skirmishing until June 12, when Grant began moving his army to cross the James River. General Early's Corps was withdrawn from the line on June 11 and was ordered to Lynchburg on June 12 to defend that city against an anticipated attack by troops under General David Hunter. Early was directed to remain in the Shenandoah Valley after striking Hunter's force.

General Early's troops began arriving at Lynchburg on June 17, and the balance arrived the next day. Hunter retired, and after an unsuccessful attempt to overtake the retreating Federals, Early proceeded into the Shenandoah Valley. Still in Grimes' Brigade, Rodes' division, this battalion took part in Early's Valley campaign of 1864. On July 6, 1864, Early crossed into Maryland and advanced on Washington, D.C. At the Battle of Monocacy River, July 9, 1864, Rodes' Division operated on the Baltimore Road while the main fighting occurred on the Washington Road to the division's right. Rodes' Division was in the van when the defenses of Washington came in sight on July 11. Finding the defenses heavily manned on the morning of July 12, Early called off a planned assault, and during the night of July 12 the army began to retire toward Virginia. Back in the Shenandoah Valley, Early's troops were engaged at Stephenson's Depot, July 20, and at Kernstown, July 24, before he moved to Martinsburg and gave his men a rest.

Early in August, 1864, the Federals began concentrating a large force under General Phil Sheridan at Harpers Ferry. On August 10 Early began a series of maneuvers to create the impression of a larger force than he had. His men were northeast of Winchester when Sheridan began to move. On September 19 contact was made, and Early concentrated to receive the attack. The Confederates were making a determined defense east of Winchester when the left came under heavy attack, and the whole line began to retire. During the initial stages of the battle General Rodes was killed as he deployed his division between Gordon's and Ramseur's divisions. These three divisions held the main line against repeated assaults, and only when the left appeared to be turned did they begin to retire to a defensive line close to the town. Again the Federals assaulted the front and left of the line. Word of a Federal column turning the right caused Early to issue orders for a general withdrawal. Upon finding that the troops moving on the right were his own men adjusting the alignment, Early tried to counter the order. It was too late. The troops continued to the rear through Winchester and rallied south of the town. From there they continued the retreat to Fisher's Hill, near Strasburg.

At Fisher's Hill, Major General Stephen D. Ramseur was placed in command of Rodes' Division. Sheridan struck Early's left and center at Fisher's Hill on September 22 and forced a general retreat. Early regrouped at Waynesboro on September 28. Here he received reinforcements and again began to move down the valley. On October 7 his troops occupied New Market. Moving to Fisher's Hill on October 12-13, Early found the enemy on the north bank of Cedar Creek. On October 19, 1864, Early launched a surprise, three-pronged attack on the Federal camp. The attack was initially successful, and the Confederates succeeded in driving the Federals from two defensive lines. Early delayed the attack on the third line and assumed the defensive. Rallying his troops, Sheridan launched a devastating attack and routed Early's army. In this battle the three divisions of the 2nd Corps were commanded by General John B. Gordon. While attempting to rally the men, General Ramseur was mortally wounded and captured. Brigadier General Bryan Grimes, as senior brigadier, was assigned to command the division. Thus, when the 2nd Corps regrouped at New Market after the Cedar Creek disaster, the 2nd Battalion N.C. Infantry was in Grimes' Brigade (commanded by Colonel David G. Cowand, 32nd Regiment N.C. Troops) Grimes' Division. Colonel Cowand commanded the brigade for the balance of the war. With the exception of minor skirmishing and a repulse of a Federal cavalry force on November 22, the army remained inactive.

On December 9 two divisions of the 2nd Corps moved under orders to return to Richmond. A few days later the Rodes-Ramseur Division, under Grimes, was ordered to return to the main army in the Richmond-Petersburg line. On December 14 it marched to Staunton and took the train for Petersburg. The brigade arrived on December 16 and went into winter quarters at Swift Creek, about three miles north of Petersburg. Here it remained until ordered to the right of the Confederate line about February 20, 1865. Grimes' Division had been placed on alert to be ready to move at a moment's notice. On February 5 the brigade was moved to Burgess' Mill but arrived too late to take part in the battle of that day. It returned to its old camp at Swift Creek after remaining a day at Burgess' Mill. On February 17 Grimes' Brigade was one of the three brigades moved to Sutherland's Depot on the right of the line. Cox's Brigade covered the division front at Swift Creek until relieved and then joined the division at Sutherland's. In mid-March, 1865, the division was ordered into the trenches in front of Petersburg. There it remained until the night of March 24 when the 2nd Corps, still under General Gordon, was massed for an attack on Fort Stedman. The sharpshooters who led the attacking force on the morning of March 25 were commanded by Colonel Hamilton A. Brown of the 1st Regiment N.C. State Troops. Although initially successful, the concentrated fire-power and man-power of the Federal army forced the Confederates to retreat.

The remnants of the battalion returned to the trenches with the rest of the brigade and division. During the general assault on the morning of April 2, 1865, the Federals reached the divisional line near Fort Mahone. Grimes' Division attacked and reoccupied its trenches only to have other portions of the line fall to the Federal assault. Retreat was necessary, and it began the night of April 2-3. Gordon's Corps acted as rear guard as the army moved to Amelia Court House. It camped five miles east of the town on April 4 as the army awaited the collection of supplies. The next day the retreat resumed and continued through the night of April 5-6. As the rear guard, Gordon's Division was subjected to attacks by Federal cavalry and infantry. At a crossing of Sayler's Creek, on April 6, Gordon's men made a stand and repulsed the assault on their front. To the south of Gordon's position the Confederates under Generals Ewell and Anderson were severely defeated and captured. The Federals then moved on Gordon's right. The pressure forced the line to break in confusion, but Gordon rallied the survivors west of the creek and rejoined the army. At Farmville on April 7 the men of Gordon's Corps went to the relief of General Mahone's Division. The Federals were held, and the army continued the retreat.

On the night of April 7-8, Gordon's Corps moved to the advance of the army. His lead elements reached Appomattox Court House in the late afternoon of April 8 and halted. Later that evening they found the Federal cavalry in their front. It was decided that an attack should be made the next morning to cut through the enemy. Gordon's men moved into position west of the town during the night. At 5:00 A.M. the advance began and drove the Federal cavalry from the crossroads. The Confederates then took up a defensive position and came under attack by Federal infantry and cavalry. Gordon held his line until word came of the truce.

A cease-fire was arranged and Gordon began to withdraw. The Army of Northern Virginia was surrendered on that date, and on April 12, 1865, 52 members of the 2nd Battalion N.C. Infantry were paroled.

FIELD AND STAFF

LIEUTENANT COLONELS

GREEN, WHARTON J.
Previously served in Company F, 12th Regiment N.C. Troops (2nd Regiment N.C. Volunteers). Discharged from that company on June 18, 1861, having received the position of Colonel in Wise's Legion. Regimental organization never completed and paid as Lieutenant Colonel from July 10, 1861. Appointed Lieutenant Colonel on December 24, 1861, to rank from December 9, 1861. Captured at Roanoke Island on February 8, 1862, and paroled at Elizabeth City, N.C., on February 8, 1862. Not reelected at reorganization of battalion on September 25, 1862. Later served as a volunteer aide on General Junius Daniel's staff.

SHOBER, CHARLES E.
Transferred from the Field and Staff, 45th Regiment N.C. Troops, upon appointment as Lieutenant Colonel to rank from October 1, 1862. Present or accounted for until he resigned June 6, 1863, by reason of "asthma."

ANDREWS, HEZEKIAH L.
Transferred from Company F of this battalion upon appointment as Major on October 1, 1862. Promoted to Lieutenant Colonel on June 6, 1863, and killed at Gettysburg, Pennsylvania, July 1, 1863.

MAJORS

ERWIN, MARCUS
Resided in Buncombe County and appointed Major to rank from August 7, 1861. Captured at Roanoke Island on February 8, 1862, and paroled at Elizabeth City, N. C., on February 21, 1862. Not reelected at reorganization of battalion on September 25, 1862.

HANCOCK, JOHN M.
Transferred from Company F of this battalion upon appointment as Major on June 6, 1863. Wounded at Gettysburg, Pennsylvania, July 1, 1863, and captured at South Mountain, Pennsylvania, July 5, 1863. Confined in hospital at Frederick, Maryland, until transferred to hospital at Baltimore, Maryland, August 10, 1863. Transferred on September 29, 1863, to Johnson's Island, Ohio, where he remained until paroled and sent to Point Lookout, Maryland, March 14, 1865, for exchange. Received in exchange at Cox's Landing, James River, Virginia, March 22, 1865.

IREDELL, JAMES JOHNSTON
Assigned to duty in this battalion from the 53rd Regiment N.C. Troops on August 10, 1863. Killed at Spotsylvania Court House, Virginia, May 12, 1864.

ADJUTANTS

McNUTT, JOHN W.
Resided in Missouri and appointed Adjutant, with the rank of 1st Lieutenant, on December 26, 1861. Also served as Assistant Quartermaster. Captured at Roanoke Island on February 8, 1862, and paroled at Elizabeth City, N.C., on February 21, 1862. Resigned in September, 1862.

GREEN, AUSTIN W.
Transferred from Company F, 12th Regiment N.C. Troops (2nd Regiment N.C. Volunteers) upon appointment as Adjutant with the rank of 1st Lieutenant, September 1, 1862. Wounded May 19, 1864. Present or accounted for through October, 1864. Paroled at Appomattox Court House, Virginia, April 9, 1865.

ASSISTANT QUARTERMASTER

BAHNSON, CHARLES F.
Transferred from Company G of this battalion upon appointment as Captain, Assistant Quartermaster, to rank from January 1, 1863. Present or accounted for on muster rolls through August, 1864. Paroled at Greensboro on April 28, 1865.

ASSISTANT COMMISSARIES OF SUBSISTENCE

SHUFORD, ANDREW HOYLE
Resided in Georgia and appointed Captain, Assistant Commissary of Subsistence, December 24, 1861, to rank from September 27, 1861. Submitted his resignation on September 30, 1862, by reason of his being 53 years old; the loss of his only son in battle; and the necessity to return home to his family. Resignation officially accepted on November 3, 1862.

COOPER, DAVID M.
Transferred from Company B of this battalion upon appointment as Captain, Assistant Commissary of Subsistence, December 1, 1862, to rank from November 30, 1862. Submitted his resignation on December 20, 1862, by reason of age and "owing to the extension of the Conscript Law, the person to whom I entrusted my business, was enrolled as a conscript and I now find my family and business entirely neglected." Resignation officially accepted on December 30, 1862.

CHAPLAIN

BROOKS, HENRY E.
Transferred from Company E of this battalion upon appointment as Chaplain to rank from January 1, 1862. Captured at Gettysburg, Pennsylvania, July 5, 1863, and confined at Fort McHenry, Maryland, August 11, 1863. Sent to City Point, Virginia, for exchange on October 5, 1863. Present or accounted for on muster rolls through August, 1864. Transfer to the Field and Staff, 44th Regiment Georgia Infantry, as Chaplain, approved on May 2, 1864, but exact date of transfer not reported.

SURGEONS

PATTERSON, FRANK
Resided in Warren County and appointed Surgeon on February 17, 1862, to rank from December 8, 1861, having served with the battalion from that time. Captured at Roanoke Island on February 8, 1862, and paroled at Elizabeth City, N.C., on February 21, 1862. Present or accounted for until he submitted his resignation on November 6, 1863, by reason of disability. Resignation officially accepted on November 20, 1863.

GREEN, WILLIAM
Resided in Culpeper County, Virginia, and appointed Surgeon to rank from October 10, 1862. Reported on Field and Staff muster roll for November-December, 1863, as present. Roll of Honor states that he was "transferred to Hardway's Battalion of Artillery."

LEACH, RICHARD V.
Resided in Virginia and appointed Surgeon to rank from July 24, 1862. Reported on Field and Staff muster rolls from January through October, 1864, as present. Paroled at Appomattox Court House, Virginia, April 9, 1865.

ASSISTANT SURGEONS

YOUNG, SAMUEL
Resided in Granville County. Captured at Roanoke Island on February 8, 1862, and paroled at Elizabeth City, N.C., on February 21, 1862. Resigned in July, 1862.

ROBINSON, CICERO F.
Transferred from Company E of this battalion upon appointment as Assistant Surgeon on September 19, 1862. Died January 1, 1863.

McQUEEN, ARCHIBALD A.
Resided in Alabama and appointed Assistant Surgeon to rank from November 13, 1861. Assigned to this battalion on August 10, 1863. Transferred to the Provost Guard, 2nd Army Corps early in 1864.

GODWIN, J. ROBINSON
Resided in Virginia and appointed Assistant Surgeon on October 14, 1862. Assigned to this battalion in February, 1863. Captured at Jacks Mountain, Pennsylvania, July 5, 1863, and confined at Fort Delaware, Delaware, until transferred to Johnson's Island, Ohio, July 18, 1863. Paroled at Johnson's Island and sent to City Point, Virginia, November 17, 1863, for exchange. Present or accounted for from November, 1863, through December, 1864.

SERGEANTS MAJOR

YOUNG, WILLIAM
Resided in Granville County and enlisted in October, 1862, for the war. "Discharged by substitute."

DANIEL, WILLIAM D.
Transferred from Company G, 12th Regiment N.C. Troops (2nd Regiment N.C. Volunteers) upon appointment as Sergeant Major, January

24, 1863. Wounded at Spotsylvania Court House, Virginia, May 12, 1864. Absent wounded until returned to duty January 19, 1865. Detailed on February 6, 1865.

QUARTERMASTER SERGEANT

KELLY, WILLIAM H.
Captured at Roanoke Island on February 8, 1862, and paroled at Elizabeth City, N.C., on February 21, 1862.

COMMISSARY SERGEANTS

ASKEW, GEORGE C.
Transferred from Company H of this battalion upon appointment as Commissary Sergeant, November-December, 1861. Discharged January 20, 1862, by reason of "old age and chronic rheumatism."

RENFROE, JOHN A.
Transferred from Company E of this battalion upon appointment as Commissary Sergeant, September-October, 1863. Transferred to 2nd Company A, 60th Regiment Georgia Infantry, April 11, 1864.

RICHARDSON, ALLEN
Transferred from Company F of this battalion upon appointment as Commissary Sergeant in September, 1864. Present or accounted for until paroled at Appomattox Court House, Virginia, April 9, 1865.

ORDNANCE SERGEANT

RUSSELL, EARL A.
Transferred from Company H of this battalion upon appointment as Ordnance Sergeant prior to September-October, 1863. Present or accounted for until paroled at Appomattox Court House, Virginia, April 9, 1865.

HOSPITAL STEWARDS

POOLE, THEODORE W.
Assigned to the battalion as Hospital Steward on August 22, 1862. Paid as such through December, 1862. Later enlisted in Company C, 1st Regiment Maryland Cavalry.

BAHNSON, HENRY THEODORE
Resided in Forsyth County and enlisted in Wayne County on January 1, 1863, for the war. Mustered in as Hospital Steward. Captured at Gettysburg, Pennsylvania, July 5, 1863, and confined at Point Lookout, Maryland, until transferred to City Point, Virginia, December 24, 1863, for exchange. Present or accounted for until transferred to Company B, 1st Battalion N.C. Sharpshooters on November 5, 1864.

CHIEF MUSICIAN

IDOL, DAVID H.
Transferred from Company G of this battalion May-October, 1863. Captured at Washington, D.C., July 13-26, 1864, and confined at Elmira, New York, until released after taking the Oath of Allegiance on May 15, 1865.

COMPANY A

This company, known as the "Brown Mountain Boys," was organized in Stokes County and enlisted May 4, 1861. It proceeded to Richmond, Virginia, where it joined General Henry A. Wise's Legion and was assigned to Colonel Green's Independent Regiment, Wise's Legion. The regiment failed to complete its organization, and the companies were reorganized as the 2nd Battalion N.C. Infantry on November 1, 1861. In January, 1862, the battalion organization was completed and this company became Company A. Prior to January, 1862, it had been referred to as Company A, Company B, and Captain Milton Smith's Company. After joining the battalion it functioned as a part of the battalion, and its history for the war period is reported as a part of the battalion history.

The information contained in the following roster of the company was compiled principally from company muster rolls which covered from July 9 through December 31, 1861; April 30 through December 31, 1862; March-April, 1863; September, 1863, through April 1, 1864; and September, 1864, through February, 1865. No company muster rolls were found for the period prior to July 9, 1861; January through April, 1862; January-February, 1863; May through August, 1863; April 2 through August, 1864; or for the period after February, 1865. In addition to the company muster rolls, Roll of Honor records, receipt rolls and hospital records, supplemented by state pension applications, United Daughters of the Confederacy records, and postwar rosters and histories, all provided useful information.

OFFICERS

CAPTAIN

SMITH, MILTON
Resided in Stokes County where he enlisted at age 28, May 4, 1861, for twelve months. Appointed Captain on June 13, 1861, to rank from date of enlistment. Captured at Roanoke Island on February 8, 1862, and paroled at Elizabeth City, N.C., on February 21, 1862. Present or accounted for on company muster rolls through October, 1864, when he was reported with the remark that he "deserted the 24th of October."

LIEUTENANTS

GUNTER, DAVID COLUMBUS, 2nd Lieutenant
Resided in Stokes County where he enlisted at age 19, May 4, 1861, for twelve months. Appointed 2nd Lieutenant on June 9, 1861, and commissioned on June 13, 1861. Died at High Point, N.C., February 9, 1862, of disease.

SMITH, EDWIN, 3rd Lieutenant
Resided in Stokes County where he enlisted at age 17, May 4, 1861, for twelve months. Mustered in as Private. Elected 3rd Lieutenant on September 25, 1862, and appointed to rank from date of election. Wounded at Gettysburg, Pennsylvania, July 1-3, 1863. Wounded a second time in June, 1864, and died of wound on June 7, 1864.

SMITH, NATHANIEL G., 2nd Lieutenant
Resided in Stokes County where he enlisted at age 21, May 4, 1861, for twelve months. Mustered in as Private. Captured at Roanoke Island on February 8, 1862, and paroled at Elizabeth City, N.C., February 21, 1862. Elected 2nd Lieutenant on September 25, 1862, and appointed to rank from date of election. Present or accounted for on company muster rolls through April 1, 1864, when he was reported as "absent on leave of absence at Stokes County, N.C."

TUCKER, JAMES B., 1st Lieutenant
Resided in Stokes County where he enlisted at age 26, May 4, 1861, for twelve months. Appointed 1st Lieutenant on June 13, 1861, to rank from date of enlistment. Captured at Roanoke Island on February 8, 1862, and paroled at Elizabeth City, N.C., on February 21, 1862. Present or accounted for on company muster rolls through February, 1865, when he was reported as "absent on furlough in Stokes County, N.C."

NONCOMMISSIONED OFFICERS
AND PRIVATES

BARNES, HIRAM, Private
Resided in Rockingham County and enlisted in Stokes County at age 48, May 4, 1861, for twelve months. Discharged November 20, 1861, for "disability."

BARNES, JAMES M., Private
Resided in Rockingham County and enlisted in Stokes County at age 23, May 4, 1861, for twelve months. Captured at Roanoke Island on February 8, 1862, and paroled at Elizabeth City, N.C., on February 21, 1862. Transferred to Company H, 23rd Battalion Virginia Infantry upon election as Captain April 1, 1863.

BARNES, JOHN F., Private
Resided in Rockingham County and enlisted in Stokes County at age 16, May 4, 1861, for twelve months. Captured at Roanoke Island on February 8, 1862, and paroled at Elizabeth City, N.C., on February 21, 1862. Transferred to Company H, 23rd Battalion Virginia Infantry on April 1, 1863.

BARNES, WILLIAM M., Private
Resided in Stokes County where he enlisted at age 18, May 4, 1861, for twelve months. Mustered in as Corporal. Captured at Roanoke Island on February 8, 1862, and paroled at Elizabeth City, N.C., on February 21, 1862. Reported as Private on April 30-October 31, 1862, muster roll with the remark: "Absent without leave. Joined Virginia State Line Troops." Later enlisted in Company H, 23rd Battalion Virginia Infantry on April 9, 1864.

BEASLEY, WILLIAM, Private
Resided in Stokes County where he enlisted at age 19, May 4, 1861, for twelve months. Captured at Roanoke Island on February 8, 1862, and paroled at Elizabeth City, N.C., on February 21, 1862. Reported on April 30-October 31, 1862, muster roll as "absent without leave. Joined

Colonel Manafees regiment Virginia State Troops."

BOYLES, JOHN H., Private
Resided in Stokes County where he enlisted at age 19, May 4, 1861, for twelve months. Captured at Roanoke Island on February 8, 1862, and paroled at Elizabeth City, N.C., on February 21, 1862. Reported on April 30-October 31, 1862, muster roll as "absent without leave." Later enlisted in Company H, 23rd Battalion Virginia Infantry on April 1, 1863.

BOYLES, WILLIAM W., Private
Resided in Stokes County where he enlisted at age 19, May 4, 1861, for twelve months. Captured at Roanoke Island on February 8, 1862, and paroled at Elizabeth City, N.C., on February 21, 1862. Reported on April 30-October 31, 1862, muster roll as "absent without leave." Later enlisted in Company H, 23rd Battalion Virginia Infantry on April 1, 1863.

BRIMON, RAWLEY, Private
Enlisted in Stokes County on September 1, 1862, for twelve months. Reported on April 30-October 31, 1862, muster roll as "absent. Taken bush furlow." Reported as absent without leave through December, 1862. Later enlisted in Company H, 23rd Battalion Virginia Infantry.

BUNDRANT, DRURY, Private
Resided in Virginia and enlisted in Stokes County at age 20, May 4, 1861, for twelve months. Mustered in as Private. Captured at Roanoke Island on February 8, 1862, and paroled at Elizabeth City, N.C., on February 21, 1862. Appointed Corporal on September 25, 1862. Present or accounted for until he is reported as a Private on the September-October, 1863, muster roll with the remark: "Absent in arrest." Reported as absent sick November, 1863, through April, 1864. Captured at Winchester, Virginia, September 19, 1864, and admitted to U.S.A. Depot Field Hospital, Winchester, the same day with "V.S. left foot, flesh wound." Transferred to U.S.A. General Hospital, West's Buildings, Baltimore, Maryland, October 19, 1864. Transferred on October 25-26, 1864, to Point Lookout, Maryland, where he was confined until paroled and sent to Venus Point, Savannah River, Georgia, October 29, 1864, for exchange. Received at Venus Point on November 15, 1864. Reported as "absent without leave" on the company muster roll for January-February, 1865.

BUNDRANT, JOEL, Private
Resided in Virginia and enlisted in Stokes County at age 18, May 4, 1861, for twelve months. Mustered in as a Private. Captured at Roanoke Island on February 8, 1862, and paroled at Elizabeth City, N.C., on February 21, 1862. Appointed Corporal, September 25, 1862. Present or accounted for until he appears on the March-April, 1863, muster roll as a Private with the remark: "Absent in arrest." Present or accounted for through February, 1865. Paroled at Appomattox Court House, Virginia, April 9, 1865.

BUNDRANT, WILLIAM, Private

Resided in Virginia and enlisted in Stokes County at age 17, May 4, 1861, for twelve months. Captured at Roanoke Island on February 8, 1862, and paroled at Elizabeth City, N.C., on February 21, 1862. Present or accounted for until reported on the November-December, 1862, muster roll as "absent on detached service at Danville, Virginia." Later enlisted in Company H, 23rd Battalion Virginia Infantry on April 1, 1863.

CARTER, HUGH, Private

Resided in Virginia and enlisted in Stokes County at age 25, May 4, 1861, for twelve months. Captured at Roanoke Island on February 8, 1862, and was paroled at Elizabeth City, N.C., on February 21, 1862. Present or accounted for until reported as "absent in arrest" on the March-April, 1863, muster roll. Company muster roll for September-October, 1863, states that he "deserted."

CHATHAM, WILLIAM J., Private

Resided in Virginia and enlisted in Stokes County at age 18, May 4, 1861, for twelve months. Captured at Roanoke Island on February 8, 1862, and was paroled at Elizabeth City, N.C., on February 21, 1862. Company muster roll for April 30-October 31, 1862, carries him as "absent without leave. Joined Colonel Manafees Regiment Virginia State Troops." Later reenlisted in this company on February 24, 1863. Captured at Gettysburg, Pennsylvania, July 4-5, 1863, while detailed to nurse the wounded. Confined at Point Lookout, Maryland, until paroled and transferred to City Point, Virginia, for exchange on March 16, 1864. Again captured on September 22, 1864, at Fisher's Hill, Virginia. Confined on October 1, 1864, at Point Lookout, Maryland, where he joined the U.S. service October 14, 1864, and was assigned to Company B, 4th Regiment U.S. Volunteer Infantry.

CHRISTIAN, CHARLES THOMAS, Private

Resided in Stokes County where he enlisted at age 21, May 4, 1861, for twelve months. Captured at Roanoke Island on February 8, 1862, and was released on parole at Elizabeth City, N.C., February 21, 1862. Detailed for duty in the Quartermaster Department from November-December, 1863, through February, 1865.

CLARK, WILLIAM, Private

Enlisted in Stokes County on September 1, 1862, for twelve months. Absent sick through December, 1862. No further records.

COBLE, JOHN D., Private

Enlisted in Stokes County on September 1, 1864, for the war. Present or accounted for until he appears on the February, 1865, muster roll as "absent sick in hospital."

COLE, BENNETT C., Private

Resided in Davidson County and enlisted in Wake County on August 10, 1864, for the war. Present or accounted for until captured near Petersburg, Virginia, March 25, 1865. Confined at Point Lookout, Maryland, until released after taking the Oath of Allegiance on June 26, 1865.

COLLINS, DRURY T., Private

Resided in Stokes County where he enlisted at age 28, May 4, 1861, for twelve months. Admitted to C.S.A. General Military Hospital No. 4, Wilmington, February 1, 1862, with "rubeola" and was returned to duty February 3, 1862. Reported as "absent without leave" on the company muster roll for April 30-October 31, 1862. Later enlisted in Company H, 23rd Battalion Virginia Infantry on April 1, 1863.

COLLINS, JOHN, Private

Resided in Stokes County where he enlisted at age 20, May 4, 1861, for twelve months. Present or accounted for on company muster rolls until February, 1865, when he was reported as "absent prisoner of war." No further records.

COLLINS, JOSEPH H., Private

Resided in Virginia and enlisted in Stokes County at age 17, May 4, 1861, for twelve months. Captured at Roanoke Island on February 8, 1862, and paroled at Elizabeth City, N.C., on February 21, 1862. Reported as absent without leave on the company muster roll for April 30-October 31, 1862. Later enlisted in Company H, 23rd Battalion Virginia Infantry on April 1, 1863.

COLLINS, LEVI P., Private

Resided in Stokes County where he enlisted at age 20, May 4, 1861, for twelve months. Reported as "absent without leave" on the company muster roll for November-December, 1861. Later enlisted in Company H, 23rd Battalion Virginia Infantry on April 1, 1863.

COLLINS, ROBERT S., Private

Resided in Virginia and enlisted in Stokes County at age 18, May 4, 1861, for twelve months. Captured at Roanoke Island on February 8, 1862, and paroled at Elizabeth City, N.C., February 21, 1862. Present or accounted for until he appears on the company muster roll for March-April, 1863, with the remark: "On detail to Stokes County, N.C."

COLLINS, RUSSELL, Private

Resided in Stokes County where he enlisted at age 25, May 4, 1861, for twelve months. Company muster roll for April 30-October 31, 1862, states that he "joined Colonel Manafees regiment Virginia State Troops." Reported as absent without leave from that date until he again appears as present on company muster roll for September-October, 1863. Present or accounted for until captured at Wilderness, Virginia, May 6, 1864. Confined at Point Lookout, Maryland, May 17, 1864, and transferred to Elmira, New York, August 10, 1864. Paroled at Elmira on October 11, 1864, and sent to Point Lookout, where he was exchanged October 29, 1864. Company muster rolls report him as "absent prisoner of war" through February, 1865.

COLLINS, WILLIAM H. H., Private

Resided in Stokes County where he enlisted at age 18, May 4, 1861, for twelve months. Captured at Roanoke Island on February 8, 1862, and paroled at Elizabeth City, N.C., on February 21,

1862. Reported as "absent without leave" on the company muster roll for April 30-October 31, 1862. Later enlisted in Company H, 23rd Battalion Virginia Infantry on April 1, 1863.

COOK, ALEX, Private
Enlisted in Wake County on September 1, 1864, for the war. Captured at Strasburg, Virginia, October 19, 1864, and confined at Point Lookout, Maryland, October 23, 1864. Paroled at Point Lookout, March 17, 1865, and sent to Aiken's Landing, James River, Virginia, for exchange.

COOPER, JOHN C., Private
Resided in Wake County and enlisted in Stokes County at age 35, December 1, 1862, for twelve months. Present or accounted for until discharged May 3, 1863, "for disability."

COOPER, WILLIAM, Private
Resided in Alamance County and enlisted in Stokes County at age 18, December 1, 1862, for twelve months. Present or accounted for until captured at Gettysburg, Pennsylvania, July 3, 1863. Confined at Fort Delaware, Delaware, July 7-12, 1863, and was transferred to Point Lookout, Maryland, October 18, 1863. Took the Oath of Allegiance and joined the U.S. service at Point Lookout on January 24, 1864. Assigned to Company A, 1st Regiment U.S. Volunteer Infantry.

COX, AUGUSTIN G., Private
Resided in Stokes County where he enlisted at age 18, September 1, 1862, for twelve months. Present or accounted for through April 1, 1864. No further records.

COX, JOHN H., 1st Sergeant
Resided in Stokes County where he enlisted at age 20, May 4, 1861, for twelve months. Mustered in as Corporal. Captured at Roanoke Island on February 8, 1862, and paroled at Elizabeth City, N.C., on February 21, 1862. Reported on company muster rolls as a Private from April 30, 1862, until November-December, 1862, when he appears as 1st Sergeant. Admitted to Jackson Hospital, Richmond, Virginia, May 18, 1864, with "v.s. r. hip, min. b." Furloughed from hospital for 60 days May 26, 1864. Reported on company muster rolls as absent sick through February, 1865.

COX, NEWEL G., Private
Resided in Stokes County where he enlisted at age 22, May 4, 1861, for twelve months. Captured at Roanoke Island on February 8, 1862, and paroled at Elizabeth City, N.C., on February 21, 1862. Present or accounted for until captured near Spotsylvania, Virginia, May 12, 1864. Confined at Point Lookout, Maryland, May 18, 1864, and was transferred to Elmira, New York, August 10, 1864. Paroled at Elmira and sent to James River, Virginia, March 14, 1865, for exchange. Received at Boulware's Wharf, James River, March 18-21, 1865.

COX, ROBERT, Private
Resided in Stokes County where he enlisted at age 19, February 24, 1863, for the war. Present or accounted for until reported on the September-October, 1863, muster roll as "present in arrest." No further records.

CRAVER, A. C., Private
Enlisted August 10, 1864, at Richmond, Virginia, for the war. Present or accounted for through February, 1865. Paroled at Appomattox Court House, Virginia, April 9, 1865.

CRAWFORD, G. W., Private
Enlisted in Wake County on September 1, 1864, for the war. Captured at Strasburg, Virginia, October 19, 1864. Confined on October 23, 1864, at Point Lookout, Maryland, where he was paroled and transferred to Aiken's Landing, James River, Virginia, March 28, 1865, for exchange.

DEARMIN, DRURY A., Private
Resided in Stokes County where he enlisted at age 16, May 1, 1861, for twelve months. Appointed 2nd Lieutenant to rank from date of enlistment. Captured at Roanoke Island on February 8, 1862, and paroled at Elizabeth City, N.C., on February 21, 1862. Not reelected at reorganization of company on September 25, 1862, and appointed 1st Sergeant. Failed to return to company until February 24, 1863, at which time he was reported as Private. September-October, 1863, muster roll reported him as "deserted." Enlisted in Company H, 23rd Battalion Virginia Infantry on October 17, 1863.

DIXON, JAMES T., Private
Resided in Alamance County and enlisted in Wake County, August 10, 1864, for the war. Captured at Strasburg, Virginia, October 19, 1864, and confined at Point Lookout, Maryland, until released after taking the Oath of Allegiance on June 26, 1865.

DOLLARHIDE, TYRE, Private
Enlisted in Stokes County, December 1, 1862, for the war. Deserted on December 14, 1862, and enlisted in Company H, 23rd Battalion Virginia Infantry on April 1, 1863.

DURHAM, J. N., Private
Enlisted in Stokes County, May 4, 1861, for twelve months. Reported on April 30-October 31, 1862, and November-December, 1862, muster rolls as "over 35 years of age." No further records.

EAST, BURRELL, Private
Previously served in Company H, 23rd Battalion Virginia Infantry. Enlisted in this company in Stokes County, December 10, 1863, for the war. Present or accounted for until captured at Petersburg, Virginia, March 25, 1865. Confined at Point Lookout, Maryland, until released after taking the Oath of Allegiance on June 11, 1865.

EAST, JOHN, Private
Resided in Stokes County where he enlisted at age 35, May 4, 1861, for twelve months. Mustered in as Sergeant and reported as Private after September-October, 1861, by reason of being absent without leave. Captured at Gettysburg, Pennsylvania, July 3-5, 1863, and confined at Fort Delaware, Delaware, until paroled on July 30, 1863, and sent to City Point, Virginia, for exchange. Died in hospital at Petersburg, Virginia, August 2, 1863, of "febris typhoides."

FAGG, HENRY H., Private
Resided in Stokes County where he enlisted at

age 22, September 1, 1862, for the war. Present or accounted for until admitted to hospital at Farmville, Virginia, June 3, 1864, with "chronic diarrhoea and debilitas." Furloughed for 60 days on June 7, 1864. Company muster rolls report him as absent sick through October, 1864, and as absent without leave from that date through February, 1865.

FAGG, JOHN H., Private

Resided in Stokes County where he enlisted at age 17, September 1, 1862, for the war. Present or accounted for until admitted to hospital at Farmville, Virginia, May 6-7, 1864, with "feb. typhoides" and "rheum chro." Transferred to Richmond, Virginia, May 21-22, 1864. Reported as absent without leave on company muster rolls after October, 1864.

FAGG, WILLIAM F., Private

Resided in Stokes County where he enlisted at age 23, September 1, 1862, for the war. Reported as absent sick from March-April, 1863, through April 1, 1864, and as absent without leave after that date.

FLIPPEN, JOHN A., Private

Resided in Stokes County where he enlisted at age 18, May 4, 1861, for twelve months. Captured at Roanoke Island on February 8, 1862, and paroled at Elizabeth City, N.C., on February 21, 1862. Company muster roll for April 30-October 31, 1862, reported him as "absent without leave. Joined Colonel Manafees regiment Virginia State Troops." Later enlisted in Company H, 23rd Battalion Virginia Infantry.

FLIPPEN, WILLIAM H., Private

Resided in Stokes County where he enlisted at age 35, May 4, 1861, for twelve months. Captured at Roanoke Island on February 8, 1862, and paroled at Elizabeth City, N.C., on February 21, 1862. Company muster rolls for April 30-October 31, 1862, and November-December, 1862, report him as "over 35 years of age." Not reported on company muster rolls until he was reported as enlisting a second time on December 10, 1863, for the war. Reported as absent sick in Stokes County from September-October, 1864, through February, 1865.

FOREST, JAMES M., Private

Resided in Stokes County where he enlisted at age 30, May 4, 1861, for twelve months. Wounded at Gettysburg, Pennsylvania, July 1-3, 1863. Present or accounted for until paroled at Appomattox Court House, Virginia, April 9, 1865.

FOULK, WILLIAM A., Private

Resided in Stokes County where he enlisted at age 20, May 4, 1861, for twelve months. Captured at Roanoke Island on February 8, 1862, and paroled at Elizabeth City, N.C., on February 21, 1862. Died at home in Stokes County on April 9, 1862.

FRANCE, ELISHA, Private

Resided in Stokes County where he enlisted at age 23, May 4, 1861, for twelve months. Captured on February 8, 1862, at Roanoke Island, where he died February 12-13, 1862.

FRANCIS, CALEB, Private

Resided in Stokes County where he enlisted at age 18, May 4, 1861, for twelve months. Captured at Roanoke Island on February 8, 1862, and paroled at Elizabeth City, N.C., February 21, 1862. Wounded at Gettysburg, Pennsylvania, July 1-3, 1863. Captured in hospital at Gettysburg and confined at DeCamp General Hospital, Davids Island, New York Harbor, July 18, 1863. Admitted to hospital on January 11, 1864, at Point Lookout, Maryland, where he was paroled and sent to City Point, Virginia, March 17, 1864, for exchange. Admitted to hospital at Richmond, Virginia, March 20, 1864, and furloughed for 30 days March 26, 1864. Company muster rolls report him as absent sick through October, 1864, and as absent without leave from that date through February, 1865.

FRANCIS, JAMES M., Sergeant

Resided in Stokes County where he enlisted at age 21, May 4, 1861, for twelve months. Mustered in as Private. Captured at Roanoke Island on February 8, 1862, and paroled at Elizabeth City, N.C., February 21, 1862. Appointed Sergeant at reorganization of company September 25, 1862. Wounded at Gettysburg, Pennsylvania, July 1-3, 1863, and captured in hospital at Gettysburg. Confined at DeCamp General Hospital, Davids Island, New York Harbor, until paroled and sent to City Point, Virginia, August 24, 1863, for exchange. Present or accounted for on company muster rolls through February, 1865.

FRANCIS, JASON M. W., Private

Resided in Stokes County where he enlisted at age 17, May 4, 1861, for twelve months. Captured at Roanoke Island on February 8, 1862, and paroled at Elizabeth City, N.C., February 21, 1862. Company muster roll for April 30-October 31, 1862, states that he "joined Colonel Manafees regiment Virginia State Troops." Enlisted in Company H, 23rd Battalion Virginia Infantry on July 27, 1863. Returned to this company September-October, 1864, and admitted to hospital at Charlottesville, Virginia, September 23, 1864, with a gunshot wound of the left foot. Transferred back to Company H, 23rd Battalion Virginia Infantry, November-December, 1864.

FRANCIS, JOEL M., Corporal

Resided in Stokes County where he enlisted at age 22, May 4, 1861, for twelve months. Mustered in as Corporal. Captured at Roanoke Island on February 8, 1862, and paroled at Elizabeth City, N.C., February 21, 1862. Reported as Private after the company reorganized September 25, 1862, but reappointed Corporal in March-April, 1863. Wounded and captured at Gettysburg, Pennsylvania, July 1-4, 1863. Confined at DeCamp General Hospital, Davids Island, New York Harbor, until paroled and sent to City Point, Virginia, for exchange. Exchanged on September 8, 1863, and admitted to hospital at Petersburg, Virginia, on the same date. Furloughed for 30 days September 16, 1863. Retired to the Invalid Corps on April 22, 1864, but rejoined the company from retirement November 28, 1864. Reported as present through December, 1864, and as absent on furlough in Stokes County on January-February, 1865, muster roll.

FRANCIS, PRESLEY, Private
Resided in Stokes County where he enlisted at age 22, May 4, 1861, for twelve months. Captured at Roanoke Island on February 8, 1862, and paroled at Elizabeth City, N.C., on February 21, 1862. Present or accounted for until captured at Beltsville, Maryland, July 12-13, 1864. Confined July 23-25, 1864, at Elmira, New York, where he died September 27, 1864, of "chronic diarrhoea."

GEORGE, JESSE B., Private
Resided in Stokes County where he enlisted at age 20, May 4, 1861, for twelve months. Captured at Roanoke Island on February 8, 1862, and paroled at Elizabeth City, N.C., on February 21, 1862. Never returned to company and later enlisted in Company H, 23rd Battalion Virginia Infantry on April 1, 1863.

GEORGE, JOHN W., Private
Resided in Stokes County where he enlisted at age 22, May 4, 1861, for twelve months. Captured at Roanoke Island on February 8, 1862, and paroled at Elizabeth City, N.C., on February 21, 1862. Company muster roll for April 30-October 31, 1862, states that he "joined Colonel Manafees regiment Virginia State Troops." Enlisted in Company H, 23rd Battalion Virginia Infantry on April 1, 1863, and deserted from that unit and re-enlisted in this company in Beaufort County, April 10, 1863, for the war. Present or accounted for on company muster rolls through February, 1865.

GEORGE, JOSEPH, Private
Resided in Stokes County where he enlisted at age 16, September 1, 1862, for the war. Present or accounted for until paroled at Appomattox Court House, Virginia, April 9, 1865.

GILMER, WILLIAM, Private
Resided in Stokes County where he enlisted at age 30, May 4, 1861, for twelve months. Captured at Roanoke Island on February 8, 1862, and paroled at Elizabeth City, N.C., February 21, 1862. Present or accounted for on company muster rolls through February, 1865.

GUNTER, JAMES M., Private
Resided in Virginia and enlisted in Stokes County at age 20, May 4, 1861, for twelve months. Present or accounted for until detailed for hospital duty June 10, 1864. September-October, 1864, muster roll reports him with the remark: "Deserted Liberty Hospital."

HARNER, A., Private
Reported on the September-October, 1864, muster roll as absent sick in hospital. Date, place, and period of enlistment not given. November-December, 1864, muster roll states that he died November 8, 1864.

HART, H. H., Private
Enlisted in Stokes County on May 4, 1861, for twelve months. Captured at Roanoke Island on February 8, 1862, and paroled at Elizabeth City,

N.C., on February 21, 1862. Company muster roll for April 30-October 31, 1862, carries the remark: "Over age. I was ordered to drop him from the rolls by Colonel Green."

HART, WILLIAMSON, Private
Resided in Stokes County where he enlisted at age 32, September 1, 1862, for twelve months. Present or accounted for until he appears on the September-October, 1863, muster roll with the remark: "Deserted May 1863." Enlisted in Company H, 23rd Battalion Virginia Infantry on June 10, 1863.

HEMMINGS, JAMES W., Private
Resided in Rockingham County and enlisted in Stokes County at age 22, May 4, 1861, for twelve months. Captured at Roanoke Island on February 8, 1862, and paroled at Elizabeth City, N.C., February 21, 1862. Company muster rolls state that he "joined Colonel Manafees regiment Virginia State Troops after being paroled." Later enlisted in Company H, 23rd Battalion Virginia Infantry on April 1, 1863.

HEMMINGS, WILLIAM C., Private
Resided in Rockingham County and enlisted in Stokes County at age 21, May 4, 1861, for twelve months. Captured at Roanoke Island on February 8, 1862, and paroled at Elizabeth City, N.C., on February 21, 1862. Reported on the company muster roll for April 30-October 31, 1862, as "absent, taken bush furlow." Later enlisted in Company H, 23rd Battalion Virginia Infantry on February 1, 1864.

HENDERSON, J. R., Private
Appears on a list of prisoners of war taken by the forces of General A. E. Burnside at Roanoke Island, dated February 15, 1862. No further records.

HICKES, ELIJAH, Drummer
Enlisted December 9, 1862, in Stokes County for twelve months. Appears as present with rank of Drummer on the company muster roll for November-December, 1862. No further records.

HILL, F., Private
Enlisted in Lenoir County, February 8, 1863, for the war. Company muster roll for March-April, 1863, states that he was absent sick in hospital at Tarboro. Appears on the September-October, 1863, muster roll as "deserted." No further records.

HILL, JAMES M., Private
Resided in Stokes County where he enlisted at age 22, May 4, 1861, for twelve months. Present or accounted for until reported on the September-October, 1863, muster roll as "absent without leave."

HILL, JAMES O., Corporal
Resided in Stokes County where he enlisted at age 22, May 4, 1861, for twelve months. Mustered in as Private. Captured at Roanoke Island on February 8, 1862, and paroled at Elizabeth City, N.C., on February 21, 1862. Appointed Corporal, January-April, 1863. Wounded at Gettysburg, Pennsylvania, July 1-3, 1863. Present or accounted for until admitted to Receiving and Wayside Hospital, Richmond, Virginia, May 27, 1864.

Transferred to Chimborazo Hospital No. 3, Richmond, May 28, 1864, with "dysentery." Returned to duty June 6, 1864.

HILL, THOMAS, Private

Born in Halifax County and resided as a farmer in Stokes County where he enlisted at age 45, May 4, 1861, for twelve months. Captured at Roanoke Island on February 8, 1862, and paroled at Elizabeth City, N.C., on February 21, 1862. Discharged November 11, 1862, by reason of "being a non-conscript." Reenlisted in Stokes County as a substitute April 30, 1863. Captured at Gettysburg, Pennsylvania, July 3, 1863, and confined at Fort Delaware, Delaware, until transferred to Point Lookout, Maryland, October 18, 1863. Paroled for exchange at Point Lookout, September 30, 1864. Admitted to General Hospital No. 24, Richmond, Virginia, with "chronic diarrhoea" and furloughed for 40 days October 11, 1864. Reported on company muster rolls as absent through February, 1865. Again captured at Dinwiddie Court House, Virginia, on April 2, 1865, and confined at Point Lookout until released after taking the Oath of Allegiance on June 21, 1865.

HILL, WILLIAM S., Private

Resided in Stokes County where he enlisted at age 20, May 4, 1861, for twelve months. Captured at Roanoke Island on February 8, 1862, and paroled at Elizabeth City, N.C., on February 21, 1862. Wounded and captured at Gettysburg, Pennsylvania, July 3, 1863. Confined at Point Lookout, Maryland, where he took the Oath of Allegiance to the U.S. and joined the U.S. service January 22, 1864. Later assigned to 1st Regiment U.S. Volunteer Infantry.

HOLE, ELI, Private

Resided in Stokes County where he enlisted at age 17, May 4, 1861, for twelve months. Captured at Roanoke Island on February 8, 1862, and paroled at Elizabeth City, N.C., February 21, 1862. Present or accounted for until he died in hospital at Wilson, N.C., May 13, 1863, of "febris typhoides."

HOOKER, JOHN W., Corporal

Resided in Virginia and enlisted in Stokes County at age 23, May 4, 1861, for twelve months. Mustered in as Private. Captured at Roanoke Island on February 8, 1862, and paroled at Elizabeth City, N.C., February 21, 1862. Appointed Corporal on December 1, 1864. Present or accounted for until captured near Petersburg, Virginia, March 25, 1865. Confined at Point Lookout, Maryland, until released after taking the Oath of Allegiance on June 27, 1865.

HUDSON, JOSEPH H., Private

Enlisted in Stokes County, September 1, 1862, for twelve months. Present or accounted for until admitted to Jackson Hospital, Richmond, Virginia, February 20, 1865, with "febris cont." Returned to duty March 17, 1865. Paroled at Appomattox Court House, Virginia, April 9, 1865.

HUNLY, HENRY H., Private

Resided in Virginia and enlisted in Stokes County at age 36, September 1, 1862, for twelve months.

Present or accounted for until he appears on the February 29-April 1, 1864, muster roll with the remark: "Died in hospital at Orange Court House, Virginia, February 22, 1864."

HURT, HENRY, Private

Resided in Virginia and enlisted at age 35, May 4, 1861, for twelve months. Roll of Honor states that he was "discharged for disability of body and mind."

JESSUP, G. W., Private

Born in Surry County and resided as a farmer in Stokes County where he enlisted at age 49, May 4, 1861, for twelve months. Discharged October 10, 1861, by reason of "chronic rheumatism."

JOHNSON, NORMAN, Private

Appears on a list of men forwarded to Provost Marshal, 8th Army Corps, from Provost Marshal, Annapolis, Maryland, dated March 31, 1865, which states that he "escaped by mixing with our prisoners and came here on Flag of Truce boat March 29, 1865." Confined at Military Prison, Baltimore, Maryland, and was released "to go North" after taking Oath of Allegiance on April 1, 1865.

JONES, AUSTIN RUSSELL, Private

Enlisted in Stokes County, September 1, 1864, for the war. Present or accounted for through February, 1865. Paroled at Appomattox Court House, Virginia, April 9, 1865.

JONES, JOHN W., Corporal

Resided in Stokes County where he enlisted at age 19, May 4, 1861, for twelve months. Mustered in as Private. Captured at Roanoke Island on February 8, 1862, and was paroled at Elizabeth City, N.C., on February 21, 1862. Appointed Corporal, March-April, 1863. Captured near Spotsylvania Court House, Virginia, May 10, 1864, and confined at Point Lookout, Maryland, May 18, 1864. Transferred on August 10, 1864, to Elmira, New York, where he remained until released after taking the Oath of Allegiance on July 3, 1865.

LANE, JAMES A., Private

Name appears as a signature to a parole of prisoners of war belonging to the Army of Northern Virginia paroled at Greensboro, May 25-26, 1865.

LANKFORD, WYATT, Private

Resided in Stokes County where he enlisted at age 27, May 4, 1861, for twelve months. Captured at Roanoke Island on February 8, 1862, and paroled at Elizabeth City, N.C., February 21, 1862. Reported on the company muster roll for November-December, 1863, as "present in arrest." Appears on muster rolls as "absent at Richmond, Virginia, undergoing sentence of General Court Martial" from that date through October, 1864. Absent without leave from September-October, 1864, through February, 1865.

LAWSON, ALLEN, Private

Resided in Guilford County and enlisted in Stokes County at age 24, December 1, 1862, for the war. Present or accounted for until captured at Spotsylvania Court House, Virginia, May 20, 1864. Confined at Point Lookout, Maryland, until transferred to Elmira, New York, July 3-6, 1864. Released at Elmira after taking the Oath of Allegiance on July 7, 1865.

LAWSON, BRAXTON R., Private
Resided in Stokes County where he enlisted at age 18, May 4, 1861, for twelve months. Present or accounted for until reported on the March-April, 1863, muster roll as absent in arrest. September-October, 1863, muster roll states that he "deserted July, 1863." No further records.

LAWSON, HAMTON, Private
Enlisted December 1, 1862, for the war. Appears as present on the company muster roll for November-December, 1862. No further records.

LAWSON, JAMES A., Private
Resided in Stokes County where he enlisted November 1, 1864, for the war. Present or accounted for on company muster rolls through February, 1865. Captured at Burkeville, Virginia, April 6, 1865, and was confined at Point Lookout, Maryland, on April 15, 1865. Released at Point Lookout after taking the Oath of Allegiance on June 28, 1865.

LAWSON, JOHN, Private
Enlisted in Stokes County, September 1, 1862, for twelve months. Reported on company muster rolls as absent sick at home through December, 1862. No further records.

LEAKE, JAMES AUSTIN, Sergeant
Resided in Stokes County where he enlisted at age 21, May 4, 1861, for twelve months. Mustered in as Private. Captured at Roanoke Island on February 8, 1862, and paroled at Elizabeth City, N.C., on February 21, 1862. Appointed Sergeant, January-April, 1863. Wounded at Gettysburg, Pennsylvania, July 1, 1863, and captured while in hospital at Gettysburg on July 1-5, 1863. Wound described as "g. s. foot." Transferred on July 21, 1863, to DeCamp General Hospital, Davids Island, New York Harbor, where he remained until paroled and sent to City Point, Virginia, for exchange on August 24, 1863. Company muster rolls report him as absent on sick leave through October, 1864, and as absent without leave from that date through February, 1865.

LINVILLE, RUEL, Private
Enlisted in Stokes County, September 1, 1862, for twelve months. Company muster roll for April 30-October 31, 1862, states that he was "absent without leave." Later enlisted in Company H, 23rd Battalion Virginia Infantry on April 1, 1863.

MABE, ANDERSON, Private
Resided in Stokes County where he enlisted at age 25, May 4, 1861, for twelve months. Captured at Roanoke Island on February 8, 1862, and paroled at Elizabeth City, N.C., on February 21, 1862. Reported on the company muster roll for April 30-October 31, 1862, as "absent—taken bush furlough." Appears on a monthly pay voucher for the period from June 30, 1863, to August 31, 1863, which states that he was "under guard to return to regiment." No further records.

MABE, EDWARDE, Private
Company muster roll for September-October,

1864, states that he "deserted the 6th of October, 1864," but does not give date or place of enlistment.

MABE, GIDEON, Private
Resided in Stokes County where he enlisted at age 24, May 4, 1861, for twelve months. Captured at Roanoke Island on February 8, 1862, and paroled at Elizabeth City, N.C., on February 21, 1862. Died March 30, 1862, in Stokes County.

MABE, ISAAC, Sergeant
Resided in Stokes County where he enlisted at age 18, May 4, 1861, for twelve months. Mustered in as Private. Captured at Roanoke Island on February 8, 1862, and paroled at Elizabeth City, N.C., on February 21, 1862. Appointed Sergeant, April-October, 1864. Captured near Spotsylvania Court House, Virginia, May 10, 1864, and confined at Point Lookout, Maryland, until transferred to Elmira, New York, August 10, 1864. Died at Elmira, August 27, 1864, of "chronic diarrhoea."

MABE, JOSEPH, Private
Born in Stokes County where he resided as a farmer and enlisted at age 35, May 4, 1861, for twelve months. Captured at Roanoke Island on February 8, 1862, and paroled at Elizabeth City, N.C., February 21, 1862. Reported as absent sick on company muster rolls from September-October, 1863, until discharged for disability on February 29, 1864.

MABE, MOSES, Private
Resided in Stokes County where he enlisted at age 27, December 1, 1862, for the war. Died of disease in hospital at Raleigh, May 10-11, 1863.

McHONE, ANDERSON, Private
Resided in Stokes County where he enlisted at age 25, May 4, 1861, for twelve months. Present or accounted for on company muster rolls through April, 1864. No further records.

McHONE, JOHN, Private
Resided in Stokes County where he enlisted at age 22, May 4, 1861, for twelve months. Captured at Roanoke Island on February 8, 1862, and paroled at Elizabeth City, N.C., February 21, 1862. Captured at Gettysburg, Pennsylvania, July 3-5, 1863, and confined at Fort McHenry, Maryland. Transferred to Fort Delaware, Delaware, July 10, 1863, and to Point Lookout, Maryland, October 18, 1863. Took the Oath of Allegiance and joined the U.S. service at Point Lookout, January 22, 1864. Assigned to Company G, 1st Regiment U.S. Volunteer Infantry.

MANRING, GABRIEL H., Private
Resided in Stokes County where he enlisted at age 20, May 4, 1861, for twelve months. Captured at Roanoke Island on February 8, 1862, and paroled at Elizabeth City, N.C., on February 21, 1862. Again captured at Gettysburg, Pennsylvania, July 5, 1863. Confined at Point Lookout, Maryland, until paroled and sent to Cox's Landing, James River, Virginia, for exchange. Received at Cox's Landing, February 14-15, 1865.

MATTHEWS, CALEB, Private
Resided in Stokes County where he enlisted at

age 22, May 4, 1861, for twelve months. Captured at Roanoke Island on February 8, 1862, and paroled at Elizabeth City, N.C., on February 21, 1862. Reported on the company muster roll for April 30-October 31, 1862, as "absent—taken bush furlow." Appears as absent without leave through December, 1862. There are no company muster rolls from that date until his death on "July 13, 1863, at Williamsport, Md."

MATTHEWS, HENDERSON, Private
Resided in Stokes County where he enlisted at age 20, June 15, 1863, for the war. "Deserted September 15, 1863."

MOOREFIELD, WILLIAM, Private
Resided in Stokes County where he enlisted at age 40, October 1, 1863, for the war. Present or accounted for until captured near Petersburg, Virginia, March 25, 1865. Confined at Point Lookout, Maryland, until released after taking the Oath of Allegiance on June 29, 1865.

MOSS, WILLIAM A., Private
Resided in Stokes County where he enlisted at age 18, May 4, 1861, for twelve months. Captured at Roanoke Island on February 8, 1862, and paroled at Elizabeth City, N.C., on February 21, 1862. Company muster roll for April 30-October 31, 1862, states that he "joined Colonel Manafees regiment Virginia State Troops." Later enlisted in Company H, 23rd Battalion Virginia Infantry on April 1, 1863.

MUCKLE, ISAAC, Private
Enlisted in Wake County, September 10, 1864, for the war. Present or accounted for through February, 1865, when he was reported as "sick on furlough in Moore County, N.C."

NELSON, R. A., Private
Resided in Stokes County where he enlisted at age 23, February 24, 1863, for the war. Died in hospital at Wilson, N.C., May 4-15, 1863, of "febris typhoides."

NUNN, ASA, Private
Resided in Stokes County where he enlisted at age 25, September 1, 1862, for the war. Did not report to company because of sickness and enlisted a second time in the company on February 24, 1863. Captured at Gettysburg, Pennsylvania, July 5, 1863, and confined at DeCamp General Hospital, Davids Island, New York Harbor, until paroled and exchanged at City Point, Virginia, September 8, 1863. Reported as absent on parole, absent sick, and absent without leave through February, 1865.

NUNN, MARTIN, Private
Resided in Stokes County where he enlisted at age 18, February 24, 1863, for the war. Reported as absent on sick leave September-October, 1863, and as absent without leave from that date through February, 1865.

OVERBEY, JOHN B., Private
Born in Halifax County, Virginia, and enlisted at Richmond, Virginia, at age 16, October 19, 1861, for twelve months. Died in hospital at Richmond on December 18, 1861, from "the effects of measles."

OWENS, FLOYD, Private
Resided in Stokes County where he enlisted at age 18, May 4, 1861, for twelve months. Captured at Roanoke Island on February 8, 1862, and paroled at Elizabeth City, N.C., February 21, 1862. Company muster roll for April 30-October 31, 1862, states that he "joined Colonel Manafees regiment Virginia State Troops." Later enlisted in Company H, 23rd Battalion Virginia Infantry on April 1, 1863.

OWENS, ISHAM, Private
Previously served in Company H, 23rd Battalion Virginia Infantry. Enlisted in this company in Stokes County at age 35, February 1, 1864, for the war. Present or accounted for through April 1, 1864.

OWENS, JESSE, Private
Resided in Stokes County and enlisted at age 24, December 1, 1862, for the war. Deserted December 14-20, 1862, and later enlisted in Company H, 23rd Battalion Virginia Infantry on April 1, 1863.

OWENS, WILLIAM, Jr., Private
Resided in Stokes County where he enlisted at age 25, May 4, 1861, for twelve months. Captured at Roanoke Island on February 8, 1862, and paroled at Elizabeth City, N.C., on February 21, 1862. Company muster roll for April 30-October 31, 1862, states that he "joined Colonel Manafees regiment Virginia State Troops." Later enlisted in Company H, 23rd Battalion Virginia Infantry on April 1, 1863.

OWENS, WILLIAM, Sr., Private
Enlisted in Stokes County, September 1, 1862, for the war. Reported on the company muster roll for April 30-October 31, 1862, with the remark: "Joined Colonel Manafees regiment Virginia State Troops." Later enlisted in Company H, 23rd Battalion Virginia Infantry on April 1, 1863.

PALMER, ELIAS, Private
Previously served in Company H, 23rd Battalion Virginia Infantry. Enlisted in this company in Stokes County at age 25, December 10, 1863, for the war. Present or accounted for on company muster rolls through April 1, 1864. No further records.

PRUITT, HARDIN, Private
Resided in Stokes County where he enlisted at age 23, May 4, 1861, for twelve months. Captured at Roanoke Island on February 8, 1862, and paroled at Elizabeth City, N.C., on February 21, 1862. Company muster roll for April 30-October 31, 1862, states that he was "detailed to work in government shop in N.C." Admitted to C.S.A. General Hospital, Charlottesville, Virginia, September 1, 1864, with "rheum. act." and was returned to duty September 6, 1864. Company muster rolls carry him as absent without leave from that date through February, 1865.

PRUITT, JAMES M., Private
Resided in Stokes County where he enlisted at age 18, May 4, 1861, for twelve months. Captured at Roanoke Island on February 8, 1862, and paroled at Elizabeth City, N.C., February 21, 1862. Company muster roll for April 30-October 31,

1862, states that he was "absent on bush furlow." Reenlisted in this company in Stokes County, December 10, 1863. Company muster rolls report that he "deserted the 29th of May 1864."

RAY, WILLIAM S., Sergeant
Resided in Stokes County where he enlisted at age 26, May 4, 1861, for twelve months. Mustered in as Sergeant. Present or accounted for until captured in hospital at Gettysburg, Pennsylvania, after the battle of July 1-3, 1863. Transferred on July 21, 1863, to DeCamp General Hospital, Davids Island, New York Harbor, where he was confined until paroled and sent to City Point, Virginia, August 24, 1863, for exchange. Present or accounted for on company muster rolls from that date through February, 1865. Paroled at Burkeville, Virginia, April 14-17, 1865.

RIGHT, JOHN E., Private
Resided in Stokes County where he enlisted at age 35, March 10, 1863, for the war. Present or accounted for through February, 1865. Paroled at Appomattox Court House, Virginia, April 9, 1865.

ROBERSON, C. N., Private
Enlisted in Stokes County, September 1, 1864, for the war. Captured at Fisher's Hill, Virginia, September 22, 1864, and confined at Point Lookout, Maryland, until paroled and transferred to Aiken's Landing, James River, Virginia, March 17, 1865, for exchange. Received at Boulware's Wharf, James River, March 19, 1865, for exchange.

RUTLEY, A. H., Private
Enlisted in Stokes County, September 1, 1862, for the war. Reported on the company muster roll for April 30-October 31, 1862, as "absent—taken bush furlow." Absent without leave through December, 1862. No further records.

SAMS, ELIJAH, Private
Enlisted in Stokes County, May 4, 1861, for twelve months. Captured at Roanoke Island on February 8, 1862, and paroled at Elizabeth City, N.C., February 21, 1862. Company muster rolls state that he "joined Colonel Manafees regiment after exchanged." Later enlisted in Company H, 23rd Battalion Virginia Infantry on April 1, 1863.

SAMS, GREEN L., Sergeant
Resided in Stokes County where he enlisted at age 17, May 4, 1861, for twelve months. Mustered in as Private. Captured at Roanoke Island on February 8, 1862, and paroled at Elizabeth City, N.C., on February 21, 1862. Appointed Sergeant September 25, 1862. Present or accounted for on company muster rolls through February, 1865. Captured at Farmville, Virginia, April 6, 1865, and confined at Point Lookout, Maryland, until released after taking the Oath of Allegiance on June 20, 1865.

SAMS, JAMES, Private
Born in Henry County, Virginia, and resided as a farmer in Stokes County where he enlisted at age 52, May 4, 1861, for twelve months. Captured at Roanoke Island on February 8, 1862, and paroled at Elizabeth City, N.C., February 21, 1862.

Discharged November 3, 1862, by reason of "being a non-conscript."

SAMS, WILLIAM A., Private
Resided in Guilford County and enlisted in Stokes County at age 17, September 1, 1862, for the war. Company muster roll for September-October, 1863, reported that he was wounded at Gettysburg, Pennsylvania. Captured at Spotsylvania Court House, Virginia, May 20, 1864, and confined at Point Lookout, Maryland, until transferred to Elmira, New York, July 6, 1864. Released at Elmira after taking the Oath of Allegiance on May 21, 1865.

SANDS, ANDERSON, Private
Resided in Stokes County where he enlisted at age 20, September 1, 1862, for the war. Present or accounted for on company muster rolls through April 1, 1864. Died at hospital in Richmond, Virginia, June 4, 1864, of "vulnus sclopet."

SANDS, JAMES, Private
Resided in Stokes County where he enlisted at age 21, May 4, 1861, for twelve months. Died March 15, 1862, in Stokes County.

SAWYER, W. S., Private
Appears on a list of prisoners of war taken by the forces of General A. E. Burnside on Roanoke Island, February 8, 1862, and released on parole at Elizabeth City, N.C., February 21, 1862.

SHAW, ALBERT G., Private
Resided in Stokes County where he enlisted at age 22, May 4, 1861, for twelve months. Captured at Roanoke Island on February 8, 1862, and paroled at Elizabeth City, N.C., February 21, 1862. Present or accounted for until detailed for hospital duty at Richmond, Virginia, December 29, 1863. Absent detailed until captured at hospital in Richmond on April 3, 1865. Paroled at Jackson Hospital, Richmond, April 20, 1865.

SHELTON, FRANKLIN, Private
Resided in Stokes County where he enlisted at age 35, November 8, 1863, for the war. Present or accounted for on company muster rolls until admitted to hospital at Danville, Virginia, June 7, 1864, with "diarrhoea chronic." Furloughed June 17, 1864. Admitted to hospital at Raleigh July 1, 1864, with "anaemia" and was returned to duty August 11, 1864. Company muster rolls report him as absent without leave from September-October, 1864, through February, 1865.

SHELTON, JAMES, Private
Enlisted in Madison County, July 4, 1861, for twelve months. Mustered in as Musician. Appears as a Private after October, 1861. Captured at Roanoke Island on February 8, 1862, and paroled at Elizabeth City, N.C., February 21, 1862. No further records.

SHELTON, WILLIAM F., Private
Resided in Stokes County where he enlisted at age 22, May 4, 1861, for twelve months. Reported on the company muster roll for April 30-October 31, 1862, as "absent without leave." Later enlisted in Company H, 23rd Battalion Virginia Infantry on April 1, 1863.

SHEPHERD, JAMES T., Private
Resided in Stokes County where he enlisted September 1, 1862, for the war. Company muster roll for April 30-October 31, 1862, reported him as "absent without leave." Later enlisted in Company H, 23rd Battalion Virginia Infantry on April 1, 1863.

SIMMONS, E. J., Private
Resided in Stokes County and enlisted at age 27, September 1, 1862, for the war. Reported as "absent sick at home" on company muster rolls through September 1, 1862. Rejoined the company February 24, 1863. Present or accounted for until captured near Spotsylvania Court House, Virginia, May 10, 1864. Confined at Point Lookout, Maryland, until transferred to Elmira, New York, August 10-14, 1864. Died at Elmira, October 2, 1864, of "chronic diarrhoea."

SIMMONS, EPHRAIM B., Private
Resided in Stokes County where he enlisted at age 20, September 1, 1862, for the war. Captured at Gettysburg, Pennsylvania, July 3-6, 1863, and confined at Fort Delaware, Delaware, July 10, 1863. Transferred on October 18, 1863, to Point Lookout, Maryland, where he died August 8, 1864.

SIMMONS, GABRIEL J., Private
Resided in Stokes County where he enlisted at age 23, May 4, 1861, for twelve months. Captured at Roanoke Island on February 8, 1862, and paroled at Elizabeth City, N.C., February 21, 1862. Reported on the company muster roll for April 30-October 31, 1862, as "absent—taken bush furlow." Returned to company November-December, 1862, and reported as absent in arrest until detailed for hospital duty at Richmond, Virginia, October 1, 1863. Absent detailed through February, 1865.

SIMMONS, GEORGE A., Private
Resided in Stokes County where he enlisted at age 17, May 4, 1861, for twelve months. Captured at Roanoke Island on February 8, 1862, and paroled at Elizabeth City, N.C., February 21, 1862. Wounded and captured while in hospital at Gettysburg, Pennsylvania, July 1-3, 1863. Admitted to Camp Letterman U.S.A. General Hospital, Gettysburg, July 27, 1863, with "g. fracture, r. thigh, up. 3rd," and died October 26, 1863.

SIMMONS, JOHN F., Private
Resided in Stokes County where he enlisted at age 28, February 24, 1863, for the war. Present or accounted for on company muster rolls until captured near Spotsylvania Court House, Virginia, May 10, 1864. Confined at Point Lookout, Maryland, until transferred to Elmira, New York, August 10-14, 1864. Died at Elmira, March 13, 1865, of "chronic diarrhoea."

SIMMONS, MATHEW E., Private
Resided in Stokes County where he enlisted at age 18, May 4, 1861, for twelve months. Reported on the company muster rolls as present through December, 1862. Enlisted in Company H, 23rd Battalion Virginia Infantry on April 1, 1863.

SIMMONS, PETER M., Private
Resided in Stokes County where he enlisted at age 23, May 4, 1861, for twelve months. Captured at Roanoke Island on February 8, 1862, and paroled at Elizabeth City, N.C., February 21, 1862. Present or accounted for until captured near Spotsylvania Court House, Virginia, May 10, 1864. Confined at Point Lookout, Maryland, until transferred to Elmira, New York, August 14, 1864. Died at Elmira on September 29, 1864, of "chronic diarrhoea."

SIMMONS, THOMAS, Private
Enlisted in Stokes County, September 1, 1862, for the war. Reported on the company muster roll for April 30-October 31, 1862, as "absent—taken bush furlow." Appears on muster rolls as absent without leave through December, 1862. No further records.

SLAUGHTER, JAMES N., Private
Resided in Stokes County where he enlisted at age 23, May 4, 1861, for twelve months. Mustered in as Sergeant and reduced to ranks November-December, 1861. Appointed Drummer, December 20, 1862; however, he again appears as Private, March-April, 1863. Present or accounted for until captured at Spotsylvania Court House, Virginia, June 10, 1864. Confined at Point Lookout, Maryland, until transferred to Elmira, New York, July 25-28, 1864. Paroled at Elmira and sent to James River, Virginia, March 2, 1865, for exchange. Admitted to Jackson Hospital, Richmond, Virginia, March 6, 1865, with "debilitas" and furloughed for 30 days on March 9, 1865.

SLAUGHTER, WILLIAM H., Private
Enlisted in Stokes County, November 28, 1864, for the war. Present or accounted for on company muster rolls through February, 1865. Paroled at Appomattox Court House, Virginia, April 9, 1865.

SMITH, CHARLES, Private
Enlisted in Stokes County, September 1, 1862, for the war. Company muster roll for April 30-October 31, 1862, states that he "deserted October 12 from camp near Drury Bluff." No further records.

SMITH, EDWARD, Sergeant
Enlisted in Stokes County at age 23, May 4, 1861, for twelve months. Mustered in as Private and appointed Sergeant, November-December, 1861. Captured at Roanoke Island on February 8, 1862, and paroled at Elizabeth City, N.C., February 21, 1862. Company muster roll for April 20-October 31, 1862, states that he was "absent without leave— joined Virginia State Line Service." No further records.

SMITH, JOHN, Private
Resided in Stokes County where he enlisted at age 18, March 14, 1863, for the war. Appears on a register of U.S.A. Depot Field Hospital, Winchester, Virginia, being admitted September 19, 1864, from the field with "v.s." and states that he died September 20, 1864.

SMITH, JOHN T., Private
Enlisted in Stokes County, September 1, 1862, for the war. Mustered in as Private and appointed Corporal September 25, 1862. Again appears as Private after November-December, 1862. Present

or accounted for through February, 1865, when he is reported as absent on sick furlough in Surry County.

SMITH, JOSHUA, Private
Resided in Stokes County where he enlisted at age 23, May 4, 1861, for twelve months. Captured at Roanoke Island on February 8, 1862, and paroled at Elizabeth City, N.C., February 21, 1862. Present or accounted for on company muster rolls through February, 1865. Paroled at Appomattox Court House, Virginia, April 9, 1865.

SMITH, LEROY, Private
Enlisted in Stokes County, September 22, 1864, for the war. Present or accounted for through February, 1865.

SMITH, MARTIN V. B., 1st Sergeant
Enlisted in Stokes County at age 25, May 4, 1861, for twelve months. Mustered in as 1st Sergeant. Captured at Roanoke Island on February 8, 1862, and paroled at Elizabeth City, N.C., February 21, 1862. Died April 7, 1862, in Stokes County.

SMITH, NOAH, Private
Enlisted in Stokes County, September 1, 1864, for the war. Captured at Fisher's Hill, Virginia, September 22, 1864, and confined at Point Lookout, Maryland, until paroled and transferred to Aiken's Landing, Virginia, March 17, 1865, for exchange. Received at Boulware's Wharf, James River, Virginia, March 19, 1865, for exchange.

SMITH, PETER, Private
Resided in Stokes County where he enlisted at age 27, September 1, 1862, for the war. Present or accounted for until captured at Fisher's Hill, Virginia, September 22, 1864. Confined at Point Lookout, Maryland, until paroled and transferred to Aiken's Landing, James River, Virginia, March 17, 1865, for exchange.

SMITH, TANDY S., Private
Resided in Stokes County where he enlisted at age 30, September 1, 1862, for the war. Company muster roll for September-October, 1863, states that he was "absent without leave." No further records.

SMITH, WILLIAM C., Private
Resided in Stokes County where he enlisted at age 17, May 4, 1861, for twelve months. Captured at Roanoke Island on February 8, 1862, and paroled at Elizabeth City, N.C., February 21, 1862. Company muster rolls report that he was captured at South Mountain, Maryland, July 6, 1863, and carry him as absent prisoner of war from that date through February, 1865.

SOUTHERN, REUBEN A., Private
Appears on company muster roll for November-December, 1862, which states that he deserted December 14, 1862. Later enlisted in Company H, 23rd Battalion Virginia Infantry on April 1, 1863.

SOUTHERN, WILLIAM, Private
Resided as a farmer in Stokes County where he enlisted at age 18, May 4, 1861, for twelve months. Captured at Roanoke Island on February 8, 1862, and paroled at Elizabeth City, N.C., February 21,

1862. Present or accounted for until again captured on October 19, 1864, at Strasburg, Virginia. Confined at Point Lookout, Maryland, until released after taking the Oath of Allegiance on May 14, 1865.

STANLY, J. H., Private
Enlisted in Stokes County at age 21, May 4, 1861, for twelve months. Present or accounted for on company muster rolls until November-December, 1861, when he was reported as "absent on sick leave." No further records.

SULLIVAN, JOHN B., Private
Enlisted in Stokes County, September 1, 1864, for the war. Present or accounted for on company muster rolls through February, 1865. Paroled at Appomattox Court House, Virginia, April 9, 1865.

THROWER, GEORGE, Private
Enlisted in Stokes County, November 28, 1864, for the war. Present or accounted for until admitted to hospital at Richmond, Virginia, on February 24, 1865, with "feb. remit." Furloughed from hospital on March 29, 1865, for 60 days.

THROWER, JAMES NEWBERN, Private
Resided in Stokes County where he enlisted at age 18, February 24, 1863, for the war. Admitted to hospital at Farmville, Virginia, June 10, 1863, with "ascites" and was furloughed for 30 days on August 20, 1863. Reported on company muster rolls as absent on sick leave through October, 1863, and as absent without leave from that date until he returned to the company in November-December, 1864. Captured near Petersburg, Virginia, March 25, 1865, and confined at Point Lookout, Maryland, where he died May 31, 1865, of "pneumonia."

THROWER, WILLIAM, Private
Resided in Stokes County where he enlisted at age 18, May 4, 1861, for twelve months. Captured at Roanoke Island on February 8, 1862, and paroled at Elizabeth City, N.C., February 21, 1862. Present or accounted for until admitted to hospital at Farmville, Virginia, June 11, 1863, with "rheumatism" and was furloughed for 60 days on July 29, 1863. Appears on company muster rolls as absent sick from that date through October, 1863, and as absent without leave until January-February, 1864, when he is reported as "present, sick in camp." Again reported as absent without leave from November-December, 1864, through February, 1865. No further records.

TILLEY, AARON B., Private
Resided in Stokes County where he enlisted at age 17, September 1, 1862, for twelve months. Present or accounted for on company muster rolls through December, 1862. Roll of Honor states that he "died June 10, 1863, at Goldsboro, N.C."

TUCKER, GABRIEL H., Private
Resided in Stokes County where he enlisted at age 21, May 4, 1861, for twelve months. Captured at Roanoke Island on February 8, 1862, and paroled at Elizabeth City, N.C., February 21, 1862. Present or accounted for on company mus-

ter rolls until January-February, 1865, when he appears as "absent without leave."

WILKES, DRURY D., Sergeant

Resided in Stokes County where he enlisted at age 18, May 4, 1861, for twelve months. Mustered in as Private. Captured at Roanoke Island on February 8, 1862, and paroled at Elizabeth City, N.C., February 21, 1862. Appointed Sergeant, September 25, 1862. Present or accounted for until transferred to Company F. 21st Regiment N.C. Troops (11th Regiment N.C. Volunteers) on March 21, 1864.

WILKES, JAMES P., Private

Resided in Virginia and enlisted in Stokes County at age 17, September 1, 1862, for the war. Killed at Gettysburg, Pennsylvania, July 1, 1863.

WILKES, JOSEPH H., Private

Resided in Stokes County where he enlisted at age 21, May 4, 1861, for twelve months. Captured at Roanoke Island on February 8, 1862, and paroled at Elizabeth City, N.C., February 21, 1862. Company muster rolls state that he "joined the Virginia State Line service after paroled" and carry him as absent without leave through November-December, 1862.

WILKES, PINKNEY, Private

Enlisted in Stokes County, September 1, 1862, for the war. Company muster roll for April 30-October 31, 1862, reported him as "absent without leave—joined Virginia State Line service."

WILKES, RUFUS V., Private

Resided in Virginia and enlisted in Stokes County at age 19, May 4, 1861, for twelve months. Captured at Roanoke Island on February 8, 1862, and paroled at Elizabeth City, N.C., February 21, 1862. Company muster rolls state that he "joined the Virginia State Line service after paroled" and report him as absent without leave through November-December, 1862.

WILLARD, JOHN, Private

Resided in Stokes County where he enlisted at age 17, May 4, 1861, for twelve months. Captured at Roanoke Island on February 8, 1862, and paroled at Elizabeth City, N.C., February 21, 1862. Company muster rolls carry him as absent without leave after paroled. Later enlisted in Company H, 23rd Battalion Virginia Infantry on April 1, 1863.

WILLIAMS, JAMES A., Private

Resided in Davidson County and enlisted in Stokes County, September 1, 1864, for the war. Present or accounted for on company muster rolls until January-February, 1865, when he appears as absent sick in hospital. Captured at Appomattox Court House, Virginia, April 3, 1865, and confined at Point Lookout, Maryland, until released after taking the Oath of Allegiance on June 21, 1865.

WILSON, H. L., Private

Appears on a list of prisoners of war taken by the forces of General A. E. Burnside on Roanoke Island, February 8, 1862, and released on parole at Elizabeth City, N.C., February 21, 1862,

with the remark: "Wounded." No further records.

WOODS, JOHN H., Private

Resided in Stokes County and enlisted in Lenoir County at age 19, February 8, 1863, for the war. Deserted in May, 1863, and reported as "present in arrest" after November-December, 1863. Captured at Spotsylvania Court House, Virginia, May 10, 1864, and confined at Point Lookout, Maryland. Transferred on August 13-14, 1864, to Elmira, New York, where he remained until released after taking the Oath of Allegiance on June 27, 1865.

COMPANY B

This company was organized in Surry County and enlisted at Dobson on August 10, 1861. It was mustered into Confederate States service at Wilmington on January 31, 1862, as Company B of this battalion. After that date it functioned as a part of the battalion, and its history for the war period is reported as a part of the battalion history.

The information contained in the following roster of the company was compiled principally from company muster rolls which included the muster-in roll, dated January 31, 1862, and muster rolls for March through June, 1862; October through December, 1862; March-April, 1863; and September, 1863, through February, 1865. No company muster rolls were found for the period prior to the date of muster-in, January 31, 1862; for February, 1862; July through September, 1862; January-February, 1863; May through August, 1863; or for the period after February, 1865. In addition to the company muster rolls, Roll of Honor records, receipt rolls, and hospital records, supplemented by state pension applications, United Daughters of the Confederacy records, and postwar rosters and histories, all provided useful information.

OFFICERS
CAPTAINS

COOPER, DAVID M.

Resided in Surry County where he enlisted at age 44, August 10, 1861, for twelve months. Appointed Captain to rank from October 25, 1861. Captured at Roanoke Island on February 8, 1862, and paroled at Elizabeth City, N.C., February 21, 1862. Transferred to the Field and Staff of this battalion upon appointment as Captain, Assistant Commissary of Subsistence, December 1, 1862.

NORMAN, LACY J.

Resided in Surry County where he enlisted at age 33, August 10, 1861, for twelve months. Appointed 1st Lieutenant to rank from October 25, 1861. Captured at Roanoke Island on February 8, 1862, and paroled at Elizabeth City, N.C., February 21, 1862. Promoted to Captain to rank from December 1, 1862. Wounded in action at Gettysburg, Pennsylvania, July 1-3, 1863, and returned to company by October, 1863. Present or accounted for with company until wounded at Cedar Creek, Virginia, October 19, 1864. Reported as absent wounded on company muster rolls through February, 1865. Paroled at Richmond, Virginia, on May 16, 1865.

LIEUTENANTS

BRAY, WILLIAM A., 2nd Lieutenant

Resided in Surry County where he enlisted at age 27, August 10, 1861, for twelve months. Mustered in as 1st Sergeant. Captured at Roanoke Island on February 15, 1862, and paroled at Elizabeth City, N.C., February 21, 1862. Elected 2nd Lieutenant on December 17, 1862, and appointed on January 15, 1863, to rank from date of election. Mortally wounded at Gettysburg, Pennsylvania, July 1, 1863, and died "same night."

GORDON, JOSEPH, 2nd Lieutenant

Resided in Surry County where he enlisted at age 32, August 10, 1861, for twelve months. Mustered in as 3rd Lieutenant to rank from October 25, 1861. Captured at Roanoke Island on February 8, 1862, and paroled at Elizabeth City, N.C., February 21, 1862. Promoted to 2nd Lieutenant to rank from December 1, 1862. Resigned on Surgeon's Certificate of Disability and resignation accepted February 10, 1863.

LAFFOON, NATHAN D., 2nd Lieutenant

Resided in Surry County where he enlisted at age 19, September 1, 1862, for the war. Mustered in as Private and elected 2nd Lieutenant on March 3, 1863. Appointed to rank from date of election. Wounded at Gettysburg, Pennsylvania, July 1-3, 1863, and captured at Smithburg, Pennsylvania, July 4, 1863. Confined at Fort Delaware, Delaware, July 8-10, 1863, and transferred to Johnson's Island, Ohio, July 18, 1863. Paroled and sent to Fort Monroe, Virginia, for exchange on September 16, 1864. Admitted to hospital at Richmond, Virginia, September 21, 1864, and furloughed October 5, 1864. Reported as absent on leave through December, 1864. Admitted to hospital at Richmond on February 25, 1865, with "bronchitis ch." and furloughed for 30 days on March 26, 1865.

SOYARS, JOSEPH, 1st Lieutenant

Resided in Surry County where he enlisted at age 33, August 10, 1861, for twelve months. Appointed 2nd Lieutenant on November 1, 1861. Captured at Roanoke Island on February 8, 1862, and paroled at Elizabeth City, N.C., February 21, 1862. Promoted to 1st Lieutenant on December 1, 1862. Wounded slightly at Gettysburg, Pennsylvania, July 1-3, 1863. Resigned July 12, 1864, while under arrest "for cowardice" and ordered to reenlist. Later enlisted in "37th Regiment Virginia Cavalry."

NONCOMMISSIONED OFFICERS AND PRIVATES

ALLEN, WILLIAM, Private

Admitted to hospital at Wilmington on July 10, 1864, with "diarrhoea acuta" and returned to duty July 15, 1864.

ANDERSON, HENRY E., Private

Enlisted in Surry County, September 18, 1861, for twelve months. Captured at Roanoke Island on February 8, 1862, and paroled at Elizabeth City, N.C., February 21, 1862. Present or accounted for until detailed as mechanic for the brigade September-October, 1863. Absent on detail through September 19, 1864, when he was captured at Winchester, Virginia. Confined at Point Lookout, Maryland, until paroled and exchanged on February 18, 1865. Reported as present on a roll of a detachment of paroled and exchanged prisoners at Camp Lee, near Richmond, Virginia, on February 23, 1865.

ASHBURN, DENSON A., Private

Resided in Surry County where he enlisted at age 28, September 1, 1862, for the war. Company muster rolls report that he deserted on October 19, 1862, near Drewry's Bluff, Virginia, and returned to the company in November, 1862. Detailed for duty in the ambulance corps from November-December, 1863, through February, 1865. Captured at Amelia Court House, Virginia, April 6, 1865, and confined at Point Lookout, Maryland, until released after taking the Oath of Allegiance on June 22, 1865.

ASHBURN, ISAAC WILLIAM, Private

Resided in Surry County where he enlisted at age 25, September 1, 1862, for the war. Company muster rolls report that he deserted October 19, 1862, near Drewry's Bluff, Virginia, and returned to the company in November, 1862. Died in hospital at Raleigh, May 29, 1863, of "pneumonia."

ASHBURN, JOHN W., Sergeant

Resided in Surry County where he enlisted at age 18, September 18, 1861, for twelve months. Mustered in as Private. Captured at Roanoke Island on February 8, 1862, and paroled at Elizabeth City, N.C., February 21, 1862. Appointed Corporal, September 25, 1862. Present or accounted for on company muster rolls through April, 1863. Roll of Honor states that he was promoted to Sergeant in June, 1863. Killed July 1, 1863, in battle at Gettysburg, Pennsylvania.

ATKINS, DANIEL W., Sergeant

Resided in Surry County where he enlisted at age 20, September 18, 1861, for twelve months. Mustered in as Private. Captured at Roanoke Island on February 8, 1862, and paroled at Elizabeth City, N.C., February 21, 1862. Appointed Sergeant, September 1, 1863. Present or accounted for through February, 1865. Admitted to hospital at Danville, Virginia, April 6, 1865, with "vul. sclop. in right arm" and furloughed for 60 days on April 8, 1865.

BADGETT, JOHN R., Private

Resided in Surry County where he enlisted at age 17, September 1, 1862, for the war as a substitute for S. W. Houser. Wounded and captured at Gettysburg, Pennsylvania, July 1-5, 1863. Admitted on July 14-24, 1863, to DeCamp General Hospital, Davids Island, New York Harbor, where he was confined until paroled and sent to City

Point, Virginia, for exchange. Received at City Point on September 8, 1863, for exchange. Admitted to hospital at Richmond, Virginia, May 28, 1864, with "v.s. right hand" and was transferred to another hospital on June 29, 1864. Present or accounted for on company muster rolls through February, 1865. Paroled at Appomattox Court House, Virginia, April 9, 1865.

BAKER, JAMES H., Corporal
Resided in Surry County where he enlisted at age 22, September 1, 1862, for the war. Mustered in as Private and appointed Corporal on September 25, 1862. Killed at Gettysburg, Pennsylvania, July 1, 1863.

BASS, HENRY, Private
Resided in Surry County where he enlisted at age 35, January 29, 1863, for the war. Wounded and captured at Gettysburg, Pennsylvania, July 1-4, 1863. Admitted on July 17-24, 1863, to DeCamp General Hospital, Davids Island, New York Harbor, where he was confined until paroled and sent to City Point, Virginia, for exchange on September 27, 1863. Admitted to hospital at Richmond, Virginia, September 28, 1863. Reported on company muster rolls as absent on parole until April 1, 1864, when he appears as absent without leave. Carried on muster rolls as such until retired to the Invalid Corps, December 13, 1864, and assigned to duty at Salisbury, N.C., with Colonel Mallett, Commandant of Conscripts.

BATES, WILLIAM, Private
Resided in Surry County where he enlisted September 1, 1862, for the war. Present or accounted for until wounded and captured while in hospital at Gettysburg, Pennsylvania, July 1-3, 1863. Admitted on July 14-17, 1863, to DeCamp General Hospital, Davids Island, New York Harbor, where he was confined until paroled and sent to City Point, Virginia, for exchange. Received at City Point on September 8, 1863, for exchange. Wounded near Spotsylvania Court House, Virginia, May 10, 1864. Present or accounted for on company muster rolls through February, 1865. Captured near Petersburg, Virginia, March 25, 1865, and confined at Point Lookout, Maryland, until released after taking the Oath of Allegiance on June 23, 1865.

BONE, JAMES, Private
Resided in Surry. County where he enlisted at age 35, January 29, 1863, for the war. Captured at Gettysburg, Pennsylvania, July 3-5, 1863, and confined at Fort Delaware, Delaware, until transferred to Point Lookout, Maryland, October 18, 1863. Paroled at Point Lookout and sent to Cox's Landing, James River, Virginia, for exchange February 13, 1865. Appears on a muster roll of a detachment of paroled and exchanged prisoners at Camp Lee, near Richmond, Virginia, dated February 18, 1865, which carries him as present.

BOWLES, WILLIAM, Private
Enlisted in Surry County on September 8, 1861, for twelve months. Company muster roll for February 28-June 30, 1862, states that he was "over 35 years."

BRAY, DAVID, Private
Enlisted in Surry County, September 18, 1861, for twelve months. Company muster roll for February 28-June 30, 1862, states that he "joined Captain Rankin's Company." Later enlisted in Company A, 1st Battalion N.C. Heavy Artillery.

BRAY, KING H., Sergeant
Resided in Surry County where he enlisted at age 38, November 14, 1863, for the war. Mustered in as Private. Company muster rolls indicate that he was acting Quartermaster Sergeant from January-February, 1864, until appointed Sergeant, November-December, 1864. Present or accounted for through February, 1865. Admitted to hospital at Richmond, Virginia, March 26, 1865, with "v.s." and was turned over to Federal Provost Marshal on April 14, 1865.

BRAY, OLIVER, Private
Born in Surry County where he resided as a farmer and enlisted at age 38, September 18, 1861, for twelve months. Captured at Roanoke Island on February 8, 1862, and paroled at Elizabeth City, N.C., February 21, 1862. Discharged on December 10, 1862, by reason of "being a nonconscript."

BRAY, ROBERT F., Private
Resided in Surry County where he enlisted at age 25, September 18, 1861, for twelve months. Mustered in as Private. Captured at Roanoke Island on February 8, 1862, and paroled at Elizabeth City, N.C., February 21, 1862. Company muster rolls give his rank as Musician from February 28, 1862, until appointed 1st Sergeant, December 17, 1862. Reduced to ranks "for bad conduct May 1, 1863." Captured near Washington, D.C., July 14, 1864, and confined at Old Capitol Prison, Washington, until transferred to Elmira, New York, July 23-25, 1864. Paroled at Elmira and sent to James River, Virginia, for exchange, March 2, 1865. Captured in hospital at Richmond, Virginia, April 3, 1865, and turned over to the Federal Provost Marshal on April 29, 1865.

BULLIN, JAMES, Private
Resided in Surry County where he enlisted at age 27, September 18, 1861, for twelve months. Captured at Roanoke Island on February 8, 1862, and paroled at Elizabeth City, N.C., February 21, 1862. Captured at Gettysburg, Pennsylvania, July 3-6, 1863, and confined at Fort Delaware, Delaware, until transferred to Point Lookout, Maryland, October 18, 1863. Paroled at Point Lookout and transferred to City Point, Virginia, March 16, 1864, for exchange. Again captured at Fisher's Hill, Virginia, on September 23, 1864. Confined at Point Lookout, where he remained until paroled and sent to Cox's Landing, James River, Virginia, February 13, 1865, for exchange. Appears on a muster roll of a detachment of paroled and exchanged prisoners at Camp Lee, near Richmond, Virginia, dated February 17, 1865, which carries him as present.

BULLIN, WILLIAM, Private
Resided in Surry County where he enlisted at age 21, September 1, 1862, for the war. Present

or accounted for on company muster rolls through February, 1865. Captured at Burkeville, Virginia, April 6, 1865, and confined at Point Lookout, Maryland, until released after taking the Oath of Allegiance on June 23, 1865.

CABLE, MILTON, Private
Resided in Alamance County and enlisted in Surry County on February 20, 1864, for the war. Present or accounted for until captured near Petersburg, Virginia, March 25, 1865. Confined at Point Lookout, Maryland, until released after taking the Oath of Allegiance on June 24, 1865.

CAVE, ALGIAS R., Private
Resided in Surry County where he enlisted at age 21, February 20, 1864, for the war. Present or accounted for until admitted to hospital at Richmond, Virginia, March 26, 1865, with "v.s. leg." Captured while in hospital on April 3, 1865, and confined at Point Lookout, Maryland, May 9, 1865.

CAVE, HENRY, Private
Resided in Surry County where he enlisted at age 38, September 18, 1861, for twelve months. Captured at Roanoke Island on February 8, 1862, and paroled at Elizabeth City, N.C., February 21, 1862. Present or accounted for until again captured on June 12, 1864, at Spotsylvania Court House, Virginia. Confined at Point Lookout, Maryland, where he remained until paroled and sent to Cox's Wharf, James River, Virginia, October 11, 1864, for exchange. Admitted to hospital at Richmond, Virginia, on October 16, 1864, but disposition from hospital is not given. Company muster rolls carry him as absent with leave from date of exchange through February, 1865.

CAVE, REUBEN, Private
Resided in Surry County where he enlisted at age 26, September 8, 1861, for twelve months. Captured at Roanoke Island on February 8, 1862, and paroled at Elizabeth City, N.C., February 21, 1862. Reported in hospital at Danville, Virginia, on May 18, 1864, with "vul. sclopeticum eye"; however, there is no other information on wound or hospitalization. Present or accounted for on company muster rolls through February, 1865. Paroled at Appomattox Court House, Virginia, April 9, 1865.

COCKERHAM, SANBURN W., Sergeant
Resided in Surry County where he enlisted at age 34, September 13, 1861, for twelve months. Mustered in as Sergeant and reduced to ranks September 25, 1862. Again appointed Sergeant, May 1, 1864. Company muster rolls state that he was wounded at Snicker's Gap, Virginia, on July 18, 1864, and carry him as absent with leave from that date through February, 1865. Admitted to hospital at Richmond, Virginia, February 17, 1865, with "pneumonia feb. typh." and was furloughed for 60 days on March 29, 1865.

COCKERHAM, WILLIAM, Private
Resided in Surry County where he enlisted at age 33, September 1, 1862, for the war. Present or accounted for on company muster rolls through January-February, 1865, when he appears as absent sick.

COE, DUDLEY, Private
Resided in Surry County where he enlisted at age 19, September 18, 1861, for twelve months. Captured at Roanoke Island on February 8, 1862, and paroled at Elizabeth City, N.C., February 21, 1862. Present or accounted for until killed July 1, 1863, at Gettysburg, Pennsylvania.

COPELAND, GIDEON, Private
Resided in Surry County where he enlisted at age 22, September 18, 1861, for twelve months. Captured at Roanoke Island on February 8, 1862, and paroled at Elizabeth City, N.C., February 21, 1862. Died in Surry County, March 12, 1862.

COPELAND, ISAAC, Private
Resided in Surry County where he enlisted at age 20, September 18, 1861, for twelve months. Captured at Roanoke Island on February 8, 1862, and paroled at Elizabeth City, N.C., on February 21, 1862. Wounded and captured at Gettysburg, Pennsylvania, July 1-5, 1863. Transferred on July 14, 1863, from hospital at Gettysburg to DeCamp General Hospital, Davids Island, New York Harbor, where he remained until paroled and sent to City Point, Virginia, for exchange. Received at City Point, September 8-16, 1863, in exchange. Absent on parole through February, 1864. Transferred to C.S. Navy, April 5, 1864.

CORDER, ENOCH, Private
Resided in Surry County where he enlisted at age 30, September 1, 1862, for the war. Died in hospital at Goldsboro on March 8, 1863, of "pleuritis."

CREED, ANDERSON, Private
Resided in Surry County where he enlisted at age 22, September 18, 1861, for twelve months. Captured at Roanoke Island on February 8, 1862, and paroled at Elizabeth City, N.C., February 21, 1862. Present or accounted for until detailed as division wagoner September-October, 1863. Detailed through February, 1865. Admitted to hospital at Danville, Virginia, June 4, 1864, with "vul. sclopeticum arm" and was "transferred June 21, 1864." Paroled at Appomattox Court House, Virginia, April 9, 1865.

CROUSE, HIRAM, Private
Resided in Surry County where he enlisted at age 29, September 1, 1862, for the war. Present or accounted for until admitted to hospital at Charlottesville, Virginia, on September 24, 1864, with "v.s. right arm." Transferred to Lynchburg, Virginia, September 26, 1864. Present or accounted for on company muster rolls through February, 1865.

DANLY, THOMAS J., Private
Transferred from Company E, 53rd Regiment N.C. Troops on October 1, 1862, in exchange for F. J. Marion. Present or accounted for through February, 1865. Paroled at Lynchburg, Virginia, April 15, 1865.

DAVIS, GABRIEL L., Private
Resided in Surry County where he enlisted at age 18, September 1, 1862, for the war. Captured at Gettysburg, Pennsylvania, July 3-4, 1863, and confined at Fort Delaware, Delaware, where he died August 11, 1863, of "chronic enteritis."

DAVIS, RALEIGH, Private
Date and place of enlistment are not given. Granted sick furlough from June 25, 1863, to August 25, 1863. Admitted to hospital at Richmond, Virginia, May 27, 1864, with "dysentery ac." Furloughed from hospital at Richmond, August 11, 1864. Paroled at Appomattox Court House, Virginia, April 9, 1865.

DAVIS, THOMAS, Private
Resided in Surry County where he enlisted at age 25, September 18, 1861, for twelve months. Captured at Roanoke Island on February 8, 1862, and paroled at Elizabeth City, N.C., on February 21, 1862. Present or accounted for on company muster rolls through February, 1865.

DONETHAN, RICHARD, Private
Resided in Surry County where he enlisted at age 18, September 18, 1861, for twelve months. Captured at Roanoke Island on February 8, 1862, and paroled at Elizabeth City, N.C., February 21, 1862. Died in hospital at Lynchburg, Virginia, on October 28, 1863, of "pneumonia."

DUNNEGAN, REUBEN, Private
Resided in Surry County where he enlisted at age 35, September 18, 1861, for twelve months. Mustered in as Corporal. Captured at Roanoke Island on February 8, 1862, and paroled at Elizabeth City, N.C., February 21, 1862. Reduced to ranks on September 25, 1862. Wounded in battle at Gettysburg, Pennsylvania, July 1-3, 1863, and captured in hospital at that place on July 5, 1863. Admitted to DeCamp General Hospital, Davids Island, New York Harbor, on July 14, 1863, with "g.s. arm" and remained there until paroled and sent to City Point, Virginia, for exchange. Received at City Point, September 27, 1863, for exchange. Company muster rolls carry him as absent on parole through February, 1864. Present or accounted for until his death in hospital at Staunton, Virginia, on October 25, 1864, of "pyaemia supervening on wound."

EDMONDS, JOHN H., Private
Resided in Surry County where he enlisted at age 17, September 18, 1861, for twelve months. Captured at Roanoke Island on February 8, 1862, and paroled at Elizabeth City, N.C., February 21, 1862. Present or accounted for on company muster rolls through February, 1865. Paroled at Appomattox Court House, Virginia, April 9, 1865.

ELLIS, JOHN, Private
Resided in Surry County where he enlisted at age 53, September 18, 1861, for twelve months. Captured at Roanoke Island on February 8, 1862, and paroled at Elizabeth City, N.C., February 21, 1862. Discharged December 10, 1862, by reason of "being a non-conscript."

EMERSON, JOHN S., Private
Resided in Surry County where he enlisted at age 26, September 1, 1862, for the war. Wounded in battle at Wilderness, Virginia, May 5, 1864, and carried on company muster rolls as absent with leave from that date through February, 1865. Admitted to hospital at Raleigh on March 20,

1865, with "scabies." Admitted to hospital at Greensboro in April, 1865. No further records.

FLINCHUM, GIDEON, Private
Resided in Surry County where he enlisted at age 22, September 1, 1862, for the war. Company muster rolls report that he "deserted September 19, 1862, and died about the first of November, 1862."

FLINCHUM, JAMES E., Private
Resided in Surry County where he enlisted at age 31, September 1, 1862, for the war. Company muster rolls report that he deserted on October 19, 1862, from near Drewry's Bluff, Virginia, and carry him as a deserter until he appears on the March-April, 1863, muster roll as "absent sick in hospital at Goldsboro." Deserted the sick camp near Kinston on May 17, 1863, and is reported as absent in arrest from November-December, 1863, through December, 1864. Captured near Petersburg, Virginia, March 25, 1865, and confined at Point Lookout, Maryland, until released after taking the Oath of Allegiance on June 26, 1865.

FLINCHUM, JONATHAN, Private
Resided in Surry County where he enlisted at age 27, September 1, 1862, for the war. Company muster rolls report that he deserted on October 19, 1862, from near Drewry's Bluff, Virginia, and carry him as a deserter until he appears on the company muster roll for March-April, 1863, as "present, sick in quarters." Deserted the sick camp near Kinston, May 17, 1863, and is reported as absent from that date until November-December, 1863, when he appears as "present in arrest." Absent in arrest at Salisbury, N.C., undergoing sentence of court-martial from January-February, 1864, until released from confinement December 1, 1864. Company muster rolls, however, carry him as absent in arrest through February, 1865.

FREEMAN, EZEKIEL, Private
Resided in Surry County where he enlisted at age 23, September 1, 1861, for twelve months. Captured at Roanoke Island on February 8, 1862, and paroled at Elizabeth City, N.C., February 21, 1862. Captured at Gettysburg, Pennsylvania, July 3-5, 1863, and confined at Fort Delaware, Delaware, until transferred to Point Lookout, Maryland, on October 18, 1863. Paroled at Point Lookout and sent to Boulware's and Cox's Wharf, James River, Virginia, February 18, 1865, for exchange. Company muster rolls carry him as absent prisoner of war through February, 1865.

FREEMAN, HUGH, Private
Resided in Surry County where he enlisted at age 19, September 18, 1861, for twelve months. Captured at Roanoke Island on February 8, 1862, and paroled at Elizabeth City, N.C., February 21, 1862. Present or accounted for until "killed May 14, 1864, near Spotsylvania Court House, Virginia, by a bomb shell."

FREEMAN, SAMUEL P., Private
Born in Surry County where he resided as a

farmer and enlisted at age 39, September 18, 1861, for twelve months. Captured at Roanoke Island on February 8, 1862, and paroled at Elizabeth City, N.C., February 21, 1862. Discharged December 10, 1862, by reason of "being a non-conscript."

FULK, AUGUSTIN, Corporal
Resided in Surry County where he enlisted at age 33, September 1, 1862, for the war. Mustered in as Private. Company muster rolls state that he deserted on October 19, 1862, from near Drewry's Bluff, Virginia, and carry him as a deserter until he is reported present on the March-April, 1863, muster roll. Appointed Corporal, November-December, 1863. Wounded at Snicker's Gap, Virginia, July 18, 1864, and reported as absent with leave from that date through December, 1864. Company muster roll for January-February, 1865, reports him as "absent without leave."

GARDNER, DANIEL A., Private
Resided in Surry County where he enlisted at age 50, August 10, 1861, for twelve months. Captured at Roanoke Island on February 8, 1862, and paroled at Elizabeth City, N.C., February 21, 1862. Discharged on November 1, 1862, and later enlisted in the 45th Regiment N.C. Troops.

GILLASPIE, JAMES LAWRANCE, Corporal
Resided in Surry County where he enlisted at age 28, August 10, 1861, for twelve months. Mustered in as Private. Captured at Roanoke Island on February 8, 1862, and paroled at Elizabeth City, N.C., on February 21, 1862. Appointed Corporal on September 25, 1862. Wounded at Gettysburg, Pennsylvania, July 1, 1863, and again at Mechanicsville, Virginia, May 30, 1864. Present or accounted for through February, 1865. Admitted to hospital at Richmond, Virginia, April 8, 1865, and paroled from hospital on April 28, 1865.

GILLASPIE, WARREN, Sergeant
Resided in Surry County where he enlisted at age 33, August 10, 1861, for twelve months. Mustered in as Corporal. Captured at Roanoke Island on February 8, 1862, and paroled at Elizabeth City, N.C., on February 21, 1862. Promoted to Sergeant in March-April, 1863. Present or accounted for on company muster rolls through February, 1865. Admitted to hospital at Richmond, Virginia, April 3, 1865, with a gunshot wound of the mouth. Captured in hospital on April 3, 1865, and paroled on April 28, 1865.

GORDON, JAMES M., Private
Resided in Surry County where he enlisted at age 36, August 10, 1861, for twelve months. Mustered in as Sergeant. Captured at Roanoke Island on February 8, 1862, and paroled at Elizabeth City, N.C., on February 21, 1862. Reduced to ranks on September 25, 1862. Appointed Sergeant on September 1, 1863, and reduced to ranks a second time on May 1, 1864, "for words and conduct unbecoming an officer." Captured near Washington, D.C., June 13, 1864, and confined at Elmira, New York, until transferred to James River, Virginia, for exchange on March 2,

1865. Admitted to hospital at Richmond, Virginia, March 7, 1865. and furloughed for 30 days March 9, 1865.

GREENWOOD, JAMES H., Private
Resided in Surry County where he enlisted at age 21, September 1, 1862, for the war. Deserted near Kinston on April 14, 1863, and deserted a second time near Summerville Ford, Virginia, December 12, 1863. Never returned to company.

GREENWOOD, WILLIAM T., Private
Resided in Surry County where he enlisted at age 23, September 1, 1862, for the war. Deserted from the hospital at Wilson, N.C., June 5, 1863, and died at his father's home in Surry County on August 22, 1863.

GRIFFITH, SAMUEL, Private
Resided as a farmer in Surry County where he enlisted at age 21, August 10, 1861, for twelve months. Captured at Roanoke Island on February 8, 1862, and paroled at Elizabeth City, N.C., on February 21, 1862. Dropped out on march to Pennsylvania and surrendered at Hancock, Maryland, July 7, 1863. Confined at Fort Delaware, Delaware, where he died September 20, 1863, of "measles."

HAINES, JAMES, Private
Resided in Surry County where he enlisted at age 34, September 18, 1861, for twelve months. Captured at Roanoke Island on February 8, 1862, and paroled at Elizabeth City, N.C., on February 21, 1862. Died at home in Surry County on June 10, 1862.

HANCOCK, JOHN, Private
Resided in Surry County where he enlisted at age 37, August 10, 1861, for twelve months. Captured at Roanoke Island on February 8, 1862, and paroled at Elizabeth City, N.C., February 21, 1862. Captured at Gettysburg, Pennsylvania, July 5, 1863, and confined at Point Lookout, Maryland, until paroled and sent to Venus Point, Savannah River, Georgia, for exchange on November 1, 1864.

HANCOCK, WILLIAM HENRY, Private
Resided in Randolph County and captured near Fayetteville, N.C., March 10, 1865. Confined at Point Lookout, Maryland, until released after taking the Oath of Allegiance on June 27, 1865.

HARRIS, JOEL, Private
Born in Surry County where he resided as a farmer and enlisted at age 57, August 10, 1861, for twelve months. Captured at Roanoke Island on February 8, 1862, and paroled at Elizabeth City, N.C., on February 21, 1862. Discharged December 22, 1862, by reason of age and "being a non-conscript."

HARRIS, MARTIN A., Private
Resided in Surry County where he enlisted at age 27, August 10, 1861, for twelve months. Captured at Roanoke Island on February 8, 1862, and paroled at Elizabeth City, N.C., February 21, 1862. Slightly wounded at Gettysburg, Pennsylvania, July 1-3, 1863, and captured at South Mountain on July 4, 1863. Confined at Fort Delaware, Dela-

ware, until released after taking the Oath of Allegiance on June 19, 1865.

HEDGECOCK, JOHN L., Private
Born in Stokes County and resided as a farmer in Surry County where he enlisted at age 57, August 10, 1861, for twelve months. Captured at Roanoke Island on February 8, 1862, and paroled at Elizabeth City, N.C., on February 21, 1862. Discharged on December 10, 1862, by reason of age and being a nonconscript.

HODGES, ANDREW J., Private
Resided in Surry County where he enlisted at age 45, September 1, 1862, for the war as a substitute for Aaron C. Woodruff. Killed at Gettysburg, Pennsylvania, July 1, 1863.

HOLT, YANCY A., Private
Resided in Surry County where he enlisted at age 32, August 10, 1861, for twelve months. Captured at Roanoke Island on February 8, 1862, and paroled at Elizabeth City, N.C., on February 21, 1862. Killed at Gettysburg, Pennsylvania, July 1, 1863.

HOLYFIELD, MARTIN R., Private
Resided in Surry County where he enlisted at age 34, August 10, 1861, for twelve months. Captured at Roanoke Island on February 8, 1862, and paroled at Elizabeth City, N.C., on February 21, 1862. Killed at Gettysburg, Pennsylvania, July 1, 1863.

HOLYFIELD, VALENTINE, Private
Born in Surry County where he resided as a farmer and enlisted at age 44, August 10, 1861, for twelve months. Captured at Roanoke Island on February 8, 1862, and paroled at Elizabeth City, N.C., on February 21, 1862. Discharged December 10, 1862, by reason of age and "being a non-conscript."

HUDSON, JAMES W., Private
Resided in Surry County where he enlisted at age 20, September 1, 1862, for the war. Died in hospital at Lynchburg, Virginia. Date of death reported as June 15, 1863, and July 15, 1863.

HUDSON, JOHN W., Private
Resided in Surry County where he enlisted at age 26, September 1, 1862, for the war. Present or accounted for until wounded at Spotsylvania Court House, Virginia, May 10-12, 1864.

HUDSON, YOUNG H., Private
Born in Halifax County, Virginia, and was by occupation a farmer when he enlisted in Surry County at age 52, August 10, 1861, for twelve months. Discharged December 22, 1862, by reason of age and "being a non-conscript."

HUTCHINS, WILLIAM, Private
Resided in Surry County where he enlisted on July 20, 1864, for the war. Present or accounted for through February, 1865. Captured near Petersburg, Virginia, March 25, 1865, and confined at Point Lookout, Maryland, until released after taking the Oath of Allegiance on June 13, 1865.

JERVIS, G. M., Private
Enlisted in Wake County on November 1, 1864, for the war. Present or accounted for until

paroled at Appomattox Court House, Virginia, April 9, 1865.

JERVIS, J. M., Private
Resided in Surry County and enlisted in Wake County on November 1, 1864, for the war. Present or accounted for until captured at Petersburg, Virginia, April 2, 1865. Confined at Point Lookout, Maryland, until released after taking the Oath of Allegiance on June 28, 1865.

JOHNSON, JESSE, Private
Joined company from conscript camp at Raleigh on September 17, 1864. Date of enlistement not reported. Present or accounted for until captured near Petersburg, Virginia, March 25, 1865. Confined at Point Lookout, Maryland, until released after taking the Oath of Allegiance on June 3, 1865.

JOHNSON, JOHN, Private
Resided in Surry County where he enlisted at age 26, September 1, 1862, for the war. "Deserted Camp Danville, Virginia, about January 20, 1863."

JONES, SILAS, Corporal
Resided in Surry County where he enlisted at age 28, August 10, 1861, for twelve months. Mustered in as Private and appointed Corporal September 1, 1863. Admitted to hospital at Charlottesville, Virginia, October 23, 1864, with gunshot "contuisi abdomen." Died in hospital at Richmond, Virginia, January 21, 1865.

JOYCE, JOHN W., Private
Resided in Surry County where he enlisted at age 27, August 10, 1861, for twelve months. Mustered in as Private. Captured at Roanoke Island on February 8, 1862, and paroled at Elizabeth City, N.C., on February 21, 1862. Appointed Corporal, March-April, 1863. Reduced to ranks by consent and detailed as wagoner and regimental teamster from September, 1863, through August, 1864. Present or accounted for on company muster rolls through February, 1865.

KEY, AUGUSTINE, Private
Resided in Surry County where he enlisted at age 22, September 1, 1862, for the war. Deserted December 14, 1862, and returned February 9, 1863. Present or accounted for until captured near Spotsylvania Court House, Virginia, May 20, 1864. Confined at Point Lookout, Maryland, until released after taking the Oath of Allegiance. Date released not reported.

KEY, HEZEKIAH, Private
Resided in Surry County where he enlisted at age 18, September 1, 1862, for the war. Present or accounted for until he "deserted near Liberty, Virginia, June 20, 1864."

KEY, JOSEPH, Private
Resided in Surry County where he enlisted at age 44, August 10, 1861, for twelve months. Captured at Roanoke Island on February 8, 1862, and paroled at Elizabeth City, N.C., on February 21, 1862. "Discharged at the end of 12 months being over age." Date of discharge reported as April 30, 1863, and May 8, 1863.

KEY, LEWIS, Private
Resided in Surry County where he enlisted at

age 25, September 1, 1862, for the war. Died in hospital at Richmond, Virginia, August 5-6, 1863, of "diarrhoea chro."

KEY, MARTIN, Private
Resided in Surry County where he enlisted at age 29, September 1, 1862, for the war. Reported as present until "slightly wounded May 10, 1864, near Spotsylvania Court House, Virginia." Reported as absent with leave from that date through February, 1865.

KEY, SAMUEL, Corporal
Resided in Surry County where he enlisted at age 24, September 1, 1862, for the war. Mustered in as Private and appointed Corporal on September 1, 1863. Wounded in forearm and right chest and captured near Washington, D.C., July 12, 1864. Died in hospital at Washington on September 27, 1864, of "exhaustion from gunshot wounds."

KIDD, JESSE, Private
Resided in Surry County where he enlisted at age 20, August 10, 1861, for twelve months. Captured at Roanoke Island on February 8, 1861, and paroled at Elizabeth City, N.C., on February 21, 1862. Wounded and captured at Gettysburg, Pennsylvania, July 1-4, 1863, and confined at DeCamp General Hospital, Davids Island, New York Harbor, until sent to City Point, Virginia, where he was exchanged on September 8, 1863. Reported as absent on parole through February, 1864. Deserted near Liberty, Virginia, June 20, 1864. Reported on November-December, 1864, muster roll as "joined from desertion." Present through February, 1865. Admitted to hospital at Richmond, Virginia, March 26, 1865, with a gunshot wound in the neck. Captured in hospital at Richmond on April 3, 1865, and sent to Newport News, Virginia, April 23, 1865. Released after taking the Oath of Allegiance on June 30, 1865.

LAFFOON, WILLIAM G., Private
Resided in Surry County where he enlisted at age 21, September 18, 1861, for twelve months. Mustered in as Sergeant. Captured at Roanoke Island on February 8, 1862, and paroled at Elizabeth City, N.C., on February 21, 1862. Promoted to 1st Sergeant, March-April, 1863. Reduced to ranks "having resigned his office of Sergeant" September-October, 1863. Captured near Spotsylvania Court House, Virginia, May 10, 1864, and confined at Point Lookout, Maryland. Transferred on August 10, 1864, to Elmira, New York, where he died November 2, 1864, of "chronic diarrhoea."

LENARD, G. W., Private
Enlisted in Surry County on August 10, 1864, for the war. Present or accounted for through February, 1865.

LINEBACK, JOSEPH, Private
Joined company from conscript camp at Raleigh, September 17, 1864. Present or accounted for until he died at Farmville, Virginia, February 24, 1865.

LINVILLE, BERRY, Private
Transferred from Company A, 28th Regiment N.C. Troops on October 23, 1862. Present or

accounted for through August, 1864, when he was reported as absent sick in hospital. Reported as absent sick through October, 1864, and as absent without leave from that date through February, 1865.

LINVILLE, DAVID, Private
Resided in Surry County where he enlisted at age 18, August 10, 1861, for twelve months. Captured at Roanoke Island on February 8, 1862, and paroled at Elizabeth City, N.C., on February 21, 1862. Present or accounted for until captured at Gettysburg, Pennsylvania, July 3-5, 1863. Confined at Fort Delaware, Delaware, where he died February 3, 1864, of "inflammation of lungs."

LINVILLE, HENRY, Private
Resided in Surry County where he enlisted at age 20, August 10, 1861, for twelve months. Captured at Roanoke Island on February 8, 1862, and paroled at Elizabeth City, N.C., on February 21, 1862. Present or accounted for until captured at Gettysburg, Pennsylvania, July 5, 1863. Confined at DeCamp General Hospital, Davids Island, New York Harbor, until paroled and exchanged at City Point, Virginia, August 28, 1863. Present or accounted for until admitted to hospital at Richmond, Virginia, February 18, 1865, with "hydrothorax." Captured in hospital at Richmond, April 3, 1865, and sent to Newport News, Virginia, April 23, 1865. Released after taking the Oath of Allegiance on June 30, 1865.

LINVILLE, MOSES, Private
Enlisted in Surry County on September 18, 1861, for twelve months. Never mustered into service.

McGEE, ALLISON, Private
Resided in Surry County where he enlisted at age 27, August 10, 1861, for twelve months. Captured at Roanoke Island on February 8, 1862, and paroled at Elizabeth City, N.C., on February 21, 1862. Present or accounted for until captured at Gettysburg, Pennsylvania, July 3-5, 1863. Confined at Fort Delaware, Delaware, until transferred to Point Lookout, Maryland, October 18, 1863. Later transferred to Elmira, New York, where he died October 1, 1864, of "pneumonia and erysipelas."

McKINNEY, DAVID, Sergeant
Born in Surry County where he resided as a farmer and enlisted at age 19, August 10, 1861, for twelve months. Mustered in as Private. Captured at Roanoke Island on February 8, 1862, and paroled at Elizabeth City, N.C., on February 21, 1862. Appointed Sergeant on September 25, 1862. Killed at Gettysburg, Pennsylvania, July 1, 1863.

McMATH, W. R., Private
Joined the company from conscript camp at Raleigh, September 17, 1864. Present or accounted for through February, 1865.

McMILLON, PLEASANT, Private
Enlisted in Surry County on September 1, 1862, for the war. Deserted soon after enlisting.

MAHONE, WILLIAM, Private
Transferred from Company E, 53rd Regiment N.C. Troops on September 1, 1862. Captured at Gettysburg, Pennsylvania, July 4-5, 1863, and

confined at Fort Delaware, Delaware, where he died April 14, 1865, of "inflammation of lungs."

MARTIN, SPENCER A., Private
Resided in Surry County where he enlisted at age 15, August 10, 1861, for twelve months. Captured at Roanoke Island on February 8, 1862, and paroled at Elizabeth City, N.C., on February 21, 1862. Discharged by reason of age and "being a non-conscript." Date of discharge reported as December 1, 1862, and February 1, 1863.

MAXWELL, HUGH H., Private
Resided in Surry County where he enlisted at age 31, September 13, 1861, for twelve months. Present or accounted for until detached for hospital service November-December, 1863. Absent detached through February, 1865. Paroled at Lynchburg, Virginia, in April, 1865.

MELTON, WILLIAM B., Sergeant
Resided in Surry County where he enlisted at age 21, September 18, 1861, for twelve months. Mustered in as Private. Captured at Roanoke Island on February 8, 1862, and paroled at Elizabeth City, N.C., February 21, 1862. Appointed Sergeant on September 25, 1862. Captured at Gettysburg, Pennsylvania, July 3-4, 1863, and confined at Fort Delaware, Delaware, until transferred to Point Lookout, Maryland, on October 18, 1863. Paroled at Point Lookout and sent to Aiken's Landing, Virginia, for exchange September 18, 1864. Admitted to hospital at Richmond, Virginia, September 22, 1864, with "ch. diarrhoea" and died September 25, 1864.

MITCHELL, WILLIAM, Private
Enlisted in Surry County, February 20, 1865, for the war. Paroled at Appomattox Court House, Virginia, April 9, 1865.

MOORE, ISAAC, Private
Resided in Surry County where he enlisted at age 34, on September 1, 1862, for the war. Company muster rolls state that he "deserted the 14th December 1862 from camp near Drewry's Bluff, Virginia." Reported as present on the March-April, 1863, muster roll. Killed in battle at Gettysburg, Pennsylvania, on July 1, 1863.

MOORE, JOHN W., Private
Resided in Surry County where he enlisted at age 19, February 20, 1864, for the war. Admitted to hospital at Richmond, Virginia, on June 1, 1864, with "v.s." and was furloughed June 17, 1864, for 30 days. Present or accounted for through February, 1865. Captured near Petersburg, Virginia, March 25, 1865, and confined at Point Lookout, Maryland, until released after taking the Oath of Allegiance on June 15, 1865.

MOORE, WYATT, Private
Resided in Surry County where he enlisted at age 33, September 13, 1861, for twelve months. Captured at Roanoke Island on February 8, 1862, and paroled at Elizabeth City, N.C., February 21, 1862. Died March 25, 1862, in Surry County.

MURRAY, J. S., Private
Provided Henry Smith as his substitute.

NICHOLS, SAMUEL J., Private
Resided in Surry County where he enlisted at age 27, October 22, 1863, for the war. Died in hospital at Orange Court House, Virginia, on February 5, 1864, of "pneumonia fever."

NORMAN, F. W., Private
Paroled at Appomattox Court House, Virginia, April 9, 1865.

NORTON, NICHOLAS, Private
Born in Surry County where he resided as a farmer and enlisted at age 34, September 13, 1861, for twelve months. Captured at Roanoke Island on February 8, 1862, and paroled at Elizabeth City, N.C., February 21, 1862. Discharged December 10, 1862, by reason of "being a non-conscript." Reenlisted in company January 1, 1865, in Wake County for the war. Admitted to hospital at Richmond, Virginia, March 10, 1865, with "pneumonia" and was transferred to Farmville, Virginia, April 1, 1865.

ONEAL, ELIAS, Private
Resided in Surry County where he enlisted at age 39, September 1, 1862, for the war. Detailed as wagoner from March-April, 1863, through April 1, 1864. Present or accounted for on company muster rolls through February, 1865. Captured at Burkeville, Virginia, on April 6, 1865, and confined at Point Lookout, Maryland, until released after taking the Oath of Allegiance on June 29, 1865.

PARSONS, JAMES C., Private
Resided in Surry County where he enlisted at age 30, September 1, 1862, for the war. Present or accounted for on company muster rolls until September-October, 1863, when he was reported as absent with the remark: "Deserted the hospital, Wilson, N.C., June 5, 1863." Appears as "present in arrest" on the November-December, 1863, muster roll. Died at Camp Terrell, Virginia, on January 19, 1864, of "pneumonia fever."

PEGRAM, ELIJAH S., Private
Company muster rolls state that he was received from the conscript camp at Raleigh, September 17, 1864, and report him as absent with leave or absent sick from that date through February, 1865. Paroled at Greensboro on May 20, 1865.

REYNOLDS, JAMES D., Private
Resided in Surry County where he enlisted at age 18, September 13, 1861, for twelve months. Captured at Roanoke Island on February 8, 1862, and paroled at Elizabeth City, N.C., February 21, 1862. Company muster roll dated October 31, 1862, reports him as "absent without leave—said to be in cavalry company."

RICHARDSON, WILLIAM, Private
Enlisted in Surry County, September 13, 1861, for twelve months. Never mustered in and "said to have joined a cavalry company."

RING, ENOCH, Private
Resided in Surry County where he enlisted at age 30, September 1, 1862, for the war. Wounded at Gettysburg, Pennsylvania, and captured in hospital at that place July 1-3, 1863. Admitted

on July 14, 1863, to DeCamp General Hospital, Davids Island, New York Harbor, where he remained until paroled and sent to City Point, Virginia, for exchange. Received at City Point, September 8, 1863, in exchange. Absent on parole until reported as present on the company muster roll dated April 1, 1864. Paroled at Appomattox Court House, Virginia, on April 9, 1865.

SAFTEN, R. T., Private
Paroled at Appomattox Court House, Virginia, April 9, 1865.

SARTIN, RICHARD, Private
Resided in Surry County where he enlisted at. age 17, September 13, 1861, for twelve months. Captured at Roanoke Island on February 8, 1862, and paroled at Elizabeth City, N.C., February 21, 1862. Present or accounted for on company muster rolls through February, 1865.

SHAW, IRA L., Private
Resided in Surry County where he enlisted at age 26, September 1, 1862, for the war. Died at hospital at Richmond, Virginia, on June 13, 1863, of "rubeola."

SHINALL, JAMES, Private
Resided in Surry County where he enlisted at age 18, September 1, 1862, for the war. Captured at Gettysburg, Pennsylvania, July 3-4, 1863, and confined at Fort Delaware, Delaware, until transferred to Hammond U.S.A. General Hospital, Point Lookout, Maryland, October 22, 1862. Disease given as "scorbutus." Paroled for exchange at Point Lookout, March 17, 1863. Admitted to hospital at Richmond, Virginia, March 20, 1864, and was furloughed for 30 days on March 26, 1864. Present or accounted for on company muster rolls from that date until admitted to hospital at Richmond, February 25, 1865. Captured in hospital at Richmond on April 3, 1865, and confined at Libby Prison, Richmond, until transferred to Newport News, Virginia, April 23, 1865. Released after taking the Oath of Allegiance on June 30, 1865.

SHORE, CALVIN R., Private
Resided in Surry County where he enlisted at age 18, September 1, 1862, for the war. Company muster rolls report that he deserted on October 19, 1862, and returned to the company in November, 1862. Present or accounted for until November-December, 1863, when he appears as absent without leave. Carried on company muster rolls as such through February, 1865.

SHORE, HENRY T., Private
Resided in Surry County where he enlisted September 1, 1862, for the war. Deserted from hospital at Raleigh, April-May, 1863, and "was shot near his home in Surry County and killed February, 1864."

SHORE, ISAAC, Private
Company muster rolls state that he was received from the conscript camp at Raleigh on September 17, 1864. Admitted to hospital at Charlottesville, Virginia, October 29, 1864, with "feb. int. tertian" and died November 11, 1864.

SHROPSHIRE, HENRY, Private
Resided in Surry County where he enlisted at age 40, September 13, 1861, for twelve months. Captured at Roanoke Island on February 8, 1862, and paroled at Elizabeth City, N.C., February 21, 1861. Died at home in Surry County in May, 1862.

SMITH, HENRY, Private
Resided in Surry County where he enlisted at age 17, September 13, 1861, for twelve months as a substitute for J. S. Murray. Mustered in as Private. Captured at Roanoke Island on February 8, 1862, and paroled at Elizabeth City, N.C., February 21, 1862. Appointed Musician, March-April, 1863. Present or accounted for on company muster rolls through February, 1865. Paroled at Appomattox Court House, Virginia, April 9, 1865, with rank of Private.

SMITH, JOHN, Private
Resided in Surry County where he enlisted at age 32, January 29, 1863, for the war. Died in hospital at Wilson, N.C., July 26, 1863, of "eresipelas."

SPEECE, EDMOND, Private
Enlisted in Wake County, September 17, 1864, for the war. Reported on company muster rolls as absent with leave through February, 1865.

STEEL, DOCTOR F., Private
Born in Surry County where he resided as a farmer and enlisted at age 45, September 18, 1861, for twelve months. Mustered in as Corporal. Reduced to ranks September 20, 1862, by reason of his being "over 45 years old." Discharged December 10, 1862, by reason of "being a nonconscript."

TEAGUE, M. R., Private
Company muster rolls report that he was received from conscript camp at Raleigh on September 17, 1864. Captured at Strasburg, Virginia, October 19, 1864, and confined at Point Lookout, Maryland, October 23, 1864. Paroled at Point Lookout and sent to Boulware's and Cox's Wharf, James River, Virginia, for exchange on February 18, 1865. Reported as present on a muster roll of a detachment of paroled prisoners at Camp Lee, near Richmond, Virginia, dated February 23, 1865.

THOMPSON, ISAAC, Private
Company muster rolls report that he was received from conscript camp at Raleigh on September 17, 1864. Killed in action near Cedar Creek, Virginia, October 19, 1864.

TICKEL, BROOKS, Private
Enlisted in Surry County, September 13, 1861, for twelve months. Company muster roll for February 28-June 30, 1862, states that he transferred to Company E, 53rd Regiment N.C. Troops.

TICKEL, LINDSAY, Private
Enlisted in Surry County on August 10, 1861, for twelve months. Transferred to Company E, 53rd Regiment N.C. Troops soon after enlisting.

VAUGHN, ROBERT S., Private
Resided in Warren County and enlisted on October 20, 1864, for the war. Present or accounted for through February, 1865. Captured

near Petersburg, Virginia, March 25, 1865, and confined at Point Lookout, Maryland, until released after taking the Oath of Allegiance on June 21, 1865.

WALL, NEWEL J., Private
Resided in Surry County where he enlisted on September 1, 1862, for the war. Present or accounted for through February, 1865. Admitted to hospital at Richmond, Virginia, March 26, 1865, with a gunshot wound of the left heel. Captured in hospital at Richmond on April 3, 1865, and transferred to Newport News, Virginia, April 23, 1865. Released after taking the Oath of Allegiance on June 30, 1865.

WATSON, JOHN H., Private
Enlisted in Surry County on August 10, 1861, for twelve months. Transferred to Company E, 53rd Regiment N.C. Troops soon after enlisting.

WHITAKER, EWELL, Private
Resided in Surry County where he enlisted at age 20, November 1, 1863, for the war. Present or accounted for through February, 1865. Captured in March-April, 1865, and confined at Point Lookout, Maryland, until released after taking the Oath of Allegiance on June 21, 1865.

WHITAKER, HENRY C., Private
Enlisted in Surry County on September 1, 1862, for the war. Wounded and captured at Gettysburg, Pennsylvania, July 1-3, 1863. Left arm amputated. Sent to hospital at Baltimore, Maryland. Paroled and sent to City Point, Virginia, for exchange on September 25, 1863. Admitted to hospital at Richmond, Virginia, September 28, 1863, and furloughed for 60 days October 5, 1863. Reported as absent on furlough until retired to the Invalid Corps on January 23, 1865. Assigned to light duty at Goldsboro.

WHITAKER, ISAIAH, Private
Resided in Surry County where he enlisted at age 40, January 29, 1863, for the war. Present or accounted for through February, 1865. Captured at Burkeville, Virginia, April 6, 1865, and confined at Point Lookout, Maryland, until released after taking the Oath of Allegiance on June 21, 1865.

WHITAKER, JASON F., Private
Resided in Surry County where he enlisted at age 18, November 1, 1863, for the war. Present or accounted for through February, 1865. Captured at Farmville, Virginia, April 6, 1865, and confined at Point Lookout, Maryland, until released after taking the Oath of Allegiance on June 21, 1865.

WHITAKER, LEVI, Private
Resided in Surry County where he enlisted at age 20, August 10, 1861, for twelve months. Captured at Roanoke Island on February 8, 1862, and paroled at Elizabeth City, N.C., February 21, 1862. Present or accounted for until captured near Spotsylvania Court House, Virginia, May 20, 1864. Confined at Point Lookout, Maryland, until transferred to Elmira, New York, July 3-6, 1864. Released at Elmira after taking the Oath of Allegiance on May 17, 1865.

WHITAKER, RICHARD, Private
Born in Surry County where he resided as a farmer and enlisted at age 39, August 10, 1861, for twelve months. Captured at Roanoke Island on February 8, 1862, and paroled at Elizabeth City, N.C., on February 21, 1862. Discharged on December 10, 1862, by reason of age and being a nonconscript.

WILLIAMS, JOHN H., Private
Enlisted in Stokes County at age 20, May 4, 1861, for twelve months. Captured at Roanoke Island on February 8, 1862, and paroled at Elizabeth City, N.C., on February 21, 1862. Wounded at Gettysburg, Pennsylvania, July 1-3, 1863. Present or accounted for through September-October, 1864, when he was reported as "absent prisoner of war." Died at Elmira, New York, October 28, 1864. Date and place of capture not reported.

WILLIAMS, JOHN I., Private
Resided in Davidson County and enlisted in Forsyth County at age 34, September 19, 1861, for twelve months. Mustered in as Corporal. Reduced to ranks January-February, 1863. Present or accounted for through February, 1865, being detailed as an ambulance driver in 1865. Paroled at Appomattox Court House, Virginia, April 9, 1865.

WILMOTH, WILLIAM R., Private
Resided in Surry County where he enlisted at age 37, August 10, 1861, for twelve months. Mustered in as Corporal. Captured at Roanoke Island on February 8, 1862, and paroled at Elizabeth City, N.C., on February 21, 1862. Reduced to ranks September 25, 1862, and discharged on May 13, 1863, by reason of age.

WOOD, BENJAMIN FRANKLIN, 1st Sergeant
Resided in Surry County where he enlisted at age 17, August 10, 1861, for twelve months. Mustered in as Private. Captured at Roanoke Island on February 8, 1862, and paroled at Elizabeth City, N.C., on February 21, 1862. Appointed Sergeant on September 25, 1862, and promoted to 1st Sergeant in May, 1863. Present or accounted for until captured at Strasburg, Virginia, October 19, 1864. Confined at Point Lookout, Maryland, until released after taking the Oath of Allegiance on June 21, 1865.

WOOD, LEE A., Private
Resided in Surry County where he enlisted at age 19, August 10, 1861, for twelve months. Captured at Roanoke Island on February 8, 1862, and paroled at Elizabeth City, N.C., on February 21, 1862. Present or accounted for until captured near Washington, D.C., July 14, 1864. Confined at Elmira, New York, until released after taking the Oath of Allegiance on June 30, 1865.

WOOD, WILLIAM H., Private
Resided in Surry County where he enlisted at age 19, January 15, 1864, for the war. Captured at Fisher's Hill, Virginia, September 22, 1864, and confined at Point Lookout, Maryland, until paroled on February 18, 1865, and sent to James River, Virginia, for exchange. Reported as present on a roll of a detachment of paroled and ex-

changed prisoners at Camp Lee, near Richmond, Virginia, dated February 23, 1865.

WOODRUFF, AARON C., Private
Provided Andrew J. Hodges as his substitute.

COMPANY C

This company was organized at Richmond, Virginia, where it enlisted on October 19, 1861, and was assigned to Green's Independent Regiment, Wise's Legion. The regiment failed to complete its organization and the companies were reorganized as the 2nd Battalion N.C. Infantry on November 1, 1861. This battalion completed its organization in January, 1862, and this company became Company C. Prior to January, 1862, the company was reported as Company A, Green's Independent Regiment, Wise's Legion. After the company joined the battalion it functioned as a part of the battalion, and its history is reported as a part of the battalion history. On November 15, 1862, this company was transferred out of the battalion and became 3rd Company G, 59th Regiment Virginia Infantry.

The following roster of the company covers only that period when the company served as Company C, 2nd Battalion N.C. Infantry. Researchers who wish to continue research for the period after November 15, 1862, when the company became 3rd Company G, 59th Regiment Virginia Infantry, should check the Compiled Military Service Records for that company on file in Record Group 109, National Archives and Records Service, Washington, D. C., and any records on file at the Virginia State Archives, Richmond, Virginia.

The information contained in the following roster of the company was compiled principally from company muster rolls which covered from the date of enlistment through June, 1862. No company muster rolls were found for the period from July, 1862, through the date of transfer, November 15, 1862. In addition to the company muster rolls, Roll of Honor records, receipt rolls, and hospital records, supplemented by state pension applications, United Daughters of the Confederacy records, and postwar rosters and histories, all provided useful information.

OFFICERS
CAPTAIN

OVERBEY, ROBERT C.
Appointed Captain to rank from July 27, 1861. Captured at Roanoke Island on February 8, 1862, and paroled at Elizabeth City, N.C., on February 21, 1862. Present or accounted for until transferred to 3rd Company G, 59th Regiment Virginia Infantry on November 15, 1862.

LIEUTENANTS

TALLEY, NATHANIEL, 2nd Lieutenant
Born in Virginia and enlisted at Richmond, Virginia, August 22, 1862, for the war. Elected 2nd Lieutenant on September 25, 1862, and appointed to rank from date of election. Transferred to 3rd

Company G, 59th Regiment Virginia Infantry on November 15, 1862.

WILLIAMSON, BAILEY PEYTON, 1st Lieutenant
Enlisted at Richmond, Virginia, October 19, 1861, for twelve months and appointed 1st Lieutenant to rank from July 24, 1861. Captured at Roanoke Island on February 8, 1862, and paroled at Elizabeth City, N.C., on February 21, 1862. Submitted his resignation on September 16, 1862, "in consideration of my having become a contractor with the Ordnance Department." Resignation accepted on September 25, 1862.

WILLIAMSON, BENJAMIN R., 2nd Lieutenant
Enlisted at Richmond, Virginia, October 19, 1861, for twelve months and appointed 2nd Lieutenant to rank from July 27, 1861. Captured at Roanoke Island on February 8, 1862, and paroled at Elizabeth City, N.C., on February 21, 1862. Died September 26, 1862, from "sting of a spider."

WILLIAMSON, EDMOND J., 1st Lieutenant
Born in Virginia and resided in Mecklenburg County, Virginia, prior to enlisting at Richmond, Virginia, October 19, 1861, for twelve months. Mustered in as Sergeant. Captured at Roanoke Island on February 8, 1862, and paroled at Elizabeth City, N.C., on February 21, 1862. Appointed 1st Lieutenant to rank from September 25, 1862. Present or accounted for until transferred to 3rd Company G, 59th Regiment Virginia Infantry on November 15, 1862.

WOOD, HENRY, Jr., 2nd Lieutenant
Enlisted at Richmond, Virginia, October 19, 1861, for twelve months. Appointed 2nd Lieutenant to rank from July 27, 1861. Captured at Roanoke Island on February 8, 1862, and paroled at Elizabeth City, N.C., on February 21, 1862. Present or accounted for until transferred to 3rd Company G, 59th Regiment Virginia Infantry on November 15, 1862.

NONCOMMISSIONED OFFICERS AND PRIVATES

ARRINGTON, WILLIAM, Private
Enlisted at Richmond, Virginia, October 19, 1861, for twelve months. Present or accounted for until transferred to 3rd Company G, 59th Regiment Virginia Infantry on November 15, 1862.

BELL, GEORGE, Private
Enlisted at Richmond, Virginia, October 19, 1861, for twelve months. Captured at Roanoke Island on February 8, 1862, and paroled at Elizabeth City, N.C., on February 21, 1862. Present or accounted for until transferred to 3rd Company G, 59th Regiment Virginia Infantry on November 15, 1862.

BELL, GREEN, Private
Enlisted at Richmond, Virginia, October 19, 1861, for twelve months. Captured at Roanoke Island on February 8, 1862, and paroled at Elizabeth City, N.C., on February 21, 1862. Present or accounted for until transferred to 3rd Company G, 59th Regiment Virginia Infantry on November 15, 1862.

BLANKS, VINCENT N., Sergeant
Enlisted at Richmond, Virginia, September 10, 1862, for the war. Mustered in as Sergeant. Transferred to 3rd Company G, 59th Regiment Virginia Infantry on November 15, 1862.

BLANKS, WILLIAM F., Private
Enlisted at Richmond, Virginia, September 10, 1862, for the war. Transferred to 3rd Company G, 59th Regiment Virginia Infantry on November 15, 1862.

BOWEN, JAMES B., Private
Enlisted at Richmond, Virginia, October 19, 1861, for twelve months. Captured at Roanoke Island on February 8, 1862, and paroled at Elizabeth City, N.C., on February 21, 1862. Present or accounted for until transferred to 3rd Company G, 59th Regiment Virginia Infantry on November 15, 1862.

BOWEN, JAMES E., Private
Enlisted at Richmond, Virginia, October 19, 1861, for twelve months. Captured at Roanoke Island on February 8, 1862, and paroled at Elizabeth City, N.C., on February 21, 1862. Present or accounted for until transferred to 3rd Company G, 59th Regiment Virginia Infantry on November 15, 1862.

BOWEN, JOHN W., Private
Enlisted at Richmond, Virginia, October 19, 1861, for twelve months. Present or accounted for until he died on January 21, 1862.

CLIBORNE, JAMES L., Sergeant
Enlisted at Richmond, Virginia, October 19, 1861, for twelve months. Mustered in as Sergeant. Captured at Roanoke Island on February 8, 1862, and paroled at Elizabeth City, N.C., on February 21, 1862. Present or accounted for until transferred to 3rd Company G, 59th Regiment Virginia Infantry on November 15, 1862.

CLIBORNE, STANLEY J., Private
Born in Chatham County and enlisted at Richmond, Virginia, October 19, 1861, for twelve months. Wounded at Roanoke Island on February 8, 1862, and died of his wounds on February 10, 1862.

DAVIS, WILLIAM H., Private
Enlisted at Richmond, Virginia, October 19, 1861, for twelve months. Present or accounted for on company muster rolls through June 30, 1862. No further records.

DUNN, J. C., Private
Resided in Halifax County and enlisted September 3, 1862, for the war. Present or accounted for on company muster rolls until reported as absent without leave February 10, 1865.

ELLIOTT, ANDREW J., Private
Enlisted at Richmond, Virginia, October 19, 1861, for twelve months. Died at Richmond, November-December, 1861.

ELLIOTT, JAMES M., Private
Enlisted at Richmond, Virginia, October 19, 1861, for twelve months. Captured at Roanoke Island on February 8, 1862, and paroled at Elizabeth City, N.C., February 21, 1862. Present or accounted

for on company muster rolls through June 30, 1862. No further records.

ELLIOTT, WILLIAM A., Private
Resided in Halifax County, Virginia, and enlisted October 19, 1861, at Richmond, Virginia, for twelve months. Captured at Roanoke Island on February 8, 1862, and paroled at Elizabeth City, N.C., February 21, 1862. Present or accounted for until transferred to 3rd Company G, 59th Regiment Virginia Infantry on November 15, 1862.

ELLIOTT, WILLIAM LEWIS, Private
Enlisted at Richmond, Virginia, October 19, 1861, for twelve months. Captured at Roanoke Island on February 8, 1862, and paroled at Elizabeth City, N.C., February 21, 1862. No further records.

FORLINES, JOHN W., Corporal
Resided in Halifax County, Virginia, and enlisted at Richmond, Virginia, October 19, 1861, for twelve months. Mustered in as Corporal. Captured at Roanoke Island on February 8, 1862, and paroled at Elizabeth City, N.C., February 21, 1862. Present or accounted for until transferred to 3rd Company G, 59th Regiment Virginia Infantry on November 15, 1862.

GLASS, DAVID D., Corporal
Resided in Halifax County, Virginia, and enlisted at Richmond, Virginia, October 19, 1861, for twelve months. Mustered in as Corporal. Captured at Roanoke Island on February 8, 1862, and paroled at Elizabeth City, N.C., February 21, 1862. Present or accounted for until transferred to 3rd Company G, 59th Regiment Virginia Infantry on November 15, 1862.

HIGHTOWER, WILLIAM H., Private
Resided in Halifax County, Virginia, and enlisted at Richmond, Virginia, October 19, 1861, for twelve months. Captured at Roanoke Island on February 8, 1862, and paroled at Elizabeth City, N.C., February 21, 1862. Present or accounted for until transferred to 3rd Company G, 59th Regiment Virginia Infantry on November 15, 1862.

HITE, EDWARD, Private
Enlisted at Richmond, Virginia, October 19, 1861, for twelve months. Captured at Roanoke Island on February 8, 1862, and paroled at Elizabeth City, N.C., February 21, 1862. Discharged October 27, 1862.

HITE, JAMES A., Private
Enlisted at Richmond, Virginia, October 19, 1861, for twelve months. Captured at Roanoke Island on February 8, 1862, and paroled at Elizabeth City, N.C., February 21, 1862. Present or accounted for until transferred to 3rd Company G, 59th Regiment Virginia Infantry on November 15, 1862.

HITE, SPENCER, Private
Enlisted at Richmond, Virginia, October 19, 1861, for twelve months. Captured at Roanoke Island on February 8, 1862, and paroled at Elizabeth City, N.C., February 21, 1862. Present or accounted for until transferred to 3rd Company G, 59th Regiment Virginia Infantry on November 15, 1862.

HUNDLEY, JOHN H., Private
Enlisted at Richmond, Virginia, October 19, 1861, for twelve months. Present or accounted for until

transferred to 3rd Company G, 59th Regiment Virginia Infantry on November 15, 1862.

HUTTON, JOBE C., Private

Enlisted in Virginia, January 1, 1862, for twelve months. Captured at Roanoke Island on February 8, 1862, and paroled at Elizabeth City, N.C., February 21, 1862. Present or accounted for until transferred to 3rd Company G, 59th Regiment Virginia Infantry on November 15, 1862.

JOHNSON, JAMES T., Corporal

Born in Mecklenburg County, Virginia, and enlisted at Richmond, Virginia, October 19, 1861, for twelve months. Mustered in as Corporal. Captured at Roanoke Island on February 8, 1862, and paroled at Elizabeth City, N.C., February 21, 1862. Present or accounted for until transferred to 3rd Company G, 59th Regiment Virginia Infantry on November 15, 1862.

JONES, EDWARD, Private

Enlisted in Virginia, January 15, 1862, for twelve months. Captured at Roanoke Island on February 8, 1862, and paroled at Elizabeth City, N.C., February 21, 1862. Present or accounted for through June 30, 1862.

KEEN, LEVI OSCAR, Private

Enlisted at Richmond, Virginia, October 19, 1861, for twelve months. Captured at Roanoke Island on February 8, 1862, and paroled at Elizabeth City, N.C., February 21, 1862. Present or accounted for until he appears on a pay voucher for the period June 30-October 22, 1862, which carries the remark: "Discharged."

LADD, JOHN W., Private

Resided in Halifax County, Virginia, and enlisted at Richmond, Virginia, October 19, 1861, for twelve months. Captured at Roanoke Island on February 8, 1862, and paroled at Elizabeth City, N.C., February 21, 1862. Present or accounted for until transferred to 3rd Company G, 59th Regiment Virginia Infantry on November 15, 1862.

McKANN, ARCHER T., Private

Resided in Halifax County, Virginia, and enlisted at Richmond, Virginia, October 19, 1861, for twelve months. Present or accounted for until transferred to 3rd Company G, 59th Regiment Virginia Infantry on November 15, 1862.

MATHEWS, WILLIAM H., Private

Born in Mecklenburg County, Virginia, and enlisted at Richmond, Virginia, October 19, 1861, for twelve months. Present or accounted for until transferred to 3rd Company G, 59th Regiment Virginia Infantry on November 15, 1862.

MOORE, ALFRED H., Sergeant

Enlisted at Richmond, Virginia, October 19, 1861, for twelve months. Mustered in as Sergeant. Captured at Roanoke Island on February 8, 1862, and paroled at Elizabeth City, N.C., February 21, 1861. Present or accounted for until transferred to 3rd Company G, 59th Regiment Virginia Infantry on November 15, 1862.

MURRAY, JAMES, Private

Enlisted at Richmond, Virginia, October 19, 1861, for twelve months. Died January 20, 1862, at Wilmington.

NEWTON, JAMES J., Private

Born in Mecklenburg County, Virginia, and was a well digger prior to his enlistment at Richmond, Virginia, October 19, 1861, for twelve months. Present or accounted for until transferred to 3rd Company G, 59th Regiment Virginia Infantry on November 15, 1862.

NUNN, CONRAD B., Private

Enlisted at Richmond, Virginia, October 19, 1861, for twelve months. Captured at Roanoke Island on February 8, 1862, and paroled at Elizabeth City, N.C., February 21, 1862. Present or accounted for through October 22, 1862. No further records.

NUNN, JAMES T., Private

Enlisted in Virginia, January 15, 1862, for twelve months. Captured at Roanoke Island on February 8, 1862, and paroled at Elizabeth City, N.C., February 21, 1862. Died April 8, 1862, in Mecklenburg County.

NUNN, JOSHUA, Private

Resided in Halifax County, Virginia, and enlisted August 27, 1862, for the war. Transferred to 3rd Company G, 59th Regiment Virginia Infantry on November 15, 1862.

OVERBEY, DITRION, Private

Resided in Halifax County, Virginia, and enlisted at Richmond, Virginia, October 19, 1861, for twelve months. Captured at Roanoke Island on February 8, 1862, and paroled at Elizabeth City, N.C., February 21, 1862. Present or accounted for until transferred to 3rd Company G, 59th Regiment Virginia Infantry on November 15, 1862.

OVERBY, LAFAYETTE L., Private

Born in Halifax County, Virginia, where he resided prior to enlisting at Richmond, Virginia, October 19, 1861, for twelve months. Present or accounted for until transferred to 3rd Company G, 59th Regiment Virginia Infantry on November 15, 1862.

PHILLIPS, JOHN TUCKER, Private

Born in Virginia and enlisted at Richmond, Virginia, October 19, 1861, for twelve months. Captured at Roanoke Island on February 8, 1862, and paroled at Elizabeth City, N.C., February 21, 1862. Present or accounted for until transferred to 3rd Company G, 59th Regiment Virginia Infantry on November 15, 1862.

REESE, BEVERLY M., Corporal

Enlisted at Richmond, Virginia, October 19, 1861, for twelve months. Mustered in as Corporal. Captured at Roanoke Island on February 8, 1862, and paroled at Elizabeth City, N.C., February 21, 1862. Present or accounted for until transferred to 3rd Company G, 59th Regiment Virginia Infantry on November 15, 1862.

RICE, LEANDER W., Private

Resided in Halifax County, Virginia, and enlisted at Richmond, Virginia, October 19, 1861, for twelve months. Present or accounted for until transferred to 3rd Company G, 59th Regiment Virginia Infantry on November 15, 1862.

RICE, WILLIAM, Private

Enlisted at Richmond, Virginia, October 19, 1861, for twelve months. Present or accounted for until transferred to 3rd Company G, 59th Regiment Virginia Infantry on November 15, 1862.

SINGLETON, GEORGE W., Private

Enlisted at Richmond, Virginia, October 19, 1861, for twelve months. Captured at Roanoke Island on February 8, 1862, and paroled at Elizabeth City, N.C., February 21, 1862. Died on March 21, 1862.

SMITH, ANDERSON P., Private

Enlisted at Richmond, Virginia, October 19, 1861, for twelve months. Captured at Roanoke Island on February 8, 1862, and paroled at Elizabeth City, N.C., February 21, 1862. Present or accounted for until transferred to 3rd Company G, 59th Regiment Virginia Infantry on November 15, 1862.

SMITH, NATHANIEL A., Private

Born in Chatham County and was a farmer prior to enlisting at Richmond, Virginia, October 19, 1861, for twelve months. Captured at Roanoke Island on February 8, 1862, and paroled at Elizabeth City, N.C., February 21, 1862. Present or accounted for until transferred to 3rd Company G, 59th Regiment Virginia Infantry on November 15, 1862.

SMITH, WILLIAM A., Private

Enlisted at Richmond, Virginia, October 19, 1861, for twelve months. Captured at Roanoke Island on February 8, 1862, and paroled at Elizabeth City, N.C., February 21, 1862. Present or accounted for until transferred to 3rd Company G, 59th Regiment Virginia Infantry on November 15, 1862.

STRANGE, E. F., Private

Resided in Halifax County, Virginia, and enlisted on August 27, 1862, for the war. Transferred to 3rd Company G, 59th Regiment Virginia Infantry on November 15, 1862.

TALLEY, JOHN H., 1st Sergeant

Enlisted at Richmond, Virginia, October 19, 1861, for twelve months. Mustered in as 1st Sergeant. Killed February 8, 1862, at Roanoke Island.

TALLEY, PEYTON R., Private

Born in Mecklenburg County, Virginia, where he resided prior to enlisting at Richmond, Virginia, October 19, 1861, for twelve months. Captured at Roanoke Island on February 8, 1862, and paroled at Elizabeth City, N.C., February 21, 1862. Present or accounted for until transferred to 3rd Company G, 59th Regiment Virginia Infantry on November 15, 1862.

THOMPSON, JOSEPH, Private

Enlisted at Richmond, Virginia, October 19, 1861, for twelve months. Captured at Roanoke Island on February 8, 1862, and paroled at Elizabeth City, N.C., February 21, 1862. No further records.

THOMPSON, WILLIAM A., Private

Enlisted at Richmond, Virginia, October 19, 1861, for twelve months. Died February 1, 1862.

WALLER, ISAAC D., Private

Enlisted at Richmond, Virginia, October 19, 1861, for twelve months. Captured at Roanoke Island on February 8, 1862, and paroled at Elizabeth City, N.C., February 21, 1862. Present or ac-

counted for until transferred to 3rd Company G, 59th Regiment Virginia Infantry on November 15, 1862.

WELLS, LATIMUS L., Private

Enlisted at Richmond, Virginia, October 19, 1861, for twelve months. Captured at Roanoke Island on February 8, 1862, and paroled at Elizabeth City, N.C., February 21, 1862. Present or accounted for until transferred to 3rd Company G, 59th Regiment Virginia Infantry on November 15, 1862.

WILKINS, LEROY S., Private

Enlisted at Richmond, Virginia, October 19, 1861, for twelve months. Captured at Roanoke Island on February 8, 1862, and paroled at Elizabeth City, N.C., February 21, 1862. Present or accounted for until transferred to 3rd Company G, 59th Regiment Virginia Infantry on November 15, 1862.

WILKINSON, DAVID, Private

Enlisted at Richmond, Virginia, October 19, 1861, for twelve months. Captured at Roanoke Island on February 8, 1862, and paroled at Elizabeth City, N.C., on February 21, 1862. Present or accounted for until transferred to 3rd Company G, 59th Regiment Virginia Infantry on November 15, 1862.

WILKINSON, EDMOND J., Private

Enlisted at Richmond, Virginia, October 19, 1861, for twelve months. Captured at Roanoke Island on February 8, 1862, and paroled at Elizabeth City, N.C., on February 21, 1862. Present or accounted for until transferred to 3rd Company G, 59th Regiment Virginia Infantry on November 15, 1862.

WILKINSON, WILLIAM, Private

Resided in Halifax County, Virginia, and enlisted at Richmond, Virginia, October 19, 1861, for twelve months. Captured at Roanoke Island on February 8, 1862, and paroled at Elizabeth City, N.C., February 21, 1862. Present or accounted for until transferred to 3rd Company G, 59th Regiment Virginia Infantry on November 15, 1862.

WILLIAMSON, HUGH L., Private

Enlisted in Virginia, January 15, 1862, for twelve months. Present or accounted for until transferred to 3rd Company G, 59th Regiment Virginia Infantry on November 15, 1862.

WILLIAMSON, WILLIAM A., Private

Enlisted at Richmond, Virginia, October 19, 1861, for twelve months. Captured at Roanoke Island on February 8, 1862, and paroled at Elizabeth City, N.C., February 21, 1862. Present or accounted for until transferred to 3rd Company G, 59th Regiment Virginia Infantry on November 15, 1862.

COMPANY D

This company was formed at Richmond, Virginia, on September 27, 1861, from a part of Captain Jesse Burtz's Company, known as the "Cherokee Georgia Mountaineers." Captain Burtz's Company had enlisted at Concord, Georgia, on July 22, 1861. The spin-off company joined Green's Independent Regiment, Wise's Legion, and became Company D. The regiment failed to complete its organization, and the companies were organized into the 2nd Battalion N.C. Infantry on November 1, 1861. When the battalion completed its organization in January, 1862, the company became Company D of the battalion. After the company joined the battalion it functioned as a part of the battalion, and its history is reported as a part of the battalion history. On April 11, 1864, this company was transferred out of the battalion and became 2nd Company E, 21st Regiment Georgia Infantry.

The following roster of the company covers only that period when the company served as Company D, 2nd Battalion N.C. Infantry. Researchers who wish to continue research for the period after April 11, 1864, when the company became 2nd Company E, 21st Regiment Georgia Infantry, should check the Compiled Military Service Records for that company on file in Record Group 109, National Archives and Records Service, Washington, D. C., and the records on file at the Georgia Archives, Atlanta, Georgia.

The information contained in the following roster of the company was compiled principally from company muster rolls which covered from the date of enlistment through December, 1861; April through October, 1862; September-October, 1863; and April, 1864. No company muster rolls were found for January through March, 1862; October, 1862, through August, 1863; or November, 1863, through March, 1864. In addition to the company muster rolls, Roll of Honor records, receipt rolls, and hospital records, supplemented by state pension applications, United Daughters of the Confederacy records, and postwar rosters and histories, all provided useful information.

OFFICERS
CAPTAIN
SMITH, EDWARD
Resided in Forsyth County, Georgia, where he enlisted on July 22, 1861, for twelve months. Appointed Captain to rank from September 27, 1861. Captured at Roanoke Island on February 8, 1862, and paroled at Elizabeth City, N.C., on February 21, 1862. Wounded at Gettysburg, Pennsylvania, July 1, 1863. Present or accounted for until transferred to 2nd Company E, 21st Regiment Georgia Infantry on April 11, 1864.

LIEUTENANTS
HARRIS, DAVID T., 3rd Lieutenant
Resided in Forsyth County, Georgia, where he enlisted on July 22, 1861, for twelve months. Appointed 3rd Lieutenant to rank from September 27, 1861. Captured at Roanoke Island on February 8, 1862, and paroled at Elizabeth City, N.C., on February 21, 1862. Present or accounted for until transferred to 2nd Company E, 21st Regiment Georgia Infantry on April 11, 1864.

HILL, JOHN W., 1st Lieutenant
Enlisted in Forsyth County, Georgia, July 22, 1861, for twelve months. Appointed 1st Lieutenant

to rank from September 27, 1861. Captured at Roanoke Island on February 8, 1862, and paroled at Elizabeth City, N.C., on February 21, 1862. April 30-October 31, 1862, muster roll carries the remark: "Defeated 25 September in reorganization as 1st Lieutenant. Gone home."

JULIAN, ROBERT M., 2nd Lieutenant
Enlisted in Forsyth County, Georgia, July 22, 1861, for twelve months. Appointed 2nd Lieutenant to rank from October 2, 1861. Captured at Roanoke Island on February 8, 1862, and paroled at Elizabeth City, N.C., on February 21, 1862. Present or accounted for until captured at Jacks Mountain, Pennsylvania, July 4, 1863. Confined at Fort Delaware, Delaware, until transferred to Johnson's Island, Ohio, July 18-20, 1863. Absent in confinement when transferred to 2nd Company E, 21st Regiment Georgia Infantry on April 11, 1864.

McCLURE, WILLIAM H., 1st Lieutenant
Resided in Forsyth County, Georgia, where he enlisted on November 28, 1861, for twelve months. Mustered in as Private and appointed Sergeant around April, 1862. Elected 1st Lieutenant at reorganization of company on September 25, 1862, and appointed to rank from date of election. Wounded at Gettysburg, Pennsylvania, July 1, 1863. Present or accounted for until transferred to 2nd Company E, 21st Regiment Georgia Infantry on April 11, 1864.

NONCOMMISSIONED OFFICERS AND PRIVATES
ASHWORTH, JOHN A., Corporal
Enlisted in Forsyth County, Georgia, July 22, 1861, for twelve months. Mustered in as Corporal. Present or accounted for until transferred to 2nd Company E, 21st Regiment Georgia Infantry on April 11, 1864.

ASHWORTH, WILLIAM, Private
Enlisted in Forsyth County, Georgia, September 1, 1862, for the war. Captured at Gettysburg, Pennsylvania, July 1-5, 1863, and confined at DeCamp General Hospital, Davids Island, New York Harbor, until sent to City Point, Virginia, August 24, 1863, for exchange. Reported as present at Camp Lee, near Richmond, Virginia, on September 7, 1863. Transferred to 2nd Company E, 21st Regiment Georgia Infantry on April 11, 1864.

BAGWELL, JOHN, Private
Enlisted in Forsyth County, Georgia, July 22, 1861, for twelve months. Captured at Roanoke Island on February 8, 1862, and paroled at Elizabeth City, N.C., on February 21, 1862. Present or accounted for until transferred to 2nd Company E, 21st Regiment Georgia Infantry on April 11, 1864.

BANISTER, COLUMBUS, Private
Enlisted in Forsyth County, Georgia, January 19, 1864, for the war. Present or accounted for until transferred to 2nd Company E, 21st Regiment Georgia Infantry on April 11, 1864.

BANISTER, JAMES, Private
Enlisted in Forsyth County, Georgia, July 22, 1861, for twelve months. Captured at Roanoke Island on February 8, 1862, and paroled at Elizabeth City,

N.C., on February 21, 1862. Present or accounted for until captured at or near Gettysburg, Pennsylvania, July 3-4, 1863. Confined in hospital at Frederick, Maryland, July 6, 1863, with a gunshot wound of the leg. Transferred to Fort Delaware, Delaware, July 9, 1863, and to Point Lookout, Maryland, October 18, 1863. Died at Point Lookout on January 8, 1864, of "pleurisy."

BARNETT, FRANCIS M., Corporal

Enlisted in Forsyth County, Georgia, July 22, 1861, for twelve months. Mustered in as Private. Captured at Roanoke Island on February 8, 1862, and paroled at Elizabeth City, N.C., February 21, 1862. Appointed Corporal, September 25, 1862. Present or accounted for on company muster rolls through October, 1862. Died at Gordon's Springs, Georgia, prior to October, 1863.

BEAM, ANDREW J., Private

Enlisted in Forsyth County, Georgia, July 22, 1861, for twelve months. Captured at Roanoke Island on February 8, 1862, and paroled at Elizabeth City, N.C., February 21, 1862. Present or accounted for on company muster rolls through October, 1862. No further records.

BLACKSTOCK, ALLEN, Private

Enlisted in Forsyth County, Georgia, July 22, 1861, for twelve months. Captured at Roanoke Island on February 8, 1862, and paroled at Elizabeth City, N.C., February 21, 1862. Reported on company muster roll for September-October, 1863, as "at home, wounded furlough." Appears on the muster roll for April 1, 1864, as "absent without leave, furlough expired." Transferred to 2nd Company E, 21st Regiment Georgia Infantry on April 11, 1864.

BLANTON, ASA, Private

Resided as a farmer prior to enlisting in Forsyth County, Georgia, July 22, 1861, for twelve months. Captured at Roanoke Island on February 8, 1862, and paroled at Elizabeth City, N.C., February 21, 1862. Discharged by Conscript Act at age 46 on October 17, 1862.

BLANTON, GRANDISON, Private

Enlisted in Forsyth County, Georgia, January 15, 1862, for twelve months. Captured at Roanoke Island on February 8, 1862, and paroled at Elizabeth City, N.C., February 21, 1862. Wounded at Gettysburg, Pennsylvania, and captured in hospital at that place July 1-3, 1863. Confined at DeCamp General Hospital, Davids Island, New York Harbor, July 20, 1863, with "g.s. hip." Paroled at DeCamp General Hospital and sent to City Point, Virginia, for exchange. Received at City Point, September 8, 1863. Admitted to hospital at Petersburg, Virginia, September 8, 1863, and furloughed for 50 days on September 16, 1863. Reported on company muster rolls as absent without leave after expiration of furlough until transferred to 2nd Company E, 21st Regiment Georgia Infantry on April 11, 1864.

BOND, JAMES W., Private

Enlisted in Forsyth County, Georgia, July 1, 1861, for twelve months. Present or accounted for on company muster rolls through October, 1861. No further records.

BREWTON, ENOCH, Private

Enlisted in Forsyth County, Georgia, September 1, 1862, for the war. Present or accounted for on company muster rolls through October, 1862. Discharged February 10, 1863, by reason of "being a minor."

BROOKS, JOHN, Private

Enlisted in Forsyth County, Georgia, September, 12, 1862, for the war. Company muster roll for April 30-October 31, 1862, carries the remark: "Substitute deserted 15 September." No further records.

CAIN, HECTOR V., Private

Born in Forsyth County, Georgia, and resided as a farmer prior to enlisting in Forsyth County on July 22, 1861, for twelve months. Discharged at age 22 on January 23, 1862, by reason of "diseased lungs produced by an attack of measles pneumonia."

CAIN, JOHN D., Private

Enlisted in Forsyth County, Georgia, July 22, 1861, for twelve months. Died November 4, 1861.

CAIN, WILLIAM J., Private

Resided in Lenoir County and enlisted in Forsyth County, Georgia, November 28, 1861, for twelve months. Present or accounted for until transferred to 2nd Company E, 21st Regiment Georgia Infantry on April 11, 1864.

CLARK, MILTON L., Private

Enlisted in Georgia on May 8, 1862, for twelve months. Present or accounted for until transferred to 2nd Company E, 21st Regiment Georgia Infantry on April 11, 1864.

COPELAND, WILLIAM C., Private

Enlisted in Forsyth County, Georgia, July 22, 1861, for twelve months. Mustered in as Corporal. Captured at Roanoke Island on February 8, 1862, and paroled at Elizabeth City, N.C., February 21, 1862. Reduced to ranks September 25, 1862. Admitted to hospital at Richmond, Virginia, July 20, 1863, with "vul. sclopm. foot" and was furloughed July 28-29, 1863. Reported on company muster rolls as absent wounded until he appears as present April 1, 1864. Transferred to 2nd Company E, 21st Regiment Georgia Infantry on April 11, 1864.

COPLAND, SYLVANUS C., Private

Enlisted in Forsyth County, Georgia, September 1, 1862, for the war. Present or accounted for until transferred to 2nd Company E, 21st Regiment Georgia Infantry on April 11, 1864.

COX, MARION L., Sergeant

Enlisted in Forsyth County, Georgia, July 22, 1861, for twelve months. Mustered in as Private. Captured at Roanoke Island on February 8, 1862, and paroled at Elizabeth City, N.C., February 21, 1862. Appointed Corporal, September 25, 1862. Company muster roll for April 1, 1864, reports him as absent without leave and gives his rank as Sergeant. Transferred to 2nd Company E, 21st Regiment Georgia Infantry on April 11, 1864.

CRAIN, HARPER, Private

Born in Pickens District, South Carolina, and enlisted in Forsyth County, Georgia, July 22, 1861, for twelve months. Present or accounted for until discharged at age 17, November 17, 1862, by reason of the Conscript Act.

CROCKER, JACOB A., Private

Enlisted in Forsyth County, Georgia, July 22, 1861, for twelve months. Mustered in as Sergeant. Captured at Roanoke Island on February 8, 1862, and paroled at Elizabeth City, N.C., February 21, 1862. Reduced to ranks September 25, 1862. Admitted to hospital at Williamsburg, Virginia, August 1, 1863, with "vul. sclopeticum" and was transferred to hospital at Petersburg, Virginia, August 17, 1863. Returned to duty August 21, 1863. Present or accounted for until transferred to 2nd Company E, 21st Regiment Georgia Infantry on April 11, 1864.

CROCKER, THOMAS E., Private

Enlisted in Forsyth County, Georgia, July 22, 1861, for twelve months. Captured at Roanoke Island on February 8, 1862, and paroled at Elizabeth City, N.C., February 21, 1862. Present or accounted for through October, 1862. No further records.

DOOLEY, JOHN H., Private

Enlisted in Forsyth County, Georgia, October 19, 1861, for twelve months. Admitted to hospital at Wilmington, February 7, 1862, with "catarrhus" and returned to duty the same day. Present or accounted for on company muster rolls until transferred to 2nd Company E, 21st Regiment Georgia Infantry on April 11, 1864.

DOOLY, JOSHUA A., Private

Born in Georgia and was by occupation a farmer prior to enlisting in Forsyth County, Georgia, October 19, 1861, for twelve months. Discharged at age 22, January 31, 1862.

DUNLAP, TYLER, Private

Enlisted in Forsyth County, Georgia, July 22, 1861, for twelve months. Company muster roll for November-December, 1861, states that he was "discharged."

DUNLAP, WADDY T., Private

Enlisted in Forsyth County, Georgia, July 22, 1861, for twelve months. Died September 30, 1861,

ELLIOTT, HIRAM, Private

Born in Lumpkin County, Georgia, and was by occupation a farmer prior to enlisting in Forsyth County, Georgia, November 28, 1861, for twelve months. Admitted to hospital at Wilmington, February 4, 1862, with "parotitis" and was returned to duty on February 13, 1862. Discharged at age 16 on December 13, 1862.

ELLIOTT, JOHN R., Sergeant

Enlisted in Forsyth County, Georgia, July 1, 1861, for twelve months. Mustered in as Private. Admitted to hospital at Wilmington, February 1, 1862, with "parotitis" and returned to duty February 4, 1862. Again admitted to same hospital on February 6, 1862, with "diarrhoea acute" and returned to duty on February 20, 1862. Appointed Sergeant, September 25, 1862. Present or accounted for until transferred to 2nd Company E, 21st Regiment Georgia Infantry on April 11, 1864.

ELLIS, THOMAS J., Musician

Enlisted in Forsyth County, Georgia, November

19, 1862, for the war. Mustered in as Musician. Present or accounted for until transferred to 2nd Company E, 21st Regiment Georgia Infantry on April 11, 1864.

FULLER, URIAH, Private

Enlisted November 19, 1862, for the war. Admitted to hospital at Richmond, Virginia, September 16, 1863, with "bronchitis chro." and was returned to duty January 23, 1864. Again admitted to hospital at Richmond on March 28, 1864, with "asthma" and was transferred to another hospital on March 30, 1864. Company muster rolls report that he was absent on sick leave until transferred to 2nd Company E, 21st Regiment Georgia Infantry on April 11, 1864.

GAINES, GREEN B., Private

Enlisted in Forsyth County, Georgia, July 22, 1861, for twelve months. Captured at Roanoke Island on February 8, 1862, and paroled at Elizabeth City, N.C., on February 21, 1862. Captured at Gettysburg, Pennsylvania, July 4, 1863, and admitted to U.S.A. General Hospital, Frederick, Maryland, July 6, 1863, with "g.s.w. arm." Transferred on August 7, 1863, to U.S.A. General Hospital, West's Buildings, Baltimore, Maryland, where he remained until sent to Fort McHenry, Maryland, on August 14, 1863. Transferred to Point Lookout, Maryland, August 22, 1863, and was admitted on October 24, 1863, to Hammond U.S.A. General Hospital at Point Lookout, where he died January 26, 1864, of "chronic diarrhoea." Died at age 19.

GENTRY, JOHN B., Private

Enlisted in Forsyth County, Georgia, July 22, 1861, for twelve months. Died January 23, 1862.

GOSS, TYRA G., Private

Enlisted in Forsyth County, Georgia, on July 22, 1861, for twelve months. Company muster rolls state that he died October 26, 1861, or November 1, 1861.

HAMBY, BENJAMIN G., Private

Enlisted in Forsyth County, November 28, 1861, for twelve months. Present or accounted for until transferred to 2nd Company E, 21st Regiment Georgia Infantry on April 11, 1864.

HARRIS, JOHN, Private

Enlisted in Forsyth County, Georgia, July 22, 1861, for twelve months. Captured at Roanoke Island on February 8, 1862, and paroled at Elizabeth City, N.C., February 21, 1862. Again captured at Funkstown, Maryland, on July 6, 1863, and admitted to U.S.A. General Hospital, Frederick, Maryland, on the same day with gunshot wound of right arm. Transferred to 2nd Company E, 21st Regiment Georgia Infantry on April 11, 1864, while absent prisoner of war.

HARRISON, ALFRED G., Private

Born in Surry County and was a blacksmith prior to enlisting in Forsyth County, Georgia, on July 22, 1861, for twelve months. Discharged January 23, 1862, at age 19, by reason of "measles complicated with general prostration and absolutely broken down health."

HARRISON, LEROY, Private

Enlisted in Forsyth County, Georgia, July 22, 1861, for twelve months. Captured at Roanoke Island on February 8, 1862, and paroled at Elizabeth City, N.C., February 21, 1862. Present or accounted for until he appears on a register of prisoners received and disposed of by the Provost Marshal General, Army of the Potomac, dated February 14, 1864, which states that he was a "Rebel deserter."

HARVEY, B. C., Private

Captured at Roanoke Island on February 8, 1862, and paroled at Elizabeth City, N.C., February 21, 1862.

HEAD, WILLIAM O., Private

Enlisted in Forsyth County, Georgia, July 22, 1861, for twelve months. Mustered in as Private. Captured at Roanoke Island on February 8, 1862, and paroled at Elizabeth City, N.C., February 21, 1862. Appointed Corporal, September 25, 1862. Wounded at Gettysburg, Pennsylvania, and captured in hospital at that place July 4, 1863. Confined at DeCamp General Hospital, Davids Island, New York Harbor, until paroled and sent to City Point, Virginia, for exchange on October 22, 1863. Admitted to hospital at Richmond, Virginia, October 29, 1863, with gunshot wound of foot and furloughed for 30 days on November 7, 1863. Transferred to 2nd Company E, 21st Regiment Georgia Infantry on April 11, 1864, while "absent without leave, exchanged prisoner."

HENDERSON, W., Private

Captured at Roanoke Island on February 8, 1862, and paroled at Elizabeth City, N.C., February 21, 1862.

HENDRIX, W., Private

Born in Elbert County, Georgia, and was a farmer prior to enlisting in Forsyth County, Georgia, January 15, 1862, for twelve months. Captured at Roanoke Island on February 8, 1862, and paroled at Elizabeth City, N.C., February 21, 1862. Discharged at age 58 on January 14, 1863, by reason of the Conscript Act.

HENSEN, WILLIAM, Private

Enlisted in Forsyth County, Georgia, July 22, 1861, for twelve months. Captured at Roanoke Island on February 8, 1862, and paroled at Elizabeth City, N.C., February 21, 1862. Wounded and captured at Gettysburg, Pennsylvania, July 3-5, 1863, and admitted to U.S.A. General Hospital, Frederick, Maryland, July 6, 1863, with "com. fract. left forearm." Transferred to Fort McHenry, Maryland, July 7, 1863, and to Fort Delaware, Delaware, July 9, 1863. Transferred to Point Lookout, Maryland, October 18, 1863, and remained absent in confinement when transferred to 2nd Company E, 21st Regiment Georgia Infantry on April 11, 1864.

HENSON, JOHN H., Private

Enlisted in Forsyth County, Georgia, July 22, 1861, for twelve months. Discharged for disability October 31, 1861.

HERNDON, CALEB J., Private

Enlisted in Forsyth County, Georgia, July 22, 1861, for twelve months. Captured at Roanoke Island on February 8, 1862, and paroled at Elizabeth City, N.C., February 21, 1862. "Deserted from the C.S. Army at Greencastle, Pennsylvania, July 6, 1863," and took the Oath of Allegiance to the U.S. at Fort Mifflin, Pennsylvania, on November 17, 1863. Oath states that he was "released, but still in employ of government."

HIGGINS, WILLIAM S., Private

Enlisted in Forsyth County, Georgia, July 22, 1861, for twelve months. Company muster rolls state that he died October 24 or November 2, 1861.

HILL, DAVID M., Private

Enlisted in Forsyth County, Georgia, July 1, 1861, for twelve months. Company muster roll for July 22-October 31, 1861, carries the remark: "David M. Hill at home not bound to come." No further records.

HILL, JAMES, Private

Born in York District, South Carolina, and was a farmer prior to enlisting in Forsyth County, Georgia, July 22, 1861, for twelve months. Discharged at age 67, January 23, 1862, by reason of "physical disability."

HILL, REUBEN, Private

Born in Lumpkin County, Georgia, and was a farmer prior to enlisting in Forsyth County, Georgia, July 22, 1861, for twelve months. Discharged at age 17, October 17, 1862, by reason of the Conscript Act.

HOOD, HENRY, Private

Enlisted in Forsyth County, Georgia, July 1, 1861, for twelve months. Company muster roll for July 22-October 31, 1861, carries him as present. No further records.

HOOD, JOHN M., Private

Enlisted in Forsyth County, Georgia, July 1, 1861, for twelve months. Company muster roll for July 22-October 31, 1861, carries him as present. No further records.

HOPE, JAMES H., Private

Enlisted in Forsyth County, Georgia, July 22, 1861, for twelve months. Present or accounted for on company muster rolls through October, 1862. No further records.

JONES, YOUNG J., Private

Born in Dawson County, Georgia, and was a farmer prior to enlisting in Forsyth County, Georgia, July 22, 1861, for twelve months. Discharged at age 27, January 27, 1862, by reason of "physical disability caused by an attack of typhoid fever." Reenlisted in company September 1, 1862, in Forsyth County, Georgia. Wounded at Gettysburg, Pennsylvania, and captured in hospital at that place July 1-5, 1863. Confined on July 20, 1863, at DeCamp General Hospital, Davids Island, New York Harbor, where he was paroled and sent to City Point, Virginia, for exchange on August 24, 1863. Company muster rolls report him as absent at home paroled or furloughed through October, 1863. Appears as present on muster rolls dated April 1, 1864. Transferred to 2nd Company E, 21st Regiment Georgia Infantry on April 11, 1864.

JULIAN, ALFRED W., Private
Enlisted in Forsyth County, Georgia, November 28, 1861, for twelve months. Captured at Roanoke Island on February 8, 1862, and paroled at Elizabeth City, N.C., February 21, 1862. Again captured at Gettysburg, Pennsylvania, July 3, 1863, and confined at Fort McHenry, Maryland, until transferred to Fort Delaware, Delaware, July 9, 1863. Transferred to Point Lookout, Maryland, on October 18, 1863. Transferred to 2nd Company E, 21st Regiment Georgia Infantry on April 11, 1864, while absent confined as prisoner of war.

JULIAN, MICHAEL S., 1st Sergeant
Enlisted July 22, 1861, in Forsyth County, Georgia, for twelve months. Mustered in as 1st Sergeant. Captured at Roanoke Island on February 8, 1862, and paroled at Elizabeth City, N.C., February 21, 1862. Again captured at Gettysburg, Pennsylvania, July 3, 1863, and confined at Fort McHenry, Maryland, until transferred to Fort Delaware, Delaware, July 9, 1863. Transferred to Point Lookout, Maryland, October 18, 1863, and remained absent in confinement when transferred to 2nd Company E, 21st Regiment Georgia Infantry on April 11, 1864.

JULIAN, SAMUEL B., Private
Born in Forsyth County, Georgia, and was a farmer prior to enlisting in Forsyth County, January 15, 1862, for twelve months. Captured at Roanoke Island on February 8, 1862, and paroled at Elizabeth City, N.C., February 21, 1862. Discharged at age 17, January 14, 1863, by reason of the Conscript Act.

LAMB, BENJAMIN, Private
Enlisted in Forsyth County, Georgia, July 22, 1861, for twelve months. Captured at Roanoke Island on February 8, 1862, and paroled at Elizabeth City, N.C., February 21, 1862. Again captured at Gettysburg, Pennsylvania, July 1-5, 1863. Confined at DeCamp General Hospital, Davids Island, New York Harbor, until paroled and sent to City Point, Virginia, for exchange on August 24, 1863. Company muster rolls report him as absent at home paroled and furloughed through October, 1863. Appears as present on the company muster roll dated April 1, 1864. Transferred to 2nd Company E, 21st Regiment Georgia Infantry on April 11, 1864.

LEDBETTER, LEWIS J., Sergeant
Enlisted in Forsyth County, Georgia, July 22, 1861, for twelve months. Mustered in as Sergeant. Captured at Roanoke Island on February 8, 1862, and paroled at Elizabeth City, N.C., February 21, 1862. Present or accounted for until transferred to 2nd Company E, 21st Regiment Georgia Infantry on April 11, 1864.

LEE, ELIHU, Private
Enlisted in Forsyth County, Georgia, July 22, 1861, for twelve months. Captured at Roanoke Island on February 8, 1862, and released on parole at Elizabeth City, N.C., February 21, 1862. Present or accounted for on company muster rolls until April 1, 1864, when he is reported with the remark: "Absent without leave—furlough expired." Transferred to 2nd Company E, 21st Regiment Georgia

Infantry, on April 11, 1864, while absent without leave.

LOWE, HIRAM, Private
Enlisted in Forsyth County, Georgia, July 22, 1861, for twelve months. Captured at Roanoke Island on February 8, 1862, and released on parole at Elizabeth City, N.C., February 21, 1862. Present or accounted for on company muster rolls through October, 1863. Appears on a register of prisoners received and disposed of by the Provost Marshal General, Army of the Potomac, dated February 14, 1864, which states that he was a "Rebel deserter" sent in by the Provost Marshal, Cavalry Corps.

McBRAYER, GEORGE W., Private
Enlisted in Forsyth County, Georgia, July 22, 1861, for twelve months. Captured at Roanoke Island on February 8, 1862, and paroled at Elizabeth City, N.C., February 21, 1862. Present or accounted for on company muster rolls through October, 1862. No further records.

McCORMACK, WILLIAM L., Private
Enlisted in Forsyth County, Georgia, November 28, 1861, for twelve months. Admitted to hospital at Wilmington, February 1, 1862, with "febris typhoides" or "parotitis" and returned to duty February 15, 1862. Present or accounted for through October, 1862. Discharged November 28, 1862.

McCORMICK, HECTOR D., Private
Born in Rockingham County and was a farmer prior to enlisting in Forsyth County, Georgia, January 15, 1862, for twelve months. Captured at Roanoke Island on February 8, 1862, and paroled at Elizabeth City, N.C., February 21, 1862. Present or accounted for through October, 1862. Discharged at age 54, January 14, 1863, by reason of Conscript Act.

MARTIN, CHARLES B., Private
Enlisted in Forsyth County, Georgia, July 22, 1861, for twelve months. Captured at Roanoke Island on February 8, 1862, and paroled at Elizabeth City, N.C., February 21, 1862. Present or accounted for on company muster rolls until April 1, 1864, when he is reported as "absent sick in hospital at Lynchburg, Virginia." No further records.

MARTIN, HUGH W., Private
Enlisted in Forsyth County, Georgia, July 22, 1861, for twelve months. Died at Richmond, Virginia, November 11, 1861.

MILFORD, WILLIAM P., Sergeant
Enlisted in Forsyth County, Georgia, November 19, 1862, for the war. Mustered in as Sergeant. Present or accounted for until transferred to 2nd Company E, 21st Regiment Georgia Infantry on April 11, 1864.

MITCHELL, GOODMAN L., Private
Enlisted in Forsyth County, Georgia, July 22, 1861, for twelve months. Present or accounted for until transferred to 2nd Company E, 21st Regiment Georgia Infantry on April 11, 1864.

MITCHELL, WILLIAM B., Private
Born in Jones County, Georgia, and was a harness maker prior to enlisting in Forsyth County, Georgia, July 22, 1861, for twelve months. Dis-

charged at age 43, January 23, 1862, by reason of disability.

MULLINEX, THOMAS P., Private
Enlisted in Forsyth County, Georgia, July 22, 1861, for twelve months. Killed in battle at Roanoke Island on February 8, 1862.

NICELER, DANIEL, Private
Enlisted in Forsyth County, Georgia, July 22, 1861, for twelve months. Died October 16, 1861.

NICHOLS, THOMAS J., Private
Enlisted in Forsyth County, Georgia, July 22, 1861, for twelve months. Captured at Roanoke Island on February 8, 1862, and paroled at Elizabeth City, N.C., February 21, 1862. Again captured at Gettysburg, Pennsylvania, July 3-5, 1863, and confined at Fort McHenry, Maryland, until transferred to Fort Delaware, Delaware, July 9, 1863. Transferred on October 18, 1863, to Point Lookout, Maryland, where he took the Oath of Allegiance and joined the U.S. service on February 22, 1864.

PORTER, JOHN W., Private
Enlisted in Forsyth County, Georgia, July 22, 1861, for twelve months. Died October 22, 1861.

PRUITT, HARVEY, Private
Enlisted in Forsyth County, Georgia, January 15, 1862, for twelve months. Captured at Roanoke Island on February 8, 1862, and paroled at Elizabeth City, N.C., February 21, 1862. Again captured at South Mountain, Maryland, July 4, 1863, and confined at Fort McHenry, Maryland, until transferred to Fort Delaware, Delaware, July 9, 1863. Paroled at Fort Delaware, July 30, 1863. Admitted to hospital at Williamsburg, Virginia, August 1, 1863, with "v.s. right hand" and transferred to another hospital August 17, 1863. Present or accounted for until transferred to 2nd Company E, 21st Regiment Georgia Infantry on April 11, 1864.

RAINES, DAVID R., Private
Enlisted in Forsyth County, Georgia, November 28, 1861, for twelve months. Captured at Roanoke Island on February 8, 1862, and paroled at Elizabeth City, N.C., February 21, 1862. Died March 26, 1862.

RAINES, WESLEY, Private
Born in Pendleton District, South Carolina, and was a farmer prior to enlisting in Forsyth County, Georgia, July 22, 1861, for twelve months. Captured at Roanoke Island on February 8, 1862, and paroled at Elizabeth City, N.C., February 21, 1862. Discharged at age 49, October 17, 1862, by reason of "being a non-conscript."

RAKESTRAW, JAMES, Private
Enlisted in Forsyth County, Georgia, November 28, 1861, for twelve months. Captured at Roanoke Island on February 8, 1862, and paroled at Elizabeth City, N.C., February 21, 1862. Present or accounted for until transferred to 2nd Company E, 21st Regiment Georgia Infantry on April 11, 1864.

RAKESTRAW, LIPHUS, Private
Enlisted in Forsyth County, Georgia, July 22, 1861, for twelve months. Captured at Roanoke Island on February 8, 1862, and paroled at Elizabeth City, N.C., February 21, 1862. Present or accounted for

until transferred to 2nd Company E, 21st Regiment Georgia Infantry on April 11, 1864.

SCOTT, ALFRED W., Corporal
Enlisted in Forsyth County, Georgia, July 22, 1861, for twelve months. Mustered in as Corporal. Killed in battle at Roanoke Island on February 8, 1862.

SEAY, EFFORD, Corporal
Enlisted in Forsyth County, Georgia, July 22, 1861, for twelve months. Mustered in as Private. Captured at Roanoke Island on February 8, 1862, and paroled at Elizabeth City, N.C., February 21, 1862. Appointed Corporal, September 25, 1862. Captured at Gettysburg, Pennsylvania, July 5, 1863, and confined at U.S.A. General Hospital, Frederick, Maryland, July 7, 1863, with "rheumatism." Transferred on September 5, 1863, to U.S.A. General Hospital, West's Buildings, Baltimore, Maryland, where he was paroled on September 25, 1863, and sent to City Point, Virginia, for exchange. Present or accounted for on company muster rolls until April 1, 1864, when he is reported as "absent without leave—exchanged prisoner." Transferred to 2nd Company E, 21st Regiment Georgia Infantry on April 11, 1864, while absent without leave.

SEAY, IRVING, Private
Enlisted in Forsyth County, Georgia, July 22, 1861, for twelve months. Died October 26, 1861.

SEAY, JOHN B., Private
Enlisted in Forsyth County, Georgia, February 23, 1863, for the war. Admitted to hospital at Farmville, Virginia, June 10-11, 1863, with "neuralgia, face" and was returned to duty July 1, 1863. Detailed for duty as a nurse in hospital at Richmond, Virginia, September 7, 1863. Absent detailed until transferred to 2nd Company E, 21st Regiment Georgia Infantry on April 11, 1864.

SEAY, RANSOM, Private
Resided in Dawson County, Georgia, and enlisted in Forsyth County, Georgia, July 22, 1861, for twelve months. Captured at Roanoke Island on February 8, 1862, and paroled at Elizabeth City, N.C., February 21, 1862. Again captured at Gettysburg, Pennsylvania, on July 4, 1863, and confined at Fort McHenry, Maryland, until sent to Fort Delaware, Delaware, July 9, 1863. Remained absent in confinement when transferred to 2nd Company E, 21st Regiment Georgia Infantry on April 11, 1864.

SHERRILL, HENRY W., Private
Enlisted in Forsyth County, Georgia, July 22, 1861, for twelve months. Captured at Roanoke Island on February 8, 1862, and paroled at Elizabeth City, N.C., February 21, 1862. Again captured near Gettysburg, Pennsylvania, July 5, 1863, and was confined at Fort McHenry, Maryland, until transferred to Fort Delaware, Delaware, July 9, 1863. Remained absent in confinement when transferred to 2nd Company E, 21st Regiment Georgia Infantry on April 11, 1864.

SHOEMAKER, ANDREW J., Private
Enlisted in Forsyth County, Georgia, October 19, 1861, for twelve months. Captured at Roanoke

Island on February 8, 1862, and paroled at Elizabeth City, N.C., February 21, 1862. Present or accounted for on company muster rolls through October, 1862. Admitted to hospital at Richmond, Virginia, October 23, 1862, with "remittent fever" and was returned to duty January 31, 1863. Died prior to October 5, 1863.

SHOEMAKER, JOHN W., Private
Enlisted in Forsyth County, Georgia, July 22, 1861, for twelve months. Captured at Roanoke Island on February 8, 1862, and paroled at Elizabeth City, N.C., February 21, 1862. Again captured at Gettysburg, Pennsylvania, on July 3, 1863, and confined at Fort McHenry, Maryland, until sent to Fort Delaware, Delaware, July 9, 1863. Transferred to Point Lookout, Maryland, October 18, 1863, and remained absent in confinement when transferred to 2nd Company E, 21st Regiment Georgia Infantry on April 11, 1864.

SHOEMAKER, OLIVER R., Private
Enlisted in Forsyth County, Georgia, September 1, 1862, for the war. Company muster roll for April 30-October 31, 1862, carries him as present. No further records.

SMITH, EDWARD R., Private
Born in Anderson District, South Carolina, and was a farmer prior to enlisting in Forsyth County, Georgia, July 22, 1861, for twelve months. Captured at Roanoke Island on February 8, 1862, and paroled at Elizabeth City, N.C., February 21, 1862. Discharged at age 17, October 17, 1862, by the Conscript Act.

SMITH, MATTHEW A., Private
Enlisted in Forsyth County, Georgia, July 22, 1861, for twelve months. Died in hospital at Wilmington, February 16, 1862, of "pneumonia."

SMITH, ROBERT H., Private
Enlisted in Forsyth County, Georgia, November 28, 1861, for twelve months. Died in hospital at Wilmington, February 7, 1862, of "febris typhoides."

STEDMAN, HENRY W., Private
Enlisted in Forsyth County, Georgia, July 22, 1861, for twelve months. Captured at Roanoke Island on February 8, 1862, and paroled at Elizabeth City, N.C., February 21, 1862. Present or accounted for until transferred to 2nd Company E, 21st Regiment Georgia Infantry on April 11, 1864.

STEWART, JOHN, Private
Enlisted in Forsyth County, Georgia, September 1, 1862, for the war. Present or accounted for until transferred to 2nd Company E, 21st Regiment Georgia Infantry on April 11, 1864.

STEWART, THOMAS J., Private
Enlisted in Forsyth County, Georgia, July 22, 1861, for twelve months. Captured at Roanoke Island on February 8, 1862, and paroled at Elizabeth City, N.C., February 21, 1862. Present or accounted for through October, 1862. No further records.

STOWERS, JOHN, Private
Enlisted November 19, 1862. Detailed as a wagoner to drive division ordnance wagon from September-October, 1863, until transferred to 2nd

Company E, 21st Regiment Georgia Infantry on April 11, 1864.

STRIPLAND, TOLIVER E. L., Private
Enlisted in Forsyth County, Georgia, July 22, 1861, for twelve months. Captured at Roanoke Island on February 8, 1862, and paroled at Elizabeth City, N.C., February 21, 1862. Present or accounted for until transferred to 2nd Company E, 21st Regiment Georgia Infantry on April 11, 1864.

THACKER, ISAAC, Private
Born in Hall County, Georgia, and was a farmer prior to enlisting in Forsyth County, Georgia, July 22, 1861, for twelve months. Captured at Roanoke Island on February 8, 1862, and paroled at Elizabeth City, N.C., February 21, 1862. Discharged at age 17, October 17, 1862, by reason of the Conscript Act. Reenlisted in company prior to July, 1863, and was captured at Gettysburg, Pennsylvania, July 5, 1863. Confined at Fort McHenry, Maryland, and transferred to Fort Delaware, Delaware, July 9, 1863. Transferred to Point Lookout, Maryland, where he was paroled and sent to City Point, Virginia, for exchange on December 24, 1863. Company muster roll for April 1, 1864, reports him as absent without leave. Remained absent without leave when transferred to 2nd Company E, 21st Regiment Georgia Infantry on April 11, 1864.

THACKER, JAMES, Private
Enlisted in Forsyth County, Georgia, July 22, 1861, for twelve months. Captured at Roanoke Island on February 8, 1862, and paroled at Elizabeth City, N.C., February 21, 1862. Again captured at Gettysburg, Pennsylvania, on July 3, 1863, and confined at Fort McHenry, Maryland, until sent to Fort Delaware, Delaware, July 9, 1863. Transferred to Point Lookout, Maryland, October 18, 1863, and remained in confinement until transferred to 2nd Company E, 21st Regiment Georgia Infantry on April 11, 1864.

THOMAS, JAMES R., Private
Resided in Dawson County, Georgia, and enlisted in Forsyth County, Georgia, July 22, 1861, for twelve months. Captured at Roanoke Island on February 8, 1862, and paroled at Elizabeth City, N.C., February 21, 1862. Present or accounted for until he is reported on the September-October, 1863, muster roll as "absent—wounded and furloughed, home—time expired." Name appears as signature to an Oath of Allegiance to the U.S. subscribed and sworn to at Chattanooga, Tennessee, March 20, 1864.

THOMAS, LEWIS, Private
Enlisted in Forsyth County, Georgia, January 19, 1864, for the war. Present or accounted for until transferred to 2nd Company E, 21st Regiment Georgia Infantry on April 11, 1864.

THOMAS, REUBEN, Private
Enlisted in Forsyth County, Georgia, July 22, 1861, for twelve months. Captured at Roanoke Island on February 8, 1862, and paroled at Elizabeth City, N.C., February 21, 1862. Present or accounted for on company muster rolls through October, 1862. No further records.

THOMAS, SAMUEL, Private

Enlisted in Forsyth County, Georgia, July 22, 1861, for twelve months. Captured at Roanoke Island on February 8, 1862, and paroled at Elizabeth City, N.C., February 21, 1862. Present or accounted for until admitted to hospital at Richmond, Virginia, July 20, 1863, with "vul. sclop. in foot." Furloughed from hospital for 40-45 days on July 28-29, 1863. Reported on company muster rolls as absent without leave after furlough expired until his name appears as signature to an Oath of Allegiance to the U.S. subscribed and sworn to at Chattanooga, Tennessee, March 20, 1864.

TRIBBLE, BENJAMIN J., Private

Enlisted in Forsyth County, Georgia, July 22, 1861, for twelve months. Admitted to hospital at Wilmington, February 6, 1862, with "pleuritis" and was returned to duty February 13, 1862. No further records.

TURNER, JOHN P., Musician

Enlisted in Forsyth County, Georgia, July 22, 1861, for twelve months. Mustered in as Private. Captured at Roanoke Island on February 8, 1862, and paroled at Elizabeth City, N.C., February 21, 1862. Wounded at Gettysburg, Pennsylvania, July 1-3, 1863, and captured in hospital at that place. Confined on July 17-24, 1863, at DeCamp General Hospital, Davids Island, New York Harbor, where he remained until paroled and sent to City Point, Virginia, for exchange on August 24, 1863. Appointed Musician September-October, 1863. Absent on parole through October, 1863, and reported as present from that date until transferred to 2nd Company E, 21st Regiment Georgia Infantry on April 11, 1864.

TURNER, M. L., Private

Enlisted in Forsyth County, Georgia, February 22, 1864. Present or accounted for until transferred to 2nd Company E, 21st Regiment Georgia Infantry on April 11, 1864.

TURNER, WILLIAM C., Private

Enlisted in Forsyth County, Georgia, July 22, 1861, for twelve months. Captured at Roanoke Island on February 8, 1862, and paroled at Elizabeth City, N.C., February 21, 1862. Present or accounted for on company muster rolls until he is reported as absent sick in hospital at Lynchburg, Virginia, on the September-October, 1863, muster roll. Absent without leave when transferred to 2nd Company E, 21st Regiment Georgia Infantry on April 11, 1864.

WAFFORD, WILLIAM H., Private

Born in Forsyth County, Georgia, and was a farmer prior to enlisting in Forsyth County, July 22, 1861, for twelve months. Captured at Roanoke Island on February 8, 1862, and paroled at Elizabeth City, N.C., February 21, 1862. Discharged at age 17, October 17, 1862, by reason of the Conscript Act.

WALDO, W. S., Corporal

Captured at Roanoke Island on February 8, 1862, and paroled at Elizabeth City, N.C., February 21, 1862. No further records.

WALLACE, WILLIAM T., Sergeant

Enlisted in Forsyth County, Georgia, July 22, 1861, for twelve months. Mustered in as Private. Captured at Roanoke Island on February 8, 1862, and paroled at Elizabeth City, N.C., February 21, 1862. Appointed Sergeant, September 25, 1862. Present or accounted for on company muster rolls through October, 1862. No further records.

WALLS, DRURY M., Private

Enlisted in Forsyth County, Georgia, November 28, 1861, for twelve months. Captured at Roanoke Island on February 8, 1862, and paroled at Elizabeth City, N.C., February 21, 1862. Captured near Gettysburg, Pennsylvania, July 3-4, 1863, and confined at Fort McHenry, Maryland, until sent to Fort Delaware, Delaware, July 9, 1863. Transferred on October 18, 1863, to Point Lookout, Maryland, where he remained until paroled and sent to City Point, Virginia, for exchange on December 24, 1863. Present or accounted for until transferred to 2nd Company E, 21st Regiment Georgia Infantry on April 11, 1864.

WELLS, WILLIAM L., Private

Enlisted in Forsyth County, Georgia, July 22, 1861, for twelve months. Mustered in as Corporal and reduced to ranks September 25, 1862. Present or accounted for until admitted to hospital at Richmond, Virginia, September 15, 1863, with "intermittent fever" and was returned to duty December 3, 1863. Reported as "absent without leave, furlough expired" when transferred to 2nd Company E, 21st Regiment Georgia Infantry on April 11, 1864.

WESTRAY, JOHN M., Private

Enlisted in Forsyth County, Georgia, July 22, 1861, for twelve months. Captured at Roanoke Island on February 8, 1862, and paroled at Elizabeth City, N.C., February 21, 1862. Died March 24, 1862.

WHITED, MILES, Private

Enlisted in Forsyth County, Georgia, November 28, 1861, for twelve months. Admitted to hospital at Wilmington, February 4, 1862, with "febris typhoides" and died February 14, 1862.

WILKINS, MARCUS L., Private

Enlisted in Forsyth County, Georgia, July 22, 1861, for twelve months. Captured at Roanoke Island on February 8, 1862, and paroled at Elizabeth City, N.C., February 21, 1862. Again captured at Gettysburg, Pennsylvania, on July 3, 1863, and confined at Fort McHenry, Maryland, until transferred to Fort Delaware, Delaware, July 7-12, 1863. Sent to Point Lookout, Maryland, October 15-18, 1863, and remained absent in confinement when transferred to 2nd Company E, 21st Regiment Georgia Infantry on April 11, 1864.

WILLIAMS, JONATHAN, Private

Enlisted in Forsyth County, Georgia, July 22, 1861, for twelve months. Killed in battle at Roanoke Island on February 8, 1862.

WILLIAMS, M. S., Private

Captured at Roanoke Island on February 8, 1862. No further records.

WOFFORD, GEORGE, Private

Enlisted in Forsyth County, Georgia, July 22, 1861, for twelve months. Captured at Roanoke Island on

February 8, 1862, and paroled at Elizabeth City, N.C., February 21, 1862. Present or accounted for on company muster rolls until transferred to 2nd Company E, 21st Regiment Georgia Infantry on April 11, 1864.

WOOD, LUKE, Private
Enlisted in Forsyth County, Georgia, July 22, 1861, for twelve months. Captured at Roanoke Island on February 8, 1862, and paroled at Elizabeth City, N.C., February 21, 1862. Present or accounted for on company muster rolls until transferred to 2nd Company E, 21st Regiment Georgia Infantry on April 11, 1864.

COMPANY E

This company, known as "The Anthony Grays," was organized in Meriwether County, Georgia, and enlisted on September 16, 1861. It was mustered into Confederate States service at Richmond, Virginia, October 31, 1861, and assigned to this battalion as Company E when the battalion was organized on November 1, 1861. After joining the battalion the company functioned as a part of the battalion, and its history is recorded as a part of the battalion history.

When the company was paroled after its capture at Roanoke Island on February 8, 1862, the men returned to Georgia to await exchange. The company was reorganized with recruits on May 16, 1862, and attached to the 55th Regiment Georgia Infantry until the original members were exchanged in August, 1862. After being declared exchanged the company was ordered to rejoin the battalion at Drewry's Bluff, which it did. On April 11, 1864, the company was transferred out of the battalion and became 2nd Company A, 60th Regiment Georgia Infantry.

The following roster of the company covers only that period when the company served as Company E, 2nd Battalion N.C. Infantry. Researchers who wish to continue research for the period after April 11, 1864, when the company became 2nd Company A, 60th Regiment Georgia Infantry, should check the Compiled Military Service Records for that company on file in Record Group 109, National Archives and Records Service, Washington, D.C., and the records on file at the Georgia Archives, Atlanta, Georgia.

The information contained in the following roster of the company was compiled principally from company muster rolls which covered from the date of enlistment through June, 1862; September through December, 1862; March-April, 1863; and September, 1863, through February, 1864. No company muster rolls were found for July-August, 1862; January-February, 1863; May through August, 1863; or March through April 11, 1864, the date of transfer. In addition to company muster rolls, Roll of Honor records, receipt rolls, and hospital records, supplemented by state pension applications, United Daughters of the Confederacy records, and postwar rosters and histories, all provided useful information.

OFFICERS
CAPTAINS

DuBOSE, WILDS S.
Enlisted in Meriwether County, Georgia, September 16, 1861, for the war. Appointed Captain to rank from date of enlistment. Captured at Roanoke Island on February 8, 1862, and paroled at Elizabeth City, N.C., on February 21, 1862. Not reelected at reorganization of company on May 16, 1862.

TUCKER, JOHN J.
Enlisted in Meriwether County, Georgia, September 16, 1861, for the war. Appointed 2nd Lieutenant to rank from date of enlistment. Captured at Roanoke Island on February 8, 1862, and paroled at Elizabeth City, N.C., on February 21, 1862. Elected Captain at reorganization of company on May 16, 1862, and appointed to rank from date of election. Captured at Jacks Mountain, Pennsylvania, July 5, 1863, and confined at Fort Delaware, Delaware. Transferred to Johnson's Island, Ohio, July 18, 1863. Absent in confinement when transferred to 2nd Company A, 60th Regiment Georgia Infantry on April 11, 1864.

LIEUTENANTS

BRAY, WILLIAM C., 1st Lieutenant
Enlisted in Meriwether County, Georgia, September 16, 1861, for the war. Appointed 1st Lieutenant to rank from date of enlistment. Captured at Roanoke Island on February 8, 1862, and paroled at Elizabeth City, N.C., on February 21, 1862. Not reelected at reorganization of company on May 16, 1862. Later enlisted in Company B, 2nd Regiment Georgia Cavalry (State Guard).

CLOPTON, JAMES F., 3rd Lieutenant
Enlisted in Meriwether County, Georgia, September 16, 1861, for twelve months. Mustered in as Private. Captured at Roanoke Island on February 8, 1862, and paroled at Elizabeth City, N.C., on February 21, 1862. Appointed 1st Sergeant on October 25, 1862, and elected 3rd Lieutenant on November 1, 1863. Appointed to rank from date of election. Present or accounted for until transferred to 2nd Company A, 60th Regiment Georgia Infantry on April 11, 1864.

GILLESPIE, ROBERT H. C., 2nd Lieutenant
Enlisted in Meriwether County, Georgia, September 16, 1861, for twelve months. Mustered in as Private. Captured at Roanoke Island on February 8, 1862, and paroled at Elizabeth City, N.C., on February 21, 1862. Appointed 1st Sergeant on September 1, 1862, and reduced to ranks September 16, 1862. Elected 3rd Lieutenant on October 19, 1862, and appointed to rank from date of election. Promoted to 2nd Lieutenant on November 1, 1863. Present or accounted for until transferred to 2nd Company A, 60th Regiment Georgia Infantry on April 11, 1864.

HUDSON, WILLIAM J., 1st Lieutenant
Elected 2nd Lieutenant at reorganization of company on May 16, 1862, and appointed to rank from date of election. Promoted to 1st Lieutenant, October 15, 1862. Present or accounted for until

captured at Smithburg, Pennsylvania, July 4, 1863. Confined at Fort Delaware, Delaware, until transferred to Johnson's Island, Ohio, July 18-20, 1863. Died at Johnson's Island on August 4, 1863, of "enteritis."

LEE, JOEL W., 1st Lieutenant
Enlisted in Meriwether County, Georgia, May 16, 1862, for the war. Appointed 1st Lieutenant on May 17, 1862, and resigned on October 14, 1862, after he provided George A. Lindsay as his substitute.

LEE, JOHN W., 1st Lieutenant
Enlisted in Meriwether County, Georgia, May 16, 1862, for the war. Elected 3rd Lieutenant at reorganization of company on May 16, 1862, and appointed to rank from date of election. Promoted to 2nd Lieutenant on October 15, 1862. Wounded at Gettysburg, Pennsylvania, July 2, 1863, and "left at Gettysburg." Appointed 1st Lieutenant to rank from August 6, 1863. Reported as absent "wounded and captured at Gettysburg" when transferred to 2nd Company A, 60th Regiment Georgia Infantry on April 11, 1864.

WILLIAMS, FRANKLIN J., 2nd Lieutenant
Enlisted in Meriwether County, Georgia, September 16, 1861, for twelve months. Appointed 2nd Lieutenant to rank from date of enlistment. Captured at Roanoke Island on February 8, 1862, and paroled at Elizabeth City, N.C., on February 21, 1862. Present or accounted for through August, 1862.

NONCOMMISSIONED OFFICERS AND PRIVATES

ADCOCK, ROBERT A., Musician
Enlisted in Meriwether County, Georgia, September 16, 1861, for twelve months. Mustered in as Private and appointed Musician in January, 1862. Captured at Roanoke Island on February 8, 1862, and paroled at Elizabeth City, N.C., February 21, 1862. Discharged September 25, 1862, for "seniority—term expired." Reenlisted November 12, 1862, as a substitute for R. M. Anthony and was assigned to this company as a Musician. Captured when left as a nurse for the wounded at Gettysburg, Pennsylvania, July 3-5, 1863. Confined at Fort Delaware, Delaware, and transferred to Point Lookout, Maryland, October 18, 1863. Absent in confinement when transferred to 2nd Company A, 60th Regiment Georgia Infantry on April 11, 1864.

ALBRIGHT, WILLIAM H., Private
Enlisted in Meriwether County, Georgia, September 16, 1861, for twelve months. Absent sick until discharged after April 30, 1862.

ANDERSON, D. M., Private
Enlisted in Meriwether County, Georgia, September 16, 1861, for twelve months. Absent sick until his death on December 24, 1861, near Richmond, Virginia.

ANTHONY, ROBERT M., Private
Enlisted in Meriwether County, Georgia, May 16, 1862, for the war. Present or accounted for on

company muster rolls until he furnished Robert A. Adcock as his substitute on November 12, 1862.

ARINGTON, E. S., Private
Enlisted in Meriwether County, Georgia, September 16, 1861, for twelve months. Captured at Roanoke Island on February 8, 1862, and paroled at Elizabeth City, N.C., February 21, 1862. Died at home in Meriwether County on March 12, 1862.

BATEMAN, HENRY C., Private
Enlisted in Meriwether County, Georgia, at age 33, May 16, 1862, for the war. Died January 19, 1863, in hospital at Goldsboro of "typhoid fever."

BLACKWOOD, GREEN W., Private
Enlisted in Meriwether County, Georgia, at age 34, May 16, 1862, for the war. Present or accounted for until transferred to 2nd Company A, 60th Regiment Georgia Infantry on April 11, 1864.

BONNER, JAMES M., Private
Enlisted in Meriwether County, Georgia, May 16, 1862, for the war. Present or accounted for until transferred to 2nd Company A, 60th Regiment Georgia Infantry on April 11, 1864.

BRAKEFIELD, EDWARD L., Private
Enlisted in Meriwether County, Georgia, at age 22, May 16, 1862, for the war. Died at Camp Randolph, Georgia, July 5, 1862.

BRAKEFIELD, HENRY N., Private
Enlisted in Meriwether County, Georgia, May 16, 1862, for the war. Captured near Gettysburg, Pennsylvania, July 3-5, 1863, and confined at Fort McHenry, Maryland, until sent to Fort Delaware, Delaware, July 9, 1863. Transferred to Point Lookout, Maryland, October 18, 1863, where he died March 15, 1864, of "diarrhoea."

BRANTLEY, A. H., Private
Enlisted in Meriwether County, Georgia, September 16, 1861, for twelve months. Absent sick until discharged for disability on February 12, 1862.

BRAZELL, JAMES W., Private
Enlisted in Meriwether County, Georgia, September 16, 1861, for twelve months. Captured at Roanoke Island on February 8, 1862, and paroled at Elizabeth City, N.C., February 21, 1862. Present or accounted for until transferred to 2nd Company A, 60th Regiment Georgia Infantry on April 11, 1864.

BRAZELL, JOHN T., Private
Enlisted in Meriwether County, Georgia, September 16, 1861, for twelve months. Captured at Roanoke Island on February 8, 1862, and paroled at Elizabeth City, N.C., February 21, 1862. Present or accounted for until transferred to 2nd Company A, 60th Regiment Georgia Infantry on April 11, 1864.

BRILEY, NAPOLEON B., Private
Enlisted in Meriwether County, Georgia, at age 22, May 10, 1862, for the war. Died on Belle Isle, near Richmond, Virginia, August 12, 1862.

BRILEY, SIDNEY H., Private
Enlisted in Meriwether County, Georgia, September 16, 1861, for twelve months. Died December 12, 1861.

BRILEY, W. G., Private
Enlisted in Meriwether County, Georgia, September 16, 1861, for twelve months. Died at White Sulphur Springs, Virginia, November 23, 1861.

BROOKS, CHARLES S., Private
Enlisted in Meriwether County, Georgia, January 5, 1862, for twelve months. Captured at Roanoke Island on February 8, 1862, and paroled at Elizabeth City, N.C., February 21, 1862. Present or accounted for until transferred to 2nd Company A, 60th Regiment Georgia Infantry on April 11, 1864.

BROOKS, HENRY E., Private
Enlisted in Meriwether County, Georgia, September 16, 1861, for twelve months. Mustered in as Private. Present or accounted for until transferred to Field and Staff of this battalion upon his appointment as Chaplain to rank from January 1, 1862.

BROOKS, JACK, Private
Enlisted in Meriwether County, Georgia, September 16, 1861, for twelve months. Company muster roll dated December 7, 1861, reports that he was "absent at home without leave." No further records.

BROOKS, JAMES M., Private
Enlisted in Meriwether County, Georgia, September 16, 1861, for twelve months. Discharged January 15, 1862, when he furnished William Davis, Sr., as his substitute.

BROOKS, RHODOM M., Private
Enlisted in Meriwether County, Georgia, at age 30, May 16, 1862, for the war. Discharged September 22, 1862, by reason of "being Superintendent, Wool Factory."

BROOKS, THOMAS J., Private
Enlisted in Meriwether County, Georgia, May 16, 1862, for the war. Present or accounted for until discharged when he furnished James L. Brown as his substitute on December 3, 1862.

BROOKS, WILLIAM P., Private
Enlisted in Meriwether County, Georgia, September 16, 1861, for twelve months. Captured at Roanoke Island on February 8, 1862, and paroled at Elizabeth City, N.C., February 21, 1862. Present or accounted for until transferred to 2nd Company A, 60th Regiment Georgia Infantry on April 11, 1864.

BROWN, JAMES L., Private
Enlisted as a substitute for Thomas J. Brooks on December 3, 1862. Present or accounted for until transferred to 2nd Company A, 60th Regiment Georgia Infantry on April 11, 1864.

BROWN, JOHN S., Private
Born in Meriwether County, Georgia, and was a mechanic prior to enlisting in Meriwether County, September 16, 1861, for twelve months. Mustered in as Private. Captured at Roanoke Island on February 8, 1862, and paroled at Elizabeth City, N.C., February 21, 1862. Appointed Musician, December 15, 1862. Present or accounted for as a Private from March-April, 1863, until transferred to C.S. Navy, April 23, 1864.

BROWN, ROBERT P., Corporal
Enlisted in Meriwether County, Georgia, September 16, 1861, for twelve months. Mustered in as Private. Captured at Roanoke Island on February 8, 1862, and paroled at Elizabeth City, N.C., February 21, 1862. Appointed Corporal October 19, 1862. Captured at Gettysburg, Pennsylvania, July 3-5, 1863. Confined at Fort McHenry, Maryland, and transferred to Fort Delaware, Delaware, July 7-12, 1863. Died in hospital at Fort Delaware on August 30, 1863, of "chronic diarrhoea."

BROWN, THOMAS, Private
Company muster rolls state that he enlisted September 1, 1862, at Richmond, Virginia, and was "dropped from roll" November-December, 1862. No further records.

BUTTS, J. T., Private
Enlisted in Meriwether County, Georgia, September 16, 1861, for twelve months. Absent sick until his death on February 4, 1862, in Meriwether County.

CALDWELL, BENJAMIN, Private
Enlisted in Meriwether County, Georgia, May 16, 1862, for the war. Present or accounted for through April, 1863. No further records.

CALDWELL, JOSEPH, Corporal
Enlisted in Meriwether County, Georgia, September 16, 1861, for twelve months. Mustered in as Corporal. Absent without leave through December, 1861. No further records.

CALDWELL, MARTIN S., Private
Enlisted in Meriwether County, Georgia, September 16, 1861, for twelve months. Company muster roll dated December 7, 1861, states that he was "absent on sick furlough." No further records.

CHAPMAN, ABNER A., Private
Enlisted in Meriwether County, Georgia, May 10, 1862, for the war. Died on July 25, 1862, at Belle Isle, near Richmond, Virginia.

CHAPMAN, JOHN H., Private
Enlisted in Meriwether County, Georgia, September 16, 1861, for twelve months. Present or accounted for until transferred to 2nd Company A, 60th Regiment Georgia Infantry on April 11, 1864.

CHRISTIAN, WILLIAM D., Private
Enlisted in Meriwether County, Georgia, September 16, 1861, for twelve months. Captured at Roanoke Island on February 8, 1862, and paroled at Elizabeth City, N.C., February 21, 1862. Discharged October 20, 1862, "for minority."

CHUNN, ANDREW J., Sergeant
Enlisted in Meriwether County, Georgia, September 16, 1861, for twelve months. Mustered in as Sergeant. Present or accounted for until transferred to 2nd Company A, 60th Regiment Georgia Infantry on April 11, 1864.

CHUNN, BENJAMIN F., Private
Enlisted in Meriwether County, Georgia, at age 31, May 16, 1862, for the war. Present or accounted for on company muster rolls until January-February, 1864, when he appears with the remark: "Furloughed from hospital August 26 for 30 days—has failed to report in person or by certificate."

Transferred to 2nd Company A, 60th Regiment Georgia Infantry on April 11, 1864.

CHUNN, JOHN T., Private

Enlisted in Meriwether County, Georgia, at age 21, May 16, 1862, for the war. Company muster rolls report that he was captured at Gettysburg, Pennsylvania, and carry him as absent paroled and at home from September-October, 1863, through February, 1864. Transferred to 2nd Company A, 60th Regiment Georgia Infantry on April 11, 1864.

CLOPTON, F. C., Private

Enlisted in Meriwether County, Georgia, September 16, 1861, for twelve months. Appears on a register of a hospital at Wilmington, which gives disease as "febris typhoides" and states that he was returned to duty on February 2, 1862. Died at Norfolk, Virginia, February 19, 1862.

COCHRAN, JAMES HAMILTON, Private

Enlisted in Meriwether County, Georgia, September 16, 1861, for twelve months. Died December 26, 1861, at Wilmington.

COX, WILLIAM M., Private

Enlisted at Camp Randolph, June 20, 1862, as a substitute for A. F. Hill. Present or accounted for until admitted to hospital on August 28, 1863, at Charlottesville, Virginia, where he died September 11, 1863, of "typhoid fever."

CREWS, ASBERRY, Private

Enlisted in Meriwether County, Georgia, September 16, 1861, for twelve months. Captured at Roanoke Island on February 8, 1862, and paroled at Elizabeth City, N.C., February 21, 1862. Present or accounted for until wounded and captured at Gettysburg, Pennsylvania, July 1-3, 1863. Died in hospital at Gettysburg, July 6, 1863, of "thigh amputated."

CREWS, W. D., Private

Enlisted in Meriwether County, Georgia, September 16, 1861, for twelve months. Reported as absent sick in hospital at White Sulphur Springs, Virginia, until his death at that place on November 30, 1861.

DAVERS, ANTHONY, Private

Enlisted at Goldsboro, February 4, 1863, for the war. Wounded and captured at Gettysburg, Pennsylvania, July 1-3, 1863. Died in hospital at Gettysburg, July 7, 1863, of "g.s. thigh (ampt)."

DAVIS, JOHN W., Private

Enlisted at Richmond, Virginia, October 19, 1861, for twelve months. Company muster roll for December 31, 1861-March, 1862, carries the remark: "Died."

DAVIS, WILLIAM, Jr., Private

Enlisted in Meriwether County, Georgia, September 16, 1861, for twelve months. Captured at Roanoke Island on February 8, 1862, and paroled at Elizabeth City, N.C., February 21, 1862. Present or accounted for until transferred to 2nd Company A, 60th Regiment Georgia Infantry on April 11, 1864.

DAVIS, WILLIAM, Sr., Private

Enlisted as a substitute for James M. Brooks on January 15, 1862. Captured at Roanoke Island on February 8, 1862, and paroled at Elizabeth City, N.C., February 21, 1862. Company muster rolls report that he "joined another company after he was exchanged" and carry him as absent without leave through December, 1862. No further records.

DAVIS, WILLIAM H., Private

Enlisted in Meriwether County, Georgia, September 16, 1861, for twelve months. Reported as absent sick until he "died January 15, 1862."

DeLOACH, MICHAEL, Private

Enlisted in Meriwether County, Georgia, at age 30, May 16, 1862, for the war. Died at Orange Court House, Virginia, December 15, 1863, "of disease."

DOUGLASS, R. D., Private

Enlisted in Meriwether County, Georgia, May 16, 1862, for the war. Reported on pay roll dated July 6, 1862, with the remark: "Name cancelled."

EVANS, JOHN W., Private

Enlisted in Meriwether County, Georgia, May 16, 1861, for the war. Absent sick until he "died at home in Meriwether County, Georgia, July 21, 1862."

FLORENCE, JAMES T., Private

Enlisted in Meriwether County, Georgia, May 10, 1862, for the war. Captured at Gettysburg, Pennsylvania, July 2-3, 1863, and confined at Fort Delaware, Delaware, where he died October 27, 1863, of "diarrhoea chronic."

FOLDS, ELISHA D., Private

Transferred to this company from Company C, 13th Regiment Georgia Infantry on January 13, 1864, in exchange for Henry I. Hudson. Present or accounted for until transferred to 2nd Company A, 60th Regiment Georgia Infantry on April 11, 1864.

FOLDS, FRANK M., Private

Enlisted in Meriwether County, Georgia, September 16, 1861, for twelve months. Captured at Roanoke Island on February 8, 1862, and paroled at Elizabeth City, N.C., February 21, 1862. Present or accounted for until transferred to 2nd Company A, 60th Regiment Georgia Infantry on April 11, 1864.

FOSTER, JAMES R., Private

Enlisted in Meriwether County, Georgia, September 16, 1861, for twelve months. Reported as absent on sick furlough on the company muster roll for September 16-October 31, 1861, dated December 7, 1861. No further records.

FOWLER, GEORGE W., Private

Enlisted in Meriwether County, Georgia, at age 27, May 16, 1862, for the war. Present or accounted for until transferred to 2nd Company A, 60th Regiment Georgia Infantry on April 11, 1864.

FOWLER, THOMAS W., Private

Enlisted in Meriwether County, Georgia, at age 34, May 16, 1862, for the war. Present or accounted for until transferred to 2nd Company A, 60th Regiment Georgia Infantry on April 11, 1864.

GARIETY, JAMES, Private

Enlisted at Richmond, Virginia, September 1,

1862, for the war. Company muster roll for November-December, 1862, reported that he was "dropped from roll."

GATES, BENJAMIN K., Private
Provided John H. Madden as his substitute on May 16, 1862.

GENTRY, GEORGE W., Corporal
Enlisted in Meriwether County, Georgia, September 16, 1861, for twelve months. Mustered in as Corporal. Reported on company muster rolls as absent without leave through December, 1861. No further records.

GORDY, JAMES T., Private
Enlisted in Meriwether County, Georgia, February 20, 1863. Reported as absent sick on the March-April, 1863, muster roll. No further records.

GORE, ASBERRY, Private
Enlisted in Meriwether County, Georgia, September 16, 1861, for twelve months. Died December 27, 1861, in Richmond, Virginia.

GRANGER, J. L., Private
Enlisted in Meriwether County, Georgia, September 16, 1861, for twelve months. Company muster roll for September 16-October 31, 1861, reports that he had "deserted and gone to the coast of Georgia." No further records.

GRANGER, ROBERT W., Private
Enlisted in Meriwether County, Georgia, at age 28, September 16, 1861, for twelve months. Present or accounted for until discharged on November 14, 1862, by reason of "chronic rheumatism."

GRANT, WILLIAMS, Private
Enlisted in Meriwether County, Georgia, September 16, 1861, for twelve months. Reported as absent without leave on the company muster roll for September 16, 1861, to October 31, 1861. No further records.

GREER, WILLIAM H., Private
Enlisted in Meriwether County, Georgia, May 16, 1862, for the war. Present or accounted for until transferred to 2nd Company A, 60th Regiment Georgia Infantry on April 11, 1864.

GRIFFIN, NEWTON, Private
Enlisted in Meriwether County, Georgia, September 16, 1861, for twelve months. Captured at Roanoke Island on February 8, 1862, and paroled at Elizabeth City, N.C., February 21, 1862. Present or accounted for until transferred to 2nd Company A, 60th Regiment Georgia Infantry on April 11, 1864.

HANEY, JOHN J., Private
Enlisted in Meriwether County, Georgia, September 16, 1861, for twelve months. Present or accounted for until transferred to 2nd Company A, 60th Regiment Georgia Infantry on April 11, 1864.

HARDIN, CHARLES D., Private
Enlisted in Meriwether County, Georgia, September 16, 1861, for twelve months. Captured at Roanoke Island on February 8, 1862, and paroled at Elizabeth City, N.C., February 21, 1862. Present or accounted for until his death in

hospital at Gordonsville, Virginia, August 30, 1863, of "pneumonia."

HARDIN, H. M., Private
Enlisted in Meriwether County, Georgia, September 16, 1861, for twelve months. Died November 13, 1861, at White Sulphur Springs, Virginia.

HARRIS, JOHN T., Private
Enlisted in Meriwether County, Georgia, at age 24, May 16, 1862, for the war. Present or accounted for until transferred to 2nd Company A, 60th Regiment Georgia Infantry on April 11, 1864.

HARRISON, JOHN H., Private
Enlisted in Meriwether County, Georgia, at age 23, September 16, 1861, for twelve months. Mustered in as Sergeant and reduced to ranks May 17, 1862. Present or accounted for until transferred to 2nd Company A, 60th Regiment Georgia Infantry on April 11, 1864.

HARRISON, SANFORD T., Corporal
Enlisted in Meriwether County, Georgia, at age 22, September 16, 1861, for twelve months. Mustered in as Private and appointed Corporal, May 17, 1862. Present or accounted for until transferred to 2nd Company A, 60th Regiment Georgia Infantry on April 11, 1864.

HATCHETT, CHARLES H., Private
Enlisted in Meriwether County, Georgia, at age 30, May 16, 1862, for the war. Discharged on November 14, 1862, by reason of "chronic rheumatism."

HATCHETT, FRANCIS M., Private
Enlisted in Meriwether County, Georgia, at age 26, May 16, 1862, for the war. Reported on company muster rolls as absent sick from September-October, 1862, through February, 1864. Transferred to 2nd Company A, 60th Regiment Georgia Infantry on April 11, 1864.

HEARD, JAMES M., Private
Enlisted in Meriwether County, Georgia, at age 29, May 16, 1862, for the war. Present or accounted for until transferred to 2nd Company A, 60th Regiment Georgia Infantry on April 11, 1864.

HICKS, ISAAC J., Private
Enlisted in Meriwether County, Georgia, at age 21, September 16, 1861, for twelve months. Present or accounted for on company muster rolls through April, 1863. No further records.

HILL, A. F., Private
Provided William M. Cox as his substitute on June 20, 1862.

HINES, ELIAS D., Private
Born in Meriwether County, Georgia, and was a farmer prior to enlisting at Richmond, Virginia, August 21, 1862, for the war. Captured at Gettysburg, Pennsylvania, July 3-4, 1863, and confined at Fort McHenry, Maryland, until transferred to Fort Delaware, Delaware, July 7-12, 1863. Transferred on October 20, 1863, to Point Lookout, Maryland, where he remained until paroled and sent to City Point, Virginia, for exchange on March 16, 1864. Transferred to 2nd Company A, 60th Regiment Georgia Infantry on April 11, 1864.

HOLT, IVERSON F., Private
Enlisted in Meriwether County, Georgia, May 16, 1862, for the war. Present or accounted for until captured at Gettysburg, Pennsylvania, July 3-5, 1863. Confined at Fort Delaware, Delaware, until transferred to Point Lookout, Maryland, October 18, 1863. Paroled and exchanged at City Point, Virginia, December 24, 1863. Present or accounted for until transferred to 2nd Company A, 60th Regiment Georgia Infantry on April 11, 1864.

HOOD, WILEY, Private
Enlisted in Meriwether County, Georgia, September 16, 1861, for twelve months. Captured at Roanoke Island on February 8, 1862, and paroled at Elizabeth City, N.C., on February 21, 1862. Died at Weldon, N.C., March 1, 1862.

HOOD, WILLIAM T., Private
Enlisted in Meriwether County, Georgia, September 16, 1861, for twelve months. Reported as absent at home on sick furlough on September 16-October 31, 1861, muster roll.

HUDSON, DAVID A., Private
Enlisted in Meriwether County, Georgia, May 16, 1862, for the war. Present or accounted for until captured at South Mountain, Pennsylvania, July 5, 1863. Confined at DeCamp General Hospital, Davids Island, New York Harbor, until paroled and sent to City Point, Virginia, for exchange on September 16, 1863. Present or accounted for until transferred to 2nd Company A, 60th Regiment Georgia Infantry on April 11, 1864.

HUDSON, HENRY I., Private
Enlisted in Meriwether County, Georgia, May 10, 1862, for the war. Present or accounted for until transferred to Company C, 13th Regiment Georgia Infantry on January 13, 1864.

INGRAM, THOMAS J., Private
Enlisted in Meriwether County, Georgia, at age 19, May 16, 1862, for the war. Died in hospital at Richmond, Virginia, August 24, 1862.

JACKSON, WILLIAM, Private
Enlisted in Meriwether County, Georgia, September 16, 1861, for twelve months. Died at White Sulphur Springs, Virginia, on November 15, 1861.

JAMES, CALVIN, Private
Enlisted in Meriwether County, Georgia, at age 28, May 16, 1862, for the war. Present or accounted for until transferred to 2nd Company A, 60th Regiment Georgia Infantry on April 11, 1864.

JAMES, WILLIAM A., Private
Enlisted in Meriwether County, Georgia, February 1, 1863, for the war. Present or accounted for until transferred to 2nd Company A, 60th Regiment Georgia Infantry on April 11, 1864.

JARRELL, JAMES W., Private
Enlisted in Meriwether County at age 29, May 16, 1862, for the war. Present or accounted for through April, 1863.

JENKINS, GEORGE W., Private
Enlisted in Meriwether County at age 29, May 16, 1862, for the war. Wounded and captured at Gettysburg, Pennsylvania, July 1-5, 1863. Confined at DeCamp General Hospital, Davids Island, New York Harbor, until paroled and sent to City

Point, Virginia, for exchange on August 24, 1863. Admitted to hospital at Richmond, Virginia, and furloughed in December, 1863. Absent on furlough when transferred to 2nd Company A, 60th Regiment Georgia Infantry on April 11, 1864.

JOHNSON, BERRY M., Corporal
Enlisted in Meriwether County, Georgia, at age 27, May 16, 1862, for the war. Mustered in as Corporal. Present or accounted for until transferred to 2nd Company A, 60th Regiment Georgia Infantry on April 11, 1864.

JONES, THOMAS, Private
Enlisted in Meriwether County, Georgia, May 16, 1862, for the war. Name reported on pay roll for May 16, 1862, with the remark: "Name cancelled."

JONES, WILLIAM C., Private
Enlisted in Meriwether County, Georgia, at age 22, May 16, 1862, for the war. Admitted to hospital at Richmond, Virginia, October, 1862, and furloughed November 18, 1862. Did not return at expiration of furlough and reported as absent without leave. Transferred to 2nd Company A, 60th Regiment Georgia Infantry on April 11, 1864, while absent without leave.

KEELING, JAMES W., Private
Enlisted in Meriwether County, Georgia, at age 22, May 16, 1862, for the war. Present or accounted for until transferred to 2nd Company A, 60th Regiment Georgia Infantry on April 11, 1864.

KEELING, WILLIAM T., 1st Sergeant
Enlisted in Meriwether County, Georgia, September 16, 1861, for twelve months. Mustered in as Private. Captured at Roanoke Island on February 8, 1862, and paroled at Elizabeth City, N.C., on February 21, 1862. Appointed 1st Sergeant on November 1, 1863. Present or accounted for until transferred to 2nd Company A, 60th Regiment Georgia Infantry on April 11, 1864.

KENEDY, BYRD F., Private
Enlisted in Meriwether County, Georgia, February 24, 1864, for the war. Transferred to 2nd Company A, 60th Regiment Georgia Infantry on April 11, 1864.

KENNEDY, JOHN T., Private
Enlisted in Meriwether County, Georgia, at age 22, May 16, 1862, for the war. Present or accounted for until transferred to 2nd Company A, 60th Regiment Georgia Infantry on April 11, 1864.

KEY, GEORGE W., Private
Enlisted in Meriwether County, Georgia, September 16, 1861, for twelve months. Captured at Roanoke Island on February 8, 1862, and paroled at Elizabeth City, N.C., on February 21, 1862. Present or accounted for until transferred to 2nd Company A, 60th Regiment Georgia Infantry on April 11, 1864.

KEY, JAMES F., Private
Born in Randolph County, Alabama, and resided as a farmer prior to enlisting in Meriwether County, Georgia, at age 14, September 16, 1861, for twelve months. Discharged January 26, 1862, by reason of "chronic dysentery."

KEY, WILLIAM H., Private
Enlisted in Meriwether County, Georgia, September 16, 1861, for twelve months. Captured at Roanoke Island on February 8, 1862, and paroled at Elizabeth City, N.C., on February 21, 1862. Present or accounted for on company muster rolls through December, 1862.

KILPATRICK, THOMAS F., Private
Enlisted in Meriwether County, Georgia, September 16, 1861, for twelve months. Captured at Roanoke Island on February 8, 1862, and paroled at Elizabeth City, N.C., on February 21, 1862. Died in hospital at Wilson, N.C., May 1, 1863, of "febris typhus."

KOON, ROBERT, Private
Enlisted in Meriwether County, Georgia, September 16, 1861, for twelve months. Present or accounted for until transferred to 2nd Company A, 60th Regiment Georgia Infantry on April 11, 1864.

LAMAR, GEORGE P., Sergeant
Enlisted in Meriwether County, Georgia, at age 21, May 16, 1862, for the war. Mustered in as Private and appointed Sergeant, October 19, 1862. Present or accounted for until transferred to 2nd Company A, 60th Regiment Georgia Infantry on April 11, 1864.

LESLEY, ERASMUS M., Private
Enlisted in Meriwether County, Georgia, June 25, 1862, for the war. Present or accounted for until transferred to 2nd Company A, 60th Regiment Georgia Infantry on April 11, 1864.

LINDSAY, GEORGE A., Private
Enlisted at Richmond, Virginia, October 15, 1862, as a substitute for Joel W. Lee. Wounded and captured at Gettysburg, Pennsylvania, July 1-3, 1863. Confined at DeCamp General Hospital, Davids Island, New York Harbor, July 20, 1863, with "g.s. knee" and remained there until paroled and sent to City Point, Virginia, for exchange. Received at City Point on September 8, 1863, for exchange. Admitted to hospital at Richmond September 25, 1863, and furloughed for 20 days on October 6, 1863. Absent with leave until detailed as a compositor and ordered to report to the Superintendent of Public Printing, Richmond, March 31, 1864. Detailed for guard duty and ordered to report to Lieutenant M. Henry in charge of Arsenal Guard, Richmond, on April 7, 1864. Transferred to 2nd Company A, 60th Regiment Georgia Infantry on April 11, 1864.

LOFTIN, F. P., Private
Enlisted in Meriwether County, Georgia, September 16, 1861, for twelve months. Company muster roll for September 16-October 31, 1861, states that he had "deserted—gone to coast."

McALISTER, JAMES, Private
Enlisted at Richmond, Virginia, September 16, 1862, for the war. Deserted from camp near Drewry's Bluff, Virginia, on October 20, 1862.

McCALLA, HUGH L., Private
Enlisted in Meriwether County, Georgia, at age 22, May 16, 1862, for the war. Mustered in as 1st Sergeant. Reduced to ranks "by request" October 22, 1862. Present or accounted for until transferred to 2nd Company A, 60th Regiment Georgia Infantry on April 11, 1864.

McCALLA, MATTHEW, Private
Enlisted in Meriwether County, Georgia, May 10, 1862, for the war. Present or accounted for until admitted to hospital at Richmond, Virginia, on January 11, 1864, with "variola dist." and was furloughed for 30 days January 28, 1864. Absent on furlough through February, 1864. Transferred to 2nd Company A, 60th Regiment Georgia Infantry on April 11, 1864.

MADDEN, JOHN H., Private
Enlisted in Meriwether County, Georgia, at age 45, May 16, 1862, for the war as a substitute for Benjamin K. Gates. Present or accounted for until transferred to 2nd Company A, 60th Regiment Georgia Infantry on April 11, 1864.

MAGOUIRK, JOHN W., Private
Enlisted in Meriwether County, Georgia, at age 23, May 16, 1862, for the war. Reported as absent sick from September-October, 1862, through March-April, 1863. No further records.

MAGOUIRK, SEBRON S., Private
Enlisted in Meriwether County, Georgia, at age 34, May 16, 1862, for the war. Present or accounted for on company muster rolls through February, 1864, when he appears with the remark: "Furloughed from hospital for forty days from 12th January—has failed to report." Transferred to 2nd Company A, 60th Regiment Georgia Infantry on April 11, 1864.

MANN, THOMAS A., Private
Enlisted in Meriwether County, Georgia, at age 22, May 16, 1862, for the war. Present or accounted for until transferred to 2nd Company A, 60th Regiment Georgia Infantry on April 11, 1864.

MEADOWS, ASA, Private
Enlisted in Meriwether County, Georgia, at age 24, May 16, 1862, for the war. Present or accounted for until transferred to 2nd Company A, 60th Regiment Georgia Infantry on April 11, 1864.

MEADOWS, JOHN, Private
Enlisted in Meriwether County, Georgia, at age 19, May 16, 1862, for the war. Died at Belle Isle, near Richmond, Virginia, July 28, 1862.

MITCHAM, J. D., Private
Enlisted in Meriwether County, Georgia, September 16, 1861, for twelve months. Died at White Sulphur Springs, Virginia, November 20, 1861.

MURRAH, CHARLES P., Private
Born in Harris County, Georgia, and was a farmer prior to enlisting in Meriwether County, Georgia, at age 18, May 16, 1862, for the war. Wounded at Gettysburg, Pennsylvania, and admitted to hospital at Richmond, Virginia, July 15, 1863, with "g.s.w. right shoulder." Transferred to Raleigh, July 24, 1863. Absent wounded through December, 1863. Transferred to 2nd Company A, 60th Regiment Georgia Infantry on April 11, 1864.

MURRAH, JAMES A., Private
Enlisted in Meriwether County, Georgia, at age 30, May 16, 1862, for the war. Mustered in as Pri-

vate. Appointed wagoner, September 1, 1862, and reduced to ranks after October, 1862. Left as a nurse for wounded at Gettysburg, Pennsylvania, and was captured at that place July 5, 1863. Confined at DeCamp General Hospital, Davids Island, New York Harbor, where he was paroled and sent to City Point, Virginia, for exchange August 24, 1863. Present or accounted for until transferred to 2nd Company A, 60th Regiment Georgia Infantry on April 11, 1864.

MURRAH, MORGAN H., Sergeant
Born in Harris County, Georgia, and was a farmer prior to enlisting in Meriwether County, Georgia, at age 18, May 16, 1862, for the war. Mustered in as Sergeant. Present or accounted for until transferred to 2nd Company A, 60th Regiment Georgia Infantry on April 11, 1864.

NALLS, GEORGE W., Private
Enlisted in Meriwether County, Georgia, September 16, 1861, for twelve months. Died November 29, 1861, at Richmond, Virginia.

OWENS, SAMUEL, Private
Enlisted in Meriwether County, Georgia, September 16, 1861, for twelve months. Company muster roll for September 16-October 31, 1861, reports that he was "absent at home without leave." No further records.

PARKER, WILLIAM A., Private
Enlisted in Meriwether County, Georgia, at age 30, May 16, 1862, for the war. Present or accounted for until transferred to 2nd Company A, 60th Regiment Georgia Infantry on April 11, 1864.

PERKINS, WILEY, Private
Enlisted in Meriwether County, Georgia, September 16, 1861, for twelve months. Company muster roll for September 16-October 31, 1861, reports that he was "absent—left without leave." No further records.

PHILLIPS, LEVI, Private
Enlisted in Meriwether County, Georgia, September 16, 1861, for twelve months. Admitted to hospital at Wilmington, February 1, 1862, with "catarrhus" and was returned to duty February 7, 1862. Company muster rolls report that he was absent on furlough, sick, through April, 1862. Present or accounted for until transferred to 2nd Company A, 60th Regiment Georgia Infantry on April 11, 1864.

POAGE, ROBERT H., Private
Enlisted in Meriwether County, Georgia, at age 29, May 16, 1862, for the war. Wounded and captured at Gettysburg, Pennsylvania, July 3, 1863. Confined at Fort McHenry, Maryland, and sent to Fort Delaware, Delaware, July 7-12, 1863. Transferred on October 18, 1863, to Point Lookout, Maryland, where he took the Oath of Allegiance January 23, 1864, and joined the U.S. service. Later assigned to Company G, 1st Regiment U.S. Volunteer Infantry.

POLLARD, CHARLES, Private
Enlisted in Meriwether County, Georgia, September 16, 1861, for twelve months. Company muster roll for September 16-October 31, 1861, reports

that he was "absent at home without leave." No further records.

RENFROE, JOHN A., Sergeant
Enlisted in Meriwether County, Georgia, at age 22, May 16, 1862, for the war. Mustered in as Corporal. Appointed Sergeant, October 1, 1862. Appointed Commissary Sergeant and transferred to the Field and Staff of this battalion September-October, 1863.

RICKLES, JAMES R., Private
Enlisted in Meriwether County, Georgia, at age 29, May 16, 1862, for the war. Wounded and captured at Gettysburg, Pennsylvania, July 1-3, 1863. Confined at DeCamp General Hospital, Davids Island, New York Harbor, July 14, 1863, with "g.s. leg" and was transferred to Fort Wood, Bedloe's Island, New York Harbor, October 24, 1863. Sent to Fortress Monroe, Virginia, January 5, 1864, and was admitted to Hammond U.S.A. General Hospital, Point Lookout, Maryland, January 10, 1864. Paroled at Point Lookout and transferred for exchange March 3, 1864. Admitted to hospital at Richmond, Virginia, March 7, 1864, and was furloughed for 60 days March 12, 1864. Transferred to 2nd Company A, 60th Regiment Georgia Infantry on April 11, 1864.

ROBINSON, CICERO F., Private
Enlisted in Meriwether County, Georgia, at age 28, May 16, 1862, for the war. Mustered in as Private. Appointed Assistant Surgeon, September 19, 1862, and transferred to the Field and Staff of this battalion.

ROWE, KINION, Private
Enlisted in Meriwether County, Georgia, at age 32, May 16, 1862, for the war. Company muster rolls report him as absent at home sick from June 11, 1862, through April, 1863. No further records.

ROWE, MARK, Private
Enlisted in Meriwether County, Georgia, September 16, 1861, for twelve months. Captured at Roanoke Island on February 8, 1862, and paroled at Elizabeth City, N.C., February 21, 1862. Left at Gettysburg, Pennsylvania, as a nurse for the wounded and was captured at that place July 3-5, 1863. Confined at Fort McHenry, Maryland, and was sent to Fort Delaware, Delaware, July 7-12, 1863. Transferred on October 18, 1863, to Point Lookout, Maryland, where he remained until paroled and sent to City Point, Virginia, for exchange on March 17, 1864. Transferred to 2nd Company A, 60th Regiment Georgia Infantry on April 11, 1864.

SEE, HARTWELL H., Private
Enlisted in Meriwether County, Georgia, May 10, 1862, for the war. Present or accounted for until transferred to 2nd Company A, 60th Regiment Georgia Infantry on April 11, 1864.

SHEPPARD, JOHN H., Corporal
Enlisted in Meriwether County, Georgia, at age 26, May 16, 1862, for the war. Mustered in as Corporal. Present or accounted for until transferred to 2nd Company A, 60th Regiment Georgia Infantry on April 11, 1864.

SISTRUNK, THOMAS L., Private
Enlisted in Meriwether County, Georgia, September 16, 1861, for twelve months. Died December 14, 1861, at White Sulphur Springs, Virginia.

SMITH, EBER D., Private
Enlisted in Meriwether County, Georgia, at age 33, May 16, 1862, for the war. Present or accounted for until transferred to 2nd Company A, 60th Regiment Georgia Infantry on April 11, 1864.

SMITH, HENRY, Private
Enlisted in Meriwether County, Georgia, at age 21, May 16, 1862, for the war. Company muster roll for November-December, 1863, reports that he was "left at Gettysburg, Pennsylvania, as nurse to wounded. Paroled and at home." Present or accounted for until transferred to 2nd Company A, 60th Regiment Georgia Infantry on April 11, 1864.

SMITH, RUSSELL, Private
Resided in Meriwether County, Georgia, where he enlisted at age 29, May 16, 1862, for the war. Present or accounted for until transferred to 2nd Company A, 60th Regiment Georgia Infantry on April 11, 1864.

SPILLER, CHARLES F., Sergeant
Enlisted in Meriwether County, Georgia, September 16, 1861, for twelve months. Mustered in as Private and appointed Sergeant, May-June, 1862. Discharged October 1, 1862, "for seniority and disability."

THORNTON, SEABORN, Private
Enlisted in Meriwether County, Georgia, May 16, 1862, for the war. Company pay roll for May 16, 1862-May 16, 1865, carries the notation: "Name canceled." No further records.

TRAMMELL, ADRIAN O., Private
Enlisted in Meriwether County, Georgia, at age 28, May 16, 1862, for the war. Company muster roll for May 16-June 30, 1862, does not report whether he was present or absent. No further records.

TUCKER, DANIEL J., Private
Enlisted in Meriwether County, Georgia, at age 34, May 16, 1862, for the war. Company muster roll for May 16-June 30, 1862, does not report whether he was present or absent. No further records.

TURNER, JAMES W., Private
Enlisted in Meriwether County, Georgia, at age 18, September 16, 1861, for twelve months. Present or accounted for until reported on the September-October, 1862, muster roll as "absent without leave—joined another company."

VAUGHN, J. H., Private
Enlisted in Meriwether County, Georgia, September 16, 1861, for twelve months. Company muster roll for September 16-October 31, 1861, reports that he was "absent at home on furlough." No further records.

WALKER, WOOLFORD, Private
Enlisted in Meriwether County, Georgia, September 16, 1861, for twelve months. Company muster roll for November-December, 1861, states that he "transferred to Captain Huff's Company Georgia Volunteers."

WARREN, SAM H., Private
Enlisted in Meriwether County, Georgia, September 16, 1861, for twelve months. Detailed at White Sulphur Springs as clerk to the Quartermaster. September-October, 1861. Absent on detached service through December, 1861. No further records.

WHITEHEAD, THOMAS, Private
Enlisted in Meriwether County, Georgia, September 16, 1861, for twelve months. Reported on the company muster roll for September 16-October 31, 1861, as "absent at home on sick furlough." No further records.

WILLIAMS, C. D., Private
Resided as a farmer in Meriwether County, Georgia, where he enlisted September 16, 1861, for twelve months. Captured at Roanoke Island on February 8, 1862, and paroled at Elizabeth City, N.C., February 21, 1862. Discharged at age 17, September 22, 1862, by reason of Conscript Law.

WILLIAMS, HOOD H., Private
Enlisted in Meriwether County, Georgia, at age 21, May 16, 1862, for the war. Died in hospital at Richmond, Virginia, August 29, 1862.

WILLIAMS, JOHN W., Sergeant
Enlisted in Meriwether County, Georgia, September 16, 1861, for twelve months. Mustered in as Private. Admitted to hospital at Wilmington, February 1, 1862, with "parotitis" and was returned to duty February 7, 1862. Appointed Sergeant, May 16-June 30, 1862. Discharged at age 17, September 30, 1862, "for minority."

WILLIAMS, LEWIS, Private
Born in Coffee County, Alabama, and was a farmer prior to enlisting in Meriwether County, Georgia, at age 30, May 16, 1862, for the war. Records in jacket indicate that he was discharged November 14, 1862, by reason of "chronic rheumatism"; however, he is present or accounted for on company muster rolls through February, 1864. Transferred to 2nd Company A, 60th Regiment Georgia Infantry on April 11, 1864.

WILLIAMS, THOMAS H., Sergeant
Enlisted in Meriwether County, Georgia, at age 31, May 16, 1862, for the war. Mustered in as Private and appointed Sergeant on November 1, 1863. Present or accounted for until transferred to 2nd Company A, 60th Regiment Georgia Infantry on April 11, 1864.

WILLIAMS, WILSON S., Private
Born in Meriwether County, Georgia, where he resided as a farmer and enlisted at age 17, September 16, 1861, for twelve months. Discharged September 22, 1862, by reason of age.

WILLINGHAM, GRIFFIN B., Sergeant
Enlisted in Meriwether County, Georgia, September 16, 1861, for twelve months. Mustered in as Sergeant. Died at White Sulphur Springs, Virginia, December 4, 1861.

WRIGHT, GEORGE W., Private
Enlisted in Meriwether County, Georgia, September 16, 1861, for twelve months. Died at White Sulphur Springs, Virginia, November 1, 1861.

COMPANY F

This company was organized in Randolph County in October, 1861, and was mustered into Confederate States service at Wilmington, New Hanover County, on January 7, 1862, as Company F of this battalion. After joining the battalion the company functioned as a part of the battalion, and its history is recorded as a part of the battalion history.

The information contained in the following roster of the company was compiled principally from company muster rolls which covered from the date of enlistment through December, 1862; March-April, 1863; September, 1863, through March, 1864; and September, 1864, through February, 1865. No company muster rolls were found for January-February, 1863; May through August, 1863; April through August, 1864; or for the period after February, 1865. In addition to the company muster rolls, Roll of Honor records, receipt rolls, and hospital records, supplemented by state pension applications, United Daughters of the Confederacy records, and postwar rosters and histories, all provided useful information.

OFFICERS
CAPTAINS

ANDREWS, HEZEKIAH L.
Resided in Randolph County and appointed Captain at age 22 to rank from November 30, 1861. Captured at Roanoke Island on February 8, 1862, and paroled at Elizabeth City, N.C., on February 21, 1862. Transferred to the Field and Staff of this battalion upon appointment as Major on October 1, 1862.

HANCOCK, JOHN M.
Resided in Randolph County and appointed 1st Lieutenant at age 23 to rank from November 30, 1861. He was not captured at Roanoke Island on February 8, 1862, and attached himself to the 54th Regiment N.C. Troops on May 15, 1862. Served with that regiment until September 3, 1862. Elected Captain at reorganization of this company on September 26, 1862, and appointed to rank from date of election. Transferred to the Field and Staff of this battalion upon appointment as Major on June 6, 1863.

LIEUTENANTS

ANDREWS, THOMAS WILBURN,
2nd Lieutenant
Resided in Randolph County where he enlisted at age 27, December 4, 1861, for twelve months. Mustered in as Sergeant. Captured at Roanoke Island on February 8, 1862, and paroled at Elizabeth City, N.C., February 21, 1862. Appointed 2nd Lieuteuant, September 25, 1862. Present or accounted for until captured at Fisher's Hill, Virginia, September 22, 1864. Confined at Fort Delaware, Delaware, until released after taking the Oath of Allegiance on June 17, 1865.

PUGH, JAMES W., 3rd Lieutenant
Resided in Randolph County where he enlisted at age 20, December 4, 1861, for twelve months. Mustered in as 1st Sergeant. Captured at Roanoke Island on February 8, 1862, and paroled at Eliza-

beth City, N.C., on February 21, 1862. Appointed Corporal at reorganization of company on September 25, 1862. Elected 3rd Lieutenant on March 8, 1863, and appointed to rank from date of election. Present or accounted for through February, 1865. Captured on April 3, 1865, in hospital at Richmond, Virginia, where he had been admitted as "wounded." Paroled on June 5, 1865.

WILLIAMS, ZIMRI J., 1st Lieutenant
Resided in Randolph County and appointed 3rd Lieutenant to rank from November 30, 1861. Captured at Roanoke Island on February 8, 1862, and paroled at Elizabeth City, N.C., on February 21, 1862. Promoted to 1st Lieutenant at reorganization of company on September 25, 1862. Present or accounted for until captured at Silver Spring, Maryland, July 13, 1864. Confined at Old Capitol Prison, Washington, D.C., until transferred to Fort Delaware, Delaware, October 23, 1864. Died at Fort Delaware on January 24, 1865, of "smallpox."

WINSLOW, HILKIAH, 2nd Lieutenant
Resided in Randolph County and appointed 2nd Lieutenant at age 26 to rank from November 30, 1861. Captured at Roanoke Island on February 8, 1862, and paroled at Elizabeth City, N.C., on February 21, 1862. Not reelected at reorganization of company on September 25, 1862.

NONCOMMISSIONED OFFICERS AND PRIVATES

ALLRIDGE, CALAWAY, Private
Enlisted in Wake County, September 7, 1864, for the war. Captured at Strasburg, Virginia, October 19, 1864, and confined at Point Lookout, Maryland, until paroled and sent to Aiken's Landing, James River, Virginia, for exchange on March 28, 1865. Admitted to hospital at Richmond, Virginia, March 30, 1865, with "febris cont." and was transferred to Camp Lee, Virginia, April 1, 1865.

ASBILL, WILLIAM, Private
Enlisted in Wake County, August 18, 1864, for the war. Wounded and captured at Winchester, Virginia, September 19, 1864, and admitted to U.S.A. Depot Field Hospital, Winchester, September 24, 1864. Transferred to U.S.A. General Hospital, West's Buildings, Baltimore, Maryland, November 15-16, 1864, with "g.s.w. left thigh and right hand" and was transferred to Point Lookout, Maryland, January 8, 1865. Released at Point Lookout after taking the Oath of Allegiance on June 4, 1865.

BARKER, JASPER M., Private
Resided in Randolph County where he enlisted at age 20, October 21, 1861, for twelve months. Captured at Roanoke Island on February 8, 1862, and paroled at Elizabeth City, N.C., February 21, 1862. Captured at Gettysburg, Pennsylvania, July 4, 1863, and was confined at Fort Delaware, Delaware. Took the Oath of Allegiance at Fort Delaware on July 27, 1863, and joined the U.S. service. Assigned to Ahl's Independent Company, Delaware Heavy Artillery.

BARKER, LEWIS S., Private
Resided in Randolph County where he enlisted

at age 16, October 20, 1861, for twelve months. Captured at Roanoke Island on February 8, 1862, and paroled at Elizabeth City, N.C., on February 21, 1862. Enlisted in Company E, 63rd Regiment N.C. Troops (5th Regiment N.C. Cavalry) on August 20, 1863, while absent without leave from this company.

BOGGS, ARRINGTON, Private
Enlisted in Randolph County, October 20, 1861, for twelve months. Company muster roll for February, 1862, to July 1, 1862, reports that he "deserted from this company and joined another."

BOON, DANIEL H., Private
Resided in Randolph County where he enlisted at age 47, March 29, 1863, as a substitute. Wounded at Gettysburg, Pennsylvania, July 1-3, 1863, and died July 10, 1863, of "g.s. right shoulder."

BRANSON, J. M., Private
Enlisted in Wake County, August 18, 1864, for the war. Captured at Winchester, Virginia, September 19, 1864, and confined at Point Lookout, Maryland. Died at Point Lookout, March 17, 1865, of "chronic diarrhoea."

BREEDLOVE, HENRY, Private
Enlisted in Randolph County, November 10, 1861, for twelve months. Present or accounted for on company muster rolls through July 1, 1862. No further records.

BUTLER, HICKMAN, Private
Resided in Randolph County where he enlisted at age 35, November 10, 1861, for twelve months. Discharged April 25, 1863, by reason of "being non-conscript."

CAGLE, D. M., Private
Enlisted in Wake County, September 22, 1864, for the war. Present or accounted for on company muster rolls through February, 1865. Captured in hospital at Richmond, Virginia, April 3, 1865, and "escaped from hospital May 4, 1865."

CAGLE, GEORGE, Private
Transferred from Company K, 54th Regiment N.C. Troops on September 3, 1862. Appointed Musician, March 1, 1863. Captured at Gettysburg, Pennsylvania, July 4, 1863, and confined at DeCamp General Hospital, Davids Island, New York Harbor, until paroled and sent to City Point, Virginia, for exchange. Received at City Point, September 8, 1863, for exchange. Reduced to ranks January-February, 1864. Present or accounted for on company muster rolls through February, 1865. Paroled at Appomattox Court House, Virginia, April 9, 1865.

CAGLE, HENRY, Corporal
Transferred from Company K, 54th Regiment N.C. Troops on September 3, 1862. Appointed Corporal, December 1, 1864. Present or accounted for on company muster rolls through February, 1865. Admitted to hospital at Danville, Virginia, April 7, 1865, with "vul. sclop. in left scalp," and was furloughed for 30 days on April 9, 1865.

CAGLE, JAMES, Private
Transferred from Company K, 54th Regiment N.C. Troops, September 3, 1862. Died in hospital

at Petersburg, Virginia, December 30, 1862, of "pneumonia typhoides."

CAGLE, LEWIS, Private
Transferred from Company K, 54th Regiment N.C. Troops on September 3, 1862. Captured at Gettysburg, Pennsylvania, July 4, 1863, and confined at DeCamp General Hospital, Davids Island, New York Harbor, until paroled and sent to City Point, Virginia, for exchange. Received at City Point on September 8, 1863, for exchange. Company muster rolls report him as absent prisoner of war until January-February, 1865, when he appears with the remark: "Died 3rd day of November, 1864, at Newton, Virginia."

CAMERON, ALEXANDER, Private
Resided in Randolph County where he enlisted at age 42, October 10, 1861, for twelve months. Captured at Roanoke Island on February 8, 1862, and paroled at Elizabeth City, N.C., February 21, 1862. Discharged December 3, 1862, by reason of "being a non-conscript."

CLARK, D. L., Private
Enlisted in Wake County, August 17, 1864, for the war. Present or accounted for on company muster rolls through February, 1865. Took the Oath of Allegiance at Washington, D.C., on May 29, 1865, and was "furnished transportation to Hamilton, Indiana."

CONNER, MILES S., Private
Resided in Randolph County where he enlisted at age 33, October 20, 1861, for twelve months. Captured at Roanoke Island on February 8, 1862, and paroled at Elizabeth City, N.C., February 21, 1862. Present or accounted for on company muster rolls through April, 1863. Roll of Honor reports that he was "killed July 1, 1863, in battle of Gettysburg."

COX, GEORGE W., Private
Enlisted in Wake County, August 18, 1864, for the war. Present or accounted for on company muster rolls through February, 1865. Paroled at Appomattox Court House, Virginia, April 9, 1865.

COX, HENRY C., Private
Resided in Randolph County where he enlisted at age 18, November 20, 1861, for twelve months. Admitted to hospital at Wilmington, February 1, 1862, with "febris typhoides" and was returned to duty on February 13, 1862. Present or accounted for on company muster rolls through April, 1863. Roll of Honor reports that he was "killed July 1, 1863, in battle at Gettysburg."

COX, JONATHAN L., Private
Resided in Randolph County and enlisted at age 35, May, 1863. Employed on extra duty with the artillery ordnance train June 29-July 31, 1863. Roll of Honor states that he "deserted August 6, 1863." Paroled at Greensboro, May 16, 1865.

COX, WILLIAM, Private
Resided in Randolph County where he enlisted at age 23, November 20, 1861, for twelve months. Captured at Roanoke Island on February 8, 1862, and paroled at Elizabeth City, N.C., February 21, 1862. Detailed as a nurse for the wounded at Gettysburg, Pennsylvania, where he was captured July 3-5, 1863. Confined at Fort Delaware, Dela-

ware, and transferred to Point Lookout, Maryland, October 18, 1863. Took the Oath of Allegiance at Point Lookout, January 25, 1864, and joined the U.S. service. Later assigned to Company B, 1st Regiment U.S. Volunteer Infantry.

CRAVEN, JAMES M., Private
Resided in Randolph County where he enlisted at age 17, November 20, 1861, for twelve months. Present or accounted for until discharged December 3, 1862, by reason of "being a non-conscript."

DAVIDSON, FELIX, Private
Born in Randolph County where he resided as a farmer and enlisted at age 28, March 1, 1862, for the war. Discharged at hospital at Richmond, Virginia, October 13, 1862, by reason of "disease of heart."

DAVIS, DOUGAN, Private
Resided in Randolph County where he enlisted at age 17, October 10, 1861, for twelve months. Present or accounted for until captured at Brandy Station, Virginia, November 8, 1863. Confined at Point Lookout, Maryland, where he died March 18, 1864, of "smallpox."

DAVIS, GREENBERRY, Private
Resided in Randolph County where he enlisted at age 45, October 10, 1861, for twelve months. Captured at Roanoke Island on February 8, 1862, and paroled at Elizabeth City, N.C., February 21, 1862. Discharged March 24, 1863, by reason of "being a non-conscript."

DAVIS, HENRY, Private
Born in Randolph County where he resided as a farmer and enlisted at age 17, October 10, 1861, for twelve months. Captured at Roanoke Island on February 8, 1862, and paroled at Elizabeth City, N.C., February 21, 1862. Discharged November 30, 1862, by reason of "being a non-conscript."

DAVIS, JESSE, Private
Resided in Randolph County where he enlisted at age 28, October 10, 1861, for twelve months. Present or accounted for until captured at Brandy Station, Virginia, November 8, 1863. Confined at Old Capitol Prison, Washington, D.C., and transferred to Point Lookout, Maryland, February 3, 1864. Took the Oath of Allegiance at Point Lookout, February 26, 1864, and joined the U.S. service.

DAVIS, JOHN W., Private
Resided in Randolph County where he enlisted at age 22, October 10, 1861, for twelve months. Captured at Roanoke Island on February 8, 1862, and paroled at Elizabeth City, N.C., February 21, 1862. Present or accounted for on company muster rolls through April 1, 1864. No further records.

DENSON, AARON, Private
Resided in Randolph County where he enlisted at age 19, November 1, 1861, for twelve months. Captured at Roanoke Island on February 8, 1862, and paroled at Elizabeth City, N.C., February 21, 1862. Present or accounted for on company muster rolls through February, 1865, when he is reported as absent sick. Paroled at Greensboro, May 16, 1865.

DENSON, JAMES, Private
Resided in Randolph County where he enlisted at age 23, November 1, 1861, for twelve months. Cap-

tured at Roanoke Island on February 8, 1862, and paroled at Elizabeth City, N.C., February 21, 1862. Present or accounted for until reported on the March-April, 1863, muster roll with the remark: "Deserted camp near Greenville, N.C., April 26, 1863." Roll of Honor states that he was "killed by Home Guards in Randolph County."

DENSON, SAMUEL, Private
Resided in Randolph County where he enlisted at age 53, November 1, 1861, for twelve months. Discharged November 30, 1862, by reason of "being a non-conscript." Reenlisted in this company April 4, 1863. Deserted April 26, 1863, and returned to the company November 15, 1863. Reported on company muster rolls as "absent in Confederate States Prison, Salisbury, N.C.," from that date until released from confinement December 1, 1864. Captured near Petersburg, Virginia, March 25, 1865, and confined at Point Lookout, Maryland. Released at Point Lookout after taking the Oath of Allegiance on May 13, 1865.

DOUGAN, THOMAS H., Sergeant
Resided in Randolph County where he enlisted at age 22, November 1, 1861, for twelve months. Mustered in as Private. Captured at Roanoke Island on February 8, 1862, and paroled at Elizabeth City, N.C., February 21, 1862. Appointed Sergeant, February 28-October 31, 1862. Present or accounted for on company muster rolls through February, 1865. Paroled at Appomattox Court House, Virginia, April 9, 1865.

ELBERSON, JOHN H., Private
Resided in Randolph County where he enlisted at age 22, October 20, 1861, for twelve months. Captured at Roanoke Island on February 8, 1862, and paroled at Elizabeth City, N.C., February 21, 1862. Present or accounted for on company muster rolls through February, 1865. Paroled at Appomattox Court House, Virginia, April 9, 1865.

ELLIOTT, SAMUEL B., Corporal
Transferred from Company K, 54th Regiment N.C. Troops, September 3, 1862. Appointed Corporal, October 1, 1862. Died in camp December 8, 1862, of "typhoid fever."

FORD, ASHWELL, Private
Resided in Randolph County where he enlisted at age 25, April 26, 1863, for the war. Captured in western Virginia, August 7, 1863, and took the Oath of Allegiance and was "sent to Wheeling, Virginia."

GORDON, JOSEPH E., Private
Resided in Davidson County and enlisted in Randolph County at age 31, October 10, 1861, for twelve months. Captured at Roanoke Island on February 8, 1862, and paroled at Elizabeth City, N.C., February 21, 1862. Deserted April 15, 1863, and was returned to camp November 1, 1863. Reported as absent in Confederate States Prison, Salisbury, N.C., through April 1, 1864. No further records.

GORDON, LINSEY D., Private
Resided in Davidson County and enlisted in Randolph County at age 27, October 10, 1861, for twelve months. Captured at Roanoke Island on

February 8, 1862, and paroled at Elizabeth City, N.C., February 21, 1862. Deserted April 15, 1863, and was returned to company December 1, 1863. Present or accounted for on company muster rolls through February, 1865. Paroled at Appomattox Court House, Virginia, April 9, 1865.

GOWEN, NELSON, Private

Resided in Guilford County and enlisted in Randolph County on November 26, 1861, for twelve months. Present or accounted for until captured near Spotsylvania Court House, Virginia, May 12, 1864. Confined at Point Lookout, Maryland, and transferred to Elmira, New York, August 12-14, 1864. Released at Elmira after taking the Oath of Allegiance on May 19, 1865.

GUYER, ANDREW D. C., Private

Resided in Davidson County and enlisted in Randolph County at age 20, October 1, 1861, for twelve months. Was not captured at Roanoke Island on February 8, 1862, and enlisted in Company A, 10th Battalion N.C. Heavy Artillery on April 25, 1862. Did not return to company when it was reorganized on September 25, 1862.

HALL, JAMES, Private

Resided in Randolph County where he enlisted at age 25, March 30, 1863, for the war. Reported on company muster rolls as absent sick from September-October, 1863, through April 1, 1864. Roll of Honor states that he "deserted from hospital." No further records.

HANCOCK, BETHUEL, Private

Enlisted in Wake County, October 12, 1864, for the war. Deserted November 10, 1864.

HANCOCK, LEVI, Private

Enlisted in Wake County, October 12, 1864, for the war. Deserted January 15, 1865. Took the Oath of Allegiance and was "furnished transportation to Indianapolis, Indiana."

HARDEN, JOHN C., Private

Paroled at Greensboro, May 17, 1865.

HELMS, H. P., Private

Paroled at Greensboro, 1865.

HILL, GREEN, Private

Born in Randolph County where he resided as a farmer prior to enlisting in Wake County at age 27, August 19, 1864, for the war. Captured at Winchester, Virginia, September 19, 1864, and confined at Point Lookout, Maryland. Paroled at Point Lookout and sent to Venus Point, Savannah River, Georgia, for exchange on October 30, 1864. Died at home in Randolph County, December 24, 1864, of "typhoid fever."

HINSON, HENRY, Private

Enlisted in Wake County, September 22, 1864, for the war. Captured September 29, 1864, at Swift Run Gap, Virginia, and confined at Point Lookout, Maryland. Paroled at Point Lookout and sent to Boulware's and Cox's Wharf, James River, Virginia, for exchange on February 18, 1865. Admitted to hospital at Richmond, Virginia, February 22, 1865, with "pneumonia" and furloughed for 60 days on March 7, 1865. Paroled at Charlotte, May 15, 1865.

HIX, CLEMENT, Private

Resided in Randolph County where he enlisted at age 40, March 30, 1863, for the war. Captured at Winchester, Virginia, September 19, 1864, and confined at Point Lookout, Maryland. Released at Point Lookout after taking the Oath of Allegiance on June 4, 1865.

HOLDER, WILLIAM, Private

Enlisted in Randolph County, March 12, 1862, for twelve months. Present or accounted for until captured or "gave himself up" at Frederick, Maryland, July 10, 1864. Confined at Old Capitol Prison, Washington, D.C., and transferred to Elmira, New York, July 23-25, 1864. Died October 4, 1864, at Elmira of "chronic diarrhoea."

HOOKER, ALEXANDER F., Private

Resided in Randolph County where he enlisted at age 35, February 6, 1863, for the war. Died in hospital at Orange Court House, Virginia, March 3, 1864, of "disease."

HOOKER, CLARKSON, Private

Resided in Randolph County where he enlisted at age 15, November 1, 1861, for twelve months. Discharged November 30, 1862, by reason of "being a non-conscript." Reenlisted in this company February 6, 1863. Present or accounted for until captured near Harpers Ferry, West Virginia, July 10, 1864, and confined at Old Capitol Prison, Washington, D.C. Transferred to Elmira, New York, July 23, 1864, and was confined at that place until released after taking the Oath of Allegiance on May 29, 1865.

HOOVER, HENRY E., Private

Resided in Randolph County where he enlisted at age 16, October 1, 1861, for twelve months. Present or accounted for until discharged November 30, 1862, by reason of "being a non-conscript."

JACKSON, L. W., Private

Paroled at Greensboro, May 5, 1865.

JAMES, MARSHALL E., Private

Resided in Randolph County where he enlisted at age 28, October 10, 1861. Mustered in as Sergeant. Captured at Roanoke Island on February 8, 1862, and paroled at Elizabeth City, N.C., February 21, 1862. Discharged February 15, 1863. Reenlisted as a substitute for Martin Kearn, April 4, 1863. Present or accounted for until captured near Spotsylvania Court House, Virginia, May 10, 1864. Confined at Point Lookout, Maryland, and transferred to Elmira, New York, August 10-14, 1864. Died at Elmira, November 22, 1864, of "pneumonia."

JARRELL, ANDERSON, Private

Enlisted in Wake County, August 18, 1864, for the war. Wounded and captured at Winchester, Virginia, September 19, 1864. Confined at U.S.A. Depot Field Hospital, Winchester, September 20, 1864, with "v.s. right hip, flesh wound." Transferred to U.S.A. General Hospital, West's Buildings, Baltimore, Maryland, October 13, 1864, and sent to Point Lookout, Maryland, October 26, 1864. Paroled at Point Lookout, October 30, 1864, and sent to Venus Point, Savannah River, Georgia, for exchange. Reported on the company muster roll for January-February, 1865, as "absent without leave in Randolph County."

JOHNSON, HENRY, Private
Captured at Winchester, Virginia, September 19, 1864, and confined at Point Lookout, Maryland, September 23, 1864. No further records.

KEARN, MARTIN, Private
Provided Marshall E. James as his substitute April 4, 1863.

KIME, ARRINGTON G., Corporal
Resided in Randolph County where he enlisted at age 21, October 20, 1861, for twelve months. Mustered in as Corporal. Died at home in Randolph County, June 5, 1862, of "typhoid fever."

KING, JOHN H., Private
Born in Randolph County where he resided as a farmer and enlisted at age 16, November 1, 1861, for twelve months. Captured at Roanoke Island on February 8, 1862, and paroled at Elizabeth City, N.C., February 21, 1862. Discharged November 30, 1862, by reason of "being a non-conscript."

KINLEY, GEORGE W., Private
Resided in Davidson County where he enlisted at age 36, March 4, 1863, for the war. Deserted April 15, 1863, and was returned to the company December 1, 1863. Company muster roll for January-February, 1864, reports that he "escaped from Division Provost Guard. Deserted." No further records.

KINLEY, MADISON, Private
Enlisted in Wake County, September 11, 1864, for the war. Present or accounted for on company muster rolls through February, 1865. Paroled at Appomattox Court House, Virginia, April 9, 1865.

KINNEY, HENDERSON, Private
Resided in Randolph County where he enlisted at age 25, February 11, 1863, for the war. Admitted to hospital at Richmond, Virginia, June 12, 1863, and was returned to duty July 13, 1863. Company muster rolls report that he deserted July 13, 1863, from the hospital and never returned to duty with the company.

LAMBETH, JOSEPH, Private
Resided in Randolph County where he enlisted at age 24, October 10, 1861, for twelve months. Captured at Roanoke Island on February 8, 1862, and paroled at Elizabeth City, N.C., February 21, 1862. Present or accounted for until he deserted and took the Oath of Allegiance at Washington, D.C., March 20, 1865. Furnished transportation to Hamilton, Indiana, after taking Oath.

LAMBETH, ZACHARIAH, Private
Resided as a farmer in Randolph County where he enlisted at age 26, October 10, 1861, for twelve months. Captured at Roanoke Island on February 8, 1862, and paroled at Elizabeth City, N.C., February 21, 1862. Present or accounted for until captured near Petersburg, Virginia, March 25-26, 1865, and confined at Point Lookout, Maryland. Released at Point Lookout after taking the Oath of Allegiance on May 12-14, 1865.

LANE, WILLIAM F., Private
Resided in Randolph County where he enlisted

at age 23, March 30, 1863, for the war. Present or accounted for on company muster rolls through April 1, 1864. Died in hospital at Gordonsville, Virginia, May 12, 1864, of "pneumonia."

LEDWELL, WHITSON C., Private
Resided in Randolph County where he enlisted at age 35, February 8, 1863, for the war. Deserted near Orange Court House, Virginia, August 6, 1863, and was returned to company November 2, 1863. Absent in confinement at Confederate States Prison, Salisbury, from January-February, 1864, until released on December 1, 1864, and ordered to return to his unit. No further records.

LEE, HENRY W., Private
Enlisted in Randolph County, October 10, 1861, for twelve months. Captured at Roanoke Island on February 8, 1862, and paroled at Elizabeth City, N.C., February 21, 1862. Company muster rolls report that he deserted from hospital at Farmville, Virginia, on July 20, 1863, and was returned to the company November 20, 1863. Reported as absent in Confederate States Prison, Salisbury, from that date until his death March 15, 1864, of "pneumonia."

LEE, RILEY, Private
Enlisted in Randolph County, October 10, 1861, for twelve months. Present or accounted for on company muster rolls through July 1, 1862. No further records.

LEWALLEN, DAWSON, Private
Resided in Randolph County where he enlisted as age 19, October 20, 1861, for twelve months. Mustered in as Corporal. Captured at Roanoke Island on February 8, 1862, and paroled at Elizabeth City, N.C., February 21, 1862. Reduced to ranks October 1, 1862. Present or accounted for until captured near Spotsylvania Court House, Virginia, May 10, 1864. Confined at Point Lookout, Maryland, where he died July 12, 1864.

LEWALLEN, ZIMRI A., Corporal
Transferred from Company K, 54th Regiment N.C. Troops on September 3, 1862, as a Private. Appointed Corporal, April-October, 1863. Present or accounted for until captured near Washington, D.C., July 13, 1864. Confined at Lincoln U.S.A. General Hospital, Washington, to serve as a nurse. Transferred to Old Capitol Prison, Washington, July 20, 1864, and to Elmira, New York, July 23-25, 1864. Confined at Elmira until released after taking the Oath of Allegiance on May 29, 1865.

LITTLE, GREEN, Private
Resided in Randolph County where he enlisted at age 50, March 26, 1863, as a substitute. Company muster roll for March-April, 1863, reports him as absent sick. Roll of Honor states that he was killed July 1, 1863, in battle at Gettysburg, Pennsylvania.

LOWDERMILK, ELKANAH, Private
Transferred from Company K, 54th Regiment N.C. Troops on September 3, 1862, as a Private. Appointed Corporal, December 25, 1862. Present or accounted for until captured at Strasburg, Virginia, October 19, 1864, and was released after taking the Oath of Allegiance on December 7, 1864.

McCOLLUM, WILLIAM W., Private
Enlisted in Randolph County at age 23, November 28, 1861, for twelve months. Deserted at Camp Belvedere, near Wilmington, January 10, 1862.

McCOLUM, NATHAN, Private
Enlisted in Randolph County, November 1, 1861, for twelve months. Deserted January 10, 1862, from Camp Belvedere, near Wilmington.

McCRARY, JOHN, Private
Enlisted in Wake County, August 10, 1864, for the war. Reported as absent sick on company muster rolls from September-October, 1864, through January-February, 1865. Captured in hospital at Richmond, Virginia, April 3, 1865, and died April 6, 1865, of "gunshot wound of right arm."

McINTYRE, GEORGE, Private
Enlisted in Wake County, September 22, 1864, for the war. Captured at Swift Run Gap, Virginia, September 29, 1864, and confined at Point Lookout, Maryland, until paroled and transferred to Aiken's Landing, Virginia, for exchange on March 17, 1865. Received at Aiken's Landing on March 19, 1865, for exchange.

MACON, GIDEON, Private
Enlisted in Wake County, September 11, 1864, for the war. Reported on company muster rolls as absent in arrest from September-October, 1864, through February, 1865. Paroled at Appomattox Court House, Virginia, April 9, 1865.

MANUS, ELI, Private
Enlisted in Randolph County, March 25, 1863, for the war. Captured at Strasburg, Virginia, October 19, 1864, and confined at Point Lookout, Maryland, until paroled and sent to Aiken's Landing, Virginia, for exchange on March 28, 1865.

MEDLEY, REDDICK, Private
Born in Edgecombe County and was a farmer prior to enlisting in Randolph County at age 50, November 1, 1861, for twelve months. Discharged December 3, 1863, by reason of "being over age."

MEDLEY, WILLIAM R., Private
Resided in Randolph County where he enlisted at age 49, November 20, 1861, for twelve months. Captured at Roanoke Island on February 8, 1862, and paroled at Elizabeth City, N.C., February 21, 1862. Roll of Honor states that he was "discharged by conscript law," but date of discharge is not shown.

MENDENHALL, JULIAN, Private
Resided in Randolph County where he enlisted at age 18, October 1, 1861, for twelve months. Was not captured with the company on Roanoke Island on February 8, 1862, and was transferred to Company A, 10th Battalion N.C. Heavy Artillery on April 26, 1862.

MOFFITT, ADAM J., Private
Transferred from Company K, 54th Regiment N.C. Troops on September 3, 1862. Present or accounted for on company muster rolls through December, 1862, when he appears as "absent on detached service at Danville, Virginia." Admitted to hospital at Danville on January 3, 1863, with "febris typnoides" and died January 6, 1863.

MOFFITT, ELIJAH K., 1st Sergeant
Transferred from Company K, 54th Regiment N.C. Troops on September 3, 1862, with rank of Sergeant. Promoted to 1st Sergeant on October 1, 1862. Present or accounted for until reduced to Sergeant when detailed as guard at Gordonsville, Virginia, February 26, 1864. Absent detailed until captured at Fisher's Hill, Virginia, September 22, 1864. Confined at Point Lookout, Maryland, until paroled and exchanged. Date of exchange not reported. Reappointed 1st Sergeant, December 1, 1864. Present or accounted for through February, 1865.

MOFFITT, KELLEY, Private
Enlisted in Randolph County on October 20, 1861, for twelve months. Present or accounted for through July 1, 1862.

MOFFITT, MANLY R., Private
Transferred from Company K, 54th Regiment N.C. Troops on September 3, 1862. Captured in hospital at Jordan Springs, Virginia, July 26, 1863, and paroled August 3, 1863. Admitted to hospital at Richmond, Virginia, September 7, 1863, with a gunshot wound and furloughed for 20 days on September 14, 1863. Reported as absent on parole on company muster rolls through February, 1864, and as absent on detached service in Randolph County through February, 1865.

MOFFITT, MATHEWS H., Sergeant
Transferred from Company K, 54th Regiment N.C. Troops on September 3, 1862. Appointed Corporal on October 1, 1862, and promoted to Sergeant on December 1, 1864. Present or accounted for on company muster rolls through February, 1865. Paroled at Appomattox Court House, Virginia, April 9, 1865.

NELSON, WILLIAM W., Private
Transferred from Company K, 54th Regiment N.C. Troops on September 3, 1862. Detailed on the Virginia Central Railroad, September-October, 1863, and reported as absent on detail on company muster rolls through February, 1865.

PERDUE, HENRY HARRISON, Private
Enlisted in Randolph County at age 18, October 20, 1861, for twelve months. Captured at Roanoke Island on February 8, 1862, and paroled at Elizabeth City, N.C., on February 21, 1862. Appointed Corporal on March 9, 1863. Deserted near Kinston, May 18, 1863, and returned to company November 15, 1863. Reduced to ranks for desertion. Present or accounted for until captured near Frederick, Maryland, July 10, 1864. Confined at Old Capitol Prison, Washington, D.C., until transferred to Elmira, New York, July 23-25, 1864. Released at Elmira after taking the Oath of Allegiance on May 29, 1865.

PHILLIPS, JOHN COLMAN, Private
Enlisted in Randolph County on October 20, 1861, for twelve months. Present or accounted for through July 1, 1862.

PIERCE, LEWIS, Private
Enlisted in Randolph County at age 45, October 10, 1861, for twelve months. Captured at Roanoke Island on February 8, 1862, and paroled at

Elizabeth City, N.C., on February 21, 1862. Discharged December 3, 1862, by reason of "being a non-conscript."

POOL, JAMES M., Private
Resided in Randolph County where he enlisted at age 21, October 10, 1861, for twelve months. Captured at Roanoke Island on February 8, 1862, and paroled at Elizabeth City, N.C., on February 21, 1862. Present or accounted for until captured at Strasburg, Virginia, October 19, 1864. Confined at Point Lookout, Maryland, until released after taking the Oath of Allegiance on June 17, 1865.

POUNDS, WILLEY L., Private
Born in Randolph County where he resided as a farmer and enlisted at age 16, November 1, 1861, for twelve months. Captured at Roanoke Island on February 8, 1862, and paroled at Elizabeth City, N.C., on February 21, 1862. Discharged November 30, 1862, by reason of "being under 18 years of age."

PRESNELL, JOHN, Private
Resided in Randolph County where he enlisted at age 34, November 1, 1861, for twelve months. Captured at Roanoke Island on February 8, 1862, and paroled at Elizabeth City, N.C., on February 21, 1862. Deserted January 19, 1863, and returned voluntarily April 1, 1863. Wounded at Gettysburg, Pennsylvania, July 1-3, 1863, and reported as absent sick until detailed for hospital duty on March 16, 1864. Paroled at Greensboro on May 25, 1865.

PRINCE, GEORGE W., Private
Name reported on March-April, 1863, muster roll with the remark: "Enlisted as a recruit—was found to belong to another company and was dropped."

PUGH, JOHN R., Corporal
Resided in Randolph County where he enlisted at age 18, November 1, 1863, for the war. Mustered in as Private and appointed Corporal on October 1, 1864. Present or accounted for on company muster rolls through February, 1865. Paroled at Greensboro on May 13, 1865.

RAMSEY, JAMES, Private
Enlisted in Wake County, September 20, 1864, for the war. Present or accounted for on company muster rolls through February, 1865. Captured at Burkeville, Virginia, April 6, 1865, and confined at Point Lookout, Maryland, where he died June 1, 1865, of "act. diarrhoea."

REDDING, ALFRED, Private
Resided in Randolph County where he enlisted at age 40, March 31, 1863, for the war. Present or accounted for until captured near Washington, D.C., July 12, 1864. Confined at Old Capitol Prison, Washington, D.C., and transferred to Elmira, New York, July 23, 1864. Died at Elmira on August 27, 1864, of "chronic diarrhoea."

REESE, JOSEPH M. D., Private
Enlisted in Randolph County, November 1, 1861, for twelve months. Present or accounted for on company muster rolls through July 1, 1862. No further records.

REEVES, A. PERRY, Private
Enlisted in Wake County, September 7-9, 1864, for the war. Captured at Fisher's Hill, Virginia, September 22, 1864, and confined at Point Lookout, Maryland, until transferred to Aiken's Landing, Virginia, for exchange on March 17, 1865. Admitted to hospital at Richmond, Virginia, March 19, 1865, and sent to Camp Lee, near Richmond, the next day.

RICH, DANIEL, Private
Resided in Randolph County where he enlisted at age 43, November 1, 1861, for twelve months. Was not captured with his company at Roanoke Island on February 8, 1862, and enlisted in Company K, 54th Regiment N.C. Troops on March 5, 1862. Transferred back to this company on September 3, 1862. Present or accounted for until captured at Gettysburg, Pennsylvania, July 3-4, 1863. Confined at Fort McHenry, Maryland, until transferred to Fort Delaware, Delaware, July 7-12, 1863. Sent to U.S. Hospital, Chester, Pennsylvania, July 25, 1863, and was transferred to Hammond General Hospital, Point Lookout, Maryland, October 2, 1863. Paroled at Point Lookout and sent to City Point, Virginia, for exchange on March 3, 1864. Present or accounted for until the November-December, 1864, muster roll reports that he "deserted November 10, 1864." Paroled at Appomattox Court House, Virginia, April 9, 1865.

RICH, JOHN M., Private
Enlisted in Randolph County, December 4, 1861, for twelve months. Company muster-in roll dated January 7, 1862, states that he was sick at home. No further records.

RICH, JOSEPH. Private
Enlisted in Wake County, September 7, 1864, for the war. Captured at Fisher's Hill, Virginia, September 22, 1864, and confined at Point Lookout, Maryland, October 1, 1864. Released at Point Lookout, May 13, 1865.

RICH, MILTON, Private
Enlisted in Randolph County, November 1, 1861, for twelve months. Company muster roll for February 8, 1862, to July 1, 1862, reports him as present. No further records.

RICHARDSON, ALLEN, Sergeant
Resided in Randolph County where he enlisted at age 22, December 4, 1861, for twelve months. Mustered in as Sergeant. Captured at Roanoke Island on February 8, 1862, and paroled at Elizabeth City, N.C., February 21, 1862. Reduced to Corporal, October 1, 1862. Reappointed Sergeant, January-April, 1863. Wounded at Gettysburg, Pennsylvania, July 1, 1863, and admitted to hospital at Richmond, Virginia, July 20, 1863, with "v.s. right arm." Transferred to Raleigh July 25, 1863, and is reported on company muster rolls as absent sick through February, 1864. Transferred to the Field and Staff of this battalion upon appointment as Commissary Sergeant in September, 1864.

RICHARDSON, ELWOOD, Private
Resided in Randolph County where he enlisted at age 19, October 20, 1861, for twelve months.

Captured at Roanoke Island on February 8, 1862, and paroled at Elizabeth City, N.C., February 21, 1862. Present or accounted for on company muster rolls through April, 1863. Roll of Honor states that he was "killed July 1, 1863, in battle at Gettysburg, Pennsylvania."

RICHARDSON, JOHN, Private
Resided in Randolph County where he enlisted at age 18, October 10, 1862, for the war. Present or accounted for on company muster rolls through February, 1865. Deserted and took the Oath of Allegiance at Washington, D.C., April 4, 1865, and was furnished transportation to Wayne County, Indiana.

RICHARDSON, JOHN R., Sergeant
Resided in Randolph County where he enlisted at age 27, October 20, 1861, for twelve months. Mustered in as Corporal. Captured at Roanoke Island on February 8, 1862, and paroled at Elizabeth City, N.C., February 21, 1862. Appointed Sergeant, October 1, 1862. Present or accounted for on company muster rolls through February, 1865. Deserted and took the Oath of Allegiance at Washington, D.C., March 29, 1865, and was furnished transportation to Hamilton County, Indiana.

RICHARDSON, PETER, Private
Resided as a blacksmith in Randolph County prior to enlisting in Wake County, September 7, 1864, for the war. Captured at Fisher's Hill, Virginia, September 22, 1864, and confined at Point Lookout, Maryland, until released after taking the Oath of Allegiance on May 14, 1865.

ROACH, SIDNEY, Private
Resided in Randolph County where he enlisted at age 20, October 20, 1861, for twelve months. Captured at Roanoke Island on February 8, 1862, and paroled at Elizabeth City, N.C., February 21, 1862. Deserted at camp near Orange Court House, Virginia, August 23, 1863, and was returned to the company December 15, 1863, "under guard." Present or accounted for on company muster rolls until he was reported on the September-October, 1864, muster roll as a prisoner of war. Reported as such through February, 1865; however, date and place of capture are not shown in records.

ROBBINS, JOHN, Private
Enlisted in Randolph County, December 4, 1861, for twelve months. Company muster-in roll, dated January 7, 1862, reports him as "sick at home." No further records.

ROBBINS, THOMAS R., Private
Resided in Randolph County where he enlisted at age 22, March 31, 1863, for the war. Died in hospital at Staunton, Virginia, July 26, 1863, of "febris typhoides."

SEXTON, JOHN, Private
Resided in Randolph County where he enlisted at age 18, October 10, 1861, for twelve months. Captured at Roanoke Island on February 8, 1862, and paroled at Elizabeth City, N.C., February 21, 1862. Died in hospital at Gettysburg, Pennsylvania, July 16, 1863, of "typhoid pneumonia."

SEXTON, MOREHEAD, Private
Resided in Randolph County where he enlisted at age 18, October 10, 1861, for twelve months. Captured at Roanoke Island on February 8, 1862, and paroled at Elizabeth City, N.C., February 21, 1862. Died at home March 10, 1862, of "typhoid fever."

SLACK, LABAN, Private
Enlisted in Wake County, August 19, 1864, for the war. Wounded and captured at Winchester, Virginia, September 19, 1864. Admitted to U.S.A. General Hospital, West's Buildings, Baltimore, Maryland, October 19, 1864, with "f.w. left thigh above the middle" and was transferred to Point Lookout, Maryland, October 25-26, 1864. Paroled and sent to Venus Point, Savannah River, Georgia, for exchange on October 30, 1864. Reported on company muster rolls as absent prisoner of war until January-February, 1865, when he appears as absent without leave.

SMITH, ALBERT, Private
Transferred from Company K, 54th Regiment N.C. Troops on September 3, 1862. Captured at Gettysburg, Pennsylvania, July 1-4, 1863, and confined at DeCamp General Hospital, Davids Island, New York Harbor, until paroled and sent to City Point, Virginia, for exchange. Received at City Point on September 8, 1863, for exchange. Reported on company muster rolls as absent on parole from that date through February, 1864, and as absent without leave through February, 1865. Paroled at Greensboro, May 16, 1865.

SMITH, DAVID N., Private
Resided in Mecklenburg County and enlisted in Wake County, September 20, 1864, for the war. Present or accounted for on company muster rolls through February, 1865. Captured at Farmville, Virginia, April 6, 1865, and confined at Point Lookout, Maryland, until released after taking the Oath of Allegiance on June 30, 1865.

SMITH, EDWIN, Private
Resided in Randolph County where he enlisted at age 24, February 8, 1863, for the war. Company muster roll for September-October, 1863, reports that he was "absent on parole in Randolph County, N.C." Reported as absent on parole through February, 1864, and as absent without leave from that date through February, 1865. Date and place of capture not shown in records.

SMITH, ELIAS A., Private
Resided in Randolph County where he enlisted at age 25, February 6, 1863, for the war. Company muster roll for March-April, 1863, reports him as "absent sick at Kinston, N.C." Roll of Honor states that he "deserted to the enemy June, 1863."

STEED, BENJAMIN FRANKLIN, Private
Resided in Randolph County where he enlisted at age 24, April 4, 1863, for the war. Wounded and captured at Gettysburg, Pennsylvania, July 1-3, 1863. Confined at DeCamp General Hospital, Davids Island, New York Harbor, until paroled and sent to City Point, Virginia, for exchange

on August 24, 1863. Reported on company muster rolls as absent on parole through February, 1864. Appointed Sergeant and detailed with Major Peter Mallett, Commandant of Conscripts, March 1, 1864. Absent detailed through December, 1864. Reported as absent without leave on the January-February, 1865, muster roll with the rank of Private.

STEED, JOHN STANLEY, Private

Enlisted in Randolph County, November 20, 1861, for twelve months. Present or accounted for on company muster rolls through July 1, 1862. No further records.

STEEL, ABNER B., Private

Enlisted in Randolph County, November 1, 1861, for twelve months. Present or accounted for on company muster rolls through July 1, 1862. No further records.

STUART, JOHN, Private

Resided in Randolph County and enlisted at age 24, March, 1863, for the war. Roll of Honor states that he "deserted to the enemy June, 1863." No further records.

TROGDEN, H. K., Private

Enlisted in Wake County, September 20, 1864, for the war. Captured at Strasburg, Virginia, October 19, 1864, and confined at Point Lookout, Maryland, until "released on Oath December 7, 1864."

TURNER, JOHN J., Private

Enlisted in Wake County, August 17, 1864, for the war. Present or accounted for on company muster rolls until January-February, 1865, when he is reported as "absent without leave in Guilford County, N.C." Paroled at Greensboro, May 20, 1865.

UPTON, ALVIS, Private

Resided as a farmer in Randolph County prior to enlisting in Wake County, September 7, 1864, for the war. Captured at Fisher's Hill, Virginia, September 22, 1864, and confined at Point Lookout, Maryland, until released after taking the Oath of Allegiance on May 12-14, 1865.

VARNER, WILLIAM PRESSLY, Private

Resided in Randolph County where he enlisted at age 21, October 10, 1861, for twelve months. Captured at Roanoke Island on February 8, 1862, and paroled at Elizabeth City, N.C., February 21, 1862. Present or accounted for until again captured at Wilderness, Virginia, on May 19, 1864. Confined at Old Capitol Prison, Washington, D.C., and transferred to Fort Delaware, Delaware, June 15-17, 1864. Released at Fort Delaware after taking the Oath of Allegiance on May 31, 1865.

VEACH, JOSEPH R. P., 1st Sergeant

Resided in Davidson County and enlisted in Randolph County at age 25, October 1, 1861, for twelve months. Mustered in as Corporal and promoted to Sergeant, October 1, 1862. Appointed 1st Sergeant, March, 1864. Present or accounted for until retired to the Invalid Corps, October 26, 1864.

VEACH, McKINDREE L., Private

Born in Davidson County and enlisted in Ran-

dolph County, October 1, 1861, for twelve months. Died in hospital at Wilmington, August 28, 1862, of "typhoid fever."

VUNCANNON, WILLIAM, Private

Enlisted in Wake County, August 19, 1864, for the war. Captured at Winchester, Virginia, September 19, 1864, and confined at Point Lookout, Maryland. Released at Point Lookout after taking the Oath of Allegiance on March 22, 1865, and was furnished transportation to Dublin, Indiana, by the Provost Marshal General, Washington, D.C., March 23, 1865.

WARD, JAMES, Private

Enlisted in Wake County, August 8, 1864, for the war. Company muster roll for November-December, 1864, reports that he "deserted November 24, 1864."

WHISTENHUNT, ALEXANDER W., Private

Resided in Randolph County where he enlisted at age 35, October 10, 1861, for twelve months. Captured at Roanoke Island on February 8, 1862, and paroled at Elizabeth City, N.C., February 21, 1862. Present or accounted for on company muster rolls until March-April, 1863, when he is reported as "absent in guard house, Greenville, N.C." Roll of Honor states that he "deserted August 22, 1863, and died in Randolph County." No further records.

WHISTENHUNT, HENRY H., Private

Resided in Randolph County where he enlisted at age 19, October 10, 1861, for twelve months. Was not captured at Roanoke Island on February 8, 1862, and attached himself to Company B, 52nd Regiment N.C. Troops. Did not return to the company when it reorganized in September, 1862.

WILSON, HUGH, Private

Resided in Randolph County where he enlisted at age 18, November 20, 1861, for twelve months. Captured at Roanoke Island on February 8, 1862, and paroled at Elizabeth City, N.C., February 21, 1862. Present or accounted for on company muster rolls through April, 1863. September-October, 1863, muster roll reports that he was "absent at home sick in Randolph County, N.C." Absent sick from that date until January-February, 1865, when he appears as "absent without leave in Randolph County." Paroled at Greensboro, May 17, 1865.

WILSON, JESSE, Private

Transferred from Company K, 54th Regiment N.C. Troops on September 3, 1862. Present or accounted for until admitted to hospital at Richmond, Virginia, March 21, 1865, with "diarrhoea ch." Captured in hospital at Richmond on April 3, 1865, and confined at Libby Prison, Richmond, until transferred to Newport News, Virginia, April 23, 1865. Admitted to Prison Hospital, Newport News, May 31, 1865, with "diarrhoea chr." and died June 24, 1865.

WOODBURN, THEODORE B., Private

Resided in Randolph County where he enlisted at age 30, March 31, 1863, for the war. Killed at Gettysburg, Pennsylvania, July 1, 1863.

WOODELL, ALLEN J., Private
Resided in Randolph County where he enlisted at age 22, March 19, 1862, for the war. Present or accounted for until captured at Brandy Station, Virginia, November 8, 1863. Confined at Old Capitol Prison, Washington, D.C., until transferred to Point Lookout, Maryland, February 3-4, 1864. Released after taking the Oath of Allegiance and joining the U. S. service on February 19, 1864.

WOODELL, BENJAMIN F., Private
Resided in Randolph County where he enlisted at age 21, November 20, 1861, for twelve months. Present or accounted for on company muster rolls through February, 1865, being reported as absent sick from September through December, 1864, and as absent without leave January-February, 1865.

WOODELL, ENOCH, Corporal
Resided in Randolph County where he enlisted at age 19, November 10, 1861, for twelve months. Mustered in as Private. Captured at Roanoke Island on February 8, 1862, and paroled at Elizabeth City, N.C., on February 21, 1862. Appointed Corporal on June 1, 1863. Wounded at Gettysburg, Pennsylvania, July 1-3, 1863. Present or accounted for until captured at Spotsylvania Court House, Virginia, May 20, 1864. Confined at Point Lookout, Maryland, until transferred to Elmira, New York, July 3-6, 1864. Transferred back to Point Lookout on October 14, 1864, and paroled for exchange on October 29, 1864. Date and place exchanged not reported, and January-February, 1865, muster roll reports him as absent prisoner of war.

WOODELL, THOMAS, Private
Transferred from Company K, 54th Regiment N.C. Troops on September 3, 1862. Present or accounted for until he died in hospital at Orange Court House, Virginia, on March 9, 1864.

WRIGHT, EMSLEY, Private
Transferred from Company K, 54th Regiment N.C. Troops on September 3, 1862. Present or accounted for until he deserted near Goldsboro on January 19, 1863.

YORK, ALFRED D., Private
Transferred from Company K, 54th Regiment N.C. Troops on September 3, 1862. Captured at Gettysburg, Pennsylvania, July 1-5, 1863, and confined at DeCamp General Hospital, Davids Island, New York Harbor, until paroled and sent to City Point, Virginia, for exchange on August 24, 1863. Declared exchanged at City Point on August 28, 1863. Reported as absent on parole through February, 1864, and as absent without leave on muster roll dated April 1, 1864. September-October, 1864, muster roll reports him as present; however, he deserted on November 10, 1864, and was brought back to the company on December 14, 1864. Present or accounted for until admitted to hospital at Farmville, Virginia, March 5, 1865, with "acute pneumonia" and died March 18, 1865.

COMPANY G

This company was organized in Forsyth County and enlisted on September 16, 1861. It was mustered into Confederate States service at Wilmington, New Hanover County, on January 18, 1862, as Company G of this battalion. After joining the battalion it functioned as a part of the battalion, and its history for the war period is recorded as a part of the battalion history.

The information contained in the following roster of the company was compiled pricipally from company muster rolls which covered from the date of enlistment through December, 1862; March-April, 1863; September, 1863, through March, 1864; and May, 1864, through February, 1865. No company muster rolls were found for January-February, 1863; May through August, 1863; April, 1864; or for the period after February, 1865. In addition to the company muster rolls, Roll of Honor records, receipt rolls, and hospital records, supplemented by state pension applications, United Daughters of the Confederacy records, and postwar rosters and histories, all provided useful information.

OFFICERS

CAPTAINS

WHEELER, WILLIAM H.
Resided in Forsyth County where he enlisted at age 24, September 19, 1861, for twelve months. Appointed Captain to rank from October 1, 1861. Captured at Roanoke Island on February 8, 1862, and paroled at Elizabeth City, N.C., on February 21, 1862. Present or accounted for until he submitted his resignation on January 27, 1863, by reason of ill health. Resignation accepted on February 7, 1863.

WHEELER, HENRY C.
Resided in Forsyth County where he enlisted at age 18, September 19, 1861, for twelve months. Mustered in as Private and appointed Sergeant early in 1862. Captured at Roanoke Island on February 8, 1862, and paroled at Elizabeth City, N.C., on February 21, 1862. Elected 1st Lieutenant when the company reorganized on September 25, 1862, and appointed to rank from date of election. Promoted to Captain on February 15, 1863. Wounded in both thighs and left arm and captured at Gettysburg, Pennsylvania, July 1, 1863. Left arm amputated July 1, 1863. Confined in hospital at Frederick, Maryland, until transferred to hospital at Baltimore, Maryland, on September 4, 1863. Transferred to Fort McHenry, Maryland, April 10, 1864, and from there to Fort Delaware, Delaware, June 15-16, 1864. Paroled at Fort Delaware, September 14, 1864, and sent to Aiken's Landing, Virginia, for exchange on September 18, 1864. Reported as absent on furlough until retired to the Invalid Corps on March 4, 1865.

LIEUTENANTS

BROWN, DEMPSEY S., 1st Lieutenant
Resided in Forsyth County where he enlisted at age 18, September 19, 1861, for twelve months.

Mustered in as Sergeant. Captured at Roanoke Island on February 8, 1862, and paroled at Elizabeth City, N.C., on February 21, 1862. Elected 2nd Lieutenant at reorganization of company on September 25, 1862, and appointed to rank from date of election. Promoted to 1st Lieutenant to rank from July 1, 1863. Present or accounted for until paroled at Appomattox Court House, Virginia, April 9, 1865.

GORRELL, RALPH, 1st Lieutenant
Resided in Forsyth County where he enlisted at age 23, September 19, 1861, for twelve months. Appointed 3rd Lieutenant and mustered in as such on January 18, 1862. Date appointment to rank from not reported on records. Captured at Roanoke Island on February 8, 1862, and paroled at Elizabeth City, N.C., on February 21, 1862. Elected 2nd Lieutenant at reorganization of company on September 25, 1862, and appointed to rank from date of election. Appointed 1st Lieutenant to rank from June 1, 1863, and killed at Gettysburg, Pennsylvania, July 1, 1863.

PAYNE, JOHN WESLEY, 1st Lieutenant
Resided in Davidson County and enlisted in Forsyth County at age 32, September 19, 1861, for twelve months. Appointed 1st Lieutenant to rank from October 1, 1861. Captured at Roanoke Island on February 8, 1862, and paroled at Elizabeth City, N.C., on February 21, 1862. Not reelected at reorganization of company on September 25, 1862.

SWAIM, COLUMBUS F., 2nd Lieutenant
Transferred from Company B, 1st Battalion N.C. Sharpshooters upon appointment as 2nd Lieutenant to rank from June 30, 1863. Present or accounted for until captured at Fisher's Hill, Virginia, September 22, 1864. Confined at Fort Delaware, Delaware, until released after taking the Oath of Allegiance on June 17, 1865.

SWAIM, JOSEPH S., 1st Lieutenant
Resided in Davidson County and enlisted in Forsyth County at age 42, September 19, 1861, for twelve months. Appointed 2nd Lieutenant to rank from October 1, 1861. Captured at Roanoke Island on February 8, 1862, and paroled at Elizabeth City, N.C., on February 21, 1862. Elected 1st Lieutenant at reorganization of company on September 25, 1862, and appointed to rank from date of election. Submitted his resignation on April 23, 1863, by reason of "health." Resignation was accepted on May 30, 1863.

NONCOMMISSIONED OFFICERS AND PRIVATES

BAHNSON, CHARLES F., 1st Sergeant
Resided in Forsyth County where he enlisted at age 23, September 19, 1861, for twelve months. Mustered in as 1st Sergeant. Captured at Roanoke Island on February 8, 1862, and paroled at Elizabeth City, N.C., February 21, 1862. Appointed Captain, Assistant Quartermaster, January 1, 1863, and transferred to the Field and Staff of this battalion.

BEESON, NEWELL W., Corporal
Resided in Davidson County and enlisted in Wake County at age 18, February 26, 1864, for the war. Mustered in as Private and appointed Corporal, December 15, 1864. Present or accounted for on company muster rolls through February, 1865. Admitted to hospital at Greensboro in March, 1865.

BENFIELD, COONROD A., Private
Resided in Catawba County and enlisted in Wake County, April 22, 1864, for the war. Present or accounted for on company muster rolls through February, 1865. Admitted to hospital at Richmond, Virginia, March 25, 1865, with "febris remit." and was captured in the hospital April 3, 1865. Confined at Libby Prison, Richmond, until transferred to Newport News, Virginia, April 23, 1865. Released after taking the Oath of Allegiance at Newport News on June 30, 1865.

BLACKBURN, ELISHA, Private
Enlisted in Wake County, August 19, 1864, for the war. Reported on the company muster roll for April 30-October 31, 1864, as "absent on furlough, wounded." Appears on muster rolls from that date through February, 1865, as absent without leave.

BODENHAMER, HEZEKIAH, Private
Resided in Forsyth County where he enlisted at age 23, September 19, 1861, for twelve months. Present or accounted for until admitted to hospital on May 27, 1863, at Richmond, Virginia, where he died June 5, 1863, of "typhoid fever."

BRATTON, CHARLES, Private
Enlisted in Wake County, September 17, 1864, for the war. Present or accounted for on company muster rolls until January-February, 1865, when he was reported as "absent on detached service."

BROWN, ISAAC N., Private
Resided in Davidson County and enlisted in Wake County at age 18, February 26, 1864, for the war. Wounded on September 19, 1864, at Winchester, Virginia, where he died September 25, 1864, of his wounds.

BROWN, J. A. J., Private
Resided in Davidson County where he enlisted at age 36, September 8, 1862, for the war. Wounded at Gettysburg, Pennsylvania, July 1, 1863, and died July 5, 1863, of his wounds.

BROWN, ROMULAS M., Private
Resided in Davidson County where he enlisted at age 18, January 1, 1864, for the war. Wounded and captured at Winchester, Virginia, September 19, 1864. Confined at U.S.A. Depot Field Hospital, Winchester, September 24, 1864, with "v.s. thigh, severe flesh wound" and was transferred to U.S.A. General Hospital, West's Buildings, Baltimore, Maryland, October 19, 1864. Sent to Point Lookout, Maryland, October 25-26, 1864, and was paroled and transferred to Venus Point, Savannah River, Georgia, for exchange on October 29, 1864. Company muster rolls report him as absent wounded or sick until admitted to hospital at Richmond, Virginia, February 24, 1865, with "scabies—feb. remit." Furloughed from hospital for 60 days on March 21, 1865.

CALHOUN, STEPHEN, Private
Resided in Forsyth County where he enlisted at age 25, September 23, 1862, for the war. Died in hospital at Goldsboro, February 24, 1863.

CARTER, FRANCIS M., Private
Resided in Davidson County and enlisted in Forsyth County at age 16, September 19, 1861, for twelve months. Captured at Roanoke Island on February 8, 1862, and paroled at Elizabeth City, N.C., February 21, 1862. Discharged by reason of the Conscript Law on November 21, 1862. Reenlisted in Davidson County, January 1, 1864. Mustered in as Corporal. Reduced to ranks "for misconduct" May 19, 1864, and pay stopped for 80 days for "absence without leave." Captured at Winchester, Virginia, September 19, 1864, and confined at Point Lookout, Maryland, until paroled and transferred to Aiken's Landing, Virginia, March 15, 1865, for exchange.

CHADWICK, CYRUS B., Private
Resided in Guilford County and enlisted in Forsyth County at age 23, September 19, 1861, for twelve months. Captured at Roanoke Island on February 8, 1862, and paroled at Elizabeth City, N.C., February 21, 1862. Present or accounted for until again captured on September 19, 1864, at Winchester, Virginia. Confined at Point Lookout, Maryland, until paroled and transferred to Aiken's Landing, Virginia, for exchange March 15, 1865. Paroled at Greensboro, May 13, 1865.

CHAMBERLAIN, CHARLES, Private
Resided in Forsyth County where he enlisted at age 27, September 8, 1862, for the war. Present or accounted for until transferred to Company A, 1st Regiment N.C. State Troops, March 13, 1864.

CLINARD, JOHN, Private
Enlisted in Forsyth County at age 21, September 19, 1861. Appears on company muster-in roll dated January 18, 1862. No further records.

CLINE, JOHN H., Private
Enlisted in Forsyth County, December 23, 1862, for the war. Deserted near Kinston, February 20, 1863.

CLODFELTER, GEORGE, Private
Resided in Forsyth County where he enlisted at age 16, September 19, 1861, for twelve months. Captured at Roanoke Island on February 8, 1862, and paroled at Elizabeth City, N.C., February 21, 1862. Discharged by Conscript Law, November 21, 1862. Reenlisted in this company January 20, 1863, for the war. Captured at Gettysburg, Pennsylvania, July 3-5, 1863, and confined at Fort Delaware, Delaware, where he died November 6, 1863, of "smallpox."

COOK, JOSIAH, Private
Enlisted in Wake County, September 16, 1864, for the war. Present or accounted for on company muster rolls through February, 1865. Paroled at Appomattox Court House, Virginia, April 9, 1865.

COOK, PHILIP, Corporal
Resided in Forsyth County where he enlisted at age 24, September 19, 1861, for twelve months. Mustered in as Private and appointed Corporal, December 1, 1863. Present or accounted for on

company muster rolls until reported on the April 30-October 31, 1864, roll with the remark: "Killed in action May 10, 1864."

COOPER, FRANKLIN, Private
Resided in Forsyth County where he enlisted at age 28, March 1, 1863, for the war. Appears on a roll of rebel prisoners of war forwarded from Harrisburg, Pennsylvania, to Philadelphia, Pennsylvania, on July 21, 1863. Company muster rolls report that he was "sick and left in the hands of the enemy" prior to September-October, 1863, and "died at Harrisburg, Pennsylvania, August 15, 1863, of fever."

CRABB, DANIEL W., Private
Enlisted in Wake County, September 10, 1864, for the war. Captured at Winchester, Virginia, September 19, 1864, and confined at Point Lookout, Maryland, until paroled and sent to Cox's Landing, James River, Virginia, for exchange February 13, 1865. Admitted to hospital at Richmond, Virginia, February 15, 1865, and is reported as present at hospital through February, 1865.

CRAVEN, HARRISON, Private
Resided in Davidson County and enlisted in Forsyth County at age 17, September 19, 1861, for twelve months. Discharged in January, 1862, and reenlisted in February, 1863, for the war. Wounded and captured at Gettysburg, Pennsylvania, July 1-5, 1863, and confined at DeCamp General Hospital, Davids Island, New York Harbor, until paroled and sent to City Point, Virginia, for exchange. Received at City Point, September 16, 1863, for exchange. Company muster rolls report him as absent wounded through February, 1864. Captured at Strasburg, Virginia, October 19, 1864, and confined at Point Lookout, Maryland, until paroled and sent to Cox's Landing, James River, Virginia, February 13, 1865, for exchange. Admitted to hospital at Richmond, Virginia, and furloughed for 30 days March 2, 1865.

CRAVEN, WILLIAM D., Sergeant
Resided in Davidson County and enlisted in Forsyth County at age 19, September 19, 1861, for twelve months. Mustered in as Private. Appointed Sergeant prior to April 30, 1864. Died July 26, 1864, in hospital at Winchester, Virginia, of "v.s. breast." Company muster roll states that he was wounded July 18, 1864, but place is not shown.

CREWS, HENRY T., Sergeant
Resided in Forsyth County where he enlisted at age 30, September 25, 1862, for the war. Mustered in as Private and appointed Sergeant, March 20, 1863. Captured at Gettysburg, Pennsylvania, July 3-5, 1863, and confined at Fort Delaware, Delaware. Died in hospital at Fort Delaware on August 29, 1863, of "hypertrophy of heart."

CRIDLEBAUGH, THOMAS, Private
Resided in Davidson County where he enlisted at age 23, September 8, 1862, for the war. Captured at Gettysburg, Pennsylvania, July 3, 1863, and confined at Fort Delaware, Delaware, until sent to U.S. Hospital, Chester, Pennsylvania, July 25, 1863. Paroled at that hospital September 17, 1863, and sent to City Point, Virginia, for exchange.

Received at City Point, September 23, 1863. Absent at home on parole until he returned to duty January-February, 1864. Captured at Strasburg, Virginia, October 19, 1864, and confined at Point Lookout, Maryland, until paroled and sent to Aiken's Landing, Virginia, March 28, 1865, for exchange.

CROUCH, JAMES ANDERSON, Private

Resided as a farmer in Davidson County where he enlisted at age 19, January 1, 1864, for the war. Captured at Fisher's Hill, Virginia, September 22, 1864, and confined at Point Lookout, Maryland, until released after taking the Oath of Allegiance on May 13, 1865.

DAVIS, ALPHEUS L., Private

Resided in Davidson County and enlisted in Forsyth County at age 18, September 18, 1861, for twelve months. Captured at Roanoke Island on February 8, 1862, and paroled at Elizabeth City, N.C., February 21, 1862. Present or accounted for until wounded and captured at Gettysburg, Pennsylvania, July 1-3, 1863. Confined at DeCamp General Hospital, Davids Island, New York Harbor, July 17, 1863, with "g.s. arm." Paroled and sent to City Point, Virginia, for exchange August 24, 1863. Present or accounted for until again captured July 10, 1864, at Harpers Ferry, West Virginia. Confined at Old Capitol Prison, Washington, D.C., and transferred to Elmira, New York, July 23-25, 1864. Died at Elmira, November 26, 1864, of "chronic diarrhoea."

DAVIS, CHARLES M., Private

Enlisted in Wake County, August 10, 1864, for the war. Reported on company muster rolls as absent sick through February, 1865.

DAVIS, EVEN, Private

Enlisted in Wake County, September 10, 1864, for the war. Admitted to hospital at Charlottesville, Virginia, September 23, 1864, with "v.s. left hand" and was furloughed on September 30, 1864. Reported on company muster rolls as absent without leave from November-December, 1864, through February, 1865.

DAVIS, JOHN R., Private

Resided in Davidson County and enlisted in Forsyth County at age 18, September 19, 1861, for twelve months. Present or accounted for until captured at Gettysburg, Pennsylvania, July 3-5, 1863, and confined at Fort McHenry, Maryland, until transferred to Fort Delaware, Delaware, July 9, 1863. Paroled at Fort Delaware and sent to City Point, Virginia, for exchange on July 30, 1863. Died August 16, 1863, at home.

DELAP, SAMUEL, Private

Enlisted in Wake County, July 15, 1864, for the war. Present or accounted for on company muster rolls through February, 1865. Deserted and took the Oath of Allegiance at Washington, D.C., March 29, 1865, and was "furnished transportation to Hancock County, Ohio."

DICKERSON, ALPHONSO, Corporal

Previously served in Company A, 9th Regiment N.C. State Troops (1st Regiment N.C. Cavalry). Enlisted in this company in Forsyth County at age 30, February 15, 1863, for the war. Mustered in as Private. Appointed Corporal on March 23, 1863. Deserted on April 26, 1863.

DISHER, HENRY, Private

Enlisted in Wake County, August 10, 1864, for the war. Present or accounted for until admitted to hospital at Richmond, Virginia, February 24, 1865. Reported on company muster rolls as absent sick through February, 1865.

ELER, L. D., Private

Enlisted in Wake County, July 15, 1864, for the war. Captured at Fisher's Hill, Virginia, September 22, 1864, and confined at Point Lookout, Maryland, until paroled and transferred to Aiken's Landing, Virginia, for exchange on March 17, 1865.

FERGERSON, JAMES, Private

Resided in Forsyth County where he enlisted at age 22, September 25, 1862, for the war. Discharged November 21, 1862, by reason of disability.

FISHEL, ANDREW, Corporal

Resided in Forsyth County where he enlisted at age 24, September 19, 1861, for twelve months. Mustered in as Corporal. Captured at Roanoke Island on February 8, 1862, and paroled at Elizabeth City, N.C., February 21, 1862. Died March 5, 1862, at Elizabeth City.

FISHEL, CHARLES, Private

Resided in Davidson County and enlisted in Forsyth County at age 19, September 19, 1861, for twelve months. Captured at Roanoke Island on February 8, 1862, and paroled at Elizabeth City, N.C., February 21, 1862. Wounded and captured at Gettysburg, Pennsylvania, July 1-3, 1863. Died of wounds August 3, 1863, at "David Isle."

FISHEL, JAMES, Private

Resided in Davidson County and enlisted in Forsyth County at age 18, June 23, 1863, for the war. Wounded and captured at Gettysburg, Pennsylvania, July 1-5, 1863. Confined at DeCamp General Hospital, Davids Island, New York Harbor, until paroled and sent to City Point, Virginia, for exchange. Received at City Point on September 16, 1863. Reported on company muster rolls as absent without leave until retired to the Invalid Corps, May 4, 1864, and assigned to hospital duty.

GRAY, ALFRED, Private

Resided in Davidson County where he enlisted at age 23, September, 1861, for twelve months. Was not captured at Roanoke Island on February 8, 1862, and attached himself to Company A, 10th Battalion N.C. Heavy Artillery on April 3, 1862. Did not return to this company when it was reorganized in September, 1862.

GRAY, SAMUEL, Private

Resided in Davidson County and enlisted in Forsyth County at age 18, September 19, 1861, for twelve months. Was not captured at Roanoke Island on February 8, 1862, and attached himself to Company A, 10th Battalion N.C. Heavy Artillery on April 3, 1862. Did not return to this company when it was reorganized in September, 1862.

HAMMER, ALVIN RANSOM, Private
Enlisted in Davidson County, February 8, 1865, for the war. Admitted to hospital at Richmond, Virginia, February 24, 1865, with "v.s." and furloughed for 60 days on March 16, 1865.

HAMMER, SOLOMON A., Private
Resided in Davidson County and enlisted in Forsyth County at age 24, September 19, 1861, for twelve months. Present or accounted for on company muster rolls until he is reported on the April 30-October 31, 1864, roll with the remark: "Absent in the hands of the enemy." Records do not indicate where he was captured. Reported as absent prisoner of war through February, 1865.

HAMPTON, JAMES A., Private
Born in Forsyth County where he resided as a farmer and enlisted at age 19, September 19, 1861, for twelve months. Captured at Roanoke Island on February 8, 1862, and paroled at Elizabeth City, N.C., February 21, 1862. Wounded at Mine Run, Virginia, November 27-28, 1863. Present or accounted for on company muster rolls from that date until reported as "absent on wounded furlough" on the April 30-October 31, 1864, roll. Admitted to hospital at Richmond, Virginia, September 10, 1864, and was furloughed for 30 days the same day. Reported as absent wounded until again admitted to hospital at Richmond, February 25, 1865, with "v.s. old, l. hip." Retired to the Invalid Corps, March 14, 1865, and detailed for light duty at hospital in Richmond. Captured at hospital in Richmond, April 3, 1865, and confined at Libby Prison, Richmond, until transferred to Newport News, Virginia, April 23, 1865. Released at Newport News after taking the Oath of Allegiance on June 30, 1865.

HAMPTON, ROBERT, Private
Enlisted in Wake County, September 17, 1864, for the war. Captured at Cedar Creek, Virginia, October 19, 1864, and confined at U.S.A. General Hospital, West's Buildings, Baltimore, Maryland, October 24, 1864, with "g.s.w. left hip, f.w." Paroled at this hospital February 16, 1865, and sent to James River, Virginia, for exchange. Admitted to hospital at Richmond, Virginia, March 4, 1865, and was captured in hospital April 3, 1865. Took the Oath of Allegiance at hospital in Richmond, July 15, 1865.

HARMON, HAMILTON VALENTINE, Corporal
Resided in Davidson County and enlisted in Forsyth County at age 27, September 19, 1861, for twelve months. Mustered in as Private. Captured at Roanoke Island on February 8, 1862, and paroled at Elizabeth City, N.C., February 21, 1862. Appointed Corporal, January-April, 1863. Present or accounted for until admitted to hospital at Richmond, Virginia, May 19, 1864, with "v.s. r. thigh" and was furloughed for 60 days on May 28, 1864. Present or accounted for until captured at Petersburg, Virginia, March 25, 1865. Admitted to U.S.A. General Hospital, West's Buildings, Baltimore, Maryland, "from Steamer *Hero of Jersey*" May 19, 1865, with "g.s.w. left temporal region of face inv. bone and loss of left eye." Transferred to Fort McHenry, Maryland, May 22, 1865, where he was released after taking the Oath of Allegiance on June 9, 1865.

HARRIS, SAMUEL H., Private
Enlisted in Wake County, September 10, 1864, for the war. Admitted to hospital at Richmond, Virginia, December 25, 1864, with "pneumonia" and was furloughed for 60 days March 10, 1865.

HAYWORTH, W. ANDREW, Private
Enlisted in Davidson County, July 28, 1864, for the war. Reported on company muster roll for April 30-October 31, 1864, as "absent on wounded furlough." Date and place wounded are not shown. Absent wounded until he appears as present on the January-February, 1865, muster roll. Paroled at Appomattox Court House, Virginia, April 9, 1865.

HEDGECOCK, ELISHA, Private
Enlisted in Wake County, September 10, 1864, for the war. Present or accounted for on company muster rolls through January-February, 1865, when he is reported as "absent on detached service." Nature of detail not given. Paroled at Appomattox Court House, Virginia, April 9, 1865.

HEDGECOCK, HENRY, Private
Enlisted in Forsyth County at age 18, September 19, 1861, for twelve months. Never mustered in.

HEDGECOCK, JOSEPH, Private
Enlisted in Forsyth County at age 32, September 19, 1861, for twelve months. Never mustered in.

HEDGECOCK, WILLIAM, Private
Resided in Davidson County and enlisted in Forsyth County at age 18, September 19, 1861, for twelve months. Present or accounted for until killed in battle at Gettysburg, Pennsylvania, July 1, 1863.

HILL, LEANDER, Private
Resided in Forsyth County where he enlisted at age 26, September 19, 1861, for twelve months. Discharged November 14, 1862, "for disability."

HODGE, JOHN H., Private
Resided in Forsyth County where he enlisted at age 18, March 2, 1863, for the war. Deserted to Greenville, N.C., April 26, 1863. Reported on company muster rolls as absent "sentenced to hard labor" from November-December, 1863, until released from confinement and returned to company December 1, 1864. Paroled at Appomattox Court House, Virginia, April 9, 1865.

IDOL, DAVID H., Musician
Resided in Guilford County and enlisted in Davidson County on November 1, 1862, for the war. Mustered in as Musician. Present or accounted for until appointed Chief Musician and transferred to the Field and Staff of this battalion, May-October, 1863.

JACKSON, WILLIAM, Private
Resided in Davidson County and enlisted in Forsyth County at age 20, September 19, 1861, for twelve months. Mustered in as Private. Captured at Roanoke Island on February 8, 1862, and paroled at Elizabeth City, N.C., February 21, 1862.

Reduced to ranks March-April, 1863. Deserted at Greenville, N.C., April 26, 1863.

JONES, JOHN, Private

Enlisted in Wake County, September 10, 1864, for the war. Admitted to hospital at Charlottesville, Virginia, October 23, 1864, with "v.s. left hand" and was furloughed November 8, 1864. Reported on company muster rolls as absent wounded through December, 1864, and as present sick January-February, 1865.

JONES, JOSEPH, Private

Enlisted in Forsyth County at age 18, September 19, 1861, for twelve months. Never mustered in.

JONES, SAMUEL, Private

Resided in Davidson County and enlisted in Forsyth County at age 41, September 19, 1861, for twelve months. Captured at Roanoke Island on February 8, 1862, and paroled at Elizabeth City, N.C., February 21, 1862. Discharged November 21, 1862, by Conscript Law.

KENNEDY, J. V., 1st Sergeant

Born in Forsyth County where he resided prior to enlisting at age 28, September, 1861, for twelve months. Mustered in as Private. Captured at Roanoke Island on February 8, 1862, and paroled at Elizabeth City, N.C., February 21, 1862. Promoted to 1st Sergeant, January 17, 1863. Wounded in battle at Gettysburg, Pennsylvania, July 1-3, 1863. Captured in hospital at Gettysburg where he died July 7, 1863, of "g.s. legs and body."

KENNEDY, JOSEPH B., Private

Resided in Davidson County where he enlisted at age 18, February 26, 1864, for the war. Present or accounted for until admitted to hospital at Richmond, Virginia, May 18, 1864, with "v.s. r. ankle." Furloughed for 60 days May 26, 1864. Absent wounded through December, 1864. Reported as absent without leave on the January-February, 1865, muster roll.

KIGER, LEVI, Private

Resided in Forsyth County where he enlisted at age 29, March 1, 1863, for the war. Present or accounted for until admitted to hospital at Richmond, Virginia, May 18, 1864, with "v.s. back" and furloughed for 60 days May 24, 1864. Reported as absent sick from that date through February, 1865. Paroled at Lynchburg, Virginia, April, 1865.

KIGER, LEWIS, Private

Resided in Forsyth County where he enlisted at age 27, March 1, 1863, for the war. Wounded and captured at Gettysburg, Pennsylvania, July 1-3, 1863, and confined until paroled and exchanged. Appears as present on a muster roll of a detachment of paroled and exchanged prisoners at Camp Lee, near Richmond, Virginia, dated September 7, 1863. Absent wounded and paroled through February, 1864. Captured at Fisher's Hill, Virginia, September 22-23, 1864, and confined at Point Lookout, Maryland, until paroled and transferred to Aiken's Landing, Virginia, for exchange on March 17, 1865.

LENARD, DAVID, Private

Enlisted in Wake County, September 10, 1864, for the war. Present or accounted for through February, 1865.

LONG, SAMUEL P., Private

Resided in Forsyth County where he enlisted at age 31, March 1, 1863, for the war. Captured at Gettysburg, Pennsylvania, July 1-4, 1863, and confined at DeCamp General Hospital, Davids Island, New York Harbor, until transferred to Fort Wood, Bedloe's Island, New York Harbor, October 24, 1863. Sent to Point Lookout, Maryland, December 17-21, 1863, and transferred to Elmira, New York, July 23-26, 1864. Died at Elmira, April 6, 1865, of "chro. diarr."

LYNN, J. J., Private

Enlisted in Wake County, August 13, 1864, for the war. Captured at Strasburg, Virginia, October 19, 1864, and confined at Point Lookout, Maryland, October 25, 1864. Paroled at Point Lookout and sent to Cox's Landing, James River, Virginia, for exchange, February 10, 1865. Admitted to hospital at Richmond, Virginia, February 15, 1865, with "diarrhoea ch." and was furloughed for 60 days on March 2, 1865. Paroled at Raleigh, May 25, 1865.

MAABB, WILLIAM, Private

Resided in Forsyth County where he enlisted at age 33, March 2, 1863, for the war. Present or accounted for until killed in battle at Mine Run, Virginia, November 28, 1863.

MARTIN, BARNET, Private

Enlisted in Forsyth County at age 19, September 19, 1861, for twelve months. Never mustered in.

MARTIN, WILLIAM, Private

Enlisted in Forsyth County at age 23, September 19, 1861, for twelve months. Never mustered in.

MITCHELL, WILLIAM, Private

Resided in Stokes County and enlisted in Forsyth County at age 21, September 19, 1861, for twelve months. Captured at Roanoke Island on February 8, 1862, and paroled at Elizabeth City, N.C., February 21, 1862. Again captured at Gettysburg, Pennsylvania, July 3-5, 1863, and confined at Fort McHenry, Maryland, until transferred to Fort Delaware, Delaware, July 9, 1863. Transferred October 18, 1863, to Point Lookout, Maryland, where he remained until paroled and sent to Boulware's and Cox's Wharf, James River, Virginia, for exchange on February 18, 1865. Paroled at Greensboro, May 18, 1865.

MOCK, ALEXANDER, Corporal

Enlisted in Forsyth County, November 1, 1862, for the war. Mustered in as Private and appointed Corporal, January-April, 1863. Company muster rolls report that he "deserted at Greencastle, Pennsylvania, June 28, 1863."

MOCK, LEWIS, Private

Resided in Forsyth County where he enlisted at age 20, September 19, 1861, for twelve months. Captured at Roanoke Island on February 8, 1862, and paroled at Elizabeth City, N.C., February 21, 1862. Wounded and captured at Gettysburg, Pennsylvania, July 1-3, 1863. Died July 10, 1863, of wounds.

MOLSINGER, MOSES, Private
Enlisted in Forsyth County at age 26, September 19, 1861, for twelve months. Never mustered in.

MOORE, A. M., Private
Enlisted in Wake County, September 10, 1864, for the war. Captured at Winchester, Virginia, September 19, 1864, and confined at Point Lookout, Maryland, until paroled and sent to Aiken's Landing, Virginia, for exchange on March 15, 1865.

MOSER, JOHN HENRY, Private
Transferred from Company B, 1st Battalion N.C. Sharpshooters, November 6, 1864. Present or accounted for on company muster rolls through February, 1865. Captured at Dinwiddie Court House, Virginia, April 3, 1865, and confined at Point Lookout, Maryland, until released after taking the Oath of Allegiance on June 8, 1865.

NIFONG, MADISON, Private
Resided in Forsyth County where he enlisted at age 33, March 1, 1863, for the war. Captured at Gaines Farm, Virginia, June 3, 1864, and confined at Point Lookout, Maryland. Transferred on July 12-17, 1864, to Elmira, New York, where he died September 29, 1864, of "scorbutis."

NORTHERN, BURGES P., Private
Resided in Forsyth County where he enlisted at age 20, September 19, 1861, for twelve months. Captured at Roanoke Island on February 8, 1862, and paroled at Elizabeth City, N.C., February 21, 1862. Present or accounted for until again captured at Cold Harbor, Virginia, May 30, 1864, and confined at Elmira, New York. Company muster rolls report him as absent prisoner of war through February, 1865. Date released from prison not shown on records.

NOTT, JOHN, Private
Enlisted in Forsyth County in February, 1863. Reported as "absent sick at Greenville" on the March-April, 1863, muster roll. No further records.

ORRELL, NAPOLEON, Sergeant
Enlisted in Forsyth County at age 32, September 19, 1861, for twelve months. Never mustered in.

PAYNE, ALFRED, Private
Resided in Davidson County and enlisted in Wake County, June 14, 1864, for the war. Wounded October 19, 1864, and reported on company muster rolls as absent wounded through December, 1864. Present or accounted for from that date until captured near Petersburg, Virginia, March 24, 1865. Confined at Point Lookout, Maryland, until released after taking the Oath of Allegiance on June 16, 1865.

PAYNE, CHARLES, Private
Resided in Davidson County and enlisted in Forsyth County at age 21, September 19, 1861, for twelve months. Captured at Roanoke Island on February 8, 1862, and paroled at Elizabeth City, N.C., February 21, 1862. Present or accounted for on company muster rolls through December, 1862. Died in hospital at Raleigh, February 11, 1863, of "pneumonia."

PAYNE, JOHN, Private
Enlisted in Forsyth County at age 23, September 19, 1861, for twelve months. Never mustered in.

PAYNE, JOSEPH, Private
Enlisted in Wake County, October 24, 1864, for the war. Present or accounted for on company muster rolls through February, 1865. Paroled at Appomattox Court House, Virginia, April 9, 1865.

PAYNE, SANFORD, Private
Enlisted in Wake County, October 25, 1864, for the war. Company muster roll for January-February, 1865, reports that he "died at Camp Rader, Virginia, February 2, 1865."

PAYNE, SOLOMON, 1st Sergeant
Resided in Davidson County and enlisted in Forsyth County at age 23, September 19, 1861, for twelve months. Mustered in as Sergeant. Captured at Roanoke Island on February 8, 1862, and paroled at Elizabeth City, N.C., February 21, 1861. Promoted to 1st Sergeant, May-August, 1863. Present or accounted for on company muster rolls through February, 1865. Captured in hospital at Richmond, Virginia, April 3, 1865, and confined at Libby Prison, Richmond, until transferred to Newport News, Virginia, April 23, 1865. Released at Newport News after taking the Oath of Allegiance on June 30, 1865.

PAYNE, THOMAS, Private
Resided in Davidson County and enlisted in Forsyth County at age 16, September 19, 1861, for twelve months. Captured at Roanoke Island on February 8, 1862, and paroled at Elizabeth City, N.C., February 21, 1862. Discharged November 11, 1862, by Conscript Law.

PEDDICORD, GEORGE, Private
Resided in Forsyth County where he enlisted at age 24, March 2, 1863, for the war. Present or accounted for until captured near Washington, D.C., July 12, 1864, and confined at Old Capitol Prison, Washington. Transferred on July 23-25, 1864, to Elmira, New York, where he died December 7, 1864, of "pneumonia."

PEDDICORD, LEWIS, Private
Resided in Forsyth County where he enlisted at age 22, March 2, 1863, for the war. Company muster rolls report that he deserted at Canterbury Creek, N.C., April 5, 1863.

PERYMAN, ROBERT, Private
Enlisted in Wake County, July 14, 1864, for the war. Present or accounted for until captured near Petersburg, Virginia, March 25, 1865. Confined at Point Lookout, Maryland, until released after taking the Oath of Allegiance on June 6, 1865.

PICKARD, AARON, Sergeant
Resided in Davidson County and enlisted in Forsyth County at age 19, September 19, 1861, for twelve months. Mustered in as Private. Captured at Roanoke Island on February 8, 1862, and paroled at Elizabeth City, N.C., February 21, 1862. Appointed Sergeant, January 14, 1863. Admitted to hospital at Richmond, Virginia, July 14, 1863, with "g.s.w. of neck" and transferred to Raleigh, July 28, 1863. Returned from furlough September-

October, 1863. Present or accounted for until reported on the April 30-October 31, 1864, muster roll with the remark: "Died 19 July 1864 from wounds received on the 18 July 1864."

PICKARD, WILSON W., Private
Enlisted in Wake County, August 12, 1864, for the war. Deserted February 17, 1865. Took the Oath of Allegiance at Washington, D.C., February 21, 1865, and was furnished transportation to Indianapolis, Indiana.

PICKARD, WILSON W., Private
Enlisted in Wake County, October 21, 1864, for the war. Deserted February 17, 1865. Took the Oath of Allegiance at Washington, D.C., February 21, 1865, and was furnished transportation to Indianapolis, Indiana.

REESE, JOHN, Private
Enlisted in Forsyth County at age 26, September 19, 1861, for twelve months. Never mustered in.

REGANS, JACOB J., Private
Enlisted in Mecklenburg County on October 28, 1864, for the war. Present or accounted for through February, 1865.

RICE, JOHN, Private
Born in Forsyth County where he resided as a farmer and enlisted at age 21, September 19, 1861, for twelve months. Captured at Roanoke Island on February 8, 1862, and paroled at Elizabeth City, N.C., on February 21, 1862. Transferred to 3rd Company G, 59th Regiment Virginia Infantry on September 20, 1862.

RICHARD, AARON, Private
Federal Provost Marshal records report him as captured at Roanoke Island on February 15, 1862. No further records.

RICHARDS, RANDLE, Private
Resided in Davidson County and enlisted in Forsyth County at age 28, September 19, 1861, for twelve months. Captured at Roanoke Island on February 8, 1862, and paroled at Elizabeth City, N.C., February 21, 1862. Killed at Gettysburg, Pennsylvania, July 1, 1863.

RIGANY, I. I., Private
Paroled at Greensboro on May 8, 1865.

ROMINGER, REUBEN, Private
Resided in Forsyth County where he enlisted at age 37, March 2, 1863, for the war. Wounded and captured at Gettysburg, Pennsylvania, July 1-4, 1863. Confined at DeCamp General Hospital, Davids Island, New York Harbor, where he died August 3, 1863.

SANFORD, HILARD, Private
Enlisted in Wake County on August 18, 1864, for the war. Present or accounted for through February, 1865.

SAUNDERS, ANDREW, Private
Enlisted in Forsyth County at age 30, September 19, 1861, for twelve months. Never mustered in.

SAUNDERS, JACOB, Private
Resided in Forsyth County where he enlisted at age 17, January 20, 1863, for the war. Captured at Gettysburg, Pennsylvania, July 5, 1863, and con-

fined at Fort Delaware, Delaware, until paroled and exchanged in February, 1865. Reported as present on a roll of paroled and exchanged prisoners at Camp Lee, near Richmond, Virginia, February 23, 1865.

SAUNDERS, PHILIP, Private
Resided in Forsyth County where he enlisted at age 17, January 20, 1863, for the war. Wounded and captured at Gettysburg, Pennsylvania, July 3, 1863. Confined at Fort Delaware, Delaware, until transferred to Point Lookout, Maryland, October 18, 1863. Paroled at Point Lookout on February 18, 1865, for exchange. Exact date exchanged not reported. Appears as present on a roll of paroled and exchanged prisoners at Camp Lee, near Richmond, Virginia, February 23, 1865.

SAUNDERS, RANDLE, Private
Resided in Forsyth County where he enlisted at age 18, September 19, 1861, for twelve months. Captured at Roanoke Island on February 8, 1862, and paroled at Elizabeth City, N.C., on February 21, 1862. Killed at Gettysburg, Pennsylvania, July 1, 1863.

SHIELDS, HARRISON, Private
Enlisted in Wake County on July 14, 1864, for the war. Killed at Winchester, Virginia, September 19, 1864.

SHIELDS, LEVI, Private
Resided in Forsyth County where he enlisted at age 18, September 19, 1861, for twelve months. Died at Tarboro, April 20, 1863.

SIKES, A. W., Private
Paroled on May 9, 1865.

SIKES, ANDERSON, Private
Resided in Davidson County and enlisted in Forsyth County at age 19, March 2, 1863, for the war. Deserted April 26, 1863.

SLATER, CHRISTIAN, Private
Resided in Davidson County and enlisted in Forsyth County at age 19, September 19, 1861, for twelve months. Captured at Roanoke Island on February 8, 1862, and paroled at Elizabeth City, N.C., February 21, 1862. Deserted at Greencastle, Pennsylvania, June 25, 1863.

SLATER, THOMAS W., Private
Enlisted in Forsyth County at age 24, September 19, 1861, for twelve months. Never mustered in.

SLATER, WILLIAM, Private
Resided in Davidson County and enlisted in Forsyth County on September 19, 1861, for twelve months. Never mustered in. Later reenlisted in Forsyth County at age 25, March 2, 1863, for the war. Captured at Gettysburg, Pennsylvania, July 4, 1863, and confined at Fort Delaware, Delaware, until paroled for exchange on July 30, 1863. Exchanged at City Point, Virginia, August 1, 1863. Present or accounted for until he died in hospital at Richmond, Virginia, June 15, 1864, of "diarrhoea acuta."

SMITH, ZEBIDEE, Private
Enlisted in Forsyth County at age 24, September 19, 1861, for twelve months. Never mustered in.

SMOCK, LOUIS, Private

Captured at Roanoke Island on February 8, 1862, and paroled at Elizabeth City, N.C., on February 21, 1862.

SNOW, HENRY M., Private

Resided in Forsyth County where he enlisted at age 22, September 19, 1861, for twelve months. Captured at Roanoke Island on February 8, 1862, and paroled at Elizabeth City, N.C., on February 21, 1862. Died at Kinston on April 2, 1863.

SNOW, WINSTON, Private

Resided in Forsyth County where he enlisted at age 18, March 2, 1863, for the war. Wounded at Spotsylvania Court House, Virginia, May 14, 1864, and died of wound May 22, 1864.

SNYDER, JAMES W., Private

Resided in Forsyth County where he enlisted at age 28, September 25, 1862, for the war. Discharged on November 14, 1862, by reason of "chronic diarrhoea."

SNYDER, WESLEY, Private

Resided in Forsyth County where he enlisted at age 24, September 19, 1861, for twelve months. Captured at Roanoke Island on February 8, 1862, and paroled at Elizabeth City, N.C., on February 21, 1862. Wounded and captured at Gettysburg, Pennsylvania, July 1-3, 1863, and died July 17, 1863.

SNYDER, WILLIAM, Private

Resided in Forsyth County where he enlisted at age 21, September 19, 1861, for twelve months. Captured at Roanoke Island on February 8, 1862, and paroled at Elizabeth City, N.C., on February 21, 1862. Wounded and captured at Gettysburg, Pennsylvania, July 3-5, 1863, and confined in hospital at Baltimore, Maryland, until paroled for exchange September 20, 1863. Exchanged at City Point, Virginia, and returned to the company after December, 1863. Captured at Spotsylvania Court House, Virginia, May 10, 1864, and confined at Point Lookout, Maryland. Transferred on July 22, 1864, to Elmira, New York, where he remained until released after taking the Oath of Allegiance on May 13, 1865.

SPURGIN, SANDFORD, Private

Enlisted in Forsyth County at age 23, September 19, 1861, for twelve months. Never mustered in.

STONE, JOSEPH, Private

Enlisted in Mecklenburg County on October 25, 1864, for the war. Federal Provost Marshal records report him as a "rebel deserter" with the remark that he took the Oath of Allegiance at Washington, D.C., March 25, 1865, and was provided transportation to Plainfield, Indiana.

STUART, FOUNTAIN, Private

Resided in Davidson County and enlisted in Wake County on September 10, 1864, for the war. Captured at Strasburg, Virginia, October 19, 1864, and confined at Point Lookout, Maryland, until released after taking the Oath of Allegiance on June 20, 1865.

TEAGUE, JACOB, Private

Resided in Davidson County and enlisted at age

18, July 6, 1863, for the war. Wounded May 29, 1864, and died of wound on July 10, 1864.

TEAGUE, JOSEPH F., Private

Resided in Davidson County and enlisted at age 36, January 20, 1863, for the war. Present or accounted for until reported as "captured August 25, 1864."

TEAGUE, ROMULUS, Private

Resided in Davidson County and enlisted in Forsyth County at age 18, September 19, 1861, for twelve months. Captured at Roanoke Island on February 8, 1862, and paroled at Elizabeth City, N.C., on February 21, 1862. Died at High Point, March 8, 1862.

TICE, COSTUN, Private

Enlisted in Forsyth County at age 26, September 19, 1861, for twelve months. Never mustered in.

TIMS, JOHN, Private

Resided in Davidson County and enlisted in Forsyth County at age 22, September 19, 1861, for twelve months. Captured at Roanoke Island on February 8, 1862, and paroled at Elizabeth City, N.C., on February 21, 1862. Transferred to Company A, 10th Battalion N.C. Heavy Artillery on August 1, 1862.

TRENTHAM, A. J., Private

Enlisted in Wake County on September 10, 1864, for the war. Captured at Fisher's Hill, Virginia, September 22, 1864, and confined at Point Lookout, Maryland, until paroled for exchange on March 17, 1865. Exchanged at Boulware's Wharf, James River, Virginia, March 19, 1865. Admitted to hospital at Richmond, Virginia, March 19, 1865, and transferred to Camp Lee, near Richmond, the next day.

WELBORN, WISDOM P., Corporal

Resided in Davidson County and enlisted in Forsyth County at age 19, September 19, 1861, for the war. Mustered in as Private. Appointed Corporal on December 17, 1862. Captured at Gettysburg, Pennsylvania, July 2, 1863, and confined at Fort Delaware, Delaware, where he died October 12, 1863.

WELCH, ALBERT H., Private

Resided in Forsyth County where he enlisted at age 35, March 2, 1863, for the war. Detailed as ambulance driver after October, 1863, and remained on detail throughout the war. Paroled at Appomattox Court House, Virginia, April 9, 1865.

WELCH, CYRUS, Private

Resided in Guilford County and enlisted in Forsyth County at age 20, September 19, 1861, for twelve months. Present or accounted for until he "deserted to the enemy February 17, 1865." Federal Provost Marshal records report him as a "rebel deserter" with the remark that he took the Oath of Allegiance at Washington, D.C., February 21, 1865, and was provided transportation to Indianapolis, Indiana.

WELCH, JONATHAN, Private

Resided in Guilford County and enlisted at age 28 in February, 1863, for the war. Wounded at Gettysburg, Pennsylvania, July 1-3, 1863, and captured in hospital at Gettysburg, July 4-5, 1863. Died in hospital at Gettysburg on July 12, 1863.

WELCH, MOSES, Sergeant

Transferred from Company A, 1st Regiment N.C. State Troops on March 13, 1864, as Private. Appointed Sergeant on September 1, 1864. Present or accounted for until paroled at Appomattox Court House, Virginia, April 9, 1865.

WILLARD, WILLIAM, Private

Enlisted in Wake County on September 15, 1864, for the war. Captured at Strasburg, Virginia, October 19, 1864, and confined at Point Lookout, Maryland, where he died May 11, 1865.

WILSON, JAMES, Private

Enlisted in Wake County on August 19, 1864, for the war. Muster roll covering period of enlistment through October 31, 1864, states that he was "absent on wounded furlough" but does not give date or place wounded. Detailed on December 2, 1864, and reported as absent on detail on company muster rolls through February, 1865.

WOOSLEY, FRANK, Private

Resided in Forsyth County where he enlisted at age 18, March 2, 1863, for the war. Captured at Gettysburg, Pennsylvania, July 3, 1863, and confined at Fort Delaware, Delaware, until paroled and sent to City Point, Virginia, for exchange on July 30, 1863. Wounded at Mine Run, Virginia, November 27-December 3, 1863. Present or accounted for until captured at Winchester, Virginia, September 19, 1864. Confined at Point Lookout, Maryland, until paroled and sent to Aiken's Landing, Virginia, for exchange on March 15, 1865. Declared exchanged on March 18, 1865.

YOUNG, JOHN H., Private

Resided in Forsyth County where he enlisted at age 18, September 19, 1861, for twelve months. Captured at Roanoke Island on February 8, 1862, and paroled at Elizabeth City, N.C., on February 21, 1862. Present or accounted for until he died in hospital at Richmond, Virginia, February 6, 1864, of "typhoid pneumonia."

ZIMMERMAN, JULIUS, Private

Resided in Forsyth County where he enlisted at age 19, September 19, 1861, for twelve months. "Died February 26, 1862, at Portsmouth, Virginia."

ZIMMERMAN, MARTIN, Private

Resided in Forsyth County where he enlisted at age 25, September 19, 1861, for twelve months. Captured at Roanoke Island on February 8, 1862, and paroled at Elizabeth City, N.C., February 21, 1862. Died at Elizabeth City on March 4, 1863.

COMPANY H

This company, known as the "Madison Guards," was organized in Madison County and enlisted at Marshall, Madison County, July 4, 1861. It was assigned to Green's Independent Regiment, Wise's Legion, at Richmond, Virginia, in August, 1861. The regiment failed to complete its organization,

and the companies were organized into the 2nd Battalion N.C. Infantry on November 1, 1862. The battalion completed its organization in January, 1862, and this company became Company H. Prior to that time it had been reported as Company A, B, and C of the battalion. After the company joined the battalion it functioned as a part of the battalion, and its history for the war period is recorded as a part of the battalion history.

The information contained in the following roster of the company was compiled principally from company muster rolls which covered from the date of enlistment through December, 1862; March-April, 1863; and September, 1863, through February, 1865. No company muster rolls were found for January-February, 1863; May through August, 1863; or for the period after February, 1865. In addition to the company muster rolls, Roll of Honor records, receipt rolls, and hospital records, supplemented by state pension applications, United Daughters of the Confederacy records, and postwar rosters and histories, all provided useful information.

OFFICERS
CAPTAINS

ALLEN, LAWRENCE M.

Enlisted in Madison County on July 4, 1861, for twelve months. Appointed Captain to rank from July 5, 1861. Captured at Roanoke Island on February 8, 1862, and paroled at Elizabeth City, N.C., on February 21, 1862. Transferred to the Field and Staff, 64th Regiment N.C. Troops upon appointment as Major to rank from May 1, 1862.

BROWN, VAN

Resided in Madison County where he enlisted at age 21, July 4, 1861, for twelve months. Appointed 2nd Lieutenant to rank from July 5, 1861. Captured at Roanoke Island on February 8, 1862, and paroled at Elizabeth City, N.C., on February 21, 1862. Elected Captain at reorganization of company on September 25, 1862, and appointed to rank from date of election. Wounded July 18, 1864, and reported as absent wounded until retired to the Invalid Corps on December 15, 1864. Ordered to report to General T. H. Holmes, commanding reserves in North Carolina.

LIEUTENANTS

ASKEW, JOSEPH W., 2nd Lieutenant

Resided in Madison County where he enlisted at age 22, July 4, 1861, for twelve months. Mustered in as Private. Captured at Roanoke Island on February 8, 1862, and paroled at Elizabeth City, N.C., on February 21, 1862. Elected 2nd Lieutenant at reorganization of company on September 25, 1862, and appointed to rank from date of election. Wounded at Gettysburg, Pennsylvania, July 1, 1863, and captured in hospital at Gettysburg, July 4-5, 1863. Died in hospital July 15, 1863.

BROWN, EDOM K., 1st Lieutenant

Resided in Madison County where he enlisted at age 40, July 4, 1861, for twelve months. Appointed 1st Lieutenant to rank from July 5, 1861. Not reelected at reorganization of company on September 25, 1862, and dropped from rolls.

CANDLER, CHARLES N., 2nd Lieutenant
Resided in Madison County where he enlisted at age 36, July 4, 1861, for twelve months. Appointed 2nd Lieutenant to rank from July 5, 1861. Captured at Roanoke Island on February 8, 1862, and paroled at Elizabeth City, N.C., on February 21, 1862. Not reelected at reorganization of company on September 25, 1862, and dropped from the rolls. Later appointed 1st Lieutenant in Company C, 64th Regiment N.C. Troops.

DUCKETT, JOSEPH N., 2nd Lieutenant
Resided in Madison County where he enlisted at age 26, July 4, 1861, for twelve months. Mustered in as Private. Captured at Roanoke Island on February 8, 1862, and paroled at Elizabeth City, N.C., on February 21, 1862. Elected 2nd Lieutenant at reorganization of company on September 25, 1862, and appointed to rank from date of election. Wounded at Gettysburg, Pennsylvania, July 1, 1863, and captured in hospital at Gettysburg, where he died July 7, 1863.

LUSK, SAMUEL A. J., 1st Lieutenant
Resided in Madison County where he enlisted at age 37, July 4, 1861, for twelve months. Mustered in as Sergeant. Captured at Roanoke Island on February 8, 1862, and paroled at Elizabeth City, N.C., on February 21, 1862. Elected 1st Lieutenant at reorganization of company on September 25, 1862, and appointed to rank from date of election. Wounded at Gettysburg, Pennsylvania, July 1, 1863. Present or accounted for through February, 1865. Submitted his resignation on February 24, 1865, by reason of age, and resignation was officially accepted on March 4, 1865.

NONCOMMISSIONED OFFICERS AND PRIVATES

AKED, J. C., Private
Died in hospital at Fayetteville, December 23, 1861.

ANDERSON, WILLIAM, Private
Enlisted in Madison County, July 4, 1861, for twelve months. He was not captured at Roanoke Island on February 8, 1862, and attached himself to Company C, 64th Regiment N.C. Troops. Did not return to company when it was reorganized in September, 1862.

ARRINGTON, LEWIS, Private
Enlisted in Madison County, July 4, 1861, for twelve months. Captured at Roanoke Island on February 8, 1862, and paroled at Elizabeth City, N.C., February 21, 1862. Company muster rolls indicate that he did not return to duty. Carried as absent without leave until dropped from the roll March-April, 1863. Later served in Company C, 64th Regiment N.C. Troops.

ARROWOOD, WILLIAM, Private
Resided in Madison County where he enlisted at age 20, July 4, 1861, for twelve months. Captured at Roanoke Island on February 8, 1862, and paroled at Elizabeth City, N.C., February 21, 1862. Present or accounted for until wounded "in hip and arm" at Mine Run, Virginia, November 30, 1863. Admitted to hospital in Charlottes-

ville, Virginia, December 2, 1863, and furloughed from the hospital on December 31, 1863. Company muster rolls report that he deserted March 1, 1864. No further records.

ASKEW, GEORGE A., Private
Resided in Madison County where he enlisted at age 21, July 4, 1861, for twelve months. Mustered in as Private. Captured at Roanoke Island on February 8, 1862, and paroled at Elizabeth City, N.C., February 21, 1862. Appointed Corporal, September 25, 1862. Present or accounted for until reported on the September-October, 1864, muster roll as being reduced to ranks and "present in arrest." Reason for reduction or arrest not shown in records. Present or accounted for through February, 1865. Captured at Burkeville, Virginia, April 7, 1865, and confined at Point Lookout, Maryland, until released after taking the Oath of Allegiance on June 23, 1865.

ASKEW, GEORGE C., Private
Born in Burke County and resided as a farmer in Madison County where he enlisted at age 51, July 4, 1861, for twelve months. Mustered in as Private. Appointed Commissary Sergeant, November-December, 1861, and transferred to the Field and Staff of this battalion.

ASKEW, THOMAS P., Private
Resided in Madison County where he enlisted at age 17, July 4, 1861, for twelve months. Mustered in as Private. Captured at Roanoke Island on February 8, 1862, and paroled at Elizabeth City, N.C., February 21, 1862. Appointed Corporal, September, 1862, and reduced to ranks November-December, 1862. Wounded and captured at Gettysburg, Pennsylvania, July 3-5, 1863, and confined at Fort Delaware, Delaware, until transferred to Point Lookout, Maryland, October 18, 1863. Admitted to Hammond General Hospital, Point Lookout, January 24, 1864, with "diarrhoea chronic" and died February 4, 1864.

ASKEW, THOMAS W., Private
Resided in Madison County where he enlisted at age 30, July 4, 1861, for twelve months. Captured at Roanoke Island on February 8, 1862, and paroled at Elizabeth City, N.C., February 21, 1862. Present or accounted for on company muster rolls through April, 1863. Roll of Honor reports that he was "killed July 1, 1863, at Gettysburg."

BAKER, JAMES G., Private
Enlisted in Madison County, July 4, 1861, for twelve months. Present or accounted for through February, 1862. No further records.

BALDING, FIDELLA A., Private
Resided in Madison County where he enlisted at age 32, July 4, 1861, for twelve months. Captured at Roanoke Island on February 8, 1862, and paroled at Elizabeth City, N.C., February 21, 1862. Transferred to Company C, 60th Regiment N.C. Troops on September 1, 1862.

BALDING, MARQUES D. L., Sergeant
Resided in Madison County where he enlisted at age 30, July 4, 1861, for twelve months. Mustered in as Sergeant. Captured at Roanoke Island on

February 8, 1862, and paroled at Elizabeth City, N.C., February 21, 1862. Transferred to Company C, 60th Regiment N.C. Troops on October 1, 1862.

BOKEN, GODFREY, Private
Resided in Madison County where he enlisted at age 20, July 4, 1861, for twelve months. Captured at Roanoke Island on February 8, 1862, and died at that place on February 10, 1862.

BRANSON, LEWIS B., Private
Enlisted in Madison County, July 4, 1861, for twelve months. Captured at Roanoke Island on February 8, 1862, and paroled at Elizabeth City, N.C., February 21, 1862. Reported on company muster rolls as absent sick from that date until dropped from the rolls March-April, 1863. Later served in Company C, 64th Regiment N.C. Troops.

BRANSON, WILLIAM H., Corporal
Resided in Madison County where he enlisted at age 24, July 4, 1861, for twelve months. Mustered in as Corporal. Captured at Roanoke Island on February 8, 1862, and paroled at Elizabeth City, N.C., February 21, 1862. Attached himself to Company C, 64th Regiment N.C. Troops while absent on parole and did not return to the company when it was reorganized in September, 1862.

BRIGHT, ADAM, Sergeant
Resided in Madison County where he enlisted at age 23, July 4, 1861, for twelve months. Mustered in as Private. Captured at Roanoke Island on February 8, 1862, and paroled at Elizabeth City, N.C., February 21, 1862. Appointed Corporal, September 25, 1862. Appointed Sergeant, January-August, 1864. Wounded and captured at Winchester, Virginia, September 19, 1864, and confined at U.S.A. Depot Field Hospital with "v.s. thigh." Transferred to U.S.A. General Hospital, West's Buildings, Baltimore, Maryland, December 20-21, 1864. Transferred to Fort McHenry, Maryland, February 10, 1865, and to Point Lookout, Maryland, February 20, 1865. Date of parole and exchange not shown. Admitted to hospital at Richmond, Virginia, March 2, 1865, and was furloughed for 30 days on March 9, 1865.

BRIGHT, JAMES, Private
Resided in Madison County where he enlisted at age 25, July 4, 1861, for twelve months. Captured at Roanoke Island on February 8, 1862, and paroled at Elizabeth City, N.C., February 21, 1862. Again captured July 1-5, 1863, at Gettysburg, Pennsylvania, and confined at DeCamp General Hospital, Davids Island, New York Harbor, until paroled and sent to City Point, Virginia, for exchange. Received at City Point on September 16, 1863, for exchange. Deserted in Madison County in June, 1864, and sent to Military Prison, Louisville, Kentucky, where he took the Oath of Allegiance on June 22, 1864, and was "to be released north of the Ohio River."

BROOKS, TERRELL A., Private
Resided in Madison County where he enlisted at age 30, July 4, 1861, for twelve months. Captured at Roanoke Island on February 8, 1862, and paroled at Elizabeth City, N.C., February 21, 1862.

Transferred to Company C, 60th Regiment N.C. Troops, September 1, 1862.

BROWN, ALBERT F., Corporal
Previously enlisted in Company A, 5th Battalion N.C. Cavalry but was never mustered in. Enlisted in this company in Madison County, July 4, 1861, for twelve months. Mustered in as Private and appointed Corporal, September 25, 1862. Captured at Gettysburg, Pennsylvania, July 3, 1863, and confined at Fort Delaware, Delaware, until transferred to Point Lookout, Maryland, October 18, 1863. Paroled at Point Lookout and sent to Cox's Landing, James River, Virginia, for exchange on February 13, 1865.

BROWN, JAMES T., Private
Resided in Madison County where he enlisted at age 21, July 4, 1861, for twelve months. Captured at Roanoke Island on February 8, 1862, and paroled at Elizabeth City, N.C., February 21, 1862. Enlisted in Company C, 64th Regiment N.C. Troops while absent on parole.

BROWN, JASON J., Sergeant
Resided in Madison County where he enlisted at age 19, July 4, 1861, for twelve months. Mustered in as Sergeant. Captured at Roanoke Island on February 8, 1862, and paroled at Elizabeth City, N.C., February 21, 1862. Present or accounted for on company muster rolls through April, 1863. Roll of Honor reports that he was "killed July 1, 1863, in battle at Gettysburg."

BROWN, JOHN, Private
Transferred from Company B, 16th Regiment N.C. Troops (6th Regiment N.C. Volunteers), August 20, 1863. Present or accounted for until discharged September 17, 1864, by reason of "being over 45 years of age."

BROWN, OBEDIAH A., Private
Enlisted in Madison County at age 18, July 4, 1861, for twelve months. Captured at Roanoke Island on February 8, 1862, and paroled at Elizabeth City, N.C., February 21, 1861. Enlisted in Company B, 60th Regiment N.C. Troops while absent on parole.

BROWN, WILEY B., Private
Resided in Madison County where he enlisted at age 27, July 4, 1861, for twelve months. Captured at Roanoke Island on February 8, 1862, and paroled at Elizabeth City, N.C., February 21, 1862. Enlisted in Company B, 60th Regiment N.C. Troops while absent on parole.

BRYANT, WILLIAM M., Private
Enlisted in Madison County, July 4, 1861, for twelve months. Captured at Roanoke Island on February 8, 1862, and paroled at Elizabeth City, N.C., February 21, 1862. Enlisted in Company C, 64th Regiment N.C. Troops while absent on parole.

BUCKNER, ABSOLEM, Private
Enlisted in Madison County, July 4, 1861, for twelve months. Captured at Roanoke Island on February 8, 1862, and paroled at Elizabeth City, N.C., February 21, 1862. Company muster roll for April 30-October 31, 1862, states that he was

"left at home being 64 years old and ordered by Colonel Green to drop from my muster rolls." Later served in Company C, 64th Regiment N.C. Troops.

BUCKNER, CHRISTOPHER S., Private
Enlisted in Madison County, July 4, 1861, for twelve months. Captured at Roanoke Island on February 8, 1862, and paroled at Elizabeth City, N.C., February 21, 1862. Enlisted in Company C, 64th Regiment N.C. Troops while absent on parole.

BUCKNER, DAVID, Private
Enlisted in Madison County, July 4, 1861, for twelve months. Captured at Roanoke Island on February 8, 1862, and paroled at Elizabeth City, N.C., February 21, 1862. Reported as present on a company muster roll for February 28, 1862. No further records.

CAMPBELL, WILLIAM, Private
Enlisted in Madison County, April 1, 1863, for the war. Assigned to this company from the conscript camp at Raleigh on September 20, 1864. Present or accounted for on company muster rolls through February, 1865.

CANDLER, JAMES M., Private
Enlisted in Madison County, July 4, 1861, for twelve months. Captured at Roanoke Island on February 8, 1862, and paroled at Elizabeth City, N.C., February 21, 1862. Present or accounted for through December, 1862.

CARVER, EWELL P., Private
Born in Haywood County and resided as a farmer in Madison County where he enlisted at age 34, July 4, 1861, for twelve months. Captured at Roanoke Island on February 8, 1862, and paroled at Elizabeth City, N.C., February 21, 1862. Discharged November 18, 1862, by reason of disability.

CARVER, JAMES M., 1st Sergeant
Resided in Madison County where he enlisted at age 19, July 4, 1862, for twelve months. Mustered in as Private and appointed Sergeant, February-April, 1863. Promoted to 1st Sergeant on November 19, 1863. Present or accounted for on company muster rolls through February, 1865. Admitted to hospital at Richmond, Virginia, April 1, 1865, with "v.s. right shoulder." Captured in hospital April 3, 1865, and died while still in hospital on June 9, 1865.

CHAMBERS, JAMES R., 1st Sergeant
Resided in Madison County where he enlisted at age 28, July 4, 1861, for twelve months. Mustered in as 1st Sergeant. He was not captured on Roanoke Island on February 8, 1862, and enlisted in Company B, 60th Regiment N.C. Troops in August, 1862.

CHURCH, SIMON, Private
Enlisted in Madison County, July 4, 1861, for twelve months. First reported on company muster roll for September-October, 1863. Present or accounted for until captured at Spotsylvania Court House, Virginia, May 10, 1864. Confined at Point Lookout, Maryland, until paroled and transferred

to Aiken's Landing, Virginia, for exchange on September 18, 1864. Furloughed from hospital at Richmond, Virginia, September 26, 1864. Reported on company muster rolls as absent with leave through December, 1864, and as absent without leave January-February, 1865.

CLONTZ, JEFFERSON, Private
Enlisted in Madison County, December 20, 1861, for twelve months. Captured at Roanoke Island on February 8, 1862, and paroled at Elizabeth City, N.C., February 21, 1862. Enlisted in Company B, 16th Regiment N.C. Troops (6th Regiment N.C. Volunteers) while absent on parole.

COGDILL, FIDELLA P., Private
Resided in Madison County where he enlisted at age 18, July 4, 1861, for twelve months. Captured at Roanoke Island on February 8, 1862, and paroled at Elizabeth City, N.C., February 21, 1862. Enlisted in Company B, 60th Regiment N.C. Troops while absent on parole.

COGDILL, JOHN R., Corporal
Resided in Madison County where he enlisted at age 19, July 4, 1861, for twelve months. First reported on company muster roll for April 30-October 31, 1862. Present or accounted for until wounded and captured at Gettysburg, Pennsylvania, July 3-5, 1863. Confined at Fort McHenry, Maryland, and sent to Fort Delaware, Delaware, July 1-12, 1863. Transferred on October 18, 1863, to Point Lookout, Maryland, where he was paroled and sent to City Point, Virginia, for exchange on December 24-25, 1863. Returned to company prior to April 1, 1864, when he was appointed Corporal. Present or accounted for until captured near Petersburg, Virginia, March 25, 1865. Confined at Point Lookout until released after taking the Oath of Allegiance on June 26, 1865.

COGDILL, WILLIAM, Corporal
Resided in Madison County where he enlisted at age 20, July 4, 1861, for twelve months. Mustered in as Private. Captured at Roanoke Island on February 8, 1862, and paroled at Elizabeth City, N.C., February 21, 1862. Appointed Corporal in April, 1864. Present or accounted for until captured near Petersburg, Virginia, March 25, 1865. Confined at Point Lookout, Maryland, until released after taking the Oath of Allegiance on June 26, 1865.

COGDILL, WILLIAM A., Private
Resided in Madison County where he enlisted at age 32, December 20, 1861, for twelve months. Present or accounted for until wounded and captured at Gettysburg, Pennsylvania, July 1-6, 1863. Confined at DeCamp General Hospital, Davids Island, New York Harbor, until paroled and sent to City Point, Virginia, for exchange, August 24, 1863. Again captured at Fisher's Hill, Virginia, September 22, 1864. Confined at Point Lookout, Maryland, until released after taking the Oath of Allegiance on October 15, 1864, and joining the U.S. service. Later assigned to Company A, 4th Regiment U.S. Volunteer Infantry.

COGDILL, WILLIAM R., Private
Enlisted in Madison County, April 15, 1864, for

the war. Present or accounted for on company muster rolls through February, 1865. Wounded at Petersburg, Virginia, March 28, 1865, and admitted to hospital at Richmond, Virginia, April 2, 1865. Captured in hospital April 3, 1865, and transferred to U.S.A. General Hospital, Point Lookout, Maryland, May 9-12, 1865. Released at that hospital after taking the Oath of Allegiance on July 25, 1865.

COGDILL, Z. T., Private
Enlisted in Madison County, April 15, 1864, for the war. Present or accounted for on company muster rolls through February, 1865. Paroled at Appomattox Court House, Virginia, April 9, 1865.

COLWELL, HENRY E., Private
Resided in Madison County where he enlisted at age 32, July 4, 1861, for twelve months. Captured at Roanoke Island on February 8, 1862, and paroled at Elizabeth City, N.C., February 21, 1862. Present or accounted for until captured at Gettysburg, Pennsylvania, July 1-4, 1863. Confined at DeCamp General Hospital, Davids Island, New York Harbor, until paroled and sent to City Point, Virginia, for exchange. Received at City Point, September 8, 1863, for exchange. Present or accounted for through February, 1865.

COLWELL, JAMES A., Private
Enlisted in Madison County, July 4, 1861, for twelve months. Captured at Roanoke Island on February 8, 1862, and paroled at Elizabeth City, N.C., February 21, 1862. Present or accounted for on company muster rolls through December, 1862. No further records.

COOK, WILLIAM R., Private
Resided in Madison County where he enlisted at age 18, July 4, 1861, for twelve months. He was not captured at Roanoke Island on February 8, 1862, and enlisted in Company B, 60th Regiment N.C. Troops, September 1, 1862.

CRANE, ANDREW J., Private
Resided in Madison County where he enlisted at age 17, July 4, 1861, for twelve months. Captured at Roanoke Island on February 8, 1862, and paroled at Elizabeth City, N.C., February 21, 1862. Present or accounted for until admitted to hospital at Farmville, Virginia, May 10-11, 1864, with "g.s. wound of left hand received 6 May 1864." Furloughed for 60 days May 20, 1864. Company muster roll for December 31, 1863-August 31, 1864 reports that he was "killed in Madison County about the 29 June 1864 by the Torries."

CRANE, WILLIAM, Private
Enlisted in Madison County, July 4, 1861, for twelve months. Captured at Roanoke Island on February 8, 1862, and paroled at Elizabeth City, N.C., February 21, 1862. Company muster roll for April 30-October 31, 1862, reports that "this man is 62 years old and left at home and ordered to be dropped from my muster roll by Colonel Green." Later enlisted in Company C, 64th Regiment N.C. Troops.

DAVIS, ANDREW J., Corporal
Resided in Madison County where he enlisted at age 23, July 4, 1861, for twelve months. Mustered in as Private. Captured at Roanoke Island on February 8, 1862, and paroled at Elizabeth City, N.C., February 21, 1862. Appointed Corporal on September 24, 1862. Present or accounted for until discharged February 2, 1863, "for disability."

DAVIS, BENJAMIN, Sergeant
Resided in Madison County where he enlisted at age 27, July 4, 1861, for twelve months. Mustered in as Private and appointed Sergeant, September 25, 1862. Present or accounted for until captured in hospital at Gettysburg, Pennsylvania, July 1-3, 1863. Confined at DeCamp General Hospital, Davids Island, New York Harbor, July 12, 1863, with "fever." Paroled at that hospital and sent to City Point, Virginia, for exchange. Received at City Point, September 16, 1863. Present or accounted for on company muster rolls through February, 1865.

DAVIS, ELISHA, Private
Resided in Madison County where he enlisted at age 21, July 4, 1861, for twelve months. Captured at Roanoke Island on February 8, 1862, and paroled at Elizabeth City, N.C., February 21, 1862. Present or accounted for on company muster rolls until admitted to hospital at Richmond, Virginia, April 14, 1864, with "chro. dia." Died in hospital at Richmond, May 23, 1864.

DAVIS, HARRISON D., Private
Resided in Madison County where he enlisted at age 18, July 4, 1861, for twelve months. Captured at Roanoke Island on February 8, 1862, and paroled at Elizabeth City, N.C., February 21, 1862. Company muster rolls report that he attached himself to another company while absent on parole but returned to duty with this company March-April, 1863. Present or accounted for until captured at South Mountain, Maryland, July 4, 1863, and confined at Fort McHenry, Maryland. Date of parole and exchange not shown and he is reported on company muster rolls as absent prisoner through October, 1863. Reported as present November-December, 1863, and as absent without leave from that date through February, 1865.

DAVIS, LORENZO D., Private
Resided in Madison County where he enlisted at age 23, July 4, 1861, for twelve months. Captured at Roanoke Island on February 8, 1862, and paroled at Elizabeth City, N.C., February 21, 1862. Present or accounted for until wounded and captured at Gettysburg, Pennsylvania, July 1-5, 1863. Confined at DeCamp General Hospital, Davids Island, New York Harbor, until paroled and sent to City Point, Virginia, for exchange. Received at City Point on September 8, 1863, for exchange. Wound described as "g.s. forehead." Absent with leave after exchanged until February, 1865, when he appears as absent without leave.

DAVIS, SOLOMON C., Private
Resided in Madison County where he enlisted at age 17, July 4, 1861, for twelve months. Captured at Roanoke Island on February 8, 1862, and

paroled at Elizabeth City, N.C., February 21, 1862. Company muster rolls state that he attached himself to another company while absent on parole but returned to this company March-April, 1863. Wounded at Gettysburg, Pennsylvania, July 1-3, 1863, and reported on company muster rolls as absent wounded and furloughed from that date until November-December, 1864, when he appears as absent without leave. Reported as absent without leave through February, 1865.

DAVIS, WILLIAM A., Private
Resided in Madison County where he enlisted at age 44, May 1, 1863, for the war. Wounded and captured at Gettysburg, Pennsylvania, July 1-4, 1863, and confined at DeCamp General Hospital, Davids Island, New York Harbor, with "g.s. leg." Paroled at that hospital and sent to City Point, Virginia, for exchange, August 24, 1863. Absent on parole through December, 1863. Present or accounted for until again captured on March 25, 1865, near Petersburg, Virginia. Confined at Point Lookout, Maryland, until released after taking the Oath of Allegiance on June 26, 1865.

DOCKERY, ALFRED L., Private
Enlisted in Madison County, July 4, 1861, for twelve months. Present or accounted for on company muster rolls until April, 1863, when he is reported as "absent sick at home." No further records.

DOCKERY, ELISHA LOGAN, Private
Resided in Madison County where he enlisted at age 34, July 4, 1861, for twelve months. Captured at Roanoke Island on February 8, 1862, and paroled at Elizabeth City, N.C., February 21, 1862. Enlisted in Company A, 5th Battalion N.C. Cavalry on May 14, 1862, while absent on parole.

DONE, JAMES, Private
Enlisted in Madison County, December 20, 1861, for twelve months. Captured at Roanoke Island on February 8, 1862, and paroled at Elizabeth City, N.C., February 21, 1862. Enlisted in Company A, 64th Regiment N.C. Troops while absent on parole.

DUCKETT, HIRAM M., Private
Resided in Madison County where he enlisted at age 31, July 4, 1861, for twelve months. Captured at Roanoke Island on February 8, 1862, and paroled at Elizabeth City, N.C., February 21, 1862. Present or accounted for until reported on the company muster roll for August 31-November 31, 1863, as "at home sick, hospital." Reported as absent without leave from that date through February, 1865.

DUCKETT, JACOB, Private
Enlisted in Madison County, July 4, 1861, for twelve months. He was not captured at Roanoke Island on February 8, 1862, and is reported on the company muster roll for April 30-October 31, 1862, with the remark: "Left at home being 64 years old and ordered to be dropped from my muster rolls by Colonel Green."

ELDER, SMITH, Private
Enlisted in Madison County, July 4, 1861, for twelve months. Captured at Roanoke Island on February 8, 1862, and paroled at Elizabeth City, N.C., February 21, 1862. Enlisted in Company C, 64th Regiment N.C. Troops while absent on parole.

EVANS, DANIEL J., Private
Resided in Madison County where he enlisted at age 19, July 4, 1861, for twelve months. Captured at Roanoke Island on February 8, 1862, and paroled at Elizabeth City, N.C., February 21, 1862. Present or accounted for until his death on December 29, 1862, at Goldsboro of "febris typhoides."

EVANS, WILLIAM M., Private
Resided in Madison County where he enlisted at age 19, July 4, 1861, for twelve months. Captured at Roanoke Island on February 8, 1862, and paroled at Elizabeth City, N.C., February 21, 1862. Present or accounted for on company muster rolls through April, 1863. Roll of Honor reports that he was killed July 1, 1863, at Gettysburg, Pennsylvania.

FLEMING, JOHN P., Private
Born in Madison County where he resided as a farmer and enlisted at age 15, July 4, 1861, for twelve months. Captured at Roanoke Island on February 8, 1862, and paroled at Elizabeth City, N.C., February 21, 1862. Discharged November 19, 1862, by reason of being a nonconscript.

FLEMING, WILLIAM J. B., Private
Resided in Madison County where he enlisted at age 19, July 4, 1861, for twelve months. Captured at Roanoke Island on February 8, 1862, and paroled at Elizabeth City, N.C., February 21, 1862. No further records.

FRANKS, JOSHUA, Private
Enlisted in Madison County, July 4, 1861, for twelve months. Captured at Roanoke Island on February 8, 1862, and paroled at Elizabeth City, N.C., February 21, 1862. Enlisted in Company B, 60th Regiment N.C. Troops while absent on parole.

FREEMAN, JAMES M., Private
Resided in Madison County where he enlisted at age 20, July 4, 1861, for twelve months. First reported on company muster roll for April 30-October 31, 1862. Present or accounted for on company muster rolls through April, 1863. Roll of Honor reports that he died July 6, 1863, in hospital at Liberty, Virginia.

FRISBY, JOSEPH H., Private
Resided in Madison County where he enlisted at age 42, July 4, 1861, for twelve months. Captured at Roanoke Island on February 8, 1862, and paroled at Elizabeth City, N.C., February 21, 1862. Present or accounted for until discharged on November 19, 1862, by reason of the Conscript Law.

GENTRY, HIRAM M., Private
Resided in Madison County where he enlisted at age 18, March 1, 1863, for the war. Admitted to

hospital at Richmond, Virginia, July 20, 1863, with "v.s. left hand" and was transferred to Raleigh, July 25, 1863. Reported as present on the company muster roll for August 31-November 31, 1863. Present or accounted for from that date until admitted to hospital at Richmond on May 25, 1864, with "gunshot wound left foot, flesh." Furloughed from the hospital on August 11, 1864. Reported as absent without leave from November-December, 1864, through February, 1865.

GILLESPIE, JAMES H., Private

Resided in Madison County where he enlisted at age 19, July 4, 1861, for twelve months. Captured at Roanoke Island on February 8, 1862, and paroled at Elizabeth City, N.C., February 21, 1862. Present or accounted for on company muster rolls until captured at Silver Spring, Maryland, July 13, 1864. Admitted to Lincoln U.S.A. General Hospital, Washington, D.C., with "contusion left thigh, slight" and transferred to Old Capitol Prison, Washington, D.C., July 26, 1864. Admitted to U.S.A. Hospital, Old Capitol Prison, August 1, 1864, with "typhoid fever" and died August 16, 1864.

GILLON, MARCUS W., Private

Resided in Madison County where he enlisted at age 18, July 4, 1861, for twelve months. First reported on company muster roll for March-April, 1863. Present or accounted for until captured July 22, 1864, in Madison County. Confined at Military Prison, Louisville, Kentucky, August 3, 1864, and transferred to Camp Chase, Ohio, the same day. Released at Camp Chase after taking the Oath of Allegiance on March 20, 1865, and joining the U.S. service. Later assigned to Company B, 6th Regiment U.S. Volunteer Infantry.

GLANCE, JACKSON W., Private

Resided in Madison County where he enlisted at age 24, July 4, 1861, for twelve months. Mustered in as Corporal. Captured at Roanoke Island on February 8, 1862, and paroled at Elizabeth City, N.C., February 21, 1862. Appointed 1st Sergeant, September 25, 1862. Present or accounted for until captured at Gettysburg, Pennsylvania, July 1-4, 1863. Confined at DeCamp General Hospital, Davids Island, New York Harbor, until paroled and sent to City Point; Virginia, for exchange on August 24, 1863. Absent on parole through October, 1863, and absent without leave from November-December, 1863 (when he was reduced to ranks) through February, 1864. Again reported as absent without leave from September-October, 1864, through February, 1865.

GLANCE, JAMES H., Private

Resided in Madison County where he enlisted at age 19, July 4, 1861, for twelve months. First reported on company muster roll for September-October, 1863. Died of wounds received at Spotsylvania Court House, Virginia, May 19, 1864.

GOWIN, DANIEL H., Private

Resided in Madison County where he enlisted at age 18, January 20, 1864, for the war. Admitted to

hospital at Farmville, Virginia, May 11, 1864, with "vul. sclop." and was returned to duty July 11, 1864. Captured at Winchester, Virginia, September 19, 1864, and confined at Point Lookout, Maryland, until released after taking the Oath of Allegiance on October 18, 1864, and joining the U.S. service.

GRIFFEE, JAMES, Private

Enlisted in Madison County, July 4, 1861, for twelve months. Captured at Roanoke Island on February 8, 1862, and paroled at Elizabeth City, N.C., February 21, 1862. Enlisted in Company C, 64th Regiment N.C. Troops while absent on parole.

HART, JOHN, Private

Enlisted in Madison County, September 20, 1864. Reported on the company muster roll for September-October, 1864, with the remark: "Deserted October 10, 1864."

HENDERSON, JOHN H., Private

Enlisted in Madison County, July 4, 1861, for twelve months. Captured at Roanoke Island on February 8, 1862, and paroled at Elizabeth City, N.C., February 21, 1862. Enlisted in Company C, 64th Regiment N.C. Troops while absent on parole.

HENLINE, WILLIAM M., Private

Resided in Madison County where he enlisted at age 37, July 4, 1861, for twelve months. Died at hospital in Richmond, Virginia, November 21, 1861.

HILL, AARON L., Sergeant

Resided in Madison County where he enlisted at age 19, July 4, 1861, for twelve months. Mustered in as Private. First reported on company muster roll for April 30-October 31, 1862. Appointed Sergeant, November 1, 1863. Captured at Spotsylvania Court House, Virginia, May 12, 1864, and confined at Point Lookout, Maryland, until released after taking the Oath of Allegiance on June 27, 1864, and joining the U.S. service. Later assigned to Company I, 1st Regiment U.S. Volunteer Infantry.

HILL, JOHN R., Private

Resided in Madison County where he enlisted at age 26, July 4, 1861, for twelve months. Mustered in as Sergeant. Captured at Roanoke Island on February 8, 1862, and paroled at Elizabeth City, N.C., February 21, 1862. Reduced to ranks when not reappointed at the reorganization of the company on September 25, 1862. Discharged November 14, 1862, by reason of "organic disease heart."

HOLCOMBE, JAMES R., Private

Enlisted in Madison County, July 4, 1861, for twelve months. Captured at Roanoke Island on February 8, 1862, and paroled at Elizabeth City, N.C., February 21, 1862. Company muster rolls state that he "refused to report" after parole and voluntarily attached himself to Company C, 64th Regiment N.C. Troops.

HOLCOMBE, MAY, Private

Enlisted in Madison County, July 4, 1861, for twelve months. Company muster roll for April 30-

October 31, 1862, reports that he was "absent at home and refuses to report." Later enlisted in Company C, 64th Regiment N.C. Troops.

HOPPERS, SAMUEL J., Private
Resided in Madison County where he enlisted at age 18, July 4, 1861, for twelve months. Mustered in as Private. Captured at Roanoke Island on February 8, 1862, and paroled at Elizabeth City, N.C., February 21, 1862. Appointed Sergeant, September 25, 1862. Reduced to ranks April-August, 1864. Present or accounted for on company muster rolls through February, 1865. Paroled at Appomattox Court House, Virginia, April 9, 1865.

HOPPERS, WILLIAM H. C., Private
Enlisted in Madison County, July 4, 1861, for twelve months. Captured at Roanoke Island on February 8, 1862, and paroled at Elizabeth City, N.C., February 21, 1862. Enlisted in Company A, 5th Battalion N.C. Cavalry, May 31, 1862. Returned to this company November-December, 1862. Present or accounted for on company muster rolls until September-October, 1864, when he is reported as "absent in arrest." Absent undergoing sentence of court-martial through December, 1864. Reported as present on the January-February, 1865, muster roll. Paroled at Appomattox Court House, Virginia, April 9, 1865.

HUDSON, AQUILLA, Private
Resided in Madison County where he enlisted at age 32, July 4, 1861, for twelve months. First reported on company muster roll for April 30-October 31, 1862. Present or accounted for on company muster rolls through April, 1863. Died in hospital in Raleigh, May 19, 1863, of "fever."

HUDSON, JOHN K., Private
Resided in Madison County where he enlisted at age 21, July 4, 1861, for twelve months. Captured at Roanoke Island on February 8, 1862, and paroled at Elizabeth City, N.C., February 21, 1862. Reported on company muster rolls as being "in the pioneer corps" from September-October, 1863, through February, 1864. Reported as absent without leave from that date through February, 1865.

JARRETT, ELI H., Private
Enlisted in Madison County, July 4, 1861, for twelve months. Captured at Roanoke Island on February 8, 1862, and paroled at Elizabeth City, N.C., February 21, 1862. Company muster roll for April 30-October 31, 1862, reports that he was "absent at home and refuses to report under pretext of not being legally exchanged." Later enlisted in Company C, 64th Regiment N.C. Troops.

JARRETT, JACOB P., Private
Enlisted in Madison County, July 4, 1861, for twelve months. Captured at Roanoke Island on February 8, 1862, and paroled at Elizabeth City, N.C., February 21, 1862. Company muster roll for April 30-October 31, 1862, reports that he was "absent at home and refuses to report under pretext of not being legally exchanged." Later enlisted in Company C, 64th Regiment N.C. Troops.

JONES, GEORGE N., Private
Resided in Madison County where he enlisted at age 35, July 4, 1861, for twelve months. Died October 19, 1861, at Camp Lee, Virginia.

JONES, JAMES A., Private
Born in Madison County where he resided as a farmer and enlisted at age 21, July 4, 1861, for twelve months. Present or accounted for until killed in battle near Spotsylvania Court House, Virginia, May 10, 1864.

KEENER, JESSE A., Private
Resided in Madison County where he enlisted at age 17, July 4, 1861, for twelve months. Captured at Roanoke Island on February 8, 1862, and paroled at Elizabeth City, N.C., February 21, 1862. Present or accounted for until again captured on September 19, 1864, at Winchester, Virginia. Confined at U.S.A. Depot Field Hospital, Winchester, with "v.s. comp. com. fracture tibia" and was transferred to U.S.A. General Hospital, West's Buildings, Baltimore, Maryland, October 13, 1864. Sent on October 18, 1864, to Point Lookout, Maryland, where he was paroled and transferred to Venus Point, Savannah River, Georgia, November 15, 1864, for exchange. Reported as absent without leave on the January-February, 1865, muster roll.

LEDFORD, ISAAC G., Private
Resided in Madison County where he enlisted at age 18, January 20, 1864, for the war. Present or accounted for on company muster rolls until reported on the January-February, 1865, muster roll as absent without leave.

LEDFORD, LEANDER E., Private
Resided in Madison County where he enlisted December 1, 1862, for the war. Captured at Gettysburg, Pennsylvania, July 1-4, 1863, and confined at DeCamp General Hospital, Davids Island, New York Harbor, until paroled and sent to City Point, Virginia, for exchange. Received at City Point on September 8, 1863, for exchange. Present or accounted for until again captured on October 19, 1864, at Strasburg, Virginia. Confined at Point Lookout, Maryland, until paroled and sent to Aiken's Landing, Virginia, for exchange on March 28, 1865.

LEDFORD, NOAH, Private
Resided in Madison County where he enlisted July 4, 1861, for twelve months. Captured at Roanoke Island on February 8, 1862, and paroled at Elizabeth City, N.C., February 21, 1862. Present or accounted for on company muster rolls through February, 1865. Captured at Petersburg, Virginia, April 2, 1865, and confined at Point Lookout, Maryland, until released after taking the Oath of Allegiance on June 28, 1865.

LEDFORD, SAMUEL E., Private
Resided in Madison County where he enlisted at age 18, July 4, 1861, for twelve months. First reported on company muster roll for March-April, 1863. Captured in hospital at Gettysburg, Pennsylvania, July 1-3, 1863, and confined at Camp Letterman U.S.A. General Hospital, Gettysburg, August 10, 1863, with "g. fract. r. ankle jt.—amp.

r. leg." Transferred September 28-29, 1863, to U.S.A. General Hospital, West's Buildings, Baltimore, Maryland, where he was paroled and sent to City Point, Virginia, for exchange on November 12, 1863. Reported as absent with leave through October, 1864, and as absent without leave from that date through February, 1865.

LEDFORD, SOLOMON, Private
Resided in Madison County where he enlisted at age 33, July 4, 1861, for twelve months. Captured at Roanoke Island on February 8, 1862, and paroled at Elizabeth City, N.C., February 21, 1862. Present or accounted for until again captured near Spotsylvania Court House, Virginia, May 10, 1864, and confined at Point Lookout, Maryland. Transferred on August 10-14, 1864, to Elmira, New York, where he was paroled and sent to James River, Virginia, for exchange, March 14, 1865.

LEE, BLACKMON, Private
Received from the conscript camp at Raleigh on September 17, 1864. Company muster rolls report him as "absent, prisoner of war" from September-October, 1864, through February, 1865. Date and place of capture not shown in records.

LEWIS, JAMES, Private
Resided in Madison County where he enlisted at age 36, July 4, 1861, for twelve months. Captured at Roanoke Island on February 8, 1862, and paroled at Elizabeth City, N.C., February 21, 1862. Present or accounted for until wounded and captured near Winchester, Virginia, September 19-25, 1864. Admitted to Field Hospital, Winchester, Virginia, October 6, 1864, with "wound in left shoulder" and was transferred to U.S.A. General Hospital, West's Buildings, Baltimore, Maryland, October 12-13, 1864. Sent on October 18, 1864, to Point Lookout, Maryland, where he was paroled and sent to Venus Point, Savannah River, Georgia, for exchange on October 30, 1864. Present or accounted for until he deserted and took the Oath of Allegiance on March 29, 1865, at Washington, D.C., and was furnished transportation to Knoxville, Tennessee.

LOGAN, HENRY, Private
Resided in Surry County where he enlisted at age 19, September 18, 1861, for twelve months. Captured at Roanoke Island on February 8, 1862, and paroled at Elizabeth City, N.C., February 21, 1862. Died March 15, 1862, in Surry County, while absent on parole.

LUSK, DAVID R., Sergeant
Born in Madison County where he resided as a farmer and enlisted at age 19, July 4, 1861, for twelve months. Mustered in as Private. Captured at Roanoke Island on February 8, 1862, and paroled at Elizabeth City, N.C., February 21, 1862. Appointed Corporal, January 1, 1863. Captured at Gettysburg, Pennsylvania, July 1-4, 1863, and confined at DeCamp General Hospital, Davids Island, New York Harbor, until paroled and sent to City Point, Virginia, for exchange. Received at City Point on September 16, 1863, for exchange. Promoted to Sergeant, January-August, 1864. Present

or accounted for until admitted to hospital at Richmond, Virginia, June 3, 1864, with "v.s. left below knee, ball passing through tibia." Furloughed from hospital for 60 days on July 16, 1864. Absent sick until retired to the Invalid Corps, March 16, 1865, and detailed for light duty at Danville, Virginia, March 31, 1865.

LUSK, VIRGIL S., Private
Enlisted in Madison County, July 4, 1861, for twelve months. Present or accounted for on company muster rolls through February, 1862. No further records.

McARTHUR, DANIEL H., Private
Received from the conscript camp at Raleigh on September 17, 1864. Died of disease at division hospital on February 9, 1865.

McGEE, ALBERT N., Private
Resided as a farmer in Surry County where he enlisted at age 23, September 13, 1861, for twelve months. Reported as absent without leave until he appears as present on the February 28-June 30, 1862, muster roll. Present or accounted for until captured at Winchester, Virginia, September 19, 1864, and confined at Point Lookout, Maryland. Paroled at Point Lookout and transferred to Aiken's Landing, Virginia, for exchange on March 15, 1865.

McNAIR, JOHN N., Private
Enlisted in Wake County, September 10, 1864, for the war. Admitted to hospital at Richmond, Virginia, January 2, 1865, and died January 9, 1865, of "colitis."

MEESE, MARTIN, Private
Enlisted in Madison County, June 28, 1864, for the war. Reported on company muster rolls as absent with leave from September-October, 1864, through February, 1865.

MILLER, ANDREW B., Private
Resided in Madison County where he enlisted at age 33, July 4, 1861, for twelve months. Captured at Roanoke Island on February 8, 1862, and paroled at Elizabeth City, N.C., February 21, 1862. Present or accounted for until again captured at Gettysburg, Pennsylvania, July 1-3, 1863. Confined at DeCamp General Hospital, Davids Island, New York Harbor, until paroled and sent to City Point, Virginia, for exchange. Received at City Point on September 8, 1863, for exchange. Absent on parole through December, 1863, and absent without leave from that date until he deserted in Madison County, March 8, 1864. Received at Knoxville, Tennessee, June 15, 1864, and transferred to Military Prison, Louisville, Kentucky, where he took the Oath of Allegiance and was released "to remain North of the Ohio River during the war" on June 24, 1864.

MILLER, SAMUEL, Private
Resided in Madison County where he enlisted at age 33, July 4, 1861, for twelve months. Captured at Roanoke Island on February 8, 1862, and paroled at Elizabeth City, N.C., February 21, 1862. Died March 6, 1862, in Madison County.

MORGAN, PREMENTOR M., Private
Resided in Madison County where he enlisted at

age 37, July 4, 1861, for twelve months. Captured at Roanoke Island on February 8, 1862, and paroled at Elizabeth City, N.C., February 21, 1862. Present or accounted for until again captured September 22. 1864, at Fisher's Hill, Virginia. Confined at Point Lookout, Maryland, until paroled and transferred to Aiken's Landing, Virginia, March 17, 1865, for exchange.

MULL, WILLIAM F., Private
Resided in Madison County where he enlisted at age 15, July 4, 1861, for twelve months. Captured at Roanoke Island on February 8, 1862, and paroled at Elizabeth City, N.C., February 21, 1862. Roll of Honor reports that he "deserted his company August 25, 1863" and was returned and sentenced to hard labor by a court-martial. Company muster rolls state that he was absent in arrest or absent undergoing sentence of court-martial from that date through October. 1864. Absent sick from November-December, 1864, through February, 1865.

OSBORN, RILLEY, Private
Received from the conscript camp at Raleigh on September 25, 1864. Present or accounted for until captured near Petersburg, Virginia, March 25, 1865. Confined at Point Lookout, Maryland, until released after taking the Oath of Allegiance on June 8, 1865. Admitted on June 12, 1865, to Jackson Hospital, Richmond, Virginia, where he died June 21, 1865.

PARRIS, MERRITT R., Private
Resided in Madison County where he enlisted at age 19, July 4, 1861, for twelve months. Captured at Roanoke Island on February 8, 1862, and paroled at Elizabeth City, N.C., February 21, 1862. Present or accounted for until again captured at Gettysburg, Pennsylvania, July 4, 1863. Confined at DeCamp General Hospital, Davids Island, New York Harbor, until paroled and sent to City Point, Virginia, for exchange. Received at City Point on September 16, 1863, for exchange. Present or accounted for until killed in action near Spotsylvania Court House, Virginia, May 15, 1864.

PEARCE, HENRY C., Private
Resided in Madison County where he enlisted at age 20, July 4, 1861, for twelve months. Captured at Roanoke Island on February 8, 1862, and paroled at Elizabeth City, N.C., February 21, 1862. Present or accounted for on company muster rolls through February, 1865. Captured at Petersburg, Virginia, April 2, 1865, and confined at Point Lookout, Maryland, until released after taking the Oath of Allegiance on June 17, 1865.

PEEK, ALFRED, Private
Enlisted in Madison County, July 4, 1861, for twelve months. Captured at Roanoke Island on February 8, 1862, and paroled at Elizabeth City, N.C., February 21, 1862. Present or accounted for on company muster rolls through February, 1862. No further records.

PEEK, JAMES M., Private
Enlisted in Madison County, July 4, 1861, for twelve months. Captured at Roanoke Island on February 8, 1862, and paroled at Elizabeth City,

N.C., February 21, 1862. Present or accounted for on company muster rolls through February, 1862. No further records.

PEEK, JOB B., Private
Enlisted in Madison County, July 4, 1861, for twelve months. Captured at Roanoke Island on February 8, 1862, and and paroled at Elizabeth City, N.C., February 21, 1862. Present or accounted for on company muster rolls through February, 1862. No further records.

PLEMMONS, JOSIAH N., Private
Resided in Madison County where he enlisted at age 20, July 4, 1861, for twelve months. Captured at Roanoke Island on February 8, 1862, and paroled at Elizabeth City, N.C., February 21, 1862. Died December 19, 1862, in Madison County.

PLEMMONS, LEVI J., Private
Enlisted in Madison County, July 4, 1861, for twelve months. He was not captured at Roanoke Island on February 8, 1862, and attached himself to Company I, 60th Regiment N.C. Troops. Returned to this company November-December, 1864, and is reported as present on company muster rolls through February, 1865. Paroled at Appomattox Court House, Virginia, April 9, 1865.

PLEMMONS, SILAS J., Private
Enlisted in Madison County, July 4, 1861, for twelve months. Captured at Roanoke Island on February 8, 1862, and paroled at Elizabeth City, N.C., February 21, 1862. Enlisted in Company B, 60th Regiment N.C. Troops while absent on parole.

PLEMMONS, THOMAS M., Private
Resided in Madison County where he enlisted at age 30, July 4, 1861, for twelve months. Captured at Roanoke Island on February 8, 1862, and paroled at Elizabeth City, N.C., February 21, 1862. Present or accounted for on company muster rolls through February, 1862. Roll of Honor reports that he died January 23, 1863, in hospital at Wilmington.

PLEMMONS, WILLIAM J., Jr., Private
Resided in Madison County where he enlisted at age 33, July 4, 1861, for the war. Captured at Roanoke Island on February 8, 1862, and paroled at Elizabeth City, N.C., February 21, 1862. Present or accounted for on company muster rolls through February, 1865. Paroled at Appomattox Court House, Virginia, April 9, 1865.

PLEMMONS, WILLIAM J., Sr., Private
Resided in Madison County where he enlisted at age 19, July 4, 1861, for twelve months. Company muster roll for November-December, 1861, reports that he died December 3, 1861.

PRICE, JOSEPH, Private
Resided in Madison County where he enlisted at age 20, July 4, 1861, for twelve months. Captured at Roanoke Island on February 8, 1862, and released at Elizabeth City, N.C., February 21, 1862. Present or accounted for on company muster rolls through February, 1865.

PRICE, PHILLIP F. L., Private
Resided in Madison County where he enlisted at

age 18, September 1, 1862, for the war. Died December 23, 1862, of "pneumonia."

PRICE, WILLIAM F., Private

Resided in Madison County where he enlisted at age 22, July 4, 1861, for twelve months. Captured at Roanoke Island on February 8, 1862, and paroled at Elizabeth City, N.C., February 21, 1862. Present or accounted for on company muster rolls until November-December, 1862, when he was reported as "absent on detached service at Danville, Virginia, doing Provost Duty." Roll of Honor states that he was killed July 1, 1863, in battle at Gettysburg, Pennsylvania.

PROFFITT, WAITSEL A., Corporal

Resided in Madison County where he enlisted at age 20, July 4, 1861, for twelve months. Mustered in as Corporal. Captured at Roanoke Island on February 8, 1862, and paroled at Elizabeth City, N.C., February 21, 1862. Transferred to Company A, 5th Battalion N.C. Cavalry upon appointment as 2nd Lieutenant of that company in October, 1862.

RAMSEY, LOUIS, Private

Enlisted in Madison County, December 20, 1861, for twelve months. Captured at Roanoke Island on February 8, 1862, and paroled at Elizabeth City, N.C., February 21, 1862. Enlisted in Company C, 64th Regiment N.C. Troops while absent on parole.

REYNOLDS, JAMES G., Private

Resided in Madison County where he enlisted at age 39, July 4, 1861, for twelve months. Present or accounted for on company muster rolls through April, 1863. Roll of Honor states that he was discharged on May 1, 1863, at Kinston.

RIGSBEE, WILLIAM, Private

Enlisted in Madison County, December 20, 1861, for twelve months. Captured at Roanoke Island on February 8, 1862, and paroled at Elizabeth City, N.C., February 21, 1862. Enlisted in Company C, 64th Regiment N.C. Troops while absent on parole.

ROBERTS, AMOS, Jr., Private

Resided in Madison County where he enlisted at age 36, December 20, 1861, for twelve months. Captured at Roanoke Island on February 8, 1862, and paroled at Elizabeth City, N.C., February 21, 1862. Present or accounted for on company muster rolls through April, 1863. Roll of Honor reports that he was discharged May 12, 1863, at Kinston.

ROBERTS, AMOS J., Private

Resided in Madison County where he enlisted at age 17, July 4, 1861, for twelve months. Captured at Roanoke Island on February 8, 1862, and paroled at Elizabeth City, N.C., February 21, 1862. Present or accounted for until wounded and captured at Gettysburg, Pennsylvania, July 1-3, 1863. Confined at DeCamp General Hospital, Davids Island, New York Harbor, with "g.s. forearm." Paroled at that hospital and sent to City Point, Virginia, where he was received September 16, 1863, for exchange. Present or accounted for until again captured on October 19, 1864, at Strasburg, Virginia, and confined at Point Lookout, Mary-

land. Released at Point Lookout after taking the Oath of Allegiance on June 17, 1865.

ROBERTS, BENJAMIN, Corporal

Resided in Madison County where he enlisted at age 33, July 4, 1861, for twelve months. Mustered in as Corporal. Captured at Roanoke Island on February 8, 1862, and paroled at Elizabeth City, N.C., February 21, 1862. Enlisted in Company C, 64th Regiment N.C. Troops while absent on parole.

ROBERTS, FRANKLIN, Private

Resided in Madison County where he enlisted at age 17, December 20, 1861, for twelve months. Captured at Roanoke Island on February 8, 1862, and died at Elizabeth City, N.C., February 21, 1862.

ROBERTS, WILLIAM F., Private

Enlisted in Madison County, November 19, 1864, for the war. Deserted to the enemy on January 15, 1865. Took the Oath of Allegiance at Washington, D.C., January 26, 1865, and was furnished transportation to Portsmouth, Virginia.

ROGERS, WILLIAM, Private

Enlisted in Madison County, December 20, 1861, for twelve months. Captured at Roanoke Island on February 8, 1862, and paroled at Elizabeth City, N.C., February 21, 1862. Enlisted in Company C, 64th Regiment N.C. Troops while absent on parole.

RUSSELL, EARL A., Sergeant

Resided in Madison County where he enlisted at age 32, July 4, 1861, for twelve months. Mustered in as Private. Captured at Roanoke Island on February 8, 1862, and paroled at Elizabeth City, N.C., February 21, 1862. Appointed Sergeant, April-October, 1862. Appointed Ordnance Sergeant prior to September-October, 1863, and transferred to the Field and Staff of this battalion.

RUSSELL, WILLIAM, Private

Resided in Madison County where he enlisted at age 26, July 4, 1861, for twelve months. Captured at Roanoke Island on February 8, 1862, and paroled at Elizabeth City, N.C., February 21, 1862. Present or accounted for until his death on April 10, 1864, at Orange Court House, Virginia.

SAMES, EDMOND, Private

Enlisted in Madison County, July 4, 1861, for twelve months. First reported on company muster roll for April 30-October, 1862, which states that he was absent sick at home. Appears as absent sick until March-April, 1863, when he is reported as being "engaged in manufacturing salt for the state." No further records.

SAMES, ZEPHANIAH, Private

Enlisted in Madison County, July 4, 1861, for twelve months. Captured at Roanoke Island on February 8, 1862, and paroled at Elizabeth City, N.C., February 21, 1862. Enlisted in Company C, 64th Regiment N.C. Troops while absent on parole.

SAWYER, JAMES T., Private

Enlisted in Madison County, July 4, 1861, for twelve months. He was not captured at Roanoke

Island on February 8, 1862, and attached himself to Company A, 5th Battalion N.C. Cavalry. Did not return when company was reorganized in September, 1862.

SAWYER, LEWIS S., Corporal
Enlisted in Madison County, July 4, 1861, for twelve months. Mustered in as Corporal. Captured at Roanoke Island on February 8, 1862, and paroled at Elizabeth City, N.C., February 21, 1862. Present or accounted for on company muster rolls through February, 1862. No further records.

SAWYER, WESLEY, Private
Enlisted in Madison County, December 20, 1861, for twelve months. He was not captured at Roanoke Island on February 8, 1862, and attached himself to Company A, 5th Battalion N.C. Cavalry. Did not return when company was reorganized in September, 1862.

SEXTON, HIRAM, Private
Resided in Madison County where he enlisted at age 19, July 4, 1861, for twelve months. Captured at Roanoke Island on February 8, 1862, and paroled at Elizabeth City, N.C., February 21, 1862. Present or accounted for on company muster rolls until reported on the September-October, 1864, roll as "present in arrest." Reported as absent in arrest undergoing sentence of court-martial from that date through February, 1865. Paroled at Appomattox Court House, Virginia, April 9, 1865.

SEXTON, PINKNEY, Private
Resided in Madison County where he enlisted at age 16, March 1, 1864, for the war. Reported as "absent, a prisoner of war" on the company muster roll for December 31, 1863-August 31, 1864. Appears as such through February, 1865. Date and place of capture are not shown in records.

SEXTON, SAMUEL J., Private
Resided in Madison County where he enlisted at age 21, July 4, 1861, for twelve months. Present or accounted for until wounded and captured at Gettysburg, Pennsylvania, July 1-3, 1863. Confined at DeCamp General Hospital, Davids Island, New York Harbor, with "elbow joint amputated." Paroled at DeCamp General Hospital and sent for exchange to City Point, Virginia, where he was received September 16, 1863. Present or accounted for until November-December, 1864, when he is reported as absent without leave. Appears as such through February, 1865.

SEYMOUR, WILLIAM D., Private
Captured at Roanoke Island on February 8, 1862, and paroled at Elizabeth City, N.C., February 21, 1862.

SIMSON, THOMAS R., Private
Received from the conscript camp at Raleigh on September 17, 1864. Present or accounted for through February, 1865.

SMART, JOSEPH, Private
Resided in Madison County where he enlisted at age 16, September 1, 1862, for the war. Present or accounted for on company muster rolls through February, 1865. Captured in hospital at Richmond, Virginia, April 3, 1865, and confined at

Libby Prison, Richmond, until transferred to Newport News, Virginia, April 23, 1865. Released at Newport News after taking the Oath of Allegiance on June 30, 1865.

SMITH, JACOB, Private
Resided in Madison County where he enlisted at age 43, July 4, 1861, for twelve months. First reported on company muster roll for April 30-October 31, 1862. Reported on the company muster roll for September-October, 1863, as being absent on sick furlough. November-December, 1863, muster roll states that he was "absent on parole at home" but does not give date or place of capture. Appears as absent without leave on all company muster rolls from that date through February, 1865.

SMITH, JASON, Private
Resided in Madison County where he enlisted at age 30, July 24, 1863, for the war. Reported on company muster rolls as absent without leave from November 16, 1863, to October 15, 1864. Present or accounted for from that date through February, 1865, when he appears as absent sick.

STANLEY, JOHN, Private
Resided in Madison County where he enlisted at age 17, July 4, 1861, for twelve months. Captured at Roanoke Island on February 8, 1862, and paroled at Elizabeth City, N.C., February 21, 1862. Present or accounted for until wounded and captured at Gettysburg, Pennsylvania, July 1-3, 1863. Confined at DeCamp General Hospital, Davids Island, New York Harbor, with "g.s. hip." Paroled at that hospital and sent to City Point, Virginia, where he was received on September 8, 1863, for exchange. Company muster rolls report him as absent on parole through October, 1863, and as absent without leave until he "deserted and went to the enemy 20 March 1864."

TAYLOR, HUGH M., Private
Resided in Madison County where he enlisted at age 21, March 1, 1863, for the war. Wounded and captured at Gettysburg, Pennsylvania, July 1-5, 1863. Confined at Fort McHenry, Maryland, until transferred to Fort Delaware, Delaware, July 7-12, 1863. Transferred to U.S.A. General Hospital, Chester, Pennsylvania, July 19, 1863, with "g.s. arm." Paroled at that hospital August 17, 1863, and sent to City Point, Virginia, for exchange. Reported as absent on parole through October, 1863, and as absent without leave from that date through October, 1864. No further records.

TAYLOR, JESSE W., Private
Resided in Madison County where he enlisted at age 24, March 1, 1863, for the war. Reported as absent sick from date of enlistment through December, 1863. Detailed as a shoemaker at Richmond, Virginia, January 9, 1864. Absent detailed through June, 1864, and reported as absent without leave from that date through February, 1865. Captured at Richmond on April 15, 1865, and took the Oath of Allegiance the same date.

THOMAS, DAVID, Private
Resided in Madison County where he enlisted at age 20, July 4, 1861, for twelve months. He was

not captured at Roanoke Island on February 8, 1862, and attached himself to another company. Returned to this company January-April, 1863. Present or accounted for until captured at Gettysburg, Pennsylvania, July 1-4, 1863. Confined at DeCamp General Hospital, Davids Island, New York Harbor, until paroled and sent to City Point, Virginia, for exchange on August 24, 1863. Reported on company muster rolls as absent on parole through October, 1863, and as absent without leave from that date until he "deserted and went to the enemy 20 March, 1864."

THOMSON, JAMES M., Private
Enlisted in Madison County, July 4, 1861, for twelve months. Captured at Roanoke Island on February 8, 1862, and paroled at Elizabeth City, N.C., February 21, 1862. Enlisted in Company C, 64th Regiment N.C. Troops while absent on parole.

TRAMMELL, ISAAC F., Private
Enlisted in Madison County, July 4, 1861, for twelve months. First reported on company muster roll for September-October, 1863. Present or accounted for through January-February, 1864, when he is reported as "present, detailed as ambulance driver." No further records.

TRAMMELL, MONTREVILLE P., Private
Resided in Madison County where he enlisted at age 23, April 20, 1863, for the war. Company muster rolls report that he was wounded and captured at Gettysburg, Pennsylvania, July 1-3, 1863, and "died a prisoner of war about the 1 October 1863."

VANKNAPP, MILES, Private
Enlisted in Madison County, December 20, 1861, for twelve months. Captured at Roanoke Island on February 8, 1862, and paroled at Elizabeth City, N.C., February 21, 1862. No further records.

WADDELL, WILLIAM J., Private
Resided in Madison County where he enlisted at age 20, July 4, 1861, for twelve months. Captured at Roanoke Island on February 8, 1862, and paroled at Elizabeth City, N.C., February 21, 1862. Roll of Honor states that he "died March 6, 1862, in Madison County, N.C."

WALDRUP, NOAH, Private
Enlisted in Madison County, December 30, 1861, for twelve months. Captured at Roanoke Island on February 8, 1862, and paroled at Elizabeth City, N.C., February 21, 1862. Enlisted in Company A, 5th Battalion N.C. Cavalry while absent on parole, May 14, 1862.

WALKER, THOMAS, Private
Enlisted in Surry County, September 13, 1861, for twelve months. Never mustered in.

WALLEN, BENJAMIN, Private
Enlisted in Madison County, December 30, 1861, for twelve months. Captured at Roanoke Island on February 8, 1862, and paroled at Elizabeth City, N.C., February 21, 1862. Reported on company muster rolls as absent without leave until March-April, 1863, when he appears with the remark: "Engaged in manufacturing salt for the state."

WAMBLE, J. B., Private
Received from conscript camp at Raleigh on September 17, 1864. Captured at Strasburg, Virginia, October 19, 1864, and confined at Point Lookout, Maryland, until released after taking the Oath of Allegiance on June 22, 1865.

WATTS, WILLIAM, Private
Resided in Madison County where he enlisted at age 18, July 4, 1861, for twelve months. Captured at Roanoke Island on February 8, 1862, and paroled at Elizabeth City, N.C., February 21, 1862. Roll of Honor states that he "died February 28, 1862, at Norfolk, Virginia."

WEST, GEORGE W., Private
Enlisted in Madison County, July 4, 1861, for twelve months. Reported as present on the company muster roll for August 12-October 31, 1861. Never mustered in. Later enlisted in Company A, 5th Battalion N.C. Cavalry.

WHIT, JAMES, Private
Enlisted in Madison County, June 28, 1864, for the war. Admitted to hospital at Charlottesville, Virginia, July 31, 1864, with "v.s. head, skull injured" and was furloughed for 30 days on August 9, 1864. Reported as absent without leave on company muster rolls from September-October, 1864, through February, 1865.

WHITE, JOHN E., Private
Enlisted in Madison County, July 4, 1861, for twelve months. Captured at Roanoke Island on February 8, 1862, and paroled at Elizabeth City, N.C., February 21, 1862. Present or accounted for on company muster rolls through April, 1863. Roll of Honor states that he was "killed July 1, 1863, in battle at Gettysburg, Pennsylvania."

WHITE, MARTIN W., Private
Resided in Madison County where he enlisted at age 26, July 4, 1861, for twelve months. Captured at Roanoke Island on February 8, 1862, and paroled at Elizabeth City, N.C., February 21, 1862. Enlisted in Company B, 60th Regiment N.C. Troops while absent on parole.

WILLIAMS, JOSEPH, Private
Enlisted in Madison County, December 30, 1861, for twelve months. Captured at Roanoke Island on February 8, 1862, and paroled at Elizabeth City, N.C., February 21, 1862. Enlisted in Company A, 5th Battalion N.C. Cavalry while absent on parole.

WILSON, WILLIAM L., Private
Resided in Madison County where he enlisted at age 23, July 4, 1861, for twelve months. Wounded and captured at Roanoke Island on February 8, 1862, and paroled at Elizabeth City, N.C., February 21, 1862. Present or accounted for until detailed for hospital duty August 22, 1863. Absent detailed through February, 1865.

WOODSON, FRANCIS M., Private
Resided in Madison County where he enlisted at age 19, July 4, 1861, for twelve months. Captured at Roanoke Island on February 8, 1862, and paroled at Elizabeth City, N.C., February 21, 1862.

Enlisted in Company B, 60th Regiment N.C. Troops while absent on parole.

WOODY, JAMES, Private

Resided in Madison County where he enlisted at age 19, July 4, 1861, for twelve months. Captured at Roanoke Island on February 8, 1862, and paroled at Elizabeth City, N.C., February 21, 1862. Enlisted in Company B, 60th Regiment N.C. Troops while absent on parole. Rejoined this company March 1, 1864, and is reported as present or accounted for through February, 1865.

WOODY, JOSEPH, Private

Resided in Madison County where he enlisted at age 19, July 4, 1861, for twelve months. Captured at Roanoke Island on February 8, 1862, and paroled at Elizabeth City, N.C., February 21, 1862. Present or accounted for on company muster rolls through February, 1865.

WORLEY, AMOS P., Private

Resided in Madison County where he enlisted at age 25, September 1, 1862, for the war. Present or accounted for on company muster rolls through February, 1865. Paroled at Appomattox Court House, Virginia, April 9, 1865.

WORLEY, B. F., Private

Enlisted in Buncombe County, November 10, 1864, for the war. Present or accounted for on company muster rolls through February, 1865. Paroled at Appomattox Court House, Virginia, April 9, 1865.

WORLEY, WILLIAM D., Private

Resided in Madison County where he enlisted at age 23, April 1, 1862, for twelve months. Present or accounted for until captured near Petersburg, Virginia, March 25, 1865, and confined at Point Lookout, Maryland. Released at Point Lookout after taking the Oath of Allegiance on June 21, 1865.

MISCELLANEOUS

The following list of names was compiled from primary records which indicate that these men served in the 2nd Battalion N.C. Infantry but do not indicate the company to which they belonged.

BALINGAR, T. J., Private

Appears on a register of General Hospital, Winchester, Virginia, dated July 20, 1864.

BROMS, JOHN M., Private

Reported as a patient in General Hospital No. 4, Wilmington, on September 9, 1864. Furloughed for 21 days on September 22, 1864.

CAVE, G., Private

Resided in Surry County. Wounded at Petersburg, Virginia, March 25, 1865, and captured at Richmond, Virginia. Admitted to hospital at Point Lookout, Maryland, May 12, 1865. Released from Point Lookout after taking the Oath of Allegiance on July 7, 1865.

LEONARD, P. W., Private

Federal Provost Marshal records report him as a "deserter from the enemy" received January 22, 1865.

LEPPIN, M. D., Lieutenant

Captured at Gettysburg, Pennsylvania, July 4, 1863, and confined at Camp Hamilton, Virginia, September 20, 1864. Forwarded "to Point of Exchange on September 21, 1864."

LOGAN, JOSEPH, 2nd Lieutenant

Captured at Roanoke Island on February 8, 1862.

STAEN, WILLIAM, Private

Paroled at Charlotte on May 12, 1865.

This battalion, commonly referred to as the Arsenal Guard, was composed of employees, detailed men, and nonconscripts who worked at the Fayetteville Arsenal and Armory. During the course of the war seven companies were raised at this manufactory and were organized into a battalion, which was officially designated the 2nd Battalion N.C. Local Defense Troops.

In September, 1861, Captain John C. Booth, commandant of the arsenal, raised for guard duty at the arsenal a company composed entirely of men who were employed in the Ordnance Department. This company was referred to as the "Ordnance Detachment" or as "Booth's Company, Ordnance Regulars, C. S. A." A second company, composed of nonconscripts and men unfit for duty, was raised for local defense and guard duty by an order of the Secretary of War dated June 20, 1863. With the organization of this company the battalion organization was also established, and the new company became Company B of the battalion. Three additional companies were organized in September, 1863, for local defense and special service. These companies were composed exclusively of employees of the arsenal and became Companies C, D, and E of the battalion. A cavalry company was authorized in February, 1864, and completed its organization in April. It was known as the "Mounted Riflemen" and became Company F of the battalion. The seventh and final company in the battalion, Company G, was organized late in 1864 and was composed of soldiers detailed for light duty.

With the exception of two companies, the battalion remained at the Fayetteville Arsenal and Armory until January, 1865. The men drilled once a week; the company officers and noncommissioned officers drilled half an hour every day. In May-June, 1864, Companies B and F were ordered to Weldon. Early in July Company B was ordered to Wilmington and arrived there July 4. On July 8 it was ordered to Camp Jackson, and the next day it was moved to Camp Lamb. From there it was moved to Smithville. On November 2 the company moved to Fort Caswell, where it remained until moved to Fort Campbell on November 27. Orders were received on December 25 to proceed to Fort Fisher, then under attack. On December 28, after the Federals withdrew, the company was ordered back to Fort Campbell. Company F was moved to Garysburg after its arrival at Weldon in May-June, 1864. From there it moved to Franklin, Virginia, on August 14, 1864. By the end of the year it was back at Garysburg. It remained in that area attached to the 4th Sub-District, 2nd Military District, for the balance of the war.

During this time the balance of the battalion remained at Fayetteville. On January 14, 1865, Lieutenant Colonel Frederick L. Childs, commanding the battalion and arsenal, was ordered to send "all" his "garrison" to Wilmington. When the battalion arrived on January 17, 1865, Childs was ordered to return to Fayetteville with his "opera-

tives" and to leave the "guards." With the fall of Fort Fisher on January 15, 1865, Company B was ordered to Fort Anderson. When Wilmington was evacuated, February 20-21, 1865, the company was sent to obstruct the navigation of the Cape Fear River. With the area in Federal hands, the company retired to Fayetteville, where it and some men from the other companies of the battalion joined Lieutenant General William J. Hardee's command. On the approach of General William T. Sherman's army, the entire command was put to the task of dismantling and moving machinery. The Federals occupied Fayetteville on March 11, 1865. The portion of the battalion that remained behind had moved to "the Gulf in Moore County." Here it remained until the surrender of General Joseph E. Johnston's army on April 26, 1865. The men who were with the army and those in Moore County were included in the surrender.

This battalion was erroneously designated the 6th Battalion-Armory Guard in Moore's *Roster* and in Clark's *Regiments*. Although it was locally referred to as the Armory Guard, it was officially designated the 2nd Battalion N.C. Local Defense Troops.

FIELD AND STAFF

LIEUTENANT COLONELS

DeLAGNEL, JULIUS A.
Assigned to Fayetteville Arsenal and Armory from the Ordnance Department, Richmond, Virginia, September-October, 1862, with the rank of Lieutenant Colonel. Relieved and ordered back to field duty on April 17, 1863.

CHILDS, FREDERICK L.
Transferred from Charleston Arsenal, Charleston, South Carolina, April 17, 1863, under orders to relieve Lieutenant Colonel DeLagnel as commander of Fayetteville Arsenal and Armory. Transferred with rank of Major and promoted to Lieutenant Colonel on November 19, 1863. Present or accounted for through December, 1864.

MAJORS

BOOTH, JOHN C.
Transferred from Company A of the battalion upon appointment as Major to rank from August 1, 1862. Died at Fayetteville on September 6-7, 1862.

TAYLOR, MATTHEW P.
Transferred from Company B of this battalion upon appointment as Major to rank from November 19, 1863. Present or accounted for through December, 1864.

ENSIGN

HANKS, WILLIAM H.
Transferred from Company C of this battalion upon appointment as Ensign, March-April, 1864. Present or accounted for through December, 1864.

SURGEON

ROBINSON, BENJAMIN
Resided in Cumberland County and appointed Medical Officer and Acting Surgeon under con-

tract dated October 1, 1861. Present or accounted for through December, 1864.

MILITARY STOREKEEPER AND PAYMASTER

DANGERFIELD, J. E. P.

Transferred from Harpers Ferry, Virginia, and appointed Military Storekeeper and Paymaster by Major Booth.

SERGEANT MAJOR

POWERS, EDWARD P.

Transferred from Company C of this battalion upon appointment as Sergeant Major on May 7, 1864. Present or accounted for through December, 1864.

ORDNANCE SERGEANT

STEPHENS, THOMAS

Assigned to the Fayetteville Arsenal and Armory as Ordnance Sergeant in May-June, 1862. Duties included ordnance, commissary, and quartermaster functions, and he served in all these capacities. Present or accounted for through December, 1864.

COMPANY A

This company was organized at Fayetteville, Cumberland County, in September, 1861, and was entirely composed of men in the Ordnance Department, Fayetteville Arsenal and Armory. The company was known as the "Ordnance Detachment" or "Booth's Company, Ordnance Regulars, C. S. A." and was assigned to guard duty at the arsenal. Since it functioned as a part of the battalion, its history is recorded as a part of the battalion history.

The information contained in the following roster of the company was compiled principally from company muster rolls for May-August, 1862; September, 1863-June, 1864; and September-December, 1864. No company muster rolls were found for May, 1862; September, 1862-August, 1863; July-August, 1864; or for the period after December, 1864. Although there are no Roll of Honor records for this company, useful information was obtained from receipt rolls, prisoner of war records, medical records, and other primary records, supplemented by state pension applications, United Daughters of the Confederacy records, and postwar rosters and histories.

OFFICERS

CAPTAINS

BOOTH, JOHN C.

Appointed Captain of Artillery, C. S. Army, to rank from March 16, 1861, and ordered to Baton Rouge, Louisiana. Ordered to assume command of the Fayetteville Arsenal and Armory on July 27, 1861. Organized this company in September, 1861, and assumed command of company as commander of the arsenal and armory. Transferred to the Field and Staff of this battalion upon appointment as Major to rank from August 1, 1862.

BOLLES, CHARLES P.

Appointed Captain of Artillery, C. S. Army, July 8, 1862, to rank from June 25, 1862, and assigned to Fayetteville Arsenal and Armory. Assigned to command this company. Remained at Fayetteville through May, 1864, when he was transferred to Tallassee, Alabama, to command the armory

under construction at that place.

HOLMES, JOHN L.

Assigned to Fayetteville Arsenal and Armory on April 11, 1864, and joined station on May 10, 1864. Date of appointment as Captain not reported. Reported as present on company muster rolls through December, 1864.

LIEUTENANTS

ASHE, SAMUEL A., 1st Lieutenant

Transferred from Company I, 18th Regiment N.C. Troops (8th Regiment N.C. Volunteers) August 25, 1863, and appointed 1st Lieutenant. Present or accounted for on company muster rolls through December, 1864.

TALLEY, ROBERT A., 2nd Lieutenant

Reported as 2nd Lieutenant, present, on July-August, 1862, muster roll. No further records.

TAYLOR, MATTHEW P., 1st Lieutenant

Assigned to company as 1st Lieutenant on June 25, 1862. Transferred to Company B of this battalion upon appointment as Captain on June 20, 1863.

NONCOMMISSIONED OFFICERS AND PRIVATES

ADCOCKS, JAMES W., Laborer

Issued clothing December 1, 1861. Discharged by reason of disability on March 5, 1862.

ANDERSON, JEFFERSON, Laborer

Enlisted in Cumberland County, September 16, 1861, for the war. Present or accounted for on company muster rolls from May-June, 1862, through August, 1862. Issued clothing on September 5, 1862.

ATKINS, WILLIAM T., Private

Attached to this company from 1st Company C, 36th Regiment N.C. Troops (2nd Regiment N.C. Artillery), August 31, 1863. Issued clothing in 1864 and on January 9, 1865.

ATKINSON, CHARLES, Laborer

Enlisted in Cumberland County, September 2, 1863, for the war. Present or accounted for on company muster rolls through December, 1864.

BAISCH, CHRISTIAN, Private

Attached to this company from Company B, 40th Regiment N.C. Troops (3rd Regiment N.C. Artillery), April 12, 1863.

BETHEA, WILLIAM C., Private

Attached to this company from Company E, 8th Regiment N.C. State Troops, January 14, 1862. Later served in Company G of this battalion.

BOND, ISREAL C., Private

Temporarily attached from Company C, 7th Regiment South Carolina Cavalry from September, 1863, through February, 1864. Later served in Company G of this battalion.

BROWN, DANIEL, Laborer

Enlisted in Cumberland County, October 11, 1861, for the war. Present or accounted for on company muster rolls from May-June, 1862, until transferred to Company B of this battalion upon appointment as 1st Sergeant of that company on November 1, 1863.

BROWN, JAMES M., Laborer
Enlisted September 21, 1864, for the war, having previously served in Company C of this battalion. Present or accounted for through December, 1864, when he was reported absent on furlough.

BRYANT, ROBERT H., Laborer
Resided in Cumberland County where he enlisted September 16, 1861, for the war. Present or accounted for through December, 1864. Captured at Piney Grove, N.C., on March 19, 1865, and confined at Point Lookout, Maryland, until released after taking the Oath of Allegiance on June 23, 1865.

BUCKNER, HENRY E., Private
Attached to this company from Company D, 41st Regiment N.C. Troops (3rd Regiment N.C. Cavalry), November 25, 1862. Died at Fayetteville on November 7, 1863.

BUIE, JAMES D., Sergeant
Attached to this company from Company D, 19th Regiment N.C. Troops (2nd Regiment N.C. Cavalry) from September, 1863, through February, 1864.

BULLARD, HENRY, Laborer
Enlisted in Cumberland County, September 11, 1863, for the war. Present or accounted for through December, 1864. Paroled at Avin's Ferry, N.C., April 26, 1865.

BULLARD, HENRY J., Laborer
Enlisted in Cumberland County, January 6, 1863, for the war. Present or accounted for through December, 1864.

BULLARD, OWEN, Laborer
Enlisted in Cumberland County, January 6, 1863, for the war. Present or accounted for through December, 1864.

BURKETT, BRYANT, Laborer
Enlisted in Cumberland County, June 1, 1863, for the war. Present or accounted for through December, 1864.

CALDER, JOHN W., Private
Temporarily attached from Company E, 26th Regiment N.C. Troops from November, 1863, through February, 1864. Later served in Company G of this battalion.

CAMERON, COLIN A., Artificer
Enlisted in Cumberland County, January 6, 1863, for the war. Mustered in as Laborer and appointed Artificer on March 24, 1864. Present or accounted for through December, 1864.

CAMPBELL, NEILL, Laborer
Resided in Cumberland County where he enlisted October 1, 1861, for the war. Present or accounted for through December, 1864. Captured at Fayetteville on March 11, 1865, and confined at Hart's Island, New York Harbor, until released after taking the Oath of Allegiance on June 18, 1865.

CARTER, JAMES, Private
Resided as a farmer in Cumberland County where he enlisted June 8, 1863, for the war. Present or accounted for through December, 1864. Captured at Fayetteville on March 11, 1865, and confined at Point Lookout, Maryland, until released after taking the Oath of Allegiance on May 13, 1865.

CLARK, JAMES M., Private
Detailed from Company B, 13th Battalion N.C. Light Artillery, November-December, 1863.

COLLINS, ALFRED N., Private
Attached to this company from Company A, 21st Regiment N.C. Troops from September-October, 1863, through February, 1864. Later served in Company G of this battalion.

CURRIE, JOSEPH A., Laborer
Enlisted in Cumberland County, June 12, 1863, for the war. Present or accounted for through December, 1864.

CURRIE, LOCHLIN W., Private
Attached to this company from Company H, 26th Regiment N.C. Troops from November-December, 1863, through February, 1864. Later served in Company G of this battalion.

CURTIS, ZENO W., Laborer
Enlisted in Cumberland County, January 5, 1863, for the war. Present or accounted for through December, 1864. Paroled at Greensboro on May 12, 1865.

DeROSSET, THOMAS C., Laborer
Transferred from Company C of this battalion May 1, 1864. Present or accounted for through December, 1864.

DUFFIE, ALEX M., Acting Corporal
Attached to this company from Company C, 3rd and 5th Regiments C.S. Infantry from September-October, 1863, through February, 1864. Later served in Company G of this battalion.

ELLIS, ARCHIBALD R., Laborer
Enlisted in Cumberland County, January 7, 1863, for the war. Present or accounted for through December, 1864.

EVANS, JAMES M., Laborer
Enlisted in Cumberland County, January 7, 1863, for the war. Present or accounted for through December, 1864.

EVANS, JOHN WILLIAM, Private
Attached to this company from Company D, 3rd Regiment N.C. State Troops, September, 1863. Present or accounted for through December, 1864.

FAIRCLOTH, GREY, Laborer
Enlisted in Cumberland County, September 4, 1863, for the war. Present or accounted for through December, 1864.

FORT, JOHN W., Laborer
Enlisted in Cumberland County, October 1, 1861, for the war. Present or accounted for through August, 1862.

FOWLER, THOMAS, Private
Temporarily attached from Company I, 2nd Regiment N.C. State Troops, January-February, 1864. Later served in Company G of this battalion.

GATES, GEORGE W., Corporal
Attached to this company from Company E, 10th Regiment N.C. State Troops (1st Regiment N.C. Artillery), July 23, 1863. Present or accounted for through February, 1864. Later served in Company G of this battalion.

GRAHAM, JAMES C., Laborer
Enlisted in Cumberland County, October 11, 1861,

for the war. Present or accounted for until transferred to the conscript camp at Raleigh on March 9, 1864.

GRIMES, WILLIAM W., Laborer
Enlisted in Cumberland County, October 1, 1861, for the war. Mustered in as Artificer. Reduced to Laborer by sentence of general court-martial, September 12, 1863, but reason for reduction not shown in records. Present or accounted for through December, 1864.

GURLEY, JOSEPH D., Laborer
Enlisted in Cumberland County, October 1, 1861, for the war. Mustered in as Artificer. Reduced to Laborer on March 23, 1864, but reason for reduction not shown in records. Present or accounted for through December, 1864.

HALL, LUTHER R., Laborer
Enlisted in Cumberland County, January 20, 1863, for the war. Present or accounted for through December, 1864.

HALL, NATHAN, Laborer
Resided in Cumberland County where he enlisted January 7, 1863, for the war. Present or accounted for through December, 1864. Captured at Fayetteville on March 13, 1865, and confined at Hart's Island, New York Harbor, until released after taking the Oath of Allegiance on June 18, 1865.

HENRY, WILLIAM, Laborer
Enlisted in Cumberland County, November 21, 1861, for the war. Present or accounted for until transferred to the conscript camp at Raleigh on March 9, 1864.

HETCHELL, WILLIAM W., Private
Attached to this company from Company A, 63rd Regiment N.C. Troops (5th Regiment N.C. Cavalry), September 30, 1863. Present or accounted for through December, 1863.

HOLLIDAY, ROBERT H., 1st Sergeant
Attached to this company from Company I, 18th Regiment N.C. Troops (8th Regiment N.C. Volunteers) from September-October, 1863, through February, 1864.

HOLMES, ARCHIBALD, Private
Attached to this company from Company A, 63rd Regiment N.C. Troops (5th Regiment N.C. Cavalry), July 23, 1863. Present or accounted for through February, 1864.

HORNE, JOHN B., Laborer
Enlisted in Cumberland County, October 11, 1861, for the war. Present or accounted for through December, 1864.

HUDSON, LEWIS H., Laborer
Enlisted in Cumberland County, September 16, 1861, for the war. Present or accounted for through December, 1864.

JOHNSON, HUGH F., Laborer
Enlisted in Cumberland County, January 14, 1863, for the war. Present or accounted for through December, 1864.

JOHNSON, JOHN, Laborer
Enlisted in Cumberland County, September 19, 1861, for the war. Present or accounted for through August, 1862.

JOHNSON, NORMAN, Laborer
Enlisted in Cumberland County, June 4, 1863, for the war. Present or accounted for through December, 1864.

LAMONT, ALEXANDER, Laborer
Enlisted in Cumberland County, January 1, 1863, for the war. Present or accounted for until transferred to the conscript camp at Raleigh on March 9, 1864.

LANIER, JOSEPH H., Laborer
Resided in Robeson County and enlisted in Cumberland County, May 4, 1863, for the war. Present or accounted for through December, 1864. Captured at Rockfish Creek, N.C., March 10, 1865, and confined at Point Lookout, Maryland, until released after taking the Oath of Allegiance on June 29, 1865.

LATTER, EDWARD N., Sergeant
Attached to this company from Company C, 18th Regiment N.C. Troops (8th Regiment N.C. Volunteers) in 1863.

LEE, JAMES E., Private
Attached to this company from Company E, 24th Regiment N.C. Troops (14th Regiment N.C. Volunteers), September 9, 1863. Present or accounted for through February, 1864. Later served in Company G of this battalion.

LITTLE, CHRISTOPHER C., Laborer
Enlisted in Cumberland County, October 1, 1861, for the war. Present or accounted for through August, 1862. Issued clothing in May, 1863. No further records.

McCALL, JOHN R., Laborer
Enlisted in Cumberland County, January 20, 1863, for the war. Present or accounted for through December, 1864.

McDONALD, ALEXANDER, Artificer
Enlisted in Cumberland County, November 21, 1861, for the war. Mustered in as Laborer and appointed Artificer on November 1, 1863. Present or accounted for through December, 1864.

McDONALD, JOHN W., Laborer
Enlisted in Cumberland County, November 21, 1861, for the war. Present or accounted for until transferred to the conscript camp at Raleigh on March 9, 1864.

McFARLAND, WILLIAM, Laborer
Enlisted in Cumberland County, December 20, 1862, for the war. Present or accounted for through December, 1864.

McGRATH, JOHN J., Private
Detailed from Company E, 10th Regiment N.C. State Troops (1st Regiment N.C. Artillery), May 23, 1862. Present or accounted for until transferred to C. S. Navy on December 7, 1863.

McILWAINE, JOHN S., Laborer
Enlisted in Cumberland County, October 11, 1861, for the war. Present or accounted for through December, 1864.

McINTOSH, WILLIAM D., Laborer
Enlisted in Cumberland County, April 12, 1864, for the war. Present or accounted for on company muster rolls until September-October, 1864, when

he is reported as present "sick." Died at Fayetteville Arsenal prior to November 28, 1864.

McKAY, JOHN A., Laborer

Enlisted in Cumberland County, November 11, 1861, for the war. Present or accounted for on company muster rolls through August, 1862. Issued clothing in May, 1863. No further records.

McLEOD, ALEXANDER, Private

Attached to this company from Company G, 33rd Regiment N.C. Troops from September-October, 1863, through December, 1863.

McLEOD, ARCHIBALD, Private

Attached to this company from Company G, 33rd Regiment N.C. Troops, January-February, 1864. Later served in Company G of this battalion.

McMILLAN, JOHN, Laborer

Enlisted in Cumberland County, June 9, 1863, for the war. Present or accounted for through December, 1864.

McNEILL, JOHN, Laborer

Enlisted in Cumberland County, January 12, 1863, for the war. Present or accounted for until reported on the January-February, 1864, muster roll with the remark: "Died."

McQUEEN, WILLIAM, Laborer

Enlisted in Cumberland County, June 8, 1863, for the war. Present or accounted for through December, 1864.

MATTHEWS, FREDERICK J., Laborer

Enlisted in Cumberland County, January 14, 1863, for the war. Present or accounted for on company muster rolls through December, 1864. Deserted at Rockfish, N.C., March 10, 1865. Took the Oath of Allegiance at Washington, D.C., April 5, 1865, and was furnished transportation to Wilmington.

MATTHEWS, JOHN J., Private

Issued clothing July 26, 1864.

MILLER, CHARLES W., Private

Attached to this company from Company B, 56th Regiment N.C. Troops from September-October, 1863, through February, 1864.

MITCHELL, W. W., Private

Attached to this company January-February, 1864.

MOFFITT, HENRY C., Laborer

Enlisted in Cumberland County, December 27, 1862, for the war. Present or accounted for through December, 1864.

MONROE, ELISHA, Laborer

Enlisted in Cumberland County, January 1, 1863, for the war. Present or accounted for through December, 1864.

MONROE, MALCOLM N., Laborer

Enlisted in Cumberland County, September 16, 1861, for the war. Present or accounted for until transferred to Company B of this battalion upon his election as 2nd Lieutenant of that company on August 31, 1863.

MONROE, NEILL L., Laborer

Enlisted in Cumberland County, October 1, 1861, for the war. Mustered in as Artificer. Reduced to Laborer on May 24, 1864. Present or accounted for through December, 1864.

MOODY, THOMAS W., Laborer

Enlisted in Cumberland County, September 7, 1863, for the war. Present or accounted for through December, 1864.

MUNROE, COLIN A., Laborer

Enlisted in Cumberland County, January 29, 1863, for the war. Present or accounted for through December, 1864.

MUNROE, JOHN A., Laborer

Enlisted in Cumberland County, October 1, 1861, for the war. Present or accounted for on company muster rolls through August, 1862. Issued clothing May, 1863.

O'QUIN, JOHN A., Laborer

Enlisted in Cumberland County, October 11, 1861, for the war. Present or accounted for through December, 1864.

PARDUE, JOHN L., Private

Attached to this company from Company E, Holcombe's Legion, South Carolina, from September-October, 1863, through February, 1864. Later served in Company G of this battalion.

PHILLIPS, BENJAMIN P., Laborer

Enlisted in Cumberland County, June 6, 1863, for the war. Present or accounted for through December, 1864.

PLUMMER, JOHN W., Laborer

Enlisted in Cumberland County, January 1, 1863, for the war. Present or accounted for through December, 1864.

PLUMMER, NATHANIEL J., Laborer

Enlisted in Cumberland County, November 21, 1861, for the war. Present or accounted for through December, 1864.

POPE, THOMAS, Laborer

Enlisted in Cumberland County, October 21, 1861, for the war. Present or accounted for on company muster rolls through August, 1862. No further records.

POPE, WILLIAM H., Laborer

Enlisted in Cumberland County, October 1, 1861, for the war. Present or accounted for on company muster rolls through August, 1862, when he is reported as absent on furlough. Issued clothing May, 1863.

RAY, DAVID J., Laborer

Enlisted in Cumberland County, October 11, 1861, for the war. Present or accounted for until transferred to Company B of this battalion upon his election as 1st Lieutenant of that company on August 31, 1863.

REED, HENRY S., Private

Attached to this company from Company F, 50th Regiment N.C. Troops on December 12, 1863. Present or accounted for through February, 1864. Later served in Company G of this battalion.

REYNOLDS, JOHN E., Private

Attached to this company from Company E, 2nd Regiment N.C. State Troops in October, 1862, and returned to that company September 8, 1863.

RITTER, JOHN T., Laborer

Enlisted in Cumberland County, September 16,

1861, for the war. Present or accounted for until transferred to Company B of this battalion upon his election as 2nd Lieutenant of that company on August 31, 1863.

RIVES, BENJAMIN F., Laborer
Enlisted in Cumberland County, January 19, 1863, for the war. Present or accounted for through December, 1864.

ROUSE, JOHN W., Private
Attached to this company from Company C, 3rd Regiment N.C. State Troops, January-February, 1864.

RUSSELL, BENJAMIN R., Laborer
Enlisted in Cumberland County, November 11, 1861, for the war. Present or accounted for on company muster rolls through August, 1862. Issued clothing in May, 1863, and on September 5, 1863.

SAUNDERS, JOHN O., Laborer
Enlisted in Cumberland County, November 21, 1861, for the war. Present or accounted for through December, 1864.

STRAUGHN, LUTHER C., Private
Transferred from Company C, 3rd Regiment N.C. State Troops, May 23, 1862. Present or accounted for until transferred to Company G of this battalion November-December, 1864.

STRICKLAND, JACOB B., Private
Transferred from Company C, 3rd Regiment N.C. State Troops, February 6, 1864. Present or accounted for until transferred to Company G of this battalion November-December, 1864.

THOMAS, GEORGE W., Laborer
Enlisted in Cumberland County, January 15, 1863, for the war. Present or accounted for through December, 1864.

THOMAS, JOSEPH, Laborer
Enlisted in Cumberland County, September 14, 1863, for the war. Present or accounted for through December, 1864.

THOMAS, JOSEPH H., Private
Attached to this company from Company F, 50th Regiment N.C. Troops on December 12, 1863. Present or accounted for through February, 1864. Later served in Company G of this battalion.

TOLAR, JOHN R., Laborer
Enlisted in Cumberland County, September 2, 1863, for the war. Present or accounted for through December, 1864.

TOLAR, THOMAS J., Laborer
Enlisted in Cumberland County, November 1, 1861, for the war. Present or accounted for through December, 1864.

UTLEY, MOSES C., Private
Attached to this company from 2nd Company C, 36th Regiment N.C. Troops (2nd Regiment N.C. Artillery), November 25, 1863. Present or accounted for through February, 1864.

WATSON, THOMAS D., Laborer
Enlisted in Cumberland County, January 5, 1863, for the war. Present or accounted for through December, 1864.

WILLIAMSON, JAMES P., Private
Attached to this company from 8th Regiment Georgia Infantry.

WOMBLE, JAMES R., Laborer
Enlisted in Cumberland County, January 7, 1863, for the war. Present or accounted for through December, 1864.

WORTH, ALBERT H., Private
Attached to this company from Company I, 22nd Regiment N.C. Troops (12th Regiment N.C. Volunteers), October 24, 1863. Present or accounted for through February, 1864. Later served in Company G of this battalion.

COMPANY B

This company was organized at Fayetteville, Cumberland County, by an order of the Secretary of War dated June 20, 1863. It was organized in July and August, 1863, for local defense and special service. The company was composed of non-conscripts and men unfit for field duty and was assigned to the battalion as Company B. Since it functioned as a part of the battalion, its history is recorded as a part of the battalion history.

The information contained in the following roster of the company was compiled principally from company muster rolls for the period from the date of enlistment through April, 1864; for July-August, 1864; and for November-December, 1864. No company muster rolls were found for May-June, 1864; September-October, 1864; or for the period after December, 1864. Although there are no Roll of Honor records for this company, useful information was obtained from receipt rolls, prisoner of war records, medical records, and other primary records, supplemented by state pension applications, United Daughters of the Confederacy records, and postwar rosters and histories.

OFFICERS
CAPTAINS

TAYLOR, MATTHEW P.
Transferred from Company A of this battalion upon appointment as Captain on June 20, 1863. Transferred to the Field and Staff of this battalion upon appointment as Major on November 19, 1863.

DeROSSET, ARMAND L.
Previously served as 1st Lieutenant, Assistant Provost Marshal at Wilmington. Appointed Captain on March 24, 1864, to rank from February 19, 1864. Present or accounted for through February, 1864.

LIEUTENANTS

MONROE, MALCOLM N., 2nd Lieutenant
Transferred from Company A of this battalion upon election as 2nd Lieutenant on August 31, 1863. Present or accounted for through December, 1864.

RAY, DAVID J., 1st Lieutenant
Transferred from Company A of this battalion upon election as 1st Lieutenant on August 31,

1863. Present or accounted for through December, 1864.

RITTER, JOHN T., 2nd Lieutenant
Transferred from Company A of this battalion upon election as 2nd Lieutenant on August 31, 1863. Present or accounted for through December, 1864.

NONCOMMISSIONED OFFICERS AND PRIVATES

AUTRY, CARLTON W., Private
Resided in Cumberland County where he enlisted on August 3, 1863, for the war. Deserted July 26, 1864, and was arrested and returned August 16, 1864. Reported on company muster rolls as being absent in confinement awaiting trial until November-December, 1864, when he appears with the remark: "Absent Military Prison in Wilmington under sentence of death for desertion." Records indicate that he was not executed and was "restored to duty" on March 5, 1865. Captured on the South Side Railroad on April 2, 1865, and confined at Hart's Island, New York Harbor, until released after taking the Oath of Allegiance on June 14, 1865. Admitted to U.S.A. Transit Hospital, New York City, June 26, 1865, with "chronic diarrhoea" and was transferred to DeCamp General Hospital, Davids Island, New York Harbor, June 30, 1865. Released at that place after again taking the Oath of Allegiance on July 22, 1865.

AUTRY, GEORGE W., Musician
Born in Sampson County and was by occupation a farmer prior to enlisting in Cumberland County at age 17, August 26, 1863, for the war. Mustered in as Private. Appointed Musician on January 1, 1864. Died in Post Hospital, Fayetteville Arsenal and Armory, March 6, 1864, of "cerebritis."

BAGGOTT, WILLIAM, Private
Resided in Sampson County and enlisted in Cumberland County, September 25, 1863, for the war. Present or accounted for on company muster rolls through December, 1864. Captured near Fayetteville on March 7, 1865, and confined at Point Lookout, Maryland, until released after taking the Oath of Allegiance on June 24, 1865.

BAKER, EVANDER, Private
Enlisted in Cumberland County, July 3, 1863, for the war. Present or accounted for on company muster rolls until reported on the November-December, 1864, roll as "absent sick in Smithville Hospital." Died in hospital at Raleigh on February 3, 1865, of "febris intermittens."

BARFIELD, STEPHEN, Private
Enlisted in Cumberland County, October 6, 1863, for the war. Discharged December 12, 1863.

BLUE, JOHN, Private
Born in Cumberland County and was by occupation a farmer prior to enlisting in Cumberland County at age 17, August 8, 1863, for the war. Present or accounted for through December, 1864.

BOONE, ABSALOM CHESTNUTT, Private
Born in Sampson County and was by occupation a farmer prior to enlisting in Cumberland County

at age 17, August 10, 1863, for the war. Present or accounted for through December, 1864.

BOWLES, WILLIAM ALEXANDER, Private
Transferred from Company C of this battalion in September-October, 1863. Present or accounted for through December, 1864.

BRADSHAW, CHARLES F., Private
Enlisted in Cumberland County, November 15, 1863, for the war. Present or accounted for on company muster rolls through December, 1864. Admitted to hospital at Raleigh on March 20, 1865, with "febris intermitt. tert." and was returned to duty on April 7, 1865.

BRADSHAW, JOHN P., Private
Enlisted in Cumberland County, November 15, 1863, for the war. Mustered in as Private. Appointed Sergeant in May-June, 1864, but reduced to ranks July 21, 1864. Present or accounted for on company muster rolls through December, 1864. Admitted to hospital at Wilmington, January 23, 1865, with "pleurodynia" and was returned to duty January 28, 1865. Paroled at Greensboro on May 15, 1865.

BRAY, THOMAS B., Private
Enlisted in Cumberland County, October 14, 1863, for the war. Present or accounted for through December, 1864. Paroled at Greensboro on May 17, 1865.

BRAY, WILLIAM, Private
Enlisted in Cumberland County, October 14, 1863, for the war. Present or accounted for through December, 1864. Paroled at Greensboro on May 17, 1865.

BROWN, DANIEL, 1st Sergeant
Transferred from Company A of this battalion upon his appointment as 1st Sergeant in this company, November 1, 1863. Present or accounted for until admitted to hospital at Fayetteville on July 27, 1864. Present or accounted for on hospital muster rolls through February, 1865.

BUNCE, HARVEY, Private
Enlisted in Cumberland County, September 25, 1863, for the war. Present or accounted for on company muster rolls until November-December, 1864, when he is reported with the remark: "Deserted. Dropped December 1, 1864, for absence without leave."

BURKE, QUINTON R., Private
Born in Chatham County and was by occupation a farmer prior to enlisting in Cumberland County at age 17, July 8, 1863, for the war. Present or accounted for through December, 1864.

BURKETT, HENRY, Private
Transferred from Company E of this battalion March-April, 1864. Present or accounted for until admitted to hospital at Fayetteville on October 16, 1864. Appears as present on muster rolls of that hospital dated February 21, 1865, and February 28, 1865.

CAMERON, JOHN B., Private
Born in Harnett County where he resided as a farmer prior to enlisting in Cumberland County at age 17, June 13, 1863, for the war. Present or

accounted for on company muster rolls through December, 1864. Admitted to hospital at Raleigh on March 20, 1865, with "febris intermitt. quot." and was returned to duty April 7, 1865.

CAVENESS, LORENZO D., Sergeant
Born in Harnett County and was by occupation a farmer prior to enlisting in Cumberland County at age 46, July 23, 1863, for the war. Mustered in as Private. Appointed Corporal on February 1, 1864, and promoted to Sergeant in May-August, 1864. Present or accounted for through December, 1864.

CLARK, JAMES M., Private
Attached to this company from Company B, 13th Battalion N.C. Light Artillery, November-December, 1863.

COLE, JOHN D., Private
Born in Moore County and was by occupation a farmer prior to enlisting in Cumberland County at age 17, August 23, 1863, for the war. Present or accounted for until admitted to hospital at Fayetteville on January 5, 1865. Reported as present on hospital muster rolls dated February 21, 1865, and February 28, 1865.

COOPER, ERASTUS, Private
Born in Duplin County and was by occupation a farmer prior to enlisting in Cumberland County at age 17, July 10, 1863, for the war. Transferred to Company F of this battalion on January 1, 1864, but was returned to this company on March 30, 1864, "having failed to procure a horse." Present or accounted for through December, 1864.

COVINGTON, ELI W., Private
Enlisted in Cumberland County, January 22, 1864, for the war. Present or accounted for on company muster rolls through December, 1864. Admitted to hospital at Raleigh on March 15, 1865, with "diarrhoea acute" and was returned to duty March 24, 1865.

CRUMPLER, WILLIAM E., Private
Born in Sampson County and was by occupation a farmer prior to enlisting in Cumberland County at age 17, July 23, 1863, for the war. Present or accounted for until reported on the March-April, 1864, muster roll as being "in confinement awaiting trial." No further records.

CULBRETH, BLACKMAN H., Private
Enlisted in Cumberland County, October 2, 1863, for the war. Present or accounted for until transferred to Company F of this battalion on January 1, 1864.

CUMMINGS, WILLIAM, Private
Enlisted in Cumberland County, September 26, 1863, for the war. Present or accounted for on company muster rolls through December, 1864. Admitted to hospital at Wilmington on February 7, 1865, with "pernio" and was returned to duty on February 13, 1865.

CURRIE, ANGUS M., Corporal
Enlisted in Cumberland County, October 14, 1863, for the war. Mustered in as Private. Appointed Corporal on November 12, 1864. Present or accounted for through December, 1864.

DEAL, BITHONE H., Private
Enlisted in New Hanover County, October 6, 1864, for the war. Present or accounted for through December, 1864.

DUNCAN, HENRY J., Private
Born in Sampson County and was by occupation a farmer prior to enlisting in Cumberland County at age 17, July 16, 1863, for the war. Present or accounted for on company muster rolls through December, 1864, when he is reported as "absent in Smithville hospital."

DUNCAN, JOSEPH D., Private
Enlisted in New Hanover County, September 28, 1864, for the war. Present or accounted for through December, 1864.

EMERSON, ISAAC M., Private
Enlisted in Cumberland County, June 8, 1864, for the war. Present or accounted for through December, 1864.

EMMERSON, MARION F., Private
Born in Chatham County and was by occupation a farmer prior to enlisting in Cumberland County at age 17, August 17, 1863, for the war. Present or accounted for through December, 1864.

EMMERSON, WILLIAM H., Corporal
Enlisted in Cumberland County, October 14, 1863, for the war. Mustered in as Private. Appointed Corporal in May-August, 1864. Present or accounted for on company muster rolls through December, 1864. Admitted to hospital at Wilmington on February 7, 1865, with "febris remittens biliosa" and was returned to duty February 13, 1865.

EWING, THOMAS M., Corporal
Born in Richmond County and was by occupation a farmer prior to enlisting in Cumberland County at age 17, July 4, 1863, for the war. Mustered in as Private and appointed Corporal on September 1, 1863. Present or accounted for until transferred to Company F of this battalion January 1, 1864.

EZZELL, DAVID, Private
Enlisted in Brunswick County, November 10, 1864, for the war. Present or accounted for through December, 1864.

EZZELL, MATTHEW JAMES, Private
Born in Sampson County and was by occupation a farmer prior to enlisting in Cumberland County at age 17, August 10, 1863, for the war. Present or accounted for through December, 1864.

FISHER, JAMES G., Private
Born in Cumberland County and was by occupation a farmer prior to enlisting in that county at age 17, June 26, 1863, for the war. Present or accounted for through December, 1864.

FISHER, JOSEPH G., Private
Enlisted in Cumberland County, April 18, 1864, for the war. Present or accounted for through December, 1864.

GARRIS, ALBERT C., Sergeant
Born in Duplin County and was by occupation a

farmer prior to enlisting in Cumberland County at age 17, August 10, 1863, for the war. Mustered in as Private. Appointed Sergeant on September 1, 1863. Present or accounted for through December, 1864.

GRICE, WILLIAM D., Private
Transferred from Company D, 10th Regiment N.C. State Troops (1st Regiment N.C. Artillery), November 5, 1864. Present or accounted for on company muster rolls through December, 1864. Admitted to hospital at Wilmington on January 23, 1865, and was returned to duty on February 1, 1865. Captured at Owensville, N.C., March 16, 1865, and was forwarded to Washington, D.C., where he took the Oath of Allegiance and was "furnished transportation to Wilmington, N.C." on April 5, 1865. Admitted to U.S.A. Transit Hospital, New York City, as a refugee, April 11, 1865, and was transferred to Decamp General Hospital, Davids Island, New York Harbor, May 3, 1865. Released at that hospital after again taking the Oath of Allegiance on June 21, 1865.

GUNTER, NAPOLEON B., Private
Enlisted in Cumberland County, April 1, 1864, for the war. Present or accounted for through December, 1864.

HALL, CHARLES H., Sergeant
Born in Sampson County and was by occupation a farmer prior to enlisting in Cumberland County at age 17, June 17, 1863, for the war. Mustered in as Private and appointed Sergeant on September 1, 1863. Present or accounted for through December, 1864.

HALL, GASTON, Private
Enlisted in Cumberland County, September 26, 1863, for the war. Discharged October 31, 1863.

HALL, JOHN R., Private
Enlisted in Cumberland County, October 24, 1863, for the war. Present or accounted for through December, 1864.

HALL, LIVINGSTON, Private
Transferred from Company D, 10th Regiment N.C. State Troops (1st Regiment N.C. Artillery), November 6, 1864. Present or accounted for on company muster rolls through December, 1864. Captured at Fayetteville on March 18, 1865, and confined at Hart's Island, New York Harbor, until released after taking the Oath of Allegiance on June 19, 1865.

HALL, WILEY, Private
Enlisted in Cumberland County, September 4, 1863, for the war. Present or accounted for on company muster rolls through December, 1864, when he was reported as "detailed as garrison woodcutter."

HANCOCK, WILLIAM H., Private
Enlisted in Cumberland County, November 11, 1863, for the war. Present or accounted for through December, 1864.

HATCH, ORREN, Private
Born in Chatham County and was by occupation a farmer prior to enlisting in Cumberland County at age 17, June 23, 1863, for the war. Present or

accounted for through December, 1864, when he was reported as "absent sick in Smithville hospital."

HERRING, ERASTUS, Private
Enlisted in Cumberland County, October 10, 1863, for the war. Present or accounted for until reported on the November-December, 1864, muster roll with the remark: "Deserted. Dropped November 1, 1864, for absence without leave."

HERRINGTON, JOHN E., Private
Born in Moore County and was by occupation a farmer prior to enlisting in Cumberland County at age 17, August 25, 1863, for the war. Present or accounted for through December, 1864.

HILLIARD, DANIEL C., Private
Born in Chatham County and was by occupation a farmer prior to enlisting in Cumblerland County at age 17, June 23, 1863, for the war. Present or accounted for through December, 1864.

HODGES, AMOS C., Private
Born in Cumberland County and was by occupation a farmer prior to enlisting in that county at age 17, June 15, 1863, for the war. Present or accounted for through December, 1864.

HOLLAND, BLUEMAN, Private
Born in Sampson County where he resided as a farmer prior to enlisting in Cumberland County at age 17, July 10, 1863, for the war. Present or accounted for on company muster rolls through December, 1864. Captured in Sampson County on March 18, 1865, and confined at Hart's Island, New York Harbor, until released after taking the Oath of Allegiance on June 18, 1865.

HOLLAND, NICHOLAS, Private
Enlisted in Cumberland County, September 24, 1863, for the war. Present or accounted for through December, 1864.

HOLT, JOHN S., Private
Enlisted in Cumberland County, September 19, 1863, for the war. Present or accounted for through December, 1864.

HOWELL, JAMES K., Private
Born in Cumberland County and was by occupation a farmer prior to enlisting in that county at age 17, August 29, 1863. Present or accounted for until reported on the March-April, 1864, muster roll as being "in confinement awaiting trial." No further records.

JOHNSON, CHARLES K., Private
Transferred from Company D, 10th Regiment N.C. State Troops (1st Regiment N.C. Artillery) November 5, 1864. Present or accounted for through December, 1864.

JOHNSON, CHARLES M., Private
Enlisted in Cumberland County, September 24, 1863, for the war. Present or accounted for through December, 1864.

JOHNSON, DANIEL J., Private
Transferred from Company D, 10th Regiment N.C. State Troops (1st Regiment N.C. Artillery), November 5, 1864. Present or accounted for through December, 1864.

JOHNSON, JOSIAH JOSEPH, Private
Enlisted in Cumberland County, February 1, 1864, for the war. Present or accounted for through December, 1864.

JOHNSON, WILLIAM D., Private
Born in Cumberland County and was by occupation a farmer prior to enlisting in that county at age 17, June 18, 1863, for the war. Died at Fayetteville Arsenal and Armory on February 13, 1864.

KELLY, MYROVER, Private
Born in Moore County and was by occupation a farmer prior to enlisting in Cumberland County at age 17, July 20, 1863, for the war. Present or accounted for until transferred to Company F of this battalion on January 1, 1864.

LAMBERT, CHASLEY M., Private
Born in Randolph County and was by occupation a farmer prior to enlisting in Cumberland County at age 17, August 24, 1863, for the war. Present or accounted for on company muster rolls through December, 1864. Admitted to hospital at Wilmington on January 23, 1865, with "feb. remitt. bil." Paroled at Greensboro on May 18, 1865.

LAMBERT, GEORGE H., Private
Born in Randolph County and was by occupation a farmer prior to enlisting in Cumberland County at age 17, August 24, 1863, for the war. Present or accounted for on company muster rolls through December, 1864. Admitted to hospital at Raleigh on March 29, 1865, with "febris intermitt. tert." and was transferred to another hospital on March 22, 1865.

LAURENCE, SION H., Private
Born in Chatham County and was by occupation a farmer prior to enlisting in Cumberland County at age 17, August 5, 1863, for the war. Present or accounted for until transferred to Company F of this battalion on January 1, 1864.

LEDBETTER, ABNER, Private
Enlisted in Cumberland County, June 1, 1864, for the war. Present or accounted for until reported on the November-December, 1864, muster roll with the remark: "Deserted. Dropped November 1. Taken up November 17. Dropped again December 17 for absence without leave."

LEIPPO, WILLIAM D., Private
Born in Marion County, South Carolina, and was by occupation a farmer prior to enlisting in Cumberland County at age 17, August 15, 1863, for the war. Present or accounted for through December, 1864.

LEWIS, HENRY H., Private
Born in Sampson County and was by occupation a farmer prior to enlisting in Cumberland County at age 17, August 10, 1863, for the war. Present or accounted for through December, 1864.

LEWIS, ROBERT L., Private
Born in Sampson County and was by occupation a farmer prior to enlisting in Cumberland County at age 17, August 10, 1863, for the war. Mustered in as Private and appointed Corporal

on September 1, 1863. Reduced to ranks in May-August, 1864. Present or accounted for through December, 1864, when he was reported as "absent sick in Smithville hospital."

McARTAN, COLIN, Private
Born in Scotland and was by occupation a farmer prior to enlisting in Cumberland County at age 17, August 10, 1863, for the war. Mustered in as Private and appointed Corporal on April 13, 1864. Reduced to ranks in May-August, 1864. Present or accounted for on company muster rolls through December, 1864. Admitted to a hospital at Wilmington on January 23, 1865, with "diarrhoea acute" and was transferred to a hospital at Goldsboro on February 12, 1865.

McARTHUR, DANIEL, Private
Born in Cumberland County and was by occupation a farmer prior to enlisting in that county at age 46, August 17, 1863, for the war. Present or accounted for on company muster rolls through March-April, 1864, when he was reported as present "in confinement awaiting trial."

McAULEY, JAMES R., Private
Enlisted in Cumberland County, October 24, 1863, for the war. Present or accounted for through December, 1864.

McDIARMID, JOSEPH A., Private
Born in Robeson County and was by occupation a student prior to enlisting in Cumberland County at age 17, June 20, 1863, for the war. Mustered in as Private and appointed Corporal on September 1, 1863. Reduced to ranks "per sentence of General Court Martial" on December 1, 1863. Present or accounted for until retired to the Invalid Corps on June 14, 1864.

McDONALD, JAMES K., Private
Born in Cumberland County and was by occupation a farmer prior to enlisting in that county at age 17, June 11, 1863, for the war. Mustered in as Private and appointed Corporal on September 1, 1863. Promoted to Sergeant on April 13, 1864. Company muster roll for July-August, 1864, carries the remark: "Deserted July 22. Reduced to ranks from Sergeant July 21." November-December, 1864, muster roll reports that he "joined from desertion."

McDUGALD, EVANDER, Private
Enlisted in Cumberland County, January 15, 1864, for the war. Present or accounted for on company muster rolls through December, 1864, when he is reported as "absent at Fayetteville hospital sick."

McGREGOR, MALCOLM J., Private
Enlisted in Cumberland County, April 25, 1864, for the war. Admitted to hospital at Wilmington on August 25, 1864, with "febris remittens biliosa" and was returned to duty October 11, 1864. Present or accounted for through December, 1864.

McGUGAN, DANIEL B., Corporal
Born in Cumberland County and was by occupation a farmer prior to enlisting in that county at age 17, June 27, 1863, for the war. Mustered in

as Private and appointed Corporal in May-August, 1864. Present or accounted for through December, 1864.

McKENZIE, JAMES M., Private
Born in Sampson County and was by occupation a farmer prior to enlisting in Cumberland County at age 17, July 10, 1863, for the war. Present or accounted for through December, 1864.

McKETHAN, JOHN G., Private
Born in Cumberland County and was by occupation a blacksmith prior to enlisting in that county at age 17, August 24, 1863, for the war. Present or accounted for through December, 1864.

McKINNAN, HECTOR T., Private
Enlisted in Cumberland County, October 13, 1863, for the war. Present or accounted for through December, 1864.

McLEAN, WILLIAM A., Private
Born in Cumberland County and was by occupation a farmer prior to enlisting in that county at age 17, June 26, 1863, for the war. Present or accounted for until reported on the March-April, 1864, muster roll as being "present in confinement awaiting trial." No further records.

McLEMORE, HAYWOOD, Private
Born in Sampson County and was by occupation a laborer prior to enlisting in Cumberland County at age 17, August 17, 1863, for the war. Present or accounted for on company muster rolls through December, 1864. Admitted to hospital at Wilmington on February 18, 1865, and was transferred to another hospital February 20, 1865.

McLEMORE, JAMES C., Private
Born in Bladen County and was by occupation a farmer prior to enlisting in Cumberland County at age 25, August 10, 1863, for the war. Present or accounted for until reported on the January-February, 1864, muster roll as being present "in confinement awaiting trial on charge of desertion." Company muster rolls state that he was "absent in confinement under sentence of General Court Martial at Bald Head, N.C.," from March-April, 1864, through December, 1864.

McMILLAN, NEILL, Private
Enlisted in Cumberland County, September 24, 1863, for the war. Present or accounted for through December, 1864.

McNEILL, HECTOR L., Private
Born in Cumberland County and was by occupation a blacksmith prior to enlisting in that county at age 17, August 11, 1863, for the war. Present or accounted for on company muster rolls through December, 1864. Admitted to hospital at Wilmington on January 23, 1865, with "diarrhoea acute" and was returned to duty January 27, 1865.

MALONE, JAMES, Private
Born in Moore County and was by occupation a farmer prior to enlisting in Cumberland County at age 17, August 3, 1863, for the war. Present or accounted for on company muster rolls through December, 1864. Died in hospital at High Point on March 29, 1865, of "pneumonia."

MARSH, JAMES, Sergeant
Born in Cumberland County and was by occupa-

tion a farmer prior to enlisting in that county at age 46, June 27, 1863, for the war. Mustered in as Private and appointed Sergeant on September 1, 1863. Attached to Company G of this battalion November-December, 1864.

MASHBURN, THOMAS, Private
Born in Chatham County and was by occupation a farmer prior to enlisting in Cumberland County at age 17, June 23, 1863, for the war. Present or accounted for through December, 1864.

MASON, JAMES C., Private
Enlisted in Cumberland County, January 22, 1864, for the war. Present or accounted for on company muster rolls through December, 1864. Admitted to hospital at Wilmington on January 21, 1865, with "rheumatism acute" and was transferred to hospital at Goldsboro on January 22, 1865.

MATTHEWS, BENJAMIN, Private
Born in Harnett County and was by occupation a farmer prior to enlisting in Cumberland County at age 17, July 13, 1863, for the war. Present or accounted for through December, 1864.

MOBLY, CHARLES M., Private
Born in Chatham County and was by occupation a farmer prior to enlisting in Cumberland County at age 17, June 26, 1863, for the war. Present or accounted for through December, 1864.

MOFFITT, JOHN H., Private
Enlisted in Cumberland County, October 6, 1863, for the war. Died in hospital at Wilmington on August 13, 1864.

MOFFITT, RANDOLPH, Private
Enlisted in Cumberland County, December 9, 1863, for the war. Present or accounted for through April, 1864. No further records.

MOORE, WILLIAM T., Private
Enlisted in Cumberland County, September 1, 1863, for the war. Present or accounted for through December, 1864.

MORGAN, JAMES A., Private
Born in Harnett County and was by occupation a farmer prior to enlisting in Cumberland County at age 17, July 16, 1863, for the war. Present or accounted for through December, 1864.

MORLEY, DANIEL J., Private
Enlisted in Cumberland County, January 22, 1864, for the war. Present or accounted for through December, 1864.

MORLEY, JOHN C., Private
Enlisted in Cumberland County, January 22, 1864, for the war. Present or accounted for through December, 1864.

MORRIS, DANIEL A., Private
Born in Moore County and was by occupation a farmer prior to enlisting in Cumberland County at age 17, August 10, 1863, for the war. Present or accounted for through December, 1864.

ODOM, JAMES W., Private
Enlisted in Cumberland County, September 5, 1863. Present or accounted for until transferred to Company F of this battalion on January 1, 1864.

PATE, ALEXANDER, Private

Born in Cumberland County and was by occupation a farmer prior to enlisting in that county at age 17, June 13, 1863, for the war. Present or accounted for through December, 1864.

PATE, JAMES, Private

Enlisted in Brunswick County, November 22, 1864, for the war. Present or accounted for through December, 1864.

PHILLIPS, ATLAS G., Private

Enlisted in Cumberland County, December 7, 1864, for the war. Present or accounted for through December 31, 1864. Admitted to hospital at Raleigh on March 20, 1865, with "abscessus" and was transferred to another hospital on March 22, 1865.

PHILLIPS, BENJAMIN Y., Private

Born in Chatham County and was by occupation a farmer prior to enlisting in Cumberland County at age 17, June 28, 1863, for the war. Present or accounted for through December, 1864.

PICKETT, WINFIELD, Private

Born in Cumberland County and was by occupation a weaver prior to enlisting in that county at age 17, July 31, 1863, for the war. Died in hospital at Fayetteville on April 15, 1864, of "empyema."

PRIEST, ALLEN, Private

Enlisted in Cumberland County, April 18, 1864, for the war. Present or accounted for through December, 1864.

RAY, GILBERT G., Private

Enlisted in Cumberland County, April 18, 1864, for the war. Present or accounted for until reported on the November-December, 1864, muster roll as absent sick in hospital at Fayetteville.

ROBINSON, ABNER, Corporal

Born in Sampson County and was by occupation a farmer prior to enlisting in Cumberland County at age 17, July 16, 1863, for the war. Mustered in as Private and appointed Corporal on February 1, 1864. Present or accounted for on company muster rolls through December, 1864. Admitted to hospital at Greensboro in April, 1865.

ROE, CHARLES A., Musician

Enlisted in Cumberland County, January 26, 1864, for the war. Mustered in as Private and appointed Musician on July 27, 1864. Present or accounted for on company muster rolls through November-December, 1864, when he was reported as "detailed at Fort Caswell."

SIMMONDS, MILES C., Private

Born in Sampson County and was by occupation a farmer prior to enlisting in Cumberland County at age 17, July 17, 1863, for the war. Present or accounted for on company muster rolls through November-December, 1864, when he was reported with the remark: "Deserted. Dropped December 1, 1864, absence without leave."

SLOAN, WILLIAM T., Private

Enlisted in Cumberland County, September 10, 1863, for the war. Present or accounted for through December, 1864.

SMITH, WHITSON, Private

Born in Moore County and was by occupation a farmer prior to enlisting in Cumberland County at age 17, June 10, 1863, for the war. Present or accounted for through December, 1864.

SMITH, WILLIAM, Private

Born in Cumberland County and was by occupation a farmer prior to enlisting in that county at age 17, June 10, 1863, for the war. Present or accounted for through December, 1864.

SMITH, WILLIAM J., Private

Born in Cumberland County and was by occupation a farmer prior to enlisting in that county at age 17, June 7, 1863, for the war. Mustered in as Private and appointed Corporal on September 1, 1863. Reduced to ranks in May-August, 1864. Present or accounted for through December, 1864.

STARLING, SOTHEY J., Private

Enlisted in Cumberland County, September 25, 1863, for the war. Present or accounted for through December, 1864.

STEDMAN, DAVID M., Private

Enlisted in Cumberland County, March 15, 1864, for the war. Present or accounted for through December, 1864.

STEWART, MURDOCK, Private

Born in Moore County and was by occupation a farmer prior to enlisting in Cumberland County at age 17, July 20, 1863, for the war. Died at Fayetteville Arsenal and Armory on October 11, 1863.

STRAUGHON, GEORGE W., Private

Enlisted in Cumberland County, November 5, 1863, for the war. Present or accounted for through April, 1864. No further records.

SUGGS, LEWIS O., Private

Enlisted in Cumberland County, October 7, 1863, for the war. Present or accounted for until reported on the November-December, 1864, muster roll with the remark: "Deserted. Dropped December 1, 1864, for absence without leave."

TALLY, GEORGE M. D., Private

Born in Chatham County and was by occupation a farmer prior to enlisting in Cumberland County at age 17, August 4, 1863, for the war. Mustered in as Private and appointed Corporal in May-August, 1864. Reduced to ranks on August 24, 1864. Present or accounted for through December, 1864. Admitted to hospital at Fayetteville on February 10, 1865, and is reported as present on hospital muster rolls through February 28, 1865.

TEW, LOUDIN, Private

Enlisted in Cumberland County, September 19, 1863, for the war. Present or accounted for through December, 1864.

THOMAS, JOHN B., Private

Enlisted in Cumberland County, December 19, 1863, for the war. Present or accounted for on company muster rolls until November-December, 1864, when he was reported with the remark: "Deserted. Dropped December 1, 1864, for absence without leave."

THOMAS, SACKFIELD F., Private

Born in Moore County and was by occupation a

farmer prior to enlisting in Cumberland County at age 17, July 6, 1863, for the war. Present or accounted for through December, 1864.

THOMPSON, WILLIAM M., Private
Enlisted in Cumberland County, February 11, 1864, for the war. Present or accounted for through December, 1864.

TURNER, CICERO, Musician
Enlisted in Cumberland County, December 12, 1863, for the war. Mustered in as Musician. Present or accounted for through December, 1864.

TYSON, AARON, Private
Born in Cumberland County and was by occupation a farmer prior to enlisting in that county at age 17, August 20, 1863, for the war. Reported on company muster rolls as absent sick from March-April, 1864, through December, 1864.

USHER, EDWIN T., Sergeant
Born in Duplin County and was by occupation a student prior to enlisting in Cumberland County at age 17, July 29, 1863, for the war. Mustered in as Private and appointed Sergeant on September 1, 1863. Present or accounted for until transferred to Company F of this battalion on March 1, 1864.

WARD, JAMES, Private
Enlisted in Cumberland County, September 5, 1863, for the war. Deserted September, 1863, and was arrested and returned October 10, 1863. Reported as "present in confinement awaiting trial on charge of desertion" from that date until March-April, 1864, when he was reported with the remark: "Deserted from Fayetteville Arsenal and Armory April 23, 1864."

WATSON, DAVID MAC, Private
Born in Moore County and was by occupation a farmer prior to enlisting in Cumberland County at age 17, July 13, 1863, for the war. Present or accounted for until transferred to Company F of this battalion on January 1, 1864.

WILLIAMS, BLACKMAN, Private
Born in Sampson County and was by occupation a farmer prior to enlisting in Cumberland County at age 17, August 20, 1863, for the war. Present or accounted for on company muster rolls through November-December, 1864, when he was reported as absent sick at Smithville hospital.

WILLIAMS, JAMES D., Private
Born in Cumberland County and was by occupation a farmer prior to enlisting in Cumberland County at age 17, August 26, 1863, for the war. Present or accounted for through December, 1864.

WOMACK, ROMALUS M., Private
Enlisted in Cumberland County, October 30, 1863, for the war. Present or accounted for through December, 1864.

COMPANY C

This company was organized at Fayetteville, Cumberland County, where it was mustered into Confederate States service on September 2, 1863. Composed exclusively of employees of the Fayetteville Arsenal and Armory, the company was organ-ized for local defense and special service and was assigned to the battalion as Company C. Since it functioned as part of the battalion, its history is recorded as a part of the battalion history.

The information contained in the following roster of the company was compiled principally from company muster rolls which covered the period from September 2, 1863 (the date of the muster-in roll), through August, 1864, and also November-December, 1864. No company muster rolls were found for September-October, 1864, or for the period after December, 1864. Although there are no Roll of Honor records for this company, useful information was obtained from receipt rolls, prisoner of war records, medical records, and other primary records, supplemented by state pension applications, United Daughters of the Confederacy records, and postwar rosters and histories.

OFFICERS
CAPTAIN

DECKER, GEORGE W.
Enlisted in Cumberland County at age 32, September 2, 1863, for the war. Appointed Captain to rank from date of enlistment. Present or accounted for through December, 1864.

LIEUTENANTS

BANKS, CHARLES R., 1st Lieutenant
Enlisted in Cumberland County at age 26, September 2, 1863, for the war. Appointed 1st Lieutenant to rank from date of enlistment. Present or accounted for through December, 1864.

GARRISON, ALONZO, 2nd Lieutenant
Enlisted in Cumberland County at age 29, September 2, 1863, for the war. Appointed 2nd Lieutenant to rank from date of enlistment. Present or accounted for through December, 1864.

ROBERTS, CHARLES E., 2nd Lieutenant
Enlisted in Cumberland County at age 27, September 2, 1863, for the war. Appointed 2nd Lieutenant to rank from date of enlistment. Present or accounted for through December, 1864.

NONCOMMISSIONED OFFICERS AND PRIVATES

ASHE, WILLIAM C., Private
Enlisted in Cumberland County at age 17, June 21, 1864, for the war. Present or accounted for through December, 1864.

BECKERDITE, AMOS F., Private
Enlisted in Cumberland County at age 29, September 2, 1863, for the war. Present or accounted for through December, 1864.

BOSWELL, THOMAS, Private
Enlisted in Cumberland County at age 25, September 2, 1863, for the war. Present or accounted for through December, 1864.

BOWLES, WILLIAM ALEXANDER, Private
Enlisted in Cumberland County at age 17, September 2, 1863, for the war. Company muster roll for September 2-October 31, 1863, reported that

he was "transferred. Joined Company B, Arsenal and Armory Battalion by enlistment."

BRANCH, JORDAN W., Private
Enlisted in Cumberland County at age 32, September 2, 1863, for the war. Present or accounted for through December, 1864.

BROOKS, RICHARD, Private
Enlisted in Cumberland County at age 28, September 2, 1863, for the war. Present or accounted for through December, 1864.

BROWN, JAMES M., Laborer
Enlisted April 23, 1864, for the war. Present or accounted for on company muster rolls through August, 1864. Later served in Company A of this battalion.

BROWN, JOHN D., Private
Enlisted in Cumberland County at age 18, September 2, 1863, for the war. Present or accounted for through December, 1864.

BRYANT, IRVIN, Private
Enlisted in Cumberland County at age 20, September 2, 1863, for the war. Present or accounted for through December, 1864.

BURCH, ANDERSON M., Private
Enlisted in Cumberland County at age 37, September 2, 1863, for the war. Present or accounted for through December, 1864.

BURKART, JEROME D., Private
Enlisted January-February, 1864, for the war, having previously served in Company E of this battalion. Present or accounted for through December, 1864.

BUTTLER, WILLIAM, Private
Enlisted in Cumberland County at age 37, September 2, 1863, for the war. Present or accounted for through December, 1864.

CALHOUN, JAMES A., Private
Enlisted in Cumberland County at age 26, September 2, 1863, for the war. Present or accounted for through December, 1864.

CAMPBELL, HENRY S., Private
Enlisted in Cumberland County at age 36, September 2, 1863, for the war. Present or accounted for through December, 1864.

CLASPY, GEORGE W., Sergeant
Enlisted in Cumberland County at age 18, September 2, 1863, for the war. Mustered in as Corporal. Appointed Sergeant on May 7, 1864. Present or accounted for through December, 1864.

CLOWE, CHARLES R., Sergeant
Enlisted in Cumberland County at age 31, September 2, 1863, for the war. Mustered in as Sergeant. Present or accounted for through December, 1864.

CLOWE, JOHN H., Corporal
Enlisted in Cumberland County at age 19, September 2, 1863, for the war. Mustered in as Private and appointed Corporal on April 27, 1864. Present or accounted for through December, 1864.

CONSIDINE, MICHAEL, Sergeant
Enlisted in Cumberland County at age 26, September 2, 1863, for the war. Mustered in as

Corporal and appointed Sergeant on May 7, 1864. Present or accounted for through December, 1864.

CORD, JOHN T., Private
Enlisted in Cumberland County at age 26, September 2, 1863, for the war. Present or accounted for through December, 1864, when he is reported with the remark: "Light duty conscript."

CURTIS, HENDERSON W., Private
Enlisted in Cumberland County at age 31, September 2, 1863, for the war. Reported as absent without leave on the company muster roll for September 2-October 31, 1863. Subsequent muster rolls state that he deserted but do not give date.

DAVIS, JESSE, Private
Enlisted in Cumberland County at age 18, September 2, 1863, for the war. Mustered in as Corporal and reduced to ranks on May 7, 1864. Present or accounted for through December, 1864.

DENNING, GURDON S., Private
Enlisted in Cumberland County at age 41, September 2, 1863, for the war. Present or accounted for through December, 1864.

DeROSSET, THOMAS C., Private
Enlisted in Cumberland County at age 18, September 2, 1863, for the war. Present or accounted for until transferred to Company A of this battalion May 1, 1864.

FAIRCLOTH, ALEX, Private
Enlisted in Cumberland County at age 17, April 11, 1864, for the war. Present or accounted for through August, 1864. No further records.

FAIRCLOTH, SAMUEL, Private
Enlisted in Cumberland County at age 38, September 2, 1863, for the war. Present or accounted for through August, 1864. No further records.

FERRINGTON, JOHN, Private
Enlisted in Cumberland County at age 45, September 2, 1863, for the war. Present or accounted for through December, 1864.

FOUST, GEORGE M., Private
Enlisted in Cumberland County at age 37, October 7, 1863, for the war. Discharged on December 11, 1863.

FRAZIER, ALBERT, Private
Enlisted in Cumberland County at age 33, September 2, 1863, for the war. Present or accounted for through December, 1864.

GALES, SOLOMON, Private
Enlisted in Cumberland County at age 33, September 2, 1863, for the war. Present or accounted for through December, 1864.

GIERSH, ALEX E., Private
Enlisted in Cumberland County at age 48, April 23, 1864, for the war. Present or accounted for until transferred to Company G of this battalion September-December, 1864.

GRAHAM, JESSE, Private
Enlisted in Cumberland County at age 38, September 2, 1863, for the war. Present or accounted for through December, 1864.

HANKS, WILLIAM H., Sergeant
Enlisted in Cumberland County at age 26, Sep-

tember 2, 1863, for the war. Mustered in as Sergeant. Present or accounted for until promoted to Ensign and transferred to the Field and Staff of this battalion in March-April, 1864.

HARRIS, PASCHAL J., Private
Enlisted in Cumberland County at age 32, September 2, 1863, for the war. Present or accounted for through December, 1864.

HENDRICKS, ALEXANDER J., Private
Enlisted in Cumberland County at age 14, March 12, 1864, for the war. Discharged and "turned over to the enrolling officer" in July-August, 1864.

HEWITT, ATHO, Private
Enlisted in Cumberland County at age 30, September 2, 1863, for the war. Present or accounted for through December, 1864.

HEWITT, JOHN W., Private
Enlisted in Cumberland County at age 26, September 2, 1863, for the war. Present or accounted for through December, 1864.

HOLLAND, HENRY C., Private
Enlisted in Cumberland County at age 21, September 2, 1863, for the war. Present or accounted for until his death on August 16, 1864, at Post Hospital, Fayetteville Arsenal and Armory.

IVEY, RICHARD, Private
Enlisted in Cumberland County at age 34, September 2, 1863, for the war. Present or accounted for through December, 1864.

JOHNSON, MATTHEW, Private
Enlisted in Cumberland County at age 25, September 2, 1863, for the war. Present or accounted for through December, 1864.

JOHNSON, ROBERT, Private
Enlisted in Cumberland County at age 36, September 2, 1863, for the war. Present or accounted for through December, 1864.

JOHNSON, WILEY F., Private
Enlisted in Cumberland County at age 19, September 2, 1863, for the war. Discharged on November 23, 1863.

JOHNSTON, BALDWIN, Private
Enlisted in Cumberland County at age 47, April 23, 1864, for the war. Present or accounted for until transferred to Company G of this battalion September-December, 1864.

JONES, DAVID, Private
Enlisted in Cumberland County at age 20, September 2, 1863, for the war. Mustered in as Sergeant. Reduced to ranks on May 7, 1864. Present or accounted for through December, 1864.

JONES, HENRY, Private
Enlisted in Cumberland County at age 31, September 2, 1863, for the war. Present or accounted for until discharged on January 21, 1864.

JONES, NATHAN, Private
Enlisted in Cumberland County at age 41, September 2, 1863, for the war. Present or accounted for through December, 1864, when he was reported as absent.

LEWIS, McLEOD D., Private
Enlisted in Cumberland County at age 26, Sep

tember 2, 1863, for the war. Present or accounted for through December, 1864.

LOCKAMAN, HENDERSON, Private
Enlisted in Cumberland County at age 34, September 2, 1863, for the war. Present or accounted for through December, 1864.

McARTHUR, NEILL A., Private
Enlisted in Cumberland County at age 28, September 2, 1863, for the war. Present or accounted for until transferred to Company G of this battalion in September-October, 1864.

McGILVRAY, EDWARD T., Private
Enlisted in Cumberland County at age 30, September 2, 1863, for the war. Present or accounted for through December, 1864.

McMILLAN, JOHN C., Private
Enlisted in Cumberland County at age 43, September 2, 1863, for the war. Present or accounted for through December, 1864.

McNEILL, JOHN C., Private
Enlisted in Cumberland County at age 36, September 2, 1863, for the war. Present or accounted for through December, 1864.

MARTIN, JOHN N., Private
Enlisted in Cumberland County at age 30, September 2, 1863, for the war. Present or accounted for through December, 1864.

MASON, ALEXANDER, Private
Enlisted in Cumberland County at age 25, September 2, 1863, for the war. Present or accounted for through December, 1864.

MERRICK, JAMES A., Private
Enlisted in Cumberland County at age 36, September 2, 1863, for the war. Present or accounted for through December, 1864.

O'BRIEN, THOMAS, Private
Enlisted in Cumberland County at age 36, September 2, 1863, for the war. Present or accounted for through December, 1864.

PARKER, JAMES, Private
Enlisted in Cumberland County at age 47, September 2, 1863, for the war. Present or accounted for through December, 1864.

POWELL, ISHAM, Private
Enlisted in Cumberland County at age 28, September 2, 1863, for the war. Present or accounted for on company muster rolls through December, 1864. Captured at South River, N.C., March 14, 1865, and took the Oath of Allegiance at Washington, D.C., April 5, 1865. Furnished transportation to Wilmington.

POWELL, JAMES, Private
Enlisted in Cumberland County at age 25, September 2, 1863, for the war. Present or accounted for on company muster rolls through December, 1864. Captured at South River, N.C., March 14, 1865, and took the Oath of Allegiance at Washington, D.C., April 5, 1865. Admitted to U.S.A. Transit Hospital, New York City, April 12, 1865, and died at that hospital on April 28, 1865.

POWERS, EDWARD P., 1st Sergeant
Previously served in Company H, 1st Regiment N.C. Infantry (6 months, 1861). Enlisted in this

company on September 2, 1863, for the war. Mustered in as 1st Sergeant. Present or accounted for until appointed Sergeant Major and transferred to the Field and Staff of this battalion on May 7, 1864.

ROBINSON, THOMAS J., Private
Enlisted in Cumberland County at age 35, September 2, 1863, for the war. Present or accounted for through December, 1864.

SCHAARMAN, PHILIP, Private
Enlisted in Cumberland County, September 2, 1863, for the war. Present or accounted for through December, 1864.

SCHILLING, JOHN L., 1st Sergeant
Enlisted in Cumberland County at age 21, September 2, 1863, for the war. Mustered in as Sergeant and appointed 1st Sergeant on May 7, 1864. Present or accounted for through December, 1864.

SELLARS, BRYANT, Private
Enlisted in Cumberland County at age 46, September 2, 1863, for the war. Reported on company muster rolls as absent without leave from the September 2-October 31, 1863, roll until May-June, 1864, when he was discharged.

SHOLAR, JOHN, Corporal
Enlisted in Cumberland County at age 35, September 2, 1863, for the war. Mustered in as Private and appointed Corporal on May 7, 1864. Present or accounted for through December, 1864.

SPONCLER, JACOB F., Sergeant
Enlisted in Cumberland County at age 33, September 2, 1863, for the war. Mustered in as Corporal and appointed Sergeant on April 27, 1864. Present or accounted for through December, 1864.

STEEL, SAMUEL H., Private
Enlisted in Cumberland County at age 45, September 2, 1863, for the war. Present or accounted for through December, 1864.

STRICKLAND, HENRY, Private
Enlisted in Cumberland County at age 35, September 2, 1863, for the war. Present or accounted for until discharged March-April, 1864.

SUNDAY, JOHN L., Private
Enlisted in Cumberland County at age 31, September 2, 1863, for the war. Present or accounted for through December, 1864.

VALENTINE, BENJAMIN S., Private
Enlisted in Cumberland County at age 20, September 2, 1863, for the war. Present or accounted for until discharged November 23, 1863.

WALKER, ALBERT W., Corporal
Enlisted in Cumberland County at age 27, September 2, 1863, for the war. Mustered in as Private and appointed Corporal on May 7, 1864. Present or accounted for through December, 1864.

WATSON, WALTER, Private
Enlisted in Cumberland County at age 31, September 2, 1863, for the war. Present or accounted for until reported as absent on the March-April, 1864, muster roll. Reported absent until July-August, 1864, when he appears with the remark: "Discharged. Englishman. Expiration of contract."

WEST, ARCHIBALD, Private
Enlisted in Cumberland County at age 28, September 2, 1863, for the war. Present or accounted for through December, 1864.

WIDDIFIELD, WILLIAM, Private
Enlisted in Cumberland County at age 26, September 2, 1863, for the war. Present or accounted for through December, 1864.

WINKLER, CHARLES A., Private
Enlisted in Cumberland County at age 23, September 2, 1863, for the war. Present or accounted for through December, 1864.

WOODWARD, WILLIAM J., Private
Enlisted in Cumberland County at age 20, September 2, 1863, for the war. Present or accounted for through December, 1864.

COMPANY D

This company was organized at Fayetteville, Cumberland County, where it was mustered into Confederate States service on September 2, 1863. Composed exclusively of employees of the Fayetteville Arsenal and Armory, the company was organized for local defense and special service and was assigned to the battalion as Company D. Since it functioned as a part of the battalion, its history is recorded as a part of the battalion history.

The information contained in the following roster of the company was compiled principally from company muster rolls which covered the period from September 2, 1863 (the date of the company muster-in roll), through August, 1864, and also November-December, 1864. No company muster rolls were found for September-October, 1864, or for the period after December, 1864. Although there are no Roll of Honor records for this company, useful information was obtained from receipt rolls, prisoner of war records, medical records, and other primary records, supplemented by state pension applications, United Daughters of the Confederacy records, and postwar rosters and histories.

OFFICERS
CAPTAIN

WEMYSS, WILLIAM PROUDFOOT
Enlisted in Cumberland County at age 29, September 2, 1863, for the war. Appointed Captain to rank from date of enlistment. Present or accounted for through December, 1864.

LIEUTENANTS

BRUFF, RICHARD W., 2nd Lieutenant
Enlisted in Cumberland County at age 36, September 2, 1863, for the war. Mustered in as Private and elected 2nd Lieutenant on October 1, 1863. Present or accounted for through December, 1864.

McDUFFIE, ROBERT H., 2nd Lieutenant
Enlisted in Cumberland County at age 27, September 2, 1863, for the war. Appointed 2nd Lieutenant to rank from date of enlistment. Died of disease on September 30, 1863.

McINNIS, MALCOLM, 2nd Lieutenant
Enlisted in Cumberland County at age 31, Sep-

tember 2, 1863, for the war. Appointed 2nd Lieutenant to rank from date of enlistment. Present or accounted for through December, 1864.

WALTON, SAMUEL J., 1st Lieutenant
Enlisted in Cumberland County at age 41, September 2, 1863, for the war. Appointed 1st Lieutenant to rank from date of enlistment. Discharged and turned over to Enrolling Officer on September 30, 1863.

WOODWARD, JAMES F., 1st Lieutenant
Enlisted in Cumberland County at age 27, September 2, 1863, for the war. Mustered in as Sergeant and elected 1st Lieutenant on October 1, 1863. Present or accounted for through December, 1864.

NONCOMMISSIONED OFFICERS AND PRIVATES

ALBRIGHT, JAMES P., Private
Enlisted in Cumberland County, April 11, 1864, for the war. Present or accounted for through December, 1864.

ALBRIGHT, JOHN P., Private
Enlisted in Cumberland County at age 38, April 11, 1864, for the war. Present or accounted for through December, 1864.

BARCLAY, WILLIAM D., Private
Enlisted in Cumberland County at age 43, September 2, 1863, for the war. Present or accounted for through December, 1864.

BARRETT, TRISTRAM S., Private
Enlisted in Cumberland County at age 59, September 2, 1863, for the war. Present or accounted for through December, 1864.

BOLTON, WILLIAM A., Private
Enlisted in Cumberland County at age 17, January 10, 1864, for the war. Present or accounted for until discharged in March-April, 1864.

BRANCH, ROBERT, Private
Enlisted in Cumberland County at age 24, September 2, 1863, for the war. Present or accounted for through December, 1864.

BROWN, JOHN B., Private
Enlisted in Cumberland County at age 46, April 23, 1864, for the war. Present or accounted for until transferred to Company G of this battalion in September-October, 1864.

BRUER, ALSTON, Private
Enlisted in Cumberland County at age 37, September 2, 1863, for the war. Present or accounted for until discharged in January-February, 1864.

BURGESS, ABSALOM C., Private
Enlisted in Cumberland County, April 11, 1864, for the war. Present or accounted for through December, 1864. Paroled at Greensboro on May 12, 1865.

BURKE, CHARLES D., Private
Enlisted in Cumberland County at age 43, September 2, 1863, for the war. Present or accounted for until discharged in March-April, 1864.

BURKETT, RICHARD, Private
Enlisted in Cumberland County at age 52, Sep-

tember 2, 1863, for the war. Reported as absent sick through December, 1863. Absent without leave from that date until discharged in March-April, 1864.

CAMERON, ALEXANDER McK., Corporal
Enlisted in Cumberland County at age 26, September 2, 1863, for the war. Mustered in as Corporal. Present or accounted for through December, 1864.

CARTER, AMOS, Private
Enlisted in Cumberland County at age 26, September 2, 1863, for the war. Present or accounted for until discharged in March-April, 1864.

CARTER, JOHN, Private
Enlisted in Cumberland County at age 29, September 2, 1863, for the war. Present or accounted for until discharged in January-February, 1864.

CLARK, NEILL, Private
Enlisted in Cumberland County at age 47, February 27, 1864, for the war. Present or accounted for until discharged in March-April, 1864.

COSTIN, WILLIAM H., Private
Enlisted in Cumberland County at age 45, September 15, 1863, for the war. Present or accounted for until reported on the March-April, 1864, muster roll with the remark: "Deserted."

COUNCIL, ABED W., Private
Enlisted in Cumberland County at age 33, September 2, 1863, for the war. Present or accounted for through December, 1864.

CULBRETH, HENRY C., Private
Enlisted in Cumberland County at age 17, May 20, 1864, for the war. Present or accounted for on company muster rolls until July-August, 1864, when he is reported as absent. Issued clothing September 6, 1864. No further records.

CULBRETH, JOHN, Private
Enlisted in Cumberland County at age 46, May 20, 1864, for the war. Present or accounted for on company muster rolls through December, 1864, when he is reported as "light duty conscript."

CULBRETH, WILLIAM H., Private
Enlisted in Cumberland County at age 22, April 11, 1864, for the war. Present or accounted for through December, 1864.

DEAL, ANDREW J., Private
Enlisted in Cumberland County at age 27, September 2, 1863, for the war. Present or accounted for until transferred to Company G of this battalion September-December, 1864.

ENGLE, JAMES D., Private
Enlisted in Cumberland County at age 17, April 23, 1864, for the war. Present or accounted for through December, 1864.

GAME, JOSEPH T., Private
Enlisted in Cumberland County at age 26, September 2, 1863, for the war. Present or accounted for until discharged in March-April, 1864.

GRIFFITH, MARION L., Private
Enlisted in Cumberland County at age 22, April 11, 1864, for the war. Present or accounted for through August, 1864. Issued clothing on September 6, 1864.

HARDIN, JOHN, Private
Enlisted in Cumberland County at age 36, April 11, 1864, for the war. Reported as absent sick on the July-August, 1864, muster roll. No further records.

HINES, CLARENCE, Private
Enlisted in Cumberland County at age 16, September 2, 1863, for the war. Present or accounted for through December, 1864.

HINES, EDWARD K., Corporal
Enlisted in Cumberland County at age 35, September 2, 1863, for the war. Mustered in as Corporal. Present or accounted for through December, 1864.

HINES, ELI J., 1st Sergeant
Enlisted in Cumberland County at age 26, September 2, 1863, for the war. Mustered in as 1st Sergeant. Present or accounted for through December, 1864.

HINES, ELI W., Private
Enlisted in Cumberland County at age 26, September 2, 1863, for the war. Present or accounted for through December, 1864.

HOLLINGSWORTH, WILLIAM J., Private
Enlisted in Cumberland County at age 16, May 20, 1864, for the war. Present or accounted for on company muster rolls through August, 1864. Issued clothing on September 6, 1864. No further records.

HORNRINE, GEORGE R., Private
Enlisted in Cumberland County at age 33, September 2, 1863, for the war. Present or accounted for through December, 1864.

HORNRINE, WILLIAM J., Private
Enlisted in Cumberland County at age 18, March 18, 1864, for the war. Present or accounted for through December, 1864.

HOWARD, THOMAS A., Private
Enlisted in Cumberland County at age 38, April 30, 1864, for the war. Present or accounted for through December, 1864.

JACKSON, PARMEANUS, Private
Enlisted in Cumberland County at age 49, September 2, 1863, for the war. Present or accounted for on company muster rolls through November-December, 1864, when he is reported as absent.

JOHNSON, FLEET, Private
Enlisted in Cumberland County at age 42, September 2, 1863, for the war. Present or accounted for on company muster rolls through December, 1864. Captured at Fayetteville on March 12, 1865, and confined at Hart's Island, New York Harbor, where he died May 29, 1865, of "meningitis."

JOHNSON, MALCOLM J., Private
Enlisted in Cumberland County at age 35, September 2, 1863, for the war. Present or accounted for on company muster rolls through December, 1864.

JOHNSON, WILLIAM J., Sergeant
Enlisted in Cumberland County at age 30, September 2, 1863, for the war. Mustered in as Corporal and appointed Sergeant on October 4, 1863. Present or accounted for through December, 1864.

JONES, ELIAS, Private
Enlisted in Cumberland County at age 57, September 2, 1863, for the war. Present or accounted for until discharged in March-April, 1864.

JONES, HARDY, Private
Enlisted in Cumberland County at age 42, September 2, 1863, for the war. Present or accounted for until discharged in January-February, 1864.

JORDAN, ALEXANDER, Private
Enlisted in Cumberland County at age 36, September 2, 1863, for the war. Present or accounted for until reported as "absent on duty" on the January-February, 1864, muster roll. Reported with this remark through August, 1864. Issued clothing September 6, 1864. No further records.

KENNEDY, JOHN W., Private
Enlisted in Cumberland County at age 45, September 2, 1863, for the war. Present or accounted for through December, 1864.

KENNET, J. F., Private
Enlisted in Cumberland County at age 36, April 11, 1864, for the war. Present or accounted for through December, 1864.

LANDA, FRANK W., Private
Enlisted in Cumberland County at age 42, September 2, 1863, for the war. Present or accounted for through December, 1864.

LEGGETT, BRYANT, Private
Enlisted in Cumberland County at age 50, September 2, 1863, for the war. Reported as absent without leave on the company muster roll for September 2-October 31, 1863. Reported as such until discharged in March-April, 1864.

McCALL, DANIEL, Private
Enlisted in Cumberland County at age 27, September 2, 1863, for the war. Present or accounted for until discharged in March-April, 1864.

McDONALD, THOMAS, Private
Enlisted in Cumberland County at age 52, September 2, 1863, for the war. Company muster roll for September 2-October 31, 1863, reports that he was absent without leave. Appears as absent from that date until discharged in March-April, 1864.

McDOUGALD, ALEXANDER C., Private
Enlisted in Cumberland County at age 34, September 2, 1863, for the war. Present or accounted for through December, 1864.

McINNIS, NEILL, Private
Enlisted in Cumberland County at age 34, September 2, 1863, for the war. Present or accounted for until discharged in March-April, 1864.

McLEAN, DUNCAN N., Private
Enlisted in Cumberland County at age 21, September 2, 1863, for the war. Present or accounted for until discharged in January-February, 1864.

McNAIR, WILLIAM C., Private
Enlisted in Cumberland County at age 39, September 2, 1863, for the war. Present or accounted for through December, 1864.

McPHAUL, JOHN, Private
Enlisted in Cumberland County at age 41, February 20, 1864, for the war. Present or accounted for through December, 1864.

MADDEN, MALACHI J., Private
Enlisted in Cumberland County at age 17, September 2, 1863, for the war. Present or accounted for until discharged in March-April, 1864.

MADDEN, RICHARD, Private
Enlisted in Cumberland County at age 47, September 2, 1863, for the war. Present or accounted for until reported on the July-August, 1864, muster roll with the remark: "Absent. Deserted."

MATTHEWS, JAMES A., Private
Enlisted in Cumberland County at age 17, April 23, 1864, for the war. Present or accounted for on company muster rolls through August, 1864. Issued clothing September 6, 1864. No further records.

MAULTSBY, DAVID SHEPHERD, Private
Enlisted in Cumberland County at age 41, September 2, 1863, for the war. Present or accounted for until transferred to Company G of this battalion September-December, 1864.

MAULTSBY, JOHN W., Private
Enlisted in Cumberland County at age 19, April 12, 1864, for the war. Present or accounted for through December, 1864.

MONROE, NEILL C., Private
Enlisted in Cumberland County at age 38, September 2, 1863, for the war. Present or accounted for through December, 1864.

MONROE, THOMAS, Private
Enlisted in Cumberland County at age 40, September 2, 1863, for the war. Present or accounted for through December, 1864.

MURDOCK, ANDREW, Sergeant
Enlisted in Cumberland County at age 34, September 2, 1863, for the war. Mustered in as Sergeant. Present or accounted for through December, 1864.

NANCE, JOHN W., Corporal
Enlisted in Cumberland County at age 36, September 2, 1863, for the war. Mustered in as Private and appointed Corporal on October 1, 1863. Present or accounted for through December, 1864.

NANCE, WASHINGTON J., Private
Enlisted in Cumberland County at age 33, September 2, 1863, for the war. Present or accounted for through December, 1864.

PALMER, ORRIN D., Private
Transferred from Company E of this battalion January 10, 1864. Present or accounted for through December, 1864, when he was reported as absent on furlough.

POWERS, MICHAEL, Private
Enlisted in Cumberland County at age 37, September 2, 1863, for the war. Reported on company muster rolls as "absent on duty" from January-February, 1864, through August, 1864. Issued clothing September 6, 1864. No further records.

PRICE, FRANCIS M., Private
Enlisted in Cumberland County at age 28, September 2, 1863, for the war. Present or accounted for until transferred to Company G of this battalion September-December, 1864.

RAY, DUNCAN K., Private
Enlisted in Cumberland County at age 28, September 2, 1863, for the war. Present or accounted for through December, 1864.

REYNOLDS, JOHN W., Private
Enlisted in Cumberland County at age 27, September 2, 1863, for the war. Present or accounted for until discharged in March-April, 1864.

RUARK, JOHN H., Sergeant
Enlisted in Cumberland County at age 25, September 2, 1863, for the war. Mustered in as Sergeant. Present or accounted for through December, 1864.

SHEETZ, SILAS, Sergeant
Enlisted in Cumberland County at age 34, September 2, 1863, for the war. Mustered in as Sergeant. Present or accounted for through December, 1864.

SOUTHERLAND, ROBERT, Corporal
Enlisted in Cumberland County at age 37, September 2, 1863, for the war. Mustered in as Corporal. Present or accounted for through December, 1864.

STRATTON, ALEXANDER, Private
Enlisted in Cumberland County at age 45, September 2, 1863, for the war. Present or accounted for through December, 1864.

VAUGHN, JAMES C., Private
Enlisted in Cumberland County at age 35, September 2, 1863, for the war. Present or accounted for through December, 1864.

VAUGHN, RUFFIN, Private
Enlisted in Cumberland County at age 30, September 2, 1863, for the war. Present or accounted for through December, 1864.

VAUGHN, STEPHEN, Private
Enlisted in Cumberland County at age 33, September 2, 1863, for the war. Present or accounted for through December, 1864.

WARD, GEORGE, Private
Enlisted in Cumberland County at age 20, September 2, 1863, for the war. Present or accounted for through December, 1864.

WATSON, HUGH L., Private
Enlisted in Cumberland County at age 35, September 2, 1863, for the war. Present or accounted for through December, 1864.

WELKER, DANIEL C., Private
Enlisted in Cumberland County at age 38, April 11, 1864, for the war. Present or accounted for through December, 1864.

WELSH, SAMUEL N., Private
Enlisted in Cumberland County at age 36, April 11, 1864, for the war. Present or accounted for until transferred to Company G of this battalion September-December, 1864.

WEMYSS, ROBERT, Private
Enlisted in Cumberland County at age 17, February 27, 1864, for the war. Present or accounted for through December, 1864.

WOODS, JAMES C., Private
Enlisted in Cumberland County at age 26, April

11, 1864, for the war. Present or accounted for through December, 1864.

WRIGHT, HIRAM, Private
Enlisted in Cumberland County at age 47, September 2, 1863, for the war. Reported on company muster rolls as absent or "absent on duty" from November-December, 1863, through December, 1864.

COMPANY E

This company was organized at Fayetteville, Cumberland County, where it was mustered into Confederate States service on September 2, 1863. Composed exclusively of employees at the Fayetteville Arsenal and Armory, the company was organized for local defense and special service and was assigned to the battalion as Company E. Since it functioned as part of the battalion, its history is recorded as a part of the battalion history.

The information contained in the following roster of the company was compiled principally from company muster rolls which covered the period from September 2, 1863 (the date of the company muster-in roll), through August, 1864, and also November-December, 1864. No company muster rolls were found for September-October, 1864, or for the period after December, 1864. Although there are no Roll of Honor records for this company, useful information was obtained from receipt rolls, prisoner of war records, medical records, and other primary records, supplemented by state pension applications, United Daughters of the Confederacy records, and postwar rosters and histories.

OFFICERS
CAPTAIN
TALLEY, MARTIN VAN BUREN
Enlisted in Cumberland County at age 22, September 2, 1863, for the war. Appointed Captain to rank from date of enlistment. Present or accounted for through December, 1864.

LIEUTENANTS
AHERN, JAMES J., 2nd Lieutenant
Enlisted in Cumberland County at age 35, September 2, 1863, for the war. Mustered in as 1st Sergeant and elected 2nd Lieutenant on December 4, 1863. Present or accounted for through December, 1864.

BATTLEY, WILLIAM T., 2nd Lieutenant
Previously served in Company H, 1st Regiment N.C. Infantry (6 months, 1861). Enlisted in this company in Cumberland County on September 2, 1863, for the war. Appointed 2nd Lieutenant to rank from date of enlistment. Present or accounted for through December, 1864.

BURKHART, JEROME D., 1st Lieutenant
Enlisted in Cumberland County at age 23, September 2, 1863, for the war. Appointed 1st Lieutenant to rank from date of enlistment. Discharged on November 30, 1863. Later enlisted in Company C of this battalion.

EPPES, ROBERT F., 1st Lieutenant
Enlisted in Cumberland County at age 42, September 2, 1863, for the war. Appointed 2nd Lieutenant to rank from date of enlistment and pro-

moted to 1st Lieutenant on December 4, 1863. Present or accounted for through December, 1864.

NONCOMMISSIONED OFFICERS AND PRIVATES

BAKER, WILLIAM H., Private
Enlisted in Cumberland County, April 23, 1864, for the war. Reported as absent without leave on the company muster roll for July-August, 1864.

BARRINGER, WILLIAM R., Private
Previously served in Company H, 1st Regiment N.C. Infantry (6 months, 1861). Enlisted in this company in Cumberland County on September 2, 1863, for the war. Present or accounted for through December, 1864.

BELL, GEORGE, Private
Enlisted in Cumberland County at age 22, September 2, 1863, for the war. Present or accounted for through December, 1864, when he was reported as absent.

BIGGS, DANIEL, Private
Enlisted in Cumberland County at age 35, April 11, 1864, for the war. Present or accounted for through December, 1864.

BLACK, JAMES K., Private
Enlisted in Cumberland County at age 42, September 2, 1863, for the war. Present or accounted for through December, 1864.

BLACKBURN, JAMES G., Private
Enlisted in Cumberland County at age 32, September 2, 1863, for the war. Present or accounted for through December, 1864.

BLOUNT, ANDREW J., Private
Enlisted in Cumberland County at age 41, September 2, 1863, for the war. Company muster roll for September 2-October 31, 1863, states that he was absent sick. Reported as absent sick until discharged in March-April, 1864.

BOSWELL, JOSEPH, Private
Enlisted in Cumberland County at age 23, September 2, 1863, for the war. Present or accounted for through December, 1864, when he was absent on furlough.

BRADY, JAMES, Private
Enlisted in Cumberland County at age 33, September 2, 1863, for the war. Present or accounted for through December, 1864.

BRAXLEY, JOHN, Private
Enlisted in Cumberland County at age 41, September 2, 1863, for the war. Present or accounted for through December, 1864.

BRUFF, JOHN K., Corporal
Enlisted in Cumberland County at age 34, September 2, 1863, for the war. Mustered in as Private and appointed Corporal on December 30, 1863. Present or accounted for through December, 1864.

BUIE, HUGH, Private
Enlisted in Cumberland County at age 17, April 23, 1864, for the war. Present or accounted for through December, 1864.

BURKETT, HENRY, Private
Enlisted in Cumberland County at age 16, No-

vember 28, 1863, for the war. Present or accounted for until transferred to Company B of this battalion in March-April, 1864.

BURKHART, GEORGE F., 1st Sergeant
Enlisted in Cumberland County at age 17, September 2, 1863, for the war. Mustered in as Sergeant and appointed 1st Sergeant on December 4, 1863. Present or accounted for through December, 1864.

CAMPBELL, JOHN, Private
Enlisted in Cumberland County at age 17, March 10, 1864, for the war. Present or accounted for until discharged in July-August, 1864.

CARMICHAEL, ARCHIBALD, Private
Enlisted in Cumberland County at age 31, September 2, 1863, for the war. Present or accounted for through December, 1864.

CARVER, JOSIAH, Private
Enlisted in Cumberland County at age 17, September 2, 1863, for the war. Present or accounted for through August, 1864.

CLOVER, R. S., Private
Enlisted in Cumberland County at age 30, November 28, 1863, for the war. Present or accounted for through April, 1864.

CLOWE, WILLIARD H., Private
Enlisted in Cumberland County at age 16, September 2, 1863, for the war. Present or accounted for through December, 1864.

CROW, NELSON M., Private
Enlisted in Cumberland County at age 34, November 28, 1863, for the war. Present or accounted for through December, 1864.

CULBRETH, SOLOMON, Private
Enlisted in Cumberland County at age 28, September 2, 1863, for the war. Present or accounted for through December, 1864.

CURTIS, JOHN M., Private
Enlisted in Cumberland County at age 40, March 10, 1864, for the war. Present or accounted for until discharged in July-August, 1864.

DRIVER, HARRISON, Private
Enlisted in Cumberland County at age 35, September 2, 1863, for the war. Present or accounted for through December, 1864.

ELLIOTT, GEORGE, Private
Enlisted in Cumberland County at age 37, September 2, 1863, for the war. Discharged prior to October 31, 1863.

EVANS, THEOPHILUS, Private
Enlisted in Cumberland County at age 44, September 2, 1863, for the war. Reported on company muster rolls as absent or "absent on duty" from date of enlistment through December, 1864.

FAIRCLOTH, STEPHEN, Private
Enlisted in Cumberland County at age 17, November 28, 1863, for the war. Reported on company muster rolls as absent or "absent without leave" from November-December, 1863, until he was discharged in March-April, 1864.

GADDIE, DOUGALD, Private
Enlisted in Cumberland County at age 43, September 2, 1863, for the war. Present or accounted

for through December, 1864, when he was reported absent.

HALE, DAVID, Private
Enlisted in Cumberland County at age 37, April 11, 1864, for the war. Present or accounted for through December, 1864, when he was reported as absent sick.

HALL, JAMES T., Corporal
Resided in Jones County and enlisted in Cumberland County at age 21, September 2, 1863, for the war. Mustered in as Corporal. Present or accounted for on company muster rolls through December, 1864. Captured at Fayetteville on March 13, 1865, and confined at Hart's Island, New York Harbor, until released after taking the Oath of Allegiance on June 18, 1865.

HARPER, CHARLES A., Private
Enlisted in Cumberland County at age 30, September 2, 1863, for the war. Present or accounted for until he died at Fayetteville on August 2, 1864.

HARPER, GEORGE S., Private
Enlisted in Cumberland County at age 27, September 2, 1863, for the war. Reported as absent sick on the muster-in roll dated September 2, 1863. Discharged prior to October 31, 1863.

HAWLEY, JOHN, Private
Enlisted in Cumberland County at age 41, September 2, 1863, for the war. Present or accounted for until discharged on January 13, 1864.

HENRY, J. B., Private
Enlisted in Cumberland County at age 24, September 2, 1863, for the war. Present or accounted for until discharged on November 9, 1863.

JACKSON, JOHN D., Private
Enlisted in Cumberland County at age 31, September 2, 1863, for the war. Reported on company muster rolls as absent or "absent on duty" through December, 1864.

JONES, OWEN D., Private
Enlisted in Cumberland County at age 17, September 14, 1863, for the war. Present or accounted for on company muster rolls until January-February, 1864, when he was reported as absent without leave. Discharged in March-April, 1864.

KENNEDY, JAMES, Private
Enlisted in Cumberland County at age 17, September 2, 1863, for the war. Present or accounted for until discharged in March-April, 1864.

KING, J. M., Private
Paroled at Greensboro on May 16, 1865.

KING, SAMUEL M., Private
Enlisted in Cumberland County at age 26, October 15, 1863, for the war. Present or accounted for through August, 1864. No further records.

KLING, SAMUEL M., Private
Enlisted in Cumberland County at age 26, April 11, 1864, for the war. Reported as present on company muster roll for November-December, 1864.

KYSER, CHARLES S., Private
Enlisted in Cumberland County at age 18, March 10, 1864, for the war. Present or accounted for through August, 1864. No further records.

KYSER, GEORGE W., Private
Resided in Jefferson County, Virginia. Captured at Fayetteville on March 13, 1865, and confined at Hart's Island, New York Harbor, until released after taking the Oath of Allegiance on June 21, 1865.

KYSER, JAMES H., Private
Enlisted in Cumberland County at age 26, April 11, 1864, for the war. Present or accounted for through December, 1864.

LINDSEY, HENRY M., Private
Enlisted in Cumberland County at age 24, September 2, 1863, for the war. Present or accounted for through December, 1864.

LLEWELLYN, WILLIAM, Private
Enlisted in Cumberland County at age 36, September 2, 1863, for the war. Present or accounted for through December, 1864.

LUMSDEN, FOUNTAIN L., Private
Enlisted in Cumberland County at age 32, September 2, 1863, for the war. Present or accounted for until discharged in March-April, 1864.

LUMSDEN, JOHN, Private
Enlisted in Cumberland County at age 17, September 2, 1863, for the war. Present or accounted for through August, 1864. No further records.

McALPIN, MALCOM, Private
Enlisted in Cumberland County at age 41, October 5, 1863, for the war. Present or accounted for until discharged on January 13, 1864.

McDUFFIE, ARCHIBALD, Corporal
Enlisted in Cumberland County at age 16, September 2, 1863, for the war. Mustered in as Private and appointed Corporal on September 15, 1863. Present or accounted for on company muster rolls through December, 1864. Took the Oath of Allegiance at Wilmington on March 30, 1865, and was released to "go North."

McMILLIAN, DANIEL G., Private
Enlisted in Cumberland County at age 16, September 2, 1863, for the war. Reported as absent without leave on the January-February, 1864, muster roll. Discharged in March-April, 1864.

McPHAIL, ALEX, Private
Enlisted in Cumberland County at age 49, April 23, 1864, for the war. Present or accounted for through December, 1864.

McPHAIL, MALCOLM, Corporal
Enlisted in Cumberland County at age 17, September 2, 1863, for the war. Mustered in as Corporal. Present or accounted for through December, 1864.

MAULTSBY, JOHN S., Private
Enlisted in Cumberland County at age 37, September 2, 1863, for the war. Present or accounted for through December, 1864.

MAY, LEVI J., Private
Enlisted in Cumberland County at age 23, February 20 1864, for the war. Present or accounted for on company muster rolls through December, 1864. Paroled at Greensboro on May 18, 1865.

MEMORY, GEORGE W., Private
Enlisted in Cumberland County at age 40, April

8, 1864, for the war. Present or accounted for on company muster rolls through June, 1864, when he is reported as absent on furlough.

MERRICK, MARSHALL T., Private
Enlisted in Cumberland County at age 16, September 2, 1863, for the war. Present or accounted for through December, 1864.

MERRICK, SHADRACK F., Sergeant
Enlisted in Cumberland County at age 33, September 2, 1863, for the war. Mustered in as Private and appointed Sergeant on December 30, 1863. Present or accounted for through December, 1864.

MITCHELL, ROBERT J., Private
Enlisted in Cumberland County at age 17, October 6, 1863, for the war. Present or accounted for until transferred to Company B, 13th Battalion N.C. Light Artillery on July 15, 1864.

MITCHELL, VALENTINE N., Private
Enlisted in Cumberland County at age 31, September 29, 1863, for the war. Present or accounted for on company muster rolls through December, 1864. Captured in Chatham County and paroled at Avins Ferry, N.C., April 25, 1865.

MONAGHAN, JOSEPH, Sergeant
Enlisted in Cumberland County at age 18, September 2, 1863, for the war. Mustered in as Sergeant. Present or accounted for through December, 1864.

MONAGHAN, THOMAS, Private
Enlisted in Cumberland County at age 15, September 2, 1863, for the war. Present or accounted for through December, 1864.

MONROE, DOUGALD, Private
Enlisted in Cumberland County at age 36, September 2, 1863, for the war. Present or accounted for through August, 1864. No further records.

NEWBURY, THOMAS B., Private
Enlisted in Cumberland County at age 23, September 2, 1863, for the war. Present or accounted for through December, 1864, when he was reported as absent.

NICHOLSON, WILLIAM W., Private
Enlisted in Cumberland County at age 37, June 23, 1864, for the war. Present or accounted for through December, 1864.

PALMER, ORRIN D., Private
Enlisted in Cumberland County at age 17, December 28, 1863, for the war. Transferred to Company D of this battalion January 10, 1864.

PARRISH, JOHN S., Private
Enlisted in Cumberland County at age 22, November 28, 1863, for the war. Present or accounted for on company muster rolls through December, 1864, when he is reported as absent sick. Paroled at Greensboro on May 15, 1865.

PARUCKER, WILLIAM, Sergeant
Enlisted in Cumberland County at age 22, September 2, 1863, for the war. Mustered in as Corporal and promoted to Sergeant on December 30, 1863. Present or accounted for through December, 1864.

SELLARS, JOHN T., Private
Enlisted in Cumberland County at age 22, Sep-

tember 2, 1863, for the war. Mustered in as Sergeant. Promoted to 1st Sergeant on December 4, 1863, and reduced to ranks on July 9, 1864. Present or accounted for through December, 1864, when he was reported as absent.

SHOLAR, WILLIAM H., Private
Enlisted in Cumberland County at age 27, September 2, 1863, for the war. Mustered in as Sergeant. Resigned his position as Sergeant on December 30, 1863. Discharged in March-April, 1864.

SIKES, JOHN A., Private
Enlisted in Cumberland County at age 25, September 2, 1863, for the war. Present or accounted for through August, 1864. No further records.

SINCLAIR, JAMES, Private
Enlisted in Cumberland County at age 16, February 6, 1864, for the war. Present or accounted for through April, 1864, when he was reported as absent. No further records.

SUITS, ROBERT L., Sergeant
Enlisted in Cumberland County at age 19, November 28, 1863, for the war. Mustered in as Private and appointed Sergeant on July 9, 1864. Present or accounted for through December, 1864.

TAYLOR, A. E., Private
Enlisted in Cumberland County at age 29, September 22, 1863, for the war. Present or accounted for until discharged in March-April, 1864.

THORNTON, JACOB L., Private
Enlisted in Cumberland County at age 35, September 2, 1863, for the war. Present or accounted for through December, 1864.

TROLLINGER, JOHN H., Private
Enlisted in Cumberland County at age 19, April 19, 1864, for the war. Present or accounted for through August, 1864, when he was reported as absent without leave. No further records.

TURLINGTON, JAMES H., Private
Enlisted in Cumberland County at age 43, September 2, 1863, for the war. Discharged on November 19, 1863.

VALENTINE, ROBERT H. C., Private
Enlisted in Cumberland County at age 16, September 2, 1863, for the war. Mustered in as Corporal and reduced to ranks on September 15, 1863. Reported as absent without leave on the company muster roll for September 2-October 31, 1863. Reported as absent without leave from that date until discharged in March-April, 1864.

VAUGHAN, JOHN, Private
Enlisted in Cumberland County at age 27, September 2, 1863, for the war. Discharged prior to October 31, 1863.

WARWICK, WILEY, Private
Enlisted in Cumberland County at age 42, September 2, 1863, for the war. Present or accounted for through December, 1864.

WATKINS, THOMAS P., Private
Enlisted in Cumberland County, July 29, 1864, for the war. Issued clothing at hospital in Fayetteville on August 12, 1864. Company muster roll for December, 1864, states that he was absent at hospital.

WEBSTER, GURDON F., Private
Enlisted in Cumberland County at age 45, September 2, 1863, for the war. Present or accounted for through December, 1864.

WELSH, JOHN W., Private
Enlisted in Cumberland County, April 23, 1864, for the war. Transferred to Company G of this battalion September-December, 1864.

WEST, HARDIE, Private
Enlisted in Cumberland County at age 36, September 2, 1863, for the war. Present or accounted for until discharged in March-April, 1864.

WHALEY, HIRAM, Private
Enlisted in Cumberland County at age 39, September 2, 1863, for the war. Present or accounted for until transferred to Company G of this battalion September-December, 1864.

WHISNANT, JOHN O., Private
Enlisted in Cumberland County at age 32, November 28, 1863, for the war. Present or accounted for through December, 1864.

WILLIFORD, JAMES, Private
Enlisted in Cumberland County, April 23, 1864, for the war. Present or accounted for through August, 1864. No further records.

WILSON, NOEL, Private
Enlisted in Cumberland County at age 27, September 2, 1863, for the war. Present or accounted for through December, 1864, when he was reported as "sick."

WOODLE, DARIUS B., Private
Enlisted in Cumberland County at age 18, September 2, 1863, for the war. Present or accounted for through December, 1864.

WOODLE, JAMES, Private
Enlisted in Cumberland County at age 20, April 11, 1864, for the war. Reported as present on the company muster roll for November-December, 1864.

WOODWARD, GEORGE W., Private
Enlisted in Cumberland County at age 18, September 2, 1863, for the war. Present or accounted for until discharged in March-April, 1864.

COMPANY F

This cavalry company, known as the "Mounted Riflemen," was organized at Fayetteville, Cumberland County, beginning in February, 1864. Organization was completed in April, 1864, and the company was assigned to the battalion as Company F. Since it functioned as a part of the battalion, its history is recorded as a part of the battalion history.

The information contained in the following roster of the company was compiled principally from company muster rolls for the period from the date of enlistment through August, 1864, and also for December, 1864. No company muster rolls were found for September-November, 1864, or for the period after December, 1864. Although there are no Roll of Honor records for this company, useful information was obtained from receipt rolls, prisoner of war records, medical records, and other primary records, supplemented by state pension applications, United Daughters of the Confederacy records, and postwar rosters and histories.

OFFICERS

CAPTAIN

STRANGE, JAMES WILLIAM

Transferred from Company D, 19th Regiment N.C. Troops (2nd Regiment N.C. Cavalry), April 26, 1864, upon election as Captain of this company on that date. Present or accounted for through December, 1864. Paroled at Bunn's House, N.C., April 20, 1865.

LIEUTENANTS

HOLLIDAY, ROBERT H., 1st Lieutenant

Enlisted in Cumberland County on May 24, 1864, for the war. Appointed 1st Lieutenant to rank from date of enlistment. Present or accounted for through December, 1864.

McMURRAY, CHRISTOPHER C., 2nd Lieutenant

Enlisted in Cumberland County on April 26, 1864, for the war. Mustered in as Private and appointed 2nd Lieutenant on May 24, 1864. Present or accounted for through December, 1864.

NONCOMMISSIONED OFFICERS AND PRIVATES

BLUE, JOHN C., Private

Enlisted in Cumberland County, May 3, 1864, for the war. Present or accounted for until admitted to hospital at Raleigh on December 18, 1864, with "febris int. ter." Transferred to Kittrells on January 1, 1865.

BLUE, MURDOCK I., Private

Enlisted in Cumberland County, September 21, 1864, for the war. Present or accounted for through December, 1864.

BOSTICK, JOHN S., Private

Enlisted in Cumberland County, October 5, 1864, for the war. Present or accounted for through December, 1864.

BOWDEN, JOHN, Private

Enlisted in Cumberland County, March 4, 1864, for the war. Present or accounted for through December, 1864.

BRADY, MANLY, Private

Enlisted in Cumberland County, February 22, 1864, for the war. Present or accounted for through December, 1864.

CAIN, WILLIAM J., Private

Enlisted in Cumberland County, April 12, 1864, for the war. Present or accounted for through December, 1864.

CAMERON, ALLEN D., Private

Enlisted in Cumberland County, May 28, 1864, for the war. Present or accounted for through December, 1864.

CAMERON, ARCHIBALD McD., Private

Enlisted in Cumberland County, May 28, 1864, for the war. Present or accounted for through December, 1864.

CAROWAY, TRISTUM T., Private

Enlisted in Cumberland County, July 25, 1864, for

the war. Present or accounted for through December, 1864.

COBLE, GEORGE A., Private

Enlisted in Cumberland County, March 21, 1864, for the war. Present or accounted for through December, 1864, when he was reported as absent at hospital.

COOPER, ERASTUS, Private

Transferred from Company B of this battalion January 1, 1864. Returned to Company B on March 30, 1864, "having failed to procure a horse."

CROMARTIE, ADDISON A., Private

Previously served in 2nd Company I, 36th Regiment N.C. Troops (2nd Regiment N.C. Artillery). Enlisted in this company July 13, 1864, in Cumberland County for the war. Present or accounted for on company muster rolls through December, 1864. Captured at Piney Grove, N.C., March 19, 1865. Confined at Point Lookout, Maryland, until released after taking the Oath of Allegiance on June 26, 1865.

CROSS, GEORGE A., Private

Enlisted in Cumberland County, April 6, 1864, for the war. Present or accounted for through December, 1864.

CULBRETH, BLACKMAN H., Sergeant

Transferred from Company B of this battalion January 1, 1864, as a Private. Appointed Corporal in May-June, 1864, and promoted to Sergeant in September-December, 1864. Present or accounted for on company muster rolls through December, 1864. Paroled at Avins Ferry, N.C., April 27, 1865.

CULBRETH, THOMAS L., Private

Enlisted in Cumberland County, June 14, 1864, for the war. Present or accounted for through December, 1864, when he is reported as present with the remark: "Horse died 18 December, 1864."

CURRIE, WILLIAM JACKSON, Private

Enlisted in Cumberland County, April 29, 1864, for the war. Present or accounted for on company muster rolls through December, 1864. Admitted to hospital at Raleigh on January 17, 1865, with "catarrhus" and was returned to duty January 29, 1865.

DEATON, THOMAS, Private

Enlisted in Cumberland County, August 25, 1864, for the war. Present or accounted for through December, 1864.

DOWD, HENRY C., Private

Enlisted in Cumberland County, April 28, 1864, for the war. Present or accounted for through December, 1864, when he was reported as absent at hospital.

DRAUGHON, JAMES R., Private

Enlisted in Cumberland County, April 19, 1864, for the war. Present or accounted for through December, 1864.

DRAUGHON, WALTER M., Sergeant

Enlisted in Cumberland County, January 22, 1864, for the war. Mustered in as Private and appointed Sergeant in May-June, 1864. Present or accounted for through December, 1864.

DUNLAP, DAVID R., Private

Enlisted in Cumberland County, September 23, 1864, for the war. Present or accounted for through December, 1864.

EWING, JAMES F., Private

Enlisted in Cumberland County, October 3, 1864, for the war. Present or accounted for through December, 1864.

EWING, THOMAS M., Sergeant

Transferred from Company B of this battalion January 1, 1864, as a Corporal. Appointed Sergeant in May-June, 1864. Present or accounted for through December, 1864, when he was reported as absent on sick furlough. Retired to the Invalid Corps on March 11, 1865. Detailed for light duty and ordered to report to the Medical Director at Raleigh on March 31, 1865.

FISHER, HENRY C., Private

Enlisted in Cumberland County, April 1, 1864, for the war. Present or accounted for through December, 1864, when he was reported as absent on detached duty at Weldon.

FOGLEMAN, JOHN F., Private

Enlisted in Cumberland County, March 21, 1864, for the war. Present or accounted for through December, 1864.

GILBERT, WILLIAM A., Private

Enlisted in Cumberland County, April 14, 1864, for the war. Present or accounted for through December, 1864.

GREEN, JAMES N., Private

Enlisted in Cumberland County, April 22, 1864, for the war. Present or accounted for through December, 1864.

GREEN, JOHN A., Private

Enlisted in Cumberland County, May 30, 1864, for the war. Present or accounted for through December, 1864.

HARDIN, JOHN C., Private

Enlisted in Cumberland County, April 26, 1864, for the war. Present or accounted for until admitted to hospital at Raleigh on December 18, 1864, with "feb int. ter." Transferred to Kittrells on January 1, 1865.

HAYES, WILLIAM J., Corporal

Enlisted in Cumberland County, April 5, 1864, for the war. Mustered in as Private and appointed Corporal in May-June, 1864. Present or accounted for through December, 1864.

JORDAN, JAMES R., Private

Enlisted in Cumberland County, November 5, 1864, for the war. Present or accounted for on company muster rolls through December, 1864. Paroled at Troy, N.C., May 22, 1865.

KELLY, DAVID W., Private

Enlisted in Cumberland County, April 29, 1864, for the war. Present or accounted for through December, 1864, when he was reported as absent on sick furlough.

KELLY, HENRY M., Private

Enlisted in Cumberland County, July 25, 1863, for the war. Reported as present on the December, 1864, muster roll. Paroled at Avins Ferry, N.C., April 24, 1865.

KELLY, JOHN McL., Private

Enlisted in Cumberland County, December 21, 1864, for the war. Present or accounted for through December, 1864.

KELLY, MYROVER, Private

Transferred from Company B of this battalion on January 1, 1864. Present or accounted for through August. 1864. No further records.

KILLETT, JULIAN A., Private

Enlisted in Cumberland County, April 25, 1864, for the war. Present or accounted for through December, 1864, when he was reported as absent on sick furlough.

LAURENCE, SION H., Private

Transferred from Company B of this battalion January 1, 1864. Present or accounted for through December, 1864.

LEACH, JAMES G., Private

Enlisted in Cumberland County, January 6, 1864, for the war. Present or accounted for through December, 1864.

LONG, JOHN A., Private

Enlisted in Cumberland County, April 4, 1864, for the war. Present or accounted for through December, 1864, when he was reported as absent on sick furlough.

McARTHUR, JOHN, Private

Enlisted in Cumberland County, March 1, 1864, for the war. Present or accounted for through December, 1864.

McCLENAHAN, WADDY, Private

Enlisted in Cumberland County, April 26, 1864, for the war. Present or accounted for through December, 1864, when he was reported as absent at hospital.

McCOLLUM, DUNCAN A., Private

Enlisted in Cumberland County, January 6, 1864, for the war. Present or accounted for through December, 1864.

McDONALD, ANGUS, Private

Enlisted in Cumberland County, January 22, 1864, for the war. Present or accounted for through December, 1864, when he was reported as absent with leave.

McLAUCHLIN, JOHN W., Private

Enlisted in Cumberland County, April 14, 1864, for the war. Present or accounted for through December, 1864.

McLENDON, WALTER J., Private

Enlisted in Cumberland County, July 25, 1864. Present or accounted for through December, 1864, when he was reported as absent at hospital.

McLEOD, DANIEL W., Private

Enlisted in Cumberland County, April 6, 1864, for the war. Present or accounted for through December, 1864.

McLEOD, MARTIN J., Private

Enlisted in Cumberland County, March 21, 1864, for the war. Present or accounted for through December, 1864, when he was reported as absent at hospital.

McMILLAN, ALEXANDER, Corporal

Enlisted in Cumberland County, March 24, 1864,

for the war. Mustered in as Private and appointed Corporal in May-June, 1864. Present or accounted for through December, 1864, when he was reported as absent at hospital.

MATTHIS, WILLIAM R., Private
Enlisted in Cumberland County, January 22, 1864, for the war. Present or accounted for through December, 1864.

MERRITT, JOSEPH, Bugler
Enlisted in Cumberland County, March 4, 1864, for the war. Mustered in as Private and appointed Bugler in May-June, 1864. Present or accounted for through December, 1864.

MONROE, CALVIN S., Private
Enlisted in Cumberland County, August 25, 1864, for the war. Present or accounted for through December, 1864.

MONROE, JOHN C., Private
Enlisted in Cumberland County, December 10, 1864, for the war. Present or accounted for through December, 1864.

MOORMAN, JOHN P., Private
Enlisted in Cumberland County, June 2, 1864, for the war. Present or accounted for through December, 1864.

MUSE, JOHN C., Private
Enlisted in Cumberland County, May 11, 1864, for the war. Present or accounted for through December, 1864.

NETTLES, JOHN G., Private
Enlisted in Cumberland County, April 25, 1864, for the war. Present or accounted for through December, 1864.

NUNNERY, AMOS, Private
Enlisted in Cumberland County, February 8, 1864, for the war. Company muster rolls state that he deserted June 14, 1864, and report him as absent until December, 1864, when he appears as "absent in confinement awaiting trial by General Court Martial."

ODOM, JAMES W., Private
Transferred from Company B of this battalion on January 1, 1864. Present or accounted for through December, 1864.

PEGRAM, WILLIAM H., Corporal
Enlisted in Cumberland County, January 6, 1864, for the war. Mustered in as Private and appointed Corporal in May-June, 1864. Present or accounted for through December, 1864.

PERKINS, S. C., Private
Enlisted in Cumberland County, May 4, 1864, for the war. Present or accounted for through December, 1864.

PETERSON, BUCKNER S., Private
Enlisted in Cumberland County, April 25, 1864, for the war. Present or accounted for through December, 1864.

PORTER, EDWARD W., Private
Furloughed from Company E, 19th Regiment N.C. Troops (2nd Regiment N.C. Cavalry) for 30 days on June 30, 1864. Attached himself to this company while on furlough. Returned to his original company in December, 1864.

REIVES, JOHN A., Private
Enlisted in Cumberland County, April 1, 1864, for the war. Present or accounted for through August, 1864. No further records.

RIVES, JOHN R., Private
Enlisted in Cumberland County, April 1, 1864, for the war. Present or accounted for through December, 1864.

SMITH, SIDNEY J., Private
Enlisted in Cumberland County, June 2, 1864, for the war. Company muster roll for July-August, 1864, states that he was "absent at hospital from accidental discharge of a gun wounding him in hand." Reported as present on the December, 1864, muster roll.

STROUD, SIDNEY S., Private
Enlisted in Cumberland County, April 22, 1864, for the war. Present or accounted for through December, 1864.

SUTTON, WILLIAM J., Sergeant
Enlisted in Cumberland County, March 13, 1864, for the war. Mustered in as Private and appointed Sergeant in May-June, 1864. Present or accounted for through December, 1864.

TAYLOR, WILLIAM H., Private
Enlisted in Cumberland County, April 25, 1864, for the war. Present or accounted for through December, 1864.

THOMPSON, GEORGE W., Private
Enlisted in Cumberland County, February 10, 1864, for the war. Present or accounted for through December, 1864, when he was reported as absent on sick furlough.

TURNER, JOHN J., Private
Enlisted in Cumberland County, September 21, 1864, for the war. Present or accounted for through December, 1864.

TYSON, ANDREW J., Private
Enlisted in Cumberland County, September 23, 1864, for the war. Present or accounted for through December, 1864.

USHER, EDWIN T., Corporal
Transferred from Company B of this battalion on March 1, 1864, as a Private. Appointed Corporal in September-December, 1864. Present or accounted for through December, 1864, when he was reported as absent at hospital.

WALKER, JOHN M., 1st Sergeant
Enlisted in Cumberland County, March 5, 1864, for the war. Mustered in as Private and appointed 1st Sergeant in May-June, 1864. Present or accounted for through December, 1864.

WATSON, DAVID MAC, Private
Transferred from Company B of this battalion January 1, 1864. Present or accounted for through December, 1864.

WILLIAMS, HENRY M., Sergeant
Enlisted in Cumberland County, March 4, 1864, for the war. Mustered in as Private and appointed Sergeant in May-June, 1864. Present or accounted for through August, 1864. No further records.

WILLIAMSON, JOHN J., Private
Enlisted in Cumberland County, January 21, 1864,

for the war. Present or accounted for through December, 1864.

WILLIAMSON, M. G., Private
Enlisted in Cumberland County, April 30, 1864, for the war. Present or accounted for through December, 1864.

COMPANY G

This company was organized at Fayetteville, Cumberland County, in late 1864. It was composed of detailed soldiers employed as artisans, mechanics, etc., light duty detailed soldiers and light duty conscripts employed as watchmen, etc., and was to be a temporary organization. Events made it a permanent one. It was assigned to the battalion as Company G. Since it functioned as a part of the battalion, its history is recorded as a part of the battalion history.

The information contained in the following roster of the company was compiled principally from the company muster roll for November-December, 1864. No company muster rolls were found for the period prior to November, 1864, or for the period after December, 1864. Although there are no Roll of Honor records for this company, useful information was obtained from receipt rolls, prisoner of war records, medical records, and other primary records, supplemented by state pension applications, United Daughters of the Confederacy records, and postwar rosters and histories.

OFFICERS
CAPTAIN

BUIE, JAMES D.
Detailed from Company D, 19th Regiment N.C. Troops (2nd Regiment N.C. Cavalry) and reported as Acting Captain of this company on the November-December, 1864, muster roll.

LIEUTENANTS

CURRIE, LOCHLIN W., 1st Lieutenant
Detailed from Company H, 26th Regiment N.C. Troops and reported as Acting 1st Lieutenant of this company on the November-December, 1864, muster roll.

GATES, GEORGE W., 2nd Lieutenant
Detailed from Company E, 10th Regiment N.C. State Troops (1st Regiment N.C. Artillery) and reported as Acting 2nd Lieutenant of this company on the November-December, 1864, muster roll.

NONCOMMISSIONED OFFICERS AND PRIVATES

BAGGETT, JOSIAH, Private
Attached to this company from Company I, 46th Regiment N.C. Troops, November-December, 1864.

BETHEA, WILLIAM C., Private
Attached to this company from Company E, 8th Regiment N.C. State Troops, November-December, 1864.

BOND, ISREAL C., 1st Sergeant
Attached to this company from Company C, 7th

Regiment South Carolina Infantry, November-December, 1864, as Acting 1st Sergeant.

BRAMBLE, JAMES H., Private
Enlisted in Cumberland County, April 11, 1864, for the war. Assigned to this company as a "light duty conscript" November-December, 1864.

BROWN, JOHN B., Private
Transferred from Company D of this battalion as a "light duty conscript," September-December, 1864, and reported as present on the November-December, 1864, muster roll.

BRYANT, WILLIAM R., Private
Reported on the November-December, 1864, muster roll with the remark: "Conscript. Discharged. Turned over to Enrolling Officer."

CADDLE, CORNEILERS D., Sergeant
Attached to this company from Company H, 26th Regiment N.C. Troops, September-December, 1864, and is reported as absent on furlough on the November-December, 1864, muster roll. Rank given as Acting Sergeant.

CALDER, JOHN W., Sergeant
Attached to this company from Company E, 26th Regiment N.C. Troops, September-December, 1864, and is reported as present on the November-December, 1864, muster roll. Rank given as Acting Sergeant.

CAMPBELL, WILLIAM FREDERICK, Private
Attached to this company from Company A, 63rd Regiment N.C. Troops (5th Regiment N.C. Cavalry), November-December, 1864.

CARVER, CALVIN, Private
Enlisted in Cumberland County, April 11, 1864, for the war. Assigned to this company as a "light duty conscript" November-December, 1864.

CLOWE, ELIJAH, Private
Enlisted in Cumberland County, April 11, 1864, for the war. Assigned to this company as a "light duty conscript" November-December, 1864.

COLLINS, ALFRED N., Private
Attached to this company from Company A, 21st Regiment N.C. Troops (11th Regiment N.C. Volunteers), November-December, 1864.

COOLY, WILLIAM J., Private
Attached to this company from Company E, 4th Regiment Georgia Cavalry, November-December, 1864. Reported as absent on the company muster roll for November-December, 1864.

DAVIS, JOHN D., Private
Attached to this company from Company E, 59th Regiment N.C. Troops (4th Regiment N.C. Cavalry), November-December, 1864.

DEAL, ANDREW J., Private
Transferred from Company D of this battalion September-December, 1864, as a "light duty conscript" and reported as absent on the November-December, 1864, muster roll.

DUFFIE, ALEX M., Corporal
Attached to this company from Company C, 3rd and 5th Regiments C.S. Infantry as Acting Corporal, November-December, 1864.

EASOM, WILLIAM, Private
Enlisted in Cumberland County, April 11, 1864,

for the war. Assigned to this company as a "light duty conscript" November-December, 1864, and reported as present on the November-December, 1864, muster roll.

EDWARDS, JOHN L., Private
Enlisted in Cumberland County, April 11, 1864, for the war. Assigned to this company as a "light duty conscript" November-December, 1864, and reported as present on the November-December, 1864, muster roll.

EVANS, JAMES M., Private
Transferred from Company A of this battalion November-December, 1864.

FORT, WILEY, Corporal
Assigned to this company as a "light duty conscript" November-December, 1864, with rank of Acting Corporal.

FOWLER, THOMAS, Private
Attached to this company from Company I, 2nd Regiment N.C. State Troops, November-December, 1864.

FRAZIER, MURDOCH, Private
Attached to this company from Company K, 10th Regiment N.C. State Troops (1st Regiment N.C. Artillery), November-December, 1864.

GIERSH, ALEX E., Private
Transferred from Company C of this battalion September-December, 1864, as a "light duty conscript" and reported as present on the November-December, 1864, muster roll.

GILLIS, JOHN A., Private
Transferred from Company A, 63rd Regiment N.C. Troops (5th Regiment N.C. Cavalry), November-December, 1864.

HERRING, ARCHIBALD T., Private
Attached to this company from Company D, 46th Regiment N.C. Troops, November-December, 1864.

HOLMES, ARCHIBALD, Private
Attached to this company from Company A, 63rd Regiment N.C. Troops (5th Regiment N.C. Cavalry), November-December, 1864.

JOHNSTON, BALDWIN, Private
Transferred from Company C of this battalion as a "light duty conscript" September-December, 1864, and reported as present on the November-December, 1864, muster roll.

JONES, EVERETT, Private
Attached to this company from Company F, 66th Regiment N.C. Troops, November-December, 1864.

JONES, JAMES, Private
Attached to this company from Company C, 3rd Regiment N.C. State Troops, November-December, 1864.

KINLAW, RALPH W., Private
Reported on the November-December, 1864, muster roll with the remark: "Conscript. Discharged. Turned over to Enrolling Officer."

LEE, JAMES E., Private
Transferred to this company from Company E, 24th Regiment N.C. Troops (14th Regiment N.C. Volunteers), November-December, 1864.

McARTHUR, NEILL A., Private
Transferred from Company C of this battalion September-December, 1864. Reported on November-December, 1864, muster roll with the remark: "Light duty conscript."

McKETHAN, DANIEL A., Private
Reported on the November-December, 1864, muster roll with the remark: "Conscript. Discharged. Turned over to Enrolling Officer."

McLEAN, JOHN A., Corporal
Detailed from Company B, 13th Battalion N.C. Light Artillery to work in Fayetteville Arsenal, March-April, 1864, and was attached to this company while on detail.

McLEOD, ARCHIBALD, Private
Attached to this company from Company G, 33rd Regiment N.C. Troops, November-December, 1864. Captured at Goldsboro, March 24, 1865, and forwarded to Washington, D.C., where he took the Oath of Allegiance on April 5, 1865, and was furnished transportation to Wilmington.

MARSH, JAMES, Sergeant
Attached to this company from Company B of this battalion from July-August, 1864, through December, 1864, as Acting Sergeant.

MASON, LEVI, Private
Transferred to this company from Company D, 51st Regiment N.C. Troops, November-December, 1864.

MAULTSBY, DAVID SHEPHERD, Private
Transferred from Company D of this battalion September-December, 1864, as a "light duty conscript" and reported as present on the November-December, 1864, muster roll.

PARDUE, JOHN L., Corporal
Attached to this company from Company E, Holcombe's Legion, South Carolina, November-December, 1864, as Acting Corporal.

PORTER, EDWARD W., Private
Furloughed from Company D, 19th Regiment N.C. Troops (2nd Regiment N.C. Cavalry), June 30, 1864, and was attached to this company while absent on furlough. Attached through December, 1864, when he was returned to his original company.

PRICE, FRANCIS M., Private
Transferred from Company D of this battalion September-December, 1864, as a "light duty conscript" and reported as present on the November-December, 1864, muster roll.

REED, HENRY S., Private
Attached to this company from Company F, 50th Regiment N.C. Troops, November-December, 1864.

SHAW, F. S., Private
Enlisted in Cumberland County, April 11, 1864, for the war. Assigned to this company as a "light duty conscript" November-December, 1864.

SPAITH, HENRY, Private
Attached to this company from Company C, 19th Mississippi Infantry, November-December, 1864.

SPIVEY, WILLIAM A., Private
Enlisted in Cumberland County, April 11, 1864,

for the war. Assigned to this company as a "light duty conscript" November-December, 1864.

STRAUGHN, LUTHER C., Private
Transferred from Company A of this battalion November-December, 1864. Reported as present on November-December, 1864, muster roll.

STRICKLAND, JACOB B., Private
Transferred from Company A of this battalion November-December, 1864. Reported as present on November-December, 1864, muster roll.

TAYLOR, WILLIAM J., Private
Reported on company muster roll for November-December, 1864, with the remark: "Company H, 51st Regiment N.C. Troops. Discharged. Ordered to his company."

THOMAS, JOSEPH H., Private
Attached to this company from Company F, 50th Regiment N.C. Troops, November-December, 1864.

WARD, JOHN, Private
Attached to this company from Company G, 1st Regiment N.C. State Troops, November-December, 1864.

WATSON, RICHARD BUCHANAN, Private
Attached to this company from Company E, 8th Regiment N.C. State Troops, November-December, 1864.

WELSH, JOHN W., Private
Transferred from Company E of this battalion September-December, 1864, as a "light duty conscript" and reported as present on the November-December, 1864, muster roll.

WELSH, SAMUEL N., Private
Transferred from Company D of this battalion September-December, 1864, as a "light duty conscript" and reported as present on the November-December, 1864, muster roll.

WHALEY, HIRAM, Private
Transferred from Company E of this battalion September-December, 1864, as a "light duty conscript" and reported as present on the November-December, 1864, muster roll.

WORTH, ALBERT H., Sergeant
Attached to this company from Company I, 22nd Regiment N.C. Troops (12th Regiment N.C. Volunteers) November-December, 1864, as Acting Sergeant.

MISCELLANEOUS

The following list of men was compiled from primary records which record the unit as the 2nd Battalion N.C. Local Defense Troops but do not give the company to which these men belonged. Those reported as being sent from Harpers Ferry, Virginia, are reported in the unit history as serving in the battalion.

ADAMS, A. C.
Reported as a mason at the Fayetteville Arsenal and Armory in December, 1862.

ALBERTSON, SAMUEL
Reported as a carpenter at the Fayetteville Arsenal and Armory in December, 1862.

ALBRIGHT, JOSEPH, Private
Appears on a muster and pay roll of detailed conscripts at the Fayetteville Arsenal and Armory for the period August 1-October 31, 1864. Muster roll carries the remark that he was detailed by order of the Conscript Bureau on July 15, 1863.

BROWN, ADAM
Sent from Harpers Ferry, Virginia, to work at the Fayetteville Arsenal and Armory.

BURKHART, PHILLIP, Jr.
Sent from Harpers Ferry, Virginia, to work at the Fayetteville Arsenal and Armory.

BUTLER, REES H.
Sent from Harpers Ferry, Virginia, to work at the Fayetteville Arsenal and Armory.

CLASBY, JAMES
Sent from Harpers Ferry, Virginia, to work at the Fayetteville Arsenal and Armory.

CLASPY, JOHN
Sent from Harpers Ferry, Virginia, to work at the Fayetteville Arsenal and Armory.

CLOWE, RICHARD
Sent from Harpers Ferry, Virginia, to work at the Fayetteville Arsenal and Armory.

COPELAND, WILLIAM
Sent from Harpers Ferry, Virginia, to work at the Fayetteville Arsenal and Armory.

DECKER, LEVI
Sent from Harpers Ferry, Virginia, to work at the Fayetteville Arsenal and Armory.

DUKE, TOLLECT
Sent from Harpers Ferry, Virginia, to work at the Fayetteville Arsenal and Armory.

FUSS, ALLAN
Sent from Harpers Ferry, Virginia, to work at the Fayetteville Arsenal and Armory.

FUSS, GEORGE
Sent from Harpers Ferry, Virginia, to work at the Fayetteville Arsenal and Armory.

FUSS, JEREMIAH
Sent from Harpers Ferry, Virginia, to work at the Fayetteville Arsenal and Armory.

HARRINGTON, TIMOTHY
Sent from Harpers Ferry, Virginia, to work at the Fayetteville Arsenal and Armory.

HERRINGTON, FRANK
Sent from Harpers Ferry, Virginia, to work at the Fayetteville Arsenal and Armory.

HERRINGTON, HERBERT
Sent from Harpers Ferry, Virginia, to work at the Fayetteville Arsenal and Armory.

HERRINGTON, HIRAM
Sent from Harpers Ferry, Virginia, to work at the Fayetteville Arsenal and Armory.

HERRINGTON, ORRIE
Sent from Harpers Ferry, Virginia, to work at the Fayetteville Arsenal and Armory.

HEWITT, WILLIAM

Sent from Harpers Ferry, Virginia, to work at the Fayetteville Arsenal and Armory.

KITZMILLER, ARCHIBALD

Sent from Harpers Ferry, Virginia, to work at the Fayetteville Arsenal and Armory.

McCLOUD, LEWIS

Sent from Harpers Ferry, Virginia, to work at the Fayetteville Arsenal and Armory.

McDONALD, ALEXANDER, Artificer

Reported as a member of the battalion in the unit history.

MARTIN, WILLIAM

Sent from Harpers Ferry, Virginia, to work at the Fayetteville Arsenal and Armory.

PRICE, BENJAMIN

Sent from Harpers Ferry, Virginia, to work at the Fayetteville Arsenal and Armory.

PRICE, JOHN

Sent from Harpers Ferry, Virginia, to work at the Fayetteville Arsenal and Armory.

2nd REGIMENT N. C. STATE TROOPS

This regiment was organized at Camp Advance, Garysburg, Northampton County, in early June, 1861, and was mustered into state service on June 19, 1861. Two of the original companies assigned to the regiment (Companies A and C) were artillery companies serving as infantry. These two companies were eventually transferred and replaced by infantry companies. When orders came for the regiment to proceed to Richmond, Virginia, on July 13, 1861, one of the original infantry companies (Company E) withdrew from the regiment because it was not sufficiently advanced in drill. This company was transferred to the 7th Regiment N.C. State Troops and became Company E of that regiment.

Four of the companies left Camp Advance for Richmond on July 15. The balance left within a day or two, and all nine companies were reported in Richmond on July 19, 1861. From Richmond the regiment proceeded to Camp Holmes, Stafford County, Virginia, by way of Fredericksburg. On July 23, 1861, it went into camp, where it remained one month. One of the artillery companies, Company C, was ordered to Fort Macon on August 21, 1861, and assigned to the garrison as a heavy artillery battery on September 1, 1861. Thus the company was transferred out of the regiment, which now contained eight companies. On August 23, 1861, the regiment changed camps and moved to Camp Potomac, King George County, where it was stationed to guard the fortifications near the mouth of Potomac Creek and to protect the citizens of the county from marauding parties of the enemy. Here the regiment was assigned to Brigadier General John G. Walker's Brigade, Aquia District, commanded by Major General Theophilus H. Holmes. In addition to this regiment, the brigade was composed of the 1st and 3rd Regiments N.C. State Troops, 30th Regiment Virginia Infantry, and the 1st Regiment Arkansas Infantry. Two additional companies joined the regiment in November, 1861, to bring it up to ten companies. Throughout the winter of 1861-1862 the regiment remained at Camp Potomac. With the exception of Company K, the activities of the various companies were not reported for this period. The Captain of Company K reported on the muster rolls that the company was stationed at Smith's Battery from September to December 26, 1861. On a return of the Aquia District filed on January 14, 1862, the regiment was reported with the remark: "batteries about Aquia and Potomac."

When General A. E. Burnside's expedition began to advance from New Bern, troops were sent to North Carolina from Virginia. This regiment received orders to march with the brigade on March 22, 1862, and entrained for Richmond on March 24. Traveling by rail, the regiment arrived at Goldsboro on March 25 and went into camp below the town on the Atlantic and North Carolina Railroad at Camp McIntosh. Here the regiment remained until detached from the brigade and ordered to Wilmington on April 30. It proceeded by train to Wilmington on May 1 and marched some 21 miles to

Confederate Point on May 2 to strengthen the fortifications at New Inlet. The regiment encamped at Camp Wyatt and Company A, originally an artillery company, was stationed at Fort St. Philip. Early in June, 1862, the regiment was ordered back to Virginia minus Company A, which was detached. This company would remain on detached service until it was transferred out of the regiment in September, 1862. A newly raised infantry company would be assigned to the regiment in September, 1862, but from June to September, 1862, the regiment consisted of nine companies.

Arriving in Richmond, Virginia, on June 17, 1862, the regiment was ordered to do picket duty near the Williamsburg road. Since its old brigade had been broken up, it was assigned to Brigadier General Samuel Garland's Brigade, Major General D. H. Hill's Division. To accommodate regimental commanders, the regiment was soon transferred to Brigadier General George B. Anderson's Brigade, Major General D. H. Hill's Division. In addition to this regiment, the brigade consisted of the 4th Regiment N.C. State Troops, 14th Regiment N.C. Troops (4th Regiment N.C. Volunteers), and 30th Regiment N.C. Troops. Although the brigade would undergo a change in commanders, the regiment served in the brigade for the balance of the war.

On the morning of June 26, 1862, the brigade moved from its camp near the Williamsburg road, about five miles from Richmond, to the Chickahominy Bridge on the Mechanicsville Turnpike. General Lee was concentrating his troops to attack the Federal right at Mechanicsville. At 4:00 P.M., June 26, 1862, Brigadier General Roswell S. Ripley's Brigade, D. H. Hill's Division, crossed the bridge to aid General A. P. Hill's troops engaged at Mechanicsville. The balance of the division followed but did not take an active part in the day's action. That night General D. H. Hill received orders to cooperate with Major General T. J. Jackson on the Cold Harbor road. General Jackson's troops were on the Confederate left. At daylight, General Hill found his route blocked and sent Garland's and Anderson's brigades to the left to turn the enemy's position. The Federals abandoned their defenses when the two brigades began to move on their flank and rear, and Hill's whole division moved on toward Cold Harbor.

In the meantime, General Jackson had been forced to change his route and was proceeding on a road that would bring his troops in behind and to the right of Hill's Division. Hill advanced his troops to Cold Harbor and then deployed them along the edge of Powhite Swamp. To his right, Jackson's troops came into position, and on their right the troops of A. P. Hill's and James Longstreet's divisions were engaging the enemy at Gaines' Mill. Jackson's and D. H. Hill's troops were ordered forward to the support of Longstreet and A. P. Hill. Anderson's Brigade was second from the end on the left of the line and met the enemy on the edge of the swamp. After a short but bloody contest, the woods were cleared of the enemy. Between the edge of the wooded swamp and the Federal position was an open field some 400 yards wide. A general attack was ordered, and the Federals withdrew under pressure from the front and the threat of the attacks on their right. Night brought an end to the contest, and the Federals made good their escape.

From Gaines' Mill the Confederates, now under general command of General Jackson, moved to cross the Chickahominy at Grapevine Bridge. The bridge had been destroyed by the enemy in his retreat, and the position was defended to delay any attempted crossing. Here the troops went into bivouac while the bridge was being rebuilt, June 28-29. On June 30 the troops advanced across the bridge and marched to White Oak Bridge over White Oak Swamp. Here a strong Federal force kept the Confederates from rebuilding the bridge and thus kept Jackson's men at bay while the battle of Frayser's Farm was raging. Following the battle the bridge was rebuilt, and Jackson's men joined forces with the right wing of the army and moved to meet the enemy at Malvern Hill. General D. H. Hill's Division was placed on the Confederate center. Late on the afternoon of July 1, 1862, a general assault was launched by Hill's division. During the assault this regiment became separated from Anderson's Brigade and joined Brigadier General Robert E. Rodes' Brigade commanded by Colonel John B. Gordon. These troops advanced across an open field with the enemy batteries some 700-800 yards distant. They reached within 200 yards of the enemy's batteries before halting and falling back. During the night the Federals retired to Harrison's Landing. The battle of Malvern Hill was the last battle of the Seven Days' Battles around Richmond, June 26-July 1, 1862. During this campaign the regiment lost 20 killed and 96 wounded.

The brigade remained in bivouac near Malvern Hill until marched back to its original camp near Richmond on July 9-10. Here it remained until marched to Malvern Hill on August 6 and returned the night of August 7. D. H. Hill's Division had been left in front of Richmond to watch McClellan's troops at Harrison's Landing while Jackson and then Longstreet moved to confront General John Pope in middle Virginia. In mid-August, General Anderson's Brigade was moved to Hanover Junction. On August 26 the brigade moved to join the division at Orange Court House. On August 28 the entire division moved to join the Army of Northern Virginia. The division reached the army at Chantilly, September 2, 1862, after the Battle of Second Manassas and crossed into Maryland on September 4-5.

Reaching Frederick, Maryland, the army halted, and General Lee determined to send Jackson to capture Harpers Ferry while Longstreet moved to Hagerstown. On September 10 D. H. Hill's Division moved out of Frederick as the rear guard of Longstreet's column. Mounting pressure from the advancing Federals, plus the necessity of protecting Jackson at Harpers Ferry, resulted in the deployment of Hill's Division along the South Mountain gaps below Boonsboro on September 13. This regiment, as part of Anderson's Brigade, saw heavy action at Fox's Gap on September 14 and withdrew the next day under general orders to concentrate at Sharpsburg. Arriving at Antietam Creek on September 15, the brigade went into position on the heights east of the creek. Later D. H. Hill's troops were moved into position on the Confederate line in front of Sharpsburg, between the troops of Jackson and Longstreet.

On the morning of September 17 the Confederate left was vigorously assaulted and the three brigades of Hill's Division on the left of his line were ordered to support Jackson's right. When the Federal attack fell on the Confederate center, Anderson's and Rodes' Brigades were in the sunken road later called the Bloody Lane. Several determined assaults were repulsed, but the Federals succeeded in enfilading the right of Rodes' Brigade. An order for the right regiment to form perpendicular to the road to protect the flank was mistakenly interpreted for a general withdrawal. As Rodes' Brigade retired, General Anderson's men held their ground until forced to retire. As the enemy moved in on their front and flank, General Anderson was mortally wounded, and the brigade was routed from its position. The remnants went into position about 200 yards in rear of the road. Here the survivors on both sides began to dig in as the battle shifted to the Confederate right. General Hill attempted to lead an assault on the Federal position with about 200 men, but it failed. This ended any serious fighting on that part of the line. The following day the troops rested on the field and retired across the Potomac during the night of September 18 and went into camp. During the Maryland campaign the regiment lost 13 killed and 36 wounded.

The Army of Northern Virginia remained in the Shenandoah Valley until the Army of the Potomac crossed the Potomac River east of the Blue Ridge. Using his cavalry, Lee sought to discover the enemy's intentions. On October 28, 1862, Longstreet's Corps moved east of the mountains to Culpeper Court House while Jackson's Corps moved closer to Winchester. D. H. Hill's Division was posted at the forks of the Shenandoah River to guard the mountain passes. General Anderson died of his wound on October 16, 1862, and on November 7, 1862, Colonel Stephen D. Ramseur, 49th Regiment N.C. Troops, was promoted to Brigadier General and assigned to command Anderson's old brigade. General Ramseur was absent wounded at the time and did not assume active command until March, 1863. In the interim, Colonel Bryan Grimes of the 4th Regiment N.C. State Troops commanded the brigade.

When the enemy's intention was discerned, Lee moved Longstreet to Fredericksburg and ordered Jackson to prepare to move. Hill's Division was pulled back and moved to Strasburg. From there the division took up the line of march to Gordonsville on November 21, and from Gordonsville it moved to Fredericksburg. On December 3 Hill's Division was sent to Port Royal below Fredericksburg to prevent any crossing of the Rappahannock River at or near that point. It remained until ordered to Fredericksburg on December 12. Arriving in the morning on December 13, the division was placed in the third defensive line. During the battle of that day the division was subjected to heavy artillery fire but saw little action. After the battle it was advanced to the second line, where it remained throughout the next day. On December 15 it went into the first line, where it remained for two days. While on the field, the regiment was never actually engaged but suffered 4 killed and 17 wounded from the artillery fire.

Following the battle the regiment went into winter quarters at Grace Church, near Fredericksburg. There it spent the winter of 1862-1863 on picket duty. In January, 1863, General D. H. Hill was ordered to report to the Adjutant General in Richmond. His division was assigned to General Edward Johnson, who was absent wounded. The senior brigadier, Robert E. Rodes, assumed command until General Johnson returned to active duty. In March, 1863, General Ramseur reported and assumed command of the brigade. On April 29, 1863, the division received orders to march to Hamilton's Crossing, below Fredericksburg. Here it was placed in position on the right of the forces in the Fredericksburg entrenchments and extended the line to Massaponax Creek. Ramseur's Brigade was placed on the south side of the creek to guard the ford near its mouth. During the 29th and 30th the brigade was subjected to occasional shelling, but no general action occurred. Concluding that the enemy activity at Massaponax Creek was a feint, the brigade was moved up to Hamilton's Crossing during the evening of April 30.

General Hooker's Federal army had moved up the left bank of the Rappahannock to cross over behind the Confederates at Fredericksburg, and General Lee was moving a portion of his army to oppose it. The two armies would meet at Chancellorsville. Jackson's Corps moved down the Orange and Fredericksburg Plank Road on May 1, in the direction of Chancellorsville. After advancing about seven miles, Ramseur's Brigade was detached and ordered to report to Major General Richard H. Anderson, whose division was engaged on the right of Jackson's column. Joining Anderson's Division, Ramseur's Brigade took part in the advance against the enemy and drove them back about two miles. Night brought an end to the attack. May 2, about sunrise, Ramseur's Brigade was relieved from duty with Anderson's Division and ordered to return Johnson's Division. The brigade rejoined the division in time to participate in Jackson's flank march. After hard marching, Jackson's Corps succeeded in reaching a point about four miles west of Chancellorsville on the exposed right flank of Hooker's army.

As the troops came up, Jackson ordered they be deployed in three lines for the attack. Four divisions of the division were placed in the first of three lines of battle. Ramseur's Brigade was placed on the right of the second line to secure the right flank of the first line. The attack began about 5:15 P.M. During the advance the brigade in front of Ramseur's failed to maintain the pace, and thus the right of the line failed to bring its full weight against the enemy positions. Soon after the advance began the second line began to catch up to the first line and the two became one as they drove in Hooker's right

flank. The advance continued until night and strong resistance forced a halt. The lines were reformed, and the brigade was placed on the right side of the Plank Road in the third line. The activities of the brigade on May 3, 1863, were reported by General Ramseur as follows (*O.R.*, S.I., Vol. XXV, pt. 1, pp. 995-997):

Saturday night our division occupied the last line of battle within the intrenchments from which the routed corps of Sigel had fled in terror. My brigade was placed perpendicular to the Plank road, the left resting on the road, General Doles on my right and Colonel [E. A.] O'Neal, commanding Rodes' brigade, on my left. I placed Colonel [F. M.] Parker, Thirtieth North Carolina, on the right of my brigade; Colonel [R. T.] Bennett, Fourteenth North Carolina, on right center; Colonel [W. R.] Cox, Second North Carolina, left center; and Colonel [Bryan] Grimes, Fourth North Carolina, on left.

Sunday, May 3, the division being, as stated, in the third line of battle, advanced about 9 o'clock to the support of the second line. After proceeding about one-fourth of a mile, I was applied to by Major [W. J.] Pegram for a support to his battery, when I detached Colonel Parker, Thirtieth North Carolina, for this purpose, with orders to advance obliquely to his front and left, and rejoin me after his support should be no longer needed, or to fight his regiment as circumstances might require. I continued to advance to the first line of breastworks, from which the enemy had been driven, and behind which I found a small portion of Paxton's brigade and Jones' brigade, of Trimble's division. . . . At the command "Forward," my brigade, with a shout, cleared the breastworks, and charged the enemy. The Fourth North Carolina (Colonel Grimes) and seven companies of the Second North Carolina (Colonel Cox) drove the enemy before them until they had taken the last line of his works, which they held under a severe, direct, and enfilading fire, repulsing several assaults on this portion of our front. The Fourteenth North Carolina (Colonel Bennett) and three companies of the Second were compelled to halt some 150 or 200 yards in rear of the troops just mentioned, for the reason that the troops on my right had failed to come up, and the enemy was in heavy force on my right flank. Had Colonel Bennett advanced, the enemy could easily have turned my right. As it was, my line was subjected to a horrible enfilade fire, by which I lost severely. I saw the danger threatening my right, and sent several times to Jones' brigade to come to my assistance; and I also went back twice myself and exhorted and ordered it (officers and men) to fill up the gap (some 500 or 600 yards) on my right, but all in vain. I then reported to General Rodes that unless support was sent to drive the enemy from my right, I would have to fall back.

In the meantime Colonel Parker, of the

Thirtieth [North Carolina], approaching my position from the battery on the right, suddenly fell upon the flank and handsomely repulsed a heavy column of the enemy who were moving to get in my rear by my right flank, some 300 or 400 of them surrendering to him as prisoners of war. The enemy still held his strong position in the ravine on my right, so that the Fourteenth [North Carolina] and the three companies of the Second [North Carolina] could not advance. The enemy discovered this situation of affairs, and pushed a brigade to the right and rear of Colonel Grimes, and seven companies of Colonel Cox's (Second [North Carolina]), with the intention of capturing their commands. This advance was made under a terrible direct fire of musketry and artillery. The move necessitated a retrograde movement on the part of Colonels Grimes and Cox, which was executed in order, but with the loss of some prisoners, who did not hear the command to retire. Colonel Bennett held his position until ordered to fall back, and, in common with all the others, to replenish his empty cartridge-boxes. The enemy did not halt at this position, but retired to his battery, from which he was quickly driven, Colonel Parker, of the Thirtieth [North Carolina], sweeping over it with the troops on my right.

During this assault and the heavy fighting at the enemy's entrenchments, the entire color guard of the regiment was either killed or wounded. When the withdrawal commenced, a portion of the regiment remained and was captured with the regimental colors. The 4th Regiment N.C. State Troops suffered a similar loss.

After refilling cartridge boxes, the brigade was ordered to the left to meet an expected enemy attack. The entire Confederate line was converging on Chancellorsville, forcing the Federals to retire. Once Chancellorsville was occupied, the division was ordered to entrench along the Plank Road. It occupied this position until Hooker's army recrossed the Rappahannock and Lee moved his army back to Fredericksburg. On May 6 the brigade encamped near Hamilton's Crossing. During the Chancellorsville campaign the regiment lost 55 killed, 155 wounded, and 49 captured.

Following the Chancellorsville campaign and the death of Jackson, the Army of Northern Virginia was divided into three corps. Ramseur's Brigade was assigned to Major General Robert E. Rodes' Division, Lieutenant General Richard S. Ewell's 2nd Corps. The brigade composition remained the same. The division left camp on June 3 and reached just beyond Culpeper Court House on June 7. Ewell's Corps, with Rodes' Division leading, was on the march to Pennsylvania. From Culpeper Court House the division moved to Brandy Station to assist the cavalry on June 9 but arrived after the battle was over. It then resumed its march toward the Shenandoah Valley. Rodes Division received orders on June 12 to proceed to Cedarville by way of Chester Gap in advance of the other two divisions of the corps. At Cedarville, Rodes received orders to move on Berryville and Martinsburg and

into Maryland, while the other two divisions of the corps moved on Winchester. Berryville was occupied on June 13, after its defenders made good their escape. On June 14 Rodes' Division deployed before the defenses in front of Martinsburg. Fearing the defenders might escape, Rodes ordered a charge. Ramseur's Brigade, being in the lead, drove the enemy at almost a run for two miles beyond the town. However, the enemy infantry escaped by taking the Shepherdstown road while the Confederates concentrated on the Federal cavalry and artillery on the Williamsport road. On June 15 Rodes heard of the victory at Winchester and moved his men to Williamsport. Ramseur's Brigade was one of three that Rodes ordered across the Potomac River. The division remained at Williamsport until the balance of the corps moved up. On June 19 Rodes' Division was put in motion and marched to Hagerstown, where it remained two days. The division resumed its march on June 22, crossed into Pennsylvania, and bivouacked at Greencastle. The next day the division moved toward Chambersburg and passed through that town on June 24. There Major General Edward Johnson's Division joined Rodes', and together they moved to Carlisle, arriving there on June 27.

On the night of June 30 Rodes' Division was at Heidlersburg, where General Ewell received orders to proceed to Cashtown or Gettysburg, as circumstances might dictate. Rodes' Division moved on the morning of July 1 for Cashtown. While en route, word came that A.P. Hill's Corps was moving on Gettysburg, and General Ewell directed Rodes to proceed toward Gettysburg. When Rodes' Division arrived on the field, A. P. Hill's men were already engaged. Rodes moved his division into position on Hill's left, placing four brigades on the line and Ramseur's Brigade in reserve. The timely arrival of Major General Jubal Early's Division, on the left of Rodes, combined with the assaults launched from Hill's and Rodes' lines, drove the enemy through the town of Gettysburg. General Ramseur reported the activities of his brigade on that and succeeding days at Gettysburg as follows (*O.R.*, S.I., Vol. XXVII, pt. 2, pp. 587-588):

July 1, in rear of the division train, as a guard on the march from Heidlersburg to Gettysburg. My brigade arrived on the field after the division had formed line of battle. I was then held in reserve to support General Doles, on the left; Colonel O'Neal, left center; or General Iverson, on the right center, according to circumstances.

After resting about fifteen minutes, I received orders to send two regiments to the support of Colonel O'Neal, and with the remaining two to support Iverson. I immediately detached the Second and Fourth North Carolina troops to support O'Neal, and with the Fourteenth and Thirtieth hastened to the support of Iverson. I found three regiments of Iverson's command almost annihilated, and the Third Alabama Regiment coming out of the fight from Iverson's right. I requested Colonel [C. A.] Battle, Third Alabama, to join me, which he cheerfully did. With these regiments (Third Alabama, Fourteenth and Thirtieth North Carolina), I turned the enemy's strong position in a body of woods, surrounded by a stone fence, by attacking en masse on his right flank, driving him back, and getting in his rear. At the time of my advance on the enemy's right, I sent to the commanding officer of the Twelfth North Carolina, of Iverson's brigade, to push the enemy in front. This was done. The enemy seeing his right flank turned, made but feeble resistance to the front attack, but ran off the field in confusion, leaving his killed and wounded and between 800 and 900 prisoners in our hands. The enemy was pushed through Gettysburg to the heights beyond, when I received an order to halt, and form line of battle in a street in Gettysburg running east and west.

Colonel Grimes of the 4th Regiment N.C. State Troops reported the movements of the 2nd and 4th Regiment N.C. State Troops on July 1, 1863, as follows (*O.R.*, S.I., Vol. XXVII, pt. 2, pp. 589-590):

On Wednesday, July 1, we were encamped near Heidlersburg, and were under arms and on the march by sunrise. About 4 P.M. arrived near the battle-field, and formed in line of battle, being on the left of our brigade. After resting a few minutes, were ordered to advance in line of battle, which was soon countermanded, and then moved by the right flank. After proceeding a few hundred yards, this regiment, together with the Second, were recalled by Major-General Rodes, and posted on a hill to repel any attack from that quarter, as at that time there were indications of an advance on the part of the enemy. This position was parallel with the road, down which the other two regiments of our brigade had moved.

After a very few minutes—the enemy not advancing, and a regiment of theirs had been seen obliquing to the left instead of advancing toward us—General Rodes ordered me with the Second Regiment to advance. After getting from under cover of the hill, we were exposed to a severe, galling, and enfilading fire from a woods to our right, which compelled me to change front toward the right. We then advanced upon the enemy, joining our brigade, and driving them in great confusion, and, but for the fatiguing and exhausting march of the day, would have succeeded in capturing a very large number of prisoners. As it was, we captured more by far than the number of men in the command; but the troops were too exhausted to move rapidly, as they could otherwise have done. We were the first to enter the town of Gettysburg, and halted to rest on the road leading to Fairfield. We remained in that position during that night and Thursday.

Ramseur's Brigade did not partake in any major fighting on July 2 and 3. General Ramseur's report on Gettysburg quoted above continued as follows:

July 2, remained in line of battle all day, with very heavy skirmishing in front. At dark, I received an order from Major-General Rodes to move by the right flank until Brigadier-General Doles' troops cleared the town, and then to advance in line of battle on the enemy's position on the Cemetery Hill. Was told that the remaining brigades of the division would be governed by my movements. Obeyed this order until within 200 yards of the enemy's position, where batteries were discovered in position to pour upon our lines direct, cross, and enfilade fires. Two lines of infantry behind stone walls and breastworks were supporting these batteries. The strength and position of the enemy's batteries and their supports induced me to halt and confer with General Doles, and, with him, to make representation of the character of the enemy's position, and ask further instructions.

In answer, received an order to retire quietly to a deep road some 300 yards in rear, and be in readiness to attack at daylight; withdrew accordingly.

July 3, remained in line all day, with severe and damaging skirmishing in front, exposed to the artillery of the enemy and our own short-range guns, by the careless use or imperfect ammunition of which I lost 7 men killed and wounded. Withdrew at night, and formed line of battle near Gettysburg, where we remained on July 4. Commenced retreat with the army on the night of the 4th instant.

On the night of July 4-5, the division began to move toward Hagerstown by way of Fairfield. On the morning of July 6 it became the rear guard of the army and was engaged in several brief skirmishes on that day. Reaching Hagerstown on July 7, a line of battle was established, but no general engagement occurred. On the night of July 14 the division recrossed the Potomac and marched to near Darkesville. During the Gettysburg campaign the regiment lost four killed, twenty-seven wounded, and one missing or captured.

When the Federal army began crossing the Potomac River east of the Blue Ridge, General Lee had to move his army east of the mountains to interpose it between the enemy and Richmond. By August 1, 1863, the Army of Northern Virginia was encamped near Orange Court House, with the Army of the Potomac at Warrenton. By August 4 Lee withdrew his army to the Rapidan River line. In October Lee attempted to turn the flank of the Federal army. The movement maneuvered the Federal commander into falling back, and on October 14 the Federal rear guard was intercepted at Bristoe Station. Failure to coordinate the attack resulted in heavy casualties to troops of A.P. Hill's Corps and in the escape of the Federal rear guard. The regiment took part in the movement with the brigade and division, but Ewell's Corps was not engaged at Bristoe Station. However, this regiment was engaged in a skirmish at Warrenton on October 13-14 and lost two killed and two wounded.

With the escape of the Federal army to Centreville, Lee retired to the upper Rappahannock River. Rodes' Division was positioned opposite Kelly's Ford. The Federal army followed the Confederates and launched an attack at Kelly's Ford on November 7. On that day this regiment was on picket duty and received the brunt of the Federal assault. The 30th Regiment N.C. Troops moved up to assist the regiment but failed to act in concert. The result was that both regiments lost approximately 290 men captured of the 800 engaged. The number of killed and wounded ranged up to 50.

Lee withdrew his army south across the upper Rapidan River toward Orange Court House, where the army went into camp. Ramseur's Brigade encamped near Morton's Ford, and companies from the regiment went on picket duty at various fords on the river. On November 26 the Federal army crossed the lower Rapidan and turned west to face Lee's army. Lee thought the Federal army was moving south to a position between the Confederate army and Richmond. He put his army in motion to strike the Federal army on its flank. The activities of Ramseur's Brigade in the move and the resulting Mine Run campaign were described in Ramseur's report as follows (*O.R.*, S.I., Vol. XXIX, pt. 1, pp. 886-887):

. . . my brigade moved with the division about 3 o'clock on the morning of November 27. Formed line of battle along ridge road leading by Zoar Church; remained here several hours, right resting near the church, left near right of Major-General Johnson's intrenchments, and then took up line of march toward Locust Grove. Met the enemy in heavy force near and this side of Locust Grove. Division was again formed in line of battle and advanced a short distance, developing the enemy in strong force; then halted, and my brigade, on the right, was thrown forward so as to connect with the left of Major-General Early's division, Brigadier-General Gordon's brigade. Remained thus in line of battle, with sharp skirmishing in front, until dark. My brigade was then moved from the right to the left of the division, partially covering a wide gap between Major-General Rodes and Major-General Johnson.

About 12 o'clock at night the division fell back from its advanced position near Locust Grove, and took up line of battle again on Mine Run. My brigade was left to cover this movement. This line was strongly and rapidly fortified, and here we awaited the onset of the enemy, November 28, 29, and 30, and December 1. This he declined to make, and during the night of the 1st retreated to the north bank of the Rapidan.

At daylight Wednesday morning, December 2, advanced with my brigade and followed the retreating enemy as far as the river, picking up some 50 or 60 stragglers. Returned to camp at Morton's Ford December 3.

Thus ended the Mine Run campaign. Both armies went into winter quarters. This regiment built winter quarters near Orange Court House and did picket duty at Mitchell's and Morton's fords during the winter of 1863-1864.

On the morning of May 4, 1864, while the Federal army under General U. S. Grant was moving across the lower Rapidan, Ramseur's Brigade was at Raccoon Ford. When the division moved to oppose the Federal advance, Ramseur's Brigade was left to guard the fords from Rapidan Station to Mitchell's Ford. It remained in position during the first day of the Battle of the Wilderness, May 5. Rejoining the corps on the evening of May 6, the brigade was placed on the extreme left of the line to protect the flank. On the morning of May 7 it was moved to the rear as a reserve. When Burnside's IX Corps appeared to be moving into the gap between Ewell's and A. P. Hill Corps, Ramseur's Brigade was sent in to check the enemy and did so. At the same time, it closed the gap between the two corps.

Late in the evening of May 7 orders came to close up on the right. Throughout the night of May 7-8 the troops moved to the right. On May 8 the division arrived on the field at Spotsylvania Court House and formed on the right of Brigadier General Benjamin G. Humphrey's Brigade, Major General Kershaw's Division, Longstreet's Corps. By a vigorous charge Ramseur's Brigade drove the enemy from Humphrey's right for half a mile. It was then recalled and placed on the right of Kershaw's Division, to the left of the famous Mule Shoe. Here they were subjected to heavy skirmishing with the enemy on May 9, 10, 11.

When the Federal assault broke through the angle of the Mule Shoe on the morning of May 12, Ramseur's Brigade was ordered to check the enemy's advance and to drive him back. To do this he formed his brigade in a line parallel to the lines the enemy had taken. This regiment formed the right-center portion of the brigade line. When the command to charge was given, the entire brigade moved forward and drove the enemy out of the captured works. This was accomplished by 7:30 A.M. on May 12, and the brigade held the lines until 3:00 A.M. on May 13, when it was withdrawn to a new line in its rear. Here it would remain until moved out on May 19. On May 15, 1864, the remnants of the 1st and 3rd Regiments N.C. State Troops were assigned to the brigade. These two regiments had been in Brigadier General George H. Steuart's Brigade, Major General Edward Johnson's Division, Ewell's Corps. Steuart's Brigade had been in position in the Mule Shoe on the morning of May 12 and had been overrun and captured. Only a few escaped. The 1st and 3rd Regiments N.C. State Troops mustered about 30 men each when they joined Ramseur's Brigade. General Ramseur was promoted to Major General and assigned to command a division on May 27, and Colonel William R. Cox of this regiment was promoted to Brigadier General and assigned to command the brigade.

After several unsuccessful attempts against the Confederate line, General Grant began to move his army eastward. Because of the increased Federal activity to the east, the 2nd Corps was ordered to reconnoiter and find out what was going on. Ewell's Corps, with Ramseur's Brigade leading, moved out of the entrenchments and engaged the rear elements of the Federal army on May 19. An attack was made but was repulsed, and with reinforcements coming up the Federals began to press Ewell's men. The Confederates held and took advantage of night to break off the engagement and retire. This move disclosed the enemy's movement, and Lee moved his army accordingly. On May 22 Ewell's Corps arrived at Hanover Junction with Longstreet's Corps. Hill's Corps arrived on the morning of May 23. From here the Army of Northern Virginia moved to the North Anna, where it blocked the Federal army once again. At North Anna, May 24-25, Ewell's Corps, now commanded by General Jubal Early, was on the Confederate right and was not engaged. Grant withdrew during the night of May 26-27 and crossed the Pamunkey River, again sidestepping to the Confederate right. Early's Corps marched some 24 miles on May 27 and entrenched between Beaver Dam Creek and Pole Green Church. Longstreet's Corps came up on Early's right and Hill's Corps extended along the left of Early's line. On May 30, under orders from General Lee, Early moved to attack the Federal left at Bethesda Church. The attack failed to turn the Federal left but did reveal that the enemy was moving to the Confederate right.

The two armies began to concentrate at Cold Harbor, and on June 1 a spirited engagement occurred. Again Lee moved to his right, and the new alignment left Early's Corps on the Confederate left. Early was ordered to move out on June 2 to strike the Federal right. The attack was led by Rodes' Division and met with partial success until Federal reinforcements arrived to drive it back. During the Battle of Cold Harbor, June 3, 1864, Early's Corps was under attack by General A. E. Burnside's IX Corps and a part of General G. K. Warren's V Corps. The men of Warren's Corps struck the line held by Rodes' Division and were repulsed. Following the battle, the armies remained in position observing and skirmishing until June 12, when Grant began moving his army to cross the James River. General Early's Corps was withdrawn from the line on June 11 and was ordered to Lynchburg on June 12 to defend that city against an anticipated attack by troops under General David Hunter. Early was directed to remain in the Shenandoah Valley after striking Hunter's force.

General Early's troops began arriving at Lynchburg on June 17. By the next day, Early's entire command was there. Hunter retired and, after an unsuccessful attempt to overtake the retreating Federals, Early proceeded into the Shenandoah Valley. Still in Cox's Brigade, Rodes' Division, this regiment took part in Early's Valley campaign of 1864. On July 6, 1864, Early crossed into Maryland and advanced on Washington, D.C. At the Battle of Monocacy River, July 9, 1864, Rodes' Division operated on the Baltimore road while the main fighting occurred on the Washington road to the division's right. Rodes' Division was in the van when the defenses of Washington came in sight on July 11. Finding the defenses heavily manned on the morning of July 12, Early called off a planned assault, and during the night of July 12 the army began to retire toward Virginia. Back in the Shenandoah Valley. Early's troops were engaged at Stephenson's Depot, July 20, and at Kernstown, July 24, before he moved to Martinsburg to give his men a rest.

Early in August, 1864, the Federals began concentrating a large force under General Phil Sheridan at Harpers Ferry. On August 10 Early began a series of maneuvers to create the impression of a larger force than he had. His men were northeast of Winchester when Sheridan began to move. On September 19 contact was made and Early concentrated to receive the attack. The Confederates were making a determined defense east of Winchester when the left came under heavy attack and the whole line began to retire. During the initial stages of the battle General Rodes was killed as he deployed his division between Gordon's and Ramseur's divisions. These three divisions held the main line against repeated assaults, and only when the left appeared to be turned did they begin to retire to a defensive line close to the town. Again the Federals assaulted the front and left of the line. Word of a Federal column turning the right caused Early to issue orders for a general withdrawal. Finding the troops moving on the right were his own men adjusting the alignment, Early tried to counter the order. It was too late. The troops continued to the rear through Winchester and rallied south of the town. From there they continued the retreat to Fisher's Hill near Strasburg.

At Fisher's Hill, Major General Stephen D. Ramseur was placed in command of Rodes' Division. Sheridan struck Early's left and center at Fisher's Hill on September 22 and forced a general retreat. Early regrouped at Waynesboro on September 28. Here he received reinforcements and again began to move down the valley. On October 7 his troops occupied New Market. Moving to Fisher's Hill on October 12-13, Early found the enemy on the north bank of Cedar Creek. On October 19, 1864, Early launched a surprise attack on the Federal camp. The attack was initially successful and the Confederates succeeded in driving the Federals from two defensive lines. Early delayed the attack on the third line and assumed the defensive. Rallying his troops, Sheridan launched a devastating counterattack and routed Early's army. In this battle the three divisions of the 2nd Corps were commanded by General John B. Gordon. While attempting to rally the men, General Ramseur was mortally wounded and captured. Brigadier General Bryan Grimes, as senior brigadier, was assigned to command the division. Thus, when the 2nd Corps regrouped at New Market after the Cedar Creek disaster, the 2nd Regiment N.C. State Troops was in Cox's Brigade, Grimes Division. With the exception of minor skirmishing and the repulse of a Federal cavalry force on November 22, the army remained inactive.

On December 9 two divisions of the 2nd Corps moved under orders to return to Richmond. A few days later the Rodes-Ramseur Division, under Grimes, was ordered to return to the main army in the Richmond-Petersburg line. On December 14 it marched to Staunton and took the train for Petersburg. The brigade arrived on December 16 and went into winter quarters at Swift Creek, about three miles north of Petersburg. Here it remained until ordered to the right of the Confederate line about February 20, 1865. Grimes' Division had been placed on alert to be ready to move at a moment's notice. On February 17 three brigades moved to Sutherland's Depot on the right of the line. Cox's Brigade covered the division front at Swift Creek until relieved and then joined the division at Sutherland's. In mid-March, 1865, the division was ordered into the trenches in front of Petersburg. There it remained until the night of March 24, when the 2nd Corps, still under General Gordon, was massed for an attack on Fort Stedman. The sharpshooters who led the attacking force on the morning of March 25 were commanded by Colonel Hamilton A. Brown of the 1st Regiment N.C. State Troops. Although initially successful, the concentrated firepower and manpower of the Federal army forced the Confederates to retreat.

The remnants of the regiment returned to the trenches with the rest of the brigade and division. During the general assault on the morning of April 2, 1865, the Federals reached the divisional line near Fort Mahone. Grimes' Division attacked and reoccupied its trenches only to have other portions of the line fall to the Federal assault. Retreat was necessary, and it began the night of April 2-3. Gordon's Corps acted as rear guard as the army moved to Amelia Court House. It camped five miles east of the town on April 4, while the army awaited the collection of supplies. The next day the retreat resumed and continued through the night of April 5-6. As the rear guard, Gordon's Division was subjected to attacks by Federal cavalry and infantry. At a crossing of Sayler's Creek, on April 6, Gordon's men made a stand and repulsed the assault on their front. To the south of Gordon's position the Confederates under Generals Ewell and Anderson were severely defeated and captured. The Federals then moved on Gordon's right. The pressure forced the line to break in confusion, but Gordon rallied the survivors west of the creek and rejoined the army. At Farmville, on April 7, the men of Gordon's Corps went to the relief of General Mahone's Division. The Federals were held and the army continued the retreat.

On the night of April 7-8 Gordon's Corps moved to the advance of the army. His lead elements reached Appomattox Court House in the late afternoon of April 8 and halted. Later that evening they found the Federal cavalry in their front. It was decided that an attack should be made the next morning to cut through the enemy. Gordon's men moved into position west of the town during the night. At 5:00 A.M. the advance began and drove the Federal cavalry from the crossroads. The Confederates then took up a defensive position and came under attack by Federal infantry and cavalry. Gordon held his line until word came of the truce. A cease-fire was arranged and Gordon began to withdraw. Cox's Brigade had not received the cease-fire order, and as it moved back the men turned and fired on an advancing Federal cavalry force. After hearing the volley, General Gordon sent word of the truce. The last shot had been fired. The Army of Northern Virginia was surrendered on that date, and on April 12, 1865, fifty-five members of the 2nd Regiment N.C. State Troops were paroled.

FIELD AND STAFF
COLONELS
TEW, CHARLES COURTENAY
Resided in Orange County as Commandant of Cadets at the Hillsboro Military Academy and served as commander of Fort Macon prior to his appointment as Colonel of this regiment to rank from May 8, 1861. Assumed command of the regiment on June 20, 1861. Present or accounted for until killed in action at Sharpsburg, Maryland, on September 17, 1862.

BYNUM, WILLIAM PRESTON
Resided in Lincoln County and appointed Lieutenant Colonel of this regiment to rank from May 8, 1861. Promoted to Colonel on April 2, 1863, to rank from September 17, 1862. Submitted his resignation in March, 1863, by reason of his "having been chosen by the Legislature of North Carolina, Solicitor of the 7th Judicial Circuit." Resignation officially accepted March 21, 1863.

COX, WILLIAM RUFFIN
Resided in Wake County and appointed Major of this regiment to rank from May 8, 1861. Promoted to Lieutenant Colonel on April 2, 1863, to rank from September 17, 1862, and promoted to Colonel to rank from March 21, 1863. Wounded five or six times at Chancellorsville, Virginia, May 3, 1863. Returned to the regiment on August 1, 1863, and admitted to hospital at Richmond, Virginia, November 8, 1863, with wounds of the face and right shoulder. Furloughed from hospital for 40 days on November 11, 1863. Appointed to temporary rank of Brigadier General on May 31, 1864, and transferred from the regiment.

COBB, JOHN P.
Transferred from Company H of this regiment upon appointment as Colonel to rank from August 30, 1864. Wounded in left leg and captured at Winchester, Virginia, on September 19, 1864. Admitted to hospital at Winchester on September 19, 1864, and left leg amputated the next day. Transferred to hospital at Baltimore, Maryland, on November 19, 1864. Confined on December 9, 1864, at Fort McHenry, Maryland, where he remained until transferred to Fort Delaware, Delaware, on January 2, 1865. Paroled at Fort Delaware on February 27, 1865, and forwarded to City Point, Virginia, for exchange. Exact date of exchange not reported, but he was admitted to hospital at Richmond, Virginia, on March 4, 1865, and furloughed for 30 days on March 7, 1865.

LIEUTENANT COLONELS
STALLINGS, WALTER S.
Transferred from Company D of this regiment upon appointment as Major on October 4, 1862, to rank from September 17, 1862. Date of appointment also reported as April 2, 1863, to rank from September 17, 1862. Promoted to Lieutenant Colonel to rank from March 21, 1863. Wounded in action at Chancellorsville, Virginia, May 3, 1863, and returned to duty with the regiment on August 1, 1863. Present or accounted for until

killed in action at Snicker's Gap, Virginia, July 18, 1864.

SCALES, JAMES TURNER

Transferred from 2nd Company E of this regiment upon appointment as Major to rank from August 30, 1864. Promoted to Lieutenant Colonel to rank from August 31, 1864. Wounded near Petersburg, Virginia, in late 1864 or early 1865. Present or accounted for until paroled at Appomattox Court House, Virginia, April 9, 1865.

MAJORS

CUNNINGHAM, JOHN W.

Appointed Major to rank from May 16, 1861, but declined the appointment. Never served with the regiment.

HOWARD, JOHN

Transferred from Company B of this regiment upon appointment as Major on September 17, 1862. Died on October 4, 1862, of wounds received at Sharpsburg, Maryland, on September 17, 1862.

HURTT, DANIEL W.

Transferred from Company I of this regiment upon appointment as Major to rank from March 21, 1863. Wounded in the wrist at Gettysburg, Pennsylvania, July 1, 1863, and admitted to hospital at Richmond, Virginia, July 20, 1863. Furloughed from hospital on July 26, 1863, for 60 days. Remained absent on furlough through July 7, 1864, when he submitted his resignation by reason of his being unfit for field duty. Resignation officially accepted on August 30, 1864.

ADJUTANTS

HUGHES, NICHOLAS COLLIN

Temporarily transferred from Company I of this regiment when detailed as Adjutant on June 25, 1861. Returned to Company I in March, 1862.

DILLINGHAM, JOHN P.

Previously served in Company I and as Captain, Assistant Quartermaster, of this regiment. Appointed Adjutant with the rank of 1st Lieutenant to rank from March 22, 1862. Present or accounted for until captured at Strasburg, Virginia, October 19, 1864. Confined on October 25, 1864, at Fort Delaware, Delaware, where he remained until released after taking the Oath of Allegiance on June 17, 1865.

ASSISTANT QUARTERMASTERS

DILLINGHAM, JOHN P.

Transferred from Company I of this regiment upon appointment as Captain, Assistant Quartermaster, to rank from July 13, 1861. Present or accounted for until dropped from the rolls on February 24, 1862. Later appointed Adjutant of this regiment.

FAIRCLOTH, WILLIAM T.

Transferred from 2nd Company C of this regiment upon appointment as Captain, Assistant Quartermaster, March 14, 1862. Present or accounted for until ordered to report to the 67th Regiment N.C. Troops on October 29, 1864, to serve as Assistant Quartermaster of that regiment. Order never carried out and he was detailed to assist the Quartermaster of Cox's Brigade on October 31, 1864. Paroled at Appomattox Court House, Virginia, April 9, 1865, as Captain, Assistant Quartermaster, of Cox's Brigade.

ASSISTANT COMMISSARY OF SUBSISTENCE

HILLIARD, LOUIS

Appointed Captain, Assistant Commissary of Subsistence, on July 19, 1861, and assigned to this regiment. Present or accounted for until the position was abolished on July 31, 1863. Later appointed Captain, Assistant Quartermaster, and assigned to the Quartermaster Department.

SURGEONS

HUGHES, JAMES B.

Resided as a physician in Craven County when appointed Surgeon, at age 28, to rank from May 16, 1861. Present or accounted for until he submitted his resignation on July 18, 1863, by reason of "business practice problems and family health." Resignation officially accepted on July 28, 1863. Later appointed Acting Assistant Surgeon at Pettigrew General Hospital No. 13, Raleigh.

JOHNSON, JAMES

Appointed Surgeon to rank from May 18, 1861, and resigned on December 27, 1861.

KIRBY, GEORGE LEONIDAS

Resided in Sampson County and appointed Assistant Surgeon on June 27, 1861, to rank from May 16, 1861. Promoted to Surgeon on March 9, 1863, to rank from August 14, 1862. Present or accounted for until captured at Kelly's Ford, Virginia, November 7, 1863. Confined at Old Capitol Prison, Washington, D.C., until transferred on November 16, 1863, to Fort McHenry, Maryland, where he remained until paroled for exchange on November 21, 1863. Exact date of exchange not reported, but he appears as present or accounted for on muster rolls through October, 1864. Relieved from duty with the regiment on December 14, 1864, and ordered to report to Surgeon F. A. Ramsey, Medical Director, Bristol, Tennessee. Furloughed for 20 days on January 12, 1865.

CARRINGTON, GEORGE W.

Appointed Assistant Surgeon to rank from July 19, 1861, and was on duty in hospital at Richmond, Virginia, when ordered to report to this regiment to serve as Surgeon on December 14, 1864. Paroled at Appomattox Court House, Virginia, April 9, 1865.

ASSISTANT SURGEONS

STITH, L. A.

Resided in Wilson County and appointed Assistant Surgeon to rank from September 2, 1861. Present or accounted for until he resigned on July 31, 1862.

COBB, WILLIAM HENRY HARRISON

Previously served in Company D of this regiment. Appointed Assistant Surgeon to rank from February 20, 1863. Present or accounted for on muster rolls through October, 1864. Transferred to the Field and Staff, 20th Regiment Georgia Infantry after October, 1864.

CHAPLAIN

WATSON, ALFRED A.

Resided in Craven County as a minister of the Protestant Episcopal Church. Appointed Chaplain of this regiment to rank from June 27, 1861. Relieved from duty with the regiment on October 15, 1862, and assigned to the post at Goldsboro. Submitted his resignation on March 2, 1863, in order "that he may undertake parochial duty in one of our parishes left vacant by the death from yellow fever of its pastor." Resignation officially accepted on March 13, 1863.

DRILLMASTER

CALDER, WILLIAM

Resided in Craven County and appointed Drillmaster at age 18, May 1, 1861. Assigned to this regiment and detailed to Company F until transferred to Company K upon appointment as 2nd Lieutenant on October 22, 1861.

SERGEANTS MAJOR

COBB, WILLIAM HENRY HARRISON

Transferred from Company H of this regiment upon appointment as Sergeant Major on July 6, 1861. Present or accounted for until transferred to Company D of this regiment upon appointment as 2nd Lieutenant to rank from October 14, 1861.

BROWN, JOHN ISAAC

Transferred from Company K of this regiment upon appointment as Sergeant Major on November 1, 1861. Wounded at Malvern Hill, Virginia, July 1, 1862, and at Sharpsburg, Maryland, September 17, 1862. Present or accounted for until transferred to 1st Company C of this regiment upon appointment as 2nd Lieutenant to rank from March 13, 1863.

WISE, JOHN M.

Transferred from Company K of this regiment upon appointment as Sergeant Major on April 16, 1863. Captured at Kelly's Ford, Virginia, November 7, 1863, and confined at Point Lookout, Maryland, until paroled for exchange on April 27, 1864. Received in exchange at City Point, Virginia, April 30, 1864. Admitted to hospital at Richmond, Virginia, May 1, 1864, and furloughed for 30 days on May 6, 1864. Present or accounted for until killed in action at Winchester, Virginia, September 19, 1864.

COLLIER, SAMUEL P.

Detailed from Company H of this regiment as acting Sergeant Major from January through May, 1864, and from September, 1864, through April, 1865.

COMMISSARY SERGEANT

WHEELER, PETER W.

Transferred from Company I of this regiment upon appointment as Commissary Sergeant on August 6, 1863. Present or accounted for until discharged on January 11, 1864, by reason of "dyspepsia."

ORDNANCE SERGEANT

MURDOCK, ALEXANDER

Transferred from Company H of this regiment upon appointment as Ordnance Sergeant on May 14, 1862. Present or accounted for until he died in hospital at Staunton, Virginia, July 1, 1864.

DRUM MAJOR

PREMPERT, HENRY C.

Transferred from Company H of this regiment upon appointment as Drum Major on March 1, 1862. Present or accounted for on muster rolls through October, 1864. Admitted to hospital at Goldsboro on February 12, 1865. Took the Oath of Allegiance at Goldsboro on March 23, 1865.

1st COMPANY A

This heavy artillery company, known as the "Rifle Rangers" and composed of New Hanover County men, was mustered into state service on April 16, 1861, as "Captain Edward Dudley Hall's Company, Artillery." After organizing at Wilmington, the company was stationed at Fort Caswell. It remained an unattached company until ordered to Camp Advance, near Garysburg, Northampton County, where it was redesignated an infantry company on June 2, 1861, and was mustered in for the war as Company A, 2nd Regiment N.C. State Troops. Being the first company to serve as Company A of the regiment, it was later referred to as 1st Company A. In April, 1862, the company was detached from the regiment and ordered to Fort St. Philip to serve as artillery. Muster rolls indicate that the company was reported as 1st Company A, 2nd Regiment N.C. State Troops through August, 1862. Beginning with the September-October, 1862, muster roll the company was reported as "Captain Calvin Barnes' Company Unattached North Carolina Artillery." It was reported as unattached until November-December, 1863, when it was assigned to the 40th Regiment N.C. Troops (3rd Regiment N.C. Artillery) as Company H. Being the second company to serve as Company H of that regiment, it was later referred to as 2nd Company H.

Since the company was originally mustered in as a heavy artillery unit and was redesignated an artillery unit after only brief service as 1st Company A of this regiment, the editor has chosen to report the company's entire period of service in the roster of 2nd Company H, 40th Regiment N.C. Troops (3rd Regiment N.C. Artillery). The reader is therefore referred to the history and roster of that company, which appears on pages 478-489 of volume I of this series.

2nd COMPANY A

This company from Surry County was organized at Raleigh in September, 1862. Soon after its organization was completed it was assigned to this regiment as Company A. Being the second company to serve as Company A of this regiment, it was later referred to as 2nd Company A. The exact date the company joined the regiment was not reported, but it appears to have joined before the end of 1862. After joining the regiment the company functioned as a part of the regiment, and its history for the war period is recorded as a part of the regimental history.

The information contained in the following roster of the company was compiled principally from company muster rolls which covered from January through October, 1863, and January through October, 1864. No company muster rolls were found for the period prior to January, 1863; for November-December, 1863; or for the period after October, 1864. In addition to the company muster rolls, Roll of Honor records, receipt rolls, and hospital records, supplemented by state pension applications, United Daughters of the Confederacy records, and postwar rosters and histories, all provided useful information.

OFFICERS

CAPTAINS

WAUGH, JAMES R.
Resided in Surry County and appointed Captain to rank from September 9, 1862. Wounded in action at Chancellorsville, Virginia, May 3, 1863, and died of wound May 28, 1863.

NORMAN, WILLIAM M.
Resided in Surry County and appointed 1st Lieutenant to rank from September 9, 1862. Promoted to Captain to rank from May 28, 1863. Present or accounted for until captured at Kelly's Ford, Virginia, November 7, 1863. Confined at Old Capitol Prison, Washington, D.C., November 8, 1863, and transferred to Johnson's Island, Ohio, November 11, 1863. Confined at Johnson's Island until released after taking the Oath of Allegiance on May 19, 1865.

LIEUTENANTS

BANNER, WILLIAM O. T., 2nd Lieutenant
Resided in Surry County and appointed 3rd Lieutenant to rank from September 9, 1862. Promoted to 2nd Lieutenant to rank from May 28, 1863. Present or accounted for until captured at Kelly's Ford, Virginia, November 7, 1863. Confined at Old Capitol Prison, Washington, D.C., November 8, 1863, and transferred to Johnson's Island, Ohio, November 11, 1863. Confined at Johnson's Island until released after taking the Oath of Allegiance on June 12, 1865.

BRAY, BENJAMIN F., 1st Lieutenant
Resided in Surry County and appointed 2nd Lieutenant to rank from September 9, 1862. Detailed with the Pioneer Corps from November 16, 1862, through October, 1863. Promoted to 1st Lieutenant to rank from May 28, 1863, while absent on detail. Wounded at Spotsylvania Court House, Virginia, May 12, 1864. Present or accounted for until captured at Sayler's Creek, Virginia, April 6, 1865. Confined at Old Capitol Prison, Washington, D.C., April 14, 1865, and transferred to Johnson's Island, Ohio, April 17, 1865. Released at Johnson's Island after taking the Oath of Allegiance on June 18, 1865.

NONCOMMISSIONED OFFICERS AND PRIVATES

ALLEN, JOHN E., Private
Resided in Sampson County and paroled at Goldsboro in 1865.

ANDREWS, WILLIAM F., Private
Resided in Stokes County and enlisted in Wake County at age 19, August 29, 1862, for the war. Detailed in the Signal Corps on December 8, 1862, and reported as absent on detail through October, 1864.

ARMFIELD, JACOB, Private
Resided in Guilford County and enlisted in Wake County at age 24, September 5, 1862, for the war. Died at Gordonsville, Virginia, December 8, 1862, of "pneumonia."

ARMFIELD, MARTIN HENDRIX, Corporal
Resided in Guilford County and enlisted in Wake County at age 20, September 5, 1862, for the war. Mustered in as Private and appointed Corporal on October 8, 1862. Wounded in the left foot at Chancellorsville, Virginia, May 3, 1863. Reported as absent wounded until detailed in the Quartermaster Department on August 29, 1864. Captured at Amelia Court House, Virginia, April 6, 1865, and confined at Point Lookout, Maryland, until released after taking the Oath of Allegiance on June 23, 1865.

ATKINS, HAUSE, Private
Resided in Guilford County and enlisted in Wake County at age 30, September 5, 1862, for the war. Deserted at Staunton, Virginia, September 17, 1862, and reported as a deserter on company muster rolls through April 1, 1864. Reported as present on muster roll for May 1-August 31, 1864. Admitted to hospital at Richmond, Virginia, February 23, 1865, with "scorbutis" and returned to duty on March 7, 1865.

ATKINS, JERRY, Private
Enlisted in Wake County on September 5, 1862, for the war. Deserted at Staunton, Virginia, September 17, 1862.

BANNER, JOHN E., Sergeant
Resided in Stokes County and enlisted in Wake County at age 27, August 20, 1862, for the war. Mustered in as Sergeant. Captured at Chancellorsville, Virginia, May 3, 1863, and paroled the next day. Captured a second time at Kelly's Ford, Virginia, November 7, 1863, and confined at Point Lookout, Maryland. Paroled at Point Lookout on November 1, 1864, and sent to Venus Point, Savannah River, Georgia, for exchange. Exact date exchanged not reported. Paroled at Appomattox Court House, Virginia, April 9, 1865.

BARKER, MARTIN V., Private
Resided in Surry County and enlisted in Wake County at age 22, September 5, 1862, for the war. Killed in action at Chancellorsville, Virginia, May 3, 1863.

BARKER, THOMAS T., Private
Resided in Surry County and enlisted in Wake County at age 21, September 5, 1862, for the war.

Deserted at Staunton, Virginia, September 17, 1862.

BARNES, STEPHEN, Private
Resided in Johnston County and paroled at Goldsboro on May 1, 1865. "Came in for parole."

BASS, S., Private
Resided in Wayne County and captured at Goldsboro on March 31, 1865. Confined at Hart's Island, New York Harbor, until released after taking the Oath of Allegiance on June 19, 1865.

BEAN, THOMAS L., Private
Resided in Montgomery County and enlisted in Wake County at age 19, August 20, 1862, for the war. Sent to hospital sick on February 3, 1863, and reported as absent sick through October, 1864.

BELL, E., Private
Resided in Duplin County and paroled at Goldsboro on May 22, 1865. "Came in for parole."

BELL, PETER, Private
Resided in Alamance County and enlisted in Wake County at age 19, September 5, 1862, for the war. Died in hospital at Richmond, Virginia, April 12, 1863, of "pneumonia."

BELTON, FRANK M., Private
Born in Patrick County, Virginia, and resided as a farmer prior to enlisting in Wake County at age 19, September 5, 1862, for the war. Discharged on April 13, 1863, by reason of "chronic valvular disease of the heart."

BLUM, G. C., Corporal
Captured at Gettysburg, Pennsylvania, July 3-4, 1863, and confined at Fort McHenry, Maryland, July 6, 1863. Transferred to Fort Delaware, Delaware, July 7-12, 1863.

BRADLEY, JOHN C., Private
Enlisted in Wake County at age 19, September 5, 1862, for the war. Killed in action at Fredericksburg, Virginia, December 13, 1862.

BRAY, THOMAS W., Private
Resided in Surry County. Captured at Farmville, Virginia, April 6, 1865, and confined at Point Lookout, Maryland, until released after taking the Oath of Allegiance on June 23, 1865.

BROWN, J. C., Private
Paroled at Greensboro on May 5, 1865.

BROWN, PINKNEY S., Private
Resided in Moore County and enlisted in Wake County at age 28, September 5, 1862, for the war. Reported as absent sick until detailed as shoemaker at Lynchburg, Virginia, January 4, 1864. Admitted to hospital at Richmond, Virginia, May 15, 1864, with a gunshot wound of the head and transferred to Camp Winder, Richmond, May 29, 1864. Reported as present on September-October, 1864, muster roll. Admitted to hospital at Richmond on March 3, 1865, with "scorbutis" and transferred to Farmville, Virginia, April 1, 1865. Paroled at Troy, North Carolina, May 23, 1865.

BURT, JAMES G., Private
Resided in Wake County where he enlisted at age 30, June 22, 1863, for the war. Company muster rolls report him as absent sick through November

10, 1863, and as absent without leave from that date through October, 1864. Paroled at Appomattox Court House, Virginia, April 9, 1865.

BYRNES, P. H., Private
Reported as a prisoner transferred from Alexandria, Virginia, September 15, 1864, and forwarded to New Bern on September 19, 1864.

CALICOTT, JAMES A., Private
Resided in Montgomery County and enlisted in Wake County at age 25, September 5, 1862, for the war. Company muster rolls state that he was sent to hospital at Winchester, Virginia, sick, in October, 1862, and carry him as absent "supposed to be dead" from May-June, 1863, until September-October, 1864, when he appears with the remark: "died of desease at Winchester. Date not known."

CALICOTT, PLEASANT C., Private
Born in Montgomery County where he resided as a farmer prior to enlisting in Wake County at age 28, September 5, 1862, for the war. Wounded in eyes and right arm at Chancellorsville, Virginia, May 3, 1863, and discharged on December 10, 1863, by reason of disability caused by wounds.

CASE, CHARLES T., Private
Resided in Greene County and enlisted in Wake County at age 19, August 9, 1862, for the war. Present or accounted for until sent to hospital sick, June 1, 1863. Reported as absent sick through February, 1864. Captured at Spotsylvania Court House, Virginia, May 20-21, 1864, and confined at Point Lookout, Maryland. Paroled at Point Lookout and transferred to Aiken's Landing, Virginia, September 18, 1864, for exchange. Exact date of exchange not reported but company muster roll for September-October, 1864, states that he was furloughed for 40 days from October 1, 1864.

CASE, WILLIAM G., Private
Resided in Greene County and enlisted in Wake County at age 26, August 9, 1862, for the war. Wounded in action at Chancellorsville, Virginia, May 3, 1863. Present or accounted for until captured at Kelly's Ford, Virginia, November 7, 1863. Confined at Point Lookout, Maryland, until paroled and sent to James River, Virginia, for exchange, February 18, 1865. Declared exchanged on February 20-21, 1865.

CLARK, GEORGE M., Private
Resided in Virginia and enlisted in Wake County at age 21, September 5, 1862, for the war. Killed in action at Chancellorsville, Virginia, May 3, 1863.

COBLE, AUSTIN C., Private
Enlisted on August 26, 1864, for the war.

COBLER, EDMOND, Private
Resided in Rockingham County and enlisted in Wake County at age 23, September 5, 1862, for the war. Present or accounted for until captured at Kelly's Ford, Virginia, November 7, 1863. Confined at Point Lookout, Maryland, where he died July 31, 1864.

COBLER, GREENVILLE, Private
Enlisted in Wake County, October 3, 1863, for the war. Present or accounted for on company muster rolls until captured at Kelly's Ford, Virginia,

November 7, 1863. Confined at Point Lookout, Maryland, where he died January 30, 1864.

COBLER, NICHOLAS, Private
Resided in Rockingham County and enlisted in Wake County at age 32, September 5, 1862, for the war. Present or accounted for until he died in hospital at Richmond, Virginia, March 28, 1863, of "pneumonia."

COLLIER, JOHN, Private
Paroled at Farmville, Virginia, April 11-21, 1865.

COMBS, WILLIAM, Private
Resided in Wilkes County and enlisted at Camp Vance, August 15, 1864, for the war. Present or accounted for until captured at Burkeville, Virginia, April 6, 1865. Confined at Point Lookout, Maryland, until released after taking the Oath of Allegiance on June 10, 1865.

COOPER, CASWELL, Private
Resided in Pitt County and enlisted in Wake County at age 44, June 23, 1863, for the war as a substitute. Present or accounted for through October, 1864. Captured at Petersburg, Virginia, April 3, 1865, and confined at Hart's Island, New York Harbor. Released after taking the Oath of Allegiance on June 18, 1865.

COX, WASHINGTON, Private
Resided in Surry County and enlisted in Wake County at age 34, September 5, 1862, for the war. Present or accounted for until he died at Mount Jackson, Virginia, December 19, 1862, of "cystitis."

DAVIS, JASPER, Private
Resided in Surry County and enlisted in Wake County at age 23, September 5, 1862, for the war. Deserted at Staunton, Virginia, September 17, 1862.

DENNIS, GEORGE T., Fifer
Resided in Montgomery County and enlisted in Wake County at age 24, August 20, 1862, for the war. Mustered in as Fifer. Died in hospital at Richmond, Virginia, March 21, 1863, of "bronchitis."

DENNIS, WILLIS M., Private
Resided in Montgomery County and enlisted in Wake County at age 25, August 20, 1862, for the war. Wounded in action at Chancellorsville, Virginia, May 3, 1863, and reported as absent on furlough through August, 1863. Present or accounted for on company muster rolls until captured at Strasburg, Virginia, October 19, 1864. Confined at Point Lookout, Maryland, until paroled and transferred to Aiken's Landing, Virginia, March 28, 1865, for exchange. Received in exchange at Boulware's Wharf, James River, Virginia, March 30, 1865.

DIX, JAMES H., Corporal
Resided as a tobacconist in Surry County prior to enlisting in Wake County at age 25, September 5, 1862, for the war. Mustered in as Corporal. Captured near Fredericksburg, Virginia, May 3, 1863, and exchanged at City Point, Virginia, May 10, 1863. Present or accounted for until captured at Winchester, Virginia, September 19, 1864. Confined at Point Lookout, Maryland, until released

after taking the Oath of Allegiance on May 13, 1865.

DOBSON, JOHN O., Private
Wounded and captured at Gettysburg, Pennsylvania, July 1-5, 1863, and died of wounds on September 3, 1863.

DUNMAN, JAMES B., Private
Resided in Stokes County and enlisted in Wake County at age 19, September 5, 1862, for the war. Deserted at Staunton, Virginia, September 17, 1862, and returned to the company in December, 1862. Reported as absent sick in hospital on January-February, 1863, muster roll. Furloughed from hospital at Liberty, Virginia, for 40 days on June 6, 1863. Company muster rolls carry him as absent without leave from date his furlough expired through October, 1864.

EDWARDS, JOSIAH, Private
Born in Johnston County where he resided prior to enlisting in Wake County at age 37, August 15, 1862, for the war. Died in hospital at Gordonsville, Virginia, April 6, 1863, of disease.

ELLIS, JEREMIAH, Private
Enlisted in Wake County at age 30, January 20, 1863, for the war. Deserted February 27, 1863.

FARRIS, JAMES F., Private
Captured at Winchester, Virginia, September 19, 1864, and confined at Point Lookout, Maryland, until paroled and transferred to Aiken's Landing, Virginia, for exchange on March 15, 1865. Received in exchange on March 18, 1865.

FLIPPIN, JOSEPH, Sergeant
Enlisted in Wake County at age 35, September 5, 1862, for the war. Mustered in as Corporal and promoted to Sergeant on October 8, 1862. Wounded in right arm at Chancellorsville, Virginia, May 2-3, 1863. Company muster rolls report him as absent wounded through February 1, 1864, and as absent without leave from that date through October, 1864. Detailed as a guard in hospital at Charlotte on November 3, 1864. Paroled at Newton, North Carolina, April 19, 1865.

FORKNER, JAMES LAWRENCE, Corporal
Born in Surry County where he resided prior to enlisting in Wake County at age 19, September 5, 1862, for the war. Mustered in as Private and appointed Corporal on October 8, 1862. Wounded in action in Chancellorsville, Virginia, May 3, 1863, and died at Mount Airy, North Carolina, June 19, 1863, of wound.

FORKNER, SAMUEL, Private
Resided in Surry County and enlisted in Wake County at age 25, September 5, 1862, for the war. Mustered in as Private and appointed Corporal on June 1, 1863. Reduced to ranks on October 28, 1863. Present or accounted for until captured at Kelly's Ford, Virginia, November 7, 1863. Confined at Point Lookout, Maryland, until paroled and exchanged at City Point, Virginia, April 27, 1864. Admitted to hospital at Richmond, Virginia, May 1, 1864, with "scorbutus" and furloughed for 30 days on May 6, 1864. Reported as absent on furlough on company muster rolls through October, 1864.

FORKNER, WILLIAM, Private

Resided in Surry County and enlisted in Wake County at age 28, September 5, 1862, for the war. Present or accounted for on company muster rolls until furloughed on February 24, 1863, by reason of sickness. Reported as absent without leave after expiration of furlough on April 1, 1863, until detailed as Provost Guard at Salisbury on August 12, 1864.

FRIAR, RICHARD K., Private

Resided in Pitt County and enlisted in Wake County at age 55, June 22, 1863, for the war as a substitute. Present or accounted for on company muster rolls until reported on May 1-August 31, 1864, muster roll with the remark that he was "absent prisoner May 18, 1864." September-October, 1864, muster roll states that he was "absent wounded May 12, 1864." Admitted to hospital at Richmond, Virginia, December 24, 1864, and detailed January 19, 1865. Admitted to hospital at Richmond on February 23, 1865, with a gunshot wound of the right arm and transferred to Farmville, Virginia, April 1, 1865.

GASKINS, H., Private

Captured at Hanover Court House, Virginia, May 27, 1862, and exchanged at Aiken's Landing, Virginia, October 6, 1862. Declared exchanged on November 10, 1862.

GATLIN, JOHN, Private

Federal Provost Marshal records indicate that he was detained at Camp Distribution. Entry dated October 3, 1864, states that he was received from City Point, Virginia, and forwarded to "R. I." October 8, 1864.

GILLICAN, A., Private

Federal Provost Marshal records indicate that he was detained at Camp Distribution on June 3, 1864, and forwarded to New Bern on June 4, 1864.

GOOCH, NATHANIEL, Private

Enlisted in Wake County on October 3, 1863, for the war. Present or accounted for until captured at Winchester, Virginia, September 19, 1864. Confined at Point Lookout, Maryland, until paroled and exchanged at Venus Point, Savannah River, Georgia, November 15, 1864.

GOODEN, S. H., Private

Enlisted in September, 1864, for the war.

GORDON, ORISON T., Private

Resided in Surry County and enlisted in Wake County at age 20, September 5, 1862, for the war. Died in hospital at Richmond, Virginia, July 31, 1863, of "pneumonia."

HALL, DAVID, Private

Born in Pittsylvania County, Virginia, and resided in Surry County prior to enlisting in Wake County at age 29, September 5, 1862, for the war. Deserted at Staunton, Virginia, September 17, 1862, and reported as absent on company muster rolls through September-October, 1863, when he was reported as present with the remark: "Charges preferred for desertion." Captured at Kelly's Ford, Virginia, November 7, 1863, and confined at Point Lookout, Maryland, where he died January 31, 1864.

HARDEN, JAMES L., Private

Resided in Halifax County where he enlisted at age 37, December 20, 1862, for the war. Captured at Fredericksburg, Virginia, May 3, 1863, and exchanged at City Point, Virginia, May 10, 1863. Company muster rolls carry him as absent sick from date of exchange through October, 1863, and as absent without leave from that date until January-February, 1864, when he was reported as present with the remark: "Sentence for General Court Martial three months hard labor under the direction of the Divisional Commander. Stoppage for absence without leave eight months and ten days." Present or accounted for on company muster rolls from that date through October, 1864. Detailed on January 6, 1865, and ordered to report to the Surgeon-in-Charge at Danville, Virginia.

HARRISS, DANIEL, Private

Enlisted in Wake County on October 3, 1863, for the war. Captured at Kelly's Ford, Virginia, November 7, 1863, and confined at Point Lookout, Maryland, November 11, 1863.

HAUSER, ADAM, Private

Born in Surry County where he resided as a farmer prior to enlisting in Wake County at age 23, September 5, 1862, for the war. Killed in action at Chancellorsville, Virginia, May 3, 1863.

HAUSER, SAMUEL P., Fifer

Born in Surry County where he resided as a farmer prior to enlisting in Wake County at age 18, September 5, 1862, for the war. Mustered in as Private. Reported as Fifer for the first time on the March-April, 1863, muster roll with the remark that he "died March 27, 1863." Hospital records indicate that he died at Staunton, Virginia, March 27, 1863, of "pneumonia."

HAYMORE, JOHN B., Corporal

Resided in Surry County and enlisted in Wake County at age 25, September 5, 1862, for the war. Mustered in as Corporal. Died April 23, 1863.

HAYMORE, WILLIAM H., Private

Resided in Surry County and enlisted in Wake County at age 24, September 5, 1862, for the war. Admitted to hospital at Richmond, Virginia, March 8, 1863, with "chronic rheumatism and enlarged knee joint" and furloughed for 30 days on June 9, 1863. Company muster rolls carry him as absent without leave after expiration of furlough. Reported as absent without leave through October, 1864.

HENDRIX, WILLIAM J., Private

Enlisted on October 3, 1863, for the war. Captured at Kelly's Ford, Virginia, November 7, 1863. Confined at Point Lookout, Maryland, where he remained until released after taking the Oath of Allegiance on January 23, 1864, to join the U.S. service. Assigned to the 1st Regiment U.S. Volunteer Infantry.

HIGH, JOEL B., Private

Resided in Nash County and enlisted in Wake County at age 38, June 23, 1863, for the war. Present or accounted for through October, 1864.

HILL, A., Private
Resided in Wayne County and paroled at Goldsboro on May 19, 1865. "Came in for parole."

HINES, HENRY, Sergeant
Resided in Surry County and enlisted in Wake County at age 22, September 5, 1862, for the war. Mustered in as Sergeant. Died at Mount Jackson, Virginia, October 7, 1862, "from an attack of measles."

HOLLIFIELD, GEORGE F., Private
Enlisted in Wake County on May 9, 1864, for the war. Present or accounted for through October, 1864. Appears on a roll of "rebel deserters" forwarded to Colonel T. Ingraham, Provost Marshal General, Defenses North of Potomac, April 18, 1865, with the remark: "Nashville, Tennessee."

HORN, JACOB H., Private
Federal Provost Marshal records report him as received at Camp Distribution from Alexandria, Virginia, on September 15, 1864, and forwarded to New Bern on September 19, 1864.

HORN, JAMES, Private
Resided in Wilson County and enlisted in Wake County at age 46, June 23, 1863, for the war as a substitute. Present or accounted for until captured at Kelly's Ford, Virginia, November 7, 1863. Confined at Point Lookout, Maryland, until paroled and exchanged at Boulware's Wharf, James River, Virginia, January 17, 1865. Appears as present on a roll of a detachment of paroled and exchanged prisoners at Camp Lee, near Richmond, Virginia, dated January 26, 1865.

HOWELL, FREEMAN, Private
Resided in Wayne County and captured at Goldsboro on March 8, 1865. Confined at Hart's Island, New York Harbor, until released after taking the Oath of Allegiance on June 18, 1865.

HURLEY, DANIEL W., Musician
Resided in Montgomery County and enlisted in Wake County at age 27, August 20, 1862, for the war. Mustered in as Musician. Killed in action at Chancellorsville, Virginia, May 3, 1863.

HUTCHINGS, JAMES L., Private
Resided in Surry County and enlisted in Wake County at age 33, September 5, 1862, for the war. Deserted at Staunton, Virginia, September 17, 1862.

JARRELL, ALBERT H., Private
Resided in Rockingham County and enlisted in Wake County at age 27, September 5, 1862, for the war. Captured at Fredericksburg, Virginia, May 3, 1863, and exchanged at City Point, Virginia, May 10, 1863. Present or accounted for until captured at Kelly's Ford, Virginia, November 7, 1863. Confined at Point Lookout, Maryland, until paroled and exchanged at Aiken's Landing, Virginia, February 18-24, 1865.

JARRETT, JOHN E., Private
Enlisted in Wake County on May 9, 1864, for the war. Present or accounted for until captured at Winchester, Virginia, September 19, 1864. Confined at Point Lookout, Maryland, where he died May 29, 1865, of "chronic diarrhoea."

JONES, JOHN R., Private
Resided in Pitt County and enlisted in Wake County at age 30, July 17, 1862, for the war. Wounded in leg at Chancellorsville, Virginia, May 3, 1863, and leg amputated. Died May 31, 1863.

KINGSBURY, WILLIAM C., Private
Resided in Stokes County and enlisted in Wake County at age 28, September 5, 1862, for the war. Died in hospital at Charlottesville, Virginia, November 2, 1862, of "phthisis."

KROUSE, JOHN H., Private
Resided in Surry County and enlisted in Wake County at age 20, September 5, 1862, for the war. Died in hospital at Mount Jackson, Virginia, in December, 1862, from "typhoid pneumonia." Date of death given as December 17, 1862, and December 29, 1862.

LACY, JOHN T., Private
Resided in Pitt County and enlisted in Wake County at age 28, August 9, 1862, for the war. Wounded in right hip and captured at Chancellorsville, Virginia, May 3, 1863. Admitted to hospital at Washington, D.C., May 11, 1863, and transferred to Old Capitol Prison, Washington, October 14, 1863. Released after taking the Oath of Allegiance on December 13, 1863.

LAMM, WILLIAM, Private
Resided in Wilson County where he enlisted at age 38, June 18, 1863, for the war. Detailed in hospital at Richmond, Virginia, September 9, 1863. Company muster rolls report him as absent on detail through October, 1864. Admitted to hospital at Petersburg, Virginia, January 1, 1865, and furloughed on January 21, 1865.

LANGFORD, PLUMMER, Private
Resided in Alamance County where he enlisted at age 43, August 20, 1863, for the war. Detailed in hospital at Richmond, Virginia, December 9, 1863. Muster rolls report him as absent on detail through April, 1864, and as present or accounted for from that date through October, 1864. Captured at Farmville, Virginia, April 6, 1865, and confined at Point Lookout, Maryland, until released after taking the Oath of Allegiance on June 16, 1865.

LEWIS, CHARLES W., 1st Sergeant
Resided in Surry County and enlisted in Wake County at age 27, August 20, 1862, for the war. Mustered in as 1st Sergeant. Present or accounted for until captured at Kelly's Ford, Virginia, November 7, 1863. Confined at Point Lookout, Maryland, until paroled for exchange on September 30, 1864. Exact date of exchange not reported, but September-October, 1864, muster roll states that he was absent on furlough which would expire on November 6, 1864. Captured at Amelia Court House, Virginia, April 6, 1865, and confined at Point Lookout until released after taking the Oath of Allegiance on June 28, 1865.

McLEAN, JOHN L., Private
Resided in Montgomery County and enlisted in Wake County at age 28, August 16, 1862, for the war. Detailed as a shoemaker in the Quartermaster Department, Richmond, Virginia, Decem-

ber 7, 1862. Reported as absent on detail through December, 1864. Captured at Richmond on April 3, 1865, and confined at Point Lookout, Maryland, until released after taking the Oath of Allegiance on June 29, 1865.

McRACKEN, LINDSEY, Private
Enlisted on February 4, 1864, for the war. Captured at Spotsylvania Court House, Virginia, May 20, 1864, and confined at Point Lookout, Maryland. Died at Point Lookout on July 15, 1864, of "remit. fever."

MANDEY, GABRIEL, Private
Captured at Fisher's Hill, Virginia, September 23, 1864, and confined at Point Lookout, Maryland, October 3, 1864.

MARTIN, ALLEN, Private
Resided in Montgomery County and enlisted in Wake County at age 22, August 9, 1862, for the war. Captured near Fredericksburg, Virginia, May 3, 1863, and exchanged at City Point, Virginia, May 10, 1863. Captured at Hagerstown, Maryland, July 12-13, 1863, and confined at Fort Delaware, Delaware, July 30, 1863. Transferred on October 18, 1863, to Point Lookout, Maryland, where he died February 9, 1864.

MARTIN, DANIEL, Private
Resided in Montgomery County and enlisted in Wake County at age 19, August 9, 1862, for the war. Present or accounted for until captured at Kelly's Ford, Virginia, November 7, 1863. Confined at Point Lookout, Maryland, until paroled and exchanged at Aiken's Landing, Virginia, February 18-24, 1865. Admitted to hospital at Richmond, Virginia, March 2, 1865, and furloughed for 30 days on March 8, 1865.

MATTHEWS, J. P., Private
Paroled at Raleigh on May 16, 1865.

MITCHEL, WILLIAM A., Sergeant
Resided in Surry County and enlisted in Wake County at age 23, September 5, 1862, for the war. Mustered in as Sergeant. Wounded in action at Chancellorsville, Virginia, May 3, 1863, and furloughed for 30 days on June 6, 1863. Company muster rolls carry him as absent without leave after expiration of furlough until January-February, 1864, when he appears as present. Present or accounted for on company muster rolls through October, 1864, when he appears with the remark: "Absent detailed in Quartermaster Department, Greensboro."

MITCHELL, THOMAS J., Private
Enlisted in Wake County at age 28, September 5, 1862, for the war. Detailed as a shoemaker in the Quartermaster Department, Richmond, Virginia, November 15, 1862. Reported as absent on detail through December, 1864.

MOORE, JESSE, Private
Resided in Surry County and enlisted in Wake County at age 22, August 20, 1862, for the war. Company muster rolls report him as absent sick from September 10, 1862, through October, 1864.

MOREFIELD, JOHN H., Private
Resided in Forsyth County and enlisted in Wake County at age 28, September 5, 1862, for the war. Present or accounted for on company muster rolls through October, 1864.

NICHOLS, J. H., Private
Took the Oath of Allegiance at Elmira, New York, May 19, 1865.

OWEN, LEVI, Private
Resided in Greene County and enlisted in Wake County at age 38, June 22, 1863, for the war. Company muster rolls report him as present through July, 1863, and absent sick from that date through October, 1864.

PASHAL, A. R., Private
Enlisted on November 30, 1864, for the war.

PATTERSON, WILLIAM, Private
Resided in Franklin County where he enlisted at age 42, August 20, 1863, for the war. Detailed in hospital at Richmond, Virginia, October 5, 1863. Absent on detail until captured in hospital at Richmond on April 3, 1865. Paroled on April 20, 1865.

PELL, JOSEPH J., Fifer
Resided in Surry County and enlisted in Wake County at age 33, September 5, 1862, for the war. Mustered in as Private. Died in hospital at Lynchburg, Virginia, December 3, 1862, of "typhoid pneumonia." Rank given on hospital records as Fifer.

PENDER, THOMAS R., Private
Resided in Alamance County where he enlisted at age 42, August 20, 1863, for the war. Present or accounted for until captured at Kelly's Ford, Virginia, November 7, 1863. Confined at Point Lookout, Maryland, where he died January 5, 1864, of "diptheria."

POOR, JOHN, Private
Born in Surry Conty where he resided prior to enlisting in Wake County at age 19, September 5, 1862, for the war. Killed in action at Chancellorsville, Virginia, May 3, 1863.

POOR, LEVI, Fifer
Born in Surry County where he resided prior to enlisting in Wake County at age 26, September 5, 1862, for the war. Mustered in as Private. Appointed Fifer, March-April, 1863. Admitted to hospital on March 1, 1863, at Richmond, Virginia, where he died March 11, 1863, of "chronic dysentery."

POOR, SAMUEL D., Private
Resided in Surry County and enlisted in Wake County at age 25, September 5, 1862, for the war. Reported as absent sick from October 20, 1862, until February 1, 1864, when he was reported as absent without leave. Reported as absent without leave until August 20, 1864, when he was reported as absent sick. Captured at Winchester, Virginia, September 19, 1864, and confined at Point Lookout, Maryland. Paroled at Point Lookout and sent to Venus Point, Savannah River, Georgia, November 1, 1864, for exchange. Date of exchange not reported.

POOR, WILLIAM F., Private
Born in Surry County where he resided prior to

enlisting in Wake County at age 21, September 5, 1862, for the war. Died in camp near Guinea Station, Virginia, February 14, 1863.

POORE, ALLEN, Private
Resided in Surry County and enlisted in Wake County at age 23, September 5, 1862, for the war. Deserted near Staunton, Virginia, September 17, 1862.

PRESCOTT, WILLOUGHBY, Private
Federal Provost Marshal records report that he was received at Camp Distribution from Alexandria, Virginia, September 15, 1864, and forwarded to New Bern on September 19, 1864.

RAGG, JOHN W., Private
Paroled at Greensboro on May 16, 1865.

RAY, JOHN W., Private
Paroled at Greensboro on May 16, 1865.

REDMAN, WASHINGTON S., Private
Resided in Stokes County and enlisted in Wake County at age 19, September 5, 1862, for the war. Captured near Fredericksburg, Virginia, May 3, 1863, and exchanged at City Point, Virginia, May 10, 1863. Present or accounted for until captured at Kelly's Ford, Virginia, November 7, 1863. Confined at Point Lookout, Maryland, until paroled and transferred to Aiken's Landing, Virginia, for exchange on February 24, 1865. Admitted to hospital at Richmond, Virginia, February 25, 1865, and furloughed for 60 days on March 20, 1865.

REECE, JOHN, Private
Born in Surry County and resided as a farmer in Rockingham County prior to enlisting in Wake County at age 25, September 5, 1862, for the war. Died in hospital near Guinea Station, Virginia, January 12, 1863.

RING, HUGUSTIN, Sergeant
Captured at Fisher's Hill, Virginia, September 22, 1864, and confined at Point Lookout, Maryland, until paroled for exchange on March 17, 1865. Received at Boulware's Wharf, James River, Virginia, March 19, 1865.

ROARK, ELI, Private
Born in Stokes County where he resided as a farmer prior to enlisting in Wake County at age 18, September 5, 1862, for the war. Discharged on April 13, 1863, by reason of "pulmonary consumption."

ROBINS, ABNER, Private
Federal Provost Marshal records report that he was received at Camp Distribution from Alexandria, Virginia, September 15, 1864, and was forwarded to New Bern on September 19, 1864.

RODGERS, B. H., Private
Enlisted in January, 1865, for the war.

RODGERS, HENRY, Private
Born in Pitt County where he resided as a farmer prior to enlisting in Wake County at age 21, July 22, 1863, for the war. Discharged on August 31, 1863, by reason of his being "incapable of performing the duties of a soldier because of a lack of physical development and want of muscular power."

ROTTENBURY, HARRIS, Private
Resided in Granville County and enlisted in Wake County at age 18, September 5, 1862, for the war. Died March 18, 1863, of disease.

SCOTT, WILLIAM F., Private
Resided in Stokes County and enlisted in Wake County at age 28, September 5, 1862, for the war. Deserted near Staunton, Virginia, September 17, 1862.

SHOFFNER, H. B., Private
Enlisted on October 10, 1864, for the war.

SIKES, GEORGE W., Private
Paroled at Greensboro on May 16, 1865.

SILLS, LEVI, Private
Resided in Montgomery County and enlisted in Wake County at age 18, August 15, 1862, for the war. Present or accounted for on company muster rolls until captured at Mechanicsville, Virginia, May 31, 1864. Confined at Point Lookout, Maryland, until transferred to Elmira, New York, July 8, 1864. Died at Elmira on December 10, 1864, of "congestion of the lungs."

SIMPSON, ALEXANDER, Private
Resided in Surry County and enlisted at age 22, September 5, 1862, for the war.

SIMPSON, ISHAM, Private
Resided in Stokes County and enlisted in Wake County at age 33, September 5, 1862, for the war. Died October 13, 1863, of disease.

SIMPSON, SANDY, Private
Enlisted in Wake County on September 5, 1862, for the war. Deserted on September 17, 1862, and reported as a deserter until August, 1863, when he was reported as present. Captured at Kelly's Ford, Virginia, November 7, 1863, and confined at Point Lookout, Maryland. Released at Point Lookout after taking the Oath of Allegiance and joining the U.S. service on January 23, 1864. Assigned to Company A, 1st Regiment U.S. Volunteer Infantry.

SIMPSON, WILLIAM L., Private
Resided in Stokes County and enlisted in Wake County at age 27, September 5, 1862, for the war. Deserted on September 17, 1862, and reported as absent through August, 1863. Present or accounted for until captured at Kelly's Ford, Virginia, November 7, 1863. Confined at Point Lookout, Maryland, until released after taking the Oath of Allegiance and joining the U.S. service on January 23, 1864. Assigned to the 1st Regiment U.S. Volunteer Infantry.

SNIPES, T. W., Private
Resided in McDowell County and enlisted in Wake County on May 9, 1864, for the war. Present or accounted for through December, 1864, when he was furloughed for 60 days.

SNODDY, JESSE A., Private
Resided in Surry County and enlisted in Wake County at age 19, September 5, 1862, for the war. Died in hospital at Lynchburg, Virginia, February 17, 1863, of "febris typhoides."

SOUTHERLAND, WILLIAM, Private
Enlisted at Camp Vance, April 11, 1864, for the war. Company muster rolls and hospital records

report him as absent sick after May 18, 1864.

SOYERS, SANDY, Private

Resided in Surry County and enlisted in Wake County at age 20, September 5, 1862, for the war. Deserted September 17, 1862, and reported as a deserter through August, 1863. Present or accounted for until captured at Kelly's Ford, Virginia, November 7, 1863. Confined at Point Lookout, Maryland, until released after taking the Oath of Allegiance and joining the U.S. service on January 23, 1864. Assigned to Company A, 1st Regiment U.S. Volunteer Infantry.

STOCKS, WILLIAM LAWRENCE, Private

Resided in Pitt County and enlisted in Wake County at age 30, July 17, 1862, for the war. Present or accounted for until captured at Kelly's Ford, Virginia, November 7, 1863. Confined at Point Lookout, Maryland, until transferred to Aiken's Landing, Virginia, for exchange on February 24, 1865.

STONE, JOHN H., Private

Resided in Surry County and enlisted in Wake County at age 28, September 5, 1862, for the war. Died in hospital at Lynchburg, Virginia, on February 25, 1863, of "phthisis pulmonalis."

THOMPSON, MARTIN, Private

Resided in Montgomery County and enlisted in Wake County at age 26, August 15, 1862, for the war. Present or accounted for on company muster rolls through October, 1864. Captured at Burkeville, Virginia, April 6, 1865, and confined at Point Lookout, Maryland. Released at Point Lookout after taking the Oath of Allegiance on June 20, 1865.

TILLEY, PETER L., Private

Born in Surry County where he resided prior to enlisting in Wake County at age 34, September 5, 1862, for the war. Died March 5, 1863.

TRIPP, WILLIAM H., Private

Resided in Pitt County and enlisted in Wake County at age 21, July 20, 1862, for the war. Present or accounted for until captured at Kelly's Ford, Virginia, November 7, 1863. Confined at Point Lookout, Maryland, until transferred to Aiken's Landing, Virginia, March 14, 1865, for exchange. Received in exchange on March 16, 1865.

WATSON, SANFORD, Private

Resided in Surry County and enlisted in Wake County at age 23, September 5, 1862, for the war. Died in hospital at Richmond, Virginia, April 15, 1863, of "typhoid pneumonia."

WHITE, RILEY, Sergeant

Resided in Guilford County and enlisted in Wake County at age 33, September 5, 1862, for the war. Mustered in as Sergeant. Present or accounted for until captured at Kelly's Ford, Virginia, November 7, 1863. Confined at Point Lookout, Maryland, until paroled and exchanged at Venus Point, Savannah River, Georgia, November 15, 1864.

WHITE, THOMAS, Private

Resided in McDowell County and enlisted in Wake County on May 9, 1864, for the war. Present or accounted for on company muster rolls through October, 1864. Captured at Burkeville, Virginia, April 6, 1865. Confined at Point Lookout, Maryland, until released after taking the Oath of Allegiance on June 21, 1865.

WHITESELL, ELI, Private

Resided in Alamance County where he enlisted at age 43, August 20, 1863, for the war. Present or accounted for until captured at Kelly's Ford, Virginia, November 7, 1863. Confined at Point Lookout, Maryland, where he died on December 28, 1863.

WILLIAMS, A. P., Private

Resided in Duplin County and paroled at Goldsboro on May 19, 1865. "Came in for parole."

WILLIAMS, J. C., Private

Paroled at Raleigh on April 20, 1865.

WILLIAMS, JOHN, Private

Captured at Spotsylvania Court House, Virginia, May 12, 1864, and confined at Point Lookout, Maryland, until transferred to Elmira, New York, on August 10, 1864. Died at Elmira on October 28, 1864, of "chronic diarrhoea."

WILSON, ANDREW, Private

Captured at Hanover Court House, Virginia, May 27, 1862, and confined at Fort Columbus, New York Harbor, June 4, 1862.

WILSON, ANDREW S., Private

Born in Surry County where he resided prior to enlisting in Wake County at age 28, September 5, 1862, for the war. Died at Jordan Springs, Virginia, July 1, 1863, of disease.

WRIGHT, WILLIS F., Private

Resided in Montgomery County and enlisted in Wake County at age 28, August 29, 1862, for the war. Present or accounted for until captured at Kelly's Ford, Virginia, November 7, 1863. Confined at Point Lookout, Maryland, where he died on August 18, 1864.

YARBER, DAVID A., Private

Resided in Montgomery County and enlisted in Wake County at age 20, August 15, 1862, for the war. Present or accounted for on company muster rolls through October, 1864. Paroled at Troy, North Carolina, May 28, 1865.

YARBER, JOSHUA, Private

Resided in Montgomery County and enlisted in Wake County at age 27, August 15, 1862, for the war. January-February, 1863, muster roll states that he was absent in hospital. Muster roll for November-December, 1863, carries him with the remark: "Absent in hospital sick, Fayetteville, North Carolina. Deserted hospital, Liberty, Virginia, March 19, 1863." Reported with the same remark on company muster rolls through October, 1864.

COMPANY B

This company was organized in Wilson County and enlisted at Wilson on May 27, 1861. It tendered its service to the state and was ordered to Camp Advance, near Garysburg, Northampton County, where it was assigned to this regiment as Company B. After joining the regiment the company functioned as a part of the regiment, and its history for the war period is recorded as a part of the regimental history.

The information contained in the following roster of the company was compiled principally from company muster rolls which covered the periods from June 8 through December, 1861; May through October, 1862; and January, 1863, through October, 1864. No company muster rolls were found for the period prior to June 8, 1861; for January-February, 1862; for November-December, 1862; or for the period after October, 1864. In addition to the company muster rolls, Roll of Honor records, receipt rolls, and hospital records, supplemented by state pension applications, United Daughters of the Confederacy records, and postwar rosters and histories, all provided useful information.

OFFICERS

CAPTAINS

HOWARD, JOHN
Resided in Wilson County and appointed Captain at age 27 to rank from May 16, 1861. Wounded in action at Sharpsburg, Maryland, September 17, 1862, and transferred to the Field and Staff of this regiment upon promotion to Major on the same date.

GORMAN, JOHN C.
Resided in Wilson County and appointed 3rd Lieutenant to rank from May 16, 1861. Promoted to 1st Lieutenant to rank from March 8, 1862. Wounded at Sharpsburg, Maryland, September 17, 1862. Promoted to Captain to rank from September 17, 1862. Wounded a second time at Fredericksburg, Virginia. Date wounded not reported. Present or accounted for until captured at Spotsylvania Court House, Virginia, May 19, 1864. Confined at Fort Delaware, Delaware, until transferred to Hilton Head, South Carolina, August 20, 1864. Paroled at Charleston Harbor, South Carolina, December 15, 1864. Wounded near Petersburg, Virginia, in April, 1865. Paroled at Raleigh on May 24, 1865.

LIEUTENANTS

BARNES, BUNYAN J., 2nd Lieutenant
Resided in Wilson County and enlisted in Northampton County at age 24, May 27, 1861, for the war. Mustered in as Sergeant. Wounded in action at Malvern Hill, Virginia, July 1, 1862. Promoted to 1st Sergeant on September 1, 1862. Appointed 2nd Lieutenant to rank from March 20, 1863. Present or accounted for with company through October, 1864, when he was reported with the remark that he was "assigned to command Companies D and C of this regiment." Captured at Petersburg, Virginia, April 2, 1865, and confined at Johnson's Island, Ohio, until released after taking the Oath of Allegiance on June 18, 1865.

BARNES, CALVIN, 1st Lieutenant
Resided in Wilson County and appointed 1st Lieutenant to rank from May 16, 1861. Trans-

ferred to 1st Company A of this regiment upon appointment as Captain on October 22, 1861. First Company A of this regiment became Company H, 40th Regiment N.C. Troops (3rd Regiment N.C. Artillery).

BOYETTE, LARRY BRYANT, 2nd Lieutenant
Resided in Wilson County where he enlisted at age 24, May 29, 1861, for the war. Mustered in as Private. Appointed 1st Sergeant on August 20, 1862. Appointed 2nd Lieutenant to rank from June 25, 1863. Present or accounted for until paroled at Appomattox Court House, Virginia, April 9, 1865.

CALDER, ROBERT E., 1st Lieutenant
Resided in New Hanover County and was a cadet at the Hillsboro Military Academy prior to being appointed a Drillmaster, 2nd Class, May 1, 1861. Served as Drillmaster with this company from May 1 to September 4, 1861, when he was appointed 2nd Lieutenant to rank from September 1, 1861. Wounded in the eye at Malvern Hill, Virginia, July 1, 1862. Reported as absent wounded on company muster rolls through December, 1862. Promoted to 1st Lieutenant to rank from September 17, 1862. Resigned because of wound on March 9, 1863.

FULGHAM, GARRY, 1st Lieutenant
Resided in Wilson County where he enlisted at age 27, May 27, 1861, for the war. Mustered in as Private. Wounded at Sharpsburg, Maryland, September 17, 1862. Appointed Sergeant, January-February, 1863. Elected 2nd Lieutenant on February 10, 1863, and appointed to rank from date of election. Promoted to 1st Lieutenant to rank from March 9, 1863. Wounded at Chancellorsville, Virginia, May 3, 1863. Present or accounted for until paroled at Appomattox Court House, Virginia, April 9, 1865.

HOWARD, WILLIAM, 2nd Lieutenant
Resided in Wilson County and appointed 2nd Lieutenant to rank from February 3, 1862. Wounded in action at Malvern Hill, Virginia, July 1-2, 1862, and resigned because of wound on March 23, 1863.

PIERCE, JOSEPH C., 1st Lieutenant
Transferred from Company D of this regiment upon appointment as 1st Lieutenant to rank from October 22, 1861. Submitted his resignation on February 22, 1862, by reason of "festula" and resignation was accepted on March 1, 1862. Later appointed Captain and Enrolling Officer, 2nd Congressional District, North Carolina.

WILLIAMS, ORREN, 2nd Lieutenant
Resided in Wilson County and appointed 2nd Lieutenant to rank from May 16, 1861. Transferred to Company G of this regiment upon appointment as 1st Lieutenant to rank from September 10, 1861.

NONCOMMISSIONED OFFICERS AND PRIVATES

ANDERSON, W. H., Private
Paroled at Greensboro on May 9, 1865.

BAITEY, E. S., Private
Paroled at Greensboro on May 16, 1865.

BAREFOOT, JAMES H., Private
Resided in Wilson County and enlisted in Northampton County at age 18, June 2, 1861, for the war. Present or accounted for until detailed as a nurse on November 28, 1863. Retired to the Invalid Corps on May 6, 1864, and assigned to military station at Wilson. Discharged on November 10, 1864, by reason of "paralysis of left arm."

BARNES, JAMES, Private
Resided in Wilson County where he enlisted at age 22, May 27, 1861, for the war. Killed in skirmish on Williamsburg Road, near Richmond, Virginia, June 21, 1862.

BARNES, WILLIAM, Private
Resided in Wilson County where he enlisted at age 27, May 27, 1861, for the war. Died in hospital at Richmond, Virginia, September 1, 1862, of "typhoid fever."

BASS, JOHN HODGE, Private
Enlisted "at camp" on October 25, 1864, for the war. Present or accounted for until paroled at Appomattox Court House, Virginia, April 9, 1865.

BASS, JORDAN, Private
Resided in Wilson County where he enlisted at age 35, February 12, 1862, for the war. Present or accounted for on company muster rolls through October, 1864.

BATTS, JOSEPH J., Private
Resided in Wilson County where he enlisted at age 21, May 27, 1861, for the war. Mustered in as Private and appointed Corporal on December 11, 1862. Wounded at Chancellorsville, Virginia, May 3, 1863, and returned to duty on September 3, 1863. Reduced to ranks on October 12, 1863. Present or accounted for until captured at Fisher's Hill, Virginia, September 22, 1864. Confined at Point Lookout, Maryland, until paroled and exchanged at Aiken's Landing, Virginia, March 17, 1865.

BATTS, WILLIAM C., Corporal
Resided in Wilson County where he enlisted at age 18, February 12, 1862, for the war. Mustered in as Private. Wounded and captured at Sharpsburg, Maryland, September 17, 1862. Exchanged at Aiken's Landing, Virginia, November 10, 1862. Appointed Corporal in April, 1863. Detailed as Provost Guard at Corps Headquarters from November 20, 1863, through October, 1864. Paroled at Appomattox Court House, Virginia, April 9, 1865.

BEGMON, E. C., Private
Resided in Wilson County. Paroled at Goldsboro in April, 1865.

BISSETT, BERRY N., Private
Resided in Wilson County where he enlisted at age 18, May 27, 1861, for the war. Captured at Boonsboro, Maryland, September 13, 1862, and confined at Fort Delaware, Delaware. Exchanged at Aiken's Landing, Virginia, October 2, 1862. Died in hospital at Richmond, Virginia, October 8-10, 1862, of "cerebritis."

BOTTOMS, GEORGE W., Private
Resided in Wilson County where he enlisted at age 19, January 20, 1862, for the war. Present or accounted for on company muster rolls through October, 1864. Captured at Burkeville, Virginia, April 6, 1865, and confined at Point Lookout, Maryland, until released after taking the Oath of Allegiance on June 23, 1865.

BOYETT, JOEL, Private
Resided in Wilson County where he enlisted at age 29, May 27, 1861, for the war. Wounded in action at Chancellorsville, Virginia, May 3, 1863. Present or accounted for on company muster rolls through October, 1864. Captured at Sutherland's Station, Virginia, April 8, 1865, and confined at Point Lookout, Maryland, until released after taking the Oath of Allegiance on June 24, 1865.

BOYETT, RANSOM, Private
Resided in Wilson County where he enlisted at age 18, May 27, 1861, for the war. Captured at Williamsport, Maryland, September 16, 1862, and confined at Fort Delaware, Delaware. Exchanged at Aiken's Landing, Virginia, October 2, 1862. Present or accounted for until captured at Winchester, Virginia, September 19, 1864. Confined at Point Lookout, Maryland, until transferred to Aiken's Landing, Virginia, March 15, 1865, for exchange.

BOYETT, THOMAS, Private
Resided in Wilson County and enlisted at Camp Potomac, Virginia, at age 24, November 11, 1861, for the war. Detailed as wagoner from July, 1862, to May 5, 1863. Wounded in action at Spotsylvania Court House, Virginia, May, 1864. Admitted to hospital at Richmond, Virginia, May 17, 1864, and furloughed for 60 days on June 3, 1864. Readmitted to hospital at Richmond on August 17, 1864, with a gunshot wound of the left hand. Remained in hospital until he was reported as a deserter on March 8, 1865. Paroled at Richmond on April 22, 1865.

BOYETTE, GEORGE T., Private
Enlisted in Wilson County, February 27, 1864, for the war. Wounded and captured at Winchester, Virginia, September 19, 1864. Died in hospital at Baltimore, Maryland, January 1, 1865.

BOYETTE, ISAAC, Private
Resided in Wilson County where he enlisted at age 26, May 27, 1861, for the war. Admitted to hospital at Staunton, Virginia, October 28, 1862, with "wounded foot." Date wounded not reported. Present or accounted for on company muster rolls through October, 1864.

BOYETTE, JAMES H., Private
Resided in Wilson County where he enlisted at age 21, April 29, 1862, for the war. Present or accounted for until captured at Winchester, Virginia, September 19, 1864. Confined at Point Lookout, Maryland, until sent to Boulware's Wharf, James River, Virginia, for exchange on January 17, 1865. Paroled at Goldsboro on May 4, 1865. "Came in for parole."

BOYETTE, JOSIAH, Corporal
Resided in Wilson County where he enlisted at age 24, May 28, 1861, for the war. Mustered in as Private and promoted to Corporal on June 1, 1864. Present or accounted for on company muster rolls through October, 1864, when he was reported with the remark: "Wounded at Cedar Creek, Virginia, October 19, 1864. Left in the enemy's hands."

BOYKIN, BENJAMIN H., Sergeant
Resided in Wilson County where he enlisted at age 23, May 28, 1861, for the war. Mustered in as Sergeant and appointed 1st Sergeant on April 28, 1863. Wounded at Chancellorsville, Virginia, May 3, 1863. Detailed at Gordonsville, Virginia, November 28, 1863, and remained absent on detail through April, 1864. Reported as Sergeant on company muster rolls after April 1, 1864. Present or accounted for on company muster rolls through October, 1864. Captured near Petersburg, Virginia, April 3, 1865, and confined at Hart's Island, New York Harbor, until released after taking the Oath of Allegiance on June 18, 1865.

BOYKIN, ELI J., Private
Resided in Wilson County where he enlisted at age 20, May 28, 1861, for the war. Died at Camp Potomac, King George County, Virginia, November 1, 1861.

BOYKIN, IRVIN, Private
Resided in Wilson County where he enlisted at age 18, January 20, 1862, for the war as a substitute for his father. Wounded at Spotsylvania Court House, Virginia, May, 1864. Detailed as a hospital guard at Lynchburg, Virginia, November 12, 1864. Reported as absent on detail through February, 1865. Paroled at Appomattox Court House, Virginia, April 9, 1865.

BOYKIN, PUMMER W., Private
Resided in Wilson County where he enlisted at age 20, May 7, 1862, for the war. Present or accounted for until he was killed at Spotsylvania Court House, Virginia, May 19, 1864.

BOYKIN, TOBIAS, Private
Resided in Wilson County and enlisted at Camp Potomac, Virginia, at age 46, November 11, 1861, for the war. Discharged on January 20, 1862, by reason of providing his son as a substitute.

BOYKIN, WILEY, Private
Born in Wilson County where he resided and enlisted at age 22, June 1, 1861, for the war. Died in camp at Fredericksburg, Virginia, March 20-23, 1863.

BOYKIN, WILLIAM, Private
Enlisted in Wilson County on May 7, 1862, for the war. Died in camp near Fredericksburg, Virginia, on March 10, 1863.

BOYKIN, WILLIAM H., Sergeant
Resided in Wilson County where he enlisted at age 19, May 28, 1861, for the war. Mustered in as Sergeant. Died at Camp Potomac, King George County, Virginia, March 8, 1862.

BOYKIN, WILLIAM M., Private
Resided in Wilson County where he enlisted at age 18, September 12, 1863, for the war. Present or accounted for until wounded and captured at Winchester, Virginia, September 19, 1864. Confined in hospitals at Baltimore, Maryland, until transferred to Fort McHenry, Maryland, December 9, 1864. Transferred to Point Lookout, Maryland, January 2-3, 1865. Released at Point Lookout after taking the Oath of Allegiance on June 3, 1865.

BRIDGERS, WILEY R., Sergeant
Resided in Wilson County where he enlisted at age 19, May 27, 1861, for the war. Mustered in as Private and appointed Sergeant on May 1, 1863. Wounded and captured at Spotsylvania Court House, Virginia, May 19, 1864. Died in hospital at Washington, D.C., June 2, 1864, of a gunshot wound of the left lung.

BROOKS, J. W., Sergeant
Paroled at Greensboro on May 12, 1865.

BROWN, I. P., Private
Paroled at Charlotte on May 25, 1865.

BROWN, S. H., Private
Paroled at Charlotte on May 25, 1865.

BRYANT, G. T., Private
Wounded and captured at Winchester, Virginia, September 19, 1864. Reported on records of field hospital at Winchester with the remark that he was transferred on October 20, 1864.

BRYANT, JOSEPH J., Private
Resided in Wilson County where he enlisted at age 33, May 27, 1861, for the war. Present or accounted for until killed at Spotsylvania Court House, Virginia, May 19, 1864.

BURRIS, BENNETT, Private
Resided in Wilson County and enlisted at age 18, June 24, 1863, for the war. Admitted to hospital soon after enlisting and did not join the company until October 26, 1863. Sent to hospital sick on November 10, 1863, and remained in hospital until detailed for hospital duty at Richmond, Virginia, March 8, 1864. Detailed as a nurse until discharged on June 11, 1864, by reason of "paralysis right side."

CARTER, JAMES, Private
Captured at Burkeville, Virginia, April 6, 1865, and confined at Point Lookout, Maryland, until released after taking the Oath of Allegiance on June 26, 1865. Residence given on Oath as Franklin County, Florida.

CARTER, LEWIS, Private
Resided in Wilson County where he enlisted at age 54, May 27, 1861, for the war. Detailed as a nurse in hospital at Fredericksburg, Virginia, August 17, 1861. Reported as absent on detail through February, 1862. Reported as present for the balance of 1862 and as absent on detail as a nurse from January through December, 1863. Returned to company on February 19, 1864. Wounded at Spotsylvania Court House, Virginia, May 12, 1864.

CARTER, WILLIAM, Private
Resided in Wilson County where he enlisted at age 21, May 27, 1861, for the war. Died in hospital at Fredericksburg, Virginia, September 1, 1861.

CHRISTMAS, NATHAN C., Private
Resided in Wilson County where he enlisted at age 27, May 27, 1861, for the war. Present or accounted for until wounded at Chancellorsville, Virginia, May 3, 1863. Reported as absent wounded until retired to the Invalid Corps on May 10, 1864. Reported as on duty at Goldsboro on October 31, 1864. Assigned to Quartermaster Department at Tarboro on December 3, 1864.

CLENDEMER, W. T., Sergeant
Paroled at Greensboro on May 16, 1865.

COLEMAN, HENRY, Private
Enlisted in Wilson County on January 6, 1864, for the war. Wounded at Spotsylvania Court House, Virginia, in May, 1864. Reported as absent wounded through October, 1864. Admitted to hospital at Richmond, Virginia, December 23, 1864, with a gunshot wound of the left thigh. Furloughed for 60 days on February 3, 1865. Paroled at Goldsboro on May 8, 1865. "Came in for parole."

COLEMAN, JOHN C., Private
Resided in Wilson County where he enlisted at age 20, May 27, 1861, for the war. Wounded at Chancellorsville, Virginia, May 3, 1863, and returned to duty on August 19, 1863. Present or accounted for until killed in action near Richmond, Virginia, June 3, 1864.

COLEMAN, JOSIAH, Private
Resided in Wilson County and enlisted in Wake County at age 30, June 24, 1863, for the war. Present or accounted for until wounded at Snicker's Gap, Virginia, in August, 1864. Retired to the Invalid Corps on December 1, 1864. Paroled at Goldsboro on May 8, 1865. "Came in for parole."

COLEMAN, WILEY, Private
Resided in Wilson County and enlisted in Wake County at age 36, June 24, 1863, for the war. Detailed for light duty in hospital at Richmond, Virginia, October 29, 1863. Reported as absent on detail through October, 1864. Captured at Petersburg, Virginia, April 3, 1865, and confined at Hart's Island, New York Harbor, until released after taking the Oath of Allegiance on June 18, 1865.

CROCKER, JACOB A., Private
Captured at South Mountain, Maryland, July 4-5, 1863, and admitted to hospital at Frederick, Maryland, July 6, 1863, with "amputated finger left hand." Transferred to Fort Delaware, Delaware, July 9, 1863. Paroled at Fort Delaware on July 30, 1863, and sent to City Point, Virginia, for exchange. Received at City Point on August 1, 1863. Reported in hospital at Petersburg, Virginia, August 18, 1863.

DAVIS, A., Private
Admitted to hospital in Richmond, Virginia, May 2, 1863, and transferred. Paroled at Goldsboro on May 8, 1865. "Came in for parole."

DAVIS, HENRY, Private
Resided in Wilson County where he enlisted at age 22, January 20, 1862, for the war. Reported as absent sick or absent on detail from March-April,

1862, until May-August, 1864, when he was reported with the remark: "Died of disease in Wilson County, North Carolina, time not known."

DAVIS, NATHAN, Private
Resided in Wilson County where he enlisted at age 23, May 28, 1861, for the war. Wounded in arm at Malvern Hill, Virginia, July 1, 1862. Present or accounted for until sent to hospital in Richmond, Virginia, April 28, 1863. Returned to company on October 9, 1863. Present or accounted for until furloughed for 60 days on June 10, 1864. Reported as absent without leave after August 10, 1864.

DAVIS, RANSOM, Private
Born in Wilson County where he resided and enlisted at age 20, May 28, 1861, for the war. Wounded in action at Chancellorsville, Virginia, May 3, 1863, and died in hospital at Richmond, Virginia, May 16, 1863.

DAVIS, RAYFORD, Private
Resided in Wilson County where he enlisted at age 20, May 28, 1861, for the war. Present or accounted for on company muster rolls through September-October, 1864, when he was reported as absent sick in hospital at Lynchburg, Virginia. Died in hospital at Lynchburg on November 29, 1864, of "pneumonia."

DAVIS, WILEY, Private
Born in Wilson County where he resided prior to enlisting at Richmond, Virginia, at age 26, July 16, 1861, for the war. Present or accounted for until he died in hospital at Richmond, February 20, 1863, of "pneumonia."

DAVIS, WILLIAM, Private
Resided in Wilson County where he enlisted at age 25, May 27, 1861, for the war. Died at Camp Potomac, King George County, Virginia, September 14, 1861, of "pneumonia."

DAVIS, WILLIAMSON, Private
Born in Wilson County where he resided and enlisted at age 31, February 3, 1862, for the war. Present or accounted for until killed at Chancellorsville, Virginia, May 3, 1863.

DEANS, ANDREW J., Private
Resided in Wilson County where he enlisted on May 9, 1862, for the war. Wounded at Chancellorsville, Virginia, May 3, 1863, and returned to duty on October 9, 1863. Present or accounted for on company muster rolls through October, 1864. Captured at Petersburg, Virginia, April 3, 1865, and confined at Hart's Island, New York Harbor, until released after taking the Oath of Allegiance on June 18, 1865.

DEANS, DAVID, Private
Resided in Wilson County where he enlisted at age 19, May 28, 1861, for the war. Captured and paroled near Sharpsburg, Maryland, September 21, 1862. Wounded in left shoulder at Gettysburg, Pennsylvania, July 2-3, 1863. Reported as absent wounded until detailed for light duty on February 23, 1864. Absent on detail through August, 1864. Reported as present on September-October, 1864, muster roll. Captured at Petersburg, Virginia, April 3, 1865, and confined at Hart's Island, New

York Harbor, until released after taking the Oath of Allegiance on June 18, 1865.

DIXON, WILEY GREY, Private

Born in Wilson County where he resided as a farmer and enlisted at age 24, February 3, 1862, for the war. Reported as absent sick from July, 1862, until detailed as a nurse in hospital at Wilson on February 1, 1863. Remained on detail until discharged on April 4, 1864, by reason of "paralysis affecting muscles of the left leg."

EATMAN, ALSEY W., Corporal

Born in Wilson County where he resided as a farmer and enlisted at age 21, May 28, 1861, for the war. Mustered in as Private and appointed Corporal on August 9, 1861. Captured and paroled near Sharpsburg, Maryland, September 21, 1862. Died in hospital at Richmond, Virginia, November 12, 1862, of disease.

EATMAN, HENRY R., Private

Born in Wilson County where he resided as a farmer and enlisted at age 20, May 28, 1861, for the war. Present or accounted for until he died in hospital at Richmond, Virginia, November 10-14, 1862, of "febris typhoides."

EATMAN, JOHN, Private

Born in Wilson County where he resided prior to enlisting at Camp Potomac, King George County, Virginia, at age 18, November 11, 1861, for the war. Present or accounted for until killed at Chancellorsville, Virginia, May 3, 1863.

EATMAN, RAYMOND, Private

Resided as a mechanic in Wilson County where he enlisted at age 29, May 28, 1861, for the war. Captured in Loudoun County, Virginia, December 6, 1862, and confined at Fort McHenry, Maryland. Paroled at Fort McHenry and transferred for exchange on December 14, 1862. Present or accounted for on company muster rolls until captured at Strasburg, Virginia, October 19, 1864. Confined at Point Lookout, Maryland, until released after taking the Oath of Allegiance on May 13, 1865.

EATMAN, TAYLOR, Private

Resided in Wilson County where he enlisted at age 18, April 29, 1862, for the war. Admitted to hospital at Richmond, Virginia, August 30, 1862, with a gunshot wound of the leg and furloughed for 35 days on September 22, 1862. Wounded at Chancellorsville, Virginia, May 3, 1863. Deserted from hospital at Richmond, May-June, 1863, and reported as absent without leave until he rejoined the company on January 29, 1864. Reported as present or absent accounted for from that date through October, 1864. Captured at Burkeville, Virginia, April 6, 1865, and confined at Point Lookout, Maryland, until released after taking the Oath of Allegiance on June 12, 1865.

EVANS, ALFRED, Private

Enlisted in Wilson County on January 12, 1864, for the war. Killed at Spotsylvania Court House, Virginia, May 12, 1864.

EVANS, HARTWELL, Private

Resided in Wilson County where he enlisted at age 23, May 28, 1861, for the war. Wounded at

Malvern Hill, Virginia, July 1, 1862, and died of wounds at Wilson in August, 1862.

EVANS, JOHN, Private

Resided in Wilson County and enlisted at Camp Potomac, King George County, Virginia, at age 35, November 11, 1861, for the war. Died in hospital at Lynchburg, Virginia, February 6, 1863, of "diarrhea chronic."

FERRELL, WILLIAM C., Private

Resided in Nash County and enlisted in Wilson County at age 21, May 28, 1861, for the war. Wounded at Malvern Hill, Virginia, July 1, 1862. Present or accounted for until transferred to Company H, 59th Regiment N.C. Troops (4th Regiment N.C. Cavalry) upon appointment as 3rd Lieutenant to rank from October 18, 1862.

FISHER, H., Private

Paroled at Salisbury on May 15, 1865.

FLORA, JOHN, Private

Resided in Wilson County where he enlisted at age 19, May 27, 1861, for the war. Present or accounted for until wounded at Chancellorsville, Virginia, May 3, 1863. Reported as absent wounded on company muster rolls through October, 1864. Admitted to hospital at Richmond, Virginia, December 24, 1864, with a gunshot wound of the right leg and furloughed for 60 days on December 31, 1864.

FLOWERS, DUNCAN, Private

Born in Edgecombe County and resided as a farmer in Wilson County where he enlisted at age 23, May 27, 1861, for the war. Died in hospital in Fredericksburg, Virginia, October 23, 1861, of "typhoid fever."

FLOWERS, EATMAN, Private

Resided in Wilson County where he enlisted at age 20, May 28, 1861, for the war. Wounded in skirmish near Richmond, Virginia, July 21, 1862, and again at Sharpsburg, Maryland, September 17, 1862. Wounded a third time at Gettysburg, Pennsylvania, July 2-3, 1863. Present or accounted for on company muster rolls through October, 1864. Captured at Harper's Farm, Virginia, April 6, 1865, and confined at Point Lookout, Maryland, until released after taking the Oath of Allegiance on June 26, 1865.

FLOWERS, GRAY L., Private

Resided in Wilson County where he enlisted at age 30, May 28, 1861, for the war. Mustered in as Private and reported as Corporal on March-April, 1862, muster roll. Killed in action at Malvern Hill, Virginia, July 1, 1862. Reported as Private on death records.

FLOWERS, JACOB H., Private

Resided in Wilson County where he enlisted at age 20, May 27, 1861, for the war. Present or accounted for until he was reported as "missing since the battle of Sharpsburg." There is no record of him after September, 1862.

FLOWERS, JAMES E., Private

Born in Wilson County where he resided as a farmer and enlisted at age 18, May 27, 1861, for the war. Present or accounted for until he died at

Harrisonburg, Virginia, October 4, 1862, of disease.

FLOWERS, RUFFIN, Private
Resided in Wilson County where he enlisted at age 25, May 28, 1861, for the war. Wounded in skirmish near Richmond, Virginia, June 21, 1862, and died of wounds in July, 1862.

FLOWERS, THOMAS, Private
Resided in Wilson County where he enlisted at age 23, May 28, 1861, for the war. Present or accounted for until paroled at Appomattox Court House, Virginia, April 9, 1865.

FLOWERS, WILEY G., Private
Born in Wilson County where he resided as a farmer and enlisted at age 19, January 20-24, 1862, for the war. Present or accounted for until killed at Chancellorsville, Virginia, May 3, 1863.

FLOWERS, WILLIAM H., Private
Resided in Wilson County where he enlisted at age 27, May 27, 1861, for the war. Present or accounted for until wounded in the leg at Gettysburg, Pennsylvania, July 2-3, 1863. Returned to company December 27, 1863. Killed at Spotsylvania Court House, Virginia, May 12, 1864.

FORBES, JOSEPH W., Sergeant
Resided in Wilson County where he enlisted at age 21, May 28, 1861, for the war. Mustered in as Private and appointed Corporal in February, 1862. Wounded at Fredericksburg, Virginia, in December, 1862, and promoted to Sergeant during that same month. Wounded at Chancellorsville, Virginia, May 3, 1863. Present or accounted for on company muster rolls through October, 1864. Captured at Petersburg, Virginia, April 3, 1865, and confined at Hart's Island, New York Harbor, until released after taking the Oath of Allegiance on June 18, 1865.

FULGHUM, JAMES HENRY, Sergeant
Resided in Wilson County where he enlisted at age 22, May 27-28, 1861, for the war. Mustered in as Private and appointed Corporal on December 1, 1862. Wounded at Chancellorsville, Virginia, May 3, 1863. Promoted to Sergeant on June 1, 1864. Present or accounted for on company muster rolls through October, 1864. Captured at Burkeville, Virginia, April 6, 1865, and confined at Point Lookout, Maryland, until released after taking the Oath of Allegiance on June 26, 1865.

FULGHUM, RAYFORD, Private
Resided in Wilson County where he enlisted at age 25, May 28, 1861, for the war. Present or accounted for until paroled at Appomattox Court House, Virginia, April 9, 1865.

FULGHUM, WILLIAM B., Private
Resided in Wilson County where he enlisted at age 21, May 28, 1861, for the war. Present or accounted for until he died in hospital at Wilson on February 17, 1863, of "diarrhea chronic."

GOODMAN, D. J., Sergeant
Paroled at Salisbury on May 18, 1865.

GOODMAN, P. O., Private
Paroled at Salisbury on May 19, 1865.

GRIFFIN, G., Private
Paroled at Goldsboro in 1865.

GRIFFIN, JAMES H., Private
Resided in Nash County and enlisted in Wilson County at age 25, August 22, 1861, for the war. Present or accounted for until detailed as a nurse in February, 1863. Returned to company on August 5, 1863. Present or accounted for until wounded at Cedar Creek, Virginia, October 19, 1864, and sent to hospital. Furloughed from hospital at Charlottesville, Virginia, November 8, 1864. Admitted to hospital at Danville, Virginia, April 5, 1865, with "debilitas."

GRISWOLD, JOHN, Private
Resided in Wilson County where he enlisted at age 23, June 27, 1861, for the war. Detailed as wagoner November-December, 1862. March-April, 1863, muster roll reports him as absent "in Castle Thunder, Richmond, Virginia, on charge of murder." Reported with the same remark on May-June, 1863, muster roll. July-August, 1863, muster roll carries him with the remark: "Deserted August 27, 1863." Absent without leave until he rejoined the company on October 21, 1864, under the amnesty proclamation of Governor Vance. Captured at Petersburg, Virginia, April 3, 1865, and confined at Hart's Island, New York Harbor, until released after taking the Oath of Allegiance on June 19, 1865.

HAMMERY, JAMES, Private
Paroled at Salisbury on May 27, 1865.

HARRELL, ASA T., Private
Captured in Norfolk County, Virginia, June 1, 1864, and confined at Elmira, New York, where he died on January 10, 1865, of "chronic diarrhoea."

HAYNES, J. B., Private
Paroled at Charlotte on May 11, 1865.

HINNANT, JAMES, Private
Born in Wilson County where he resided as a farmer and enlisted at age 19, January 26, 1862, for the war. Wounded at Chancellorsville, Virginia, May 3, 1863, and died of wound on May 9, 1863.

HINNANT, JOHN W., Private
Born in Wilson County where he resided and enlisted at age 28, May 27, 1861, for the war. Wounded at Chancellorsville, Virginia, May 3, 1863, and died of wound May 4-6, 1863.

HINNANT, JONATHAN, Private
Born in Wilson County where he resided as a farmer and enlisted at age 22, May 28, 1861, for the war. Mustered in as Sergeant. Reported as Private after December, 1861. Wounded at Gettysburg, Pennsylvania, July 2-3, 1863, and captured at Williamsport, Maryland, July 14, 1863. Wound described on Federal Hospital Registers as "gunshot wound of left eye, destruction of ball." Admitted to hospital at Hagerstown, Maryland, in July, 1863, and transferred to hospital at Baltimore, Maryland, August 7, 1863. Paroled at Baltimore and sent to City Point, Virginia, for exchange on August 23, 1863. Company muster rolls report him as absent wounded until detailed for light duty at Petersburg, Virginia, January 26, 1864. Admitted to hospital at Farmville, Virginia, June 20, 1864, and furloughed for 40 days on July

8, 1864. Retired to the Invalid Corps on November 11, 1864.

JEFFERSON, JOSEPH, Private

Resided in Wilson County where he enlisted at age 34, January 20, 1862, for the war. Killed at Malvern Hill, Virginia, July 1, 1862.

JOYNER, REDDICK, Private

Resided in Wilson County where he enlisted at age 28, May 29, 1861, for the war. Mustered in as Private and appointed Musician on April 1, 1862. Reduced to ranks while absent without leave from May 18 to July 22, 1863. Present or accounted for until captured at Spotsylvania Court House, Virginia, May 20, 1864. Confined at Point Lookout, Maryland, until transferred to Elmira, New York, July 3, 1864. Released at Elmira after taking the Oath of Allegiance on June 16, 1865.

KALE, WILLIAM R., Private

Resided in Norfolk County, Virginia, where he was captured on June 1, 1864. Confined at Point Lookout, Maryland, until transferred to Elmira, New York, July 25, 1864. Released at Elmira after taking the Oath of Allegiance on May 29, 1865.

KELLEY, MACK C., Private

Resided in Wilson County where he enlisted at age 31, May 28, 1861, for the war. Present or accounted for until killed at Sharpsburg, Maryland, September 17, 1862.

KENNEL, H. G., Private

Paroled at Greensboro on May 15, 1865.

KINNS, ISAAC, Private

Captured at Falling Waters, Maryland, July 14, 1863. Admitted to hospital at Baltimore, Maryland, August 3, 1863. Paroled at Baltimore on August 23, 1863, and delivered at City Point, Virginia, August 24, 1863, in exchange.

KLUTTZ, W. C., Private

Paroled at Salisbury on May 11, 1865.

LAMB, HARRIS, Private

Resided in Wilson County where he enlisted at age 25, May 27, 1861, for the war. Transferred to Company D of this regiment on November 10, 1861.

LAMB, LARRY L., Private

Resided in Wilson County where he enlisted at age 25, May 28, 1861, for the war. Present or accounted for until wounded near Warrenton, Virginia, October 15, 1863. Died in hospital at Richmond, Virginia, December 19, 1863, of "gunshot wound in hip and typhoid fever."

LAMB, SIMON D., Private

Born in Wilson County where he resided and enlisted at age 22, May 28, 1861, for the war. Present or accounted for until he died in hospital at Wilson on May 20, 1863, of disease.

LAMB, SPIAS, Private

Born in Wilson County where he resided as a farmer and enlisted at age 22, June 1, 1861, for the war. Died at Camp Potomac, King George County, Virginia, December 31, 1861, of "inflamation of the brain."

LEACH, E., Private

Paroled at Leesburg, Virginia, October 2, 1862.

LOGAN, WILLIAM, Private

Captured at Murfreesboro, Tennessee, December 30, 1862, and paroled at Fort Delaware, Delaware, September 14, 1864.

McCARTY, JAMES, Private

Captured at Burkeville, Virginia, April 6, 1865, and confined at Point Lookout, Maryland, April 17, 1865.

MADDRY, CHARLES, Private

Enlisted in Wilson County on February 27, 1864, for the war. Present or accounted for until paroled at Appomattox Court House, Virginia, April 9, 1865.

MANN, JOHN, Private

Name reported on receipt roll for clothing issued during the second quarter of 1864. Paroled at Farmville, Virginia, April 11-21, 1865.

MARSHALL, GEORGE W., Private

Resided in Wilson County where he enlisted at age 20, May 27, 1861, for the war. Present or accounted for on company muster rolls until captured at Old Church, Virginia, May 30, 1864. Confined at Point Lookout, Maryland, until transferred to Elmira, New York, July 9, 1864. Released at Elmira after taking the Oath of Allegiance on June 30, 1865.

MARTIN, G., Private

Resided in Wilson County. Paroled at Goldsboro on May 15, 1865. "Came in for parole."

MAYS, W. T., Private

Paroled at Salisbury on May 12, 1865.

MEARS, WILLIAM R., Private

Resided in Wilson County where he enlisted at age 22, January 27, 1862, for the war. Present or accounted for until killed at Chancellorsville, Virginia, May 3, 1863.

MEEKS, HENRY, Private

Resided in Wilson County where he enlisted at age 45, May 27, 1861, for the war. Detailed at Goldsboro on May 15, 1862. Records indicate that he was detailed as artificer and carpenter. Muster rolls carry him as absent on detail through October, 1864. Detail extended by order on January 21, 1865.

MERCER, HENRY, Private

Resided in Wilson County where he enlisted at age 18, May 28, 1861, for the war. Wounded at Sharpsburg, Maryland, September 17, 1862. Died near Winchester, Virginia, October 15, 1862, of wound.

MILLS, A. W., Private

Paroled at Salisbury on May 27, 1865.

MOORE, ALFRED, Private

Resided in Wilson County where he enlisted at age 23, May 28, 1861, for the war. Mustered in as Corporal and reduced to ranks in January, 1862. Deserted May 10, 1863, and arrested in March, 1864. Sentenced to one year hard labor at Richmond, Virginia, April 9, 1864. Captured at Wadesboro, Virginia, September 27, 1864, and confined at Point Lookout, Maryland, until released after taking the Oath of Allegiance on May 14, 1865.

MOORE, NATHANIEL, Jr., Private
Resided in Wilson County where he enlisted at age 22, May 29, 1861, for the war. Mustered in as Corporal and promoted to Sergeant on April 1, 1862. Reduced to ranks on September 9, 1862. Wounded at Chancellorsville, Virginia, May 3, 1863, and returned to duty on August 10, 1863. Present or accounted for on company muster rolls through October, 1864, when he appears with the remark: "Wounded in hospital at Lynchburg, Virginia."

MOORE, NATHANIEL, Sr., Private
Resided in Wilson County and enlisted "at camp" at age 36, December 1, 1862, for the war. Present or accounted for until captured at Kelly's Ford, Virginia, November 7, 1863. Confined at Point Lookout, Maryland, until paroled and exchanged at Venus Point, Savannah River, Georgia, November 15, 1864. Captured at Burkeville, Virginia, April 6, 1865, and confined at Point Lookout, Maryland, until released after taking the Oath of Allegiance on June 29, 1865.

MOORE, SIMON, Private
Resided in Wilson County where he enlisted at age 21, May 28, 1861, for the war. Present or accounted for until paroled at Appomattox Court House, Virginia, April 9, 1865.

MOOSE, F. D., Private
Paroled at Salisbury on May 28, 1865.

MORRIS, DEMPSEY, Private
Resided in Wilson County where he enlisted at age 24, January 31, 1862, for the war. Wounded at Chancellorsville, Virginia, May 3, 1863. Present or accounted for until killed at Spotsylvania Court House, Virginia, May 12, 1864.

MORRIS, WILEY, Private
Resided in Wilson County where he enlisted at age 22, May 27, 1861, for the war. Present or accounted for until he died at Camp McIntosh, Wayne County, April 10, 1862.

MOSLEY, J., Private
Resided in Wilson County and paroled at Goldsboro in 1865.

MURRAY, JOHN H., Private
Born in Wilson County where he resided prior to enlisting in Northampton County at age 37, June 29, 1861, for the war. Died at Camp Potomac, King George County, Virginia, September 16, 1861, of "inflamation of brain."

ODOM, RICHARD, Private
Resided in Wilson County where he enlisted at age 23, May 30, 1861, for the war. Wounded in skirmish near Richmond, Virginia, June 21, 1862. Reported as absent wounded on company muster rolls until he died on January 16, 1864, of "phthisis pulmonalis."

OSBORNE, J., Private
Captured at Gettysburg, Pennsylvania, July 1-3, 1863, and confined at Point Lookout, Maryland, where he died February 18, 1864.

OUTLAW, GRADY, Private
Enlisted in December, 1864, for the war.

OWENS, HAMLET H., Private
Resided in Wilson County where he enlisted at age 18, January 20, 1862, for the war. Died at Richmond, Virginia, in July, 1862.

OWENS, MORRISON T., Private
Born in Wilson County where he resided as a farmer and enlisted at age 21, May 29, 1861, for the war. Wounded at Malvern Hill, Virginia, July 1, 1862. Wounded and captured at Sharpsburg, Maryland, September 17, 1862. Paroled at Shepherdstown, Maryland, September 30, 1862. Died at Winchester, Virginia, October 10, 1862, of wound.

PARKER, JOSIAH H., Private
Resided in Nash County and enlisted in Wilson County at age 21, May 27, 1861, for the war. Wounded at Sharpsburg, Maryland, September 17, 1862. Present or accounted for until captured at Kelly's Ford, Virginia, November 7, 1863. Confined at Point Lookout, Maryland, until transferred to Aiken's Landing, Virginia, February 24, 1865, for exchange.

PEEL, MATTHEW T., Private
Resided in Wilson County where he enlisted at age 22, May 28, 1861, for the war. Discharged October 31, 1861.

PENINGTON, RUFUS, Private
Enlisted in October, 1864, for the war.

PITTMAN, CANNON, Private
Enlisted in Wake County on June 24, 1863, for the war. Reported for duty with the company on February 24, 1864, from hospital at Wilson. Killed at Spotsylvania Court House, Virginia, May 12, 1864.

PRIDGERS, SAMUEL, Private
Resided in Wilson County where he enlisted at age 21, May 27, 1861, for the war. Died at Fredericksburg, Virginia, August 8, 1861.

PUCKETT, JAMES H., Private
Received pay on March 11, 1864, for service covering the period December 31, 1863, to February 29, 1864.

PUCKETT, L. H., Private
Paroled at Salisbury on May 27, 1865.

REDWINE, G. A., Private
Paroled at Salisbury on May 3, 1865.

RENIKE, JOHN, Private
Resided in Wilson County where he enlisted at age 27, May 27, 1861, for the war. Present or accounted for on company muster rolls through October, 1864, being detailed as blacksmith from May, 1863, through October, 1864. Paroled at Appomattox Court House, Virginia, April 9, 1865.

RENIS, J., Private
Paroled at Salisbury on May 27, 1865.

RENTFROW, JOHN T., Private
Resided in Wilson County where he enlisted at age 24, May 28, 1861, for the war. Present or accounted for until he died at Wilson on December 18, 1862, of disease.

RENTFROW, PERRY, Private
Resided in Wilson County and enlisted in Wake

County at age 24, June 18, 1863, for the war. Present or accounted for on company muster rolls through October, 1864. Captured at Burkeville, Virginia, April 6, 1865, and confined at Point Lookout, Maryland, until released after taking the Oath of Allegiance on June 17, 1865.

RETCHEY, HENRY J., Private
Paroled at Salisbury on May 11, 1865.

ROBINSON, JOHN, Private
Resided in Wilson County where he enlisted at age 25, May 27, 1861, for the war. Wounded in the knee and permanently disabled at Malvern Hill, Virginia, July 1, 1862. Detailed as hospital guard January, 1863. Retired to the Invalid Corps on April 29, 1864.

ROE, WILLIAM, Private
Resided in Wilson County where he enlisted at age 22, January 21, 1862, for the war. Present or accounted for on company muster rolls through October, 1864. Deserted and surrendered to Federal forces February 23, 1865. Took the Oath of Allegiance at Washington, D.C., and was provided transportation to Philadelphia, Pennsylvania.

ROSE, HAYWOOD, Private
Resided in Wilson County where he enlisted at age 21, May 27, 1861, for the war. Wounded at Chancellorsville, Virginia, May 3, 1863. Present or accounted for on company muster rolls through October, 1864. Captured at Farmville, Virginia, April 6, 1865, and confined at Point Lookout, Maryland, until released after taking the Oath of Allegiance on June 17, 1865.

ROSE, WILLIAM T., Private
Resided in Wilson County where he enlisted at age 18, May 28, 1861, for the war. Wounded at Sharpsburg, Maryland, September 17, 1862. Wounded in the left arm at Hagerstown, Maryland, in July, 1863. Reported as absent wounded on company muster rolls and hospital records until furloughed from hospital at Richmond, Virginia, for 60 days on January 26, 1865.

ROUNDTREE, THADDEUS, Private
Resided in Wilson County where he enlisted at age 28, May 27, 1861, for the war. Discharged at Wilson on April 14, 1863, by reason of "phthisis pulmonalis." Died at Wilson in May, 1863.

SCOTT, ARNOLD B., Private
Resided in Wilson County and enlisted in Northampton County at age 18, July 9, 1861, for the war. Died at Camp Holmes, Virginia, August 1, 1861.

SHERRILL, J., Private
Admitted to hospital at Richmond, Virginia, February 25, 1865. Captured in hospital at Richmond on April 3, 1865, and turned over to the Provost Marshal on April 14, 1865.

SIMPSON, BENJAMIN GRIFFIN, Private
Resided in Wilson County where he enlisted at age 22, April 29, 1862, for the war. Wounded at Chancellorsville, Virginia, May 3, 1863. Returned to duty on August 24, 1863. Present or accounted for on company muster rolls until captured at

Winchester, Virginia, September 19, 1864. Confined at Point Lookout, Maryland, until paroled and transferred for exchange to Aiken's Landing, Virginia, on March 15, 1865. Paroled at Goldsboro on May 9, 1865. "Came in for parole."

SKINNER, JESSE L., Corporal
Resided in Wilson County where he enlisted at age 26, April 29, 1862, for the war. Mustered in as Private and appointed Corporal on October 12, 1863. Captured at Kelly's Ford, Virginia, November 7, 1863. Confined at Point Lookout, Maryland, until paroled and transferred for exchange to Aiken's Landing, Virginia, on February 24, 1865. Captured in hospital at Richmond, Virginia, April 3, 1865, and transferred to Newport News, Virginia, April 24, 1865.

SKINNER, VAN BUREN, Private
Born in Wilson County where he resided as a farmer and enlisted at age 23, May 7, 1862, for the war. Died in hospital at Staunton, Virginia, November 9, 1862, of "carditis."

STOKES, WILLIAM, Private
Captured at Gettysburg, Pennsylvania, July 3, 1863, and confined at Fort Delaware, Delaware. Transferred to Point Lookout, Maryland, October 18, 1863. Reported on a roll at Point Lookout as a "prisoner who arrived at this station under assumed name, or who assumed one for the purpose of being transferred, exchanged or released."

STOTT, ADDISON, Private
Resided in Wilson County where he enlisted at age 22, May 28, 1861, for the war. Died in camp in Stafford County, Virginia, August 4, 1861, of "typhoid fever."

STOTT, WILEY, Private
Resided in Wilson County and enlisted in Wake County at age 18, June 24, 1863, for the war. Reported to the company on October 9, 1863, being absent sick in hospital from date of enlistment until the day he joined the company. Furloughed for 30 days at Lynchburg, Virginia, December 4, 1863. Detailed to light duty in hospital at Richmond, Virginia, February 4, 1864. Returned to company by August, 1864. September-October, 1864, muster roll states that he was "absent wounded in hospital at Lynchburg, Virginia." Paroled at Appomattox Court House, Virginia, April 9, 1865.

STOTTS, BUNYAN, Private
Enlisted in Wilson County on February 27, 1864, for the war. Present or accounted for until paroled at Appomattox Court House, Virginia, April 9, 1865.

STRICKLAND, ANDREW J., Private
Born in Nash County and was by occupation a farmer prior to enlisting at Richmond, Virginia, at age 17, November 19, 1863, for the war. Killed at Spotsylvania Court House, Virginia, May 12, 1864.

STRICKLAND, BERRY, Private
Resided in Wilson County where he enlisted at age 20, May 27, 1861, for the war. Wounded at Chancellorsville, Virginia, May 3, 1863. Present or accounted for on company muster rolls until

captured at Harper's Farm, Virginia, April 6, 1865. Confined at Point Lookout, Maryland, until released after taking the Oath of Allegiance on June 20, 1865.

STRICKLAND, WESLEY, Private

Born in Nash County and resided as a farmer in Wilson County where he enlisted at age 25, May 27, 1861, for the war. Wounded in the hand at Sharpsburg, Maryland, September 17, 1862. Present or accounted for until admitted to hospital at Charlottesville, Virginia, June 16, 1864. Furloughed for 60 days on September 13, 1864. Admitted to hospital at Richmond, Virginia, November 12, 1864, and retired to the Invalid Corps on January 26, 1864. Admitted to hospital at Richmond, February 23, 1865, with "debilitas" and died March 25, 1865.

TATUM, HENRY, Private

Enlisted in Wilson County on January 6, 1864, for the war. Present or accounted for until captured at Winchester, Virginia, September 19, 1864. Admitted to hospital at Baltimore, Maryland, December 21, 1864, with "bronchitis chronic, very slight." Transferred to Fort McHenry, Maryland, February 10, 1865. Transferred to Point Lookout, Maryland, for exchange on February 20, 1865.

TAYLOR, A. H., Private

Paroled at Farmville, Virginia, April 11-21, 1865.

TAYLOR, FREDERICK, Private

Resided in Wilson County where he enlisted at age 38, April 29, 1862, for the war. Died in hospital at Richmond, Virginia, in August, 1862.

TAYLOR, JESSE M., Private

Resided in Wilson County where he enlisted at age 19, May 27, 1861, for the war. Mustered in as 1st Sergeant and reduced to ranks on September 9, 1861. Present or accounted for until transferred to Company H, 7th Regiment Confederate Cavalry on December 9, 1863.

TAYLOR, WILLIAM H., Private

Resided in Wilson County where he enlisted at age 22, May 27, 1861, for the war. Present or accounted for on company muster rolls until he was "furloughed from camp, September 18, 1864, for 30 days." Admitted to hospital at Charlottesville, Virginia, on December 20, 1864, with "lumbago." Transferred to Lynchburg, Virginia, on April 9, 1865. Readmitted to hospital at Charlottesville on April 12, 1865, and returned to duty April 14, 1865.

THOMPSON, J. G., Private

Paroled at Salisbury on May 27, 1865.

THOMPSON, RAIFORD, Private

Born in Wilson County where he resided and enlisted at age 18, May 7, 1862, for the war. Wounded and captured at Sharpsburg, Maryland, September 17, 1862. Paroled on September 27, 1862. Died of wound on October 10, 1862.

THORN, MARTIN RAMSEY, Private

Transferred from Company D of this regiment, March-April, 1862. Paroled at Leesburg, Virginia, October 2, 1862. May 1-October 31, 1862, muster roll states that he was "left sick at Culpeper Court House." Reported as such on muster rolls until March-April, 1863, muster roll reports him with the remark that he "died near Lovelleville, Virginia, in October, 1862."

THORNELL, MARTIN V., Private

Resided in Wilson County where he enlisted at age 24, May 27, 1861, for the war. Present or accounted for on company muster rolls until captured at Spotsylvania Court House, Virginia, May 8, 1864. Confined at Point Lookout, Maryland, until released after taking the Oath of Allegiance on June 6, 1865.

TODD, ELBERT, Sergeant

Resided in Wilson County where he enlisted at age 22, May 27, 1861, for the war. Mustered in as Private and appointed Corporal on December 1, 1862. Promoted to Sergeant on April 10, 1863. Present or accounted for on company muster rolls through October, 1864, being reported as absent wounded from May 1-August 31, 1864, muster roll through October, 1864. Paroled at Appomattox Court House, Virginia, April 9, 1865.

TODD, WILEY J., Private

Enlisted in Wilson County on May 29, 1861, for the war. Killed at Chancellorsville, Virginia, May 3, 1863.

TODD, WILSON, Private

Resided in Wilson County where he enlisted at age 26, May 7, 1862, for the war. Wounded at Chancellorsville, Virginia, May 3, 1863. Returned to company on September 12, 1863. Detailed on detached service December 18, 1863, through February, 1864. May 1-August 31, 1864, muster roll states that he was "absent wounded and in hospital at Wilson, North Carolina." Reported absent wounded through October, 1864.

TREVATHAN, MATHEW G., Private

Resided in Wilson County where he enlisted at age 33, June 20, 1862, for the war. Wounded at Chancellorsville, Virginia, May 3, 1863. Present or accounted for on company muster rolls until captured at Winchester, Virginia, September 19, 1864. Confined at Point Lookout, Maryland, until transferred to James River, Virginia, for exchange on February 10, 1865. Appears as present on a roll of a detachment of paroled and exchanged prisoners at Camp Lee, near Richmond, Virginia, dated February 17, 1865.

TREVATHAN, SANDERS M., Private

Enlisted in Wilson County on May 5, 1862, for the war. First reported on company muster roll for May 1-August 31, 1864. Reported as present with the remark: "In hospital at Staunton, Virginia. Has returned to duty." September-October, 1864, muster roll carries him as "absent wounded at Cedar Creek and sent to hospital." Admitted to hospital at Richmond, Virginia, December 24, 1864, with a gunshot wound of the right arm. Furloughed for 60 days on March 1, 1865.

VIMMEL, J., Private

Resided in Wilson County and paroled at Goldsboro in 1865.

WATSON, DeWITT, Sergeant
Resided in Wilson County where he enlisted at age 22, May 27, 1861, for the war. Mustered in as Private and appointed Corporal on April 1, 1862. Promoted to Sergeant on September 1, 1862. Present or accounted for until killed at Spotsylvania Court House, Virginia, May 19, 1864.

WATSON, E., Private
Resided in Wilson County and paroled at Goldsboro in 1865.

WEARET, W. A., Private
Paroled at Salisbury on May 15, 1865.

WELLS, J., Private
Admitted to hospital at Richmond, Virginia, on February 25, 1865. Retired "February 24."

WELLS, JESSE L., Private
Resided in Wilson County where he enlisted at age 18, May 29, 1861, for the war. Present or accounted for until he died in hospital at Lynchburg, Virginia, on January 29, 1863, of "variola."

WELLS, JOHN G., Private
Resided in Wilson County where he enlisted at age 19, May 27, 1861, for the war. Present or accounted for on company muster rolls through August, 1864, when he was reported as "absent wounded at Charlestown and sent to hospital." Admitted to hospital at Richmond, Virginia, September 13, 1864, and furloughed for 45 days on the same date. Paroled at Appomattox Court House, Virginia, April 9, 1865.

WELLS, WATSON, Private
Resided in Wilson County where he enlisted at age 29, May 29, 1861, for the war. Wounded at Sharpsburg, Maryland, September 17, 1862, and died of wound at Mount Jackson, Virginia, October 5, 1862.

WHITTY, H., Private
Paroled at Greensboro on May 13, 1865.

WIGGS, BALLARD, Private
Transferred from Company H, 7th Regiment Confederate Cavalry on December 15, 1863. Reported as absent without leave on company muster rolls through April 1, 1864. Transferred to Company H of this regiment in April, 1864.

WILLIAMSON, JOSEPH D., Corporal
Resided in Wilson County where he enlisted at age 18, May 28, 1861, for the war. Mustered in as Corporal. Died at Fredericksburg, Virginia, August 8, 1861, of "typhoid fever."

WILLIAMSON, LEVI T., Private
Resided in Wilson County where he enlisted at age 23, May 27, 1861, for the war. Wounded at Chancellorsville, Virginia, May 3, 1863. Returned to company on September 9, 1863. Present or accounted for on company muster rolls until transferred to Company A, 55th Regiment N.C. Troops on May 3, 1864.

WILLIFORD, JOHN T., Sergeant
Resided in Wilson County where he enlisted at age 18, May 27, 1861, for the war. Mustered in as Corporal and promoted to Sergeant on February 1, 1862. Wounded at Malvern Hill, Virginia, July 1, 1862, and died at home of wound in October, 1862.

WILSON, GEORGE W., Private
Born in Wilson County where he resided as a farmer and enlisted at age 23, May 7, 1862, for the war. Died in hospital at Richmond, Virginia, September 20-22, 1862, of "typhoid fever."

WILSON, JOHN W., Private
Resided in Wilson County where he enlisted at age 28, May 7, 1862, for the war. Present or accounted for on company muster rolls until captured at Kelly's Ford, Virginia, November 7-8, 1863. Died in hospital at Washington, D.C., January 11, 1864, of "typhoid pneumonia."

WINBORN, STEPHEN, Private
Resided in Wilson County where he enlisted at age 18, May 29, 1861, for the war. Present or accounted for on company muster rolls through October, 1864, being detailed as a wagoner from May-June, 1863, through October, 1864.

WINSTEAD, JORDAN COFIELD, Corporal
Resided in Wilson County and enlisted in Northampton County at age 18, June 12, 1861, for the war. Mustered in as Private and appointed Corporal on September 1, 1862. Wounded at Fredericksburg, Virginia, December 13, 1862, and reported as absent wounded on company muster rolls through October, 1864. Hospital records indicate that he was detailed as a cook in General Military Hospital No. 2, Wilson, August 17, 1863. Hospital records carry him as present through December, 1864. Records also show that he served as a nurse during the same period.

WOMBLE, JOHN G., Private
Resided in Wilson County where he enlisted at age 22, May 27, 1861, for the war. Present or accounted for until captured at Gettysburg, Pennsylvania, July 3, 1863. Confined at Fort Delaware, Delaware, until transferred to Point Lookout, Maryland, October 15-18, 1863. Paroled at Point Lookout and transferred to City Point, Virginia, for exchange on March 17, 1864. Received at City Point in exchange on March 20, 1864. Present or accounted for on company muster rolls through October, 1864. Captured at Burkeville, Virginia, April 6, 1865, and confined at Point Lookout Maryland, until released after taking the Oath of Allegiance on June 21, 1865.

1st COMPANY C

Organized in Carteret County, this company, known as the "Topsail Rifles," was organized soon after Lincoln's election and tendered its service to the state on May 21, 1861. It was ordered to Fort Macon, where it served as a heavy artillery company. On June 4, 1861, it was ordered to Camp Advance, near Garysburg, Northampton County, where it was mustered into state service as Company C of this regiment. On August 21, 1861, the company was ordered back to Fort Macon, where it was assigned to the garrison as a heavy artillery company on September 1, 1861, and designated Company H, 10th Regiment N.C. State Troops (1st Regiment N.C. Artillery). Because it was the first company to serve as Company C, 2nd Regiment N.C. State Troops, it was later referred to as 1st Company C of the regiment.

Since the company was originally mustered in as a heavy artillery company and was redesignated an artillery company after only brief service as 1st Company C of this regiment, the editor has chosen to report the entire period of service in the roster of Company H, 10th Regiment N.C. State Troops (1st Regiment N.C. Artillery). The reader is therefore referred to the history and roster of that company which appears on pages 124-137 of volume I of this series.

2nd COMPANY C

This company, known as the "Rip Van Winkles," was organized in Wayne County and enlisted at Goldsboro on June 17, 1861. The company was accepted into state service August 21, 1861, at Camp Mason and transferred to Confederate States service on September 23, 1861. It was assigned to this regiment as Company C in September, 1861. Since it was the second company to serve as Company C, it was later referred to as 2nd Company C. Although assigned to the regiment, in September, 1861, the company was ordered to Hyde County, where it was stationed at Middleton. It remained in Hyde County until ordered to rejoin the regiment. The exact date the company joined the regiment was not reported, but its November-December, 1861, muster roll reports the station as Camp Potomac, Virginia, the regimental camp. After joining the regiment the company functioned as a part of the regiment, and its history for the war period is recorded as a part of the regimental history.

The information contained in the following roster of the company was compiled principally from company muster rolls which covered from the muster-in roll, dated August 21, 1861, through December, 1861; March through October, 1862; and January, 1863, through October, 1864. No company muster rolls were found for January-February, 1862; November-December, 1862; or for the period after October, 1864. In addition to the company muster rolls, Roll of Honor records, receipt rolls, and hospital records, supplemented by state pension applications, United Daughters of the Confederacy records, and postwar rosters and histories, all provided useful information.

OFFICERS
CAPTAINS

ROBERTS, GIDEON M.

Born in Wayne County where he resided as a physician and enlisted at age 34 for the war. Appointed Captain to rank from July 16, 1861. Present or accounted for until he submitted his resignation on October 10, 1862, by reason of "dyspepsia, disease of kidneys, and debility resulting therefrom." Resignation accepted November 5, 1862, to take effect November 8, 1862.

WHITFIELD, NATHAN B.

Transferred from Company H of this regiment upon appointment as Captain to rank from February 1, 1863. Wounded at Chancellorsville, Virginia, May 3, 1863. Returned to regiment on August 5, 1863. Present or accounted for until killed at Spotsylvania Court House, Virginia, May 12, 1864.

LIEUTENANTS

BRITT, GEORGE W., 1st Lieutenant

Born in Wayne County where he resided as a farmer and enlisted at age 20, June 17, 1861, for the war. Mustered in as 1st Sergeant. Appointed 2nd Lieutenant to rank from April 7, 1862, and promoted to 1st Lieutenant to rank from February 1, 1863. Present or accounted for until wounded and captured at ·Winchester, Virginia, September 19, 1864. Died in hospital near Winchester on October 17, 1864.

BROWN, JOHN ISAAC, 2nd Lieutenant

Transferred from the Field and Staff of this regiment upon appointment as 2nd Lieutenant to rank from March 13, 1863. Wounded at Chancellorsville, Virginia, May 3, 1863. Submitted his resignation July 20, 1863, having been appointed 1st Lieutenant in Company F, 1st Battalion N.C. Local Defense Troops. Resignation accepted September 1, 1863, to take effect from July 20, 1863.

COGDELL, DAVID, 3rd Lieutenant

Born in Wayne County where he resided as a farmer and enlisted at age 41 for the war. Appointed 3rd Lieutenant to rank from May 16, 1861. Resigned December 9, 1861.

CROW, THOMAS W., 1st Lieutenant

Born in Duplin County and resided as a farmer in Wayne County where he enlisted at age 23, June 17, 1861, for the war. Mustered in as Private and appointed 2nd Lieutenant to rank from November 18, 1861. Promoted to 1st Lieutenant to rank from May 6, 1862. Died October· 21, 1862.

FAIRCLOTH, WILLIAM T., 1st Lieutenant

Resided in Wayne County and appointed 1st Lieutenant to rank from May 16, 1861. Present or accounted for until transferred to the Field and Staff of this regiment upon appointment as Captain, Assistant Quartermaster, March 14, 1862.

JONES, JOEL, 3rd Lieutenant

Born in Duplin County and resided as a farmer in Wayne County where he enlisted at age 21, June 17, 1861, for the war. Mustered in as Private and appointed Corporal on April 13, 1862. Wounded at Boonsboro, Maryland, September 14, 1862. Appointed 3rd Lieutenant to rank from March 13, 1863. Wounded at Chancellorsville, Virginia, May 3, 1863, and died of wound on July 3, 1863.

JONES, THADDEUS, 2nd Lieutenant

Born in Duplin County where he resided as a farmer prior to enlisting in Wayne County at age 26, June 17, 1861, for the war. Mustered in as Private. Appointed Sergeant, March-April, 1863. Wounded at Chancellorsville, Virginia, May 3, 1863. Appointed 2nd Lieutenant to rank from October 1, 1863. Present or accounted for on company muster rolls until reported on the May 1-August 31, 1864, muster roll as "absent wounded July 18, 1864." Admitted to hospital at Charlottesville, Virginia, July 25, 1864, with a gunshot wound of the right arm and transferred to Mount Olive, N.C., to await furlough on August 3, 1864. Company muster roll for September-October, 1864, states that he was "absent wounded since October 19, 1864." Admitted to hospital at Lynchburg, Virginia, in October, 1864, with a gunshot wound of the right hand. Admitted to hospital at Richmond, Virginia, February 24, 1865, and furloughed for 30 days on March 21, 1865.

LOFTIN, WILLIAM W., 3rd Lieutenant
Resided in Duplin County and appointed 3rd Lieutenant to rank from May 16, 1861. Died October 28-29, 1861, of "typhoid fever."

WILLIAMSON, STEPHEN, 2nd Lieutenant
Born in Duplin County and resided as a schoolteacher in Wayne County where he enlisted at age 34, June 17, 1861, for the war. Mustered in as Corporal and promoted to 1st Sergeant on April 30, 1862. Appointed 2nd Lieutenant to rank from May 6, 1862. Admitted to hospital at Richmond, Virginia, September 1, 1862, with "remittent fever" and returned to duty September 16, 1862. Admitted to hospital at Richmond a second time on November 4, 1862, with "V.S." and returned to duty on November 24, 1862. Dropped from the rolls on January 30, 1863.

NONCOMMISSIONED OFFICERS AND PRIVATES

ADAMS, WILLIAM B., Private
Born in Johnston County and resided as a laborer in Wayne County where he enlisted at age 45, June 17, 1861, for the war. Died at Fredericksburg, Virginia, January 23, 1862, of disease.

ANDERSON, JAMES, Private
Born in Wayne County where he resided as a laborer and enlisted at age 18, June 17, 1861, for the war. Present or accounted for on company muster rolls until captured at Kelly's Ford, Virginia, November 7, 1863. Confined at Old Capitol Prison, Washington, D.C., until transferred to Point Lookout, Maryland, February 3-4, 1864. Remained at Point Lookout, until paroled and transferred to Aiken's Landing, Virginia, February 24, 1865, for exchange.

BASS, JETHRO B., Private
Born in Wayne County where he resided and enlisted at age 25, July 27, 1861, for the war. Present or accounted for on company muster rolls through October, 1864. Captured at Petersburg, Virginia, April 3, 1865, and confined at Hart's Island, New York Harbor, where he died June 3, 1865, of "phthisis."

BENFIELD, A. A., Private
Enlisted in Wake County on May 2, 1864, for the war. September-October, 1864, muster roll reports him as "missing since battle Winchester, September 19, 1864."

BENNETT, JOHN J., Corporal
Resided in Duplin County where he enlisted at age 21, February 15, 1862, for the war. Mustered in as Private and appointed Corporal, March-April, 1863. Captured near Fredericksburg, Virginia, May 3, 1863, and paroled and exchanged at City Point, Virginia, May 10, 1863. Wounded at Gettysburg, Pennsylvania, July 2-3, 1863. Present or accounted for on company muster rolls until wounded at Cold Harbor, Virginia, and admitted to hospital at Richmond, Virginia, May 22, 1864. Died in hospital at Richmond on June 2, 1864.

BENNETT, SEBRON L., Private
Born in Duplin County where he resided as a farmer prior to enlisting in Wayne County at age 21, June 17, 1861, for the war. Mustered in as Corporal and reduced to ranks on September 27, 1862. Wounded at Chancellorsville, Virginia, May 3, 1863, and reported as "absent on surgeon's certificate" on company muster rolls through October, 1864. Furloughed from hospital at Richmond, Virginia, December 24, 1864, for 60 days.

BENSON, W. O., Private
Enlisted October 1, 1864, for the war.

BINGHAM, R. M., Private
Enlisted in Wake County on April 22, 1864, for the war. Admitted to hospital at Charlottesville, Virginia, July 25, 1864, with "diarrhoea chronic" and died August 2, 1864.

BISHOP, E. R., Private
Name reported on company muster roll for the period May 1-October 31, 1862, but date, place, and period of enlistment not reported. Died at Charlottesville, Virginia, October 13, 1862.

BLACK, ELI, Private
Born in Davidson County where he resided prior to enlisting in Wake County at age 29, July 8, 1862, for the war. Died at Guinea Station, Virginia, February 17, 1863, of disease.

BLACKWELL, BENJAMIN H., Private
Born in Wayne County where he resided as a laborer and enlisted at age 25, June 17, 1861, for the war. Captured at South Mountain, Maryland, in September, 1862, and confined at Fort Delaware, Delaware. Transferred to Aiken's Landing, Virginia, October 2, 1862, and declared exchanged on November 10, 1862. Present or accounted for until he died in hospital at Richmond, Virginia, April 27, 1864, of "phthisis pulmonalis."

BROCK, DAVID J., Private
Born in Wayne County where he resided as a laborer and enlisted at age 18, June 20, 1861, for the war. Present or accounted for on company muster rolls until reported on May 1-October 31, 1862, muster roll with the remark that he was "absent, taken prisoner in Maryland." January-February, 1863, muster roll states that he "took Oath of Allegiance to the U. S. Government, September 12, 1862."

BROCK, ROBERT, Private
Born in Duplin County where he resided as a laborer prior to enlisting in Wake County at age 20, September 9, 1861, for the war. Wounded in skirmish near Seven Pines, Virginia, June 20-21, 1862. Reported as absent wounded through

December, 1863, and absent on Certificate of Permanent Disability until retired to the Invalid Corps on November 22, 1864.

BROCK, ROBERT T., Private
Resided in Duplin County and enlisted at Camp Potomac, King George County, Virginia, at age 26, March 6, 1862, for the war. Wounded at Fredericksburg, Virginia, December 13, 1862. Company muster rolls report him as absent wounded through December, 1863, and as absent without leave from January through October, 1864.

BRUCE, R. E., Private
Wounded and captured at Winchester, Virginia, September 19, 1864. Died in hospital near Winchester of a gunshot wound of the chest on September 30, 1864.

BRYANT, WILLIAM D., Private
Enlisted in Wake County on May 19, 1864, for the war. Present or accounted for until captured at Farmville, Virginia, April 6, 1865. Confined at Point Lookout, Maryland, where he died June 24, 1865, of "diarrhea chronic."

CHAMBERS, WILLIAM J., Private
Enlisted in Wake County at age 19, July 12, 1862, for the war. Present or accounted for until admitted to hospital at Richmond, Virginia, May 22, 1864, with a gunshot wound. Furloughed for 60 days on June 7, 1864. Captured at Fisher's Hill, Virginia, September 22, 1864. Confined at Point Lookout, Maryland, until paroled and transferred for exchange to Aiken's Landing, Virginia, on March 17, 1865.

CHERRY, LEMUEL, Corporal
Born in Duplin County where he resided as a farmer prior to enlisting in Wayne County at age 22, July 2, 1861, for the war. Wounded at Sharpsburg, Maryland, September 17, 1862. Promoted to Corporal on March 1, 1863. Wounded at Chancellorsville, Virginia, May 3, 1863. Present or accounted for until captured at Kelly's Ford, Virginia, November 7, 1863. Confined at Point Lookout, Maryland, until transferred to Aiken's Landing, Virginia, February 24, 1865, for exchange.

CHERRY, WILLIAM A., Private
Born in Duplin County where he resided as a student prior to enlisting in Wayne County at age 18, July 2, 1861, for the war. Wounded at Gettysburg, Pennsylvania, July 1-3, 1863. Returned to duty on October 30, 1863. Wounded a second time May-June, 1864. Furloughed from hospital at Richmond, Virginia, November 21, 1864, for 60 days. Federal Provost Marshal records for March, 1865, report him as a "deserter from the enemy" with the remark that he took the Oath of Allegiance and was furnished transportation to Wilmington, March 24, 1865.

CHERRY, WILLIS W., Private
Born in Duplin County where he resided as a farmer prior to enlisting in Wayne County at age 24, June 17, 1861, for the war. Present or accounted for until discharged on April 28, 1862, by reason of his having provided a substitute.

COBLE, J. S., Private
Resided in Alamance County and enlisted in Wake County on May 5, 1864, for the war. Wounded June 18, 1864, and furloughed from hospital at Richmond, Virginia, September 11, 1864, for 60 days. Captured at Petersburg, Virginia, April 3, 1865, and confined at Hart's Island, New York Harbor, until released after taking the Oath of Allegiance on June 17, 1865.

COGDELL, LEWIS D., Private
Born in Wayne County and resided as a student prior to enlisting in Wake County at age 20, August 16, 1861, for the war. Died in hospital at Lynchburg, Virginia, February 1, 1863, of "diarrhoea chronic."

CREACH, BLOUNT, Private
Born in Duplin County where he resided as a laborer and enlisted at age 30, July 30, 1861, for the war. Died at Richmond, Virginia, September 3, 1862.

CREWS, M. C., Private
Paroled at Greensboro on May 23, 1865.

DALE, JOHN A., Private
Born in Duplin County where he resided prior to enlisting in Wayne County at age 22, September 24, 1861, for the war. Died at Guinea Station, Virginia, February 1, 1863.

DANIEL, N. K., Private
Born in Cumberland County and resided as a farmer prior to enlisting in Wake County on July 12, 1862, for the war. Died at Winchester, Virginia, October 24, 1862.

DAVIS, ELIJAH, Private
Resided in Duplin County where he enlisted at age 26, February 15, 1862, for the war. Wounded in skirmish at Leesburg, Virginia, in September, 1862. Paroled at Leesburg on October 2, 1862. Admitted to hospital at Richmond, Virginia, October 14, 1862, with a gunshot wound of the left hand and furloughed for 30 days on October 18, 1862. Present or accounted for until November 27, 1863, when he failed to return from a 30 day furlough. Reported as absent without leave on company muster rolls through October, 1864. Paroled April 3, 1865.

DAVIS, HENRY B., Private
Born in Duplin County where he resided as a farmer prior to enlisting in Wayne County at age 30, June 17, 1861, for the war. Present or accounted for until captured at Falling Waters, Maryland, July 14, 1863. Confined at Point Lookout, Maryland, until paroled for exchange on November 1, 1864. Date exchanged not reported. Captured at Petersburg, Virginia, April 3, 1865, and confined at Hart's Island, New York Harbor, until released after taking the Oath of Allegiance on June 17, 1865.

DEAL, JOHN A., Private
Enlisted in Wayne County on September 23, 1861, for the war. Reported as present on company muster roll through October 31, 1861.

DEAVER, WILLIAM, Private
Born in Duplin County where he resided as a

farmer prior to enlisting in Wayne County at age 18, June 24, 1861, for the war. Present or accounted for until wounded and captured at Gettysburg, Pennsylvania, July 1-5, 1863. Confined at DeCamp General Hospital, Davids Island, New York Harbor, until paroled and transferred for exchange. Exchanged at City Point, Virginia, September 16, 1863. Company muster rolls report him as absent wounded through December, 1863, and as present or accounted for from January through October, 1864. Captured near Petersburg, Virginia, April 4, 1865, and confined at Hart's Island, New York Harbor, until released after taking the Oath of Allegiance on June 19, 1865.

ELLIS, EPHRAIM, Private
Born in Wayne County where he resided as a laborer and enlisted at age 19, June 17, 1861, for the war. Reported as absent sick from October 10, 1862, through May-June, 1863, when he was reported with the remark: "Absent left at hospital, Winchester, October 15, 1862. Supposed to be dead." Claim for balance of pay due filed October 21, 1863, but date and place of death not reported. Roll of Honor carries the remark: "Court Martialed for absence without leave and sentenced. Deserted May 13, 1863."

ELLIS, THOMAS C., Sergeant
Born in Orange County where he resided as a clerk prior to enlisting in Wake County at age 20, September 14, 1861, for the war. Mustered in as Private and appointed Corporal on October 1, 1862. Promoted to Sergeant on March 1, 1863. Wounded at Chancellorsville, Virginia, May 3, 1863, and furloughed from hospital at Richmond, Virginia, for 60 days on June 18, 1863. Reported as absent wounded through February 9, 1864, when he was "detailed by the Medical Board to assist the Enrolling Officer of Orange County until March 10." Reported as present on muster roll dated April 1, 1864. Captured near Spotsylvania Court House, Virginia, May 12, 1864. Confined at Point Lookout, Maryland, until transferred to Elmira, New York, August 10-14, 1864. Released at Elmira after taking the Oath of Allegiance on June 14, 1865.

EVERETT, ROBERT, Private
Born in Wayne County where he resided as a farmer and enlisted at age 26, July 6, 1861, for the war. Mustered in as Sergeant and reduced to ranks on October 1, 1862. Present or accounted for until captured at Manassas Gap, Virginia, July 20, 1863. Confined at Point Lookout, Maryland, until transferred to Fort Monroe, Virginia, March 2, 1864. Took the Oath of Allegiance at Fort Monroe on March 3, 1864, and was "employed in Quartermaster Department, Fort Monroe."

FISHER, BENJAMIN, Private
Enlisted in Wake County on February 12, 1864, for the war. Present or accounted for on company muster rolls through October, 1864, when he was reported with the remark that he deserted August 29, 1864. Paroled at Gordonsville, Virginia, June 17, 1865.

FISHER, JOHN, Private
Born in New Jersey and resided as a laborer in

Wayne County where he enlisted at age 19, June 25, 1861, for the war. Deserted November 24, 1862, and returned to company in April, 1863. Captured near Fredericksburg, Virginia, May 3, 1863, and paroled and exchanged at City Point, Virginia, May 10, 1863. Deserted May 15, 1863. Arrested and returned from desertion September 10, 1863. Deserted again on December 10, 1863. Captured and sentenced by court-martial "to twelve months hard labor and to miss no fights and to receive only half pay or allowance." Sentence of court-martial remitted by special order on April 7, 1864. Deserted April 24, 1864, and reported as absent "in desertion" through October, 1864.

FOREHAND, THEOPHILUS, Private
Born in Wayne County where he resided as a farmer and enlisted on February 6, 1862, for the war. Died in hospital at Lynchburg, Virginia, March 18, 1863, of "diarrhoea chronic."

FULGHUM, WILLIAM GWYER, Musician
Enlisted at Camp Potomac, Virginia, February 14, 1862, for the war. Mustered in as Musician. Detailed at C.S. Military Prison, Danville, Virginia, March 2, 1863, by reason of "wound in side." Company muster rolls report him as absent on detail through October, 1864.

GILBERT, EUGENE F., Private
Born in Connecticut and resided as a jeweler in Wayne County where he enlisted at age 25, July 19, 1861, for the war. Discharged June 17, 1862.

GLISSON, HARRY J., Private
Born in Duplin County where he resided as a farmer prior to enlisting in Wayne County at age 40, June 17, 1861, for the war. Mustered in as Private and appointed Corporal on March 1, 1863. Wounded and captured at Chancellorsville, Virginia, May 3, 1863. Paroled and exchanged at City Point, Virginia, June 12, 1863. Present or accounted for on company muster rolls through October, 1864, when he was reported as "absent wounded since October 19, 1864." Paroled at Goldsboro on May 15, 1865. "Came in for parole."

GLISSON, JOHN, Private
Born in Duplin County where he resided as a laborer prior to enlisting in Wayne County at age 35, June 17, 1861, for the war. Present or accounted for until admitted to hospital at Richmond, Virginia, May 22, 1864, with a gunshot wound. Furloughed for 60 days on June 17, 1864. Hospital records indicate that he remained in hospital at Richmond through January, 1865. Admitted to hospital at Richmond on March 6, 1865, with a gunshot wound of the left leg. Captured in hospital at Richmond on April 3, 1865, and transferred to Newport News, Virginia, April 23, 1865. Released after taking the Oath of Allegiance at Newport News on June 14, 1865.

GLOVER, HENRY H., Private
Resided in Mecklenburg County and enlisted in Wake County on April 20, 1864, for the war. Wounded July 18, 1864, and reported as absent in hospitals at Richmond, Virginia, and Charlotte through January, 1865. Captured at Farmville, Virginia, April 6, 1865, and confined at Point

Lookout, Maryland, until released after taking the Oath of Allegiance on June 27, 1865.

GODWIN, EDMOND E., Private
Born in Sampson County and resided as a laborer in Wayne County where he enlisted at age 35, June 17, 1861, for the war. Wounded and captured at Chancellorsville, Virginia, May 3, 1863, and paroled and exchanged on May 13, 1863. Reported as absent wounded through October, 1864. Paroled at Goldsboro in 1865.

GOODMAN, EDWARD, Private
Born in Sampson County and resided as a farmer prior to enlisting in Wayne County at age 26, July 13, 1861, for the war. Died in hospital at Mount Jackson, Virginia, October 31, 1862, of "meningitis."

GOUGH, JAMES T., Private
Born in Duplin County where he resided as a farmer prior to enlisting in Wayne County at age 24, February 3, 1862, for the war. Died in hospital at Richmond, Virginia, March 21, 1863, of "chronic diarrhoea."

GOUGH, JOHN H., Private
Born in Duplin County where he resided as a farmer prior to enlisting in Wayne County at age 19, June 24, 1861, for the war. Died at Mount Jackson, Virginia, November 14, 1862, of "diarrhoea chronic."

GOUGH, ROBERT W., Private
Resided in Duplin County and enlisted in Wayne County at age 20, February 3, 1862, for the war. Detailed as a nurse in February, 1863. Reported as absent on detail through October, 1864. Captured at Petersburg, Virginia, April 3, 1865, and confined at Hart's Island, New York Harbor, until released after taking the Oath of Allegiance on June 17, 1865.

GRADY, TIMOTHY, Private
Resided in Duplin County and enlisted in Wayne County on May 12, 1862, for the war. Detailed as a nurse on March 21, 1863. Reported as absent on detail through June, 1863, and as present from that date through October, 1864. Captured at Petersburg, Virginia, April 3, 1865, and confined at Hart's Island, New York Harbor, until released after taking the Oath of Allegiance on June 17, 1865.

GRANTHAM, MARSHALL P., Sergeant
Born in Wayne County where he resided as a clerk and enlisted at age 18, June 20, 1861, for the war. Mustered in as Sergeant. Discharged on February 9, 1862, by reason of his having provided a substitute.

GUFFORD, SETH, Private
Resided in Duplin County where he enlisted at age 18, February 15, 1862, for the war. Present or accounted for until captured at Kelly's Ford, Virginia, November 7, 1863. Confined at Point Lookout, Maryland, where he died February 13, 1865, of "diarrhoea chronic."

HAGER, A. M., Private
Captured at Gettysburg, Pennsylvania, July 3, 1863, and confined at Fort Delaware, Delaware, where he died October 26, 1863, of "scurvy."

HAGER, W., Private
Paroled at Charlotte on May 16, 1865.

HALL, WILLIAM H., Private
Enlisted in Wake County on April 22, 1864, for the war. Wounded July 18, 1864, and reported as absent wounded on company muster rolls through October, 1864.

HARDISON, LEMUEL, Private
Born in Duplin County where he resided as a cooper prior to enlisting in Wayne County at age 33, June 17, 1861, for the war. Admitted to hospital at Danville, Virginia, September 6, 1862, with "phthisis pulmonalis." Hospital records indicate that he was detailed as a nurse at Richmond, Virginia, March 26, 1864. Reported on hospital muster rolls of Jackson Hospital, Richmond, through February, 1865. Captured in hospital at Richmond on April 3, 1865, and paroled on May 15, 1865.

HARDISON, THOMAS J., Private
Born in Wayne County and resided as a farmer in Duplin County prior to enlisting in Wayne County at age 21, June 17, 1861, for the war. Captured and paroled near Fredericksburg, Virginia, May 4, 1863. Captured at Manassas Gap, Virginia, July 24, 1863. Confined at Point Lookout, Maryland, until paroled and sent to City Point, Virginia, for exchange on March 3, 1864. Present or accounted for until captured at Winchester, Virginia, September 19, 1864. Confined at Point Lookout until released after taking the Oath of Allegiance on June 27, 1865.

HARRELL, FURNEY, Private
Born in Sampson County and resided as a laborer in Wayne County where he enlisted at age 24, July 9, 1861, for the war. Present or accounted for until detailed as a teamster prior to October, 1862. Reported as absent on detail through October, 1864. Paroled at Appomattox Court House, Virginia, April 9, 1865.

HARRON, JOHN, Private
Resided in Mecklenburg County and enlisted in Wake County on April 22, 1864, for the war. Captured at Fisher's Hill, Virginia, October 19, 1864, and confined at Point Lookout, Maryland, until released after taking the Oath of Allegiance on May 12-14, 1865.

HARTMAN, ADAM, Private
Resided in Davidson County where he enlisted on September 27, 1863, for the war. Present or accounted for until wounded on July 18, 1864. Died of wound in hospital at Mount Jackson, Virginia.

HERRING, ALEXANDER, Private
Born in Duplin County where he resided as a farmer prior to enlisting in Wayne County at age 22, July 19, 1861, for the war. Wounded and captured at Chancellorsville, Virginia, May 3, 1863. Confined at Old Capitol Prison, Washington, D.C., until paroled on June 25, 1863. Exchanged at City Point, Virginia. Admitted to hospital at Petersburg, Virginia, June 30, 1863, and furloughed for 40 days on July 14, 1863. Returned to duty on October 16, 1863. Present or accounted for on company muster rolls until reported on the May 1-August 31, 1864, muster roll with the

remark that he was "absent wounded and a prisoner, May 19, 1864." Reported with the same remark on September-October, 1864, muster roll.

HERRING, JAMES F., Private
Resided in Duplin County and enlisted in Wayne County at age 20, February 5, 1862, for the war. Company muster rolls report that he was absent sick from October 18, 1862, until he returned to the company on January 10, 1864. Detailed on February 26, 1864. Reported as absent without leave after May 4, 1864.

HERRING, NATHANIEL, Private
Born in Duplin County where he resided as a farmer prior to enlisting in Wayne County at age 25, July 2, 1861, for the war. "Never mustered into service."

HERRING, WILLIAM, Private
Resided in Duplin County and enlisted in Wayne County at age 26, February 5, 1862, for the war. Captured near Fredericksburg, Virginia, May 3, 1863, and paroled and exchanged at City Point, Virginia, May 10, 1863. Present or accounted for on company muster rolls through October, 1864. Federal Provost Marshal records indicate that he was reported on March 19, 1865, with the remark: "Deserted from the enemy." Took the Oath of Allegiance and was furnished transportation to Wilmington, March 24, 1865.

HINES, JEREMIAH, Private
Born in Lenoir County and resided as a farmer in Wayne County where he enlisted at age 24, June 24, 1861, for the war. Present or accounted for on company muster rolls until he was killed at Spotsylvania Court House, Virginia, May 12, 1864.

HINLY, WILLIAM, Private
Confined at Fort Delaware, Delaware, until transferred to Aiken's Landing, Virginia, October 2, 1862. Declared exchanged November 10, 1862.

HINSON, JESSE, Private
Born in Wayne County where he resided as a farmer and enlisted at age 15, May 1, 1862, for the war. Discharged on September 29, 1862, by reason of "extreme youth and a delicate constitution."

HOLMES, ELIAS H., Private
Born in Greene County and resided as a laborer in Duplin County prior to enlisting in Wayne County at age 19, June 17, 1861, for the war. Present or accounted for until he "deserted November 24, 1862." Returned to company, September-October, 1863. Confined at Castle Thunder, Richmond, Virginia, in October, 1863, under sentence for desertion. Remained in confinement until he died on September 2, 1864, of "anasarca."

HOPKINS, WILLIS H., Private
Resided in Wake County where he enlisted at age 21, July 1, 1863, for the war. Present or accounted for until wounded on May 6, 1864. Retired to the Invalid Corps on November 3, 1864.

HUNTER, A. R., Private
Captured at Salisbury on April 12, 1865, and con-

fined at Camp Chase, Ohio, where he took the Oath of Allegiance on June 13, 1865. Residence given on Oath as Forsyth County and age as 26.

JENNETT, NATHANIEL G. B., Private
Born in Wayne County where he resided as a farmer and enlisted at age 21, July 15, 1861, for the war. Wounded in shoulder at Cold Harbor, Virginia, June 27, 1862, and reported as absent wounded until transferred to hospital duty on December 16, 1863. Absent on detail until captured at Petersburg, Virginia, April 3, 1865. Confined at Hart's Island, New York Harbor, until released after taking the Oath of Allegiance on June 17, 1865.

JONES, CHARLES Y. F., 1st Sergeant
Born in Duplin County where he resided as a farmer prior to enlisting in Wayne County at age 29, June 17, 1861, for the war. Mustered in as Sergeant and appointed 1st Sergeant on May 7, 1862. Died November 4, 1862, of disease.

JONES, COUNCIL B., Private
Resided in Duplin County where he enlisted at age 18, February 15, 1862, for the war. Present or accounted for until captured at Wilderness, Virginia, May 8, 1864. Confined at Point Lookout, Maryland, where he died July 20, 1864.

JONES, JAMES T., Sergeant
Born in Duplin County where he resided as a laborer prior to enlisting in Wayne County at age 21, June 24, 1861, for the war. Mustered in as Private. Captured at Sharpsburg, Maryland, September 17, 1862, and confined at Fort Delaware, Delaware, until paroled and exchanged at Aiken's Landing, Virginia, November 10, 1862. Appointed Corporal on March 1, 1863, and promoted to Sergeant on May 19, 1863. Present or accounted for until captured at Winchester, Virginia, September 19, 1864. Confined at Point Lookout, Maryland, until released after taking the Oath of Allegiance on June 28, 1865.

JONES, RUEL, Private
Born in Duplin County and was by occupation a laborer when he enlisted in Wake County at age 18, September 12, 1861, for the war. Died August 2, 1862, of disease.

KELLY, WILLIAM L., Private
Born in Sampson County and resided as a farmer in Duplin County prior to enlisting in Wayne County at age 18, July 24, 1861, for the war. Wounded at Chancellorsville, Virginia, May 3, 1863, and reported as absent wounded until detailed in hospital at Richmond, Virginia, November 28, 1863. Transferred to hospital at Goldsboro on March 22, 1864, as a guard. Reported as present on hospital muster rolls at Goldsboro through November, 1864. Admitted to hospital at Richmond, Virginia, December 24, 1864, and returned to duty December 27, 1864. Retired to the Invalid Corps on December 31, 1864. Assigned to light duty at Richmond, Virginia, February 28, 1865. Captured at Goldsboro on April 8, 1865, and confined at Military Prison, Camp Hamilton, Virginia, April 25, 1865. Transferred to Newport News, Virginia, May 1, 1865,

and released after taking the Oath of Allegiance on June 30, 1865.

KING, JAMES, Private
Born in Wayne County where he resided as a farmer and enlisted at age 18, June 20, 1861, for the war. Present or accounted for until captured at Gettysburg, Pennsylvania, July 3, 1863. Confined at Fort Delaware, Delaware, until transferred to Point Lookout, Maryland, October 15-18, 1863. Died at Point Lookout on October 21, 1863, of "pneumonia."

KING, JOHN C., Private
Born in Sampson County and resided as a farmer in Wayne County where he enlisted at age 22, July 15, 1861, for the war. Wounded at South Mountain, Maryland, September 14-15, 1862. Present or accounted for until reported as "missing in action" at Chancellorsville, Virginia, May 3, 1863.

KING, JOHN T., Private
Born in Wayne County where he resided as a farmer and enlisted at age 20, June 20, 1861, for the war. Killed in action at Chancellorsville, Virginia, May 4, 1863.

KING, JOSEPH G., Private
Born in Alabama and resided as a mechanic in Wayne County where he enlisted at age 24, June 17, 1861, for the war. Detailed as regimental teamster May 1-October 31, 1862, through August, 1864. Present or accounted for on company muster rolls through October, 1864.

KIRBY, AUGUSTUS, Private
Captured at Hanover Court House, Virginia, May 23, 1864, and confined at Point Lookout, Maryland. Federal Provost Marshal records report him on a roll of prisoners of war at Point Lookout desirous of taking the Oath of Allegiance with the remark that he was born in Germany and that he "has no interest south. Would like to go to our navy." Age reported on roll as 20.

KNOX, ARCHIBALD, Private
Born in Bertie County and resided as a mechanic in Duplin County prior to enlisting in Wayne County at age 31, June 8, 1861, for the war. Died in hospital at Farmville, Virginia, March 24, 1863, of "pneumonia."

KNOX, GARDNER, Private
Resided in Greene County and enlisted in Wake County at age 27, June 24, 1863, for the war. Present or accounted for until captured at Spotsylvania Court House, Virginia, May 20, 1864. Confined at Point Lookout, Maryland, until transferred to Elmira, New York, July 3, 1864. Died at Elmira on February 28, 1865, of "diarrhoea."

KORNEGAY, JAMES H., Private
Born in Wayne County where he resided as a farmer and enlisted at age 31, June 24, 1861, for the war. Wounded at South Mountain, Maryland, September 14-15, 1862, and died of wounds. Date of death reported as September 30, 1862, and October 6, 1862.

KORNEGAY, LEWIS T., Private
Born in Duplin County where he resided as a farmer prior to enlisting in Wake County at age

18, September 10, 1861, for the war. Present or accounted for until wounded at Spotsylvania Court House, Virginia, May 12, 1864. Reported as absent wounded on company muster rolls through October, 1864. Reported on a receipt roll for clothing issued November 14, 1864, with the remark that he was "on way to command." Admitted to hospital at Charlottesville, Virginia, December 20, 1864, with a gunshot wound of the right leg and returned to duty March 28, 1865.

LAMBERT, CALVIN, Private
Resided in Duplin County and enlisted in Wayne County at age 29, February 4, 1862, for the war. Present or accounted for on company muster rolls until he was left in hospital at Leesburg, Virginia, August 25, 1862, sick. May-June, 1863, muster roll reports him with the remark: "Supposed to be dead."

LANE, JOHN D., Private
Resided in Randolph County prior to enlisting in Wake County on July 21, 1862, for the war. Present or accounted for until wounded October 19, 1864. Captured at Sutherland Station, Virginia, April 7, 1865, and confined at Point Lookout, Maryland, until released after taking the Oath of Allegiance on June 28, 1865.

LAWTON, JOHN M., Private
Reported on a register of prisoners of war, Department of the Cumberland, with the remark that he was captured at Stone's River, Tennessee.

LENTER, WILLIAM, Private
Resided in Cherokee County and reported on Federal Provost Marshal records as a deserter received at Jonesboro, Tennessee, September 28, 1864. Took the Oath of Allegiance at Knoxville, Tennessee, October 7, 1864.

LONG, ALEXANDER M., Private
Resided in Person County prior to enlisting in Wake County at age 23, July 15, 1862, for the war. Present or accounted for until captured at Gettysburg, Pennsylvania, July 1-5, 1863. Confined at DeCamp General Hospital, Davids Island, New York Harbor, July 17-24, 1863. Transferred on October 24, 1863, to Fort Wood, Bedloe's Island, New York Harbor, where he remained until transferred to Point Lookout, Maryland, December 17, 1863. Released at Point Lookout after taking the Oath of Allegiance and joining the U.S. service on January 26, 1864.

LONG, CHARLES C., Private
Born in Person County and resided as a laborer in Wayne County where he enlisted at age 26, July 17, 1861, for the war. Wounded at Chancellorsville, Virginia, May 3, 1863, and reported as absent wounded until detailed on April 20, 1864. Detailed as a guard in hospital at Goldsboro through July 7, 1864, when he was detailed as a cook in hospital at Goldsboro. Company muster rolls report him as absent wounded through October, 1864. Paroled at Greensboro on May 1, 1865.

LONG, JOHN H., Private
Born in Person County where he resided as a farmer prior to enlisting in Wake County at age 24, July 15, 1862, for the war. Present or ac-

counted for until captured at Gettysburg, Pennsylvania, July 1-4, 1863. Confined at DeCamp General Hospital, Davids Island, New York Harbor, July 17-24, 1863. Paroled and sent to City Point, Virginia, where he was exchanged on September 8, 1863. Company muster rolls report him as absent sick through October, 1864. Discharged at Staunton, Virginia, December 28, 1864, by reason of "curvature of the spine with phthisis pulmonalis."

LONG, JOSEPH, Private
Resided in Edgecombe County and enlisted in Wake County at age 25, July 4, 1862, for the war. Present or accounted for until he deserted on March 15, 1863. Returned from desertion, November-December, 1863. Company muster roll for November-December, 1863, carries the remark: "Court martial sentenced to be drummed out of the regiment with his head shaven and sent to Richmond to work on fortification to a ball and chain during the war." Reported as absent under sentence through October, 1864.

McCAN, ALFRED P., Private
Enlisted in Wake County on October 3, 1863, for the war. Captured at Kelly's Ford, Virginia, November 7, 1863, and confined at Point Lookout, Maryland, where he died December 27, 1863.

MANNING, CORNELIUS, Private
Born in Cork County, Ireland, and resided as a laborer in Wayne County where he enlisted at age 37, July 5, 1861, for the war. Wounded at Sharpsburg, Maryland, September 17, 1862, and killed at Chancellorsville, Virginia, May 3, 1863.

MARTIN, RIGDEN J., Private
Born in Wayne County where he resided and enlisted at age 18, April 27, 1862, for the war. Present or accounted for until killed at Chancellorsville, Virginia, May 3, 1863.

MARTIN, WILLIAM B., Private
Born in Wayne County where he resided as a farmer and enlisted at age 22, June 17, 1861, for the war. Wounded at South Mountain, Maryland, September 14-15, 1862, and died of wound October 16, 1862.

MATTHEWS, JAMES R., Private
Resided in Wayne County and enlisted in Wake County at age 20, July 15, 1862, for the war. Captured at South Mountain, Maryland, September 15, 1862, and confined at Fort Delaware, Delaware, until paroled and exchanged at Aiken's Landing, Virginia, November 10, 1862. Never returned to the company and reported as absent without leave from November, 1862, through October, 1864.

MATTHEWS, JAMES T., Private
Resided in Sampson County and enlisted in Wake County on July 15, 1862, for the war. Wounded and captured at Chancellorsville, Virginia, May 3, 1863. Confined at Washington, D.C., until sent to City Point, Virginia, on May 10, 1863. Exchanged on May 13, 1863. Never returned to the company and reported as absent without leave through October, 1864.

MAZINGO, GEORGE D., Private
Born in Duplin County where he resided as a farmer prior to enlisting in Wayne County at age 18, June 17, 1861, for the war. Wounded at Chancellorsville, Virginia, May 3, 1863, and died of wound in hospital at Richmond, Virginia, on May 14, 1863.

MAZINGO, IVY, Private
Born in Lenoir County and resided as a ditcher in Wayne County where he enlisted at age 52, June 17, 1861, for the war. Reported as present until October 10, 1862, when he was reported as absent sick. May-June, 1863, muster roll states that he was "sent to hospital at Winchester, October 20, 1862. Supposed to be dead."

MAZINGO, ROBERT J., Private
Born in Wayne County where he resided as a laborer and enlisted at age 18, June 17, 1861, for the war. Present or accounted for on company muster rolls through October, 1864, when he was reported as "absent wounded since August 10, 1864." Name reported on a register of effects of deceased soldiers turned over to the Quartermaster Department in 1865. Date, place, and cause of death not reported.

MORGAN, FRANCIS M., Private
Resided in Edgecombe County and enlisted in Wake County at age 30, July 4, 1862, for the war. Present or accounted for until captured at Burkeville, Virginia, April 6, 1865. Confined at Point Lookout, Maryland, until released after taking the Oath of Allegiance on June 6, 1865.

NASH, JOHN W., Private
Enlisted in Wake County on July 15, 1862, for the war. Captured at South Mountain, Maryland, September 15, 1862, and confined at Fort Delaware, Delaware. Transferred to Aiken's Landing, Virginia, October 2, 1862, and declared exchanged on November 10, 1862. March-April, 1863, muster roll carries him with the remark: "Absent. Sent to hospital-Winchester, October 10, 1862." May-June, 1863, muster roll carries him with the remark: "Absent. Taken prisoner Sharpsburg and sent to hospital very sick. Supposed to be dead."

OVERMAN, JOHN W., Private
Enlisted in Wayne County on April 23, 1862, for the war. Died at Richmond, Virginia, August 1, 1862.

OVERMAN, JOSEPH R., Private
Born in Wayne County where he resided as a farmer and enlisted at age 17, June 26, 1861, for the war. Wounded at Chancellorsville, Virginia, May 3, 1863. Reported as absent wounded until detailed as ambulance driver, January-February, 1864. May 1-August 31, 1864, muster roll reports him as "Absent. In hospital wounded at Staunton, Virginia." Reported as present on September-October, 1864, muster roll. Captured at Goldsboro on March 30, 1865, and confined at Hart's Island, New York Harbor, until released after taking the Oath of Allegiance on June 19, 1865.

OVERMAN, THOMAS C., Sergeant
Born in Wayne County where he resided as a blacksmith and enlisted at age 21, June 20, 1861,

for the war. Mustered in as Corporal. Wounded at Malvern Hill, Virginia, July 1, 1862. Promoted to Sergeant on March 1, 1863. Admitted to hospital at Richmond, Virginia, April 7, 1863, with "typhoid fever" and died April 16, 1863.

PARNELLE, JOSEPH F., Private
Born in Wayne County where he resided as a laborer and enlisted at age 21, July 4, 1861, for the war. Present or accounted for until he died near Goldsboro on April 29, 1862.

PARRISH, JOHN S., Private
Paroled at Greensboro on May 15, 1865.

PEEBLES, ROBERT B., Private
Resided in Pitt County prior to enlisting in Wayne County at age 42, December 4, 1861, for the war. Present or accounted for on company muster rolls through October, 1864. Captured near Farmville, Virginia, April, 9, 1865, and confined at Newport News, Virginia, until released after taking the Oath of Allegiance on June 30, 1865.

PERRY, REDDIN, Private
Enlisted in Wake County on July 15, 1862, for the war. Present or accounted for until he died in hospital at Richmond, Virginia, February 2, 1863, of "pneumonia typhoides."

PHILLIPS, WILLIS R., Private
Born in Wayne County where he resided as a laborer and enlisted at age 19, June 17, 1861, for the war. Present or accounted for until reported on May-June, 1863, muster roll with the remark: "Absent. Left at hospital, Winchester, October 20, 1862. Supposed to be dead."

PIERCE, ANDREW F., Private
Resided in Wayne County where he enlisted at age 27, April 1, 1862, for the war as a substitute. Captured at Boonsboro, Maryland, September 15, 1862, and confined at Fort Delaware, Delaware, until paroled for exchange on October 2, 1862. Declared exchanged at Aiken's Landing, Virginia, November 10, 1862. Returned to company June 1, 1863. Wounded at Gettysburg, Pennsylvania, July 2-3, 1863. Reported as absent wounded through August, 1863. Present or accounted for on company muster rolls through June 30, 1864. Hospital records indicate that he was furloughed from hospital in Richmond, Virginia, June 3, 1864, for 60 days and received an extension of the furlough to November 6, 1864. Reported as absent without leave after November 6, 1864. He returned on January 18, 1865, and was sentenced by court-martial to 30 days punishment "to do police duty in regimental camp every alternate day from sunrise to sunset, to ride a wooden horse four hours each of the remaining alternate day."

PRICE, CALEB B., 1st Sergeant
Born in Duplin County where he resided as a schoolteacher prior to enlisting in Wayne County at age 23, July 9, 1861, for the war. Mustered in as Corporal and promoted to Sergeant on April 13, 1862. Promoted to 1st Sergeant on March 1, 1863. Present or accounted for on company muster rolls through October, 1864. Captured near Peters-

burg, Virginia, April 4, 1865, and confined at Hart's Island, New York Harbor, until released after taking the Oath of Allegiance on June 19, 1865.

PRICE, ENOCH, Private
Born in Duplin County where he resided as a farmer prior to enlisting in Wayne County at age 18, June 17, 1861, for the war. Died September 23, 1861.

PRICE, FRANCIS M., Corporal
Resided in Wayne County where he enlisted on August 21, 1861, for the war. Mustered in as Private and appointed Corporal on May 1, 1863. Present or accounted for on company muster rolls until captured at Kelly's Ford, Virginia, November 7, 1863. Confined at Old Capitol Prison, Washington, D.C., until transferred to Point Lookout, Maryland, February 3, 1864. Paroled at Point Lookout and sent to James River, Virginia, for exchange on February 18, 1865. Exchanged at Boulware's and Cox's Wharf, James River, February 20-21, 1865.

PRICE, JOEL, Sergeant
Born in Duplin County where he resided as a farmer prior to enlisting in Wayne County at age 24, June 17, 1861, for the war. Mustered in as Private. Wounded at Malvern Hill, Virginia, July 1, 1862, and furloughed from hospital at Richmond, Virginia, July 8, 1862, for 60 days. Returned to duty on September 17, 1862. Appointed Corporal on October 1, 1862, and promoted to Sergeant on March 13, 1863. Present or accounted for until killed at Strasburg, Virginia, September 23, 1864.

PRICE, JOSHUA, Private
Born in Duplin County where he resided and enlisted at age 20, February 22, 1862, for the war. Captured at Sharpsburg, Maryland, September 17, 1862, and confined at Fort Delaware, Delaware, until paroled for exchange on October 2, 1862. Exchanged at Aiken's Landing, Virginia, November 10, 1862. Admitted to hospital at Richmond, Virginia, where he died November 18-20, 1862.

PRICE, ROBERT D., Private
Born in Wayne County where he resided as a farmer and enlisted at age 18, June 17, 1861, for the war. Killed at Chancellorsville, Virginia, May 3, 1863.

PRICE, STEPHEN J., Sergeant
Born in Duplin County and resided as a schoolteacher in Wayne County where he enlisted at age 20, June 17, 1861, for the war. Mustered in as Private and appointed Corporal on April 13, 1862. Promoted to Sergeant on May 7, 1862. Died in hospital in Richmond, Virginia, November 10-14, 1862.

PROCTOR, AARON, Private
Born in Edgecombe County and resided as a laborer in Wayne County where he enlisted at age 30, June 17, 1861, for the war. Discharged at Staunton, Virginia, April 4, 1863, by reason of "phthisis pulmonalis."

PROCTOR, JOHN, Private
Federal Provost Marshal records indicate he was

confined at Fort McHenry, Maryland, September 26, 1862, and transferred to Fort Monroe, Virginia, for exchange on October 2, 1862. Exchanged at Aiken's Landing, Virginia, November 9, 1862.

RAINS, J. H., Private
Federal Provost Marshal records report him as being sent from Gettysburg, Pennsylvania, to the Provost Marshal, New York City, July 21, 1863.

REAVES, HENRY, Private
Born in Wayne County where he resided as a farmer and enlisted at age 28, June 17, 1861, for the war. Died at Goldsboro on April 18, 1862.

REAVES, WILLIAM H., Private
Born in Lenoir County and resided as a laborer in Wayne County where he enlisted at age 18, June 29, 1861, for the war. Present or accounted for until wounded at Gettysburg, Pennsylvania, July 2-3, 1863. Furloughed from hospital at Richmond, Virginia, July 28, 1863, and returned from furlough October 30, 1863. Present or accounted for until captured at White's Tavern, Virginia, August 10, 1864. Confined at Old Capitol Prison, Washington, D.C., until transferred to Elmira, New York, August 28, 1864. Died at Elmira on January 29, 1865, of "variola."

ROBERTSON, I. N., Private
Federal Provost Marshal records report that he was captured at Williamsburg, Virginia, May 5, 1862, and exchanged at Aiken's Landing, Virginia, August 5, 1862.

RODGERS, JAMES R., Private
Resided in Duplin County and enlisted in Wayne County at age 24, February 7, 1862, for the war. Wounded and captured at Chancellorsville, Virginia, May 3-4, 1863. Paroled and exchanged at Aiken's Landing, Virginia, May 13, 1863. Present or accounted for until captured at Kelly's Ford, Virginia, November 7, 1863. Confined at Old Capitol Prison, Washington, D.C., and transferred to Point Lookout, Maryland, February 3, 1864. Paroled at Point Lookout and sent to James River, Virginia, for exchange on October 11, 1864. Received in exchange on October 15, 1864. Federal Provost Marshal records report him as "deserter from the enemy" received March 19, 1865, from Bermuda Hundred, Virginia. Sent to Washington, where he took the Oath of Allegiance on March 24, 1865, and was furnished transportation to Wilmington.

ROGERS, ALEXANDER, Private
Born in Duplin County where he resided as a farmer and enlisted at age 20, February 15, 1862, for the war. Killed at Sharpsburg, Maryland, September 17, 1862.

SECRIST, CONRAD, Private
Born in Davidson County and resided as a farmer prior to enlisting at age 17 for the war. Date and place of enlistment not reported on muster roll. Died in hospital at Lynchburg, Virginia, September 28, 1862, of "diarrhoea chronic."

SENTER, RANDALL J., Private
Born in Harnett County and resided as a laborer in Duplin County prior to enlisting in Wayne

County at age 27, June 24, 1861, for the war. Present or accounted for until transferred to the C.S. Navy on April 10, 1864.

SULLIVAN, MERRILL, Private
Resided in Duplin County where he enlisted at age 21, March 4, 1862, for the war. Present or accounted for until wounded and captured at Gettysburg, Pennsylvania, July 1-3, 1863. Confined at DeCamp General Hospital, Davids Island, New York Harbor, until paroled on August 24, 1863, and sent to City Point, Virginia, for exchange. Received at City Point on August 28, 1863. Present or accounted for until captured at Sheperdstown, Virginia, August 27, 1864. Confined at Camp Chase, Ohio, until released after taking the Oath of Allegiance on May 15, 1865.

SUMMERLIN, CHARLES H., Private
Resided in Duplin County prior to enlisting in Wayne County at age 29, May 1, 1862, for the war. Wounded and captured at Gettysburg, Pennsylvania, July 2-3, 1863. Died at Fort Delaware, Delaware, September 8, 1863, of "typhoid fever."

SUMMERLIN, DENNIS J., Private
Born in Duplin County where he resided as a laborer prior to enlisting in Wayne County at age 35, July 13, 1861, for the war. Wounded and captured at Gettysburg, Pennsylvania, July 1-4, 1863. Confined at DeCamp General Hospital, Davids Island, New York Harbor, until paroled and exchanged at City Point, Virginia, September 8, 1863. Present or accounted for on company muster rolls until captured at Winchester, Virginia, September 19, 1864. Confined at Point Lookout, Maryland, until paroled and sent to Venus Point, Savannah River, Georgia, for exchange on November 1, 1864. Received in exchange on November 15, 1864. Captured near Petersburg, Virginia, April 4, 1865, and confined at Hart's Island, New York Harbor, until released after taking the Oath of Allegiance on June 19, 1865.

SUMMERLIN, JOHN F., Private
Born in Duplin County where he resided as a laborer prior to enlisting in Wayne County at age 22, July 13, 1861, for the war. Captured near Fredericksburg, Virginia, May 3, 1863, and paroled and sent to City Point, Virginia, for exchange on May 10, 1863. Declared exchanged on May 13, 1863. Present or accounted for on company muster rolls through October, 1864, when he was reported as "absent, taken prisoner September 19, 1864."

SUMMERLIN, PINKNEY H., Private
Resided in Duplin County where he enlisted at age 25, February 15, 1862, for the war. Died at Mount Olive, N.C., December 7, 1862, of disease.

SWINSON, NATHANIEL M., Private
Resided in Duplin County and enlisted in Wayne County at age 23, February 15, 1862, for the war. Captured at Boonsboro, Maryland, September 15, 1862, and confined at Fort Delaware, Delaware, until sent to Aiken's Landing, Virginia, October 2, 1862, for exchange. Declared exchanged on November 10, 1862. Present or accounted for on company

muster rolls through October, 1864. Captured near Petersburg, Virginia, April 4, 1865, and confined at Hart's Island, New York Harbor, until released after taking the Oath of Allegiance on June 19, 1865.

TAYLOR, OSHEABUD B., Private
Born in Duplin County where he resided as a laborer prior to enlisting in Wayne County at age 21, June 17, 1861, for the war. Wounded at Sharpsburg, Maryland, September 17, 1862. Returned to company in November, 1862. Wounded at Gettysburg, Pennsylvania, July 2-3, 1863, and furloughed from hospital at Richmond, Virginia, for 30 days on October 20, 1863. Furlough extended on March 10, 1864. Reported as absent in hospital at Richmond on company muster roll through October, 1864.

TEW, B. T., Private
Enlisted in Wake County on July 15, 1862, for the war. Furloughed from hospital at Liberty, Virginia, January 16, 1863, for 60 days and "died at home in May, 1863."

TEW, OSBORN, Private
Enlisted in Wake County on July 15, 1862, for the war. Wounded and captured at Sharpsburg, Maryland, September 17, 1862. Paroled on September 30, 1862. Died of wounds in October, 1862.

TEW, W. R., Private
Born in Sampson County and enlisted in Wake County on July 15, 1862, for the war. Present or accounted for until he died in hospital at Richmond, Virginia, February 2, 1863, of "febris typhoides."

TURNAGE, JESSE J., Private
Born in Duplin County and resided as a shoemaker in Wayne County where he enlisted at age 40, June 27, 1861, for the war. Present or accounted for until discharged on April 29, 1862, by reason of his having provided a substitute.

TURNAGE, JOHN W., Private
Born in Duplin County and resided as a farmer in Wayne County where he enlisted at age 31, June 17, 1861, for the war. Present or accounted for until furloughed for 25 days on October 25, 1862. Failed to return to company at expiration of furlough and reported as absent without leave until "arrested and brought back from desertion September 10, 1863." Present or accounted for on company muster rolls from that date through October, 1864.

UNDERHILL, JOHN J., Private
Born in Wayne County where he resided as a farmer and enlisted at age 18, June 17, 1861, for the war. Wounded in the leg at Chancellorsville, Virginia, May 3, 1863, and reported as absent wounded through October, 1864.

VANN, WILLIAM K., Private
Enlisted in Wayne County on December 4, 1861, for the war. Reported on the November-December, 1861, muster roll with the remark that he was "absent last muster."

WARD, ALFRED, Private
Resided in Randolph County and enlisted in

Wake County on July 21, 1862, for the war. Remained at Camp Holmes, Raleigh, until assigned to company, May 1-August 31, 1864. Present or accounted for until captured at Strasburg, Virginia, October 19, 1864. Confined at Point Lookout, Maryland, until released after taking the Oath of Allegiance on June 21, 1865.

WHITEHURST, R., Private
Enlisted in Wake County on June 7, 1864, for the war. Present or accounted for until captured at Winchester, Virginia, September 19, 1864. Confined at Point Lookout, Maryland, where he died on April 11, 1865, of "chronic diarrhoea."

WIGGS, PATRICK H., Private
Resided in Franklin County and enlisted in Wake County at age 18, July 16, 1862, for the war. Present or accounted for until wounded in the right leg at Spotsylvania Court House, Virginia, May 12, 1864. Died in hospital at Kittrell's, N.C., January 17, 1865, of "abscessus chronic."

WILLIAMS, NOAH, Private
Federal Provost Marshal records report him on a register of enlisted men, rebel deserters, and refugees detained at Camp Distribution on September 15, 1864. Remarks on register indicate that he was received from Alexandria, Virginia, and forwarded to New Bern on September 19, 1864.

WILLIAMS, W. A., Private
Captured in hospital at Richmond, Virginia, April 3, 1865.

WILSON, JOSEPH E., Private
Born in Duplin County and resided as a farmer in Wayne County where he enlisted at age 18, June 17, 1861, for the war. Present or accounted for on company muster rolls until admitted to hospital at Farmville, Virginia, on May 6, 1864. Furloughed from hospital for 40 days on June 21, 1864. Hospital records report disease as "dysentery of three weeks standing," "debility," and "morbi varii." Admitted to hospital at Goldsboro, September 22, 1864, and returned to duty October 7, 1864. Hospital records indicate that he was ordered to report at or near Staunton, Virginia. Paroled at Staunton on April 30, 1865.

WINDERS, CHARLES A., Private
Born in Duplin County where he resided as a farmer prior to enlisting in Wayne County at age 20, July 2, 1861, for the war. Present or accounted for until he died on July 25, 1862.

WINDERS, EDWARD, Private
Born in Duplin County where he resided as a farmer prior to enlisting in Wayne County at age 19, June 17, 1861, for the war. Captured at Fredericksburg, Virginia, May 3, 1863, and paroled for exchange May 4, 1863. Sent to City Point, Virginia, where he was declared exchanged on May 13, 1863. Present or accounted for until wounded at Spotsylvania Court House, Virginia, May 12, 1864. Admitted to hospital at Richmond, Virginia, May 15, 1864, and died of wounds on May 29, 1864.

WINDERS, HENRY J., Private
Born in Duplin County where he resided as a

farmer prior to enlisting in Wayne County at age 24, July 2, 1861, for the war. Wounded in head at Cold Harbor, Virginia, June 27, 1862, and never returned to the company. May-June, 1863, muster roll reports him as "absent. Supposed to be dead. Missing at Cold Harbor and not heard from since."

WINDERS, SAMUEL R., 1st Sergeant

Born in Duplin County where he resided as a farmer prior to enlisting in Wayne County at age 21, June 17, 1861, for the war. Mustered in as Sergeant and promoted to 1st Sergeant on November 4, 1862. Present or accounted for until he died on January 30, 1863.

YARBOROUGH, A., Private

Admitted to hospital at Greensboro in March, 1865.

COMPANY D

This company was organized in Wayne County and enlisted at Goldsboro on May 29, 1861. It tendered its service to the state and was ordered to Camp Advance, near Garysburg, Northampton County, where it was assigned to this regiment as Company D. After joining the regiment the company functioned as a part of the regiment, and its history for the war period is recorded as a part of the regimental history.

The information contained in the following roster of the company was compiled principally from company muster rolls for July 16, 1861, through December, 1861; March, 1862, through March, 1864; and May through October, 1864. No company muster rolls were found for the period prior to July 16, 1861; for January-February, 1862; for April, 1864; or for the period after October, 1864. In addition to the company muster rolls, Roll of Honor records, receipt rolls, and hospital records, supplemented by state pension applications, United Daughters of the Confederacy records, and postwar rosters and histories, all provided useful information.

OFFICERS

CAPTAINS

STALLINGS, WALTER S.

Resided in Wilson County and appointed Captain at age 27 to rank from July 16, 1861. Present or accounted for until transferred to the Field and Staff of this regiment upon appointment as Major on October 4, 1862, to rank from September 17, 1862.

APPLEWHITE, ISAAC C.

Resided in Wilson County and appointed 1st Lieutenant at age 27 to rank from May 16, 1861. Wounded at Sharpsburg, Maryland, September 17, 1862. Promoted to Captain on October 4, 1862, to rank from September 17, 1862. Submitted his resignation on July 15, 1863, by reason of wounds received at Sharpsburg. Resignation officially accepted on July 28, 1863.

MANLY, MATTHIAS E.

Resided in Craven County and appointed 3rd

Lieutenant at age 16 to rank from May 16, 1861. Promoted to 1st Lieutenant on October 4, 1862, to rank from September 17, 1862. Wounded in the arm and captured at Chancellorsville, Virginia, May 3, 1863. Confined at Old Capitol Prison, Washington, D.C., May 6, 1863. Promoted to Captain while a prisoner of war in confinement at Old Capitol Prison on July 28, 1863. Transferred from Old Capitol Prison to Fort McHenry, Maryland, September 24, 1863. Transferred on September 29, 1863, from Fort McHenry to Johnson's Island, Ohio, where he remained until forwarded to City Point, Virginia, February 24, 1865, for exchange. Date exchanged not reported.

LIEUTENANTS

APPLEWHITE, WILLIAM HENRY, 2nd Lieutenant

Resided in Wilson County and enlisted in Wayne County at age 20, May 29, 1861, for the war. Mustered in as Sergeant and promoted to 1st Sergeant on December 2, 1862. Appointed 2nd Lieutenant to rank from March 13, 1863. Wounded at Chancellorsville, Virginia, May 3, 1863. Returned to con.pany on August 10, 1863. Present or accounted for until captured at Strasburg, Virginia, October 19, 1864. Confined at Fort Delaware, Delaware, until released after taking the Oath of Allegiance on June 17, 1865.

COBB, WILLIAM HENRY HARRISON, 2nd Lieutenant

Transferred from the Field and Staff of this regiment upon appointment as 2nd Lieutenant to rank from October 14, 1861. Resigned March 6, 1863, upon appointment as Assistant Surgeon and was assigned to the Field and Staff of this regiment.

PIERCE, JOSEPH C., 2nd Lieutenant

Appointed 2nd Lieutenant at age 20 to rank from May 16, 1861. Present or accounted for until transferred to Company B of this regiment upon appointment as 1st Lieutenant to rank from October 22, 1861.

YELVERTON, WYATT E., 1st Lieutenant

Resided in Wilson County and enlisted in Northampton County at age 19, June 20, 1861, for the war. Mustered in as 1st Sergeant. Appointed 2nd Lieutenant to rank from December 2, 1862. Promoted to 1st Lieutenant to rank from July 28, 1863. Wounded at Spotsylvania Court House, Virginia, May 12, 1864, and wounded a second time at Cedar Creek, Virginia, October 19, 1864. Present or accounted for until captured at Sayler's Creek, Virginia, April 6, 1865. Confined at Old Capitol Prison, Washington, D.C., until transferred to Johnson's Island, Ohio, April 21, 1865. Released at Johnson's Island after taking the Oath of Allegiance on June 20, 1865.

NONCOMMISSIONED OFFICERS AND PRIVATES

ALLEN, JAMES G., Private

Resided in Johnston County and enlisted in Wake County at age 36, September 8, 1862, for the war as a substitute. Absent sick on furlough from April 28, 1863, to September 17, 1863, and reported as absent without leave from that date until he appears as present on May 1-August 31, 1864, muster roll. Reported as "absent wounded at Winchester, in hospital" on company muster roll for September-October, 1864.

ALLEN, WILLIAM A., Private
Resided in Edgecombe County and enlisted in Wayne County at age 20, May 29, 1861, for the war. Died in hospital at Fredericksburg, Virginia, on September 8, 1861.

AMERSON, JOHN G., Private
Resided in Wilson County and enlisted in Wayne County at age 19, April 18, 1862, for the war. Wounded at Chancellorsville, Virginia, May 3, 1863. Absent on furlough through December, 1863. Detailed for light duty on March 6, 1864, and assigned to General Hospital No. 3 at Goldsboro as a nurse and guard. Remained on detail until retired to the Invalid Corps on December 22, 1864. Paroled at High Point, May 1, 1865.

AMERSON, WARREN, Private
Born in Wilson County where he resided prior to enlisting in Wayne County at age 22, May 29, 1861, for the war. Present or accounted for until killed at Chancellorsville, Virginia, May 3, 1863.

BAKER, EVANS, Private
Born in Wilson County where he resided as a farmer prior to enlisting in Wayne County at age 39, April 12, 1862, for the war. Present or accounted for until admitted to hospital at Richmond, Virginia, December 31, 1862, with "variola." Died in hospital on January 11, 1863.

BAKER, JAMES, Private
Resided in Wilson County and enlisted in Wayne County at age 19, May 29, 1861, for the war. Present or accounted for until he left the company at Leesburg, Virginia, on September 7, 1862, sick. Discharged from hospital at Liberty, Virginia, March 4, 1863, and failed to return to the company. May 1-August 31, 1864, muster roll states that he was "absent in hospital sick last heard from."

BAREFOOT, STEPHEN, Private
Enlisted in Wilson County on April 7, 1864, for the war. Deserted on June 22, 1864.

BARNES, JACOB, Private
Resided in Wilson County and enlisted in Wayne County at age 26, May 29, 1861, for the war. Wounded at Chancellorsville, Virginia, May 3, 1863. Attached to hospital at Wilson, August 14, 1863, as a nurse. Company muster rolls report him as absent wounded in hospital at Wilson through October, 1864. Paroled at Greensboro on April 29, 1865.

BARNES, JESSE, Corporal
Resided in Wilson County and enlisted in Wayne County at age 19, May 29, 1861, for the war. Mustered in as Corporal. Captured near Sharpsburg, Maryland, and paroled on September 20, 1862. Captured a second time near Fredericksburg, Virginia, May 3, 1863, and paroled and exchanged

at City Point, Virginia, May 10, 1863. Wounded at Gettysburg, Pennsylvania, July 1-3, 1863. Present or accounted for until captured at Kelly's Ford, Virginia, November 7, 1863. Confined at Old Capitol Prison, Washington, D.C. Died in hospital at Washington on February 11, 1864, of "typhoid fever."

BARNES, MARTIN V., Private
Resided in Wilson County where he enlisted at age 19, February 20, 1862, for the war. Present or accounted for until captured at Kelly's Ford, Virginia, November 7, 1863. Confined at Point Lookout, Maryland, until paroled and transferred for exchange to Aiken's Landing, Virginia, February 24, 1865. Date exchanged not reported. Paroled at Goldsboro on May 15, 1865.

BARNES, STEPHEN J., Private
Resided in Wilson County where he enlisted at age 34, June 18, 1863, for the war. Present or accounted for until captured at Kelly's Ford, Virginia, November 7, 1863. Confined at Point Lookout, Maryland, where he died January 31, 1864, of "chronic diarrhoea."

BARNES, WASHINGTON LAWRENCE, Sergeant
Resided in Wilson County where he enlisted at age 23, August 28, 1861, for the war. Mustered in as Private and appointed Sergeant on December 1, 1862. Present or accounted for until captured at Kelly's Ford, Virginia, November 7, 1863. Confined at Old Capitol Prison, Washington, D.C., until transferred to Point Lookout, Maryland, February 3, 1864. Died at Point Lookout on May 13, 1864, of "typhoid fever."

BARRATT, D., Private
Died in hospital at Richmond, Virginia, on May 5, 1864, of "hepititis."

BARROW, JAMES G., Private
Born in Wayne County where he resided as an artist and enlisted at age 22, June 18, 1861, for the war. Present or accounted for until killed at Chancellorsville, Virginia, May 3, 1863.

BASS, JONATHAN B., Private
Resided in Wayne County where he enlisted at age 22, May 31, 1861, for the war. Present or accounted for until captured at Kelly's Ford, Virginia, November 7, 1863. Confined to Point Lookout, Maryland, until released after taking the Oath of Allegiance and joining the U.S. service on June 25, 1864. Assigned to Company D, 1st Regiment U.S. Volunteer Infantry.

BASS, PATRICK, Private
Resided in Wayne County where he enlisted at age 22, May 29, 1861, for the war. Present or accounted for on company muster rolls through October, 1864.

BOSWELL, ALFRED F., Private
Resided in Wilson County and enlisted in Wayne County at age 22, May 29, 1861, for the war. Present or accounted for until captured at Spotsylvania Court House, Virginia, May 20, 1864. Confined at Point Lookout, Maryland, until transferred to Elmira, New York, July 3, 1864. Released at Elmira after taking the Oath of Allegiance on June 30, 1865.

BOYCE, JOHN, Private
Resided in Wilson County and enlisted in Virginia at age 28, February 23, 1862, for the war. Present or accounted for until he died in hospital at Wilson, April 21, 1864, of "varioloid."

BOYKIN, COUNCIL, Private
Resided in Wilson County where he enlisted on April 7, 1864, for the war. Wounded at Cedar Creek, Virginia, October 19, 1864. Paroled at Goldsboro on May 8, 1865. "Came in for parole."

BURRIS, WILLIAM, Private
Resided in Wilson County where he enlisted at age 27, June 3, 1861, for the war. Reported as absent sick on company muster rolls through May, 1862. Roll of Honor states that he was "discharged July, 1861."

CAHO, JOSEPH M., Private
Resided in Wayne County where he enlisted at age 35, May 28, 1861, for the war. Mustered in as Sergeant and detailed as acting hospital steward in February, 1862. Reported as acting hospital steward on company muster rolls through October, 1864; however, he was reduced to ranks July-August, 1863. Elected to the General Assembly in August, 1864.

CARR, JOHN B., Private
Captured at Burkeville, Virginia, April 6, 1865, and confined at Point Lookout, Maryland, until released after taking the Oath of Allegiance on June 26, 1865.

COLEY, BENJAMIN, Private
Resided in Wayne County where he enlisted at age 24, May 29, 1861, for the war. Reported as absent on sick furlough on company muster rolls through December, 1861. Roll of Honor states that he "died April, 1861, at home."

CORBETT, RICHARD, Private
Born in Johnston County and resided as a farmer in Wayne County where he enlisted at age 18, May 31, 1861, for the war. Died in hospital at Fredericksburg, Virginia, August 15, 1861.

DARDIN, PATRICK, Private
Resided in Wayne County where he enlisted at age 22, May 29, 1861, for the war. Present or accounted for until killed in action at Boonsboro, Maryland, September 14, 1862.

DARDIN, WILLIAM J., Private
Resided in Wayne County where he enlisted at age 25, May 29, 1861, for the war. Deserted January 10, 1863, and returned to company in December, 1863. Sentenced by court-martial in January, 1864, and reported on company muster rolls for the balance of 1864 as "undergoing sentence of Court Martial at Salisbury, North Carolina." Paroled at Greensboro on May 4, 1865.

DAVIS, JOHN E., Corporal
Resided in Wayne County and enlisted at Richmond, Virginia, at age 22, July 17, 1862, for the war. Mustered in as Private and promoted to Corporal on June 1, 1863. Present or accounted for on company muster rolls through October, 1864. Captured at Burkeville, Virginia, April 6, 1865, and confined at Point Lookout, Maryland,

until released after taking the Oath of Allegiance on June 12, 1865.

DAVIS, T. H., Private
Paroled at Salisbury on May 2, 1865. Residence given on parole as Cleveland County.

DAVIS, W. P., Private
Born in Wayne County where he enlisted at age 26, May 29, 1861, for the war. Died at Camp Advance, Northampton County, July 1, 1861.

DUNBAR, A., Private
Reported on regimental return for May, 1862, with the remark that he was discharged by sentence of general court-martial on May 6, 1862.

EASON, ABNER, Private
Resided in Wilson County and enlisted in Wayne County at age 24, May 29, 1861, for the war. Present or accounted for until captured at Spotsylvania Court House, Virginia, May 12, 1864. Confined at Point Lookout, Maryland, until transferred to Elmira, New York, August 10-14, 1864. Released at Elmira after taking the Oath of Allegiance on June 14, 1865.

EASON, N. T., Private
Resided in Wilson County where he enlisted at age 29, May 1, 1862, for the war. Killed at Sharpsburg, Maryland, September 17, 1862.

EASON, WILLIAM M., Private
Resided in Wilson County where he enlisted at age 23, May 1, 1862, for the war. Wounded and captured at Sharpsburg, Maryland, September 17, 1862. Paroled on September 30, 1862. July-August, 1863, muster roll carries the remark that he was "wounded in battle September 17, 1862. Not heard from since. Supposed to be dead." Date of death not reported; however, he was buried in Elmwood Cemetery, Shepherdstown, West Virginia.

EATMAN, BURTIS, Private
Resided in Wayne County where he enlisted at age 30, May 29, 1861, for the war. Died in hospital at Camp Advance, Northampton County, July 15, 1861.

EDMUNDSON, JAMES T., Musician
Resided in Wayne County where he enlisted at age 18, June 7, 1861, for the war. Mustered in as Musician. Present or accounted for until paroled at Appomattox Court House, Virginia, April 9, 1865.

EDWARDS, LEVI R., Sergeant
Resided in Wilson County and enlisted in Wayne County at age 20, May 29, 1861, for the war. Mustered in as Sergeant. Wounded at Gaines' Mill, Virginia, June 27, 1862. Present or accounted for until detailed as a nurse in hospital at Richmond, Virginia, March 8, 1863. Returned to company in October, 1863, and reported as present through October, 1864. Admitted to hospital at Richmond, December 24, 1864, with "catarrhus" and returned to duty on February 6, 1865. Captured at Farmville, Virginia, April 6, 1865, and confined at Point Lookout, Maryland, until released after taking the Oath of Allegiance on June 12, 1865.

ELLIS, CALVIN, Private

Resided in Wilson County and enlisted in Wayne County at age 18, May 29, 1861, for the war. Captured at Williamsport, Maryland, September 16, 1862, and confined at Fort Delaware, Delaware, until transferred to Aiken's Landing, Virginia, October 2, 1862, for exchange. Declared exchanged on November 10, 1862. Present or accounted for until captured at Kelly's Ford, Virginia, November 7, 1863. Confined at Point Lookout, Maryland, until transferred to Aiken's Landing, Virginia, for exchange on February 24, 1865. Date exchanged not reported. Paroled at Goldsboro on May 15, 1865. "Came in for parole."

ELLIS, JAMES, Private

Resided in Wilson County and enlisted in Wayne County at age 22, July 2, 1861, for the war. Present or accounted for until he died in hospital at Staunton, Virginia, October 17, 1862, of "febris typhoides."

FAIRCLOTH, ARCHER, Private

Enlisted in Sampson County on May 19, 1864, for the war. Captured at Beltsville, Maryland, July 12-13, 1864, and confined at Elmira, New York. Paroled at Elmira on October 11, 1864, and sent to Point Lookout, Maryland, for exchange. Exchanged from Point Lookout on October 29, 1864.

FAUCETT, S. W., Private

Paroled at Greensboro on May 19, 1865.

FELTON, SHADRACK, Sergeant

Resided in Wilson County and enlisted in Wayne County at age 22, May 29, 1861, for the war. Mustered in as Private. Wounded at Malvern Hill, Virginia, July 1, 1862, and reported absent wounded through October, 1862. Appointed Corporal on December 1, 1862. Wounded at Chancellorsville, Virginia, May 3, 1863. Promoted to Sergeant on June 1, 1863. Present or accounted for on company muster rolls until captured at Strasburg, Virginia, October 19, 1864. Confined at Point Lookout, Maryland, October 25, 1864. Date released not given.

FORT, JOHN WILLIAM, Private

Resided in Wayne County and enlisted in Wilson County at age 18, June 2, 1862, for the war. Wounded at Chancellorsville, Virginia, May 3, 1863. Wounded a second time on June 2, 1864. Present or accounted for until paroled at Appomattox Court House, Virginia, April 9, 1865.

FOWLER, HENRY, Private

Resided in Wilson or Wayne counties and enlisted in Wayne County at age 39, May 31, 1861, for the war. Detailed as ambulance driver, May 1-October 31, 1862, and remained on detail until assigned to hospital duty as a nurse on March 6, 1864. Detailed in hospital at Richmond, Virginia, until returned to the company in August, 1864. Detailed as brigade teamster October 21, 1864. Captured at Chesterfield Court House, Virginia, April 4, 1865, and confined at Hart's Island, New York Harbor, until released after taking the Oath of Allegiance on June 19, 1865.

FULLER, HENRY M., Private

Resided in Nash County and enlisted in Wayne County at age 24, August 19, 1861, for the war. Present or accounted for on company muster rolls through October, 1864, being absent without leave from August 27, 1863, to October 24, 1863.

GARDNER, BALDWIN P., Private

Resided in Wilson County and enlisted in Wayne County at age 19, May 30, 1861, for the war. Present or accounted for until he transferred to the C.S. Navy on February 1, 1862.

GARRIS, WILEY, Private

Resided in Pitt County where he enlisted at age 20, September 8, 1862, for the war. Killed at Fredericksburg, Virginia, December 13, 1862.

GAY, THEOPHILUS, Private

Resided in Greene County and enlisted in Wayne County at age 20, May 29, 1861, for the war. Present or accounted for until captured at Mechanicsville, Virginia, May 30, 1864. Confined at Point Lookout, Maryland, until released after taking the Oath of Allegiance and joining the U.S. service on June 25, 1864. Assigned to Company F, 1st Regiment U.S. Volunteer Infantry.

GAY, WILEY R., Private

Resided in Greene County and enlisted in Wayne County at age 21, July 1, 1861, for the war. Present or accounted for until killed in action either at Boonsboro, Maryland, on September 14, 1862, or at Sharpsburg, Maryland, on September 17, 1862.

GODIN, MOSES, Private

Resided in Wayne County where he enlisted at age 23, May 29, 1861, for the war. Died in hospital at Camp Advance, Northampton County, June 12, 1861.

GRIFFIN, DAVID, Private

Resided in Wilson County where he enlisted at age 27, February 1, 1862, for the war. Present or accounted for until detailed in the Medical Department, Richmond, Virginia, February 28, 1863. Hospital records indicate that he served in hospitals at Richmond through November, 1863, and at Danville, Virginia, from November, 1863, through October, 1864. Captured at Richmond on April 3, 1865, and confined at Newport News, Virginia, until released after taking the Oath of Allegiance on June 30, 1865.

GRIFFIN, LUNDY M., Private

Resided in Wilson County where he enlisted on April 7, 1864, for the war. Wounded July 18, 1864, and admitted to hospital at Charlottesville, Virginia, July 25, 1864. Returned to duty on August 29, 1864. Captured at Burkeville, Virginia, April 6, 1865, and confined at Point Lookout, Maryland, until released after taking the Oath of Allegiance on June 27, 1865.

GURGANUS, WILLIAM B., Private

Resided in Greene County and enlisted in Wayne County at age 24, May 31, 1861, for the war. Wounded at Chancellorsville, Virginia, May 3, 1863. Present or accounted for on company muster rolls through October, 1864.

HALE, W. O., Private
Appears on a list of wounded prisoners sent to the Provost Marshal, New York, July 21, 1863, from Gettysburg, Pennsylvania.

HARR, JOHN, Private
Captured at Strasburg, Virginia, October 19, 1864, and confined at Point Lookout, Maryland, October 25, 1864.

HART, WILLIAM, Private
Born in Germany. Federal Provost Marshal records state that he was captured either at Westminister, Maryland, on June 20, 1863; at Harrisburg, Pennsylvania, on June 29, 1863; or at Gettysburg, Pennsylvania, on July 3, 1863. Confined at Fort Delaware, Delaware, where he took the Oath of Allegiance and joined the U.S. service. Assigned to the 1st Regiment Connecticut Cavalry.

HAYNES, BETHEL, Private
Enlisted in Wilson County on June 18, 1863, for the war. Died in hospital at Richmond, Virginia, August 13, 1864, of disease.

HAYS, GEORGE E., Private
Federal Provost Marshal records report him as a "rebel deserter" with remarks that he was captured at Westminister, Maryland, on July 1, 1863. Confined at Fort Delaware, Delaware, where he "joined the 1st Regiment Connecticut Cavalry."

HEATH, S., Private
Name reported on return for November, 1862, with the remark that he was conscripted on November 2, 1862, at Strasburg, Virginia.

HILL, WILLIAM, Private
Captured at Gettysburg, Pennsylvania, July 3, 1863, and confined at Fort Delaware, Delaware. Transferred to Point Lookout, Maryland, October 18, 1863, and paroled for exchange on February 18, 1865.

HINSON, RANDOLPH M., Private
Enlisted in Randolph County on July 17, 1862, for the war. First reported on company muster roll for May 1-August 31, 1864, when he appears with the remark: "Deserted July 28, 1864."

HOOKS, JAMES M., Private
Resided in Wayne County and enlisted in Virginia at age 18, March 8, 1862, for the war. Present or accounted for until killed at Spotsylvania Court House, Virginia, May 12, 1864.

HOWARD, BENJAMIN A., Sergeant
Resided in Wilson County and enlisted in Wayne County at age 18, May 29, 1861, for the war. Mustered in as Private. Wounded at Sharpsburg, Maryland, September 17, 1862. Appointed Corporal on August 22, 1862. Promoted to Sergeant on June 1, 1864. Present or accounted for until paroled at Appomattox Court House, Virginia, April 9, 1865.

ISAACS, HARVEY, Private
Resided in Watauga County where he enlisted on April 29, 1864, for the war. Present or accounted for until captured at Burkeville, Virginia, April 6, 1865. Confined at Point Lookout, Maryland, until released after taking the Oath of Allegiance on June 28, 1865.

JOHNSON, FRANCIS M., Private
Resided in Wayne County where he enlisted at age 27, June 12, 1861, for the war. "Arm broken accidentally December, 1861." Detailed for hospital duty on February 28, 1863, and assigned to the Provost Guard at Danville, Virginia. Reported as present on a muster roll of the Provost Guard at Danville dated September 30, 1864.

JONES, CALVIN W., Private
Resided in Wilson County and enlisted in Virginia on January 28, 1864, for the war. Present or accounted for until captured at Petersburg, Virginia, April 3, 1865. Confined at Hart's Island, New York Harbor, until released after taking the Oath of Allegiance on June 21, 1865.

JONES, HENRY J., Corporal
Resided in Wilson County and enlisted in Northampton County at age 21, July 18, 1861, for the war. Mustered in as Private and appointed Corporal on April 10, 1863. Present or accounted for until he was mortally wounded on July 18, 1864. Died July 22, 1864.

JONES, JESSE M., Private
Resided in Wayne County where he enlisted at age 19, May 29, 1861, for the war. Admitted to hospital at Danville, Virginia, May 18, 1864, with a gunshot wound of the shoulder. Date wounded not reported. Present or accounted for until captured at Petersburg, Virginia, April 3, 1865. Confined at Hart's Island, New York Harbor, until released after taking the Oath of Allegiance on June 19, 1865.

JONES, JOSIAH M., Private
Resided in Wayne County where he enlisted at age 18, May 29, 1861, for the war. Died at Camp Potomac, King George County, Virginia, December 25, 1861.

KEITH, SIMEON, Private
Enlisted in Wake County on December 4, 1862, for the war. Deserted March 28, 1863, and returned from desertion on October 27, 1863. Wounded at Spotsylvania Court House, Virginia, May 12, 1864. Reported as absent wounded on company muster rolls through October, 1864.

KIMMERLY, SAMP, Private
Paroled at Greensboro on May 16, 1865.

KITTRELL, KENDRICK, Private
Resided in Pitt County and enlisted in Wayne County at age 22, May 29, 1861, for the war. Wounded at Chancellorsville, Virginia, May 3, 1863, and discharged by reason of wound on December 5, 1863.

LAIN, C. J., Private
Paroled at Salisbury on May 27, 1865.

LAMB, HARRIS, Private
Transferred from Company B of this regiment on November 10, 1861. Reported as Musician on company muster rolls from March-April, 1862, through May-June, 1863, and as Private thereafter. Present or accounted for until paroled at Appomattox Court House, Virginia, April 9, 1865.

LAMB, JESSE, Private
Enlisted in Wilson County on April 7, 1864, for

the war. Present or accounted for on company muster rolls through October, 1864.

LAMB, LAWRENCE B., Private
Resided in Wilson County where he enlisted at age 20, June 18, 1863, for the war. Present or accounted for until paroled at Appomattox Court House, Virginia, April 9, 1865.

LAMB, MATTHEW T., Private
Resided in Wilson County where he enlisted at age 19, June 13, 1861, for the war. Captured near Fredericksburg, Virginia, May 3, 1863, and paroled and exchanged at City Point, Virginia, May 13, 1863. Present or accounted for until captured at Kelly's Ford, Virginia, November 7, 1863. Confined at Point Lookout, Maryland, until paroled and transferred for exchange to Aiken's Landing, Virginia, February 24, 1865.

LANE, C. J., Private
Resided in Iredell County and paroled at Salisbury on May 27, 1865.

LANE, JOHN A. R., Private
Enlisted in Randolph County on July 21, 1862, for the war. First reported on company muster roll for May 1-August 31, 1864. Wounded and captured at Winchester, Virginia, September 19, 1864. Confined at Point Lookout, Maryland, until paroled on October 30, 1864, and sent to Venus Point, Savannah River, Georgia, for exchange. Received in exchange on November 15, 1864. Paroled at Greensboro on May 10, 1865.

LANE, M. T., Private
Resided in Wilson County and paroled at Goldsboro on May 16, 1865. "Came in for parole."

LASSITER, CHARLES, Private
Resided in Wilson County and enlisted in Wayne County at age 22, April 12, 1862, for the war. Wounded at Fredericksburg, Virginia, December 13, 1862, and returned to duty February 13, 1863. Admitted to hospital at Lynchburg, Virginia, where he died March 18, 1863, of "pneumonia."

LEGGETT, ALFRED, Private
Captured at Goldsboro on March 23, 1865, and confined at Fort Monroe, Virginia, until released after taking the Oath of Allegiance on April 5, 1865.

LEWIS, KINDRED S., Sergeant
Resided in Edgecombe County and enlisted in Wayne County at age 20, May 29, 1861, for the war. Mustered in as Corporal. Captured at Frederick, Maryland, September 12, 1862, and confined at Fort Delaware, Delaware, until paroled for exchange on October 2, 1862. Declared exchanged at Aiken's Landing, Virginia, November 10, 1862. Promoted to Sergeant on December 1, 1862. Killed at Chancellorsville, Virginia, May 3, 1863.

LONDON, O. C., Private
Paroled at Greensboro on May 2, 1865.

LUCAS, JAMES, Private
Resided in Wilson County and enlisted in Wayne County at age 21, May 29, 1861, for the war. Wounded and captured at Chancellorsville, Virginia, May 3, 1863. Confined at Old Capitol Pri-

son, Washington, D.C., until paroled on June 10, 1863. Exact date of exchange not reported; however, he was admitted to hospital at Petersburg, Virginia, June 12, 1863, and furloughed for 30 days on June 17, 1863. Present or accounted for until captured at Kelly's Ford, Virginia, November 7, 1863. Confined at Point Lookout, Maryland, until paroled and transferred for exchange to James River, Virginia, January 17, 1865. Reported as present on a roll of a detachment of paroled and exchanged prisoners at Camp Lee, near Richmond, Virginia, dated January 26, 1865.

McDONOUGH, PETER, Private
Resided in Wayne County where he enlisted at age 29, May 29, 1861, for the war. Captured near Fredericksburg, Virginia, May 3, 1863, and paroled and exchanged at City Point, Virginia, May 10, 1863. Present or accounted for until left sick at Shippensburg, Pennsylvania, where he was captured on June 24, 1863. Confined at Fort Delaware, Delaware, until transferred to Point Lookout, Maryland, October 18, 1863. Paroled and exchanged in September, 1864. Issued clothing on November 29, 1864.

McKELL, MURPHY, Private
Resided in Wilson County and enlisted in Wayne County at age 20, July 3, 1861, for the war. Present or accounted for until captured at Kelly's Ford, Virginia, November 7, 1863. Confined at Old Capitol Prison, Washington, D.C., until transferred to Point Lookout, Maryland, February 3-4, 1864. Paroled at Point Lookout and transferred for exchange to Aiken's Landing, Virginia, February 24, 1865.

MANN, JONATHAN, Private
Resided in Wilson County and enlisted in Wayne County at age 18, May 29, 1861, for the war. Captured at South Mountain, Maryland, September 15, 1862, and confined at Fort Delaware, Delaware, until paroled for exchange on October 2, 1862. Declared exchanged at Aiken's Landing, Virginia, November 10, 1862. Present or accounted for on company muster rolls through October, 1864.

MARCO, SAMUEL, Private
Resided in Wilson County and enlisted in Wayne County at age 23, June 3, 1861, for the war. Mustered in as Corporal and reduced to ranks August 27, 1862. Present or accounted for until transferred to the C.S. Navy on December 30, 1863.

MATHEWS, WILLIAM, Private
Resided in Wilson County where he enlisted on April 7, 1864, for the war. Present or accounted for on company muster rolls and hospital records through January, 1865. Paroled at Goldsboro in 1865.

MAYO, EDWARD J., 1st Sergeant
Resided in Wayne County where he enlisted at age 20, May 29, 1861, for the war. Mustered in as Sergeant and promoted to 1st Sergeant on March 13, 1863. Present or accounted for on company muster rolls through October, 1864. Captured at Burkeville, Virginia, April 6, 1865, and confined at Point Lookout, Maryland, where

he died on June 21, 1865, of "dysentery chronic."

MEARS, WILLIAM J. L., Private
Resided in Wilson County and enlisted in Wayne County at age 21, May 29, 1861, for the war. Present or accounted for until paroled at Appomattox Court House, Virginia, April 9, 1865.

MITCHELL, JAMES, Private
Resided in Greene County and enlisted in Wayne County at age 18, May 29, 1861, for the war. Present or accounted for until paroled at Appomattox Court House, Virginia, April 9, 1865.

MONDAY, WILLIAM, Private
Resided in Wayne County where he enlisted at age 24, May 29, 1861, for the war. Deserted on February 10, 1863, and rejoined the company from desertion on September 10, 1863. Present or accounted for on company muster rolls through October, 1864. Captured at Petersburg, Virginia, April 3, 1865, and confined at Hart's Island, New York Harbor, until released after taking the Oath of Allegiance on June 18, 1865.

MOORE, AMARIAH BIGGS, Private
Resided in Wilson County and enlisted in Wayne County at age 24, May 29, 1861, for the war. Wounded at Malvern Hill, Virginia, July 1, 1862. Reported as absent wounded on company muster rolls through October, 1864.

MOORE, THOMAS B. A., Private
Resided in Wilson County and enlisted in Wayne County at age 23, May 29, 1861, for the war. Wounded and captured at South Mountain, Maryland, September 14, 1862. Paroled and exchanged at Aiken's Landing, Virginia, November 10, 1862. Reported as absent on furlough after he was exchanged until he died on November 29, 1863, of disease.

MOORE, WILLIAM B., Private
Born in Edgecombe County and resided in Wilson County prior to enlisting in Wayne County at age 30, May 29, 1861, for the war. Killed in action at Chancellorsville, Virginia, May 3, 1863.

MUMFORD, THOMAS, Private
Resided in Wilson County and enlisted in Wayne County at age 24, May 29, 1861, for the war. Wounded and captured at South Mountain, Maryland, September 14, 1862, and paroled and exchanged at Aiken's Landing, Virginia, November 10, 1862. Present or accounted for on company muster rolls through October, 1864. Captured at Burkeville, Virginia, April 6, 1865, and confined at Point Lookout, Maryland, until released after taking the Oath of Allegiance on June 29, 1865.

MUMFORD, WILEY, Private
Resided in Wilson County and enlisted in Wayne County at age 21, May 29, 1861, for the war. Wounded at Spotsylvania Court House, Virginia, May 12, 1864. Reported as absent wounded on company muster rolls through October, 1864. Admitted to hospital at Danville, Virginia, April 5, 1865, with "debilitas" and furloughed for 60 days on April 9, 1865.

MUMFORD, WILLIAM, Private
Resided in Wayne County where he enlisted on

July 16, 1861, for the war. Wounded at Chancellorsville, Virginia, May 3, 1863. Absent wounded until detailed for Provost Guard at Gordonsville, Virginia, October 24, 1863. Remained on detail through March, 1864. Present or accounted for on company muster rolls from that date through October 8, 1864. Paroled at Appomattox Court House, Virginia, April 9, 1865.

OVERMAN, WILLIAM A., Private
Born in Wayne County where he resided as a farmer and enlisted at age 29, June 12, 1861, for the war. Lost left arm in battle at Fredericksburg, Virginia, December 13, 1862. Reported as absent wounded until discharged on January 16, 1864.

OWENS, ELISHA, Sergeant
Resided in Wilson County and enlisted in Wayne County at age 33, May 29, 1861, for the war. Mustered in as Corporal. Promoted to Sergeant on March 13, 1863. Present or accounted for on company muster rolls through October, 1864. Paroled at Goldsboro on May 9, 1865. "Came in for parole."

OWENS, HENRY, Private
Born in Wilson County where he resided as a farmer and enlisted at age 38, June 18, 1863, for the war. Present or accounted for until discharged at Orange Court House, Virginia, September 23, 1863, by reason of "anemia and debility of long standing, and of obscure disease of the kidneys and general cochexia."

PAGE, IRVIN JACKSON, Private
Born in Edgecombe County and resided as a farmer in Wilson County where he enlisted at age 33, May 14, 1862, for the war. Present or accounted for until he died March 13-14, 1863, of disease.

PARISH, NATHAN T., Private
Resided in Wilson County and enlisted in Wayne County at age 25, May 29, 1861, for the war. Deserted January 10, 1863, and returned to company in March, 1864. Muster rolls from March through October, 1864, state that he was absent undergoing sentence of court-martial. Released from confinement on December 1, 1864.

PATE, JAMES A., Private
Born in Wayne County where he resided as a farmer and enlisted at age 31, June 2, 1861, for the war. Present or accounted for until he "died at camp before Richmond, Virginia, July 21, 1862."

PEACOCK, CASWELL C., Private
Resided in Wayne County where he enlisted at age 24, May 29, 1861, for the war. Present or accounted for on company muster rolls through October, 1864.

PETWAY, SETH M., Private
Resided in Wilson County and enlisted in Virginia on February 1, 1864, for the war. Present or accounted for until captured at Spotsylvania Court House, Virginia, May 12, 1864. Confined at Point Lookout, Maryland, until transferred to Elmira, New York, August 10-14, 1864. Paroled at Elmira on October 11, 1864, and sent to Point Lookout for exchange. Exchanged on October 29, 1864. Captured at Farmville, Virginia, April 6,

1865, and confined at Point Lookout until released after taking the Oath of Allegiance on June 14, 1865.

PIERCE, LOVIT, Private

Resided in Wayne County where he enlisted at age 29, May 28, 1861, for the war. Captured near Sharpsburg, Maryland, and paroled September 21, 1862. Present or accounted for on company muster rolls until captured at Kelly's Ford, Virginia, November 7, 1863. Confined at Point Lookout, Maryland, until transferred to Aiken's Landing, Virginia, for exchange on March 17, 1865. Declared exchanged on March 19, 1865.

PITMAN, CASWELL, Private

Resided in Wayne County where he enlisted at age 23, May 29, 1861, for the war. Wounded at Sharpsburg, Maryland, September 17, 1862, and reported as absent wounded until retired to the Invalid Corps on April 28, 1864. Assigned to light duty at Goldsboro and was reported there as late as October 31, 1864.

PITMAN, JAMES, Private

Resided in Wilson County where he enlisted at age 18, in January, 1862, for the war. Died at Wilson on June 7, 1862.

POPE, BENJAMIN H., Private

Born in Wayne County where he enlisted at age 18, May 29, 1861, for the war. Wounded at Gaines' Mill, Virginia, June 27, 1862. Present or accounted for until he died in hospital at Richmond, Virginia, June 5, 1863, of "pneumonia typhoid."

POPE, LAWRENCE, Private

Born in Wayne County where he resided as a farmer and enlisted at age 20, May 29, 1861, for the war. Wounded at Malvern Hill, Virginia, July 1, 1862, and died of wound in hospital at Richmond, Virginia, July 20, 1862.

REASON, RALEIGH, Private

Born in Wilson County where he resided as a farmer prior to enlisting in Wayne County at age 17, May 29, 1861, for the war. Detailed as ambulance driver in February, 1863, and reported as absent on detail on company muster rolls through October, 1864. Captured at Waynesboro, Virginia, March 2, 1865, and confined at Fort Delaware, Delaware, until released after taking the Oath of Allegiance on June 19, 1865.

RICHARDSON, INCIL, Private

Resided in Wayne County where he enlisted at age 21, May 29, 1861, for the war. Died in hospital at Camp Potomac, King George County, Virginia, September 14, 1861.

RODGERS, JAMES M., Private

Resided in Wilson County and enlisted in Wayne County at age 18, May 31, 1861, for the war. November-December, 1861, muster roll reports him as "under sentence of Court Martial." Deserted April 28, 1862.

ROPER, JOHN, Private

Resided in Wilson County where he enlisted at age 29, April 12, 1862, for the war. Died in hospital at Mount Jackson, Virginia, November 26, 1862, of "pneumonia."

ROPER, ROBINSON, Private

Resided in Wilson County where he enlisted at age 24, June 3, 1861, for the war. Died in hospital at Richmond, Virginia, April 3, 1863, of "pneumonia."

ROUNDTREE, FRANKLIN, Private

Resided in Wilson County where he enlisted at age 23, August 19, 1861, for the war. Present or accounted for on company muster rolls through December 4, 1862, and reported as absent sick from that date through October, 1863, when he was reported with the remark: "Died of disease. No official report of his death."

SAULS, FREDERICK, Private

Resided in Wayne County and enlisted at Richmond, Virginia, at age 21, June 17, 1862, for the war. Killed in action at South Mountain, Maryland, September 14, 1862.

SCOTT, JOHN D., Private

Resided in Wilson County where he enlisted at age 30, June 18, 1863, for the war. Present or accounted for on company muster rolls through October, 1864.

SEXTON, E., Private

Died in hospital at Richmond, Virginia, February 12, 1864, of "diarrhoea chronic."

SLATER, E. S., Private

Federal Provost Marshal records indicate that he "gave himself up at Bloody Run, Pennsylvania, June 23, 1863." Confined at Fort Mifflin, Pennsylvania, July 2, 1863, and released after taking the Oath of Allegiance on June 3, 1864.

SMITH, WILLIAM, Private

Resided in Pitt County where he enlisted at age 30, September 8, 1862, for the war. Captured near Fredericksburg, Virginia, May 3, 1863, and paroled and exchanged at City Point, Virginia, May 13, 1863. Never returned to the company and reported as absent without leave on company muster rolls through October, 1864.

SPURLE, H. W., Private

Captured at Gettysburg, Pennsylvania, July 3, 1863, and confined at Fort Delaware, Delaware, where he died October 9, 1863.

STEEL, WILLIAM H., Private

Enlisted in Randolph County on September 9, 1863, for the war. First reported on company muster roll for May 1-August 31, 1864. September-October, 1864, muster roll states that he was "absent wounded since fight at Fisher's Hill, Virginia, September 22, 1864." Paroled at Greensboro on May 16, 1865.

STRICKLAND, GIDEON, Private

Resided in Wayne County where he enlisted at age 19, June 2, 1861, for the war. Deserted at Gettysburg, Pennsylvania, July 1, 1863, and captured on July 3, 1863. Confined at Fort Delaware, Delaware, where he was reported as "dead."

TAYLOR, J., Private

Paroled at Salisbury on May 22, 1865.

TEADY, R., Private

Captured at Gettysburg, Pennsylvania, July 3, 1863, and confined at Fort Delaware, Delaware, July 7-12, 1863.

THOMAS, GEORGE, Private
Resided in Wayne County where he enlisted at age 21, May 29, 1861, for the war. Discharged on January 28, 1862, upon being transferred to the C.S. Navy.

THOMPSON, JOHN H., Private
Resided in Wayne County where he enlisted at age 25, May 29, 1861, for the war. Present or accounted for until he died in hospital at Goldsboro on January 8, 1864, of disease.

THORN, MARTIN RAMSEY, Private
Resided in Wilson County where he enlisted at age 40, February 1, 1862, for the war. Transferred to Company B of this regiment March-April, 1862.

WALSTON, GOLDEN, Private
Resided in Wilson County where he enlisted at age 16, March 21, 1862, for the war. Present or accounted for on company muster rolls through August, 1863, when he was reported as "sent to hospital sick September 1, 1862. Now in North Carolina, deserter." Paroled at Goldsboro on May 9, 1865. "Came in for parole."

WARD, BENJAMIN S., Private
Resided in Wilson County and enlisted in Wake County at age 37, June 18, 1863, for the war. Detailed for hospital duty in Richmond, Virginia, August 27, 1863. Company muster rolls and hospital records indicate that he was absent on detail through February, 1865.

WARD, HENRY, Private
Resided in Wayne County where he enlisted at age 20, May 29, 1861, for the war. Captured and paroled near Sharpsburg, Maryland, September 20, 1862. Present or accounted for until captured near Fredericksburg, Virginia, May 3, 1863. Paroled and exchanged at City Point, Virginia, May 10, 1863. Present or accounted for on company muster rolls through October, 1864. Captured at Petersburg, Virginia, April 3, 1865, and confined at Hart's Island, New York Harbor, until released after taking the Oath of Allegiance on June 18, 1865.

WEBB, FRANKLIN, Private
Resided in Wilson County and enlisted in Wayne County at age 18, April 1, 1862, for the war. Wounded at Chancellorsville, Virginia, May 3, 1863. Reported as absent wounded until detailed for Provost Guard at Tarboro, January 20, 1864. Reported as absent on detail on company muster rolls through October, 1864. Admitted to hospital at Richmond, Virginia, February 27, 1865, with gunshot wound of right thigh and returned to duty on March 7, 1865. Paroled at Appomattox Court House, Virginia, April 9, 1865.

WEBB, NATHAN, Private
Resided in Wilson County and enlisted at Camp Potomac, King George County, Virginia, at age 40, October 11, 1861, for the war. Present or accounted for until captured at Spotsylvania Court House, Virginia, May 20, 1864. Confined at Point Lookout, Maryland, until transferred to Elmira, New York, July 3, 1864. Died at Elmira on October 2, 1864, of "scorbutis."

WILLIAMS, JAMES, Private
Resided in Wayne County where he enlisted at age 20, May 29, 1861, for the war. Died at Camp Advance, Northampton County, July 18, 1861.

WILSON, DANIEL, Private
Captured at Gettysburg, Pennsylvania, July 3, 1863, and confined at Fort Delaware, Delaware. Transferred to Point Lookout, Maryland, October 15-18, 1863. Paroled at Point Lookout and sent to James River, Virginia, for exchange, February 18, 1865. Declared exchanged on February 20-21, 1865.

WOODS, JOHN S., Private
Paroled at Greensboro on May 8, 1865.

1st COMPANY E

This company was organized in Nash County and enlisted at Wilson on May 25, 1861. It tendered its service to the state and was ordered to Camp Advance, near Garysburg, Northampton County, where it was assigned to this regiment as Company E and mustered into state service on June 19, 1861. When the regiment received marching orders on July 13, 1861, this company was withdrawn because it was not sufficiently organized or trained for the expected campaign. At that time, the company was transferred to the 7th Regiment N.C. State Troops, then in process of being formed, and assigned as Company E of that regiment. Since it was the first company to serve as Company E of this regiment, it was later referred to as 1st Company E. The company served in the 7th Regiment N.C. State Troops during the remainder of the war, and its history and roster will be reported in volume IV of this series.

2nd COMPANY E

This company, known as the "Guilford Guards," was organized in Guilford County and enlisted at Greensboro and Hillsdale, Guilford County, July 23-24, 1861. The company tendered its service to the state and was mustered into state service at Raleigh on September 20, 1861, as Company E of this regiment. Soon after muster-in, the company was ordered to Hyde County and stationed at Fort Hall. There it remained until ordered to the regiment. The exact date the company joined the regiment was not reported, but the November-December, 1861, muster roll reports that the company was at the regimental station at Camp Potomac, Virginia. After joining the regiment the company functioned as a part of the regiment, and its history for the war period is recorded as a part of the regimental history. Since the company was the second to serve as Company E in this regiment, it was later referred to as 2nd Company E.

The information contained in the following roster of the company was compiled principally from company muster rolls which covered from the muster-in roll, dated September 20, 1861, through December, 1861; March-April, 1862; September-October, 1862; January, 1863, through March, 1864;

and May through October, 1864. No company muster rolls were found for January-February, 1862; May through August, 1862; November-December, 1862; April, 1864; or for the period after October, 1864. In addition to the company muster rolls, Roll of Honor records, receipt rolls, and hospital records, supplemented by state pension applications, United Daughters of the Confederacy records, and postwar rosters and histories, all provided useful information.

OFFICERS
CAPTAINS
MOREHEAD, JOHN H.
  Born in Guilford County where he resided and was appointed Captain at age 27 to rank from May 16, 1861. Present or accounted for until transferred to the Field and Staff, 45th Regiment N.C. Troops upon appointment as Lieutenant Colonel to rank from April 3, 1862.

GORRELL, HENRY CLAY
  Born in Guilford County where he resided as a druggist and was appointed 1st Lieutenant at age 22 to rank from May 16, 1861. Promoted to Captain to rank from April 3, 1862. Killed in action on the Williamsburg Road, near Richmond, Virginia, June 21, 1862.

SCALES, JAMES TURNER
  Born in Henry County, Virginia, and was by occupation a lawyer when he was appointed 3rd Lieutenant at age 23 to rank from May 16, 1861. Promoted to 2nd Lieutenant on January 24, 1862, and to 1st Lieutenant on April 3, 1862. Promoted to Captain to rank from June 21, 1862. Admitted to hospital at Richmond, Virginia, November 9, 1863, with a gunshot wound in the head. Returned to duty November 28, 1863. Date and place he was wounded not reported. Wounded at Spotsylvania Court House, Virginia, May 17, 1864. Present or accounted for until transferred to the Field and Staff of this regiment upon appointment as Major on August 30, 1864.

LIEUTENANTS
FRALEY, JOHN T., 2nd Lieutenant
  Born in Rowan County and resided as a farmer in Davie County prior to enlisting in Guilford County at age 19, July 26, 1861, for the war. Mustered in as Private and appointed Corporal on December 1, 1861. Promoted to Sergeant on April 19, 1862, and appointed 2nd Lieutenant to rank from September 23, 1862. Present or accounted for until he died of wounds received in battle at Spotsylvania Court House, Virginia, May 15, 1864.

HOBSON, JAMES M., 1st Lieutenant
  Born in Rockingham County and resided as a student in Davie County prior to enlisting in Guilford County at age 21, July 26, 1861, for the war. Mustered in as Private. Elected 2nd Lieutenant February 3, 1862, and appointed to rank from date of election. Promoted to 1st Lieutenant to rank from June 21, 1862. Wounded at Chancellorsville, Virginia, May 3, 1863. Present or ac-

counted for until captured at Spotsylvania Court House, Virginia, May 8, 1864. Confined at Point Lookout, Maryland, until transferred to Fort Delaware, Delaware, June 23, 1864. Forwarded to Hilton Head, South Carolina, August 20, 1864, and transferred to Fort Pulaski, Georgia, in October, 1864. Transferred back to Hilton Head in December, 1864, and back to Fort Delaware on March 12, 1865. Released to Fort Delaware after taking the Oath of Allegiance on June 10, 1865.

HOBSON, JOHN M., 2nd Lieutenant
  Born in Rockingham County and resided as a student in Davie County prior to enlisting in Guilford County at age 19, July 24, 1861. Mustered in as 1st Sergeant. Appointed 2nd Lieutenant to rank from April 19, 1862. Wounded at Chancellorsville, Virginia, May 3, 1863, and returned to duty July 5, 1863. Present or accounted for on company muster rolls through October, 1864. Captured at Petersburg, Virginia, April 2, 1865, and confined at Old Capitol Prison, Washington, D.C., until transferred to Johnson's Island, Ohio, April 9, 1865. Released at Johnson's Island after taking the Oath of Allegiance on June 18, 1865.

MOREHEAD, JOSEPH M., 2nd Lieutenant
  Born in Guilford County where he resided as a student and was appointed 2nd Lieutenant, at age 21, to rank from May 16, 1861. Submitted his resignation on January 18, 1862, by reason of his having "for three years been afflicted with a spinal affliction which as by the necessary exposure of camp life became much aggravated." Resignation officially accepted January 24, 1862.

NONCOMMISSIONED OFFICERS AND PRIVATES
ADAMS, ASA, Private
  Enlisted in Guilford County on November 14, 1861, for the war. Deserted in December, 1861.

ADAMS, JAMES, Private
  Resided in Guilford County and enlisted in Wake County at age 37, July 7, 1863, for the war. Present or accounted for until captured at Fisher's Hill, Virginia, September 22, 1864. Confined at Point Lookout, Maryland, until transferred to Aiken's Landing, Virginia, for exchange on March 17, 1865. Declared exchanged on March 19, 1865. Paroled at Greensboro on May 11, 1865.

ADCOCK, B. F., Private
  Resided in Chatham County and enlisted in Wake County at age 20, July 15, 1862, for the war. Present or accounted for until transferred to the C.S. Navy on April 5, 1864.

AUTRY, RAYFORD, Private
  Resided in Sampson County and enlisted in Wake County at age 30, July 15, 1862, for the war. Wounded at Chancellorsville, Virginia, May 3, 1863. Present or accounted for until captured at Petersburg, Virginia, April 3, 1865. Confined at Hart's Island, New York Harbor, until released after taking the Oath of Allegiance on June 21, 1865.

BABISTON, PERDEE, Private
Resided in Columbus County where he enlisted at age 18, August 31, 1863, for the war. Present or accounted for on company muster rolls through October, 1864. Captured at Petersburg, Virginia, **April 3, 1865, and confined at Hart's Island, New York Harbor, until released after taking the Oath of Allegiance on June 18, 1865.**

BAGGOT, NAYLOR, Private
Resided in Sampson County and enlisted in Wake County at age 23, July 15, 1862, for the war. Killed at Chancellorsville, Virginia, May 3, 1863.

BAINES, JAMES F., Sergeant
Born in Pittsylvania County, Virginia, and resided as a farmer in Guilford County where he enlisted at age 19, July 24, 1861, for the war. Mustered in as Private and promoted to Corporal on October 1, 1862. Promoted to Sergeant in December, 1862. Present or accounted for until he was "killed in battle of Cedar Creek, Virginia, October 19, 1864."

BASS, B. D., Private
Resided in Sampson County and enlisted in Wake County at age 24, July 15, 1862, for the war. Captured and paroled at Leesburg, Virginia, October 2, 1862. Present or accounted for until he died March 26, 1863.

BAYNES, EATON, Private
Resided in Guilford County where he enlisted at age 40, August 24, 1863, for the war. Present or accounted for until he "died of disease August 9, 1864."

BELL, WILLIAM, Private
Born in Guilford County where he resided as a wheelwright and enlisted at age 37, July 24, 1861, for the war. Present or accounted for on company muster rolls through October, 1864. Paroled at Greensboro on May 13, 1865.

BENSON, THOMAS E., Private
Born in Guilford County where he resided as a farmer and enlisted at age 19, July 12, 1861, for the war. Present or accounted for until he "died in hospital at Guinea Station, Virginia, February 1, 1863."

BOOTH, JOHN T., Sergeant
Born in Stokes County and resided as a farmer in Guilford County where he enlisted at age 20, July 23, 1861, for the war. Mustered in as Private and appointed Corporal on October 1, 1862. Promoted to Sergeant in March, 1863. Present or accounted for on company muster rolls through October, 1864.

BOOTH, ROBERT, Private
Resided in Guilford County where he enlisted on February 24, 1862, for the war. Present or accounted for until he "died at home in Guilford County, October 10, 1862."

BRASSWELL, C. R., Private
Resided in Edgecombe County and paroled at Goldsboro on May 18, 1865. "Came in for parole."

BROWER, D. F., Private
First reported on company muster rolls on the September-October, 1862, muster roll. Date, place, and period of enlistment not reported. Captured at Middletown, Maryland, September 15, 1862, and confined at Fort Delaware, until transferred for exchange to Aiken's Landing, Virginia, October 2, 1862. Declared exchanged on November 10, 1862. Admitted to hospital at Richmond, Virginia, in October, 1862, and died October 20, 1862, of "dysenteria chronic."

BULLARD, LOVE, Private
Born in Sampson County where he resided as a farmer and enlisted at age 24, July 15, 1862, for the war. Captured and paroled near Sharpsburg, Maryland, September 23, 1862. Died in Sampson County on November 1, 1862, of disease.

BULLARD, THOMAS, Private
Resided in Sampson County and enlisted in Wake County at age 21, July 15, 1862, for the war. Killed at Chancellorsville, Virginia, on May 3, 1863.

BURKE, JAMES, Private
Resided in Chatham County and enlisted in Wake County at age 35, July 15, 1862, for the war. Present or accounted for until killed at Spotsylvania Court House, Virginia, May 12, 1864.

CAIN, JOHN J., Private
Born in Rowan County and resided as a farmer in Guilford County where he enlisted at age 21, July 24, 1861, for the war. Captured at Williamsport, Maryland, September 16, 1862, and confined at Fort Delaware, Delaware, until transferred to Aiken's Landing, Virginia, October 2, 1862, for exchange. Declared exchanged on November 10, 1862. Present or accounted for on company muster rolls until he "deserted June 26, 1863, in Pennsylvania."

CARTER, HARRISON, Private
Resided in Sampson County and enlisted at age 22, July 15, 1862, for the war. Died in camp near Winchester, Virginia, September 25-27, 1862.

CARTER, HENRY, Private
Resided in Sampson County and enlisted in Wake County at age 18, July 15, 1862, for the war. Captured and paroled at Leesburg, Virginia, October 2, 1862. Present or accounted for on company muster rolls through October, 1864.

CHUNN, THOMAS, Private
Captured at South Mountain, Maryland, July 5, 1863, and confined at Fort Delaware, Delaware, until paroled and sent to City Point, Virginia, July 30, 1863, for exchange. Date exchanged not reported. Admitted to hospital at Petersburg, Virginia, August 1, 1863, with "diarrhoea chronic" and furloughed for 30 days on August 12, 1863.

COBLE, DAVID P., Private
Born in Guilford County where he resided as a farmer and enlisted at age 21, August 20, 1861, for the war. Died at Fredericksburg, Virginia, in March, 1862.

CODY, MURPHY, Private
Born in Randolph County and resided as a farmer in Lincoln County prior to enlisting in Guilford County at age 39, August 27, 1861, for the war. Wounded at Chancellorsville, Virginia,

May 3, 1863. Reported as absent wounded through November, 1863, and as absent without leave from that date until September, 1864, when he returned to the company. Sentenced by court-martial on February 11, 1865, to "grub stumps for 30 days." Captured at Petersburg, Virginia, April 3, 1865, and confined at Hart's Island, New York Harbor, until released after taking the Oath of Allegiance on June 17, 1865.

COFFEY, MICHAEL, Private
Born in Guilford County where he resided as a farmer and enlisted at age 31, July 24, 1861, for the war. Wounded at Mechanicsville, Virginia, June 27, 1862. Reported as absent wounded until detailed for hospital duty at Richmond, Virginia, May 11, 1863. Remained on detail through February, 1864. Present or accounted for on company muster rolls until wounded and captured at Winchester, Virginia, September 19, 1864. Confined in hospital until transferred to Point Lookout, Maryland, January 1, 1865. Released at Point Lookout after taking the Oath of Allegiance on June 24, 1865.

COLLY, LUTHER R., Sergeant
Born in Charlotte County, Virginia, and resided as a wheelwright in Guilford County where he enlisted at age 26, July 24, 1861, for the war. Mustered in as Private. Wounded at Malvern Hill, Virginia, July 1, 1862. Returned to company in September, 1862. Wounded at Gettysburg, Pennsylvania, July 1-3, 1863. Appointed Sergeant on June 6, 1864. Present or accounted for until paroled at Appomattox Court House, Virginia, April 9, 1865.

COPELAND, C. S., Private
Born in Guilford County where he resided as a farmer and enlisted at age 37, July 23, 1861, for the war. Wounded at Malvern Hill, Virginia, July 1, 1862, and admitted to hospital at Richmond, Virginia, where he died September 3, 1862, of wounds and "bronchitis."

CORE, WILLIAM, Private
Born in Craven County and resided as a farmer in Guilford County where he enlisted at age 22, July 6, 1861, for the war. Wounded at Malvern Hill, Virginia, July 1, 1862, and discharged.

CRUTCHFIELD, ALGELIN S., Private
Enlisted in Wake County on June 6, 1863, for the war. First reported on company muster roll for May 1-August 31, 1864, when he appears with the remark that he "deserted to the enemy July 10, 1864."

DILLON, JONATHAN, Private
Born in Guilford County where he resided as a farmer and enlisted at age 21, July 22, 1861, for the war. Present or accounted for on company muster rolls until captured in Mechanicsville, Virginia, May 31, 1864. Confined at Point Lookout, Maryland, until transferred to Elmira, New York, July 9, 1864. Released at Elmira after taking the Oath of Allegiance on May 17, 1865.

DOROTHY, JAMES, Private
Born in Orange County and resided as a farmer in Guilford County where he enlisted at age 30,

August 21, 1861, for the war. Captured at Sharpsburg, Maryland, September 17, 1862, and paroled near Keedysville, Maryland, September 20, 1862. Captured near Fredericksburg, Virginia, May 4, 1863, and took the Oath of Allegiance to "remain within any of the loyal states."

DUDLEY, JOHN, Private
Resided in Sampson County and enlisted in Wake County at age 30, July 15, 1862, for the war. Mustered in as Private and appointed Corporal, March-April, 1863. Wounded at Gettysburg, Pennsylvania, July 2-3, 1863. Reduced to ranks on October 31, 1863. Present or accounted for until captured at Fisher's Hill, Virginia, September 22, 1864. Confined at Point Lookout, Maryland, until paroled and transferred for exchange to James River, Virginia, February 13, 1865. Declared exchanged February 14-15, 1865.

DUNBAR, SOLOMON, Private
Reported on November-December, 1861, muster roll with the remark that he "transferred September 30, 1861." Reported as present on March-April, 1862, muster roll. Sentenced by court-martial on April 29, 1862. Served in the 17th Regiment N.C. Troops (1st Organization).

DUNCAN, JAMES A., Corporal
Born in Guilford County where he resided and enlisted at age 20, February 22, 1862, for the war. Mustered in as Private. Wounded at Sharpsburg, Maryland, September 17, 1862. Detailed for hospital duty at Richmond, Virginia, April 18, 1863. Transferred to Lynchburg, Virginia, for assignment in hospital as a guard on July 1, 1863. Absent on detail through August, 1863. Appointed Corporal on October 31, 1863. Present or accounted for on company muster rolls until wounded and captured at Winchester, Virginia, September 19, 1864. Confined at Point Lookout, Maryland, until paroled and transferred for exchange to Venus Point, Savannah River, Georgia, October 31, 1864. Declared exchanged at Venus Point on November 15, 1864. Admitted to hospital at Richmond, Virginia, February 25, 1865, with a gunshot wound of the left arm and right hip. Retired to the Invalid Corps on March 16, 1865, and assigned to light duty at Jackson Hospital, Richmond, March 31, 1865. Captured in hospital at Richmond on April 3, 1865, and confined at Newport News, Virginia, until released after taking the Oath of Allegiance on June 30, 1865.

ELLINGTON, ARMSTEAD, Private
Born in Granville County and resided as a farmer in Guilford County where he enlisted at age 35, July 23, 1861, for the war. Killed in action at Gaines' Mill, Virginia, June 27, 1862.

ESTIS, WILLIAM, Private
Resided in Moore County and enlisted at age 30, July 15, 1862, for the war. Died in hospital at Richmond, Virginia, November 6, 1862, of "chronic enteritis."

FAIRCLOTH, EVANS, Private
Resided in Sampson County and enlisted in Wake County at age 25, July 15, 1862, for the war. Present or accounted for until he died at

Boonsboro, Maryland, September 24, 1862, of disease.

FARRINGTON, LOTON W., Private
Born in Guilford County where he resided as a farmer and enlisted at age 27, July 24, 1861, for the war. Present or accounted for until discharged on November 2, 1863, by reason of "an infection of the lung."

FITTS, HENRY, Private
Born in Mecklenburg County, Virginia, and resided as a farmer in Guilford County where he enlisted at age 30, July 23, 1861, for the war. Reported as absent sick from March-April, 1862, until he was detailed for hospital duty at Richmond, Virginia, January 16, 1864. Remained in hospital as a patient until detailed as a nurse on April 28, 1864. Reported as absent without leave from 3rd Division General Hospital, Camp Winder, Richmond, after September, 1864.

FITTS, JOHN H., Private
Born in Mecklenburg County, Virginia, and resided as a farmer in Guilford County where he enlisted at age 19, July 23, 1861, for the war. Died at Winchester, Virginia, in October, 1862, of "typhoid fever."

FITZGERALD, THOMAS F., Private
Born in Caswell County and resided as a farmer in Guilford County where he enlisted at age 18, July 24, 1861, for the war. Died at Aquia Creek, Virginia, in February, 1862, of "brain fever."

FITZGERALD, WILLIAM F., Private
Born in Pittsylvania County, Virginia, and resided as a farmer in Guilford County where he enlisted at age 34, August 27, 1861, for the war. Killed at Malvern Hill, Virginia, July 1, 1862.

FOSTER, SAMUEL, Private
Born in Rockingham County and resided as a farmer in Guilford County where he enlisted at age 42, July 24, 1861, for the war. Reported as absent sick from March-April, 1862, through December, 1862, and as absent without leave from January, 1863, through October, 1864. Captured and paroled at Anderson, South Carolina, May 8, 1865.

FOULKES, JAMES, Private
Born in Caswell County and resided as a farmer in Guilford County where he enlisted at age 18, July 24, 1861, for the war. Admitted to hospital at Charlottesville, Virginia, September 25, 1862, with "contusio" and furloughed October 21, 1862. Present or accounted for on company muster rolls through July-August, 1863, when he appears with the remark: "Absent in arrest at Division Headquarters for desertion, August 13, 1863. Has been tried." September-October, 1863, muster roll reports that he was "shot for desertion, September 16, 1863."

FOWLER, D. B., Private
Resided in Sampson County and enlisted in Wake County at age 26, July 15, 1862, for the war. Present or accounted for until he died at Winchester, Virginia, October 31, 1862, of disease.

FOWLER, WARREN, Private
Born in Guilford County where he resided as a

farmer and enlisted at age 26, August 21, 1861, for the war. Wounded at Fredericksburg, Virginia, December 13, 1862, and arm amputated. Reported as absent wounded through August, 1863, and as absent on detail in Quartermaster Department, Greensboro, from September, 1863, through October, 1864. Retired to the Invalid Corps on **December 1, 1864, and stationed at Greensboro. Paroled at Greensboro on May 4, 1865.**

FRALEY, MILAS J., Private
Resided in Davie County where he enlisted at age 23, September 1, 1862, for the war. Died in camp near Fredericksburg, Virginia, March 17, 1863.

GARRETT, HENRY T., Private
Born in Guilford County where he resided as a farmer and enlisted at age 33, August 21, 1861, for the war. Present or accounted for on company muster rolls through October, 1864. Captured at Petersburg, Virginia, April 3, 1865, and confined at Hart's Island, New York Harbor, until released after taking the Oath of Allegiance on June 17, 1865.

GORRELL, RALPH, Private
Born in Guilford County where he resided as a farmer and enlisted at age 18, July 22, 1861, for the war. Deserted at Orange Court House, Virginia, August 6, 1863, and returned to company on May 1, 1864. Present or accounted for on company muster rolls through October, 1864.

GRAY, WESLEY, Private
Born in Guilford County where he resided as a farmer and enlisted at age 17, August 26, 1861, for the war. Wounded near Richmond, Virginia, June 21, 1862. Died of wound in July, 1862.

GRONELL, B., Private
Paroled by President Jefferson Davis on August 3, 1864, for service in Winder's Legion.

HACKETT, LEAVEN W., Sergeant
Born in Guilford County where he resided as a farmer and enlisted at age 18, July 29, 1861, for the war. Mustered in as Private and appointed Corporal, March-April, 1863. Detailed on Provost Guard from March 23, 1863, through August, 1863. Present or accounted for on company muster rolls through October, 1864, as Corporal. Paroled at Appomattox Court House, Virginia, April 9, 1865, with the rank of Sergeant.

HAIR, JOHN C., Private
Resided in Sampson County and enlisted in Wake County at age 33, July 15, 1862, for the war. Captured and paroled at Leesburg, Virginia, October 2, 1862. Company muster rolls report him as absent without leave from January-February, 1863, through May-August, 1864, when he was reported with the remark: "Died of disease. Date not known."

HALL, LOFTIN, Private
Resided in Sampson County and enlisted in Wake County at age 28, July 15, 1862, for the war. Present or accounted for on company muster rolls through October, 1864.

HANHILL, HENRY G., Private
Paroled at Fairfax Court House, Virginia, Octo-

ber 19, 1862, and forwarded to the Provost Marshal, Washington, D.C.

HARRIS, WASHINGTON, Sergeant
Born in Guilford County where he resided as a farmer and enlisted at age 26, July 24, 1861, for the war. Mustered in as Private and appointed Sergeant in September, 1861. Present or accounted for until he died in hospital at Petersburg, Virginia, July 16-17, 1862, of disease.

HAWLEY, REDDICK, Private
Captured and paroled at Leesburg, Virginia, October 2, 1862. Admitted to hospital at Richmond, Virginia, October 31, 1862, and furloughed for 30 days on November 10-12, 1862.

HEATH, E. A. J., Sergeant
Born in Guilford County where he resided as a carpenter and enlisted at age 22, July 24, 1861, for the war. Mustered in as Corporal and promoted to Sergeant on August 25, 1862. Died of disease on October 24, 1862.

HODSON, ELI, Private
Born in Guilford County where he resided as a farmer and enlisted at age 18, July 22, 1861, for the war. Present or accounted for until discharged on August 13, 1862, by reason of "pulmonary phthisis."

HOLBROOK, JOHN, Private
Born in Guilford County where he resided as a farmer and enlisted at age 18, July 22, 1861, for the war. Died in camp on July 20-21, 1862, of "typhoid fever."

HOLLY, B., Private
Enlisted in Wake County on July 5, 1862, for the war. Died October 31, 1862.

HOLLY, JOHN A., Private
Resided in Sampson County and enlisted in Wake County at age 31, July 15, 1862, for the war. Died in October, 1862.

HOLLY, R., Private
Enlisted in Wake County on July 15, 1862, for the war. Died in hospital at Staunton, Virginia, November 3, 1862, of "diarrhoea chronic."

HOLLY, REDDICK, Private
Resided in Sampson County and enlisted in Wake County at age 28, July 15, 1862, for the war. Wounded at Chancellorsville, Virginia, May 3, 1863, and died of wounds in hospital at Richmond, Virginia, June 25, 1863.

HOWARD, H. A., Private
Paroled at Morganton on May 15, 1865.

HOWLETT, ASA, Private
Born in Guilford County where he resided as a farmer and enlisted at age 22, July 24, 1861, for the war. Died in December, 1861.

HUFFMAN, ESTELL S., Private
Born in Carroll County, Virginia, and resided as a farmer in Guilford County where he enlisted at age 21, August 2, 1861, for the war. Died in January, 1862, of "brain fever."

HUGHES, MILTON T., Private
Enlisted in Wake County on May 18, 1864, for the war. Captured at Harpers Ferry, West Virginia, July 8, 1864, and confined at Elmira, New York.

Paroled at Elmira on February 20, 1865, and sent to James River, Virginia, for exchange. Date of exchange not reported; however, he was admitted to hospital at Richmond, Virginia, March 3, 1865, and furloughed for 30 days on March 11, 1865.

JACKSON, BALLARD, Private
Resided in Sampson County and enlisted in Wake County at age 24, July 15, 1862, for the war. Detailed in hospital at Richmond, Virginia, April 13, 1863. Furloughed from hospital for 30 days on August 15, 1863. Failed to return at expiration of furlough and reported as absent without leave through October, 1864.

JACKSON, HENRY, Private
Born in Moore County and resided as a farmer in Guilford County where he enlisted at age 35, August 3, 1861, for the war. Died in camp near Richmond, Virginia, July 22, 1862, of "typhoid fever."

JEFFREYS, J. C., Private
Enlisted in Wake County on July 15, 1862, for the war. January-February, 1863, muster roll carries him with the remark: "Docked one months pay by sentence of Regimental Court Martial."

JEFFREYS, SAMUEL H., Private
Resided in Granville County and enlisted in Wake County at age 53, July 15, 1862, for the war as a substitute. Killed at Chancellorsville, Virginia, May 3, 1863.

JOHNSON, GEORGE, Private
Resided in Duplin County and enlisted in Wake County at age 25, July 15, 1862, for the war. Reported as absent without leave from August 20, 1862, through November-December, 1863, when he was reported with the remark: "Assigned to another company in regiment." Company to which assigned not reported.

JONES, H. M., Private
Born in Randolph County and resided as a farmer in Guilford County where he enlisted at age 19, July 23, 1861, for the war. Present or accounted for until he died in camp near Richmond, Virginia, July 27, 1862, of "typhoid fever."

KING, ALFRED, Private
Born in Guilford County where he resided as a farmer and enlisted at age 30, August 19, 1861, for the war. Wounded at Chancellorsville, Virginia, May 3, 1863. Reported as absent wounded until detailed as "body maker" in ambulance shop, Richmond, Virginia, January 21, 1864. Reported on company muster rolls as absent on detail through October, 1864. Paroled at Greensboro on May 11, 1865.

KING, THOMAS W., Private
Resided in Guilford County where he enlisted at age 18, February 22, 1862, for the war. Admitted to hospital on July 3, 1863, at Gettysburg, Pennsylvania, where he was captured on July 5, 1863. Confined at Fort Delaware, Delaware, where he volunteered to enter the cavalry service of the U.S. Army in August, 1863, but was rejected by the surgeon. Released after taking the Oath of Allegiance on May 10, 1865.

KIRKMAN, JOHN, Private

Enlisted in Guilford County on February 10, 1862, for the war. Died April 30, 1862.

KIRKMAN, JOHN C., Private

Enlisted in Wake County on May 17, 1864, for the war. Admitted to hospital at Richmond, Virginia, June 1, 1864, with "rubeola." Furloughed for 60 days on July 22, 1864. Readmitted to hospital at Richmond, Virginia, October 31, 1864, with "pneumonia." Returned to duty November 28, 1864. Federal Provost Marshal records report him as a rebel deserter received at Washington, D.C., April 12, 1865, from City Point, Virginia. Took the Oath of Allegiance and was provided transportation to Howard County, Indiana.

KIRKMAN, JOHN M., Sergeant

Born in Guilford County where he resided as a miner and enlisted at age 22, July 20, 1861, for the war. Mustered in as Private and appointed Sergeant on August 20, 1862. Present or accounted for until admitted to hospital at Richmond, Virginia, May 17, 1864, with a gunshot wound of the left side and chest. Died in hospital June 5, 1864.

LEE, JOHN W., Corporal

Born in Guilford County where he resided as a shoemaker and enlisted at age 23, July 23, 1861, for the war. Mustered in as Private and appointed Corporal, March-April, 1863. Present or accounted for until discharged on September 5, 1863, by reason of "dropsy consequent from Bright's Disease of the kidneys."

LEWIS, SEARLS M., Private

Born in Guilford County where he resided as a farmer and enlisted at age 20, July 24, 1861, for the war. Mustered in as Private and appointed Corporal on October 1, 1862. Reduced to ranks March-April, 1863. Wounded at Chancellorsville, Virginia, May 3, 1863, and died in hospital at Richmond, Virginia, June 15, 1863, of wound.

LIVENGOOD, HENDERSON, Private

Born in Davidson County and resided as a farmer in Davie County where he enlisted at age 25, March 24, 1862, for the war. Died in Davie County on July 8, 1862.

LOCKAMY, HUEY, Private

Resided in Sampson County and enlisted in Orange County, Virginia, February 26, 1864, for the war. Present or accounted for until captured at Harper's Farm, Virginia, April 6, 1865. Confined at Point Lookout, Maryland, until released after taking the Oath of Allegiance on June 24, 1865.

LOCKAMY, MOSES, Private

Resided in Sampson County and enlisted in Wake County at age 28, July 15, 1862, for the war. Captured and paroled at Leesburg, Virginia, October 2, 1862. Reported as absent without leave on company muster rolls through October, 1864.

LOWMAN, JOSHUA, Private

Enlisted in Wake County on June 14, 1864, for the war. Deserted July 9, 1864, and captured by Federal forces at Frederick, Maryland, July 12,

1864. Confined at Elmira, New York, where he died February 18, 1865, of "chronic diarrhoea."

LOYD, JESSE, Private

Born in Guilford County where he resided as a farmer and enlisted at age 17, July 23, 1861, for the war. Present or accounted for until he deserted on August 6, 1863. Reported as absent without leave on company muster rolls through October, 1864.

McLEAN, JAMES M., Sergeant

Born in Guilford County where he resided as a farmer and enlisted at age 32, July 24, 1861, for the war. Mustered in as Sergeant. Present or accounted for until killed at Gaines' Mill, Virginia, June 27, 1862.

McLEAN, JOHN R., 1st Sergeant

Born in Guilford County where he resided as a mason and enlisted at age 28, July 25, 1861, for the war. Mustered in as Sergeant and promoted to 1st Sergeant on April 19, 1862. Died in hospital at Richmond, Virginia, August 8, 1862, of "typhoid fever."

McLEMORE, LOFTON H., Private

Born in Sampson County where he resided as a farmer prior to enlisting in Wake County at age 20, July 15, 1862, for the war. Wounded at Chancellorsville, Virginia, May 3, 1863. Reported as absent sick until discharged on April 24, 1864, by reason of "phthisis pulmonalis affecting both lungs."

MANNING, W. A., Private

Resided in Pitt County and enlisted in Wake County at age 23, July 15, 1862, for the war. Admitted to hospital at Richmond, Virginia, September 6, 1862, with "measles." Reported on company muster rolls as absent sick through October, 1864.

MARLO, GEORGE, Private

Enlisted in Guilford County on November 14, 1861, for the war. Reported as present on November-December, 1861, muster roll.

MARLOW, JOHN, Private

Resided in Guilford County and enlisted at age 20, in November, 1861, for the war.

MARSHALL, THOMAS N., Private

Enlisted in Wake County on August 28, 1862, for the war. First reported on company muster roll for the period May 1-August 31, 1864. September-October, 1864, muster roll reports him as "absent wounded since July 18, 1864." Paroled at Greensboro on May 10, 1865.

MAXWELL, ALEXANDER T., Private

Resided in Sampson County and enlisted in Wake County at age 24, July 15, 1862, for the war. Present or accounted for until captured at Kelly's Ford, Virginia, November 7, 1863. Confined at Point Lookout, Maryland, where he died January 6, 1864.

MAXWELL, DUNCAN C., Private

Resided in Sampson County and enlisted at age 25, July 15, 1862, for the war. Died at Winchester, Virginia, October 25, 1862.

MAY, J. D., Private
Wounded and captured at Gettysburg, Pennsylvania, July 1-4, 1863. Confined at DeCamp General Hospital, Davids Island, New York Harbor, where he died July 21, 1863, of a gunshot wound.

MAY, NATHANIEL A., Private
Resided in Guilford County where he enlisted at age 24, February 24, 1862, for the war. Present or accounted for until detailed for hospital duty at Richmond, Virginia, March 1, 1864. Assigned to duty as a nurse at Jackson Hospital, Richmond, April 6, 1864. Reported as absent on detail through October, 1864.

MAY, OLIVER, Private
Born in Guilford County where he resided as a farmer and enlisted at age 47, August 5, 1861, for the war. Died in hospital at Richmond, Virginia, August 5, 1862.

MITCHELL, B. B., Private
Reported on September-October, 1862, muster roll as "absent on road." Date, place, and period of enlistment not reported. Admitted to hospital at Richmond, Virginia, October 29, 1862, with "chronic dysentery." Returned to duty on November 10, 1862.

MOST, G. H., Private
Paroled at Salisbury on May 16, 1865.

MURRAY, ALSAY H., Private
Born in Guilford County where he resided as a carpenter and enlisted at age 20, August 13, 1861, for the war. Died in hospital at Richmond, Virginia, August 16, 1862.

NAYLOR, JOSEPH, Private
Resided in Sampson County and enlisted in Wake County at age 34, July 15, 1862, for the war. Captured and paroled at Leesburg, Virginia, October 2, 1862. Wounded at Chancellorsville, Virginia, May 3, 1863, and arm amputated. Reported as absent wounded on company muster rolls through October, 1864.

NEWELL, RICHARD, Private
Born in Person County and resided as a carpenter in Guilford County where he enlisted at age 36, July 23, 1861, for the war. Present or accounted for until killed in action on August 22, 1864.

PAGE, S. B., Private
Born in Sampson County where he resided as a farmer prior to enlisting in Wake County at age 25, July 15, 1862, for the war. Present or accounted for until discharged on April 13, 1863, by reason of "valvular disease of the heart and chronic pluritis from which he was suffering before enlistment."

PARISH, DRURY, Private
Born in Guilford County where he resided as a farmer and enlisted at age 20, July 23, 1861, for the war. Captured near Fredericksburg, Virginia, May 3, 1863, and paroled and exchanged at City Point, Virginia, May 13, 1863. Present or accounted for until captured at Strasburg, Virginia, October 19, 1864. Confined at Point Lookout, Maryland, until released after taking the Oath of Allegiance on May 14, 1865.

PARISH, HENRY, Private
Enlisted in Virginia on April 1, 1864, for the war. Paroled at Greensboro on May 15, 1865.

PARKER, JOSEPH L., Private
Resided in Sampson County and enlisted in Wake County at age 29, July 15, 1862, for the war. Present or accounted for until he died in Sampson County of disease on April 23, 1863.

PATTERSON, ARCHIBALD, Private
Resided in Moore County and enlisted in Wake County at age 34, July 15, 1862, for the war. Admitted to hospital at Richmond, Virginia, October 26, 1862, and furloughed for 40 days on November 15, 1862. Reported as absent sick and as absent without leave on company muster rolls through August, 1864, when he was reported with the remark: "Died of disease, date not known."

PEGRAM, JOHN W., Private
Resided as a farmer in Guilford County where he enlisted at age 30, July 30, 1861, for the war. Admitted to hospital at Richmond, Virginia, June 10, 1864, with a gunshot wound and returned to duty on July 6, 1864. Present or accounted for until captured at Woodstock, Virginia, October 20, 1864. Confined at Point Lookout, Maryland, until released after taking the Oath of Allegiance on May 14, 1865.

PEGRAM, LINDSEY, Private
Resided in Guilford County where he enlisted at age 19, February 27, 1862, for the war. Died at Winchester, Virginia, October-November, 1862.

PEOPLES, ALBERT G., Private
Born in Guilford County where he resided as a farmer and enlisted at age 30, July 23, 1861, for the war. Wounded at Chancellorsville, Virginia, May 3, 1863. Returned to company on October 24, 1863. Admitted to hospital at Richmond, Virginia, in November, 1863, and died November 19, 1863, of "apoplexia."

PETERSON, FLEET, Private
Resided in Sampson County and enlisted in Wake County on July 15, 1862, for the war. Captured near Sharpsburg, Maryland, and paroled near Keedysville, Maryland, September 20, 1862. Admitted to hospital at Staunton, Virginia, in November, 1862, and died in hospital on November 29, 1862, of "febris typhoides."

PHIPPS, DANIEL W., Private
Born in Guilford County where he resided as a farmer and enlisted at age 30, August 26, 1861, for the war. Admitted to hospital at Richmond, Virginia, July 28, 1862, with "typhoid fever." Died in hospital on August 8, 1862.

PHIPPS, J., Private
Name reported on return for December, 1862, with the remark that he returned from missing in action on December 1.

PITCHFORD, JAMES L., Private
Resided in Guilford County and enlisted in Wake County at age 28, July 15, 1862, for the war. Present or accounted for until wounded at Cedar Creek, Virginia, October 19, 1864. Captured in hospital at Richmond, Virginia, April 3, 1865, and confined in Newport News, Virginia, until

released after taking the Oath of Allegiance on June 30, 1865.

PUGH, ALVIS, Private

Born in Orange County and resided as a farmer in Guilford County where he enlisted at age 22, July 22, 1861, for the war. Wounded at Gaines' Mill, Virginia, June 27, 1862, and discharged on June 30, 1862, by reason of "the loss of the last three fingers of his left hand."

RAYNOR, HINTON, Private

Born in Sampson County where he resided prior to enlisting in Wake County at age 19, July 15, 1862, for the war. Killed at Chancellorsville, Virginia, May 3, 1863.

RAYNOR, SAMUEL, Private

Resided in Sampson County and enlisted in Wake County at age 22, July 15, 1862, for the war. Died at Staunton, Virginia, October 23, 1862, of "febris typhoides."

REYNOLDS, JOHN E., Private

Born in Marion District, South Carolina, and resided as a gunsmith in Cumberland County prior to enlisting in Guilford County at age 25, August 14, 1861, for the war. Wounded at Sharpsburg, Maryland, September 17, 1862, and detailed at Fayetteville in October, 1862. Temporarily attached to Company A, 2nd Battalion N.C. Local Defense Troops while on detail at Fayetteville. Absent on detail through September, 1863, when he was returned to the company. Captured at Raccoon Ford, Virginia, January 7, 1864, and confined at Old Capitol Prison, Washington, D.C., until released after taking the Oath of Allegiance on March 22, 1864.

REYNOLDS, PETER, Private

Born in Guilford County where he resided as a farmer and enlisted at age 19, August 1, 1861, for the war. Wounded at Malvern Hill, Virginia, July 1, 1862. Present or accounted for on company muster rolls through October, 1864.

ROBERTSON, HENRY, Private

Born in Cabarrus County and resided as a farmer in Guilford County where he enlisted at age 24, August 23, 1861, for the war. Killed at Malvern Hill, Virginia, July 1, 1862.

ROYAL, ALBERT, Sergeant

Resided in Sampson County and enlisted in Wake County at age 23, July 15, 1862, for the war. Mustered in as Private. Captured at Sharpsburg, Maryland, September 17, 1862, and confined at Fort McHenry, Maryland, until sent to Fort Monroe, Virginia, October 17, 1862, for exchange. Exact date exchanged not reported; however, he was admitted to hospital at Richmond, Virginia, October 23, 1862, and returned to duty August 24, 1863. Present or accounted for on company muster rolls through October, 1864, as Private. Captured at Petersburg, Virginia, April 3, 1865, and confined at Hart's Island, New York Harbor, until released after taking the Oath of Allegiance on June 17, 1865. Rank given on prisoner of war records as Sergeant.

RYAN, ROBERT F., Corporal

Born in Guilford County where he resided as a

farmer and enlisted at age 23, July 23, 1861, for the war. Mustered in as Corporal. Present or accounted for until killed at Gaines' Mill, Virginia, June 27, 1862.

SAFRET, M. A., Private

Paroled at Greensboro on May 2, 1865.

SCOTT, WILLIAM T., Private

Born in Guilford County where he resided as a trimmer and enlisted at age 30, July 26, 1861, for the war. Present or accounted for until wounded at Winchester, Virginia, September 19, 1864. Captured at Farmville, Virginia, April 6, 1865, and confined at Point Lookout, Maryland, until released after taking the Oath of Allegiance on June 20, 1865.

SHEPHERD, WILSON, Private

Resided in Richmond County. Captured near Petersburg, Virginia, October 27, 1864, and confined at Point Lookout, Maryland, until released after taking the Oath of Allegiance on June 20, 1865.

SHEPPARD, WILLIAM E., Private

Born in Guilford County where he resided as a farmer and enlisted at age 20, July 11, 1861, for the war. Present or accounted for until he died in hospital at Richmond, Virginia, July 31, 1862, of "typhoid fever."

SILLS, JOHN, Private

Enlisted in Wake County on June 6, 1863, for the war. First reported on company muster roll for the period May 1-August 31, 1864. Muster rolls indicate that he was wounded July 18, 1864. Present or accounted for until paroled at Appomattox Court House, Virginia, April 9, 1865.

SILVY, ALBERT, Private

Born in Guilford County where he resided as a farmer and enlisted at age 21, June 29, 1861, for the war. Wounded at Sharpsburg, Maryland, September 17, 1862. Died at Guinea Station, Virginia, April 3, 1863, of "smallpox."

SIMMONS, AMAZIAH, Private

Resided in Columbus County and enlisted in Wake County at age 42, July 15, 1862, for the war. Present or accounted for until killed at Spotsylvania Court House, Virginia, May 8, 1864.

SIMMONS, ASHFORD, Private

Resided in Sampson County and enlisted in Wake County at age 28, July 15, 1862, for the war. Captured at Sharpsburg, Maryland, September 17, 1862, and confined at Fort Delaware, Delaware, until transferred to Aiken's Landing, Virginia, October 2, 1862, for exchange. Declared exchanged on November 10, 1862. Discharged on October 26, 1863, by reason of "tuberculosis." Captured in hospital at Richmond, Virginia, April 3, 1865, and confined at Newport News, Virginia, until released after taking the Oath of Allegiance on June 30, 1865.

SIMMONS, F. R., Private

Resided in Sampson County and enlisted on July 15, 1862, for the war. Died in hospital at Richmond, Virginia, on October 5, 1862, of "measles and diarrhoea."

SIMMONS, MILES, Private
Resided in Sampson County and enlisted on July 15, 1862, for the war. Died at Mount Jackson, Virginia, October 26, 1862.

SMITH, H. H., Private
Captured at Gettysburg, Pennsylvania, July 1-4, 1863, and confined at DeCamp General Hospital, Davids Island, New York Harbor, until paroled for exchange. Declared exchanged at City Point, Virginia, September 16, 1863.

SMITH, MARCELLUS, Sergeant
Born in Guilford County where he resided as a farmer and enlisted at age 19, July 24, 1861, for the war. Mustered in as Private and appointed Corporal in April, 1862. Promoted to Sergeant on August 25, 1862. Killed at Chancellorsville, Virginia, May 3, 1863.

SMITH, MILTON M., Private
Born in Guilford County where he resided as a farmer and enlisted at age 33, July 27, 1861, for the war. Present or accounted for until he died in camp on January 1, 1863.

SMITH, SPARKMAN, Private
Enlisted July 15, 1862, for the war. Died in hospital at Culpeper Court House, Virginia, September 29, 1862, of "febris typhoides."

SMITH, WILLIAM D., 1st Sergeant
Born in Guilford County where he resided as a farmer and enlisted at age 30, July 23, 1861, for the war. Mustered in as Sergeant and promoted to 1st Sergeant on August 9, 1862. Present or accounted for on company muster rolls until October, 1864, when he was reported as "absent wounded since September 4, 1864." Captured at Farmville, Virginia, April 6, 1865, and confined at Point Lookout, Maryland, until released after taking the Oath of Allegiance on June 20, 1865.

SOMERS, JOHN R., Private
Born in Guilford County where he resided as a farmer and enlisted at age 18, July 23, 1861, for the war. Present or accounted for until killed near Richmond, Virginia, June 21, 1862.

SOUTHARD, ANDERSON, Private
Born in Alamance County and resided as a farmer in Guilford County where he enlisted at age 25, July 26, 1861, for the war. Died in hospital at Richmond, Virginia, July 30, 1862, of "typhoid pneumonia."

SOUTHARD, DANIEL, Private
Born in White County, Tennessee, and resided as a farmer in Guilford County where he enlisted at age 19, July 31, 1861, for the war. Present or accounted for until he died in hospital at Richmond, Virginia, November 26, 1862, of "bronchitis acute."

SOUTHARD, EMSLEY, Private
Born in Alamance County and resided as a farmer in Guilford County where he enlisted at age 23, July 24, 1861, for the war. Died in camp near Richmond, Virginia, July 5, 1862, of "fever."

STACK, T., Private
Admitted to U.S. Army Field Hospital, Winchester, Virginia, September 19, 1864, with a gunshot wound of the thigh. Transferred on September 23, 1864.

STANLY, NATHAN H., Private
Born in Guilford County where he resided as a farmer and enlisted at age 19, July 22, 1861, for the war. Mustered in as Private. Wounded at Gaines' Mill, Virginia, June 27, 1862. Appointed Corporal, March-April, 1863. Deserted August 6, 1863, and returned from desertion October 28, 1864. Reduced to ranks by reason of desertion. Captured at Petersburg, Virginia, April 3, 1865, and confined at Hart's Island, New York Harbor, until released after taking the Oath of Allegiance on June 17, 1865.

STEEL, GEORGE CALVIN, Private
Born in Orange County and resided as a laborer in Guilford County where he enlisted at age 34, August 5, 1861, for the war. Present or accounted for until killed in action at Spotsylvania Court House, Virginia, May 8, 1864.

STEWART, C. J., Private
Resided in Sampson County and enlisted in Wake County at age 35, July 15, 1862, for the war. Company muster rolls report him as absent sick through October, 1863.

STEWART, DUNCAN J., Private
Enlisted in Wake County on July 15, 1862, for the war. First reported on company muster roll for January-February, 1864. Muster rolls cover through October, 1864, and report him as "absent without leave in Sampson County."

TATUM, JOHN HAWKINS, Private
Born in Guilford County where he resided as a farmer and enlisted at age 26, July 24, 1861, for the war. Wounded at Spotsylvania Court House, Virginia, May 12, 1864. Reported as absent wounded on company muster rolls through October, 1864. Retired to the Invalid Corps on December 23, 1864. Paroled at Greensboro on May 5, 1865.

TAYLOR, ANDREW, Private
Resided in Guilford County where he enlisted at age 21, February 22, 1862, for the war. Killed in action at Malvern Hill, Virginia, July 1, 1862.

TAYLOR, EDWARD, Corporal
Born in Guilford County where he resided as a farmer and enlisted at age 30, August 2, 1861, for the war. Mustered in as Corporal. Present or accounted for until he died in camp near Richmond, Virginia, July 24, 1862.

TAYLOR, S., Private
Admitted to hospital at Richmond, Virginia, February 26, 1863. Paroled at Goldsboro on May 8, 1865. "Came in for parole." Residence given on roll as Wilson County.

TAYLOR, THOMAS, Private
Born in Richmond, Virginia, and resided as a shoemaker in Guilford County where he enlisted at age 52, July 23, 1861, for the war. Died at Wilmington on June 27, 1862, of "typhoid fever."

TEW, HOLLY, Private
Resided in Sampson County and enlisted in Wake County at age 24, July 15, 1862, for the war. Captured and paroled at Leesburg, Virginia, October 2, 1862. Admitted to hospital at Richmond, Virginia, October 29, 1862, with "febris typhoides."

Transferred on December 19, 1862, to Danville, Virginia, where he died January 31, 1863, of "diarrhoea."

THOMAS, ROBERT, Private
Born in Guilford County where he resided as a farmer and enlisted at age 22, July 23, 1861, for the war. Present or accounted for until discharged on July 28, 1862, by reason of "a chronic diarrhoea which has reduced him to nearly a skeleton and he now has dropsy."

THOMPSON, JOHN, Private
Resided in Davie County where he enlisted at age 28, March 27, 1862, for the war. Wounded at Malvern Hill, Virginia, July 1, 1862. Present or accounted for on company muster rolls through October, 1864. Captured in hospital at Richmond, Virginia, April 3, 1865, and confined at Newport News, Virginia, until released after taking the Oath of Allegiance on June 30, 1865.

THOMPSON, WILLIAM A., Sergeant
Born in Guilford County where he resided as a farmer and enlisted at age 20, August 14, 1861, for the war. Mustered in as Private. Wounded at Ellerson's Mill, Virginia, June 26, 1862. Appointed Corporal on October 1, 1862. Wounded at Fredericksburg, Virginia, December 13, 1862, and leg amputated. Promoted to Sergeant, January-February, 1863. Died in hospital at Richmond, Virginia, June 1, 1863.

TURNER, DANIEL, Private
Born in Montgomery County and resided as a farmer in Guilford County where he enlisted at age 18, June 24, 1861, for the war. Wounded at Gettysburg, Pennsylvania, July. 1-3, 1863. Reported as absent wounded on company muster rolls through October, 1863, and as absent without leave from that date until September 15, 1864, when he returned to duty. Admitted to hospital at Richmond, Virginia, February 24, 1865. Captured on April 3, 1865, and confined at Newport News, Virginia, until released after taking the Oath of Allegiance on June 30, 1865.

USREY, SAMUEL W., Private
Born in Granville County where he resided as a farmer prior to enlisting in Wake County at age 24, July 15, 1862, for the war. Wounded and captured at Chancellorsville, Virginia, May 3, 1863. Confined in hospital at Washington, D.C., until transferred to Old Capitol Prison, Washington, May 27, 1863. Paroled on June 10, 1863, and sent to City Point, Virginia, for exchange. Declared exchanged on June 12, 1863. Reported as absent wounded until detailed in hospital at Richmond, Virginia, February 22, 1864. Company muster rolls report him as absent on detail through October, 1864.

WALKER, A., Private
Enlisted July 15, 1862, for the war. Reported on September-October, 1862, muster roll with the remark: "Dead." Place of enlistment not reported. Died at Culpeper Court House, Virginia, October 13, 1862, of "disease."

WALLS, BURGESS, Private
Born in Guilford County where he resided as a

farmer and enlisted at age 21, August 14, 1861, for the war. Deserted at Wilmington on June 15, 1862, and reported as a deserter on company muster rolls through October, 1864.

WARD, JOSHUA, Private
Resided in Columbus County where he enlisted at age 40, August 31, 1863, for the war. Wounded at Spotsylvania Court House, Virginia, May 12, 1864. Present or accounted for until paroled at **Lynchburg, Virginia, April 15, 1865.**

WARREN, JOHN THOMAS, Private
Resided in Sampson County and enlisted in Wake County at age 23, July 15, 1862, for the war. Wounded at Chancellorsville, Virginia, May 3, 1863. Present or accounted for until paroled at Appomattox Court House, Virginia, April 9, 1865.

WESTBROOKS, ALFRED, Private
Paroled at Greensboro on May 15, 1865.

WESTBROOKS, WARREN, Private
Resided in Sampson County and enlisted in Wake County at age 30, July 15, 1862, for the war. September-October, 1862, muster roll reports him as "absent on road." Federal Provost Marshal records indicate that he was paroled on September 26, 1862, but do not give place of capture or parole. Company muster rolls from January, 1863, through October, 1864, report that he was left sick at Leesburg, Virginia, in September, 1862, and was not heard from after that date.

WHITE, P., Private
Admitted to hospital at Richmond, Virginia, on May 9, 1863, with a gunshot wound and transferred on June 24, 1863.

WHITE, WILLIAM P., Private
Resided in Granville County and enlisted in Wake County at age 23, July 15, 1862, for the war. Admitted to hospital at Richmond, Virginia, October 29, 1862, with "chronic dysentery." Returned to duty on November 10, 1862. Company muster rolls carry him as absent without leave from January-February, 1863, until January-February, 1864, when he appears with the remark: "Dropped by order. First substitute January, 1863. **His name continued on rolls til this date.**"

WHITT, DAVID, Private
Born in Granville County where he resided as a farmer and enlisted at age 23, August 20, 1861, for the war. Present or accounted for until he "died of wounds May 21, 1864."

WHITT, NEWTON, Private
Enlisted in Wake County on May 17, 1864, for the war. Wounded July 18, 1864, and reported as absent wounded on company muster rolls through October, 1864. Paroled at Greensboro on May 9, 1865.

WHITTINGTON, CALVIN, Private
Born in Guilford County where he resided as a farmer prior to enlisting in Wake County at age 22, September 19, 1861, for the war. Present or accounted for until transferred to the C.S. Navy in January, 1862.

WILKERSON, CHARLES G., Private
Resided in Edgecombe County. Captured at Ame-

lia Court House, Virginia, April 3, 1865, and confined at Point Lookout, Maryland, until released after taking the Oath of Allegiance on June 22, 1865.

WILLIAMS, JACOB, Private
Resided in Sampson County and enlisted in Wake County at age 26, July 15, 1862, for the war. Captured at Sharpsburg, Maryland, September 17, 1862, and confined at Fort Delaware, Delaware, until paroled and exchanged at Aiken's Landing, Virginia, November 10, 1862. Captured near Fredericksburg, Virginia, May 3, 1863, and paroled and exchanged at City Point, Virginia, May 13, 1863. Present or accounted for on company muster rolls through October, 1864. Captured in hospital at Richmond, Virginia, April 3, 1865, and confined at Newport News, Virginia, until released after taking the Oath of Allegiance on June 30, 1865.

WILLIAMS, ROBERT, Private
Resided in Sampson County and enlisted in Wake County at age 28, July 15, 1862, for the war. Wounded at Chancellorsville, Virginia, May 3, 1863, and reported as absent wounded through December, 1863. Present or accounted for until he "died of wounds May 15, 1864."

WILSON, DANIEL J., Private
Resided in Sampson County and enlisted in Wake County at age 24, July 15, 1862, for the war. Wounded at Chancellorsville, Virginia, May 3, 1863. Reported as absent sick on company muster rolls through October, 1864.

WILSON, HENRY, Private
Resided in Mississippi and enlisted at Camp Price at age 17, March 24, 1862, for the war. Discharged October 7-8, 1862, by reason of age.

WOOD, MILTON, Private
Born in Guilford County where he resided as a gunsmith and enlisted at age 26, August 12, 1861, for the war. Detailed as gunsmith in Guilford County on March 15, 1862, and reported as absent on detail through April 1, 1864. Present or accounted for until captured at Strasburg, Virginia, September 23, 1864. Confined at Point Lookout, Maryland, until released after taking the Oath of Allegiance on May 12-14, 1865.

WORK, HENRY A., Private
Born in Wilson County and resided as a farmer in Guilford County where he enlisted at age 24, August 5, 1861, for the war. Wounded at Chancellorsville, Virginia, May 3, 1863, and detailed in Quartermaster Department at Charlotte, November-December, 1863. Absent on detail through October, 1864. Federal Provost Marshal records report him as a deserter from the enemy received February 23, 1865, at Washington, D.C. Took the **Oath of Allegiance and was provided transportation to Oil City, Pennsylvania, February 27, 1865.**

WRENCH, JOHN, Private
Resided in Sampson County and enlisted in Wake County at age 28, July 15, 1862, for the war. Captured and paroled in Maryland on September 23, 1862. Present or accounted for on company muster rolls until wounded and captured at Win-

chester, Virginia, September 19, 1864. Confined in hospital at Baltimore, Maryland, until transferred to Point Lookout, Maryland, January 1-2, 1865. Released at Point Lookout after taking the Oath of Allegiance on June 26, 1865.

WRIGHT, B. F., Private
Enlisted in Wake County on May 17, 1864, for the war. Wounded July 18, 1864, and reported as absent wounded on company muster rolls through October, 1864.

WRIGHT, RICHARD, Private
Born in Columbus County where he resided as a farmer and enlisted at age 40, August 31, 1863, for the war. Discharged on November 10, 1863, by reason of "dyspepsia, enlargement of the kidneys and nervous irritability following a severe attack of typhoid fever."

YARBOROUGH, A. C., Private
Resided as a farmer prior to enlisting in Wake County at age 23, August 15, 1862, for the war. Died in hospital at Richmond, Virginia, April 1, 1863, of "variola dist."

COMPANY F

This company was organized in Craven County and enlisted at New Bern on May 27, 1861. It tendered its service to the state and was ordered to Camp Advance, near Garysburg, Northampton County, where it was assigned to this regiment as Company F. After joining the regiment the company functioned as a part of the regiment, and its history for the war period is recorded as a part of the regimental history.

The information contained in the following roster of the company was compiled principally from company muster rolls for July 16, 1861, through December, 1861; March through October, 1862; January through April, 1863; July through December, 1863; March, 1864; and May through October, 1864. No company muster rolls were found for the period prior to July 16, 1861; for January-February, 1862; November-December, 1862; May-June, 1863; January-February, 1864; April, 1864; or for the period after October, 1864. In addition to the company muster rolls, Roll of Honor records, receipt rolls, and hospital records, supplemented by state pension applications, United Daughters of the Confederacy records, and postwar rosters and histories, all provided useful information.

OFFICERS
CAPTAINS
COLE, HUGH L.
Resided in Craven County and appointed Captain at age 23 to rank from May 16, 1861. Present or accounted for until he resigned on October 21, 1862. Later appointed Major of this regiment to rank from April 9, 1863, but did not accept the appointment. However, he was appointed Captain and Enrolling Officer of the 1st Congressional District and later served as Captain of Company D, McRae's Battalion N.C. Cavalry.

CHADWICK, NATHANIEL MACON
Resided in Craven County and appointed 1st

Lieutenant at age 21 to rank from May 16, 1861. Promoted to Captain to rank from October 21, 1862. Captured at Chancellorsville, Virginia, May 3, 1863, and confined at Old Capitol Prison, Washington, D.C., until paroled on May 18, 1863. Exact date of exchange not reported; however, he appears as present on July-August, 1863, muster roll. Present or accounted for on company muster rolls until captured at Winchester, Virginia, September 19, 1864. Confined at Fort Delaware, Delaware, until released after taking the Oath of Allegiance on June 17, 1865.

LIEUTENANTS

BREWER, WILLIAM CHRISTOPHER, 1st Lieutenant

Resided in Craven County where he enlisted at age 18, May 27, 1861, for the war. Mustered in as Private and appointed Corporal on November 26, 1861. Appointed 2nd Lieutenant to rank from February 10, 1863. Wounded at Chancellorsville, Virginia, May 3, 1863. Promoted to 1st Lieutenant on October 25, 1863, to rank from July 31, 1863. Present or accounted for until captured at Woodstock, Virginia, October 20, 1864. Confined at Fort Delaware, Delaware, until released after taking the Oath of Allegiance on June 17, 1865.

CLARK, HENRY J. B., Jr., 2nd Lieutenant

Resided in Craven County and appointed 2nd Lieutenant at age 19 to rank from May 16, 1861. Present or accounted for until killed in a railroad accident on the Raleigh and Gaston Railroad near Forestville, N.C., October 28, 1862.

HERITAGE, FURNIFOLD G., 1st Lieutenant

Resided in Craven County where he enlisted at age 20, May 27, 1861, for the war. Mustered in as Corporal and appointed Sergeant, January-April, 1862. Appointed 1st Lieutenant to rank from February 10, 1863. Captured at Chancellorsville, Virginia, May 3, 1863, and confined at Old Capitol Prison, Washington, D.C., until paroled on May 18, 1863. Killed at Gettysburg, Pennsylvania, July 1, 1863.

WETHERINGTON, RODERICK S., 1st Lieutenant

Resided in Craven County and appointed 2nd Lieutenant at age 21 to rank from May 16, 1861. Wounded and captured at Sharpsburg, Maryland, September 17, 1862, and paroled. Died of wound September 20, 1862. Promoted to 1st Lieutenant on October 21, 1862, after his death.

NONCOMMISSIONED OFFICERS AND PRIVATES

ABBOTT, WILLIAM, Private

Resided in McDowell County and enlisted at Camp Vance on October 4, 1863, for the war. Assigned to this company on May 1, 1864. Present or accounted for until wounded at Cedar Creek, Virginia, October 19, 1864. Captured in hospital at Petersburg, Virginia, April 3, 1865, and confined at Hart's Island, New York Harbor, until released after taking the Oath of Allegiance on June 18, 1865.

ACLIN, THOMAS, Private

Resided in Craven County where he enlisted at age 21, May 27, 1861, for the war. Discharged on August 14, 1861.

ADAMS, JAMES A., Private

Resided in Craven County where he enlisted at age 21, May 27, 1861, for the war. Transferred to the C.S. Navy in December, 1861.

ADCOCK, WYATT, Private

Resided in Anson County and enlisted in Wake County at age 34, August 15, 1862, for the war. Killed at Sharpsburg, Maryland, September 17, 1862.

ARNOLD, ALLEN J., Private

Resided in Craven County where he enlisted at age 19, May 27, 1861, for the war. Killed at Chancellorsville, Virginia, May 3, 1863.

ARTHUR, JESSE, Sergeant

Resided in Craven County where he enlisted at age 29, May 27, 1861, for the war. Mustered in as Private and appointed Sergeant on March 1, 1863. Wounded at Chancellorsville, Virginia, May 3, 1863. Present or accounted for on company muster rolls through October, 1864, being absent sick from November 7, 1863, through October, 1864. Paroled at Lynchburg, Virginia, in April, 1865.

ASKINS, JAMES A., Private

Resided in Craven County where he enlisted at age 26, May 24, 1861, for the war. Reported as absent sick at home from June 19, 1861, through April, 1862, and as absent without leave from April, 1862, through April, 1863.

AVERITT, JAMES, Private

Resided in Craven County where he enlisted at age 40, May 27, 1861, for the war. Present or accounted for until he died in hospital at Goldsboro on April 3, 1862, of disease.

AVERITT, WILLIAM J., Private

Resided in Craven County where he enlisted at age 21, May 27, 1861, for the war. Present or accounted for until he died in camp near Garysburg, July 21, 1861, of disease.

BARRINGTON, NATHAN, Private

Resided in Craven County where he enlisted at age 29, May 27, 1861, for the war. Mortally wounded at Hagerstown, Maryland, July 13, 1863.

BENNETT, PRESLEY, Private

Resided in Anson County and enlisted in Wake County at age 22, August 15, 1862, for the war. Wounded at South Mountain, Maryland, September 14-15, 1862. Wounded at Chancellorsville, Virginia, May 3, 1863. Reported as absent wounded on company muster rolls through April 1, 1864. Captured at Strasburg, Virginia, October 19, 1864, and confined at Point Lookout, Maryland, until released after taking the Oath of Allegiance on June 4, 1865.

BEXLEY, SAMUEL, Private

Resided in Craven County where he enlisted at age 39, June 29, 1861, for the war. Present or accounted for until he died in hospital at Lynchburg, Virginia, on December 12, 1862, of "diarrhoea chronic."

BLOUNT, MILES, Corporal
Resided in Craven County where he enlisted at age 22, May 27, 1861, for the war. Mustered in as Corporal. Wounded at Fredericksburg, Virginia, December 13, 1862. Present or accounted for until transferred to the C.S. Navy on September 3, 1863.

BOWERS, W. H., Private
Resided in Northampton County and enlisted in Wake County at age 33, August 15, 1862, for the war. Killed at Sharpsburg, Maryland, September 17, 1862.

BRINKLEY, JAMES, Private
Resided in Craven County where he enlisted at age 21, May 27, 1861, for the war. Wounded at Malvern Hill, Virginia, July 1, 1862. Present or accounted for until paroled at Appomattox Court House, Virginia, April 9, 1865.

BRINKLEY, REDDING, Private
Resided in Craven County where he enlisted at age 19, May 27, 1861, for the war. Wounded at Malvern Hill, Virginia, July 1, 1862, and detailed for duty as a cooper in Medical Purveyor's Office, Charlotte, October 30, 1863. Reported as absent on detail through October, 1864. Paroled at Charlotte on May 3, 1865.

BRYAN, DAVID, Private
Resided in Sampson County and enlisted in Wake County at age 30, August 15, 1862, for the war. Captured at South Mountain, Maryland, September 14, 1862, and confined at Fort Delaware, Delaware, until paroled and exchanged at Aiken's Landing, Virginia, November 10, 1862. Admitted to hospital at Richmond, Virginia, after exchanged and furloughed for 60 days on March 24, 1863. Failed to return from furlough and reported as absent without leave on company muster rolls through October, 1864.

BUTLER, WILLIAM BRICE, Private
Resided in Craven County where he enlisted at age 40, May 27, 1861, for the war. Killed at Chancellorsville, Virginia, May 3, 1863.

CARROLL, WILLIAM R., Private
Resided in Sampson County and enlisted in Wake County at age 19, August 15, 1862, for the war. Wounded at South Mountain, Maryland, September 14, 1862. Present or accounted for on company muster rolls until captured at Kelly's Ford, Virginia, November 7, 1863. Confined at Point Lookout, Maryland, until released after taking the Oath of Allegiance on June 26, 1865.

CARTER, JOHN W., Private
Resided in Sampson County and enlisted in Wake County at age 33, August 15, 1862, for the war. Admitted to hospital at Charlottesville, Virginia, February 10, 1863, with "dysenteria acute." Furloughed for 30 days on March 5, 1863, and died in Sampson County on March 30, 1863.

CHAMPION, WILLIAM, Private
First reported on May 1-August 31, 1864, muster roll with the remark that he enlisted at Raleigh, but date of enlistment not reported. September-October, 1864, muster roll carries the notation: "Cancelled." Federal Provost Marshal records indicate that he was captured at Petersburg, Vir-

ginia, April 3, 1865, and confined at Hart's Island, New York Harbor, where he died on June 17, 1865, of "phthisis."

CHAMPION, WILLIAM G., Private
Enlisted in Wake County on April 15, 1864, for the war. September-October, 1864, muster roll carries the remark: "Cancelled."

CHILDERS, NOAH A., Private
Enlisted in Wake County on May 9, 1864, for the war. Present or accounted for until wounded and captured at Strasburg, Virginia, October 19, 1864. Confined at Point Lookout, Maryland, until transferred for exchange to Venus Point, Savannah River, Georgia, October 29, 1864. Declared exchanged at Venus Point on November 15, 1864.

CHILDRESS, WILLIAM F., Private
Enlisted in Wake County on May 9, 1864, for the war. Admitted to hospital at Charlottesville, Virginia, September 26, 1864, with "debilitas" and furloughed for 30 days on October 5, 1864.

CHRISTOPHER, D., Private
Enlisted in Wake County on May 9, 1864, for the war. September-October, 1864, muster roll carries the remark: "Cancelled."

CLARK, J. S., Private
Resided in Anson County and enlisted in Wake County at age 29, August 15, 1862, for the war. Killed at Fredericksburg, Virginia, December 13, 1862.

COLLIGUE, WILLIAM J., Private
Captured at Petersburg, Virginia, April 3, 1865, and confined at Hart's Island, New York Harbor, until released after taking the Oath of Allegiance on June 19, 1865.

COUCH, J. W. A., Private
Captured at Gettysburg, Pennsylvania, July 5, 1863, and confined at DeCamp General Hospital, Davids Island, New York Harbor, until paroled and exchanged at City Point, Virginia, September 16, 1863.

COWARD, WILLIAM W., Private
Resided in Craven County where he enlisted at age 23, May 27, 1861, for the war. May 1-August 31, 1864, muster roll carries him with the remark: "Died of wounds received at Wilderness, Virginia."

COX, P. H., Private
Paroled at Greensboro on May 18, 1865.

DAUGHERTY, RICHARD J., Private
Resided in Craven County where he enlisted at age 26, May 27, 1861, for the war. Wounded at Malvern Hill, Virginia, July 1, 1862. Died in hospital at Mount Jackson, Virginia, November 21, 1862, of "febris typhoides."

DAVIS, JAMES S., Private
Enlisted in Craven County on May 29, 1861, for the war. Discharged at Camp Advance, Northampton County, July 9, 1861, by reason of "physical disability." Later reenlisted at Raleigh on April 15, 1864, for the war. Wounded at Cedar Creek, Virginia, October 19, 1864. Present or accounted for on company muster rolls through October, 1864.

DAVIS, JOSEPH L., Private
Resided in Craven County and enlisted at age 24,

May 27, 1861, for the war. "Discharged June, 1861, at Camp Advance, Virginia."

DAWSON, ROBERT, Private
Resided in Sampson County and enlisted in Wake County at age 27, August 15, 1862, for the war. Captured and paroled at Leesburg, Virginia, October 2, 1862. Wounded at Chancellorsville, Virginia, May 3, 1863, and died of wounds at Richmond, Virginia, July 23, 1863.

DEAL, JOSEPH W., Private
Enlisted in Craven County on May 27, 1861, for the war. Present or accounted for on company muster rolls through December, 1861.

DEAL, LEVI W., Private
Born in Edgecombe County and resided in Craven County where he enlisted at age 18, June 29, 1861, for the war. Present or accounted for until killed at Chancellorsville, Virginia, May 3, 1863.

DICKSON, PHILIP, Corporal
Resided in Craven County where he enlisted at age 23, May 27, 1861, for the war. Mustered in as Corporal. Died at Camp Holmes, Virginia, August 8, 1861, of disease.

DONALD, JOHN, Private
Resided in Craven County where he enlisted at age 30, May 27, 1861, for the war. Wounded and captured at Sharpsburg, Maryland, September 17, 1862, and paroled prior to September 30, 1862, when he was paid at Richmond, Virginia. Reported as absent without leave on company muster rolls after January-February, 1863.

DOWNER, FRANCIS M., Private
Resided in Anson County and enlisted in Wake County at age 22, August 15, 1862, for the war. Wounded at Chancellorsville, Virginia, May 3, 1863, and died in hospital at Richmond, Virginia, on July 23, 1863, of wound.

DREW, JOHN, Sergeant
Resided in Halifax County and enlisted in Craven County at age 28, May 27, 1861, for the war. Mustered in as Private and appointed Sergeant on March 1, 1863. Wounded at Spotsylvania Court House, Virginia, May 19, 1864. September-October, 1864, muster roll reports him as "absent prisoner, May 18, 1864."

EAST, BENJAMIN FRANKLIN, Private
Enlisted October 1, 1864, for the war.

ECKLING, THOMAS, Private
Enlisted in Craven County on May 27, 1861, for the war. Discharged on August 14, 1861, by reason of disability.

EDWARDS, I. E., Private
Paroled at Greensboro on May 13, 1865.

EDWARDS, J. R., Private
Resided in Anson County and enlisted in Wake County at age 20, August 15, 1862, for the war. Missing in action at Sharpsburg, Maryland, September 17, 1862, and later reported as dead.

EVANS, TYSON, Private
Enlisted in Wake County on May 9, 1864, for the war. Captured at Winchester, Virginia, September 19, 1864, and confined at Point Lookout, Maryland, until paroled and transferred to Aiken's

Landing, Virginia, March 15, 1865, for exchange. Declared exchanged on March 18, 1865. Admitted to hospital at Richmond, Virginia, March 19, 1865, with "diarrhoea chronic" and furloughed for 30 days on March 23, 1865.

EVANS, WILLIAM, Private
Enlisted in Wake County on May 9, 1864, for the war. Present or accounted for on company muster rolls through October, 1864. Admitted to hospital on March 21, 1865, at Petersburg, Virginia, where he was captured April 3, 1865. Died in hospital at Danville, Virginia. Hospital records give two dates of death: April 17, 1865, "from the effects of a burn," and April 22, 1865, of "ambustio from explosion."

FAIRCLOTH, EVLIN, Private
Resided in Sampson County and enlisted in Wake County at age 26, August 15, 1862, for the war. Missing in action at Sharpsburg, Maryland, September 17, 1862, and later reported as dead.

FAIRCLOTH, IRVIN, Private
Resided in Sampson County and enlisted in Wake County at age 35, August 15, 1862, for the war. Died in hospital at Mount Jackson, Virginia, November 5, 1862, of "erysipelas."

FILLINGIN, BOCHERIAS, Private
Resided in Craven County where he enlisted at age 24, June 3, 1861, for the war. Discharged at Camp Advance, Northampton County, July 9, 1861, by reason of "physical disability."

FLAKE, ROBERT J., Private
Resided in Anson County and enlisted in Wake County at age 28, August 15, 1862, for the war. Captured and paroled near Keedysville, Maryland, September 20, 1862. Present or accounted for on company muster rolls through October, 1864, being detailed as Provost Guard from January through October, 1864. Paroled at Appomattox Court House, Virginia, April 9, 1865.

FLIBERS, THOMAS B., Private
Resided in Craven County where he enlisted at age 21, May 27, 1861, for the war. Killed at Chancellorsville, Virginia, May 3, 1863.

FONTAINE, J. R., Private
Captured in hospital at Petersburg, Virginia, April 3, 1865. Hospital records indicate that he was suffering from a gunshot wound of the shoulder. Last reported on a hospital roll for Fair Ground Post Hospital, Petersburg, May 25, 1865.

FULCHER, SILAS, Corporal
Resided in Craven County where he enlisted at age 20, May 27, 1861, for the war. Mustered in as Private and appointed Corporal on March 1, 1863. Wounded at Spotsylvania Court House, Virginia, May 19, 1864. Present or accounted for on company muster rolls through October, 1864, being reported as absent wounded after May 19, 1864.

GADDY, JOHN, Private
Born in Anson County where he resided as a farmer prior to enlisting in Wake County at age 24, August 15, 1862, for the war. Discharged at Lynchburg, Virginia, July 11, 1863, by reason

of "phthisis pulmonalis, cavity in apex of right lung."

GANEY, HIRAM, Private
Born in Sampson County where he resided prior to enlisting in Wake County at age 19, August 15, 1862, for the war. Killed at Chancellorsville, Virginia, May 3, 1863.

GILLESPIE, DANIEL D., Private
Paroled at Greensboro in April, 1865.

GLOVER, WILLIAM, Private
Born in Craven County where he resided as a farmer and enlisted at age 23, May 30, 1861, for the war. Discharged at Camp Wyatt, near Wilmington, June 1, 1862, by reason of "incipient phthisis pulmonalis, with an hereditary predisposition and excited by three attacks of acute pneumonia within the past six months."

GREGORY, JAMES, Private
Resided in Bertie County and enlisted in Wake County at age 23, August 15, 1862, for the war. Reported as absent without leave from September 10, 1862, through October, 1864.

GRIFFIN, LEVI, Private
Resided in Craven County where he enlisted at age 18, May 27, 1861, for the war. Died at Fredericksburg, Virginia, in August, 1861, of disease.

GULLEDGE, WILLIAM JACKSON, Private
Resided in Anson County and enlisted in Wake County at age 32, August 15, 1862, for the war. Present or accounted for on company muster rolls through October, 1864. Took the Oath of Allegiance at Hart's Island, New York Harbor, on June 19, 1865. Date and place he was captured not reported.

HANEL, WILLIAM W., Private
Captured at Kelly's Ford, Virginia, November 7, 1863, and confined at Point Lookout, Maryland, until released after taking the Oath of Allegiance on June 26, 1865.

HARDISON, ELIJAH H., Private
Born in Craven County where he resided and enlisted at age 23, May 27, 1861, for the war. Killed at Sharpsburg, Maryland, September 17, 1862.

HARDISON, ISHAM, Private
Enlisted in Craven County on August 11, 1861, for the war. Died at Goldsboro on May 10, 1862.

HARRELL, J. P., Private
Resided in Bertie County and enlisted in Wake County at age 25, August 15, 1862, for the war. Reported as absent without leave on company muster rolls from September 10, 1862, through October, 1864.

HAWKINS, FURNEY, Private
Born in Craven County where he enlisted on May 27, 1861, for the war. Died at Goldsboro on April 10, 1862.

HAWKINS, GILES, Private
Resided in Craven County where he enlisted at age 26, May 27, 1861, for the war. Wounded and captured at South Mountain, Maryland, September 14, 1862. Confined at Fort McHenry, Maryland, until paroled and sent to Fort Monroe, Virginia, October 13, 1862, for exchange. Exact date

of exchange not reported. Admitted to hospital at Richmond, Virginia, October 24, 1862. Furloughed for 35 days on November 10, 1862. Reported as absent without leave after January, 1863.

HAWKINS, HENRY T., Private
Resided in Craven County where he enlisted at age 24, May 27, 1861, for the war. Wounded at Cold Harbor, Virginia, June 27, 1862. Wounded in the left wrist and left thigh at Chancellorsville, Virginia, May 3, 1863, and reported as absent wounded until detailed in hospital at Goldsboro in September, 1864. Temporarily assigned to duty with the Enrolling Officer for Lenoir County prior to February, 1865. Captured on the Southside Railroad, Virginia, April 6, 1865, and confined at Newport News, Virginia, until released after taking the Oath of Allegiance on June 30, 1865.

HEATH, RICHARD T., Private
Resided in Craven County where he enlisted at age 25, May 27, 1861, for the war. Present or accounted for until captured at Kelly's Ford, Virginia, November 7, 1863. Confined at Point Lookout, Maryland, where he died April 24, 1865, of "chronic dysentery."

HEFFNER, M. H., Private
Enlisted in Wake County on May 9, 1864, for the war. September-October, 1864, muster roll reports him with the remark: "Cancelled." Paroled at Newton, N. C., April 19, 1865.

HERITAGE, WILLIAM M., Sergeant
Resided in Craven County where he enlisted at age 22, May 27, 1861, for the war. Mustered in as Sergeant. Discharged in October, 1861.

HILL, W. A., Private
Wounded and captured at Winchester, Virginia, September 19, 1864. Federal Provost Marshal records indicate that he was transferred to another hospital on October 22, 1864.

HOLDER, H. H., Private
Resided in Anson County and enlisted in Wake County at age 33, August 15, 1862, for the war. Detailed as a blacksmith at Richmond, Virginia, December 21, 1863, and reported as absent detailed through October, 1864. Captured in hospital at Richmond, April 3, 1865, and paroled on April 18, 1865.

HOLLY, ROLAND, Private
Resided in Sampson County and enlisted in Wake County at age 34, August 15, 1862, for the war. Died at Staunton, Virginia, December 20, 1862, of disease.

HUDSON, MILES W., Private
Resided in Cumberland County and enlisted in Wake County at age 17, August 15, 1862, for the war. Died in hospital at Staunton, Virginia, June 4, 1863, of "phthisis pulmonalis."

HUDSON, PHAROAH, Private
Resided in Sampson County and enlisted in Wake County at age 23, August 15, 1862, for the war. Captured at South Mountain, Maryland, September 14, 1862, and confined at Fort Delaware, Delaware, until paroled and exchanged at Aiken's Landing, Virginia, November 10, 1862. Present or accounted for on company muster rolls through

October, 1864, being "absent wounded at Sinker's Ford, Virginia, August 18, 1864." Captured at Petersburg, Virginia, April 3, 1865, and confined at Hart's Island, New York Harbor, until released after taking the Oath of Allegiance on June 18, 1865.

HUMPHREY, JESSE, Private
Resided in Craven County where he enlisted at age 23, May 27, 1861, for the war. Died in hospital at Fredericksburg, Virginia, August 28, 1861, of disease.

HUMPHREY, WILLIAM J., Private
Enlisted in Craven County on May 27, 1861, for the war. May 1-October 31, 1862, muster roll states that he "died on march from Richmond to Culpeper."

INGRAHAM, _____, Private
Resided in Anson County and enlisted at age 23, August 15, 1862, for the war. Discharged on date of enlistment by providing William Newton as his substitute.

JACKSON, ABRAM, Private
Resided in Craven County where he enlisted at age 23, June 4, 1861, for the war. Discharged at Fredericksburg, Virginia, September-October, 1861.

JACKSON, BENNETT, Private
Resided in Sampson County and enlisted in Wake County at age 32, August 15, 1862, for the war. Killed at Chancellorsville, Virginia, May 3, 1863.

JACKSON, CHURCHILL, Private
Resided in Craven County where he enlisted at age 22, May 30, 1861, for the war. Died in hospital at Fredericksburg, Virginia, September-October, 1861.

JACKSON, L. S., Private
Enlisted in Wake County on August 15, 1862, for the war. Missing in action at Chancellorsville, Virginia, May 3, 1863.

JACOBSON, WILLIAM, Private
Born in Craven County where he resided and enlisted at age 21, May 27, 1861, for the war. Killed at Chancellorsville, Virginia, May 3, 1863.

JANS, D. W., Private
Paroled at Greensboro on May 16, 1865.

JOHNSON, DAVID, Musician
Resided in Craven County where he enlisted at age 16, May 27, 1861, for the war. Mustered in as Musician. Present or accounted for until paroled at Appomattox Court House, Virginia, April 9, 1865.

JOHNSON, GEORGE, Private
Resided in Duplin County and enlisted in Wake County at age 30, August 15, 1862, for the war. Present or accounted for until detailed on guard duty in hospital at Lynchburg, Virginia, March 27, 1864. Died in hospital at Lynchburg on December 6, 1864, of "pneumonia."

JOHNSON, STEPHEN, Private
Resided in Craven County where he enlisted at age 18, May 27, 1861, for the war. Wounded at Sharpsburg, Maryland, September 17, 1862, and reported as absent wounded through December, 1863.

JONES, N. G., Private
Born in Anson County where he resided as a farmer prior to enlisting in Wake County at age 19, August 15, 1862, for the war. Discharged at Richmond, Virginia, October 24, 1862, by reason of "deafness."

KORNEGAY, JOHN, Sergeant
Resided in Craven County where he enlisted at age 19, May 27, 1861, for the war. Mustered in as Private and appointed Sergeant on March 1, 1862. Present or accounted for until captured near Fredericksburg, Virginia, May 3, 1863. Confined at Washington, D.C., until paroled and exchanged at City Point, Virginia, May 10, 1863. Present or accounted for until captured at Kelly's Ford, Virginia, November 7, 1863. Confined at Point Lookout, Maryland, until paroled and transferred for exchange to Aiken's Landing, Virginia, February 24, 1865. Exact date of exchange not reported.

LANCASTER, STEPHEN, Private
Resided in Craven County where he enlisted at age 25, May 27, 1861, for the war. Mustered in as Private and appointed Corporal on August 31, 1861. Promoted to Sergeant on November 26, 1861. Reduced to ranks March-April, 1863. Wounded at Spotsylvania Court House, Virginia, May 12, 1864, and reported as absent wounded on company muster rolls through October, 1864.

LANE, DANIEL, 1st Sergeant
Resided in Craven County where he enlisted at age 21, May 27, 1861, for the war. Mustered in as Sergeant and promoted to 1st Sergeant on March 1, 1863. Present or accounted for on company muster rolls through October, 1864, when he was reported as "absent wounded furlough." Paroled at Appomattox Court House, Virginia, April 9, 1865.

LAUGHINGHOUSE, THOMAS, Private
Resided in Craven County where he enlisted at age 23, May 27, 1861, for the war. Captured at Sharpsburg, Maryland, September 17, 1862, and paroled near Keedysville, Maryland, September 20, 1862. Present or accounted for on company muster rolls through October, 1864.

LEE, WILLIAM, Private
Resided in Sampson County and enlisted in Wake County at age 34, August 15, 1862, for the war. Died of disease in Sampson County on January 15, 1863.

LEWIS, J. D., Private
Resided in Anson County and enlisted in Wake County at age 18, August 15, 1862, for the war. Killed at Chancellorsville, Virginia, May 3, 1863.

LONG, JAMES M., Private
Resided in Anson County and enlisted in Wake County at age 24, August 15, 1862, for the war. Detailed as Provost Guard at Lynchburg, Virginia, January 15, 1863. Reported as absent on detail at Lynchburg until detailed at Danville, Virginia, in July, 1864. Reported as absent on detail on company muster rolls through October, 1864. Admitted to hospital at Richmond, Virginia, February 27, 1865, with "varicose veins." Captured in hospital at Richmond on April 3, 1865.

LUTHER, CALVIN, Private
Resided in Sampson County and enlisted in Wake County at age 30, August 15, 1862, for the war. Company muster rolls report him as absent without leave from September 10, 1862, through October, 1864.

McCAFFETY, SOUTHEY, Private
Born in Craven County where he resided as a farmer and enlisted at age 30, May 27, 1861, for the war. Wounded at South Mountain, Maryland, September 14-15, 1862. Discharged at Richmond, Virginia, October 21, 1863, by reason of "wound received at South Mountain in his right forearm by which the ulna was fractured. The wound has healed but the fracture has not united."

McCAIN, GEORGE W., Private
Enlisted in Wake County on June 6, 1864, for the war. Wounded in the right lung and right leg and captured at Winchester, Virginia, September 19, 1864. Confined in hospitals until paroled for exchange at Fort McHenry, Maryland, February 10, 1865. Admitted to hospital at Richmond, Virginia, March 4, 1865, and furloughed for 60 days on March 9, 1865. Admitted to hospital at Charlotte on April 10, 1865, and furloughed on April 14, 1865.

McCOY, JOHN E., Private
Resided in Craven County where he enlisted at age 20, May 27, 1861, for the war. Captured and paroled at Leesburg, Virginia, October 2, 1862. Killed in skirmish near Warrenton, Virginia, October 14, 1863.

McCURRY, J., Private
Captured at Strasburg, Virginia, October 19, 1864, and confined at Point Lookout, Maryland, until paroled and transferred for exchange to James River, Virginia, February 10, 1865. Received in exchange at Cox's Landing, James River, February 14-15, 1865.

McGUGAN, E. F., Private
Resided in Anson County and enlisted in Wake County at age 18, August 15, 1862, for the war. Died at Richmond, Virginia, January 26, 1863, of "pneumonia."

MARLEY, W. H., Private
Resided in Sampson County and enlisted in Wake County at age 34, August 15, 1862, for the war. Present or accounted for until detailed for hospital duty at Richmond, Virginia, September 13, 1863. Reported as absent on detail through April, 1864. Captured at Harrisonburg, Virginia, September 23-25, 1864, and confined at Point Lookout, Maryland. Paroled at Point Lookout and transferred for exchange to Aiken's Landing, Virginia, March 17, 1865. Declared exchanged on March 19, 1865.

MAY, BENJAMIN F., Sergeant
Born in Pitt County and resided in Craven County where he enlisted at age 23, May 27, 1861, for the war. Mustered in as Private and appointed Sergeant on November 26, 1861. Present or accounted for until killed at Chancellorsville, Virginia, May 3, 1863.

MAY, JOHN D., 1st Sergeant
Resided in Craven County where he enlisted at age 32, May 27, 1861, for the war. Mustered in as 1st Sergeant. Company muster rolls carry him as present through December, 1861. Roll of Honor states that he was "discharged by substitute."

MAY, JOSEPH E., Corporal
Enlisted in Craven County on November 9, 1861, for the war. Mustered in as Private and appointed Corporal, March-April, 1863. Present or accounted for until captured at Kelly's Ford, Virginia, November 7, 1863. Confined at Point Lookout, Maryland, until transferred for exchange to Aiken's Landing, Virginia, February 18-24, 1865.

MEADOWS, WILLIAM CALLOWAY, Private
Enlisted in Wake County on May 9, 1864, for the war. Wounded at Cedar Creek, Virginia, October 19, 1864. Captured at Petersburg, Virginia, April 3, 1865, and confined at Hart's Island, New York Harbor, until released after taking the Oath of Allegiance on June 19, 1865.

MILLER, JONATHAN, Private
Resided in Northampton County and enlisted in Wake County at age 35, August 15, 1862, for the war. Reported as absent without leave from April 25, 1863, through October, 1864.

MILLER, JOSIAH, Private
Paroled near Keedysville, Maryland, September 20, 1862. Admitted to hospital at Richmond, Virginia, April 19, 1863, with "incised wound left foot." Transferred to Huguenot Springs, Virginia, April 20, 1863. Reported as present on hospital records through April, 1863.

MOORE, B. F., Private
Enlisted in September, 1864, for the war.

MORTON, ROBERT S., Private
Resided in Anson County and enlisted in Wake County at age 26, August 15, 1862, for the war. Detailed as guard in hospital at Richmond, Virginia, April 10, 1864. Reported as absent on detail through October, 1864. Captured in hospital at Richmond, April 3, 1865, and paroled on April 24, 1865.

MOTEN, M., Private
Born in Anson County where he resided as a farmer prior to enlisting in Wake County at age 28, August 15, 1862, for the war. Discharged at Danville, Virginia, April 2, 1863, by reason of "phthisis pulmonalis."

NEWTON, WILLIAM, Private
Born in Anson County where he resided as a farmer prior to enlisting in Wake County at age 40, August 15, 1862, for the war as a substitute for _____ Ingraham. Discharged at Richmond, Virginia, October 28, 1862, by reason of "double hernia and threatened paralysis of the left arm."

PAGE, ERASMUS F., Private
Transferred from Company A, 10th Regiment N.C. State Troops (1st Regiment N.C. Artillery), September 29, 1864. Present or accounted for until paroled at Appomattox Court House, Virginia, April 9, 1865.

PARRISH, AMOS T., Private
Resided in Craven County where he enlisted at age 22, May 27, 1861, for the war. Wounded at Chancellorsville, Virginia, May 3, 1863. Reported as absent wounded through February 1, 1864, and as absent without leave from that date through October, 1864.

PATE, HENRY E., Private
Resided in Northampton County and enlisted in Wake County at age 32, August 15, 1862, for the war. Wounded and captured at Chancellorsville, Virginia, May 3, 1863. Confined in hospital near Alexandria, Virginia, until sent to City Point, Virginia, for exchange on June 25, 1863. Exact date of exchange not reported. Admitted to hospital at Petersburg, Virginia, July 1, 1863. Reported as absent on furlough through November 1, 1863, and as absent without leave from that date through October, 1864.

PETERSON, JOHN, Private
Resided in Craven County where he enlisted at age 20, May 27, 1861, for the war. Wounded at Fredericksburg, Virginia, December 13, 1862, and died of wound in hospital at Richmond, Virginia, June 18, 1863.

PHILLIPS, ELBERT, Private
Resided in Craven County where he enlisted at age 20, June 5, 1861, for the war. Present or accounted for until captured at Kelly's Ford, Virginia, November 7, 1863. Confined at Point Lookout, Maryland, until paroled and transferred for exchange to Aiken's Landing, Virginia, September 18, 1864. Admitted to hospital at Richmond, Virginia, September 22, 1864, with "chronic diarrhoea" and furloughed for 60 days on September 27, 1864.

POTEAT, JOHN A., Private
Enlisted in Wake County on May 9, 1864, for the war. Present or accounted for until paroled at Appomattox Court House, Virginia, April 9, 1865.

POWERS, JAMES H., Private
Born in Craven County where he resided and enlisted at age 18, May 27, 1861, for the war. Killed at Malvern Hill, Virginia, July 1, 1862.

POWERS, LEVI P., Private
Resided in Craven County where he enlisted at age 25, May 27, 1861, for the war. Died at Camp Advance, Northampton County, July 3, 1861.

PRESLEY, G. W. H., Private
Born in Anson County where he resided as a farmer prior to enlisting in Wake County at age 26, August 15, 1862, for the war. Discharged at Lynchburg, Virginia, January 21, 1863, by reason of "pulmonary tuberculosis."

REEL, JAMES MADISON, Sergeant
Resided in Craven County where he enlisted at age 22, May 27, 1861, for the war. Mustered in as Private. Wounded at Chancellorsville, Virginia, May 3, 1863. Appointed Sergeant on May 25, 1864. Present or accounted for until captured at Winchester, Virginia, September 19, 1864. Confined at Point Lookout, Maryland, until paroled and transferred for exchange to Aiken's Landing, Virginia,

March 15, 1865. Declared exchanged on March 18 1865.

REGISTER, MILES, Private
Resided in Sampson County and enlisted in Wake County at age 30, August 15, 1862, for the war. Admitted to hospital at Richmond, Virginia, May 24, 1864, with a gunshot wound and furloughed for 60 days on August 12, 1864. Present or accounted for on company muster rolls through October, 1864.

REGISTER, RUFUS, Private
Resided in Sampson County and enlisted in Wake County at age 28, August 15, 1862, for the war. Reported as absent without leave from September, 1862, through October, 1864.

RIGGINS, MOSES T., Private
Born in Warren County where he resided as a farmer prior to enlisting in Wake County at age 37, August 15, 1862, for the war. Discharged at Orange Court House, Virginia, April 25, 1864, by reason of disability.

RIGGS, HAYWOOD, Private
Resided in Craven County where he enlisted at age 24, May 27, 1861, for the war. Captured and paroled at Warrenton, Virginia, September 29, 1862. Wounded at Chancellorsville, Virginia, May 3, 1863, and right arm amputated below the elbow. Reported as absent wounded on company muster rolls through December, 1863.

RIGGS, WILLIAM R., Private
Resided in Craven County where he enlisted at age 19, May 27, 1861, for the war. Mortally wounded at Malvern Hill, Virginia, July 1, 1862.

ROUSE, BENJAMIN F., Private
Resided in Craven County where he enlisted at age 26, May 27, 1861, for the war. Killed at Chancellorsville, Virginia, May 3, 1863.

ROUSE, EDWARD J., Private
Resided in Craven County where he enlisted at age 29, May 27, 1861, for the war. Died at Camp Potomac, Virginia, September 25, 1861, of disease.

ROUSE, THOMAS B., Private
Resided in Craven County where he enlisted at age 18, May 27, 1861, for the war. Captured at Sharpsburg, Maryland, September 17, 1862, and paroled at Keedysville, Maryland, September 20, 1862. Wounded at Gettysburg, Pennsylvania, July 3, 1863, when his leg was shot off. Captured in hospital at Gettysburg, July 3-4, 1863, and confined in hospital at Baltimore, Maryland, until paroled and sent to City Point, Virginia, November 12, 1863, for exchange. Admitted to hospital at Richmond, Virginia, November 16, 1863. Company muster rolls report him as absent wounded through October, 1864.

SATTERWHITE, THOMAS P., Private
Resided in McDowell County and enlisted in Wake County on May 1, 1864, for the war. Present or accounted for on company muster rolls through October, 1864. Captured at Petersburg, Virginia, April 3, 1865, and confined at Hart's Island, New York Harbor, until released after taking the Oath of Allegiance on June 19, 1865.

SELLERS, ELIJAH, Private
Resided in Anson County and enlisted in Wake County at age 30, August 15, 1862, for the war. Killed at South Mountain, Maryland, September 14, 1862.

SHEW, WILEY, Private
Enlisted in Wake County on March 1, 1864, for the war. Reported as absent wounded "since June 2, 1864." Admitted to hospital at Danville, Virginia, June 4, 1864, and furloughed on June 7, 1864. Company muster rolls report him as absent wounded through October, 1864.

SHIPP, JOHN, Private
Resided in Sampson County and enlisted in Wake County at age 33, August 15, 1862, for the war. Present or accounted for on company muster rolls through October, 1864.

SHUTE, BECTON H., Private
Resided in Craven County where he enlisted at age 20, May 27, 1861, for the war. Killed at Malvern Hill, Virginia, July 1, 1862.

SHUTE, JAMES N., Private
Resided in Craven County where he enlisted at age 36, May 27, 1861, for the war. Discharged at Fredericksburg, Virginia, September-October, 1861.

SHUTE, WILLIAM H., Private
Resided in Craven County where he enlisted at age 29, May 27, 1861, for the war. Killed at Chancellorsville, Virginia, May 3, 1863.

SIMMONS, GILLEAD, Private
Resided in Sampson County and enlisted in Wake County at age 19, August 15, 1862, for the war. Captured near Fredericksburg, Virginia, May 3, 1863, and paroled and exchanged at City Point, Virginia, May 10, 1863. Present or accounted for until wounded at Winchester, Virginia, September 19, 1864. Admitted to hospital at Charlottesville, Virginia, October 29, 1864, and returned to duty on January 5, 1865. Admitted to hospital at Richmond, Virginia, February 27, 1865, and captured in hospital on April 3, 1865. Confined at Newport News, Virginia, until released after taking the Oath of Allegiance on June 30, 1865.

SIMMONS, W. L., Private
Resided in Sampson County and enlisted in Wake County at age 23, August 15, 1862, for the war. Captured at Sharpsburg, Maryland, September 17, 1862, and confined at Fort Delaware, Delaware, until paroled and exchanged at Aiken's Landing, Virginia, November 10, 1862. Admitted to hospital at Richmond, Virginia, October 7, 1862, and transferred to Camp Lee, near Richmond, October 31, 1862. Company muster rolls report him as absent without leave through April, 1863.

SIMONS, TURNER, Private
Resided in Craven County where he enlisted at age 18, June 29, 1861, for the war. Reported as absent sick on company muster rolls through October, 1862, and as absent without leave from January, 1863, through December, 1863.

SIMPKINS, NOAH, Private
Resided in Craven County where he enlisted at age 18, May 27, 1861, for the war. Killed at Chancellorsville, Virginia, May 3, 1863.

SLACK, F., Private
Wounded and captured at Winchester, Virginia, September 19, 1864, and died in hospital on September 23, 1864.

STEVENSON, JOHN W., Sergeant
Born in Craven County where he resided and enlisted at age 18, May 27, 1861, for the war. Mustered in as Private and appointed Corporal in February, 1862. Promoted to Sergeant in November, 1862. Died in hospital at Richmond, Virginia, March 23, 1863, of "pneumonia."

STREET, PAXTON, Private
Born in Craven County where he resided as a farmer and enlisted at age 33, October 26, 1861, for the war. Died in hospital at Richmond, Virginia, June 3, 1863, of "gastro enteritis."

SUTTON, DAVID, Private
Resided in Craven County where he enlisted at age 34, May 27, 1861, for the war. Wounded and captured at South Mountain, Maryland, September 14, 1862, and confined in hospital at Frederick, Maryland, until transferred to Baltimore, Maryland, November 28, 1862. Paroled and exchanged at City Point, Virginia, February 18, 1863. Reported as absent wounded or in hospital at Danville, Virginia, until retired to the Invalid Corps on November 3, 1864.

TAYLOR, ABEL, Private
Enlisted in Craven County on October 4, 1861, for the war. Captured at Sharpsburg, Maryland, September 17, 1862, and paroled near Keedysville, Maryland, September 20, 1862. Died in hospital at Richmond, Virginia, November 21, 1862, of "typhoid fever and smallpox."

TAYLOR, ANDREW J., 1st Sergeant
Born in Jones County and resided in Craven County where he enlisted at age 28, May 27, 1861, for the war. Mustered in as Private and appointed Sergeant on July 29, 1861. Promoted to 1st Sergeant in February, 1862. Killed at Sharpsburg, Maryland, September 17, 1862.

TAYLOR, BRYAN, Private
Born in Craven County where he resided and enlisted at age 28, May 27, 1861, for the war. Died in hospital at Petersburg, Virginia, April 1, 1862, of disease.

TAYLOR, LEWIS G., Private
Resided in Craven County where he enlisted at age 23, May 27, 1861, for the war. Wounded at Malvern Hill, Virginia, July 1, 1862. Reported as absent wounded through February, 1863, and as present until detailed "as herdsman at Division Headquarters" on April 1, 1864. Absent on detail through October, 1864. Paroled at Appomattox Court House, Virginia, April 9, 1865.

TEER, JAMES A., Private
Resided in Craven County where he enlisted at age 35, May 27, 1861, for the war. Mustered in as Sergeant and reduced to ranks November 26, 1861. Mortally wounded at Chancellorsville, Virginia, May 3, 1863, and died in hospital at Richmond, Virginia, June 22, 1863, of wound.

TEW, L., Private
Enlisted in Wake County on August 15, 1862, for

the war. Captured at Sharpsburg, Maryland, September 17, 1862, and confined at Fort Delaware, Delaware, until paroled and exchanged at Aiken's Landing, Virginia, November 10, 1862. Died in hospital at Richmond, Virginia, October 26, 1862.

THIGPEN, BRYAN, Private
Resided in Duplin County and enlisted in Wake County at age 23, August 15, 1862, for the war. Company muster roll dated October 31, 1862, states that he was "absent sick in hospital at Winchester." Reported as absent without leave after November 1, 1862.

TINER, LINDSEY S., Private
Resided in Johnston County and enlisted in Wake County at age 24, August 15, 1862, for the war. Company muster rolls report him as "missing" after the battle at Sharpsburg, Maryland, September 17, 1862. Federal Provost Marshal records indicate that he was paroled on September 25, 1862.

WAUL, A. G., Private
Born in Anson County where he resided as a farmer prior to enlisting in Wake County at age 28, August 15, 1862, for the war. Discharged November 2, 1863, by reason of "spinal irritation, disease kidneys, dyspepsia, synovitis (chronic) affecting right knee joint."

WEBB, THOMAS H., Private
Resided in Anson County and enlisted in Wake County at age 34, August 15, 1862, for the war. Killed at South Mountain, Maryland, September 14, 1862.

WEST, URIAH, Private
Resided as a farmer in Sampson County prior to enlisting in Wake County at age 30, August 15, 1862, for the war. Wounded at Chancellorsville, Virginia, May 3, 1863, and returned to duty from hospital at Raleigh on June 2, 1864. Captured at Harper's Farm, Virginia, April 6, 1865, and confined at Point Lookout, Maryland, until released after taking the Oath of Allegiance on June 21, 1865.

WETHERINGTON, ABNER M., Private
Resided in Craven County where he enlisted at age 26, May 27, 1861, for the war. Present or accounted for until wounded at Spotsylvania Court House, Virginia, May 12, 1864. Captured at Core Creek, near New Bern, July 27, 1864. Confined at Fort Monroe, Virginia, until transferred to Point Lookout, Maryland, August 12, 1864. Transferred August 16, 1864, to Elmira, New York, where he remained until released after taking the Oath of Allegiance on June 3, 1865.

WETHERINGTON, JAMES, Private
Resided in Craven County where he enlisted at age 25, May 27, 1861, for the war. Wounded at Chancellorsville, Virginia, May 3, 1863. Reported as absent wounded through January, 1864, and as absent without leave after that date.

WETHERINGTON, JAMES R., Private
Resided in Craven County where he enlisted at age 25, May 27, 1861, for the war. Died at Camp Potomac, Virginia, December 25, 1861, of disease.

WETHERINGTON, RUEL, Private
Resided in Craven County where he enlisted at age 35, May 27, 1861, for the war. Discharged at Camp Advance, Northampton County, July 9, 1861, by reason of "physical disability."

WETHERINGTON, WILLIAM H., Private
Resided in Craven County where he enlisted at age 28, May 27, 1861, for the war. Wounded at Chancellorsville, Virginia, May 3, 1863, and reported as absent wounded through December, 1863.

WHITE, BENJAMIN F., Private
Born in Jones County and resided in Craven County where he enlisted at age 19, May 27, 1861, for the war. Killed at South Mountain, Maryland, September 14, 1862.

WHITE, EDWARD, Private
Resided in Craven County where he enlisted at age 21, May 27, 1861, for the war. Reported as present on company muster rolls through December, 1861. Roll of Honor states that he was "discharged by substitute."

WIGGINS, JAMES, Corporal
Resided in Craven County where he enlisted at age 27, May 27, 1861, for the war. Mustered in as Private and appointed Corporal on March 1, 1863. Federal Provost Marshal records indicate that he was paroled on May 4, 1863, but do not give date and place of capture or date and place of exchange. Present or accounted for on company muster rolls through December, 1863, when he was reported as "absent sick."

WILLIAMS, JAMES M., Private
Resided in Craven County where he enlisted at age 27, May 27, 1861, for the war. Present or accounted for on company muster rolls through April, 1862.

WILLIAMS, JEREMIAH, Private
Resided in Craven County where he enlisted at age 23, May 27, 1861, for the war. Discharged at Richmond, Virginia, August 22, 1861, by reason of disability.

WILLIAMS, MATTHEW J., Private
Enlisted in Craven County on May 27, 1861, for the war. Present or accounted for on company muster rolls through August, 1863. Reported as absent without leave from September-October, 1863, through October, 1864.

WILLIAMS, WILLIAM H., Private
Resided in Anson County and enlisted in Wake County at age 30, August 15, 1862, for the war. Wounded in the leg and arm at Chancellorsville, Virginia, May 3, 1863, and furloughed from hospital on June 11, 1863, for 60 days. Reported absent wounded on company muster rolls until detailed in hospital at Richmond, Virginia, February 25, 1864. Detailed as a guard in General Hospital at Camp Winder, Richmond. Retired to the Invalid Corps on September 28, 1864, and assigned to light duty at Richmond as a guard. Captured in hospital at Richmond on April 3, 1865, and paroled on April 18, 1865.

WILLIS, ABISHA M., Private

Resided in Craven County where he enlisted at age 27, May 27, 1861, for the war. Present or accounted for on company muster rolls through December, 1863, when he was reported as "absent without leave."

WILLIS, ABNER, Private

Born in Craven County where he resided as a farmer and enlisted at age 21, May 27, 1861, for the war. Present or accounted for until wounded at Spotsylvania Court House, Virginia, May 12, 1864. Reported as absent wounded until retired to the Invalid Corps on March 27, 1865.

WILLIS, ASA, Private

Resided in Craven County where he enlisted at age 28, May 27, 1861, for the war. Admitted to hospital at Richmond, Virginia, September 27, 1862, with a wound of the hand. Date and place wounded not reported. Returned to duty on October 25, 1862. Wounded at Gettysburg, Pennsylvania, July 3, 1863, and captured in hospital at Gettysburg on July 5, 1863. Federal Provost Marshal records last report him as being in Letterman General Hospital, Gettysburg, on August 10, 1863. Company muster rolls carry him as absent prisoner through October, 1864.

WOODS, RICHARD H., Private

Resided in Craven County where he enlisted at age 22, May 27, 1861, for the war. Killed at Malvern Hill, Virginia, July 1, 1862.

WOODS, WILLIAM F., Private

Born in Craven County where he resided and enlisted at age 21, May 27, 1861, for the war. Mustered in as Corporal and reduced to ranks on April 15, 1862. Captured and paroled at Warrenton, Virginia, September 29, 1862. Killed at Chancellorsville, Virginia, May 3, 1863.

COMPANY G

This company, known as the "Jones Rifle Guards," was organized in Jones County and enlisted at Trenton on May 24, 1861. It tendered its service to the state and was ordered to Camp Advance, near Garysburg, Northampton County, where it was assigned to this regiment as Company G. After joining the regiment the company functioned as a part of the regiment, and its history for the war period is recorded as a part of the regimental history.

The information contained in the following roster of the company was compiled principally from company muster rolls for July 16, 1861, through December, 1861; March-April, 1862; July-October, 1862; January, 1863, through March, 1864; and May through October, 1864. No company muster rolls were found for the period prior to July 16, 1861; for January-February, 1862; May-June, 1862; November-December, 1862; April, 1864; or for the period after October, 1864. In addition to the company muster rolls, Roll of Honor records, receipt rolls, and hospital records, supplemented by state pension applications, United Daughters of the

Confederacy records, and postwar rosters and histories, all provided useful information.

OFFICERS
CAPTAINS

SAWYER, HARVEY A.

Resided in Jones County and appointed Captain at age 23 to rank from May 16, 1861. Wounded in the left leg and neck at Malvern Hill, Virginia, July 1, 1862, and died in hospital at Richmond, Virginia, July 13, 1862.

WILLIAMS, ORREN

Transferred from Company B of this regiment upon appointment as 1st Lieutenant to rank from September 10, 1861. Promoted to Captain to rank from July 13, 1862. Wounded in the arm on June 4, 1864, and furloughed June 6, 1864. Submitted his resignation on September 21, 1864, by reason of "nervous prostration." Resignation officially accepted on December 12, 1864.

LIEUTENANTS

DICKERSON, WILLIAM J., 1st Lieutenant

Resided in Jones County and appointed 2nd Lieutenant to rank from May 16, 1861. Wounded at Malvern Hill, Virginia, July 1, 1862. Promoted to 1st Lieutenant to rank from July 13, 1862. Present or accounted for until captured at Kelly's Ford, Virginia, November 7, 1863. Confined at Old Capitol Prison, Washington, D.C., until transferred to Johnson's Island, Ohio, November 11, 1863. Confined at Johnson's Island until released after taking the Oath of Allegiance on June 13, 1865.

GORDON, DAVID T., 2nd Lieutenant

Paroled at Charlotte on May 17, 1865.

JONES, ROBERT H., 2nd Lieutenant

Resided in Jones County and appointed 3rd Lieutenant to rank from May 16, 1861. Promoted to 2nd Lieutenant to rank from July 13, 1862. Present or accounted for until paroled at Appomattox Court House, Virginia, April 9, 1865.

KOONCE, SIMON E., 1st Lieutenant

Resided in Jones County and appointed 1st Lieutenant at age 35 to rank from May 16, 1861. Resigned on September 10, 1861.

SAWYER, HIRAM A., 2nd Lieutenant

Resided in Jones County where he enlisted at age 21, May 24, 1861, for the war. Mustered in as 1st Sergeant. Elected 2nd Lieutenant on July 13, 1862, and appointed to rank from August 6, 1862. Wounded at Chancellorsville, Virginia, May 3, 1863, and detailed on enrolling duty in North Carolina for the balance of the war.

NONCOMMISSIONED OFFICERS AND PRIVATES

ADAMS, GEORGE W., Private

Resided in Jones County where he enlisted at age 25, May 24, 1861, for the war. Present or accounted for until captured at Kelly's Ford, Virginia, November 7, 1863. Confined at Point Lookout, Maryland, until released after taking the Oath of

Allegiance and joining the U.S. service on February 17, 1864. Unit to which assigned not reported.

ALLIGOOD, STEPHEN H., Private

Resided in Jones County where he enlisted at age 23, May 24, 1861, for the war. Present or accounted for on company muster rolls through October, 1864, when he was reported with the remark: "Pioneer now detailed as herdsman." Paroled at Appomattox Court House, Virginia, April 9, 1865.

ANDREWS, BRYANT, Private

Born in Jones County and enlisted in New Hanover County on May 5, 1862, for the war. Wounded at Malvern Hill, Virginia, July 1, 1862, and died of wound on July 15, 1862.

ANDREWS, DANIEL F., Private

Resided in Jones County where he enlisted at age 22, May 24, 1861, for the war. Present or accounted for until captured at Kelly's Ford, Virginia, November 7, 1863. Confined at Point Lookout, Maryland, until released after taking the Oath of Allegiance and joining the U.S. service on February 10, 1864. Assigned to Company E, 1st Regiment U.S. Volunteer Infantry.

BALDWIN, DAVID W., Private

Enlisted in Wake County on April 22, 1864, for the war. Wounded and captured at Winchester, Virginia, September 19, 1864. Died in hospital at Winchester on October 22, 1864, of "gangrene of stump and exhaustion."

BANKS, JAMES H., Private

Enlisted in December, 1864, for the war. Captured at Kinston on March 19, 1865, and paroled.

BARNES, JAMES E., Private

Resided in Jones County where he enlisted at age 19, May 24, 1861, for the war. Wounded at Malvern Hill, Virginia, July 1, 1862. Present or accounted for until wounded and captured at Cedar Creek, Virginia, October 19, 1864. Confined in hospital at Baltimore, Maryland, until transferred to Fort McHenry, Maryland, May 9, 1865. Released after taking the Oath of Allegiance on June 9, 1865.

BARNES, JAMES R., Private

Enlisted in Wake County at age 37, August 29, 1862, for the war. Wounded at Chancellorsville, Virginia, May 3, 1863. Reported as absent on furlough through October, 1863, and as absent without leave after that date.

BARNES, JOHN, Private

Born in Jones County where he resided prior to enlisting in Wayne County at age 27, April 11, 1862, for the war. Killed at Malvern Hill, Virginia, July 1, 1862.

BARNHART, HENRY, Private

Enlisted in Wake County on April 26, 1864, for the war. Died in hospital at Staunton, Virginia, August 12, 1864.

BARWICK, WILLIAM M., Private

Enlisted in June, 1864, for the war. Captured at Kinston on March 18, 1865, and paroled.

BENDER, FRANK J., Private

Resided in Jones County where he enlisted at age 22, May 24, 1861, for the war. Died in hospital at Fredericksburg, Virginia, September 12, 1861.

BISHOP, AMOS, Private

Transferred from Company B, 59th Regiment N.C. Troops (4th Regiment N.C. Cavalry) on April 15, 1864. Admitted to hospital at Richmond, Virginia, on May 22, 1864, with a gunshot wound and furloughed for 60 days on June 3, 1864.

BISHOP, CALEB Q., Private

Resided in Jones County where he enlisted at age 32, May 24, 1861, for the war. Present or accounted for until captured at Kelly's Ford, Virginia, November 7, 1863. Confined at Point Lookout, Maryland, until released after taking the Oath of Allegiance and joining the U.S. service on February 17, 1864. Unit to which assigned not reported.

BISHOP, WILLIAM H., Sergeant

Resided in Jones County where he enlisted at age 21, May 24, 1861, for the war. Mustered in as Private and appointed Corporal in November, 1862. Promoted to Sergeant on December 1, 1862. Wounded at Chancellorsville, Virginia, May 3, 1863. Present or accounted for until captured at Kelly's Ford, Virginia, November 7, 1863. Confined at Point Lookout, Maryland, until paroled and transferred for exchange to Aiken's Landing, Virginia, February 24, 1865.

BLACK, ALEXANDER, Private

Enlisted in Wake County on June 4, 1864, for the war. Killed at Cedar Creek, Virginia, October 19, 1864.

BOONE, J. R., Private

Paroled at Greensboro on May 19, 1865.

BOWLES, WILLIAM H., Private

Enlisted in Wake County on April 8, 1864, for the war. Reported as absent sick on company muster rolls through October, 1864. Admitted to hospital at Charlottesville, Virginia, December 22, 1864, with "debility" and returned to duty December 24, 1864.

BRADSHAW, NATHANIEL J., Private

Resided in Jones County where he enlisted at age 22, May 24, 1861, for the war. Died at Camp Holmes, Stafford County, Virginia, August 6, 1861.

BRATCHER, STANLEY, Private

Resided in Jones County where he enlisted at age 19, May 24, 1861, for the war. Present or accounted for until captured at Kelly's Ford, Virginia, November 7, 1863. Confined at Point Lookout, Maryland, until released after taking the Oath of Allegiance and joining the U.S. service on February 17, 1864. Assigned to Company E, 1st Regiment U.S. Volunteer Infantry.

BROOKS, C. S., Private

Paroled at Farmville, Virginia, April 11-21, 1865.

BRYSON, WILLIAM, Private

Captured at Gettysburg, Pennsylvania, July 3, 1863, and confined at Fort Delaware, Delaware, July 7-12, 1863.

BURRUSS, SOLOMON, Private

Enlisted in Wake County on April 22, 1864, for the war. Reported as absent sick on company muster rolls through October, 1864. Paroled at Salisbury on May 15, 1865.

COBB, MICAJAH, Private
Resided in Wilson County and enlisted in Wake County at age 29, September 3, 1862, for the war. Captured and paroled at Paris, Virginia, November 5, 1862. Died in hospital at Richmond, Virginia, December 20, 1862, of "variola."

COBLE, J. F., Private
Paroled at Greensboro on May 23, 1865.

COBLE, JOHN A., Private
Paroled at Greensboro on May 20, 1865.

COX, JAMES, Private
Resided in Jones County where he enlisted at age 50, May 24, 1861, for the war. Admitted to hospital at Richmond, Virginia, August 18, 1862, with "diarrhoea, gastritis." Furloughed from hospital for 30 days on September 28, 1862. Reported as absent without leave on company muster rolls from January, 1863, through December, 1863, when he was reported with the remark: "Deserted August 19, 1862."

COX, JAMES E., Private
Resided in Jones County where he enlisted at age 18, May 24, 1861, for the war. Died in hospital at Fredericksburg, Virginia, September 15, 1861.

COX, JOHN W., Private
Resided in Jones County where he enlisted at age 20, May 24, 1861, for the war. Present or accounted for until wounded and captured at Kelly's Ford, Virginia, November 7, 1863. Admitted to hospital at Washington, D.C., November 9, 1863, and died of wound on December 28, 1863.

CUMBO, JAMES H., Private
Resided in Jones County where he enlisted at age 20, May 24, 1861, for the war. Present or accounted for until captured at Kelly's Ford, Virginia, November 7, 1863. Confined at Point Lookout, Maryland, until transferred for exchange to Aiken's Landing, Virginia, February 24, 1865.

DILLAHUNT, ALEXANDER C., Private
Born in Jones County where he resided and enlisted at age 18, May 24, 1861, for the war. Mustered in as Sergeant and reduced to ranks in December, 1861. Present or accounted for until killed at Gettysburg, Pennsylvania, July 1, 1863.

DIXON, FERDINAND MINOR, Private
Resided in Jones County where he enlisted at age 22, May 24, 1861, for the war. Present or accounted for on company muster rolls through October, 1864, when he appears as absent in hospital at Charlottesville, Virginia, "wounded."

DUDLEY, GARDNER, Private
Resided in Jones County where he enlisted at age 26, May 24, 1861, for the war. Detailed for hospital duty April 24, 1863, and assigned to hospital at Tarboro. Reported on company muster rolls as absent on detail through March, 1864, and as absent sick from that date through October, 1864.

DUDLEY, WILLIAM J., Private
Resided in Jones County where he enlisted at age 17, May 24, 1861, for the war. Discharged on August 19, 1861, by reason of disability.

EATMAN, THOMAS J., Private
Resided in Jones County where he enlisted at age 26, May 24, 1861, for the war. Discharged September 1, 1861. Later appointed Chaplain and assigned to the Field and Staff, 33rd Regiment N.C. Troops.

ERNANDEZ, B. T., Sergeant
Born in Mexico and resided as a trimmer in Jones County where he enlisted on May 24, 1861, for the war. Killed at Malvern Hill, Virginia, July 1, 1862.

FITZGERALD, JOHN B., Private
Resided in Caswell County and enlisted in Wake County at age 20, September 2, 1862, for the war. Present or accounted for until wounded and captured at Winchester, Virginia, September 19, 1864. Confined in hospital at Baltimore, Maryland, until transferred to Point Lookout, Maryland, January 8, 1865. Released at Point Lookout after taking the Oath of Allegiance on June 3, 1865.

FOY, ENOCH, Sergeant
Born in Jones County where he resided as a farmer and enlisted at age 23, May 24, 1861, for the war. Mustered in as Sergeant. Discharged on May 26, 1862, by reason of "physical disability."

FRITZ, HIRAM, Private
Resided in Davidson County. Reported on a register of detailed men with the remark that the papers requesting his detail were received from Lynchburg, Virginia, December 11, 1864. Request was approved, but the records do not give the nature of the detail or the place, date, or period of his enlistment. Captured near Petersburg, Virginia, March 25, 1865, and confined at Point Lookout, Maryland, until released after taking the Oath of Allegiance on June 26, 1865.

GAINES, WILLIAM, Private
Captured at Sharpsburg, Maryland, September 17, 1862, and paroled and exchanged at Aiken's Landing, Virginia, November 10, 1862.

GODFREY, ARCHY, Private
First reported on May 1-August 31, 1864, muster roll with the remark that he enlisted in Wake County for the war, but date of enlistment not reported. Admitted to hospital at Richmond, Virginia, December 27, 1864, with "debilitas" and returned to duty on January 17, 1865. Federal Provost Marshal records indicate that he was received at Washington, D.C., April 12, 1865, from the Provost Marshal General, Army of the Potomac, as a "rebel deserter." Took the Oath of Allegiance and provided transportation to Beltsville, Maryland.

GOODING, LEWIS FRANKLIN, Private
Resided in Jones County where he enlisted at age 22, May 24, 1861, for the war. Wounded at Malvern Hill, Virginia, July 1, 1862, and detailed as a nurse in Richmond, Virginia, on April 28, 1863. Absent on detail until retired to the Invalid Corps on September 7, 1864.

GOODING, WILLIAM, Private
Resided in Jones County where he enlisted at age 21, May 24, 1861, for the war. Died in camp at Pratt's Point, King George County, Virginia, October 26, 1861.

GRAY, THOMAS A., Sergeant
Paroled at Greensboro on May 29, 1865.

GREEN, DAVID J., Private
Resided in Jones County where he enlisted at age 17, May 24, 1861, for the war. Wounded at Malvern Hill, Virginia, July 1, 1862, and again at Chancellorsville, Virginia, May 3, 1863. Reported as absent wounded on company muster rolls through October, 1863. Detailed in the Quartermaster Department, Richmond, Virginia, January 14, 1864. Retired to the Invalid Corps on May 2, 1864, and assigned to light duty at Goldsboro as Provost Guard. Reported as present at Goldsboro on February 7, 1865.

GREEN, JAMES F., Private
Born in Jones County where he resided as a farmer and enlisted at age 25, May 24, 1861, for the war. Discharged on January 1, 1862, by reason of "disease of the spine."

GRIMES, J. W., Private
Captured at Hatcher's Run, Virginia, April 2, 1865, and confined at Hart's Island, New York Harbor, until released after taking the Oath of Allegiance on June 19, 1865.

HALL, DREW, Private
Resided in Jones County where he enlisted at age 28, May 24, 1861, for the war. Detailed as a nurse in hospital at Wilmington on March 5, 1863. Reported as absent on detail on company muster rolls through March, 1864. Present or accounted for with the company through October, 1864. Paroled at Farmville, Virginia, April 11-21, 1865.

HAMMOND, EDWARD, Private
Resided in Jones County and enlisted in Spotsylvania County, Virginia, at age 51, April 17, 1863, for the war. Present or accounted for until he died in hospital at Richmond, Virginia, January 19, 1864, of "diarrhoea chronic."

HANCOCK, IRA, Private
Resided in Jones County where he enlisted at age 19, May 24, 1861, for the war. Present or accounted for until captured at Kelly's Ford, Virginia, November 7, 1863. Confined at Point Lookout, Maryland, until paroled and transferred for exchange to Aiken's Landing, Virginia, February 24, 1865. Admitted to hospital on April 8, 1865, at Raleigh, where he was captured and paroled on April 13, 1865.

HANCOCK, JOHN A., Private
Resided in Jones County where he enlisted at age 20, May 24, 1861, for the war. Died in camp on November 20, 1861.

HARDIN, W. D., Private
Paroled at Greensboro on May 29, 1865.

HARPER, DANIEL, Private
Resided in Jones County and enlisted "at camp" at age 44, February 17, 1863, for the war as a substitute. Present or accounted for until captured at Kelly's Ford, Virginia, November 7, 1863. Confined at Point Lookout, Maryland, until released after taking the Oath of Allegiance and joining the U.S. service on February 17, 1864. Unit to which he was assigned not reported.

HARRIS, JAMES H., Private
Born in Brunswick County and enlisted in Wake County on July 15, 1862, for the war. Wounded at Chancellorsville, Virginia, May 3, 1863, and died of wound the next day.

HARRIS, JOHN H., Private
Resided in Wake County where he enlisted at age 29, August 15, 1862, for the war. Wounded at Chancellorsville, Virginia, May 3, 1863, and died the next day.

HASTY, SAMUEL W., Private
Resided in Richmond County and enlisted in Wake County at age 30, July 17, 1862, for the war. Present or accounted for on company muster rolls through October, 1864. Captured in hospital at Richmond, Virginia, April 3, 1865, and confined at Point Lookout, Maryland, where he died June 19, 1865, of "bronchitis."

HAWKINS, ANDREW J., Private
Resided in Jones County where he enlisted at age 24, May 24, 1861, for the war. Present or accounted for until captured at Spotsylvania Court House, Virginia, May 20, 1864. Confined at Point Lookout, Maryland, until transferred to Elmira, New York, July 3-6, 1864. Paroled at Elmira on October 11, 1864, and sent back to Point Lookout. Record at Point Lookout states that he was exchanged on October 29, 1864.

HAWKINS, FRANCIS, Private
Born in Jones County where he resided as a farmer and enlisted at age 25, May 24, 1861, for the war. Discharged July 15, 1862, by reason of his having "lost an arm by an accidental explosion of a shell."

HAY, ROBERT S., Musician
Resided in Jones County where he enlisted at age 16, May 24, 1861, for the war. Mustered in as Musician. Wounded at Sharpsburg, Maryland, September 17, 1862. Discharged on November 6, 1862, by reason of his being a minor.

HAYWOOD, LEWIS G., Private
Born in Lenoir County and resided in Jones County where he enlisted at age 34, May 24, 1861, for the war. Present or accounted for until detailed in hospital at Richmond, Virginia, March 5, 1863. Died in hospital at Richmond on March 29, 1863, of "febris typhoides."

HEATH, BECTON R., Private
Resided in Jones County where he enlisted at age 23, May 24, 1861, for the war. Present or accounted for until wounded and captured at Chancellorsville, Virginia, May 3, 1863. Confined at Old Capitol Prison, Washington, D.C., until paroled and sent to City Point, Virginia, for exchange, June 10, 1863. Present or accounted for until captured at Kelly's Ford, Virginia, November 7, 1863. Confined at Point Lookout, Maryland, until paroled and transferred for exchange to Aiken's Landing, Virginia, February 24, 1865. Reported as paid in hospital at Richmond, Virginia, on March 2, 1865.

HEATH, JOHN T., Private
Resided in Jones County where he enlisted at age 28, May 24, 1861, for the war. Mustered in as Private and appointed Corporal in June, 1863. Present or accounted for until captured at Kelly's Ford, Virginia, November 7, 1863. Confined at

Point Lookout, Maryland, until transferred to Elmira, New York, August 18, 1864. Paroled at Elmira and sent to James River, Virginia, for exchange, March 10, 1865. Reported as Private on prisoner of war records.

HIGGINS, WILLIAM G., Private
Resided in Jones County where he enlisted at age 23, May 24, 1861, for the war. Killed at Malvern Hill, Virginia, July 1, 1862.

HOLLINGSWORTH, A. P., Private
Resided in Sampson County and paroled at Goldsboro on May 25, 1865. "Came in for parole."

HORN, WILSON, Private
Resided in Onslow County and enlisted at age 28 on August 15, 1862, for the war. Company muster rolls state that he deserted on November 23, 1862, when he "fell out of the march near New Market, Virginia." Claim for balance of pay due filed by his mother on May 9, 1863, with the remark that he died at home. Date and cause of death not reported.

HUDSON, ANDREW J., Private
Resided in Sampson County and enlisted in Wake County at age 27, September 2, 1862, for the war. Present or accounted for on company muster rolls through October, 1864.

HUGGINS, ABRAM, Private
Resided in Jones County and enlisted in New Hanover County at age 28, May 1, 1862, for the war. Admitted to hospital at Richmond, Virginia, May 15, 1864. May 1-August 31, 1864, muster roll reports him with the remark: "Absent on wounded furlough." Present or accounted for on company muster rolls through October, 1864.

HUGGINS, FELIX, Private
Resided in Jones County where he enlisted at age 32, May 24, 1861, for the war. Present or accounted for until captured at Kelly's Ford, Virginia, November 7, 1863. Confined at Point Lookout, Maryland, until transferred for exchange to Cox's Landing, James River, Virginia, February 13, 1865. Admitted to hospital at Richmond, Virginia, February 15, 1865, and transferred the next day.

HUGGINS, HENRY B., Private
Enlisted in Northampton County on July 18, 1861, for the war. July 1-October 31, 1862, muster roll states that he was "absent wounded by the explosion of a bomb shell at Camp Wyatt." Detailed as a nurse at Lexington, Virginia, February 15, 1863. Died in hospital at Lexington on June 16, 1863, of "typhoid pneumonia."

HUGGINS, HENRY C., 1st Sergeant
Born in Jones County where he resided as a farmer and enlisted at age 24, May 24, 1861, for the war. Mustered in as Corporal and promoted to Sergeant July-October, 1862. Promoted to 1st Sergeant in January-February, 1863. Wounded at Chancellorsville, Virginia, May 3, 1863, and discharged on December 12, 1863, by reason of "a wound received at Chancellorsville through the shoulder."

HUGGINS, HENRY C., Jr., Private
Enlisted in Northampton County on July 18, 1861, for the war. Present or accounted for on

company muster rolls through December, 1861.

HUGGINS, ISAAC, Private
Resided in Jones County where he enlisted at age 20, May 24, 1861, for the war. Wounded at Chancellorsville, Virginia, May 3, 1863. Reported as absent wounded through December, 1863, and as present until detailed and ordered to report for duty to the Provost Marshal at Liberty, Virginia, on September 17, 1864. Reported as absent on detail on company muster rolls through October, 1864.

HYMAN, JOHN M., Hospital Steward
Resided in Jones County where he enlisted at age 31, May 24, 1861, for the war. Mustered in as Private and appointed Hospital Steward on August 1, 1861. Died in February, 1862.

JONES, HARDY N., Sergeant
Resided in Jones County where he enlisted at age 17, May 24, 1861, for the war. Mustered in as Private and appointed Corporal, March-April, 1863. Present or accounted for as Corporal on company muster rolls through October, 1864. Captured at Burkeville, Virginia, April 6, 1865, and confined at Point Lookout, Maryland, until released after taking the Oath of Allegiance on June 28, 1865. Reported as Sergeant on Federal Provost Marshal records.

JONES, J. J., Private
Name reported on return for December, 1862, with the remark that he was on duty as a Provost Guard.

JONES, JAMES M., Private
Resided in Jones County where he enlisted at age 17, May 24, 1861, for the war. Died in hospital at Fredericksburg, Virginia, January 12, 1862.

JONES, JOHN P., Corporal
Resided in Jones County where he enlisted at age 22, May 24, 1861, for the war. Mustered in as Private and appointed Corporal, July-August, 1863. Present or accounted for until captured at Kelly's Ford, Virginia, November 7, 1863. Confined at Point Lookout, Maryland, where he died on April 13, 1865, of "smallpox."

JONES, JOHN R., Private
Resided in Jones County where he enlisted at age 16, May 24, 1861, for the war. Wounded at Malvern Hill, Virginia, July 1, 1862. Present or accounted for until captured at Kelly's Ford, Virginia, November 7, 1863. Confined at Point Lookout, Maryland, until transferred for exchange to Aiken's Landing, Virginia, February 24, 1865. Reported as present on a roll of a detachment of paroled and exchanged prisoners at Camp Lee, near Richmond, Virginia, on February 23, 1865. Captured on the Wilmington Road on March 10, 1865, and sent to Provost Marshal at New Bern. Transferred to Point Lookout, where he was received on March 30, 1865. Record at Point Lookout states that he was captured near Jacksonville on March 8, 1865. Released at Point Lookout after taking the Oath of Allegiance on June 28, 1865.

JONES, WILLIAM, Corporal
Born in Jones County where he resided as a farmer and enlisted at age 22, May 24, 1861, for the war.

Mustered in as Private and appointed Corporal, November-December, 1862. Wounded at South Mountain, Maryland, September 14-15, 1862, and captured at Sharpsburg, Maryland, September 17, 1862. Confined at Fort McHenry, Maryland, and sent to Fort Monroe, Virginia, October 17, 1862, for exchange. Admitted to hospital at Richmond, Virginia, October 24, 1862, and furloughed for 30 days on November 6, 1862. Reported as absent wounded on company muster rolls through October, 1864. Admitted to hospital at Richmond, February 25, 1865, with a gunshot wound of the right thigh and retired to the Invalid Corps on March 23, 1865, by reason of gunshot wound received at South Mountain, Maryland.

JONES, WILLIAM S., Private
Resided in Jones County where he enlisted at age 26, May 24, 1861, for the war. Died at Camp Advance, Northampton County, July 1-13, 1861.

JORDAN, FRANCIS M., Private
Resided in Jones County where he enlisted at age 25, May 24, 1861, for the war. Present or accounted for until killed in skirmish at Bristoe Station, Virginia, October 14, 1863.

KAGGER, J. L., Private
Captured at Gettysburg, Pennsylvania, July 5, 1863, and confined at DeCamp General Hospital, Davids Island, New York Harbor, until paroled on August 24, 1863, and exchanged at City Point, Virginia, on August 28, 1863.

KARRIKER, WILEY, Private
Enlisted in Wake County on April 26, 1864, for the war. Wounded and captured at Winchester, Virginia, September 19, 1864. Confined in hospital at Baltimore, Maryland, until transferred to Point Lookout, Maryland, January 2, 1865. Paroled at Point Lookout and transferred for exchange to Boulware's Wharf, James River, Virginia, January 17, 1865. Admitted to hospital at Richmond, Virginia, January 22, 1865, and furloughed for 60 days on January 24, 1865.

KILLINGSWORTH, IVY, Private
Resided in Jones County where he enlisted at age 23, May 24, 1861, for the war. Accidentally killed by the explosion of a bombshell at Camp Wyatt, near Wilmington, June 1, 1862.

KILPATRICK, D. N., Private
Paroled at Greensboro on May 12, 1865.

KINCEY, CHRISTOPHER, Private
Resided in Jones County where he enlisted at age 33, May 24, 1861, for the war. Killed at Cold Harbor, Virginia, July 27, 1862.

KINCEY, JAMES M., Private
Resided in Jones County where he enlisted at age 19, May 24, 1861, for the war. Died at Front Royal, Virginia, November 23, 1862.

KING, LEWIS, Sergeant
Resided in Jones County where he enlisted at age 21, May 24, 1861, for the war. Mustered in as Private. Wounded at Malvern Hill, Virginia, July 1, 1862. Promoted to Corporal in November, 1862, and to Sergeant on December 1, 1862. Present or accounted for until wounded and captured at Kelly's Ford, Virginia, November 7, 1863. Ad-

mitted to hospital at Washington, D.C., November 9, 1863, and transferred to Old Capitol Prison, Washington, January 6, 1864. Transferred on February 3, 1864, to Point Lookout, Maryland, where he was paroled and sent to Venus Point, Savannah River, Georgia, November 1, 1864, for exchange. Issued clothing on November 17, 1864, as a "paroled prisoner."

KISER, JOHN L., Private
Resided in Cabarrus County and enlisted in Wake County on April 26, 1864, for the war. Admitted to hospital at Charlottesville, Virginia, June 16, 1864, with "febris continua" and returned to duty on July 15, 1864. Federal Provost Marshal records indicate that he was admitted to hospital at Winchester, Virginia, October 6, 1864, with "rheumatism." Date and place captured not reported. Transferred to hospital at Baltimore, Maryland, October 12, 1864, and transferred from hospital to Point Lookout, Maryland, October 18, 1864. Paroled at Point Lookout, October 30, 1864, and sent to Venus Point, Savannah River, Georgia, for exchange. Declared exchanged at Venus Point on November 15, 1864. Admitted to hospital at Richmond, Virginia, April 1, 1865, with "chronic rheumatism." Captured in hospital at Richmond on April 3, 1865, and confined at Newport News, Virginia, until released after taking the Oath of Allegiance on June 30, 1865.

KOONCE, CALVIN H., Private
Resided in Jones County where he enlisted at age 22, May 24, 1861, for the war. Mustered in as Corporal. Captured at Sharpsburg, Maryland, September 17, 1862, and confined at Fort Delaware, Delaware, until paroled and exchanged at Aiken's Landing, Virginia, November 10, 1862. Reduced to ranks in November, 1862. Wounded at Chancellorsville, Virginia, May 3, 1863. Present or accounted for until captured at Kelly's Ford, Virginia, November 7, 1863. Confined at Point Lookout, Maryland, until paroled for exchange on September 18, 1864. Appears as present on a muster roll of a detachment of paroled and exchanged prisoners at Camp Lee, near Richmond, Virginia, dated October 11, 1864.

KOONCE, ELIJAH B., Private
Resided in Jones County where he enlisted at age 18, May 24, 1861, for the war. Wounded at Gettysburg, Pennsylvania, July 2-3, 1863, and died of wound on July 7, 1863.

KOONCE, EMANUEL F. B., Corporal
Resided in Jones County and enlisted in Wayne County at age 26, April 17, 1862, for the war. Mustered in as Private and appointed Corporal, January-February, 1863. Killed at Chancellorsville, Virginia, May 3, 1863.

KOONCE, JOHN PARSON, Private
Resided in Jones County where he enlisted at age 20, May 24, 1861, for the war. Wounded at Malvern Hill, Virginia, July 1, 1862, and furloughed from hospital at Richmond, Virginia, for 40 days on July 19, 1862. Discharged February 17, 1863, on providing Daniel Harper as his substitute.

KOONCE, MICHAEL, Private
Enlisted in Wake County on April 8, 1864, for the war. Present or accounted for until reported on the September-October, 1864, muster roll with the remark: "Absent missing since the battle of Cedar Creek, October 19, 1864."

KOONCE, RICHARD H., Private
Resided in Jones County where he enlisted at age 20, April 11, 1862, for the war. Mustered in as Private and appointed Corporal on October 1, 1862. Discharged on April 17, 1863, after providing a substitute. Later he enlisted in Company I, 27th Regiment N.C. Troops. Transferred back to this company on November 5, 1863. Captured at Mechanicsville, Virginia, May 30, 1864, and confined at Point Lookout, Maryland. Transferred on July 8, 1864, to Elmira, New York, where he remained until released after taking the Oath of Allegiance on June 30, 1865.

KOONCE, WILLIAM B., Private
Born in Jones County where he resided and enlisted at age 26, May 24, 1861, for the war. Wounded at South Mountain, Maryland, September 14, 1862, and died of wound.

LANDY, F., Private
Resided in Wilson County and paroled at Goldsboro on May 17, 1865. "Came in for parole."

LANE, WILLIAM A., Private
Resided in Forsyth County and enlisted in Wake County at age 27, August 28, 1862, for the war. Wounded at Chancellorsville, Virginia, May 3, 1863. Present or accounted for until captured at Spotsylvania Court House, Virginia, May 20, 1864. Confined at Point Lookout, Maryland, until released after taking the Oath of Allegiance and joining the U.S. service on June 7, 1864. Assigned to Company E, 1st Regiment U.S. Volunteer Infantry.

LANIER, HARRIS, Private
Resided in Onslow County and enlisted in Wake County on August 28, 1862, for the war. Killed at Chancellorsville, Virginia, May 3, 1863.

LENTZ, ABRAM, Private
Enlisted in Wake County on April 1, 1864, for the war. Captured at Winchester, Virginia, September 19, 1864, and confined at Point Lookout, Maryland, until transferred for exchange to Aiken's Landing, Virginia, March 15, 1865. Declared exchanged on March 18, 1865.

LENTZ, JOHN, Private
Resided in Cabarrus County and enlisted in Wake County on April 26, 1864, for the war. Captured at Petersburg, Virginia, April 3, 1865, and confined at Hart's Island, New York Harbor, until released after taking the Oath of Allegiance on June 17, 1865.

LINDSAY, THOMAS J., Private
Resided in Orange County and enlisted in Wake County on May 3, 1864, for the war. Admitted to hospital at Richmond, Virginia, June 3, 1864, with a gunshot wound of the leg and furloughed on June 17, 1864. Admitted to hospital at Raleigh on June 27, 1864, and furloughed. Readmitted to

hospital at Raleigh on September 27, 1864, and transferred to Kittrell's on January 1, 1865.

LOCKEY, HENRY J., Private
Resided in Jones County where he enlisted at age 30, May 27, 1861, for the war. Killed at Malvern Hill, Virginia, July 1, 1862.

LOW, NATHANIEL, Private
Paroled at Greensboro on May 28, 1865.

McDANIEL, JOHN, Sergeant
Resided in Jones County where he enlisted at age 23, May 24, 1861, for the war. Mustered in as Corporal. Wounded and captured at South Mountain, Maryland, September 14-15, 1862. Admitted to hospital at Frederick, Maryland, October 22, 1862, and transferred to hospital at Baltimore, Maryland, November 12, 1862. Sent to Fort McHenry, Maryland, November 17, 1862, and paroled and exchanged at City Point, Virginia, November 21, 1862. Admitted to hospital at Petersburg, Virginia, November 21, 1862, with gunshot wound in the eyes. Hospital records indicate that he lost both eyes. Furloughed for 90 days on November 29, 1862. Promoted to Sergeant in December, 1862. Company muster rolls report him as absent wounded through October, 1864.

McKNIGHT, JOHN, Private
Resided in Jones County where he enlisted at age 46, May 24, 1861, for the war. July 1-October 31, 1862, muster roll reports him as "absent sick in Richmond." Hospital record states that he was furloughed for 40 days on September 29, 1862. Reported as absent without leave on company muster rolls through December, 1863, when he was reported with the remark: "Died August 19, 1862." Roll of Honor reports him with the remark: "Deserted."

MORRISON, DANIEL, Private
Resided in Texas and enlisted in Wake County at age 37, September 7, 1862, for the war. May-June, 1863, muster roll reports him with remark: "Died of wounds received at Chancellorsville, Virginia, May, 1863." Roll of Honor states that he was "killed May 3, 1863, in battle of Chancellorsville."

OLIVER, ISAAC H., Private
Resided in Jones County where he enlisted at age 21, May 24, 1861, for the war. Died in hospital on December 17, 1861.

O'NEAL, B., Private
Resided in Craven County. Captured at Petersburg, Virginia, April 3, 1865, and confined at Hart's Island, New York Harbor, until released after taking the Oath of Allegiance on June 17, 1865.

OWENS, EDWARD M., Private
Resided in Jones County where he enlisted at age 26, May 24, 1861, for the war. Present or accounted for until transferred to Company I, 27th Regiment N.C. Troops on November 5, 1863.

OWENS, GEORGE, Private
Resided in Jones County where he enlisted at age 20, May 24, 1861, for the war. Died of wounds

received by the accidental explosion of a shell on June 1, 1862.

OWENS, JOSIAH, Private
Enlisted in Wake County on April 8, 1864, for the war. Captured at Fisher's Hill, Virginia, September 22, 1864. Confined at Point Lookout, Maryland, until paroled and sent to Venus Point, Savannah River, Georgia, October 30, 1864, for exchange. Declared exchanged at Venus Point on November 15, 1864.

PARHAM, ALEX, Private
Captured in hospital at Richmond, Virginia, April 3, 1865, and transferred to Newport News, Virginia, April 23, 1865.

PASCHAL, ROBERT T., Private
Resided in Rockingham County and enlisted in Wake County at age 19, September 3, 1862, for the war. Present or accounted for until captured at Kelly's Ford, Virginia, November 7, 1863. Confined at Point Lookout, Maryland, until paroled and transferred for exchange to Aiken's Landing, Virginia, February 24, 1865. Admitted to hospital at Richmond, Virginia, where he was paid on March 2, 1865. Paroled at Greensboro on May 5, 1865.

PEACOCK, JACOB, Private
Enlisted in Wake County on April 26, 1864, for the war. May 1-August 31, 1864, muster roll states that he "deserted July 14, 1864, near Poolsville, Maryland." Federal Provost Marshal records indicate that he was captured July 18, 1864, and confined at Old Capitol Prison, Washington, D.C. Transferred on July 23-25, 1864, to Elmira, New York, where he died September 4, 1864, of "chronic diarrhoea."

PERRY, ANDREW, Private
Resided in Alamance County and enlisted in Wake County at age 34, August 28, 1862, for the war. Deserted August 29, 1862.

POLK, JOHN RICHARDSON, Private
Resided in Cabarrus County and enlisted in Wake County at age 32, April 27, 1864, for the war. Present or accounted for on company muster rolls through October, 1864. Captured at Burkeville, Virginia, April 6, 1865, and confined at Point Lookout, Maryland, until released after taking the Oath of Allegiance on June 17, 1865.

POLLOCK, WILLIAM H., Corporal
Resided in Jones County where he enlisted at age 21, May 24, 1861, for the war. Mustered in as Corporal. Wounded at Malvern Hill, Virginia, July 1, 1862, and died of wound on August 10, 1862.

POTTER, M. CHOEL, Private
Captured at Jordan Springs, Virginia, July 26, 1863, and paroled on August 2, 1863.

RHODES, BENJAMIN F., Private
Resided in Jones County where he enlisted at age 21, May 24, 1861, for the war. Discharged on August 19, 1861, by reason of disability. Roll of Honor states that he "died August 31, 1861."

RHODES, BRANTLEY F., Private
Enlisted in Jones County on May 24, 1861, for the war. Discharged on August 19, 1861. Later

enlisted in Company K, 19th Regiment N.C. Troops (2nd Regiment N.C. Cavalry).

RHODES, EVIN, Private
Captured at Kinston on March 19, 1865, and confined at New Bern.

RHODES, GEORGE W., Private
Resided in Jones County where he enlisted at age 21, May 24, 1861, for the war. Wounded at Fredericksburg, Virginia, December 13, 1862, and returned to duty on February 3, 1863. Admitted to hospital at Richmond, Virginia, May 24, 1864, with a gunshot wound and furloughed for 40 days on July 23, 1864. Present or accounted for on company muster rolls through October, 1864. Captured at Petersburg, Virginia, April 3, 1865, and confined at Point Lookout, Maryland, until released after taking the Oath of Allegiance on June 17, 1865.

RHODES, JOHN H., Private
Resided in Jones County and enlisted in New Hanover County at age 18, May 5, 1862, for the war. Present or accounted for until captured at Kelly's Ford, Virginia, November 7, 1863. Confined at Point Lookout, Maryland, until paroled for exchange on September 30, 1864. Exact date of exchange not reported. Reported as present on a roll of a detachment of paroled and exchanged prisoners at Camp Lee, near Richmond, Virginia, dated October 11, 1864. Captured at Petersburg, Virginia, April 3, 1865, and confined at Hart's Island, New York Harbor, until released after taking the Oath of Allegiance on June 17, 1865.

RHODES, RICHARD, Private
Resided in Jones County and enlisted in Wayne County at age 19, April 17, 1862, for the war. Died at Richmond, Virginia, July 18, 1862.

ROBERSON, JOHN, Private
Enlisted in Wake County on April 28, 1864, for the war. Present or accounted for on company muster rolls through October, 1864.

ROBERTSON, J. A., Private
Resided in Pitt County. Admitted to hospital at Charlottesville, Virginia, June 16, 1864, with "acute diarrhoea" and transferred to Convalescent Camp, June 18, 1864. Captured at Petersburg, Virginia, April 3, 1865, and confined at Hart's Island, New York Harbor, until released after taking the Oath of Allegiance on June 17, 1865.

SANDEFORD, ELLIOT, Private
Resided in Wake County. Captured at Farmville, Virginia, April 6, 1865, and confined at Point Lookout, Maryland, until released after taking the Oath of Allegiance on June 20, 1865.

SAUNDERS, J., Private
Captured at Gettysburg, Pennsylvania, July 3, 1863, and confined at Fort Delaware, Delaware. Transferred on October 18, 1863, to Point Lookout, Maryland, where he remained until paroled and sent for exchange to James River, Virginia, February 18, 1865. Received in exchange at Boulware's Wharf, James River, February 20-21, 1865.

SAUNDERS, JOHN S., Private
Resided in Caswell County and enlisted in Wake County at age 25, September 2, 1862, for the war.

Wounded at Chancellorsville, Virginia, May 3, 1863. Present or accounted for on company muster rolls through October, 1864. Paroled at Appomattox Court House, Virginia, April 9, 1865.

SAWYER, ANDREW F., 1st Sergeant

Resided in Jones County where he enlisted on May 24, 1861, for the war. Mustered in as Sergeant. Wounded at Chancellorsville, Virginia, May 3, 1863. Promoted to 1st Sergeant, November-December, 1863. Present or accounted for until killed at Fisher's Hill, Virginia, September 22, 1864.

SHELFER, EVERETT, Private

Resided in Jones County where he enlisted at age 21, May 24, 1861, for the war. Wounded at Cold Harbor, Virginia, June 28, 1862, and died of wound.

SHELFER, JOHN, Private

Born in Jones County where he resided prior to enlisting in Wayne County at age 25, April 11, 1862, for the war. Died in hospital at Richmond, Virginia, January 15, 1863, of "variola."

SMITH, CALVIN D., Private

Enlisted in the fall of 1864 for the war. Paroled at Greensboro on May 23, 1865.

SMITH, E. L., Corporal

Paroled at Goldsboro on May 4, 1865.

STAFFORD, WARNER, Private

Resided in Alamance County and enlisted in Wake County at age 30, September 3, 1862, for the war. Left sick at Bunker Hill, Virginia, October 29, 1862, and captured the next day. Paroled at Provost Marshal General Office, Army of the Potomac, October 30, 1862, and was "permitted to proceed to and remain within any of the loyal states."

STALLINGS, JOHN R., Private

Resided in Edgecombe County and enlisted in Wake County on April 28, 1864, for the war. Present or accounted for on company muster rolls through October, 1864. Captured at Burkeville, Virginia, April 6, 1865, and confined at Point Lookout, Maryland, until released after taking the Oath of Allegiance on June 20, 1865.

STANLY, BRYAN, Private

Resided in Jones County where he enlisted at age 18, May 24, 1861, for the war. Died in camp on November 4, 1861.

SWIFT, G. R., Private

Enlisted in Wake County on April 26, 1864, for the war. May 1-August 31, 1864, muster roll states that he "deserted July 14, 1864, near Poolsville, Maryland."

TAGER, L., Private

Captured at Fisher's Hill, Virginia, September 22, 1864, and sent to Point Lookout, Maryland, October 1, 1864.

TAYLOR, WILLIAM, Private

Resided in Wilson County and paroled at Goldsboro in 1865.

TRIVITT, ANDREW, Private

Enlisted in Wake County for the war. First reported on May 1-August 31, 1864, muster roll, but the date of enlistment was not reported.

Appears on that muster roll with the remark: "Deserted July 29 near Martinsburg, Virginia."

TURNER, JOHN E., Private

Resided in Jones County where he enlisted at age 26, May 24, 1861, for the war. Died at Camp Advance, Northampton County, July 15, 1861.

TUTTLE, FRANCIS J., Private

Enlisted in Wake County on April 8, 1864, for the war. Present or accounted for on company muster rolls through October, 1864.

TUTTLE, MARTIN LEE, Private

Enlisted in Wake County on April 8, 1864, for the war. Wounded and captured at Spotsylvania Court House, Virginia, May 12, 1864. Confined in hospital at Washington, D.C., until transferred to Old Capitol Prison, Washington, December 4, 1864. Transferred on December 16, 1864, to Elmira, New York, where he remained until paroled for exchange on February 13, 1865. Received in exchange at Boulware's Wharf, James River, Virginia, February 20-21, 1865. Admitted to hospital at Richmond, Virginia, February 21, 1865, and furloughed on February 25, 1865.

WARTERS, EDWARD H., Private

Resided in Jones County where he enlisted at age 17, May 24, 1861, for the war. Present or accounted for until captured at Kelly's Ford, Virginia, November 7, 1863. Confined at Point Lookout, Maryland, until released after taking the Oath of Allegiance and joining the U.S. Army on February 11, 1864. Unit to which assigned not reported.

WARTERS, WILLIAM H., Private

Born in Jones County where he resided and enlisted at age 20, May 24, 1861, for the war. Captured at South Mountain, Maryland, September 14, 1862, and confined at Fort Delaware, Delaware, until paroled and exchanged at Aiken's Landing, Virginia, October 6, 1862. Declared exchanged on November 10, 1862. Admitted to hospital at Richmond, Virginia, October 8, 1862, and transferred to Goldsboro on October 16, 1862. Readmitted to hospital at Richmond on November 24, 1862, with rheumatism and transferred to Huguenot Springs, Virginia, November 30, 1862. Died in hospital at Lexington, Virginia, April 17, 1863.

WARTERS, WILLIAM M., Private

Resided in Jones County where he enlisted at age 29, May 24, 1861, for the war. Killed at Malvern Hill, Virginia, July 1, 1862.

WESTBROOK, CURTIS, Private

Resided in Jones County where he enlisted at age 40, May 24, 1861, for the war. Present or accounted for on company muster rolls until captured at Kelly's Ford, Virginia, November 7, 1863. Confined at Point Lookout, Maryland, until paroled and sent to Aiken's Landing, Virginia, May 3, 1864, for exchange. Declared exchanged on May 8, 1864, and admitted to hospital at Richmond, Virginia, on the same day with "rheumatism acute." Furloughed for 30 days on May 12, 1864. May 1-August 31, 1864, muster roll reports him as absent with the remark: "Enlisted by Colonel J. N. Whitford in the 67th Regiment

N.C. Troops." Reported with same remark on September-October, 1864, muster roll. No record of his being officially transferred.

WESTBROOK, FREEMAN S., Private
Resided in Jones County where he enlisted at age 18, May 24, 1861, for the war. July 1-October 31, 1862, muster roll reports him with the remark: "Died July 18, 1862."

WESTBROOK, JAMES H., Private
Born in Jones County where he resided and enlisted at age 21, May 24, 1861, for the war. Present or accounted for until he died in hospital at Martinsburg, Virginia, June 24, 1863.

WESTBROOK, JOSIAH, Private
Resided in Jones County where he enlisted at age 23, May 24, 1861, for the war. Present or accounted for until captured at Kelly's Ford, Virginia, November 7, 1863. Confined at Point Lookout, Maryland, until paroled and sent for exchange to Venus Point, Savannah River, Georgia, October 30, 1864. Declared exchanged at Venus Point on November 15, 1864.

WESTBROOK, WILLIAM H. H., Private
Resided in Jones County where he enlisted at age 28, May 24, 1861, for the war. Wounded in skirmish at Bristoe Station, Virginia, October 14, 1863. Killed near Spotsylvania Court House, Virginia, May 14, 1864.

WHALEY, CURTIS, Private
Resided in Jones County and enlisted at Camp Potomac, Virginia, at age 46, February 3, 1862, for the war. Died of disease September 8-15, 1862.

WHITE, AUGUSTUS W., Private
Resided in Jones County where he enlisted at age 20, May 24, 1861, for the war. Wounded at Chancellorsville, Virginia, May 3, 1863. Returned to the company by September, 1863. Present or accounted for until wounded and admitted to hospital at Richmond, Virginia, May 22, 1864. Date and place wounded not reported. Company muster rolls carry him as absent wounded through October, 1864. Admitted to hospital on April 10, 1865, at Raleigh, where he was captured on April 13, 1865. Paroled at Raleigh on April 20, 1865.

WHITE, JAMES F., Private
Born in Jones County where he resided as a merchant and enlisted at age 22, May 24, 1861, for the war. Mustered in as Private and promoted to Corporal, July-October, 1862. Promoted to Sergeant on October 1, 1862. Reduced to ranks on December 1, 1862. Wounded at Fredericksburg, Virginia, December 13, 1862, and reported as absent wounded through October, 1863. While absent wounded he was captured on the Wilmington and Warsaw Railroad, July 3-5, 1863. Confined at Fort Monroe, Virginia, until exchanged at City Point, Virginia, July 17, 1863. Present or accounted for until discharged on January 16, 1864, by reason of "a gunshot wound of the left forearm received at the battle of Fredericksburg, December 13, 1862, injuring the radius and the radial bone."

WHITEHEAD, J. W., Private
Resided in Wilson County and paroled at Goldsboro on May 17, 1865. "Came in for parole."

WHORTON, JOSEPH, Private
Resided in Jones County where he enlisted at age 17, May 24, 1861, for the war. Present or accounted for until "accidentally wounded while on picket June 23, 1862." Died from wound on August 1, 1862.

WILLIAMS, IVEY J., Private
Resided in Jones County where he enlisted at age 19, May 24, 1861, for the war. Died in camp November 1-20, 1861.

WILLIAMS, JACOB, Private
Enlisted in Wake County on April 22, 1864, for the war. Admitted to hospital at Richmond, Virginia, June 10, 1864, with a gunshot wound and furloughed for 30 days on July 30, 1864. Reported as absent on sick furlough on September-October, 1864, muster roll.

WILLIAMS, JOHN, Private
Resided in Edgecombe County and enlisted in Wake County on April 8, 1864, for the war. Captured at Fisher's Hill, Virginia, September 22, 1864, and confined at Point Lookout, Maryland, until paroled and sent to Venus Point, Savannah River, Georgia, November 1, 1864, for exchange. Captured at Petersburg, Virginia, April 3, 1865, and confined at Hart's Island, New York Harbor, until released after taking the Oath of Allegiance on June 17, 1865.

WILLIAMS, LEWIS H., Private
Born in Jones County where he resided as a merchant and enlisted at age 25, May 24, 1861, for the war. Captured at Boonsboro, Maryland, September 15, 1862, and confined at Fort Delaware, Delaware, until paroled and exchanged at Aiken's Landing, Virginia, October 6, 1862. Declared exchanged on November 10, 1862. Admitted to hospital on October 18, 1862, at Richmond, Virginia, where he died on October 28, 1862, of "febris typhoides."

WILLIFORD, THOMAS, Private
Resided in Jones County where he enlisted at age 17, May 24, 1861, for the war. Wounded at Gettysburg, Pennsylvania, July 1-3, 1863, and captured in hospital at Gettysburg on July 4-5, 1863. Died in hospital at Gettysburg on August 5, 1863, of "amputated left shoulder."

WILSON, DAVID, Private
Enlisted in Wake County on June 4, 1864, for the war. Deserted near Charlottesville, Virginia, June 16, 1864, and returned to company on September 26, 1864. Sent to hospital on October 29, 1864. Paroled at Greensboro on May 5, 1865.

WILSON, I. F., Private
Retired to Invalid Corps on November 26, 1864, by reason of his being "unfit for field service." Detailed for light duty at Richmond, Virginia, December 30, 1864, and transferred to Danville, Virginia. Paroled at Greensboro on May 8, 1865.

WINSTEAD, J. W., Private
Enlisted in Wake County on May 3, 1864, for the war. Present or accounted for on company muster rolls through October, 1864. Paroled at Winchester, Virginia, on April 27, 1865.

WYNN, J., Private
Resided in Edgecombe County and paroled at Goldsboro on May 19, 1865. "Came in for parole."

YOUNG, HENRY H., Private
Resided in Franklin County and enlisted in Wake County at age 32, September 2, 1862, for the war. Present or accounted for on company muster rolls through October, 1864. Paroled at Appomattox Court House, Virginia, April 9, 1865.

COMPANY H

This company was organized in Wayne County and enlisted at Goldsboro on May 27, 1861. It tendered its service to the state and was ordered to Camp Advance, near Garysburg, Northampton County, where it was assigned to this regiment as Company H. After joining the regiment the company functioned as a part of the regiment, and its history for the war period is recorded as a part of the regimental history.

The information contained in the following roster of the company was compiled principally from company muster rolls for June 5, 1861, through October, 1861; March through October, 1862; January, 1863, through March, 1864; and May through August, 1864. No company muster rolls were found for the period prior to June 5, 1861; for November, 1861, through February, 1862; November-December, 1862; April, 1864; or for the period after August, 1864. In addition to the company muster rolls, Roll of Honor records, receipt rolls, and hospital records, supplemented by state pension applications, United Daughters of the Confederacy records, and postwar rosters and histories, all provided useful information.

OFFICERS
CAPTAINS

WASHINGTON, JAMES A.
Resided in Wayne County and appointed Captain at age 29 to rank from May 16, 1861. Resigned on April 22, 1863, upon appointment as Lieutenant Colonel of the 50th Regiment N.C. Troops. Transferred to the Field and Staff of that regiment.

COBB, JOHN P.
Resided in Wayne County and appointed 2nd Lieutenant to rank from May 16, 1861. Promoted to 1st Lieutenant to rank from April 22, 1862, and promoted to Captain to rank from May 10, 1862. Wounded at Malvern Hill, Virginia, July 1, 1862. Wounded at Chancellorsville, Virginia, May 3, 1863, and returned to duty on August 1, 1863. Wounded at Cold Harbor, Virginia, June 2, 1864. Transferred to the Field and Staff of this regiment upon appointment as Colonel to rank from August 30, 1864.

LIEUTENANTS

BRIDGES, A. H., Lieutenant
Reported as a patient in General Hospital No. 1, Kittrell's, N.C., for the week ending April 7, 1865, with the remark: "Returned to duty."

COBB, BRYAN W., 1st Lieutenant
Resided in Wayne County where he enlisted at age 20, May 27, 1861, for the war. Mustered in as Sergeant and promoted to 1st Sergeant, March-April, 1862. January-February, 1863, muster roll states that he was promoted to Captain of Company I, 66th Regiment N.C. Troops; however, there is no indication that he served as such. Reduced to ranks April 17, 1863, and detailed at Goldsboro. Reappointed Sergeant when he returned to the company on May 11, 1863. Appointed 1st Sergeant from that date. Wounded at Gettysburg, Pennsylvania, July 1, 1863, and reported as absent wounded through August, 1863. Appointed 2nd Lieutenant to rank from October 8, 1863. Wounded at Spotsylvania Court House, Virginia, May 12, 1864. Wounded at Winchester, Virginia, September 19, 1864. Promoted to 1st Lieutenant to rank from October 12, 1864. Wounded at Cedar Creek, Virginia, October 19, 1864. Reported in hospital at Lynchburg, Virginia, for the week ending October 31, 1864, with the remark that he was admitted with a wound of the head. Admitted to hospital at Richmond, Virginia, March 27, 1865, with "vul. contusum abdomen." Hospital records indicate that the wound was received in battle and that he was returned to duty on April 2, 1865.

GULLICK, JAMES WHARTON, 3rd Lieutenant
Resided in Wayne County and appointed 3rd Lieutenant at age 26 to rank from May 16, 1861. Wounded at Malvern Hill, Virginia, July 1, 1862, and reported as absent wounded on company muster rolls until he resigned on August 18, 1863, by reason of wound.

MUNRO, DONALD D., 1st Lieutenant
Resided in Wayne County and appointed 1st Lieutenant to rank from May 16, 1861. Appointed Captain by the C.S. War Department to rank from April 22, 1862, but the appointment was not recognized by the state of North Carolina and he continued to serve as 1st Lieutenant. Captured at Sharpsburg, Maryland, September 17, 1862, and paroled near Keedysville, Maryland, September 20, 1862. Reported as absent on leave until detailed for light duty at Richmond, Virginia, November 23, 1863. Returned to company May-August, 1864. From April, 1862, through June, 1864, he was reported as 1st Lieutenant by the company and as Captain by the C.S. War Department. On June 8, 1864, he requested appointment as Lieutenant Colonel of the regiment, basing his claim to the appointment under his appointment as Captain by the War Department. The request for appointment to Lieutenant Colonel and his request to appear before an Examining Board were denied, and the case of the appointment to Captain became the central issue. He contended he was appointed by the War Department and therefore his appointment was valid, but the officers of the regiment contended that it was a State Troops unit and therefore the Governor was the only one who could appoint officers. The War Department resolved the case by stipulating that all officers to be appointed in the future would be appointed by the War Department and not by the governor of North Carolina but that all officers who were in position as appoint-

ments from the state of North Carolina would remain as such. On September 9, 1864, he tendered his resignation as Captain. The resignation was accepted on October 12, 1864, and he was dropped from the rolls. On September 22, 1864, he submitted a request to withdraw his resignation, but it was not acted upon.

WHITFIELD, NATHAN B., 3rd Lieutenant
Resided in Wayne County where he enlisted at age 21, May 27, 1861, for the war. Mustered in as Corporal and appointed 3rd Lieutenant to rank from May 20, 1862. Captured at Sharpsburg, Maryland, September 17, 1862, and paroled and exchanged at Aiken's Landing, Virginia, November 10, 1862. Present or accounted for until transferred to 2nd Company C of this regiment upon appointment as Captain to rank from February 1, 1863.

NONCOMMISSIONED OFFICERS AND PRIVATES

BAKER, JACOB BRONAUGH, Private
Resided in Wayne County where he enlisted at age 23, May 27, 1861, for the war. Present or accounted for until discharged on April 9, 1862.

BAKER, WILLIAM, Private
Born in Johnston County where he resided as a farmer prior to enlisting in Wake County at age 27, September 3, 1862, for the war. Discharged February 13, 1863, by reason of "phthisis pulmonalis succeeding variola."

BEST, RIGDON G., 1st Sergeant
Born in Wayne County where he resided as a clerk and enlisted at age 24, May 29, 1861, for the war. Mustered in as 1st Sergeant. Discharged January 1, 1862, upon providing a substitute.

BEST, WILLIAM BRIGHT, Sergeant
Born in Wayne County where he resided as a farmer and enlisted at age 20, May 27, 1861, for the war. Mustered in as Corporal and promoted to Sergeant on May 14, 1862. Transferred to Company D, 50th Regiment N.C. Troops upon appointment as 2nd Lieutenant on June 6, 1862.

BLACKMAN, J. M., Private
Name reported on undated roll of prisoners of war captured by the Army of the Ohio. Place captured not reported.

BLACKMAN, JOHN A., Private
Resided in Johnston County and enlisted in Wake County at age 23, September 3, 1862, for the war. Wounded at Chancellorsville, Virginia, May 3, 1863. Present or accounted for on company muster rolls through August, 1864, when he appears with the remark: "Detailed by order of General Early to thresh wheat in the valley." Paroled at Raleigh on May 13, 1865.

BLACKMAN, YOUNG C., Private
Resided in Sampson County and enlisted in Wake County at age 34, July 22, 1862, for the war. Wounded at Chancellorsville, Virginia, May 3, 1863, and died of wound in hospital at Richmond, Virginia, May 14, 1863.

BOGER, GEORGE C., Private
Enlisted at Camp Vance on May 9, 1864, for the war. Assigned to this company on May 20, 1864. Wounded and captured at Winchester, Virginia, September 19, 1864. Admitted to hospital on September 19, 1864, at Winchester, where he remained until transferred to Frederick, Maryland, January 18, 1865. Transferred to hospital at Baltimore, Maryland, January 19, 1865, and paroled and sent to James River, Virginia, for exchange on February 16, 1865. Admitted to hospital at Richmond, Virginia, March 4, 1865, and furloughed for 60 days on March 12, 1865.

BOSTON, URIAH, Private
Enlisted in Camp Vance on May 9, 1864, for the war. Died in hospital at Lynchburg, Virginia, on July 2, 1864, of "typhoid pneumonia."

BRIDGERS, GREEN, Private
Enlisted in Wake County on May 15, 1864, for the war. Captured at Strasburg, Virginia, October 19, 1864, and confined at Point Lookout, Maryland. Released at Point Lookout after taking the Oath of Allegiance on June 3, 1865.

BROCKEN, W., Private
Resided in Wilson County and paroled at Goldsboro on May 4, 1865. "Came in for parole."

BROOKS, J. L., Private
Paroled at Greensboro on May 12, 1865.

BUDD, JAMES W., Private
Resided in Wayne County where he enlisted at age 31, May 27, 1861, for the war. Discharged on August 21, 1861, by reason of disability.

CARRAWAY, THOMAS D., Sergeant
Born in Wayne County where he resided prior to enlisting in Northampton County at age 24, June 17, 1861, for the war. Mustered in as Private and appointed Corporal on May 14, 1862. Promoted to Sergeant on October 1, 1862. Killed at Chancellorsville, Virginia, May 3, 1863.

CARTER, LEVI, Private
Resided in Wayne County where he enlisted at age 45, May 27, 1861, for the war. Present or accounted for until captured at Kelly's Ford, Virginia, November 7, 1863. Confined at Point Lookout, Maryland, until transferred for exchange to Aiken's Landing, Virginia, February 24, 1865.

CASEY, ELIJAH, Private
Resided in Wayne County where he enlisted at age 22, May 27, 1861, for the war. Wounded at Malvern Hill, Virginia, July 1, 1862, and reported in various hospitals at Richmond and Danville, Virginia, until returned to duty on August 2, 1863. Present or accounted for until captured at Winchester, Virginia, September 19, 1864. Confined at Point Lookout, Maryland, until paroled and transferred for exchange to Aiken's Landing, Virginia, March 15, 1865. Declared exchanged at Boulware's Wharf, Virginia, March 18, 1865.

CASEY, JOSHUA J., Private
Resided in Wayne County and enlisted in Northampton County at age 24, June 10, 1861,

for the war. Wounded at Malvern Hill, Virginia, July 1, 1862, and reported as absent wounded until retired to the Invalid Corps on September 26, 1864. Ordered to report for light duty to General Winder at Richmond, Virginia, November 15, 1864. Paroled at Goldsboro on May 18, 1865. "Came in for parole."

COBB, WILLIAM HENRY HARRISON, Private
Resided in Wayne County where he enlisted at age 20, July 6, 1861. for the war. Enlisted as Private and transferred to the Field and Staff of this regiment upon appointment as Sergeant Major on July 6, 1861, the date of his enlistment.

COLLIER, SAMUEL P., Private
Transferred from Company A, 10th Regiment N.C. State Troops (1st Regiment N.C. Artillery) January 16, 1864. Reported on company muster rolls as a Private with the remark that he was acting Sergeant Major. Present or accounted for on company muster rolls through August, 1864. Paroled at Appomattox Court House, Virginia, April 9, 1865.

CORBETT, WARREN, Private
Resided in Johnston County and enlisted in Wayne County at age 30, May 27, 1861, for the war. Captured at Sharpsburg, Maryland, September 17, 1862, and paroled and exchanged at Aiken's Landing, Virginia, November 10, 1862. Wounded at Fredericksburg, Virginia, December 13, 1862. Admitted to hospital at Richmond, Virginia, and furloughed for 40 days on January 8, 1863. Present or accounted for on company muster rolls through August, 1864. Paroled at Appomattox Court House, Virginia, April 9, 1865.

CORBETT, WILLIAM A., Private
Born in Johnston County where he resided as a farmer prior to enlisting in Wayne County at age 23, May 27, 1861, for the war. Died in hospital at Fredericksburg, Virginia, August 10, 1861.

COTTON, AMOS, Private
Resided in Wayne County where he enlisted at age 28, May 27, 1861, for the war. Wounded at Chancellorsville, Virginia, May 3, 1863. Present or accounted for until captured at Winchester, Virginia, September 19, 1864. Confined at Point Lookout, Maryland, until released after taking the Oath of Allegiance and joining the U.S. service on October 17, 1864. Assigned to Company C, 4th Regiment U.S. Volunteer Infantry.

COTTON, JOSHUA, Private
Resided in Wayne County where he enlisted at age 26, May 27, 1861, for the war. Present or accounted for on company muster rolls through August, 1864. Captured at Petersburg, Virginia, April 3, 1865, and confined at Hart's Island, New York Harbor, until released after taking the Oath of Allegiance on June 18, 1865.

CRAWFORD, LEWIS K., Corporal
Born in Pitt County where he resided prior to enlisting in Wayne County at age 19, May 27, 1861, for the war. Mustered in as Private. Captured at South Mountain, Maryland, September 14, 1862, and confined at Fort Delaware, Delaware,

until paroled and exchanged at Aiken's Landing, Virginia, November 10, 1862. Appointed Corporal on October 10, 1862. Wounded at Chancellorsville, Virginia, May 3, 1863, and died of wound on May 10, 1863.

CROOM, JOHN C., Private
Resided in Wayne County where he enlisted at age 30, May 27, 1861, for the war. Wounded at Malvern Hill, Virginia, July 1, 1862. Present or accounted for until captured at Kelly's Ford, Virginia, November 7, 1863. Confined at Point Lookout, Maryland, until released after taking the Oath of Allegiance and joining the U.S. service on February 1, 1864. Assigned to Company E, 1st Regiment U.S. Volunteer Infantry.

DAILY, JOHN, Private
Resided in Maryland and enlisted near Richmond, Virginia, at age 25, July 9, 1862, for the war. Deserted from camp near Richmond on July 11, 1862.

DAILY, JOHN W., 1st Sergeant
Resided in Wayne County and enlisted in Northampton County at age 19, June 17, 1861, for the war. Mustered in as Private and appointed Corporal on April 24, 1862. Wounded at Malvern Hill, Virginia, July 1, 1862. Promoted to Sergeant on July 4, 1862. Wounded at Chancellorsville, Virginia, May 3, 1863. Promoted to 1st Sergeant on October 8, 1863. Present or accounted for until wounded and captured at Winchester, Virginia, September 19, 1864. Confined in hospital at Baltimore, Maryland, until transferred to Point Lookout, Maryland, October 26, 1864. Paroled at Point Lookout on October 30, 1864, and sent to Venus Point, Savannah River, Georgia, for exchange. Declared exchanged at Venus Point on November 15, 1864. Captured at Petersburg, Virginia, April 3, 1865, and confined at Hart's Island, New York Harbor, until released after taking the Oath of Allegiance on June 18, 1865.

DALE, EVANS, Private
Born in Duplin County where he resided as a farmer prior to enlisting in Wayne County at age 19, May 27, 1861, for the war. Died in hospital at Fredericksburg, Virginia, August 26, 1861.

DAVIS, HARRISON D., Private
Captured at Gettysburg, Pennsylvania, July 3, 1863, and confined at Fort Delaware, Delaware, July 7-12, 1863. Took the Oath of Allegiance and joined the U.S. service on August 30, 1863. Assigned to Company G, 1st Regiment Connecticut Cavalry.

DEANS, JAMES W., Private
Born in Wayne County where he resided as a laborer and enlisted at age 34, May 27, 1861, for the war. Wounded at Malvern Hill, Virginia, July 1, 1862, and died of wound on July 14, 1862.

DeFORD, EPAMINONDAS WILLIAM, 1st Sergeant
Resided in Wayne County and enlisted in Northampton County at age 27, June 20, 1861, for the war. Mustered in as Private and appointed Corporal on January 1, 1862. Promoted to Sergeant on June 24, 1862, and to 1st Sergeant on April 6,

1863. Killed at Chancellorsville, Virginia, May 3, 1863.

ELLIXSON, JAMES S., Private

Resided in Person County and enlisted in Wake County at age 46, August 26, 1862, for the war as a substitute. Deserted on April 10, 1863, and returned from desertion on August 22, 1863. Captured at Kelly's Ford, Virginia, November 7, 1863, and confined at Point Lookout, Maryland, until released after taking the Oath of Allegiance and joining the U.S. service on January 26, 1864. Unit to which assigned not reported.

ELMORE, JAMES W., Sergeant

Resided in Wayne County and enlisted in Northampton County at age 24, June 5, 1861, for the war. Mustered in as Private and appointed Corporal on June 7, 1862. Promoted to Sergeant on November 1, 1862. Wounded at Chancellorsville, Virginia, May 3, 1863, and died of wound May 29-30, 1863.

FIELDS, CALVIN S., Private

Resided in Wayne County and enlisted in Wake County at age 30, July 15, 1862, for the war. Wounded at Chancellorsville, Virginia, May 3, 1863, and died of wound at Richmond, Virginia, June 3, 1863.

FLADUNG, ANTONE, Private

Born in Germany and resided in Wayne County where he enlisted at age 27, May 27, 1861, for the war. Killed at Chancellorsville, Virginia, May 3, 1863.

FOGLEMAN, A., Private

Captured at Harrisonburg, Virginia, September 27, 1864, and confined in hospital until transferred to Point Lookout, Maryland, October 28, 1864. Paroled at Point Lookout and sent to Venus Point, Savannah River, Georgia, for exchange on October 29, 1864. Received at Venus Point on November 15, 1864. Paroled at Greensboro on May 24, 1865.

GAME, EDWIN, Private

Resided in Johnston County and enlisted in Wayne County at age 36, May 27, 1861, for the war. Discharged on February 20, 1862, on providing a substitute.

GARDNER, HENRY C., Corporal

Resided in Wayne County and enlisted in Northampton County at age 19, June 18, 1861, for the war. Mustered in as Private. Wounded at Gettysburg, Pennsylvania, July 1, 1863. Appointed Corporal on June 1, 1864. Present or accounted for on company muster rolls through August, 1864. Federal Provost Marshal records report him as a "rebel deserter" received at Washington, D.C., April 10, 1865. Took the Oath of Allegiance and was provided transportation to New Bern.

GILLISPIE, J. H., Private

Died in hospital at Lynchburg, Virginia. Date and cause of death not reported. Effects received January 6, 1864.

GLADVILLE, WILLIAM C., Private

Resided in Wake County where he enlisted at age 47, August 20, 1862, for the war as a substitute.

Present or accounted for until killed at Cedar Creek, Virginia, October 19, 1864.

GOODWYN, RICHARD J., Sergeant

Born in Lunenburg County, Virginia, and resided as a jeweler prior to enlisting in Wayne County at age 21, May 27, 1861, for the war. Mustered in as Sergeant. Killed at Malvern Hill, Virginia, July 1, 1862.

GRADY, GILES, Private

Resided in Duplin County and enlisted in Wayne County at age 27, May 27, 1861, for the war. Present or accounted for until captured at Kelly's Ford, Virginia, November 7, 1863. Confined at Point Lookout, Maryland, until paroled and exchanged at Aiken's Landing, Virginia, February 24, 1865. Declared exchanged on March 5, 1865.

GRADY, LEWIS, Private

Born in Wayne County where he resided as a farmer and enlisted at age 21, May 27, 1861, for the war. Wounded at Chancellorsville, Virginia, May 3, 1863, and died of wound on May 20, 1863.

GRADY, LEWIS H., Private

Born in Duplin County where he resided as a farmer prior to enlisting in New Hanover County at age 20, May 9, 1862, for the war. Killed at Malvern Hill, Virginia, July 1, 1862.

GRADY, NATHAN W., Private

Resided in Wayne County and enlisted in New Hanover County at age 19, May 9, 1862, for the war. Wounded at Malvern Hill, Virginia, July 1, 1862. Reported as absent wounded until detailed at Camp of Instruction, Raleigh, February 21, 1863. Company muster rolls report him as absent detailed through August, 1864. Retired to the Invalid Corps on December 29, 1864, and assigned to duty at Goldsboro on February 2, 1865.

GRADY, SIMEON, Private

Resided in Duplin County and enlisted in Wayne County at age 21, May 27, 1861, for the war. Wounded and captured at Chancellorsville, Virginia, May 3, 1863. Confined in hospital at Washington, D.C., until transferred to Old Capitol Prison, Washington, May 27, 1863. Paroled and exchanged at City Point, Virginia, June 12, 1863. Present or accounted for until captured at Kelly's Ford, Virginia, November 7, 1863. Confined at Point Lookout, Maryland, until paroled and transferred for exchange to Aiken's Landing, Virginia, February 24, 1865. Declared exchanged on March 5, 1865.

GRADY, WILLIAM, Private

Resided in Wayne County where he enlisted at age 19, October 28, 1861, for the war. Wounded at Chancellorsville, Virginia, May 3, 1863, and returned to duty July 20, 1863. Present or accounted for until captured at Kelly's Ford, Virginia, November 7, 1863. Confined at Point Lookout, Maryland, until released after taking the Oath of Allegiance and joining the U.S. service on January 26, 1864. Unit to which assigned not reported.

GRANT, ALLEN, Private

Born in Wayne County where he resided as a farmer prior to enlisting at Camp Potomac, King

George County, Virginia, at age 37, October 14, 1861, for the war. Died in camp near Richmond, Virginia, July 29, 1862, of disease.

GRANT, JOHN C., Private

Resided in Wayne County where he enlisted at age 35, May 27, 1861, for the war. Detailed as teamster May-June, 1863, and reported as absent on detail through August, 1864. Captured at Petersburg, Virginia, April 3, 1865, and confined at Hart's Island, New York Harbor, until released after taking the Oath of Allegiance on June 19, 1865.

GURLEY, RUFUS FRANK, Sergeant

Resided in Wayne County where he enlisted at age 21, May 27, 1861, for the war. Mustered in as Private. Captured at Sharpsburg, Maryland, September 17, 1862, and confined at Fort Delaware, Delaware, until paroled and exchanged at Aiken's Landing, Virginia, October 2, 1862. Declared exchanged on November 10, 1862. Promoted to Corporal on December 1, 1862. Paroled on May 4, 1863. Date and place captured and place exchanged not reported. Promoted to Sergeant, November-December, 1863. Present or accounted for until captured at Spotsylvania Court House, Virginia, May 19-20, 1864. Confined at Point Lookout, Maryland, until transferred to Elmira, New York, July 6, 1864. Released at Elmira after taking the Oath of Allegiance on June 30, 1865.

HAM, HIRAM J., Private

Resided in Wayne County where he enlisted at age 19, May 29, 1861, for the war. Discharged October 12, 1861.

HARDELL, ISHAM, Private

Resided in Stanly County and enlisted in Wayne County at age 19, May 27, 1861, for the war. Deserted June 14, 1862, but was captured and returned to the company. Deserted a second time on February 12, 1863. He was recaptured and escaped on September 3, 1863. Returned to the company under guard on January 21, 1864, and reported as present until he deserted a third time in July, 1864.

HARRELL, JOHN W., Private

Resided in Wayne County where he enlisted at age 24, May 29, 1861, for the war. Discharged on July 6, 1861, and returned to the company on September 3, 1861. Discharged a second time on December 17, 1861.

HARRISON, FRANKLIN M., Sergeant

Resided in Wayne County where he enlisted at age 27, May 29, 1861, for the war. Mustered in as Private and appointed Corporal on July 4, 1862. Reduced to ranks on December 1, 1862. Appointed Sergeant on November 1, 1863. Present or accounted for on company muster rolls through August, 1864. Captured at Burkeville, Virginia, April 6, 1865, and confined at Point Lookout, Maryland, until released after taking the Oath of Allegiance on June 27, 1865.

HEINNEMANN, MICHAEL, Private

Resided in Wayne County and enlisted at age 22, May 27, 186-, for the war. Discharged on July 9, 1862, by reason of having provided a substitute.

HENRY, ROBERT W., Sergeant

Resided in Wayne County where he enlisted at age 26, May 27, 1861, for the war. Mustered in as Corporal and promoted to Sergeant on January 1, 1862. Wounded and captured at Sharpsburg, Maryland, September 17, 1862. Paroled on September 27, 1862. Died of wound received at Sharpsburg but date and place of death not reported.

HERRING, JOSEPH R., Sergeant

Born in Wayne County where he resided as a farmer and enlisted at age 21, May 27, 1861, for the war. Mustered in as Private and appointed Corporal on January 7, 1862. Promoted to Sergeant on June 15, 1862. Killed at Sharpsburg, Maryland, September 17, 1862.

HINES, EDWIN, Private

Born in Wayne County where he resided and enlisted at age 30, May 27, 1861, for the war. Died at Camp Advance, Northampton County, July 9, 1861.

HINES, RICHARD B., Private

Born in Wayne County where he resided as a laborer and enlisted at age 25, May 27, 1861, for the war. Captured at Sharpsburg, Maryland, September 17, 1862, and confined at Fort McHenry, Maryland, until transferred for exchange to Fort Monroe, Virginia, October 17, 1862. Admitted to hospital on October 31, 1862, at Richmond, Virginia, where he died November 8, 1862, of "febris typhoides."

HINES, SAMUEL, Private

Born in Wayne County where he resided as a farmer and enlisted at age 21, June 26, 1861, for the war. Present or accounted for until killed at Sharpsburg, Maryland, September 17, 1862.

HINES, WILLIAM A., Private

Born in Wayne County where he resided as a farmer prior to enlisting in Craven County at age 18, February 21, 1862, for the war. Killed at Malvern Hill, Virginia, July 1, 1862.

HINSON, JAMES H., Private

Resided in Wayne County where he enlisted at age 35, May 27, 1861, for the war. Present or accounted for until admitted to hospital at Richmond, Virginia, on June 1, 1864, with a gunshot wound of the head. Died in hospital of wound on June 9, 1864.

HOGG, JAMES M., Private

Born in Johnston County where he resided as a laborer prior to enlisting in Wayne County at age 21, May 27, 1861, for the war. Killed at Cold Harbor, Virginia, June 27, 1862.

HOLLAND, JOHN GRAY, Private

Born in Johnston County where he resided prior to enlisting in Craven County at age 22, February 21, 1862, for the war. Present or accounted for until killed at Chancellorsville, Virginia, May 3, 1863.

HOLMES, WASHINGTON H., Private

Resided in Johnston County and enlisted in Wake County at age 20, September 3, 1862, for the war. Present or accounted for on company muster rolls through August, 1864.

HOWELL, HENRY A., Private

Resided in Wayne County where he enlisted at age 30, May 27, 1861, for the war. Present or accounted for until discharged on June 10, 1862, by reason of disability.

HOWELL, JOHN R., Musician

Enlisted at Camp Advance, Northampton County, at age 22, June 21, 1861, for the war. Mustered in as Private and appointed Musician, September-October, 1861. Present or accounted for until captured at Kelly's Ford, Virginia, November 7, 1863. Confined at Point Lookout, Maryland, until released after taking the Oath of Allegiance and joining the U.S. Army on February 1, 1864. Assigned to Company E, 1st Regiment U.S. Volunteer Infantry.

HOWELL, NEEDHAM, Private

Resided in Wayne County prior to enlisting in Northampton County at age 19, June 21, 1861, for the war. Mustered in as Private and appointed Musician, May-October, 1862. Reported as Musician through October, 1863, and as Private after that date. Captured at Kelly's Ford, Virginia, November 7, 1863, and confined at Point Lookout, Maryland, until released after taking the Oath of Allegiance and joining the U.S. service on February 1, 1864. Assigned to Company E, 1st Regiment U.S. Volunteer Infantry.

JELKS, CINCINNATUS, Private

Resided at Petersburg, Virginia, and enlisted in Wayne County at age 21, May 29, 1861, for the war. Present or accounted for until captured near Washington, D.C., July 12, 1864. Confined at Old Capitol Prison, Washington, until transferred to Elmira, New York, July 23, 1864. Released at Elmira after taking the Oath of Allegiance on May 29, 1865.

JELKS, THOMAS R., Private

Resided in Virginia and enlisted in Wayne County at age 23, May 29, 1861, for the war. Captured at Sharpsburg, Maryland, September 17, 1862, and paroled near Sharpsburg on September 27, 1862, with the remark: "Permitted to proceed to and remain in any of the loyal states."

JOHNSON, SIDNEY, Private

Resided in Wake County and enlisted in Northampton County at age 20, June 24, 1861, for the war. Deserted near Fredericksburg, Virginia, on August 23, 1861.

JORDAN, C., Private

Resided in Wilson County and paroled at Goldsboro in 1865.

JOURNEY, JAMES M., Private

Resided in Iredell County and enlisted at Camp Vance on August 19, 1862, for the war. Assigned to the company on May 22, 1864. Captured at Petersburg, Virginia, April 3, 1865, and confined at Hart's Island, New York Harbor, until released after taking the Oath of Allegiance on June 19, 1865.

JULIN, _____, Private

Paroled at Greensboro on May 11, 1865.

KENNEDY, JOHN W., Private

Resided in Wayne County where he enlisted at age 19, March 6, 1862, for the war as a substitute for Luther S. Kennedy. Captured at Fredericksburg, Virginia, May 3, 1863, and paroled and exchanged at City Point, Virginia, May 13, 1863. Wounded at Kelly's Ford, Virginia, November 7, 1863. Reported as absent wounded on company muster rolls through August, 1864. Furloughed for 40 days at Lynchburg, Virginia, September 1, 1864. Captured at Petersburg, Virginia, April 3, 1865, and confined at Hart's Island, New York Harbor, until released after taking the Oath of Allegiance on June 19, 1865.

KENNEDY, LUTHER S., Private

Resided in Wayne County where he enlisted at age 22, May 27, 1861, for the war. Present or accounted for until discharged on May 8, 1862, upon providing John W. Kennedy as his substitute. Later served in Company E, 61st Regiment N.C. Troops.

LEWIS, LORENZO DOW, Private

Born in Rockingham County and was by occupation a blacksmith when he enlisted in Wake County at age 19, April 7, 1864, for the war. Discharged on April 25, 1864, by reason of "an injury to the spine from a fall from a horse producing partial paralysis of lower limbs and a dislocation of radius of left arm at elbow joint."

LINDSAY, JULIEN, Private

Paroled at Greensboro on May 11, 1865.

LISSON, RICHARD, Private

Resided in Wayne County where he enlisted at age 39, May 27, 1861, for the war. Mustered in as Private and appointed Corporal on March 1, 1863. Promoted to Sergeant on May 11, 1863. Present or accounted for on company muster rolls as a Sergeant through October, 1863. Reported as Private on November-December, 1863, muster roll with the remark that he was killed at Kelly's Ford, Virginia, November 7, 1863.

MARLOW, BENNETT, Private

Born in Edgecombe County where he resided as a farmer prior to enlisting in Wayne County at age 23, May 27, 1861, for the war. Wounded at Kelly's Ford, Virginia, November 7, 1863. Present or accounted for until discharged on November 25, 1864, by reason of "ascites sodeminatis."

MARLOW, FRANKLIN, Private

Born in Edgecombe County where he resided as a laborer prior to enlisting in Wayne County at age 28, February 20, 1862, for the war. Captured at Sharpsburg, Maryland, September 17, 1862, and paroled near Keedysville, Maryland, September 20, 1862. Died at Winchester, Virginia, September 25, 1862.

MASSINGALE, ROBERT M., Private

Resided in Johnston County and enlisted in Wake County at age 34, September 3, 1862, for the war. Captured near Fredericksburg, Virginia, May 3, 1863, and paroled and exchanged at City Point, Virginia, May 13, 1863. Died at Camp Lee, near Richmond, Virginia, May 15, 1863, of disease.

MASSINGALE, WARREN TROY, Private

Resided in Johnston County and enlisted in Wake County at age 27, September 3, 1862, for the war.

Died in hospital at Richmond, Virginia, December 12, 1862.

MATTOX, JAMES, Private

Resided in Wayne County where he enlisted at age 29, May 27, 1861, for the war. Present or accounted for on company muster rolls through August, 1864, being detailed as a Pioneer from May-June, 1863, through August, 1864. Federal Provost Marshal records report him as a "rebel deserter" received at Washington, D.C., April 12, 1865. Took the Oath of Allegiance and was provided transportation to Goldsboro.

MINCEY, JESSE, Private

Resided in Wayne County where he enlisted at age 19, May 29, 1861, for the war. Wounded at Chancellorsville, Virginia, May 3, 1863, and reported as absent wounded until detailed as hospital guard at Lynchburg, Virginia, on November 28, 1863. Reported as absent on detail on company muster rolls through August, 1864. Federal Provost Marshal records indicate that he was captured near Harpers Ferry, West Virginia, July 8, 1864, and confined at Old Capitol Prison, Washington, D.C. Transferred to Elmira, New York, July 23-25, 1864. Paroled at Elmira on March 14, 1865, and sent to James River, Virginia, for exchange. Received in exchange at Boulware's Wharf, James River, March 18-21, 1865. Paroled at Goldsboro on May 19, 1865. "Came in for parole."

MITCHELL, JAMES C., Private

Resided in Johnston County and enlisted in Wayne County at age 24, January 1, 1862, for the war as a substitute. Wounded at Chancellorsville, Virginia, May 3, 1863, and reported as absent wounded until detailed on Provost Guard at Goldsboro in September, 1863. Company muster rolls report him as absent on detail through August, 1864. Admitted to hospital at Richmond, Virginia, December 23, 1864, and returned to duty on December 31, 1864. Detailed in hospital at Danville, Virginia, January 13, 1865. Captured at Goldsboro on March 24, 1865, and sent to Washington, D.C., where he arrived on April 5, 1865. Took the Oath of Allegiance and was provided transportation to Goldsboro.

MOORE, JOSEPHUS, Private

Enlisted in Wake County on May 19, 1864. Admitted to hospital at Danville, Virginia, June 4, 1864, with a gunshot wound of the arm. Furloughed from hospital June 7-8, 1864. Captured at Strasburg, Virginia, October 19, 1864, and confined at Point Lookout, Maryland, until paroled for exchange on March 28, 1865. Transferred for exchange to Aiken's Landing, Virginia.

MOORE, M. P., Private

Captured at Gettysburg, Pennsylvania, July 1-4, 1863, and confined at DeCamp General Hospital, Davids Island, New York Harbor, where he died on November 16, 1863, of "gunshot wound."

MUNDAY, G. H., Private

Paroled at Burkeville, Virginia, April 14-17, 1865.

MURDOCK, ALEXANDER, Sergeant

Resided in Rowan County and enlisted in Wayne County at age 30, May 27, 1861, for the war. Mus-

tered in as Sergeant. Transferred to the Field and Staff of this regiment upon appointment as Ordnance Sergeant on May 14, 1862.

NETHERCUTT, DAVID R., Private

Born in Brunswick County and resided as a farmer in Wayne County where he enlisted at age 35, May 27, 1861, for the war. Died at Camp Potomac, Virginia, October 1, 1861.

OUTLAW, FREDERICK R., Private

Resided in Duplin County and enlisted in Wayne County at age 20, February 20, 1862, for the war. Present or accounted for until captured at Kelly's Ford, Virginia, November 7, 1863. Confined at Point Lookout, Maryland, until paroled and transferred for exchange to Aiken's Landing, Virginia, March 14, 1865. Received in exchange at Boulware's Wharf, James River, Virginia, March 16, 1865. Paroled at Goldsboro on May 23, 1865. "Came in for parole."

OUTLAW, JOSEPH A., Private

Born in Wayne County and resided as a farmer in Duplin County prior to enlisting in Wayne County at age 20, February 20, 1862, for the war. Died in hospital at Richmond, Virginia, December 16, 1862, of "pneumonia typhoides."

OUTLAW, JUNIUS, Private

Transferred from Company G, 55th Regiment N.C. Troops on January 10, 1864. Present or accounted for until captured at Winchester, Virginia, September 19, 1864. Confined at Point Lookout, Maryland, until paroled and transferred for exchange to James River, Virginia, February 13, 1865. Exact date of exchange not reported. Appears as present on a muster roll of a detachment of paroled and exchanged prisoners at Camp Lee, near Richmond, Virginia, dated February 18, 1865.

PARKER, BRYANT, Private

Born in Duplin County where he resided as a laborer prior to enlisting in Wayne County at age 19, April 14, 1862, for the war. Killed at Malvern Hill, Virginia, July 1, 1862.

PARKER, EDWARD SANDERS, Corporal

Born in Cumberland County and resided as a lawyer in Wayne County where he enlisted at age 22, May 27, 1861, for the war. Mustered in as Private and appointed Corporal on July 31, 1861. Present or accounted for until transferred to the Field and Staff, 50th Regiment N.C. Troops upon appointment as Captain, Commissary of Subsistence, April 16, 1862.

PARKER, JACQUELINE, Private

Born in Duplin County and resided as a farmer in Wayne County where he enlisted at age 20, May 29, 1861, for the war. Discharged on March 22, 1863, by reason of disability.

PARNELL, HENRY, Private

Born in Wayne County where he resided as a farmer and enlisted at age 32, May 27, 1861, for the war. Died at Camp Potomac, Virginia, December 29, 1861.

PARNELL, THOMAS H., Private

First reported on company muster roll for the period May 1-August 31, 1864. Date and place enlisted not reported; however, the muster roll carries the remark: "Deserted July, 1864, near Washington, D.C. Assigned to company on May 20, 1864." Federal Provost Marshal records indicate that he was captured near Washington on July 13, 1864, and confined at Old Capitol Prison, Washington, July 15, 1864. Transferred to Elmira, New York, July 23-25, 1864. Paroled at Elmira and sent to Point Lookout, Maryland, October 11, 1864. Received at Point Lookout on October 14, 1864, and exchanged on October 29, 1864.

PATE, GEORGE DUNCAN, Private
Resided in Wayne County and enlisted in Wake County at age 22, July 15, 1862, for the war. Reported as present or accounted for on company muster rolls until admitted to hospital at Farmville, Virginia, June 11, 1863, with "debilitas." Furloughed from hospital for 60 days on July 8-10, 1863. Reported as absent without leave on company muster rolls after his furlough expired until April 1, 1864, when he was reported with the remark: "Deserted to the enemy while on sick furlough in North Carolina."

PEEL, ADDISON, Sergeant
Resided in Wayne County and enlisted in Northampton County at age 21, June 17, 1861, for the war. Mustered in as Private and appointed Corporal on December 1, 1862. Wounded at Chancellorsville, Virginia, May 3, 1863. Promoted to Sergeant, November-December, 1863. Present or accounted for on company muster rolls through August, 1864. Federal Provost Marshal records report him as a "rebel deserter" received at Washington, D.C., April 10, 1865, with the remark that he took the Oath of Allegiance and was furnished transportation to New Bern.

PENDANT, W., Private
Paroled at Greensboro on May 9, 1865.

PICKET, WILEY, Private
Enlisted in Wake County on April 7, 1864, for the war. May 1-August 31, 1864, muster roll reports him as absent with the remark: "On wounded furlough, N.C." Date and place wounded not reported. Claim for pay due deceased soldiers filed by his father on September 13, 1864, with the remark that his son died at Richmond, Virginia.

PIKE, NATHAN R., Private
Born in Wayne County where he resided as a farmer prior to enlisting in Northampton County at age 22, June 18, 1861, for the war. Killed at Malvern Hill, Virginia, July 1, 1862.

PIKE, WILLIAM B., Private
Resided in Wayne County where he enlisted at age 21, May 27, 1861, for the war. Captured near Fredericksburg, Virginia, May 3, 1863, and paroled and exchanged at City Point, Virginia, May 13, 1863. Present or accounted for on company muster rolls through August, 1864. Paroled at Appomattox Court House, Virginia, on April 9, 1865.

POPE, JAMES A., Private
Born in Wayne County where he resided and enlisted at age 21, May 27, 1861, for the war. Died in hospital at Fredericksburg, Virginia, on August 24, 1861.

PREMPERT, HENRY C., Private
Resided in Wayne County where he enlisted at age 35, May 27, 1861, for the war. Mustered in as Sergeant and reduced to ranks on December 1, 1861. Transferred to the Field and Staff of this regiment upon appointment as Drum Major on March 1, 1862.

RANSOM, G., Private
Captured at Fisher's Hill, Virginia, September 22, 1864, and confined at Point Lookout, Maryland, October 1, 1864.

RAY, ALBERT, Private
Enlisted in Wake County on May 14, 1864, for the war. Admitted to hospital at Charlottesville, Virginia, June 16, 1864, with "acute diarrhoea." Admitted to hospital at Raleigh on September 9, 1864, with "rheumatism chronic" and furloughed for 60 days from hospital on March 29, 1865.

RAY, WILLIAM HENDERSON, Private
Enlisted in Wake County on May 14, 1864, for the war. May 1-August 31, 1864, muster roll reports him as "on sick furlough in North Carolina." Register of Medical Director's Office, Richmond, Virginia, dated February 3, 1865, carries him with the remark: "Dis. permt."

REEVES, JAMES, Private
Born in Wayne County where he resided as a cooper and enlisted at age 20, May 29, 1861, for the war. Present or accounted for until transferred to Company C, 61st Regiment N.C. Troops on May 31, 1862.

RODGERS, G. C., Private
Wounded and captured at Winchester, Virginia, September 19, 1864. Federal Provost Marshal records indicate that he was transferred from field hospital on October 29, 1864.

ROLLINS, JAMES, Private
Resided in Wayne County where he enlisted at age 21, May 27, 1861, for the war. Present or accounted for until captured at Kelly's Ford, Virginia, November 7, 1863. Confined at Point Lookout, Maryland, until released after taking the Oath of Allegiance and joining the U.S. service on January 26, 1864. Unit to which assigned not reported.

ROLLINS, RICHARD, Corporal
Resided in Wayne County where he enlisted at age 23, May 27, 1861, for the war. Mustered in as Private and appointed Corporal, November-December, 1863. Present or accounted for on company muster rolls through August, 1864, when he appears as "absent on wounded furlough in North Carolina." Date and place wounded not reported. Admitted to hospital at Richmond, Virginia, May 31, 1864, and furloughed for 60 days on June 13, 1864. Received clothing on December 12, 1864.

ROUSE, WILLIAM JACKSON, Private
Resided in Wayne County where he enlisted at age 36, May 27, 1861, for the war. Present or accounted for until "discharged December 31, 1861, by substitute."

ROY, THOMAS L., Private
Born in England and enlisted at age 26 at Richmond, Virginia, on May 10, 1863, for the war.

Deserted at Brandy Station, Virginia, June 14, 1863. Took the Oath of Allegiance at Washington, D.C., July 7, 1863, and was provided transportation to Philadelphia, Pennsylvania, July 16, 1863.

SANDERSON, JOHN W., Private
Born in Wayne County where he resided as a wheelwright prior to enlisting in Wake County at age 32, July 15, 1862, for the war. Wounded at Chancellorsville, Virginia, May 3, 1863, and died of wound May 17, 1863.

SASSER, LARKIN P., Private
Born in Wayne County where he resided as a laborer and enlisted at age 22, May 27, 1861, for the war. Died at Fredericksburg, Virginia, August 4, 1861.

SAULS, WILLOUGHBY, Private
Born in Wayne County where he resided as a laborer and enlisted at age 25, May 27, 1861, for the war. Wounded at Chancellorsville, Virginia, May 3, 1863, and discharged on December 5, 1863, by reason of wound received at Chancellorsville.

SINGLETON, GEORGE W., Private
Resided in Wayne County where he enlisted at age 22, May 27, 1861, for the war. Admitted to hospital at Richmond, Virginia, June 3, 1864, with a gunshot wound. Transferred to hospital at Greensboro and furloughed on June 7, 1864. Captured at Fisher's Hill, Virginia, September 22, 1864, and confined at Point Lookout, Maryland, until paroled and transferred for exchange to Boulware's Wharf, James River, Virginia, January 17, 1865. Exact date exchanged not reported; however, he appears as present on a roll of a detachment of paroled and exchanged prisoners at Camp Lee, near Richmond, dated January 26, 1865. Captured at Goldsboro on April 3, 1865, and paroled.

SMITH, A. C., Private
Resided in New Hanover County and paroled at Goldsboro on May 11, 1865. "Came in for parole."

SMITH, ISAAC S., Private
Born in Wayne County where he resided as a farmer and enlisted at age 19, May 28, 1861, for the war. Wounded in left wrist and right hip at Chancellorsville, Virginia, May 3, 1863, and reported as absent wounded on company muster rolls through August, 1864. Applied for retirement to Invalid Corps on November 3, 1864. Application approved by the Surgeon General on January 5, 1865.

SMITH, J. S., Private
Admitted to hospital at Richmond, Virginia, December 24, 1864, with a gunshot wound of the right thigh and returned to duty on December 28, 1864. Admitted to hospital at Richmond on January 16, 1865, with "colitis acute" and died January 20, 1865.

SMITH, WILLIAM R., Private
Born in Wayne County where he resided and enlisted at age 21, May 27, 1861, for the war. Died at Camp Advance, Northampton County, June 28, 1861.

SMITHY, JOSEPH H., Private
Resided in Person County and enlisted in Wake

County at age 34, September 1, 1862, for the war. Present or accounted for until he died at Gordonsville, Virginia, December 10, 1862, of "pleuritis."

SMITHY, THOMAS G., Private
Resided in Rockingham County and enlisted in Wake County at age 34, September 1, 1862, for the war. Present or accounted for until captured at Kelly's Ford, Virginia, November 7, 1863, and confined at Point Lookout, Maryland. Released at Point Lookout after taking the Oath of Allegiance and joining the U.S. service on January 26, 1864. Assigned to the 1st Regiment U.S. Volunteer Infantry.

SPICER, JOSHUA, Private
Enlisted at Camp Vance on May 12, 1864, for the war. Reported on May 1-August 31, 1864, muster roll with the remark that he was "absent, sick at hospital." Admitted to hospital at Charlottesville, Virginia, July 25, 1864, with "diarrhoea chronic" and transferred to Lynchburg, Virginia, the next day.

STANLEY, ELI, Private
Resided in Johnston County and enlisted in Wake County at age 29, September 3, 1862, for the war. Deserted on April 10, 1863, and returned from desertion on October 25, 1863. Sentenced by court-martial to five years hard labor February 4, 1864. Released from confinement on December 1, 1864. Paroled at Raleigh on May 15, 1865.

STIGALL, WILLIAM L., Private
Resided in Person County and enlisted in Wake County at age 24, September 1, 1862, for the war. Present or accounted for until killed at Spotsylvania Court House, Virginia, May 12, 1864.

SUTHERLAND, WILLIAM H., Private
Born in Wayne County where he resided as a farmer and enlisted at age 24, May 27, 1861, for the war. Killed at Chancellorsville, Virginia, May 3, 1863.

SUTTON, WILLIAM, Private
Born in Duplin County where he resided as a farmer prior to enlisting in Wayne County at age 22, May 27, 1861, for the war. Died in hospital at Fredericksburg, Virginia, September 4, 1861.

TALTON, IREDELL, Private
Born in Johnston County where he resided as a farmer prior to enlisting in Wayne County at age 20, May 27, 1861, for the war. Wounded in the right arm at Chancellorsville, Virginia, May 3, 1863, and reported as absent wounded until discharged on February 28, 1864, by reason of wound.

TALTON, MACK, Private
Resided in Johnston County and enlisted in Wayne County at age 40, May 27, 1861, for the war. Wounded at Gettysburg, Pennsylvania, July 1, 1863, and reported as absent wounded until detailed as hospital guard at Goldsboro on March 26, 1864. Discharged from the hospital on April 5, 1864, and ordered to return to duty. Admitted to hospital at Farmville, Virginia, on May 6, 1864, with a gunshot wound. Transferred to Richmond, Virginia, May 21, 1864. Attached to hospital at Richmond as a guard on July 1, 1864. Furloughed from hospital on January 23,

1865. Captured in hospital at Richmond on April 3, 1865, and paroled on April 20, 1865.

TAYLOR, HAYWOOD, Private
Resided in Duplin County where he enlisted at age 34, June 26, 1861, for the war. Wounded at Chancellorsville, Virginia, May 3, 1863, and died of wound at Richmond, Virginia, on May 19, 1863.

TAYLOR, NOAH, Private
Born in Wayne County where he resided as a laborer and enlisted at age 25, May 27, 1861, for the war. Died at Camp Advance, Northampton County, July 18, 1861.

THOMPSON, DAVID J., Private
Resided in Wayne County where he enlisted at age 27, May 27, 1861, for the war. Captured near Fredericksburg, Virginia, May 3, 1863, and paroled and exchanged at City Point, Virginia, May 13, 1863. Present or accounted for on company muster rolls until transferred to Company G, 55th Regiment N.C. Troops on January 13, 1864.

THOMPSON, HAYS F., Private
Resided in Wayne County where he enlisted at age 22, May 27, 1861, for the war. Present or accounted for until killed at Chancellorsville, Virginia, May 3, 1863.

TIGHLMAN, JACKSON, Private
Resided in Wayne County where he enlisted at age 38, May 27, 1861, for the war. Present or accounted for until captured at Strasburg, Virginia, October 19, 1864. Confined at Point Lookout, Maryland, until paroled and transferred for exchange to Boulware's Wharf, James River, Virginia, January 17, 1865. Declared exchanged on January 21, 1865.

TINDALL, DAVID, Private
Born in Duplin County and resided in Lenoir County prior to enlisting in Wayne County at age 45, May 27, 1861, for the war. Died at Fredericksburg, Virginia, November 9, 1861.

TINDALL, JOHN L., Private
Born in Lenoir County where he resided as a farmer prior to enlisting in Wayne County at age 18, May 27, 1861, for the war. Wounded at Cold Harbor, Virginia, June 27, 1862, and died of wound on June 29, 1862.

TOLER, SAUNDERS, Private
Resided in Wayne County where he enlisted at age 25, May 27, 1861, for the war. Captured at Sharpsburg, Maryland, September 17, 1862, and confined at Fort Delaware, Delaware, until paroled and exchanged at Aiken's Landing, Virginia, October 6, 1862. Declared exchanged on November 10, 1862. Admitted to hospital at Richmond, Virginia, October 31, 1862, and transferred to Danville, Virginia, December 26, 1862. Issued clothing in hospital at Danville on April 13, 1863. Detailed as Provost Guard at Goldsboro prior to January 1, 1864, when he was reported as present at Goldsboro. Returned to duty on April 30, 1864. Admitted to hospital at Richmond. December 24, 1864, with "ulcer leg" and returned to duty January 12, 1865. Furloughed for 60 days on February 14, 1865.

WADKINS, WILLIAM J., Private
Enlisted in Wake County on May 3, 1864, for the war. Admitted to hospital at Richmond, Virginia, June 29, 1864, with a gunshot wound and furloughed for 30 days on August 4, 1864. Reported as a deserter by the Bureau of Conscripts on February 24, 1865.

WARD, RUFUS, Private
Resided in Wayne County and enlisted at Camp Potomac, Virginia, at age 31, December 29, 1861, for the war as a substitute. Present or accounted for until he "deserted February 17, 1863, from camp near Fredericksburg, Virginia."

WATSON, NEILL, Private
Born in Lenoir County where he resided as a railroad hand prior to enlisting in Northampton County at age 21, May 30, 1861, for the war. Present or accounted for until discharged on November 30, 1863, by reason of "disability from a gunshot wound." Date and place wounded not reported.

WEATHERMAN, W. L., Private
Resided in Iredell County and enlisted at Camp Vance on May 16, 1864, for the war. Reported on May 1-August 31, 1864, muster roll as "absent on 60 days furlough from July 26, 1864." Admitted to hospital at Richmond, Virginia, October 31, 1864, with a gunshot wound of the left hand and returned to duty on December 16, 1864. Captured at Petersburg, Virginia, April 3, 1865, and confined at Hart's Island, New York Harbor, until released after taking the Oath of Allegiance on June 19, 1865.

WHICKER, JULIUS H., Private
Enlisted in Wake County on May 14, 1864, for the war. Reported on May 1-August 31, 1864, muster roll with the remark that he "deserted July 28, 1864, near Martinsburg, Virginia."

WHICKER, WILLIAM J., Private
Resided in Forsyth County and enlisted in Wake County on May 14, 1864, for the war. Admitted to hospital at Charlottesville, Virginia, July 25, 1864, with a gunshot wound of the right hand and furloughed on July 29, 1864. Captured at Strasburg, Virginia, October 19, 1864, and confined at Point Lookout, Maryland, until released after taking the Oath of Allegiance on June 30, 1865.

WHITEHEAD, HENRY J., Private
Born in Wayne County where he resided and enlisted at age 19, May 27, 1861, for the war. Died at Camp Advance, Northampton County, July 18, 1861.

WHITFIELD, LEMUEL H., Private
Resided in Wayne County where he enlisted at age 21, February 20, 1862, for the war. Wounded and captured at Chancellorsville, Virginia, May 3, 1863, and confined in hospital at Washington, D.C., until transferred to Old Capitol Prison. Washington, June 16, 1863. Paroled at Old Capitol Prison on June 25, 1863, and sent to City Point, Virginia, for exchange. Received in exchange at City Point on June 30, 1863. Admitted to hospital at Petersburg, Virginia, June 30, 1863, with "debilitas" and returned to duty on August 3,

1863. Present or accounted for on company muster rolls until discharged on November 1, 1864, by reason of disability.

WHITFIELD, LEWIS D. H., Private
Resided in Wayne County where he enlisted at age 19, February 20, 1862, for the war. Present or accounted for on company muster rolls through August, 1864, when he appears with the remark: "Absent wounded and sent to hospital August 22, 1864." Admitted to hospital at Richmond, Virginia, September 13, 1864, and furloughed for 60 days on the same day. Admitted to hospital at Richmond on December 16, 1864, with a gunshot wound of the left thigh and returned to duty of February 17, 1865. Hospital records report the wound as "old." Readmitted to hospital at Richmond on February 25, 1865, with same wound and captured in hospital on April 3, 1865. Transferred to Newport News, Virginia, and released after taking the Oath of Allegiance on June 30, 1865.

WIGGS, ASHLEY, Private
Born in Wayne County where he resided and enlisted at age 25, May 27, 1861, for the war. Wounded and captured at Chancellorsville, Virginia, May 3, 1863. Confined in hospital at Washington, D.C., until transferred to Old Capitol Prison, Washington, June 11, 1863. Paroled at Old Capitol Prison on June 25, 1863, and sent to City Point, Virginia, for exchange. Exact date exchanged not reported. Admitted to hospital at Petersburg, Virginia, on July 1, 1863, and returned to duty on the same day. Present or accounted for until killed at Spotsylvania Court House, Virginia, May 19, 1864.

WIGGS, BALLARD, Private
Transferred from Company B of this regiment in April, 1864. Wounded and captured at Winchester, Virginia, September 19, 1864. Confined in hospital at Baltimore, Maryland, until transferred to Point Lookout, Maryland, October 27, 1864. Paroled at Point Lookout and sent to Venus Point, Savannah River, Georgia, October 30, 1864, for exchange. Received in exchange at Venus Point on November 15, 1864. Paroled at Goldsboro on May 9, 1865. "Came in for parole."

WIGGS, BLACKMAN, Private
Resided in Wayne County where he enlisted at age 31, October 20, 1861, for the war. Present or accounted for until wounded and captured at Winchester, Virginia, September 19, 1864. Confined in hospital at Baltimore, Maryland, until transferred to Point Lookout, Maryland, on October 17, 1864. Paroled at Point Lookout on October 31, 1864, and sent to Venus Point, Savannah River, Georgia, for exchange. Received in exchange at Venus Point on November 15, 1864.

WIGGS, JOHN, Private
Resided in Wayne County and enlisted in Wake County at age 20, August 19, 1862, for the war. Wounded at Chancellorsville, Virginia, May 3, 1863. Present or accounted for on company muster rolls through August, 1864. Captured at Petersburg, Virginia, April 3, 1865, and confined

at Hart's Island, New York Harbor, until released after taking the Oath of Allegiance on June 18, 1865.

WIGGS, WILLIAM, Private
Resided in Wayne County and enlisted in Wake County at age 18, July 1, 1863, for the war. Present or accounted for on company muster rolls through August, 1864, when he appears with the remark: "On wounded furlough in North Carolina." Date and place wounded not reported. Died in hospital at Harrisonburg, Virginia, on December 6, 1864, of "diarrhoea chronic."

WILLIAMS, GEORGE, Private
Born in Wayne County where he resided prior to enlisting in New Hanover County at age 18, May 9, 1862, for the war. Wounded at Malvern Hill, Virginia, July 1, 1862. Present or accounted for until he died in hospital at Richmond, Virginia, January 23, 1863, of "variola."

WILLIAMS, JACOB, Private
Resided in Wayne County where he enlisted at age 25, May 27, 1861, for the war. Wounded at Gettysburg, Pennsylvania, July 1, 1863. Detailed on Provost Guard at Corps Headquarters from November-December, 1863, through October, 1864. Paroled at Appomattox Court House, Virginia, April 9, 1865.

WILLIAMS, ROBIN, Private
Enlisted in Orange County, Virginia, on March 29, 1864, for the war. Reported on May 1-August 31, 1864, muster roll with the remark that he was "on wounded furlough in North Carolina." Date and place wounded not reported. Paroled at Appomattox Court House, Virginia, April 9, 1865.

WISE, MERRITT P., Private
Resided in Wayne County where he enlisted at age 27, January 22, 1862, for the war. Wounded at Chancellorsville, Virginia, May 3, 1863, and returned to duty on September 1, 1863. Present or accounted for on company muster rolls through August, 1864.

COMPANY I

This company, known as the "Beaufort Rifles" and the "Beauregard Rifles," was organized in Craven County and enlisted at New Bern on May 29, 1861. It tendered its service to the state and was ordered to Camp Advance, near Garysburg, Northampton County, where it was assigned to this regiment as Company I. After joining the regiment the company functioned as a part of the regiment, and its history for the war period is recorded as a part of the regimental history.

The information contained in the following roster of the company was compiled principally from company muster rolls for July 5, 1861, through December, 1861; March through October, 1862; January, 1863, through March, 1864; and May through October, 1864. No company muster rolls were found for the period prior to July 5, 1861; for January-February, 1862; November-December, 1862; April, 1864; or for the period after October, 1864. In addition to the company muster rolls, Roll of Honor records, receipt rolls, and hospital records, supplemented by state pension applications, United Daughters of the Confederacy records, and postwar rosters and histories, all provided useful information.

OFFICERS

CAPTAINS

HURTT, DANIEL W.

Resided in Craven County and appointed Captain to rank from May 16, 1861. Wounded at Sharpsburg, Maryland, September 17, 1862. Transferred to the Field and Staff of this regiment upon appointment as Major to rank from March 21, 1863.

TAYLOR, SYLVESTER

Resided in Craven County and appointed 3rd Lieutenant to rank from May 16, 1861. Promoted to 2nd Lieutenant to rank from March 22, 1862, and to 1st Lieutenant to rank from January 22, 1863. Promoted to Captain to rank from March 21, 1863. Wounded at Chancellorsville, Virginia, May 3, 1863. Present or accounted for until he died on February 12, 1864, of "smallpox."

LIEUTENANTS

BRYAN, EDWARD K., 1st Lieutenant

Resided in Craven County and appointed 2nd Lieutenant to rank from May 16, 1861. Promoted to 1st Lieutenant to rank from October 30, 1862. Submitted his resignation on January 10, 1863, by reason of his having been appointed as Adjutant of the 31st Regiment N.C. Troops. Resignation officially accepted on January 22, 1863.

DILLINGHAM, JOHN P., 1st Lieutenant

Resided in Craven County and appointed 1st Lieutenant to rank from May 16, 1861. Transferred to the Field and Staff of this regiment upon appointment as Captain, Assistant Quartermaster, to rank from July 13, 1861.

GILBERT, ROBERT J., 1st Lieutenant

Resided in Craven County where he enlisted at age 23, May 29, 1861, for the war. Mustered in as Private. Appointed 2nd Lieutenant to rank from January 1, 1863, and promoted to 1st Lieutenant to rank from March 21, 1863. Reported as "absent on leave" on September-October, 1863, muster roll and as "absent without leave since November 18, 1863" on November-December, 1863, muster roll. Dropped from the rolls on March 23, 1864, by reason of "prolonged absence."

HARRIS, W. L., Lieutenant

Paroled at Greensboro on April 29, 1865.

HUGHES, NICHOLAS COLLIN, 1st Lieutenant

Resided in Craven County and appointed 1st Lieutenant to rank from May 16, 1861. Detailed as Adjutant of the regiment on June 25, 1861, and reported on company muster rolls as absent on detail. Temporarily transferred to the Field and Staff while on detail. Resigned October 30, 1862, upon being appointed Assistant Adjutant General on General Pettigrew's staff.

SAMUEL, J. W., 1st Lieutenant

Paroled at Greensboro on May 22, 1865.

WATSON, ISRAEL B., 2nd Lieutenant

Born in Hyde County where he resided as a merchant prior to enlisting in Craven County at age 25, May 30, 1861, for the war. Mustered in as Private. Captured at Sharpsburg, Maryland, September 17, 1862, and confined at Fort Delaware, Delaware, until paroled and exchanged at Aiken's Landing, Virginia, November 10, 1862. Appointed Corporal on December 2, 1862, and elected 2nd Lieutenant on January 12, 1863. Appointed 2nd Lieutenant to rank from January 22, 1863. Present or accounted for until captured at Kelly's Ford, Virginia, November 7, 1863. Confined at Old Capitol Prison, Washington, D.C., until transferred to Johnson's Island, Ohio, November 11, 1863. Released at Johnson's Island after taking the Oath of Allegiance on June 13, 1865.

NONCOMMISSIONED OFFICERS AND PRIVATES

ALDRIDGE, PARROTT A., Private

Resided in Craven County where he enlisted at age 20, May 29, 1861, for the war. Died January 17, 1862.

ATTMORE, ISAAC TAYLOR, Sergeant

Resided in Craven County where he enlisted at age 22, May 29, 1861, for the war. Mustered in as Private and promoted to Sergeant in June, 1863. Present or accounted for until killed at Spotsylvania Court House, Virginia, May 12, 1864.

AUSTIN, JOHN W., Private

Resided in Craven County where he enlisted at age 37, May 29, 1861, for the war. Present or accounted for on company muster rolls through October, 1864. Paroled at Appomattox Court House, Virginia, April 9, 1865.

AVERY, JOHN Q., Private

Resided in Craven County where he enlisted at age 28, May 29, 1861, for the war. Company muster rolls indicate that he was captured at Sharpsburg, Maryland, September 19, 1862, and that he took the Oath of Allegiance to the United States. There are no Federal Provost Marshal records on file in his service jacket. Roll of Honor states that he "deserted while the army was in Maryland, September, 1862."

BALL, SAMUEL R., Private

Resided in Craven County where he enlisted at age 21, June 3, 1861, for the war. Present or accounted for until captured at Kelly's Ford, Virginia, November 7, 1863. Confined at Point Lookout, Maryland, until paroled and transferred for exchange to Aiken's Landing, Virginia, February 24, 1865.

BARR, ALLEY C., Private

Captured near Petersburg, Virginia, March 25, 1865, and confined at Point Lookout, Maryland, until released after taking the Oath of Allegiance on June 23, 1865.

BARROW, JOSEPH B. G., Corporal
Resided in Craven County where he enlisted at age 31, May 30, 1861, for the war. Mustered in as Private and appointed Corporal on October 24, 1861. Present or accounted for until he died in hospital at Danville, Virginia, December 2, 1862, of "chronic diarrhoea."

BEAMAN, STEPHEN T., Private
Resided in Sampson County and enlisted in Wake County at age 34, August 15, 1862, for the war. Present or accounted for until he died in hospital at Lynchburg, Virginia, June 14, 1863, of "anasarca."

BECTON, EDWARD T., Private
Resided in Craven County where he enlisted at age 18, May 29, 1861, for the war. Detailed in hospital at Fredericksburg, Virginia, September 11, 1861, and remained on detail through February, 1862. Detailed as a nurse at Winchester, Virginia, September 15, 1862, and remained on detail through February, 1863. Detailed as a nurse in hospital at Lexington, Virginia, from February, 1863, through June, 1863. Present or accounted for on company muster rolls until captured at Kelly's Ford, Virginia, November 7, 1863. Confined at Point Lookout, Maryland, until paroled and sent to James River, Virginia, for exchange on February 18, 1865. Received at Boulware's Wharf, James River, February 20-21, 1865, in exchange. Reported as present on a roll of paroled and exchanged prisoners at Camp Lee, near Richmond, Virginia, dated February 23, 1865.

BELL, TYRELL R., Private
Born in Johnston County where he resided prior to enlisting in Wake County at age 43, September 4, 1863, for the war. Died in hospital at Staunton, Virginia, November 4, 1863, of "diarrhoea."

BIVINS, WILLIAM, Private
Enlisted in Wake County on May 14, 1864, for the war. Died in hospital at Richmond, Virginia, July 26, 1864, of "phthisis pulmonalis."

BLALOCK, YANCEY, Private
Enlisted in Wake County on April 26, 1864, for the war. Killed in action near Richmond, Virginia, on June 2, 1864.

BLAND, JOHN L., Corporal
Resided in Craven County where he enlisted at age 38, May 29, 1861, for the war. Mustered in as Corporal. Died at Camp Potomac, Virginia, October 21-23, 1861.

BLANEY, GEORGE W., Private
Born in Craven County and resided in Lenoir County prior to enlisting in Craven County at age 36, May 29, 1861, for the war. Died in camp on December 4, 1861, of "pneumonia."

BOWERS, JOHN R., Private
Resided in Craven County where he enlisted at age 31, June 10, 1861, for the war. Deserted from Camp Advance, Northampton County, July 13, 1861.

BRASWELL, BAKER W., Private
Resided in Edgecombe County and enlisted in

Wake County on July 8, 1863, for the war. Present or accounted for until captured at Kelly's Ford, Virginia, November 7, 1863. Confined at Point Lookout, Maryland, until paroled and sent to Venus Point, Savannah River, Georgia, November 1, 1864, for exchange. Paroled at Goldsboro on May 18, 1865. "Came in for parole."

BROCK, EDWARD A., Private
Born in Duplin County and resided as a carpenter in Lenoir County prior to enlisting in Craven County at age 44, May 31, 1861, for the war. Present or accounted for until discharged on June 17, 1862, by reason of "disease of the heart and a constitution worn out in good work waiting the sick of the regiment night and day for the last year."

BROOKS, EDWARD J., 1st Sergeant
Resided in Lenoir County and enlisted in Craven County at age 19, June 6, 1861, for the war. Mustered in as Private. Wounded and captured at Sharpsburg, Maryland, September 17, 1862. Confined at Fort McHenry, Maryland, until paroled and sent to Fort Monroe, Virginia, for exchange on December 8, 1862. Declared exchanged at City Point, Virginia, December 10, 1862. Appointed Corporal on February 1, 1863, and promoted to 1st Sergeant on June 28, 1863. Present or accounted for until captured at Kelly's Ford, Virginia, November 7, 1863. Confined at Point Lookout, Maryland, until paroled and sent to Cox's Landing, James River, Virginia, for exchange on February 13, 1865. Exact date of exchange not reported. Appears as present on a roll of a detachment of paroled and exchanged prisoners at Camp Lee, near Richmond, Virginia, dated February 18, 1865.

BRYAN, JAMES T., Private
Born in Craven County where he resided as a seaman and enlisted at age 20, June 14, 1861, for the war. Wounded at Malvern Hill, Virginia, July 1, 1862, and died of wound on July 28, 1862.

BRYAN, JOHN H., Private
Resided in Craven County where he enlisted at age 22, May 29, 1861, for the war. Present or accounted for until killed at Fredericksburg, Virginia, on December 13, 1862.

BRYAN, WILLIAM G., Jr., 1st Sergeant
Born in Craven County where he resided and enlisted at age 27, May 31, 1861, for the war. Mustered in as 1st Sergeant. Wounded at Fredericksburg, Virginia, December 13, 1862, and died in hospital at Richmond, Virginia, March 6, 1863, of "pneumonia."

BUCK, RICHARD A., Private
Resided in Craven County and enlisted at Camp Potomac, Virginia, at age 30, February 20, 1862, for the war as a substitute for Nathan Tisdale. Wounded at South Mountain, Maryland, September 14, 1862, and captured. Paroled on October 3, 1862. Died of wounds in October, 1862.

BUDD, JOSEPH H., Private
Resided in Craven County where he enlisted at age 23, May 31, 1861, for the war. Died in hospi-

tal at Fredericksburg, Virginia, September 14, 1861.

CLODFELTER, DANIEL A., Private
Resided in Davidson County and enlisted in Wake County at age 24, August 18, 1862, for the war. Present or accounted for until captured in Frederick County, Virginia, October 20, 1864. Confined at Old Capitol Prison, Washington, D.C., until transferred to Elmira, New York, on February 3, 1865. Paroled at Elmira and sent to James River, Virginia, for exchange on March 14, 1865. Declared exchanged at Boulware's Wharf, James River, on March 18-21, 1865. Paroled at Greensboro on May 4, 1865.

CLODFELTER, HAMILTON L., Private
Resided in Davidson County and enlisted in Wake County at age 30, March 10, 1863, for the war. Present or accounted for on company muster rolls through October, 1864. Paroled at Greensboro on May 4, 1865.

COLEY, G. D., Private
Enlisted in Wake County on May 23, 1864, for the war. Company muster rolls report him as absent wounded from July 18, 1864, through October, 1864. Paroled at Statesville on May 19, 1865.

COMPTON, ALBERT A., Private
Resided in Orange County and enlisted in Wake County at age 32, August 18, 1862, for the war. Detailed as a nurse in hospital at Richmond, Virginia, March 22, 1863. Died in hospital at Richmond on April 12, 1863, of "laryngitis chronic."

COOK, ANDREW J., Musician
Resided in Craven County where he enlisted at age 18, May 29, 1861, for the war. Mustered in as Musician. Captured at South Mountain, Maryland, September 14, 1862, and "reported to have taken the Oath of Allegiance to the U.S."

COOK, WILLIAM W., Private
Resided in Craven County where he enlisted at age 31, May 29, 1861, for the war. Discharged on September 1, 1861, by reason of physical inability.

CROSS, JAMES, Private
Resided in Craven County where he enlisted at age 23, June 3, 1861, for the war. Died at Camp Potomac, Virginia, October 27-28, 1861.

CROUCH, JOHN R., Private
Resided in Davidson County and enlisted in Wake County at age 21, August 18, 1862, for the war. Wounded at Gettysburg, Pennsylvania, July 2-3, 1863. Present or accounted for until captured at Mechanicsville, Virginia, May 31, 1864. Confined at Point Lookout, Maryland, until transferred to Elmira, New York, July 8, 1864. Died at Elmira on October 26, 1864, of "typhoid pneumonia."

CUNNINGHAM, ROBERT H., Private
Resided in Maryland and enlisted in King George County, Virginia, at age 18, February 6, 1862, for the war. Transferred to the Maryland Line on October 10, 1862.

DIXON, WILLIAM A., Private
Resided in Edgecombe County and enlisted in Wake County at age 18, July 8, 1862, for the war. Reported as missing after May 12, 1864.

DOWTY, ISAAC P., Corporal
Resided in Craven County where he enlisted at age 22, May 29, 1861, for the war. Mustered in as Private. Wounded at Sharpsburg, Maryland, September 17, 1862, and at Chancellorsville, Virginia, May 3, 1863. Severely wounded at Gettysburg, Pennsylvania, July 1-3, 1863. Promoted to Corporal on September 15, 1863. Company muster rolls report him as absent in hospital through October, 1864. Captured at Burkeville, Virginia, April 6, 1865, and confined at Point Lookout, Maryland, until released after taking the Oath of Allegiance on June 12, 1865.

DUDLEY, CHURCHILL G., Corporal
Resided in Pitt County and enlisted in Craven County at age 20, June 3, 1861, for the war. Mustered in as Corporal. Died in hospital at Leesburg, Virginia, October 15, 1862.

DUKE, ROBERT, Private
Resided in Orange County and enlisted in Wake County at age 33, January 27, 1863, for the war. Present or accounted for until he "deserted from camp on February 27, 1863."

ELLIS, HENRY, Private
Resided in Craven County where he enlisted at age 22, June 12, 1861, for the war. Wounded at Spotsylvania Court House, Virginia, May 12, 1864. Captured in hospital at Richmond, Virginia, April 3, 1865, and confined at Newport News, Virginia, until released after taking the Oath of Allegiance on June 30, 1865.

ESSICK, RANSOM, Private
Resided in Randolph County and enlisted in Wake County at age 20, August 18, 1862, for the war. Wounded at Chancellorsville, Virginia, May 3, 1863, and died of wound the next day.

FELTON, PETER F., Private
Resided in Craven County where he enlisted at age 44, June 1, 1861, for the war. Detailed as a nurse at Gordonsville, Virginia, October 1, 1862, and reported as absent on detail through June 23, 1863. Present or accounted for until captured at Kelly's Ford, Virginia, November 7, 1863. Confined at Point Lookout, Maryland, until transferred for exchange to James River, Virginia, February 13, 1865. Received at Cox's Landing, James River, Virginia, February 14-15, 1865, in exchange. Captured at High Bridge, Virginia, April 6, 1865, and confined at Point Lookout until released after taking the Oath of Allegiance on June 27, 1865.

FORD, REDDIN, Private
Born in Edgecombe County where he resided as a farmer prior to enlisting in Wake County at age 37, July 8, 1863, for the war. Discharged on October 23, 1863, by reason of "epilepsia."

FOWLER, THOMAS, Private
Resided in Harnett County and enlisted in Wake County at age 35, December 13, 1862, for the war. Reported as present or accounted for on company muster rolls until sent to hospital sick, June 4, 1863. Company muster rolls carry him as

absent without leave from November 1, 1863, through October, 1864. Appears on a muster roll of Company A, 2nd Battalion N.C. Local Defense Troops, for January-February, 1864, as present with the remark: "Joined by order of the Medical Examining Board at Fayetteville, N.C. Temporarily attached." Reported as present on a roll of detailed men at Fayetteville dated June 30, 1864. Appears as present on muster roll of Company G, 2nd Battalion N.C. Local Defense Troops, for November-December, 1864, with the remark: "Company I, 2nd Regiment N.C. State Troops."

FULGHUM, GEORGE W., Private
Resided in Craven County and enlisted in Northampton County at age 19, July 4, 1861, for the war. Present or accounted for on company muster rolls through October, 1864. Paroled at Appomattox Court House, Virginia, April 9, 1865.

FULP, A. C., Private
Paroled at Greensboro on May 22, 1865.

GARDNER, HARVEY C., Private
Resided in Pitt County and enlisted in Craven County at age 21, June 10, 1861, for the war. Killed at Gettysburg, Pennsylvania, July 2-3, 1863.

GASKINS, LEWIS, Private
Resided in Craven County where he enlisted at age 21, May 29, 1861, for the war. Roll of Honor states that he "died of wounds received by accidental explosion of a shell in Camp Wyatt, New Hanover County, June, 1862."

GLOVER, WILLIAM B., Private
Resided in Northampton County and enlisted in Wake County at age 30, August 18, 1862, for the war. Died in hospital at Guinea Station, Virginia, February 24, 1863, of "smallpox."

GOODFRIEND, SAMUEL, Private
Resided in Craven County where he enlisted at age 21, May 29, 1861, for the war. Company muster rolls report him as "missing," "taken prisoner," and "deserter" during the Maryland campaign of September, 1862.

GRAVES, A., Private
Enlisted in Wake County on February 3, 1864, for the war. Deserted on July 28, 1864.

GRAY, CALEB B., Private
Resided in Craven County where he enlisted at age 19, May 29, 1861, for the war. Captured at Boonsboro, Maryland, September 17, 1862, and confined at Fort Delaware, Delaware, until paroled and exchanged at Aiken's Landing, Virginia, October 2, 1862. Declared exchanged on November 10, 1862. Reported on May-June, 1863, muster roll with the remark that he "deserted in Maryland, September 17, 1862."

GREEN, JOSEPH, Private
Resided in Craven County where he enlisted at age 22, May 29, 1861, for the war. Died at Camp Potomac, Virginia, October 24, 1861.

GREEN, WILLIAM R., Private
Born in Halifax County where he resided as a farmer prior to enlisting in Wayne County at age 32, April 20, 1862, for the war. Wounded at Sharpsburg, Maryland, September 17, 1862, and discharged on August 26, 1863, by reason of wound in left arm.

GRIFFIN, THOMAS, Private
Resided in Edgecombe County and enlisted in Wake County at age 33, July 8, 1863, for the war. Present or accounted for until captured at Kelly's Ford, Virginia, November 7-8, 1863. Confined at Point Lookout, Maryland, from Old Capitol Prison, Washington, D.C., February 8, 1864. Paroled at Point Lookout and sent to Venus Point, Savannah River, Georgia, for exchange. Declared exchanged on November 15, 1864.

GRISHAM, SILAS, Private
Resided in Randolph County and enlisted in Wake County on August 30, 1862, for the war. Died in hospital at Guinea Station, Virginia, April 1, 1863, of "smallpox."

GUTHRIE, JOHN L., Private
Resided in Carteret County and enlisted in Craven County at age 27, May 29, 1861, for the war. Deserted in March, 1862.

HAINES, DANIEL W., Private
Resided in Craven County where he enlisted at age 24, June 5, 1861, for the war. Mustered in as Sergeant. Detailed in machine shop at Wilmington on June 1, 1862. Reported as absent on detail through October, 1864. Reduced to ranks in September, 1863.

HALL, GEORGE W., Sergeant
Resided in Craven County where he enlisted at age 21, May 29, 1861, for the war. Mustered in as Corporal and promoted to Sergeant, May-June, 1863. Captured at Gettysburg, Pennsylvania, July 1-4, 1863, and confined at DeCamp General Hospital, Davids Island, New York Harbor. Transferred on December 17, 1863, to Point Lookout, Maryland, where he was released after taking the Oath of Allegiance on February 6, 1864.

HALL, JOHN J., Private
Resided in Craven County where he enlisted at age 22, June 6, 1861, for the war. May-August, 1863, muster rolls report him as present with the remark: "Acting Quartermaster." Present or accounted for until reported as "missing since May 19, 1864."

HANCOCK, HORATIO, Private
Resided in Craven County where he enlisted at age 19, May 29, 1861, for the war. Reported as present or accounted for until reported as absent without leave on October 17, 1863. Reported as absent without leave through October, 1864.

HANCOCK, JAMES W., Private
Resided in Craven County where he enlisted at age 29, May 29, 1861, for the war. Detailed to work on gunboats at Wilmington in June, 1862, and reported as absent on detail through October, 1864.

HARDISON, GEORGE W., Private
Resided in Craven County where he enlisted at age 24, May 29, 1861, for the war. Discharged on September 12, 1861, by reason of "physical inability."

HEATH, BENJAMIN J., Private

Resided in Lenoir County and enlisted in Craven County at age 26, June 6, 1861, for the war. Present or accounted for on company muster rolls through December 8, 1863. Reported as absent without leave from that date through October, 1864.

HEATHCOCK, SAMUEL W., Private

Enlisted in Wake County on May 23, 1864, for the war. Company muster rolls state that he was left near Washington, D.C., July 12, 1864, sick. Federal Provost Marshal records do not indicate where and when he was captured, but his name appears on a roll of prisoners who took the Oath of Allegiance at Elmira, New York, July 7, 1865.

HERITAGE, PHILIP W., Private

Resided in Craven County where he enlisted at age 34, January 18, 1862, for the war. Killed at Malvern Hill, Virginia, July 1, 1862.

HERRITAGE, JOHN L., Private

Born in Craven County where he resided as a druggist and enlisted at age 23, June 14, 1861, for the war. Discharged September 24, 1862, by reason of "asthma, deafness, and rheumatism."

HILL, JONATHAN, Private

Resided in Lenoir County where he enlisted at age 19, April 20, 1862, for the war. Died in hospital at Gordonsville, Virginia, June 17, 1863, of "pneumonia."

HILL, NATHANIEL, Private

Resided in Edgecombe County and enlisted in Wake County at age 23, July 8, 1863, for the war. Present or accounted for until captured at Kelly's Ford, Virginia, November 7, 1863. Confined at Point Lookout, Maryland, until paroled and sent to Aiken's Landing, Virginia, May 3, 1864. Received in exchange at Aiken's Landing on May 8, 1864. Company muster rolls report him as absent prisoner of war through October, 1864.

HOOVER, JOHN J., Private

Resided in Craven County where he enlisted at age 23, June 7, 1861, for the war. Present or accounted for on company muster rolls through October, 1864.

HOWELL, CULLEN, Private

Resided in Randolph County and enlisted in Wake County at age 32, August 18, 1862, for the war. Captured at Martinsburg, Virginia, July 20, 1863, and confined at Fort McHenry, Maryland, until transferred to Point Lookout, Maryland, October 22, 1863. Paroled at Point Lookout and transferred for exchange to City Point, Virginia, March 16, 1864. Received in exchange at City Point on March 20, 1864. Company muster rolls report him as absent sick through October, 1864.

IVES, JOHN P., Private

Resided in Craven County where he enlisted at age 28, June 3, 1861, for the war. Wounded and captured at South Mountain, Maryland, September 14, 1862. Reported on a roll at Fort McHenry, Maryland, October 17, 1862, with the remark that he was sent to Fort Monroe, Virginia, for exchange. Admitted to hospital at Richmond, Virginia, and furloughed for 50 days on November 1, 1862. Present or accounted for until captured at Spotsylvania Court House, Virginia, May 19, 1864. Admitted to hospital at Washington, D.C., May 29, 1864, with a gunshot wound of the left leg. Transferred to Old Capitol Prison, Washington, July 26, 1864, and to Elmira, New York, August 12, 1864. Sent from Elmira to Point Lookout, Maryland, October 11-14, 1864. Paroled at Point Lookout on October 29, 1864. Date exchanged not reported. Admitted to hospital at Richmond on February 25, 1865, and transferred to Farmville, Virginia, April 1, 1865. Paroled at Lynchburg, Virginia, April 15, 1865.

JONES, G., Private

Captured at Gettysburg, Pennsylvania, July 1-3, 1863, and transferred to the Provost Marshal on December 2, 1863.

JONES, JOHN H., Private

Resided as a shoemaker in Craven County where he enlisted at age 24, May 29, 1861, for the war. Wounded at Sharpsburg, Maryland, September 17, 1862. Present or accounted for on company muster rolls through August, 1864, when he appears with the remark: "Died of wounds received at Spotsylvania Court House." Reported on a Register of General Hospital, Winchester, Virginia, dated July 20, 1864, with the remark that he was suffering from a gunshot wound of the breast.

KILLEBREW, ROBERT, Private

Born in Edgecombe County where he resided prior to enlisting in Wake County at age 36, July 8, 1863, for the war. Died in hospital at Charlottesville, Virginia, December 1, 1863, of "pneumonia."

KIMBALL, WILLIAM, Private

Resided in Orange County. Federal Provost Marshal records indicate that he was captured in Orange County, but date of capture not reported. Released at Louisville, Kentucky, after taking the Oath of Allegiance on July 27, 1864.

KOPPEL, JACOB, Private

Resided in New Hanover County where he enlisted at age 19, May 29, 1862, for the war. Company muster rolls report him as absent prisoner and deserter after the Maryland campaign of September, 1862.

LOCK, JAMES W., Private

Resided in Craven County where he enlisted at age 18, May 29, 1861, for the war. Captured and paroled near Sharpsburg, Maryland, September 27, 1862. Requested "not to be returned by exchange or parole" and was "permitted to proceed and remain in any of the loyal states."

LOCK, JOHN, Private

Signed pay voucher for pay from July 1, 1863, through February 29, 1864, giving this unit. Admitted to hospital at Richmond, Virginia, April 13, 1864, wounded. Furloughed for 60 days on April 14, 1864. Hospital register states that he was injured in September, 1862, and gives nature of disability as "amputation of right thigh at upper third, permanent disability."

McCALL, JOHN, Private

Enlisted in Wake County for the war. First reported on May 1-August 31, 1864, muster roll, but date of enlistment not reported. Reported on that muster roll with the remark: "Deserted." Appears on September-October, 1864, muster roll with the remark that he "deserted August, 1864."

McCOLLUM, DANIEL P., Musician
Resided in Craven County where he enlisted at age 15, May 29, 1861, for the war. Mustered in as Musician. Present or accounted for on company muster rolls through October, 1864. Paroled at Burkeville, Virginia, April 14-17, 1865.

McCOTTER, THOMAS Y., Private
Resided in Craven County where he enlisted at age 20, May 29, 1861, for the war. Present or accounted for until captured near Washington, D.C., July 12, 1864. Confined at Old Capitol Prison, Washington, until transferred to Elmira, New York, July 23-25, 1864. Paroled at Elmira and sent to James River, Virginia, March 10, 1865, for exchange. Declared exchanged at Boulware's Wharf, James River, March 15, 1865.

McLACKLAN, EDWARD T., Corporal
Resided in Craven County where he enlisted at age 20, May 29, 1861, for the war. Mustered in as Private and appointed Corporal on November 1, 1862. Killed at Gettysburg, Pennsylvania, July 2-3, 1863.

MEDLIN, JOEL R., Private
Resided in Halifax County and enlisted in Northampton County at age 21, July 15, 1861, for the war. Captured at Frederick, Maryland, September 12, 1862, and confined at Fort Delaware, Delaware, until paroled and exchanged at Aiken's Landing, Virginia, October 2, 1862. Declared exchanged on November 10, 1862. Admitted to hospital on October 13, 1862, at Richmond, Virginia, where he died on October 27, 1862, of "febris cont."

MERCER, JESSE, Private
Resided in Edgecombe County and enlisted in Wake County at age 20, July 8, 1863, for the war. Killed at Spotsylvania Court House, Virginia, May 12, 1864.

MORRIS, JAMES H., Private
Resided in Craven County where he enlisted at age 29, May 29, 1861, for the war. Company muster roll for May 1-October 31, 1862, states that he was "wounded at the battle of Sharpsburg and prisoner." Reported on company muster rolls through June, 1863, as absent with the remark that he took the Oath of Allegiance. Also reported as a deserter.

MORRIS, WILLIAM, Private
Resided in Wayne County. Federal Provost Marshal records report him as a "rebel deserter" confined at Knoxville, Tennessee, March 29, 1865. Took the Oath of Allegiance on April 3, 1865, "to remain north of the Ohio River during the war."

MOZINGO, THOMAS A., Sergeant
Resided in Craven County where he enlisted at age 20, May 29, 1861, for the war. Mustered in as Private. Wounded at Chancellorsville, Virginia, May 3, 1863. Appointed Corporal on June 28,

1863. Wounded at Gettysburg, Pennsylvania, July 1-3, 1863. Promoted to Sergeant on September 1, 1863. Present or accounted for until captured at Kelly's Ford, Virginia, November 7, 1863, and confined at Point Lookout, Maryland. Paroled at Point Lookout and exchanged at Cox's Landing, James River, Virginia, February 14-15, 1865. Admitted to hospital at Richmond, Virginia, February 15, 1865, and transferred the next day.

MURDOCK, DAVID, Private
Resided in Davidson County and enlisted in Wake County at age 33, August 28, 1862, for the war. Present or accounted for until he died in hospital at Richmond, Virginia, October 17, 1863, of "typhoid fever."

NANTY, G., Private
Paroled at Charlotte on May 24, 1865.

NEWSOM, ENSLY, Private
Born in Randolph County where he resided as a farmer prior to enlisting in Wake County at age 20, August 21, 1862, for the war. Present or accounted for until discharged on September 12, 1863, by reason of "the loss of his left hand by the accidental discharge of his musket December 29, 1862."

NOLL, DAVID, Private
Resided in Craven County where he enlisted at age 20, May 29, 1861, for the war. Present or accounted for until he "deserted August, 1862."

OLIVER, JAMES, Private
Resided in Northampton County and enlisted in Wake County at age 30, August 17, 1862, for the war. Present or accounted for until furloughed for 30 days from hospital at Guinea Station, Virginia, April 28, 1863. Never returned from furlough.

OWENS, JOHN, Private
Enlisted in Wake County on June 6, 1864, for the war. Deserted June 16, 1864.

PHALLER, JOHN D., Private
Resided in Craven County where he enlisted at age 29, June 3, 1861, for the war. Detailed as guard in hospital at Richmond, Virginia, in October, 1862, and remained on detail through October, 1864.

PITT, AARON A., Sergeant
Resided in Edgecombe County where he enlisted at age 25, June 25, 1861, for the war. Mustered in as Private. Wounded and captured in skirmish near Richmond, Virginia, June 21, 1862. Confined in hospital at Fort Columbus, New York Harbor, until sent to Fort Monroe, Virginia, July 31, 1862. Date and place exchanged not reported. Reported as present on May 1-October 31, 1862, muster roll. Promoted to Corporal on June 28, 1863, and to Sergeant on September 1, 1863. Captured at Kelly's Ford, Virginia, November 7, 1863, and confined at Point Lookout, Maryland, where he died November 9, 1864, of "congestive intermittent fever."

PITT, BRYAN, Private
Resided in Edgecombe County and enlisted in Wake County at age 39, July 8, 1863, for the war.

Present or accounted for until captured at Kelly's Ford, Virginia, November 7, 1863. Confined at Point Lookout, Maryland, until paroled and sent to Aiken's Landing, Virginia, February 24, 1865, for exchange. Admitted to hospital at Richmond, Virginia, March 5, 1865, and furloughed for 30 days the next day.

PITT, JAMES, Private
Resided in Edgecombe County and enlisted in Craven County at age 20, June 25, 1861, for the war. Mustered in as Private. Wounded at Malvern Hill, Virginia, July 1, 1862. Appears as Corporal after September-October, 1863. Admitted to hospital at Richmond, Virginia, May 22, 1864, with a gunshot wound and furloughed for 60 days on June 3, 1864. September-October, 1864, muster roll reports him with the remark: "Died September 26, 1864, of wounds received at Fisher's Hill, Virginia, September 22, 1864."

POWELL, ALBERT B., Sergeant
Resided in Craven County where he enlisted at age 19, June 26, 1861, for the war. Mustered in as Private. Captured at Sharpsburg, Maryland, September 17, 1862, and paroled on September 23, 1862. Wounded at Chancellorsville, Virginia, May 3, 1863. Appointed Sergeant on September 1, 1863. Captured at Kelly's Ford, Virginia, November 7, 1863, and confined at Point Lookout, Maryland. Paroled at Point Lookout and sent to James River, Virginia, February 13, 1865, for exchange. Declared exchanged February 14-15, 1865. Reported on a roll of a detachment of paroled and exchanged prisoners at Camp Lee, near Richmond, Virginia, dated February 18, 1865.

POWELL, ALEXANDER MILNE, Private
Resided in Tennessee and enlisted in Orange County, Virginia, at age 16, September 1, 1863, for the war. Present or accounted for on company muster rolls through October, 1864, being reported as absent "orderly at brigade headquarters" from April, 1864, through October, 1864. Paroled at Appomattox Court House, Virginia, April 9, 1865.

POWERS, DAVID, Private
Resided in Johnston County and enlisted in Wake County at age 43, September 4, 1863, for the war. Wounded at Spotsylvania Court House, Virginia, September 12, 1864. Present or accounted for on company muster rolls through October, 1864. Paroled at Appomattox Court House, Virginia, April 9, 1865.

PRICE, ASHLEY, Private
Resided in Johnston County and enlisted in Wake County at age 42, September 4, 1863, for the war. Died in hospital at Lynchburg, Virginia, November 1, 1863, of "dysenteria chronic."

RAWLS, ALFRED D., Private
Resided in Craven County where he enlisted at age 18, May 29, 1861, for the war. Present or accounted for until captured at Spotsylvania Court House, Virginia, May 12, 1864. Confined at Point Lookout, Maryland, until transferred to Elmira, New York, August 14, 1864. Released at Elmira after taking the Oath of Allegiance on June 14, 1865.

RAWLS, JOHN F., Private
Resided in Craven County where he enlisted at age 19, June 11, 1861, for the war. Wounded at Chancellorsville, Virginia, May 3, 1863. Present or accounted for until he "died of wounds received at Spotsylvania Court House, Virginia."

RAY, JOHN D., Private
Enlisted in Wake County on April 29, 1864, for the war. Present or accounted for on company muster rolls through October, 1864. Admitted to hospital at Richmond, Virginia, January 5, 1865, and furloughed for 60 days on January 8, 1865.

REID, MALON, Private
Enlisted in Wake County on June 7, 1861, for the war. Reported on September-October, 1864, muster roll as "absent wounded and taken prisoner September 19, 1864."

RIDGE, WILLIAM, Private
Enlisted in Wake County for the war. First reported on company muster roll for May 1-August 31, 1864. Reported on that muster roll as "absent sick since August 17, 1864." Reported with same remark on September-October, 1864, muster roll. Issued clothing at General Hospital, Liberty, Virginia, October 21, 1864.

ROBINSON, JOHN, Private
Resided in Person County and enlisted in Wake County at age 31, July 15, 1862, for the war. Present or accounted for until captured at Kelly's Ford, Virginia, November 7, 1863. Confined at Point Lookout, Maryland, until paroled for exchange on May 3, 1864. Declared exchanged at Aiken's Landing, Virginia, May 8, 1864. Paroled at Greensboro on May 5, 1865.

ROSE, JOSEPH, Private
Resided in Craven County where he enlisted at age 19, June 6, 1861, for the war. Present or accounted for until he "deserted while on his way to join his regiment, September, 1862."

SALTER, EDWARD H., Sergeant
Born in Craven County where he resided and enlisted at age 29, May 29, 1861, for the war. Mustered in as Sergeant. Wounded at Chancellorsville, Virginia, May 3, 1863, and died the next day.

SCHAFFER, JOHN G., Private
Resided in Craven County where he enlisted at age 21, May 29, 1861, for the war. Present or accounted for until he "deserted August, 1862."

SILVERBERG, BERNARD, Private
Resided in Craven County where he enlisted at age 25, June 3, 1861, for the war. Mustered in as Private and appointed Quartermaster Sergeant on July 10, 1861. Present or accounted for until he deserted on January 3, 1863. Reduced to ranks for desertion and reported as absent through June, 1863. Roll of Honor states that he was "reduced to ranks for misconduct and desertion."

SMAW, EDWARD S., Private
Born in Beaufort County and resided in Craven County prior to enlisting in Northampton County at age 19, June 20, 1861, for the war. Wounded at Sharpsburg, Maryland, September 17, 1862, and died of wound October 1, 1862.

SMITH, JOHN B., Private

Enlisted in Wake County on April 27, 1864, for the war. Deserted May 22, 1864, and reported as a deserter on muster rolls through October, 1864. Appears on a register of effects of deceased soldiers dated 1864.

SMITH, JOHN H., Private

Resided in Craven County where he enlisted at age 22, May 29, 1861, for the war. Captured at Gettysburg, Pennsylvania, July 3-4, 1863, and confined at Fort Delaware, Delaware. Released at Fort Delaware after taking the Oath of Allegiance and joining the U.S. service on September 22, 1863. Assigned to Company G, 3rd Regiment Maryland Cavalry.

SOMMERS, GEORGE, Private

Resided in Randolph County and enlisted in Wake County at age 28, August 18, 1862, for the war. Deserted April 10, 1863.

SPARROW, STEPHEN P., Sergeant

Resided in Hyde County and enlisted in Craven County at age 20, May 29, 1861, for the war. Mustered in as Sergeant. Present or accounted for until transferred to Captain William H. Spencer's Company (Independent Cavalry) upon appointment as 2nd Lieutenant to rank from February 7, 1863.

STEWART, WILLIAM W., Private

Enlisted in Wake County on June 1, 1864, for the war. Captured at Winchester, Virginia, September 19, 1864, and confined at Point Lookout, Maryland. Paroled at Point Lookout and transferred for exchange to Aiken's Landing, Virginia, March 15, 1865. Declared exchanged on March 18, 1865.

ST. JOHN, JOHN, Private

Resided in Craven County where he enlisted at age 30, May 29, 1861, for the war. Present or accounted for until he "deserted August, 1862."

STONE, WILLIAM JACKSON, Private

Resided in Davidson County and enlisted in Wake County at age 33, August 18, 1862, for the war. Present or accounted for until captured at Kelly's Ford, Virginia, November 7, 1863. Confined at Point Lookout, Maryland, where he died July 18, 1864.

STYRON, JOSEPH H., Private

Resided in Craven County where he enlisted at age 18, June 10, 1861, for the war. Present or accounted for until killed at Sharpsburg, Maryland, September 17, 1862.

SWINDELL, ANSON M., Private

Resided in Craven County where he enlisted at age 26, May 29, 1861, for the war. Wounded at Spotsylvania Court House, Virginia, May 12-14, 1864. Returned to duty on December 20, 1864. Admitted to hospital at Richmond, Virginia, February 25, 1865, with "ascites" and transferred to Farmville, Virginia, April 1, 1865. Paroled at Lynchburg, Virginia, April 15, 1865.

TEASLEY, ALGERNON, Private

Resided in Orange County and enlisted in Wake County at age 31, February 14, 1863, for the war. Deserted February 27, 1863.

TILLEY, JAMES, Private

Resided in Davidson County and enlisted in Wake County at age 31, July 31, 1862, for the war. Present or accounted for until killed at Spotsylvania Court House, Virginia, May 12, 1864.

TISDALE, NATHAN, Private

Resided in Craven County where he enlisted at age 19, May 29, 1861, for the war. Present or accounted for until discharged on February 20, 1862, upon providing Richard A. Buck as his substitute. Later enlisted in 1st Company H, 40th Regiment N.C. Troops (3rd Regiment N.C. Artillery).

TRADER, GEORGE W., Private

Born in Accomac County, Virginia, and resided in Carteret County prior to enlisting in Craven County at age 27, May 31, 1861, for the war. Died in camp on December 22, 1861, of "pneumonia."

TRUITT, WILLIAM, Private

Resided in Craven County where he enlisted at age 24, June 1, 1861, for the war. Discharged on October 4, 1861, by reason of "physical inability."

VAUGHN, JOHN, Private

Resided in Greene County and enlisted in Wake County at age 32, August 18, 1862, for the war. Present or accounted for until captured at Kelly's Ford, Virginia, November 7, 1863. Confined at Point Lookout, Maryland, until paroled and transferred for exchange to Aiken's Landing, Virginia, February 24, 1865.

VAUGHN, JOSHUA, Private

Resided in Greene County and enlisted in Wake County at age 20, August 18, 1862, for the war. Furloughed from hospital at Guinea Station, Virginia, for 60 days July 16, 1863, and never returned to the company.

VOGLER, GEORGE E., Private

Resided in Craven County where he enlisted at age 23, June 24, 1861, for the war. Captured at South Mountain, Maryland, September 14, 1862, and confined at Fort Delaware, Delaware, until paroled and exchanged at Aiken's Landing, Virginia, October 2, 1862. Declared exchanged on November 10, 1862. Reported as absent on company muster rolls through June, 1863.

WADE, JOHN H., Corporal

Resided in Craven County where he enlisted at age 21, May 29, 1861, for the war. Mustered in as Private. Wounded at Chancellorsville, Virginia, May 3, 1863. Appointed Corporal on September 1, 1863. Present or accounted for until reported as "absent missing since May 8, 1864."

WALKER, WILLIAM A., Private

Resided in Craven County where he enlisted at age 24, May 31, 1861, for the war. Captured and paroled near Keedysville, Maryland, September 20, 1862. Captured at Frederick, Maryland, July 4, 1863, and confined at Fort Delaware, Delaware, until released after taking the Oath of Allegiance and joining the U.S. service on September 22, 1863. Assigned to Company G, 3rd Regiment Maryland Cavalry. Roll of Honor carries the following remark: "Taken prisoner at Boonsboro; exchanged and soon after deserted; returned at Fredericksburg where he deserted again; was arrested at Chancellorsville, April 11, 1863, and released. Deserted at Williamsport, Maryland, June 17, 1863."

WALLACE, CALVIN R., Private

Resided in Johnston County and enlisted in Wake County at age 40, September 4, 1863, for the war. Present or accounted for until captured at Kelly's Ford, Virginia, November 7, 1863. Confined at Point Lookout, Maryland, until paroled and sent to James River, Virginia, February 13, 1865, for exchange. Received at Cox's Landing, James River, February 14-15, 1865, in exchange.

WATKINS, JOHN O., Private

Resided in Union County. Captured at Aberdeen Church, Virginia, April 3, 1865, and confined at Point Lookout, Maryland, until released after taking the Oath of Allegiance on June 21, 1865.

WHEELER, PETER W., Sergeant

Born in Newark, New Jersey, and resided as a teacher in Craven County where he enlisted at age 21, June 7, 1861, for the war. Mustered in as Sergeant. Present or accounted for until transferred to the Field and Staff of this regiment upon appointment as Commissary Sergeant on August 6, 1863.

WHIRLAN, A. B., Private

Captured and paroled at Raleigh on April 12, 1865.

WHITE, FRANCIS J., Private

Resided in Randolph County and enlisted in Wake County at age 33, July 17, 1862, for the war. Present or accounted for until captured at Kelly's Ford, Virginia, November 7, 1863. Confined at Point Lookout, Maryland, until paroled and sent to Venus Point, Savannah River, Georgia, November 1, 1864, for exchange. Received at Venus Point in exchange on November 15, 1864. Paroled at Greensboro on May 10, 1865.

WHITLOW, JOHN, Private

Resided in Randolph County and enlisted in Wake County at age 26, August 19, 1862, for the war. Roll of Honor carries the remark: "Sent to hospital November 15, 1862, and not heard from since."

WILLIS, ROBERT W., Private

Resided in Carteret County and enlisted in Craven County at age 19, May 31, 1861, for the war. Detailed to work on gunboats at Wilmington in May, 1862, and remained absent on detail through August, 1863. Captured at Kelly's Ford, Virginia, November 7, 1863, and confined at Point Lookout, Maryland, until released after taking the Oath of Allegiance and joining the U.S. service on January 24, 1864. Unit to which assigned not reported.

WITTIE, AUGUST, Private

Resided in Craven County where he enlisted at age 31, May 31, 1861, for the war. Wounded at Chancellorsville, Virginia, May 3, 1863. Reported as absent sick until attached to hospital at Goldsboro as a nurse on September 7, 1863. Reported

as absent detailed until he appears on the May 1-August 31, 1864, muster roll as "absent within the enemy's lines." Reported on September-October, 1864, muster roll with the remark that he "deserted to the enemy."

WOOD, JONATHAN D., Private

Resided in Craven County where he enlisted at age 22, May 29, 1861, for the war. Deserted in March, 1862. Roll of Honor states that he was "at New Bern when the enemy occupied it, and still remains there. Reported to be a deserter."

WOODRUFF, JOSHUA, Private

Enlisted in Wake County on June 25, 1863, for the war. Present or accounted for on company muster rolls through October, 1864, being reported as absent without leave from March 22, 1864, through October, 1864.

COMPANY K

This company, known as the "Elm City Rifles" and "Elm City Cadets," was organized in Craven County and enlisted at New Bern on June 3, 1861. It tendered its service to the state and was ordered to Camp Advance, near Garysburg, Northampton County, where it was assigned to this regiment as Company K. After joining the regiment the company functioned as a part of the regiment, and its history for the war period is recorded as a part of the regimental history.

The information contained in the following roster of the company was compiled principally from company muster rolls for July 16, 1861, through December, 1861; March-April, 1862; July through October, 1862; January, 1863, through March, 1864; and May through October, 1864. No company muster rolls were found for the period prior to July 16, 1861; for January-February, 1862; May-June, 1862; November-December, 1862; April, 1864; or for the period after October, 1864. In addition to the company muster rolls, Roll of Honor records, receipt rolls, and hospital records, supplemented by state pension applications, United Daughters of the Confederacy records, and postwar rosters and histories, all provided useful information.

OFFICERS
CAPTAINS

LEWIS, GEORGE C.

Resided in Craven County and appointed Captain at age 22 to rank from May 16, 1861. Wounded at Ellerson's Mill, Virginia, June 26, 1862. Submitted his resignation on November 26, 1862, by reason of "ill health." Resignation dated October 20, 1862, and officially accepted to take effect from October 21, 1862.

MILLER, ALEXANDER

Resided in Craven County and appointed 1st Lieutenant at age 21 to rank from May 16, 1861. Promoted to Captain to rank from October 21, 1862. Present or accounted for until captured at Kelly's Ford, Virginia, November 7, 1863. Confined at Old Capitol Prison, Washington, D.C., until transferred to Johnson's Island, Ohio, November 11, 1863. Remained at Johnson's Island until released after taking the Oath of Allegiance on June 13, 1865.

LIEUTENANTS

CALDER, WILLIAM, 2nd Lieutenant
Transferred from the Field and Staff of this regiment upon appointment as 2nd Lieutenant to rank from October 22, 1861. Present or accounted for until transferred to the Field and Staff, 1st Battalion N.C. Heavy Artillery upon appointment as Adjutant with the rank of 1st Lieutenant to rank from July 21, 1863.

HANCOCK, RICHARD D., 1st Lieutenant
Resided in Craven County and appointed 2nd Lieutenant at age 18 to rank from May 16, 1861. Promoted to 1st Lieutenant to rank from October 21, 1862. Wounded at Chancellorsville, Virginia, May 3, 1863. Present or accounted for on company muster rolls through October, 1864. Paroled at Appomattox Court House, Virginia, April 9, 1865.

HELLEN, JOSEPH FULFORD, 3rd Lieutenant
Resided in Craven County and appointed 3rd Lieutenant at age 19 to rank from May 16, 1861. Present or accounted for until transferred to 2nd Company H, 40th Regiment N.C. Troops (3rd Regiment N.C. Artillery) upon appointment as 2nd Lieutenant in November, 1861.

STREET, WILLIAM J., 2nd Lieutenant
Resided in Craven County where he enlisted at age 19, June 7, 1861, for the war. Mustered in as 1st Sergeant. Reduced to ranks on October 1, 1861, and reappointed 1st Sergeant on November 1, 1861. Wounded at Sharpsburg, Maryland, September 17, 1862. Appointed 2nd Lieutenant to rank from November 1, 1862. Wounded at Chancellorsville, Virginia, May 3, 1863, and again at Spotsylvania Court House, Virginia, May 12, 1864. Reported as absent wounded through September, 1864. Paroled at Appomattox Court House, Virginia, April 9, 1865.

NONCOMMISSIONED OFFICERS AND PRIVATES

AUMAN, DEMPSEY, Private
Enlisted in Wake County at age 32, August 29, 1862, for the war. Died at Harrisonburg, Virginia, November 29, 1862, of disease.

BALL, ANDREW F., Private
Resided in Craven County where he enlisted at age 18, June 5, 1861, for the war. Discharged at Fredericksburg, Virginia, in September, 1861. Appears on an account for burial of soldiers at Fredericksburg dated October 4, 1861.

BELL, WILLIAM B., Sergeant
Resided in Craven County where he enlisted at age 22, June 3, 1861, for the war. Mustered in as Sergeant. Wounded at Chancellorsville, Virginia, May 3, 1863. Present or accounted for until captured at Kelly's Ford, Virginia, November 7, 1863. Confined at Point Lookout, Maryland, until paroled and transferred for exchange to Aiken's Landing, Virginia, February 24, 1865. Paroled at Appomattox Court House, Virginia, April 9, 1865.

BRINSON, JOSEPH W., Private
Resided in Craven County where he enlisted at age 22, June 11, 1861, for the war. Wounded at Malvern Hill, Virginia, July 1, 1862, and died in hospital at Richmond, Virginia, August 25, 1862, of "amputation of right leg (secondary operation) immediate cause of death hectic fever."

BRITT, LEVI, Private
Enlisted in Wake County at age 21, August 29, 1862, for the war. Present or accounted for until captured at Kelly's Ford, Virginia, November 7, 1863. Confined at Point Lookout, Maryland, until paroled and transferred for exchange to Aiken's Landing, Virginia, February 24, 1865. Admitted to hospital at Richmond, Virginia, February 25, 1865. Paid on March 6, 1865.

BROCK, RICHARD J., Private
Resided in Craven County where he enlisted at age 23, June 3, 1861, for the war. Present or accounted for until captured at Kelly's Ford, Virginia, November 7, 1863. Confined at Point Lookout, Maryland, until paroled and sent to Venus Point, Savannah River, Georgia, October 29, 1864, for exchange.

BROOKS, WILLIAM R., Private
Resided in Craven County where he enlisted at age 24, June 3, 1861, for the war. Present or accounted for on company muster rolls through October, 1864. Captured at Amelia Court House, Virginia, April 6, 1865, and confined at Point Lookout, Maryland, until released after taking the Oath of Allegiance on June 24, 1865.

BROWN, JOHN ISAAC, 1st Sergeant
Resided in Craven County where he enlisted at age 20, June 3, 1861, for the war. Mustered in as Sergeant and appointed 1st Sergeant on October 1, 1861. Transferred to the Field and Staff of this regiment upon appointment as Sergeant Major on November 1, 1861.

BUDD, NATHANIEL F., Private
Resided in Lenoir County where he enlisted at age 19, July 1, 1861, for the war. Captured at Fredericksburg, Virginia, May 3, 1863, and paroled and exchanged at City Point, Virginia, May 13, 1863. Present or accounted for until wounded at Spotsylvania Court House, Virginia, May 8, 1864. Died of wound on May 20, 1864.

BURCH, CALVIN, Private
Born in Craven County where he resided and enlisted at age 20, June 3, 1861, for the war. Wounded at Chancellorsville, Virginia, May 3, 1863, and died the next day.

BURKE, WILLIAM A., Private
Enlisted on November 1, 1864, for the war.

BYRD, BENJAMIN, Private
Enlisted in Wake County on May 20, 1864, for the war. Present or accounted for on company muster rolls through October, 1864.

CALHOUN, GEORGE C., Private
Resided in Craven County and enlisted at Fredericksburg, Virginia, at age 18, February 3, 1863, for the war. Died in hospital at Richmond, Virginia, June 3, 1863, of "meningitis following epilepsy."

CARSON, CALVIN, Private

Enlisted in Montgomery County on September 11, 1862, for the war. Killed at Chancellorsville, Virginia, May 3, 1863.

CARTER, CHARLES, Sergeant

Resided in Craven County where he enlisted at age 19, June 7, 1861, for the war. Mustered in as Corporal and promoted to Sergeant on May 10, 1863. Present or accounted for until captured at Kelly's Ford, Virginia, November 7, 1863. Confined at Point Lookout, Maryland, until paroled and sent to Venus Point, Savannah River, Georgia, October 30, 1864, for exchange. Declared exchanged at Venus Point on November 15, 1864. Captured at Amelia Court House, Virginia, April 6, 1865, and confined at Point Lookout until released after taking the Oath of Allegiance on June 26, 1865.

CARTER, WILLIAM N., Private

Born in Craven County where he resided prior to enlisting in Wayne County at age 18, May 1, 1862, for the war. Captured at South Mountain, Maryland, September 16, 1862, and exchanged at Aiken's Landing, Virginia, October 6, 1862. Died in camp on March 12, 1863, of disease.

CHERRY, FREDERICK J., Corporal

Resided in Edgecombe County and enlisted in Craven County at age 21, June 4, 1861, for the war. Mustered in as Private. Captured at Sharpsburg, Maryland, September 17, 1862, and confined at Fort Delaware, Delaware, until paroled and exchanged at Aiken's Landing, Virginia, October 2, 1862. Declared exchanged on November 10, 1862. Promoted to Corporal in November, 1862. Killed at Chancellorsville, Virginia, May 3, 1863.

CHERRY, WILLIAM B., Private

Resided in Edgecombe County and enlisted in Craven County at age 26, June 12, 1861, for the war. Present or accounted for until killed at Spotsylvania Court House, Virginia, May 12, 1864.

COOK, BENJAMIN M., Sergeant

Resided in Craven County where he enlisted at age 20, June 5, 1861, for the war. Mustered in as Sergeant. Killed at Chancellorsville, Virginia, May 3, 1863.

COWLING, GEORGE W., Private

Resided in Virginia and enlisted in Craven County at age 21, June 3, 1861, for the war. Present or accounted for until he "died July, 1862, of wounds received in battle at Malvern Hill, Virginia, July 1, 1862."

CUTHRELL, DAVID B., Private

Resided in Craven County and enlisted at age 21, June 3, 1861, for the war. Died July 11, 1861.

CUTHRELL, SAMUEL, Private

Resided in Craven County where he enlisted at age 22, June 3, 1861, for the war. Captured at Sharpsburg, Maryland, September 17, 1862, and paroled near Keedysville, Maryland, September 20, 1862. Admitted to hospital at Richmond, Virginia, October 29, 1862, and furloughed for 30 days on November 9, 1862. Died at Raleigh on December 1, 1862.

DAVENPORT, HAYWOOD, 1st Sergeant

Resided in Washington County and enlisted in Craven County at age 18, June 3, 1861, for the war. Mustered in as Corporal. Wounded and captured at South Mountain, Maryland, September 14-15, 1862. Date paroled was not reported. Promoted to 1st Sergeant on November 1, 1862. Wounded at Chancellorsville, Virginia, May 3, 1863. Present or accounted for until captured at Kelly's Ford, Virginia, November 7, 1863. Confined at Point Lookout, Maryland, until paroled and sent to Cox's Landing, James River, Virginia, February 13, 1865, for exchange. Captured at Burkeville, Virginia, April 6, 1865, and confined at Point Lookout until released after taking the Oath of Allegiance on June 11, 1865.

DICKENS, ROBERT, Private

Resided in Guilford County and enlisted in Wake County on May 5, 1864, for the war. Present or accounted for on company muster rolls through October, 1864. Captured on the Southside Railroad, near Petersburg, Virginia, April 2, 1865. Confined at Hart's Island, New York Harbor, until released after taking the Oath of Allegiance on June 17, 1865.

DIXON, BENJAMIN A., Private

Enlisted in Wake County on May 15, 1864, for the war. Captured at Strasburg, Virginia, October 19, 1864, and confined at Point Lookout, Maryland, until paroled and exchanged at Boulware's Wharf, James River, Virginia, March 30, 1865.

DIXON, LUCAS J., Private

Resided in Craven County where he enlisted at age 26, June 3, 1861, for the war. Discharged in September, 1861, by reason of disability.

DOUGHERTY, RICHARD T., Private

Resided in Lenoir County and enlisted in Northampton County at age 35, July 16, 1861, for the war. Discharged in January, 1862, upon providing William West as his substitute.

DOWDY, JOHN W., Private

Resided in Craven County and enlisted in Wayne County at age 18, May 1, 1862, for the war. Captured at Boonsboro, Maryland, September 14-16, 1862, and paroled and exchanged at Aiken's Landing, Virginia, October 6, 1862. Present or accounted for until captured at Kelly's Ford, Virginia, November 7, 1863. Confined at Point Lookout, Maryland, until paroled and exchanged at Aiken's Landing, February 25, 1865. Captured at Petersburg, Virginia, April 3, 1865, and confined at Hart's Island, New York Harbor, until released after taking the Oath of Allegiance on June 17, 1865.

DOWDY, RICHARD P., Private

Resided in Craven County where he enlisted at age 21, June 4, 1861, for the war. Captured at Sharpsburg, Maryland, September 17, 1862, and paroled at Keedysville, Maryland, September 20, 1862. Wounded in the left leg at Chancellorsville, Virginia, May 3, 1863. Reported as absent in hospital at Wilson through October, 1863, and in hospital at Goldsboro from October, 1863, through November, 1864. Retired to the Invalid Corps on December 22, 1864, and assigned to light duty in hospital at Goldsboro on January 30, 1865. Paroled at High Point on May 1, 1865.

EVANS, LEWIS H., Private

Resided in Lenoir County and enlisted in Wayne County at age 21, July 1, 1861, for the war. Present or accounted for on company muster rolls through October, 1864. Retired to the Invalid Corps on September 17, 1864, and ordered to report for light duty at Gordonsville, Virginia, December 3, 1864.

FIELDS, CHARLES M., Private

Resided in Craven County where he enlisted at age 18, June 4, 1861, for the war. Captured at South Mountain, Maryland, September 14, 1862, and exchanged at Aiken's Landing, Virginia, October 6, 1862. Declared exchanged on November 10, 1862. Transferred to the C.S. Navy on January 29, 1863.

FOSCUE, WILLIAM F., Private

Resided in Virginia and enlisted in Craven County at age 36, June 24, 1861, for the war. Present or accounted for until transferred to the C.S. Navy on May 7, 1862.

FRANCIS, J. H. C., Private

Paroled at Raleigh on April 19, 1865.

FULFORD, ANSON B., Corporal

Resided in Carteret County and enlisted in Craven County at age 20, June 9, 1861, for the war. Mustered in as Private and appointed Corporal on October 1, 1861. Captured at South Mountain, Maryland, September 15, 1862, and confined at Fort Delaware, Delaware, until paroled and sent to Aiken's Landing, Virginia, October 2, 1862, for exchange. Declared exchanged on November 10, 1862. Present or accounted for until captured at Kelly's Ford, Virginia, November 7, 1863. Confined at Point Lookout, Maryland, where he died on February 11, 1864.

FULFORD, WILLIAM B., Private

Resided in Carteret County and enlisted in Craven County at age 18, June 3, 1861, for the war. Present or accounted for until wounded at Chancellorsville, Virginia, May 3, 1863. Reported as absent wounded through August, 1863. Present or accounted for from that date until captured at Kelly's Ford, Virginia, November 7, 1863. Confined at Point Lookout, Maryland, until paroled and transferred for exchange to Aiken's Landing, Virginia, February 24, 1865.

FULK, CHARLES A., Private

Enlisted in Wake County at age 26, August 29, 1862, for the war. Captured near Fredericksburg, Virginia, May 3, 1863, and paroled and exchanged at City Point, Virginia, May 10, 1863. Present or accounted for until captured at Kelly's Ford, Virginia, November 7, 1863. Confined at Point Lookout, Maryland, where he died December 15, 1864, of "chronic dysentery."

FULK, DAVID EDWARD, Private

Enlisted in Wake County at age 24, August 29, 1862, for the war. Present or accounted for until captured at Kelly's Ford, Virginia, November 7, 1863. Confined at Point Lookout, Maryland, where he died on December 7, 1864, of "remittent fever."

HAINES, JAMES, Private

Resided in Edgecombe County and enlisted in Wake County on May 9, 1864, for the war. Present or accounted for on company muster rolls through October, 1864. Admitted to hospital at Richmond, Virginia, March 17, 1865, with "diarrhoea acute." Captured in hospital at Richmond on April 3, 1865, and confined at Newport News, Virginia, until released after taking the Oath of Allegiance on June 30, 1865.

HALL, HENRY L., Private

Resided in Craven County where he enlisted at age 20, June 3, 1861, for the war. Wounded at Malvern Hill, Virginia, July 1, 1862. Wounded and captured at South Mountain, Maryland, September 14-29, 1862. Confined at Fort McHenry, Maryland, until paroled and exchanged at City Point, Virginia, December 4, 1862. Admitted to hospital at Petersburg, Virginia, December 4, 1862, and furloughed for 40 days on December 19, 1862. Detailed as messenger at Petersburg through August, 1863, and as armorer at Goldsboro in October, 1863. Transferred to Company B, 10th Regiment N.C. State Troops (1st Regiment N.C. Artillery) on November 4, 1863.

HANCOCK, JAMES, Private

Resided in Craven County where he enlisted at age 18, June 15, 1861, for the war. Present or accounted for until killed at Cold Harbor, Virginia, June 2, 1864.

HANCOCK, ROBERT, Private

Enlisted in Craven County on June 3, 1861, for the war. Reported as present through September, 1861, and as absent sick in New Bern through December, 1861.

HARGET, CHARLES F., Private

Resided in Craven County where he enlisted at age 20, June 3, 1861, for the war. Wounded at Malvern Hill, Virginia, July 1, 1862. Present or accounted for on company muster rolls through October, 1864. Paroled at Farmville, Virginia, April 11-21, 1865.

HARPER, SPENCER H., Private

Resided in Edgecombe County and enlisted in Craven County at age 19, June 3, 1861, for the war. Present or accounted for on company muster rolls through October, 1864, being reported as absent sick from July, 1862, through April, 1863; as absent without leave from April, 1863, through December, 1863; and as absent sick from January, 1864, through October, 1864. Admitted to hospital at Richmond, Virginia, on March 6, 1865, with "burn left foot." Furloughed for 60 days on March 16, 1865.

HAWKINS, A. T., Private

Died at Goldsboro in May, 1862.

HIGGINS, WILEY F., Private

Born in Craven County where he resided as a clerk prior to enlisting in Northampton County at age 21, July 16, 1861, for the war. Present or accounted for until transferred to Company A, 1st Battalion N.C. Local Defense Troops upon appointment as 2nd Lieutenant to rank from March 28, 1863.

HORN, GARY, Private

Resided in Johnston County and enlisted in Wake County at age 24, September 1, 1862, for the war. Present or accounted for until captured at Kelly's Ford, Virginia, November 7, 1863. Confined at Point Lookout, Maryland, until paroled and sent to Venus Point, Savannah River, Georgia, October 30, 1864, for exchange. Declared exchanged at Venus Point on November 15, 1864.

HOWARD, SOLOMON, Private

Resided in Craven County where he enlisted at age 24, June 3, 1861, for the war. Present or accounted for until admitted to hospital at Charlottesville, Virginia, February 11, 1864, with "pneumonia." Transferred to Lynchburg, Virginia, May 3, 1864. Reported as absent without leave on September-October, 1864, muster roll.

HUDSON, Z., Private

Resided in Halifax County and paroled at Salisbury on May 2, 1865.

HUGHES, HENRY J., Private

Resided in Nassau and enlisted in Craven County at age 19, June 6, 1861, for the war. Present or accounted for until captured at Chancellorsville, Virginia, May 3, 1863. Paroled at Old Capitol Prison, Washington, D.C., May 19, 1863. Present or accounted for until captured at Kelly's Ford, Virginia, November 7, 1863. Confined at Point Lookout, Maryland, until paroled and transferred for exchange to Boulware's Wharf, James River, Virginia, February 18, 1865. Admitted to hospital at Greensboro on April 1, 1865.

HUMPHREY, DANIEL E., Private

Resided in Onslow County and enlisted in Northampton County at age 19, July 5, 1861, for the war. Captured at Chancellorsville, Virginia, and paroled on May 4, 1863. Present or accounted for until captured at Kelly's Ford, Virginia, November 7, 1863. Confined at Point Lookout, Maryland, until paroled and sent to James River, Virginia, February 13, 1865, for exchange. Reported as present on a roll of a detachment of paroled and exchanged prisoners at Camp Lee, near Richmond, Virginia, dated February 18, 1865. Paroled at Goldsboro on May 6, 1865. "Came in for parole."

HUMPHREY, ROBERT W., Private

Resided in Onslow County and enlisted in Craven County at age 21, June 21, 1861, for the war. Wounded and captured at Chancellorsville, Virginia, May 3, 1863. Confined in hospital at Washington, D.C., until transferred to Old Capitol Prison, Washington, June 16, 1863. Paroled and sent to City Point, Virginia, June 25, 1863, for exchange. Exact date of exchange not reported. Present or accounted for until captured at Kelly's Ford, Virginia, November 7, 1863. Confined at Point Lookout, Maryland, until paroled and sent to James River, Virginia, February 13, 1865, for exchange. Reported as present on a roll of a detachment of paroled and exchanged prisoners at Camp Lee, near Richmond, Virginia, dated February 18, 1865. Paroled at Goldsboro on May 6, 1865. "Came in for parole."

HYMAN, SAMUEL O., Private

Born in Craven County where he resided and enlisted at age 21, June 3, 1861, for the war. Present or accounted for until killed at Chancellorsville, Virginia, May 3, 1863.

IVES, FREEMAN E., Corporal

Resided in Craven County where he enlisted at age 21, June 3, 1861, for the war. Mustered in as Private and appointed Corporal on May 15, 1863. Present or accounted for until captured at Kelly's Ford, Virginia, November 7, 1863. Confined at Point Lookout, Maryland, until paroled and transferred for exchange to Aiken's Landing, Virginia, February 24, 1865.

JOHNSON, WILLIAM A., Private

Resided in Craven County where he enlisted at age 18, June 3, 1861, for the war. Wounded at Malvern Hill, Virginia, July 1, 1862, and died of wound in hospital at Richmond, Virginia, July 12, 1862.

JONES, CHRISTOPHER M., Private

Born in Jones County where he resided as a farmer prior to enlisting in Wake County at age 20, September 1, 1862, for the war. Wounded at Chancellorsville, Virginia, May 3, 1863, and reported as absent until returned to duty from hospital at Raleigh on December 2, 1864. Applied for retirement to Invalid Corps on December 12, 1864, but application was returned because it was improperly filled out.

JONES, FRANCIS E., Private

Resided in Jones County and enlisted in Wake County at age 24, September 1, 1862, for the war. Died in hospital at Richmond, Virginia, January 1, 1863, of "typhoid fever."

JONES, GEORGE W., Private

Resided in Craven County where he enlisted at age 29, June 14, 1861, for the war. Present or accounted for until transferred to the C.S. Navy on May 7, 1862.

JONES, JAMES L., Sergeant

Resided in Craven County where he enlisted at age 20, June 7, 1861, for the war. Mustered in as Corporal and promoted to Sergeant on September 1, 1861. Captured near Fredericksburg, Virginia, May 3, 1863, and paroled and exchanged at City Point, Virginia, May 10, 1863. Present or accounted for until captured at Kelly's Ford, Virginia, November 7, 1863. Confined at Point Lookout, Maryland, until paroled and transferred for exchange to Aiken's Landing, Virginia, February 24, 1865. Paroled at Thomasville, N.C., May 1, 1865.

JONES, JAMES R., Private

Resided in Jones County and enlisted in Wake County at age 27, September 1, 1862, for the war. Company muster rolls report him as absent sick from November 20, 1862, through February, 1864, and as absent without leave from that date through October, 1864.

JONES, STEPHEN W., Private

Resided in Craven County where he enlisted at age 18, June 3, 1861, for the war. Reported on July 1-October 31, 1862, muster roll with the remark: "Absent. Captured South Mountain. (Took the Oath of Allegiance)." Roll of Honor carries him with the remark: "Taken prisoner in battle at Boonsboro and took the Oath of Allegiance to the U.S. Government."

KOONCE, JAMES H., Sergeant

Resided in Jones County and enlisted in Craven County at age 20, June 3, 1861, for the war. Mustered in as Corporal and promoted to Sergeant prior to his death at Fredericksburg, Virginia, on August 18, 1861.

LAMB, GEORGE W., Private

Resided in Chowan County and enlisted in Craven County at age 20, June 6, 1861, for the war. Reported on July 1-October 31, 1862, muster roll with the remark: "Absent captured and taken the Oath of Allegiance." Roll of Honor reports him with the remark: "Taken prisoner in battle at Boonsboro, Maryland, and took the Oath of Allegiance to the U.S."

LAND, JAMES KENNETH, Private

Resided in Virginia and enlisted in Craven County at age 20, June 3, 1861, for the war. Captured at South Mountain, Maryland, September 14, 1862, and confined at Fort Delaware, Delaware, until paroled and exchanged at Aiken's Landing, Virginia, October 2, 1862. Declared exchanged on November 10, 1862. Present or accounted for until detailed for guard duty at Lynchburg, Virginia, October 6, 1864. Paroled at Lynchburg on April 13, 1865.

LANDEN, LUCIUS C., Private

Resided in Edgecombe County and enlisted in Craven County at age 24, June 12, 1861, for the war. Wounded and captured at Chancellorsville, Virginia, May 3, 1863, and paroled and exchanged at City Point, Virginia, May 10, 1863. Present or accounted for until wounded at Gettysburg, Pennsylvania, July 1, 1863. Reported as absent wounded until detailed at Staunton, Virginia, March 8, 1864. Absent on detail through August, 1864. Reported as present on September-October, 1864, company muster roll. Federal Provost Marshal records report him as a "deserter from the enemy" received by the Provost Marshal General, Army of the Potomac, February 24, 1865, and sent to the Provost Marshal General, Washington, D.C., February 26, 1865. Took the Oath of Allegiance and was provided transportation to New Bern.

LANE, LEONIDAS, Private

Resided in Pitt County and enlisted in Craven County at age 18, June 3, 1861, for the war. Died in September, 1862.

LANE, WILLIAM, Private

Resided in Craven County and enlisted in Lenoir County at age 25, April 18, 1862, for the war. Present or accounted for until captured at Kelly's Ford, Virginia, November 7, 1863. Confined at Point Lookout, Maryland, until paroled and transferred for exchange to Aiken's Landing, Virginia, February 24, 1865.

LEA, ELLIS, Private

Paroled at Greensboro on May 16, 1865.

LEATHERMAN, A. C., Private

Enlisted in Wake County on May 14, 1864, for the war. Present or accounted for on company muster rolls through October, 1864.

LEE, ABRAHAM, Private

First reported on company muster roll for July 1-October 31, 1862, as "absent sick at Richmond." Date, place, and period of enlistment not reported. Furloughed from hospital at Richmond, October 11, 1862. Reported as absent sick on company muster rolls through February, 1864.

LEE, SHADRACK, Private

Resided in Craven County where he enlisted at age 22, June 11, 1861, for the war. Killed at Malvern Hill, Virginia, July 1, 1862.

LEWIS, JOHN, Private

Resided in Craven County where he enlisted at age 30, June 3, 1861, for the war. Wounded at Malvern Hill, Virginia, July 1, 1862, and at Chancellorsville, Virginia, May 3, 1863. Present or accounted for until captured at Kelly's Ford, Virginia, November 7, 1863. Confined at Point Lookout, Maryland, until paroled and transferred for exchange to Aiken's Landing, Virginia, February 24, 1865.

McMANN, PATRICK, Private

Resided in Craven County where he enlisted at age 35, June 3, 1861, for the war. Died in hospital at Richmond, Virginia, February 2, 1862.

MARTIN, JOHN B., Private

Resided in Craven County where he enlisted at age 22, June 3, 1861, for the war. Present or accounted for until captured at Strasburg, Virginia, October 19, 1864. Confined at Point Lookout, Maryland, until paroled and transferred for exchange to Aiken's Landing, Virginia, March 28, 1865. Received in exchange at Boulware's Wharf, James River, Virginia, March 30, 1865.

MASON, FRANCIS M., Private

Born in Craven County where he resided as a farmer and enlisted at age 21, June 5, 1861, for the war. Wounded at Sharpsburg, Maryland, September 17, 1862, and captured. Paroled on September 27, 1862, and exchanged on November 12, 1862. Reported as absent wounded until discharged on April 21, 1863, by reason of wound.

MATTHEWS, JOHN E., Private

Resided in Craven County where he enlisted at age 18, June 4, 1861, for the war. July 1-October 31, 1862, muster roll reports him as "absent, captured at New Bern." Regimental return for May, 1862, reports him as "prisoner in New Bern, N.C., March, 1862." Present or accounted for until captured at Kelly's Ford, Virginia, November 7, 1863. Confined at Point Lookout, Maryland, until transferred for exchange on February 13, 1865. Received in exchange at Cox's Landing, James River, Virginia, February 14-15, 1865. Captured at Burkeville, Virginia, April 6, 1865, and confined at Point Lookout until released after taking the Oath of Allegiance on June 29, 1865.

MERRITT, JOHN F., Private

Resided in Craven County and enlisted at age 22, June 21, 1861, for the war. Died July 10, 1861.

MERRITT, LEMUEL J., Private

Resided in Craven County where he enlisted at age 31, June 12, 1861, for the war. Wounded at Malvern Hill, Virginia, July 1, 1862. Wounded at

Chancellorsville, Virginia, May 3, 1863, and died of wound on May 5, 1863.

MILLER, DAVID, Private

Resided in Ashe County and enlisted in Wake County on May 19, 1864, for the war. Present or accounted for on company muster rolls through October, 1864. Admitted to hospital at Farmville, Virginia, January 2, 1865, and furloughed for 60 days on March 17, 1865. Furlough papers carry the remark: "Mental aberration from excesive use of tobacco and nostalgia."

MITCHELL, JAMES H., Private

Resided in Stokes County and enlisted in Wake County at age 34, August 29, 1862, for the war. Present or accounted for until captured at Kelly's Ford, Virginia, November 7, 1863. Confined at Point Lookout, Maryland, until "exchanged January 17, 1864." Admitted to hospital at Richmond, Virginia, in June, 1864, and furloughed on January 24, 1865.

MOORE, LEONIDAS J., Private

Resided in Greene County and enlisted in Craven County at age 18, June 7, 1861, for the war. Wounded at Chancellorsville, Virginia, May 3, 1863. Reported as absent wounded on company muster rolls through April, 1864. Detailed at Salisbury on July 11, 1864. Detailed as clerk in Quartermaster Department, Charlotte, November 26, 1864. Paroled at Charlotte on May 3, 1865.

MOSER, WILLIAM, Private

Resided as a farmer in Stokes County prior to enlisting in Wake County at age 29, September 1, 1862, for the war. Wounded at Chancellorsville, Virginia, May 3, 1863, and died on March 8, 1864, of "bronchitis chronic."

MURPHY, HENDRICK H., Private

Resided in Lenoir County and enlisted in Craven County at age 21, February 13, 1862, for the war. Present or accounted for on company muster rolls through October, 1862, and reported as absent without leave from January, 1863, through October, 1864.

OLIVER, JAMES D., Private

Resided in Beaufort County and enlisted in Craven County at age 24, June 3, 1861, for the war. Wounded at Ellerson's Mill, Virginia, June 26, 1862. Present or accounted for until captured at Wilderness, Virginia, May 8, 1864. Confined at Point Lookout, Maryland, until transferred to Elmira, New York, August 10, 1864. Released at Elmira after taking the Oath of Allegiance on June 14, 1865.

OLIVER, THOMAS K., Private

Resided in Craven County where he enlisted at age 18, June 3, 1861, for the war. Present or accounted for until discharged November-December, 1861.

O'NEAL, BARTHOLOMEW, Private

Resided in Beaufort County and enlisted in Craven County at age 20, June 3, 1861, for the war. Wounded at Malvern Hill, Virginia, July 1, 1862. Present or accounted for until captured at Kelly's Ford, Virginia, November 7, 1863. Confined at Point Lookout, Maryland, until paroled and ex-

changed in October, 1864. Reported as present on a roll of a detachment of paroled and exchanged prisoners at Camp Lee, near Richmond, Virginia, dated October 11, 1864.

O'NEAL, JAMES BRYAN, Private

Resided in Beaufort County and enlisted in Craven County at age 19, June 3, 1861, for the war. Wounded at Chancellorsville, Virginia, May 3, 1863. Present or accounted for until captured at Kelly's Ford, Virginia, November 7, 1863. Confined at Point Lookout, Maryland, until paroled and transferred for exchange on September 18, 1864.

O'NEAL, OWEN, Private

Resided in Beaufort County and enlisted in Craven County at age 21, June 3, 1861, for the war. Present or accounted for until captured at Kelly's Ford, Virginia, November 7, 1863. Confined at Point Lookout, Maryland, until paroled and sent to Venus Point, Savannah River, Georgia, October 30, 1864, for exchange. Received in exchange at Venus Point on November 15, 1864. Paroled at Greensboro on April 28, 1865.

O'NEILL, HENRY C., Private

Resided in Beaufort County and enlisted in Craven County at age 24, June 3, 1861, for the war. Died January 15, 1862.

OSTEIN, ROBERT, Private

Resided in Craven County and enlisted at age 32 in February, 1862, for the war as a substitute. Transferred to the C.S. Navy on May 7, 1862.

PACE, DANCY, Private

Resided in Wake County where he enlisted on April 19, 1864, for the war. Present or accounted for on company muster rolls through October, 1864. Captured and paroled at Raleigh on May 23, 1865.

PALMER, HENRY L., Private

Resided in Craven County where he enlisted at age 20, June 10, 1861, for the war. Died May 21, 1862.

PARKER, EDWARD J., Musician

Resided in Virginia and enlisted in Craven County at age 20, June 3, 1861, for the war. Mustered in as Musician. Admitted to hospital at Richmond, Virginia, May 19, 1864, with a gunshot wound. Date and place wounded not reported. Furloughed for 60 days on June 10, 1864. Present or accounted for on company muster rolls through October, 1864.

PARSONS, CALVIN, Private

Resided in Montgomery County and enlisted in Wake County at age 34, September 1, 1862, for the war. Killed at Chancellorsville, Virginia, May 3, 1863.

PERRY, THOMAS G., Private

Resided in Virginia and enlisted in Wake County at age 46, August 29, 1862, for the war. Wounded at Chancellorsville, Virginia, May 3, 1863. Died in hospital at Richmond, Virginia, on May 15, 1863.

PHILLIPS, ELISHA, Private

Enlisted in February, 1862, for the war. Discharged on May 17, 1862, by reason of "first measles, second erysipelas, third typhoid fever and pneumonia, and finally phthisis and under which he is now suffering." Claim for balance of pay due a deceased soldier was filed by his mother on March 9, 1863. Place, date, and cause of death not reported.

PHILLIPS, OWEN C., Private
Resided in Carteret County and enlisted in Craven County at age 20, June 9, 1861, for the war. Killed at Malvern Hill, Virginia, July 1, 1862.

PHILLIPS, RICHARD G., Private
Resided in Rockingham County and enlisted in Wake County at age 30, August 29, 1862, for the war. Killed at Chancellorsville, Virginia, May 3, 1863.

PITMAN, JOHN C., Private
Enlisted in Wake County on May 9, 1864, for the war. Killed at Snicker's Ferry, Virginia, July 18, 1864.

PITTMAN, CHARLES M., Private
Born in Edgecombe County where he resided prior to enlisting in Craven County at age 21, June 3, 1861, for the war. Died in hospital at Richmond, Virginia, March 7, 1863, of "pneumonia."

PITTMAN, JOHN N., Private
Resided in Craven County where he enlisted at age 20, June 3, 1861, for the war. Died on August 24, 1861.

PITTS, LEVI A., Private
Resided in Guilford County and enlisted in Craven County at age 24, June 3, 1861, for the war. Detailed in navy yard at Wilmington in May, 1862, and reported as absent on detail through October, 1864. Paroled at Greensboro on May 29, 1865.

PIVER, FRANCIS J., Private
Born in Craven County where he resided as a clerk prior to enlisting in Wayne County at age 20, May 1, 1862, for the war. Wounded at Chancellorsville, Virginia, May 3, 1863. Discharged on December 19, 1863, by reason of "a gunshot wound received at Chancellorsville by which both parietal bones of the skull were fractured. He has partially lost the use of his lower limbs from this wound."

POWERS, J., Private
Died in hospital at Richmond, Virginia, July 29, 1862, of "amputation of right arm."

PRIDDY, WILLIAM F., Private
Resided in Stokes County and enlisted in Wake County at age 18, August 29, 1862, for the war. Killed at Chancellorsville, Virginia, May 3, 1863.

PRUITT, WILLIAM, Private
Enlisted in Wake County on September 1, 1862, for the war. Admitted to hospital at Richmond, Virginia, October 31, 1862, with "debility" and furloughed for 30 days on December 31, 1862. Reported as absent sick through December, 1863. Sentenced by court-martial on January 30, 1864, and confined at Salisbury where he died on December 4, 1864, of "pneumonia."

RAE, WILLIAM W., Private
Enlisted in Wake County on November 1, 1863, for the war. Captured at Harrisonburg, Virginia, September 23, 1864, and confined at Point Lookout, Maryland, until paroled and transferred for

exchange to Aiken's Landing, Virginia, March 17, 1865. Received in exchange at Boulware's Wharf, James River, Virginia, March 19, 1865.

REEVES, SANDERS, Private
Enlisted in Wake County on May 4, 1864, for the war. Present or accounted for on company muster rolls through October, 1864. Captured at Petersburg, Virginia, April 3, 1865, and confined at Hart's Island, New York Harbor, where he died on May 9, 1865, of "typhoid fever."

RICE, ROBERT, Private
Resided in Craven County where he enlisted at age 18, February 11, 1862, for the war. Reported on July 1-October 31, 1862, muster roll as absent with the remark: "Captured at South Mountain." January-February, 1863, muster roll reports him with the remark: "Prisoner and swore allegiance to U.S. Government." Reported with same remark through August, 1863. Roll of Honor reports him with the remark: "Taken prisoner in battle at Boonsboro, Maryland, and took the Oath of Allegiance to the United States."

ROBINSON, ELISHA R., Private
Resided in Jones County and enlisted in Craven County at age 34, June 3, 1861, for the war. Wounded at Malvern Hill, Virginia, July 1, 1862, and at Chancellorsville, Virginia, May 3, 1863. Present or accounted for until retired to the Invalid Corps on November 7, 1864. Stationed at Richmond, Virginia, on light duty on November 25, 1864. Present or accounted for on various records through March, 1865.

RODMAN, HARDY, Private
Resided in Craven County where he enlisted at age 19, June 3, 1861, for the war. Present or accounted for until wounded and captured at Kelly's Ford, Virginia, November 7, 1863. Confined in hospital at Washington, D.C., until transferred to Old Capitol Prison, Washington, December 7, 1863. Released after taking the Oath of Allegiance at Washington on March 22, 1864.

RUTLEDGE, WILLIAM R., Private
Resided in Stokes County and enlisted in Wake County at age 20, August 29, 1862, for the war. Wounded at Chancellorsville, Virginia, May 3, 1863. Present or accounted for on company muster rolls through October, 1864, being reported as absent without leave after July 9, 1863.

SEARLES, JESSE H., Private
Resided in Craven County where he enlisted at age 23, June 3, 1861, for the war. Wounded at Malvern Hill, Virginia, July 1, 1862, and died of wound on July 11, 1862.

SESSELCAMP, WILLIAM, Private
Resided in Craven County and enlisted at Camp Potomac, Virginia, at age 30, March 5, 1862, for the war. Company muster roll for July 1-October 31, 1862, states that he was absent "captured at South Mountain and taken the Oath." Reported as such on remaining muster rolls. Roll of Honor states that he was "taken prisoner in battle at Boonsboro and took the Oath of Allegiance to the U.S."

SHAW, ALFRED, Private

Resided in Ashe County and enlisted in Wake County on August 15, 1862, for the war. First reported on company muster roll for May 1-August 31, 1864. Captured at Strasburg, Virginia, October 19, 1864, and confined at Point Lookout, Maryland, until released after taking the Oath of Allegiance on June 20, 1865.

SHINES, JOSEPH B., Private

Resided in Craven County where he enlisted at age 19, June 17, 1861, for the war. Captured near Fredericksburg, Virginia, May 3, 1863, and paroled and exchanged at City Point, Virginia, May 13, 1863. Wounded at Gettysburg, Pennsylvania, July 1-3, 1863. Present or accounted for until captured at Kelly's Ford, Virginia, November 7, 1863. Confined at Point Lookout, Maryland, until paroled and sent to James River, Virginia, February 18, 1865, for exchange. Received in exchange at Boulware's Wharf, James River, February 20-21, 1865. Admitted to hospital at Richmond, Virginia, February 27, 1865, and furloughed on March 8, 1865.

SHIPP, JOHN T., Private

Resided in Beaufort County and enlisted in Craven County at age 18, June 4, 1861, for the war. Wounded at Gettysburg, Pennsylvania, July 2-3, 1863. Detailed for light duty on March 8, 1864. Assigned to duty in hospital at Richmond, Virginia, and reported on muster rolls of Jackson Hospital, Richmond, through February, 1865. Captured at Richmond on April 3, 1865, and turned over to the Provost Marshal on April 20, 1865.

SIMPSON, JOHN R., Private

Resided in Hyde County and enlisted in Craven County at age 19, June 13, 1861, for the war. Wounded at Malvern Hill, Virginia, July 1, 1862. Present or accounted for on company muster rolls through October, 1864. Admitted to hospital at Richmond, Virginia, March 26, 1865, and retired to the Invalid Corps on March 27, 1865.

SIMPSON, T. T., Private

Enlisted on October 15, 1864, for the war.

SISK, KELLY W., Private

Born in Stokes County where he resided prior to enlisting in Wake County at age 34, August 29, 1862, for the war. Killed at Chancellorsville, Virginia, May 3, 1863.

SLEEPER, LOUIS, Private

Resided in Craven County and enlisted at Camp Potomac, Virginia, at age 34, March 5, 1862, for the war. Detailed as a nurse in hospital at Richmond, Virginia, December 8, 1862. Admitted to General Hospital, Staunton, Virginia, March 30, 1863, and detailed as ward master at that hospital on November 22, 1863. Reported as absent on detail through October, 1864.

SMITHWICK, JOHN, Private

Born in Craven County where he resided and enlisted at age 21, June 3, 1861, for the war. Wounded at Malvern Hill, Virginia, July 1, 1862. Wounded at Chancellorsville, Virginia, May 3, 1863, and died of wound on May 5, 1863.

SPARROW, WILLIAM T., Private

Resided in Craven County where he enlisted at age 36, June 21, 1861, for the war. Discharged on December 6, 1861.

SQUIRES, CHARLES V., Private

Resided in Craven County where he enlisted at age 22, June 3, 1861, for the war. Furloughed from hospital at Richmond, Virginia, for 30 days on October 31, 1862, and reported as absent sick or absent without leave on company muster rolls through April, 1864, when appears with the remark: "Absent without leave, reported to be in the enemy's lines."

SQUIRES, GEORGE W., Private

Resided in Craven County where he enlisted at age 22, June 4, 1861, for the war. Died in regimental hospital on October 5, 1861. Date of death also reported as September 21, 1861.

STEWART, W. B., Private

Paroled at Charlotte on May 3, 1865.

STREET, SAMUEL R., Corporal

Resided in Craven County where he enlisted at age 18, June 10, 1861, for the war. Mustered in as Private. Wounded at Malvern Hill, Virginia, July 1, 1862. Appointed Corporal on May 10, 1863. Present or accounted for until captured at Kelly's Ford, Virginia, November 7, 1863. Confined at Point Lookout, Maryland, until paroled and sent to Venus Point, Savannah River, Georgia, October 30, 1864, for exchange. Received at Venus Point in exchange on November 15, 1864. Paroled at High Point on May 1, 1865.

TUCKER, ANDREW, Private

Enlisted in Wake County on May 18, 1864, for the war. Reported on September-October, 1864, muster roll as "missing since September 19, 1864."

TUCKER, WRIGHT, Private

Enlisted in Wake County on May 5, 1864, for the war. Wounded and captured at Winchester, Virginia, September 19, 1864. Confined in hospital until transferred to Point Lookout, Maryland, October 18, 1864. Paroled at Point Lookout and sent to Venus Point, Savannah River, Georgia, October 30, 1864, for exchange. Received at Venus Point in exchange on November 15, 1864. Admitted to hospital at Richmond, Virginia, March 6, 1865, with "erysipelas" and transferred to Farmville, Virginia, April 1, 1865.

VICKERS, JOHN, Private

Born in Orange County where he resided as a farmer prior to enlisting in Craven County at age 21, June 9, 1861, for the war. Wounded at Malvern Hill, Virginia, July 1, 1862. Discharged on March 14, 1863, by reason of "a wound received at Malvern Hill, July 1, 1862, from a ball which fractured the ileum."

WARNER, SWAIN, Private

Enlisted in Wake County on August 29, 1862, for the war. Deserted on October 12, 1862.

WELLS, W., Private

Captured at Gettysburg, Pennsylvania, July 3, 1863. Confined at Point Lookout, Maryland, where he died on February 24, 1864, of smallpox.

WEST, WILLIAM, Private
Resided in Lenoir County and enlisted in Craven County at age 23, February 1, 1862, for the war. Wounded at Malvern Hill, Virginia, July 1, 1862, and died in hospital at Richmond, Virginia, July 5, 1862.

WHITEHURST, LEROY, Private
Resided in Pitt County and enlisted in Craven County at age 30, June 4, 1861, for the war. Captured at South Mountain, Maryland, September 14, 1862, and confined at Fort Delaware, Delaware, until paroled and exchanged at Aiken's Landing, Virginia, October 6, 1862. Declared exchanged on November 10, 1862. Killed at Chancellorsville, Virginia, May 3, 1863.

WILLIAMS, BRYAN B., Sergeant
Resided in Craven County where he enlisted at age 22, June 5, 1861, for the war. Mustered in as Sergeant. Discharged on February 4, 1862, upon providing Robert Ostein as his substitute.

WILLIAMS, EUGENE M., Private
Resided in Craven County and enlisted in Wayne County at age 18, May 1, 1862, for the war. Present or accounted for until transferred to the C.S. Navy on October 13, 1862.

WILLIS, BENJAMIN, Private
Resided in Craven County where he enlisted at age 23, June 12, 1861, for the war. Present or accounted for until he died of disease on December 15, 1862.

WISE, JOHN M., Sergeant
Resided in Craven County where he enlisted at age 19, June 12, 1861, for the war. Mustered in as Private and appointed Corporal in September, 1861. Promoted to Sergeant on October 1, 1861. Captured at South Mountain, Maryland, September 15, 1862, and confined at Fort Delaware, Delaware, until paroled and exchanged at Aiken's Landing, Virginia, October 2, 1862. Declared exchanged November 10, 1862. Present or accounted for until transferred to the Field and Staff of this regiment upon promotion to Sergeant Major on April 16, 1863.

WOOD, JOHN A., Private
Resided in Orange County. Captured at Aberdeen Church, Virginia, April 3, 1865, and confined at Point Lookout, Maryland, until released after taking the Oath of Allegiance on June 22, 1865.

WOOD, LEMUEL S., Sergeant
Resided in Craven County where he enlisted at age 19, June 3, 1861, for the war. Mustered in as Private and promoted to Sergeant on May 10, 1863. Present or accounted for until captured at Kelly's Ford, Virginia, November 7, 1863. Confined at Point Lookout, Maryland, until paroled and transferred for exchange to Aiken's Landing, Virginia, March 14, 1865. Received in exchange at Boulware's Wharf, James River, Virginia, March 16, 1865. Admitted to hospital at Richmond, Virginia, on the same day.

MISCELLANEOUS

The following list of men was compiled from primary records which record the unit as the 2nd Regiment N.C. State Troops but do not give the company to which they belonged.

ADAMS, JOHN H., Drummer
Took the Oath of Allegiance at the office of the Provost Marshal General, Army of the Potomac, near Antietam Creek, Maryland, October 3, 186-.

ALLEN, G. W., Private
Confined at Castle Thunder, Richmond, Virginia, April 20, 1864, on charges of desertion.

BARTON, L., Private
Resided in Randolph County. Captured at Hatcher's Run, Virginia, April 1, 1865, and confined at Hart's Island, New York Harbor, until released on June 18, 1865.

BOGG, I. H., Sergeant
Paroled by Colonel D. M. Evans, 20th Regiment New York Cavalry on April 28, 1865.

BOITNOTT, I. H., Private
Paroled near Winchester, Virginia, and parole forwarded on October 4, 1862.

BOST, W. H., Private
Captured near Fredericksburg, Virginia, May 3, 1863, and paroled and exchanged at City Point, Virginia, May 10, 1863.

BURGESS, A. C., Private
Paroled at Greensboro on May 12, 1865.

CASTEEN, S., Corporal
Federal Provost Marshal records report him as a "rebel deserter" received at Fort Monroe, Virginia, July 23, 1864, from Beaufort. Forwarded July 24, 1864, with the remark: "Discharged."

CRUMP, G. T. C., Private
Paroled at Richmond, Virginia, April 28, 1865.

DOHERTY, RICHARD, Private
Paroled at Leesburg, Virginia, October 2, 1862.

DONNOUGH, P., Private
Paroled at Richmond, Virginia, May 18, 1865.

EMBER, R. W., Private
Captured at Raleigh on April 18, 1865.

EPPERMAN, RAYMOND, Private
Captured near Winchester, Virginia, December 2-6, 1862.

FORCLOTH, L., Private
Captured at Fredericksburg, Virginia, May 4, 1863, and paroled and exchanged at City Point, Virginia, May 10, 1863.

FRANCIS, J. J., Private
Captured in hospital at Richmond, Virginia, April 3, 1865. Died on April 9, 1865, of "gunshot wound of left shoulder and neck."

GROVER, J. L., Private
Captured near Fredericksburg, Virginia, May 3, 1863, and paroled and exchanged at City Point, Virginia, May 13, 1863.

HAIGLER, WILLIAM, Private
Paroled on September 27, 1862.

HANN, A., Private
Paroled on May 4, 1863.

HAWKINS, W. H., Private
Captured at Hanover Court House, Virginia, May 27, 1862, and confined at Fort Columbus, New York Harbor, June 4, 1862.

HIGGINS, JAMES, Corporal
Captured at Fredericksburg, Virginia, May 3, 1863, and paroled and exchanged at City Point, Virginia, May 10, 1863.

HOLCOMB, WILLIAM, Private
Captured in hospital at Richmond, Virginia, April 3, 1865, and transferred to Newport News, Virginia, April 23, 1865.

HUDSON, B., Private
Captured at Fredericksburg, Virginia, May 3, 1863, and paroled and exchanged at City Point, Virginia, May 10, 1863.

INGRAHAM, JOSEPH, Private
Resided in Stokes County. Took the Oath of Allegiance at Danville, Virginia, September 5, 1865.

JOHNSON, I. I., Private
Paroled at Winchester, Virginia, and parole forwarded on October 4, 1862.

JONES, J. M., Private
Resided in Wayne County. Took the Oath of Allegiance at Hart's Island, New York Harbor, June 19, 1865.

KESTLER, V. W., Corporal
Captured near Fredericksburg, Virginia, May 3, 1863, and paroled and exchanged at City Point, Virginia, May 13, 1863.

KETCHEY, HENRY J., Private
Paroled at Salisbury on May 11, 1865.

McKINE, WILLIAM, Private
Federal Provost Marshal records report him as a "rebel deserter" received at Washington, D.C., March 25, 1865. Took the Oath of Allegiance and was provided transportation to Picksboro, Indiana.

MAY, DEBY F., Private
Paroled at Salisbury on June 24, 1865.

MEADOWS, A., Private
Federal Provost Marshal records report him as a "rebel deserter" received at Camp Distribution from Beaufort, South Carolina, July 23, 1864, and "discharged" July 24, 1864.

MENDBUN, S., Private
Paroled at Richmond, Virginia, May 18, 1865.

MILLSAPS, J. L., Private
Paroled at Salisbury on May 27, 1865.

MORGAN, E., Private
Paroled at Greensboro on May 16, 1865.

O'COLLINS, STERLING, Private
Captured at Hanover Court House, Virginia, May 27, 1862, and confined at Fort Columbus, New York Harbor, June 4, 1862.

PANYEAR, GEORGE W., Private
Admitted to hospital at Petersburg, Virginia, March 17, 1865. Captured in hospital on April 3,

1865. Took the Oath of Allegiance at Newport News, Virginia, June 15, 1865.

PRIOR, G. W., Private
Captured at Petersburg, Virginia, April 2, 1865, and admitted to U.S. Army General Hospital, Fort Monroe, Virginia, April 13, 1865, with "rheumatism." Returned to Military Prison on May 6, 1865. Transferred to Newport News, Virginia, May 9, 1865.

RANNON, J. E., Sergeant
Captured near Fredericksburg, Virginia, May 3, 1863, and paroled and exchanged at City Point, Virginia, May 10, 1863.

RAYSER, G. W., Private
Federal Provost Marshal records report him as a "rebel deserter" received at Washington, D.C., June 28, 1865, with the remark that transportation was furnished to Baltimore, Maryland.

REGISTER, RUFUS, Private
Claim for balance of pay due filed by his mother on September 28, 1863, with the remark that he died at Gordonsville, Virginia.

REHOLEE, J. W., Private
Captured near Fredericksburg, Virginia, May 3, 1863, and paroled and exchanged at City Point, Virginia, May 13, 1863.

ROBERTSON, JOHN, Private
Federal Provost Marshal records report him as a "rebel deserter" sent to Alexandria, Virginia, February 16, 1864.

SAYLES, L., Private
Captured at Fredericksburg, Virginia, May 3, 1863, and paroled and exchanged at City Point, Virginia, May 13, 1863.

SESSINO, M., Private
Paroled near Keedysville, Maryland, September 20, 1862.

SIKES, J. H., Private
Captured at Fredericksburg, Virginia, May 3, 1863, and paroled and exchanged at City Point, Virginia, May 13, 1863.

SMITH, S. J., Private
Wounded and captured at Sharpsburg, Maryland, September 17, 1862, and "died at Mr. Samuel Bealer's house."

SNOW, J. A., 1st Lieutenant
Paroled at Richmond, Virginia, May 18, 1865.

STAFFORD, JAMES, Private
Paroled on October 30, 1862.

STEP, E. L., Private
Paroled at Winchester, Virginia, and parole forwarded on October 4, 1862.

TURNER, T. J., Private
Wounded and captured at Gettysburg, Pennsylvania, July 1-3, 1863. Died at Gettysburg on August 1, 1863, of "gunshot wound back."

3rd REGIMENT N. C. STATE TROOPS

This regiment began organizing at Garysburg, Northampton County, in late May, 1861, when the companies assigned to the regiment began reporting. These companies were organized from partially organized volunteer companies which had elected their officers and from regular enlistments under officers appointed by the governor. Since the regiment was a State Troops organization, all original commissions dated from May 16, 1861, and that date was given as the organizational date. Actually, the regiment was not organized until June, 1861, when the regimental officers and companies assembled at Camp Clarendon, Garysburg. As the regiment assembled, the companies were organized and drilled. After all the companies arrived, the regiment began regimental drills.

On July 17, 1861, three companies of the regiment left for Richmond, Virginia, and arrived there the next day. Three additional companies arrived at Richmond on July 22, and the balance of the regiment arrived on July 23. Their stay was not long, because the regiment left Richmond for the Aquia District on July 24. Arriving at Brooke's Station, Aquia District, on the same date, the regiment went into camp at Camp Clark, near the station. It remained at Camp Clark until August 14, when it was moved to Camp Howe, near the mouth of Aquia Creek, to act in defense of the batteries in that area.

When the regiment was assigned to the Aquia District it was ordered to report to General Theophilus H. Holmes, commanding. As the number of troops increased in the district they were brigaded, and this regiment was assigned to Brigadier General John G. Walker's Brigade. In addition to this regiment, the brigade consisted of the 1st and 2nd Regiments N.C. State Troops, 30th Regiment Virginia Infantry, and the 1st Regiment Arkansas Infantry. On August 31 and September 1, 1861, the companies were mustered into Confederate States service to date from their respective dates of enlistment. The regiment remained at Camp Howe through October, 1861, and moved sometime in November-December, 1861, to Camp Price, Aquia Creek, where it remained for the balance of its stay in the Aquia District.

During its stay the companies of the regiment continued to drill and at times were assigned special duties, but not all the companies reported their activities. Company A was reported at Battery No. 1 from September 1, 1861, through December, 1861. Company D reported that it was stationed at Sims Point, picketing three miles up the Potomac, on August 31, and did not return to the regiment until October 12. Company H reported that it commenced artillery drill at Battery No. 2, Aquia Creek, on January 1, 1862, and the company commander remarked on the January-February, 1862, muster roll that "said drill does not interfere with the company's duties in the regiment."

When General A. E. Burnside's expedition against New Bern began to advance from that town, troops were sent to North Carolina from Virginia. This regiment received orders to move on March 22, 1862, and marched to Brooke's Station, four miles from Camp Price, on March 23. The next day the regiment, with the brigade, entrained for Richmond. Arriving on the same day, the troops proceeded by rail to Petersburg and from there by rail to Goldsboro. Arriving on March 25, the regiment went into camp below Goldsboro on the Wilmington and Weldon Railroad, where it remained for three nights. From there it was moved to Camp McIntosh, three or four miles from Goldsboro on the Atlantic and North Carolina Railroad.

The entire brigade assembled at Camp McIntosh, where it remained until ordered to Petersburg, Virginia. The regiment left Goldsboro May 29 and arrived at Petersburg the next day. On June 1 the regiment was moved to Richmond and ordered to move down the Williamsburg Road and set up its camp. From June 3 to June 26 the regiment was on picket duty on the Williamsburg Road. The companies usually rotated the duty, but on June 15 the entire regiment was engaged in a skirmish near Seven Pines. While on the Williamsburg Road, the regiment was assigned to a new brigade commanded by Brigadier General Roswell S. Ripley, Major General D. H. Hill's Division. In addition to this regiment, Ripley's Brigade consisted of the 1st Regiment N.C. State Troops and the 44th and 48th Regiments Georgia Infantry.

On the morning of June 26, 1862, the brigade moved from its camp near the Williamsburg Road, about five miles from Richmond, to the Chickahominy Bridge on the Mechanicsville Turnpike. General Robert E. Lee was concentrating his troops to attack the Federal right at Mechanicsville. At 4:00 P.M., June 26, 1862, the brigade crossed the bridge to aid General A. P. Hill's troops engaged at Mechanicsville. This regiment and the 48th Regiment Georgia Infantry were ordered to the left of Brigadier General William D. Pender's Brigade under orders to attack the Federal artillery positions. The men made the charge in good order at the double-quick and succeeded in reaching a ravine within 80 yards of the enemy's position. Here the attack bogged down. Under cover of night the regiments withdrew and rejoined the brigade in the rear. Reforming, the regiment took up a position in a skirt of woods about 300 yards from the enemy artillery position. In its first battle the regiment lost 8 killed and 39 wounded.

During the night of June 26-27 the Federals withdrew to Gaines' Mill, and at 2:00 A.M. on June 27 the regiment took up march to Mechanicsville. The regiment rested at Mechanicsville until 11:00 A.M., when it moved to the positions at Gaines' Mill. Arriving about 3:00 P.M., the regiment was held on the left in reserve to prevent a flank attack. Here it was subjected to heavy artillery fire. Seven companies of the regiment joined Brigadier General Samuel Garland's Brigade in the attack on the Federal right. The remaining three companies had

481

not been notified of the move, and because of the dense undergrowth did not see the other companies **move off. Lieutenant Colonel William L. DeRosset** later withdrew the companies as the firing ceased. The three companies rejoined the regiment the following morning. During the battle the regiment lost 1 killed and 15 wounded.

From Gaines' Mill, the Confederates, now under general command of General T. J. Jackson, moved to cross the Chickahominy at Grapevine Bridge. The bridge had been destroyed by the enemy in his retreat, and the crossing was defended to delay any attempted crossing. Here the troops went into bivouac while the bridge was being rebuilt, June 28-29. On June 30 the troops advanced across the bridge and marched to White Oak Bridge over White Oak Swamp. Here a strong Federal force kept the Confederates from rebuilding the bridge and thus kept Jackson's men at bay while the battle of Frayser's Farm was raging. Following the battle the bridge was rebuilt, and Jackson's men joined forces with the right wing of the army and moved to meet the enemy at Malvern Hill. General D. H. Hill's Division was placed on the Confederate center. Lieutenant Colonel William L. DeRosset described the regiment's activities during the ill-fated assault on Malvern Hill in his report (*O.R.*, S.I., Vol. XI, pt. 2, pp. 657-659), written on July 11, 1862, as follows:

> . . . The line was being formed, an advance was ordered, and my regiment moved forward through a dense jungle up the hill to a road just in front of and within 600 yards of the enemy's batteries. From the fact that several of my companies had to move by a flank and file around the thickets, when we reached the road they were in considerable confusion. Here, after firing several rounds, we learned that a regiment of our own troops was in advance of us, and an order to cease firing was given. They were then ordered to lie down to protect themselves. While in this position, with little or no protection but what the naked ground afforded, we were exposed to a most terrific fire of every description, as the wounds testify, from the enemy, and I fear several volleys were fired into us by a regiment of our own troops in the rear, from which we suffered much.
>
> About 6 p.m. a request came from Captain [Hamilton A.] Brown, commanding First N.C., to re-enforce him, as he was hotly pressed. Colonel [Gaston] Meares gave the order to move by the left flank, and led off down the road, followed by myself and about 100 men. About the same time that this movement was made the order was given on the right to fall back, which we did not hear, and which accounts for the small number of men which went with us.
>
> Our gallant colonel had not moved more than 30 paces before he was instantly killed by the fragment of a shell in the head. No more cool, brave, and able officer lived, and his loss to the regiment and his country is irreparable. His body was carried from the field immediately and sent to his family in N.C., under charge of Adjt W. A. Cumming.

Our loss was heavy: Killed, 23; wounded, 112; missing, 7.

The brigade remained in bivouac near Malvern Hill until it returned to its camp near Richmond on July 9-10. Here it remained until it marched to Malvern Hill on August 6 and returned the night of August 7. D. H. Hill's Division had been left in front of Richmond to watch McClellan's troops at Harrison's Landing, while Jackson and then Longstreet moved to confront General John Pope in middle Virginia. On August 19 General Ripley's Brigade moved by rail to Orange Court House, arriving the next day. The balance of Hill's Division moved up and joined Ripley's Brigade and then proceeded to join the Army of Northern Virginia on August 28. The division reached the army at Chantilly on September 2 (after the battle of Second Manassas) and crossed into Maryland on September 4-5. Upon reaching Frederick the army halted, and General Lee determined to send Jackson to capture Harpers Ferry while Longstreet moved to Hagerstown. On September 10 D. H. Hill's Division moved out of Frederick as the rear guard of Longstreet's column. Mounting pressure from the advancing Federals, plus the necessity of protecting Jackson at Harpers Ferry, resulted in the deployment of Hill's Division on the South Mountain gaps below Boonsboro on September 13. This regiment, still in Ripley's Brigade, saw heavy action at Fox's Gap on September 14 and withdrew the next day under the general orders to concentrate at Sharpsburg. Arriving at Antietam Creek on September 15, the brigade went into position on the heights east of the creek. Here the brigade bivouacked until the evening of the next day, when it was moved to the extreme left of General Hill's line, to the right of General Jackson's line.

On the morning of September 17 the Federals advanced against Jackson's line. During the seesaw battle, Ripley's Brigade was ordered to close to his left and advance. In the charge General Ripley was wounded, and Colonel George Doles assumed command of the brigade. The brigade advanced as far as the Miller cornfield, when the entire advance was forced to retire. The brigade withdrew and went into position west of the Hagerstown Road. The fighting then shifted to the Confederate center, and the troops on the left established a new line. The fighting continued on the center and right until the Federals discontinued their efforts to drive the Confederates from the field. The troops rested on the field the following day, and retired across the Potomac during the night of September 18. During the Maryland campaign the regiment lost 46 killed and 207 wounded.

The Army of Northern Virginia remained in the Shenandoah Valley until the Army of the Potomac crossed over east of the Blue Ridge. Using his cavalry, Lee sought to discover the enemy's intentions. On October 28, 1862, Longstreet's Corps moved east of the mountains to Culpeper Court House, while Jackson's Corps moved closer to Winchester. D. H. Hill's Division was posted at the forks of the Shenandoah River to guard the mountain passes. The brigade crossed the river on October 31 and camped at Upperville until November 3, when it retired to Ashby's Gap. Anticipating an attack, the troops were ordered in line of battle and spent the night at Ashby's Gap. The gap was evacuated the next morning, and the men marched to Front Royal. On November 7, 1862, Colonel Doles was promoted to Brigadier General and assumed command of the brigade.

When the enemy's intention was discerned, Lee moved Longstreet to Fredericksburg and ordered Jackson to prepare to move. Hill's Division was pulled back, and on November 21 the regiment left Strasburg in the column of march for Gordonsville. At Gordonsville the company clerk of Company I reported on the November-December, 1862, muster roll that "at this point very many were sent to the various hospitals, having ailments of every nature and description consequent upon being overworked in marching, being badly clothed, half fed and without shoes." From Gordonsville the division moved to Fredericksburg. On December 3 Hill's Division was sent to Port Royal, below Fredericksburg, to prevent any crossing at or near that point. Here it remained until ordered to Fredericksburg on December 12. The division arrived in the morning of December 13 and was placed in the third line of battle. During the Battle of Fredericksburg, December 13, 1862, the division was subjected to heavy artillery fire but saw little action. After the battle it was moved up to the second line, where it remained throughout the next day. On December 15 it went into the first line, where it remained through December 16. While on the field, the regiment was never actually engaged but suffered 3 wounded from the artillery fire.

Following the battle, the regiment went into camp on the Richmond-Fredericksburg Turnpike and later established winter quarters on the Rappahannock River near Port Royal. There it spent the winter on picket duty. On January 19, 1863, the regiment was transferred to Brigadier General William B. Taliaferro's Brigade, Major General Isaac R. Trimble's Division, Jackson's Corps. General Taliaferro was transferred on February 20, 1863, and Brigadier General Raleigh E. Colston was assigned to command the brigade. In addition to this regiment, the brigade consisted of the 1st Regiment N.C. State Troops and the 10th, 23rd, and 37th Regiments Virginia Infantry.

On April 29, 1863, the division received orders to march to Hamilton's Crossing, below Fredericksburg. General Hooker's Federal army had moved up the left bank of the Rappahannock to cross over behind the Confederates at Fredericksburg, and General Lee was moving to oppose it. Jackson's Corps moved down the Orange and Fredericksburg Plank Road on May 1 in the direction of Chancellorsville. It reached the Confederate position that evening, and early the next day Jackson's men started the flank march which carried them to a point about four miles west of Chancellorsville on the exposed right flank of Hooker's army. General Colston was in command of the division, which was placed in the second of three lines preparatory to the advance. The brigade was commanded by the senior colonel and was on the right of the

divisional line. Soon after the advance started the second line began to catch up to the first line, and the two became one as they drove in Hooker's right flank. The advance continued until both darkness and strong resistance forced a halt.

During the night the lines were reformed and the brigade was placed on the left side of the plank road in the second line. Early the next morning, May 3, the brigade was moved to the right and sent in to support the first line. As the battle raged, a threatened Federal flank attack was met and driven back. During this action the brigade lost four commanders, including Lieutenant Colonel Stephen D. Thruston of this regiment, wounded. Under these repeated attacks, supported by heavy artillery fire, and the pressure exerted on the Federal left and center by troops under Lee, the Federal army began to retire. Once over the strong Federal entrenchments, which had been the object of attack, the Confederates converged on Chancellorsville. From there the remnants of the brigade were ordered to advance on the left of the United States Ford Road. Finding the enemy strongly posted, the troops were ordered to retire and went into position in the vicinity of the Chancellor house. The next morning the entire brigade was ordered to entrench on the right and perpendicular to the United States Ford Road. Here it remained for two days. Finding the Federal army had recrossed the Rappahannock River on May 6, Lee moved his army back to Fredericksburg.

Colston's Brigade was left at United States Ford, where the men supervised the movement of Federal ambulances sent over to care for the Federal wounded. Upon the completion of this task, the brigade left this regiment on picket duty and rejoined the division at Hamilton's Crossing, below Fredericksburg, on May 15. The regiment rejoined the brigade on May 22. During the Chancellorsville campaign the regiment lost 39 killed, 175 wounded, and 17 missing.

Following the Chancellorsville campaign and the death of Jackson, the Army of Northern Virginia was divided into three corps. Colston's Brigade was assigned to Major General Edward Johnson's Division, Lieutenant General Richard S. Ewell's 2nd Corps. On May 28 General Colston was relieved from duty, and Brigadier General George H. Steuart was assigned to command the brigade. Thus, for the coming campaign, the regiment would be in Steuart's Brigade, Johnson's Division, Ewell's Corps.

The division left camp near Hamilton's Crossing on June 5 and moved with the corps in the direction of Winchester, crossing the Blue Ridge at Chester Gap. At daylight on the morning of June 13 the division left camp at Cedarville and moved down the Winchester and Front Royal turnpike toward Winchester. General Ewell sent Major General Jubal Early's Division down the Valley turnpike to gain the heights west of Winchester. Johnson's Division proceeded to within four miles of Winchester, where it encountered the enemy. The division was deployed with the Stonewall and Steuart's brigades on the right of the road, while the other two brigades of the division were deployed on the left. The brigades on the right advanced under cover of a woods to a position nearer town and halted. Here the two brigades remained until the morning of June 14, when they were moved farther to the right. Johnson's mission was to engage the enemy's attention on the right while Early moved in on the left to deliver the main attack.

After nightfall, Johnson received orders to proceed farther to the right and get behind the town to cut the Federal line of retreat. Steuart's Brigade was ordered to move, together with another brigade and artillery supports. Moving by way of Jordan Springs, Johnson succeeded in getting his men into position at Stephenson's just as the Federals charged. With the aid of the Stonewall Brigade, Johnson succeeded in routing the Federals and captured between 2,300 and 2,600 prisoners. In this action at Winchester and Stephenson's the regiment lost 4 killed and 10 wounded.

On June 18 the regiment, with the brigade, crossed the Potomac River at Shepherdstown and camped on the old battlefield at Sharpsburg. From this camp the division march via Hagerstown and Chambersburg to within three miles of Carlisle, Pennsylvania. Steuart's Brigade had been ordered to McConnellsburg from Greencastle to collect horses, cattle, and other supplies. It rejoined the division near Carlisle. On June 29 the division moved to Greenville and then to Gettysburg, where it arrived too late to participate in the action on July 1. That evening the division moved through Gettysburg and formed line of battle facing south.

Late the next day, after a heavy artillery engagement, the division advanced over Rock Creek to assault the Federal positions on Culp's Hill. The brigade was on the extreme left of the advancing line. This regiment was placed on the right of the brigade and advanced up the hill toward the enemy's breastworks. As the brigade advanced, the three regiments on the left of this regiment gained and occupied the first line of enemy entrenchments. This regiment maintained its exposed position, replenishing its cartridge boxes from those of the dead and wounded. At this time the 1st Regiment N.C. State Troops was sent in to support the regiment, and a general assault on the second line of entrenchments was planned. Efforts to take the second line failed, but the Confederates successfully defended their position against repeated attacks. During the night of July 2-3, the 1st Regiment N.C. State Troops was withdrawn, and members of the 3rd Regiment N.C. State Troops alternated positions with troops behind the breastworks during the night. The next day, July 3, the brigade was formed at right angles to the breastworks to attack a Federal force on the left. Again this regiment was placed on the right. During the advance the left of the brigade did not maintain its position, and the right of the brigade, being in advance, suffered concentrated fire, wavered, and fell back. The whole line retired and rallied behind a stone wall which ran parallel to the breastworks. Here it remained about an hour until withdrawn to Rock Creek, where it remained the rest of the day.

Failure to break the Federal center by the Pickett-Pettigrew charge during the afternoon of July 3 necessitated withdrawal. Johnson's Division was withdrawn across Rock Creek and retired through the town to a position north and west of Gettysburg during the night of July 3-4. On July 5 the division started the march back to Virginia by way of Waynesboro to Hagerstown. Here a line of battle was established, but no general engagement occurred. On the night of July 13 the division re-crossed the Potomac and marched to a point near Martinsburg. During the Gettysburg campaign the regiment lost 29 killed and 127 wounded.

From Martinsburg the division moved on July 15 to Darkesville, then back to Martinsburg to destroy the Baltimore & Ohio Railroad and repel an enemy advance. When the Federal army began crossing the Potomac River east of the Blue Ridge, General Lee had to move his army east of the mountains to interpose it between the enemy and Richmond. By August 1, 1863, the Army of Northern Virginia was encamped near Orange Court House, with the Army of the Potomac at Warrenton. By August 4 Lee withdrew his army to the Rapidan River line, and in October he attempted to turn the flank of the Federal army. The movement maneuvered the Federal commander into falling back, and on October 14 the Federal rear guard was intercepted at Bristoe Station. Failure to coordinate the attack resulted in heavy casualties to troops of A. P. Hill's Corps and the escape of the Federal rear guard. The regiment took part in the movement as part of the brigade and division, but Ewell's Corps was not engaged at Bristoe Station.

With the escape of the Federal army to Centreville, Lee retired to the upper Rappahannock River. The Federal army soon followed and overran Lee's positions at Rappahannock Bridge on November 7. Lee withdrew his army south across the upper Rapidan River, toward Orange Court House. Here the army went into camp, and companies from the regiment went on picket duty at various fords on the river. On November 26 the Federal army crossed the lower Rapidan and turned west to face Lee's army. Lee thought the Federal army was heading south and moved to strike it on its flank. On November 27 the two armies met at Payne's Farm. The regiment's activities during this sharp engagement were reported by Colonel Stephen D. Thruston (O.R., S.I., Vol., XXIX, pt. 1, pp. 866-867) as follows:

My regiment immediately moved forward in as perfect order as the thick undergrowth and nature of the ground would admit, meeting the enemy just where their line crossed the road. Here the action was quite sharp for a short time, when the men with a yell charged the position, driving in confusion three strong lines of the enemy before them. The pursuit was followed for about 800 yards, when I discovered the enemy turning my left.

I immediately changed front, but three companies on the right, not hearing the command, did not follow the movement, and afterward formed on the First North Carolina Regiment, on my right. With six companies, my left company having been thrown out previously to aid the Thirty-seventh Virginia, I changed my front so as to meet the flanking party, but being largely outnumbered, retired to the field beyond the road, where a temporary work had been thrown up of rails and such material as could be hastily gotten together. Here I met the brigade commander, and being soon joined by the Thirty-seventh Virginia, was ordered to remain in that position, with sharpshooters thrown well forward. I remained here until an order was received to form in line with the rest of the brigade on the road. This being done, rested for four or five hours, when we moved on beyond Mine Run, and bivouacked for the night.

The losses of the regiment were reported as 99 men men killed, wounded, and captured.

This action proved to General Lee that the Federals were advancing toward him, not southward. He therefore withdrew his army to Mine Run and entrenched to await attack. General Meade moved his army up and began entrenching opposite the Confederate line. Finding the Federal left flank exposed, Lee determined to strike it. However, General Meade, discovering that his flank was exposed, decided to withdraw. When Lee's men began to advance on the morning of December 2 they found that the entire Federal army had withdrawn across the Rapidan. Thus ended the Mine Run campaign. Both armies went into winter quarters. This regiment built winter quarters near Pisgah Church and did picket duty at Mitchell's and Morton's fords during the winter of 1863-1864.

On the morning of May 4, 1864, while the Federal army under General U. S. Grant was moving across the lower Rapidan, Steuart's Brigade was on picket along the upper Rapidan. About noon the brigade was put in motion toward the Old Turnpike, along which Johnson's Division advanced as the lead element of Ewell's Corps. The night of May 4-5 was spent in bivouac some two and one-half miles east of Locust Grove. Contact was made with the enemy as the column moved forward on May 5, and Ewell began to deploy his troops. Before his deployment was completed, the enemy launched a surprise attack which routed one brigade and seriously threatened the destruction of another. General Steuart's Brigade moved in on the left of the threatened brigade, while General Ewell advanced fresh troops directly into the threatened area. The whole line moved foward to repulse the Federal advance. In the counterattack Steuart's Brigade captured the 146th Regiment New York Infantry and two guns. Efforts to storm a heavily entrenched Federal line failed, and Ewell's men retired and established their own line. This ended the fighting on this part of the long Confederate line.

It was quiet on the brigade front on May 6, and on May 7 it was discovered that the enemy had retired. Late in the evening of May 7 orders came to close up on the right. Throughout the night of May 7-8 the troops moved to the right. On May 8 the brigade marched to Spotsylvania Court House, where Lee had placed his army to confront Grant's advance. Late in the evening of May 8 the brigade

was put into position on the right side of the salient and was firmly entrenched when dawn broke on the morning of May 9. Johnson's Division was placed in that portion of the Confederate line which resembled an inverted V and became known as the Mule Shoe. Steuart's Brigade was on the right side of the Mule Shoe, and on May 10, when the left side was attacked, Steuart's men faced to the rear and advanced to recapture the line.

The initial success of the Federal attack forced the Confederates to strengthen their lines on May 11. As the morning of May 12 began to dawn, a heavy fog lay close to the ground. It began to lift slightly about 4:30 A.M. The noise of activity during the night had led Generals Johnson and Steuart to expect an attack. They had their men as ready as possible and anticipated the momentary return of the artillery, which had been withdrawn the previous evening. However, before the artillery arrived the Federals advanced in column formation, broke through the Confederate lines, and captured most of Johnson's Division. The Confederates succeeded in stopping the attackers and in driving them back, but the captured men had already been taken to the rear. Because so many of the men had been captured, including General Steuart, Steuart's Brigade ceased to exist as a unit. All but about 30 men of the 3rd Regiment N.C. State Troops were captured.

The survivors of the three Virginia regiments in Steuart's Brigade were consolidated with two other Virginia brigades of the division into a brigade. The two North Carolina regiments (1st and 3rd Regiment N.C. State Troops) were assigned to Brigadier General Stephen D. Ramseur's Brigade, Major General Robert E. Rodes' Division, Ewell's Corps, on May 15, 1864. General Ramseur was promoted to Major General and assigned to command a division, and Colonel William R. Cox, 2nd Regiment N.C. State Troops, was promoted to Brigadier General and assigned to command Ramseur's old brigade. Thus, the 3rd Regiment N.C. State Troops was brigaded with the 1st, 2nd, 4th Regiment N.C. State Troops, 14th Regiment N.C. Troops (4th Regiment N.C. Volunteers), and the 30th Regiment N.C. Troops. The ranks of the regiment would increase as men returned or were assigned from conscript camps, but it would never reach regimental size again.

The survivors of Johnson's Division remained with the 2nd Corps following the action of May 12. General Grant made several attempts to break or turn the Confederate line and failed. As he began moving to the east, the 2nd Corps was ordered to reconnoiter and find out if Grant's army was on the move. Ewell's Corps, with Ramseur's Brigade leading, moved out of the entrenchments and engaged the rear elements of the Federal army on May 19. An attack was made but was repulsed, and with reinforcements coming up the Federals began to press Ewell's men. The Confederates held and took advantage of night to break off the engagement and retire. This move disclosed the enemy's movement, and Lee moved his army accordingly. On May 22 Ewell's Corps arrived at Hanover Junction with Longstreet's Corps. Hill's Corps arrived on the morning of May 23. From here the Army of Northern Virginia moved to the North Anna, where it blocked the Federal army once again. At North Anna, May 24-25, Ewell's Corps, now commanded by General Jubal Early, was on the Confederate right and was not engaged. Grant withdrew during the night of May 26-27 and crossed the Pamunkey River, again sidestepping to the Confederate right. Early's Corps marched some 24 miles on May 27 and entrenched between Beaver Dam Creek and Pole Green Church. Longstreet's Corps came up on Early's right, and Hill's Corps extended along the left of Early's line. On May 30, under orders from General Lee, Early moved to attack the Federal left at Bethesda Church. The attack failed to turn the Federal left but did reveal that the enemy was moving to the Confederate right.

The two armies began to concentrate at Cold Harbor, and on June 1 a spirited engagement occurred. Again Lee moved to his right and the new alignment left Early's Corps on the Confederate left. Early was ordered to move out on June 2 to strike the Federal right. The attack was led by Rodes' Division and met with partial success until Federal reinforcements arrived to drive it back. During the Battle of Cold Harbor, June 3, 1864, Early's Corps was under attack by General A. E. Burnside's IX Corps and a part of General G. K. Warren's V Corps. The men of Warren's Corps struck the line held by Rodes' Division and were repulsed. Following the battle the armies remained in position observing and skirmishing until June 12, when Grant began moving his army to cross the James River. General Early's Corps was withdrawn from the line on June 11 and was ordered to Lynchburg on June 12 to defend that city against an anticipated attack by troops under General David Hunter. Early was directed to remain in the Shenandoah Valley after striking Hunter's force.

General Early's troops began arriving at Lynchburg on June 17. The next day the balance of Early's troops arrived and General Hunter retired. After an unsuccessful attempt to overtake the retreating Federals, Early proceeded into the Shenandoah Valley. Still in Cox's Brigade, Rodes' Division, this regiment took part in Early's Valley campaign of 1864. On July 6, 1864, Early crossed into Maryland and advanced on Washington, D.C. At the Battle of Monocacy River, July 9, 1864, Rodes' Division operated on the Baltimore road while the main fighting occurred on the Washington road to the division's right. Rodes' Division was in the van when the defenses of Washington came in sight on July 11. Finding the defenses heavily manned on the morning of July 12, Early called off a planned assault, and during the night of July 12 the army began to retire toward Virginia. Back in the Shenandoah Valley, Early's troops were engaged at Stephenson's Depot, July 20, and at Kernstown, July 24, before he moved to Martinsburg to give his men a rest.

Early in August, 1864, the Federals began concentrating a large force under General Phil Sheridan at Harpers Ferry. On August 10 Early began a series of maneuvers to create the impression of a larger force than he had. His men were northeast of Winchester when Sheridan began to move. On September 19 contact was made, and Early concentrated to receive the attack. The Confederates were making a determined defense east of Winchester when the left came under heavy attack, and the whole line began to retire. During the inital stages of the battle, General Rodes was killed as he deployed his division between Gordon's and Ramseur's divisions. These three divisions held the main line against repeated assaults, and only when the left appeared to be turned did they begin to retire to a defensive line close to the town. Again the Federals assaulted the front and left of the line. Word of a Federal column turning the right caused Early to issue orders for a general withdrawal. Finding the troops moving on the right were his own men adjusting the alignment, Early tried to counter the order. It was too late. The troops continued to the rear through Winchester and rallied south of the town. From there they continued the retreat to Fisher's Hill, near Strasburg.

At Fisher's Hill, Major General Stephen D. Ramseur was placed in command of Rodes' Division. Sheridan struck Early's left and center at Fisher's Hill on September 22 and forced a general retreat. Early regrouped at Waynesboro on September 28. Here he received reinforcements and again began to move down the valley. On October 7 his troops occupied New Market. Moving to Fisher's Hill on October 12-13, Early found the enemy on the north bank of Cedar Creek. On October 19, 1864, Early launched a surprise, three-pronged attack on the Federal camp. The attack was initially successful, and the Confederates succeeded in driving the Federals from two defensive lines. Early delayed the attack on the third line and assumed the defensive. Rallying his troops, Sheridan launched a devastating attack and routed Early's army. In this battle the three divisions of the 2nd Corps were commanded by General John B. Gordon. While attempting to rally the men, General Ramseur was mortally wounded and captured. Brigadier General Bryan Grimes, as senior brigadier, was assigned to command the division. Thus, when the 2nd Corps regrouped at New Market after the Cedar Creek disaster, the 3rd Regiment N.C. State Troops was in Cox's Brigade, Grimes' Division. With the exception of minor skirmishing and a repulse of the Federal cavalry on November 22, the army remained inactive.

On December 9 two divisions of the 2nd Corps moved under orders to return to Richmond. A few days later Rodes'-Ramseur's Division, under Grimes, was ordered to return to the main army in the Richmond-Petersburg line. The company clerk of Company I recorded activities of the regiment for the months of November and December, 1864, on the November-December, 1864, muster roll as follows:

This company was encamped near New Market, Valley of Va., from the 31 of Oct to the 10 Nov. without anything of interest occurring. On that day it moved with Early's command in a heavy reconnoissence down to Newtown, on the 12. Returned to New Market on Nov. 15. The sharpshooters were again engaged on the 22 Nov. near Mt. Jackson, Va., with the enemy's cavalry. Returned to old camp the same day. Dec. 14 it marched for Staunton and took the cars for Petersburg, arriving Dec. 16. Dec. 19 began to build winter Quarters 3½ miles North of Petersburg where we are now pleasantly situated.

The brigade went into winter quarters at Swift Creek, about three miles north of Petersburg. Here it remained until ordered to the right of the Confederate line about February 20, 1865. Grimes' Division had been placed on alert to be ready to move at a moment's notice. On February 17 three brigades moved to Sutherland's Depot on the right of the line. Cox's Brigade covered the division front at Swift Creek until relieved, and then joined the division at Sutherland's. In mid-March, 1865, the division was ordered into the trenches in front of Petersburg. There it remained until the night of March 24 when the 2nd Corps, still under General Gordon, was massed for an attack on Fort Stedman. The sharpshooters who led the attacking force on the morning of March 25 were commanded by Colonel Hamilton A. Brown of the 1st Regiment N.C. State Troops. Although initially successful, the concentrated firepower and manpower of the Federal army forced the Confederates to retreat.

The remnants of the regiment returned to the trenches with the rest of the brigade and division. During the general assault on the morning of April 2, 1865, the Federals reached the divisional line near Fort Mahone. Grimes' Division attacked and reoccupied its trenches, only to have other portions of the line fall to the Federal assault. Retreat was necessary, and it began the night of April 2-3. Gordon's Corps acted as rear guard as the army moved to Amelia Court House. It camped five miles east of the town on April 4, while the army awaited the collection of supplies. The retreat resumed the next day and continued through the night of April 5-6. As the rear guard, Gordon's Division was subjected to attacks by Federal cavalry and infantry. At a crossing of Sayler's Creek, on April 6, Gordon's men made a stand and repulsed the assault on their front. To the south of Gordon's position, the Confederates under Generals Ewell and Anderson were severely defeated and captured. The Federals then moved on Gordon's right. The pressure forced the line to break in confusion, but Gordon rallied the survivors west of the creek and rejoined the army. At Farmville, on April 7, the men of Gordon's Corps went to the relief of General Mahone's Division. The Federals were held, and the army continued the retreat.

On the night of April 7-8 Gordon's Corps moved to the advance of the army. His lead elements reached Appomattox Court House in the late afternoon of April 8 and halted. Later that evening they found the Federal cavalry in their front. It was decided that an attack would be made the next morning to cut through the enemy. Gordon's men moved into position west of the town during the night. At 5:00 A.M. the advance began and drove the Federal cavalry from the crossroads. The Confederates then took up a defensive position and came under attack by Federal infantry and cavalry. Gordon held his line until word came of the truce. A cease-fire was arranged, and Gordon began to withdraw. Cox's Brigade had not received the cease-fire order, and, as it moved back, the men turned and fired on an advancing Federal cavalry force. After hearing the volley, General Gordon sent word of the truce. The last shot had been fired. The Army of Northern Virginia was surrendered on that date, and on April 12, 1865, 58 members of the 3rd Regiment N.C. State Troops were paroled.

FIELD AND STAFF

COLONELS

MEARES, GASTON

Born in New Hanover County where he resided when appointed Colonel to rank from May 16, 1861. Killed at Malvern Hill, Virginia, July 1, 1862.

DeROSSET, WILLIAM LORD

Resided in New Hanover County when appointed Major to rank from May 16, 1861. Promoted to Lieutenant Colonel to rank from April 26, 1862, and promoted to Colonel to rank from July 1, 1862. Wounded severely in the thigh and hip at Sharpsburg, Maryland, September 17, 1862. Absent on leave from September, 1862, and submitted his resignation on September 7, 1863, by reason of his being unfit for field service. Resignation officially accepted on October 3, 1863.

THRUSTON, STEPHEN D.

Transferred from Company B of this regiment upon appointment as Major to rank from July 1, 1862. Promoted to Lieutenant Colonel March 26, 1863, to rank from December 10, 1862. Wounded at Chancellorsville, Virginia, May 3, 1863. Promoted to Colonel to rank from October 3, 1863. Wounded at Spotsylvania Court House, Virginia, May 10, 1864, and at Winchester, Virginia, September 19, 1864. Absent wounded in hospital at Wilmington until returned to duty on January 8, 1865. Detailed for court-martial duty at Wilmington on February 25, 1865. Examined at Raleigh on April 10, 1865, and declared "permanently disabled for field service."

LIEUTENANT COLONELS

COWAN, ROBERT H.

Resided in New Hanover County and appointed Lieutenant Colonel to rank from May 16, 1861. Transferred to the Field and Staff of the 18th Regiment N.C. Troops (8th Regiment N.C. Volunteers) upon appointment as Colonel to rank from April 26, 1862.

SAVAGE, EDWARD

Transferred from Company D of this regiment upon appointment as Major to rank from April 26, 1862. Wounded at Ellerson's Mill, Virginia, June 26, 1862. Promoted to Lieutenant Colonel to rank from July 1, 1862. Submitted his resignation August 25, 1862, by reason of "physical inability to properly discharge the duties of my office." Resignation officially accepted December 10, 1862.

PARSLEY, WILLIAM MURDOCK

Transferred from Company F of this regiment upon appointment as Major to rank from December 10, 1862. Promoted to Lieutenant Colonel to rank from October 3, 1863. Captured near Spotsylvania Court House, Virginia, May 12, 1864, and confined at Fort Delaware, Delaware. Transferred to Hilton Head, South Carolina, June 25, 1864, and exchanged at Charleston, South Carolina, on August 3, 1864. Killed near Farmville, Virginia, April 6, 1865.

MAJOR

ENNETT, WILLIAM T.

Transferred from Company E of this regiment upon appointment as Major to rank from October 3, 1863. Captured near Spotsylvania Court House, Virginia, May 12, 1864, and confined at Fort Delaware, Delaware. Transferred to Hilton Head, South Carolina, June 25, 1864, and exchanged at Charleston, South Carolina, on August 3, 1864. Returned to regiment and paroled at Appomattox Court House, Virginia, April 9, 1865.

ADJUTANTS

CUMMING, WILLIAM A.

Transferred from Company D of this regiment upon appointment as Adjutant with the rank of 1st Lieutenant to rank from November 27, 1861. Resigned as Adjutant when appointed Captain, Assistant Commissary of Subsistence of this regiment on December 12, 1862, to rank from October 10, 1862.

JAMES, THEODORE C.

Transferred from Company C, 59th Regiment N.C. Troops (4th Regiment N.C. Cavalry) upon appointment as Adjutant with the rank of 1st Lieutenant on March 14, 1863, to rank from January 26, 1863. Wounded at Gettysburg, Pennsylvania, July 3, 1863, and returned to duty January 10, 1864. Wounded at Wilderness, Virginia, May 5, 1864, and retired to the Invalid Corps on December 15, 1864.

ASSISTANT QUARTERMASTERS

ATKINSON, ROGER P.

Transferred from 1st Company A, 36th Regiment N.C. Troops (2nd Regiment N.C. Artillery) upon appointment as Captain, Assistant Quartermaster, on July 19, 1861. Dropped from rolls on February 24, 1862, by reason of his not having filed his bond. Reappointed on May 21, 1862, but declined commission. Dropped from the rolls October 25, 1862.

NORTHROP, WILLIAM HARRISS

Transferred from Company F of this regiment upon appointment as Captain, Assistant Quartermaster, to rank from August 8, 1862. Resigned January 23, 1863, by reason of inability to execute bond.

LANGDON, RICHARD F.

Transferred from Company E, 1st Regiment N.C. State Troops upon appointment as Captain, Assistant Quartermaster, to rank from January 29, 1863. Present or accounted for until assigned to command of ordnance train for Rodes' Division on **September 15, 1864. Reported as such through** March 10, 1865. Paroled at Salisbury on May 1, 1865.

ASSISTANT COMMISSARIES OF SUBSISTENCE

WILLIS, HARDY BRYAN

Transferred from Company F of this regiment upon appointment as Captain, Assistant Commissary of Subsistence, to rank from October 29, 1861. Dropped from the rolls on August 2, 1862.

CUMMING, WILLIAM A.

Promoted from Adjutant, with the rank of 1st Lieutenant, of this regiment upon appointment as Captain, Assistant Commissary of Subsistence, on December 12, 1862, to rank from October 10, 1862. Resigned May 26, 1863.

SURGEONS

McREE, JAMES FERGUS

Resided as a physician in New Hanover County and appointed Surgeon to rank from May 16, 1861. Present or accounted for until detailed as Surgeon at Salisbury in May, 1863.

WASHINGTON, WALKER

Served as Surgeon from June 30 to September 30, 1863. "Transferred to post duty."

STEWART, WILLIAM F.

Assigned to the regiment as Surgeon on August 13, 1863, and transferred to Charlotte Court House, Virginia, by order of the Surgeon General in November, 1863.

HERNDON, DABNEY

Served as Surgeon to this regiment while on duty with the 1st Regiment N.C. State Troops, February-April, 1864.

CROMWELL, BENJAMIN M.

Assigned to the regiment as Surgeon and reported on April 6, 1864. Captured at Winchester, Virginia, September 19, 1864, and confined at Old Capitol Prison, Washington, D.C. Transferred to Fort Delaware, Delaware, December 7, 1864, and transferred to Fort Monroe, Virginia, December 9, 1864. Forwarded for exchange on January 6, 1865. Furloughed on January 13, 1865. Returned to the regiment and paroled at Appomattox Court House, Virginia, April 9, 1865.

ASSISTANT SURGEONS

BLACK, KENNETH A.

Resided in Cumberland County as a physician and appointed Assistant Surgeon to rank from May 16, 1861. Submitted his resignation on October 16, 1862, by reason of "chronic bronchitis which threatens consumption (or incipient phthisis) and frequent attacks of intermittent fever." Resignation officially accepted October 22, 1862.

WALKER, JOSHUA C.

Resided in New Hanover County and appointed 2nd Assistant Surgeon to rank from May 16, 1861. The rank of 2nd Assistant Surgeon was dropped on August 20, 1861, and he was appointed Assistant Surgeon to rank from September 2, 1861. Present or accounted for until transferred to hospital duty on March 30, 1863.

WOOD, THOMAS F.

Transferred from Company I, 18th Regiment N.C. Troops (8th Regiment N.C. Volunteers) upon appointment as Assistant Surgeon to rank from February 4, 1863. Present or accounted for until paroled at Appomattox Court House, Virginia, April 9, 1865.

CHAPLAINS

TERRY, ROBERT E.
Resided in New Hanover County as rector of St. John's Episcopal Church, Wilmington, when appointed Chaplain to rank from December 24, 1861. Not reported on Field and Staff muster rolls as having served with the regiment.

VAUGHAN, MAURICE HAMILTON
Resided in Pasquotank County as a minister of the Protestant Episcopal Church and appointed Chaplain of this regiment on March 13, 1862, to rank from February 1, 1862. Previously served as Chaplain on the Field and Staff of the 17th Regiment N.C. Troops (1st Organization). Present or accounted for until relieved from duty with this regiment and assigned to duty at Goldsboro on November 15, 1862.

PATTERSON, GEORGE
Resided in Washington County as a minister of the Protestant Episcopal Church and appointed Chaplain of this regiment on February 11, 1863, to rank from December 30, 1862. Present or accounted for until relieved from duty with this regiment and assigned to duty at Chimborazo Hospital, Richmond, Virginia, November 5, 1864.

ENSIGN

BUTLER, HIRAM B.
Transferred from Company C of this regiment upon appointment as Ensign on April 28, 1864. Present or accounted for until paroled at Appomattox Court House, Virginia, April 9, 1865.

SERGEANTS MAJOR

THURSTON, WILLIAM J. Y.
Transferred from Company D of this regiment upon appointment as Sergeant Major on August 30, 1861. Present or accounted for until transferred to Company C of this regiment upon appointment as 2nd Lieutenant to rank from July 1, 1862.

CLARKE, JAMES FOREMAN
Transferred from Company I of this regiment upon appointment as Sergeant Major in July, 1862. Present or accounted for until transferred to Company G of this regiment upon appointment as 2nd Lieutenant to rank from September 17, 1862.

MILLS, SAMUEL A.
Transferred from Company E of this regiment upon appointment as Sergeant Major on February 10, 1863. Wounded at Chancellorsville, Virginia, May 3, 1863. Transferred back to Company E of this regiment upon appointment as 2nd Lieutenant on June 13, 1863.

McREE, ROBERT C.
Enlisted in Culpeper County, Virginia, October 26, 1863, for the war. Appointed Sergeant Major to rank from date of enlistment. Wounded at Spotsylvania Court House, Virginia, May 10, 1864, and died of wound on June 6, 1864.

TAYLOR, KINCHEN R.
Transferred from Company A of this regiment upon appointment as Sergeant Major on November 1, 1864. Present or accounted for until paroled at Appomattox Court House, Virginia, April 9, 1865.

QUARTERMASTER SERGEANTS

HAGARTY, JAMES
Transferred from Company F of this regiment upon appointment as Quartermaster Sergeant on August 1, 1861. Died at Camp Howe, Virginia, January 6, 1862, of "pneumonia."

TAYLOR, KINCHEN R.
Transferred from Company A of this regiment upon appointment as Quartermaster Sergeant on February 1, 1862. Present or accounted for until reduced to ranks and returned to Company A on October 1, 1864.

COMMISSARY SERGEANTS

REAVES, EDWARD C.
Transferred from Company F of this regiment upon appointment as Commissary Sergeant on August 24, 1861. Died at Fredericksburg, Virginia, November 1, 1861, of "pneumonia."

HOLLAND, JOHN LEWIS
Transferred from Company B of this regiment upon appointment as Commissary Sergeant on November 20, 1863. Present or accounted for through December, 1864. Captured at Farmville, Virginia, April 6, 1865, and confined at Point Lookout, Maryland, until released after taking Oath of Allegiance on June 28, 1865.

ORDNANCE SERGEANT

CLARKE, WALTER
Transferred from Company I of this regiment upon appointment as Ordnance Sergeant on August 28, 1862. Present or accounted for on muster rolls through December, 1864.

HOSPITAL STEWARDS

BLACK, JOHN
Enlisted in Wake County on July 18, 1861, for the war. Appointed Hospital Steward to rank from date of enlistment and assigned to this regiment. Present or accounted for until transferred to Company K of this regiment upon appointment as 2nd Lieutenant to rank from January 17, 1862.

WILLIAMS, GEORGE B.
Enlisted in New Hanover County on January 15, 1862, for the war. Appointed Hospital Steward to rank from date of enlistment and assigned to this regiment. Present or accounted for until he died in hospital at Charlottesville, Virginia, September 23, 1864, of "diarrhoea acute."

CHIEF MUSICIAN

CLARK, THOMAS
Transferred from Company F of this regiment upon appointment as Chief Musician on January 1, 1864. Present or accounted for until reduced to ranks and returned to Company F on December 18, 1864.

COMPANY A

This company, known as the "Greene County Riflemen," enlisted at Snow Hill, Greene County, April 23, 1861. It tendered its service to the state and was ordered to Garysburg, Northampton County, where it was assigned to this regiment as Company A. After joining the regiment the company functioned as a part of the regiment, and its history for the war period is recorded as a part of the regimental history.

The information contained in the following roster of the company was compiled principally from company muster rolls which covered from the muster-in roll, dated September 1, 1861, through December, 1864. No company muster rolls were found for the period prior to September 1, 1861, or for the period after December, 1864. In addition to the company muster rolls, Roll of Honor records, receipt rolls, and hospital records, supplemented by state pension applications, United Daughters of the Confederacy records, and postwar rosters and histories, all provided useful information.

OFFICERS

CAPTAINS

DRYSDALE, ROBERT H.
Resided in Greene County and appointed Captain at age 27 to rank from May 16, 1861. Died at Camp Price, Virginia, January 16, 1862, of "pneumonia."

BEST, HENRY H.
Resided in Greene County and appointed 1st Lieutenant at age 26 to rank from May 16, 1861. Promoted to Captain to rank from January 16, 1862. Submitted his resignation on August 14, 1862, by reason of "having been officially informed of his election to a seat in the lower house of the next legislature of North Carolina." Resignation officially accepted September 1, 1862, to take effect September 7, 1862.

ALBRITTON, JAMES HENRY
Resided in Greene County and appointed 2nd Lieutenant at age 21 to rank from May 16, 1861. Promoted to 1st Lieutenant to rank from January 16, 1862. Wounded at Malvern Hill, Virginia, July 1, 1862. Promoted to Captain to rank from September 7, 1862, while on sick furlough at home. Returned to company by January-February, 1863. Reported on March 1-May 15, 1863, muster roll as "in hospital, Richmond, sick since May 3, 1863." Returned to company and was wounded at Gettysburg, Pennsylvania, July 2, 1863. Reported as absent wounded until detailed as Enrolling Officer in Halifax County on January 19, 1864. Detail not reported to the company and he was reported on company muster rolls for 1864 as absent without leave. Officially detailed for enrolling service on March 29, 1865. Paroled at Greensboro on May 1, 1865.

LIEUTENANTS

BEST, BENJAMIN JAMES, 3rd Lieutenant
Resided in Greene County where he enlisted at age 20, April 23, 1861, for the war. Mustered in as 1st Sergeant. Appointed 3rd Lieutenant to rank from January 21, 1862. Submitted his resignation on July 11, 1862, by reason of his "having been seriously injured by a railroad accident last March, and being entirely unfit for active service in consequence thereof." Resignation officially accepted August 5, 1862.

BRYANT, HENRY, 2nd Lieutenant
Resided in Greene County where he enlisted at age 24, April 23, 1861, for the war. Mustered in as Corporal and promoted to Sergeant on February 28, 1862. Promoted to 1st Sergeant on October 1, 1862. Appointed 2nd Lieutenant to rank from February 20, 1863. Wounded at Wilderness, Virginia, May 5, 1864, and reported as absent wounded on company muster rolls through December, 1864. Admitted to hospital at Richmond, Virginia, February 25, 1865, and returned to duty on March 7, 1865. Paroled at Charlotte on May 27, 1865.

DARDEN, JOSEPH H., 1st Lieutenant
Born in Greene County where he resided as a farmer and enlisted at age 19, April 23, 1861, for the war. Mustered in as Sergeant and promoted to 1st Sergeant on August 6, 1862. Appointed 2nd Lieutenant to rank from September 7, 1862. Promoted to 1st Lieutenant to rank from February 20, 1863. Wounded at Chancellorsville, Virginia, May 3, 1863. Wounded a second time at Payne's Farm, Virginia, November 27, 1863. Captured at Wilderness, Virginia, May 10, 1864, and confined at Fort Delaware, Delaware. Transferred to Hilton Head, South Carolina, August 20, 1864, and from there to Fort Pulaski, Georgia, October 21, 1864. Returned to Hilton Head on December 26, 1864, and sent to Fort Delaware on March 12, 1865. Released at Fort Delaware after taking the Oath of Allegiance on June 16, 1865.

LANE, CHRISTOPHER C., 3rd Lieutenant
Born in Greene County where he resided as a farmer and enlisted at age 22, April 23, 1861, for the war. Mustered in as Corporal and promoted to Sergeant on September 1, 1861. Appointed 3rd Lieutenant to rank from September 17, 1862. Wounded at Gettysburg, Pennsylvania, July 2, 1863. Captured at Wilderness, Virginia, May 10, 1864, and confined at Fort Delaware, Delaware. Transferred to Hilton Head, South Carolina, August 20, 1864, and from there to Fort Pulaski, Georgia, on October 20, 1864. Died at Fort Pulaski on December 8, 1864, of "chronic diarrhoea."

SPEIGHT, ARTHUR W., 3rd Lieutenant
Resided in Greene County where he enlisted at age 20, April 23, 1861, for the war. Mustered in as Sergeant and promoted to 1st Sergeant on February 28, 1862. Appointed 3rd Lieutenant to rank from August 6, 1862. Killed at Sharpsburg, Maryland, September 17, 1862.

WILLIAMS, WILLIAM G., 1st Lieutenant
Resided in Greene County where he enlisted at age 25, April 23, 1861, for the war. Served as 1st Sergeant until appointed 3rd Lieutenant to rank from May 16, 1861. Promoted to 2nd Lieutenant to rank from January 16, 1862. Promoted to 1st Lieutenant to rank from September 7, 1862. Wounded at Sharpsburg, Maryland, September 17,

1862. Submitted his resignation on February 8, 1863, by reason of "being wounded in the battle of Sharpsburg, I am disabled in such a manner that I cannot undergo the hardships of active service, and my general health will not admit of it." Resignation officially accepted on February 20, 1863. Elected 2nd Lieutenant in Company A, Salisbury Prison Guard on February 21, 1863, and appointed as such.

NONCOMMISSIONED OFFICERS AND PRIVATES

ADCOCK, M. J., Private
Captured October 3, 1862, and paroled and exchanged at Aiken's Landing, Virginia, November 10, 1862.

ALBRITTON, BENJAMIN F., Private
Born in Greene County where he resided as a farmer and enlisted at age 20, April 23, 1861, for the war. Discharged at Camp McIntosh, near Goldsboro, May 17, 1862, by reason of gunshot wound received accidentally while on provost duty on January 25, 1862.

ALBRITTON, CHARLES H., Private
Resided in Greene County and enlisted in Wayne County at age 25, May 13, 1862, for the war. Wounded at Gettysburg, Pennsylvania, July 2, 1863, and captured at Gettysburg on July 4, 1863. Confined at DeCamp General Hospital, Davids Island, New York Harbor, until paroled and sent to City Point, Virginia, for exchange on October 22, 1863. Declared exchanged on October 28, 1863. Furloughed from hospital at Richmond, Virginia, on October 31, 1863, for 60 days. Reported as absent wounded and at home in North Carolina on company muster rolls through December, 1864. Reported on a payroll of Captain Croon's Company, N.C. Local Defense Troops, dated November 30, 1864, with the remark that he was employed as a guard at Tarboro from November 1 through December 1, 1864.

ALDRIDGE, JAMES P., Private
Resided in Greene County and enlisted in Wayne County at age 21, May 13, 1862, for the war. Killed at Chancellorsville, Virginia, May 3, 1863.

ALDRIDGE, JOHN H., Private
Resided in Greene County and enlisted in Wayne County at age 25, May 13, 1862, for the war. Wounded at Payne's Farm, Virginia, November 27, 1863. Captured near Spotsylvania Court House, Virginia, May 12, 1864, and confined at Point Lookout, Maryland. Transferred to Elmira, New York, August 10, 1864. Paroled at Elmira and sent to James River, Virginia, February 13, 1865, for exchange. Received at Boulware's Wharf, James River, February 20-21, 1865. Reported as present on a roll of a detachment of paroled and exchanged prisoners at Camp Lee, near Richmond, Virginia, dated February 23, 1865.

ALDRIDGE, JOHN T., Corporal
Resided in Greene County and enlisted in Craven County at age 21, June 7, 1861, for the war. Mustered in as Private and appointed Corporal on October 30, 1863. Killed at Payne's Farm, Virginia, November 27, 1863.

ALLEN, GEORGE, Private
Captured in hospital at Gettysburg, Pennsylvania, July 1-3, 1863, and "died October 2, 1863."

ALLEN, JOHN, Private
Resided in Greene County where he enlisted at age 21, April 23, 1861, for the war. Present or accounted for until wounded at Spotsylvania Court House, Virginia, May 12, 1864. Reported as absent wounded from that date through December, 1864.

APPLEWHITE, THOMAS J., Private
Resided in Wilson County and enlisted in Wayne County at age 21, May 13, 1862, for the war. Present or accounted for until captured at Spotsylvania Court House, Virginia, May 12, 1864. Confined at Point Lookout, Maryland, until transferred to Elmira, New York, August 10, 1864. Released at Elmira after taking the Oath of Allegiance on June 19, 1865.

ASWELL, JOHN B., Drummer
Resided in Greene County and enlisted in Wayne County at age 18, May 13, 1862, for the war. Mustered in as Drummer. Died in hospital at Richmond, Virginia, December 21, 1862, of "pneumonia."

BAKER, BLANEY, Private
Resided in Greene County where he enlisted at age 21, April 25, 1861, for the war. Present or accounted for until wounded at Chancellorsville, Virginia, May 3, 1863. Died of wound on May 25, 1863.

BAUGHN, JOHN, Private
Resided in Greene County and enlisted at age 23, May 13, 1862, for the war. Roll of Honor states that he "died August 20, 1862, at Richmond."

BEAMAN, JOHN DOBBS, Private
Resided in Greene County and enlisted at Richmond, Virginia, at age 35, July 17, 1862, for the war. Wounded at Sharpsburg, Maryland, September 17, 1862, and died of wound on October 1, 1862.

BEST, JAMES HIRAM, Private
Resided in Greene County and enlisted in Wayne County at age 19, May 13, 1862, for the war. Captured at Sharpsburg, Maryland, September 17, 1862, and confined at Fort Delaware, Delaware, until paroled and exchanged at Aiken's Landing, Virginia, November 10, 1862. Wounded at Wilderness, Virginia, May 5, 1864. Present or accounted for on company muster rolls through December, 1864. Captured at Farmville, Virginia, April 6, 1865, and confined at Newport News, Virginia, until released after taking the Oath of Allegiance on June 27, 1865.

BEST, JOHN R., Private
Resided in Greene County and enlisted in Wayne County at age 18, May 13, 1862, for the war. Wounded at Ellerson's Mill, Virginia, June 26, 1862. Reported as absent wounded through December, 1862. Wounded a second time at Winchester, Virginia, June 15, 1863. Detailed as a nurse in hospital at Goldsboro in September, 1863, and reported as absent through December, 1863. Returned to duty on March 14, 1864. Wounded at Wilderness, Virginia, May 5, 1864. Reported as absent wounded on company muster rolls through

October, 1864, and as present on November-December, 1864, muster roll. Paroled at Appomattox Court House, Virginia, April 9, 1865.

BILLIPS, WILLIAM G., Private
Born in Edgecombe County where he resided as a farmer prior to enlisting in Greene County at age 24, April 23, 1861, for the war. Present or accounted for until wounded at Winchester, Virginia, June 15, 1863. Reported as absent wounded and unfit for duty on company muster rolls from date of wound through December, 1864. Papers filed for retirement to Invalid Corps on March 4, 1865.

BLACKBURN, A. J., Private
Enlisted in Wake County on October 26, 1863, for the war. Reported on November-December, 1863, muster roll with the remark: "sent to rear sick, November 6, 1863. Not heard from since." Reported with same remark on company muster rolls through December, 1864.

BLACKBURN, J. C., Private
Enlisted in Wake County on October 26, 1863, for the war. Captured near Spotsylvania Court House, Virginia, May 12, 1864, and confined at Point Lookout, Maryland, where he died on July 28, 1864.

BLACKBURN, J. N., Private
Enlisted in Wake County on October 26, 1863, for the war. Captured at Spotsylvania Court House, Virginia, May 12, 1864, and confined at Point Lookout, Maryland. Released at Point Lookout after taking the Oath of Allegiance and joining the U.S. service on June 15, 1864. Assigned to Company E, 1st Regiment U.S. Volunteer Infantry.

BLANEY, DAVID, Private
Admitted to hospital at Richmond, Virginia, on September 30, 1862, with "bronchitis." Returned to duty on October 29, 1862.

BOWDEN, CHARLES A., Private
Resided in Greene County where he enlisted at age 23, April 27, 1861, for the war. Died at Goldsboro on May 4, 1862, of disease.

BRAND, JOHN, Private
Resided in Greene County and enlisted at Richmond, Virginia, at age 25, July 17, 1862, for the war. Reported on company muster roll for May 15-August 11, 1863, with the remark that he was "absent without leave since July 12, 1863." Federal Provost Marshal records indicate that he was captured July 30, 1863, and took the Oath of Allegiance.

BREWER, WILEY, Private
Enlisted in Wake County on October 26, 1863, for the war. Captured at Spotsylvania Court House, Virginia, May 12, 1864, and confined at Point Lookout, Maryland. Transferred on August 10, 1864, to Elmira, New York, where he died on November 15, 1864, of "chronic diarrhoea."

BRITT, A., Private
Captured in hospital at Richmond, Virginia, April 3, 1865. Reported as a patient at Jackson Hospital, Richmond, May 28, 1865.

BRITT, BENJAMIN R., Private
Resided in Greene County where he enlisted at age 18, April 23, 1861, for the war. Wounded at Payne's Farm, Virginia, November 27, 1863, and reported as absent wounded until retired to the Invalid Corps on January 9, 1865. Assigned to light duty at Tarboro on February 18, 1865. Admitted to hospital at Richmond, Virginia, February 24, 1865, and returned to duty on March 2, 1865. Admitted to hospital at Danville, Virginia, April 9, 1865, with a gunshot wound in right hand.

BRITT, JAMES, Private
Resided in Greene County and enlisted at Richmond, Virginia, at age 18, July 17, 1862, for the war. Killed at Gettysburg, Pennsylvania, July 2, 1863.

BRITT, JOHN, Private
Resided in Greene County where he enlisted at age 19, April 23, 1861, for the war. Wounded at Chancellorsville, Virginia, May 2, 1863. Killed at Gettysburg, Pennsylvania, July 2, 1863.

BRYANT, WILLIAM M., Sergeant
Resided in Greene County where he enlisted at age 18, April 23, 1861, for the war. Mustered in as Private. Wounded at Ellerson's Mill, Virginia, June 26, 1862, and again at Sharpsburg, Maryland, September 17, 1862. Reported as absent wounded through December, 1862. Wounded at Chancellorsville, Virginia, May 3, 1863. Appointed Sergeant to rank from September 1, 1863. Captured near Spotsylvania Court House, Virginia, May 12, 1864, and confined at Point Lookout, Maryland. Transferred to Elmira, New York, August 8, 1864. Paroled at Elmira and sent to James River, Virginia, March 14, 1865, for exchange. Received at Boulware's Wharf, James River, March 18-21, 1865.

BUTTS, JOHN, Private
Resided in Greene County where he enlisted at age 23, April 23, 1861, for the war. Killed at Chancellorsville, Virginia, May 2-3, 1863.

BUTTS, NATHAN, Private
Resided in Greene County where he enlisted at age 20, April 23, 1861, for the war. Killed at Sharpsburg, Maryland, September 17, 1862.

BUTTS, WILLIS J., Private
Resided in Greene County where he enlisted at age 33, April 23, 1861, for the war. Present or accounted for until wounded at Gettysburg, Pennsylvania, July 2, 1863. Captured in hospital at Gettysburg on July 4, 1863, and confined at De-Camp General Hospital, Davids Island, New York Harbor, until transferred to Fort Wood, Bedloe's Island, New York Harbor, October 24, 1863. **Paroled at Fort Wood and sent to Fort Monroe,** Virginia, January 5, 1864, for exchange. Admitted to hospital at Point Lookout, Maryland, January 10, 1864, and sent to City Point, Virginia, March 3, 1864, for exchange. Admitted to hospital at Richmond, Virginia, March 7, 1864, and furloughed for 60 days on March 12, 1864. Reported as absent wounded on company muster rolls through December, 1864.

CAIN, JAMES O., Private
Admitted to U.S. Army General Hospital, Frederick, Maryland, in September, 1862, and trans-

ferred on September 19, 1862.

CARMON, JOHN F., Private

Resided in Greene County where he enlisted at age 22, April 23, 1861, for the war. Killed in action at Sharpsburg, Maryland, September 17, 1862.

CARR, WILLIAM A., Private

Resided in Greene County and enlisted in Wayne County at age 18, July 4, 1861, for the war. Present or accounted for until transferred to Company E, 5th Regiment N.C. State Troops upon appointment as 2nd Lieutenant on May 13, 1863.

CASWELL, LEWIS A., Private

Resided in Greene County where he enlisted at age 32, April 23, 1861, for the war. Died in hospital at Staunton, Virginia, November 13, 1862, of "febris typhoides."

CAUDLE, S. J., Private

Enlisted in Wake County on October 13, 1863, for the war. Reported as absent sick on company muster rolls from December, 1863, through December, 1864.

CHRISTIAN, N. C., Private

Resided in Wayne County. Paroled at Goldsboro in 1865.

CHURCHILL, LEROY P., Private

Resided in Greene County and enlisted at Richmond, Virginia, at age 35, July 17, 1862, for the war. Wounded at Sharpsburg, Maryland, September 17, 1862. Captured at Spotsylvania Court House, Virginia, May 12, 1864, and confined at Point Lookout, Maryland. Transferred to Elmira, New York, August 10, 1864. Paroled at Elmira and sent to James River, Virginia, February 20, 1865, for exchange. Admitted to hospital at Baltimore, Maryland, while en route to be exchanged on February 22, 1865. Died in hospital at Baltimore on March 24, 1865, of "inflammation of lungs."

CHURCHWELL, S. C., Private

Resided in Greene County and enlisted in Wayne County at age 25, May 13, 1862, for the war. Died in hospital at Richmond, Virginia, on August 10, 1862.

COLE, J. L., Private

Enlisted in Wake County on October 21, 1863, for the war. Killed in action on May 10, 1864.

CONNER, WILLIAM, Private

Enlisted in Craven County at age 31, May 25, 1861, for the war. Reported on muster-in roll dated September 11, 1861, as "laundress." Not reported on rolls after September 11, 1861.

DAIL, JOHN J., Private

Resided in Greene County where he enlisted at age 21, April 23, 1861, for the war. Killed at Sharpsburg, Maryland, September 17, 1862.

DAIL, JOHN T., Private

Resided in Greene County and enlisted in Wayne County at age 18, May 13, 1862, for the war. Wounded at Sharpsburg, Maryland, September 17, 1862. Died at home in North Carolina on March 11, 1863, "of wounds received in battle at Sharpsburg, September 17, 1862."

DAIL, PERRY, Private

Resided in Greene County where he enlisted at age 23, April 23, 1861, for the war. Died at Goldsboro on May 5, 1862, of disease.

DAIL, WILLIAM HAYWOOD, Private

Resided in Greene County where he enlisted at age 20, April 23, 1861, for the war. Present or accounted for on company muster rolls through December, 1864, being absent on detached service in brigade commissary department from August 3, 1863, through December, 1864. Captured at Burkeville, Virginia, April 6, 1865, and confined at Point Lookout, Maryland, until released after taking the Oath of Allegiance on June 26, 1865.

DAVIS, BURTON, Private

Resided in Greene County where he enlisted at age 26, April 25, 1861, for the war. Wounded at Ellerson's Mill, Virginia, June 26, 1862. Sent to hospital at Richmond, Virginia, and reported as absent wounded on company muster rolls through December, 1862, when his name was dropped because he had not been heard from since he was sent to hospital.

DIXON, BENJAMIN F., Private

Resided in Greene County where he enlisted at age 23, April 27, 1861, for the war. Present or accounted for until captured near Spotsylvania Court House, Virginia, May 12, 1864. Confined at Point Lookout, Maryland, until transferred to Elmira, New York, August 10, 1864. Paroled at Elmira and sent to James River, Virginia, March 10, 1865, for exchange. Received at Boulware's Wharf, James River, March 15, 1865, in exchange.

DIXON, WILLIS, Private

Resided in Greene County and enlisted at Camp Price, Virginia, at age 25, February 10, 1862, for the war. Died at Richmond, Virginia, August 15, 1862.

DULA, ANDERSON, Private

Resided in Wilkes County and enlisted in Wake County on October 26, 1863, for the war. Captured at Kelly's Ford, Virginia, November 8, 1863, and confined at Old Capitol Prison, Washington, D.C., until released after taking the Oath of Allegiance on March 18, 1864. Sent to Philadelphia, Pennsylvania.

DUNN, JAMES B., Private

Resided in Lenoir County and enlisted at Camp Price, Virginia, at age 17, March 16, 1862, for the war. Killed at Chancellorsville, Virginia, May 3, 1863.

EASON, WILLIAM, Private

Enlisted in Wayne County at age 19, July 15, 1861, for the war. Present or accounted for until wounded at Gettysburg, Pennsylvania, July 2, 1863. Captured in hospital at Gettysburg on July 4, 1863, and confined at DeCamp General Hospital, Davids Island, New York Harbor, until paroled and sent to City Point, Virginia, September 27, 1863, for exchange. Reported as absent wounded until returned to company in August, 1864. Captured at Winchester, Virginia, September, 19, 1864, and confined at Point Lookout, Maryland, until paroled and sent to Aiken's

Landing, Virginia, March 15, 1865, for exchange. Received at Boulware's Wharf, James River, Virginia, March 18, 1865, in exchange.

EDWARDS, DANIEL W., Corporal
Born in Greene County where he resided as a student prior to enlisting in Craven County at age 21, May 30, 1861, for the war. Mustered in as Corporal. Discharged on February 1, 1862, by reason of "incipient phthisis."

EDWARDS, JOSEPH A., Private
Resided in Greene County where he enlisted at age 21, April 23, 1861, for the war. Killed at Chancellorsville, Virginia, May 3, 1863.

EDWARDS, ROBERT A., 1st Sergeant
Resided in Greene County where he enlisted at age 18, April 23, 1861, for the war. Mustered in as Private and appointed Corporal on July 19, 1861. Promoted to Sergeant July 14-October 31, 1862. Promoted to 1st Sergeant on February 20, 1863. Wounded at Gettysburg, Pennsylvania, July 2, 1863, and captured in hospital at Gettysburg on July 4, 1863. Transferred to U.S. Army General Hospital, West's Buildings, Baltimore, Maryland, October 15, 1863. Paroled and sent to City Point, Virginia, November 12, 1863, for exchange. Admitted to hospital at Richmond, Virginia, November 15, 1863, and company muster rolls report him as absent wounded and absent at home in Greene County on parole through December, 1864.

FLORA, JAMES, Private
Resided in Greene County where he enlisted at age 25, April 30, 1861, for the war. Detailed as teamster in Ordnance Train on August 20, 1863, and reported as absent on detail on company muster rolls through December, 1864. Captured at Salisbury on April 12, 1865, and confined at Camp Chase, Ohio, May 2, 1865. Released at Camp Chase after taking the Oath of Allegiance on June 13, 1865.

FORREST, BENJAMIN F., Private
Resided in Greene County where he enlisted at age 18, April 23, 1861, for the war. Died in camp near Richmond, Virginia, July 12, 1862, of disease.

GAY, JOHN WESLEY, Private
Resided in Greene County where he enlisted at age 25, April 27, 1861, for the war. Wounded at Gettysburg, Pennsylvania, July 2, 1863. Wounded a second time at Spotsylvania Court House, Virginia, May 10, 1864. Reported as absent wounded on company muster rolls through December, 1864.

GRADY, HENRY, Sergeant
Resided in Greene County where he enlisted at age 23, April 23, 1861, for the war. Mustered in as Corporal and appointed Sergeant on July 1, 1862. Wounded at Sharpsburg, Maryland, September 17, 1862, and died at home in Greene County on December 8, 1862.

GRANGER, PHILIP B., Private
Resided in Greene County where he enlisted at age 26, April 23, 1861, for the war. Captured in Maryland on September 12, 1862, and paroled and

exchanged by September 30, 1862, the date he was paid as a paroled and exchanged prisoner at Richmond, Virginia. Captured at Fredericksburg, Virginia, May 3-4, 1863, and confined at Old Capitol Prison, Washington, D.C., where he was paroled to go north on May 12, 1863.

GRANT, JOHN, Private
Resided in Greene County and enlisted in Wayne County at age 18, May 13, 1862, for the war. Captured at Frederick, Maryland, September 12, 1862, and confined at Fort Delaware, Delaware, until paroled and exchanged at Aiken's Landing, Virginia, November 10, 1862. Wounded at Chancellorsville, Virginia, May 2, 1863. Wounded at Gettysburg, Pennsylvania, July 2, 1863, and captured at Waterloo, Pennsylvania, July 5, 1863. Confined at Fort Delaware until transferred to Point Lookout, Maryland, October 18, 1863. Paroled at Point Lookout and transferred to Aiken's Landing on February 24, 1865, for exchange. Declared exchanged at Aiken's Landing on March 5, 1865.

HALL, JOHN, Private
Enlisted in Craven County at age 25, April 23, 1861, for the war. Reported on muster-in roll dated September 1, 1861, with the remark: "laundress."

HALL, ROBERT, Private
Enlisted in Wake County on October 26, 1863, for the war. Captured at Spotsylvania Court House, Virginia, May 12, 1864, and confined at Point Lookout, Maryland, where he died on July 13, 1864.

HAM, JAMES, Private
Resided in Greene County where he enlisted at age 19, April 27, 1861, for the war. Captured at Frederick, Maryland, September 12, 1862, and confined at Fort Delaware, Delaware, until paroled and exchanged at Aiken's Landing, Virginia, November 10, 1862. Wounded at Gettysburg, Pennsylvania, July 2, 1863, and captured in hospital at Gettysburg on July 4, 1863. Admitted to hospital at Baltimore, Maryland, July 11, 1863, and transferred to hospital at Chester, Pennsylvania, July 18, 1863. Sent to Point Lookout, Maryland, October 2, 1863. Paroled at Point Lookout and sent to City Point, Virginia, March 3, 1864, for exchange. Declared exchanged at City Point on March 6, 1864. Admitted to hospital at Richmond, Virginia, March 7, 1864, and furloughed. Reported on company muster rolls as absent wounded on furlough through December, 1864.

HAM, JAMES R. S., Private
Resided in Greene County where he enlisted at age 21, April 27, 1861, for the war. Captured and paroled at Paris, Virginia, November 5, 1862. Died at Paris on November 20, 1862.

HAM, WILLIAM H., Corporal
Resided in Greene County where he enlisted at age 21, April 27, 1861, for the war. Mustered in as Private. Wounded at Malvern Hill, Virginia, July 1, 1862. Wounded at Chancellorsville, Virginia, May 3, 1863. Wounded a third time at

Payne's Farm, Virginia, November 27, 1863. Appointed Corporal January-April, 1864. Captured near Spotsylvania Court House, Virginia, May 12, 1864, and confined at Point Lookout, Maryland. Transferred to Elmira, New York, August 10, 1864. Released at Elmira after taking the Oath of Allegiance on June 14, 1865.

HARDY, BENJAMIN MOSES, Private
Resided in Greene County where he enlisted at age 20, April 25, 1861, for the war. Died at Camp Howe, Virginia, September 20, 1861, of disease.

HARDY, SETH T., Corporal
Resided in Greene County where he enlisted at age 21, April 25, 1861, for the war. Mustered in as Private and appointed Corporal on February 28, 1862. Present or accounted for until he died at Gordonsville, Virginia, September 11, 1862, of "typhoid fever."

HARPER, H. D., Private
Resided in Greene County and enlisted in Wayne County at age 35, May 13, 1862, for the war. Wounded at Sharpsburg, Maryland, September 17, 1862, and died of wound near Staunton, Virginia, September 22, 1862.

HART, JESSE E., Private
Resided in Greene County where he enlisted at age 24, April 23, 1861, for the war. Present or accounted for until killed at Sharpsburg, Maryland, September 17, 1862.

HART, MACON M., Private
Resided in Greene County where he enlisted at age 18, April 23, 1861, for the war. Died in hospital at Fredericksburg, Virginia, September 5, 1861, of disease.

HEATH, HAYWOOD, Private
Resided in Greene County where he enlisted at age 24, April 23, 1861, for the war. Present or accounted for until captured at Winchester, Virginia, September 19, 1864. Confined at Point Lookout, Maryland, until paroled and exchanged at Aiken's Landing, Virginia, March 18, 1865.

HEATH, JAMES P., Private
Resided in Greene County where he enlisted at age 26, April 23, 1861, for the war. Present or accounted for on company muster rolls until captured at Spotsylvania Court House, Virginia, May 12, 1864. Confined at Point Lookout, Maryland, until transferred to Elmira, New York, August 10, 1864. Paroled at Elmira on March 10, 1865, and sent to James River, Virginia, for exchange. Received at Boulware's Wharf, James River, March 15, 1865, in exchange.

HEATH, JOHN R., Sergeant
Resided in Wayne County where he enlisted at age 23, April 23, 1861, for the war. Mustered in as Private. Wounded at Malvern Hill, Virginia, July 1, 1862. Appointed Corporal on October 1, 1862, and promoted to Sergeant on January 10, 1863. Killed at Gettysburg, Pennsylvania, July 2, 1863.

HEATH, JOSIAH, Private
Resided in Greene County where he enlisted at age 25, April 23, 1861, for the war. Present or

accounted for until killed at Malvern Hill, Virginia, July 1, 1862.

HEATH, RICHARD, Private
Enlisted in Wayne County on May 13, 1862, for the war. Wounded at Sharpsburg, Maryland, September 17, 1862. Reported as absent wounded and unfit for duty on company muster rolls from date wounded through December, 1864.

HILL, JOHN R., Private
Enlisted in Wayne County on May 13, 1862, for the war. Wounded at Chancellorsville, Virginia, May 3, 1863. Wounded at Payne's Farm, Virginia, November 27, 1863. Present or accounted for on company muster rolls through December, 1864. Paroled at Appomattox Court House, Virginia, April 9, 1865.

HILL, JOSEPH PATRICK, Private
Resided in Greene County where he enlisted at age 21, April 23, 1861, for the war. Wounded at Sharpsburg, Maryland, September 17, 1862. Returned to company in March, 1863. Wounded at Gettysburg, Pennsylvania, July 2, 1863, and captured in hospital at Gettysburg on July 4, 1863. Admitted to hospital at Baltimore, Maryland, July 11, 1863, and transferred to hospital at Chester, Pennsylvania, July 18, 1863. Paroled and sent to City Point, Virginia, August 17, 1863, for exchange. Declared exchanged at City Point on August 20, 1863. Present or accounted for on company muster rolls through December, 1864, being detailed in Pioneer Corps from January through October, 1864. Paroled at Appomattox Court House, Virginia, April 9, 1865.

HILL, REUBEN, Private
Resided in Greene County and enlisted in Wayne County at age 18, May 13, 1862, for the war. Wounded at Mechanicsville, Virginia, June 27, 1862. Died at Gordonsville, Virginia, September 1-6, 1862, of disease.

HILL, THOMAS W., Private
Resided in Greene County and enlisted in Wayne County at age 25, May 13, 1862, for the war. Captured at Frederick, Maryland, September 12, 1862, and confined at Fort Delaware, Delaware, until paroled and exchanged at Aiken's Landing, Virginia, November 10, 1862. Killed at Chancellorsville, Virginia, May 3, 1863.

HOBBS, WILLIAM, Private
Resided in Greene County where he enlisted at age 20, April 23, 1861, for the war. Present or accounted for until killed at Gettysburg, Pennsylvania, July 2, 1863.

HOLMES, JAMES THOMAS, Private
Born in Greene County and resided as a student in Wayne County where he enlisted at age 17, July 11, 1861, for the war. Discharged on May 15, 1862, by reason of "chronic rheumatism."

HOOD, ELIAS, Private
Enlisted in Wayne County at age 21, June 9, 1861, for the war. Reported on muster roll dated September 1, 1861, with the remark: "laundress." Not reported on muster rolls after that date.

HOOKER, PRESTON B., Private
Resided in Greene County and enlisted in Wayne

County at age 30, May 13, 1862, for the war. Captured in Maryland on September 12, 1862, and paroled near Keedysville, Maryland, September 20, 1862. Died in hospital at Richmond, Virginia, June 12-13, 1863, of "pneumonia."

HORTON, WILLIAM J., Private
Resided in Greene County where he enlisted at age 18, April 27, 1861, for the war. Present or accounted for on company muster rolls through December, 1864. Federal Provost Marshal records report him as a "deserter from the enemy" received at City Point, Virginia, March 19, 1865. Sent to Provost Marshal General, Washington, D.C., March 21, 1865. Took the Oath of Allegiance and was provided transportation to New Bern on March 24, 1865.

JENNING, J. J., Private
Enlisted in Wake County on October 26, 1863, for the war. Deserted on November 12, 1863, and dropped from the rolls.

JOHNSON, WILLIAM E., Private
Paroled at Raleigh on May 26, 1865.

JOLLY, ROBERT, Private
Resided in Greene County and enlisted in Wayne County at age 25, May 13, 1862, for the war. Captured at Frederick, Maryland, September 12, 1862, and confined at Fort Delaware, Delaware, until paroled and exchanged at Aiken's Landing, Virginia, November 10, 1862. Wounded at Gettysburg, Pennsylvania, July 2, 1863, and captured in hospital at Gettysburg on July 4, 1863. Confined at DeCamp General Hospital, Davids Island, New York Harbor, until paroled and sent to City Point, Virginia, August 24, 1863, for exchange. Declared exchanged at City Point on August 28, 1863. Reported on December 31, 1863-August 31, 1864, muster roll with the remark: "deserted November 1, 1863. Dropped from rolls."

JONES, BENJAMIN, Private
Resided in Lenoir County and enlisted in Wayne County at age 27, July 8, 1861, for the war. Present or accounted for on company muster rolls through December, 1864. Paroled at Appomattox Court House, Virginia, April 9, 1865.

JONES, HENRY, Private
Resided in Greene County where he enlisted at age 26, April 23, 1861, for the war. Admitted to hospital at Richmond, Virginia, July 4, 1862, with "typhoid fever." Died in hospital. Date of death reported as July 10, 1862, and August 20, 1862.

JONES, HENRY G., Private
Resided in Greene County where he enlisted at age 24, April 25, 1861, for the war. Died in hospital at Richmond, Virginia, July 2, 1862.

JONES, JAMES F., Private
Resided in Greene County where he enlisted at age 26, April 25, 1861, for the war. Wounded at Malvern Hill, Virginia, July 1, 1862. Killed at Chancellorsville, Virginia, May 3, 1863.

JONES, JAMES R. P., Private
Resided in Greene County where he enlisted at age 26, April 23, 1861, for the war. Killed at Cold Harbor, Virginia, June 27, 1862.

JONES, LEWIS H., Private
Resided in Franklin County and enlisted in Wayne County on April 4, 1862, for the war. Detailed as teamster on August 5, 1863, and reported as absent on detail on company muster rolls through December, 1864. Captured at Waynesboro, Virginia, March 2, 1865, and confined at Fort Delaware, Delaware, until released after taking the Oath of Allegiance on June 19, 1865.

JONES, WILLIAM H., Private
Resided in Greene County and enlisted in Wayne County at age 19, May 13, 1862, for the war. Present or accounted for until killed at Sharpsburg, Maryland, September 17, 1862.

KEARNEY, THOMAS, Private
Resided in Greene County and enlisted in Wayne County at age 25, May 13, 1862, for the war. Present or accounted for until captured at Gettysburg, Pennsylvania, July 3, 1863. Confined at Fort Delaware, Delaware, until transferred to Point Lookout, Maryland, October 18, 1863. Paroled at Point Lookout and transferred to James River, Virginia, February 18, 1865, for exchange. Declared exchanged at Boulware's Wharf, James River, February 20-21, 1865. Reported as present on a roll of a detachment of paroled and exchanged prisoners at Camp Lee, near Richmond, Virginia, dated February 23, 1865.

KILPATRICK, HENRY C., Sergeant
Resided in Lenoir County and enlisted in Wayne County at age 21, July 8, 1861, for the war. Mustered in as Private and appointed Corporal prior to being promoted to Sergeant on October 1, 1862. Wounded at Chancellorsville, Virginia, May 3, 1863. Killed at Gettysburg, Pennsylvania, July 2, 1863.

KNIGHT, JAMES S., Private
Resided in Wayne County and enlisted in Virginia at age 17, September 15, 1861, for the war. Wounded at Chancellorsville, Virginia, May 3, 1863. Admitted to hospital at Richmond, Virginia, May 11, 1863, with a gunshot wound and transferred to Goldsboro on May 23, 1863. Company muster rolls report him as absent wounded and absent in hospital at Goldsboro through December, 1864.

LANE, WILLIAM, Private
Resided in Greene County and enlisted in Wayne County at age 30, May 13, 1862, for the war. Present or accounted for until wounded at Gettysburg, Pennsylvania, July 2, 1863. Captured at Waterloo, Pennsylvania, July 5, 1863, and confined at Fort Delaware, Delaware. Transferred on October 18, 1863, to Point Lookout, Maryland, where he died on February 3, 1864.

LAWRENCE, PETER, Private
Resided in Greene County where he enlisted at age 24, April 25, 1861, for the war. Wounded at Sharpsburg, Maryland, September 17, 1862. Captured in hospital at Gettysburg, Pennsylvania, July 5, 1863, and confined at DeCamp General Hospital, Davids Island, New York Harbor, until paroled and sent to City Point, Virginia, September 27, 1863, for exchange. Admitted to hospital

at Richmond, Virginia, September 28, 1863, and furloughed on October 10, 1863. Captured at Spotsylvania Court House, Virginia, May 12, 1864, and confined at Point Lookout, Maryland. Transferred to Elmira, New York, August 10, 1864. Paroled at Elmira and sent to James River, Virginia, March 14, 1865, for exchange. Received at Boulware's Wharf, James River, March 18-21, 1865, in exchange. Furloughed from hospital at Richmond on March 29, 1865, for 60 days.

McEWING, E. A., Private

Paroled at Charlotte on May 6, 1865.

MARLER, NATHAN, Private

Resided in Greene County where he enlisted at age 21, April 25, 1861, for the war. Wounded at Gettysburg, Pennsylvania, July 2, 1863. Captured at Spotsylvania Court House, Virginia, May 12, 1864, and confined at Point Lookout, Maryland. Transferred to Elmira, New York, July 3, 1864. Died at Elmira on January 9, 1865, of "variola."

MEARS, JOHN L., Private

Resided in Greene County where he enlisted at age 20, April 25, 1861, for the war. Captured and paroled near Fredericksburg, Virginia, May 4, 1863. Wounded at Gettysburg, Pennsylvania, July 2, 1863. Captured at Spotsylvania Court House, Virginia, May 12, 1864, and confined at Point Lookout, Maryland. Transferred to Elmira, New York, July 3, 1864. Released at Elmira after taking the Oath of Allegiance on May 29, 1865.

MILLER, L. L., Private

Paroled at Greensboro on May 16, 1865.

MITCHELL, BARNEY E., Private

Resided in Greene County where he enlisted at age 22, April 25, 1861, for the war. Wounded at Sharpsburg, Maryland, September 17, 1862. Wounded a second time at Chancellorsville, Virginia, May 3, 1863. Company muster rolls report him as absent wounded from May, 1863, through December, 1864. Paroled at High Point on May 1, 1865.

MOORE, ARTHUR, Private

Resided in Greene County where he enlisted at age 20, April 25, 1861, for the war. Wounded at Malvern Hill, Virginia, July 1, 1862. Detailed for medical service on September 3, 1863, and assigned to hospital at Wilmington as a nurse on October 8, 1863. Company muster rolls report him as absent on detail through December, 1864. Reported on a list of employees in hospitals at Wilmington which states that he was last examined in January, 1865, and declared unfit for field service by reason of "gunshot wound of right forearm."

MOORE, JOHN, Private

Resided in Greene County where he enlisted at age 23, April 25, 1861, for the war. Wounded at Gettysburg, Pennsylvania, July 2, 1863, and reported as absent wounded until detailed in medical service on April 28, 1864. Detailed as a guard in hospital at Richmond, Virginia, May 17, 1864. Assigned to Fourth Division, General Hospital, Camp Winder, Richmond, and hospital records indicate that he served as a guard at that hospital through January, 1865. Reported as a

guard at Jackson Hospital, Richmond, March 23, 1865. Captured at Jackson Hospital, Richmond, April 3, 1865, and paroled on April 20, 1865.

MOORE, OLLIN, Sergeant

Resided in Greene County and enlisted in Wayne County at age 18, May 13, 1862, for the war. Mustered in as Private. Captured in Maryland, September 12, 1862, and confined at Fort Delaware, Delaware, until paroled and exchanged at Aiken's Landing, Virginia, November 10, 1862. Appointed Corporal on September 1, 1863. Promoted to Sergeant, January-May, 1864. Captured at Spotsylvania Court House, Virginia, May 12, 1864, and confined at Point Lookout, Maryland, until transferred to Elmira, New York, August 10, 1864. Remained at Elmira until released after taking the Oath of Allegiance on July 11, 1865.

MOORE, WILLIAM, Private

Enlisted in Wake County on October 26, 1863, for the war. Deserted November 12, 1863.

OXLEY, CHARLES, Private

Resided in Lenoir County and enlisted in Wayne County at age 22, July 8, 1861, for the war. Present or accounted for until killed at Malvern Hill, Virginia, July 1, 1862.

OXLEY, STEPHEN, Private

Resided in Lenoir County and enlisted in Wayne County at age 20, July 8, 1861, for the war. Wounded at Chancellorsville, Virginia, May 3, 1863. Present or accounted for through December, 1864. Federal Provost Marshal records report him as a deserter from the enemy who was received at Washington, D.C., March 21, 1865. Took the Oath of Allegiance and was provided transportation to New Bern.

PATE, GEORGE B., Corporal

Resided in Greene County where he enlisted at age 18, April 23, 1861, for the war. Mustered in as Private and appointed Corporal on January 1, 1863. Wounded at Chancellorsville, Virginia, May 3, 1863, and left arm amputated. Reported as absent on furlough until retired to the Invalid Corps on December 1, 1864.

PATE, OWEN J., Sergeant

Resided in Greene County where he enlisted at age 23, April 23, 1861, for the war. Mustered in as Private and appointed Corporal, February 28, 1862. Wounded at Sharpsburg, Maryland, September 17, 1862, and promoted to Sergeant on October 1, 1862. Transferred to Company C, 1st Battalion N.C. Local Defense Troops upon appointment as 2nd Lieutenant to rank from January 6, 1863.

PATRICK, JOHN, Private

Resided in Greene County and enlisted in Wayne County on May 13, 1862, for the war. Wounded in action at Malvern Hill, Virginia, July 1, 1862. Transferred to Company C, 1st Battalion N.C. Local Defense Troops upon appointment as 2nd Lieutenant on January 10, 1863.

PEEBLES, ALLEN, Private

Paroled at Greensboro on May 11, 1865.

PHILLIPS, ASA, Private
Resided in Greene County where he enlisted at age 23, April 25, 1861, for the war. Wounded in action at Chancellorsville, Virginia, May 3, 1863, and died of wound on May 17, 1863.

PRICE, JAMES W., Private
Resided in Greene County and enlisted at Camp Price, Virginia, at age 35, February 14, 1862, for the war. Present or accounted for until captured at Spotsylvania Court House, Virginia, May 12, 1864. Confined at Point Lookout, Maryland, until transferred to Elmira, New York, August 10, 1864. Remained at Elmira until released after taking the Oath of Allegiance on July 11, 1865.

PRIDGEN, HENRY R., Corporal
Resided in Greene County where he enlisted at age 23, April 23, 1861, for the war. Mustered in as Private. Wounded at Gettysburg, Pennsylvania, July 2, 1863, and captured in hospital at Gettysburg on July 4, 1863. Confined at DeCamp General Hospital, Davids Island, New York Harbor, until paroled and exchanged at City Point, Virginia, August 28, 1863. Appointed Corporal, January-May, 1864. Captured at Spotsylvania Court House, Virginia, May 12, 1864, and confined at Point Lookout, Maryland, until transferred to Elmira, New York, August 10, 1864. Remained at Elmira until paroled on February 20, 1865, and sent to James River, Virginia, for exchange.

RADFORD, LEMUEL J., Private
Resided in Greene County where he enlisted at age 20, April 27, 1861, for the war. Captured in Maryland, September 12, 1862, and confined at Fort Delaware, Delaware, until paroled and exchanged at Aiken's Landing, Virginia, November 10, 1862. Killed at Chancellorsville, Virginia, May 3, 1863.

RADFORD, MILES, Private
Resided in Greene County and enlisted in Wayne County at age 25, May 13, 1862, for the war. Captured in Maryland, September 12, 1862, and confined at Fort Delaware, Delaware, until paroled and exchanged at Aiken's Landing, Virginia, November 10, 1862. Died at Guinea Station, Virginia, April 11, 1863.

RANDOLPH, JOHN T., Private
Resided in Greene County and enlisted in Wayne County at age 30, May 13, 1862, for the war. Wounded at Sharpsburg, Maryland, September 17, 1862. Admitted to hospital at Richmond, Virginia, July 12, 1863, with "contused wound of knee." Date and place wounded not reported. Present or accounted for until captured at Spotsylvania Court House, Virginia, May 12, 1864. Confined at Point Lookout, Maryland, until transferred to Elmira, New York, August 10, 1864. Remained at Elmira until released after taking the Oath of Allegiance on June 27, 1865.

RANDOLPH, MATHEW, Sergeant
Resided in Greene County and enlisted at Camp Price, Virginia, at age 23, February 14, 1862, for the war. Mustered in as Private and appointed Corporal on February 1, 1862. Promoted to Sergeant on September 1, 1863. Captured at Spotsylvania Court House, Virginia, May 12, 1864, and confined at Point Lookout, Maryland, where he died July 11, 1864.

RANDOLPH, ROBERT, Private
Resided in Greene County and enlisted in Craven County at age 25, May 7, 1861, for the war. Present or accounted for until killed at Sharpsburg, Maryland, September 17, 1862.

RANDOLPH, W. M., Private
Resided in Greene County and enlisted at Richmond, Virginia, at age 35, July 17, 1862, for the war. Present or accounted for until captured at Spotsylvania Court House, Virginia, May 12, 1864. Confined at Point Lookout, Maryland, until transferred to Elmira, New York, August 15, 1864. Paroled at Elmira on October 11, 1864, and exchanged at Venus Point, Savannah River, Georgia, November 15, 1864. Paroled at Appomattox Court House, Virginia, April 9, 1865.

REDDICK, JAMES T., Private
Resided in Greene County where he enlisted at age 28, April 25, 1861, for the war. Died at Richmond, Virginia, August 10, 1862.

REDDICK, WILLIAM T., Private
Resided in Greene County where he enlisted at age 21, April 27, 1861, for the war. Died at Fredericksburg, Virginia, October 25, 1861.

REEVES, LOGAN, Private
Enlisted in Wake County on October 26, 1863, for the war. Reported on the November-December, 1863, muster roll with the remark: "Sent to rear sick from Brandy Station. Not heard from since."

RILEY, HENRY, Private
Paroled at Greensboro on May 5, 1865.

ROUSE, L. I., Private
Hospital record for General Hospital No. 4, Wilmington, dated October 6, 1864, reported him as fit for retirement or detail with the remark: "compd. comut. fracture of femur."

ROUSE, LEMUEL G., Private
Resided in Greene County where he enlisted at age 18, April 23, 1861, for the war. Present or accounted for until wounded at Payne's Farm, Virginia, November 27, 1863. Reported as absent wounded on company muster rolls through December, 1864.

RUBLE, JACOB, Private
Resided in Greene County where he enlisted at age 23, April 23, 1861, for the war. Killed at Malvern Hill, Virginia, July 1, 1862.

RUFF, BENJAMIN A., Private
Resided in Greene County and enlisted in Wayne County at age 25, May 13, 1862, for the war. Wounded at Gettysburg, Pennsylvania, July 2, 1863, and captured in hospital at Gettysburg on July 4, 1863. Paroled and exchanged at City Point, Virginia, August 20, 1863. Captured at Spotsylvania Court House, Virginia, May 12, 1864, and confined at Point Lookout, Maryland, until transferred to Elmira, New York, August 10, 1864. Released at Point Lookout after taking the Oath of Allegiance on June 17, 1865.

RUFF, JOHN, Private
Resided in Greene County and enlisted in
Craven County at age 26, June 20, 1861, for the
war. Present or accounted for until captured at
Spotsylvania Court House, Virginia, May 12,
1864. Confined at Point Lookout, Maryland,
until transferred to Elmira, New York, August
10, 1864. Released at Elmira after taking the
Oath of Allegiance on June 23, 1865.

RYLAND, KINCHEN, Private
Resided in Greene County where he enlisted at
age 20, April 25, 1861, for the war. Present or
accounted for until he died at Scottsville, Virginia, January 31, 1863, of "typhoid pneumonia."

SAULS, PATRICK, Private
Resided in Greene County and enlisted in Wayne
County at age 25, May 13, 1862, for the war.
Died near Strasburg, Virginia, November 13,
1862.

SEWARD, WILLIAM M., Private
Federal Provost Marshal records carry him as a
deserter with the remark that he took the Oath
of Allegiance on March 19, 1865, at City Point,
Virginia.

SHIRLEY, GEORGE, Private
Resided in Greene County and enlisted in Wayne
County at age 18, May 13, 1862, for the war.
Wounded at Spotsylvania Court House, Virginia,
May 12, 1864. Present or accounted for until
captured at Winchester, Virginia, September 19,
1864. Confined at Point Lookout, Maryland, until
paroled for exchange on March 15, 1865. Declared
exchanged at Boulware's Wharf, James River,
Virginia, March 18, 1865.

SHIRLEY, ROBERT, Private
Resided in Greene County where he enlisted at
age 20, April 23, 1861, for the war. Wounded at
Malvern Hill, Virginia, July 1, 1862, and at
Gettysburg, Pennsylvania, July 2, 1863. Captured
at Spotsylvania Court House, Virginia, May 12,
1864, and confined at Point Lookout, Maryland.
Paroled for exchange in February, 1865. Admitted
to hospital at Richmond, Virginia, March 21,
1865, and transferred the next day.

SHIRLEY, WILLIAM, Private
Resided in Greene County where he enlisted at
age 23, April 26, 1861, for the war. Present or
accounted for until captured at Spotsylvania
Court House, Virginia, May 12, 1864. Confined
at Point Lookout, Maryland, until transferred to
Elmira, New York, August 10, 1864. Released at
Elmira after taking the Oath of Allegiance on
June 23, 1865.

SKINNER, WILLIAM H., Private
Resided in Greene County where he enlisted at
age 21, April 27, 1861, for the war. Present or
accounted for until captured at Spotsylvania
Court House, Virginia, May 12, 1864. Confined
at Point Lookout, Maryland, until transferred to
Elmira, New York, August 10, 1864. Released at
Elmira after taking the Oath of Allegiance on
June 27, 1865.

SMITH, J. A., Private
Captured at Fort Fisher on December 25, 1864,

and confined at Fort Monroe, Virginia, December
29, 1864.

SMITH, JAMES, Private
Captured at Gettysburg, Pennsylvania, July 5,
1863, and exchanged at City Point, Virginia,
September 27, 1863.

SPEIGHT, ABRAM L., Sergeant
Resided in Greene County where he enlisted at
age 18, April 23, 1861, for the war. Mustered in as
Private and appointed Corporal on July 1, 1862.
Promoted to Sergeant on September 1, 1863.
Transferred to Company H, 9th Regiment N.C.
State Troops (1st Regiment N.C. Cavalry), De-
cember 30, 1863.

SPIVEY, BENJAMIN F., Sergeant
Resided in Greene County where he enlisted at
age 21, April 23, 1861, for the war. Mustered in
as Corporal and promoted to Sergeant on July 1,
1861. Killed on June 26, 1862, at Ellerson's Mill,
Virginia.

SUGG, RICHARD M., Corporal
Resided in Greene County and enlisted in Wayne
County at age 18, May 13, 1862, for the war.
Mustered in as Private and appointed Corporal
on October 30, 1862. Wounded at Chancellorsville,
Virginia, May 3, 1863, and at Winchester, Vir-
ginia, September 19, 1864. Present or accounted
for until paroled at Appomattox Court House,
Virginia, April 9, 1865.

SUGGS, DARBY WILLIAM, Private
Enlisted in Craven County at age 22, May 20,
1861, for the war. Reported on muster roll dated
September 1, 1861, with the remark: "Laundress."

SUGGS, DICK, Private
Enlisted in Greene County at age 28, April 23,
1861, for the war. Reported on muster roll dated
September 1, 1861, with the remark: "Laundress."

SUGGS, JAMES HENRY, Private
Resided in Greene County where he enlisted at
age 20, April 23, 1861, for the war. Present or
accounted for until killed at Sharpsburg, Maryland, September 17, 1862.

TAYLOR, BLOUNT, Private
Resided in Greene County where he enlisted at
age 26, April 27, 1861, for the war. Present or
accounted for until captured at Spotsylvania
Court House, Virginia, May 12, 1864. Confined
at Point Lookout, Maryland, until transferred to
Elmira, New York, July 25, 1864. Died at Elmira
on July 4, 1865, of "variola."

TAYLOR, JAMES H. C., Private
Resided in Greene County where he enlisted at
age 20, April 27, 1861, for the war. Wounded at
Chancellorsville, Virginia, May 2, 1863. Present
or accounted for until captured at Spotsylvania,
Court House, Virginia, May 12, 1864. Confined
at Point Lookout, Maryland, until transferred to
Elmira, New York, August 10, 1864. Released at
Elmira after taking the Oath of Allegiance on
June 12, 1865.

TAYLOR, JAMES W., Private
Resided in Greene County and enlisted at Richmond, Virginia, at age 30, July 17, 1862, for the

war. Captured in Maryland, September 12, 1862, and confined at Fort Delaware, Delaware, until paroled and exchanged at Aiken's Landing, Virginia, November 10, 1862. Present or accounted for until captured at Spotsylvania Court House, Virginia, May 12, 1864. Confined at Point Lookout, Maryland, until transferred to Elmira, New York, August 10, 1864. Released at Elmira after taking the Oath of Allegiance on June 23, 1865.

TAYLOR, JOHN W., Sergeant
Resided in Greene County where he enlisted at age 19, April 23, 1861, for the war. Mustered in as Private and appointed Corporal on January 10, 1863. Wounded at Chancellorsville, Virginia, May 2, 1863, and returned to duty on May 27, 1863. Wounded at Gettysburg, Pennsylvania, July 2, 1863, and captured in hospital at Gettysburg on July 4, 1863. Confined in hospital at Davids Island, New York Harbor, July 17-24, 1863. Promoted to Sergeant on September 1, 1863, while a prisoner of war. Paroled and exchanged at City Point, Virginia, September 16, 1863. Wounded at Cedar Creek, Virginia, October 19, 1864, and reported as absent wounded through December, 1864.

TAYLOR, KINCHEN R., Private
Resided in Greene County where he enlisted at age 18, April 23, 1861, for the war. Transferred to the Field and Staff of this regiment upon appointment as Quartermaster Sergeant on January 15, 1862. Returned to company October 1, 1864, as Private. Transferred back to the Field and Staff of this regiment upon appointment as Sergeant Major on November 1, 1864.

TAYLOR, THEOPHILUS E., Private
Resided in Wayne County where he enlisted at age 28, May 13, 1862, for the war. Present or accounted for until captured at Spotsylvania Court House, Virginia, May 12, 1864. Confined at Point Lookout, Maryland, until transferred to Elmira, New York, August 10, 1864. Released at Elmira after taking the Oath of Allegiance on June 27, 1865.

TAYLOR, WILLIAM ROBERT, Private
Resided in Greene County and enlisted in Craven County at age 20, July 7, 1861, for the war. Died at Gordonsville, Virginia, February 15, 1863, of "pneumonia."

TAYLOR, WILLIAM S., Private
Resided in Greene County where he enlisted at age 23, April 23,. 1861, for the war. Present or accounted for until transferred to Company K, 33rd Regiment N.C. Troops upon appointment as 2nd Lieutenant on February 15, 1862.

TIMBERLAKE, GEORGE W., Sergeant
Resided in Lenoir County and enlisted in Wayne County at age 23, July 8, 1861, for the war. Mustered in as Private and appointed Corporal on October 1, 1862. Promoted to Sergeant on February 20, 1863. Wounded at Gettysburg, Pennsylvania, July 2, 1863, and leg amputated. Captured in hospital at Gettysburg on July 4, 1863. Confined July 17-24, 1863, at DeCamp General Hospital, Davids Island, New York Harbor,

where he died August 8, 1863, of gunshot wound."

TIMBERLAKE, SIDNEY P., Private
Resided in Greene County where he enlisted at age 23, May 7, 1861, for the war. Wounded at Chancellorsville, Virginia, May 2-3, 1863. Present or accounted for until he died in hospital at Orange Court House, Virginia, December 31, 1863.

TURNAGE, JOSEPH, Musician
Resided in Greene County where he enlisted at age 25, April 27, 1861, for the war. Mustered in as Private and appointed Musician, September 1, 1861. Present or accounted for until paroled at Appomattox Court House, Virginia, April 9, 1865.

TUTON, JOHN, Private
Resided in Greene County where he enlisted at age 23, April 23, 1861, for the war. Present or accounted for until paroled at Appomattox Court House, Virginia, April 9, 1865.

TUTON, WALTER J., Private
Resided in Lenoir County and enlisted in Wayne County at age 18, July 8, 1861, for the war. Discharged October 26, 1861, by reason of disability.

TYLER, MOSES, Private
Enlisted in Craven County at age 40, April 23, 1861, for the war. Reported on muster roll dated September 1, 1861, with the remark: "Laundress."

TYSON, GEORGE, Private
Resided in Greene County and enlisted at Richmond, Virginia, at age 21, July 17, 1862, for the war. Captured in Maryland, September 12, 1862, and confined at Fort Delaware, Delaware, until paroled and exchanged at Aiken's Landing, Virginia, November 10, 1862. Killed at Fredericksburg, Virginia, December 13, 1862.

VAUGHAN, JOHN, Private
Enlisted in Wayne County on May 13, 1862, for the war. Present or accounted for until reported on July 14-October 31, 1862, muster roll with the remark: "Died from disease Richmond, date not known."

WAINWRIGHT, JOHN, Private
Resided in Greene County and enlisted in Wayne County at age 25, May 13, 1862, for the war. Wounded at Chancellorsville, Virginia, May 3, 1863. Present or accounted for until captured at Spotsylvania Court House, Virginia, May 12, 1864. Confined at Point Lookout, Maryland, until transferred to Elmira, New York, August 10, 1864. Died at Elmira on November 18, 1864, of "remittent fever."

WALKER, T., Private
Paroled at Raleigh on April 20, 1865.

WARD, JOHN, Private
Born in Greene County where he resided as a farmer and enlisted at age 30, April 27, 1861, for the war. Discharged on December 1, 1861, by reason of disability.

WARD, RICHARD, Private
Resided in Greene County where he enlisted at

age 20, April 27, 1861, for the war. Wounded at Chancellorsville, Virginia, May 2, 1863, and returned to duty on May 27, 1863. Wounded at Gettysburg, Pennsylvania, July 2, 1863, and captured in hospital at Gettysburg on July 4, 1863. Confined at DeCamp General Hospital, Davids Island, New York Harbor, July 17-24, 1863. Paroled and exchanged at City Point, Virginia, October 28, 1863. Reported as absent wounded through August, 1864. Retired to the Invalid Corps on December 1, 1864, and assigned to light duty at Danville, Virginia, January 15, 1865.

WARD, SPIRIOUS, Private
Resided in Greene County where he enlisted at age 22, April 23, 1861, for the war. Present or accounted for until captured at Cedar Creek, Virginia, October 19, 1864. Confined at Point Lookout, Maryland, until released after taking the Oath of Allegiance on June 21, 1865.

WASDON, G., Private
Captured at Chancellorsville, Virginia, May 3, 1863, and paroled at Old Capitol Prison, Washington, D. C., May 19, 1863.

WEASON, WILLIAM, Private
Captured at Winchester, Virginia, September 19, 1864, and confined at Point Lookout, Maryland, September 23, 1864.

WELLS, GEORGE, Private
Resided in Greene County where he enlisted at age 23, April 27, 1861, for the war. Present or accounted for until he died in hospital at Winchester, Virginia, December 21, 1862, of disease.

WEST, HENRY H., Private
Born in Greene County where he resided and enlisted at age 18, April 27, 1861, for the war. Wounded and captured at Sharpsburg, Maryland, September 17, 1862. Confined in hospital at Frederick, Maryland, with a gunshot wound of the right hip. Died in hospital at Frederick on July 6, 1863.

WEST, RICHARD CASWELL, Private
Resided in Greene County where he enlisted at age 19, April 23, 1861, for the war. Captured at Boonsboro, Maryland, September 15, 1862, and confined at Fort Delaware, Delaware, until paroled and exchanged at Aiken's Landing, Virginia, November 10, 1862. Transferred to Company E, 5th Regiment N.C. State Troops upon appointment as 2nd Lieutenant on April 1, 1863.

WEST, RUFUS, Private
Resided in Greene County where he enlisted at age 22, April 27, 1861, for the war. Died in hospital at Richmond, Virginia, December 25, 1862, of "pneumonia."

WEST, WINBORN, Private
Resided in Greene County where he enlisted at age 26, April 27, 1861, for the war. Wounded at Gaines' Mill, Virginia, June 27, 1862. Present or accounted for until killed at Gettysburg, Pennsylvania, July 2, 1863.

WILLIAMS, HOPKIN, Sergeant
Resided in Lenoir County and enlisted in Wayne

County at age 20, July 8, 1861, for the war. Mustered in as Private and appointed Corporal on October 1, 1862. Promoted to Sergeant on January 1, 1863. Wounded at Chancellorsville, Virginia, May 3, 1863, and died of wound on May 6, 1863.

WOOTEN, JAMES M., Private
Resided in Greene County where he enlisted at age 18, April 27, 1861, for the war. Present or accounted for until killed at Chancellorsville, Virginia, May 3, 1863.

YANDLE, W. A., Private
Paroled at Charlotte on May 6, 1865.

COMPANY B

This company was organized in Duplin County and began enlisting on May 31, 1861. It tendered its service to the state late in June, 1861, and was ordered to Garysburg, Northampton County, where it was assigned to this regiment as Company B. After joining the regiment the company functioned as a part of the regiment, and its history for the war period is recorded as a part of the regimental history.

The information contained in the following roster of the company was compiled principally from company muster rolls which covered from the muster-in roll, dated August 31, 1861, through December, 1864. No company muster rolls were found for the period prior to August 31, 1861, or for the period after December, 1864. In addition to the company muster rolls, Roll of Honor records, receipt rolls, and hospital records, supplemented by state pension applications, United Daughters of the Confederacy records, and postwar rosters and histories, all provided useful information.

OFFICERS
CAPTAINS

THRUSTON, STEPHEN D.
Resided in Brunswick County where he enlisted at age 28, May 18, 1861, for the war. Appointed captain to rank from May 16, 1861. Present or accounted for until transferred to the Field and Staff of this regiment upon appointment as Major on July 1, 1862.

BROWN, JOHN BADGER
Resided in New Hanover County where he enlisted on May 23, 1861, for the war. Appointed 1st Lieutenant to rank from May 16, 1861. Wounded at Malvern Hill, Virginia, July 1, 1862, and promoted to Captain to rank from same date. Present or accounted for until wounded at Spotsylvania Court House, Virginia, May 10, 1864. Reported as absent wounded through October, 1864. November-December, 1864, muster roll reports him as present

LIEUTENANTS

COWAN, THOMAS, Jr., 1st Lieutenant
Resided in Brunswick County and appointed 2nd Lieutenant to rank from May 16, 1861. Promoted to 1st Lieutenant on July 1, 1862. Wounded and

captured at Sharpsburg, Maryland, September 17, 1862, and died in hospital at Washington, D.C., October 4, 1862.

GILLESPIE, SHADE G., 2nd Lieutenant
Born in Duplin County where he resided as a farmer and enlisted at age 27, June 12, 1861, for the war. Mustered in as 1st Sergeant and appointed 2nd Lieutenant to rank from July 1, 1862. Killed at Sharpsburg, Maryland, September 17, 1862.

KELLY, THOMAS J., 2nd Lieutenant
Resided in Duplin County and appointed 2nd Lieutenant to rank from September 17, 1862. Wounded at Gettysburg, Pennsylvania, July 2, 1863, and captured in hospital at Gettysburg on July 4, 1863. Died in hospital on July 9, 1863.

MURRAY, WILLIAM H., 2nd Lieutenant
Resided in New Hanover County and appointed 2nd Lieutenant to rank from July 24, 1863. Roll of Honor carries him with the remark: "Captured in the battle of Gettysburg, July 2, 1863."

WARD, GEORGE W., 1st Lieutenant
Resided in Duplin County and appointed 3rd Lieutenant to rank from May 16, 1861. Wounded at Sharpsburg, Maryland, September 17, 1862. Promoted to 2nd Lieutenant on September 21, 1862, and to 1st Lieutenant on October 9, 1862. Wounded at Payne's Farm, Virginia, November 27, 1863, and at Spotsylvania Court House, Virginia, May 12, 1864. Returned to duty on August 27, 1864. Present or accounted for on company muster rolls through December, 1864. Furloughed for 18 days on February 25, 1865.

NONCOMMISSIONED OFFICERS AND PRIVATES

ALPHIN, ALEXANDER, Private
Born in Duplin County where he resided as a farmer and enlisted at age 22, June 4, 1861, for the war. Died in hospital at Goldsboro on May 24, 1862, of dysentery.

ARNETT, WILLIAM, Private
Born in Duplin County where he resided as a farmer and enlisted at age 24, February 15, 1862, for the war. Died in hospital at Lynchburg, Virginia, January 15, 1863, of "phthisis pulmonalis."

AVERHEART, L. F., Private
Furloughed from hospital at Richmond, Virginia, March 9, 1865.

BAISDEN, BRANTLY, Private
Resided in Duplin County where he enlisted at age 30, May 31, 1861, for the war. Discharged April 8, 1862, by reason of disability.

BAKER, G. F., Private
Paroled at Charlotte on May 3, 1865.

BALL, JOHN O., Private
Resided in Duplin County where he enlisted at age 19, June 4, 1861, for the war. Present or accounted for until reported as "missing since Gettysburg fight July 2, 1863." Reported as present on a roll of a detachment of paroled and exchanged prisoners at Camp Lee, near Richmond,

Virginia, dated September 15, 1863. Captured at Spotsylvania Court House, Virginia, May 12, 1864, and confined at Point Lookout, Maryland, until transferred to Elmira, New York, August 10, 1864. Paroled at Elmira and sent to James River, Virginia, for exchange on February 20, 1865. Admitted to hospital at Richmond on March 2, 1865, and transferred to Camp Lee the next day.

BASS, GEORGE W., Private
Resided in Duplin County where he enlisted on January 21, 1862, for the war. Present or accounted for until killed in action at Gettysburg, Pennsylvania, July 2, 1863.

BATCHELOR, JOHN D., Corporal
Resided in Duplin County where he enlisted on July 15, 1862, for the war. Mustered in as Private. Wounded at Sharpsburg, Maryland, September 17, 1862, and appointed Corporal on July 2, 1863. Killed in action at Payne's Farm, Virginia, November 27, 1863.

BISHOP, ISAAC T., Private
Resided in Duplin County where he enlisted at age 19, June 17, 1861, for the war. Wounded in action at Sharpsburg, Maryland, September 17, 1862, and detailed as a guard in hospital at Petersburg, Virginia, March 10, 1863. Ordered back to his company on March 4, 1864. Captured at Spotsylvania Court House, Virginia, May 12, 1864, and confined at Point Lookout, Maryland, until transferred to Elmira, New York, August 8, 1864. Remained at Elmira until released after taking the Oath of Allegiance on June 30, 1865.

BOSTICK, JAMES W., Private
Resided in Duplin County where he enlisted on July 15, 1862, for the war. Wounded at Sharpsburg, Maryland, September 17, 1862, and paroled at Leesburg, Virginia, October 2, 1862. Reported on September-October, 1863, muster roll with the remark: "Died. Missing. Supposed killed at Sharpsburg, Maryland, September 17, 1862."

BOSTICK, JOHN C., Private
Resided in Duplin County where he enlisted on July 15, 1862, for the war. Wounded at Sharpsburg, Maryland, September 17, 1862. Captured at Fredericksburg, Virginia, May 3, 1863. Paroled and exchanged at City Point, Virginia, May 10, 1863. Wounded at Gettysburg, Pennsylvania, July 2, 1863, and captured the next day. Confined on July 7-12, 1863, at Fort Delaware, Delaware, where he died on August 2, 1863, of "chronic diarrhoea."

BOSTICK, JOSEPH W., Private
Resided in Duplin County where he enlisted on July 15, 1862, for the war. Killed at Sharpsburg, Maryland, September 17, 1862.

BOSTICK, SAMUEL T., Private
Born in Duplin County where he resided as a farmer and enlisted at age 27, June 8, 1861, for the war. Detailed as a nurse in hospital at Fredericksburg, Virginia, October 31, 1861. Remained on duty as a nurse until detailed as Ward Master at General Hospital No. 8, Richmond, Virginia, on September 1, 1862. Discharged on November 28, 1862, by reason of "pulmonalis phthisis of several months standing."

BOWEN, DURHAM, Private

Born in Sampson County and resided as a farmer in Duplin County where he enlisted on February 22, 1862, for the war. Detailed for hospital duty on March 10, 1863, and assigned to duty at Raleigh. Discharged on February 3, 1864, by reason of "phthisis pulmonalis."

BOYLES, DAVID, Private

Enlisted on November 15, 1864, for the war.

BRADSHAW, WILLIAM D., Private

Resided in Duplin County where he enlisted at age 28, June 8, 1861, for the war. Wounded at Mechanicsville, Virginia, June 26, 1862. Present or accounted for until captured at Spotsylvania Court House, Virginia, May 12, 1864. Confined at Point Lookout, Maryland, until transferred to Elmira, New York, July 25, 1864. Remained at Elmira until released after taking the Oath of Allegiance on June 10, 1865.

BRINSON, FIELDS W., Private

Resided in Duplin County where he enlisted at age 19, June 17, 1861, for the war. Present or accounted for until captured near Spotsylvania Court House, Virginia, May 12, 1864. Confined at Point Lookout, Maryland, until transferred to Elmira, New York, August 10, 1864. Died at Elmira on March 23, 1865, of "pneumonia."

BRINSON, HILLARY T., Private

Resided in Duplin County where he enlisted at age 18, July 1, 1861, for the war. Wounded at Malvern Hill, Virginia, July 1, 1862. Present or accounted for on company muster rolls through December, 1864. Admitted to hospital at Richmond, Virginia, December 17, 1864, and furloughed for 60 days on January 26, 1865.

BRINSON, JONATHAN, Private

Born in Duplin County where he resided as a farmer and enlisted at age 45, June 28, 1861, for the war. Reported as absent sick from December 25, 1861, through February, 1862, and from July 25, 1862, until discharged on February 20, 1864, by reason of "bronchitis" and "advanced age."

BROWN, DANIEL M., Private

Born in Duplin County where he resided and enlisted on July 15, 1862, for the war. Died in hospital at Richmond, Virginia, June 4, 1863, of "febris typhoides."

BROWN, JACOB, Private

Born in Duplin County where he resided as a farmer and enlisted at-age 51, March 7, 1862, for the war. Discharged May 15, 1862, by reason of "old age, general debility, and an impaired constitution, the result of a severe attack of typhoid fever."

BROWN, JOHN D., Private

Resided in Duplin County where he enlisted at age 21, June 1, 1861, for the war. Mustered in as Musician and reduced to ranks on July 2, 1863. Wounded at Gettysburg, Pennsylvania, July 2, 1863, and leg amputated. Captured in hospital at Gettysburg, July 3-5, 1863, and died in hospital on July 18, 1863.

CARMODY, JOHN W., Private

Paroled at Appomattox Court House, Virginia, April 9, 1865.

CARPENTER, PHILLIP, Private

Enlisted on December 1, 1864, for the war.

CARR, JOHN R., Private

Resided in Duplin County where he enlisted on July 15, 1862, for the war. Killed at Chancellorsville, Virginia, May 3, 1863.

CARROLL, STEPHEN S., 1st Sergeant

Previously served in Company I, 9th Regiment N.C. State Troops (1st Regiment N.C. Cavalry). Enlisted in this company in Duplin County on February 4, 1862, for the war. Mustered in as Private and appointed Sergeant on July 1, 1862. Promoted to 1st Sergeant on November 1, 1862. Killed at Gettysburg, Pennsylvania, July 2, 1863.

CHAMBERS, DAVID FRANCES, Private

Born in Duplin County where he resided as a farmer and enlisted at age 34, July 15, 1862, for the war. Wounded at Sharpsburg, Maryland, September 17, 1862. Reported as absent wounded until detailed in hospital at Lynchburg, Virginia, December 2, 1864. Admitted to hospital at Richmond, Virginia, February 23, 1865, and returned to duty March 24, 1865. Captured at Burkeville, Virginia, April 6, 1865, and confined at Newport News, Virginia, until released after taking the Oath of Allegiance on June 27, 1865.

CHAMBERS, WILLIAM D., Private

Resided in Duplin County where he enlisted at age 18, June 25, 1861, for the war. Present or accounted for until wounded at Payne's Farm, Virginia, November 27, 1863. Returned to duty on March 29, 1864. Captured at Spotsylvania Court House, Virginia, May 12, 1864, and confined at Point Lookout, Maryland, until transferred to Elmira, New York, August 10, 1864. Remained at Elmira until released after taking the Oath of Allegiance on July 19, 1865.

CHESHIRE, R. J., Private

Resided in Bladen County. Captured at Farmville, Virginia, April 6, 1865, and confined at Newport News, Virginia, until released after taking the Oath of Allegiance on June 15, 1865.

COLE, WILLIAM F., Private

Resided in Duplin County where he enlisted on February 15, 1862, for the war. Detailed for hospital duty from March 10, 1863, through August, 1864, and served as a nurse and a guard in several hospitals at Richmond, Virginia, during that time. Paroled at Appomattox Court House, Virginia, April 9, 1865.

COTTLE, JAMES B., Private

Resided in Duplin County where he enlisted at age 23, July 4, 1861, for the war. Present or accounted for until captured at Payne's Farm, Virginia, November 27-28, 1863. Confined at Old Capitol Prison, Washington, D.C., until transferred to Point Lookout, Maryland, February 3, 1864. Paroled at Point Lookout on February 24, 1865, and transferred for exchange to Aiken's Landing, Virginia. Admitted to hospital at Richmond, Virginia, February 26, 1865, and furloughed for 30 days on March 6, 1865.

COTTLE, THOMAS, Private
Resided in Duplin County where he enlisted at age 19, June 5, 1861, for the war. Died in hospital at Petersburg, Virginia, August 5, 1861, of "typhoid fever."

DAIL, ALLEN B., Private
Born in Duplin County where he resided as a farmer and enlisted at age 19, June 13, 1861, for the war. Wounded at Sharpsburg, Maryland, September 17, 1862, and discharged on March 10, 1863, by reason of "a gunshot wound in right arm rendering him unfit for service."

DAVIS, JOHN A., Private
Enlisted on December 1, 1864, for the war.

DAVIS, WILLIAM, Private
Resided in Duplin County where he enlisted at age 23, June 8, 1861, for the war. Wounded at Malvern Hill, Virginia, July 1, 1862, and at Payne's Farm, Virginia, November 27-28, 1863. Captured at Spotsylvania Court House, Virginia, May 12, 1864, and confined at Point Lookout, Maryland, until transferred to Elmira, New York, August 10, 1864. Remained at Elmira until released after taking the Oath of Allegiance on June 27, 1865.

DEAL, ANSON W., Private
Resided in Duplin County where he enlisted on July 15, 1862, for the war. Killed at Sharpsburg, Maryland, September 17, 1862.

DEAL, WILLIAM W., Private
Resided in Duplin County where he enlisted at age 40, June 17, 1861, for the war. Detailed for hospital duty on January 23, 1863, and assigned as a nurse at Petersburg, Virginia. Remained on detail through March 1, 1864. Wounded at Spotsylvania Court House, Virginia, May 10, 1864, and died of wound at Richmond, Virginia, May 26, 1864.

DOBSON, HEZEKIAH, Corporal
Resided in Duplin County where he enlisted on March 1, 1862, for the war. Mustered in as Private and appointed Corporal, July 14-October 31, 1862. Killed in action at Chancellorsville, Virginia, May 3, 1863.

DREW, BRYANT W., Private
Resided in Sampson County and enlisted in Duplin County at age 21, June 10, 1861, for the war. Wounded at Payne's Farm, Virginia, November 27-28, 1863. Present or accounted for on company muster rolls through December, 1864. Paroled at Appomattox Court House, Virginia, April 9, 1865.

DUDLEY, ROBERT, Private
Resided in Duplin County where he enlisted on July 15, 1862, for the war. Admitted to hospital at Richmond, Virginia, July 25, 1862, and furloughed for 20 days on October 26, 1862. Detailed as ambulance driver on January 2, 1863, and died of disease at Guinea Station, Virginia, May 26-27, 1863.

DUFF, BENJAMIN, Private
Born in Duplin County where he resided and enlisted on February 15, 1862, for the war. Died in hospital at Richmond, Virginia, September 14, 1862, of "debility, diptheria."

DUFF, JOHN J., Private
Born in Duplin County where he resided as a farmer and enlisted on February 15, 1862, for the war. Died in hospital at Petersburg, Virginia, June 10, 1862, of "dysentery" and "pneumonia."

EDWARDS, AMOS, Private
Resided in Duplin County where he enlisted on February 15, 1862, for the war. Wounded at Mechanicsville, Virginia, June 26, 1862. Captured at Payne's Farm, Virginia, November 28, 1863, and confined at Old Capitol Prison, Washington, D.C., until transferred to Point Lookout, Maryland, February 3, 1864. Released at Point Lookout after taking the Oath of Allegiance and joining the U.S. service on June 7, 1864. Assigned to Company H, 1st Regiment U.S. Volunteer Infantry.

EDWARDS, HENRY, Private
Resided in Duplin County where he enlisted at age 25, May 31, 1861, for the war. Present or accounted for until detailed with 2nd Corps Supply Train on April 1, 1864. Absent on detail through December, 1864. Captured at Waynesboro, Virginia, March 2, 1865, and confined at Fort Delaware, Delaware, until released after taking the Oath of Allegiance on June 19, 1865.

EDWARDS, HEZEKIAH, Private
Born in Duplin County where he resided as a farmer and enlisted at age 38, June 4, 1861, for the war. Died at Camp Howe, Virginia, December 21, 1861, of "typhoid pneumonia."

EZZELL, LOVETT J., Private
Born in Duplin County where he resided as a farmer and enlisted at age 35, June 17, 1861, for the war. Detailed for hospital duty on March 10, 1863, and remained on detail until discharged on April 20, 1864, by reason of "chronic enlargement of right leg."

FREDERICK, ALFRED E., Sergeant
Resided in Duplin County where he enlisted on February 15, 1862, for the war. Mustered in as Private. Wounded at Mechanicsville, Virginia, June 26, 1862. Appointed Corporal on July 2, 1863, and wounded at Gettysburg, Pennsylvania, July 2-3, 1863. Promoted to Sergeant on February 1, 1864. Captured near Spotsylvania Court House, Virginia, May 12, 1864, and confined at Point Lookout, Maryland, until transferred to Elmira, New York, August 10, 1864. Died at Elmira on December 4, 1864, of "pneumonia."

FREDERICK, FELIX R., Sergeant
Resided in Duplin County where he enlisted at age 25, June 17, 1861, for the war. Mustered in as Sergeant. Present or accounted for until killed in action at Winchester, Virginia, June 15, 1863.

FREDERICK, JOHN W., Private
Resided in Duplin County where he enlisted at age 23, June 17, 1861, for the war. Died at Camp Howe, Virginia, November 28, 1861, of "inflammation of brain."

GAVIN, WILLIAM C., Private
Resided in Duplin County where he enlisted on

April 7, 1862, for the war. Wounded September 17, 1862. Wounded at Payne's Farm, Virginia, November 27, 1863, and reported on company muster rolls as absent wounded until detailed in the quartermaster department at Magnolia, North Carolina, September 17, 1864. Retired to the Invalid Corps, December 15, 1864.

GORE, MAJOR W., Private
Resided in Duplin County where he enlisted on July 15, 1862, for the war. Admitted to hospital on September 30, 1862, at Richmond, Virginia, where he died on December 5, 1862, of "pneumonia."

GRADY, BRYANT F., Private
Born in Duplin County where he resided as a farmer and enlisted at age 19, February 15, 1862, for the war. Died in hospital at Richmond, Virginia, August 15, 1862, of wounds received at Cold Harbor, Virginia.

GRADY, NEEDHAM, Private
Resided in Duplin County where he enlisted on February 15, 1862, for the war. Present or accounted for until wounded and captured at Gettysburg, Pennsylvania, July 2-3, 1863. Confined at Fort Delaware, Delaware, until transferred to Point Lookout, Maryland, October 18, 1863. Died at Point Lookout, December 27, 1863, of "typhoid pneumonia."

GREENE, JAMES M., Private
Name appears on a receipt roll for clothing issued November 18, 1864, with the remark: "On way to command." Paroled at Appomattox Court House, Virginia, April 9, 1865.

GRIFFEN, DANIEL J., Private
Resided in Lenoir County where he enlisted at age 40, June 12, 1861, for the war. Wounded at Sharpsburg, Maryland, September 17, 1862, and died of his wound on October 1, 1862, at Frederick, Maryland.

GUY, OWEN, Private
Resided in Duplin County where he enlisted on July 15, 1862, for the war. Died in hospital at Winchester, Virginia, October 30, 1862, of "disease."

HALL, EDWARD, Private
Resided in Duplin County where he enlisted at age 21, June 17, 1861, for the war. Present or accounted for until killed in battle at Payne's Farm, Virginia, November 27, 1863.

HALL, WILLIAM, Private
Resided in Duplin County where he enlisted on March 7, 1862, for the war. Present or accounted for until captured at Spotsylvania Court House, Virginia, May 12, 1864. Confined at Point Lookout, Maryland, until transferred to Elmira, New York, August 10, 1864. Released at Elmira after taking the Oath of Allegiance on June 27, 1865.

HANCHEY, JAMES W., Private
Resided in Duplin County where he enlisted on January 21, 1862, for the war. Present or accounted for until captured at Spotsylvania Court House, Virginia, May 12, 1864. Confined at Point Lookout, Maryland, until transferred to Elmira,

New York, August 10, 1864. Died at Elmira, March 20, 1865, of "variola."

HANCHEY, JOHN OBED, Private
Born in Duplin County where he resided and enlisted on January 21, 1862, for the war. Died in hospital at Richmond, Virginia, September 9, 1862, of "typhoid fever."

HARVEL, WILLIAM W., Corporal
Born in Duplin County where he resided as a farmer and enlisted at age 24, June 10, 1861, for the war. Mustered in as Corporal. Killed in battle near Richmond, Virginia, June 26, 1862.

HENDERSON, RILEY, Private
Born in Duplin County where he resided and enlisted on July 15, 1862, for the war. Died in hospital at Lynchburg, Virginia, December 12, 1862, of "diarrhoea chronic."

HOLLAND, JOHN LEWIS, Sergeant
Resided in Duplin County where he enlisted at age 25, June 10, 1861, for the war. Mustered in as Private and appointed Sergeant, May 15, 1863. Appointed Commissary Sergeant and transferred to the Field and Staff of this regiment on November 20, 1863.

HOUSTON, ROBERT B., 1st Sergeant
Resided in Duplin County where he enlisted on February 3, 1862, for the war. Mustered in as a Private and appointed Sergeant on February 1, 1863. Promoted to 1st Sergeant on July 2, 1863. Appointed 2nd Lieutenant and transferred to Company D of this regiment on February 1, 1864.

HOWARD, JAMES N., Private
Born in Duplin County where he resided as a farmer and enlisted on February 7, 1862, for the war. Discharged at age 33, August 18, 1863, by reason of disability.

HUNTER, CHARLES R., Private
Transferred from Company A, 38th Regiment N.C. Troops in exchange for Benjamin Franklin Pearsall on March 13, 1863. Wounded May 3, 1863, and reported as absent wounded through November, 1863. Again wounded on May 10, 1864, at Spotsylvania Court House, Virginia. Returned to company November-December, 1864. Deserted on March 18, 1865, and took the Oath of Allegiance on the same day.

HUNTER, HOSEA W., Private
Resided in Duplin County where he enlisted at age 18, June 17, 1861, for the war. Present or accounted for until captured at Spotsylvania Court House, Virginia, May 12, 1864. Confined at Point Lookout, Maryland, until released after taking the Oath of Allegiance and joining the U.S. service on June 6, 1864. Assigned to Company K, 1st Regiment U.S. Volunteer Infantry.

HUNTER, JOHN E., Private
Resided in Duplin County where he enlisted on March 7, 1862, for the war. Present or accounted for until killed at Winchester, Virginia, June 15, 1863.

INGLE, THADEUS, Private
Paroled at Greensboro on May 23, 1865.

JAMES, EVERETT, Private
Resided in Duplin County where he enlisted on

July 15, 1862, for the war. Mortally wounded at Sharpsburg, Maryland, September 17, 1862.

JAMES, HINTON, Private
Resided in Duplin County where he enlisted on July 15, 1862, for the war. Died in Duplin County on June 11, 1863, of disease.

JAMES, JOSHUA, Private
Resided in Duplin County where he enlisted on July 15, 1862, for the war. Died in hospital at Richmond, Virginia, April 19, 1863, of "typhoid fever."

JAMES, W. A., Private
Captured at Gettysburg, Pennsylvania, July 1-4, 1863, and confined at DeCamp General Hospital, Davids Island, New York Harbor, July 17-24, 1863.

JOHNSON, AMOS J., Sergeant
Resided in Duplin County where he enlisted at age 20, June 17, 1861, for the war. Mustered in as Private and appointed Corporal on September 1, 1861. Promoted to Sergeant on June 15, 1863. Captured at Spotsylvania Court House, Virginia, May 12, 1864, and confined at Point Lookout, Maryland, until transferred to Elmira, New York, August 10, 1864. Remained at Elmira until released after taking the Oath of Allegiance on June 27, 1865.

JOHNSON, GEORGE A., Private
Resided in Duplin County where he enlisted at age 30, June 8, 1861, for the war. Deserted on May 1, 1862. Roll of Honor states that he was "drummed out of the company."

JOHNSON, LUTHER F., Private
Born in Sampson County and resided as a farmer in Duplin County where he enlisted at age 25, June 10, 1861, for the war. Mustered in as Sergeant and reduced to ranks on September 1, 1861. Discharged on April 10, 1862, by reason of "chronic hepatitis producing general debility."

JOHNSON, MILTON H., Private
Resided in Duplin County where he enlisted at age 31, June 10, 1861, for the war. Wounded at Malvern Hill, Virginia, July 1, 1862, and died of wound on August 17, 1862.

JOHNSON, ROBERT M., Private
Resided in Duplin County where he enlisted on July 15, 1862, for the war. Reported as absent without leave after January 1, 1863.

JONES, JOHN A., Corporal
Resided in Duplin County where he enlisted at age 20, June 17, 1861, for the war. Mustered in as Private and appointed Corporal on May 5, 1863. Killed at Gettysburg, Pennsylvania, July 2, 1863.

JONES, MATTHEW, Private
Resided in Duplin County where he enlisted at age 18, June 17, 1861, for the war. Wounded at Sharpsburg, Maryland, September 17, 1862. Wounded and captured at Gettysburg, Pennsylvania, July 3, 1863, and confined at Point Lookout, Maryland, where he died on January 4, 1864.

JONES, NATHAN J., Private
Born in Duplin County where he resided as a farmer and enlisted at age 26, June 5, 1861, for the war. Died in hospital at Lynchburg, Virginia, January 30, 1863, of "pleuritis."

JONES, THOMAS G., 1st Sergeant
Resided in Duplin County where he enlisted at age 23, June 8, 1861, for the war. Mustered in as Corporal and promoted to Sergeant on July 2, 1863. Promoted to 1st Sergeant on April 15, 1864. Present or accounted for on company muster rolls through December, 1864. Paroled at Appomattox Court House, Virginia, April 9, 1865.

KELLY, DANIEL M., Private
Born in Moore County where he resided and enlisted on July 15, 1862, for the war. Wounded and captured at Sharpsburg, Maryland, September 17, 1862. Admitted to U.S.A. General Hospital, Frederick, Maryland, October 3, 1862, with "fractura thigh" and died at that hospital June 19, 1863.

KENNEDY, JOHN W., Musician
Resided in Duplin County where he enlisted March 7, 1862, for the war. Mustered in as Private. Appointed Musician on April 17, 1864. Present or accounted for through December, 1864.

LANIER, AMOS, Private
Resided in Duplin County where he enlisted on July 15, 1862, for the war. Mustered in as Private and appointed Corporal on April 5, 1864. Reduced to ranks November-December, 1864. Deserted and took the Oath of Allegiance at Bermuda Hundred, Virginia, March 18, 1865, and was sent to the Provost Marshal General, Washington, D.C. Received in Washington, March 24, 1865, and was furnished transportation to Wilmington, N.C.

LANIER, BLANEY W., Private
Resided in Duplin County where he enlisted on February 15, 1862, for the war. Present or accounted for until wounded in battle at Wilderness, Virginia, May 5, 1864. Admitted to hospital at Richmond, Virginia, May 7, 1864, with "v.s. right foot." Reported as absent wounded until retired to the Invalid Corps on November 30, 1864, and assigned to duty with Surgeon Hines at Raleigh.

LANIER, ELI, Private
Resided in Duplin County where he enlisted on July 15, 1862, for the war. Wounded at Winchester, Virginia, June 15, 1863, and reported as absent wounded through December, 1863. Captured near Spotsylvania Court House, Virginia, May 10-12, 1864. Confined at Point Lookout, Maryland, until transferred to Elmira, New York, July 8, 1864. Released at Elmira after taking the Oath of Allegiance on May 29, 1865.

LANIER, HOSEA G., Corporal
Resided in Duplin County where he enlisted at age 18, June 17, 1861, for the war. Mustered in as Private. Present or accounted for until wounded September 17, 1862. Appointed Corporal, February 1, 1864. Captured near Spotsylvania Court House, Virginia, May 12, 1864, and confined at Point Lookout, Maryland. Transferred to Elmira, New York, August 10, 1864, and was released after taking the Oath of Allegiance on June 23, 1865.

LANIER, JOHN W., Private
Resided in Duplin County where he enlisted on July 15, 1862, for the war. Reported as absent

sick from October 20, 1862, until November-December, 1864, when company muster roll states that he was present. Deserted and took the Oath of Allegiance at Bermuda Hundred, Virginia, March 19, 1865. Sent to the Provost Marshal General, Washington, D. C. Received in Washington, March 24, 1865, and was furnished transportation to Wilmington, N.C.

LANIER, LEWIS, Private
Resided in Sampson County where he enlisted at age 32, June 17, 1861, for the war. Present or accounted for until captured near Spotsylvania Court House, Virginia, May 18, 1864. Confined at Point Lookout, Maryland, until transferred to Elmira, New York, August 10, 1864. Died at Elmira, January 13, 1865, of "variola."

McDONALD, JOHN, Private
Resided in Moore County where he enlisted on July 20, 1862, for the war. Wounded and captured at Sharpsburg, Maryland, September 17, 1862. Admitted to U.S.A. General Hospital, Frederick, Maryland, October 22, 1862, with "fractura left leg" and remained there until paroled and sent to City Point, Virginia, for exchange on February 15, 1863. Admitted to hospital at Petersburg, Virginia, February 18, 1863, and was furloughed for 60 days March 1, 1863. Present or accounted for as absent sick until detailed April 28, 1864. Reported as absent detailed at Staunton and at Gordonsville, Virginia, from that date through December, 1864. Appears on a roll of enlisted men of different commands belonging to the Army of Northern Virginia who were not present with their commands for parole and were afterwards taken by Captain F. C. Cox, A.A.G. of the Cavalry Corps of the Army of Northern Virginia, to be paroled according to the terms of the surrender at Appomattox Court House, Virginia, April 9, 1865.

McGOWAN, CHARLES B., Private
Resided in Duplin County where he enlisted on July 15, 1862, for the war. Present or accounted for until captured near Spotsylvania Court House, Virginia, May 12, 1864. Confined at Point Lookout, Maryland, and transferred to Elmira, New York, August 10, 1864. Paroled on October 11, 1864, and transferred for exchange. Died at Fort Monroe, Virginia, October 29-31, 1864.

McLAUCHLIN, NEIL L., Private
Resided in Moore County where he enlisted on July 15, 1862, for the war. Captured at Spotsylvania Court House, Virginia, May 12, 1864, and confined at Point Lookout, Maryland, until transferred to Elmira, New York, August 14, 1864. Died at Elmira on August 24, 1864, of "chronic diarrhoea."

McLAUCHLIN, ROBERT A., Private
Resided in Moore County where he enlisted on July 15, 1862, for the war. Wounded at Gettysburg, Pennsylvania, July 2, 1863, and captured in hospital at Gettysburg, July 3-4, 1863. Confined at DeCamp General Hospital, Davids Island, New York Harbor, July 18, 1863. Paroled and sent to City Point, Virginia, for exchange on August 24, 1863. Received in exchange on August 28, 1863.

Reported as absent "paroled prisoner" from date of exchange through March 1, 1864. Company muster rolls report him as absent without leave after March 1, 1864.

MASHBURN, HENRY R., Private
Resided in Duplin County where he enlisted at age 20, June 17, 1861, for the war. Admitted to hospital at Richmond, Virginia, September 6, 1862, with a gunshot wound and furloughed for 30 days on October 10, 1862. Present or accounted for until wounded at Wilderness, Virginia, May 5, 1864. Company muster rolls report him as absent wounded through December, 1864. Roll of Honor reports him with the remark: "Wounded, right arm amputated. Retired October 19, 1864."

MASHBURN, HOSEA Q., Private
Resided in Duplin County where he enlisted on March 23, 1862, for the war. Detailed for hospital duty on March 10, 1863, and assigned to hospital at Raleigh. Remained on detail through December, 1863, when he returned to company. Captured near Spotsylvania Court House, Virginia, May 12, 1864, and confined at Point Lookout, Maryland, until transferred to Elmira, New York, August 14, 1864. Paroled at Elmira on October 11, 1864, and exchanged at Venus Point, Savannah River, Georgia, November 15, 1864. Captured at Petersburg, Virginia, April 3, 1865, and confined at Hart's Island, New York Harbor, until released after taking the Oath of Allegiance on June 17, 1865.

MATHIS, DANIEL J., Private
Resided in Duplin County where he enlisted at age 25, June 17, 1861, for the war. Wounded at Gettysburg, Pennsylvania, July 2, 1863, and captured in hospital at Gettysburg, July 3-4, 1863. Confined in hospital at Chester, Pennsylvania, until paroled for exchange on August 17, 1863. Received in exchange at City Point, Virginia, August 20, 1863. Died at Orange Court House, Virginia, April 18, 1864, of disease.

MATHIS, JOSEPH L., Private
Born in Sampson County and resided as a blacksmith in Duplin County where he enlisted on February 5, 1862, for the war. Discharged on August 15, 1863, by reason of "rheumatism."

MERCER, JOSHUA D., Private
Born in Duplin County where he resided and enlisted on January 21, 1862, for the war. Died at home in Duplin County on September 20, 1862, of "dysentery."

MEREADDY, JOHN T., Private
Born in Duplin County where he resided as a farmer and enlisted on February 15, 1862, for the war. Died at Fredericksburg, Virginia, April 1, 1862, of "pneumonia."

MIDDLETON, ISAAC J., Private
Resided in Duplin County where he enlisted on February 13, 1862, for the war. Mortally wounded at Sharpsburg, Maryland, September 17, 1862.

MITCHELL, WILLIAM J., Private
Born in Duplin County where he resided as a farmer and enlisted at age 23, June 4, 1861, for the war. Died at Camp Howe, Virginia, December 10, 1861, of "typhoid pneumonia."

MONROE, ARCHIBALD B., Private
Born in Moore County where he resided and enlisted on July 15, 1862, for the war. Died in hospital at Richmond, Virginia, September 25, 1862, of "typhoid fever."

MOORE, ARTHUR, Private
Resided in Greene County. Admitted to hospital at Richmond, Virginia, March 21, 1865, with "variola." Captured in hospital at Richmond on April 3, 1865, and confined at Newport News, Virginia, until released after taking the Oath of Allegiance on June 30, 1865.

MURRAY, DANIEL H., Private
Resided in Duplin County where he enlisted on July 15, 1862, for the war. Admitted to hospital at Richmond, Virginia, September 17, 1862, with "rheumatism" and discharged from the service on November 28, 1862.

NETHERCUTT, LOFTIN, Private
Resided in Duplin County where he enlisted at age 23, May 31, 1861, for the war. Wounded at Malvern Hill, Virginia, July 1, 1862. Captured at Payne's Farm, Virginia, November 28, 1863, and confined at Old Capitol Prison, Washington, D.C. Died in hospital at Washington on February 10, 1864, of "phthisis pulmonalis."

NORRIS, DAVID, Private
Paroled at Greensboro on May 19, 1865.

OUTLAW, WILLIAM H., Private
Resided in Duplin County where he enlisted on February 15, 1862, for the war. Died in hospital at Goldsboro on May 2, 1862, of "typhoid fever."

PAGE, WILLIAM, Private
Resided in Duplin County where he enlisted on March 7, 1862, for the war. Present or accounted for until captured near Spotsylvania Court House, Virginia, May 12, 1864. Confined at Point Lookout, Maryland, until transferred to Elmira, New York, August 10, 1864. Remained at Elmira until released after taking the Oath of Allegiance on June 23, 1865.

PARKER, JONATHAN, Private
Resided in Duplin County where he enlisted at age 20, June 4, 1861, for the war. Wounded at Spotsylvania Court House, Virginia, May 10, 1864, and reported as absent wounded through December, 1864. Returned to duty from hospital at Richmond, Virginia, February 1, 1865.

PARKER, ROBERT A., Private
Born in Sampson County where he resided and enlisted at age 24, June 17, 1861, for the war. Killed in action at Malvern Hill, Virginia, July 1, 1862.

PEARSALL, BENJAMIN FRANKLIN, Private
Resided in Duplin County where he enlisted on July 15, 1862, for the war. Transferred to Company A, 38th Regiment N.C. Troops on March 13, 1863, in exchange for Charles R. Hunter.

PERNELL, MILES, Private
Resided in Duplin County where he enlisted on February 3, 1862, for the war. Present or accounted for until paroled at Appomattox Court House, Virginia, April 9, 1865.

PETERSON, NATHAN, Private
Born in Sampson County where he resided prior to enlisting in Duplin County on February 4, 1862, for the war. Died at Winchester, Virginia, October 31, 1862, of disease.

PICKETT, JOHN Q., Private
Born in Duplin County where he resided as a farmer and enlisted at age 21, May 31, 1861, for the war. Wounded at Sharpsburg, Maryland, September 17, 1862, and discharged on January 20, 1863, by reason of wound.

PICKETT, WILLIAM H., Private
Resided in Duplin County where he enlisted at age 23, June 4, 1861, for the war. Mustered in as Sergeant. Wounded at Mechanicsville, Virginia, June 26, 1862. Reduced to ranks on May 15, 1863. Wounded at Gettysburg, Pennsylvania, July 2, 1863, and captured in hospital at Gettysburg, July 3-4, 1863. Confined at DeCamp General Hospital, Davids Island, New York Harbor, until paroled and exchanged at City Point, Virginia, September 8, 1863. Captured near Spotsylvania Court House, Virginia, May 12, 1864, and confined at Point Lookout, Maryland, until transferred to Elmira, New York, August 10, 1864. Remained at Elmira until released after taking the Oath of Allegiance on June 21, 1865.

RAY, ARCHIBALD B., Private
Born in Moore County where he resided and enlisted on July 15, 1862, for the war. Died in hospital at Richmond, Virginia, September 17, 1862, of "dysentery chronic."

REEVES, LAOMI, Private
Born in Duplin County where he resided as a farmer and enlisted on July 15, 1862, for the war. Wounded and captured at Sharpsburg, Maryland, September 17, 1862. Died in hospital at Frederick, Maryland, November 6, 1862.

REGISTER, LEWIS S., Private
Resided in Duplin County where he enlisted on February 15, 1862, for the war. Wounded at Mechanicsville, Virginia, June 26, 1862. Present or accounted for until wounded at Wilderness, Virginia, May 6, 1864. Present or accounted for on company muster rolls through December, 1864.

RIVENBARK, WILLIAM T., Private
Resided as a farmer in Duplin County where he enlisted on February 15, 1862, for the war. Present or accounted for until wounded at Spotsylvania Court House, Virginia, May 8, 1864. Reported as absent wounded from that date through December, 1864.

ROBINSON, OLIVER P., Private
Resided in Duplin County where he enlisted on July 15, 1862, for the war. Present or accounted for until captured at Payne's Farm, Virginia, November 28, 1863. Confined at Old Capitol Prison, Washington, D. C., until transferred to Fort Delaware, Delaware, June 15, 1864. Paroled and sent to Aiken's Landing, Virginia, for exchange on September 30, 1864. Furloughed from hospital at Richmond, Virginia, for 60 days on October 11, 1864. Captured at Farmville, Virginia, April 6, 1865, and confined at Newport

News, Virginia, until released after taking the Oath of Allegiance on June 15, 1865.

ROGERS, DAVID J., Private

Resided in Duplin County where he enlisted on January 21, 1862, for the war. Wounded at Chancellorsville, Virginia, May 3, 1863, and at Snicker's Gap, Virginia, July 18, 1864. Present or accounted for until paroled at Appomattox Court House, Virginia, April 9, 1865.

ROGERS, WILLIAM P. D., Private

Born in Duplin County where he resided as a farmer and enlisted at age 22, July 25, 1861, for the war. Discharged on April 10, 1862, by reason of "chronic gastritis and rheumatism."

SANDERSON, CALVIN, Private

Resided in Duplin County where he enlisted at age 28, June 25, 1861, for the war. Wounded at Gettysburg, Pennsylvania, July 2, 1863, and captured at Waterloo, Pennsylvania, July 5, 1863. Confined at Point Lookout, Maryland, where he died on December 28, 1864, of "acute diarrhoea."

SANDLIN, HENRY CURTIS, Corporal

Resided in Duplin County where he enlisted at age 18, June 4, 1861, for the war. Mustered in as Corporal. Mortally wounded at Chancellorsville, Virginia, May 3, 1863, and died two days later.

SHALER, ISHAM, Private

Born in Duplin County where he resided as a farmer and enlisted at age 19, June 4, 1861, for the war. Discharged on October 22, 1861, by reason of "congenital hernia."

SHAW, JOHN H., Musician

Resided in Duplin County where he enlisted on January 21, 1862, for the war. Mustered in as Musician. Present or accounted for until paroled at Appomattox Court House, Virginia, April 9, 1865.

SHAW, JOSEPH A., Private

Resided in Duplin County where he enlisted at age 19, June 22, 1861, for the war. Detailed as shoemaker at Richmond, Virginia, November 23, 1862. Company muster rolls report him as absent on detail through December, 1864. Captured at Burkeville, Virginia, April 6, 1865, and confined at Newport News, Virginia, until released after taking the Oath of Allegiance on June 20, 1865.

SHAW, LEWIS J., Corporal

Resided in Duplin County where he enlisted on February 8, 1862, for the war. Mustered in as Private and appointed Corporal on May 3, 1863. Wounded at Chancellorsville, Virginia, May 3, 1863. Company muster rolls report him as absent wounded through December, 1864. Captured at Harper's Farm, Virginia, April 6, 1865, and confined at Point Lookout, Maryland, until released after taking the Oath of Allegiance on June 20, 1865.

SHERN, JOHN, Private

Detailed on extra duty at Kelly's Ford, Virginia, August 1-September 30, 1863.

SMITH, DANIEL, Private

Born in New Hanover County where he resided prior to enlisting in Northampton County at age 18, July 20, 1861, for the war. Wounded at Mechanicsville, Virginia, June 26, 1862. Died in hospital at Wilmington on October 10, 1862, of "yellow fever."

SMITH, STEPHEN, Private

Resided in New Hanover County and enlisted in Northampton County at age 36, July 20, 1861, for the war. Captured near Yanceyville, Virginia, May 3, 1863, and took the Oath of Allegiance at Washington, D.C., June 24, 1863.

SOUTHERLAND, COOPER, Private

Resided in Duplin County where he enlisted at age 20, June 8, 1861, for the war. Killed at Malvern Hill, Virginia, July 1, 1862.

STALLINGS, SHADE W., Private

Born in Duplin County where he resided as a farmer and enlisted at age 19, June 8, 1861, for the war. Wounded at Malvern Hill, Virginia, July 1, 1862, and reported as absent wounded until detailed for hospital duty on January 20, 1863. Assigned as a nurse in hospital of 2nd Corps, June 20, 1863. Company muster rolls report him as absent on detail through December, 1864. Captured at Farmville, Virginia, April 6, 1865, and confined at Point Lookout, Maryland, until released after taking the Oath of Allegiance on June 20, 1865.

STEWART, FORNEY, Private

Born in Duplin County where he resided and enlisted on March 25, 1862, for the war. Died in hospital at Winchester, Virginia, October 14, 1862, of "dysentery."

STEWART, PATRICK, Private

Resided in Duplin County where he enlisted at age 15, February 21, 1862, for the war. Discharged September 25, 1862, by reason of "general delicacy of health and tender years."

STRICKLAND, JOHN SAMUEL, Private

Resided in Duplin County where he enlisted at age 22, June 5, 1861, for the war. Present or accounted for until wounded and captured at Cedar Creek, Virginia, October 19, 1864. Confined at Point Lookout, Maryland, until paroled and sent for exchange to Venus Point, Savannah River, Georgia, October 30, 1864. Received in exchange on November 15, 1864. Paroled at Appomattox Court House, Virginia, April 9, 1865.

SULLIVAN, BRYANT H., Private

Born in Duplin County where he resided as a farmer and enlisted at age 22, June 18, 1861, for the war. Wounded at Sharpsburg, Maryland, September 17, 1862. Discharged on January 20, 1863, by reason of gunshot wound.

SUMNER, ASA, Private

Resided in Duplin County where he enlisted at age 21, June 17, 1861, for the war. Wounded at Chancellorsville, Virginia, May 2-3, 1863, and left leg amputated. Company muster rolls report him as absent wounded through December, 1864.

SUMNER, MARTIN, Private

Resided in Duplin County where he enlisted at age 26, June 17, 1861, for the war. Wounded at Payne's Farm, Virginia, November 27-28, 1863. Captured near Spotsylvania Court House, Virginia, May 12, 1864, and confined at Point Lookout, Maryland, until transferred to Elmira, New York, August 10, 1864. Remained at Elmira until released after taking the Oath of Allegiance on July 7, 1865.

SUMNER, ROBERT B., Private

Resided in Duplin County where he enlisted at age 23, June 17, 1861, for the war. Mustered in as Corporal and reduced to ranks September-October, 1861, "for drunkeness." Wounded at Sharpsburg, Maryland, September 17, 1862, and captured and paroled by September 30, 1862. Company muster rolls report him as absent without leave through December, 1864. Detailed on January 19, 1865.

SUTTON, ELIAS, Private

Born in Sampson County and resided in Duplin County where he enlisted on February 7, 1862, for the war. Wounded and captured at Sharpsburg, Maryland, September 17, 1862. Died at Frederick, Maryland, October 1, 1862.

TEACHEY, DANIEL WILLIAM, Private

Resided in Duplin County where he enlisted on July 15, 1862, for the war. Mortally wounded at Sharpsburg, Maryland, September 17, 1862.

THIGPEN, AMOS, Private

Born in Duplin County where he resided as a farmer and enlisted on March 7, 1862, for the war. Wounded and captured at Sharpsburg, Maryland, September 17, 1862. Died at Frederick, Maryland, November 19, 1862.

THIGPEN, BRYANT, Private

Born in Duplin County where he resided as a farmer and enlisted on February 15, 1862, for the war. Discharged on April 15, 1862, by reason of "rheumatism and general physical inertia."

THIGPEN, BYTHEL, Private

Resided in Duplin County where he enlisted at age 26, June 11, 1861, for the war. Wounded at Malvern Hill, Virginia, July 1, 1862. Captured near Spotsylvania Court House, Virginia, May 12, 1864, and confined at Point Lookout, Maryland, until transferred to Elmira, New York, August 10, 1864. Died at Elmira on April 19, 1865, of "general debility."

THIGPEN, JESSE J., Private

Resided in Duplin County where he enlisted on March 7, 1862, for the war. Mortally wounded at Sharpsburg, Maryland, September 17, 1862.

THIGPEN, KINSEY W., Private

Resided in Duplin County where he enlisted at age 25, June 11, 1861, for the war. Died near Richmond, Virginia, March 7, 1862, of "typhoid pneumonia."

THOMPSON, JOHN J., Private

Born in Duplin County where he resided as a farmer and enlisted on June 10, 1862, for the war. Wounded at Chancellorsville, Virginia, May 3, 1863, and discharged on March 17, 1864, by reason of "an old gunshot fracture of left radius."

THOMPSON, WILLIAM H., Private

Paroled at Greensboro on May 19, 1865.

TUCKER, JOHN W., Private

Born in Duplin County where he resided as a

farmer and enlisted on March 7, 1862, for the war. Wounded at Malvern Hill, Virginia, July 1, 1862, and discharged on January 20, 1863, by reason of wound.

TURNER, H. W., Private

Paroled at Salisbury on May 23, 1865.

VAUGHN, JOHN, Private

Admitted to Federal hospital on May 18, 1865, with "pneumonia" and transferred to a second hospital on May 20, 1865.

WARNER, LEWIS, Private

Resided in Moore County where he enlisted on July 15, 1862, for the war. Company muster rolls report him as absent sick from July 25, 1862, until he was "dropped" in October, 1864.

WHALEY, JOHN J., Sergeant

Resided in Duplin County where he enlisted at age 26, June 11, 1861, for the war. Mustered in as Sergeant. Wounded at Sharpsburg, Maryland, September 17, 1862. Captured and paroled near Sharpsburg, September 17-27, 1862. Captured a second time near Sharpsburg on September 28, 1862, and confined at Fort McHenry, Maryland, until paroled for exchange on October 13, 1862. Declared exchanged at Aiken's Landing, Virginia, November 10, 1862. Present or accounted for until transferred to Company I, 9th Regiment N.C. State Troops (1st Regiment N.C. Cavalry), July 13, 1864.

WHITE, J. C., Private

Paroled at Greensboro on May 5, 1865.

WHITEFIELD, THOMAS J., Sergeant

Resided in Duplin County where he enlisted on February 10, 1862, for the war. Mustered in as Private and appointed Corporal on June 15, 1863. Promoted to Sergeant on April 15, 1864. Captured near Spotsylvania Court House, Virginia, May 12, 1864, and confined at Point Lookout, Maryland, until transferred to Elmira, New York, August 10, 1864. Paroled at Elmira on March 14, 1865, and sent to James River, Virginia, for exchange. Received in exchange at Boulware's Wharf, James River, March 18-21, 1865.

WHITFIELD, NEEDHAM H., Private

Resided in Duplin County where he enlisted on February 10, 1862, for the war. Captured at Gettysburg, Pennsylvania, July 2-4, 1863, and confined at DeCamp General Hospital, Davids Island, New York Harbor, until paroled and exchanged at City Point, Virginia, September 8, 1863. Company muster rolls report him as absent sick from September, 1863, through December, 1864.

WICKLAND, J., Private

Paroled at Goldsboro in 1865.

WILEY, LEWIS M., Private

Born in Duplin County where he resided as a farmer and enlisted at age 29, June 10, 1861, for the war. Wounded at Malvern Hill, Virginia, July 1, 1862. Discharged on March 28, 1863, by reason of "gunshot wound of the right hip joint."

WILKINS, ISAAC DAVID, Private

Resided in Duplin County where he enlisted at age 24, June 11, 1861, for the war. Wounded at

Sharpsburg, Maryland, September 17, 1862. Detailed for hospital duty on March 16, 1863, and assigned to hospital at Petersburg, Virginia. Returned to company in September, 1864, and remained with company until retired to the Invalid Corps on January 19, 1865.

WILLIAMS, JACOB, Sergeant
Born in Duplin County where he resided as a farmer and enlisted at age 29, July 1, 1861, for the war. Mustered in as Private and appointed Sergeant on September 1, 1861. Wounded at Malvern Hill, Virginia, July 1, 1862. Discharged on November 18, 1862, by reason of wound.

WILLIAMS, WILLIAM B., Private
Born in Duplin County where he resided as a farmer and enlisted on January 20, 1862, for the war. Wounded through both legs at Malvern Hill, Virginia, July 1, 1862. Died at Petersburg, Virginia, May 7, 1863, of disease.

WORLEY, FRANCIS M., Private
Born in Duplin County where he resided as a farmer and enlisted at age 18, January 20, 1862, for the war. Killed at Sharpsburg, Maryland, September 17, 1862.

WORLEY, PATRICK B., Private
Resided in Duplin County where he enlisted on January 20, 1862, for the war. Wounded at Gettysburg, Pennsylvania, July 2, 1863, and returned to duty on October 15, 1863. Captured near Spotsylvania Court House, Virginia, May 12, 1864, and confined at Point Lookout, Maryland, until transferred to Elmira, New York, on August 10, 1864. Paroled at Elmira on February 13, 1865, and sent to Point Lookout for exchange. Received in exchange at Boulware's Wharf, James River, Virginia, February 20-21, 1865. Reported as present on a roll of a detachment of paroled and exchanged prisoners at Camp Lee, near Richmond, Virginia, on February 23, 1865.

COMPANY C

This company was organized in Cumberland County and enlisted at Fayetteville on May 29, 1861. It tendered its service to the state and was ordered to Garysburg, Northampton County, where it was assigned to this regiment as Company C. After joining the regiment the company functioned as a part of the regiment, and its history for the war period is recorded as a part of the regimental history.

The information contained in the following roster of the company was compiled principally from company muster rolls which covered from September, 1861, through December, 1864, and included an undated muster-in roll. No company muster rolls were found for the period prior to September, 1861, or for the period after December, 1864. In addition to the company muster rolls, Roll of Honor records, receipt rolls, and hospital records, supplemented by state pension applications, United Daughters of the Confederacy records, and postwar rosters and histories, all provided useful information.

OFFICERS
CAPTAINS

MALLETT, PETER
Born in North Carolina and resided as a merchant in New York when the war started. Returned to Cumberland County to raise a company and was appointed Captain to rank from May 16, 1861. Present or accounted for until transferred upon appointment as Major, Assistant Adjutant General, May 23, 1862, to serve as Commandant of Conscripts for North Carolina.

HORNE, HENRY W.
Resided in Cumberland County where he enlisted at age 25, May 23, 1861, for the war. Appointed 2nd Lieutenant to rank from May 16, 1861, and promoted to 1st Lieutenant on November 22, 1861. Promoted to Captain to rank from May 23, 1862. Wounded at Sharpsburg, Maryland, September 17, 1862. Present or accounted for until captured near Spotsylvania Court House, Virginia, May 12, 1864. Confined at Fort Delaware, Delaware, until transferred to Hilton Head, South Carolina, August 20, 1864. Transferred to Fort Pulaski, Georgia, after October 20, 1864, and back to Hilton Head on November 19, 1864. Returned to Fort Delaware on March 12, 1865, and was released at Fort Delaware after taking the Oath of Allegiance on June 16, 1865.

LIEUTENANTS

BAKER, GEORGE B., 2nd Lieutenant
Transferred from 2nd Company B, 36th Regiment N.C. Troops (2nd Regiment N.C. Artillery) upon appointment as 2nd Lieutenant on May 10, 1862. Wounded at Malvern Hill, Virginia, July 1, 1862. Transferred to Conscript Bureau at Raleigh upon appointment as 1st Lieutenant on July 14, 1862.

GRAHAM, NEIL A., 2nd Lieutenant
Born in Cumberland County where he resided and enlisted at age 26, May 29, 1861, for the war. Mustered in as Sergeant and promoted to 1st Sergeant, November-December, 1861. Appointed 2nd Lieutenant to rank from July 1, 1862. Wounded at Sharpsburg, Maryland, September 17, 1862. Admitted to hospital at Richmond, Virginia, October 13, 1862, and furloughed for 60 days on October 23, 1862. Reported as absent wounded through December, 1863. Returned to company in January, 1864. Present or accounted for until paroled at Appomattox Court House, Virginia, April 9, 1865.

MALLETT, CHARLES PETER, 1st Lieutenant
Resided in Cumberland County where he enlisted at age 16, June 4, 1861, for the war. Appointed 3rd Lieutenant to rank from May 16, 1861, and promoted to 2nd Lieutenant on November 22, 1861. Promoted to 1st Lieutenant on May 23, 1862. Wounded at Malvern Hill, Virginia, July 1, 1862. Present or accounted for until captured near Spotsylvania Court House, Virginia, May 12, 1864. Confined at Fort Delaware, Delaware, until transferred to Hilton Head, South Carolina, August 20, 1864. Transferred to Fort Pulaski, Georgia, after October 20, 1864, and

returned to Hilton Head on November 19, 1864. Transferred on March 12, 1865, to Fort Delaware, where he was released after taking the Oath of Allegiance on June 1, 1865.

MURPHY, THOMAS D., 2nd Lieutenant

Resided in Cumberland County where he enlisted at age 22, May 29, 1861, for the war. Mustered in as Corporal and promoted to Sergeant, November-December, 1861. Wounded at Ellerson's Mill, Virginia, June 26, 1862. Promoted to 1st Sergeant in July, 1862. Appointed 2nd Lieutenant to rank from December 1, 1863. Killed at Winchester, Virginia, September 19, 1864.

SPEARMAN, EDWARD, 1st Lieutenant

Resided in Cumberland County where he enlisted at age 47, June 7, 1861, for the war. Appointed 1st Lieutenant to rank from May 16, 1861, and resigned on November 22, 1861.

THURSTON, WILLIAM J. Y., 2nd Lieutenant

Transferred from the Field and Staff of this regiment upon appointment as 2nd Lieutenant to rank from July 1, 1862. Submitted his resignation on November 6, 1863, and it was officially accepted on December 1, 1863.

NONCOMMISSIONED OFFICERS AND PRIVATES

ABOK, J., Private

Captured in hospital at Gettysburg, Pennsylvania, July 1-3, 1863.

ALPHIN, JOHN W., Private

Resided in Cumberland County where he enlisted at age 30, June 6, 1861, for the war. Captured and paroled at Paris, Virginia, November 5, 1862. Company muster roll for May 15-August 11, 1863, states that he was wounded in battle at Gettysburg, Pennsylvania. Present or accounted for from that date until admitted to hospital at Richmond, Virginia, June 27, 1864, with gunshot wound. Returned to duty August 24, 1864. Captured at Winchester, Virginia, September 19, 1864, and confined at Point Lookout, Maryland. Paroled at Point Lookout and transferred to Aiken's Landing, James River, Virginia, for exchange on March 15, 1865.

ARNETT, ALLEN, Private

Enlisted in Cumberland County, May-June, 1861. Detailed as a nurse and assigned to hospital duty October 20, 1861. Detailed as a nurse at various hospitals from that date through January, 1865.

ARNETT, ALLEN, Jr., Private

Resided in Cumberland County where he enlisted at age 26, February 19, 1862, for the war. Wounded at Spotsylvania Court House, Virginia, and admitted to hospital at Richmond, Virginia, May 8, 1864, with "v.s. right shoulder." Furloughed from hospital May 26, 1864, and reported as absent wounded until November-December, 1864. Detailed as a guard at hospital at Petersburg, Virginia, January 8, 1865. Retired to the Invalid Corps, January 19, 1865, and assigned to duty with Post Surgeon at Fayetteville.

ARNETT, ALLEN, Sr., Private

Resided in Cumberland County where he enlisted at age 45, June 15, 1861, for the war. Present or accounted for through December, 1864.

ARNETT, HENRY, Private

Resided in Cumberland County where he enlisted at age 48, June 12, 1861, for the war. Discharged May 25, 1862.

ARNETT, JAMES B., Private

Resided in Cumberland County where he enlisted at age 24, May 29, 1861, for the war. Mustered in as Corporal and reduced to ranks May 1-July 14, 1862. Wounded in battle near Richmond, Virginia, July 1, 1862. Mortally wounded in battle at Payne's Farm, Virginia, November 27-28, 1863.

ARNETT, NEILL H., Private

Resided in Cumberland County where he enlisted at age 21, February 19, 1862, for the war. Present or accounted for until captured at Spotsylvania Court House, Virginia, May 12, 1864. Confined at Point Lookout, Maryland, until transferred to Elmira, New York, August 8, 1864. Released at Elmira after taking the Oath of Allegiance on June 27, 1865.

ARNOLD, H., Private

Admitted to hospital at Richmond, Virginia, March 7, 1865, with "debilitas" and furloughed for 30 days on March 8, 1865.

ASHLEY, W. H., Private

Admitted to hospital at Charlottesville, Virginia, June 17, 1864, with gunshot wound of left hand and was furloughed for 30 days on July 4, 1864.

AUTRY, DAVID, 1st Sergeant

Resided in Cumberland County where he enlisted at age 19, May 29, 1861, for the war. Mustered in as Private and appointed Corporal May 1-July 14, 1862. Promoted to Sergeant July 14-November 1, 1862, and to 1st Sergeant on December 1, 1863. Wounded and captured at Gettysburg, Pennsylvania, July 2-3, 1863. Confined at Fort Delaware, Delaware, until transferred to Point Lookout, Maryland, October 18, 1863. Paroled at Point Lookout and sent to James River, Virginia, for exchange October 11, 1864. Paroled at Appomattox Court House, Virginia, April 9, 1865.

AUTRY, GEORGE, Private

Resided in Cumberland County where he enlisted at age 21, May 29, 1861, for the war. Wounded at Sharpsburg, Maryland, September 17, 1862. Wounded and captured at Gettysburg, Pennsylvania, July 3, 1863. Confined at Fort Delaware, Delaware, until transferred to Point Lookout, Maryland, October 18, 1863. Paroled at Point Lookout and sent to James River, Virginia, for exchange, February 18, 1865. Reported as present on a muster roll of a detachment of paroled and exchanged prisoners at Camp Lee, near Richmond, Virginia, dated February 23, 1865.

BAILEY, JESSE, Private

Born in Moore County where he resided as a farmer and enlisted on July 20, 1862, for the war. Died in hospital at Winchester, Virginia, November 1, 1862.

BAILEY, JOHN, Private

Resided in Moore County where he enlisted on July 20, 1862, for the war. Wounded in battle at

Gettysburg, Pennsylvania, July 1-3, 1863. Wounded and captured at Mine Run, Virginia, November 28, 1863. Confined at Old Capitol Prison, Washington, D.C., until transferred to Fort Delaware, Delaware, June 15, 1864. Released at Fort Delaware after taking the Oath of Allegiance on June 19, 1865.

BARBER, ALEXANDER, Private
Resided in Cumberland County where he enlisted at age 24, July 1, 1861, for the war. Wounded in battle near Richmond, Virginia, July 1, 1862. Admitted to hospital at Richmond, July 4, 1862, with "gunshot wound in hip" and died July 24, 1862.

BAYNE, HENRY, Private
Resided in Moore County where he enlisted at age 47, February 26, 1862, for the war. Company muster rolls state that he "deserted August, 1862." Reported on company muster rolls with this remark until February, 1863, when he appears with the remark: "Supposed to be at Castle Thunder." No further records.

BAYNE, JOEL, Private
Born in Cumberland County where he resided as a farmer and enlisted at age 24, March 17, 1862, for the war. Discharged by reason of disability on August 18, 1862.

BAYNE, PATRICK, Corporal
Resided in Cumberland County where he enlisted at age 19, March 17, 1862, for the war. Mustered in as Private. Wounded at Sharpsburg, Maryland, September 17, 1862. Appointed Corporal on December 1, 1863. Wounded in battle at Wilderness, Virginia, May 5, 1864, and died of his wounds on May 31, 1864, in hospital at Staunton, Virginia.

BEDSOLE, TRAVIS, Private
Resided in Cumberland County where he enlisted on July 18, 1862, for the war. Wounded at Sharpsburg, Maryland, September 17, 1862, and again at Chancellorsville, Virginia, on May 3, 1863. Captured at Harrisonburg, Virginia, October 2, 1864, and confined at Point Lookout, Maryland. Paroled at Point Lookout and sent to Aiken's Landing, Virginia, for exchange, March 17, 1865.

BENOY, ALEXANDER, Private
Resided in Cumberland County where he enlisted at age 35, June 15, 1861, for the war. Detailed as hospital guard at Richmond, Virginia, April 9, 1863. Absent detailed through January, 1865.

BISHOP, EDWIN F., Private
Born in Cumberland County where he resided as a laborer and enlisted at age 16, June 9, 1861, for the war. Died in hospital at Aquia Creek, Virginia, September 20, 1861.

BISHOP, HENRY, Private
Resided in Cumberland County where he enlisted at age 32, June 4, 1861, for the war. Wounded in battle at Ellerson's Mill, Virginia, June 26, 1862. Present or accounted for until he deserted and took the Oath of Allegiance at Bermuda Hundred, Virginia, March 19, 1865. Sent to the Provost Marshal General, Washington, D.C., and was furnished transportation from Washington

to Wilmington, N.C., March 24, 1865.

BLANCHARD, YOUNG, Private
Born in Cumberland County where he resided as a farmer and and enlisted at age 28, May 29, 1861, for the war. Killed in battle at Malvern Hill, Virginia, July 1, 1862.

BRADY, CHARLES, Private
Resided in Cumberland County where he enlisted at age 17, June 3, 1861, for the war. Mustered in as Private and appointed Musician, March-April, 1862. Reduced to ranks December 17, 1864. Paroled at Lynchburg, Virginia, April 13, 1865.

BRADY, NATHAN, Private
Born in Cumberland County where he resided as a laborer and enlisted at age 19, July 1, 1861, for the war. Discharged December 6, 1861, by reason of "physical inability."

BRADY, ROBERT, Private
Resided in Cumberland County where he enlisted at age 18, May 29, 1861, for the war. Present or accounted for until captured at Gettysburg, Pennsylvania, July 4, 1863. Confined at Fort McHenry, Maryland, until transferred to Fort Delaware, Delaware, July 7-12, 1863. Took the Oath of Allegiance and joined the U.S. service September 5, 1863. Assigned to Company E, 3rd Regiment Maryland Cavalry.

BRAMBLE, KINCHEN G., Private
Born in Bladen County and resided as a farmer in Cumberland County where he enlisted at age 27, May 29, 1861, for the war. Died in hospital at Richmond, Virginia, February 9, 1862, of "convulsions and cramps."

BREECE, JAMES, Private
Enlisted in Cumberland County on July 18, 1862, for the war. Present or accounted for until transferred to Company E, 8th Regiment N.C. State Troops, April 10, 1863.

BROOKS, G. W., Private
Paroled at Greensboro on May 9, 1865.

BROWN, ALEXANDER W., Private
Resided in Moore County where he enlisted on July 20, 1862, for the war. Captured at Frederick, Maryland, September 15, 1862, and confined at Fort Delaware, Delaware. Paroled and transferred to Aiken's Landing, Virginia, for exchange, October 2, 1862. Declared exchanged at Aiken's Landing on November 10, 1862. Company muster rolls carry him as absent prisoner through February, 1863, and report him as a deserter after that date.

BRYANT, JOHN C., Private
Resided in Cumberland County where he enlisted at age 35, February 19, 1862, for the war. Wounded at Sharpsburg, Maryland, September 17, 1862. Company muster rolls state that he was captured May 12, 1864, and report him as absent prisoner from that date through December, 1864.

BUTLER, DANIEL, Private
Born in Cumberland County where he resided as a farmer and enlisted at age 18, June 15, 1861, for the war. Wounded in battle at Malvern Hill, Virginia, July 1, 1862. Absent wounded until discharged March 19, 1863, by reason of disability

caused by "gunshot wound of the left forearm."

BUTLER, HIRAM B., Sergeant

Resided in Cumberland County where he enlisted at age 23, June 17, 1861, for the war. Mustered in as Private and appointed Corporal, July 14-November 1, 1862. Wounded at Chancellorsville, Virginia, May 3, 1863. Admitted to hospital at Richmond, Virginia, May 10, 1863, with "vulnus sclopeticum thigh, left" and was returned to duty July 17, 1863. Promoted to Sergeant, November-December, 1863. Appointed Ensign on April 28, 1864, and transferred to the Field and Staff of this regiment.

BYRD, THOMAS R., Private

Resided in Cumberland County where he enlisted at age 19, June 4, 1861, for the war. Present or accounted for until admitted to hospital on September 2, 1862, at Richmond, Virginia, where he died October 1, 1862, of "debility, diarrhoea chronic."

CALCUTT, GEORGE T., Private

Resided in Cumberland County where he enlisted at age 48, February 19, 1862, for the war. Wounded in battle near Richmond, Virginia, July 1, 1862. Again wounded in battle at Boonsboro, Maryland, September 14, 1862. Present or accounted for until captured near Spotsylvania Court House, Virginia, May 12, 1864. Confined at Point Lookout, Maryland, until transferred to Elmira, New York, August 10, 1864. Paroled at Elmira and sent to James River, Virginia, for exchange, February 13, 1865.

CAMERON, J. F., Private

Resided in Cumberland County and enlisted in Moore County on July 20, 1862, for the war. Reported as absent sick on company muster roll for July 14-November 1, 1862. Reported as sick from that date until he appears on the muster roll for May 15-August 11, 1863, with the remark: "Dead but no official report received."

CARROLL, PETER J., Private

Resided in Cumberland County where he enlisted at age 20, May 29, 1861, for the war. Captured and paroled at Paris, Virginia, November 5, 1862. Deserted January 26, 1863, and was returned to duty August 23, 1863. Captured at Raccoon Ford, Virginia, September 28, 1863, and confined at Old Capitol Prison, Washington, D.C. Released after taking the Oath of Allegiance at Old Capitol Prison on December 13, 1863.

CARTER, JAMES C., Private

Resided in Cumberland County where he enlisted on July 18, 1862, for the war. Reported as a deserter on company muster roll for May 1-May 15, 1863. Returned from desertion in June, 1864. Captured at Cedar Creek, Virginia, October 19, 1864, and confined at Point Lookout, Maryland. Paroled at Point Lookout and transferred to Aiken's Landing, Virginia, for exchange, March 17, 1865.

CARVER, JAMES B., Private

Roll of Honor states that he resided in Cumberland County and enlisted at age 43, June 21, 1861.

CAVANAUGH, THOMAS, Private

Resided in Cumberland County where he enlisted at age 23, June 4, 1861, for the war. Deserted August, 1862.

CHAMBERS, HENRY, Private

Enlisted in Cumberland County on January 5, 1862, for the war. Discharged May 25, 1862.

COBBS, CALVIN, Private

Paroled at Greensboro on May 13, 1865.

COLE, JOHN A., Private

Resided in Cumberland County and enlisted in Moore County on July 20, 1862, for the war. Wounded at Sharpsburg, Maryland, September 17, 1862. Detailed to nurse wounded at Gettysburg, Pennsylvania, and was captured in the hospital at Gettysburg, July 1-3, 1863. Admitted to U.S.A. General Hospital, West's Buildings, Baltimore, Maryland, September 25, 1863, with "debility." Transferred on December 2, 1863, to Marine Hospital, Baltimore, where he died on December 9, 1863.

CREEL, ROBERT, Private

Born in Cumberland County where he resided as a farmer and enlisted at age 17, June 3, 1861, for the war. Died April 30, 1862, at Goldsboro.

CRIBB, JOHN W. W., Private

Born in Bladen County and resided in Cumberland County where he enlisted at age 20, May 29, 1861, for the war. Died in hospital at Richmond, Virginia, July 29, 1861.

DAUGHTRY, THOMAS C., Private

Resided in Cumberland County where he enlisted at age 22, March 17, 1862, for the war. Admitted to hospital at Richmond, Virginia, June 25, 1862, with "dysentery" and died June 29, 1862.

DAVIS, LAUCHLIN, Private

Born in Cumberland County where he resided and enlisted at age 20, June 13, 1861, for the war. Died September 15, 1861, at Fredericksburg, Virginia.

DAVIS, WILLIAM G., Corporal

Resided in Cumberland County where he enlisted at age 22, February 19, 1862, for the war. Mustered in as Private. Wounded in battle near Richmond, Virginia, July 1, 1862. Appointed Corporal on December 1, 1863. Paroled at Appomattox Court House, Virginia, April 9, 1865.

DAWKINS, WILLIAM W., Private

Resided in Cumberland County where he enlisted at age 28, July 3, 1861, for the war. Mortally wounded in battle at Malvern Hill, Virginia, July 1, 1862.

EDGE, L., Private

Died in hospital at Lynchburg, Virginia, August 30, 1862, of "febris typhoides."

EDGE, WILLIAM JAMES, Private

Resided in Cumberland County where he enlisted at age 21, February 25, 1862, for the war. Reported as a deserter on company muster roll for July 14-November 1, 1862. Returned from desertion June 11, 1864. Wounded at Snicker's Gap, Virginia, July 18, 1864. Absent wounded until retired to the Invalid Corps, December 1, 1864, and assigned to duty with the commandant of the post at Richmond, Virginia. Admitted to hospital at Charlottesville, Virginia, December 20, 1864, and was furloughed January 21, 1865.

EDWARDS, EDWARD JACKSON, Private
Born in Cumberland County where he resided as a farmer and enlisted at age 18, June 17, 1861, for the war. Wounded at Chancellorsville, Virginia, May 3, 1863, and admitted to hospital at Richmond, Virginia, May 10, 1863, with "ampt. right forearm." Absent wounded until discharged December 23, 1863, by reason of amputation of right forearm.

ELAM, WILLIAM C., Private
Resided in Cumberland County where he enlisted at age 25, May 29, 1861, for the war. Mustered in as 1st Sergeant and reduced to ranks November-December, 1861. Discharged December 22, 1861.

ELLIS, JESSE M., Private
Resided in Cumberland County where he enlisted on July 18, 1862, for the war. Captured at Boonsboro, Maryland, September 15, 1862, and confined at Fort Delaware, Delaware. Paroled at Fort Delaware and sent to Aiken's Landing, Virginia, for exchange on October 2, 1862. Admitted to hospital at Richmond, Virginia, October 20, 1862, and furloughed for 30 days on October 21, 1862. Reported on company muster rolls as absent prisoner until January-February, 1863, when he appears with the remark: "Dead. No official report of death."

EMERY, GEORGE CHARLES, Private
Resided in Cumberland County where he enlisted at age 46, May 29, 1861, for the war. Wounded in battle near Richmond, Virginia, July 1, 1862. Captured at Raccoon Ford, Virginia, September 25, 1863. Confined at Old Capitol Prison, Washington, D.C., where he was released after taking the Oath of Allegiance on March 14, 1864. Sent to New York after taking Oath.

FAIRCLOTH, WILLIAM, Private
Born in Cumberland County where he resided as a farmer and enlisted at age 21, June 21, 1861, for the war. Wounded at Gettysburg, Pennsylvania, July 2-3, 1863, and captured in hospital at Gettysburg, July 4-5, 1863. Confined at DeCamp General Hospital, Davids Island, New York Harbor, until paroled and exchanged at City Point, Virginia, August 28, 1863. Detailed in Quartermaster Department at Fayetteville early in 1864 and reported as absent on detail on company muster rolls through December, 1864.

FIELDS, A. M., Private
Resided in Moore County where he enlisted on July 20, 1862, for the war. Wounded at Sharpsburg, Maryland, September 17, 1862. Present or accounted for until captured near Spotsylvania Court House, Virginia, May 12, 1864. Confined at Point Lookout, Maryland, until transferred to Elmira, New York, August 10, 1864. Died at Elmira on February 13, 1865, of "variola."

FISHER, J. A., Private
Enlisted on October 8, 1863, for the war. Cap-

tured near Spotsylvania Court House, Virginia, May 15, 1864, and confined at Point Lookout, Maryland. Died at Point Lookout on June 17, 1864.

FISHER, WILLIAM S., Private
Resided in Cumberland County where he enlisted at age 32, June 4, 1861, for the war. Wounded at Payne's Farm, Virginia, November 27-28, 1863, and furloughed on December 4, 1863. Detailed to Captain Samuel B. Waters' Company, Provost Guard, Raleigh, February 4, 1864. Reported as absent on detail through December, 1864.

FLOWERS, JAMES E., Private
Resided in Cumberland County where he enlisted at age 15, May 29, 1861, for the war. Captured and confined at Old Capitol Prison, Washington, D.C., September 16, 1862. Paroled and exchanged at Aiken's Landing, James River, Virginia, November 10, 1862. Captured at Gettysburg, Pennsylvania, July 3, 1863, and confined at Fort Delaware, Delaware, until released after taking the Oath of Allegiance on June 19, 1865.

FLOWERS, THOMAS, Private
Resided in Cumberland County where he enlisted at age 44, May 29, 1861, for the war. Wounded at Malvern Hill, Virginia, July 1, 1862. Captured and confined at Old Capitol Prison, Washington, D.C., September 16, 1862. Paroled and exchanged at Aiken's Landing, James River, Virginia, November 10, 1862. Killed at Gettysburg, Pennsylvania, July 2-3, 1863.

GILES, HIRAM R., Private
Resided in Cumberland County where he enlisted at age 22, May 29, 1861, for the war. Present or accounted for on company muster rolls through December, 1864, being reported as absent sick from June, 1863, through October, 1864. Wounded and admitted to hospital at Farmville, Virginia, April 7, 1865. Paroled at Farmville, April 11-21, 1865.

GILES, W. H., Private
Resided in Cumberland County where he enlisted at age 20, May 31, 1861, for the war. Present or accounted for until killed at Gettysburg, Pennsylvania, July 2-3, 1863.

GODFREY, MATTHEW, Private
Resided in Cumberland County where he enlisted at age 26, February 26, 1862, for the war. Died at Goldsboro on April 16, 1862, of disease.

GODWIN, ASA, Private
Resided in Cumberland County where he enlisted at age 40, May 29, 1861, for the war. Discharged on August 7, 1861, by reason of disability.

GOULD, DAVID J., Private
Resided in Cumberland County where he enlisted at age 21, May 29, 1861, for the war. Mustered in as Sergeant. Present or accounted for until captured at Gettysburg, Pennsylvania, July 3, 1863. Reduced to ranks November-December, 1863. Date of release from prison not shown. Company muster rolls report him as absent prisoner until he was admitted to hospital at Richmond, Virginia, on May 1, 1864, with "diarrhoea chronic." Furloughed from the hospital for 60 days on

May 8, 1864. Present or accounted for through December, 1864. Deserted and took the Oath of Allegiance at Bermuda Hundred, Virginia, March 10, 1865. Transferred to the Provost Marshal General, Washington, D.C., and was furnished transportation from Washington to Canton, Ohio, on March 13, 1865.

GOULD, JOHN W., Private
Enlisted in Cumberland County, January 1, 1863, for the war as a substitute for John W. Lett. Discharged by reason of disability January 23, 1864.

GRIMES, D. L., Private
Resided in Cumberland County where he enlisted at age 24, February 5, 1862, for the war. Mustered in as Private and appointed Corporal, May 1-July 14, 1862. Reduced to ranks April 16, 1863. Wounded at Payne's Farm, Virginia, November 27-28, 1863. Absent wounded through December, 1864. Paroled at Appomattox Court House, Virginia, April 9, 1865.

GUITON, THOMAS W., Private
Resided in Cumberland County where he enlisted July 18, 1862, for the war. Captured and paroled at Warrenton, Virginia, September 29, 1862. Present or accounted for until again captured near Spotsylvania Court House, Virginia, May 12, 1864. Confined at Point Lookout, Maryland, and transferred to Elmira, New York, August 10, 1864. Paroled at Elmira and sent to James River, Virginia, for exchange on March 2, 1865. Admitted to hospital at Richmond, Virginia, March 7, 1865, with "debilitas" and was furloughed for 30 days on March 9, 1865.

HALL, JAMES A., Private
Born in Bladen County and resided as a farmer in Cumberland County where he enlisted at age 20, May 29, 1861, for the war. Wounded in battle at Ellerson's Mill, Virginia, on June 26, 1862. Died of his wounds in hospital at Richmond, Virginia, on June 29, 1862.

HARTMAN, J. W., Private
Resided in Cumberland County where he enlisted at age 59, July 1, 1861, for the war. Detailed as a nurse at Fredericksburg, Virginia, March 15, 1862. Deserted April 26, 1862.

HILL, ELBURTON, Private
Resided in Cumberland County where he enlisted at age 29, June 3, 1861, for the war. Admitted to hospital at Richmond, Virginia, October 22, 1862, and detailed in hospital at Richmond on March 16, 1863. Reported as absent on detail on company muster rolls through December, 1864.

HODGES, ARCHIBALD, Private
Born in Bladen County and resided as a laborer in Cumberland County where he enlisted at age 19, June 14, 1861, for the war. Died at Richmond, Virginia, September 26, 1861.

HODGES, B. W., Private
Enlisted in Cumberland County at age 20, May 29, 1861, for the war. Deserted on June 16, 1861.

HOLLINGSWORTH, DAVID T., Private
Resided in Cumberland County where he enlisted at age 26, March 4, 1862, for the war. Mus-

tered in as Sergeant and reduced to ranks January 31, 1863. Killed at Chancellorsville, Virginia, May 3, 1863.

HOLLINGSWORTH, ENOCH, Private
Born in Cumberland County where he resided as a farmer and enlisted at age 15, June 15, 1861, for the war. Killed at Malvern Hill, Virginia, July 1, 1862.

HOLLINGSWORTH, JONATHAN, Private
Resided in Cumberland County where he enlisted at age 18, June 15, 1861, for the war. Present or accounted for until detailed for light duty in hospital at Staunton, Virginia, August 9, 1863. Remained on detail until transferred for light duty to the Fayetteville Arsenal and Armory on April 9, 1864. Returned to company in September, 1864, and was captured at Strasburg, Virginia, October 19, 1864. Confined at Point Lookout, Maryland, until paroled and exchanged at Cox's Landing, James River, Virginia, February 14-15, 1865.

HORNE, J. B., Private
Resided in Cumberland County where he enlisted on July 18, 1862, for the war. Wounded and captured at Sharpsburg, Maryland, September 17, 1862. Died in hospital at Frederick, Maryland, September 26, 1862.

HORNE, WILLIAM B., Private
Resided in Cumberland County where he enlisted on July 18, 1862, for the war. Present or accounted for until captured near Spotsylvania Court House, Virginia, May 12, 1864. Confined at Point Lookout, Maryland, until transferred to Elmira, New York, August 10, 1864. Remained at Elmira until released after taking the Oath of Allegiance on June 30, 1865.

HOWARD, WILLIAM H., Private
Resided in Cumberland County where he enlisted at age 30, May 31, 1861, for the war. Discharged on August 7, 1861, by reason of disability.

HUSEY, CALVIN, Private
Resided in Cumberland County where he enlisted on July 18, 1862, for the war. Died near Middletown, Virginia, November 20, 1862.

HUSSEY, SAMUEL, Private
Resided in Cumberland County where he enlisted at age 21, June 3, 1861, for the war. Captured at Gettysburg, Pennsylvania, July 5, 1863, and confined at Fort Delaware, Delaware. Remained at Fort Delaware until released after taking the Oath of Allegiance on June 19, 1865.

HUTHMACHER, ANDREW, Private
Resided in Cumberland County where he enlisted at age 26, May 29, 1861, for the war. Deserted at Richmond, Virginia, July 23, 1861.

JACKSON, JOSHUA, Private
Resided in Cumberland County where he enlisted at age 42, March 15, 1862, for the war. Wounded at Malvern Hill, Virginia, July 1, 1862. Died in hospital at Liberty, Virginia, September 27, 1862, of "scorbutus."

JACKSON, KELLY W., Private
Paid bounty at Wilmington on March 11, 1862.

JOHNSON, JAMES M., Private

Resided in Cumberland County where he enlisted at age 27, February 17, 1862, for the war. Wounded at Sharpsburg, Maryland, September 17, 1862, and furloughed from hospital at Richmond, Virginia, for 30 days on October 10, 1862. Wounded and captured at Gettysburg, Pennsylvania, July 1-3, 1863. Sent to General Hospital on September 29, 1863. No further records.

JOHNSON, RUFUS, Private

Resided in Cumberland County where he enlisted on July 18, 1862, for the war. Wounded at Sharpsburg, Maryland, September 17, 1862. Present or accounted for until captured near Spotsylvania Court House, Virginia, May 12, 1864. Confined at Point Lookout, Maryland, until transferred to Elmira, New York, August 10, 1864. Remained at Elmira until released after taking the Oath of Allegiance on June 16, 1865.

JOHNSON, WILLIAM, Private

Resided in Cumberland County where he enlisted on July 18, 1862, for the war. Wounded at Payne's Farm, Virginia, November 27-28, 1863. Present or accounted for until paroled at Appomattox Court House, Virginia, April 9, 1865.

JONES, ALLEN, Private

Resided in Cumberland County where he enlisted at age 26, May 29, 1861, for the war. Wounded at Gettysburg, Pennsylvania, July 2-3, 1863, and captured in hospital at Gettysburg, July 4-5, 1863. Confined in hospital at Baltimore, Maryland, until transferred to Fort McHenry, Maryland, March 2, 1864. Transferred on July 21, 1864, to Point Lookout, Maryland, where he was paroled. Received in exchange at Venus Point, Savannah River, Georgia, November 15, 1864. Captured at Rockfish, N.C., March 10, 1865, and sent to Washington, D.C., where he took the Oath of Allegiance on April 5, 1865.

JONES, JAMES, Private

Resided in Cumberland County where he enlisted at age 21, July 1, 1861, for the war. Wounded at Sharpsburg, Maryland, September 17, 1862, and at Gettysburg, Pennsylvania, July 2-3, 1863. Present or accounted for until detailed at Fayetteville Arsenal and Armory on March 24, 1864. Assigned to Company G, 2nd Battalion N.C. Local Defense Troops while on detail at Fayetteville. Returned to company November-December, 1864. Detailed again on January 23, 1865.

JONES, WILLIAM H., Private

Born in Harnett County and resided as a laborer in Cumberland County where he enlisted at age 17, February 17, 1862, for the war. Wounded at Malvern Hill, Virginia, July 1, 1862. Reported as absent wounded until discharged on February 27, 1864.

KING, DAVID D., Sergeant

Resided in Cumberland County where he enlisted at age 25, June 7, 1861, for the war. Mustered in as Private and appointed Corporal, May 1-July 14, 1862. Captured at Chancellorsville, Virginia, May 3, 1863, and paroled and exchanged at City Point, Virginia, May 10, 1863. Wounded

at Gettysburg, Pennsylvania, July 2-3, 1863, and captured at Waterloo, Pennsylvania, July 5, 1863. Confined at Fort Delaware, Delaware, until transferred to Point Lookout, Maryland, October 15-18, 1863. Promoted to Sergeant while absent in confinement on December 1, 1863. Died at Point Lookout on December 4, 1863.

KONTZ, MICHAEL, Private

Paroled at Greensboro on May 8, 1865.

LASHLEY, WILLIAM H., Private

Resided in Cumberland County where he enlisted at age 36, June 10, 1861, for the war. Present or accounted for until wounded and captured at Cedar Creek, Virginia, October 19, 1864. Confined at Point Lookout, Maryland, until paroled and exchanged at Venus Point, Savannah River, Georgia, November 15, 1864. Admitted to hospital at Fayetteville on December 14, 1864, and reported as present in the hospital on February 28, 1865.

LEDBETTER, A. L., Private

Resided in Moore County and enlisted in Cumberland County at age 22, March 4, 1862, for the war. Wounded at Chancellorsville, Virginia, May 3, 1863, and at Payne's Farm, Virginia, November 27-28, 1863. Captured near Spotsylvania Court House, Virginia, May 12, 1864, and confined at Point Lookout, Maryland, until transferred to Elmira, New York, August 10, 1864. Paroled at Elmira on March 10, 1865, and exchanged at Boulware's Wharf, James River, Virginia, March 15, 1865.

LETT, JOHN W., Private

Provided John W. Gould as his substitute.

LOOKVILLE, F. D., Private

Paroled at Greensboro on May 8, 1865.

LOVITT, JOSHUA, Private

Resided in Cumberland County where he enlisted at age 34, June 4, 1861, for the war. Died February 24, 1862.

McCALL, NEILL, Private

Resided in Cumberland County where he enlisted on July 18, 1862, for the war. Present or accounted for until captured near Spotsylvania Court House, Virginia, May 12, 1864. Confined at Point Lookout, Maryland, until transferred to Elmira, New York, August 10, 1864. Died at Elmira on December 15, 1864, of "pneumonia."

McCORMACK, ROBERT S., Private

Resided in Cumberland County where he enlisted at age 44, June 11, 1861, for the war. Discharged at Garysburg on July 16, 1861.

McDONALD, D. C., Private

Resided in Moore County where he enlisted on July 20, 1862, for the war. Died at Danville, Virginia, on January 5, 1863, of "pneumonia."

McDONALD, M. A., Private

Resided in Moore County where he enlisted on July 20, 1862, for the war. Died at Raleigh on April 19, 1863, of "pneumonia."

McDONALD, NORMAN, Private

Resided in Moore County where he enlisted on July 20, 1862, for the war. Died near Winchester, Virginia, December 15, 1862, of disease.

McDOUGALD, HUGH, Private

Born in Scotland and resided as a farmer in Cumberland County where he enlisted at age 28, July 9, 1861, for the war. Discharged on May 12, 1862, by reason of "pulmonary phthisis and general inertia."

McKEATHAN, EZEKIEL, Private

Resided in Cumberland County where he enlisted at age 32, March 10, 1862, for the war. Died in hospital at Petersburg, Virginia, June 22, 1862, of "pneumonia."

McKINNON, D. R., Private

Resided in Moore County where he enlisted on July 20, 1862, for the war. Wounded at Sharpsburg, Maryland, September 17, 1862, and at Chancellorsville, Virginia, May 3, 1863. Died in hospital at Richmond, Virginia, June 29, 1863.

McLAMB, WILLIAM, Private

Resided in Cumberland County where he enlisted at age 28, March 5, 1862, for the war. Wounded at Chancellorsville, Virginia, May 3, 1863, and reported as absent wounded on company muster rolls from May 3, 1863, through December, 1864.

McLEAN, JOHN, Private

Resided in Moore County where he enlisted on July 20, 1862, for the war. Wounded at Sharpsburg, Maryland, September 17, 1862. Present or accounted for until detailed for guard duty at Gordonsville, Virginia, December 23, 1863. Reported as absent on detail on company muster rolls through December, 1864.

McPHATTER, ONSLOW, Private

Resided in Moore County where he enlisted at age 18, February 26, 1862, for the war. Wounded at Gettysburg, Pennsylvania, July 2-3, 1863. Captured near Spotsylvania Court House, Virginia, May 12, 1864, and confined at Point Lookout, Maryland. Released at Point Lookout after taking the Oath of Allegiance and joining the U.S. service on June 18, 1864. Assigned to Company K, 1st Regiment U.S. Volunteer Infantry.

MANKER, STEPHEN H., Private

Resided in Cumberland County where he enlisted at age 23, May 29, 1861, for the war. Killed at Sharpsburg, Maryland, September 17, 1862.

MASON, JOHN D., Private

Resided in Cumberland County where he enlisted at age 21, February 19, 1862, for the war. Captured at Fredericksburg, Virginia, May 3, 1863, and paroled and exchanged at City Point, Virginia, May 10, 1863. Deserted on September 27, 1863, and surrendered to the enemy the next day at Raccoon Ford, Virginia. Confined at Old Capitol Prison, Washington, D.C., until released after taking the Oath of Allegiance on December 13, 1863.

MASON, WILLIAM, Private

Resided in Cumberland County where he enlisted on July 18, 1862, for the war. Mortally wounded at Sharpsburg, Maryland, September 17, 1862.

MEDLIN, JOHN C., Private

Resided in Cumberland County where he enlisted at age 17, May 29, 1861, for the war. Mortally wounded at Sharpsburg, Maryland, September 17, 1862.

MITCHELL, MAJOR, Private

Resided in Cumberland County where he enlisted at age 30, May 29, 1861, for the war. Wounded at Gettysburg, Pennsylvania, July 2-3, 1863, and captured at Waterloo, Pennsylvania, July 5, 1863. Confined at Fort Delaware, Delaware, until transferred to Point Lookout, Maryland, October 15-18, 1863. Paroled at Point Lookout on February 18, 1865, and sent to James River, Virginia, for exchange. Received in exchange at Boulware's Wharf, James River, February 18, 1865. Reported as present on a roll of a detachment of paroled and exchanged prisoners at Camp Lee, near Richmond, Virginia, February 23, 1865.

MONTGOMERY, DANIEL J., Corporal

Resided in Cumberland County where he enlisted at age 18, May 29, 1861, for the war. Mustered in as Private. Wounded at Malvern Hill, Virginia, July 1, 1862. Promoted to Corporal on April 16, 1863. Killed at Gettysburg, Pennsylvania, July 2-3, 1863.

MOORE, WILLIAM P., Private

Resided in Robeson County where he enlisted at age 22, February 28, 1862, for the war. Killed at Malvern Hill, Virginia, July 1, 1862.

MORRISON, HENRY, Private

Born in Ireland and resided as a laborer in Cumberland County where he enlisted at age 23, May 29, 1861, for the war. Present or accounted for until he transferred to the C.S. Navy on February 1, 1862.

MULLINS, JOHN T., Sergeant

Resided in Cumberland County where he enlisted at age 34, May 29, 1861, for the war. Mustered in as Corporal. Promoted to Sergeant, May 1-July 14, 1862, and reduced to ranks July 14-November 1, 1862. Reappointed Sergeant on January 31, 1863. Present or accounted for until captured at Spotsylvania Court House, Virginia, May 12, 1864. Confined at Point Lookout, Maryland, until transferred to Elmira, New York, August 10, 1864. Paroled at Elmira on March 2, 1865, and sent to James River, Virginia, for exchange. Admitted to hospital at Richmond, Virginia, March 7, 1865, and furloughed for 30 days on March 9, 1865.

NAGLE, JOHN, Private

Resided in Cumberland County where he enlisted at age 27, June 4, 1861, for the war. Deserted in August, 1862.

NEAL, PLEASANT, Private

Resided in Cumberland County where he enlisted at age 34, May 31, 1861, for the war. Wounded at Gettysburg, Pennsylvania, July 2-3, 1863, and captured at South Mountain, Pennsylvania, July 4, 1863. Confined at Fort Delaware, Delaware, until released after taking the Oath of Allegiance on June 19, 1865.

NEWELL, EDWARD R., Private

Resided in Cumberland County where he enlisted at age 20, May 29, 1861, for the war. Present or accounted for until captured at Spotsylvania Court House, Virginia, May 12, 1864. Confined at Point Lookout, Maryland, until transferred to Elmira, New York, August 10, 1864. Remained at Elmira until released after taking the Oath of Allegiance on June 16, 1865.

NEWELL, FRANCIS, Private
Resided in Cumberland County where he enlisted at age 47, March 4, 1862, for the war. Wounded at Malvern Hill, Virginia, July 1, 1862. Admitted to hospital at Richmond, Virginia, July 4, 1862, with gunshot wounds of the leg and shoulder and furloughed for 60 days on September 3, 1862. Reported as absent wounded on company muster rolls from July, 1862, through December, 1864. Assigned to Captain Samuel B. Waters' Company, Provost Guard, Raleigh, February 13, 1864, and reported on rolls of that company through January, 1865.

NOWELL, LEMUEL, Private
Resided in Cumberland County where he enlisted at age 36, May 29, 1861, for the war. Wounded at Malvern Hill, Virginia, July 1, 1862, and killed at Sharpsburg, Maryland, September 17, 1862.

OLIPHANT, PETER N., Private
Born in Cumberland County where he resided as a printer and enlisted at age 19, June 6, 1861, for the war. Mustered in as Musician and reduced to ranks May 1-July 14, 1862. Wounded and captured at Sharpsburg, Maryland, September 17, 1862, and died in field hospital near Sharpsburg prior to September 29, 1862.

PARKER, ROBERT M., Private
Born in Bladen County and resided in Cumberland County where he enlisted at age 34, May 29, 1861, for the war. Killed at Malvern Hill, Virginia, July 1, 1862.

PERNELL, WILLIAM J., Private
Resided in Cumberland County where he enlisted at age 26, June 28, 1861, for the war. Died in hospital at Richmond, Virginia, in 1862.

PETH, W. H., Private
Resided in Wayne County. Paroled at Goldsboro in 1865.

POPE, JAMES W., Private
Resided in Cumberland County where he enlisted at age 18, March 19, 1862, for the war. Died near Richmond, Virginia, July 18, 1862, of disease.

PORTER, ARCHIBALD, Private
Resided in Cumberland County where he enlisted at age 40, March 15, 1862, for the war. Wounded at Malvern Hill, Virginia, July 1, 1862. Present or accounted for on company muster rolls through December, 1864. Admitted to hospital at Richmond, Virginia, December 10, 1864, with a gunshot wound of the right arm. Returned to duty on March 23, 1865. Captured at Farmville, Virginia, April 6, 1865, and confined at Newport News, Virginia, until released after taking the Oath of Allegiance on June 27, 1865.

POWELL, DAVID, Private
Resided in Cumberland County where he enlisted at age 29, May 29, 1861, for the war. Mustered in as Sergeant and reduced to Corporal, March-April, 1862. Reduced to Private, May 1-July 14, 1862. Wounded at Malvern Hill, Virginia, July 1,

1862. Deserted August 20, 1862.

PRIDGEN, DAVID J., Private
Resided in Cumberland County where he enlisted at age 40, May 29, 1861, for the war. Present or accounted for until discharged on May 24, 1862.

PRIDGEN, JOHN HENRY, Private
Resided in Cumberland County where he enlisted at age 19, May 29, 1861, for the war. Deserted November 7, 1862, and returned August 20, 1863. Captured at Payne's Farm, Virginia, November 28, 1863, and confined at Old Capitol Prison, Washington, D.C., until released after taking the Oath of Allegiance on March 19, 1864. Sent to Philadelphia, Pennsylvania.

RAY, A. A., Private
Resided in Moore County where he enlisted on July 20, 1862, for the war. Captured at Frederick, Maryland, September 13, 1862, and confined at Fort Delaware, Delaware. Paroled at Fort Delaware and sent to Aiken's Landing, James River, Virginia, for exchange, October 2, 1862. Died in hospital at Richmond, Virginia, June 29, 1863, of "phthisis pulmo."

RAY, ANGUS, Private
Resided in Cumberland County and enlisted in Moore County on July 20, 1862, for the war. Captured at Frederick, Maryland, September 13, 1862, and confined at Fort Delaware, Delaware. Paroled at Fort Delaware and sent to Aiken's Landing, James River, Virginia, for exchange, October 2, 1862. Present or accounted for until captured near Spotsylvania Court House, Virginia, May 12, 1864. Confined at Point Lookout, Maryland, and transferred to Elmira, New York, August 10, 1864. Died at Elmira, July 10, 1865, of "chronic diarrhoea."

RAY, J. C., Private
Enlisted in Moore County on July 20, 1862, for the war. Reported on company muster rolls as absent sick until he is carried on the May 15-August 11, 1863, muster roll with the remark: "Dead but no official report received."

RICHARDSON, D. A., Private
Captured in hospital at Richmond, Virginia, April 3, 1865.

RIGGS, C., Private
Confined at DeCamp General Hospital, Davids Island, New York Harbor, July 17-24, 1863.

RILEY, CALVIN P., Private
Resided in Cumberland County where he enlisted on July 18, 1862, for the war. Wounded in battle at Winchester, Virginia, June 15, 1863. Captured near Spotsylvania Court House, Virginia, May 12, 1864, and confined at Point Lookout, Maryland. Transferred on August 10, 1864, to Elmira, New York, where he died November 26, 1864, of "chronic diarrhoea."

RILEY, JOHN, Private
Born in Ireland and resided as a laborer in Cumberland County where he enlisted at age 19, May 29, 1861, for the war. Present or accounted for until discharged and transferred to the C.S. Navy on January 29, 1862.

ROBERTSON, DANIEL, Sergeant

Resided in Cumberland County where he enlisted at age 26, July 9, 1861, for the war. Mustered in as Private. Wounded in battle near Richmond, Virginia, July 1, 1862. Appointed Corporal, July 14-November 1, 1862, and promoted to Sergeant, November-December, 1863. Captured near Spotsylvania Court House, Virginia, May 10, 1864, and confined at Point Lookout, Maryland. Transferred to Elmira, New York, August 10, 1864. Released at Elmira after taking the Oath of Allegiance on June 27, 1865.

ROUSE, JOHN W., Private

Resided in Cumberland County where he enlisted at age 16, June 15, 1861, for the war. Wounded in battle near Richmond, Virginia, July 1, 1862. Again wounded at Chancellorsville, Virginia, May 3, 1863. Reported on company muster rolls as absent without leave or absent sick from that date until temporarily attached to Company A, 2nd Battalion N.C. Local Defense Troops, January-February, 1864. Absent detached from that date through December, 1864. Retired to the Invalid Corps on February 17, 1865, and assigned to light duty with the Superintendent of the Bureau of Conscripts at Fayetteville on March 9, 1865.

ROUSE, JOSHUA, Private

Resided in Cumberland County where he enlisted at age 17, June 6, 1861, for the war. Present or accounted for until wounded and captured at Gettysburg, Pennsylvania, July 1-3, 1863. Admitted to U.S.A. General Hospital, Frederick, Maryland, July 6, 1863, with "g.s.w.f., right arm." Confined at Fort McHenry, Maryland, July 9, 1863, and was transferred to Fort Delaware, Delaware, the same day. Sent from Fort Delaware on October 15-18, 1863, to Point Lookout, Maryland, where he was confined until paroled and sent to James River, Virginia, for exchange on February 18, 1865. Reported as present on a muster roll of a detachment of paroled and exchanged prisoners at Camp Lee, near Richmond, Virginia, dated February 23, 1865.

SANDERSON, JOHN, Private

Resided in Cumberland County where he enlisted at age 25, June 21, 1861, for the war. Present or accounted for until killed in battle at Gettysburg, Pennsylvania, July 2, 1863.

SEAWELL, SIMON McNEILL, Private

Born in Moore County where he resided and enlisted on July 20, 1862, for the war. Wounded at Sharpsburg, Maryland, September 17, 1862. Present or accounted for until again wounded at Chancellorsville, Virginia, May 3, 1863. Reported as absent wounded until detailed for hospital duty on August 6, 1863. Absent on detail until retired to the Invalid Corps, October 26, 1864. Assigned as a hospital guard at Richmond, Virginia, from that date through January, 1865.

SESSOMS, WILLIAM JAMES, Private

Resided in Cumberland County where he enlisted at age 18, May 29, 1861, for the war. Admitted to hospital at Danville, Virginia, June 29, 1862, with "typhoides febris" and was returned to duty

August 20, 1862. Again admitted to hospital at Richmond, Virginia, October 14, 1862, with "caries tibia." Reported as absent sick from that date until detailed for hospital duty April 6, 1863. Absent on detail at various hospitals in Richmond until captured in hospital at Richmond on April 3, 1865. Paroled on April 18, 1865, at Richmond.

SHARPE, A., Private

Paroled at Salisbury on May 23, 1865.

SHERAN, JAMES, Private

Captured at Raccoon Ford, Virginia, and confined at Old Capitol Prison, Washington, D. C. Took the Oath of Allegiance on December 13, 1863, at Old Capitol Prison and was sent north.

SHIELDS, J. M., Private

Paroled at Greensboro on May 22, 1865.

SINCLAIR, DUNCAN F., Private

Born in Cumberland County and resided as a farmer in Moore County where he enlisted at age 30, July 20, 1862, for the war. Present or accounted for until discharged January 26, 1863, by reason of disability caused by "chronic plurisy with empyema."

SMITH, ANGUS, Private

Resided in Cumberland County where he enlisted on July 18, 1862, for the war. Wounded at Sharpsburg, Maryland, September 17, 1862. Present or accounted for until again wounded at Chancellorsville, Virginia, on May 3, 1863. Wounded and captured at Gettysburg, Pennsylvania, July 1-5, 1863. Confined at Fort McHenry, Maryland, and transferred to Fort Delaware, Delaware, July 9, 1863. Died at Fort Delaware, October 8, 1863.

SMITH, DANIEL, Private

Resided in Harnett County and enlisted in Bladen County on July 17, 1862, for the war. Wounded at Sharpsburg, Maryland, September 17, 1862. Present or accounted for until again wounded at Chancellorsville, Virginia, May 3, 1863. Admitted to hospital at Richmond, Virginia, May 12, 1863, with gunshot wound of thigh and died May 24, 1863.

SMITH, JAMES D., Private

Resided in Cumberland County where he enlisted at age 18, June 15, 1861, for the war. Present or accounted for until admitted to hospital at Danville, Virginia, September 28, 1862, with "debilitas." Died at that hospital November 12, 1862, of "chronic diarrhoea."

SMITH, WILLIAM J., Private

Resided in Cumberland County where he enlisted at age 23, March 8, 1862, for the war. Present or accounted for until wounded at Chancellorsville, Virginia, May 3, 1863. Present or accounted for as absent wounded from that date until captured at Fisher's Hill, Virginia, September 22, 1864. Confined at Point Lookout, Maryland, where he took the Oath of Allegiance and joined the U.S. service on October 16, 1864. Later assigned to Company E, 4th Regiment U.S. Volunteer Infantry.

SPRINGS, EZEKIEL D., Private

Born in Cumberland County where he resided as a farmer and enlisted at age 16, June 15, 1861, for the war. Died February 22, 1862, at Camp Howe, Stafford County, Virginia.

SPRINGS, THOMAS, Private
Resided in Cumberland County where he enlisted at age 21, May 29, 1861, for the war. Present or accounted for until wounded in battle at Malvern Hill, Virginia, July 1, 1862. Absent wounded through December, 1862. Detailed for hospital duty from January-February, 1863, through December, 1863. Present or accounted for through December, 1864. Paroled at Appomattox Court House, Virginia, April 9, 1865.

STERLING, JONATHAN, Private
Born in Cumberland County where he resided as a farmer and enlisted at age 34, March 8, 1862, for the war. Discharged July 10, 1862, by reason of disability caused by "phthisis pulmonalis."

STRAUGHN, LUTHER C., Private
Resided in Cumberland County where he enlisted at age 32, June 1, 1861, for the war. Mustered in as Private and appointed Corporal, August 3, 1861. Reduced to ranks March-April, 1862. Temporarily attached to Company A, 2nd Battalion N.C. Local Defense Troops, May 23, 1862. Absent detached through December, 1864.

STRICKLAND, JACOB B., Private
Born in Cumberland County where he resided as a farmer and enlisted at age 21, May 29, 1861, for the war. Mustered in as Corporal and reduced to ranks August 3, 1861. Reappointed Corporal November-December, 1861, and promoted to Sergeant, July 14-November 1, 1862. Wounded at Sharpsburg, Maryland, September 17, 1862. Absent wounded from that date until reported as present on the November-December, 1863, muster roll, with rank of Private. Attached to Company A, 2nd Battalion N.C. Local Defense Troops, January 28, 1864. Absent detached through December, 1864.

STRICKLAND, R., Private
Killed at Sharpsburg, Maryland, September 17, 1862.

SWEENEY, PATRICK, Private
Resided in Cumberland County where he enlisted at age 33, May 29, 1861, for the war. Present or accounted for until he deserted in August, 1862. Returned August 23, 1863, and again deserted September-October, 1863. No further records.

THOMAS, B. A., Private
Resided in Moore County where he enlisted on July 20, 1862, for the war. Died in hospital at Richmond, Virginia, December 29, 1862.

THOMAS, W. H., Private
Resided in Cumberland County where he enlisted at age 44, July 8, 1861, for the war. Discharged on May 24, 1862.

TOLAR, SIMEON RANDALL, Corporal
Resided in Cumberland County where he enlisted at age 18, February 18, 1862, for the war. Mustered in as Private. Captured and confined at Old Capitol Prison, Washington, D.C., September 16, 1862. Paroled and exchanged at Aiken's Landing, **James River, Virginia, September 27, 1862. Appointed Corporal on December 1, 1863.**

Wounded at Payne's Farm, Virginia, November 27-28, 1863. Returned to duty on December 15, 1863, and reported as absent sick from February 22, 1864, through December, 1864. Wounded in foot on December 3, 1864, and furloughed from hospital at Richmond, Virginia, for 60 days on February 14, 1865.

TRAILER, J. B., Private
Paroled at Charlotte on May 3, 1865.

TYSON, CORNELIUS, Private
Resided in Cumberland County where he enlisted at age 21, May 29, 1861, for the war. Deserted at Sharpsburg, Maryland, September 17, 1862, and took the Oath of Allegiance on September 27, 1862.

VUNCANNON, WILLIAM, Private
Resided in Moore County where he enlisted at age 35, February 26, 1862, for the war. Present or accounted for until captured near Spotsylvania Court House, Virginia, May 12, 1864. Confined at Point Lookout, Maryland, until transferred to Elmira, New York, August 10, 1864. Died at Elmira on July 7, 1865, of "chronic diarrhoea."

WALLACE, JOHN McL., Private
Resided in Cumberland County where he enlisted at age 20, June 15, 1861, for the war. Present or accounted for until captured near Spotsylvania Court House, Virginia, May 12, 1864. Confined at Point Lookout, Maryland, until released after taking the Oath of Allegiance and joining the U.S. service on June 18, 1864. Assigned to Company D, 1st Regiment U.S. Volunteer Infantry.

WALLS, JAMES, Private
Resided in Cumberland County where he enlisted at age 43, May 29, 1861, for the war. Died in hospital at Richmond, Virginia, November 22, 1862, of "variola."

WATKINS, JOHN M., Private
Resided in Cumberland County where he enlisted at age 34, May 29, 1861, for the war. Mustered in as Sergeant. Wounded at Malvern Hill, Virginia, July 1, 1862, and died of wound. Reduced to ranks after he was wounded.

WEST, DANIEL H., Private
Resided in Cumberland County where he enlisted at age 18, January 25, 1862, for the war. Wounded at Chancellorsville, Virginia, May 3, 1863, and furloughed from hospital for 30 days on May 16, 1863. Present or accounted for until admitted to hospital at Richmond, Virginia, May 8, 1864, with a gunshot wound of the right hand. Returned to company September-October, 1864. Deserted March 18, 1865, and took the Oath of Allegiance on March 21, 1865.

WILLIFORD, DAVID, Corporal
Resided in Cumberland County where he enlisted at age 18, February 25, 1862, for the war. Mustered in as Private. Wounded at Gettysburg, **Pennsylvania, July 2-3, 1863. Appointed Corporal on December 1, 1863. Wounded at Spotsylvania Court House, Virginia, May 10, 1864.** Furloughed from hospital at Charlottesville, Virginia, for 60 days on May 27, 1864. Reported as absent wounded on company muster rolls through December, 1864.

WILLIFORD, HENRY J., Private
Resided in Cumberland County where he enlisted on July 18, 1862, for the war. Wounded at Chancellorsville, Virginia, May 3, 1863, and at Gettysburg, Pennsylvania, July 2-3, 1863. Captured at Spotsylvania Court House, Virginia, May 12, 1864, and confined at Point Lookout, Maryland, until transferred to Elmira, New York, August 10, 1864. Paroled at Elmira on March 2, 1865, and sent to James River, Virginia, for exchange. Admitted to hospital at Richmond, Virginia, March 6, 1865, and furloughed for 30 days on March 9, 1865.

WILLIFORD, SION, Private
Resided in Cumberland County where he enlisted at age 21, February 25, 1862, for the war. Present or accounted for until captured at Spotsylvania Court House, Virginia, May 12, 1864. Confined at Point Lookout, Maryland, until transferred to Elmira, New York, August 10, 1864. Remained at Elmira until released after taking the Oath of Allegiance on June 19, 1865.

WILLIFORD, THOMAS, Private
Resided in Cumberland County where he enlisted at age 26, February 25, 1862, for the war. Died in hospital at Richmond, Virginia, July 24, 1862, of "febris typhoid."

WILSON, GEORGE W., Private
Resided in Cumberland County where he enlisted at age 23, May 29, 1861, for the war. Wounded at Gettysburg, Pennsylvania, July 2, 1863, and captured at Gettysburg on July 3, 1863. Died in hospital at Chester, Pennsylvania, July 23, 1863, of "gunshot wound abdomen."

WREN, J. M., Private
Paroled at Greensboro on April 28, 1865.

WRINK, P., Private
Captured at Gettysburg, Pennsylvania, July 3, 1863, and confined at Fort Delaware, Delaware, July 7-12, 1863.

COMPANY D

This company was organized in New Hanover County and enlisted at Wilmington on May 27, 1861. It tendered its service to the state and was ordered to Garysburg, Northampton County, where it was assigned to this regiment as Company D. After joining the regiment the company functioned as a part of the regiment, and its history for the war period is recorded as a part of the regimental history.

The information contained in the following roster of the company was compiled principally from company muster rolls which covered from the date of enlistment through December, 1864. No company muster rolls were found for the period after December, 1864. In addition to the company muster rolls, Roll of Honor records, receipt rolls, and hospital records, supplemented by state pension applications, United Daughters of the Confederacy records, and postwar rosters and histories, all provided useful information.

OFFICERS

CAPTAINS

SAVAGE, EDWARD
Resided in New Hanover County and appointed Captain at age 40 to rank from May 16, 1861. Transferred to the Field and Staff of this regiment upon appointment as Major to rank from April 26, 1862.

MEARES, EDWARD G.
Resided in New Hanover County and appointed 2nd Lieutenant at age 19 to rank from May 16, 1861. Promoted to 1st Lieutenant to rank from November 27, 1861, and promoted to Captain to rank from April 26, 1862. Killed at Sharpsburg, Maryland, September 17, 1862.

VAN BOKKELEN, JOHN F. S.
Resided in New Hanover County and appointed 2nd Lieutenant at age 19 to rank from May 16, 1861. Promoted to 1st Lieutenant to rank from April 26, 1862, and promoted to Captain to rank from September 17, 1862. Wounded at Chancellorsville, Virginia, May 3, 1863. Admitted to hospital June 13, 1863, at Richmond, Virginia, where he died on June 22, 1863, of "int. fever."

COWAN, JOHN
Transferred from Company I, 18th Regiment N.C. Troops (8th Regiment N.C. Volunteers) upon appointment as 2nd Lieutenant to rank from January 14, 1862. Promoted to 1st Lieutenant to rank from September 17, 1862, and promoted to Captain to rank from June 22, 1863. Captured at Wilderness, Virginia, May 10, 1864, and confined at Fort Delaware, Delaware. Transferred to Hilton Head, South Carolina, August 20, 1864, and forwarded to Fort Pulaski, Georgia, October 21, 1864. Returned to Hilton Head by December 26, 1864, and to Fort Delaware by March 12, 1865. Released at Fort Delaware after taking the Oath of Allegiance on May 26, 1865.

LIEUTENANTS

BARR, WILLIAM H., 2nd Lieutenant
Resided in New Hanover County where he enlisted at age 37, May 27, 1861, for the war. Mustered in as Sergeant. Wounded at Sharpsburg, Maryland, September 17, 1862, and appointed 2nd Lieutenant to rank from that date. Wounded at Chancellorsville, Virginia, May 3, 1863. Submitted his resignation on January 30, 1864, by reason of not being able to support his family on the pay that he was receiving. Resignation officially accepted February 10, 1864.

BIVINS, WILLIAM J., 1st Lieutenant
Resided in New Hanover County where he enlisted at age 26, May 27, 1861, for the war. Mustered in as 1st Sergeant and appointed 2nd Lieutenant to rank from May 7, 1862. Wounded at Sharpsburg, Maryland, September 17, 1862. Promoted to 1st Lieutenant to rank from June 22, 1863. Company muster rolls and hospital records report him as absent wounded from September, 1862, through February, 1865.

CUMMING, WILLIAM A., 1st Lieutenant
Resided in New Hanover County and appointed

1st Lieutenant to rank from May 16, 1861. Transferred to the Field and Staff of this regiment upon appointment as Adjutant with the rank of 1st Lieutenant on November 27, 1861.

HOUSTON, ROBERT B., 2nd Lieutenant
Transferred from Company B of this regiment upon appointment as 2nd Lieutenant to rank from February 1, 1864. Admitted to hospital at Wilmington on June 15, 1864, with "febris remittens" and returned to duty on November 28, 1864. Reported as absent sick through February, 1865.

NONCOMMISSIONED OFFICERS AND PRIVATES

ADAMS, ALLEN G., Private
Resided in Pitt County and enlisted in Wake County at age 23, July 15, 1862, for the war. Wounded at Sharpsburg, Maryland, September 17, 1862. Deserted near Port Royal, Virginia, March 20, 1863.

ADAMS, CHURCHILL D., Private
Resided in Pitt County where he enlisted at age 22, July 15, 1862, for the war. Wounded at Sharpsburg, Maryland, September 17, 1862, and never reported to the company after that date.

ADAMS, GEORGE B., Private
Resided in Pitt County where he enlisted at age 18, July 15, 1862, for the war. Wounded at Chancellorsville, Virginia, May 2, 1863. Died in hospital at Lynchburg, Virginia, on May 30, 1863, of "typhoid fever."

ADAMS, JOHN D., Private
Resided in Pitt County where he enlisted on July 15, 1862, for the war. Present or accounted for until transferred to Company G of this regiment on November 11, 1863, in exchange for R. B. Wood.

ALLEN, IVEY, Private
Resided in Pitt County where he enlisted at age 34, July 15, 1862, for the war. Present or accounted for on company muster rolls until November-December, 1863, when he was reported as absent "sick in hospital (wounded), Richmond, Virginia." Date of return to duty not shown. Captured at Spotsylvania Court House, Virginia, May 12, 1864, and confined at Point Lookout, Maryland. Transferred to Elmira, New York, August 10, 1864. Paroled at Elmira and sent to James River, Virginia, for exchange, February 13, 1865.

ALLEN, LEWIS, Private
Resided in Pitt County where he enlisted at age 28, July 15, 1862, for the war. Deserted March 20, 1863, and returned to duty August 30, 1863. Wounded at Payne's Farm, Virginia, November 27, 1863. Admitted to hospital at Charlottesville, Virginia, December 4, 1863, with gunshot wound and was returned to duty January 30, 1864. Company muster roll for September-October, 1864, states that he was absent "wounded and captured October 19, 1864." Admitted to hospital at Charlottesville, Virginia, November 22, 1864, with "v.s. left thigh" and was furloughed December 6,

1864. Reported as absent wounded through December, 1864.

AUSTIN, Z., Private
Captured near Spotsylvania Court House, Virginia, May 12, 1864, and confined at Point Lookout, Maryland, May 18, 1864.

AVERY, CHARLES O., Private
Born in Bladen County where he resided as a farmer prior to enlisting in New Hanover County at age 23, May 27, 1861, for the war. Present or accounted for until wounded near Richmond, Virginia, July 1, 1862. Again wounded in battle at Sharpsburg, Maryland, September 17, 1862. Discharged February 10, 1863, by reason of disability caused by wounds.

BALDREE, ARNOLD T., Private
Resided in Pitt County where he enlisted at age 30, July 15, 1862, for the war. Wounded and captured at Sharpsburg, Maryland, September 17, 1862. Admitted to U.S.A. General Hospital, Frederick, Maryland, October 15, 1862, with "wound in the left thigh." Transferred to U.S.A. General Hospital, Baltimore, Maryland, February 10, 1863, and was transferred to Fort McHenry, **Maryland, February 14-15, 1863. Paroled and sent** to City Point, Virginia, for exchange, February 18, 1863. Admitted to hospital at Petersburg, Virginia, February 18, 1863, and was furloughed for 40 days on March 1, 1863. Reported on company muster rolls as absent wounded through October, 1863, and as absent without leave after that date.

BALDREE, ELIAS A., Private
Resided in Pitt County and enlisted in Wake County on July 15, 1862, for the war. Wounded at Sharpsburg, Maryland, September, 1862, and died of his wounds November 17, 1862.

BALDREE, RICHARD H., Corporal
Resided in Pitt County where he enlisted at age 27, July 15, 1862, for the war. Mustered in as Private and appointed Corporal November 1, 1862. Present or accounted for until he "deserted May 27, 1863, while in camp near Hamilton's Crossing."

BEASELEY, JACOB, Private
Resided in New Hanover County where he enlisted at age 23, May 27, 1861, for the war. Present or accounted for until captured at Spotsylvania Court House, Virginia, May 12, 1864. Confined at Point Lookout, Maryland, until paroled and sent to Aiken's Landing, James River, Virginia, for exchange, March 17, 1865.

BEASLEY, PYROM P., Private
Resided in New Hanover County where he enlisted at age 25, May 29, 1861, for the war. Wounded in battle at Mechanicsville, Virginia, June 26, 1862. Present or accounted for until detailed as a pioneer in Gordon's Division, January 10, 1864. Absent detailed through August, 1864. Present or accounted for through December, 1864. Deserted, took the Oath of Allegiance, and was furnished transportation from Washington, D.C., to Wilmington on April 6, 1865.

BEAVERS, GALEN, Private
Resided in Wake County where he enlisted at

age 34, July 15, 1862, for the war. Wounded in battle at Chancellorsville, Virginia, May 3, 1863, and died on May 15, 1863.

BELL, BENJAMIN C., Private
Resided in Pitt County where he enlisted on July 15, 1862, for the war. Discharged July 20, 1862.

BEST, RICHARD W., Private
Resided in Wayne County where he enlisted at age 26, July 15, 1862, for the war. Wounded at Sharpsburg, Maryland, September 17, 1862. Absent wounded through December, 1862. Present or accounted for until again wounded at Chancellorsville, Virginia, on May 3, 1863. Received a flesh wound in battle at Payne's Farm, Virginia, November 27-28, 1863. Present or accounted for until killed in battle at Wilderness, Virginia, May 5, 1864.

BEST, ROBERT S., Private
Resided in Wayne County where he enlisted at age 31, July 15, 1862, for the war. Present or accounted for until wounded at Chancellorsville, Virginia, May 3, 1863. Absent wounded through August, 1863. Present or accounted for until again wounded at Payne's Farm, Virginia, November 27, 1863. Died of his wounds in hospital at Gordonsville, Virginia, January 18, 1864.

BEST, WILLIAM H., Private
Resided in Wayne County where he enlisted at age 19, July 15, 1862, for the war. Captured and paroled at Frederick, Maryland, September 27, 1862. Absent sick from that date until reported as present on the November-December, 1862, muster roll. Present or accounted for until wounded and captured at Gettysburg, Pennsylvania, July 1-4, 1863. Confined at DeCamp General Hospital, Davids Island, New York Harbor, July 17-24, 1863. Paroled at that hospital and sent to City Point, Virginia, for exchange on August 24, 1863. Reported on company muster rolls as absent wounded and at home in North Carolina from that date through December, 1864.

BLAKE, WILLIAM, Private
Born in New Hanover County where he resided as a farmer and enlisted at age 21, May 27, 1861, for the war. Discharged July 20, 1861, by reason of disability caused by "predisposition to phthisis pulmonalis and muscular weakness."

BONEY, JOHN B., Private
Born in New Hanover County where he resided as a farmer and enlisted at age 23, March 3, 1862, for the war. Discharged April 16, 1862, by reason of disability caused by "mental and physical inertia and epileptic fits."

BOYLAN, GEORGE W., 1st Sergeant
Resided in New Hanover County where he enlisted at age 26, May 27, 1861, for the war. Mustered in as Sergeant. Accidentally wounded at Malvern Hill, Virginia, July 20, 1862. Absent wounded through December, 1862. Appointed 1st Sergeant on January 1, 1863. Present or accounted for until killed in battle at Chancellorsville, Virginia, May 2, 1863.

BRANCH, DENNIS J., Private
Resided in Pitt County where he enlisted at age 23, July 15, 1862, for the war. Wounded at Sharpsburg, Maryland, September 17, 1862. Died in hospital at Richmond, Virginia, December 19, 1862.

BRANCH, JAMES F., Private
Resided in Pitt County where he enlisted at age 20, July 15, 1862, for the war. Present or accounted for until captured at Winchester, Virginia, September 19, 1864. Confined at Point Lookout, Maryland, until released after taking the Oath of Allegiance on June 3, 1865.

BRANCH, RICHARD H., Private
Resided in Pitt County and enlisted at age 22, July 15, 1862, for the war.

BRIDGER, GEORGE E., Private
Resided in New Hanover County where he enlisted at age 20, May 27, 1861, for the war. Mustered in as Corporal and reduced to ranks January 1, 1863. Present or accounted for until wounded at Chancellorsville, Virginia, May 2, 1863. Reported as absent wounded until he deserted at Raccoon Ford, Virginia, February 8, 1864.

BROWN, JAMES, Private
Enlisted in Randolph County on June 27, 1861, for the war. Detailed as regimental wagonmaster, or regimental teamster, from January-April, 1862, through December, 1864. Paroled at Troy, N.C., May 23, 1865.

BRYLEY, BURTON, Private
Born in Pitt County where he resided as a farmer and enlisted at age 33, July 15, 1862, for the war. Discharged September 2, 1862, by reason of disability caused by "phthisis pulmonalis."

BULLOCK, J. B., Private
Paroled at Appomattox Court House, Virginia, April 9, 1865.

BULLOCK, JOHN, Private
Enlisted in Wake County on August, 31, 1864, for the war. Present or accounted for until reported on the November-December, 1864, muster roll as being "on detached service."

BURNS, FRANCIS, Private
Born in Ireland and resided in New Hanover County where he enlisted at age 27, May 27, 1861, for the war. Present or accounted for until his death on March 22, 1862, in hospital at Fredericksburg, Virginia.

BYRD, CHRISTOPHER, Private
Born in Wayne County and resided as a farmer in Pitt County where he enlisted on July 15, 1862, for the war. Reported as absent sick from August 19, 1862, until discharged on August 8, 1863, by reason of disability caused by "pulmonary consumption developed by repeated attacks of pneumonia, marasmas."

BYRD, MICHAEL, Corporal
Resided in Duplin County and enlisted in New Hanover County at age 26, May 27, 1861, for the war. Mustered in as Private and appointed Corporal, January 1, 1863. Wounded in battle at Winchester, Virginia, June 15, 1863. Present or accounted for through December, 1864.

CANNON, SIMON, Private

Resided in Pitt County where he enlisted at age 27, July 15, 1862, for the war. Muster rolls report that he was left in Richmond, Virginia, August 19, 1862, sick. Furloughed from hospital at Richmond on October 3, 1862. Muster roll for January-February, 1863, states that he died in North Carolina in October, 1862.

CARROLL, ADAM, Private

Resided in Pitt County where he enlisted at age 30, July 15, 1862, for the war. Muster rolls report that he was left in Richmond, Virginia, August 19, 1862, sick. Admitted to hospital at Richmond on September 8, 1862, with "typhoid fever" and was furloughed September 12, 1862. Muster roll for January-February, 1863, states that he died in North Carolina of disease on November 15, 1862.

CARTER, BRANCH S., Private

Resided in Duplin County and enlisted in New Hanover County at age 39, May 27, 1861, for the war. Present or accounted for until detailed as a shoemaker in the Quartermaster Department at Richmond, Virginia, on November 15, 1862. Absent detailed through December, 1864.

CARTER, ENOCH, Private

Born in Duplin County where he resided prior to enlisting in New Hanover County at age 22, May 27, 1861, for the war. Present or accounted for until his death on June 28, 1862, at Richmond, Virginia, of disease.

CARTER, JOHN W., Private

Resided in Robeson County and enlisted in New Hanover County at age 25, May 27, 1861, for the war. Wounded at Payne's Farm, Virginia, November 27, 1863. Present or accounted for on company muster rolls through December, 1864.

CASTEEN, JACOB, Private

Born in New Hanover County where he resided as a farmer and enlisted at age 19, May 27, 1861, for the war. Died in hospital at Richmond, Virginia, June 20, 1862, of "typhoid fever."

CASTEEN, JOHN, Sergeant

Born in New Hanover County where he resided as a laborer and enlisted at age 19, May 27, 1861, for the war. Mustered in as Private and discharged at Fredericksburg, Virginia, August 14, 1861, by reason of disability. Reenlisted in New Hanover County on February 18, 1862, for the war. Mustered in as Private and wounded at Malvern Hill, Virginia, July 1, 1862. Appointed Sergeant on July 4, 1863. Present or accounted for until captured near Spotsylvania Court House, Virginia, May 12, 1864. Confined at Point Lookout, Maryland, until transferred to Elmira, New York, August 10, 1864. Remained at Elmira until released after taking the Oath of Allegiance on July 3, 1865.

CHASE, ROBERT, Private

Resided in Sampson County and enlisted in New Hanover County at age 18, May 27, 1861, for the war. Present or accounted for until captured near Spotsylvania Court House, Virginia, May 12, 1864. Confined at Point Lookout, Maryland, until transferred to Elmira, New York, August 10, 1864. Remained at Elmira until released after taking the

Oath of Allegiance on June 27, 1865.

CLARKSON, HENRY J., Private

Resided in Georgia and enlisted in New Hanover County at age 21, May 27, 1861, for the war. Captured at South Mountain, Maryland, September 14, 1862, and confined at Fort Delaware, Delaware, until paroled and exchanged at Aiken's Landing, James River, Virginia, November 10, 1862. Deserted on June 25, 1863, and surrendered to the enemy at Chambersburg, Pennsylvania, in June, 1863. Confined at Old Capitol Prison, Washington, D.C., October 2, 1863, and released after taking the Oath of Allegiance on October 7, 1863.

COOK, WILLIAM, Private

Resided in New Hanover County where he enlisted at age 33, May 27, 1861, for the war. Transferred to the C.S. Navy on May 16, 1862.

COREY, SAMUEL, Private

Resided in Pitt County where he enlisted at age 30, July 15, 1862, for the war. Deserted near Port Royal, Virginia, March 20, 1863.

COSTIN, ZEPHANIAH, Private

Resided in New Hanover County where he enlisted at age 18, May 27, 1861, for the war. Present or accounted for until captured near Spotsylvania Court House, Virginia, May 12, 1864. Confined at Point Lookout, Maryland, until released after taking the Oath of Allegiance and joining the U.S. service in June, 1864. Assigned to Company I, 1st Regiment U.S. Volunteer Infantry.

DANIELS, JAMES MATTHEW, Private

Resided in Wayne County where he enlisted at age 20, July 15, 1862, for the war. Present or accounted for until admitted to hospital on August 11, 1863, and reported as absent sick from that date through December, 1864.

DAVIS, JOEL P., Private

Resided in Pitt County and enlisted in Wayne County on July 15, 1862, for the war. Captured at Frederick, Maryland, in September, 1862, and paroled at Frederick on September 27, 1862. Wounded at Payne's Farm, Virginia, November 27, 1863, and captured near Spotsylvania Court House, Virginia, May 12, 1864. Confined at Point Lookout, Maryland, until paroled and exchanged at Boulware's Wharf, James River, Virginia, March 18, 1865.

DICKSEY, JESSE J., Private

Resided in New Hanover County where he enlisted at age 18, June 7, 1861, for the war. Captured at Gettysburg, Pennsylvania, July 3, 1863, and confined at Fort Delaware, Delaware, until released after taking the Oath of Allegiance on May 5, 1865.

DUNN, NEWMAN, Private

Resided in Pitt County where he enlisted at age 22, July 15, 1862, for the war. Died near Port Royal, Virginia, March 2, 1863, of disease.

ENGLISH, CHARLES D., Private

Enlisted in New Hanover County on March 1, 1862, for the war. Captured at Frederick, Maryland, September 14, 1862, and paroled and exchanged at Aiken's Landing, James River, Virginia, November 10, 1862. Wounded at Gettysburg, Pennsylvania, July 3, 1863, and captured at Gettysburg July 3-4, 1863. Confined at DeCamp General Hospital, Davids Island, New York Harbor, until paroled and exchanged at City Point, Virginia, September 16, 1863. Captured near Spotsylvania Court House, Virginia, May 12, 1864, and confined at Point Lookout, Maryland, until transferred to Elmira, New York, August 10, 1864. Released at Elmira after taking the Oath of Allegiance on June 27, 1865.

ENGLISH, GEORGE W., Private

Resided in Duplin County and enlisted in New Hanover County at age 22, May 28, 1861, for the war. Wounded at Sharpsburg, Maryland, September 17, 1862. Present or accounted for until captured near Spotsylvania Court House, Virginia, May 12, 1864. Confined at Point Lookout, Maryland, until transferred to Elmira, New York, August 10, 1864. Paroled at Elmira and exchanged at Boulware's Wharf, James River, Virginia, March 18-21, 1865.

ENGLISH, JAMES W., Private

Born in Duplin County where he resided as a laborer prior to enlisting in New Hanover County at age 23, May 27, 1861, for the war. Wounded in arm and "right eye destroyed by shell" at Sharpsburg, Maryland, September 17, 1862. Discharged on February 28, 1863, by reason of wounds.

EVANS, JOHN WILLIAM, Private

Resided in Cumberland County where he enlisted at age 24, July 15, 1862, for the war. Captured and paroled at Warrenton, Virginia, September 29, 1862. Reported as absent sick from April, 1863, through January, 1864, when he was assigned to the Fayetteville Arsenal and Armory. Attached to Company A, 2nd Battalion N.C. Local Defense Troops at the Fayetteville Arsenal and Armory from January through December, 1864.

EVANS, WILLIAM Y., Private

Born in Orange County where he resided as a laborer prior to enlisting in Northampton County at age 28, June 11, 1861, for the war. Died in Wake County on January 25, 1862, of "acute hepatitis."

FLEMING, JOHN M., Private

Resided as a farmer in Pitt County where he enlisted at age 28, July 15, 1862, for the war. Wounded at Sharpsburg, Maryland, September 17, 1862, and returned to duty March 27, 1863. Wounded at Payne's Farm, Virginia, November 27-28, 1863, and captured at Mine Run, Virginia, November 28, 1863. Confined at Old Capitol Prison, Washington, D.C., until transferred to Point Lookout, Maryland, February 3, 1864. Paroled at Point Lookout on February 18, 1865, and exchanged at Boulware's Wharf, James River, Virginia, February 20-21, 1865. Reported as present on a roll of paroled and exchanged prisoners at Camp Lee, near Richmond, Virginia, February 23, 1865.

FORBES, ROBERT G., Private

Resided in Pitt County where he enlisted at age 28, July 15, 1862, for the war. Captured and paroled at Warrenton, Virginia, September 29, 1862. Died November 4, 1862.

FORNES, JOHN, Private

Resided in Pitt County where he enlisted at age

30, July 15, 1862, for the war. Died at Gordonsville, Virginia, May 8, 1864, of "febris typhoides."

FREDERICK, E., Private

Resided in Duplin County and enlisted in New Hanover County at age 24, May 27, 1861, for the war. Present or accounted for until captured near Spotsylvania Court House, Virginia, May 12, 1864. Confined at Point Lookout, Maryland, until transferred to Elmira, New York, August 10, 1864. Died at Elmira on January 22, 1865, of "variola."

FREDERICK, PATRICK, Private

Resided in Duplin County and enlisted in New Hanover County at age 21, May 27, 1861, for the war. Present or accounted for until captured near Spotsylvania Court House, Virginia, May 12, 1864. Confined at Point Lookout, Maryland, until transferred to Elmira, New York, August 10, 1864. Released at Elmira after taking the Oath of Allegiance on June 21, 1865.

FREDERICKS, JAMES R., Private

Resided in Duplin County and enlisted in New Hanover County at age 22, May 27, 1861, for the war. Present or accounted for until paroled at Appomattox Court House, Virginia, April 9, 1865.

GARVEY, JAMES, Private

Resided in New Hanover County where he enlisted at age 23, May 27, 1861, for the war. Wounded at Malvern Hill, Virginia, July 1, 1862, and at Sharpsburg, Maryland, September 17, 1862. Present or accounted for until captured near Spotsylvania Court House, Virginia, May 12, 1864. Confined at Point Lookout, Maryland, until transferred to Elmira, New York, August 15, 1864. Released at Elmira after taking the Oath of Allegiance on June 19, 1865.

GILMORE, JAMES W., Private

Born in Augusta, Georgia, and resided in New Hanover County where he enlisted at age 21, May 31, 1861, for the war. Wounded at Malvern Hill, Virginia, July 1, 1862. Killed at Sharpsburg, Maryland, September 17, 1862.

GORDON, WILLIAM K., Private

Resided in New Hanover County where he enlisted at age 27, May 27, 1861, for the war. Reported on November-December, 1862, muster roll with the remark: "Supposed to have shot himself to keep out of action December 13. In hospital at Richmond." Admitted to hospital at Richmond, Virginia, December 14, 1862, and deserted from hospital on December 27, 1862.

GRUBB, SOLOMON M., Corporal

Resided in Davidson County and enlisted in New Hanover County at age 36, May 27, 1861, for the war. Mustered in as Private and appointed Corporal on November 1, 1862. Wounded at Chancellorsville, Virginia, May 2-3, 1863. Present or accounted for on company muster rolls through December, 1864. Admitted to hospital at Richmond, Virginia, March 25, 1865, with "rheumatismus ch." Captured in hospital at Richmond on April 3, 1865, and confined at Newport News, Virginia, until released after taking the Oath of Allegiance on June 30, 1865.

GULLY, JONATHAN B., Private

Resided in Johnston County and enlisted in New

Hanover County at age 36, May 27, 1861, for the war. Wounded and captured at Sharpsburg, Maryland, September 17, 1862. Confined in hospital at Frederick, Maryland, until transferred to hospital at Baltimore, Maryland, March 4, 1863. Paroled and exchanged at Fort Monroe, Virginia, March 13, 1863. Admitted to hospital at Petersburg, Virginia, March 18, 1863, and furloughed for 60 days April 6, 1863. Detailed as a nurse at Wilmington on March 8, 1864. Reported on company muster rolls as absent on detail from March through December, 1864.

HALL, JOHN, Private
Paroled at Farmville, Virginia, April 11-21, 1865.

HANCHEY, WILLIAM H., Corporal
Resided in New Hanover County where he enlisted at age 31, May 27, 1861, for the war. Mustered in as Private. Present or accounted for until captured at Frederick, Maryland, on September 13, 1863. Confined at Fort Delaware, Delaware, until paroled and sent to Aiken's Landing, James River, Virginia, for exchange on October 2, 1862. Appointed Corporal, September 1, 1863. Present or accounted for until killed in battle at Payne's Farm, Virginia, on November 27, 1863.

HARLOW, WILLIAM SHEPARD, Sergeant
Resided in New Hanover County where he enlisted at age 43, May 27, 1861, for the war. Mustered in as Corporal. Appointed Sergeant, November-December, 1861. Company muster roll for May 15-August 11, 1863, states that he was absent sick. Reported as absent from that date through December, 1864. Died February 20, 1865, in hospital at Raleigh of "phthisis."

HARRELL, JOSEPH HOLIDAY, Private
Resided in New Hanover County where he enlisted at age 27, May 27, 1861, for the war. Wounded in battle at Sharpsburg, Maryland, on September 17, 1862. Absent wounded through December, 1862. Present or accounted for until again wounded on May 3, 1863, in battle at Chancellorsville, Virginia. Admitted to hospital at Richmond, Virginia, on May 22, 1863, with "gunshot wound thigh" and transferred to hospital at Wilmington, May 31, 1863. Furloughed from hospital on June 27, 1863, and reported as absent wounded through November, 1863. Captured at Spotsylvania Court House, Virginia, May 12, 1864, and confined at Point Lookout, Maryland. Transferred to Elmira, New York, August 10, 1864, and was confined at that place until released after taking the Oath of Allegiance on June 19, 1865.

HARRINGTON, DAVID, Private
Born in Jones County where he resided prior to enlisting in New Hanover County at age 19, May 27, 1861, for the war. Present or accounted for until his death on January 10, 1862, in regimental hospital at Aquia Creek, Virginia.

HARRINGTON, EDWARD A., Private
Resided in Tennessee and enlisted in New Hanover County at age 26, May 27, 1861, for the war. Mustered in as Private and appointed Sergeant on November 1, 1862. Reduced to ranks July 4, 1863. Present or accounted for until captured at Gettys-

burg, Pennsylvania, July 3-5, 1863. Confined at Fort McHenry, Maryland, where he took the Oath of Allegiance and joined the U.S. service on September 22, 1863. Assigned to the 3rd Regiment Maryland Cavalry.

HARRINGTON, WILEY FRANKLIN, Private
Resided in Pitt County where he enlisted at age 23, July 15, 1862, for the war. Muster rolls report that he was left at Richmond, Virginia, on August 19, 1862, sick. Admitted to hospital at Richmond on September 8, 1862, with "typhoid fever" and was furloughed September 12, 1862. Absent sick from that date through December, 1862. Reported as absent without leave after December, 1862.

HARRIS, JAMES H., Private
Enlisted in Pitt County on July 15, 1862, for the war. Company muster roll for July 14-October 31, 1862, reports that he was left in Frederick, Maryland, sick.

HARRIS, WILLIAM H., Private
Resided in Pitt County and enlisted in Wake County at age 34, July 15, 1862, for the war. Captured at Frederick, Maryland, September 12, 1862, and confined at Fort Delaware, Delaware. Paroled at Fort Delaware and sent to Fort Monroe, Virginia, for exchange on December 15, 1862. Present or accounted for until captured on November 28, 1862, at Mine Run, Virginia, and confined at Old Capitol Prison, Washington, D.C. Transferred on February 3, 1864, to Point Lookout, Maryland, where he was confined until released after taking the Oath of Allegiance and joining the U.S. service on October 12, 1864.

HART, MATTHEW, Private
Resided in Pitt County where he enlisted at age 34, July 15, 1862, for the war. Wounded at Boonsboro, Maryland, on September 14-15, 1862, and at Chancellorsville, Virginia, May 3, 1863. Present or accounted for until captured at Spotsylvania Court House, Virginia, May 12, 1864. Confined at Point Lookout, Maryland, until transferred to Elmira, New York, on August 10, 1864. Released at Elmira after taking the Oath of Allegiance on June 27, 1865.

HETHCOCK, ALEXANDER, Private
Resided in Halifax County and enlisted in Northampton County at age 36, June 10, 1861, for the war. Present or accounted for until killed at Gettysburg, Pennsylvania, July 2, 1863.

HETHCOCK, WILLIAM, Private
Resided in Halifax County and enlisted in Northampton County at age 28, June 10, 1861, for the war. Captured at Frederick, Maryland, in September, 1862, and paroled on September 23, 1862. Deserted on May 27, 1863, and returned September-October, 1863. Deserted again on February 8, 1864, and surrendered to the enemy February 10, 1864. Sent to Alexandria, Virginia, February 16, 1864.

HIGHSMITH, RICHARD P., Private
Resided in New Hanover County where he enlisted at age 23, May 27, 1861, for the war. Captured at Boonsboro, Maryland, September 15, 1862, and paroled and exchanged at Aiken's Landing, James River, Virginia, November 10, 1862.

Company muster rolls report him as absent sick from November, 1862, through December, 1864. Claim for balance of pay due a deceased soldier filed by his widow on March 4, 1865. Date and place of death not reported.

HINES, JOHN W., Private
Resided in New Hanover County where he enlisted at age 18, May 29, 1861, for the war. Wounded at Chancellorsville, Virginia, May 2, 1863, and at Winchester, Virginia, June 15, 1863. Present or accounted for on company muster rolls through December, 1864. Captured in hospital at Richmond, Virginia, April 3, 1865, and paroled on April 24, 1865.

HINES, LEWIS W., Private
Born in New Hanover County where he resided as a laborer and enlisted at age 44, May 28, 1861, for the war. Discharged on March 14, 1863, by reason of "plea of old age."

HOLMES, BENJAMIN, Private
Resided in Beaufort County where he enlisted at age 50, July 15, 1862, for the war as a substitute for William Tucker. Wounded at Sharpsburg, Maryland, September 17, 1862. Died in hospital at Richmond, Virginia, December 25, 1862, of "pneumonia."

HOWARD, WILLIAM A., Private
Born in Onslow County where he resided prior to enlisting in New Hanover County at age 24, May 27, 1861, for the war. Died near Winchester, Virginia, October 3, 1862, of disease.

HUGGINS, WILLIAM H., Private
Transferred from Company I, 44th Regiment N.C. Troops on February 24, 1863. Wounded and admitted to hospital at Richmond, Virginia, May 28, 1864. Returned to duty June 3, 1864. Captured near Farmville, Virginia, April 6, 1865, and confined at Newport News, Virginia, until released after taking the Oath of Allegiance on June 27, 1865.

HUTCHINSON, WILLIAM K., Private
Resided in Duplin County and enlisted in New Hanover County at age 21, May 27, 1861, for the war. Wounded at Malvern Hill, Virginia, July 1, 1862. Deserted November 3, 1862, and returned to duty August 23, 1863. Deserted at Warrenton, Virginia, October 1, 1863, and surrendered to the enemy at Warrenton on November 4, 1863. Confined at Old Capitol Prison, Washington, D.C., until released after taking the Oath of Allegiance on March 15, 1864.-

JAMES, ROBERT, Private
Resided in New Hanover County where he enlisted at age 21, May 27, 1861, for the war. Killed at Chancellorsville, Virginia, May 3, 1863.

JERNIGAN, JESSE RUFUS, Sergeant
Resided in Wayne County where he enlisted at age 26, July 15, 1862, for the war. Mustered in as Private. Wounded at Sharpsburg, Maryland, September 17, 1862. Appointed Sergeant June 26, 1863. Killed at Wilderness, Virginia, May 5, 1864.

JOLLY, WILLIAM, Private
Resided in Pitt County where he enlisted at age 32, July 15, 1862, for the war. Captured at Fred-

icksburg, Virginia, May 3, 1863, and paroled and exchanged at City Point, Virginia, May 23, 1863. Captured near Spotsylvania Court House, Virginia, May 12, 1864, and confined at Point Lookout, Maryland, until transferred to Elmira, New York, August 10, 1864. Released at Elmira after taking the Oath of Allegiance on June 27, 1865.

JOYNER, CHARLES, Private
Born in Pitt County where he resided as a farmer prior to enlisting in Wake County at age 21, July 15, 1862, for the war. Discharged October 5, 1862, by reason of "anemia and general debility."

JOYNER, J. W. H., Private
Captured at Winchester, Virginia, September 19, 1864, and confined at Point Lookout, Maryland, until paroled and exchanged at Aiken's Landing, James River, Virginia, March 18, 1865.

KEETER, ELIJAH, Private
Resided in New Hanover County where he enlisted at age 22, May 27, 1861, for the war. Transferred to the C.S. Navy on April 18, 1864.

KING, CHARLES C., Private
Resided in New Hanover County where he enlisted at age 20, May 27, 1861, for the war. Mustered in as Private and appointed Corporal April 30-July 14, 1862. Reduced to ranks on October 1, 1862. Deserted near Port Royal, Virginia, March 20, 1863, and surrendered to the enemy April 23, 1863. Confined at Old Capitol Prison, Washington, D.C., until released after taking the Oath of Allegiance on April 29, 1863.

KING, ISAAC W., Private
Born in New Hanover County where he resided as a laborer and enlisted at age 23, May 27, 1861, for the war. Mustered in as Sergeant and promoted to 1st Sergeant on May 7, 1862. Wounded at Malvern Hill, Virginia, July 1, 1862. Reduced to ranks on November 1, 1862, by reason of his "being disabled from wound." Discharged near Port Royal, Virginia, March 4, 1863, by reason of "paralysis of the shoulder."

KNOWLES, WILLIAM, Private
Born in Duplin County and enlisted in New Hanover County on March 4, 1862, for the war. Discharged at age 42 on June 18, 1862, by reason of "hernia."

KORNEGAY, LUKE, Private
Resided in Duplin County and enlisted in New Hanover County at age 23, May 27, 1861, for the war. Wounded at Malvern Hill, Virginia, July 1, 1862, and at Sharpsburg, Maryland, September 17, 1862. Wounded a third time at Chancellorsville, Virginia, May 2, 1863, and a fourth time at Payne's Farm, Virginia, November 27, 1863. Killed in action at Snicker's Gap, Virginia, July 18, 1864.

LAMON, MALCOM A., Sergeant
Resided in Robeson County and enlisted in New Hanover County at age 24, May 27, 1861, for the war. Mustered in as Corporal and promoted to Sergeant April 30-July 14, 1862. Present or accounted for on company muster rolls until reported on May 15-August 11, 1863, muster roll with the remark: "Deserted June 26, 1863, while in Pennsylvania."

McCLENNY, JOHN H., Private
Resided in Wayne County where he enlisted at age 22, July 15, 1862, for the war. Wounded at South Mountain, Maryland, September 14, 1862, and reported as absent on company muster rolls from September, 1862, through December, 1864.

MacCUMBER, FLORNEY NOAH, Private
Resided in New Hanover County where he enlisted at age 24, May 27, 1861, for the war. Present or accounted for until captured near Spotsylvania Court House, Virginia, May 12, 1864. Confined at Point Lookout, Maryland, until transferred to Elmira, New York, August 10, 1864. Paroled at Elmira on February 13, 1865, and exchanged at Boulware's Wharf, James River, Virginia, February 20-21, 1865. Captured at Goldsboro on March 24, 1865, and sent to Washington, D.C., where he took the Oath of Allegiance on April 5, 1865.

McCUMBER, ORRIN, Private
Resided in New Hanover County where he enlisted at age 23, May 27, 1861, for the war. Wounded at Ellerson's Mill, Virginia, June 26, 1862. Present or accounted for until captured near Spotsylvania Court House, Virginia, May 12, 1864. Confined at Point Lookout, Maryland, until transferred to Elmira, New York, August 10, 1864. Released at Elmira after taking the Oath of Allegiance on June 27, 1865.

McDONALD, ISAAC W., Private
Resided in Onslow County and enlisted in New Hanover County at age 21, May 21, 1861, for the war. Deserted March 18, 1862, from Camp Price, Virginia.

McGEE, GEORGE W., Private
Enlisted in Randolph County on June 28, 1861, for the war. Discharged May 12-13, 1862.

McGLAWHORN, ALFRED, Private
Resided in Pitt County where he enlisted at age 22, July 15, 1862, for the war. Present or accounted for until captured near Spotsylvania Court House, Virginia, May 12, 1864. Confined at Point Lookout, Maryland, until transferred to Elmira, New York, August 10, 1864. Released at Elmira after taking the Oath of Allegiance on June 19, 1865.

McGLAWHORN, LUKE, Private
Resided in Pitt County where he enlisted at age 23, July 15, 1862, for the war. Wounded at Winchester, Virginia, June 15, 1863. Present or accounted for until captured near Spotsylvania Court House, Virginia, May 12, 1864. Confined at Point Lookout, Maryland, until transferred to Elmira, New York, August 10, 1864. Released at Elmira after taking the Oath of Allegiance on July 3, 1865.

McGOWN, GEORGE W., Private
Resided in Pitt County where he enlisted at age 27, July 15, 1862, for the war. Captured at Frederick, Maryland, in September, 1862, and paroled and exchanged at Aiken's Landing, James River, Virginia, November 10, 1862. Deserted from camp at Hamilton's Crossing, Virginia, May 27, 1863.

McKINLASS, JAMES, Private
Resided in Wayne County and enlisted in New Hanover County at age 24, May 27, 1861, for the war. Company muster roll for April 30-July 14, 1862, carries him with the remark: "Discharged, whipped and drummed out of service by sentence of Court Martial May 7, 1862." Roll of Honor reports him with the remark: "Received 39 lashes for desertion and was drummed out of the regiment May, 1862."

McNEAL, A. B., Private
Enlisted in Wake County on August 8, 1864, for the war. Present or accounted for until paroled at Appomattox Court House, Virginia, April 9, 1865.

McNEAL, D. G., Private
Enlisted in Wake County on August 8, 1864, for the war. Present or accounted for until paroled at Appomattox Court House, Virginia, April 9, 1865.

MANNING, ABRAM, Private
Resided in Pitt County where he enlisted at age 35, July 15, 1862, for the war. Present or accounted for until killed at Gettysburg, Pennsylvania, July 3, 1863.

MANNING, LILLINGTON M., Private
Resided in Pitt County where he enlisted at age 28, July 15, 1862, for the war. Wounded at Gettysburg, Pennsylvania, July 2, 1863, and captured in hospital at Gettysburg July 4-5, 1863. Admitted to hospital July 16, 1863, at Chester, Pennsylvania, where he remained until transferred to Point Lookout, Maryland, October 2, 1863. Paroled at Point Lookout on March 17, 1865, and exchanged at Boulware's Wharf, James River, Virginia, March 19, 1865.

MANNING, SAMUEL, Private
Resided in Pitt County where he enlisted at age 26, July 15, 1862, for the war. Died in hospital at Lynchburg, Virginia, February 19, 1863, of "phthisis pulmonalis."

MANNING, THEOPHILUS, Private
Resided in Pitt County where he enlisted at age 24, July 15, 1862, for the war. Wounded at Winchester, Virginia, June 15, 1863. Present or accounted for until captured near Spotsylvania Court House, Virginia, May 12, 1864. Confined at Point Lookout, Maryland, until transferred to Elmira, New York, August 10, 1864. Paroled at Elmira on March 17, 1865, and sent to Aiken's Landing, James River, Virginia, for exchange.

MEEKS, NATHANIEL, Private
Resided in Pitt County where he enlisted at age 35, July 15, 1862, for the war. Died in hospital at Lynchburg, Virginia, September 12, 1862, of "febris typhoides."

MILLS, CALVIN, Private
Resided in Pitt County where he enlisted at age 20, July 15, 1862, for the war. Wounded at Sharpsburg, Maryland, September 17, 1862. Present or accounted for until transferred to Company I, 44th Regiment N.C. Troops on February 24, 1863.

MILLS, SAMUEL, Private
Resided in Pitt County where he enlisted at age 24, July 15, 1862, for the war. Wounded at Sharpsburg, Maryland, September 17, 1862. Reported as absent sick from February, 1863, through January, 1864, and as absent without leave from January through December, 1864.

MOORE, GEORGE B., Private

Born in Pitt County where he resided as a farmer and enlisted at age 24, July 15, 1862, for the war. Discharged on October 1, 1862, by reason of "phthisis pulmonalis and general debility."

MOORE, JOHN ALLEN, Private

Born in Pitt County where he resided as a farmer and enlisted at age 28, July 15, 1862, for the war. Wounded at Sharpsburg, Maryland, September 17, 1862. Discharged on March 19, 1863, by reason of "wound of the arm producing anchylosis."

MOORE, WARREN, Private

Resided in Pitt County where he enlisted on July 15, 1862, for the war. Admitted to hospital at Richmond, Virginia, September 8, 1862, with "typhoid fever." Furloughed from hospital on October 14, 1862. Reported as absent with leave and absent sick on company muster rolls from September, 1862, through December, 1864.

MUSGRAVE, CRAWFORD E., Private

Resided in Wayne County where he enlisted at age 24, July 15, 1862, for the war. Wounded and captured at Sharpsburg, Maryland, September 17, 1862. Paroled on September 27, 1862, but never returned to company. Reported on November-December, 1863, muster roll with the remark: "wounded September 17, 1862. Nothing has been heard of him since by his family or anyone else. It is the opinion of the company commander that he is dead in Maryland from the wounds received."

MUSGRAVE, LOUIS J., Private

Resided in Wayne County where he enlisted at age 23, July 15, 1862, for the war. Captured at Frederick, Maryland, in September, 1862, and paroled on September 26, 1862. Present or accounted for until captured at Payne's Farm, Virginia, November 27, 1863. Confined at Old Capitol Prison, Washington, D.C., until transferred to Point Lookout, Maryland, February 3, 1864. Paroled at Point Lookout on February 24, 1865, and exchanged at Aiken's Landing, James River, Virginia. Admitted to hospital at Richmond, Virginia, February 25, 1865, and paid on March 6, 1865.

NEEDHAM, ELIAS, Private

Enlisted in Randolph County on June 27, 1861, for the war. Present or accounted for until admitted to hospital at Richmond, Virginia, May 31, 1863, with "pneumonia." Furloughed from hospital for 30 days July 9, 1863. Reported as absent sick on company muster rolls from May, 1863, through December, 1864.

NEEDHAM, JAMES, Private

Enlisted in Randolph County on June 27, 1861, for the war. Wounded at Chancellorsville, Virginia, May 2, 1863, and returned to duty in August, 1863. Wounded at Wilderness, Virginia, May 5, 1864, and reported as absent wounded on company muster rolls from May through December, 1864.

NEELE, JOSEPH E., Private

Born in Monroe County, Virginia, and resided as a laborer in New Hanover County where he enlisted at age 42, June 10, 1861, for the war. Wounded at Sharpsburg, Maryland, September 17, 1862. Wounded a second time at Gettysburg, Penn-

sylvania, July 2, 1863, and captured in hospital at Gettysburg July 4-5, 1863. Confined at DeCamp General Hospital, Davids Island, New York Harbor, until paroled and exchanged at City Point, Virginia, August 28, 1863. Wounded at Wilderness, Virginia, May 6, 1864, and died in hospital at Gordonsville, Virginia, June 23, 1864.

NELSON, LEMUEL, Private

Resided in Pitt County where he enlisted at age 21, July 15, 1862, for the war. Died in hospital at Richmond, Virginia, July 4, 1863, of "febris typhoides."

NEWSOM, ALFRED, Private

Resided in Duplin County and enlisted in New Hanover County at age 21, May 27, 1861, for the war. Wounded accidentally June 14, 1863. Present or accounted for until paroled at Appomattox Court House, Virginia, April 9, 1865.

NEWSOM, JAMES, Private

Enlisted in Wake County on August 31, 1864, for the war. Deserted September 25, 1864.

NEWSOM, JOSHUA J., Musician

Enlisted in Wayne County on May 12, 1862, for the war. Mustered in as Musician. Died in hospital at White Sulphur Springs, Virginia, September 29, 1862.

NEWSOM, OWEN, Private

Resided in Duplin County and enlisted in New Hanover County at age 22, May 29, 1861, for the war. Present or accounted for until paroled at Appomattox Court House, Virginia, April 9, 1865.

NOBLES, JAMES, Private

Resided in Pitt County where he enlisted at age 21, July 15, 1862, for the war. Died in September, 1862.

NOLIN, WILLIAM H., Private

Enlisted in New Hanover County on June 21, 1861, for the war. Deserted from Camp Price, Virginia, March-April, 1862.

PADGETT, HINTON, Private

Resided in Duplin County and enlisted in New Hanover County at age 38, May 27, 1861, for the war. Sent to hospital at Fredericksburg, Virginia, March 18, 1862, and never heard from again. Later reported dead.

PARKER, JESSE, Private

Resided in Pitt County where he enlisted at age 26, July 15, 1862, for the war. Died in hospital at Richmond, Virginia, August 25, 1862, of disease.

PENN, CHARLES, Private

Resided in New Hanover County where he enlisted at age 27, May 27, 1861, for the war. Deserted from Camp Price, Virginia, in February, 1862.

PLYLER, A., Private

Paroled at Charlotte on May 15, 1865.

RINGOLD, LOCKETT, Private

Resided in Pitt County where he enlisted at age 34, July 15, 1862, for the war. Left sick at Leesburg, Virginia, September 7, 1862, and never returned to the company. Later reported dead.

ROCHELLE, JOHN T., Private

Resided in Duplin County and enlisted in New Hanover County at age 19, May 27, 1861, for the war. Wounded at Mechanicsville, Virginia, June 26, 1862, and at Chancellorsville, Virginia, May 2, 1863. Present or accounted for until captured near Spotsylvania Court House, Virginia, May 12, 1864. Confined at Point Lookout, Maryland, until released after taking the Oath of Allegiance and joining the U.S. service on June 6, 1864. Assigned to Company K, 1st Regiment U.S. Volunteer Infantry.

ROCHELLE, NAPOLEON B., Private
Born in Onslow County where he resided prior to enlisting in New Hanover County at age 25, May 27, 1861, for the war. Wounded at Sharpsburg, Maryland, September 17, 1862, and died of wound on September 27, 1862.

ROUSE, ASA, Private
Resided in Duplin County and enlisted in New Hanover County at age 25, May 27, 1861, for the war. Wounded at Payne's Farm, Virginia, November 27, 1863. Sent to hospital May 1, 1864, and returned to duty January 10, 1865. Captured at Farmville, Virginia, April 6, 1865, and confined at Newport News, Virginia, until released after taking the Oath of Allegiance on June 27, 1865.

ROUSE, GEORGE W., Private
Resided in New Hanover County where he enlisted at age 32, May 27, 1861, for the war. Captured at South Mountain, Maryland, September 15, 1862, and paroled and exchanged at Aiken's Landing, James River, Virginia, November 10, 1862. Killed at Winchester, Virginia, June 15, 1863.

SLAUGHTER, CANNON, Private
Resided in Pitt County where he enlisted at age 29, July 15, 1862, for the war. Left at Richmond, Virginia, August 19, 1862, sick. Absent sick until returned to duty from hospital at Danville, Virginia, on March 27, 1863. Wounded in battle at Chancellorsville, Virginia, May 3, 1863. Reported as absent wounded from that date through December, 1864.

SMITH, HAGAN H., Private
Resided in Duplin County and enlisted in New Hanover County at age 34, May 27, 1861, for the war. Present or accounted for until killed in battle at Chancellorsville, Virginia, May 23, 1863.

SMITH, WILLIAM H., Private
Resided in New Hanover County where he enlisted at age 35, May 27, 1861, for the war. Discharged on August 7, 1861, by reason of disability.

SMITH, WILLIAM J., Private
Transferred from Company I, 44th Regiment N.C. Troops in February, 1864. Died at Richmond, Virginia, on August 19, 1864, of gunshot wound in right hip.

SPRINGS, SETH J., Sergeant
Born in New Hanover County where he resided as a carpenter and enlisted at age 43, May 27, 1861, for the war. Mustered in as Sergeant. Discharged December 8, 1861, by reason of "old age and debility from disease."

STINE, WILLIAM T., Private
Resided in Onslow County and enlisted in New Hanover County at age 24, May 27, 1861, for the war. Wounded at Sharpsburg, Maryland, Septem-

ber 17, 1862, and at Wilderness, Virginia, May 5, 1864. Present or accounted for until captured at New Market, Virginia, December 10, 1864. Took the Oath of Allegiance on December 15, 1864.

STOKES, JOHN W., Private
Resided in New Hanover County where he enlisted at age 36, May 27, 1861, for the war. Reported on November-December, 1862, muster roll with the remark: "Supposed to have shot himself for the purpose of shirking engagement December 13." Company muster roll for February 28-May 15, 1863, carries him with the remark: "Deserted on March 20, 1863, near Port Royal. Gone to enemy. Supposed drowned." Roll of Honor carries him with the remark: "Died March, 1863. Drowned in attempting to swim the Rappahannock to the enemy."

STOKES, WILLIAM B., Private
Resided in Pitt County where he enlisted at age 24, July 15, 1862, for the war. Killed at Sharpsburg, Maryland, September 17, 1862.

STONE, W., Private
Issued clothing on March 31, 1864.

TAYLOR, JOHN, Private
Born in Lenoir County and resided as a laborer in New Hanover County where he enlisted at age 31, May 27, 1861, for the war. Discharged on November 23, 1861, by reason of "ascites."

TEEL, WILLIAM E., Private
Resided in Pitt County and enlisted in Wake County on July 15, 1862, for the war. Present or accounted for until captured near Spotsylvania Court House, Virginia, May 12, 1864. Confined at Point Lookout, Maryland, until transferred to Elmira, New York, August 10, 1864. Paroled at Elmira on October 11, 1864, and exchanged at Venus Point, Savannah River, Georgia, November 15, 1864. Wounded and captured at Farmville, Virginia, April 7, 1865. Admitted to hospital at Farmville and right arm amputated. Died at Farmville on May 4, 1865.

TERRY, S. HILLSMAN, Private
Enlisted in Orange County, Virginia, February 28, 1864, for the war. Present or accounted for through December, 1864. Admitted to hospital at Richmond, Virginia, February 25, 1865, with a gunshot wound of the right leg. Transferred to Farmville, Virginia, April 1, 1865. Paroled at Lynchburg, Virginia, April 13, 1865.

THURSTON, WILLIAM J. Y., Private
Born in New Hanover County where he resided as a farmer and enlisted at age 22, June 12, 1861, for the war. Transferred to the Field and Staff of this regiment upon appointment as Sergeant Major on August 30, 1861.

TINDALL, JESSE, 1st Sergeant
Resided in New Hanover County where he enlisted at age 34, May 27, 1861, for the war. Mustered in as Private and appointed Corporal in December, 1861. Wounded at Sharpsburg, Maryland, September 17, 1862. Promoted to Sergeant January 1, 1863, and to 1st Sergeant on May 2, 1863. Appointed 2nd Lieutenant to rank from September 17, 1863, but was not commissioned by reason of

being "incompetent." Present or accounted for as 1st Sergeant for balance of war. Captured at Winchester, Virginia, September 19, 1864, and confined at Point Lookout, Maryland, until paroled for exchange on March 15, 1865. Exchanged at Boulware's Wharf, James River, Virginia, March 18, 1865.

TOTTAN, JOHN H., Private
Paroled at Greensboro on May 8, 1865.

TRIPP, CALEB, Private
Resided in Pitt County where he enlisted at age 23, July 15, 1862, for the war. Deserted from camp near Hamilton's Crossing, Virginia, May 27, 1863.

TUCKER, WILLIAM, Private
Resided in Pitt County and enlisted at age 34, July 15, 1862, for the war. Discharged upon providing Benjamin Holmes as his substitute effective from his date of enlistment.

VANN, MARION, Corporal
Resided in Sampson County and enlisted in New Hanover County at age 19, May 27, 1861, for the war. Mustered in as Corporal. Wounded at Sharpsburg, Maryland, September 17, 1862, and died of wound October 10, 1862.

WALLACE, WILLIAM, Private
Enlisted in Randolph County on June 20, 1861, for the war. Wounded at Wilderness, Virginia, May 5, 1864. Reported as absent wounded from May, 1864, through December, 1864. Paroled at Greensboro on May 16, 1865.

WEATHERINGTON, SPIVER W., Private
Resided in Pitt County where he enlisted at age 34, July 15, 1862, for the war. Deserted on March 29, 1863.

WIGGS, ALEXANDER W., Sergeant
Resided in New Hanover County where he enlisted at age 22, May 27, 1861, for the war. Mustered in as Private. Wounded at Sharpsburg, Maryland, September 17, 1862. Appointed Sergeant on May 2, 1863. Wounded at Gettysburg, Pennsylvania, July 3, 1863, and captured at Gettysburg on July 4-5, 1863. Confined on July 17-24, 1863, at DeCamp General Hospital, Davids Island, New York Harbor, where he remained until paroled and exchanged at City Point, Virginia, September 16, 1863. Detailed as a guard at Goldsboro on March 8, 1864. Remained on detail until retired to the Invalid Corps on January 9, 1865. Assigned to light duty at Goldsboro on February 11, 1865.

WILLIAMS, ELIAS, Private
Born in Randolph County where he enlisted on June 27, 1861, for the war. Died at Fredericksburg, Virginia, November 8, 1861, of "typhoid pneumonia."

WILLIAMS, SIMEON, Private
Resided in Pitt County where he enlisted on July 15, 1862, for the war. Died in hospital at Richmond, Virginia, September 8, 1862, of "typhoid fever."

WILLIAMS, STEPHEN LEVI T., Private
Resided in Pitt County where he enlisted at age 27, July 15, 1862, for the war. Wounded near Spotsylvania Court House, Virginia, May 10, 1864. Killed at Cedar Creek, Virginia, October 19, 1864.

WILLOUGHBY, ROBERT T., Private
Resided as a farmer in Pitt County where he enlisted at age 26, July 15, 1862, for the war. Sent to hospital in April, 1863, and reported as absent sick from April through October, 1863. Reported as absent without leave from November, 1863, through December, 1864.

WOOD, DAVID W., Corporal
Resided in New Hanover County where he enlisted at age 18, May 27, 1861, for the war. Mustered in as Private and appointed Corporal on May 2, 1863. Wounded at Gettysburg, Pennsylvania, July 1-3, 1863. Wounded near Richmond, Virginia, June 2, 1864, and reported as absent wounded from June through December, 1864.

WOOD, JOHN L., Private
Resided in New Hanover County where he enlisted at age 22, May 27, 1861, for the war. Died at Petersburg, Virginia, August 1, 1861, of disease.

WOOTEN, THOMAS, Private
Enlisted in Wake County on September 3, 1864, for the war. Present or accounted for until paroled at Appomattox Court House, Virginia, April 9, 1865.

COMPANY E

This company, known as the "Onslow Greys," was enlisted in Onslow County on May 13, 1861. It tendered its service to the state and was ordered to Garysburg, Northampton County, where it was assigned to this regiment as Company E. After joining the regiment the company functioned as part of the regiment, and its history for the war period is recorded as a part of the regimental history.

The information contained in the following roster of the company was compiled principally from company muster rolls which covered from the muster-in roll, dated August 31, 1861, through December, 1864. No company muster rolls were found for the period prior to August 31, 1861, or for the period after December, 1864. In addition to the company muster rolls, Roll of Honor records, receipt rolls, and hospital records, supplemented by state pension applications, United Daughters of the Confederacy records, and postwar rosters and histories, all provided useful information.

OFFICERS
CAPTAINS

REDD, MARCUS LaFAYETTE
Resided in Onslow County when appointed Captain at age 36 to rank from May 16, 1861. Resigned on December 12, 1861.

ENNETT, WILLIAM T.
Resided in Onslow County when appointed 1st Lieutenant at age 23 to rank from May 16, 1861. Promoted to Captain to rank from December 12, 1861. Wounded at Sharpsburg, Maryland, September 17, 1862, and at Chancellorsville, Virginia, May 3, 1863. Transferred to the Field and Staff of this regiment upon appointment as Major to rank from October 3, 1863.

PORTER, ELISHA

Resided in Onslow County when appointed 3rd Lieutenant at age 27 to rank from May 16, 1861. Promoted to 2nd Lieutenant to rank from December 12, 1861, and to 1st Lieutenant to rank from February 24, 1863. Wounded at Chancellorsville, Virginia, May 3, 1863. Furloughed from hospital at Richmond, Virginia, for 90 days July 20, 1863. Detailed as Enrolling Officer in Onslow County while on furlough. Promoted to Captain to rank from October 3, 1863, but remained on detail and did not return to company. Company muster rolls report him as absent on enrolling service through December, 1864. Retired to the Invalid Corps on February 24, 1865, and assigned as Enrolling Officer in Wake County on March 1, 1865.

SANDERLIN, GEORGE W.

Paroled at Appomattox Court House, Virginia, April 9, 1865.

LIEUTENANTS

GURGANUS, ANDREW J., 2nd Lieutenant

Resided in Onslow County where he enlisted at age 22, May 13, 1861, for the war. Mustered in as Private and appointed Corporal July 14-October 31, 1862. Promoted to Sergeant February 24, 1863, and appointed 2nd Lieutenant to rank from February 1, 1864. Captured near Spotsylvania Court House, Virginia, May 12, 1864, and confined at Fort Delaware, Delaware, until transferred to Hilton Head, South Carolina, August 20, 1864. Transferred from Hilton Head to Fort Pulaski, Georgia, October 21, 1864, and back to Hilton Head after December 26, 1864. Forwarded to Fort Delaware on March 12, 1865, and released at Fort Delaware after taking the Oath of Allegiance on June 16, 1865.

KING, JOHN E., 2nd Lieutenant

Resided in Onslow County where he enlisted at age 30, May 13, 1861, for the war. Mustered in as Sergeant and appointed 2nd Lieutenant to rank from December 1, 1863. Present or accounted for until captured near Spotsylvania Court House, Virginia, May 12, 1864. Confined at Fort Delaware, Delaware, until transferred to Hilton Head, South Carolina, August 20, 1864. Transferred from Hilton Head to Fort Pulaski, Georgia, October 21, 1864, and back to Hilton Head after December 26, 1864. Forwarded on March 12, 1865, to Fort Delaware, where he took the Oath of Allegiance on June 10, 1865. Died at Fort Delaware on June 15, 1865, of "chronic dysentery."

MILLS, SAMUEL A., 2nd Lieutenant

Resided in Onslow County where he enlisted at age 23, May 13, 1861, for the war. Mustered in as Sergeant and reduced to Corporal on July 25, 1861. Promoted to Sergeant July 14-October 31, 1862. Wounded at Sharpsburg, Maryland, September 17, 1862. Transferred to the Field and Staff of this regiment upon appointment to Sergeant Major on February 10, 1863. Transferred back to this company upon appointment as 2nd Lieutenant to rank from June 13, 1863. Resigned December 28, 1863, by reason of gunshot wound of right hand received at Chancellorsville, Virginia, May 3, 1863.

MOORE, LEANDER, 1st Lieutenant

Resided in Onslow County when appointed 2nd Lieutenant at age 40 to rank from May 16, 1861. Promoted to 1st Lieutenant to rank from December 12, 1861. Wounded at Malvern Hill, Virginia, July 1, 1862. Admitted to hospital at Richmond, Virginia, July 28, 1862, with "dysentery" and furloughed on July 28, 1862. Dropped on February 24, 1863, for prolonged absence.

OATES, JOHN P., 2nd Lieutenant

Resided in Onslow County where he enlisted at age 24, May 13, 1861, for the war. Mustered in as Sergeant and promoted to 1st Sergeant February 24, 1863. Appointed 2nd Lieutenant to rank from October 3, 1863. Killed at Payne's Farm, Virginia, November 27, 1863.

SIDBURY, AMOS C., 2nd Lieutenant

Resided in Onslow County where he enlisted at age 20, July 8, 1861, for the war. Mustered in as Sergeant and appointed 2nd Lieutenant to rank from January 14, 1862. Wounded at Chancellorsville, Virginia, May 3, 1863, and died of wound on June 14, 1863.

STOKELY, JOHN W., 1st Lieutenant

Resided in Onslow County where he enlisted at age 23, May 13, 1861, for the war. Mustered in as Sergeant and promoted to 1st Sergeant August 19, 1862. Appointed 2nd Lieutenant to rank from February 24, 1863, and promoted to 1st Lieutenant to rank from October 3, 1863. Captured at Spotsylvania Court House, Virginia, May 12, 1864, and confined at Fort Delaware, Delaware. Released at Fort Delaware after taking the Oath of Allegiance on June 16, 1865.

NONCOMMISSIONED OFFICERS AND PRIVATES

AMAN, ELIJAH, Private

Resided in Onslow County where he enlisted at age 21, January 28, 1862, for the war. Present or accounted for until killed on May 3, 1863, in battle at Chancellorsville, Virginia.

AMAN, ROBERT, Private

Resided in Onslow County where he enlisted at age 21, August 27, 1861, for the war. Present or accounted for until his death on March 16, 1862, at Fredericksburg, Virginia.

AMAN, ROBERT T., Private

Born in Onslow County where he resided and enlisted at age 19, May 13, 1861, for the war. Present or accounted for until his death on February 4, 1862, at Camp Price, Virginia.

AMAN, THOMAS F., Private

Born in Onslow County where he resided and enlisted at age 18, June 29, 1861, for the war. Present or accounted for until his death on April 27, 1862, at Goldsboro.

AUTAWAY, WILLIAM E., Private

Resided in New Hanover County and enlisted in Wake County at age 32, July 15, 1862, for the war. Company muster rolls state that he was left in Maryland, sick, on September 12, 1862, and died September 17, 1862.

BARBER, JEREMIAH, Private
Born in Moore County where he resided as a farmer prior to enlisting in Wake County at age 21, July 15, 1862, for the war. Present or accounted for until his death on February 19, 1863, in hospital at Richmond, Virginia, of "diarrhoea chronic."

BARBER, WILLIAM, Private
Resided in Moore County and enlisted in Wake County at age 24, July 15, 1862, for the war. Present or accounted for until reported as missing at Chancellorsville, Virginia, on May 3, 1863. Reported as missing until August 1, 1863, when he deserted.

BARBER, WILLIAM R., Private
Resided in Moore County and enlisted in Wake County at age 26, July 15, 1862, for the war. Present or accounted for until admitted to hospital at Charlottesville, Virginia, on April 27, 1863, with "chronic diarrhoea." Reported as absent sick until August 1, 1863, when he appears as absent without leave. Date of return to company not shown. Captured on May 12, 1864, at Spotsylvania Court House, Virginia, and confined at Point Lookout, Maryland. Transferred to Elmira, New York, August 10, 1864, and died March 29, 1865, of "chronic diarrhoea."

BISHOP, JACOB, Private
Born in Onslow County where he resided and enlisted at age 21, May 13, 1861, for the war. Present or accounted for until wounded on September 17, 1862, in battle at Sharpsburg, Maryland. Died of his wounds on October 21, 1862, at Winchester, Virginia.

BLAKE, JOHN F., Private
Resided in Onslow County where he enlisted at age 33, May 13, 1861, for the war. Present or accounted for until wounded on September 17, 1862, at Sharpsburg, Maryland. Admitted to hospital at Richmond, Virginia, on September 27, 1862, with "wound neck, side, and hand." Returned to duty November 12, 1862. Detailed for hospital duty March 18, 1863. Absent detailed through December, 1864.

BOLTON, MERRIWEATHER L., Private
Enlisted in Onslow County at age 26, May 13, 1861, for the war. Discharged July 18, 1861.

BRADY, W. M., Private
Resided in Moore County and enlisted in Wake County at age 25, July 15, 1862, for the war. Killed on September 17, 1862, at Sharpsburg, Maryland.

BREECE, JAMES, Private
Resided in Onslow County where he enlisted at age 18, January 23, 1862, for the war. Wounded on September 17, 1862, at Sharpsburg, Maryland. Present or accounted for through December, 1864. Paroled at Appomattox Court House, Virginia, on April 9, 1865.

BREECE, JOSEPH, Private
Resided in Onslow County where he enlisted at age 32, May 13, 1861, for the war. Reported as absent sick on December 25, 1861. Absent sick from that date through December, 1862. Detailed for hospital duty on March 18, 1863. Absent detailed through October, 1863. Furloughed April 1, 1864. Reported as absent on sick furlough from that date through December, 1864.

BREECE, RICHARD T., Private
Born in Onslow County where he resided as a fisherman and enlisted at age 35, May 13, 1861, for the war. Discharged October 17, 1862, by reason of disability.

BREECE, WILLIAM R., Private
Born in Onslow County where he resided as a farmer and enlisted at age 21, May 13, 1861, for the war. Killed on September 17, 1862, in battle at Sharpsburg, Maryland.

BRINSON, G. W., Private
Transferred to this company from Company H, 41st Regiment N.C. Troops (3rd Regiment N.C. Cavalry) on December 1, 1863. Captured on May 12, 1864, at Spotsylvania Court House, Virginia, and confined at Point Lookout, Maryland. Transferred to Elmira, New York, August 10, 1864. Paroled at Elmira and sent to James River, Virginia, for exchange, on February 20, 1865. Admitted to hospital at Richmond, Virginia, on March 2, 1865, and was transferred to Camp Lee, near Richmond, on March 3, 1865.

BROWN, J. J., Private
Born in Pitt County where he resided prior to enlisting in Wake County at age 33, July 15, 1862, for the war. Died September 11, 1862, in hospital at Richmond, Virginia, of "febris typhoides."

BROYLEY, W. M., Private
Enlisted in Wake County on July 15, 1862, for the war. Present or accounted for until wounded at Winchester, Virginia, on June 15, 1863. Reported as absent wounded from that date through December, 1864.

BRYAN, B. F., Private
Resided in Pitt County and enlisted in Wake County at age 19, July 15, 1862, for the war. Reported as absent sick from August 28, 1862, through February, 1863. Wounded May 3, 1863, at Chancellorsville, Virginia. Reported as absent wounded or absent sick from that date through December, 1864.

BRYAN, J. C., Private
Resided in Martin County and enlisted in Wake County at age 22, July 15, 1862, for the war. Reported as absent sick from September 24, 1862, through February, 1863. Mortally wounded May 3, 1863, at Chancellorsville, Virginia.

BRYAN, JAMES H., Private
Resided in Pitt County and enlisted in Wake County at age 19, July 15, 1862, for the war. Reported as absent sick from September 24, 1862, through February, 1863. Present or accounted for until captured May 12, 1864, near Spotsylvania Court House, Virginia. Confined at Point Lookout, Maryland, and transferred to Elmira, New York, August 10, 1864. Released after taking the Oath of Allegiance on June 30, 1865, at Elmira.

BRYANT, F. J., Private
Resided in Pitt County and enlisted in Wake County at age 23, July 15, 1862, for the war. Re-

ported as absent sick from September 23, 1862, through December, 1864.

BULLOCK, J. B., Private
Resided in Pitt County and enlisted in Wake County at age 19, July 15, 1862, for the war. Reported as absent sick from September 20, 1862, through February, 1863. Wounded May 3, 1863, at Chancellorsville, Virginia. Hospital records describe wound as "gunshot wound right arm amputated." Absent wounded until detailed for hospital duty on February 7, 1864. Discharged March 18, 1864, by reason of being permanently disabled.

BULLOCK, SIMPSON, Private
Resided in Pitt County and enlisted in Wake County at age 23, July 15, 1862, for the war. Killed September 17, 1862, in battle at Sharpsburg, Maryland.

BUNTING, W. T., Private
Resided in Pitt County and enlisted in Wake County at age 30, July 15, 1862, for the war. Present or accounted for until reported as absent sick on May 1, 1863. Absent sick until discharged on July 26, 1864, by reason of "excessive dropsy (ascites)."

CANADY, JAMES J., Private
Resided in Onslow County where he enlisted at age 22, May 13, 1861, for the war. Reported as absent sick from September-October, 1861, through February, 1862. Wounded in battle at Malvern Hill, Virginia, on July 1, 1862. Company muster roll for December 31, 1863-August 31, 1864, states that he was "wounded in battle May 5, 1864." Present or accounted for through December, 1864, when he was reported as absent sick. Paroled April 15, 1865, at Lynchburg, Virginia.

CAPPS, THOMAS J., Private
Resided in Onslow County where he enlisted at age 19, May 13, 1861, for the war. Mustered in as Corporal and reduced to ranks on August 31, 1861. Present or accounted for through December, 1864. Captured on March 2, 1865, at Waynesboro, Virginia, and confined at Fort Delaware, Delaware. Released at Fort Delaware after taking the Oath of Allegiance on June 19, 1865.

CARPENTER, ROBERT, Private
Resided in Moore County and enlisted in Wake County at age 38, July 15, 1862, for the war. Reported as absent sick from August 21, 1862, through December, 1862. Killed August 25, 1863, in railroad accident near Louisa Court House, Virginia.

COOPER, GABRIEL, Corporal
Resided in Onslow County where he enlisted at age 20, May 13, 1861, for the war. Mustered in as Private. Reported as absent sick from September 27, 1862, through December, 1862. Appointed Corporal on March 1, 1863. Wounded May 3, 1863, at Chancellorsville, Virginia. Died July 1, 1863, of his wounds.

COSTON, HIRAM D., Musician
Born in Onslow County where he resided as a carpenter and enlisted at age 30, May 13, 1861, for the war. Mustered in as Musician. Died

February 5, 1862, at Camp Price, Virginia.

COX, A. L., Private
Resided in Moore County and enlisted in Wake County at age 30, July 15, 1862, for the war. Reported as absent sick from May 1, 1863, until returned to duty on August 22, 1863. Captured at Mine Run, Virginia, on November 28, 1863, and confined at Old Capitol Prison, Washington, D.C. Transferred to Point Lookout, Maryland, on February 3, 1864. Paroled at Point Lookout and transferred to Aiken's Landing, James River, Virginia, February 24, 1865, for exchange. Admitted to hospital at Richmond, Virginia, on February 25, 1865. Received pay on March 6, 1865, at hospital at Richmond.

CREEL, J. J., Private
Resided in Onslow County and enlisted in Wake County at age 32, July 15, 1862, for the war. Reported as absent sick from September 25, 1862, through December, 1862. Present or accounted for until captured on May 12, 1864, at Spotsylvania Court House, Virginia. Confined at Point Lookout, Maryland, until transferred to Elmira, New York, on August 10, 1864. Released at Elmira after taking the Oath of Allegiance on June 23, 1865.

CUMMINGS, JOHN, Private
Born in Pitt County where he resided prior to enlisting in Wake County at age 31, July 15, 1862, for the war. Died September 15, 1862, in hospital at Richmond, Virginia, of "febris remittens."

CURTIS, REUBEN, Private
Born in Onslow County where he resided and enlisted at age 18, May 13, 1861, for the war. Present or accounted for until his death on January 26, 1862, at Camp Price, Virginia.

DAVIS, SAMUEL, Private
Born in Onslow County where he resided and enlisted at age 37, May 13, 1861, for the war. Present or accounted for until his death on March 18, 1862, at Fredericksburg, Virginia.

DEAL, ISAAC, Private
Born in Onslow County where he resided as a farmer and enlisted at age 45, January 28, 1862, for the war. Discharged November 28, 1862, by reason of disability caused by "loss of teeth and entire absorption of alveoler processes of superior maxillary bone, and chronic rheumatism."

DEAL, JOHN, Private
Resided in Onslow County where he enlisted at age 18, March 25, 1863, for the war. Wounded May 3, 1863, at Chancellorsville, Virginia. Absent wounded through December, 1863. Captured May 12, 1864, at Spotsylvania Court House, Virginia, and confined at Point Lookout, Maryland. Transferred from Point Lookout to Elmira, New York, on August 10, 1864. Released at Elmira after taking the Oath of Allegiance on June 27, 1865.

DUNN, BENNETT, Private
Resided in Edgecombe County and enlisted in Wake County at age 26, July 15, 1862, for the war. Present or accounted for until wounded on May 3, 1863, in battle at Chancellorsville, Virginia.

Wounded and captured at Gettysburg, Pennsylvania, July 1-4, 1863. Confined at DeCamp General Hospital, Davids Island, New York Harbor, until paroled September 27, 1863, and sent to City Point, Virginia, for exchange. Wound described as "f.w. and amputation of leg." Admitted to hospital at Richmond, Virginia, on September 28, 1863. Reported as absent sick through December, 1864.

EDENS, EZEKIEL L., Private
Born in Onslow County where he resided as a farmer and enlisted at age 24, May 13, 1861, for the war. Wounded and captured at Sharpsburg, Maryland, September 17, 1862. Paroled on September 30, 1862, and died of wound on October 23, 1862.

EDENS, JAMES A., Private
Resided in Onslow County where he enlisted at age 28, May 13, 1861, for the war. Wounded at Malvern Hill, Virginia, July 1, 1862, and killed at Chancellorsville, Virginia, May 3, 1863.

EDENS, JAMES H., Private
Born in Onslow County where he resided as a farmer and enlisted at age 36, May 13, 1861, for the war. Wounded at Malvern Hill, Virginia, July 1, 1862, and discharged on March 24, 1863, by reason of wound received at Malvern Hill.

EDENS, JAMES T., Private
Resided in Onslow County where he enlisted at age 26, May 13, 1861, for the war. Wounded at Payne's Farm, Virginia, November 27, 1863. Present or accounted for until paroled at Appomattox Court House, Virginia, April 9, 1865.

EDENS, JOHN H., Private
Resided in Onslow County where he enlisted at age 26, May 13, 1861, for the war. Discharged on July 12, 1861.

ENNETT, NATHANIEL S., Private
Resided in Onslow County where he enlisted at age 22, May 13, 1861, for the war. Present or accounted for until killed at Chancellorsville, Virginia, May 3, 1863.

ENNETT, THOMAS, Private
Resided in Onslow County where he enlisted at age 22, May 13, 1861, for the war. Discharged on August 9, 1861.

EVERETT, CALEB N., Private
Born in Onslow County where he resided as a farmer and enlisted at age 27, May 13, 1861, for the war. Mustered in as Sergeant and reduced to ranks on August 18, 1861. Present or accounted for until discharged on August 19, 1862, by reason of disability.

EVERETT, THOMAS J., Private
Resided in Onslow County where he enlisted at age 38, May 13, 1861, for the war. Wounded at Chancellorsville, Virginia, May 3, 1863, and reported as absent wounded from May, 1863, through December, 1864.

EVERETT, WILLIAM T., Private
Born in Onslow County where he resided and enlisted at age 23, May 13, 1861, for the war. Died on May 7, 1862, of "pneumonia."

EVERETT, WOODMAN S., Corporal
Born in Onslow County where he resided as a farmer and enlisted at age 33, May 13, 1861, for the war. Mustered in as Private and appointed Corporal on August 19, 1862. Killed at Sharpsburg, Maryland, September 17, 1862.

FARR, GEORGE S., Private
Born in Onslow County where he resided as a farmer and enlisted at age 52, May 18, 1862, for the war. Discharged on March 24, 1863, by reason of "physical disability."

FARR, HENRY JACKSON, Private
Resided in Onslow County where he enlisted at age 18, May 13, 1861, for the war. Wounded at Payne's Farm, Virginia, November 27, 1863. Present or accounted for on company muster rolls through December, 1864. Captured at Burkeville, Virginia, April 6, 1865, and confined at Newport News, Virginia. Released after taking the Oath of Allegiance on June 15, 1865.

FARR, RICHARD E., Private
Born in Onslow County where he resided as a farmer and enlisted at age 23, May 13, 1861, for the war. Wounded at Malvern Hill, Virginia, July 1, 1862, and discharged on March 24, 1863, by reason of wound received at Malvern Hill.

FIELDS, KINCHEN E., Private
Resided in Chatham County and enlisted in Wake County at age 50, July 15, 1862, for the war. Died in hospital at Richmond, Virginia, December 9, 1862, of "variola."

FORD, J. R., Private
Resided in Pitt County and enlisted in Wake County at age 18, July 15, 1862, for the war. Present or accounted for until he deserted July 1, 1863, when he failed to report to regiment from hospital at Lynchburg, Virginia.

FOX, ALBERT C., Private
Captured in Lenoir County on April 15, 1865, and confined at Louisville, Kentucky, April 29, 1865. Transferred to Camp Chase, Ohio, May 2, 1865. Released after taking the Oath of Allegiance on June 13, 1865. Age reported on Oath as 17.

FOY, GEORGE W., Private
Born in Onslow County where he resided and enlisted at age 21, May 13, 1861, for the war. Died on August 28, 1862, of consumption.

FRESHWATER, WILLIAM H., Private
Born in Onslow County where he resided and enlisted at age 22, May 13, 1861, for the war. Died in hospital at White Sulphur Springs, Virginia, April 1, 1862.

GIDDINS, ANDREW J. P., Private
Resided in Onslow County where he enlisted at age 24, May 13, 1861, for the war. Wounded and captured at Gettysburg, Pennsylvania, July 3, 1863. Confined at DeCamp General Hospital, Davids Island, New York Harbor, until paroled and exchanged at City Point, Virginia, September 8, 1863. Captured at Spotsylvania Court House, Virginia, May 12, 1864, and confined at Point Lookout, Maryland, until transferred to Aiken's Landing, James River, Virginia, March 15, 1865, for exchange. Declared exchanged on March 18, 1865.

GILLIKIN, ISAIAH, Private

Born in Onslow County where he resided and enlisted at age 18, March 15, 1862, for the war. Wounded at Ellerson's Mill, Virginia, June 26, 1862. Died in hospital at Richmond, Virginia, September 4, 1862, of "febris typhoides."

GORNTO, JOHN R., Sergeant

Resided in Onslow County where he enlisted at age 18, May 13, 1861, for the war. Mustered in as Private and appointed Corporal on October 31, 1862. Promoted to Sergeant on February 10, 1863. Wounded and captured at Gettysburg, Pennsylvania, July 3, 1863. Died of wound on August 1, 1863.

GRANT, BENJAMIN L., Private

Resided in Onslow County where he enlisted at age 18, March 24, 1862, for the war. Mustered in as Musician. Present or accounted for on company muster rolls through December, 1864, as Musician. Paroled as Private at Appomattox Court House, Virginia, April 9, 1865.

GREEN, EDWARD, Private

Resided in Onslow County where he enlisted at age 21, May 13, 1861, for the war. Died in hospital at Fredericksburg, Virginia, October 27, 1861.

HANNA, W. S., Private

Resided in Guilford County and enlisted in Wake County at age 27, July 15, 1862, for the war. Captured at Frederick, Maryland, September 12, 1862, and paroled and exchanged at Aiken's Landing, James River, Virginia, November 10, 1862. Died on March 15, 1863.

HANSLEY, JERRY M., Private

Resided in Onslow County where he enlisted at age 18, May 13, 1861, for the war. Wounded at Chancellorsville, Virginia, May 3, 1863. Captured at Spotsylvania Court House, Virginia, May 12, 1864, and confined at Point Lookout, Maryland, until transferred to Elmira, New York, August 10, 1864. Released at Elmira after taking the Oath of Allegiance on June 27, 1865.

HANSLEY, JOHN T., Private

Resided in Onslow County where he enlisted at age 18, May 13, 1861, for the war. Wounded and captured at Gettysburg, Pennsylvania, July 3, 1863. Confined at Fort Delaware, Delaware, until transferred to Point Lookout, Maryland, October 18, 1863. Paroled at Point Lookout on March 14, 1865, and transferred to Aiken's Landing, James River, Virginia, for exchange. Received in exchange at Boulware's Wharf, James River, March 16, 1865.

HARDISON, A. JACKSON, Private

Born in Onslow County where he enlisted at age 22, January 28, 1862, for the war. Died at Richmond, Virginia, August 8, 1862, of "consumption."

HARDISON, E. H., Private

Resided in Onslow County where he enlisted at age 18, May 2, 1862, for the war. Wounded at Malvern Hill, Virginia, July 1, 1862, and died of wound on July 10, 1862.

HARDISON, ELZA, Private

Resided in Onslow County where he enlisted at

age 18, February 20, 1862, for the war. Wounded at Chancellorsville, Virginia, May 3, 1863, and at Spotsylvania Court House, Virginia, May 10, 1864. Present or accounted for on company muster rolls through December, 1864.

HARDISON, FRANKLIN, Private

Resided in Onslow County where he enlisted at age 33, July 15, 1862, for the war. Wounded at Payne's Farm, Virginia, November 27, 1863. Present or accounted for on company muster rolls through December, 1864.

HARDISON, JOSEPH, Corporal

Resided in Onslow County where he enlisted at age 21, May 13, 1861, for the war. Mustered in as Private. Wounded at Chancellorsville, Virginia, May 3, 1863. Appointed Corporal in 1864 prior to being captured at Spotsylvania Court House, Virginia, May 12, 1864. Confined at Point Lookout, Maryland, until transferred to Elmira, New York, August 10, 1864. Released from Elmira after taking the Oath of Allegiance on June 27, 1865.

HARDISON, ROBERT J., Private

Resided in Onslow County where he enlisted at age 23, May 13, 1861, for the war. Discharged on August 10, 1861.

HARDISON, SAMUEL J., Private

Born in Onslow County where he resided and enlisted at age 32, May 13, 1861, for the war. Died at Wilmington January 16, 1862.

HEADY, WILLIAM, Private

Resided in Onslow County where he enlisted at age 36, July 6, 1861, for the war. Wounded and captured at Sharpsburg, Maryland, September 17, 1862. Confined at Fort McHenry, Maryland, until paroled and exchanged at. City Point, Virginia, November 21, 1862. Wounded at Gettysburg, Pennsylvania, July 3, 1863, and captured in hospital at Gettysburg July 4-5, 1863. Confined in hospital at Chester, Pennsylvania, until paroled and exchanged at City Point on September 23, 1863. Captured at Spotsylvania Court House, Virginia, May 12, 1864, and confined at Point Lookout, Maryland, until transferred to Elmira, New York, August 10, 1864. Paroled at Elmira on February 9, 1865, and exchanged at Boulware's Wharf, James River, Virginia, February 20-21, 1865. Admitted to hospital at Richmond, Virginia, February 21, 1865, with "debilitas." Furloughed from hospital for 60 days March 2, 1865.

HICKS, ROBERT T. J., Musician

Resided in Onslow County and enlisted in New Hanover County at age 18, February 24, 1862, for the war. Mustered in as Musician. Present or accounted for until he "deserted July 8, 1863, while in Maryland."

HOBBS, ANDREW J., Private

Born in Onslow County where he resided and enlisted at age 33, May 13, 1861, for the war. Killed at Sharpsburg, Maryland, September 17, 1862.

HOBBS, EDWARD J., Private

Born in Onslow County where he resided and enlisted at age 27, May 13, 1861, for the war.

Wounded at Ellerson's Mill, Virginia, June 26, 1862, and died of wound July 19, 1862.

HOBBS, ELVA H., Private

Born in Onslow County where he resided as a farmer and enlisted at age 22, May 13, 1861, for the war. Discharged at Petersburg, Virginia, December 14, 1862, by reason of "phthisis pulmonalis."

HOBBS, JOSEPH E., Private

Resided in Onslow County where he enlisted at age 33, May 13, 1861, for the war. Wounded at Sharpsburg, Maryland, September 17, 1862. Captured at Spotsylvania Court House, Virginia, May 12, 1864, and confined at Point Lookout, Maryland. Transferred to Elmira, New York, August 10, 1864. Released at Elmira after taking the Oath of Allegiance on June 30, 1865.

HOBBS, PIRAM P., Private

Born in Onslow County where he resided as a farmer and enlisted at age 27, May 13, 1861, for the war. Discharged on February 19, 1863, by reason of "contraction of the flexor muscles of the left forearm from rheumatism."

HOBBS, THOMAS A. J., Corporal

Resided in Onslow County and enlisted in Guilford County at age 23, May 2, 1862, for the war. Mustered in as Private and appointed Corporal on October 31, 1862. Captured at Spotsylvania Court House, Virginia, May 10, 1864, and confined at Point Lookout, Maryland. Transferred to Elmira, New York, August 10, 1864. Released from Elmira after taking the Oath of Allegiance on June 27, 1865.

HOBBS, WILLIAM N., Private

Resided in Onslow County where he enlisted at age 20, May 13, 1861, for the war. Wounded at Ellerson's Mill, Virginia, June 26, 1862. Reported as absent wounded until detailed for hospital duty on April 1, 1863. Absent on detail until returned to company September-October, 1864. Present or accounted for through December, 1864.

HORN, DAVID W., Private

Resided in Onslow County where he enlisted age 23, May 13, 1861, for the war. Died on August 12, 1861.

HORN, JACOB R., Private

Born in Onslow County where he resided as a farmer and enlisted at age 50, May 13, 1861, for the war. Discharged on November 8, 1861, by reason of disability.

HORN, OWEN H., Private

Resided in Onslow County where he enlisted at age 18, May 13, 1861, for the war. Wounded and captured at Chancellorsville, Virginia, May 3, 1863. Paroled and exchanged at City Point, Virginia, May 13, 1863. Wounded at Wilderness, Virginia, May 5, 1864. Present or accounted for through December, 1864. Captured at Farmville, Virginia, April 6, 1865, and confined at Newport News, Virginia. Released after taking the Oath of Allegiance on June 27, 1865.

HOWARD, JOHN W., Private

Resided in Onslow County where he enlisted at age 27, May 13, 1861, for the war. Discharged in October, 1861.

HUNSUCKER, GASTON D., Private

Resided in Moore County and enlisted in Wake County at age 23, July 15, 1862, for the war. Captured at Chancellorsville, Virginia, May 3, 1863, and paroled at Washington, D.C., May 19, 1863. Wounded at Gettysburg, Pennsylvania, July 3, 1863, and captured at Gettysburg July 4-5, 1863. Confined in hospital at Chester, Pennsylvania, until paroled and exchanged at City Point, Virginia, September 23, 1863. Captured near Spotsylvania Court House, Virginia, May 20, 1864, and confined at Point Lookout, Maryland. Transferred July 3, 1864, to Elmira, New York, where he remained until paroled on March 2, 1865. Admitted to hospital at Richmond, Virginia, March 6, 1865, with "debilitas." Furloughed from hospital March 9, 1865, for 30 days.

JACKSON, BENJAMIN B., Private

Born in Moore County where he resided as a farmer prior to enlisting in Wake County at age 34, July 15, 1862, for the war. Killed September 17, 1862, in battle at Sharpsburg, Maryland.

JARVIS, DEXTER B., Corporal

Born in Onslow County where he resided as a farmer and enlisted at age 23, May 13, 1861, for the war. Mustered in as Private and appointed Corporal on February 17, 1862. Present or accounted for until his death on January 10, 1863.

JARVIS, SAMUEL, Private

Born in Onslow County where he resided and enlisted at age 26, May 13, 1861, for the war. Present or accounted for until his death on September 13, 1862, in hospital at Richmond, Virginia, of "febris typhoides."

JENKINS, EDMUND, Private

Resided in Onslow County where he enlisted at age 29, May 13, 1861, for the war. Died December 13, 1861, at Camp Howe, Aquia Creek, Virginia, of "erysipelas supposed to have been caused by injuries received about the head."

JENKINS, JOSEPH R., Sergeant

Resided in Onslow County where he enlisted at age 18, May 13, 1861, for the war. Mustered in as Corporal and appointed Sergeant on January 14, 1862. Wounded July 1, 1862, at Malvern Hill, Virginia. Present or accounted for until killed on May 3, 1863, in battle at Chancellorsville, Virginia.

JENKINS, LEWIS R., Private

Resided in Onslow County where he enlisted at age 25, May 13, 1861, for the war. Present or accounted for until killed on July 1, 1862, in battle at Malvern Hill, Virginia.

JENKINS, UZZA, Corporal

Resided in Onslow County where he enlisted at age 23, May 13, 1861, for the war. Mustered in as Private. Present or accounted for until wounded on July 3, 1863, at Gettysburg, Pennsylvania. Absent wounded through August, 1863. Received a flesh wound of November 27-28, 1863, at Mine Run, Virginia. Muster rolls state that he was wounded on May 5, 1864, and report him as absent wounded through August, 1864. Appointed Corporal September-October, 1864. Present or accounted for through December, 1864. Captured on April 6, 1865, at Burkeville, Virginia. Confined at Newport News, Virginia, until released after taking the Oath of Allegiance on June 27, 1865.

JENKINS, WILLIAM H., Sergeant
Resided in Onslow County where he enlisted at age 21, May 13, 1861, for the war. Mustered in as Private. Wounded and captured on September 17, 1862, at Sharpsburg, Maryland. Paroled September 20, 1862. Appointed Corporal on May 4, 1863, and promoted to Sergeant November-December, 1863. Wounded on November 27, 1863, in battle at Payne's Farm, Virginia. Reported as absent wounded, or absent sick, from that date through December, 1864. Returned to duty from hospital at Wilmington on February 10, 1865. Captured on April 3, 1865, in hospital at Richmond, Virginia.

JONES, L. H., Private
Captured April 6, 1865, at Burkeville, Virginia, and confined at Newport News, Virginia. Took the Oath of Allegiance on June 27, 1865, at Newport News.

KIMBREL, W. B., Private
Born in Moore County where he resided as a farmer prior to enlisting in Wake County at age 21, July 15, 1862, for the war. Muster roll states that he was left in Maryland, sick, on September 12, 1862. Prisoner of war records report that he was captured at Antietam, Maryland, and was sent from Fort McHenry, Maryland, to Fort Monroe, Virginia, for exchange on October 17, 1862. Received at Aiken's Landing, Virginia, on October 19, 1862. Discharged November 12, 1862, by reason of disability caused by "anaemia and debility."

KING, EDWARD H., 1st Sergeant
Resided in Onslow County and enlisted in Wayne County at age 18, May 11, 1862, for the war. Mustered in as Private and appointed Corporal on January 10, 1863. Wounded May 3, 1863, at Chancellorsville, Virginia. Admitted to hospital at Richmond, Virginia, on May 6, 1863, with "gunshot wound left hand." Absent wounded until reported as present November-December, 1863. Promoted to Sergeant on August 1, 1863, while absent wounded. Captured near Spotsylvania Court House, Virginia, on May 12, 1864. Confined at Point Lookout, Maryland, until transferred to Elmira, New York, on August 10, 1864. Paroled at Elmira on October 11, 1864, and sent to Point Lookout to be forwarded for exchange. Promoted to 1st Sergeant, September-October, 1864. Reported as absent sick on the November-December, 1864, muster roll. Paroled at Appomattox Court House, Virginia, April 9, 1865.

KING, GEORGE W., Private
Born in Onslow County where he enlisted at age 18, July 2, 1861, for the war. Died January 7, 1862, in hospital at Camp Price, Stafford County, Virginia.

KING, JOHN R., Private
Resided in Onslow County and enlisted in New Hanover County at age 21, June 15, 1861, for the war. Present or accounted for until wounded on September 17, 1862, at Sharpsburg, Maryland. Admitted to hospital at Richmond, Virginia, on September 25, 1862, and furloughed on October 30, 1862. Absent wounded through December, 1862. Present or accounted for until captured near Spotsylvania Court House, Virginia, on May 12, 1864. Confined at Point Lookout, Maryland, until transferred to Elmira, New York, on August 10, 1864. Released at Elmira after taking the Oath of Allegiance on June 27, 1865.

KING, JOHN W., Private
Born in Onslow County where he resided as a farmer and enlisted at age 18, July 2, 1861, for the war. Reported as absent sick from November-December, 1861, until July, 1862. Killed on September 17, 1862, in battle at Sharpsburg, Maryland.

KING, THOMAS E., Private
Resided in Onslow County where he enlisted at age 25, May 13, 1861, for the war. Reported as absent sick from November 9, 1862, through February, 1863. Wounded on May 3, 1863, at Chancellorsville, Virginia. Absent wounded through October, 1863. Received a flesh wound at Mine Run, Virginia, November 27-28, 1863. Captured May 12, 1864, near Spotsylvania Court House, Virginia, and confined at Point Lookout, Maryland. Transferred to Elmira, New York, July 23, 1864. Released at Elmira after taking the Oath of Allegiance on May 17, 1865.

KING, WILLIAM, Private
Born in Onslow County where he enlisted at age 33, July 2, 1861, for the war. Died on February 2, 1862, at Camp Price, Stafford County, Virginia.

McCAULEY, S. H., Private
Born in Moore County where he resided prior to enlisting in Wake County at age 26, July 15, 1862, for the war. Died October 10, 1862, of wounds received in battle at Sharpsburg, Maryland, September 17, 1862.

McKETHAN, NEILL, Private
Resided in Moore County prior to enlisting in Wake County at age 20, July 15, 1862, for the war. Company muster rolls state that he was sent to the rear on September 17, 1862, while the company was in Maryland and was "supposed deserted." Appears on a parole of prisoners of war dated Office of the Provost Marshal General, Army of the Potomac, October 3, 1862. No further records.

McLEMORE, JOHN H., Private
Resided in Moore County prior to enlisting in Wake County at age 30, July 15, 1862, for the war. Wounded at Sharpsburg, Maryland, on September 17, 1862. Present or accounted for until reported as absent sick from April 6, 1863, through August, 1863. Captured at Spotsylvania Court House, Virginia, May 20, 1864, and confined at Point Lookout, Maryland. Transferred to Elmira, New York, on July 6, 1864. Released at Elmira after taking the Oath of Allegiance on July 11, 1865.

McLEOD, NEILL, Private

Enlisted in Wake County on July 15, 1862, for the war. Muster rolls state that he was "missing since September 17, 1862." Appears on a parole of prisoners of war dated Office of the Provost Marshal General, Army of the Potomac, September 27, 1862. Also appears on a roll of prisoners of war at Fort McHenry, Maryland, dated October 14, 1862, which states that he was paroled and sent to Aiken's Landing, James River, Virginia, for exchange. This roll states that he was captured on October 1, 1862, at Antietam, Maryland. Admitted to hospital at Richmond, Virginia, on October 24, 1862, with "wound of right hip" and was furloughed on December 20, 1862, for 50 days. Present or accounted for until captured near Spotsylvania Court House, Virginia, May 12, 1864. Confined at Point Lookout, Maryland, until transferred to Elmira, New York, on August 10, 1864. Died December 10, 1864, at Elmira of "pneumonia."

MANNING, A. A., Private

Resided in Pitt County and enlisted in Wake County at age 21, July 15, 1862, for the war. Died on September 23, 1862, in hospital at Warrenton, Virginia, of "rubeola."

MARSHALL, BENJAMIN D., Private

Born in Onslow County where he resided and enlisted at age 23, May 13, 1861, for the war. Mustered in as Musician and reduced to ranks August 31, 1861. Present or accounted for until his death on August 28, 1862, of "pneumonia."

MARSHALL, JOHN R., Private

Resided in Onslow County where he enlisted at age 24, May 13, 1861, for the war. Discharged on July 16, 1861. Reenlisted in Wake County on July 15, 1862, for the war. Wounded at Sharpsburg, Maryland, September 17, 1862. Admitted to hospital at Richmond, Virginia, on September 28, 1862, with "gun wound in shoulder." Absent wounded until detailed for hospital duty on March 1, 1863. Absent detailed until admitted to hospital at Richmond on April 7, 1863, with "hernia and debility." Returned to duty August 18, 1863. Reported as present on the August, 1863, muster roll. Absent sick from October 15, 1863, until detailed as a nurse at hospital at Lynchburg, Virginia, on December 10, 1864. Paroled in April, 1865, at Lynchburg.

MARSHBURN, DANIEL, Private

Born in Onslow County where he resided as a farmer and enlisted at age 19, June 29, 1861, for the war. Died on May 1, 1862, of "pneumonia."

MARSHBURN, HOSEA, Private

Born in Onslow County where he resided and enlisted at age 30, January 29, 1862, for the war. Died at Petersburg, Virginia, on June 8, 1862, of "chronic diarrhoea."

MELTON, LORENZO, Private

Resided in Onslow County and enlisted in Stafford County, Virginia, at age 19, February 2, 1862, for the war. Wounded at Ellerson's Mill, Virginia, June 26, 1862. Deserted October 1, 1863, and surrendered to the enemy at Fort Mon-

roe, Virginia, April 24, 1864. Released April 25, 1864, and sent to the Federal Quartermaster Department as a "government employee."

MILLIS, DAVID H., Sergeant

Resided in Onslow County where he enlisted at age 20, May 13, 1861, for the war. Mustered in as Private and appointed Corporal on July 1, 1863. Wounded at Wilderness, Virginia, May 5, 1864, and promoted to Sergeant, September-October, 1864. Paroled at Appomattox Court House, Virginia, April 9, 1865. Admitted to hospital at Farmville, Virginia, April 14, 1865, with a gunshot wound of the left thigh and transferred to another hospital on June 1, 1865.

MOORE, ELIJAH, Private

Resided in Onslow County where he enlisted at age 38, January 28, 1862, for the war. Discharged on August 19, 1862, by reason of disability.

MOORE, WESLEY W., Private

Resided in Onslow County where he enlisted on March 24, 1862, for the war. Wounded at Gettysburg, Pennsylvania, July 3, 1863, and captured in hospital at Gettysburg July 4-5, 1863. Confined at DeCamp General Hospital, Davids Island, New York Harbor, until paroled and exchanged at City Point, Virginia, August 28, 1863. Transferred to C.S. Navy April 5, 1864.

NIXON, H. W., Private

Paroled at Appomattox Court House, Virginia, April 9, 1865.

PARISH, DAVID, Private

Resided in Moore County and enlisted in Wake County at age 18, July 15, 1862, for the war. Captured in Maryland in September, 1862, and paroled at Keedysville, Maryland, September 20, 1862. Deserted February 1, 1863.

PARKER, HENRY, Private

Born in Pitt County where he resided as a farmer prior to enlisting in Wake County at age 21, July 15, 1862, for the war. Discharged on November 18, 1862, by reason of "carditis, inflammation of bronchitia."

PARKER, WILLIAM E., Private

Resided in Pitt County and enlisted in Wake County at age 26, July 15, 1862, for the war. Killed at Chancellorsville, Virginia, May 3, 1863.

PARSONS, W. H., Private

Paroled at Farmville, Virginia, April 11-21, 1865.

PASCHAL, ROBERT, Private

Resided in Moore County and enlisted in Wake County at age 31, July 15, 1862, for the war. Wounded at Chancellorsville, Virginia, May 3, 1863. Present or accounted for through December, 1864. Paroled at Hart's Island, New York Harbor, June 21, 1865.

PATRICK, GEORGE W., Private

Resided in Onslow County where he enlisted at age 21, July 2, 1861, for the war. Wounded at Malvern Hill, Virginia, July 1, 1862, and at Chancellorsville, Virginia, May 3, 1863. Detailed for light duty on December 23, 1863, and reported as absent on detail through December, 1864. Captured in hospital at Richmond, Virginia,

April 3, 1865, and paroled on April 24, 1865.

PHILLIPS, A. W., Private

Resided in Moore County and enlisted in Wake County at age 29, July 15, 1862, for the war. Wounded at Sharpsburg, Maryland, September 17, 1862. Detailed for light duty on December 4, 1863, at Raleigh. Remained on detail at Raleigh until detailed as a nurse at Lynchburg, Virginia, August 5, 1864. Returned to duty with company September-October, 1864. Admitted to hospital at Richmond, Virginia, December 24, 1864, and returned to duty on March 24, 1865. Captured at Burkeville, Virginia, April 6, 1865, and confined at Newport News, Virginia. Released after taking the Oath of Allegiance on June 27, 1865.

PHILLIPS, D. C., Private

Resided in Moore County and enlisted in Wake County at age 22, July 15, 1862, for the war. Killed at Sharpsburg, Maryland, September 17, 1862.

PHILLIPS, D. C., Private

Resided in Moore County and enlisted in Wake County at age 24, July 15, 1862, for the war. Wounded at Sharpsburg, Maryland, September 17, 1862. Captured at Spotsylvania Court House, Virginia, May 12, 1864, and confined at Point Lookout, Maryland. Paroled at Point Lookout on March 14, 1865, and exchanged at Boulware's Wharf, James River, Virginia, March 16, 1865.

PHILLIPS, JOHN W., Private

Resided in Moore County and enlisted in Wake County at age 33, July 15, 1862, for the war. Wounded at Sharpsburg, Maryland, September 17, 1862. Deserted on February 1, 1863.

PHILLIPS, LEWIS S., Private

Born in Moore County where he resided prior to enlisting in Wake County at age 34, July 15, 1862, for the war. Wounded and captured at Sharpsburg, Maryland, September 17, 1862. Died in hospital at Frederick, Maryland, October 30, 1862.

PHILLIPS, WILLIAM, Private

Born in Onslow County where he resided as a farmer and enlisted at age 25, January 28, 1862, for the war. Discharged on May 26, 1862, by reason of "atrophy of the entire muscular system producing anemia and debility."

PINER, JAMES M., Private

Resided in Onslow County where he enlisted at age 23, May 13, 1861, for the war. Mustered in as Private and appointed Corporal January-February, 1862. Reduced to ranks October 31, 1862. Captured at Spotsylvania Court House, Virginia, May 20, 1864, and confined at Point Lookout, Maryland. Transferred to Elmira, New York, July 3, 1864. Died at Elmira on March 4, 1865.

POLLOCK, FRANCIS M., Private

Resided in Onslow County where he enlisted at age 24, May 13, 1861, for the war. Died at home on July 24, 1861.

PORTER, ELI, Private

Born in Pitt County and resided in Onslow County where he enlisted at age 33, March 24, 1862, for the war. Wounded at Sharpsburg, Maryland, September 17, 1862, and died of wound on January 10, 1863.

REDD, FRANCIS M., Private

Resided in Onslow County where he enlisted at age 18, May 13, 1861, for the war. Mustered in as Private and appointed Corporal on December 6, 1861. Wounded at Chancellorsville, Virginia, May 3, 1863. Promoted to Sergeant on May 4, 1863. Furloughed for 60 days on August 1, 1863, and reported as absent wounded from August, 1863, through December, 1864. Reduced to ranks for prolonged absence.

REDD, JACOB, Private

Resided in Onslow County where he enlisted at age 23, March 25, 1863, for the war. Died in hospital at Danville, Virginia, June 6, 1863, of "diarrhoea chronic."

REDD, SIGLEE, Private

Resided in Onslow County where he enlisted at age 25, May 13, 1861, for the war. Mustered in as Corporal and reduced to ranks on December 6, 1861. Reappointed Corporal on March 1, 1863. Wounded at Chancellorsville, Virginia, May 3, 1863, and at Payne's Farm, Virginia, November 27, 1863. Present or accounted for until transferred to Company H, 41st Regiment N.C. Troops (3rd Regiment N.C. Cavalry), December 5, 1863.

RICHARDSON, AULEY, Private

Resided in Onslow County where he enlisted at age 39, January 28, 1862, for the war. Wounded at Sharpsburg, Maryland, September 17, 1862, and at Wilderness, Virginia, May 5, 1864. Present or accounted for through December, 1864.

ROGERS, JAMES H., Private

Born in Onslow County where he resided and enlisted at age 23, May 13, 1861, for the war. Wounded at Malvern Hill, Virginia, July 1, 1862, and died of wound at Richmond, Virginia, July 12, 1862.

SAUNDERS, JAMES, Private

Born in Onslow County where he resided and enlisted at age 36, January 28, 1862, for the war. Died at Goldsboro on May 26, 1862, of "jaundice."

SAUNDERS, SHEPARD, Private

Born in Onslow County where he resided and enlisted at age 40, March 18, 1862, for the war. Killed at Malvern Hill, Virginia, July 1, 1862.

SCREWS, WILLIAM, Private

Resided in Onslow County where he enlisted at age 26, May 13, 1861, for the war. Discharged on July 12, 1861.

SEWELL, DANIEL H., Private

Born in Onslow County where he resided and enlisted at age 20, January 28, 1862, for the war. Wounded at Malvern Hill, Virginia, July 1, 1862, and died of wound on August 17, 1862.

SEWELL, THOMAS E., Private

Resided in Onslow County where he enlisted at age 18, January 28, 1862, for the war. Died August 7, 1862, of "diarrhoea."

SHERRILL, E. G., Private
Paroled at Salisbury on May 12, 1865.

SHIELDS, NEIL M., Private
Resided in Wake County and enlisted in Wake County at age 20, July 15, 1862, for the war. Deserted November 3, 1863.

SHIELDS, R. D., Private
Born in Moore County where he resided as a farmer prior to enlisting in Wake County at age 22, July 15, 1862, for the war. Discharged on September 28, 1862, by reason of "phthisis pulmonalis and extreme debility."

SIDBURY, LEMUEL H., Corporal
Born in Onslow County where he resided and enlisted at age 23, May 13, 1861, for the war. Mustered in as Corporal. Died in hospital in Stafford County, Virginia, January 30, 1862.

SINCLAIR, T. W., Private
Resided in Moore County and enlisted in Wake County at age 29, July 15, 1862, for the war. Died at home on July 1, 1863.

SMITH, NEIL R., Private
Resided in Moore County and enlisted in Wake County at age 22, July 15, 1862, for the war. Left sick in Maryland on September 17, 1862, and took the Oath of Allegiance at Hagerstown, Maryland, October 7, 1862.

SPARKMAN, CHARNEY, Private
Born in Onslow County where he resided and enlisted at age 18, May 13, 1861, for the war. Wounded at Ellerson's Mill, Virginia, June 26, 1862, and died of wound July 8-9, 1862.

TAYLOR, W. H., Private
Born in Pitt County where he resided as a farmer prior to enlisting in Wake County at age 27, July 15, 1862, for the war. Discharged on May 29, 1863, by reason of "staphyloma of the cornea of left eye, the other eye is also diseased." Rejoined the company on October 4, 1864, and died December 6, 1864, of "pneumonia."

THOMAS, WARREN A., Private
Resided in Pitt County and enlisted in Wake County at age 27, July 15, 1862, for the war. Wounded at Sharpsburg, Maryland, September 17, 1862. Reported as absent wounded until detailed in hospital at Lynchburg, Virginia, November 25, 1864. Paroled at Lynchburg on April 15, 1865.

THOMPSON, BRYANT W., Private
Born in Onslow County where he resided and enlisted at age 27, May 13, 1861, for the war. Mortally wounded at Cold Harbor, Virginia, June 27, 1862.

TIPPITT, LOTT W., Sergeant
Resided in Onslow County where he enlisted at age 34, May 13, 1861, for the war. Mustered in as Private. Wounded at Cold Harbor, Virginia, June 27, 1862. Appointed Corporal on December 31, 1863. Captured near Spotsylvania Court House, Virginia, May 12, 1864, and confined at Point Lookout, Maryland, until transferred to Elmira, New York, August 10, 1864. Paroled at Elmira on October 11, 1864, and exchanged at Venus Point, Savannah River, Georgia, Novem-

ber 14, 1864. Promoted to Sergeant, September-October, 1864. Present or accounted for through December, 1864.

TULL, LEMUEL H., Private
Resided in Onslow County where he enlisted at age 39, May 13, 1861, for the war. Discharged October 6-7, 1861.

VANN, THOMAS N., Private
Resided in Moore County and enlisted in Wake County at age 34, July 15, 1862, for the war. Accidentally wounded at Fredericksburg, Virginia, December 10, 1862. Killed at Chancellorsville, Virginia, May 3, 1863.

WALKER, JOSEPH, Private
Resided in Chatham County and enlisted in Wake County at age 30, July 15, 1862, for the war. Left in hospital at Richmond, Virginia, August 17, 1862, and never returned to company.

WALTON, AMOS, Private
Born in Onslow County where he resided as a farmer and enlisted at age 21, January 28, 1862, for the war. Discharged on May 8, 1862, by reason of "sore leg of several years standing."

WALTON, JESSE W., Private
Born in Onslow County where he resided and enlisted at age 21, May 13, 1861, for the war. Wounded at Malvern Hill, Virginia, July 1, 1862, and died of wound at Richmond, Virginia, July 29, 1862.

WESTON, RICHARD, Private
Resided in Onslow County where he enlisted at age 28, May 13, 1861, for the war. Wounded at Payne's Farm, Virginia, November 27, 1863. Captured near Spotsylvania Court House, Virginia, May 12, 1864, and confined at Point Lookout, Maryland. Transferred to Elmira, New York, August 10, 1864. Died at Elmira on September 23, 1864, of "remittent fever and erysipelas."

WHITEHURST, J. R., Private
Resided in Pitt County and enlisted in Wake County at age 19, July 15, 1862, for the war. Died at Richmond, Virginia, April 21, 1863, of "bronchitis."

WHITEHURST, W. A., Private
Resided in Pitt County and enlisted in Wake County at age 33, July 15, 1862, for the war. Died at Richmond, Virginia, September 7, 1862, of "typhoid fever."

WILFONG, CHARLES F., Private
Captured at Lenoir on April 15, 1865, and confined at Camp Chase, Ohio, where he died on May 26, 1865, of "pneumonia."

WILLIAMS, BENJAMIN, Private
Born in Onslow County where he resided and enlisted at age 30, May 13, 1861, for the war. Wounded at Malvern Hill, Virginia, July 1, 1862, and died of wound at Richmond, Virginia, July 11, 1862.

WILLIAMS, BRICE F., Private
Resided in Onslow County where he enlisted at age 26, May 13, 1861, for the war. Wounded at Chancellorsville, Virginia, May 3, 1863. Captured near Spotsylvania Court House, Virginia,

May 12, 1864, and confined at Point Lookout, Maryland. Transferred to Elmira, New York, August 10, 1864. Paroled at Elmira on March 14, 1865, and exchanged at Boulware's Wharf, James River, Virginia, March 18-21, 1865.

WILLIAMS, EDWARD STANLEY, 1st Sergeant
Born in Onslow County where he resided as a farmer and enlisted at age 33, May 13, 1861, for the war. Mustered in as 1st Sergeant. Discharged on August 19, 1862, by reason of disability.

WILLIAMS, HILL, Sergeant
Resided in Onslow County where he enlisted at age 25, January 30, 1862, for the war. Mustered in as Private. Wounded at Malvern Hill, Virginia, July 1, 1862. Appointed Corporal on August 1, 1863. Wounded at Payne's Farm, Virginia, November 27, 1863. Captured near Spotsylvania Court House, Virginia, May 12, 1864, and confined at Point Lookout, Maryland. Transferred to Elmira, New York, August 10, 1864. Promoted to Sergeant September-October, 1864, while a prisoner of war. Paroled at Elmira on March 14, 1865, and exchanged at Boulware's Wharf, James River, Virginia, March 18-21, 1865. Captured in hospital at Raleigh on April 13, 1865.

WILLIAMS, JAMES R., Private
Resided in New Hanover County and enlisted in Onslow County at age 22, May 13, 1861, for the war. Captured near Spotsylvania Court House, Virginia, May 12, 1864, and confined at Point Lookout, Maryland. Transferred to Elmira, New York, August 10, 1864. Released at Elmira after taking the Oath of Allegiance on June 27, 1865.

WILSON, JOHN, Private
Born in Germany and resided as a bridge carpenter in Onslow County where he enlisted at age 34, May 13, 1861, for the war. Discharged on January 29, 1862, and transferred to the C.S. Navy.

YOPP, ROBERT W., Private
Resided in Onslow County where he enlisted at age 35, May 13, 1861, for the war. Wounded at Sharpsburg, Maryland, September 16, 1862, and at Chancellorsville, Virginia, May 3, 1863. Wounded a third time at Payne's Farm, Virginia, November 27, 1863. Captured near Spotsylvania Court House, Virginia, May 12, 1864, and confined at Point Lookout, Maryland. Transferred to Elmira, New York, August 10, 1864. Paroled at Elmira on March 2, 1865, and sent to James River, Virginia, for exchange. Admitted to hospital at Richmond, Virginia, March 11, 1865, and furloughed for 30 days the next day.

COMPANY F

This company was organized in New Hanover County and enlisted at Wilmington on June 6, 1861. It tendered its service to the state and was ordered to Garysburg, Northampton County, where it was assigned to this regiment as Company F. After joining the regiment the company functioned as a part of the regiment, and its history is recorded as a part of the regimental history.

The information contained in the following roster of the company was compiled principally from company muster rolls which covered from July 2, 1861, through December, 1864, and included a muster-in roll dated April 19, 1862. No company muster rolls were found for the period prior to July 2, 1861, or for the period after December, 1864. In addition to the company muster rolls, Roll of Honor records, receipt rolls, and hospital records, supplemented by state pension applications, United Daughters of the Confederacy records, and postwar rosters and histories, all provided useful information.

OFFICERS
CAPTAINS

PARSLEY, WILLIAM MURDOCK
Resided in New Hanover County and appointed Captain to rank from May 16, 1861. Wounded at Malvern Hill, Virginia, July 1, 1862. Present or accounted for until transferred to the Field and Staff of this regiment upon appointment as Major to rank from December 10, 1862.

RADCLIFFE, ROBERT S.
Resided in New Hanover County and appointed 2nd Lieutenant to rank from May 16, 1861. Promoted to 1st Lieutenant to rank from November 30, 1861. Wounded at Sharpsburg, Maryland, September 17, 1862. Promoted to Captain to rank from December 10, 1862, while absent on wounded furlough. Appointed Enrolling Officer, 4th Congressional District, August 13, 1863, and transferred from the company on August 19, 1863.

CANTWELL, JOHN L.
Previously served in Company A, 13th Battalion N.C. Infantry and on the Field and Staff, 51st Regiment N.C. Troops. Appointed Captain of this company to rank from November 13, 1863. Captured at Spotsylvania Court House, Virginia, May 12, 1864, and confined at Fort Delaware, Delaware. Transferred to Hilton Head, South Carolina, August 20, 1864, and to Fort Pulaski, Georgia, October 21, 1864. Returned to Hilton Head on December 26, 1864, and sent back to Fort Delaware on March 12, 1865. Released at Fort Delaware after taking the Oath of Allegiance on May 26, 1865.

LIEUTENANTS

CRAPON, GEORGE M., 2nd Lieutenant
Resided in New Hanover County where he enlisted at age 21, June 7, 1861, for the war. Mustered in as Corporal and promoted to Sergeant on October 1, 1861. Promoted to 1st Sergeant on April 1, 1863. Wounded at Chancellorsville, Virginia, May 3, 1863. Appointed 2nd Lieutenant to rank from November 17, 1863. Captured at Wilderness, Virginia, May 10, 1864, and confined at Fort Delaware, Delaware. Transferred to Hilton Head, South Carolina, August 20, 1864, and to Fort Pulaski, Georgia, October 20, 1864. Sent back to Hilton Head on December 26, 1864, and returned to Fort Delaware March 20, 1865. Released at Fort Delaware after taking the Oath of Allegiance on June 16, 1865.

GARRISON, EDWARD J., 1st Lieutenant
Resided in New Hanover County where he enlisted at age 21, June 6, 1861, for the war. Mustered in as Sergeant and promoted to 1st Sergeant, January-February, 1862. Wounded at Ellerson's Mill, Virginia, June 26, 1862. Appointed 2nd Lieutenant to rank from August 8, 1862, and promoted to 1st Lieutenant to rank from December 10, 1862. Killed at Gettysburg, Pennsylvania, July 2, 1863.

McCLAMMY, CHARLES W., 2nd Lieutenant
Resided in New Hanover County where he enlisted at age 24, June 6, 1861, for the war. Mustered in as Sergeant. Promoted to 1st Sergeant, January-February, 1863. Appointed 2nd Lieutenant to rank from March 23, 1863. Captured at Wilderness, Virginia, May 10, 1864, and confined at Fort Delaware, Delaware. Released at Fort Delaware after taking the Oath of Allegiance on June 16, 1865.

NORTHROP, WILLIAM HARRISS, 2nd Lieutenant
Resided in New Hanover County and appointed 2nd Lieutenant to rank from February 18, 1862. Transferred to the Field and Staff of this regiment upon appointment as Captain, Assistant Quartermaster, August 8, 1862.

PICKETT, ISAAC J., 1st Lieutenant
Resided in New Hanover County and appointed 2nd Lieutenant to rank from December 10, 1862. Never commissioned as such so he did not report to company. Appointed 1st Lieutenant to rank from November 13, 1863, and commissioned. Captured at Wilderness, Virginia, May 10, 1864, and confined at Fort Delaware, Delaware. Released at Fort Delaware after taking the Oath of Allegiance on June 16, 1865.

POTTER, HENRY W., 2nd Lieutenant
Resided in New Hanover County where he enlisted at age 25, June 6, 1861, for the war. Mustered in as Corporal and appointed Sergeant on August 18, 1861. Promoted to 1st Sergeant on November 1, 1862, and appointed 2nd Lieutenant to rank from November 20, 1862. Killed at Gettysburg, Pennsylvania, July 2, 1863.

RUNCIMAN, JOHN W., 3rd Lieutenant
Resided in New Hanover County and appointed 3rd Lieutenant to rank from May 16, 1861. Died at Wilmington on April 6, 1862, of "pneumonia."

SUMMERSETT, CHRISTOPHER H., 2nd Lieutenant
Resided in New Hanover County where he enlisted at age 27, June 6, 1861, for the war. Mustered in as Sergeant and promoted to 1st Sergeant on September 14, 1861. Appointed 2nd Lieutenant to rank from May 10, 1862. Dropped on November 20, 1862, "for continuous absence without leave."

WILLIS, HARDY BRYAN, 1st Lieutenant
Resided in New Hanover County and appointed 1st Lieutenant at age 27 to rank from May 16, 1861. Transferred to the Field and Staff of this regiment upon appointment as Captain, Assistant Commissary of Subsistence, to rank from October 29, 1861.

NONCOMMISSIONED OFFICERS AND PRIVATES

ALDRIDGE, GEORGE W., Sergeant
Resided in New Hanover County where he enlisted at age 20, February 24, 1862, for the war. Mustered in as Private and appointed Corporal on October 31, 1862. Promoted to Sergeant on March 1, 1863. Present or accounted for until captured at Gettysburg, Pennsylvania, July 3-5, 1863. Confined at Fort Delaware, Delaware, until released after taking the Oath of Allegiance on June 19, 1865.

ALLEN, JOHN CALVIN, Private
Resided in Moore County where he enlisted at age 25, July 15, 1862, for the war. Reported as absent sick from August, 1862, through February, 1863. Wounded May 3, 1863, at Chancellorsville, Virginia, and reported as absent wounded from that date through December, 1864.

ANDERSON, ANDREW J., Private
Resided in New Hanover County where he enlisted at age 19, June 6, 1861, for the war. Accidentally wounded on June 27, 1862. Died December 10, 1862, in Wilmington of "yellow fever."

ATKINSON, BENJAMIN, Private
Resided in New Hanover County where he enlisted at age 20, June 10, 1861, for the war. Absent sick from August, 1862, through December, 1862. Present or accounted for until he "gave himself up" near Bloomfield, Pennsylvania, on June 29, 1863. Confined at Fort Mifflin, Pennsylvania, on July 1, 1863, and escaped from that place on January 15, 1864. No further records.

BELL, GEORGE J. M., Sergeant
Born in New Hanover County where he resided and enlisted at age 20, June 6, 1861, for the war. Mustered in as Private and appointed Corporal on October 1, 1861. Present or accounted for until promoted to Sergeant on April 10, 1862. Killed on September 17, 1862, at Sharpsburg, Maryland.

BELL, ROBERT N., 1st Sergeant
Resided in New Hanover County where he enlisted at age 27, June 28, 1861, for the war. Mustered in as 1st Sergeant. Transferred to Company G of this regiment upon appointment as 2nd Lieutenant to rank from September 17, 1861.

BERRY, CHARLES W., Private
Born in Hanover, Germany, and resided as a tailor in New Hanover County where he enlisted at age 27, March 10, 1862, for the war. Present or accounted for until detailed to the Quartermaster Department at Richmond, Virginia, on September 10, 1862, as a tailor. Absent detailed in Quartermaster Department, or in hospitals at Wilmington or Richmond, from that date through December, 1864.

BISHOP, GEORGE W., Private
Resided in New Hanover County where he enlisted at age 18, June 6, 1861, for the war. Present or accounted for until wounded on June 27, 1862, at Cold Harbor, Virginia. Absent wounded through February, 1863. Captured July 3, 1863, at Gettysburg, Pennsylvania, and confined at

Fort Delaware, Delaware. Transferred to Point Lookout, Maryland, October 18, 1863. Paroled at Point Lookout and sent to James River, Virginia, for exchange on February 18, 1865. Reported as present on a muster roll of a detachment of paroled and exchanged prisoners at Camp Lee, near Richmond, Virginia, dated February 23, 1865.

BISHOP, HENRY M., Private
Resided in New Hanover County where he enlisted at age 18, June 6, 1861, for the war. Present or accounted for until wounded on July 2, 1863, at Gettysburg, Pennsylvania. Admitted to hospital at Richmond, Virginia, on July 20, 1863, with "gunshot wound left leg (flesh)" and was furloughed September 16, 1863. Reported as absent wounded from that date through December, 1864. Paroled April 9, 1865, at Appomattox Court House, Virginia.

BRADSHAW, JOHN H., Private
Resided in Wayne County where he enlisted at age 34, July 15, 1862, for the war. Present or accounted for until killed on November 27, 1863, in battle at Payne's Farm, Virginia.

BRADSHAW, WILLIAM, Private
Killed at Mine Run, Virginia, November 27-28, 1863.

BRAFFORD, EDWARD, Private
Resided in Wayne County where he enlisted at age 35, July 15, 1862, for the war. Reported as absent sick from April 29, 1863, through October, 1863. Present or accounted for until captured on May 12, 1864, near Spotsylvania Court House, Virginia. Confined at Point Lookout, Maryland, until transferred to Elmira, New York, August 10, 1864. Released at Elmira after taking the Oath of Allegiance on June 19, 1865.

BRANTLEY, GEORGE W., Private
Resided in New Hanover County where he enlisted at age 26, June 10, 1861, for the war. Present or accounted for until admitted to hospital at Richmond, Virginia, on May 8, 1863, with "hernia." Returned to duty September 23, 1863. Present or accounted for until captured on May 12, 1864, at Spotsylvania Court House, Virginia. Confined at Point Lookout, Maryland, until transferred to Elmira, New York, July 12, 1864. Paroled at Elmira and sent to James River, Virginia, for exchange on March 2, 1865. Admitted to hospital at Richmond on March 2, 1865, and furloughed for 30 days on March 8, 1865.

BREWER, MARTIN, Private
Resided in Moore County where he enlisted at age 22, July 15, 1862, for the war. Captured at Frederick, Maryland, on September 13, 1862, and confined at Fort Delaware, Delaware. Paroled at Fort Delaware and sent to Aiken's Landing, Virginia, for exchange, October 2, 1862. Present or accounted for until captured on May 12, 1864, near Spotsylvania Court House, Virginia. Confined at Point Lookout, Maryland, until transferred to Elmira, New York, on August 10, 1864. Released at Elmira after taking the Oath of Allegiance on June 30, 1865.

BRITT, ENOCH, Private
Resided in Wayne County where he enlisted at age 21, July 15, 1862, for the war. Wounded at Sharpsburg, Maryland, September 17, 1862. Died in hospital at Mt. Jackson, Virginia, November 22, 1862, of "diarrhoea chronic."

BRITT, KINCHEN, Private
Resided in Wayne County where he enlisted at age 20, July 15, 1862, for the war. Wounded and captured September 17, 1862, at Sharpsburg, Maryland. Admitted to U.S.A. General Hospital, Philadelphia, Pennsylvania, September 27, 1862, with "gunshot wound, cheek, r.s." Transferred to U.S.A. General Hospital, Ladies Home, New York City, on March 17, 1863. Transferred to Fort Delaware, Delaware, in September, 1863. Released at Fort Delaware after taking the Oath of Allegiance on June 19, 1865.

BROOKS, H., Private
Paroled May 20, 1865, at Salisbury.

BROWN, JOHN, Private
Paroled May 15, 1865, at Morganton.

BROWN, L., Private
Paroled May 15, 1865, at Morganton.

BYRD, JOHN B., Corporal
Resided in New Hanover County where he enlisted at age 22, June 6, 1861, for the war. Mustered in as Private and appointed Corporal in August, 1862. Present or accounted for until wounded on September 17, 1862, in battle at Sharpsburg, Maryland. Died of his wounds on September 24, 1862, at Mt. Jackson, Virginia.

BYRD, JOSEPH T., Private
Resided in New Hanover County where he enlisted at age 35, November 26, 1861, for the war. Wounded September 17, 1862, at Sharpsburg, Maryland. Present or accounted for through December, 1864. Deserted and took the Oath of Allegiance at Headquarters, Army of the James, on March 19, 1865. Forwarded to the Provost Marshal General, Washington, D.C., and furnished transportation from Washington to Wilmington on March 24, 1865. Admitted to Mansfield General Hospital, Morehead City, N.C., April 22, 1865, and died April 22, 1865, of "erysipelas."

BYRD, ROBERT J., Private
Resided in New Hanover County where he enlisted at age 28, March 3, 1862, for the war. Accidentally wounded June 10, 1862, while on picket duty near Richmond, Virginia. Absent wounded through February, 1863. Muster rolls report that he was left sick in camp near Port Royal, Virginia, on April 29, 1863. Absent sick from that date through December, 1864.

CANADY, JOHN, Private
Born in Ireland and resided in New Hanover County where he enlisted at age 43, June 7, 1861, for the war. Died January 4, 1862, at Wilmington.

CARTER, NICHOLAS, Private
Resided in Wayne County where he enlisted at age 25, July 15, 1862, for the war. Present or accounted for until wounded on May 3, 1863, at Chancellorsville, Virginia. Hospital records give

nature of wound as "gunshot thigh with erysipelas and pneumonia" and state that he was furloughed from hospital at Richmond, Virginia, for 30 days on June 2, 1863. Present or accounted for until captured on May 12, 1864, near Spotsylvania Court House, Virginia. Confined at Point Lookout, Maryland, until transferred to Elmira, New York, August 10, 1864. Released at Elmira after taking the Oath of Allegiance on June 27, 1865.

CASTEEN, ALONZO, Private

Resided in New Hanover County where he enlisted at age 24, June 24, 1861, for the war. Present or accounted for until accidentally wounded on September 16, 1862, at Sharpsburg, Maryland. Absent wounded through December, 1862. Deserted from camp near Port Royal, Virginia, on April 15, 1863, and took the Oath of Allegiance at the Office of the Provost Marshal General, Army of the Potomac, on April 22, 1863. Confined at Old Capitol Prison, Washington, D.C., on April 24, 1863.

CHANDLER, PETER H., Private

Resided in New Hanover County where he enlisted at age 18, June 17, 1861, for the war. Present or accounted for until killed at Chancellorsville, Virginia, May 3, 1863.

CHARLES, ANDREW, Private

Enlisted in Davidson County on October 18, 1863, for the war. Captured near Spotsylvania Court House, Virginia, May 12, 1864, and confined at Point Lookout, Maryland. Transferred to Elmira, New York, August 10, 1864. Died at Elmira on September 9, 1864, of "chronic diarrhoea."

CHARLES, LEVIN, Private

Resided in Davidson County where he enlisted on October 18, 1863, for the war. Captured at Mine Run, Virginia, November 28, 1863, and confined at Old Capitol Prison, Washington, D.C. Released after taking the Oath of Allegiance on March 19, 1864.

CLARK, THOMAS, Private

Resided in New Hanover County where he enlisted at age 32, June 12, 1861, for the war. Mustered in as Fifer. Appointed 1st Musician, September-October, 1861, and served as such until reported as Musician after July, 1862. Transferred to the Field and Staff of this regiment upon appointment as Chief Musician on January 1, 1864. Reduced to ranks and returned to the company on December 18, 1864. Deserted to the enemy March 18, 1865, and took the Oath of Allegiance at Washington, D.C., March 24, 1865.

CLIFF, ELIAS, Private

Born in Brunswick County and resided in New Hanover County where he enlisted at age 37, June 6, 1861, for the war. Died at Camp Howe, Virginia, December, 14, 1861, of "heart disease."

COLE, RYLAND R., Private

Born in Moore County where he resided as a farmer and enlisted on July 15, 1862, for the war. Died in hospital at Richmond, Virginia, September 10, 1862, of "fever cont. and typhoid."

COLLINS, JOHN, Private

Resided in New Hanover County where he

enlisted at age 37, June 12, 1861, for the war. Absent sick from February 12, 1862, until returned to duty after April, 1862. Reported on November-December, 1862, muster roll with the remark: "Absent without leave since July 1, 1862." February 28-May 13, 1863, muster roll reports him with the remark: "Left sick at camp near Port Royal, Virginia, April 29, 1863." Admitted to hospital at Richmond, Virginia, May 8, 1863, with "rheumatismus acute" and returned to duty August 19, 1863. Company muster rolls report him as absent sick until August 20, 1863, and as absent without leave after that date.

COOPER, JOHN W., Private

Resided in New Hanover County where he enlisted at age 29, June 12, 1861, for the war. Captured September 17, 1862, at Sharpsburg, Maryland, and paroled September 20, 1862, near Keedysville, Maryland. Admitted to hospital at Richmond, Virginia, on November 4, 1862, with "febris remitten." Absent sick through May, 1863. Deserted June 27, 1863, while the company was in Pennsylvania. Confined at Fort Mifflin, Pennsylvania, on July 1, 1863. Took the Oath of Allegiance at Fort Mifflin on November 17, 1863. Oath states that he was "released but still in the employ of government."

COURTNEY, PATRICK, Private

Born in Ireland and resided as a laborer in New Hanover County where he enlisted at age 48, June 12, 1861, for the war. Reported as absent sick from March, 1862, until discharged November 2, 1862, by reason of disability caused by "chronic inflammation of kidneys and bladder in connection with his age."

COX, JOHN W., Private

Resided in Wayne County where he enlisted at age 30, July 15, 1862, for the war. Provided Jackson Evans as his substitute; however, the substitute was not accepted. Reported as present from January-February, 1863, until discharged in April, 1863, "after paying $500. because he belonged to the Society of Friends."

CRAIG, EDWARD, Corporal

Resided in New Hanover County where he enlisted at age 18, June 6, 1861, for the war. Mustered in as Private and appointed Corporal on November 17, 1863. Present or accounted for until wounded November 27, 1863, in battle at Payne's Farm, Virginia. Absent wounded from that date until September-October, 1864, when he was detailed in the enrolling office at Wilmington. Absent detailed through December, 1864.

CRAIG, HENRY, Private

Resided in New Hanover County where he enlisted at age 42, June 6, 1861, for the war. Reported as absent sick from August 17, 1862, through December, 1862. Present or accounted for from that date until killed May 5, 1864, at Wilderness, Virginia.

CRAWFORD, CHARLES H., Private

Resided in New Hanover County where he enlisted at age 33, January 17, 1862, for the war.

Present or accounted for until transferred to the C.S. Navy on April 13, 1864.

CROOM, ISAAC, Private
Born in Wayne County and resided as a mason in New Hanover County where he enlisted at age 26, June 6, 1861, for the war. Present or accounted for until admitted to hospital at Richmond, Virginia, on November 14, 1862, with "pneumonia." Absent wounded until discharged March 17, 1863, by reason of disability caused by "phthisis pul."

CURTIS, CHARLES, Private
Resided in New Hanover County where he enlisted on February 19, 1862, for the war. Deserted June 27, 1863, while the company was in Pennsylvania. Confined at Fort Mifflin, Pennsylvania, July 1, 1863, and released after taking the Oath of Allegiance on November 17, 1863.

CURTIS, WASHINGTON, Private
Enlisted in New Hanover County at age 23, February 19, 1862, for the war.

DAVIS, CALVIN, Private
Resided in Robeson County and enlisted in New Hanover County at age 23, March 8, 1862, for the war. Wounded September 17, 1862, at Sharpsburg, Maryland. Absent wounded through December, 1862. Deserted March 17, 1863, and was returned to duty August 5, 1863. Present or accounted for until captured May 12, 1864, near Spotsylvania Court House, Virginia. Confined at Point Lookout, Maryland, where he died on July 17, 1864.

DAVIS, STEPHEN, Private
Resided in Moore County where he enlisted at age 20, July 15, 1862, for the war. Captured at Frederick, Maryland, on September 13, 1862, and confined at Fort Delaware, Delaware. Paroled at Fort Delaware and sent to Aiken's Landing, James River, Virginia, for exchange on October 2, 1862. Declared exchanged on November 10, 1862. Reported as absent without leave from that date through February, 1863. Present or accounted for until killed on November 27, 1863, at Payne's Farm, Virginia.

DONNIGAN, ASHLEY, Private
Issued clothing on February 20, 1864; March 1, 1864; and April 20, 1864. Captured May 12, 1864, near Spotsylvania Court House, Virginia. Confined at Point Lookout, Maryland, until transferred to Elmira, New York, on July 25, 1864. Died February 28, 1865, at Elmira of "variola."

ELDRIDGE, JOHN H., Private
Resided in New Hanover County where he enlisted at age 19, June 6, 1861, for the war. Present or accounted for until reported as absent without leave on February 15, 1862. Returned to duty March-April, 1862. Deserted June 13, 1862. No further records.

EVANS, JACKSON, Private
Negro. Enlisted July 15, 1862, as a substitute for John W. Cox. Captured and paroled at Keedysville, Maryland, on September 20, 1862. Dropped from rolls November-December, 1862.

EVANS, JOHN, Private
Enlisted in Wayne County on July 15, 1862, for the war. Captured September 17, 1862, at Sharpsburg, Maryland. No further records.

EVANS, JUNIUS G., Private
Resided in New Hanover County where he enlisted at age 32, June 17, 1861, for the war. Never reported. Died in Brunswick County in November, 1861.

FARROW, CHARLES H., Sergeant
Resided in New Hanover County where he enlisted at age 20, June 6, 1861, for the war. Mustered in as Private and appointed Corporal on October 31, 1862. Present or accounted for until wounded at Sharpsburg, Maryland, September 17, 1862. Absent wounded through October, 1862. Captured at Fredericksburg, Virginia, May 3, 1863. Paroled and sent to City Point, Virginia, for exchange on May 10, 1863. Wounded on July 3, 1863, at Gettysburg, Pennsylvania. Absent wounded through October, 1863. Promoted to Sergeant on November 17, 1863. Present or accounted for until admitted to hospital at Richmond, Virginia, on May 8, 1864, with "gunshot wound stomach." Date returned to duty not shown. Reported as present on company muster roll for December 31, 1863-August 31, 1864. Killed October 19, 1864, in battle at Cedar Creek, Virginia.

FINK, JOHN A., Private
Paroled at Salisbury on May 25, 1865.

FLOYD, THOMAS D., Private
Resided in New Hanover County where he enlisted at age 21, June 10, 1861, for the war. Present or accounted for until wounded on November 27, 1863, at Payne's Farm, Virginia. Absent wounded until detailed and assigned to Captain Samuel B. Waters' Company, Provost Guard, Raleigh, on March 9, 1864. Absent detailed through January, 1865. Paroled at Raleigh on May 16, 1865.

GENTRY, W. H., Private
Enlisted on October 3, 1864, for the war.

GIBBS, J. R., Private
Paroled at Morganton on May 29, 1865.

GILDEA, PATRICK, Private
Resided in New Hanover County where he enlisted at age 20, June 15, 1861, for the war. Wounded at Malvern Hill, Virginia, July 1, 1862. Present or accounted for until he "deserted while on picket on the Rappahannock River, Virginia, April 17, 1863."

GOODMAN, CURTIS, Private
Captured at Winchester, Virginia, September 19, 1864, and confined at Point Lookout, Maryland. Paroled on March 15, 1865, and exchanged at Aiken's Landing, James River, Virginia, March 18, 1865.

GREEN, JOHN, Private
Enlisted in Randolph County on August 21, 1864, for the war. Deserted soon after assigned to company.

HAGA, ABSALOM, Private
Enlisted in Forsyth County on October 29, 1863,

for the war. Captured at Spotsylvania Court House, Virginia, May 12, 1864, and confined at Point Lookout, Maryland. Released at Point Lookout after taking the Oath of Allegiance and joining the U.S. service on May 26, 1864.

HAGARTY, JAMES, Private
Resided in New Hanover County where he enlisted at age 24, June 11, 1861, for the war. Transferred to the Field and Staff of this regiment upon appointment as Quartermaster Sergeant on August 1, 1861.

HAMILTON, SAMUEL, Private
Captured near Washington, N. C., February 10, 1864, and confined at Point Lookout, Maryland. Paroled at Point Lookout on March 15, 1865, and exchanged at Boulware's Wharf, James River, Virginia, March 18, 1865.

HANCOCK, JOHN M., Private
Resided in Moore County and enlisted in Wayne County at age 30, July 15, 1862, for the war. Captured at Frederick, Maryland, September 12, 1862, and paroled and exchanged at Aiken's Landing, James River, Virginia, November 10, 1862. Wounded at Payne's Farm, Virginia, November 27-28, 1863. Reported as absent wounded on company muster rolls from December, 1863, through December, 1864. Captured at Burkeville, Virginia, April 6, 1865, and confined at Point Lookout, Maryland. Released at Point Lookout after taking the Oath of Allegiance on June 27, 1865.

HARDIN, CORNELIUS, Private
Resided in Robeson County and enlisted at Camp Howe, Virginia, at age 24, November 20, 1861, for the war. Wounded at Chancellorsville, Virginia, May 3, 1863, and sent to hospital. Deserted from hospital at Lynchburg, Virginia, August 13, 1863, and never returned to company.

HARDIN, JESSE, Private
Resided in Robeson County and enlisted in New Hanover County at age 22, March 14, 1862, for the war. Wounded at Gettysburg, Pennsylvania, July 2, 1863, and captured in hospital at Gettysburg July 4-5, 1863. Confined in hospital at Chester, Pennsylvania, until paroled on September 17, 1863. Exchanged at City Point, Virginia, September 23, 1863. Returned to company in September, 1864. Admitted to hospital at Richmond, Virginia, December 23, 1864, with "scabies," and returned to duty on February 7, 1865. Captured at Farmville, Virginia, April 6, 1865, and confined at Newport News, Virginia. Released at Newport News after taking Oath of Allegiance on June 27, 1865.

HARDIN, WILLIAM, Private
Resided in New Hanover County where he enlisted at age 18, June 12, 1861, for the war. Deserted on August 10, 1862, and died in hospital at Black and Whites, Virginia, March 30, 1863, of "pleuritis."

HARRELL, A. STROUD, Private
Enlisted in Forsyth County on October 29, 1863, for the war. Deserted on November 17, 1863.

HAWKINS, JAMES H., Private
Resided in New Hanover County where he enlisted at age 23, June 6, 1861, for the war. Killed at Sharpsburg, Maryland, September 17, 1862.

HENRY, W. B., Private
Paroled at Salisbury on May 27, 1865.

HEWETT, JAMES HENRY, Sergeant
Resided in New Hanover County where he enlisted at age 20, June 6, 1861, for the war. Mustered in as Private. Captured at Boonsboro, Maryland, September 15, 1862, and confined at Fort Delaware, Delaware. Paroled at Fort Delaware on October 2, 1862, and exchanged at Aiken's Landing, James River, Virginia, November 10, 1862. Appointed Corporal on March 1, 1863. Wounded at Gettysburg, Pennsylvania, July 3, 1863, and captured in hospital at Gettysburg, July 4-5, 1863. Confined at DeCamp General Hospital, Davids Island, New York Harbor, until paroled on September 27, 1863. Admitted to hospital at Richmond, Virginia, September 28, 1863, and detailed for guard duty on December 2, 1863, for the 60 days. Promoted to Sergeant, January-August, 1864. Present or accounted for through December, 1864.

HICKS, JAMES H., Private
Resided in New Hanover County where he enlisted at age 19, June 10, 1861, for the war. Present or accounted for until captured at Spotsylvania Court House, Virginia, May 12, 1864. Confined at Point Lookout, Maryland, until transferred to Elmira, New York, August 10, 1864. Released at Elmira after taking the Oath of Allegiance on May 19, 1865.

HIGHTOWER, ROBERT A., Private
Resided in Duplin County and enlisted in New Hanover County at age 19, December 17, 1861, for the war. Deserted April 15, 1863, and took the Oath of Allegiance at Washington, D. C., April 29, 1863.

HOLMES, DAVID E., Private
Resided in New Hanover County where he enlisted at age 19, June 6, 1861, for the war. Deserted on May 8, 1862.

JARRELL, HIRAM, Private
Resided in New Hanover County where he enlisted at age 32, June 6, 1861, for the war. Wounded at Mechanicsville, Virginia, June 26, 1862. Present or accounted for until captured at Mine Run, Virginia, November 30, 1863. Confined at Old Capitol Prison, Washington, D.C. Released after taking the Oath of Allegiance on March 19, 1864.

JULIAN, TOBIAS C., Private
Enlisted in Randolph County on August 21, 1864, for the war. Sent to hospital on October 4, 1864, and never returned to company. Paroled at Greensboro on May 11, 1865.

JUSTICE, ARCHUS H., Private
Resided in New Hanover County where he enlisted at age 18, June 6, 1861, for the war. Killed at Sharpsburg, Maryland, September 17, 1862.

JUSTICE, ELIJAH, Private
Resided in New Hanover County where he enlisted at age 18, June 6, 1861, for the war. Present or accounted for until reported as "missing since battle of Gettysburg, Pennsylvania, July 2, 1863."

KEEN, JOSEPH L., Jr., Private
Enlisted in New Hanover County, March 1, 1862, for the war. Transferred to Company K, 36th Regiment N. C. Troops (2nd Regiment N.C. Artillery), March 1, 1862.

KEITH, RALEY, Private
First reported on September-October, 1864, muster roll. Date of enlistment given as July 15, 1861, but place and period of enlistment not reported. Carried on the muster roll with the remark: "Absent without leave since enlistment."

KELLY, THOMAS, Private
Enlisted at Richmond, Virginia, July 19, 1861, for the war. Reported as absent sick after February 17, 1862.

KING, JAMES MADISON, Private
Resided in New Hanover County where he enlisted at age 19, June 12, 1861, for the war. Captured at Boonsboro, Maryland, September 15, 1862, and confined at Fort Delaware, Delaware. Paroled at Fort Delaware on October 2, 1862, and exchanged at Aiken's Landing, James River, Virginia, November 10, 1862. Wounded at Gettysburg, Pennsylvania, July 2, 1863, and captured in hospital at Gettysburg July 4-5, 1863. Confined in hospital at Chester, Pennsylvania, until transferred to Point Lookout, Maryland, October 2, 1863. Paroled at Point Lookout on October 11, 1864, and exchanged at Cox's Landing, James River, October 15, 1864.

LANE, WILLIAM H., Private
Resided in New Hanover County where he enlisted at age 19, June 6, 1861, for the war. Mortally wounded at Sharpsburg, Maryland, September 17, 1862.

LAURENS, HIRAM, Private
Resided in New Hanover County where he enlisted at age 45, June 6, 1861, for the war. Detailed as clerk in Commissary Department in October, 1862, and reported as absent on detail through December, 1864. Paroled at Appomattox Court House, Virginia, April 9, 1865.

LYNCH, JOHN, Private
Born in Ireland and resided as a sailmaker in New Hanover County where he enlisted at age 22, June 19, 1861, for the war. Present or accounted for until transferred to the C.S. Navy on February 1, 1862.

McDONALD, DAVIS, Private
First reported on September-October, 1864, muster roll. Date, place, and period of enlistment not reported. Carried on muster roll with the remark: "Wounded at Winchester, Virginia, September 19, 1864. Supposed taken prisoner." Reported with same remark on November-December, 1864, muster roll. No further records.

McDONOUGH, JOHN, Private
Enlisted at Richmond, Virginia, July 19, 1861, for the war. Reported as absent sick after February 18, 1862.

MARSHALL, JOHN H., Musician
Resided in New Hanover County where he enlisted at age 18, June 10, 1861, for the war. Mustered in as Private and appointed Musician, January-February, 1862. Absent without leave after July 3, 1863.

MARTIN, HAYWOOD, Private
Resided in Wayne County and enlisted in Wake County at age 25, July 15, 1862, for the war. Captured at Sharpsburg, Maryland, September 17, 1862, and paroled to remain "in any of the loyal states" on September 27, 1862.

MONTGOMERY, GEORGE T., Private
Resided in New Hanover County where he enlisted at age 20, April 15, 1862, for the war. Wounded at Sharpsburg, Maryland, September 17, 1862, and at Payne's Farm, Virginia, November 27, 1863. Present or accounted for until reported as missing since the battle at Winchester, Virginia, September 19, 1864.

MONTGOMERY, JOHN, Private
Resided in New Hanover County where he enlisted at age 22, June 21, 1861, for the war. Wounded at Gettysburg, Pennsylvania, July 2, 1863, and "left at hospital."

MONTGOMERY, JOHN J., Private
Born in Brunswick County and enlisted in New Hanover County on April 15, 1862, for the war. Killed at Mechanicsville, Virginia, June 26, 1862.

MONTGOMERY, WILLIAM A., 1st Sergeant
Resided in New Hanover County where he enlisted at age 23, June 6, 1861, for the war. Mustered in as Corporal and reduced to ranks April 30-July 14, 1862. Appointed Sergeant on September 1, 1863, and promoted to 1st Sergeant on November 17, 1863. Killed at Spotsylvania Court House, Virginia, May 12, 1864.

MOORE, ALEXANDER, Private
Resided in Robeson County where he enlisted at age 36, February 24, 1862, for the war. Died in hospital at Richmond, Virginia, September 26-27, 1862, of disease.

MOORE, ASA W., Private
Resided as a navigator in New Hanover County where he enlisted at age 18, June 8, 1861, for the war. Wounded at Sharpsburg, Maryland, September 17, 1862, and paroled on September 30, 1862. Captured at Spotsylvania Court House, Virginia, May 12, 1864, and confined at Point Lookout, Maryland. Transferred to Elmira, New York, August 10, 1864. Released at Elmira and transferred to Point Lookout for exchange on October 11, 1864. Remained at Point Lookout until released after taking the Oath of Allegiance on May 15, 1865.

MORGAN, JOHN, Private
Resided in Wayne County where he enlisted at age 32, July 15, 1862, for the war. Wounded at Payne's Farm, Virginia, November 27, 1863, and reported as absent wounded from November, 1863, through December, 1864.

MORGAN, JOHN M., Private

Resided in Moore County where he enlisted at age 30, July 15, 1862, for the war. Left sick at Frederick, Maryland, September 9, 1862, and never returned to company.

MURRAY, MICHAEL, Private

Born in Duplin County and resided as a painter in New Hanover County where he enlisted at age 28, June 6, 1861, for the war. Discharged on June 14, 1862, by reason of disability.

NELSON, HIRAM, Private

Resided in Guilford County and assigned to the company in August, 1864. Captured at Winchester, Virginia, September 20, 1864, and confined at Point Lookout, Maryland. Released after taking the Oath of Allegiance on May 12, 1865.

NIXON, WILLIAM, Private

Resided in Randolph County where he enlisted on August 21, 1864, for the war. Present or accounted for until captured at Burkeville, Virginia, April 6, 1865. Confined at Newport News, Virginia, where he died June 18, 1865, of "diarrhoea chronic."

NOLIN, WILLIAM, Private

Born in Fairfield District, South Carolina, and resided as a laborer in New Hanover County where he enlisted at age 30, June 6, 1861, for the war. Discharged on September 13, 1861, by reason of "nephritis and general debility."

NORTHROP, HENRY F., Private

Born at St. Augustine, Florida, and resided as a machinist in New Hanover County where he enlisted at age 18, February 25, 1862, for the war. Wounded at Sharpsburg, Maryland, September 17, 1862, and paroled on September 30, 1862. Detailed in railroad shop at Wilmington on November 16, 1863, and reported as absent on detail through December, 1864.

NUTT, H. H., Private

Enlisted in Forsyth County on October 29, 1863, for the war. Deserted on November 17, 1863.

ORMSBY, ASA D., Corporal

Resided in New Hanover County where he enlisted at age 19, June 19, 1861, for the war. Mustered in as Private. Wounded at Mechanicsville, Virginia, June 27, 1862. Appointed Corporal on October 31, 1862. Missing in action at Chancellorsville, Virginia, May 3, 1863.

ORRELL, JACOB D., Private

Resided in New Hanover County where he enlisted at age 18, February 19, 1862, for the war. Wounded at Malvern Hill, Virginia, July 1, 1862. Absent wounded and on furlough until retired to the Invalid Corps on May 18, 1864.

ORRELL, JAMES S., Private

Resided in New Hanover County where he enlisted at age 27, July 15, 1861, for the war. Present or accounted for on company muster rolls through December, 1864. Deserted to the enemy on February 24, 1865, and took the Oath of Allegiance at Washington, D.C., February 27, 1865.

OWEN, HARBIN, Private

Captured at Spotsylvania Court House, Virginia,

May 12, 1864, and confined at Point Lookout, Maryland. Transferred to Elmira, New York, August 10, 1864. Died at Elmira on October 10, 1864, of "chronic diarrhoea."

PARISH, NELSON, Private

Resided in Moore County where he enlisted at age 30, July 15, 1862, for the war. Wounded at Wilderness, Virginia, May 5, 1864. Present or accounted for through December, 1864. Admitted to hospital at Richmond, Virginia, April 1, 1865. Captured in hospital at Richmond on April 3, 1865. Died in hospital on June 14, 1865.

PAVYO, THOMAS L., Private

Resided in New Hanover County where he enlisted at age 26, June 6, 1861, for the war. Wounded at Sharpsburg, Maryland, September 17, 1862. Deserted and surrendered to the enemy at Bloomfield, Pennsylvania, June 29, 1863. Confined July 1, 1863, at Fort Mifflin, Pennsylvania, where he remained until released after taking the Oath of Allegiance on December 20, 1863.

PEEBLES, SELBURN, Private

Resided in Forsyth County where he enlisted on October 29, 1863, for the war. Captured near Spotsylvania Court House, Virginia, May 12, 1864, and confined at Point Lookout, Maryland. Transferred to Elmira, New York, August 10, 1864. Remained at Elmira until released after taking the Oath of Allegiance on July 26, 1865.

PEUGH, JOHN H., Private

Born at Mobile, Alabama, and resided as a pattern maker in New Hanover County where he enlisted at age 18, June 6, 1861, for the war. Wounded at Ellerson's Mill, Virginia, June 26, 1862. Discharged on July 24, 1862, by reason of "amputation of right forearm."

PHILLIPS, J., Private

Resided in Moore County where he enlisted at age 33, July 15, 1862, for the war. Left sick at Frederick, Maryland, September 9, 1862, and never returned to company.

PHILLIPS, J. R., Private

Resided as a farmer in Moore County where he enlisted at age 35, July 15, 1862, for the war. Wounded at Sharpsburg, Maryland, September 17, 1862. Deserted on November 17, 1862, and returned to the company in March, 1864. Captured at Wilderness, Virginia, May 6, 1864, and confined at Point Lookout, Maryland. Transferred to Elmira, New York, July 25, 1864. Released at Elmira after taking the Oath of Allegiance on May 29, 1865.

PICKETT, WILLIAM H., Private

Resided in New Hanover County where he enlisted at age 21, June 6, 1861, for the war. Mustered in as Private and appointed Corporal July 2-August 31, 1861. Reduced to ranks April 30-July 14, 1862. Wounded at Sharpsburg, Maryland, September 17, 1862, and at Chancellorsville, Virginia, May 3, 1863. Captured at Gettysburg, Pennsylvania, July 3, 1863, and confined at Fort Delaware, Delaware. Released after taking the Oath of Allegiance and joining the U.S. service October, 1863. Assigned to Company F, 1st Regiment Connecticutt Cavalry.

PITTMAN, HEZEKIAH, Private
Resided in Onslow County and enlisted in New Hanover County at age 24, February 22, 1862, for the war. Deserted on May 20, 1862.

POTTER, MILES, Private
Resided in New Hanover County where he enlisted at age 27, June 17, 1861, for the war. Killed at Sharpsburg, Maryland, September 17, 1862.

POWERS, MATHEW, Private
Born in Moore County where he resided prior to enlisting in Robeson County at age 33, July 15, 1862, for the war. Killed at Sharpsburg, Maryland, September 17, 1862.

PRESTON, ALLEN, Private
Resided in Forsyth County where he enlisted on October 29, 1863, for the war. Muster roll for November-December, 1863, states that he had been absent without leave since December 7, 1863. Company muster roll for December 31, 1863, to August 31, 1864, states that he was absent and had been "sent to Richmond under sentence of Court Martial." Reported as present from that date through December, 1864. Captured at Burkeville, Virginia, April 6, 1865, and confined at Newport News, Virginia. Released after taking the Oath of Allegiance at Newport News on June 15, 1865.

PREVATT, ALFRED, Private
Resided in Robeson County where he enlisted at age 28, May 14, 1862, for the war. Died December 4, 1862, in hospital at Liberty, Virginia.

PREVATT, ELI, Private
Born in Robeson County where he resided as a farmer and enlisted at age 26, May 14, 1862, for the war. Present or accounted for until killed on May 3, 1863, at Chancellorsville, Virginia.

PREVATT, JAMES P., Corporal
Resided in Robeson County where he enlisted at age 26, February 24, 1862. Mustered in as Private and appointed Corporal on November 17, 1863. Present or accounted for until captured May 12, 1864, at Spotsylvania Court House, Virginia. Confined at Point Lookout, Maryland, until transferred to Elmira, New York, August 10, 1864. Released at Elmira after taking the Oath of Allegiance on June 19, 1865.

PREVATT, THOMAS, Corporal
Resided in New Hanover County where he enlisted at age 20, June 13, 1861, for the war. Mustered in as Private and appointed Corporal on November 17, 1863. Present or accounted for until captured May 12, 1864, near Spotsylvania Court House, Virginia. Confined at Point Lookout, Maryland, until released after taking the Oath of Allegiance on June 17, 1865.

QUINN, EDWARD R., Private
Resided in New Hanover County where he enlisted at age 21, April 15, 1862, for the war. Reported on company muster rolls as absent sick from December 27, 1862, through December, 1864. Appears on a register of deaths and account of money and clothing received in C.S.A. General Military Hospital No. 4, Wilmington, dated December 9, 1864. No further records.

REAVES, EDWARD C., Private
Resided in New Hanover County where he enlisted at age 18, June 11, 1861, for the war. Transferred to the Field and Staff of this regiment upon appointment as Commissary Sergeant, August 24, 1861.

REAVES, JULIUS F. A., Private
Resided in New Hanover County where he enlisted at age 18, June 6, 1861, for the war. Present or accounted for until reported as absent sick on the muster roll for December 31, 1863-August 31, 1864. Absent sick through December, 1864.

REAVES, THOMAS, Private
Resided in Wayne County and enlisted in Duplin County at age 21, June 15, 1862, for the war. Absent sick from August 19, 1862, through December, 1862. Present or accounted for until wounded and captured at Gettysburg, Pennsylvania, July 1-3, 1863. Confined at DeCamp General Hospital, Davids Island, New York Harbor, July 17-24, 1863, with "f.w. in back and side." Paroled at DeCamp General Hospital and sent to City Point, Virginia, for exchange. Received at City Point on September 16, 1863. Present or accounted for through December, 1864. Captured at Burkeville, Virginia, on April 6, 1865, and confined at Newport News, Virginia. Released after taking the Oath of Allegiance on June 27, 1865.

ROBBINS, ROBERT F., Private
Resided in New Hanover County where he enlisted at age 21, June 21, 1861, for the war. Present or accounted for until wounded at Gettysburg, Pennsylvania, July 3, 1863. Admitted to U.S.A. hospital at Gettysburg, July 3, 1863, with "gunshot in head, serious."

RODDY, PATRICK, Private
Resided in New Hanover County where he enlisted at age 23, June 17, 1861, for the war. Wounded at Chancellorsville, Virginia, May 3, 1863, and admitted to hospital at Richmond, Virginia, May 9, 1863. Furloughed from hospital on June 14, 1863, for 50 days. Company muster rolls carry him as absent wounded and on furlough from that date until he appears on the December 31, 1863-August 31, 1864, muster roll with the remark: "Left at Corps Hospital near Spotsylvania." Reported on November-December, 1864, muster roll as "absent prisoner since May, 1864."

ROWE, WILLIAM L., Private
Enlisted in New Hanover County on January 17, 1862, for the war. Mortally wounded at Sharpsburg, Maryland, September 17, 1862.

RUSS, JOHN, Private
Born in New Hanover County where he resided as a harness maker and enlisted at age 24, June 6, 1861, for the war. Mustered in as Private and appointed Corporal April 30-July 14, 1862. Discharged as a Private on July 24, 1862, by reason of "phthisis pulmonalis."

SAMPSON, JOHN W., Private
Resided in New Hanover County where he enlisted at age 28, June 4, 1861, for the war. Wounded at Chancellorsville, Virginia, May 3, 1863, and at Payne's Farm, Virginia, November 27, 1863. Captured near Spotsylvania Court House, Virginia,

May 12, 1864, and confined at Point Lookout, Maryland. Transferred to Elmira, New York, August 10, 1864. Released at Elmira after taking the Oath of Allegiance on May 19, 1865.

SANDERS, BRITTON, Private
Resided in Moore County where he enlisted at age 30, July 15, 1862, for the war. Present or accounted for until captured at Spotsylvania Court House, Virginia, May 12, 1864. Confined at Point Lookout, Maryland, until transferred to Elmira, New York, August 10, 1864. Released at Elmira after taking the Oath of Allegiance on July 7, 1865.

SANDERS, JESSE, Private
Resided in Moore County where he enlisted at age 33, July 15, 1862, for the war. Wounded at Gettysburg, Pennsylvania, July 3, 1863, and captured in hospital at Gettysburg, July 4-5, 1863. Confined in hospital at Chester, Pennsylvania, until paroled and exchanged at City Point, Virginia, on September 23, 1863. Company muster rolls carry him as absent "said to be at home" from November-December, 1863, through October, 1864. Reported as "absent without leave in North Carolina" on November-December, 1864, muster roll.

SANDERS, JOHN, Private
Resided in Moore County where he enlisted at age 25, July 15, 1862, for the war. Captured at Frederick, Maryland, September 13, 1862, and confined at Fort Delaware, Delaware, until paroled and exchanged at City Point, Virginia, November 10, 1862. Wounded and captured at Chancellorsville, Virginia, May 3, 1863, and paroled and exchanged at City Point on May 10, 1863. Never returned to company.

SELL, DAVID, Private
Resided in Forsyth County where he enlisted on October 29, 1863, for the war. Wounded and captured at Payne's Farm, Virginia, November 27-28, 1863. Confined at Old Capitol Prison, Washington, D.C. Released after taking the Oath of Allegiance on March 19, 1864.

SELL, JACOB, Private
Enlisted in Forsyth County on October 29, 1863, for the war. Wounded at Payne's Farm, Virginia, November 27, 1863, and reported as absent wounded on company muster rolls through December, 1864. Paroled at Greensboro on May 13, 1865.

SELLERS, JOSEPH D., 1st Sergeant
Resided in New Hanover County where he enlisted at age 26, June 6, 1861, for the war. Mustered in as Private and appointed Corporal October 31, 1862. Promoted to Sergeant on November 1, 1862. Wounded at Chancellorsville, Virginia, May 3, 1863. Captured near Spotsylvania Court House, Virginia, May 12, 1864, and confined at Point Lookout, Maryland. Transferred to Elmira, New York, August 10, 1864. Promoted to 1st Sergeant September-October, 1864, while a prisoner of war. Released at Elmira after taking the Oath of Allegiance on May 15, 1865.

SHAY, JOHN, Private
Resided in New Hanover County where he enlisted at age 25, June 19, 1861, for the war. Reported as absent sick after February 19, 1862, and as deserted after June 20, 1862.

SHEFFIELD, ISAAC E., Private
Resided in Moore County where he enlisted at age 25, July 15, 1862, for the war. Wounded at Sharpsburg, Maryland, September 17, 1862. Reported as absent on furlough in North Carolina on company muster rolls from April, 1863, through December, 1864.

SHEFFIELD, JOHN, Private
Born in Moore County where he resided and enlisted at age 27, July 15, 1862, for the war. Died in hospital at Richmond, Virginia, August 30, 1862, of "typhoid fever."

SHEPHERD, JOHN F., Private
Born in Pennsylvania and resided as a seaman in New Hanover County where he enlisted at age 28, December 9, 1861, for the war. Transferred to the C.S. Navy on February 20, 1862.

SIMMS, WILLIAM JAMES, Private
Resided in New Hanover County where he enlisted at age 31, June 6, 1861, for the war. Died at Strasburg, Virginia, November 28, 1862, of disease.

SIMPSON, ISAAC, Private
Resided in New Hanover County where he enlisted at age 26, June 10, 1861, for the war. Deserted in Pennsylvania on June 27, 1863. Took the Oath of Allegiance at Washington, D.C., August 31, 1864.

SIMPSON, JAMES W., Sergeant
Resided in New Hanover County where he enlisted at age 23, June 6, 1861, for the war. Mustered in as Private and appointed Corporal April 30-July 14, 1862. Promoted to Sergeant on October 31, 1862. Wounded at Gettysburg, Pennsylvania, July 2, 1863, and captured at Gettysburg on July 3, 1863. Confined at Fort Delaware, Delaware, until transferred to Point Lookout, Maryland, October 15-18, 1863. Died at Point Lookout on November 22, 1863.

SMITH, HIRAM, Private
Resided in Moore County where he enlisted at age 25, July 15, 1862, for the war. Wounded at Chancellorsville, Virginia, May 2, 1863. Detailed for hospital duty on September 23, 1863, and reported as absent on detail on company muster rolls through December, 1864.

SMITH, JAMES E., Sergeant
Resided in New Hanover County where he enlisted at age 20, June 6, 1861, for the war. Mustered in as Private and appointed Corporal on November 1, 1862. Promoted to Sergeant on November 17, 1863. Captured near Spotsylvania Court House, Virginia, May 12, 1864, and confined at Point Lookout, Maryland. Paroled at Point Lookout on March 15, 1865, and exchanged at Boulware's Wharf, James River, Virginia, March 18, 1865.

SMITH, PETER H., Private

Resided in New Hanover County where he enlisted at age 27, June 6, 1861, for the war. Mustered in as Private and appointed Corporal April 30-July 14, 1862. Wounded at Sharpsburg, Maryland, September 17, 1862, and left leg amputated below knee. Reduced to ranks October 31, 1862. Reported on company muster rolls as absent wounded from September, 1862, through December, 1864.

SMITH, THOMAS, Private

Resided in Brunswick County and enlisted in New Hanover County at age 24, June 7, 1861, for the war. Wounded at Sharpsburg, Maryland, September 17, 1862, and captured at Sharpsburg after the battle. Paroled at Sharpsburg on September 27, 1862, and exchanged at Aiken's Landing, James River, Virginia, November 10, 1862. Absent on furlough until detailed in railroad shop at Wilmington on December 10, 1863. Returned to company in August, 1864, and captured at Winchester, Virginia, September 19, 1864. Confined at Point Lookout, Maryland, until paroled on February 13, 1865. Exchanged at Cox's Landing, James River, February 14-15, 1865. Captured on April 13, 1865, in hospital at Raleigh, where he died May 3, 1865.

SMITH, THOMAS J., Private

Resided in New Hanover County where he enlisted at age 24, July 6, 1861, for the war. Wounded at Gettysburg, Pennsylvania, July 2, 1863, and captured at Waterloo, Pennsylvania, July 5, 1863. Confined at Fort Delaware, Delaware, until transferred to Point Lookout, Maryland, October 15-18, 1863. Paroled at Point Lookout on February 18, 1865, and exchanged at Cox's Landing, James River, Virginia, February 20-21, 1865. Captured at Farmville, Virginia, April 6, 1865, and confined at Newport News, Virginia. Released after taking the Oath of Allegiance on June 25, 1865.

SPIVEY, JOSIAH, Private

Resided in Randolph County where he enlisted on January 16, 1864, for the war. Captured at Spotsylvania Court House, Virginia, May 12, 1864, and confined at Point Lookout, Maryland. Transferred to Elmira, New York, July 28, 1864. Released at Elmira after taking the Oath of Allegiance on May 29, 1865.

SPOONER, WILLIAM T., Private

Resided in New Hanover County where he enlisted at age 24, June 6, 1861, for the war. Captured at Waterloo, Pennsylvania, July 5, 1863, and confined at Fort Delaware, Delaware. Transferred to Point Lookout, Maryland, October 15-18, 1863. Paroled at Point Lookout on February 18, 1865, and exchanged at Cox's Landing, James River, Virginia, February 20-21, 1865.

SPRINGS, LEMUEL, Private

Resided in New Hanover County where he enlisted at age 25, June 6, 1861, for the war. Died at Richmond, Virginia, April 28, 1862.

STEPHENS, JAMES E., Private

Resided in New Hanover County where he en-

listed at age 34, June 12, 1861, for the war. Detailed as a nurse October 1, 1861, and remained on detail until returned to company in September, 1863. Sent to hospital October 8, 1863, and reported as absent sick until detailed as a brick maker at C.S. Armory, Macon, Georgia, April 4, 1864. Detail extended on September 3, 1864, and again on January 24, 1865. Admitted to hospital at Greensboro on February 4, 1865, with "diarrhoea chronic" and furloughed on February 14, 1865.

TERRY, CALVIN S., Private

Resided in New Hanover County where he enlisted at age 27, June 15, 1861, for the war. Detailed in Ordnance Department at Richmond, Virginia, March 4, 1862. Reported as absent on detail through December, 1864. Detail extended on February 11, 1865.

THOMPSON, THOMAS, Private

Born in New Hanover County where he resided as a farmer and enlisted at age 35, June 10, 1861, for the war. Discharged on October 24, 1861, by reason of disability.

TILLOTSON, WILLIAM H., Private

Enlisted on October 3, 1864, for the war.

TYNER, BENJAMIN, Private

Enlisted in New Hanover County on May 14, 1862, for the war. Died in camp near Richmond, Virginia, August 20, 1862, of "typhoid fever."

UTLEY, HENRY C., Musician

Resided in New Hanover County where he enlisted at age 19, June 6, 1861, for the war. Mustered in as Musician. Died in hospital at Richmond, Virginia, January 10, 1863, of "variola."

WADE, JOHN M., Musician

Resided as a machinist in New Hanover County where he enlisted at age 19, February 19, 1862, for the war. Mustered in as Private. Admitted to hospital on December 6, 1862, and returned to duty on April 22, 1863. Admitted to hospital a second time on July 22, 1863, and returned to duty in August, 1863. Appointed Musician on October 8, 1863, and reported as absent without leave after July 30, 1864.

WALSH, COLEMAN, Private

Enlisted at Richmond, Virginia, at age 28, July 15, 1861, for the war. Deserted on August 15, 1862.

WEEKS, THOMAS O., Private

Resided in New Hanover County where he enlisted at age 21, June 6, 1861, for the war. Present or accounted for until wounded and captured at Gettysburg, Pennsylvania, July 2-3, 1863. Confined at Fort Delaware, Delaware, where he took the Oath of Allegiance and joined the U.S. service August 30, 1863. Assigned to Company F, 1st Regiment Connecticut Cavalry.

WHITE, JOHN A., Corporal

Resided in New Hanover County where he enlisted at age 18, June 22, 1861, for the war. Mustered in as Private. Wounded at Chancellorsville, Virginia, May 2, 1863, and returned to duty on January 4, 1864. Appointed Corporal, January-May, 1864. Captured at Spotsylvania Court House,

Virginia, May 12, 1864, and confined at Point Lookout, Maryland. Transferred to Elmira, New York, August 10, 1864. Released at Elmira after taking the Oath of Allegiance on May 29, 1865.

WILLIAMS, GEORGE W., Private
Resided in Brunswick County and enlisted in New Hanover County at age 18, June 24, 1861, for the war. Wounded at Chancellorsville, Virginia, May 3, 1863, and returned to duty in January, 1864. Captured at Winchester, Virginia, September 19, 1864, and confined at Point Lookout, Maryland. Paroled at Point Lookout on October 30, 1864, and exchanged at Venus Point, Savannah River, Georgia, November 15, 1864.

WILLIAMS, GIBSON, Private
Resided in New Hanover County where he enlisted at age 27, June 20, 1861, for the war. Wounded and captured at Sharpsburg, Maryland, September 17, 1862. Paroled at Sharpsburg on September 27, 1862, and exchanged at Aiken's Landing, James River, Virginia, November 10, 1862. Admitted to hospital at Richmond, Virginia, and furloughed on November 14, 1862, for 30 days. Reported as absent on furlough in North Carolina on company muster rolls from November, 1862, through December, 1864.

WILLIAMS, NATHAN, Private
Resided in Wake County where he enlisted at age 30, July 15, 1862, for the war. Reported as absent sick from August, 1862, through December, 1864.

WILSON, JOHN A., Private
Resided in New Hanover County where he enlisted at age 20, June 6, 1861, for the war. Discharged July 9-15, 1861.

WRIGHT, A. S., Private
Enlisted in Guilford County on October 29, 1863, for the war. Wounded at Payne's Farm, Virginia, November 27, 1863, and reported as absent wounded from November, 1863, through December, 1864. Paroled at Greensboro on May 5, 1865.

WRIGHT, WILLIAM E., Private
Resided in New Hanover County where he enlisted at age 39, June 27, 1861, for the war. Discharged on July 15, 1861, by reason of disability.

YOPP, FRANKLIN V. B., Sergeant
Resided in New Hanover County where he enlisted at age 27, June 7, 1861, for the war. Mustered in as Sergeant. Discharged on August 1, 1861, by reason of disability.

COMPANY G

This company was organized in Onslow County and enlisted at Jacksonville on July 1, 1861. It tendered its service to the state and was ordered to Garysburg, Northampton County, where it was assigned to this regiment as Company G. After joining the regiment the company functioned as a part of the regiment, and its history for the war period is recorded as a part of the regimental history.

The information contained in the following roster of the company was compiled principally from company muster rolls which covered from the date of enlistment through December, 1864. No company muster rolls were found for the period after December, 1864. In addition to the company muster rolls, Roll of Honor records, receipt rolls, and hospital records, supplemented by state pension applications, United Daughters of the Confederacy records, and postwar rosters and histories, all provided useful information.

OFFICERS
CAPTAINS

RHODES, EDWARD H.
Resided in Onslow County and appointed Captain at age 30 to rank from May 16, 1861. Present or accounted for until killed at Sharpsburg, Maryland, September 17, 1862.

ARMSTRONG, EDWARD HALL
Born in New Hanover County where he resided as a farmer and enlisted at age 21, February 1, 1862, for the war. Appointed Sergeant on February 10, 1862, and promoted to 1st Sergeant on April 10, 1862. Appointed 2nd Lieutenant to rank from July 1, 1862, and promoted to Captain to rank from September 17, 1862. Present or accounted for until wounded at Spotsylvania Court House, Virginia, May 12, 1864. Died June 7, 1864, of wound.

METTS, JAMES ISAAC
Enlisted in Wayne County on May 15, 1862, for the war. Mustered in as Sergeant and promoted to 1st Sergeant on July 1, 1862. Appointed 2nd Lieutenant to rank from September 17, 1862, and detailed as Acting Adjutant for the regiment on November 4, 1862. Wounded at Gettysburg, Pennsylvania, July 2, 1863, and captured at Gettysburg, July 4-5, 1863. Confined at Johnson's Island, Ohio, August 24, 1863. Promoted to 1st Lieutenant to rank from September 16, 1863, and to Captain to rank from June 7, 1864, while in confinement as a prisoner of war. Paroled at Johnson's Island on September 16, 1864, and received at Military Prison, Camp Hamilton, Virginia, September 20, 1864. Forwarded for exchange on September 21, 1864. Admitted to hospital at Richmond, Virginia, September 22, 1864, and furloughed two days later. Assumed duties as Captain on December 17, 1864. Paroled at Appomattox Court House, Virginia, April 9, 1865.

LIEUTENANTS

BELL, ROBERT N., 2nd Lieutenant
Transferred from Company F of this regiment upon appointment as 2nd Lieutenant to rank from September 17, 1861. Resigned on May 30, 1862.

CLARKE, JAMES FOREMAN, 2nd Lieutenant
Transferred from the Field and Staff of this regiment upon appointment as 2nd Lieutenant to rank from September 17, 1862. Wounded at Payne's Farm, Virginia, November 27, 1863. Submitted resignation on February 21, 1864, by reason of "chronic rheumatism." Resignation officially accepted on March 11, 1864.

GORNTO, SOLOMON, 1st Lieutenant
Resided in Onslow County and appointed 1st Lieutenant at age 30 to rank from May 16, 1861. Resigned on January 2, 1862.

HENDERSON, LEWIS J., 2nd Lieutenant
Resided in Onslow County where he enlisted at age 18, July 1, 1861, for the war. Mustered in as Sergeant and promoted to 1st Sergeant on September 17, 1862. Wounded at Gettysburg, Pennsylvania, July 2, 1863, and captured at Gettysburg, July 4-5, 1863. Confined at DeCamp General Hospital, Davids Island, New York Harbor, until paroled and exchanged at City Point, Virginia, September 8, 1863. Appointed 2nd Lieutenant to rank from September 16, 1863. Captured at Spotsylvania Court House, Virginia, May 12, 1864, and confined at Fort Delaware, Delaware. Transferred to Hilton Head, South Carolina, August 20, 1864, and from there to Fort Pulaski, Georgia, October 21, 1864. Transferred back to Hilton Head on December 26, 1864, and from there to Fort Delaware on March 12, 1865. Released at Fort Delaware after taking the Oath of Allegiance on June 16, 1865.

HENDERSON, THOMAS B., 2nd Lieutenant
Resided in Onslow County and appointed 2nd Lieutenant at age 18 to rank from May 16, 1861. Resigned on September 10, 1861.

QUINCE, WILLIAM H., 1st Lieutenant
Resided in New Hanover County and appointed 2nd Lieutenant at age 24 to rank from May 16, 1861. Promoted to 1st Lieutenant on February 21, 1862, to rank from January 2, 1862. Killed at Sharpsburg, Maryland, September 17, 1862.

RHODES, ANTHONY H., 1st Lieutenant
Born in Duplin County and resided as a farmer in Onslow County where he enlisted at age 24, July 1, 1861, for the war. Mustered in as 1st Sergeant. Appointed 2nd Lieutenant to rank from April 10, 1862, and promoted to 1st Lieutenant to rank from September 17, 1862. Submitted his resignation on June 2, 1863, and dropped from the rolls on September 16, 1863. Reenlisted as a Private on September 29, 1863, for the war. Transferred to Company C, 59th Regiment N.C. Troops (4th Regiment N.C. Cavalry) October 8, 1863.

NONCOMMISSIONED OFFICERS AND PRIVATES

ADAMS, J. A., Private
Died at Winchester, Virginia, November 4, 1862.

ADAMS, JOHN D., Private
Transferred from Company D of this regiment November 11, 1863. Captured at Spotsylvania Court House, Virginia, May 12, 1864, and confined at Point Lookout, Maryland. Transferred August 8, 1864, to Elmira, New York, where he died October 6, 1864, of "chronic diarrhoea."

ADAMS, JOHN Q., Private
Transferred from Company F, 10th Regiment N.C. State Troops (1st Regiment N.C. Artillery) November 11, 1863. Never reported to company.

AMAN, GEORGE, Private
Resided in Onslow County where he enlisted at age 26, July 1, 1861, for the war. Wounded at Ellerson's Mill, Virginia, June 26, 1862. Reported as absent wounded from June, 1862, until declared "unfit for duty on account of rheumatism" January-February, 1863. Reported as absent sick through December, 1864.

AMAN, PINKNEY, Private
Born in Onslow County where he resided and enlisted at age 21, July 1, 1861, for the war. Wounded at Sharpsburg, Maryland, September 17, 1862, and died at Winchester, Virginia, September 20, 1862.

AMAN, THOMAS, Corporal
Born in Onslow County where he resided and enlisted at age 27, July 1, 1861, for the war. Mustered in as Corporal. Died at home on January 25, 1862, of disease.

AMAN, WILLIAM H., Private
Born in Onslow County where he resided and enlisted at age 23, July 1, 1861, for the war. Died at Goldsboro on April 14, 1862, of disease.

AVERY, LEWIS A., Sergeant
Resided in Onslow County where he enlisted at age 22, July 1, 1861, for the war. Mustered in as Sergeant. Reduced to Corporal when detailed on April 29, 1862, "at Tar River bridge." Promoted back to Sergeant on August 12, 1862, after rejoining company. Wounded at Sharpsburg, Maryland, September 17, 1862, and at Chancellorsville, Virginia, May 3, 1863. Wounded a third time at Payne's Farm, Virginia, November 27, 1863. Present or accounted for until paroled at Appomattox Court House, Virginia, April 9, 1865.

BARBER, MARCUS DeL., Private
Resided in Onslow County where he enlisted at age 21, July 1, 1861, for the war. Wounded at Malvern Hill, Virginia, July 1, 1862. Captured and paroled at Warrenton, Virginia, September 29, 1862. Sent to hospital on November 26, 1862, and deserted from hospital at Lynchburg, Virginia, February 19, 1863.

BASS, CHARLES THOMAS, Private
Resided in Sampson County and enlisted at age 34, July 23, 1862, for the war. Mortally wounded at Sharpsburg, Maryland, September 17, 1862.

BATCHELOR, WILLIAM N., Private
Resided in Onslow County where he enlisted at age 22, July 1, 1861, for the war. Deserted at Greencastle, Pennsylvania, June 17, 1863, and surrendered to the enemy. Confined at Fort Delaware, Delaware, until released after taking the Oath of Allegiance and joining the U.S. service on September 22, 1863. Assigned to the 3rd Regiment Maryland Cavalry.

BELL, ISAIAH, Private
Born in Onslow County where he resided and enlisted at age 30, July 1, 1861, for the war. Killed at Sharpsburg, Maryland, September 17, 1862.

BLOODGOOD, JAMES, Private
Resided in Onslow County where he enlisted at

age 29, July 1, 1861, for the war. Present or accounted for until he "deserted to the enemy about January 15, 1864."

BOYKIN, JAMES, Private
Resided in Sampson County and enlisted at age 21, July 23, 1862, for the war. Discharged on August 19, 1862.

BRADSHAW, N. SLOAN, Private
Born in Sampson County where he resided and enlisted at age 24, July 15, 1862, for the war. Died in hospital at Lynchburg, Virginia, December 3, 1862, of "gangrene."

BRITT, LEWIS, Private
Resided in Wayne County where he enlisted at age 34, July 15, 1862, for the war. Died in hospital at Richmond, Virginia, September 9, 1862, of "dysentery consqn. typhoid fever."

BROWN, LOVET, Private
Resided in Wayne County where he enlisted at age 33, July 15, 1862, for the war. Wounded at Chancellorsville, Virginia, May 3, 1863. Killed at Wilderness, Virginia, May 5, 1864.

BROWN, OLIVER, Private
Resided in Onslow County where he enlisted at age 25, July 1, 1861, for the war. Wounded at Chancellorsville, Virginia, May 3, 1863. Captured at Gettysburg, Pennsylvania, July 3, 1863, and confined at Fort Delaware, Delaware. Transferred October 18, 1863, to Point Lookout, Maryland, where he remained until paroled on November 1, 1864. Exchanged at Venus Point, Savannah River, Georgia, November 15, 1864. Reported on November-December, 1864, muster roll as "sick in Onslow County."

CAIN, JAMES S., Private
Born in Sampson County where he resided as a farmer and enlisted at age 28, July 23, 1862, for the war. Captured and paroled on October 1, 1862. Died in hospital at Richmond, Virginia, December 9, 1862, of "general dropsy."

CAIN, RICHARD, Private
Born in Sampson County where he resided as a farmer and enlisted at age 29, July 23, 1862, for the war. Died in hospital at Richmond, Virginia, December 30, 1862, of "variola conf."

CANADY, WILLET M., Musician
Resided in Onslow County where he enlisted at age 20, January 28, 1862, for the war. Mustered in as Private and appointed Musician March-April, 1862. Present or accounted for until left as a nurse with the wounded at Gettysburg, Pennsylvania, on July 3. 1863, Never returned to company.

CAPPS, ABNER, Private
Resided in Wayne County where he enlisted at age 29, July 15, 1862, for the war. Wounded and captured at Sharpsburg, Maryland, September 17, 1862, and paroled at Keedysville, Maryland, September 20, 1862. Wounded at Payne's Farm, Virginia, November 27, 1863. Captured at Mine Run, Virginia, May 7, 1864, and confined at Point Lookout, Maryland. Transferred to Elmira, New York, August 8, 1864. Released at Elmira

after taking the Oath of Allegiance on June 30, 1865.

CAPPS, WINSLOW, Private
Resided in Onslow County where he enlisted at age 23, July 1, 1861, for the war. Wounded at Chancellorsville, Virginia, May 3, 1863, and died in hospital at Richmond, Virginia, June 26, 1863, of gunshot wound.

CARR, MICHAEL, Private
Resided in Sampson County where he enlisted at age 27, July 23, 1862, for the war. Wounded at Sharpsburg, Maryland, September 17, 1862, and returned to company in September, 1863. Wounded at Wilderness, Virginia, May 5, 1864, and reported as absent wounded through December, 1864.

CARTER, WILLIAM M., Private
Resided in Wake County where he enlisted at age 29, July 15, 1862, for the war. Reported as absent sick from August, 1862, through December, 1864. Paroled at Raleigh on April 22, 1865.

CHESNUT, BEDFORD B., Private
Resided in Sampson County where he enlisted at age 28, July 15, 1862, for the war. Captured at Gettysburg, Pennsylvania, July 3, 1863, and confined at Point Lookout, Maryland. Paroled at Point Lookout on March 14, 1865, and transferred to Aiken's Landing, James River, Virginia, for exchange.

CHESNUT, JOHN E., Private
Resided in Sampson County where he enlisted at age 28, July 23, 1862, for the war. Detailed as a nurse in hospital at Farmville, Virginia, in December, 1862, by reason of "chronic bronchitis and constitutional debility." Remained on detail until returned to duty on October 18, 1864. Paroled at Appomattox Court House, Virginia, April 9, 1865.

CONWAY, ELIJAH H., Private
Resided in Onslow County where he enlisted at age 40, July 1, 1861, for the war. Wounded at Malvern Hill, Virginia, July 1, 1862, and died in hospital at Richmond, Virginia, August 1, 1862.

CONWAY, NICHOLAS J., Private
Resided in Onslow County where he enlisted at age 33, July 1, 1861, for the war. Captured at Sharpsburg, Maryland, September 17, 1862, and took the Oath of Allegiance at Fort McHenry, Maryland, November 16, 1862.

CONWAY, WILLIAM A., Private
Born in Onslow County where he resided as a farmer and enlisted at age 29, July 1, 1861, for the war. Discharged on May 26, 1862, by reason of "chronic rheumatism."

COTTLE, LEWIS J., Private
Resided in Onslow County where he enlisted at age 45, January 28, 1862, for the war. Wounded at Chancellorsville, Virginia, May 3, 1863, and reported as absent wounded through December, 1863. Captured at Spotsylvania Court House, Virginia, May 12, 1864, and confined at Point Lookout, Maryland. Transferred August 10, 1864, to Elmira, New York, where he died on February 1, 1865, of "variola."

COVILLE, WILLIAM F., Corporal

Resided in Onslow County where he enlisted at age 19, July 1, 1861, for the war. Mustered in as Private. Wounded at Ellerson's Mill, Virginia, June 26, 1862, and appointed Corporal on August 12, 1862. Wounded at Sharpsburg, Maryland, September 17, 1862. Wounded at Gettysburg, Pennsylvania, July 2, 1863, and captured in hospital at Gettysburg July 4-5, 1863. Confined at DeCamp General Hospital, Davids Island, New York Harbor, until paroled and exchanged. Admitted to hospital September 28, 1863, at Richmond, Virginia, where he remained until transferred to hospital at Wilmington in February, 1864. Transferred in March, 1864, to hospital at Raleigh, where he remained on detail until captured and paroled on April 13, 1865.

CULLAM, W. E., Private

Captured near Spotsylvania Court House, Virginia, May 12, 1864, and confined at Point Lookout, Maryland. Transferred to Elmira, New York, August 10, 1864. Released at Elmira after taking the Oath of Allegiance on June 30, 1865.

CURRIN, DAVID, Private

Born in Onslow County where he resided and enlisted at age 21, July 1, 1861, for the war. Killed at Sharpsburg, Maryland, September 17, 1862.

DAVIS, BENJAMIN, Private

Resided in Onslow County where he enlisted at age 26, January 28, 1862, for the war. Wounded and captured at Sharpsburg, Maryland, on September 17, 1862. Paroled at Fort Delaware, Delaware, and sent to Fort Monroe, Virginia, for exchange in December, 1862. Present or accounted for until he "deserted to the enemy about January 20, 1864."

DAWSON, LEONARD, Private

Born in Onslow County where he resided and enlisted at age 26, July 1, 1862, for the war. Died December 20, 1861, at Camp Howe, Virginia.

DENTON, J. M., Private

Paroled on May 16, 1865, at Morganton, N.C.

DIXON, JAMES W., Private

Resided in Onslow County where he enlisted at age 28, July 1, 1861, for the war. Present or accounted for until captured at Gettysburg, Pennsylvania, on July 3, 1863. Confined at Fort Delaware, Delaware, until transferred to Point Lookout, Maryland, on October 18, 1863. Paroled March 17, 1864, at Point Lookout and sent to City Point, Virginia, for exchange. Reported as absent without leave from that date through August, 1864. Present or accounted for through December, 1864. Captured in hospital at Richmond, Virginia, April 3, 1865, and confined at Libby Prison, Richmond, on April 14, 1865. Transferred to Newport News, Virginia, April 23, 1865. Released at Newport News after taking the Oath of Allegiance on June 30, 1865.

EUBANKS, AARON, Private

Resided in Onslow County where he enlisted at age 23, July 1, 1861, for the war. Present or accounted for until captured on May 12, 1864, near

Spotsylvania Court House, Virginia. Confined at Point Lookout, Maryland, and transferred to Elmira, New York, on August 10, 1864. Released at Elmira after taking the Oath of Allegiance on July 11, 1865.

EUBANKS, ELISHA P., Private

Born in Onslow County where he resided as a farmer and enlisted at age 23, July 1, 1861, for the war. Wounded September 17, 1862, at Sharpsburg, Maryland, and died September 20, 1862.

EUBANKS, JOHN M., Private

Resided in Onslow County where he enlisted at age 33, July 1, 1861, for the war. Wounded July 1, 1862, in battle near Richmond, Virginia. Present or accounted for until again wounded on May 3, 1863, at Chancellorsville, Virginia. Absent wounded through December, 1863. Company muster roll for December 31, 1863-August 31, 1864, reports that he was "taken prisoner May 1, 1864, improperly paroled and now at home in N.C." Absent without leave from that date through December, 1864.

EZZEL, ALEXANDER H., Private

Resided in Sampson County where he enlisted at age 27, July 23, 1862, for the war. Reported as absent sick from February 11, 1863, through December, 1863. Captured May 12, 1864, near Spotsylvania Court House, Virginia. Confined at Point Lookout, Maryland, until transferred to Elmira, New York on August 10, 1864. Died May 23, 1865, at Elmira, of "chronic diarrhoea."

EZZELL, E. M., Private

Born in Sampson County where he resided and enlisted at age 17, July 23, 1862, for the war. Died of "typhoid fever" August 25, 1862, in hospital at Gordonsville, Virginia.

FAISON, JAMES C., Private

Born in Sampson County where he resided as a farmer and enlisted at age 34, July 23, 1862, for the war. Killed September 17, 1862, at Sharpsburg, Maryland.

FLOWERS, BENNETT, Private

Paroled on May 11, 1865, at Goldsboro.

GARY, ALFRED, Private

Born in Onslow County where he resided and enlisted at age 44, July 1, 1861, for the war. Died November 8, 1861, at Fredericksburg, Virginia.

GRANT, JAMES H., Private

Resided in Wayne County where he enlisted at age 28, July 15, 1862, for the war. Present or accounted for until reported as absent sick on April 29, 1863. Absent sick through December, 1864.

GURGANUS, LOUIS J., Corporal

Born in Onslow County where he resided and enlisted at age 20, July 1, 1861, for the war. Mustered in as Private and appointed Corporal in August, 1861. Died January 7, 1862, at Camp Howe, Virginia.

HANKS, JOHN W., Private

Resided in Chatham County where he enlisted at age 18, February 19, 1862, for the war. Wounded on July 1, 1862, in battle near Richmond, Virginia. Wounded and captured at Sharpsburg,

Maryland, on September 17, 1862. Admitted to U.S.A. hospital, Smoketown, Maryland, on October 5, 1862, with "wound of left leg." Transferred to Fort McHenry, Maryland, where he was paroled and sent to Aiken's Landing, Virginia, for exchange on October 25, 1862. Declared exchanged November 10, 1862. Furloughed for 30 days on November 12, 1862. Present or accounted for until appointed Drillmaster with the rank of 2nd Lieutenant on September 25, 1863, and ordered to Raleigh.

HARDISON, ELZA H., Private
Born in Onslow County where he resided and enlisted at age 22, July 1, 1861, for the war. Present or accounted for until killed on July 1, 1862, in battle at Malvern Hill, Virginia.

HASKINS, DAVID B., Private
Born in Onslow County where he resided and enlisted at age 21, July 1, 1861, for the war. Present or accounted for until May 3, 1863, in battle at Chancellorsville, Virginia.

HENDERSON, HILLORY E., Private
Resided in Onslow County where he enlisted at age 19, July 1, 1861, for the war. Present or accounted for until wounded on September 17, 1862, at Sharpsburg, Maryland. Furloughed from hospital at Richmond, Virginia, for 30 days on October 8, 1862. Reported as absent without leave from expiration of furlough through December, 1862. Returned January, 1863, and wounded at Gettysburg, Pennsylvania, July 2, 1863. Transferred to Company K, 19th Regiment N.C. Troops (2nd Regiment N.C. Cavalry) September 29, 1863.

HENDERSON, JAMES B., Private
Resided in Onslow County where he enlisted at age 23, July 1, 1861, for the war. Died in hospital at Fredericksburg, Virginia, September 1, 1861, of disease.

HERRING, JAMES O., Private
Resided in Sampson County where he enlisted at age 28, July 23, 1862, for the war. Mortally wounded at Sharpsburg, Maryland, September 17, 1862.

HEWITT, ABRAM, Private
Born in Onslow County where he resided and enlisted at age 42, October 4, 1861, for the war. Died at Camp Howe, Virginia, January 9, 1862, of disease.

HEWITT, THEODORE F., Private
Resided in Onslow County where he enlisted at age 17, January 28, 1862, for the war. Wounded at Chancellorsville, Virginia, May 3, 1863, and at Payne's Farm, Virginia, November 27, 1863. Captured near Spotsylvania Court House, Virginia, May 12, 1864, and confined at Point Lookout, Maryland. Transferred to Elmira, New York, August 10, 1864. Paroled at Elmira on October 14, 1864, and exchanged on October 29, 1864. Reported as absent sick in Onslow County on November-December, 1864, muster roll.

HIGGINS, BENJAMIN F., Private
Resided in Onslow County where he enlisted at age 19, July 1, 1861, for the war. Wounded at Sharpsburg, Maryland, September 17, 1862, and

at Chancellorsville, Virginia, May 2, 1863. Captured near Spotsylvania Court House, Virginia, May 12, 1864, and confined at Point Lookout, Maryland. Transferred to Elmira, New York, August 10, 1864. Paroled at Elmira on March 2, 1865, and exchanged at Aiken's Landing, James River, Virginia. Admitted to hospital at Richmond, Virginia, March 7, 1865, and furloughed on March 9, 1865, for 30 days.

HILL, JAMES, Private
Resided in Onslow County where he enlisted at age 20, January 28, 1862, for the war. Wounded and captured at Sharpsburg, Maryland, September 17, 1862. Paroled on September 27, 1862. Never returned to company and reported on the September-October, 1863, muster roll with the remark: "Died. Wounded in battle Sharpsburg September 17, 1862. Not heard from since. Supposed to be dead."

HILL, OWEN C., 1st Sergeant
Resided in Onslow County where he enlisted at age 21, July 1, 1861, for the war. Mustered in as Sergeant. Captured at Sharpsburg, Maryland, September 17, 1862, and paroled and exchanged at Aiken's Landing, James River, Virginia, November 10, 1862. Wounded at Chancellorsville, Virginia, May 3, 1863, and at Gettysburg, Pennsylvania, July 2, 1863. Promoted to 1st Sergeant in November, 1863, and wounded at Payne's Farm, Virginia, November 27, 1863. Captured near Spotsylvania Court House, Virginia, May 12, 1864, and confined at Point Lookout, Maryland. Transferred to Elmira, New York, August 10, 1864. Released at Elmira after taking the Oath of Allegiance on June 23, 1865.

HOLLAND, BRYAN, Private
Transferred from Company F, 10th Regiment N.C. State Troops (1st Regiment N.C. Artillery) March 20, 1864. Never reported to company.

HOLLINGSWORTH, JAMES, Private
Resided in Sampson County where he enlisted at age 20, July 23, 1862, for the war. Wounded at Cedar Creek, Virginia, October 19, 1864. Admitted to hospital at Danville, Virginia, November 14, 1864, and furloughed on November 24, 1864, for 60 days.

HOLLOMAN, JOSIAH, Private
Resided in Wayne County where he enlisted at age 18, July 15, 1862, for the war. Wounded at Payne's Farm, Virginia, November 27, 1863. Transferred to Company F, 10th Regiment N.C. State Troops (1st Regiment N.C. Artillery) March 22, 1864.

HOLLOMAN, NATHAN, Private
Born in Wayne County where he resided and enlisted at age 36, July 15, 1862, for the war. Died in hospital at Richmond, Virginia, February 2, 1863, of "variola conf."

HOOD, NATHAN B., Private
Resided in Wayne County where he enlisted at age 19, July 15, 1862, for the war. Present or accounted for until transferred to Company F, 10th Regiment N.C. State Troops (1st Regiment N.C. Artillery) November 11, 1863.

HOOD, ROBERT B., Private

Resided in Wayne County where he enlisted at age 33, July 15, 1862, for the war. Present or accounted for until transferred to Company F, 10th Regiment N.C. State Troops (1st Regiment N.C. Artillery) November 11, 1863.

JOHNSON, RIGDEN, Private

Resided in Wake County where he enlisted at age 24, July 15, 1862, for the war. Absent without leave after August 20, 1862.

JONES, JOHN B., Private

Resided in Onslow County where he enlisted at age 43, July 1, 1861, for the war. Wounded at Chancellorsville, Virginia, May 3, 1863. Captured at Spotsylvania Court House, Virginia, May 12, 1864, and confined at Point Lookout, Maryland. Transferred to Elmira, New York, August 10, 1864. Paroled at Elmira on February 20, 1865, and transferred for exchange. Admitted to hospital at Richmond, Virginia, February 26, 1865, and returned to duty on March 1, 1865.

JONES, JOSEPH W., Private

Resided in Onslow County where he enlisted at age 33, July 1, 1861, for the war. Detailed as a guard at Augusta, Georgia, July 18, 1863, and reported as absent on detail through December, 1864.

JONES, WILLIAM C., Private

Resided in Craven County and enlisted in Onslow County at age 19, July 1, 1861, for the war. Captured and paroled at Chancellorsville, Virginia, May 4, 1863. Wounded at Gettysburg, Pennsylvania, July 2, 1863. Captured at Spotsylvania Court House, Virginia, May 12, 1864, and confined at Point Lookout, Maryland. Transferred to Elmira, New York, August 10, 1864. Released at Elmira after taking the Oath of Allegiance on June 12, 1865.

KELLUM, JOSIAH, Private

Born in Onslow County where he resided as a farmer and enlisted at age 25, July 1, 1861, for the war. Killed at Sharpsburg, Maryland, September 17, 1862.

KELLUM, WILLIAM E., Private

Resided in Onslow County where he enlisted at age 24, July 1, 1861, for the war. Wounded at Malvern Hill, Virginia, July 1, 1862, and at Gettysburg, Pennsylvania, July 2, 1863. Present or accounted for until missing after battle at Spotsylvania Court House, Virginia, May 12, 1864.

KELLY, THOMAS O., Private

Resided in Sampson County where he enlisted at age 24, July 23, 1862, for the war. Discharged on September 9, 1862.

KETCHUM, JACKSON J., Private

Resided in Onslow County where he enlisted at age 26, July 1, 1861, for the war. Left leg amputated after railroad accident at Hanover Junction, Virginia, February 12, 1862. Detailed as a shoemaker at Raleigh on March 4, 1863. Reported as absent on detail through December, 1864.

KETCHUM, JAMES P., Sergeant

Resided in Onslow County where he enlisted at age 28, July 1, 1861, for the war. Mustered in as Private and appointed Sergeant on September 17, 1862. Wounded at Chancellorsville, Virginia, May 3, 1863, and at Gettysburg, Pennsylvania, July 2-3, 1863. Captured at Spotsylvania Court House, Virginia, May 12, 1864, and confined at Point Lookout, Maryland. Transferred to Elmira, New York, August 10, 1864. Paroled at Elmira on October 11, 1864, and exchanged on October 29, 1864. Reported as absent on sick furlough on November-December, 1864, muster roll.

LANGLEY, JAMES P., Private

Resided in Onslow County where he enlisted at age 21, July 1, 1861, for the war. Wounded at Chancellorsville, Virginia, May 3, 1863, and at Gettysburg, Pennsylvania, July 2, 1863. Captured in hospital at Gettysburg July 4-5, 1863. Confined in DeCamp General Hospital, Davids Island, New York Harbor, until paroled and transferred for exchange on October 24, 1863. Confined in various hospitals until exchanged at City Point, Virginia, March 20, 1864. Admitted to hospital at Richmond, Virginia, March 20, 1864, and furloughed on March 29, 1864, for 60 days. Reported as absent "permanently disabled" on company muster rolls through December, 1864.

LILES, SAMUEL, Private

Resided in Wake County where he enlisted at age 31, July 23, 1862, for the war. Left sick at Frederick, Maryland, September 10, 1862, and never returned to company.

LITTLETON, ARETUS, Private

Resided in Onslow County where he enlisted at age 19, July 1, 1861, for the war. Discharged on October 5, 1861.

LITTLETON, ELISHA A., Private

Resided in Onslow County where he enlisted at age 23, July 1, 1861, for the war. Present or accounted for until killed at Gettysburg, Pennsylvania, July 2, 1863.

LITTLETON, WILLOUGHBY S., Private

Born in Onslow County where he resided and enlisted at age 21, July 1, 1861, for the war. Died at Camp Howe, Virginia, September 23, 1861, of disease.

LLOYD, GEORGE, Private

Captured at Mechanicsville, Virginia, May 30, 1864, and confined at Elmira, New York, where he took the Oath of Allegiance on November 15, 1864.

McCULLEN, ORREN, Private

Resided in Sampson County where he enlisted at age 34, July 23, 1862, for the war. Wounded at Chancellorsville, Virginia, May 3, 1863. Captured near Spotsylvania Court House, Virginia, May 12, 1864, and confined at Point Lookout, Maryland. Transferred to Elmira, New York, August 10, 1864. Paroled at Elmira on March 2, 1865, and sent to James River, Virginia, for exchange. Admitted to hospital at Richmond, Virginia, March 7, 1865, and furloughed from hospital on March 9, 1865, for 30 days. Paroled at Raleigh on April 22, 1865.

MASHBURN, FRANCIS, Private
Born in Onslow County where he resided and enlisted at age 18, July 1, 1861, for the war. Died at Camp Howe, Virginia, December 15, 1861, of disease.

MASHBURN, JAMES H., Private
Resided in Onslow County where he enlisted at age 31, July 1, 1861, for the war. Wounded at Ellerson's Mill, Virginia, June 26, 1862. Detailed as a shoemaker at Richmond, Virginia, November 23, 1862, and returned to company in January, 1863. Reported as absent sick from March 5, 1863, through December, 1863. Detailed as a shoemaker at Richmond on January 1, 1864, and remained on detail until returned to company November-December, 1864. Paroled at Lynchburg, Virginia, April 14, 1865.

MASHBURN, JOHN, Private
Resided in Onslow County where he enlisted at age 22, July 1, 1861, for the war. Died in hospital at Fredericksburg, Virginia, September 1, 1861, of disease.

MATHIS, JOHN D., Private
Resided in Onslow County where he enlisted at age 20, July 1, 1861, for the war. Present or accounted for until he died at Lynchburg, Virginia, November 21, 1863, of "pneumonia."

MEADOWS, RAYMOND, Private
Resided in Onslow County where he enlisted at age 19, July 1, 1861, for the war. Wounded at Malvern Hill, Virginia, July 1, 1862, and at Payne's Farm, Virginia, November 27, 1863. Captured at Spotsylvania Court House, Virginia, May 12, 1864, and confined at Point Lookout, Maryland. Transferred August 10, 1864, to Elmira, New York, where he died October 20, 1864, of "typhoid fever."

MERITT, GEORGE W., Private
Born in Duplin County and resided as a farmer in Onslow County where he enlisted at age 18, March 17, 1862, for the war. Discharged on May 26, 1862, by reason of "scrofulous affections and debility."

MILLS, WILLIAM H., Private
Resided in Onslow County where he enlisted at age 18, July 1, 1861, for the war. Discharged at Camp Howe, Virginia, December ·7, 1861, by reason of disability.

MORTON, ARCHIBALD, Private
Born in Onslow County where he resided as a farmer and enlisted at age 19, January 28, 1862, for the war. Died at Goldsboro on April 11, 1862.

MORTON, EDWARD, Private
Resided in Onslow County where he enlisted at age 18, January 28, 1862, for the war. Killed at Malvern Hill, Virginia, July 1, 1862.

MORTON, GEORGE, Private
Resided in Onslow County where he enlisted at age 18, January 28, 1862, for the war. Died at Goldsboro on April 19, 1862.

MORTON, HILLORY, Private
Born in Onslow County where he resided and enlisted at age 20, January 28, 1862, for the war.

Died in hospital at Danville, Virginia, August 24, 1862, of "phagedenic ulcer."

MORTON, ISAAC, Private
Born in Onslow County where he resided as a farmer and enlisted at age 18, January 28, 1862, for the war. Wounded at Ellerson's Mill, Virginia, June 26, 1862, and "totally disabled." Reported as absent wounded on company muster rolls through December, 1864.

MORTON, JACOB, Private
Resided in Onslow County where he enlisted at age 22, January 28, 1862, for the war. Present or accounted for until paroled at Appomattox Court House, Virginia, April 9, 1865.

O'BRYAN, WILLIAM, Private
Resided in Chatham County where he enlisted at age 40, February 27, 1862, for the war. Detailed as a guard in hospital at Richmond, Virginia, November 5, 1862, and remained on detail until detailed as a miner on August 1, 1863. Returned to detail as guard in hospital on February 2, 1864. Died in hospital at Richmond on June 10, 1864.

ODOM, ALVIN, Private
Born in Sampson County where he resided as a farmer and enlisted at age 34, July 23, 1862, for the war. Died in hospital at Richmond, Virginia, September 11, 1862, of "typhoid fever."

ODOM, RUFFIN, Private
Resided in Onslow County and enlisted in Orange County, Virginia, on March 15, 1864, for the war. Captured at Spotsylvania Court House, Virginia, May 12, 1864, and confined at Point Lookout, Maryland. Transferred to Elmira, New York, August 10, 1864. Paroled at Elmira on October 11, 1864, and exchanged on October 29, 1864.

OLIVER, DAVID, Private
Born in Onslow County where he resided as a farmer and enlisted at age 21, July 1, 1861, for the war. Killed at Sharpsburg, Maryland, September 17, 1862.

O'REILLY, PATRICK, Private
Captured at Wilderness, Virginia, May 12, 1864, and confined at Point Lookout, Maryland. Released after taking the Oath of Allegiance and joining the U.S. service on May 30, 1864.

OWENS, DEMPSEY, Private
Resided in Onslow County where he enlisted at age 24, July 1, 1861, for the war. Present or accounted for until killed at Gettysburg, Pennsylvania, July 2, 1863.

OWENS, NATHANIEL S., Private
Resided in Onslow County where he enlisted at age 38, July 1, 1861, for the war. Wounded at Ellerson's Mill, Virginia, June 26, 1862. Detailed as a guard in hospital at Richmond, Virginia, April 17, 1863. Reported as absent on detail until returned to company September, 1864. Paroled at Farmville, Virginia, April 11-21, 1865.

PACKER, LEWIS, Private
Resided in Sampson County where he enlisted at age 32, July 23, 1862, for the war. Absent sick from June 3, 1863, through December, 1863.

Captured on May 12, 1864, at Spotsylvania Court House, Virginia. Confined at Old Capitol Prison, Washington, D.C., until transferred to Fort Delaware, Delaware, on June 15, 1864. Released at Fort Delaware after taking the Oath of Allegiance on June 19, 1865.

PARISH, PINKNEY, Private

Resided in Wake County where he enlisted at age 25, July 15, 1862, for the war. Reported on company muster rolls as absent without leave or absent sick from August, 1862, through December, 1864, when he appears with the remark: "Absent on wounded furlough in Wake County, N.C."

PETERSON, PATRICK, Private

Resided in Sampson County where he enlisted at age 28, July 23, 1862, for the war. Admitted to hospital at Richmond, Virginia, on October 3, 1862, and was returned to duty on January 16, 1863. Died in hospital at Guinea Station, Virginia, on April 7, 1863.

PHILLIPS, AARON, Private

Born in Onslow County where he resided and enlisted at age 20, July 1, 1861, for the war. Present or accounted for until his death on March 10, 1862, at Camp Howe, Virginia.

PHILLIPS, BRICE P., Private

Born in Onslow County where he resided and enlisted at age 20, August 27, 1861, for the war. Present or accounted for until his death on September 29, 1862, at Richmond, Virginia.

PHILLIPS, HENRY, Private

Resided in Onslow County where he enlisted at age 18, July 1, 1861, for the war. Present or accounted for until killed on July 1, 1862, at Malvern Hill, Virginia.

PHILLIPS, LEVI, Private

Resided in Onslow County where he enlisted at age 18, August 27, 1861, for the war. Present or accounted for until admitted to hospital at Richmond, Virginia, on November 18, 1862. Returned to duty January 21, 1863. Present or accounted for until wounded on July 2, 1863, in battle at Gettysburg, Pennsylvania. Returned to duty in August, 1863. Present or accounted for until captured on May 12, 1864, near Spotsylvania Court House, Virginia. Confined at Point Lookout, Maryland, until transferred to Elmira, New York, on August 10, 1864. Released at Elmira after taking the Oath of Allegiance on June 27, 1865.

PIPKIN, GEORGE W., Private

Resided in Wayne County where he enlisted at age 22, July 15, 1862, for the war. Wounded and captured on September 17, 1862, at Sharpsburg, Maryland. Took the Oath of Allegiance on September 27, 1862, at the Office of the Provost Marshal General, Army of the Potomac, camped near Sharpsburg, "requesting not to be exchanged or paroled."

PIPKIN, JOHN W., Private

Born in Wayne County where he resided and enlisted at age 29, July 15, 1862, for the war. Present or accounted for until his death on March 19, 1863, at Guinea Station, Virginia.

POOL, HOWARD, Private

Resided in Wake County where he enlisted at age 32, July 23, 1862, for the war. Present or accounted for until captured at Sharpsburg, Maryland, on September 17, 1862. Confined at Fort McHenry, Maryland, until paroled and sent to Aiken's Landing, Virginia, for exchange on October 17, 1862. Admitted to hospital at Richmond, Virginia, on October 23, 1862, with "debility" and was furloughed for 25 days on November 10, 1862. Reported on company muster rolls as absent without leave after expiration of furlough.

POOL, SIMEON, Private

Resided in Wake County where he enlisted at age 19, July 23, 1862, for the war. Admitted to hospital at Danville, Virginia, August 20, 1862, with "chronic rheumatism" and deserted from the hospital on December 1, 1862. No further records.

POOLE, JACKSON T., Private

Resided in Onslow County where he enlisted at age 34, July 1, 1861, for the war. Present or accounted for until wounded July 1, 1862, near Richmond, Virginia. Wounded and captured September 17, 1862, at Sharpsburg, Maryland. Confined at U.S.A. hospital at Frederick, Maryland, with "wound left thigh" until transferred to U.S.A. General Hospital, Baltimore, Maryland, on October 25, 1862. Sent on December 8, 1862, to Fort McHenry, Maryland, where he was paroled the same day and sent to City Point, Virginia, for exchange. Admitted to hospital at Petersburg, Virginia, in December, 1862, and furloughed for 40 days on December 19, 1862. Absent wounded until reported on the February 28-May 15, 1863, muster roll with the remark: "Died in N.C. about April 15, 1863."

RAY, JOHN, Private

Born in Orange County and resided in Chatham County where he enlisted at age 24, March 15, 1862, for the war. Killed September 17, 1862, at Sharpsburg, Maryland.

RAY, MARION, Private

Resided in Chatham County and enlisted in Wayne County at age 18, March 28, 1862, for the war. Reported as absent without leave from August 20, 1862, until September-October, 1863, when muster roll carries the remark: "Deserted. Absent without leave since August 20, 1862. Supposed to have deserted."

REAGAN, PETER, Private

Enlisted on October 30, 1863, for the war as a substitute. Present or accounted for until captured on May 12, 1864, near Spotsylvania Court House, Virginia. Confined at Point Lookout, Maryland, May 18, 1864, but date of release from prison is not shown in records. Reported on company muster rolls as absent, prisoner of war, through December, 1864.

REECE, BENJAMIN F., Private

Resided in Onslow County where he enlisted at age 18, July 1, 1861, for the war. Present or accounted for until wounded on June 26, 1862, near Richmond, Virginia. Accidentally wounded on December 12, 1862, near Fredericksburg, Virginia. Present or accounted for until again wounded on July 2, 1863, at Gettysburg, Pennsylvania. Absent wounded through August, 1863. Wounded November 27, 1863, in battle at Payne's Farm, Virginia. Returned to duty January 6, 1864. Present or accounted for through December, 1864.

REECE, WILLIAM, Private

Resided in Onslow County where he enlisted at age 32, January 28, 1862, for the war. Mustered in as Private and appointed Corporal on August 12, 1862. Present or accounted for until wounded on May 2, 1863, at Chancellorsville, Virginia. Absent wounded until returned to duty in August, 1863. Reduced to ranks December 31, 1863-August 31, 1864. Wounded in battle at Wilderness, Virginia, on May 5, 1864. Absent wounded until reported as present November-December, 1864. Admitted to hospital at Richmond, Virginia, on March 15, 1865, with "parotitis." Captured in the hospital at Richmond on April 3, 1865, and confined at Libby Prison, Richmond, on April 14, 1865. Transferred April 23, 1865, to Newport News, Virginia, where he was released after taking the Oath of Allegiance on June 30, 1865.

RICH, ALBERT, Private

Resided in Sampson County where he enlisted at age 20, July 23, 1862. Captured on September 15, 1862, at Boonsboro, Maryland. Confined at Fort Delaware, Delaware, until paroled on October 2, 1862, and sent to Aiken's Landing, James River, Virginia, for exchange. Admitted to hospital at Richmond, Virginia, October 9, 1862, with "pleurisy" and was furloughed for 30 days on October 30, 1862. Returned to duty in January, 1863. Wounded May 3, 1863, in battle at Chancellorsville, Virginia. Present or accounted for until captured on May 12, 1864, near Spotsylvania Court House, Virginia. Confined at Point Lookout, Maryland, until transferred to Elmira, New York, August 10, 1864. Released at Elmira after taking the Oath of Allegiance on June 23, 1865.

RIGGS, ALBERT, Private

Born in Onslow County where he resided as a farmer and enlisted at age 18, July 1, 1861, for the war. Present or accounted for until his death on August 31, 1862, at Richmond, Virginia.

RIGGS, BARRUS, Private

Resided in Onslow County where he enlisted at age 22, July 1, 1861, for the war. Present or accounted for until wounded on July 18, 1864, in battle at Snicker's Gap, Virginia. Admitted to hospital at Charlottesville, Virginia, on July 26, 1864, with "gunshot wound right hand" and was furloughed for 60 days on August 12, 1864. Returned to duty in October, 1864. Present or accounted for through December, 1864. Paroled at Appomattox Court House, Virginia, April 9, 1865.

RIGGS, BASIL M., Private

Resided in Onslow County where he enlisted at age 19, July 1, 1861, for the war. Mustered in as Drummer and reduced to ranks March-April,

1862. Present or accounted for until wounded July 1, 1862, near Richmond, Virginia. Absent wounded until returned to duty January-February, 1863. Present or accounted for until again wounded and captured at Gettysburg, Pennsylvania, July 1-3, 1863. Date of parole and exchange not shown in records. Company muster rolls report him as being absent wounded and on parole from September-October, 1863, until admitted to hospital at Richmond, April 10, 1864, with "gunshot wound of neck." Absent sick through August, 1864. Captured September 22, 1864, at Fisher's Hill, Virginia. Confined at Point Lookout, Maryland, until paroled and sent to Aiken's Landing, James River, Virginia, for exchange on March 17, 1865.

RIGGS, EDWARD W. O., Private

Resided in Onslow County where he enlisted at age 33, July 1, 1861, for the war. Present or accounted for until captured on September 17, 1862, at Sharpsburg, Maryland. Confined at Fort Delaware, Delaware, until paroled on October 2, 1862, and sent to Aiken's Landing, James River, Virginia, for exchange. Declared exchanged November 10, 1862. Present or accounted for until wounded and captured July 1-3, 1863, at Gettysburg, Pennsylvania. Transferred from hospital at Gettysburg to U.S.A. General Hospital, West's Buildings, Baltimore, Maryland, on July 28, 1863. Paroled at that hospital, September 25, 1863, and sent to City Point, Virginia, for exchange. Reported as absent on parole until returned to duty September-October, 1864. Absent sick November-December, 1864. Captured April 6, 1865, at Chesterfield, Virginia, and confined at Point Lookout, Maryland. Released at Point Lookout after taking the Oath of Allegiance on June 17, 1865.

RIGGS, GEORGE C., Private

Resided in Onslow County where he enlisted at age 18, July 1, 1861, for the war. Present or accounted for until wounded September 17, 1862, at Sharpsburg, Maryland. Absent wounded until returned to duty November 16, 1862. Present or accounted for until wounded on November 27, 1863, at Payne's Farm, Virginia. Captured May 30, 1864, while on picket duty at Mechanicsville, Virginia. Confined at Point Lookout, Maryland, until transferred to Elmira, New York, July 8, 1864. Released at Elmira after taking the Oath of Allegiance on June 12, 1865.

RIGGS, ISAAC N., Private

Born in Onslow County where he resided and enlisted at age 23, July 1, 1861, for the war. Present or accounted for until wounded July 1, 1862, at Malvern Hill, Virginia. Admitted to hospital at Richmond, Virginia, July 4, 1862, with "gunshot wound in hip" and died July 9, 1862.

RIGGS, JOHN B., Private

Resided in Onslow County where he enlisted at age 19, July 1, 1861, for the war. Present or accounted for until wounded July 1, 1862, near Richmond, Virginia. Again wounded September

17, 1862, at Sharpsburg, Maryland. Present or accounted for until wounded July 2, 1863, in battle at Gettysburg, Pennsylvania. Reported as absent sick from July 26, 1863, until returned to duty September-October, 1863. Died February 15, 1864.

ROBERSON, EDWIN B., Private

Resided in Onslow County where he enlisted at age 26, July 1, 1861, for the war. Present or accounted for until wounded on July 1, 1862, at Malvern Hill, Virginia. Absent wounded through February, 1863. Present or accounted for until wounded November 27, 1863, at Payne's Farm, Virginia. Returned to duty after December, 1863. Captured May 12, 1864, at Spotsylvania Court House, Virginia. Confined at Point Lookout, Maryland, until transferred to Elmira, New York, August 14, 1864. Released at Elmira after taking the Oath of Allegiance on June 23, 1865

ROBERSON, L. B., Private

Born in Sampson County where he resided and enlisted at age 33, July 23, 1862, for the war. Wounded May 3, 1863, at Chancellorsville, Virginia, and died May 18, 1863.

SANDLIN, ROBERT, Private

Resided in Onslow County where he enlisted at age 18, July 1, 1861, for the war. Present or accounted for until captured on May 12, 1864, at Spotsylvania Court House, Virginia. Confined at Point Lookout, Maryland, until transferred to Elmira, New York, August 14, 1864. Released at Elmira after taking the Oath of Allegiance on June 21, 1865.

SCOTT, JOHN H., Private

Resided in Onslow County where he enlisted at age 28, July 1, 1861, for the war. Mustered in as Private and appointed Corporal on January 8, 1862. Reduced to ranks March-April, 1862. Present or accounted for through December, 1864. Muster rolls report that he was detailed as a teamster, butcher, and forage master at various dates during this time. Admitted to hospital at Farmville, Virginia, on April 7, 1865. Captured in hospital and paroled April 11-21, 1865.

SCREWS, WILLIAM, Private

Resided in Onslow County where he enlisted at age 28, January 28, 1862, for the war. Wounded at Malvern Hill, Virginia, July 1, 1862, and at Gettysburg, Pennsylvania, July 2, 1863. Captured in hospital at Gettysburg July 4-5, 1863, and confined in hospital at Chester, Pennsylvania, until paroled on August 17, 1863. Exchanged at City Point, Virginia, August 20, 1863. Present or accounted for through December, 1864. Paroled at Burkeville, Virginia, April 14-17, 1865.

SELLERS, AMOS, Private

Resided in Sampson County where he enlisted at age 28, July 23, 1863, for the war. Furloughed on December 2, 1862, and reported as absent sick from that date through December, 1864.

SEWELL, CHARLES W., Private

Resided in Onslow County where he enlisted at age 23, July 1, 1861, for the war. Wounded at Malvern Hill, Virginia, July 1, 1862. Deserted

from Orange Court House, Virginia, August 20, 1862.

SHEPARD, BASIL M., Private

Resided in Onslow County where he enlisted at age 30, July 1, 1861, for the war. Wounded at Sharpsburg, Maryland, September 17, 1862. Wounded and captured at Gettysburg, Pennsylvania, July 3, 1863. Confined at Fort Delaware, Delaware, until released after taking the Oath of Allegiance on June 19, 1865.

SHEPARD, JACKSON L., Private

Resided in Onslow County where he enlisted at age 23, July 1, 1861, for the war. Wounded at Chancellorsville, Virginia, May 3, 1863, and wounded and captured at Gettysburg, Pennsylvania, July 3, 1863. Confined at Fort Delaware, Delaware, until transferred to Point Lookout, Maryland, October 15-18, 1863. Died at Point Lookout on September 11, 1864.

SHEPPARD, JAMES, Private

Born in Onslow County where he resided and enlisted at age 25, July 1, 1861, for the war. Wounded at Chancellorsville, Virginia, May 3, 1863, and at Payne's Farm, Virginia, November 27, 1863. Captured at Mine Run, Virginia, November 28, 1863, and confined at Old Capitol Prison, Washington, D.C. Died in hospital at Washington on January 7, 1864, of "variola confluent."

SIMPSON, WILLIAM A., Private

Resided in Onslow County where he enlisted at age 19, July 1, 1861, for the war. Present or accounted for until captured at Spotsylvania Court House, Virginia, May 12, 1864. Confined at Point Lookout, Maryland, until transferred to Elmira, New York, August 10, 1864. Died at Elmira on December 5, 1864, of "chronic diarrhoea."

SMITH, BASIL, Private

Born in Onslow County where he resided and enlisted at age 18, July 1, 1861, for the war. Killed at Malvern Hill, Virginia, July 1, 1862.

SMITH, JOSIAH P., Sergeant

Resided in Onslow County where he enlisted at age 23, July 1, 1861, for the war. Mustered in as Corporal and promoted to Sergeant on April 10, 1862. Captured at Fredericksburg, Virginia, May 4, 1863, and paroled and exchanged at City Point, Virginia, May 10, 1863. Wounded at Gettysburg, Pennsylvania, July 2, 1863, and captured in hospital at Gettysburg July 4-5, 1863. Confined in hospital at Chester, Pennsylvania, until paroled on September 17, 1863. Exchanged at City Point, Virginia, September 23, 1863. Wounded and captured at Fisher's Hill, Virginia, September 22, 1864. Confined at Point Lookout, Maryland, until released after taking the Oath of Allegiance on June 20, 1865.

SMITH, RUFUS, Private

Resided in Wake County where he enlisted at age 30, July 15, 1862, for the war. Died in hospital at Richmond, Virginia, September 27, 1862, of "typhoid fever."

SMITH, SAMUEL A., Private

Resided in Wake County where he enlisted at

age 23, July 15, 1862, for the war. Sent to hospital July 14-October 31, 1862, and reported on February 28-May 15, 1863, muster roll with the remark: "Died in hospital Richmond, date not known."

SMITH, WILLIAM B., Private
Born in Onslow County where he resided and enlisted at age 21, July 1, 1861, for the war. Present or accounted for until killed at Ellerson's Mill, Virginia, on June 26, 1862.

SOLOMONS, JOHN J., Corporal
Resided in Onslow County where he enlisted at age 18, July 1, 1861, for the war. Mustered in as Private and appointed Corporal on January 25, 1862. Wounded on July 1, 1862, at Malvern Hill, Virginia. Present or accounted for until admitted to hospital at Richmond, Virginia, on March 25, 1863, with "pneumonia." Returned to duty in August, 1863. Wounded on November 27, 1863, at Payne's Farm, Virginia. Absent wounded through December, 1864.

SPEIGHT, RICHARD R., Corporal
Resided in Onslow County where he enlisted at age 31, July 1, 1861, for the war. Mustered in as Corporal and reduced to ranks April 30-July 14, 1862. Wounded on May 3, 1863, at Chancellorsville, Virginia. Present or accounted for until again wounded on November 27, 1863, at Payne's Farm, Virginia. Absent wounded through December, 1863. Wounded June 3, 1864, in action near Richmond, Virginia. Died in hospital at Richmond on June 5, 1864. Company muster roll for December 31, 1863-August 31, 1864, gives his rank as Corporal.

SPIVERY, L., Private
Paroled at Goldsboro on May 11, 1865.

SUTTON, ISAAC, Private
Resided in Sampson County where he enlisted at age 24, July 23, 1862, for the war. Present or accounted for until killed on July 2, 1863, at Gettysburg, Pennsylvania.

SUTTON, JOSEPH, Private
Born in Sampson County where he resided and enlisted at age 26, July 23, 1862, for the war. Killed September 17, 1862, at Sharpsburg, Maryland.

SUTTON, WILLIAM M., Private
Resided in Sampson County where he enlisted at age 28, July 23, 1862, for the war. Furloughed from hospital at Richmond, Virginia, for 40 days on September 29, 1862. Absent sick from that date until returned to duty November-December, 1863. Present or accounted for until captured on May 12, 1864, near Spotsylvania Court House, Virginia. Confined at Point Lookout, Maryland, until transferred to Elmira, New York, on August 10, 1864. Released at Elmira after taking the Oath of Allegiance on June 21, 1865.

SWINSON, JAMES, Private
Resided in Onslow County where he enlisted at age 23, July 1, 1861, for the war. Died January 9, 1862, at Camp Howe, Virginia.

TATUM, HILLORY S., Private
Born in Sampson County where he resided as a

farmer and enlisted at age 26, July 23, 1862, for the war. Captured September 15, 1862, at Boonsboro, Maryland. Confined at Fort Delaware, Delaware, until paroled and sent to Aiken's Landing, James River, Virginia, for exchange on October 2, 1862. Admitted to hospital at Richmond, Virginia, October 9, 1862, and died November 25, 1862, of "variola."

TAYLOR, JOSEPH W., Private
Resided in Onslow County where he enlisted at age 22, July 1, 1861, for the war. Mustered in as Sergeant and reduced to ranks January-February, 1862. Present or accounted for until wounded on June 26, 1862, near Richmond, Virginia. Reported as present on the July 14-October 31, 1862, muster roll. Detailed as a shoemaker at Richmond, November 23, 1862. Absent detailed until he "deserted to the enemy about December 26, 1863."

THOMPSON, WILLIAM M., Private
Resided in Wayne County where he enlisted at age 28, July 15, 1862, for the war. Present or accounted for until wounded July 2, 1863, at Gettysburg, Pennsylvania. Returned to duty September-October, 1863. Present or accounted for until captured May 12, 1864, near Spotsylvania Court House, Virginia. Confined at Point Lookout, Maryland, until transferred to Elmira, New York, August 10, 1864. Released at Elmira after taking the Oath of Allegiance on June 27, 1865.

TROTT, NEWTON, Private
Resided in Onslow County where he enlisted at age 18, July 1, 1861, for the war. Died September 1, 1861, in hospital at Fredericksburg, Virginia.

WATERS, ALLEN, Private
Resided in Onslow County where he enlisted at age 19, July 1, 1861, for the war. Discharged October 5, 1861.

WEBSTER, ROBERT M., Private
Born in Chatham County where he resided and enlisted at age 21, February 20, 1862, for the war. Discharged June 28, 1862, by reason of disability caused by "phthisis pulmonalis."

WELLS, JAMES L., Private
Born in Onslow County where he resided and enlisted at age 21, July 1, 1861, for the war. Present or accounted for until killed on June 26, 1862, at Ellerson's Mill, Virginia.

WENBERRY, JOHN E., Private
Resided in Onslow County where he enlisted at age 19, July 1, 1861, for the war. Present or accounted for until wounded on July 1, 1862, at Malvern Hill, Virginia. Wounded again on September 17, 1862, at Sharpsburg, Maryland. Returned to duty in January, 1863. Wounded May 3, 1863, at Chancellorsville, Virginia. Returned to duty September-October, 1863. Wounded November 27, 1863, at Payne's Farm, Virginia. Captured on June 10, 1864, at Spotsylvania Court House, Virginia. Confined at Point Lookout, Maryland, where he died August 26, 1864, of "erysipelas."

WHARTON, DANIEL N., Private
Born in Onslow County where he resided and enlisted at age 19, July 1, 1861, for the war. Died

at home in Onslow County on November 10, 1861.

WIGGINS, JOHN C., Private

Transferred to this company from Company F, 10th Regiment N.C. State Troops (1st Regiment N.C. Artillery) on November 13, 1863. Captured on May 12, 1864, at Spotsylvania Court House, Virginia. Confined at Point Lookout, Maryland, until transferred to Elmira, New York, on July 23, 1864. Died at Elmira on November 15, 1864, of "chronic diarrhoea."

WIGGINS, LEWIS H., Private

Born in Sampson County where he resided and enlisted at age 34, July 23, 1862, for the war. Reported as absent sick from November 7, 1862, until returned to duty on May 5, 1863. Killed in battle at Gettysburg, Pennsylvania, July 2, 1863.

WILDER, GEORGE C., Private

Resided in Wake County where he enlisted at age 26, July 15, 1862, for the war. Reported as absent sick from November 7, 1862, until returned to duty on February 13, 1863. Present or accounted for until captured on May 12, 1864, near Spotsylvania Court House, Virginia. Confined at Point Lookout, Maryland, until transferred to Elmira, New York, August 10, 1864. Paroled at Elmira and sent to James River, Virginia, for exchange on March 14, 1865. Admitted to hospital at Richmond, Virginia, on March 18, 1865, and transferred to Camp Lee, near Richmond, the next day.

WILKINS, WILLIAM L., Corporal

Resided in Onslow County where he enlisted at age 18, March 17, 1862, for the war. Mustered in as a Private. Present or accounted for until wounded on May 3, 1863, at Chancellorsville, Virginia. Admitted to hospital at Richmond, Virginia, on May 6, 1863, with "gunshot wound right finger." Returned to duty in August, 1863. Appointed Corporal, January-August, 1864. Wounded at Wilderness, Virginia, May 5, 1864, and returned to duty November-December, 1864. Captured at Farmville, Virginia, April 6, 1865, and confined at Newport News, Virginia. Released after taking the Oath of Allegiance on June 27, 1865.

WILLIAMS, ANDREW J., Private

Born in Onslow County where he resided and enlisted at age 34, July 1, 1861, for the war. Died at Camp Howe, Virginia, December 23, 1861.

WILSON, WILLIAM G., Private

Born in Onslow County where he resided and enlisted at age 20, July 1, 1861, for the war. Died at Camp Howe, Virginia, January 3, 1862.

WOOD, BASIL M., Private

Resided in Onslow County where he enlisted at age 44, January 28, 1862, for the war. Reported on April 30-July 14, 1862, muster roll with the remark: "Dead or deserted. Left in hospital at Fredericksburg March 11, 1862. Not heard from since." Casualty list states that he was killed at Malvern Hill, Virginia, July 1, 1862.

WOOD, WILLIS F., Private

Born in Onslow County where he resided as a farmer and enlisted at age 18, July 1, 1861, for the war. Killed at Malvern Hill, Virginia, July 1, 1862.

WOODALL, W. W., Private

Resided in Wake County where he enlisted at age 34, July 15, 1862, for the war. Wounded and captured at Sharpsburg, Maryland, September 17, 1862, and paroled at Sharpsburg on September 27, 1862. Confined at Fort Delaware, Delaware, until sent for exchange on March 28, 1863. Detailed on hospital duty at Richmond, Virginia, April 17, 1863. Relieved from duty in hospital at Richmond on July 1, 1863, and ordered to duty in hospital at Lynchburg, Virginia. Detailed as a guard in hospital at Lynchburg until ordered to Raleigh in January, 1864. Assigned to Captain Samuel B. Waters' Company, Provost Guard, Raleigh, January 15, 1864, and reported on rolls of that company through January, 1865.

YATES, JOSIAH, Private

Resided in Onslow County where he enlisted at age 20, January 28, 1862, for the war. Wounded at Malvern Hill, Virginia, July 1, 1862, and died in hospital at Richmond, Virginia, July 5, 1862.

YOUNG, JOHN R., Corporal

Resided in Onslow County where he enlisted at age 38, August 27, 1861, for the war. Mustered in as Private and appointed Corporal on February 10, 1862. Wounded at Sharpsburg, Maryland, September 17, 1862. Returned to duty on October 20, 1862. Wounded at Gettysburg, Pennsylvania, July 2, 1863, and captured in hospital at Gettysburg July 4-5, 1863. Died in hospital at Gettysburg on July 25, 1863.

COMPANY H

This company, known as the "Bladen Volunteers," was organized in Bladen County and enlisted on May 10, 1861. It tendered its service to the state and was ordered to Garysburg, Northampton County, where it was assigned to this regiment as Company H. After joining the regiment the company functioned as a part of the regiment, and its history for the war period is recorded as a part of the regimental history.

The information contained in the following roster of the company was compiled principally from company muster rolls which covered from June 25, 1861, through February, 1863, and from May 15, 1863, through December, 1864. No company muster rolls were found for the period prior to June 25, 1861; for March through May 15, 1863; or for the period after December, 1864. In addition to the company muster rolls, Roll of Honor records, receipt rolls, and hospital records, supplemented by state pension applications, United Daughters of the Confederacy records, and postwar rosters and histories, all provided useful information.

OFFICERS
CAPTAINS

SIKES, THEODORE M.

Resided in Bladen County where he enlisted at

age 32, May 23, 1861, for the war. Appointed Captain to rank from May 16, 1861. Submitted his resignation on September 9, 1862, by reason of "pulmonary weakness and general physical debility." Resignation officially accepted October 29, 1862.

GALLOWAY, SWIFT

Resided in Brunswick County and appointed 2nd Lieutenant to rank from October 1, 1861. Wounded severely in left thigh at Malvern Hill, Virginia, July 1, 1862. Promoted to 1st Lieutenant to rank from September 17, 1862, and to Captain to rank from October 29, 1862, while absent wounded. Furloughed from hospital at Richmond, Virginia, December 9, 1862, for 90 days. Reported as absent wounded until detailed for duty at Salisbury on September 14, 1863. Raised a company for local defense at Salisbury in February, 1864, and elected captain of the company. Declined commission on the grounds that he was still Captain of this company. Local defense company became Captain E. D. Snead's Company, N.C. Local Defense Troops. Remained on detail at Salisbury for the balance of the war. Last reported as admitted to hospital at Danville on April 5, 1865.

LIEUTENANTS

ALLEN, RICHARD P., 2nd Lieutenant

Resided in Bladen County where he enlisted at age 21, May 23, 1861, for the war. Appointed 2nd Lieutenant to rank from May 16, 1861. Resigned on September 13, 1861.

DeROSSET, ARMAND L., 1st Lieutenant

Resided in New Hanover County and appointed 2nd Lieutenant to rank from October 1, 1861. Wounded at Sharpsburg, Maryland, September 17, 1862, and promoted to 1st Lieutenant to rank from October 29, 1862. Admitted to hospital at Richmond, Virginia, in May, 1863, with "contusion shell." Furloughed on May 16, 1863, for 30 days. Detailed as Assistant Provost Marshal at Wilmington on June 9, 1863, and transferred effective May 30, 1863. Later appointed Captain of Company B, 2nd Battalion N.C. Local Defense Troops.

DUNN, JOSEPH S., 1st Lieutenant

Resided in Randolph County and enlisted in Bladen County on May 23, 1861, for the war. Appointed 1st Lieutenant to rank from May 16, 1861. Resigned on October 5, 1861. Later enlisted in Company F, 46th Regiment N.C. Troops.

KEMP, WILLIAM JAMES, 3rd Lieutenant

Born in Bladen County where he resided and enlisted at age 25, May 23, 1861, for the war. Appointed 3rd Lieutenant to rank from May 16, 1861. Resigned on September 13, 1861.

LOWDERMILK, ZEMERIAH HADLEY, 2nd Lieutenant

Born in Randolph County where he resided as a farmer and enlisted at age 21, June 29, 1861, for the war. Mustered in as Private and appointed Corporal on July 23, 1861. Promoted to Sergeant on January 25, 1862. Admitted to hospital at

Richmond, Virginia, with a gunshot wound on July 2, 1862, and returned to duty on August 28, 1862. Appointed 2nd Lieutenant to rank from September 17, 1862. Wounded at Chancellorsville, Virginia, May 3, 1863. Present or accounted for until captured at Spotsylvania Court House, Virginia, May 12, 1864. Confined at Fort Delaware, Delaware, until transferred to Hilton Head, South Carolina, August 20, 1864. Forwarded to Fort Pulaski, Georgia, October 21, 1864, and returned to Hilton Head on December 26, 1864. Transferred back to Fort Delaware on March 12, 1865. Released at Fort Delaware after taking the Oath of Allegiance on June 1, 1865.

LYON, ROBERT H., 2nd Lieutenant

Born in Bladen County where he resided as a clerk and enlisted at age 19, May 12, 1861, for the war. Mustered in as 1st Sergeant and reduced to Sergeant effective July 23, 1861. Appointed 2nd Lieutenant to rank from October 29, 1862. Present or accounted for until captured at Spotsylvania Court House, Virginia, May 12, 1864. Confined at Fort Delaware, Delaware, until transferred to Hilton Head, South Carolina, August 20, 1864. Forwarded to Fort Pulaski, Georgia, October 21, 1864, and returned to Hilton Head on December 26, 1864. Transferred back to Fort Delaware on March 12, 1865. Released at Fort Delaware after taking the Oath of Allegiance on June 7, 1865.

McNAIR, DUNCAN E., 1st Lieutenant

Resided in Robeson County and appointed 1st Lieutenant to rank from October 11, 1861. Present or accounted for until killed at Sharpsburg, Maryland, September 17, 1862.

NONCOMMISSIONED OFFICERS AND PRIVATES

ALDRIDGE, RANSOM, Private

Resided in Randolph County where he enlisted at age 30, July 17, 1862, for the war. Wounded September 17, 1862, at Sharpsburg, Maryland. Returned to duty January-February, 1863. Wounded May 3, 1863, at Chancellorsville, Virginia. Absent wounded through October, 1863. Present or accounted for until captured on May 12, 1864, near Spotsylvania Court House, Virginia. Confined at Point Lookout, Maryland, until transferred to Elmira, New York, on August 10, 1864. Died March 3, 1865, at Elmira of "variola."

ALSTON, ALLEN, Private

Enlisted in Bladen County on May 10, 1861, for the war. Never reported for duty.

BAKER, DUNCAN, Private

Resided in Columbus County where he enlisted at age 35, February 15, 1862, for the war. Wounded on July 1, 1862, at Malvern Hill, Virginia. Returned to duty January-February, 1863. Mortally wounded on May 3, 1863, at Chancellorsville, Virginia.

BALDWIN, DAVID W., Musician

Resided in Columbus County where he enlisted on February 15, 1862, for the war. Mustered in as

Musician. Admitted to hospital at Richmond, Virginia, on September 2, 1862, with "typhoid fever" and furloughed on September 29, 1862. Returned to duty January-February, 1863. Present or accounted for until his death on April 20, 1863.

BALDWIN, HAYNES, Private
Resided in Columbus County where he enlisted at age 33, February 15, 1862, for the war. Wounded at Gettysburg, Pennsylvania, July 1-3, 1863. Reported as absent wounded on company muster rolls through August, 1864. Subsequent rolls state that he was captured on July 2, 1863, or May 12, 1864; however, there are no prisoner of war records to substantiate this report.

BALDWIN, JOSEPH, Private
Resided in Columbus County where he enlisted at age 26, February 15, 1862, for the war. Present or accounted for until wounded on July 2, 1863, at Gettysburg, Pennsylvania. Admitted to hospital at Richmond, Virginia, on July 12, 1863, with "gunshot wound of left hand with fracture of metacarpal bone." Absent wounded through December, 1863. Present or accounted for from that date until sent to the hospital at Staunton, Virginia, on November 28, 1864. Absent sick through December, 1864.

BALDWIN, ROBERT H., Private
Enlisted in Wilkes County on October 17, 1863, for the war. Deserted on November 15, 1863, at Raccoon Ford, Virginia.

BAREFOOT, WILLIAM, Private
Resided in Columbus County where he enlisted at age 24, February 15, 1862, for the war. Captured at Boonsboro, Maryland, on September 16, 1862. Confined at Fort Delaware, Delaware, until paroled and sent to Aiken's Landing, James River, Virginia, for exchange on October 2, 1862. Declared exchanged on November 10, 1862, and reported as absent without leave from that date until he returned to duty in January-February, 1863. Present or accounted for until he deserted on August 20, 1863, and was shot for desertion on September 5, 1863.

BARKER, JESSE H., Private
Born in Randolph County where he enlisted on July 17, 1862, for the war. Present or accounted for until admitted to hospital at Richmond, Virginia, on November 26, 1862. Died in that hospital on December 22, 1862, of "typhoid fever."

BARNHILL, DOYLE O., Private
Born in Bladen County where he resided as a farmer and enlisted at age 26, May 10, 1861, for the war. Killed on July 1, 1862, in battle at Malvern Hill, Virginia.

BARNHILL, HENRY H., Private
Resided in Bladen County where he enlisted at age 20, May 15, 1861, for the war. Present or accounted for until captured on September 15, 1862, at South Mountain, Maryland. Received at Aiken's Landing, James River, Virginia, for exchange on October 6, 1862. Declared exchanged on November 10, 1862, and reported as absent without leave from that date until returned to duty

January-February, 1863. Present or accounted for until detailed as a gunsmith at the C.S. Armory at Richmond, Virginia, on January 28, 1864. Absent detailed through December, 1864.

BEDSOLE, JOHN R., Private
Enlisted in Columbus County on February 15, 1862, for the war. Wounded in battle at Malvern Hill, Virginia, on July 1, 1862. Present or accounted for until he deserted on August 20, 1863. Shot for desertion on September 5, 1863.

BENSON, ARCHIBALD T., Corporal
Resided in Bladen County where he enlisted at age 20, May 28, 1861, for the war. Mustered in as Private and appointed Corporal on September 17, 1862. Present or accounted for until killed on July 2, 1863, in battle at Gettysburg, Pennsylvania.

BENSON, FRANCIS, Private
Resided in Bladen County where he enlisted at age 24, May 18, 1861, for the war. Present or accounted for until he deserted on August 20, 1863. Shot for desertion on September 5, 1863.

BENSON, THOMAS W. L., Private
Resided in Bladen County where he enlisted at age 23, May 11, 1861, for the war. Present or accounted for until wounded and captured at Sharpsburg, Maryland, on September 17-18, 1862. Confined at Fort Delaware, Delaware, until paroled and sent to Aiken's Landing, James River, Virginia, for exchange on October 2, 1862. Declared exchanged November 10, 1862. Present or accounted for until reported as "in arrest at Brigade Guard House" on the January-February, 1863, muster roll. Reported with this remark through May, 1863. Admitted to hospital at Richmond, Virginia, on June 8, 1863, with "typhoid fever." Transferred on June 17, 1863, to hospital at Danville, Virginia, where he deserted on August 15, 1863. Reported as absent sick through December, 1864.

BENSON, WILLIAM W., Private
Resided in Bladen County where he enlisted at age 20, June 4, 1861, for the war. Present or accounted for until wounded September 17, 1862, at Sharpsburg, Maryland. Reported as absent wounded through December, 1862. Returned to duty January-February, 1863, and deserted on June 4, 1863, at Hamilton's Crossing, Virginia.

BLIZZARD, EZEKIEL V. B., Private
Born in Bladen County where he resided as a farmer and enlisted at age 18, May 25, 1861, for the war. Present or accounted for until killed in battle at Sharpsburg, Maryland, on September 17, 1862.

BLIZZARD, HAYNES P., Private
Resided in Bladen County where he enlisted at age 22, May 10, 1861, for the war. Mustered in as Corporal and reduced to ranks on July 1, 1861, for "insubordination." Present or accounted for until mortally wounded on July 1, 1862, at Malvern Hill, Virginia.

BRADY, ISAAC, Private
Resided in Randolph County where he enlisted

at age 31, July 17, 1862, for the war. Never reported for duty.

BRADY, JOHN, Private

Resided in Randolph County where he enlisted at age 26, June 17, 1862, for the war. Present or accounted for until wounded on July 1, 1863, at Gettysburg, Pennsylvania. Reported as absent wounded until November-December, 1863, when the muster roll states that he was absent without leave. Subsequent rolls state that he deserted on July 10, 1863.

BRADY, JOSEPH M., Private

Resided in Randolph County where he enlisted at age 21, July 17, 1862, for the war. Company muster roll for July 14-October 31, 1862, reports that he was detailed as a teamster in the Quartermaster Department. Detailed through August, 1863. Present or accounted for until wounded November 27-28, 1863, at Payne's Farm, Virginia. Absent wounded through December, 1863. Captured on May 12, 1864, near Spotsylvania Court House, Virginia. Confined at Point Lookout, Maryland, until transferred to Elmira, New York, on August 10, 1864. Released at Elmira after taking the Oath of Allegiance on June 30, 1865.

BRADY, WILLIAM W., Private

Resided in Randolph County where he enlisted at age 21, June 17, 1862, for the war. Present or accounted for until killed in battle on May 3, 1863, at Chancellorsville, Virginia.

BROWN, GEORGE, Private

Resided in Wake County where he enlisted at age 23, July 15, 1862, for the war. Absent sick from September 18, 1862, until detailed for hospital duty on September 3, 1863. Detailed as a nurse at hospital at Richmond, Virginia, from that date through January, 1865.

BROWN, J. M., Private

Captured in hospital at Richmond, Virginia, on April 3, 1865, and turned over to the Provost Marshal on April 20, 1865.

BROWN, JESSE, Private

Resided in Randolph County where he enlisted at age 21, July 17, 1862, for the war. Wounded on September 17, 1862, at Sharpsburg, Maryland. Died in hospital at Winchester, Virginia, on October 5, 1862.

BUIE, DAVID J., Private

Resided in Bladen County where he enlisted at age 24, May 10, 1861, for the war. Wounded at Malvern Hill, Virginia, July 1, 1862. Deserted from camp at Skinker's Neck, Virginia, April 4, 1863, and took the Oath of Allegiance at Washington, D.C., April 26, 1863.

BUIE, FRANCIS M., Private

Resided in Bladen County where he enlisted at age 21, May 25, 1861, for the war. Deserted from camp at Skinker's Neck, Virginia, April 10, 1863, and "drowned in attempting to get to the enemy."

BUIE, JOSIAH S., Corporal

Born in Bladen County where he resided as a farmer and enlisted at age 28, May 30, 1861, for the war. Mustered in as Private and appointed Corporal on July 21, 1861. Killed at Sharpsburg, Maryland, September 17, 1862.

BUIE, WILLIAM W., Private

Resided in Bladen County where he enlisted at age 35, February 12, 1862, for the war. Wounded at Gettysburg, Pennsylvania, July 2-3, 1863. Captured near Spotsylvania Court House, Virginia, May 12, 1864, and confined at Point Lookout, Maryland. Transferred on August 10, 1864, to Elmira, New York, where he remained until released after taking the Oath of Allegiance on June 30, 1865.

BURKE, PATRICK, Private

Resided in Bladen County where he enlisted at age 32, May 28, 1861, for the war. Killed at Chancellorsville, Virginia, May 3, 1863.

BURR, BARNEY, Private

Resided in Randolph County where he enlisted at age 20, July 17, 1862, for the war. Reported as absent sick from June 1, 1863, through December, 1864. Paroled at Greensboro on May 17, 1865.

BUSH, THOMAS J., Private

Resided in Bladen County where he enlisted at age 22, June 24, 1861, for the war. Mustered in as Corporal and reduced to ranks on July 21, 1861. Absent sick from October, 1862, through August, 1863. Present or accounted for until admitted to hospital at Richmond, Virginia, June 16, 1864, with a gunshot wound of the left leg. Furloughed from hospital June 22, 1864, for 40 days. Reported as absent wounded through December, 1864.

BUTLER, JAMES A., Private

Resided in Wake County where he enlisted at age 26, July 15, 1862, for the war. Killed at Winchester, Virginia, June 15, 1863.

BUTLER, WILLIAM, Private

Resided in Wake County where he enlisted at age 24, July 15, 1862, for the war. Mortally wounded at Sharpsburg, Maryland, September 17, 1862.

CAIN, ALLEN W., Private

Resided in Bladen County where he enlisted at age 27, May 10, 1861, for the war. Present or accounted for until captured at Gettysburg, Pennsylvania, July 3, 1863. Confined at Fort Delaware, Delaware, until transferred to Point Lookout, Maryland, October 18, 1863. Paroled at Point Lookout on March 14, 1865, and exchanged at Boulware's Wharf, James River, Virginia, March 16, 1865.

CAIN, JOHN S., Private

Resided in Bladen County where he enlisted at age 20, May 15, 1861, for the war. Mustered in as Private and appointed Corporal, September 17, 1862. Reduced to ranks on April 18, 1863. Wounded at Chancellorsville, Virginia, May 3, 1863. Present or accounted for until he deserted in Pennsylvania on June 25, 1863.

CALLAHAN, DENNIS H., Private

Resided in Bladen County where he enlisted at age 27, May 10, 1861, for the war. Detailed as a nurse in hospital at Goldsboro from March 26, 1862, through December, 1862. Returned to company in January, 1863. Wounded and captured at Gettysburg, Pennsylvania, July 3, 1863. Confined in hospital at Chester, Pennsylvania, until transferred to Point Lookout, Maryland, October 2, 1863. Released at Point Lookout after taking the Oath of Allegiance and joining the U.S. service on January 23, 1864. Assigned to Company A, 1st Regiment U.S. Volunteer Infantry.

CAMPBELL, JOHN A. C., Private
Resided in Alexander County where he enlisted on July 18, 1862, for the war. Deserted from Camp Holmes, Raleigh, soon after enlisting. Later returned and joined the company on October 17, 1863. Captured at Mine Run, Virginia, November 28, 1863, and confined at Old Capitol Prison, Washington, D.C. Released after taking the Oath of Allegiance on March 18, 1864, and sent to Philadelphia, Pennsylvania.

CAMPBELL, JOSEPH A. L., Private
Resided in Alexander County where he enlisted on July 18, 1862, for the war. Deserted from Camp Holmes, Raleigh, soon after enlisting. Later returned and joined the company on October 17, 1863. Captured on Rapidan River, Virginia, November 28, 1863, and confined at Old Capitol Prison, Washington, D.C. Released after taking the Oath of Allegiance on March 22, 1864, and sent to Philadelphia, Pennsylvania.

CASHWELL, GEORGE W., Private
Resided in Bladen County where he enlisted at age 30, May 13, 1861, for the war. Present or accounted for until killed at Chancellorsville, Virginia, May 3, 1863.

CHEEK, GEORGE W., Private
Enlisted in Randolph County on July 17, 1862, for the war. Paroled at Leesburg, Virginia, October 2, 1862. Reported on January-February, 1863, muster roll with the remark: "Left sick at Leesburg, Virginia, September 1, 1862. Never heard from since. Supposed to be dead."

CLARKE, DUNCAN R., Private
Resided in Bladen County where he enlisted at age 19, May 15, 1861, for the war. Wounded at Chancellorsville, Virginia, May 3, 1863. Deserted August 20, 1863, and shot for desertion on September 5, 1863.

CLOUTS, J. W., Private
Paroled at Morganton on May 16, 1865.

COBLE, ELI GRAHAM, Private
Resided in Randolph County where he enlisted at age 23, July 17, 1862, for the war. Present or accounted for until captured near Spotsylvania Court House, Virginia, May 12, 1864. Confined at Point Lookout, Maryland, until transferred to Elmira, New York, August 10, 1864. Released at Elmira after taking the Oath of Allegiance on June 30 1865.

COLLUM, ARCHIBALD, Private
Resided in Bladen County where he enlisted at age 34, May 28, 1861, for the war. Wounded at Sharpsburg, Maryland, September 17, 1862, and reported as absent wounded until detailed for hospital duty April 13, 1864. Detailed as a guard in hospital at Richmond, Virginia, until returned to duty on October 11, 1864. Present or accounted

for until paroled at Appomattox Court House, Virginia, April 9, 1865.

CORBETT, NAPOLEON B., Private
Resided in Bladen County where he enlisted at age 30, July 15, 1862, for the war. Present or accounted for until transferred to Company E, 18th Regiment N.C. Troops (8th Regiment N.C. Volunteers) May 11, 1863.

COSBY, A., Private
Enlisted in New Hanover County on March 26, 1862, for the war. Deserted on March 30, 1862.

COX, ALEXANDER M., Private
Born in Randolph County where he resided and enlisted at age 18, July 17, 1862, for the war. Died in hospital at Richmond, Virginia, September 16, 1862, of "febris typhoides."

COX, ELI, Private
Resided in Randolph County where he enlisted at age 23, July 17, 1862, for the war. Died at Gordonsville, Virginia, September 12, 1862, of disease.

COX, GEORGE H., Sergeant
Resided in Randolph County and enlisted in Bladen County at age 19, June 29, 1861, for the war. Mustered in as Private and appointed Sergeant on January 1, 1862. Wounded at Gettysburg, Pennsylvania, July 2-3, 1863, and "left on the field." Died on July 25, 1863, of wounds.

COX, HENRY, Private
Born in Randolph County where he resided as a farmer and enlisted at age 25, July 17, 1862, for the war. Discharged on December 22, 1862, by reason of "rheumatism with Bright's Disease of kidney"

CRAVEN, BENJAMIN, Private
Resided in Randolph County where he enlisted at age 25, July 17, 1862, for the war. Present or accounted for until captured near Spotsylvania Court House, Virginia, May 12, 1864. Confined at Point Lookout, Maryland, until transferred to Elmira, New York, August 10, 1864. Died at Elmira on February 18, 1865, of "pneumonia."

CRAVEN, ROBERT F., Private
Born in Randolph County where he resided as a farmer and enlisted at age 27, July 17, 1862, for the war. Captured at Frederick, Maryland, September 12, 1862, and paroled and exchanged at Aiken's Landing, James River, Virginia, November 10, 1862. Died in hospital at Lynchburg, Virginia, December 22, 1862, of "hydrothorax."

CREACH, JOHN M., Private
Resided in Columbus County and enlisted in Bladen County at age 21, May 30, 1861, for the war. Wounded at Chancellorsville, Virginia, May 3, 1863. Wounded at Gettysburg, Pennsylvania, July 2, 1863, and captured in hospital at Gettysburg July 5, 1863. Confined in hospital at Chester, Pennsylvania, until transferred to Point Lookout, Maryland, October 2, 1863. Paroled at Point Lookout on March 14, 1865, and exchanged at Boulware's Wharf, James River, Virginia, March 16, 1865.

CROOM, JESSE, Private
Admitted to hospital at Richmond, Virginia, February 16, 1865, with "febris typhoides" and died March 30, 1865.

CUNIGIM, FRANCIS M., Private
Born at Washington, Georgia, and resided as a farmer in Bladen County where he enlisted at age 42, May 29, 1861, for the war. Died in camp near Richmond, Virginia, August 17, 1862.

CUNIGIM, JOHN R., Private
Enlisted in Bladen County on May 30, 1861, for the war. Discharged on May 26, 1862.

CUTTS, WILLIAM H., Private
Resided in Bladen County where he enlisted at age 22, May 10, 1861, for the war. Mustered in as Corporal and reduced to ranks July 23, 1861. Wounded at Chancellorsville, Virginia, May 3, 1863. Present or accounted for on company muster rolls through December, 1864.

DALTON, I., Private
Paroled at Greensboro on May 16, 1865.

DANIEL, WILLIAM J., Private
Born in Bladen County where he resided and enlisted at age 19, May 18, 1861, for the war. Wounded and captured at Gettysburg, Pennsylvania, July 3, 1863. Died in hospital at Baltimore, Maryland, July 22, 1863, of "febris typhoides."

EDWARDS, DANIEL, Private
Resided in Bladen County where he enlisted at age 25, May 29, 1861, for the war. Present or accounted for on company muster rolls through December, 1864. Captured at High Bridge, Virginia, April 6, 1865, and confined at Newport News, Virginia. Released after taking the Oath of Allegiance on June 25, 1865.

ELLIOTT, SIMPSON, Private
Born in Randolph County where he resided as a cooper and enlisted at age 23, July 17, 1862, for the war. Died at home on November 14, 1862, of "consumption."

ELLIS, JAMES, Private
Resided in Columbus County where he enlisted at age 32, February 10, 1862, for the war. Wounded at Sharpsburg, Maryland, September 17, 1862. Deserted on August 20, 1863, and shot for desertion on September 5, 1863.

EVERETT, DANIEL J., Private
Resided in Bladen County where he enlisted at age 18, May 25, 1861, for the war. Wounded at Malvern Hill, Virginia, July 1, 1862. Present or accounted for until captured at Morton's Ford, Virginia, January 18, 1864. Confined at Old Capitol Prison, Washington, D.C., until released after taking the Oath of Allegiance on March 15, 1864.

EVERETT, HAYS B., Sergeant
Resided in Bladen County where he enlisted at age 18, May 18, 1861, for the war. Mustered in as Private. Wounded at Malvern Hill, Virginia, July 1, 1862, and at Chancellorsville, Virginia, May 3, 1863. Appointed Corporal on October 31, 1863. Wounded at Payne's Farm, Virginia, November 27, 1863. Promoted to Sergeant in January-August, 1864. Captured near Spotsylvania Court House, Virginia, May 12, 1864, and confined at Point Lookout, Maryland. Transferred to Elmira, New York, August 10, 1864. Released after taking the Oath of Allegiance on June 30, 1865.

EVERETT, ROBERT A., Private
Resided in Bladen County where he enlisted at age 36, May 10, 1861, for the war. Died in hospital at Fredericksburg, Virginia, October 24, 1861, of disease.

FAIRCLOTH, SOLOMON, Private
Resided in Bladen County where he enlisted at age 30, July 15, 1861, for the war. Reported as absent sick after November, 1862, and never returned to company.

FIELDS, ROBERT, Private
Resided in Randolph County where he enlisted at age 23, July 17, 1862, for the war. Died in hospital at Lynchburg, Virginia, January 9, 1863, of "pneumonia."

GALLAHORN, AARON, Private
Resided in Bladen County where he enlisted at age 23, June 29, 1861, for the war. Died October 23, 1861.

GALLAHORN, ZEBEDEE, Private
Resided in Randolph County and enlisted in Bladen County at age 25, June 29, 1861, for the war. Wounded on June 26, 1862, at Ellerson's Mill, Virginia, and died July 1, 1862.

GOFF, JOHN, Private
Resided in Bladen County where he enlisted at age 44, May 19, 1861, for the war. Present or accounted for until wounded on July 1, 1862, near Richmond, Virginia. Returned to duty in January-February, 1863. Muster roll for February 28-May 15, 1863, states that he was detailed for hospital duty at Raleigh. Absent detailed at that place until detailed as a shoemaker at Wilmington on August 25, 1863. Absent detailed until admitted to hospital at Richmond on January 8, 1864, with "variola conft." Reported as absent sick from that date through December, 1864.

GRIZZARD, JAMES, Private
Resided in Bladen County where he enlisted at age 40, May 10, 1861, for the war. Died November 14, 1861, at Fredericksburg, Virginia.

HALES, SIMON, Private
Resided in Bladen County where he enlisted at age 34, July 15, 1862, for the war. Present or accounted for until wounded on May 2, 1863, at Chancellorsville, Virginia. Admitted to hospital at Richmond, Virginia, on May 20, 1863, with "gunshot wound left hand." Reported as absent wounded or absent sick through August, 1864. Captured at Harrisonburg, Virginia, October 2, 1864, and confined at Point Lookout, Maryland. Released at Point Lookout after taking the Oath of Allegiance on June 4, 1865.

HALL, WILLIAM, Private
Enlisted in Yadkin County, October 27, 1863, for the war. Deserted on November 25, 1863, near Morton's Ford, Virginia.

HARGROVE, DAVID J., Sergeant
Resided in Bladen County where he enlisted at age 21, May 11, 1861, for the war. Mustered in as Private and appointed Sergeant on September 17, 1862. Present or accounted for until captured near Spotsylvania Court House, Virginia, on May 12, 1864. Confined at Point Lookout, Mary-

land, until transferred to Elmira, New York, on August 10, 1864. Released at Elmira after taking the Oath of Allegiance on June 30, 1865.

HARGROVE, HENRY, Private
Resided in Bladen County where he enlisted at age 24, May 20, 1861, for the war. Present or accounted for until captured on July 1-3, 1863, at Gettysburg, Pennsylvania. Confined at Letterman General Hospital, Gettysburg, where he served as a nurse until transferred to Point Lookout, Maryland, September 9, 1863. Paroled at Point Lookout, for exchange, on September 30, 1863. Admitted to hospital at Richmond, Virginia, on October 6, 1864. Reported as absent through December, 1864.

HARGROVE, JOHN O., Private
Born in Bladen County where he resided as a farmer and enlisted at age 21, May 18, 1861, for the war. Present or accounted for until killed on July 1, 1862, at Malvern Hill, Virginia.

HINSHAW, JESSE, Private
Born in Yadkin County where he resided as a farmer and enlisted at age 30, October 27, 1863, for the war. Present or accounted for until discharged on March 14, 1864, by reason of disability caused by "a state of mental inbecility bordering on idiocy, and also a caracature of spine."

HOLCOMB, L. B., Private
Enlisted in Yadkin County on October 27, 1863, for the war. Deserted on November 15, 1863, at Raccoon Ford, Virginia.

HOLLINGSWORTH, JOHN, Private
Resided in Bladen County where he enlisted at age 23, May 21, 1861, for the war. Detailed as a teamster in the Quartermaster Department on July 15, 1861. Absent detailed through December, 1864.

HOLOMAN, NATHAN P., Private
Resided in Wake County where he enlisted at age 32, July 15, 1862, for the war. Present or accounted for until wounded and captured at Gettysburg, Pennsylvania, July 1-3, 1863. Confined at U.S.A. hospitals at Gettysburg until transferred to U.S.A. General Hospital, West's Buildings, Baltimore, Maryland, on October 14, 1863. Paroled at that hospital and sent to City Point, Virginia, for exchange, on November 12, 1863. Reported as absent on parole, or absent on furlough, until retired to the Invalid Corps on December 1, 1864.

HOOKER, ISHAM, Private
Resided in Randolph County where he enlisted at age 37, June 29, 1861, for the war. Present or accounted for until detailed as a nurse at hospital at Raleigh on March 26, 1863. Absent detailed until returned to duty on June 2, 1864. Reported as absent sick from July 20, 1864, through December, 1864.

INSCORE, JAMES R., Private
Enlisted in Yadkin County on October 27, 1863, for the war. Deserted November 15, 1863, at Raccoon Ford, Virginia.

JOHNSON, ABNER, Private
Born in Bladen County where he resided and enlisted at age 25, May 11, 1861, for the war. Mustered in as Private and appointed Sergeant on June 28, 1861. Reduced to ranks on January 31, 1862. Killed on September 17, 1862, at Sharpsburg, Maryland.

JOHNSON, ISHAM, Private
Enlisted in Randolph County on July 17, 1862, for the war. Never reported for duty.

JONES, THOMAS B., Corporal
Resided in Randolph County where he enlisted at age 28, July 17, 1862, for the war. Mustered in as Private. Present or accounted for until admitted to hospital at Richmond, Virginia, on May 8, 1863, with "debility." Returned to duty September-October, 1863. Wounded at Payne's Farm, Virginia, November 27-28, 1863. Appointed Corporal, January-May, 1864. Captured on May 12, 1864, near Spotsylvania Court House, Virginia. Confined at Point Lookout, Maryland, until transferred to Elmira, New York, on August 10, 1864. Paroled at Elmira on October 11, 1864, and sent to Point Lookout to be forwarded for exchange.

KELLY, WILLIAM H., Private
Resided in Bladen County where he enlisted at age 20, June 24, 1861, for the war. Present or accounted for until he deserted on August 20, 1863. Shot for desertion on September 5, 1863.

KEMP, JOSEPH R., Corporal
Resided in Bladen County where he enlisted at age 18, May 10, 1861, for the war. Mustered in as Private. Deserted on June 4, 1863, at Hamilton's Crossing, Virginia, and returned on August 14, 1863. Appointed Corporal, January-August, 1864. Captured at Spotsylvania Court House, Virginia, May 12, 1864, and confined at Point Lookout, Maryland. Transferred August 10, 1864, to Elmira, New York, where he died February 15, 1865, of "variola."

KIRKMAN, JOHN H., Private
Resided in Bladen County and enlisted in Randolph County at age 24, July 17, 1862, for the war. Admitted to hospital at Richmond, Virginia, on September 16, 1862, with "debility" and was returned to duty on November 13, 1862. Present or accounted for until wounded on July 2, 1863, at Gettysburg, Pennsylvania. Absent wounded from that date through December, 1864. Paroled at Greensboro on May 10, 1865.

KIRKMAN, THOMAS H., Private
Resided in Randolph County where he enlisted at age 21, July 17, 1862, for the war. Never reported for duty.

LAMBERT, JOHN D., Private
Resided in Randolph County where he enlisted at age 18, July 17, 1862, for the war. Wounded on September 17, 1862, and furloughed for 40 days. Present or accounted for from expiration of furlough until killed in battle at Gettysburg, Pennsylvania, on July 2, 1863.

LAMBERT, JOHN F., Private
Resided in Randolph County where he enlisted at age 23, July 17, 1862, for the war. Reported as absent sick from September 10, 1862, until he deserted on April 1, 1863.

LANGLEY, JOSIAH, Private

Resided in Randolph County where he enlisted at age 21, July 17, 1862, for the war. Present or accounted for until wounded on May 3, 1863, at Chancellorsville, Virginia. Died May 15, 1863, of his wounds.

LANIER, GEORGE W., Private

Resided in Bladen County where he enlisted at age 21, May 10, 1861, for the war. Mustered in as Corporal. Present or accounted for until wounded and captured on May 3, 1863, at Chancellorsville, Virginia. Admitted to Lincoln U.S.A. General Hospital, Washington, D.C., on May 7, 1863, with "gunshot wound, flesh left shoulder." Transferred to Old Capitol Prison, Washington, on June 16, 1863. Paroled at Old Capitol Prison and sent to City Point, Virginia, for exchange, June 25, 1863. Admitted to hospital at Petersburg, Virginia, on June 30, 1863, and returned to duty on August 17, 1863. Reported on company muster rolls as absent wounded and on furlough until he deserted on January 1, 1864. Reduced to ranks November-December, 1863.

LEONARD, WILLIAM M., Private

Resided in Randolph County where he enlisted at age 26, July 17, 1862, for the war. Present or accounted for until wounded and captured on May 3, 1863, at Chancellorsville, Virginia. Admitted to Lincoln U.S.A. General Hospital, Washington, D.C., on May 9, 1863, and was transferred to Old Capitol Prison, Washington, on June 25, 1863. Paroled at Old Capitol Prison and sent to City Point, Virginia, for exchange, June 25, 1863. Returned to duty prior to November-December, 1863. Reported as absent sick from May 15, 1864, through December, 1864. Deserted and took the Oath of Allegiance at Washington on March 24, 1865, and furnished transportation to Wilmington.

LEWIS, JOHN D., Private

Resided in Bladen County where he enlisted at age 26, May 10, 1861, for the war. Discharged November 15, 1861.

LOWDERMILK, JOHN H., Private

Resided in Randolph County where he enlisted at age 20, June 29, 1861, for the war. Present or accounted for until wounded on July 1, 1862, at Malvern Hill, Virginia. Absent on wounded furlough until September, 1862. Present or accounted for until wounded on July 2, 1863, at Gettysburg, Pennsylvania. Absent wounded until detailed December 9, 1863, for post duty at Raleigh. Attached to Captain Samuel B. Waters' Company, Provost Guard, Raleigh, on March 8, 1864. Absent detailed through January, 1865.

McDUFFIE, PETER N., Private

Enlisted in Bladen County on May 10, 1861, for the war. Reported as absent sick until he appears on the September-October, 1861, muster roll with the remark: "Dropped from list. Never regularly enlisted but accounted for on former muster roll."

McGEE, HAYS, Private

Resided in Bladen County where he enlisted at age 19, May 18, 1861, for the war. Present or

accounted for until admitted to hospital at Richmond, Virginia, on May 2, 1863, with "pneumonia." Returned to duty on July 30, 1863. Present or accounted for until mortally wounded on November 27-28, 1863, at Payne's Farm, Virginia.

McGHEE, WILLIAM, Private

Resided in Bladen County where he enlisted at age 22, May 20, 1861, for the war. Died August 5, 1861, at Brook's Station, Virginia.

McKENZIE, HIRAM, Private

Resided in Bladen County where he enlisted at age 34, May 16, 1861, for the war. Present or accounted for until wounded July 1, 1862, at Malvern Hill, Virginia. Transferred to the "2nd Battery Maryland Artillery" on July 15, 1862.

McLEOD, JOHN N., Private

Resided in Bladen County where he enlisted at age 18, May 28, 1861, for the war. Present or accounted for until captured at Frederick, Maryland, on September 12, 1862. Confined at Fort Delaware, Delaware, until paroled and sent to Aiken's Landing, Virginia, for exchange, on October 2, 1862. Declared exchanged on November 10, 1862, and reported as absent without leave from that date until he returned to duty in January-February, 1863. Wounded May 2, 1863, at Chancellorsville, Virginia. Returned to duty in November-December, 1863. Captured on May 12, 1864, near Spotsylvania Court House, Virginia. Confined at Point Lookout, Maryland, until transferred to Elmira, New York, on August 14, 1864. Died at Elmira on February 3, 1865, of "variola."

McMILLAN, DUGALD J., Private

Resided in Bladen County where he enlisted at age 28, May 11, 1861, for the war. Present or accounted for until admitted to hospital at Richmond, Virginia, on September 9, 1862, with "debility." Furloughed from the hospital on October 29, 1862, and reported as absent sick through December, 1862. Absent without leave from January 1, 1863, until he returned to duty in August, 1863. Wounded November 27-28, 1863, at Payne's Farm, Virginia. Absent wounded through December, 1863. Captured on May 12, 1864, near Spotsylvania Court House, Virginia. Confined at Point Lookout, Maryland, until transferred to Elmira, New York, on August 10, 1864. Paroled at Elmira and sent to James River, Virginia, for exchange, February 20, 1865. Admitted to hospital at Richmond March 3, 1865, with "debilitas" and furloughed for 30 days on March 14, 1865.

MAHAFFY, WILLIAM A., Private

Resided in Wilkes County where he enlisted on October 17, 1863, for the war. Present or accounted for until captured at Mine Run, Virginia, on November 28, 1863. Confined at Old Capitol Prison, Washington, D.C., until released after taking Oath of Allegiance on March 19, 1864. Sent to Philadelphia, Pennsylvania.

MARTIN, ALEXANDER, Private

Resided in Wayne County where he enlisted at

age 23, July 15, 1862, for the war. Killed September 17, 1862, at Sharpsburg, Maryland.

MATHEWS, CORNELIUS, Private

Resided in Bladen County where he enlisted at age 15, May 24, 1861, for the war. Present or accounted for until reported as absent without leave on February 11, 1862. Absent from that date until he appears on the February 28-May 15, 1863, muster roll with the remark: "Deserted from Camp at Skinker's Neck, Virginia, and went to N.C."

MATHIS, JOSHUA, Private

Resided in Bladen County where he enlisted at age 23, May 23, 1861, for the war. Present or accounted for until admitted to hospital at Charlottesville, Virginia, on May 6, 1863, with "ulcus." Died the same day.

MEARES, JOHN, Private

Resided in Bladen County where he enlisted at age 23, May 28, 1861, for the war. Present or accounted for until wounded on June 26, 1862, at Ellerson's Mill, Virginia. Returned to duty January-February, 1863. Admitted to hospital at Richmond, Virginia, May 3, 1863, with "diarrhoea acute" and transferred to Wilmington on July 17, 1863. Furloughed from hospital at Wilmington on September 18, 1863, for 30 days. Wounded at Mine Run, Virginia, November 27-28, 1863, and reported as absent wounded through December, 1864.

MELVIN, SAMUEL, Private

Resided in Bladen County where he enlisted at age 19, July 15, 1862, for the war. Present or accounted for until admitted to hospital at Richmond, Virginia, on November 21, 1862, with "febris int." Transferred to hospital at Lynchburg, Virginia, the same day. Reported as absent sick from that date through December, 1864.

MESHAW, CHRISTOPHER C., Private

Resided in Bladen County where he enlisted at age 17, October 7; 1861, for the war. Present or accounted for until wounded on July 1, 1862, near Richmond, Virginia. Reported as absent sick from that date until he appears on the February 28-May 15, 1863, muster roll with the remark: "Left at Amosville, Virginia, August 28, 1862. Supposed to have died."

MESHAW, DANIEL W., Private

Resided in Bladen County where he enlisted at age 33, May 18, 1861, for the war. Died at Fredericksburg, Virginia, November 9, 1861.

MESHAW, JAMES W., Private

Resided in Bladen County where he enlisted at age 36, May 10, 1861, for the war. Wounded on July 1, 1862, near Richmond, Virginia. Present or accounted for until his death on August 12, 1863, at Gordonsville, Virginia, of "febris typhoides."

MILLER, DAVID D., Private

Born in Bladen County where he resided and enlisted at age 22, May 16, 1861, for the war. Present or accounted for until killed on June 26, 1862, at Ellerson's Mill, Virginia.

MITCHELL, C. J., Private

Enlisted in New Hanover County on March 22, 1862, for the war. Never reported for duty.

MONEY, LEWIS, Private

Enlisted in Yadkin County on October 27, 1863, for the war. Deserted November 25, 1863, near Morton's Ford, Virginia.

MOORE, DAVID, Private

Resided in Bladen County where he enlisted at age 20, July 15, 1862, for the war. Captured at Sharpsburg, Maryland, and confined at U.S.A. General Hospital, Frederick, Maryland, on September 28, 1862, with "gunshot wound." Transferred on November 3, 1862, to Fort McHenry, Maryland, where he was paroled and sent to City Point, Virginia, for exchange on November 12, 1862. Admitted to hospital at Petersburg, Virginia, on November 21, 1862, and was furloughed for 60 days on November 29, 1862. Company muster rolls report that he deserted on June 4, 1863; however, his name appears on hospital records from November, 1863, through July, 1864. Hospital records give his disease as "anasarca and debility" and state that he had been disabled since December 1, 1862.

MORAN, MICHAEL, Private

Resided in Cumberland County and enlisted in Bladen County at age 31, May 10, 1861, for the war. Deserted July 22, 1861, at Richmond, Virginia.

NEEDHAM, ELIJAH, Private

Resided in Randolph County where he enlisted at age 23, July 17, 1862, for the war. Wounded on September 17, 1862, at Sharpsburg, Maryland. Absent wounded until he returned to duty on January 21, 1863. Present or accounted for through December, 1864. Captured on April 6, 1865, at Burkeville, Virginia, and confined at Newport News, Virginia. Released at Newport News after taking the Oath of Allegiance on June 30, 1865.

PARISH, BENJAMIN J., Private

Resided in Wake County where he enlisted at age 26, July 15, 1862, for the war. Died September 15, 1862, at Raleigh.

PARISH, NATHAN, Private

Resided in Wake County where he enlisted at age 28, July 15, 1862, for the war. Captured and paroled at Headquarters, Army of the Potomac, on May 4, 1863. Forwarded to Washington, D.C., the same day. Sent from Washington to City Point, Virginia, for exchange on May 10, 1863. Reported on company muster rolls as absent without leave from June 1, 1863, until reported as captured at Mine Run, Virginia, on December 3, 1863. Confined at Old Capitol Prison, Washington, until transferred to Point Lookout, Maryland, on February 3, 1864. Released at Point Lookout after taking the Oath of Allegiance on June 3, 1865.

PARKER, DANIEL D., Private

Resided in Bladen County where he enlisted at age 19, May 28, 1861, for the war. Present or accounted for until captured on May 3, 1863, at Chancellorsville, Virginia. Paroled at Office of the Provost Marshal General, Army of the Potomac, on May 4, 1863. Wounded and captured July 1-3, 1863, at Gettysburg, Pennsylvania. Confined at Fort Delaware, Delaware, until transferred to Point Lookout, Maryland, October 15-18, 1863. Paroled at Point Lookout and sent to Venus Point, Savannah River, Georgia, for exchange, on November 1, 1864. Reported on company muster rolls as absent prisoner through December, 1864.

PHILLIPS, WILLIAM D., Private

Resided in Yadkin County where he enlisted on October 27, 1863, for the war. Present or accounted for until captured at Morton's Ford, Virginia, on January 18, 1864. Confined at Old Capitol Prison, Washington, D.C., until released after taking the Oath of Allegiance on March 15, 1864. Sent to Philadelphia, Pennsylvania.

POPE, ALEXANDER C., Private

Resided in Randolph County where he enlisted at age 18, July 17, 1862, for the war. Present or accounted for until captured on May 12, 1864, near Spotsylvania Court House, Virginia. Confined at Point Lookout, Maryland, until transferred to Elmira, New York, on August 10, 1864. Released at Elmira after taking the Oath of Allegiance on June 23, 1865.

PORTER, TRAVIS L., Private

Resided in Bladen County where he enlisted at age 20, May 18, 1861, for the war. Present or accounted for until wounded on July 1, 1862, at Malvern Hill, Virginia. Reported as absent sick until January-February, 1863, when he appears as present. Captured on July 3, 1863, at Gettysburg, Pennsylvania. Confined at Fort Delaware, Delaware, until transferred to Point Lookout, Maryland, October 15-18, 1863. Admitted to U.S.A. Smallpox Hospital, Point Lookout, on December 16, 1863, and died on December 23, 1863.

PRESNELL, DANIEL, Sergeant

Resided in Randolph County and enlisted in Bladen County at age 31, June 29, 1861, for the war. Mustered in as Private and appointed Sergeant on September 17, 1862. Present or accounted for until killed on July 2, 1863, at Gettysburg, Pennsylvania.

PRIDGEN, JAMES L., Corporal

Born in Bladen County where he resided as a farmer and enlisted at age 23, July 4, 1861, for the war. Mustered in as Private and appointed Corporal on January 31, 1862. Present or accounted for until killed on September 17, 1862, at Sharpsburg, Maryland.

REAVIS, ASA, Private

Enlisted in Yadkin County on October 27, 1863, for the war. Deserted on November 15, 1863, at Raccoon Ford, Virginia.

REAVIS, DAVID, Private

Enlisted in Yadkin County on October 27, 1863, for the war. Deserted November 15, 1863, at Raccoon Ford, Virginia.

ROBINSON, JAMES R., Private

Resided in Bladen County where he enlisted at age 27, July 4, 1861, for the war. Present or ac-

counted for until wounded and captured July 1-3, 1863, at Gettysburg, Pennsylvania. Confined in U.S.A. hospital at Gettysburg with "gunshot wound in arm and back" until transferred to DeCamp General Hospital, Davids Island, New York Harbor, on July 18, 1863. Paroled at De-Camp General Hospital and sent to City Point, Virginia, for exchange, August 24, 1863. Reported as absent wounded and on sick furlough through December, 1864. Admitted to hospital at Wilmington on February 24, 1865, with "debilitas." Sent to Colonel Mallett "for light duty" on March 24, 1865.

ROUSE, WILLIAM, Private

Resided in Bladen County where he enlisted at age 18, May 10, 1861, for the war. Company muster rolls report him as absent sick from October, 1862, until his death on April 10, 1863, at Guinea Station, Virginia.

RUSS, FRANKLIN, Private

Enlisted in Bladen County on May 10, 1861, for the war. Died June 22, 1861, at Wilmington "on his way to the army."

RUSS, OLIN M., Private

Resided in Bladen County where he enlisted at age 21, June 11, 1861, for the war. Present or accounted for until captured on July 3, 1863, at Gettysburg, Pennsylvania. Confined at Fort Delaware, Delaware, until transferred to Point Lookout, Maryland, on October 18, 1863. Paroled at Point Lookout and sent to James River, Virginia, for exchange. Received at Cox's Landing, James River, February 14-15, 1865, for exchange. Admitted to hospital at Richmond, Virginia, on February 15, 1865, with "scurvy" and was furloughed for 60 days on March 16, 1865.

RUSS, WILLIAM H., Private

Resided in Bladen County where he enlisted at age 26, May 11, 1861, for the war. Present or accounted for until mortally wounded on July 1, 1862, at Malvern Hill, Virginia.

SALMONS, WILLIAM, Private

Resided in Bladen County where he enlisted at age 20, May 20, 1861, for the war. Present or accounted for until wounded on July 1, 1862, at Malvern Hill, Virginia. Returned to duty from hospital at Richmond, Virginia, on October 20, 1862. Present or accounted for until wounded and captured at Gettysburg, Pennsylvania, July 1-3, 1863. Confined at U.S.A. hospital at Gettysburg with "gunshot wound, thigh, fracture." Transferred to U.S.A. General Hospital, West's Buildings, Baltimore, Maryland, on November 3, 1863. Transferred from that hospital to Hammond U.S.A. General Hospital, Point Lookout, Maryland, on January 10, 1864. Paroled at Hammond U.S.A. General Hospital and sent to City Point, Virginia, for exchange on April 27, 1864. Admitted to hospital at Richmond on May 1, 1864, and was furloughed for 30 days on May 12, 1864. Absent wounded until retired to the Invalid Corps on January 9, 1865, and assigned to duty with the Post Surgeon at Fayetteville.

SASSER, BENJAMIN, Private

Resided in Columbus County where he enlisted

at age 51, February 15, 1862, for the war. Present or accounted for until discharged on May 26, 1862.

SCURRY, THOMAS J., Private

Resided in Bladen County and enlisted at Camp Price, Virginia, at age 37, February 12, 1862, for the war. Present or accounted for until discharged on May 26, 1862.

SELLARS, AZARIAH R., Private

Resided in Bladen County where he enlisted at age 19, May 10, 1861, for the war. Mustered in as Corporal and reduced to ranks on July 23, 1861. Present or accounted for until wounded at Malvern Hill, Virginia, on July 1, 1862. Absent wounded until returned to duty January-February, 1863. Captured at Gettysburg, Pennsylvania, July 5, 1863, and confined in U.S.A. Hospital at Gettysburg until transferred to U.S.A. General Hospital, West's Buildings, Baltimore, Maryland, on August 11, 1863. Transferred to Point Lookout, Maryland, September 15-16, 1863. Paroled at Point Lookout and sent to James River, Virginia, for exchange, February 18, 1865. Received at Boulware's and Cox's Wharf, James River, February 20-21, 1865.

SELLARS, CALVIN S., Private

Resided in Bladen County where he enlisted at age 18, May 12, 1861, for the war. Present or accounted for until killed on July 2, 1863, at Gettysburg, Pennsylvania.

SHAKELFORD, T. W., Private

Resided in Onslow County. Paroled May 6, 1865, at Goldsboro.

SHORE, DANIEL, Private

Enlisted October 27, 1863, in Yadkin County for the war. Company muster rolls report that he deserted on November 25, 1863, near Morton's Ford, Virginia. Died February 11, 1864.

SIKES, CHARLES B., Private

Resided in Columbus County and enlisted in Wayne County at age 27, May 15, 1862, for the war. Captured at Sharpsburg, Maryland, on September 17, 1862. Paroled and exchanged at Aiken's Landing, Virginia, on November 10, 1862. Present or accounted for until wounded and captured at Gettysburg, Pennsylvania, July 1-3, 1863. Transferred from U.S.A. General Hospital, Chester, Pennsylvania, to Hammond U.S.A. General Hospital, Point Lookout, Maryland, October 2, 1863. Paroled at that hospital and sent to City Point, Virginia, for exchange, April 27, 1864. Died at hospital at Richmond, Virginia, on June 10, 1864, of "diarrhoea chronic."

SIKES, DAVID A., 1st Sergeant

Resided in Randolph County where he enlisted at age 22, June 29, 1861, for the war. Mustered in as Private and appointed Sergeant on July 23, 1861. Present or accounted for until wounded at Sharpsburg, Maryland, on September 17, 1862. Returned to duty January-February, 1863. Wounded at Gettysburg, Pennsylvania, July 1-3, 1863. Returned to duty in November-December, 1863. Captured on May 12, 1864, near Spotsylvania Court House, Virginia. Confined at Point Lookout, Maryland, until transferred to Elmira,

New York, on August 10, 1864. Released at Elmira after taking the Oath of Allegiance on May 19, 1865. Promoted to 1st Sergeant while absent prisoner of war, September-October, 1864.

SIKES, JAMES M., 1st Sergeant

Resided in Columbus County and enlisted in Bladen County at age 25, May 30, 1861, for the war. Mustered in as Sergeant and appointed 1st Sergeant on July 23, 1861. Present or accounted for until wounded on September 17, 1862, at Sharpsburg, Maryland. Absent wounded until returned to duty January-February, 1863. Wounded and captured July 1-3, 1863, at Gettysburg, Pennsylvania. Transferred from U.S.A. hospital at Gettysburg to U.S.A. General Hospital, Chester, Pennsylvania, on July 17, 1863. Paroled at that hospital and sent to City Point, Virginia, for exchange, September 17, 1863. Absent wounded until returned to duty in August, 1864. Retired to the Invalid Corps on September 9, 1864.

SIKES, ROBERT J., Private

Resided in Columbus County where he enlisted at age 18, February 15, 1862. Captured September 15, 1862, at South Mountain, Maryland. Paroled and exchanged on November 10, 1862, at Aiken's Landing, Virginia. Present or accounted for until wounded and captured at Gettysburg, Pennsylvania, July 1-3, 1863. Transferred from U.S.A. Hospital at Gettysburg to U.S.A. General Hospital, Chester, Pennsylvania, July 16, 1863. Paroled at that hospital on September 17, 1863, and sent to City Point, Virginia, for exchange. Absent wounded through December, 1863. Furloughed on June 1, 1864, and reported as absent sick from that date through December, 1864.

SIKES, WILLIAM H., Corporal

Resided in Columbus County and enlisted in Bladen County at age 21, May 30, 1861, for the war. Mustered in as Private. Present or accounted for until wounded on May 2, 1863, at Chancellorsville, Virginia. Returned to duty May 15, 1863. Wounded and captured July 1-3, 1863, at Gettysburg, Pennsylvania. Transferred from U.S.A. Hospital at Gettysburg to U.S.A. General Hospital, Chester, Pennsylvania, July 16, 1863. Paroled at that hospital and sent to City Point, Virginia, for exchange, September 17, 1863. Absent on parole through December, 1863. Appointed Corporal, January-May, 1864. Killed May 5, 1864, at Wilderness, Virginia.

SIMMONS, WILLIAM B., Private

Resided in Bladen County where he enlisted at age 19, July 15, 1862, for the war. Captured at Frederick, Maryland, on September 12, 1862. Paroled and exchanged on November 10, 1862, at Aiken's Landing, Virginia. Deserted November 1, 1862, while on parole. Enlisted in 2nd Company I, 36th Regiment N.C. Troops (2nd Regiment N.C. Artillery) on June 10, 1863. Returned to this company April 6, 1864. Deserted March 19, 1865, and took the Oath of Allegiance at Washington, D.C., on March 24, 1865.

SIMPSON, JOHN O., Private
Enlisted in Bladen County, June 5, 1861, for the war. Deserted June 6, 1861, at Wilmington.

SIZEMORE, ABRAM, Private
Resided in Yadkin County where he enlisted October 27, 1863, for the war. Captured November 28, 1863, at Mine Run, Virginia. Confined at Old Capitol Prison, Washington, D.C., where he was released after taking the Oath of Allegiance on March 22, 1864. Sent to New York.

SMITH, JENKINS, Private
Resided in Bladen County where he enlisted at age 20, July 15, 1862, for the war. Captured September 17, 1862, at Sharpsburg, Maryland, and paroled on September 20, 1862. Deserted November 1, 1862. Enlisted in 2nd Company I, 36th Regiment N.C. Troops (2nd Regiment N.C. Artillery) on June 10, 1863. Ordered to return to this company on November 20, 1863; however, he never reported for duty.

SMITH, JOHN A., Private
Resided in Bladen County where he enlisted at age 31, July 15, 1861, for the war. Present or accounted for until captured on May 12, 1864, near Spotsylvania Court House, Virginia. Confined at Point Lookout, Maryland, until transferred to Elmira, New York, on August 10, 1864. Released at Elmira after taking the Oath of Allegiance on June 12, 1865.

SMITH, WILLIAM, Private
Resided in Bladen County where he enlisted at age 24, May 10, 1861, for the war. Present or accounted for until admitted to hospital at Richmond, Virginia, on December 15, 1862, with "gunshot wound in breast." Reported on hospital records through February 28, 1863. Reported on company muster roll for February 28-May 15, 1863, as "absent without leave." Reported as absent without leave from that date until he deserted on December 1, 1863.

SPEARMAN, GEORGE W., Private
Resided in Bladen County where he enlisted at age 22, July 15, 1862, for the war. Died at Frederick, Maryland, September 12, 1862.

SPRINGS, AARON, Private
Resided in Bladen County where he enlisted at age 34, May 10, 1861, for the war. Mustered in as Private and appointed Corporal on July 23, 1861. Present or accounted for until reduced to ranks on April 1, 1864. Captured May 12, 1864, near Spotsylvania Court House, Virginia. Confined at Point Lookout, Maryland, until transferred to Elmira, New York, on August 10, 1864. Died at Elmira, March 11, 1865, of "chronic diarrhoea."

STANTON, PRESNELL, Private
Resided in Randolph County and enlisted in Bladen County at age 22, June 29, 1861, for the war. Discharged in August, 1861.

STEPHENS, JOHN J., Private
Resided in Bladen County where he enlisted at age 24, May 13, 1861, for the war. Died July 31, 1861, at Petersburg, Virginia.

STONE, LEWIS L., Private
Resided in Wilkes County where he enlisted on

October 17, 1863, for the war. Captured at Mine Run, Virginia, November 28, 1863, and confined at Old Capitol Prison, Washington, D.C. Released at Old Capitol Prison, March 19, 1864, after taking the Oath of Allegiance. Sent to Philadelphia, Pennsylvania.

STONE, WILLIAM F., Private
Enlisted in Wilkes County on October 17, 1863, for the war. Reported as absent sick from June 21, 1864, through December, 1864.

STOUT, CALVIN N., Private
Resided in Randolph County where he enlisted at age 26, July 17, 1862, for the war. Wounded September 17, 1862, at Sharpsburg, Maryland. Reported as absent wounded until he deserted January 1, 1863. Paroled at Greensboro on May 16, 1865.

STRIDER, JAMES M. A., Sergeant
Resided in Randolph County and enlisted in Bladen County on June 29, 1861, for the war. Mustered in as Private and appointed Corporal on April 19, 1863. Wounded at Gettysburg, Pennsylvania, July 1-3, 1863. Returned to duty September-October, 1863. Appointed Sergeant, January-August, 1864. Captured near Spotsylvania Court House, Virginia, May 12, 1864. Confined at Point Lookout, Maryland, until transferred to Elmira, New York, on August 10, 1864. Died at Elmira on October 13, 1864, of "remittent fever."

SUE, ALEXANDER, Private
Resided in Bladen County where he enlisted at age 25, May 10, 1861, for the war. Mustered in as Sergeant. Present or accounted for until captured at Boonsboro, Maryland, September 14-15, 1862. Paroled September 20, 1862. Reduced to ranks on January 1, 1863, for being absent without leave. Admitted to hospital at Wilmington with a gunshot wound on January 13, 1863, and confined in jail at Wilmington on February 1, 1863. Returned to company and deserted to the enemy in King George County, Virginia, in March, 1863. Took the Oath of Allegiance at Washington, D. C., March 16, 1863, and agreed to "remain within any of the loyal states."

THOMAS, M. T., Private
Captured at Wilderness, Virginia, May 8, 1864, and confined at Point Lookout, Maryland. Transferred August 10, 1864, to Elmira, New York, where he remained until paroled on February 20, 1865.

THOMAS, R. G., Private
Captured at Richmond, Virginia, April 3, 1865, and confined at Newport News, Virginia. Died at Newport News on June 24, 1865, of "chronic diarrhoea."

THOMPSON, DAVID M., Private
Resided in Randolph County where he enlisted at age 19, July 17, 1862, for the war. Wounded at Chancellorsville, Virginia, May 3, 1863, and at Gettysburg, Pennsylvania, July 2-3, 1863. Present or accounted for until he deserted on December 1, 1863.

THORNBURG, MARTIN, Private
Resided in Randolph County where he enlisted

at age 28, July 17, 1862, for the war. Present or accounted for until he deserted on February 10, 1864. Paroled at Greensboro on May 17, 1865.

VESTAL, JOHN R., Private

Born in Randolph County where he resided and enlisted at age 23, July 17, 1862, for the war. Died in hospital at Mt. Jackson, Virginia, November 21, 1862, of "pneumonia."

VUNCANNON, ALSON G., Private

Resided in Randolph County where he enlisted at age 20, July 17, 1862, for the war. Wounded at Sharpsburg, Maryland, September 17, 1862, and died at Winchester, Virginia, October 1, 1862, of wound.

VUNCANNON, WILLIAM, Private

Resided in Randolph County where he enlisted at age 30, July 17, 1862, for the war. Wounded at Sharpsburg, Maryland, September 17, 1862, and at Gettysburg, Pennsylvania, July 2-3, 1863. Present or accounted for until reported missing in action at Spotsylvania Court House, Virginia, May 12, 1864.

WALKER, JAMES P., Private

Transferred from Company E, 18th Regiment N.C. Troops (8th Regiment N.C. Volunteers) May 11, 1863. Reported as absent sick from May 16, 1863, until he returned to company November-December, 1863. Admitted to hospital at Williamsburg, Virginia, March 22, 1864, with "paralysis of right foot." Transferred to hospital at Petersburg, Virginia, May 7, 1864, and from there to Wilmington on May 31, 1864. Furloughed from hospital at Wilmington on June 21, 1864, for 60 days. Extension of furlough recommended and application for retirement forwarded on September 13, 1864.

WARNER, W. C., Private

Captured July 30, 1863, and admitted to hospital at Winchester, Virginia.

WARREN, JOHN A., Private

Born in Bladen County and resided in Columbus County where he enlisted at age 30, February 10, 1862, for the war. Died at Goldsboro on April 14, 1862.

WARREN, JOHN BENJAMIN, Private

Resided in Columbus County where he enlisted at age 23, February 15, 1862, for the war. Died in hospital at Danville, Virginia, July 2, 1862, of "febris typhoides."

WATSON, WILLIAM D., Corporal

Resided in Bladen County where he enlisted at age 19, May 18, 1861, for the war. Mustered in as Private. Admitted to hospital at Richmond, Virginia, July 1, 1862, with "feb. typhoid" and furloughed August 26, 1862, for 40 days. Returned to company January-February, 1863. Admitted to hospital at Richmond on May 22, 1863, with "continued fever and anemia" and furloughed June 9, 1863, for 40 days. Returned to company September-October, 1863. Appointed Corporal, January-May, 1864. Killed at Wilderness, Virginia, May 5, 1864.

WILLARD, FRANCIS H., Private

Enlisted in Yadkin County on October 27, 1863,

for the war. Deserted at Raccoon Ford, Virginia, November 15, 1863.

WILLETT, JOSEPH J., Private

Resided in Randolph County where he enlisted at age 31, July 17, 1862, for the war. Captured at Boonsboro, Maryland, September 15, 1862, and paroled and exchanged at Aiken's Landing, James River, Virginia, November 10, 1862. Died at home on April 16, 1863.

WILLIAMS, JOHN T., Private

Resided in Randolph County and enlisted in Bladen County at age 19, June 29, 1861, for the war. Present or accounted for until killed at Gettysburg, Pennsylvania, July 2-3, 1863.

WILLIAMS, SHERLEY S., Private

Resided in Bladen County where he enlisted at age 23, May 18, 1861, for the war. Wounded at Chancellorsville, Virginia, May 3, 1863, and died May 24, 1863.

WILLIAMS, ZIMRI J., Private

Resided in Randolph County where he enlisted at age 21, July 17, 1862, for the war. Wounded at Chancellorsville, Virginia, May 3, 1863, and at Winchester, Virginia, June 15, 1863. Present or accounted for until paroled at Appomattox Court House, Virginia, April 9, 1865.

WREN, THOMAS, Private

Enlisted in Randolph County at age 26, July 17, 1862, for the war. Reported on July 14-October 31, 1862, muster roll with the remark: "Absent. Never has reported. Left in North Carolina sick." Never joined the company and reported as a deserter.

YORK, JOHN, Private

Resided in Randolph County where he enlisted at age 18, July 17, 1862, for the war. Wounded at Gettysburg, Pennsylvania, July 2-3, 1863, and reported as "left in the hands of the enemy." Claim for pay due deceased soldier filed on September 6, 1864, by his mother. Place of death reported on claim as "Potomac River."

YOUNG, WILLIAM FRANKLIN, Private

Resided in Wake County and enlisted in Randolph County at age 23, July 17, 1862, for the war. Captured at Frederick, Maryland, September 12, 1862, and paroled and exchanged at Aiken's Landing, James River, Virginia, November 10, 1862. Present or accounted for until captured at Spotsylvania Court House, Virginia, May 12, 1864. Confined at Point Lookout, Maryland, until transferred to Elmira, New York, August 10, 1864. Died at Elmira on April 24, 1865, of "chronic diarrhoea."

YOUNG, WILLIAM H., Private

Resided in Wake County and enlisted in Randolph County at age 21, July 17, 1862, for the war. Captured at Frederick, Maryland, September 12, 1862, and paroled and exchanged at Aiken's Landing, James River, Virginia, November 10, 1862. Wounded at Gettysburg, Pennsylvania, July 2-3, 1863, and captured at Gettysburg July 4-5, 1863. Confined at DeCamp General Hospital, Davids Island, New York Harbor, until paroled and exchanged at City Point, Virginia, September 8,

1863. Captured at Spotsylvania Court House, Virginia, May 12, 1864, and confined at Point Lookout, Maryland. Paroled at Point Lookout on March 15, 1865, and exchanged at Boulware's Wharf, James River, Virginia, March 18, 1865. Admitted to hospital at Richmond, Virginia, March 18, 1865, and transferred to Camp Lee, near Richmond, the next day.

COMPANY I

This company, known as "Jeff Davis' Rifles," was organized in Beaufort County and enlisted at Washington on May 10, 1861. It tendered its service to the state and was ordered to Garysburg, Northampton County, where it was assigned to this regiment as Company I. After joining the regiment the company functioned as a part of the regiment, and its history for the war period is recorded as a part of the regimental history.

The information contained in the following roster of the company was compiled principally from company muster rolls which covered from the date of muster-in, August 31, 1861, through December, 1864. No company muster rolls were found for the period prior to August 31, 1861, or for the period after December, 1864. In addition to the company muster rolls, Roll of Honor records, receipt rolls, and hospital records, supplemented by state pension applications, United Daughters of the Confederacy records, and postwar rosters and histories, all provided useful information.

OFFICERS
CAPTAINS

CARMER, JOHN R.

Resided in Beaufort County where he enlisted at age 46, May 10, 1861, for the war. Appointed Captain to rank from May 16, 1861. Submitted his resignation on May 5, 1862, by reason of "continued ill health." Resignation officially accepted on May 12, 1862.

CRAIGE, ARCHIBALD

Resided in Beaufort County where he enlisted at age 36, May 10, 1861, for the war. Appointed 2nd Lieutenant to rank from May 16, 1861, and promoted to Captain to rank from July 1, 1862. Wounded at Sharpsburg, Maryland, September 17, 1862. Reported as absent wounded when he submitted his resignation on September 28, 1863, by reason of "wounds received September 17, 1862." Resignation officially accepted on October 9, 1863.

STONE, IRVING C.

Born in New York and resided as a teacher in Beaufort County where he enlisted at age 24, May 10, 1861, for the war. Mustered in as Sergeant and promoted to 1st Sergeant in July, 1862. Appointed 2nd Lieutenant to rank from August 1, 1862. Wounded at Chancellorsville, Virginia, May 3, 1863, and promoted to 1st Lieutenant to rank from June 1, 1863. Promoted to Captain to rank from October 9, 1863. Captured at Spotsylvania Court House, Virginia, May 12, 1864, and confined at Fort Delaware, Delaware. Released at Fort

Delaware after taking the Oath of Allegiance on June 16, 1865.

LIEUTENANTS

ALLEN, HENRY P., 2nd Lieutenant

Born in Beaufort County where he resided as a post master and enlisted at age 39, May 10, 1861, for the war. Mustered in as 1st Sergeant and appointed 2nd Lieutenant to rank from August 1, 1862. Transferred to Captain S. B. Waters' Independent Company N.C. Troops on October 2, 1862, upon appointment as 1st Lieutenant.

BARROW, THADDEUS P., 2nd Lieutenant

Resided in Beaufort County where he enlisted at age 21, May 10, 1861, for the war. Mustered in as Private and appointed Corporal on January 1, 1863. Promoted to Sergeant, March-April, 1863. Wounded at Chancellorsville, Virginia, May 3, 1863. Appointed 2nd Lieutenant to rank from October 9, 1863. Captured at Spotsylvania Court House, Virginia, May 12, 1864, and confined at Fort Delaware, Delaware. Transferred to Hilton Head, South Carolina, August 20, 1864, and to Fort Pulaski, Georgia, October 20, 1864. Returned to Hilton Head on December 26, 1864, and transferred back to Fort Delaware on March 12, 1865. Released at Fort Delaware after taking the Oath of Allegiance on June 16, 1865.

CRAIGE, CICERO H., 1st Lieutenant

Resided in New Hanover County and enlisted in Wayne County at age 20, March 31, 1862, for the war. Mustered in as Private and appointed 2nd Lieutenant to rank from July 1, 1862. Promoted to 1st Lieutenant to rank from October 9, 1863. Wounded at Spotsylvania Court House, Virginia, May 10, 1864, and died July 9, 1864, of wound.

GAYLARD, WILLIAM R., 1st Lieutenant

Resided in Beaufort County and enlisted in Craven County at age 23, July 3, 1861, for the war. Appointed 3rd Lieutenant to rank from May 16, 1861, and promoted to 2nd Lieutenant to rank from May 25, 1862. Promoted to 1st Lieutenant to rank from July 1, 1862. Wounded at Sharpsburg, Maryland, September 17, 1862. Reported as absent wounded when he submitted his resignation on May 15, 1863, by reason of "gunshot wound in knee joint of left leg . . . causing stiffness and rendering necessary the use of crutches for locomotion." Resignation officially accepted on June 1, 1863.

WATERS, SAMUEL B., 1st Lieutenant

Resided in Beaufort County and appointed 1st Lieutenant at age 26 to rank from May 16, 1861. Present or accounted for until transferred to the Field and Staff, 18th Regiment N.C. Troops (8th Regiment N.C. Volunteers) upon appointment as Adjutant with the rank of 1st Lieutenant on May 25, 1862.

WATSON, JOHN W., 2nd Lieutenant

Resided in Beaufort County where he enlisted at age 24, May 10, 1861, for the war. Mustered in as Private and appointed Corporal, July 14-November 1, 1862. Promoted to Sergeant on January 1, 1863. Wounded at Gettysburg, Pennsylvania, July 2-3, 1863. Appointed 2nd Lieutenant to rank from July 29, 1863. Wounded and captured at Winchester, Virginia, September 19, 1864. Confined in hospital at Baltimore, Maryland, until transferred to Fort Delaware, Delaware, January 1, 1865. Paroled at Fort Delaware on February 27, 1865, and transferred for exchange.

NONCOMMISSIONED OFFICERS AND PRIVATES

ADAMS, HARDY H., Private
Born in Wake County where he resided as a farmer and enlisted at age 27, July 15, 1862, for the war. Reported as absent sick from August 25, 1862, until his death on November 30, 1862, in North Carolina.

ALLEN, CHARLES E., Private
Born in Wake County where he resided as a farmer and enlisted at age 29, July 15, 1862, for the war. Captured at Frederick, Maryland, and died on September 18, 1862.

ALLEN, GEORGE T., Corporal
Resided in Beaufort County where he enlisted at age 24, May 10, 1861, for the war. Mustered in as Private and appointed Corporal on June 1, 1863. Present or accounted for until wounded and captured at Gettysburg, Pennsylvania, July 1-3, 1863. Transferred from U.S.A. Hospital at Gettysburg to U.S.A. General Hospital, Chester, Pennsylvania, July 11-16, 1863. Paroled at that hospital and sent to City Point, Virginia, for exchange, on September 17, 1863. Admitted to hospital at Richmond, Virginia, September 23, 1863, with "gunshot wound neck and face" and furloughed for 40 days on October 2, 1863. Absent wounded until "commissioned December 1, 1863, by Governor Vance in a company formed to guard prisoners at Salisbury, N.C."

ALLEN, JAMES FRANKLIN, Private
Resided in Franklin County and enlisted in Wake County at age 23, July 15, 1862, for the war. Captured at Frederick, Maryland, September 12, 1862, and paroled and exchanged November 10, 1862, at Aiken's Landing, Virginia. Present or accounted for until wounded on May 3, 1863, at Chancellorsville, Virginia. Admitted to hospital at Richmond, Virginia, May 13, 1863, with "gunshot wound left arm" and furloughed for 60 days on June 27, 1863. Absent wounded from that date through December, 1864.

ALLEN, JOHN T., Private
Resided in Beaufort County where he enlisted at age 18, May 10, 1861, for the war. Present or accounted for until killed in battle at Sharpsburg, Maryland, on September 17, 1862.

ALLEN, THOMAS A., Private
Resided in Wake County where he enlisted at age 25, July 15, 1862, for the war. Absent sick from September 10, 1862, until returned to duty January-February, 1863. Present or accounted for until again reported as absent sick from July 27, 1863, until he returned to duty November-December, 1864. Paroled at Burkeville, Virginia, April 14-17, 1865.

ARCHIBALD, HENRY J., Private
Resided in Beaufort County where he enlisted at age 23, May 10, 1861, for the war. Died September 12, 1862, near Richmond, Virginia, of disease.

BALL, ASHLEY, Private
Resided in Beaufort County where he enlisted at age 22, February 20, 1862, for the war. Reported as absent from December 24, 1862, until he appears on the December 31, 1863-August 31, 1864, muster roll with the remark: "Deserted January 16, 1864, and joined the enemy at Washington, N.C."

BARNETT, PELEG M., Private
Resided in Beaufort County where he enlisted at age 22, May 10, 1861, for the war. Present or accounted for until wounded at Sharpsburg, Maryland, on September 17, 1862. Died of his wounds on October 30, 1862, in hospital at Winchester, Virginia.

BARNETT, WILLIAM S., Sergeant
Resided in Beaufort County where he enlisted at age 29, May 10, 1861, for the war. Mustered in as Private and appointed Corporal on March 1, 1863. Promoted to Sergeant on December 1, 1863. Present or accounted for until captured at Spotsylvania Court House, Virginia, on May 12, 1864. Confined at Point Lookout, Maryland, until transferred to Elmira, New York, on August 8, 1864. Released at Elmira after taking the Oath of Allegiance on June 27, 1865.

BELL, SAMUEL, Private
Resided in Wake County where he enlisted at age 37, July 15, 1862, for the war. Wounded at Sharpsburg, Maryland, September 17, 1862, and died October 1, 1862, at Frederick, Maryland.

BELVIN, THOMAS H., Private
Resided in Wake County where he enlisted at age 31, July 15, 1862, for the war. Present or accounted for until wounded at Chancellorsville, Virginia, on May 3, 1863. Again wounded on November 27, 1863, at Payne's Farm, Virginia. Present or accounted for until wounded at Winchester, Virginia, September 19, 1864. Absent wounded through December, 1864.

BENNETT, CHARLES, Private
Resided in Beaufort County where he enlisted at age 27, May 10, 1861, for the war. Reported as absent sick from August 19, 1862, until returned to duty on September 20, 1862. Absent without leave from December 21, 1862, until he appears on the company muster roll for February 28-May 15, 1863, with the remark: "Deserted May 10, 1863, and supposed reenlisted in some Louisiana regiment."

BISHOP, IRA T., Private
Resided in Beaufort County where he enlisted at age 19, May 10, 1861, for the war. Present or accounted for until captured near Spotsylvania Court House, Virginia, on May 12, 1864. Confined at Point Lookout, Maryland, until transferred to Elmira, New York, on August 8, 1864. Released at Elmira after taking the Oath of Allegiance on June 19, 1865.

BOLT, JOHN, Private
Born in England and resided in Beaufort County

where he enlisted at age 35, May 10, 1861, for the war. Transferred to the C.S. Navy on January 22, 1862.

BRANTON, HENRY H., Private

Resided in Wake County where he enlisted at age 21, July 15, 1862, for the war. Present or accounted for until captured near Spotsylvania Court House, Virginia, on May 12, 1864. Confined at Point Lookout, Maryland, until transferred to Elmira, New York, on August 8, 1864. Died at Elmira on November 24, 1864, of "chronic diarrhoea."

BRINKLEY, WILLIAM S., Private

Resided in Wake County where he enlisted at age 32, July 15, 1862, for the war. Present or accounted for until captured at Frederick, Maryland, on September 12, 1862. Confined at Fort Delaware, Delaware, until paroled for exchange on December 15, 1862. Present or accounted for until captured near Spotsylvania Court House, Virginia, on May 12, 1864. Confined at Point Lookout, Maryland, until transferred to Elmira, New York, on August 8, 1864. Paroled at Elmira and sent to James River, Virginia, for exchange, February 13, 1865. Reported as present on a muster roll of a detachment of paroled and exchanged prisoners at Camp Lee, near Richmond, Virginia, dated February 23, 1865.

BROOKS, DANIEL S., Private

Resided in Beaufort County where he enlisted at age 27, May 10, 1861, for the war. Mustered in as Private and appointed Corporal on January 1, 1863. Present or accounted for until wounded on May 3, 1863, at Chancellorsville, Virginia. Reduced to ranks after December, 1863. Reported as absent wounded until detailed as a commissary agent in Beaufort County on May 1, 1864. Absent detailed until reported as absent without leave on December 20, 1864.

BROWN, ANDERTON, Private

Enlisted in Wake County on October 27, 1863, for the war. Wounded and captured at Mine Run, Virginia, November 27, 1863. Confined at 1st Division General Hospital, Alexandria, Virginia, where he died December 14, 1863, "of wound."

CAHOON, JAMES, Private

Born in Hyde County and resided as a seaman in Beaufort County where he enlisted at age 26, May 10, 1861, for the war. Transferred to the C.S. Navy on January 29, 1862.

CASH, ELKINS, Private

Resided in Wake County where he enlisted at age 36, July 15, 1862, for the war. Admitted to hospital at Richmond, Virginia, April 4, 1863, with "cont. fever" and was transferred to the hospital at Danville, Virginia, on April 20, 1863. Furloughed from that hospital for 30 days on May 13, 1863. Died May 23, 1863, at Danville, of disease.

CHAPMAN, JOHN, Private

Born in New York and resided as a seaman in Beaufort County where he enlisted at age 24, May 10, 1861, for the war. Transferred to the C.S. Navy on January 29, 1862.

CHAUNCEY, S. C., Private

Resided in Beaufort County where he enlisted at age 25, March 5, 1862, for the war. Present or accounted for until killed in battle at Chancellorsville, Virginia, on May 3, 1863.

CIVILS, JOSHUA, Private

Born in Beaufort County where he resided and enlisted at age 22, May 10, 1861, for the war. Present or accounted for until killed in battle at Sharpsburg, Maryland, on September 17, 1862.

CLARKE, JAMES FOREMAN, Sergeant

Resided in Beaufort County where he enlisted at age 19, May 10, 1861, for the war. Mustered in as Corporal and appointed Sergeant, January-February, 1862. Wounded near Richmond, Virginia, on July 1, 1862. Promoted to Sergeant Major and transferred to the Field and Staff of this regiment July 14-November 1, 1862.

CLARKE, WALTER, Corporal

Resided in Beaufort County where he enlisted at age 21, May 10, 1861, for the war. Mustered in as Corporal. Appointed Ordnance Sergeant and transferred to the Field and Staff of this regiment on August 28, 1862.

CONGLETON, ANDREW S., Private

Born in Beaufort County where he resided and enlisted at age 20, May 10, 1861, for the war. Present or accounted for until wounded at Sharpsburg, Maryland, on September 17, 1862. Died of his wounds on October 6, 1862, at Winchester, Virginia.

CROSS, THOMAS, Private

Resided in Wake County where he enlisted at age 38, July 15, 1862, for the war. Present or accounted for until wounded at Sharpsburg, Maryland, on September 17, 1862. Died of his wounds on October 15, 1862, at Frederick, Maryland.

CUTLER, ASA R., Private

Resided in Beaufort County and enlisted in Wayne County at age 27, April 18, 1862, for the war. Present or accounted for until wounded at Sharpsburg, Maryland, on September 17, 1862. Reported as absent wounded or absent sick from that date until detailed as a nurse in hospital at Liberty, Virginia, on December 22, 1863. Absent detailed through December, 1864. Paroled at Farmville, Virginia, April 11-21, 1865.

DANIELS, BANA, Private

Resided in Beaufort County where he enlisted at age 21, May 10, 1861, for the war. Present or accounted for until reported on the December 31, 1863-August 31, 1864, muster roll as being "in Beaufort County on a wounded furlough." Absent wounded through December, 1864. Date wounded not reported.

DANIELS, SAMUEL H., Private

Resided in Beaufort County where he enlisted at age 23, May 10, 1861, for the war. Present or accounted for until wounded on June 27, 1862, near Richmond, Virginia. Returned to duty January-February, 1863. Admitted to hospital at Richmond on May 2, 1863, with "gunshot wound, hip." Absent sick through December, 1863. Captured near Spotsylvania Court House, Virginia, May 12, 1864. Confined at Point Lookout, Maryland, until transferred to Elmira, New York, on August 10, 1864. Released at Elmira after taking the Oath of Allegiance on June 3, 1865.

DAVIS, HENRY L., Private
Transferred from 2nd Company G, 36th Regiment N.C. Troops (2nd Regiment N.C. Artillery) on February 1, 1862. Present or accounted for through December, 1864. Captured at Farmville, Virginia, April 6, 1865. Confined at Point Lookout, Maryland, until released after taking the Oath of Allegiance on June 26, 1865.

DAVIS, J. HYMAN, Private
Resided in Beaufort County where he enlisted at age 24, May 10, 1861, for the war. Died January 12, 1862, at Aquia Creek, Virginia.

DAVIS, JAMES H., Private
Born in Beaufort County where he resided and enlisted at age 18, May 10, 1861, for the war. Mortally wounded July 1, 1862, near Richmond, Virginia.

DAVIS, JOHN J., Private
Resided in Beaufort County where he enlisted at age 22, May 10, 1861, for the war. Present or accounted for until killed at Chancellorsville, Virginia, on May 2, 1863.

DAVIS, JOSEPH B., Private
Resided in Beaufort County where he enlisted at age 22, May 10, 1861, for the war. Present or accounted for until wounded at Sharpsburg, Maryland, September 17, 1862. Returned to duty January-February, 1863. Wounded at Chancellorsville, Virginia, May 3, 1863, and at Mine Run, Virginia, November 27-28, 1863. Absent wounded through December, 1863. Captured near Spotsylvania Court House, Virginia, May 12, 1864. Confined at Point Lookout, Maryland, until transferred to Elmira, New York, on August 10, 1864. Paroled at Elmira and sent to James River, Virginia, for exchange, March 14, 1865. Admitted to hospital at Richmond, Virginia, March 18, 1865.

DAVIS, WESLEY, Private
Resided in Wake County where he enlisted at age 36, July 15, 1862, for the war. Present or accounted for until killed at Gettysburg, Pennsylvania, July 3, 1863.

DAW, JOHN W., Private
Resided in Beaufort County where he enlisted at age 26, May 10, 1861, for the war. Died January 15, 1862, at Aquia Creek, Virginia.

DAY, JOHN W., 1st Sergeant
Resided in Beaufort County where he enlisted at age 23, May 10, 1861, for the war. Mustered in as Private and appointed Corporal, November-December, 1862. Promoted to Sergeant on March 1, 1863, and to 1st Sergeant on March 1, 1864. Present or accounted for until captured near Spotsylvania Court House, Virginia, on May 12, 1864. Confined at Point Lookout, Maryland, until transferred to Elmira, New York, August 10, 1864. Paroled at Elmira on February 13, 1865, and exchanged at Boulware's Wharf, James River, Virginia, February 20-21, 1865. Admitted to

hospital at Richmond, Virginia, on February 20, 1865, and was furloughed for 30 days on March 6, 1865.

ELMORE, A. C., Private
Enlisted in Wake County on October 27, 1863, for the war. Deserted at Raccoon Ford, Virginia, November 20, 1863.

ELMORE, JOSEPH R., Private
Enlisted in Wake County on October 27, 1863, for the war. Deserted at Raccoon Ford, Virginia, November 20, 1863. Federal Provost Marshal records report him as a "rebel deserter" confined at Knoxville, Tennessee, January 14, 1865. Released after taking the Oath of Allegiance on January 15, 1865.

FERRELL, WILLIAM B., Private
Resided in Wake County where he enlisted at age 23, July 15, 1862, for the war. Wounded at Sharpsburg, Maryland, September 17, 1862. Present or accounted for until captured at Spotsylvania Court House, Virginia, May 12, 1864. Confined at Point Lookout, Maryland, until transferred to Elmira, New York, August 10, 1864. Released at Elmira after taking the Oath of Allegiance on June 14, 1865.

FLYNN, WILLIAM S., Sergeant
Resided in Beaufort County where he enlisted at age 18, May 10, 1861, for the war. Mustered in as Private. Wounded at Malvern Hill, Virginia, July 1, 1862. Captured at Boonsboro, Maryland, September 14, 1862, and paroled and exchanged at Aiken's Landing, James River, Virginia, November 10, 1862. Appointed Corporal on March 1, 1863. Wounded at Payne's Farm, Virginia, November 27, 1863, and promoted to Sergeant on March 11, 1864. Transferred to Company I, 2nd Regiment N.C. Junior Reserves upon appointment as Captain on September 20, 1864.

FORBES, SAMUEL HARVEY, Sergeant
Resided in Beaufort County where he enlisted at age 30, May 10, 1861, for the war. Mustered in as Sergeant. Present or accounted for until transferred to 2nd Company G, 36th Regiment N.C. Troops (2nd Regiment N.C. Artillery) February 1, 1862.

FORT, DAVID FOSTER, Private
Resided in Wake County where he enlisted at age 22, July 15, 1862, for the war. Wounded at Gettysburg, Pennsylvania, July 2, 1863, and captured in hospital at Gettysburg July 4-5, 1863. Confined at DeCamp General Hospital, Davids Island, New York Harbor, until paroled and exchanged at City Point, Virginia, September 28, 1863. Detailed on March 11, 1864, and assigned to Captain Samuel B. Waters' Company, Provost Guard, Raleigh. Reported on rolls of Captain Waters' Company through January, 1865.

GASKILL, WILLIAM A., Private
Born in Beaufort County where he resided as a seaman and enlisted at age 23, May 10, 1861, for the war. Discharged on November 6, 1861, by reason of "epilepsy."

GAYLARD, AUGUSTUS, Sergeant
Born in Beaufort County where he resided and

enlisted at age 20, May 10, 1861, for the war. Mustered in as Private and appointed Corporal, July 14-November 1, 1862. Wounded at Sharpsburg, Maryland, September 17, 1862, and died at Richmond, Virginia, October 16, 1862. Promoted to Sergeant, November-December, 1862, before his death was reported to the company.

GLENN, DUNCAN C., Private
Born in Orange County and resided as a farmer in Wake County where he enlisted at age 35, July 15, 1862, for the war. Died in hospital at Richmond, Virginia, September 1, 1862.

GLENN, PAUL PRY, Private
Resided in Wake County where he enlisted at age 28, July 15, 1862, for the war. Wounded at Chancellorsville, Virginia, May 3, 1863. Wounded at Gettysburg, Pennsylvania, July 2, 1863, and captured at Gettysburg July 4-5, 1863. Confined at DeCamp General Hospital, Davids Island, New York Harbor, until paroled and exchanged at City Point, Virginia, August 28, 1863. Wounded September 22, 1864. Present or accounted for until paroled at Burkeville, Virginia, April 14-17, 1865.

GLENN, WILLIAM R., Private
Resided in Wake County where he enlisted at age 26, July 15, 1862, for the war. Wounded at Chancellorsville, Virginia, May 3, 1863, and at Payne's Farm, Virginia, November 27, 1863. Admitted to hospital at Richmond, Virginia, December 1, 1863, and furloughed from hospital on January 12, 1864, for 60 days. Reported as absent wounded through December, 1864.

GOOCH, CHARLES H., Private
Resided in Wake County where he enlisted at age 34, July 15, 1862, for the war. Captured at Williamsport, Maryland, September 15, 1862, and paroled and exchanged at Aiken's Landing, James River, Virginia, November 10, 1862. Detailed as wagoner on February 1, 1863. Absent on detail when captured at Spotsylvania Court House, Virginia, May 12, 1864. Confined at Point Lookout, Maryland, until transferred to Elmira, New York, August 6, 1864. Released at Elmira after taking the Oath of Allegiance on June 12, 1865.

GORHAM, JAMES S., Sergeant
Born in Beaufort County where he resided and enlisted at age 20, May 10, 1861, for the war. Mustered in as Private and appointed Sergeant, July 14-August 31, 1862. Wounded at Sharpsburg, Maryland, September 17, 1862, and died October 1, 1862.

GRAY, WINSLOW, Private
Resided as a farmer in Wake County where he enlisted at age 27, July 15, 1862, for the war. Wounded and captured at Sharpsburg, Maryland, September 17, 1862. Confined at Fort Delaware, Delaware, until paroled on March 28, 1863. Sent to Fort Monroe, Virginia, for exchange. Admitted to hospital at Richmond, Virginia, May 2, 1863, and transferred to Lynchburg, Virginia, May 7, 1863. Discharged on July 6, 1863, by reason of "general imbecility of mind and body."

GREASON, ELI W., Private
Enlisted in Wake County on October 28, 1863,

for the war. Died at Orange Court House, Virginia, November 21, 1863, of disease.

GURGANUS, B. S., Private
Resided in Beaufort County where he enlisted at age 26, February 28, 1862, for the war. Died at Richmond, Virginia, August 15, 1862.

HAILEY, JOHN SIDNEY, Private
Resided in Wake County where he enlisted at age 22, July 15, 1862, for the war. Wounded at Gettysburg, Pennsylvania, July 2, 1863, and captured at Gettysburg July 4-5, 1863. Confined in hospital at Chester, Pennsylvania, until transferred to Point Lookout, Maryland, October 4, 1863. Paroled at Point Lookout on March 3, 1864, and exchanged at City Point, Virginia, March 6, 1864. Captured at Burkeville, Virginia, April 6, 1865, and confined at Newport News, Virginia. Released at Newport News after taking the Oath of Allegiance on June 27, 1865.

HARRISON, DAVID BRYANT, Private
Resided in Wake County where he enlisted at age 26, July 15, 1862, for the war. Captured at Frederick, Maryland, September 12, 1862, and paroled and exchanged at Aiken's Landing, James River, Virginia, November 10, 1862. Died in hospital at Richmond, Virginia, February 15, 1863, of "smallpox."

HARRISON, LOFTIN, Private
Resided in Wake County where he enlisted at age 28, July 15, 1862, for the war. Wounded at Winchester, Virginia, June 15, 1863. Reported as absent wounded until he "deserted January 16, 1864."

HARRISON, PHILANDER A., Private
Resided in Wake County where he enlisted at age 30, July 15, 1862, for the war. Captured at Frederick, Maryland, September 12, 1862, and paroled and exchanged at Aiken's Landing, James River, Virginia, November 10, 1862. Wounded at Gettysburg, Pennsylvania, July 2-3, 1863, and captured in hospital at Gettysburg July 4-5, 1863. Confined at DeCamp General Hospital, Davids Island, New York Harbor, until paroled and exchanged at City Point, Virginia, September 16, 1863. Reported as absent wounded until he "deserted January 16, 1864."

HENDON, G. A., Private
Resided in Wake County where he enlisted at age 26, July 15, 1862, for the war. Left sick at Frederick, Maryland, September 10, 1862, and reported as absent without leave after December 21, 1862. Reported on November-December, 1863, muster roll with the remark: "Deserted December 21, 1862, supposed dead."

HENDRICK, J. PHILLIP, Private
Enlisted on August 21, 1864, for the war. Wounded and captured at Winchester, Virginia, September 19, 1864. Confined at Point Lookout, Maryland, until paroled on October 31, 1864. Exchanged at Venus Point, Savannah River, Georgia, November 15, 1864. Paroled at Greensboro on May 10, 1865.

HIGH, CHRISTOPHER C., Private
Resided in Wake County where he enlisted at age 26, July 15, 1862, for the war. Detailed as a shoe-

maker at Richmond, Virginia, November 22, 1862, and reported as absent on detail through December, 1864. Paroled at Winchester, Virginia, April 21, 1865.

HIGH, JAMES, Private
Resided in Wake County where he enlisted at age 27, July 15, 1862, for the war. Captured at Frederick, Maryland, September 12, 1862, and paroled and exchanged at Aiken's Landing, James River, Virginia, November 9, 1862. Admitted to hospital at Richmond, Virginia, May 30, 1863, with "irratatis spinalis" and transferred to Raleigh on July 28, 1863. Reported as absent sick until detailed as a shoemaker at Raleigh on July 28, 1864. Absent on detail through December, 1864.

HINTON, JOSEPH J., Private
Born in Beaufort County where he resided and enlisted at age 35, May 10, 1861, for the war. Wounded at Sharpsburg, Maryland, September 17, 1862, and died at Winchester, Virginia, October 23, 1862.

HODGES, JOHN W., Private
Resided in Beaufort County where he enlisted at age 20, February 28, 1862, for the war. Wounded at Ellerson's Mill, Virginia, June 26, 1862. Absent sick until detailed as nurse at Wilson on March 1, 1863. Absent on detail as a nurse until detailed as a guard at Raleigh on October 16, 1863. Assigned to Captain Samuel B. Waters' Company, Provost Guard, Raleigh, and reported on rolls of that company through January, 1865.

HODGIN, WILLIAM V., Private
Resided in Chatham County and enlisted in Wake County on October 31, 1863, for the war. Captured at Spotsylvania Court House, Virginia, May 12, 1864, and confined at Point Lookout, Maryland. Released at Point Lookout after taking the Oath of Allegiance on June 27, 1865.

HOLLOMAN, ELIJAH, Private
Enlisted in Wake County on October 27, 1863, for the war. Deserted on March 12, 1864.

HOLLOMAN, JOHN, Private
Enlisted in Wake County on October 27, 1863, for the war. Wounded at Wilderness, Virginia, May 5, 1864, and reported as absent wounded through December, 1864.

HOSIER, JAMES E., Private
Resided in Beaufort County where he enlisted at age 22, May 10, 1861, for the war. Wounded June 27, 1862. Present or accounted for until transferred to Company C, 13th Regiment Virginia Cavalry on March 1, 1863.

HUTSPETH, ROBERT H., Private
Resided in Wake County where he enlisted at age 24, July 15, 1862, for the war. Captured at Frederick, Maryland, September 12, 1862, and paroled and exchanged at City Point, Virginia, December 18, 1862. Wounded at Payne's Farm, Virginia, November 27, 1863, and at Cedar Creek, Virginia, October 19, 1864. Captured at Burkeville, Virginia, April 6, 1865, and confined at Newport News, Virginia. Released at Newport News after taking the Oath of Allegiance.

IRELAND, AMOS, Sergeant
Resided in Beaufort County where he enlisted at age 22, May 10, 1861, for the war. Mustered in as Private and appointed Corporal, November-December, 1862. Wounded at Chancellorsville, Virginia, May 2, 1863. Promoted to Sergeant on June 1, 1863, and died of wound at Richmond, Virginia, July 7, 1863.

IRELAND, ARCHIBALD A., Private
Resided in Beaufort County where he enlisted at age 18, May 10, 1861, for the war. Present until admitted to hospital at Richmond, Virginia, May 10, 1863, with "ulcus." Furloughed for 30 days on July 16, 1863. Reported as absent without leave after August 15, 1863.

IRELAND, JO. W., Private
Resided in Beaufort County and enlisted in Wayne County at age 23, April 29, 1862, for the war. Wounded at Malvern Hill, Virginia, July 1, 1862. Deserted from hospital at Wilson on April 9, 1863.

JACKSON, MATTHEW W., Private
Born in Wake County where he resided and enlisted at age 33, July 15, 1862, for the war. Died in hospital at Gordonsville, Virginia, September 2, 1862, of "typhoid fever."

JOAB, W. A., Private
Enlisted in Wake County on August 21, 1864, for the war. Captured at Winchester, Virginia, September 19, 1864, and confined at Point Lookout, Maryland. Paroled at Point Lookout on March 15, 1865, and exchanged at Boulware's Wharf, James River, Virginia, March 18, 1865. Paroled on May 4, 1865.

JONES, EDWIN G., Private
Born in Beaufort County where he resided and enlisted at age 25, May 10, 1861, for the war. Killed at Sharpsburg, Maryland, September 17, 1862.

JONES, MAC M., Private
Resided in Wake County where he enlisted at age 32, July 15, 1862, for the war. Captured in Maryland in September, 1862, and paroled on September 27, 1862. Died in Wake County on March 15, 1864, of disease.

JONES, NORFLEET B., Private
Resided in Wake County where he enlisted at age 24, July 15, 1862, for the war. Captured at Williamsport, Maryland, September 15, 1862, and paroled and exchanged at Aiken's Landing, James River, Virginia, November 10, 1862. Wounded at Wilderness, Virginia, May 5, 1864, and wounded and captured at Winchester, Virginia, September 19, 1864. Died of wound in field hospital near Winchester on September 21, 1864.

KEITH, ANDERSON C., Private
Resided in Wake County where he enlisted at age 26, July 15, 1862, for the war. Captured in Maryland in September, 1862, and paroled and exchanged November 12, 1862. Wounded at Gettysburg, Pennsylvania, July 2, 1863, and captured July 3, 1863. Died in hospital at Gettysburg on August 1, 1863.

KING, AISGALL, Private
Resided in Wake County where he enlisted at age

25, July 15, 1862, for the war. Wounded at Gettysburg, Pennsylvania, July 2-3, 1863. Present or accounted for until captured at Spotsylvania Court House, Virginia, May 12, 1864. Confined at Point Lookout, Maryland, until transferred to Elmira, New York, August 10, 1864. Died at Elmira on March 29, 1865, of "variola."

KING, DAVID A., Private

Born in Wake County where he resided and enlisted at age 36, July 15, 1862, for the war. Killed at Sharpsburg, Maryland, September 17, 1862.

LANGLEY, B. A., Private

Resided in Beaufort County where he enlisted at age 22, May 10, 1861, for the war. Present or accounted for until his leg was broken in a collision on the railroad near Halifax, N. C., in April, 1862. Hospital records state that his leg was later amputated on May 15, 1863. Reported on company muster rolls as absent disabled through December, 1864. Transferred from the hospital at Charlottesville, Virginia, to Raleigh, April 6, 1865.

LANIER, JOHN, Private

Resided in Beaufort County where he enlisted at age 22, May 10, 1861, for the war. Present or accounted for until wounded on May 3, 1863, at Chancellorsville, Virginia. Died of his wounds on May 17, 1863.

LASSITER, WESLEY, Private

Resided in Wake County where he enlisted at age 34, July 15, 1862, for the war. Captured near Fredericksburg, Virginia, May 3, 1863, and paroled and exchanged at City Point, Virginia, May 13, 1863. Killed at Gettysburg, Pennsylvania, July 3, 1863.

LATHAM, JAMES H., Private

Resided in Beaufort County where he enlisted at age 19, May 10, 1861, for the war. Reported as absent sick from August 19, 1862, through December, 1862, and again from May 2, 1863, through July, 1863. Present or accounted for from that date until his death on March 1, 1864, at Orange Court House, Virginia, of disease.

LEGGETT, BARTLETT, Musician

Negro. Enlisted in Beaufort County at age 42, May 10, 1861, for the war. Mustered in as Musician. Present or accounted for through December, 1864.

LEGGETT, MARSHALL W., Private

Born in Beaufort County where he resided as a farmer and enlisted at age 25, May 10, 1861, for the war. Discharged November 21, 1861, by reason of disability caused by "injury to the spine received by a fall."

LEWELL, JAMES H., Private

Paroled at Raleigh on April 20, 1865.

LEWIS, B. T., Private

Resided in Beaufort County where he enlisted at age 22, May 10, 1861, for the war. Present or accounted for until wounded on July 1, 1862, near Richmond, Virginia. Captured at Boonsboro, Maryland, September 15, 1862. Paroled and exchanged at Aiken's Landing, Virginia, November 10, 1862. Reported as absent without leave until he deserted on May 10, 1863.

LILLY, E. G., Musician

Born in Beaufort County. Company muster rolls do not give date, place, or period of enlistment but report that he died at Fredericksburg, Virginia, on August 4, 1861.

LITCHFIELD, GEORGE A., Private

Resided in Hyde County and enlisted in Wayne County at age 22, April 5, 1862, for the war. Present or accounted for until transferred to Company E, 4th Regiment N.C. State Troops on August 1, 1863.

LONG, MONTGOMERY, Private

Resided in Beaufort County where he enlisted at age 32, May 16, 1861, for the war. Discharged August 13, 1861, by reason of disability.

LOWRY, W. G., Private

Born in Wake County where he resided as a farmer and enlisted at age 35, July 15, 1862, for the war. Died November 30, 1862, at Gordonsville, Virginia, from disease.

McDEVITT, WILLIAM P., 1st Sergeant

Resided in Beaufort County where he enlisted at age 41, May 10, 1861, for the war. Mustered in as Sergeant. Present or accounted for until wounded on June 27, 1862, near Richmond, Virginia. Absent sick until reported as absent without leave on December 21, 1862. Promoted to 1st Sergeant while absent sick and was reduced to ranks on January 1, 1863. Returned to duty February 28-May 15, 1863. Again appointed Sergeant on September 1, 1863, and promoted to 1st Sergeant on December 1, 1863. Captured on December 30, 1863, near Washington, D.C. Confined at Point Lookout, Maryland, until paroled and sent to City Point, Virginia, for exchange on April 27, 1864. Admitted to hospital at Richmond on May 1, 1864, with "diarrhoea chronic" and was furloughed for 30 days on May 12, 1864. Died July 1, 1864, at Washington, N.C., of disease.

MACON, ISAAC, Private

Enlisted in Wake County, August 21, 1864, for the war. Captured at Winchester, Virginia, September 19, 1864. Confined at Point Lookout, Maryland, where he died October 11, 1864, of "chronic diarrhoea."

MARTIN, W. H., Private

Resided in Wake County where he enlisted at age 33, July 15, 1862, for the war. Present or accounted for until wounded at Chancellorsville, Virginia, on May 2, 1863. Killed at Gettysburg, Pennsylvania, on July 3, 1863.

MEDLIN, H. R., Private

Resided in Wake County where he enlisted at age 33, July 15, 1862, for the war. Present or accounted for until wounded at Chancellorsville, Virginia, on May 3, 1863. Died at Chancellorsville on May 17, 1863, of his wounds.

MEDLIN, W. HENRY, Private

Resided in Wake County where he enlisted at age 38, July 15, 1862, for the war. Present or accounted for until wounded and captured at Sharpsburg, Maryland, on September 17-18, 1862. Paroled and exchanged at City Point, Virginia, December 18, 1862. Admitted to hospital at Petersburg, Virginia, December 18, 1862, with "gunshot wound right thigh and left ankle." Furloughed for 60 days on

January 17, 1863. Reported as absent sick until detailed to Captain Samuel B. Waters' Company, Provost Guard, Raleigh, on March 8, 1864. Absent detailed through December, 1864.

MERRILL, DANIEL, Private
Born in New York and resided as a seaman in Beaufort County where he enlisted at age 27, May 10, 1861, for the war. Present or accounted for until transferred to the C.S. Navy on January 22, 1862.

MURRAY, ALVIN, Private
Enlisted in Wake County on August 21, 1864, for the war. Present or accounted for until reported as absent sick on November 10, 1864. Absent sick through December, 1864. Paroled at Appomattox Court House, Virginia, April 9, 1865.

NEAL, JONATHAN, Corporal
Resided in Hyde County and enlisted in Beaufort County at age 18, May 10, 1861, for the war. Mustered in as Private. Present or accounted for until wounded at Sharpsburg, Maryland, on September 17, 1862. Absent wounded until returned to duty January-February, 1863. Appointed Corporal on December 1, 1863. Present or accounted for through December, 1864. Paroled at Appomattox Court House, Virginia, April 9, 1865.

NEAL, LEMUEL, Private
Born in Beaufort County and resided in Hyde County prior to enlisting in Beaufort County at age 22, May 10, 1861, for the war. Present or accounted for until wounded at Malvern Hill, Virginia, on July 1, 1862. Died at Richmond, Virginia, on August 5, 1862, of his wounds.

NIPPER, JACOB, Private
Resided in Wake County where he enlisted at age 24, July 15, 1862, for the war. Wounded and captured at Sharpsburg, Maryland, September 17, 1862. Date of parole and exchange not shown on records. Company muster rolls report him as absent prisoner until admitted to hospital at Richmond, Virginia, on May 2, 1863, with "gunshot wound." Returned to duty May 15-August 11, 1863. Present or accounted for until he appears as absent sick from September through December, 1864. Paroled at Lynchburg, Virginia, on April 15, 1865.

NORMAN, JAMES F., Private
Enlisted in Wake County on October 27, 1863, for the war. Deserted November 20, 1863.

PADGETT, ASA J., Private
Resided in Beaufort County where he enlisted at age 21, May 10, 1861, for the war. Present or accounted for until detailed as a pioneer on February 1, 1863. Absent on detail through December, 1863. Captured at Spotsylvania Court House, Virginia, May 12, 1864. Confined at Point Lookout, Maryland, until transferred to Elmira, New York, on August 10, 1864. Died at Elmira on September 12, 1864, of "typhoid fever."

PADGETT, LEWIS H., Private
Born in Beaufort County where he resided as a farmer and enlisted at age 22, May 10, 1861, for the war. Present or accounted for until wounded in picket skirmish on Williamsburg Road near

Richmond, Virginia, on June 22, 1862. Discharged July 28, 1862, by reason of disability caused by wound.

PARISH, HILLSMAN, Private
Born in Wake County and resided as a seaman in Beaufort County where he enlisted at age 20, May 10, 1861, for the war. Present or accounted for until transferred to the C.S. Navy on January 29, 1862.

PATRICK, THOMAS L., Private
Resided in Craven County where he enlisted at age 20, July 22, 1861, for the war. Present or accounted for until wounded at Sharpsburg, Maryland, on September 17, 1862. Absent wounded until returned to duty on January 20, 1863. Wounded at Chancellorsville, Virginia, May 3, 1863, and died of his wounds in hospital at Richmond, Virginia, on May 28, 1863.

PERDUE, MAJOR, Private
Enlisted in Wake County on October 27, 1863, for the war. Wounded at Mine Run, Virginia, November 27-28, 1863. Deserted March 20, 1864.

PHILLIPS, JOSEPH L., Private
Paroled at Charlotte on May 24, 1865.

PINNIX, GEORGE, Private
Enlisted in Wake County on October 27, 1863, for the war. Deserted November 23, 1863, at Morton's Ford, Virginia.

PINNIX, WILLIAM, Private
Enlisted in Wake County on November 1, 1863, for the war. Deserted November 23, 1863, at Morton's Ford, Virginia.

POTTER, SAMUEL, Private
Resided in Beaufort County where he enlisted at age 35, May 10, 1861, for the war. Present or accounted for until reported on the May 15-August 11, 1863, muster roll as absent sick. Detailed for hospital duty at Richmond, Virginia, September 9, 1863. Absent detailed until returned to duty in December, 1863. Captured near Spotsylvania Court House, Virginia, May 12, 1864. Confined at Point Lookout, Maryland, until transferred to Elmira, New York, on August 10, 1864. Released at Elmira after taking the Oath of Allegiance on June 27, 1865.

QUINN, LEWIS C., Private
Temporarily attached to this company from Company K, 10th Regiment N.C. State Troops (1st Regiment N.C. Artillery) when his company was captured at Fort Hatteras on August 29, 1861. Returned to that company after it was exchanged in February, 1862.

RAY, ELISHA B., Private
Born and resided in Wake County. Date, place, or period of enlistment is not shown on records. Died in hospital at Richmond, Virginia, on October 1, 1862, of disease.

RAY, JAMES, Private
Resided in Wake County where he enlisted at age 21, July 15, 1862, for the war. Wounded and captured at South Mountain or Antietam, Maryland, September 15-17, 1862. Died of "gunshot" at U.S.A. General Hospital, Frederick, Maryland, on October 15, 1862.

RAY, THOMAS N., Private
Born in Granville County and resided as a farmer in Wake County where he enlisted at age 31, July 15, 1862, for the war. Discharged October 26, 1862, by reason of disability caused by "enlarged stomach and liver of several months standing, and dilitation of the heart."

RAY, WILLIS, Private
Resided in Wake County where he enlisted at age 25, July 15, 1862, for the war. Captured at Frederick, Maryland, on September 12, 1862. Paroled and exchanged November 10, 1862, at Aiken's Landing, James River, Virginia. Present or accounted for until wounded and captured at Gettysburg, Pennsylvania, July 2, 1863. Died of wounds on July 7, 1863, at Gettysburg.

REDDISH, GARRETT, Private
Resided in Wake County where he enlisted at age 28, July 15, 1862, for the war. Wounded at Payne's Farm, Virginia, November 27, 1863. Present or accounted for through December, 1864. Captured at Burkeville, Virginia, April 6, 1865, and confined at Newport News, Virginia. Released at Newport News after taking the Oath of Allegiance on June 27, 1865.

REDDISH, WILLIAM, Private
Resided in Wake County where he enlisted at age 32, July 15, 1862, for the war. Died in hospital at Richmond, Virginia, May 7, 1863, of disease.

RESPESS, RICHARD F., Private
Resided in Beaufort County where he enlisted at age 20, May 10, 1861, for the war. Present or accounted for until captured near Washington, N.C., February 10, 1864. Confined at Point Lookout, Maryland, where he died February 28, 1864, of "nostalgia."

RESPESS, WILLIAM O., Private
Resided in Beaufort County where he enlisted at age 20, May 10, 1861, for the war. Present or accounted for until transferred to Company K, 10th Regiment N.C. State Troops (1st Regiment N.C. Artillery) May 5, 1862.

RICHARDSON, HORATIO N., Private
Resided in Beaufort County where he enlisted at age 31, May 10, 1861, for the war. Wounded at Ellerson's Mill, Virginia, June 26, 1862. Admitted to hospital at Richmond, Virginia, May 2, 1863, and transferred to Lynchburg, Virginia, May 11, 1863. Detailed as a nurse in hospital at Lynchburg on November 22, 1863. Returned to company prior to May, 1864. Captured at Spotsylvania Court House, Virginia, May 12, 1864, and confined at Point Lookout, Maryland. Transferred on August 10, 1864, to Elmira, New York, where he remained until paroled on October 11, 1864. Exchanged at Venus Point, Savannah River, Georgia, November 15, 1864.

ROSS, GEORGE W., Private
Born in Beaufort County where he resided and enlisted at age 20, May 10, 1861, for the war. Wounded at Sharpsburg, Maryland, September 17, 1862, and died from wound on October 30, 1862.

RUSSELL, BENJAMIN F., Corporal
Resided in Hyde County and enlisted in Beaufort

County at age 30, February 20, 1862, for the war. Mustered in as Private and appointed Corporal, January-April, 1864. Present or accounted for until captured at Spotsylvania Court House, Virginia, May 12, 1864. Confined at Point Lookout, Maryland, and transferred to Elmira, New York, August 10, 1864. Released at Elmira after taking the Oath of Allegiance on July 11, 1865.

SADLER, R. B., Private
Enlisted in Beaufort County, March-April, 1862, for the war. Never reported to company since he "enlisted improperly."

SADLER, S. R., Private
Enlisted in Beaufort County, March-April, 1862, for the war. Never reported to company since he "enlisted improperly."

SATCHWELL, WILLIAM BENJAMIN, Private
Born in Beaufort County where he resided and enlisted at age 18, May 10, 1861, for the war. Died in hopital at Richmond, Virginia, September 29, 1862, of "dysenteria chronic."

SAWYER, JESSE, Private
Resided in Beaufort County where he enlisted at age 23, May 10, 1861, for the war. Wounded at Sharpsburg, Maryland, September 17, 1862. Admitted to hospital at Richmond, Virginia, May 2, 1863, with "diarrhoea acuta." Transferred on May 9, 1863, and died in hospital at Wilson on September 9, 1863, of "phthisis pulmonalis."

SAWYER, WILLIAM C., Private
Born in Beaufort County where he resided and enlisted at age 28, May 10, 1861, for the war. Captured and paroled at Paris, Virginia, November 5, 1862. Killed at Chancellorsville, Virginia, May 3, 1863.

SAWYER, WILLIAM J., Private
Born in Beaufort County where he resided and enlisted at age 19, June 28, 1861, for the war. Died in hospital at Fredericksburg, Virginia, August 25, 1861, of disease.

SAWYER, ZION W., Private
Born in Beaufort County where he resided and enlisted at age 23, May 10, 1861, for the war. Died in hospital at Richmond, Virginia, June 26, 1862, of "rubeola."

SCHRADER, J. H., Private
Captured in hospital at Richmond, Virginia, April 3, 1865, and "escaped from hospital April 20, 1865."

SCOTT, JAMES, Private
Born in Wake County where he resided and enlisted at age 30, July 15, 1862, for the war. Died in hospital at Richmond, Virginia, December 28, 1862, of "variola."

SHALLINGTON, WILLIAM E., Private
Resided in Beaufort County where he enlisted at age 21, May 10, 1861, for the war. Mustered in as Corporal and reduced to ranks July 14-November 1, 1862. Transferred to Captain William H. Spencer's Company (Independent Cavalry) upon appointment as 1st Lieutenant to rank from January 7, 1863.

SHEPPARD, JOHN, Private
Resided in Beaufort County where he enlisted

at age 27, May 10, 1861, for the war. Present or accounted for until transferred to C.S. Navy February 20, 1862.

SMITH, ALFRED, Private
Enlisted in Wake County on August 21, 1864, for the war. Captured at Winchester, Virginia, September 19, 1864, and confined at Point Lookout, Maryland. Paroled at Point Lookout on March 15, 1865, and exchanged at Boulware's Wharf, James River, Virginia, March 18, 1865. Paroled at Salisbury on May 24, 1865.

SNEAD, ROBERT, Private
Resided in Wake County where he enlisted at age 29, July 15, 1862, for the war. Deserted December 21, 1862.

SPIKES, WILLIAM, Private
Born in Wake County where he resided and enlisted at age 32, July 15, 1862, for the war. Died in hospital at Lynchburg, Virginia, December 3, 1862, of "pneumonia."

STAILY, DAVID J., Private
Enlisted in Wake County on August 21, 1864, for the war. Paroled at Appomattox Court House, Virginia, April 9, 1865.

STAILY, JOSEPH B., Private
Enlisted in Wake County on August 21, 1864, for the war. Wounded and captured at Winchester, Virginia, September 19, 1864. Confined at Point Lookout, Maryland, until paroled on October 30, 1864. Exchanged at Venus Point, Savannah River, Georgia, November 15, 1864. Paroled at Greensboro on May 5, 1865.

STANLY, JAMES, Private
Resided in Wake County where he enlisted at age 33, July 15, 1862, for the war. Wounded at Gettysburg, Pennsylvania, July 2, 1863, and captured in hospital at Gettysburg July 4-5, 1863. Died in hospital at Gettysburg July 16, 1863, of wound.

STEWART, JOHN W., Private
Resided in Beaufort County and enlisted in Craven County at age 20, June 28, 1861, for the war. Wounded at Ellerson's Mill, Virginia, June 26, 1862, and at Sharpsburg, Maryland, September 17, 1862. Wounded a third time at Gettysburg, Pennsylvania, July 2, 1863. Deserted to the enemy at Washington, N.C., January 1, 1864, and took the Oath of Allegiance at Fort Monroe, Virginia, May 10, 1864.

STONE, BERRY, Private
Resided in Beaufort County where he enlisted at age 48, May 10, 1861, for the war. Detailed in Commissary Department, June 1, 1862, and returned to company in December, 1862. Detailed as a nurse in hospital at Petersburg, Virginia, March 16, 1863, and remained on detail until returned to company in October, 1864. Reported as present with the company until detailed on January 23, 1865. Admitted to hospital at Richmond, Virginia, March 3, 1865, and furloughed for 60 days.

SURRATT, WHITSON H., Private
Enlisted in Wake County on August 21, 1864, for the war. Captured at Winchester, Virginia, September 19, 1864, and confined at Point Lookout, Maryland. Died at Point Lookout on January 8, 1865, of "typhoid fever."

SWINDELL, J. W., Private
Resided in Beaufort County where he enlisted at age 26, January 8, 1862, for the war. Died in hospital at Richmond, Virginia, April 20, 1862, of disease.

TAYLOR, ANDREW, Private
Born in Louisiana and resided as a mechanic in Beaufort County where he enlisted at age 23, May 10, 1861, for the war. Present or accounted for until transferred to C.S. Navy on January 22, 1862.

TAYLOR, GEORGE, Private
Born in Edgecombe County and resided in Wake County where he enlisted at age 25, July 15, 1862, for the war. Died in hospital at Lynchburg, Virginia, May 13, 1863, of disease.

THOMASON, PRESLEY Y., Private
Resided in Wake County where he enlisted at age 24, July 15, 1862, for the war. Captured in Maryland in September, 1862, and paroled and exchanged at Aiken's Landing, James River, Virginia, November 10, 1862. Present or accounted for until captured at Spotsylvania Court House, Virginia, May 12, 1864. Confined at Point Lookout, Maryland, until transferred to Elmira, New York, August 10, 1864. Released at Elmira after taking the Oath of Allegiance on June 27, 1865.

TILLEY, JOHN B., Private
Resided in Wake County where he enlisted at age 28, July 15, 1862, for the war. Captured in Maryland in September, 1862, and "confined September 28, 1862." Admitted to hospital at Richmond, Virginia, October 14, 1862, and furloughed February 23, 1863, for 30 days. Died in hospital at Orange Court House, Virginia, November 25, 1863, of disease.

TILLEY, STEPHEN D., Private
Resided in Wake County where he enlisted at age 26, July 15, 1862, for the war. Reported as absent sick from December, 1862, through December, 1863. Present or accounted for on company muster rolls through December, 1864. Captured at Farmville, Virginia, April 6, 1865, and confined at Newport News, Virginia. Released at Newport News after taking the Oath of Allegiance on June 15, 1865.

TINGLE, BERNIE S., Private
Resided in Beaufort County where he enlisted at age 21, May 10, 1861, for the war. Wounded at Sharpsburg, Maryland, September 17, 1862. Present or accounted for until captured at Spotsylvania Court House, Virginia, May 12, 1864. Confined at Point Lookout, Maryland, until transferred to Elmira, New York, August 10, 1864. Released at Elmira after taking the Oath of Allegiance on June 27, 1865.

TOOKER, CHARLES, Private
Resided in Beaufort County where he enlisted at age 44, May 10, 1861, for the war. Mustered in as Sergeant and reduced to ranks when transferred to C.S. Navy on February 11, 1862.

WALLACE, SAMUEL, Private
Enlisted in Wake County on October 27, 1863, for the war. Deserted on November 17, 1863.

WALLING, WILLIAM, Private
Resided in Beaufort County where he enlisted at age 32, May 10, 1861, for the war. Mustered in as Private and appointed Corporal, January-February, 1862. Captured in Maryland in September, 1862, and paroled on September 30, 1862. Promoted to Sergeant, November-December, 1862. Reduced to ranks January 1, 1863, and deserted May 10, 1863.

WALTERS, ASA W., Private
Resided in Beaufort County where he enlisted at age 21, May 10, 1861, for the war. Present or accounted for until captured at Winchester, Virginia, September 19, 1864. Confined at Point Lookout, Maryland, until paroled on March 15, 1865. Exchanged at Boulware's Wharf, James River, Virginia, March 18, 1865.

WARD, JAMES, Private
Born in New Hanover County and resided as a seaman in Beaufort County where he enlisted at age 27, July 18, 1861, for the war. Present or accounted for until transferred to the C.S. Navy January 22, 1862.

WARD, JAMES H., Private
Born in Pasquotank County and resided as a seaman in Beaufort County where he enlisted at age 34, May 10, 1861, for the war. Present or accounted for until transferred to the C.S. Navy January 22, 1862.

WARREN, MILES C., Private
Resided in Beaufort County where he enlisted at age 30, February 25, 1862, for the war. Wounded in May, 1864. Present or accounted for on company muster rolls through December, 1864. Captured at Farmville, Virginia, April 6, 1865, and confined at Newport News, Virginia. Released at Newport News after taking the Oath of Allegiance on June 27, 1865.

WARREN, THOMAS H., Private
Resided in Beaufort County where he enlisted at age 28, February 25, 1862, for the war. Wounded at Winchester, Virginia, September 19, 1864. Present or accounted for on company muster rolls through December, 1864.

WHITLEY, ANDREW M., Private
Resided in Beaufort County where he enlisted at age 23, May 10, 1861, for the war. Mustered in as Private and appointed Corporal in January-February, 1862. Detailed in Commissary Department on July 12, 1862, and reduced to ranks. Reported as absent on detail through July, 1863, and as absent sick from August, 1863, through December, 1864.

WILKINSON, DAVID B., Sergeant
Resided in Beaufort County where he enlisted at age 18, May 10, 1861, for the war. Mustered in as Private. Wounded at Ellerson's Mill, Virginia, June 26, 1862. Appointed 1st Sergeant on February 1, 1863. Wounded at Gettysburg, Pennsylvania, July 2-3, 1863, and captured at Waterloo, Pennsylvania, July 5, 1863. Confined at Fort Delaware, Delaware, until transferred to Point Lookout, Maryland, October 15-18, 1863. Reduced to Sergeant, November-December, 1863, while absent in confinement. Paroled at Point Lookout on October 30, 1864, and exchanged at Venus Point, Savannah River, Georgia, November 10, 1864. Captured at Farmville, Virginia, April 6, 1865, and confined at Point Lookout. Released at Point Lookout after taking the Oath of Allegiance on June 21, 1865.

WILKINSON, SAMUEL J., Private
Resided as a teacher in Beaufort County where he enlisted at age 20, May 10, 1861, for the war. Wounded at Chancellorsville, Virginia, May 3, 1863, and reported as absent wounded from May, 1863, until he returned to the company September-October, 1864. Captured and paroled at Farmville, Virginia, April 11-21, 1865.

WILLIAMS, J. J., Private
Captured at South Mountain, Maryland, September 12, 1862, and paroled and exchanged at Aiken's Landing, James River, Virginia, November 10, 1862.

WINDLEY, HORACE A., Private
Born in Beaufort County where he resided and enlisted at age 23, May 10, 1861, for the war. Died in hospital at Richmond, Virginia, September 6, 1862, of "febris typhoides."

WINDLEY, WILLIAM BARROW, Private
Resided in Beaufort County where he enlisted at age 28, May 10, 1861, for the war. Mustered in as Private. Wounded at Mechanicsville, Virginia, June 26, 1862. Appointed Corporal, July 14-November 1, 1862,'' and promoted to Sergeant, November-December, 1862. Reduced to ranks February 1, 1863, after having been appointed 1st Lieutenant in Captain Edward S. Swindell's Company (Partisan Rangers) to rank from January 20, 1863.

WINDLEY, WYRIOTT A., Sergeant
Born in Beaufort County where he resided and enlisted at age 26, May 10, 1861, for the war. Mustered in as Private and appointed Sergeant, July 14-September 30, 1862. Died in hospital at Richmond, Virginia, September 30, 1862, of "typhoid fever."

WINFIELD, SAMUEL T., Private
Resided in Beaufort County where he enlisted at age 22, May 10, 1861, for the war. Present or accounted for until wounded at Wilderness, Virginia, May 5, 1864. Died of wound on June 5, 1864.

WINFIELD, WILLIAM D., Private
Born in Beaufort County where he resided as a carpenter and enlisted at age 26, May 10, 1861, for the war. Discharged July 24, 1862, by reason of "blindness."

WINFREE, W. H. T., Private
Born in Wilkes County and resided as a carpenter in Wake County where he enlisted at age 29, July 15, 1862, for the war. Discharged December 6, 1862, by reason of "pulmonary tuberculosis."

WINSTEAD, S. S., Private

Captured at Frederick, Maryland, September 12, 1862, and paroled and exchanged at Aiken's Landing, James River, Virginia, November 10, 1862. Issued clothing at Richmond, Virginia, November 23, 1863.

WOODARD, JOHN H. W., Sergeant

Resided in Beaufort County where he enlisted at age 26, May 10, 1861, for the war. Mustered in as Corporal and promoted to Sergeant, January-February, 1862. Reduced to ranks May 15, 1863. Wounded and captured at Gettysburg, Pennsylvania, July 3, 1863. Confined at Fort Delaware, Delaware, until transferred to Point Lookout, Maryland, October 15-18, 1863. Paroled at Point Lookout on March 3, 1864, and exchanged at City Point, Virginia, March 6, 1864. Reappointed Sergeant to rank from December 1, 1863. Reported on company muster rolls as absent without leave from June 1, 1864, through December, 1864. Captured at Farmville, Virginia, April 6, 1865, and confined at Newport News, Virginia. Released at Newport News after taking the Oath of Allegiance on June 27, 1865.

WOOLARD, WILSON B., Private

Born in Beaufort County where he resided and enlisted at age 22, May 10, 1861, for the war. Died in hospital at Harrisonburg, Virginia, December 29, 1862, of disease.

YERBY, JAMES, Private

Resided in Wake County where he enlisted at age 38, July 15, 1862, for the war. Present or accounted for until captured at Spotsylvania Court House, Virginia, May 12, 1864. Confined at Point Lookout, Maryland, until transferred to Elmira, New York, August 10, 1864. Paroled at Elmira on February 13, 1865, and exchanged at Boulware's Wharf, James River, Virginia, February 20-21, 1865. Reported as present at Camp Lee, near Richmond, Virginia, February 23, 1865.

COMPANY K

This company, known as the "Holly Shelter Volunteers," was organized in New Hanover County and enlisted at Dogwood Grove on June 1, 1861. It tendered its service to the state and was ordered to Garysburg, Northampton County, where it was assigned to this regiment as Company K. After joining the regiment the company functioned as a part of the regiment, and its history for the war period is recorded as a part of the regimental history.

The information contained in the following roster of the company was compiled principally from company muster rolls which covered from the date of enlistment through December, 1864. No company muster rolls were found for the period after December, 1864. In addition to the company muster rolls, Roll of Honor records, receipt rolls, and hospital records, supplemented by state pension applications, United Daughters of the Confederacy records, and postwar rosters and histories, all provided useful information.

OFFICERS

CAPTAINS

WILLIAMS, DAVID

Resided in New Hanover County and appointed Captain to rank from May 16, 1861. Present or accounted for until killed at Sharpsburg, Maryland, September 17, 1862.

ARMSTRONG, THOMAS E.

Resided in New Hanover County and appointed 1st Lieutenant to rank from May 16, 1861. Promoted to Captain to rank from September 17, 1862. Killed at Chancellorsville, Virginia, May 3, 1863.

POWERS, KINCHEN

Born in New Hanover County and resided as a farmer in Onslow County prior to enlisting in New Hanover County at age 34, June 1, 1861, for the war. Mustered in as Sergeant and appointed 2nd Lieutenant to rank from August 1, 1862. Promoted to 1st Lieutenant to rank from October 9, 1862, and to Captain to rank from May 3, 1863. Present or accounted for on company muster rolls through December, 1864. Wounded and captured at Appomattox Court House, Virginia, April 9, 1865. Confined in hospital at Baltimore, Maryland, until transferred to Fort McHenry, Maryland, May 9, 1865. Released at Fort McHenry after taking the Oath of Allegiance on June 10, 1865.

LIEUTENANTS

BANNERMAN, ALEXANDER W., 2nd Lieutenant

Resided in New Hanover County and appointed 2nd Lieutenant to rank from May 16, 1861. Resigned on January 13, 1862. Later served in Company C, 59th Regiment N.C. Troops (4th Regiment N.C. Cavalry).

BLACK, JOHN, 2nd Lieutenant

Transferred from the Field and Staff of this regiment upon appointment as 2nd Lieutenant to rank from January 17, 1862. Resigned on July 14, 1862, by reason of "bronchitis and a tendency to phthisis pulmonalis."

CASTINE, ANDREW J., 1st Lieutenant

Resided in Onslow County and enlisted in New Hanover County at age 20, June 1, 1861, for the war. Mustered in as Corporal and promoted to Sergeant, May-June, 1862. Appointed 2nd Lieutenant to rank from October 10, 1862. Wounded at Chancellorsville, Virginia, May 3, 1863, and promoted to 1st Lieutenant to rank from date wounded. Wounded at Wilderness, Virginia, May 5, 1864. Present or accounted for on company muster rolls through December, 1864.

HAND, JOHN P., 3rd Lieutenant

Resided in New Hanover County and appointed 3rd Lieutenant to rank from May 16, 1861. Resigned on January 10, 1862.

HAND, SAMUEL P., 2nd Lieutenant

Resided in New Hanover County where he enlisted at age 28, June 5, 1861, for the war. Mustered in as Private and appointed Sergeant, January-February, 1862. Wounded at Sharpsburg,

Maryland, September 17, 1862. Appointed 2nd Lieutenant to rank from May 3, 1863. Wounded at Gettysburg, Pennsylvania, July 2, 1863, and captured in hospital at Gettysburg July 4-5, 1863. Confined at DeCamp General Hospital, Davids Island, New York Harbor, until paroled on October 22, 1863. Exchanged at City Point, Virginia, October 28, 1863. Reported as absent wounded and absent sick from October, 1863, through March, 1865.

ORMSBY, GEORGE M., 2nd Lieutenant
Born in New Hanover County where he resided as a farmer and enlisted at age 21, June 1, 1861, for the war. Mustered in as Corporal and promoted to Sergeant on August 1, 1862. Wounded at Sharpsburg, Maryland, September 17, 1862. Appointed 2nd Lieutenant to rank from September 17, 1862. Wounded at Chancellorsville, Virginia, May 3, 1863, and returned to duty in September, 1863. Admitted to hospital at Richmond, Virginia, May 17, 1864, with a gunshot wound and transferred on May 29, 1864. Admitted to hospital at Wilmington on June 7, 1864, and returned to duty on August 10, 1864. Reported **as absent sick after October 12, 1864, and furloughed from hospital at Richmond on March 28,** 1865, for 30 days.

WILLIAMS, ANDREW J., 1st Lieutenant
Resided in New Hanover County where he enlisted at age 23, June 1, 1861, for the war. Mustered in as Sergeant and appointed 3rd Lieutenant to rank from January 22, 1862. Promoted to 2nd Lieutenant to rank from July 14, 1862, and to 1st Lieutenant to rank from September 17, 1862. Died at Shepherdstown, Virginia, October 9, 1862, of "typhoid fever."

NONCOMMISSIONED OFFICERS AND PRIVATES

ALLEN, WILLIAM M., Private
Enlisted in Transylvania County on September 24, 1863, for the war. Captured at Mine Run, Virginia, on November 28, 1863. Confined at Old Capitol Prison, Washington, D.C., until released after taking the Oath of Allegiance on March 18, 1864. Sent to Philadelphia, Pennsylvania.

ANDERSON, WILLIAM W., Private
Resided in New Hanover County where he enlisted at age 23, May 1, 1862, for the war. Killed in battle at Sharpsburg, Maryland, September 17, 1862.

ATKINS, W. T., Private
Issued clothing on May 27, 1864.

BANKS, BERRY P., Private
Enlisted in Yancey County at age 37, March 1, 1865, for the war.

BANNERMAN, DAVID W., Musician
Resided in New Hanover County where he enlisted at age 22, June 1, 1861, for the war. Mustered in as Musician. Present or accounted for until his death on January 16, 1862, in New Hanover County.

BARLOW, MARTIN, Private
Resided in Wake County where he enlisted at age 24, July 15, 1862, for the war. Died December 15, 1862, in hospital at Richmond, Virginia.

BLAKE, JOHN B., Private
Resided in New Hanover County where he enlisted at age 23, June 5, 1861, for the war. Present or accounted for until wounded at Sharpsburg, Maryland, September 17, 1862. Absent wounded until he returned to duty January-February, 1863. Wounded at Gettysburg, Pennsylvania, on July 2, 1863. Present or accounted for until captured near Spotsylvania Court House, Virginia, May 12, 1864. Confined at Point Lookout, Maryland, until transferred to Elmira, New York, on August 8, 1864. Paroled at Elmira and sent to James River, Virginia, for exchange on March 2, 1865. Admitted to hospital at Richmond, Virginia, March 7, 1865, with "debilitas" and was furloughed for 30 days on March 9, 1865.

BLAKE, STEPHEN G., Private
Resided in New Hanover County where he enlisted at age 25, June 10, 1861, for the war. Present or accounted for until wounded on July 1, 1862, near Richmond, Virginia. Died of his wound on July 11, 1862, at Richmond.

BLOODWORTH, TIMOTHY J., Private
Resided in New Hanover County where he enlisted at age 21, June 1, 1861, for the war. Present or accounted for until killed in battle at Sharpsburg, Maryland, September 17, 1862.

BLOODWORTH, WILLIAM A., Sergeant
Resided in New Hanover County where he enlisted at age 39, June 1, 1861, for the war. Mustered in as Sergeant. Present or accounted for until wounded at Sharpsburg, Maryland, September 17, 1862. Promoted to 1st Sergeant, July 14-October 31, 1862, and reduced to Sergeant, November-December, 1862. Killed in battle at Chancellorsville, Virginia, on May 3, 1863.

BORDEAUX, RICHARD HENRY, 1st Sergeant
Resided in New Hanover County where he enlisted at age 19, June 1, 1861, for the war. Mustered in as Private and appointed Corporal on August 1, 1862. Promoted to Sergeant on March 4, 1863, and to 1st Sergeant on October 1, 1863. Present or accounted for through December, 1864. Admitted to hospital at Greensboro, January 10, 1865, with "debilitas" and was transferred to another hospital on January 21, 1865.

BOSEMAN, JAMES, Private
Resided in Northampton County and enlisted at Camp Price, Virginia, at age 19, February 13, 1862. Reported as absent sick from August 20, 1863, through December, 1864. Admitted to hospital at Richmond, Virginia, February 22, 1865. Captured in hospital at Richmond on April 3, 1865.

BOWDEN, HINTON J., Private
Resided in New Hanover County where he enlisted at age 21, June 1, 1861, for the war. Present or accounted for until killed in battle at Sharpsburg, Maryland, September 17, 1862.

BOWDEN, MORRIS C., Private
Resided in New Hanover County where he en-

listed at age 18, June 1, 1861, for the war. Present or accounted for until captured near Spotsylvania Court House, Virginia, May 12, 1864. Confined at Point Lookout, Maryland, until transferred to Elmira, New York, on August 8, 1864. Paroled at Elmira and sent to James River, Virginia, for exchange on March 2, 1865. Admitted to hospital at Richmond, Virginia, on March 7, 1865, and furloughed for 30 days on March 9, 1865.

BOWDEN, RICHARD T., Private
Born in New Hanover County where he resided as a mechanic and enlisted at age 27, June 5, 1861, for the war. Present or accounted for until discharged on May 20, 1862, by reason of disability caused by "atrophy of the heart and general inertia with adhesion of the pleura."

BOWEN, KINCHEN, Corporal
Resided in New Hanover County where he enlisted at age 25, June 1, 1861, for the war. Mustered in as Private and appointed Corporal on March 19, 1863. Present or accounted for until wounded at Chancellorsville, Virginia, May 3, 1863. Returned to duty before August, 1863. Present or accounted for until wounded and captured at Fisher's Hill, Virginia, September 22, 1864. Transferred from field hospital at Winchester, Virginia, to U.S.A. General Hospital, West's Buildings, Baltimore, Maryland, October 12, 1864. Wound described as "gunshot would left leg and right foot." Transferred to Point Lookout, Maryland, October 17, 1864. Paroled at Point Lookout and sent to Venus Point, Savannah River, Georgia, for exchange, October 31, 1864. Exchanged at Venus Point on November 15, 1864.

BRINKLEY, WILLIAM A., Private
Resided in Wake County where he enlisted at age 23, July 15, 1862, for the war. Reported on company muster rolls as absent sick from September 5, 1862, through May 15, 1861. Absent without leave from that date until furloughed by the Medical Examining Board on August 15, 1864. Absent on furlough from that date through December, 1864.

BRITT, ALEXANDER A., Private
Resided in Wake County where he enlisted at age 25, July 15, 1862, for the war. Present or accounted for until wounded at Gettysburg, Pennsylvania, on July 2, 1863. Admitted to hospital at Richmond, Virginia, July 19, 1863, with "gunshot wound left hand." Reported as absent wounded through August, 1863. Present or accounted for until October 28, 1864, when he is reported as absent without leave. Absent without leave from that date through December, 1864. Admitted to hospital at Raleigh on January 31, 1865, and returned to duty on February 14, 1865. Captured at Burkeville, Virginia, April 6, 1865. Confined at Newport News, Virginia, where he died June 26, 1865.

BROWN, ISAAC H., Private
Resided in New Hanover County where he enlisted at age 22, June 1, 1861, for the war. Present or accounted for until wounded on July 1, 1862, near Richmond, Virginia. Again wounded on September 17, 1862, at Sharpsburg, Maryland. Returned to duty January-February, 1863. Wounded and captured at Gettysburg, Penn-

sylvania, July 1-3, 1863. Transferred from the U.S.A. Hospital at Gettysburg to DeCamp General Hospital, Davids Island, New York Harbor, on July 18, 1863. Paroled at that hospital and sent to City Point, Virginia, for exchange. Received at City Point on September 16, 1863. Absent on furlough from that date through December, 1864. Company muster rolls state that he lost his right arm from his wounds at Gettysburg.

BROWN, WILLIAM J., Private
Resided in New Hanover County where he enlisted at age 18, June 1, 1861, for the war. Present or accounted for until wounded at Sharpsburg, Maryland, September 17, 1862. Returned to duty January-February, 1863. Wounded at Chancellorsville, Virginia, on May 3, 1863. Reported as absent sick from June 15, 1863, until he appears as absent without leave on December 1, 1864.

BROWN, ZACHARIAH, Private
Resided in Duplin County and enlisted in New Hanover County at age 35, February 1, 1862, for the war. Died May 7, 1862, at Goldsboro.

BUNN, DALLAS, Private
Resided in Wake County where he enlisted at age 19, July 15, 1862, for the war. Absent sick from August 27, 1862, through February, 1863. Reported as absent without leave on the August, 1863, muster roll. Shot for desertion on September 5, 1863.

BUNN, GEORGE A., Private
Resided in Wake County where he enlisted at age 27, July 15, 1862, for the war. Reported as absent sick from August 27, 1862, through February, 1863. Present or accounted for until captured at Strasburg, Virginia, on October 19, 1864. Confined at Point Lookout, Maryland, until paroled and transferred to Aiken's Landing, James River, Virginia, for exchange on March 17, 1865.

BUNN, JAMES D., Private
Resided in Wake County where he enlisted at age 19, July 15, 1862, for the war. Captured at Chancellorsville, Virginia, on May 3, 1863, and paroled the next day. Present or accounted for until reported on the August 11-31, 1863, muster roll as absent without leave. Shot for desertion on September 5, 1863.

BUNN, WESLEY, Private
Resided in Wake County where he enlisted at age 33, July 15, 1862, for the war. Captured at Sharpsburg, Maryland, September 17, 1862, and paroled October 5, 1862. Requested not to be exchanged and was permitted to "proceed to and remain in any of the loyal states."

CARTER, ELDRIDGE, Private
Resided in Harnett County where he enlisted at age 34, July 15, 1862, for the war. Died on September 20, 1862, at Warrenton, Virginia.

CARTER, JAMES H., Private
Resided in New Hanover County where he enlisted at age 23, June 10, 1861, for the war. Present or accounted for until wounded and captured at Gettysburg, Pennsylvania, July 1-3, 1863. Confined at Fort Delaware, Delaware, until transferred to Point Lookout, Maryland, on October 18, 1863. Died at Point Lookout on October 20, 1863.

CASTEEN, COUNCIL W., Private

Resided in New Hanover County where he enlisted at age 30, June 1, 1861, for the war. Mustered in as Corporal. Reduced to ranks in October, 1861. Absent sick from October, 1861, through February, 1862. Wounded in battle at Chancellorsville, Virginia, on May 3, 1863. Absent wounded through December, 1863. Admitted to hospital at Wilmington on June 21, 1864, with "gunshot wound." Appears on a register of deaths and account of money and clothing received at that hospital dated December 9, 1864; however, date of death is not given.

CHADWICK, ROBERT, Private

Resided in New Hanover County where he enlisted at age 18, June 5, 1861, for the war. Present or accounted for until wounded at Chancellorsville, Virginia, May 3, 1863. Reported as absent without leave on the May 15-August 11, 1863, muster roll. Present or accounted for from that date until captured near Spotsylvania Court House, Virginia, May 12, 1864. Confined at Point Lookout, Maryland, until transferred to Elmira, New York, on August 14, 1864. Released at Elmira after taking the Oath of Allegiance on June 12, 1865.

COLE, JOHN H., Private

Resided in New Hanover County where he enlisted at age 34, June 1, 1861, for the war. Discharged September 10, 1861.

COWAN, GEORGE H., Private

Resided in New Hanover County where he enlisted at age 21, June 1, 1861, for the war. Wounded and captured at Sharpsburg, Maryland, on September 17, 1862. Died October 24, 1862, in U.S.A. General Hospital, Frederick, Maryland.

COWAN, RICHARD O., Private

Resided in New Hanover County where he enlisted at age 22, June 1, 1861, for the war. Present or accounted for until wounded at Malvern Hill, Virginia, July 1, 1862. Absent wounded until he returned to duty November-December, 1863. Discharged on July 1, 1864.

COWAN, ROBERT M., Private

Resided in New Hanover County where he enlisted at age 26, June 10, 1861, for the war. Present or accounted for until killed in battle at Sharpsburg, Maryland, September 17, 1862,

COWAN, THOMAS J., Private

Resided in New Hanover County where he enlisted at age 19, June 1, 1861, for the war. Present or accounted for until wounded at Chancellorsville, Virginia, May 3, 1863. Returned to duty in September-October, 1863. Absent sick from November 7, 1863, until he returned to duty April 7, 1864. Captured near Spotsylvania Court House, Virginia, May 12, 1864. Confined at Point Lookout, Maryland, until transferred to Elmira, New York, August 10, 1864. Paroled at Elmira and sent to James River, Virginia, for exchange, March 2, 1865. Admitted to hospital at Richmond, Virginia, March 9, 1865. Captured in hospital at Richmond on April 3, 1865, and paroled on May 3, 1865.

COWAN, WILLIAM W., Corporal

Resided in New Hanover County where he enlisted at age 21, June 1, 1861, for the war. Mustered in as Private and appointed Corporal on May 18, 1863. Present or accounted for until captured near Spotsylvania Court House, Virginia, May 12, 1864. Confined at Point Lookout, Maryland, until transferred to Elmira, New York, August 10, 1864. Returned to Point Lookout, October 11, 1864. Paroled for exchange at Point Lookout on October 29, 1864. Issued clothing November 17, 1864. Reported on company muster rolls as absent prisoner through December, 1864. Paroled at Appomattox Court House, Virginia, April 9, 1865.

CROOM, JESSE J., Private

Resided in New Hanover County where he enlisted at age 25, June 1, 1861, for the war. Died April 8, 1862, at Goldsboro.

CROOM, WILLIAM A., Private

Resided in New Hanover County where he enlisted at age 24, June 1, 1861, for the war. Died June 23, 1861, at Wilmington.

CURRIE, BENJAMIN P., Private

Resided in New Hanover County where he enlisted at age 31, June 1, 1861, for the war. Mustered in as Corporal and reduced to ranks on August 1, 1861. Present or accounted for until reported on the February 28-May 15, 1862, muster roll as being absent detailed as a nurse at Wilmington. Absent detailed in various hospitals at Wilmington from that date through January, 1865.

DEAL, JAMES M., Private

Resided in Duplin County where he enlisted at age 35, February 1, 1862, for the war. Present or accounted for until captured near Spotsylvania Court House, Virginia, May 12, 1864. Confined at Point Lookout, Maryland, until transferred to Elmira, New York, August 10, 1864. Returned on October 14, 1864, to Point Lookout, where he was paroled for exchange October 29, 1864. Reported as absent prisoner through December, 1864.

DeBOSE, ANTHONY, Private

Resided in New Hanover County where he enlisted at age 31, June 1, 1861, for the war. Wounded at Malvern Hill, Virginia, on July 1, 1862. Returned to duty January-February, 1863. Detailed as a hospital guard at Wilmington, March 16, 1863, because of disability caused by "gunshot wound fracturing tibia of right leg." Detailed until November-December, 1864, when he was reported as present on the company muster roll. Paroled at Appomattox Court House, Virginia, April 9, 1865.

DOCKERY, ELIJAH H., Private

Captured at Gettysburg, Pennsylvania, July 4, 1863. Confined at Fort Delaware, Delaware, where he took the Oath of Allegiance and joined the U.S. service on July 27, 1863. Assigned to Ahl's Independent Company, Delaware Heavy Artillery.

ELLIS, WILLIAM H., Private

Resided in Wake County where he enlisted at

age 35, July 15, 1862, for the war. Reported as absent sick from September 5, 1862, until his death on April 14, 1863, at Richmond, Virginia, of "pneumonia."

ENNIS, JOHN A., Private

Resided in Harnett County where he enlisted at age 29, July 15, 1862, for the war. Present or accounted for until wounded at Snicker's Gap, Virginia, July 18, 1864. Reported as absent wounded from that date through December, 1864.

EVANS, LEWIS T., Private

Resided in New Hanover County where he enlisted at age 23, June 1, 1861, for the war. Present or accounted for until wounded on July 1, 1862, near Richmond, Virginia. Returned to duty July 23, 1862. Present or accounted for until wounded in battle at Spotsylvania Court House, Virginia, May 12, 1864. Returned to duty in August, 1864. Company muster roll for September-October, 1864, states that he was missing in action on October 19, 1864, and was "supposed to be a prisoner of war." Reported with same remark through December, 1864.

FERRELL, CORDA B., Private

Resided in Wake County where he enlisted at age 30, July 15, 1862, for the war. Company muster roll for July 14-October 31, 1862, reports that he was absent without leave. Reported as being absent in arrest from that date until he "deserted brigade guard November 8, 1863." Prisoner of war records state that he was captured November 9, 1863, at Culpeper, Virginia, and confined at Old Capitol Prison, Washington, D.C. Released at Old Capitol Prison after taking the Oath of Allegiance on March 15, 1864, and was sent to Philadelphia, Pennsylvania.

FOY, GEORGE W., Private

Resided in New Hanover County where he enlisted at age 21, May 16, 1862, for the war. Present or accounted for until wounded at Gettysburg, Pennsylvania, July 2, 1863. Returned to duty September-October, 1863. Captured near Spotsylvania Court House, Virginia, May 12, 1864. Confined at Point Lookout, Maryland, until transferred to Elmira, New York, August 10, 1864. Released at Elmira after taking the Oath of Allegiance on June 30, 1865.

FUTCH, CHARLES F., Private

Resided in New Hanover County where he enlisted at age 30, June 1, 1861, for the war. Present or accounted for until killed at Gettysburg, Pennsylvania, July 2, 1863.

FUTCH, HANSON M., Private

Resided in New Hanover County where he enlisted at age 20, June 1, 1861, for the war. Present or accounted for until reported as absent without leave on the August 11-31, 1863, muster roll. Absent in arrest at Castle Thunder, Richmond, Virginia, from September 1, 1863, until his death on December 17, 1863, of "variola." Muster rolls state that he was in Castle Thunder under sentence of death.

FUTCH, JOHN, Private

Resided in New Hanover County and enlisted in Harnett County at age 26, February 1, 1862, for the war. Present or accounted for until reported as absent without leave on the August 11-31, 1863, muster roll. Shot for desertion on September 5, 1863.

FUTCH, WILEY, Private

Resided in New Hanover County and enlisted in Harnett County at age 34, February 1, 1862, for the war. Present or accounted for until killed in battle at Ellerson's Mill, Virginia, June 26, 1862.

GARRIS, JAMES R., Private

Resided in New Hanover County where he enlisted at age 23, June 1, 1861, for the war. Present or accounted for until wounded at Sharpsburg, Maryland, September 17, 1862. Returned to duty November-December, 1862. Present or accounted for until captured on May 12, 1864, near Spotsylvania Court House, Virginia. Confined at Point Lookout, Maryland, until transferred to Elmira, New York, August 10, 1864. Released after taking the Oath of Allegiance on June 12, 1865.

GARRIS, JOHN W., Private

Resided in New Hanover County where he enlisted at age 25, June 1, 1861, for the war. Present or accounted for until captured and paroled at Paris, Virginia, November 5, 1862. Admitted to hospital at Richmond, Virginia, on November 26, 1862, with "contusio foot." Returned to duty January-February, 1863. Killed at Chancellorsville, Virginia, May 2, 1863.

GIDEONS, ARCHIBALD, Private

Born in New Hanover County where he resided as a farmer and enlisted at age 18, February 28, 1862, for the war. Wounded at Sharpsburg, Maryland, September 17, 1862. Absent wounded from that date until discharged on February 15, 1864, by reason of disability caused by his wounds.

GIDEONS, ROBERT, Private

Resided in New Hanover County where he enlisted at age 24, March 1, 1862, for the war. Wounded at Sharpsburg, Maryland, on September 17, 1862. Returned to duty January-February, 1863. Wounded at Chancellorsville, Virginia, May 3, 1863. Returned to duty November-December, 1863. Detailed for hospital duty at Richmond, Virginia, April 21, 1864. Absent detailed through December, 1864.

GIDEONS, WILLIAM, Private

Resided in New Hanover County where he enlisted at age 22, April 28, 1862, for the war. Detailed as a pioneer from January 25, 1863, until October 29, 1864. Present or accounted for from that date through December, 1864. Deserted March 30, 1865, and took the Oath of Allegiance at Washington, D.C., on April 6, 1865. Transportation furnished to Wilmington.

GURGANUS, ALFRED, Private

Resided in New Hanover County and enlisted at Camp Howe, Virginia, at age 34, August 30, 1861, for the war. Present or accounted for until reported as absent sick on August 19, 1862. Admitted to hospital at Richmond, Virginia, on September 8, 1862, with "epileptic convul." and furloughed for 30 days on October 3, 1862. Died in New Hanover County on November 1, 1862.

GURGANUS, JAMES A., Private
Resided in New Hanover County where he enlisted at age 29, May 16, 1862, for the war. Died on November 6, 1862, at Paris, Virginia.

HAM, J. O., Private
Captured at Mockey Ferry, Virginia, May 28, 1864. Confined at Point Lookout, Maryland, until transferred to Elmira, New York, July 9, 1864. Paroled for exchange at Elmira on October 11, 1864.

HARRIS, JOHN W., Private
Enlisted in New Hanover County on July 3, 1861, for the war. Present or accounted for until killed in battle at Chancellorsville, Virginia, on May 3, 1863.

HEATH, GEORGE H., Private
Enlisted on July 15, 1862, for the war. Deserted December 15, 1862.

HENDERSON, M. W., Private
Paroled at Greensboro on May 15, 1865.

HERRING, CALBERT M., Private
Enlisted in New Hanover County on June 26, 1864, for the war. Present or accounted for until reported as missing in action on September 19, 1864, "supposed to be a prisoner of war." Company muster rolls report him as absent with that remark through December, 1864.

HERRING, HENRY H., Private
Resided in Wake County where he enlisted at age 33, July 15, 1862, for the war. Muster rolls state that he was left sick at Antietam, Maryland, on September 13, 1862, and died September 18, 1862.

HIGHSMITH, RICHARD E., Private
Born in New Hanover County where he resided as a farmer and enlisted at age 48, February 24, 1862, for the war. Present or accounted for until discharged on September 8, 1863, by reason of disability caused by "chronic rheumatism."

HINES, JACOB, Private
Resided in New Hanover County where he enlisted at age 18, February 1, 1862, for the war. Present or accounted for until wounded and captured at Gettysburg, Pennsylvania, July 2-4, 1863. Confined at Fort Delaware, Delaware, until paroled and sent to Aiken's Landing, Virginia, for exchange, September 14-18, 1864. Reported as absent on parole or absent sick from that date through December, 1864.

HODGE, CHARLES, Private
Enlisted in Caldwell County on September 26, 1863, for the war. Deserted on February 20, 1864.

HOLMES, JAMES D., Private
Resided in Wake County where he enlisted at age 27, July 15, 1862, for the war. Died December 15, 1862, at Staunton, Virginia.

HORREL, AMERICUS V., Private
Resided in New Hanover County where he enlisted at age 18, July 15, 1862, for the war. Deserted August 20, 1863. Captured at Harrisonburg, Virginia, October 6, 1864, and confined at Point Lookout, Maryland. Released at Point Lookout after taking the Oath of Allegiance on May 13, 1865.

HORRELL, JAMES B., Private
Resided in New Hanover County where he en-

listed at age 35, July 15, 1862, for the war. Detailed as a shoemaker on November 15, 1862, and remained on detail through December, 1864.

HOWARD, GEORGE E., Private
Resided in New Hanover County where he enlisted at age 19, June 1, 1861, for the war. Present or accounted for until captured at Gettysburg, Pennsylvania, July 3-4, 1863. Confined at Fort Delaware, Delaware, where he died October 18, 1863, of "typhoid fever."

HUBBARD, MARK T., Private
Resided in Wake County where he enlisted at age 23, July 15, 1862, for the war. Present or accounted for until he died at Guinea Station, Virginia, March 28, 1863.

JAMES, GEORGE, Private
Resided in New Hanover County where he enlisted at age 21, June 1, 1861, for the war. Died at Richmond, Virginia, August 25, 1862, of disease.

JOHNSON, I. B., Private
Paroled at Warrenton, Virginia, September 29, 1862.

JOHNSON, LEVI, Private
Enlisted in Yadkin County on October 27, 1863, for the war. Deserted November 1, 1863.

JOHNSTON, JESSE V., Private
Resided in Wake County where he enlisted at age 32, July 15, 1862, for the war. Wounded at Gettysburg, Pennsylvania, July 2-3, 1863. Captured in "Western Virginia" on July 30, 1863, and took the Oath of Allegiance.

JOHNSTON, JOSIAH S., Private
Resided in New Hanover County where he enlisted at age 40, March 19, 1862, for the war. Present or accounted for until captured near Spotsylvania Court House, Virginia, May 12, 1864. Confined at Point Lookout, Maryland, until transferred to Elmira, New York, August 10, 1864. Released at Elmira after taking the Oath of Allegiance on June 16, 1865.

JONES, ALLEN H., Private
Enlisted in Granville County on September 27, 1863, for the war. Sent to hospital January 15, 1864, and reported as absent sick through December, 1864.

JONES, JOHN, Private
Resided in New Hanover County where he enlisted at age 18, June 1, 1861, for the war. Died in hospital at Richmond, Virginia, July 28, 1862.

JONES, JONAS, Private
Resided in New Hanover County where he enlisted at age 19, April 26, 1862, for the war. Wounded at Sharpsburg, Maryland, September 17, 1862, and at Gettysburg, Pennsylvania, July 2, 1863. Reported as absent wounded from July, 1863, through December, 1864.

KEITH, GEORGE A., Private
Resided in Wake County where he enlisted at age 28, July 15, 1862, for the war. Present or accounted for until reported as "missing from line of battle at Fredericksburg, Virginia, December 15, 1862."

KENION, JOSEPH B., Private
Enlisted in New Hanover County at age 30,

March 1, 1862, for the war. Killed at Malvern Hill, Virginia, July 1, 1862.

LANE, THOMAS J., Private

Resided in New Hanover County where he enlisted at age 19, June 1, 1861, for the war. Present or accounted for until captured at Spotsylvania Court House, Virginia, May 12, 1864. Confined at Point Lookout, Maryland, until transferred to Elmira, New York, August 10, 1864. Paroled at Elmira on October 11, 1864, and exchanged on October 29, 1864. Admitted to hospital at Macon, Georgia, November 15, 1864, and reported as absent sick through December, 1864. Paroled at Appomattox Court House, Virginia, April 9, 1865.

LANIER, JAMES M., Private

Resided in Duplin County and enlisted in New Hanover County at age 22, February 19, 1862, for the war. Present or accounted for until captured at Gettysburg, Pennsylvania, July 3, 1863. Confined at Fort Delaware, Delaware, until transferred to Point Lookout, Maryland, October 18, 1863. Paroled at Point Lookout on February 18, 1865, and exchanged at Boulware's Wharf, James River, Virginia, February 20-21, 1865. Reported as present at Camp Lee, near Richmond, Virginia, February 23, 1865.

LANIER, JOHN A., Private

Resided in New Hanover County where he enlisted at age 18, August 12, 1861, for the war. Admitted to hospital at Richmond, Virginia, July 20, 1863, with a gunshot wound of the right hip. Reported as absent wounded and absent sick from July, 1863, through October, 1864. Appears as present on November-December, 1864, muster roll. Paroled at Appomattox Court House, Virginia, April 9, 1865.

LANIER, THOMAS H., Private

Resided in New Hanover County where he enlisted on February 1, 1862, for the war. Present or accounted for until captured at Spotsylvania Court House, Virginia, May 12, 1864. Confined at Point Lookout, Maryland, until transferred to Elmira, New York, August 10, 1864. Released at Elmira after taking the Oath of Allegiance on June 27, 1865.

LANIER, WILLIAM E., Private

Resided in New Hanover County where he enlisted at age 24, June 1, 1861, for the war. Present or accounted for through August, 1864, when he was reported as absent "wounded August 21, 1864, near Charlestown." Wounded and captured at Winchester, Virginia, September 19, 1864. Escaped from hospital at Winchester October 25, 1864. Admitted to hospital at Richmond, Virginia, November 6, 1864, and furloughed for 60 days. Reported as absent wounded through December, 1864.

LEE, GEORGE W. B., Sergeant

Resided in New Hanover County where he enlisted at age 22, June 1, 1861, for the war. Mustered in as Private and appointed Corporal September 17, 1862. Promoted to Sergeant on March 19, 1863. Wounded at Gettysburg, Pennsylvania, July 2, 1863, and captured at South Mountain,

Maryland, July 4, 1863. Confined at Fort Delaware, Delaware, until paroled on July 30, 1863. Exchanged at City Point, Virginia, August 1, 1863. Present or accounted for through December, 1864.

LEE, JAMES C., 1st Sergeant

Resided in New Hanover County where he enlisted at age 27, June 1, 1861, for the war. Mustered in as 1st Sergeant. Killed at Malvern Hill, Virginia, July 1, 1862.

LEE, PEYTON L., Corporal

Resided in New Hanover County where he enlisted at age 25, August 12, 1861, for the war. Mustered in as Private and appointed Corporal, April 30-July 14, 1862. Wounded accidentally at Richmond, Virginia, July 14-October 31, 1862. Reduced to ranks February 28-May 15, 1863. Wounded at Chancellorsville, Virginia, May 3, 1863. Reappointed Corporal on May 16, 1863. Reported as absent wounded from May, 1863, through December, 1864.

McDONALD, J. D., Private

Captured at Winchester, Virginia, September 19, 1864, and confined at Point Lookout, Maryland. Paroled at Point Lookout on March 15, 1865, and exchanged at Boulware's Wharf, James River, Virginia, March 18, 1865.

MALLABY, REUBEN, Private

Resided in Wake County where he enlisted at age 21, July 15, 1862, for the war. Died at Strasburg, Virginia, December 1, 1862.

MALPASS, JOHN W., Private

Resided in New Hanover County and enlisted in Wayne County at age 26, May 16, 1862, for the war. Deserted May 23, 1863, and returned from desertion January 23, 1864. Wounded at Wilderness, Virginia, May 5, 1864. Reported as absent wounded until retired to the Invalid Corps on March 14, 1865. Paroled at Richmond, Virginia, April 23, 1865.

MATHEWS, NICODEMUS, Private

Resided in New Hanover County where he enlisted at age 19, July 4, 1861, for the war. Died in camp near Richmond, Virginia, August 11, 1862.

MEDLIN, WILLIAM S., Private

Resided in Wake County where he enlisted at age 28, July 15, 1862, for the war. Died in hospital at Richmond, Virginia, September 8, 1862, of "typhoid fever."

MEEKS, BRANTLY B., Private

Resided in New Hanover County where he enlisted at age 25, June 10, 1861, for the war. Discharged on August 12, 1861, by reason of "inability."

MEEKS, FELIX M., Private

Resided in New Hanover County where he enlisted at age 26, June 1, 1861, for the war. Present or accounted for until wounded at Wilderness, Virginia, May 5, 1864. Reported as absent wounded from May, 1864, through December, 1864.

MILLS, EDWARD J., Private

Resided in New Hanover County where he enlisted at age 30, June 1, 1861, for the war. Killed at

Malvern Hill, Virginia, July 1, 1862.

MILLS, JAMES L., Private

Enlisted in New Hanover County on July 4, 1861, for the war. Wounded at Sharpsburg, Maryland, September 17, 1862. Present or accounted for until paroled at Appomattox Court House, Virginia, April 9, 1865.

MILLS, TIMOTHY W., Private

Resided in New Hanover County where he enlisted at age 20, June 1, 1861, for the war. Discharged on August 12, 1861, by reason of "inability." Reenlisted on October 8, 1861, for the war. Present or accounted for until captured at Spotsylvania Court House, Virginia, May 12, 1864. Confined at Point Lookout, Maryland, until transferred to Elmira, New York, August 10, 1864. Released at Elmira after taking the Oath of Allegiance on June 27, 1865.

MOORE, DAVID, Private

Resided in New Hanover County where he enlisted at age 21, June 10, 1861, for the war. Killed at Sharpsburg, Maryland, September 17, 1862.

MOORE, TIMOTHY, Private

Resided in New Hanover County where he enlisted at age 23, June 10, 1861, for the war. Wounded at Gettysburg, Pennsylvania, July 2-3, 1863, and captured in hospital at Gettysburg July 4, 1863. Confined at DeCamp General Hospital, Davids Island, New York Harbor, until paroled and exchanged at City Point, Virginia, September 8, 1863. Present or accounted for until captured at Spotsylvania Court House, Virginia, May 12, 1864. Confined at Point Lookout, Maryland, until transferred to Elmira, New York, August 10, 1864. Released at Elmira after taking the Oath of Allegiance on June 12, 1865.

MOTT, MOSES D., Private

Resided in New Hanover County where he enlisted at age 22, August 12, 1861, for the war. Wounded and captured at Sharpsburg, Maryland, September 17, 1862. Paroled on September 30, 1862. Captured at Shepherdstown, West Virginia, November 25, 1863, and confined at Fort McHenry, Maryland, until paroled January 31, 1863. Exchanged at City Point, Virginia, February 2, 1863. Killed at Gettysburg, Pennsylvania, July 2, 1863.

MURRAY, ASA G., Corporal

Resided in New Hanover County where he enlisted at age 20, June 1, 1861, for the war. Mustered in as Private and appointed Corporal, November-December, 1861. Killed at Sharpsburg, Maryland, September 17, 1862.

NEWTON, WILLIAM B., Private

Resided in New Hanover County where he enlisted at age 46, July 7, 1861, for the war. Discharged on August 12, 1861, by reason of "inability."

ORMSBY, GEORGE WILLIAM, Private

Resided in New Hanover County where he enlisted at age 34, March 13, 1862, for the war. Wounded at Gettysburg, Pennsylvania, July 2-3, 1863, and captured at Gettysburg July 3, 1863. Confined at Fort Delaware, Delaware, until transferred to Point Lookout, Maryland, October 15-18, 1863. Paroled at Point Lookout on March 14, 1865, and exchanged at Boulware's Wharf, James River, Virginia, March 16, 1865. Admitted to hospital at Richmond, Virginia, March 16, 1865, and transferred the next day.

ORMSBY, ROBERT S., Private

Resided in New Hanover County where he enlisted at age 20, June 1, 1861, for the war. Killed at Ellerson's Mill, Virginia, June 26, 1862.

ORMSBY, THOMAS P., Private

Resided in New Hanover County where he enlisted at age 23, June 1, 1861, for the war. Detailed as courier from January, 1863, through December, 1864. Paroled at Appomattox Court House, Virginia, April 9, 1865.

PADGETT, JACOB B., Private

Resided in New Hanover County where he enlisted at age 26, June 1, 1861, for the war. Died in hospital at Fredericksburg, Virginia, March 23, 1862.

PADGETT, JOHN W., Private

Resided in New Hanover County where he enlisted at age 27, June 1, 1861, for the war. Died in Richmond, Virginia, September 13, 1862, of "febris typhoides."

PADGETT, McRAE, Private

Resided in New Hanover County where he enlisted at age 22, June 1, 1861, for the war. Killed at Chancellorsville, Virginia, May 3, 1863.

PADGETT, NELSON M., Private

Resided in New Hanover County where he enlisted at age 18, June 1, 1861, for the war. Died at home on March 27, 1863.

PEAR, JAMES, Private

Confined at Fort Mifflin, Pennsylvania, July 2, 1863, as a "rebel deserter." Provost Marshal records state that he was captured at Martinsburg, Virginia, and was released December 21, 1863.

PIERCE, ARCHIBALD, Private

Resided in New Hanover County where he enlisted at age 34, April 22, 1862, for the war. Reported as absent sick from July, 1862, through December, 1864.

PIERCE, JOHN, Private

Resided in New Hanover County and enlisted at age 48, February 1, 1862, for the war. Roll of Honor carries the remark: "Discharged by substitute."

PIERCE, JOSEPH, Private

Resided in New Hanover County and enlisted at age 23, February 1, 1862, for the war.

PIERCE, WILLIAM D., Private

Resided in New Hanover County and enlisted at age 26, May 2, 1863, for the war. Roll of Honor reports him as a substitute with the remark: "Taken prisoner in Pennsylvania."

PIGFORD, JACOB L., Private

Born in New Hanover County where he resided as a farmer and enlisted at age 21, June 1, 1861, for the war. Wounded at Malvern Hill, Virginia, July 1, 1862, and furloughed July 12, 1862, for 40 days. Wounded at Gettysburg, Pennsylvania,

July 3, 1863, and captured in hospital at Gettysburg July 4-5, 1863. Confined at DeCamp General Hospital, Davids Island, New York Harbor, until paroled and exchanged at City Point, Virginia, September 16, 1863. Reported as absent wounded until retired to the Invalid Corps on March 25, 1865.

PINER, JOHN, Private
Enlisted in New Hanover County on January 28, 1862, for the war. Discharged on April 23, 1862, after providing William D. Piner as his substitute.

PINER, JOSEPH, Private
Enlisted in New Hanover County on January 28, 1862, for the war. Captured at Mine Run, Virginia, December 1-4, 1863, and confined at Old Capitol Prison, Washington, D.C. Transferred to Point Lookout, Maryland, February 3, 1864. Paroled at Point Lookout on September 18, 1864, and exchanged at Varina, Virginia, September 22, 1864.

PINER, ROBERT, Private
Resided in New Hanover County where he enlisted at age 20, June 1, 1861, for the war. Wounded at Malvern Hill, Virginia, July 1, 1862. Returned to duty November-December, 1862. Present or accounted for until wounded at Wilderness, Virginia, May 5, 1864. Returned to duty September-October, 1864. Captured at Farmville, Virginia, April 6, 1865, and confined at Newport News, Virginia. Released after taking the Oath of Allegiance on June 30, 1865.

PINER, WILLIAM D., Private
Enlisted in Wayne County on April 23, 1862, for the war as a substitute for John Piner. Captured at Gettysburg, Pennsylvania, July 5, 1863, and confined at Fort Delaware, Delaware. Transferred to Point Lookout, Maryland, October 18, 1863. Paroled at Point Lookout on February 18, 1865, and exchanged at Boulware's Wharf, James River, Virginia, February 20-21, 1865. Reported as present at Camp Lee, near Richmond, Virginia, February 23, 1865.

PLAYER, RICHARD L., Sergeant
Resided in New Hanover County where he enlisted at age 27, July 4, 1861, for the war. Mustered in as Private and appointed Corporal, October 10, 1862. Captured at Fredericksburg, Virginia, May 3, 1863, and paroled and exchanged at City Point, Virginia, May 13, 1863. Promoted to Sergeant, May 16, 1863. Present or accounted for until captured at Spotsylvania Court House, Virginia, May 12, 1864. Confined at Point Lookout, Maryland, until transferred to Elmira, New York, August 10, 1864. Paroled at Elmira on October 11, 1864, and exchanged at Venus Point, Savannah River, Georgia, November 15, 1864. Captured at Farmville, Virginia, April 6, 1865, and confined at Newport News, Virginia. Released after taking the Oath of Allegiance on June 30, 1865.

PLAYER, WILLIAM B., Sergeant
Resided in New Hanover County where he enlisted at age 30, June 1, 1861, for the war. Mustered in as Private and appointed Corporal,

August 1, 1861. Wounded at Malvern Hill, Virginia, July 1, 1862, and at Sharpsburg, Maryland, September 17, 1862. Promoted to Sergeant, September 17, 1862, and to 1st Sergeant, November 1, 1862. Captured at Fredericksburg, Virginia, May 3, 1863, and paroled and exchanged at City Point, Virginia, May 13, 1862. Wounded at Gettysburg, Pennsylvania, July 2, 1863. Reduced to Sergeant, October 1, 1863. Present or accounted for through December, 1864. Captured at Burkeville, Virginia, April 6, 1865, and confined at Newport News, Virginia. Released after taking the Oath of Allegiance on June 30, 1865.

PLAYER, WILLIAM JACKSON, Private
Resided in New Hanover County where he enlisted at age 18, June 1, 1861, for the war. Discharged on May 20, 1862, by reason of "inability."

POOL, GEORGE, Private
Enlisted in Granville County on August 20, 1863, for the war. Captured at Mine Run, Virginia, November 28, 1863, and confined at Old Capitol Prison, Washington, D.C. Transferred on July 23, 1864, to Elmira, New York, where he died October 14, 1864, of "scorbutis."

POWERS, HANSON, Private
Resided in New Hanover County and enlisted in Northampton County at age 18, June 27, 1861, for the war. Discharged June 1, 1863, by reason of disability.

PRICE, THOMAS A., Private
Resided in New Hanover County where he enlisted at age 20, June 1, 1861, for the war. Discharged on February 18, 1862, by reason of disability.

PRIVETT, KEARNEY, Private
Resided in Wake County where he enlisted at age 19, July 15, 1862, for the war. Captured at Sharpsburg, Maryland, September 17, 1862, and paroled and exchanged at City Point, Virginia, November 10, 1862. Shot for desertion on September 5, 1863.

RAINER, JOHN N., Private
Resided in New Hanover County where he enlisted at age 18, June 1, 1861, for the war. Wounded near Richmond, Virginia, on July 1, 1862. Returned to duty January 17, 1863. Reported as absent without leave on the August 11-31, 1863, muster roll. Shot for desertion on September 5, 1863.

RAINER, STEPHEN D., Private
Enlisted in New Hanover County at age 30, July 1, 1862, for the war. Discharged July 10, 1862.

RAMSEY, ROBERT T., Private
Resided in New Hanover County and enlisted in Wayne County at age 25, May 16, 1862, for the war. Present or accounted for until wounded at Gettysburg, Pennsylvania, July 2, 1863. Absent wounded through December, 1864.

RAMSEY, THOMAS J., Private
Resided in New Hanover County where he enlisted at age 21, June 1, 1861, for the war. Present or accounted for until wounded at Sharpsburg, Maryland, September 17, 1862. Returned to duty November-December, 1862. Wounded and cap-

tured at Gettysburg, Pennsylvania, July 1-4, 1863. Confined at DeCamp General Hospital, Davids Island, New York Harbor, until paroled and sent to City Point, Virginia, for exchange. Exchanged at City Point on September 16, 1863. Absent on medical furlough through December, 1864.

RAY, BURWELL J., Private
Resided in Wake County where he enlisted at age 30, July 15, 1862, for the war. Absent sick from August 27, 1862, through December, 1864.

RICHARDSON, WILLIAM W., Private
Resided in New Hanover County where he enlisted at age 46, February 1, 1862, for the war. Killed at Malvern Hill, Virginia, July 1, 1862.

RIVENBARK, ROBERT, Corporal
Resided in New Hanover County where he enlisted at age 26, June 1, 1861, for the war. Mustered in as Private. Wounded at Sharpsburg, Maryland, September 17, 1862. Returned to duty January-February, 1863. Wounded at Chancellorsville, Virginia, May 3, 1863. Absent wounded until returned to duty September-October, 1863. Appointed Corporal, January 1, 1864. Wounded at Wilderness, Virginia, May 5, 1864. Absent wounded through December, 1864.

RIVENBARK, WASHINGTON L., Corporal
Born in New Hanover County where he resided as a farmer and enlisted at age 18, June 1, 1861, for the war. Mustered in as Private. Wounded at Malvern Hill, Virginia, July 1, 1862. Appointed Corporal on September 17, 1862. Absent wounded from July 1, 1862, until discharged on December 10, 1862, by reason of disability caused by a "gunshot wound of the forearm."

ROBBINS, ZACHARIAH, Private
Resided in New Hanover County where he enlisted at age 18, June 1, 1861, for the war. Present or accounted for until killed at Chancellorsville, Virginia, May 3, 1863.

ROCHELLE, BLANEY J., Private
Resided in New Hanover County where he enlisted at age 30, June 1, 1861, for the war. Present or accounted for until wounded at Chancellorsville, Virginia, May 3, 1863. Died of his wounds on May 16, 1863, at Richmond, Virginia.

ROCHELLE, EDWARD G., Private
Born in New Hanover County where he resided as a farmer and enlisted at age 18, February 1, 1862, for the war. Discharged May 20, 1862, by reason of disability.

ROCHELLE, EPHRAIM J., Private
Resided in New Hanover County where he enlisted at age 34, May 2, 1862, for the war. Wounded at Malvern Hill, Virginia, July 1, 1862. Absent wounded through December, 1864.

ROCHELLE, ISAAC, Private
Resided in New Hanover County where he enlisted at age 21, June 1, 1861, for the war. Wounded at Ellerson's Mill, Virginia, June 26, 1862. Admitted to hospital at Richmond, Virginia, June 27, 1862, with gunshot wound and died on August 10, 1862.

ROCHELLE, ROBERT H., Private
Resided in New Hanover County where he en-

listed at age 20, June 1, 1861, for the war. Present or accounted for until killed at Malvern Hill, Virginia, July 1, 1862.

ROOKS, WILLIAM S., Private
Resided in New Hanover County where he enlisted at age 31, June 1, 1861, for the war. Died October 18, 1861, at Camp Howe, Virginia.

ROSS, ADAM, Private
Resided in New Hanover County where he enlisted at age 20, June 5, 1861, for the war. Present or accounted for until wounded on July 1, 1862, near Richmond, Virginia. Wounded at Sharpsburg, Maryland, September 17, 1862, and died in hospital at Petersburg, Virginia, October 4, 1862.

ROSS, LUKE W., Private
Resided in Pitt County where he enlisted at age 34, July 15, 1862, for the war. Killed at Sharpsburg, Maryland, September 17, 1862.

ROWE, JOHN W., Sergeant
Resided in New Hanover County where he enlisted at age 20, June 10, 1861, for the war. Mustered in as Private. Appointed Corporal on March 4, 1863, and promoted to Sergeant on January 1, 1864. Present or accounted for until captured near Spotsylvania Court House, Virginia, May 12, 1864. Confined at Point Lookout, Maryland, until transferred to Elmira, New York, on August 10, 1864. Paroled at Elmira and sent to James River, Virginia, for exchange on February 13, 1865.

SAUNDERS, ROBERT TATE, Sergeant
Born in New Hanover County where he resided as a mechanic and enlisted at age 27, June 1, 1861, for the war. Mustered in as Sergeant. Wounded in battle near Richmond, Virginia, July 1, 1862. Absent wounded until discharged on March 19, 1863, by reason of disability.

SCARBORO, GEORGE D., Private
Resided in Wake County where he enlisted at age 20, July 15, 1862, for the war. Died at Richmond, Virginia, September 10, 1862, of "measles."

SELLERS, JORDAN, Private
Born in Sampson County and resided as a farmer in New Hanover County where he enlisted at age 52, February 12, 1862, for the war. Discharged on May 20, 1862, by reason of "old age, deafness, and general debility."

SHEPARD, GEORGE W., Private
Resided in New Hanover County where he enlisted at age 18, June 1, 1861, for the war. Present or accounted for until wounded at Malvern Hill, Virginia, July 1, 1862. Reported as absent wounded from that date through December, 1864.

SIKES, JOHN J., Private
Resided in New Hanover County where he enlisted at age 24, July 1, 1861, for the war. Wounded at Ellerson's Mill, Virginia, June 26, 1862. Died in hospital at Richmond, Virginia, September 30, 1862, of "typhoid fever."

SMILEY, ALONZO N., Private
Resided in New Hanover County where he enlisted at age 25, June 1, 1861, for the war. Wounded at Malvern Hill, Virginia, July 1, 1862. Killed at Gettysburg, Pennsylvania, July 2, 1863.

SMITH, WILLIAM A., Private

Resided in Harnett County where he enlisted at age 26, July 15, 1862, for the war. Reported as absent sick from September, 1862, through December, 1864.

SPENCE, JAMES, Private

Resided in Harnett County where he enlisted at age 21, July 15, 1862, for the war. Wounded at Sharpsburg, Maryland, September 17, 1862. Detailed as a nurse in hospital at Raleigh on March 23, 1864, and remained on detail until returned to company September, 1864. Captured at Farmville, Virginia, April 6, 1865, and confined at Newport News, Virginia. Released after taking the Oath of Allegiance on June 30, 1865.

SPENCER, EDMUND, Private

Resided in Harnett County where he enlisted at age 31, July 15, 1862, for the war. Died at home on October 8, 1862, of disease.

STELL, WILLIAM R., Private

Resided in Harnett County and enlisted in Wake County at age 28, July 15, 1862, for the war. Reported as absent sick from August, 1862, until he deserted August 11, 1863.

STOKES, WILEY, Private

Born in New Hanover County where he resided as a farmer and enlisted at age 24, June 5, 1861, for the war. Wounded at Malvern Hill, Virginia, July 1, 1862. Discharged on December 10, 1862, by reason of "gunshot wound in left shoulder."

STROUD, WILLIAM, Private

Resided in South Carolina and enlisted at Camp Price, Virginia, at age 21, February 13, 1862, for the war. Deserted near Goldsboro on April 12, 1862.

TAYLOR, ALFRED A., Private

Resided in New Hanover County where he enlisted at age 23, June 1, 1861, for the war. Present or accounted for until captured at Spotsylvania Court House, Virginia, May 12, 1864. Confined at Point Lookout, Maryland, where he died August 8, 1864.

TUTER, JAMES A., Private

Resided in Harnett County where he enlisted at age 18, July 15, 1862, for the war. Reported as absent sick after he enlisted until he deserted August 11, 1863.

WALLER, SQUIRE, Private

Resided as a farmer in Forsyth County where he enlisted on October 27, 1863, for the war. Wounded at Spotsylvania Court House, Virginia, May 10, 1864. Captured at Strasburg, Virginia, October 19, 1864, and confined at Point Lookout, Maryland. Released after taking the Oath of Allegiance on May 14, 1865.

WALTON, ELISHA E., Private

Resided in Onslow County and enlisted in Wayne County at age 19, May 16, 1862, for the war. Present or accounted for until captured near Spotsylvania Court House, Virginia, May 12, 1864. Confined at Point Lookout, Maryland, until transferred to Elmira, New York, August 10, 1864. Paroled at Elmira on February 20, 1865, and sent to James River, Virginia, for exchange. Admitted to hospital at Richmond, Virginia, March 3, 1865.

WALTON, JOHN D., Private

Resided in Onslow County and enlisted in Wayne County at age 21, May 16, 1862, for the war. Captured at Fredericksburg, Virginia, May 3, 1863, and paroled and exchanged at City Point, Virginia, May 13, 1863. Wounded at Payne's Farm, Virginia, November 27, 1863. Captured at Spotsylvania Court House, Virginia, May 12, 1864, and confined at Point Lookout, Maryland. Transferred to Elmira, New York, August 10, 1864. Released after taking the Oath of Allegiance on June 21, 1865.

WARD, ALEXANDER, Private

Resided in New Hanover County where he enlisted at age 18, June 1, 1861, for the war. Killed at Sharpsburg, Maryland, September 17, 1862.

WATKINS, DANIEL, Private

Resided in Wake County where he enlisted at age 26, July 15, 1862, for the war. Wounded at Chancellorsville, Virginia, May 3, 1863, and died from wound May 25, 1863.

WATKINS, PATRICK BUNYAN, Musician

Resided in New Hanover County where he enlisted at age 18, June 1, 1861, for the war. Mustered in as Musician. Present or accounted for on company muster rolls through December, 1864. Paroled at Appomattox Court House, Virginia, April 9, 1865.

WATKINS, SILAS C., Private

Resided in New Hanover County where he enlisted at age 21, June 1, 1861, for the war. Present or accounted for until wounded at Payne's Farm, Virginia, November 27, 1863. Captured at Mine Run, Virginia, December 3, 1863, and confined at Old Capitol Prison, Washington, D.C. Transferred to Point Lookout, Maryland, February 3, 1864. Paroled at Point Lookout on October 30, 1864, and exchanged at Venus Point, Savannah River, Georgia, November 15, 1864.

WAY, ROBERT F., Private

Paroled at Greensboro on May 9, 1865.

WELLS, HENRY, Private

Resided in New Hanover County and enlisted in Wayne County at age 31, May 16, 1862, for the war. Died in hospital at Richmond, Virginia, September 10, 1862, of "typhoid fever."

WELLS, JACOB, Private

Resided in New Hanover County where he enlisted at age 33, June 1, 1861, for the war. Died at Richmond, Virginia, September 18, 1862.

WESLEY, JOHN, Private

Enlisted July 15, 1862, for the war. Reported on February 28-May 15, 1862, muster roll with the remark: "Left in Maryland September 18, 1862. Said to have taken the Oath of Allegiance to the Government of the U.S."

WHITE, GIDEON L., Private

Resided in New Hanover County and enlisted in Northampton County at age 30, June 27, 1861, for the war. Discharged on May 20, 1862, by reason of general debility.

WILLIAMS, RANSOM, Private
Enlisted in Mitchell County on October 6, 1863, for the war. Deserted February 20, 1864.

WOOD, MURDOCK, Corporal
Resided in New Hanover County where he enlisted at age 24, June 1, 1861, for the war. Mustered in as Private and appointed Corporal on January 1, 1863. Wounded at Chancellorsville, Virginia, May 3, 1863, and died of wound May 17, 1863.

WOOTTEN, AMOS, Private
Resided in New Hanover County where he enlisted at age 25, April 17, 1862, for the war. Died at home on October 19, 1862.

MISCELLANEOUS

The following list of names was compiled from primary records which record the unit in which these men served as the 3rd Regiment N.C. State Troops but do not give the company to which they belonged.

ALEXANDER, A. C., Private
Captured at Fredericksburg, Virginia, May 3, 1863, and paroled and exchanged at City Point, Virginia, May 10, 1863.

ANDERSON, G. W., Private
Received at Washington, D.C., April 21, 1865, from City Point, Virginia, and provided transportation to Duncanville, Pennsylvania.

BEUBON, CHARLES, Private
Resided in Greene County, Tennessee, and took the Oath of Allegiance at Chattanooga, Tennessee, May 26, 1865.

CAMMACK, G. W., Private
Resided in Guilford County. Captured at Kelly's Ford, Virginia, November 8, 1863, and confined at Old Capitol Prison, Washington, D.C. Took the Oath of Allegiance at Washington on March 15, 1864, and sent to Philadelphia, Pennsylvania.

CLENYAWENS, J., Private
Reported on undated roll of prisoners of war.

COLEMAN, G. W., Private
Paroled on September 27, 1862.

COULTER, J. T., Private
Paroled on May 3, 1865.

FITZPATRICK, F. M., Private
Confined at Fort McHenry, Maryland, January 5, 1863.

HARRIE, JAMES, Private
Took the Oath of Allegiance at Washington, D.C., April 12, 1865, and sent to Goldsboro.

HARVEY, J. W., Private
Captured at Fredericksburg, Virginia, May 3, 1863, and paroled and exchanged at City Point, Virginia, May 18, 1863.

HERINX, JAMES, Private
Captured as a "rebel deserter" and forwarded by the Provost Marshal General, Army of the Potomac, September 25, 1863.

HEWITT, J., Private
Federal Provost Marshal records carry him as a "deserter from the enemy" received March 16,

1865, by the Provost Marshal General, Army of the Potomac, Bermuda Hundred, Virginia. Took the Oath of Allegiance at Washington, D.C., March 24, 1865.

JONES, EDMUND, Private
Took the Oath of Allegiance near Alexandria, Virginia, May 10, 1865.

KELLEY, C., Private
Reported on undated roll of prisoners of war.

LAMMLN, I. L., Private
Captured and paroled near Kinston on December 14, 1862.

LITTLE, S. C., Private
Enlisted on March 10, 1865, for the war.

MARS, JOHN L., Private
Captured near Fredericksburg, Virginia, May 3, 1863, and paroled and exchanged at City Point, Virginia, May 13, 1863.

PERDERRICK, G., Sergeant
Paroled at Richmond, Virginia, April 24, 1865.

PORTER, D. D., Private
Captured near Fredericksburg, Virginia, May 3, 1863, and paroled and exchanged at City Point, Virginia, May 13, 1863.

ROCHESTER, LEWIS, Private
Reported as a "deserter" on Federal Provost Marshal records dated April 14, 1865, with the remark that he be provided transportation to Suffolk, Virginia.

SMITH, J., Private
Resided in Duplin County and paroled at Goldsboro on May 29, 1865. "Came in for parole."

SMITH, JAMES, Private
Died in hospital at Sharpsburg, Maryland, and was "buried on the battlefield at Antietam."

STERLINGS, S. W., Private
Reported on undated roll of prisoners of war at Petersburg, Virginia.

STONE, W., Private
Died in hospital at Sharpsburg, Maryland, and was buried on field.

TEACHER, T., Private
Reported on a roll of prisoners of war dated September 30, 1862.

THIFTON, K., Private
Died in hospital near Sharpsburg, Maryland.

THOMAS, G. L., Private
Paroled at Leesburg, Virginia, October 2, 1862.

TIDGY, D. W., Private
Reported on a roll of prisoners of war dated September 20, 1862.

TYRONS, SAMUEL, Private
Paroled at Leesburg, Virginia, October 2, 1862.

VANHOY, JOHN A., Private
Resided in Yadkin County and took the Oath of Allegiance at Knoxville, Tennessee, June 11, 1864. Sent to Jeffersonville, Indiana.

WILLIAMS, GEORGE B., Private
Employed as hospital steward at Camp McIntosh, Wayne County, March 31-July 1, 1862.

INDEX

This index contains citations for individuals listed in the foregoing unit rosters and for all persons and places mentioned in the unit histories. Except in instances where a signature or family information was available, personal names are spelled as they were recorded in Confederate records. Corrupted spellings of some names are included with cross-references to the spelling under which the name appears.

Blow, Richard, 103
Blue, John, 348
Blue, John C., 365
Blue, Murdock I., 365
Blum, G. C., 383
Blum, James A., 70
Blunt. See Blount
Boage. See Boger, Bogue
Boan. See Bone
Bodenhamer, Hezekiah, 320
Boger. See also Bogue
Boger, George C., 452
Bogett. See Boyett
Bogg, I. H., 479
Boggs, Arrington, 311
Boggs, Lewis, 181
Boggs, Stanford, 181
Bogue. See also Boger
Bogue, John J., 145
Bohnson. See Bahnson
Boitnott, I. H., 479
Boken. See also Baker, Barker
Boken, Godfrey, 330
Bolan, Peter, 246
Bolles. See also Bowles, Boyles
Bolles, Charles P., 343
Bolt, John, 579
Bolton, Lemuel, 203
Bolton, Merriweather L., 534
Bolton, William A., 358
Bond, Francis Wayland, 144
Bond, Isreal C., 343, 368
Bond, James D., 193
Bond, James W., 294
Bond, Marmaduke N., 47
Bonds, Newton, 9
Bone. See also Bayne, Boon, Boone, Done
Bone, James, 280
Boney, John B., 524
Boney, Timothy W., 122
Bonner, James M., 302
Boon. See also Bone, Boone
Boon, Daniel H., 311
Boon, William R., 41
Boone. See also Bone, Boon
Boone, Absalom Chestnutt, 348
Boone, Alsan, 224
Boone, Daniel, 193
Boone, J. B. F., 3
Boone, J. R., 442
Boone, James D., 143, 203
Boone, John W., 203
Boone, Joseph, 47
Boone, Solon G., 203
Boone, Thomas D., 201
Boone, W. F., 203
Boonsboro, Maryland, 136, 373 482
Booth, John C., 342-343
Booth, John T., 422
Booth, Robert, 422
Boothe, Merritt, 212
Bordeaux. See also Bourdeaux
Bordeaux, A. J., 9

Bordeaux, Richard Henry, 590
Borland, Andrew J., 181
Boseman, James, 590
Bosh. See Baisch
Bosman. See Boseman
Boss. See Bass, Bost
Bost. See also Best, Boston, Most
Bost, W. H., 479
Bostick, James W., 502
Bostick, John C., 502
Bostick, John S., 365
Bostick, Joseph W., 502
Bostick, Samuel T., 502
Boston. See also Bost, Bustin
Boston, John, 224
Boston, Uriah, 452
Boswell. See also Brasswell, Braswell
Boswell, Alfred F., 413
Boswell, John A., 181
Boswell, Joseph, 361
Boswell, Thomas, 354
Boswick. See Bostick
Bottoms, George W., 391
Bouchelle, Thomas S., 155
Bouge. See Bogue
Bouie. See Bowie, Buie
Bourdeaux. See also Bordeaux
Bourdeaux, F. M., 169
Bowden. See also Bowen, Bowins
Bowden, B. B., 98
Bowden, Charles A., 492
Bowden, Hinton J., 590
Bowden, James B., 103
Bowden, John, 203, 365
Bowden, Morris C., 590
Bowden, Richard T., 591
Bowe. See Bowie, Buie
Bowen. See also Bowden, Bowins
Bowen, Charles C., 113
Bowen, Durham, 503
Bowen, James B., 290
Bowen, James E., 290
Bowen, John W., 290
Bowen, Kinchen, 591
Bowen, Lawrence, 224
Bowers, John R., 463
Bowers, W. H., 433
Bowie. See also Buie
Bowie, J. H., 224
Bowins. See also Bowden, Bowen
Bowins, Charles B., 98
Bowles. See also Bolles, Boyles
Bowles, William, 280
Bowles, William Alexander, 348, 354
Bowles, William H., 442
Boyakin. See Boykin
Boyce, John, 414
Boyce, Martin, 62
Boyd. See also Boyett, Boyette
Boyd, Abner, 86
Boyd, Perry L., 52
Boyd, S. H., 260
Boyd, T. B., 3, 15
Boyett. See also Boyd, Boyette

Boyett, Joel, 391
Boyett, John W., 122
Boyett, Ransom, 391
Boyett, Thomas, 391
Boyette. See also Boyd, Boyett
Boyette, George T., 391
Boyette, Isaac, 391
Boyette, James H., 391
Boyette, Josiah, 392
Boyette, Larry Bryant, 390
Boykin, Benjamin H., 392
Boykin, Council, 414
Boykin, Eli J., 392
Boykin, Irvin, 392
Boykin, James, 556
Boykin, Pummer W., 392
Boykin, Tobias, 392
Boykin, Wiley, 392
Boykin, William, 392
Boykin, William H., 392
Boykin, William M., 392
Boylan, David L., 169
Boylan, George W., 524
Boyle. See Ball
Boyles. See also Bolles, Bowles
Boyles, David, 503
Boyles, John H., 267
Boyles, Marcus W., 181
Boyles, William W., 267
Boyt. See Boyd, Boyett, Boyette
Brabble, E. C., 260-261
Bracey, William, 203
Brack. See also Brock
Brack, Reaves, 156
Braddy. See also Brady, Bradley
Braddy, Kinchen J., 31
Bradford. See Brafford
Bradley. See also Braddy, Brady
Bradley, James D., 47
Bradley, John C., 383
Bradley, Robert H., 5
Bradshaw, Charles F., 348
Bradshaw, Jefferson, 103
Bradshaw, John H., 545
Bradshaw, John P., 348
Bradshaw, N. Sloan, 556
Bradshaw, Nathaniel J., 442
Bradshaw, W. F., 169
Bradshaw, William, 103, 545
Bradshaw, William D., 503
Brady. See also Braddy, Bradley
Brady, Charles, 513
Brady, Isaac, 567
Brady, James, 361
Brady, John, 568
Brady, John W., 193
Brady, Joseph M., 568
Brady, Manly, 365
Brady, Nathan, 513
Brady, Robert, 513
Brady, W. M., 534
Brady, William W., 568
Brafford, Edward, 545
Bragg, J. S., 181
Bragley. See Broyley

liman, Holoman
Holloman, Elijah, 583
Holloman, John, 583
Holloman, Josiah, 558
Holloman, Nathan, 558
Hollon. *See* Holland
Holloway, Daniel H., 160
Holloway, John, 239
Hollowman. *See* Hollemon, Holliman, Holloman, Holoman
Holly. *See also* Hailey, Hawley
Holly, B., 425
Holly, H., 172
Holly, John A., 425
Holly, R., 425
Holly, Reddick, 425
Holly, Roland, 435
Holly, William D., 172
Hollyfield. *See* Hollifield, Holyfield
Holmes. *See also* Helms
Holmes, Archibald, 345, 369
Holmes, Benjamin, 528
Holmes, David E., 548
Holmes, Elias H., 406
Holmes, James D., 594
Holmes, James Thomas, 495
Holmes, John J., 185
Holmes, John L., 343
Holmes, T. L., 17
Holmes, Theophilus H., 136, 372, 481
Holmes, Thomas J., 133
Holmes, Washington H., 455
Holoman. *See also* Hollemon, Holliman, Holloman
Holoman, Nathan P., 571
Holt, Alexander, 216
Holt, Elbert F., 216
Holt, George W., 196
Holt, Iverson F., 306
Holt, John S., 350
Holt, Yancy A., 284
Holton, T. F., 17
Holyfield. *See also* Hollifield
Holyfield, Martin R., 284
Holyfield, Valentine, 284
Honrine. *See* Hornrine
Hood, David W., 117
Hood, Elias, 495
Hood, Henry, 296
Hood, John M., 296
Hood, Nathan B., 558
Hood, Robert B., 559
Hood, Wiley, 306
Hood, Wiley R., 185
Hood, William T., 306
Hooker. *See also* Tooker
Hooker, Alexander F., 313
Hooker, Clarkson, 313
Hooker, Isham, 571
Hooker, John W., 272
Hooker, Joseph, 67, 137, 374-375, 483
Hooker, Nathan, 92

Hooker, Preston B., 495
Hooker, W. B., 99, 133
Hookerton, North Carolina, 259
Hooks, J. Z., 257
Hooks, James M., 416
Hoots, W. A., 80
Hoover, Henry E., 313
Hoover, John J., 466
Hope. *See also* Houpe
Hope, H., 227
Hope, James H., 296
Hope, Joseph A., 185
Hope, Thomas L., 54
Hopkins, Joseph, 172
Hopkins, Luke, 227
Hopkins, William, 148
Hopkins, William P., 239
Hopkins, Willis H., 406
Hoppers, Samuel J., 335
Hoppers, William H. C., 335
Hord. *See* Hoard
Horn. *See also* Horne
Horn, David W., 538
Horn, Gary, 474
Horn, Jacob H., 386
Horn, Jacob R., 538
Horn, James, 386
Horn, Owen H., 538
Horn, Samuel J., 206
Horn, Wilson, 445
Horne. *See also* Horn
Horne, Henry Ruffin, 42
Horne, Henry W., 511
Horne, J. B., 516
Horne, John B., 345
Horne, William B., 516
Horner. *See* Harner
Horney. *See also* Harney
Horney, P. P., 148
Hornrine, George R., 359
Hornrine, William J., 359
Horny. *See* Harney, Horney
Horrel. *See also* Harrel, Harrell, Howel, Howell
Horrel, Americus V., 594
Horrell, James B., 594
Horton, William J., 496
Horward. *See* Howard
Hosier, James E., 583
Hoskins. *See also* Adkins, Askins, Atkin, Atkins, Gaskins, Haskins
Hoskins, Blake B., 148
Hoskins, George O., 148
Houghman, D., 196
Houghton. *See also* Haughton
Houghton, William R., 63
Houpe. *See also* Hope
Houpe, J. F., 185
Houri. *See* Howey
House. *See* Shouse
Housen. *See* Houser, Howser
Houser. *See also* Hauser, Howser
Houser, A. Monroe, 54
Houser, Absalom Josephus, 54, 180
Houser, Charles T. J., 185

Houser, J. Workman, 54
Houston. *See also* Huson
Houston, Alfred, 121
Houston, Edward W., 124
Houston, H. C., 17, 124
Houston, Robert B., 505, 523
Houston, William, 124
Hovis, Laban L., 54
How. *See* Ham
Howard, A. Z., 27
Howard, B. S., 124
Howard, Benjamin A., 416
Howard, Franklin, 94
Howard, George E., 594
Howard, H. A., 425
Howard, J., 160
Howard, J. Edward, 38
Howard, James N., 505
Howard, John, 380, 390
Howard, John W., 538
Howard, Solomon, 474
Howard, Thomas, 17
Howard, Thomas A., 359
Howard, Thomas P., 185
Howard, W. D., 17
Howard, W. F., 38
Howard, William, 390
Howard, William A., 528
Howard, William H., 516
Howard, William M., 180
Howard's Grove, Richmond, Virginia, 1
Howe, John C., 206
Howel, A., 11
Howell. *See also* Harrel, Harrell, Hoell, Horrel, Horrell, Howel
Howell, Abner, 250
Howell, C. D., 172
Howell, Cullen, 466
Howell, Edmund, 11
Howell, Eli, 5
Howell, Freeman, 386
Howell, Henry A., 456
Howell, James, 100
Howell, James A., 11
Howell, James K., 142, 350
Howell, John R., 456
Howell, Needham, 456
Howell, Stephen M., 227
Howell, William, 104
Howey, G. W., 17
Howitt. *See* Hewett
Howlett, Asa, 425
Howser. *See also* Hauser, Houser
Howser, W. T., 17
Hoyle, Lemuel J., 54
Hubbard, Josiah, 239
Hubbard, Mark T., 594
Hubbard, Wyatt, 250
Huckerty, John, 185
Hucks. *See* Hux
Hudson. *See also* Huson
Hudson, Andrew J., 445
Hudson, Aquilla, 335
Hudson, B., 480

Veach, Joseph R. P., 318
Veach, McKindree L., 318
Veneble, Isaac, 243
Venters, George W., 135
Venters, W. G., 126
Vestal, D. A., 75
Vestal, J. W., 75
Vestal, John R., 577
Vestal, William, 75
Vestal, William P. D., 76
Vick, Britton C., 209
Vick, Elias R., 209
Vickers, John, 478
Vickers, Linsey, 165
Vimmel, J., 399
Vincent, Perry, 210
Vinson, Andrew, 132
Vinson, Drewry D., 210
Vinson, John, 106
Vistall, J. W., 153
Vogler, George E., 469
Vuncannon, Alson G., 577
Vuncannon, William, 318, 521, 577
Vuncanon, I. J. M., 210

W

Wacaster, Adolphus, 57
Waddell. See also Wardell, Woodall,
   Woodell, Woodle
Waddell, William J., 340
Wade, John H., 469
Wade, John M., 553
Wadell. See Waddell, Wardell,
   Woodall, Woodell, Woodle
Wadkins. See also Watkins
Wadkins, William J., 460
Wafford. See also Wofford
Wafford, William H., 300
Wagner, J. W., 14
Wagoner, David, 233
Wagoner, Henry, 76
Wagoner, Reuben, 233
Wagoner, William, 76
Wagstaff, John W., 178
Wainwright, John, 500
Wakefield, S. D., 40
Wald. See Waul
Walden, George W., 76
Waldo, W. S., 300
Waldrup, Noah, 340
Waley. See Fraley, Whaley
Walker, A., 430
Walker, Albert W., 357
Walker, E. M., 14
Walker, Edward DeCoin, Jr., 178
Walker, James, 165
Walker, James A., 64, 66, 153
Walker, James P., 577
Walker, Jesse J., 243
Walker, John G., 136, 372, 481
Walker, John M., 367
Walker, John W., 178
Walker, Joseph, 542
Walker, Joseph M., 153, 178

Walker, Joshua C., 488
Walker, Leroy Pope, 1-2
Walker, Samuel J., 178
Walker, T., 500
Walker, Thomas, 340
Walker, Washington H., 178
Walker, William A., 469
Walker, Woolford, 309
Wall. See also Walls, Waul
Walls, Hansel J., 210
Wall, James, 244
Wall, M. T., 179
Wall, Newel J., 288
Wall, Robert D., 101
Wallace. See also Wallice
Wallace, Calvin R., 470
Wallace, John McL., 521
Wallace, Samuel, 588
Wallace, William, 532
Wallace, William T., 300
Wallen, Benjamin, 340
Waller, Haywood, 126
Waller, Isaac D., 292
Waller, Squire, 599
Wallice. See also Wallace
Wallice, James H., 50
Walling, William, 588
Wallis. See Wallace, Wallice
Walls. See also Wall, Waul, Wells
Walls, Burgess, 430
Walls, Drury M., 300
Walls, James, 521
Walsh, Alfred, 165
Walsh, Coleman, 553
Walsh, William, 165
Walston. See also Watson, Wilson
Walston, Golden, 420
Walston, Jarrett, 255
Walston, John, 8
Walston, Levi, 101
Walston, Phillip, 101
Walt, George F., 244
Walters. See also Walton, Warters,
   Waters
Walters, Asa W., 588
Walters, Hardy, 132
Walton. See also Walters
Walton, Amos, 542
Walton, Elisha E., 599
Walton, J. T., 40
Walton, James R., 153
Walton, Jesse W., 542
Walton, John D., 599
Walton, John M., 40
Walton, Samuel J., 358
Walton, Seth, 200
Wamack. See also Wammock, Wo-
   mack
Wamack, W. T., 40
Wamble. See also Womble
Wamble, J. B., 340
Wamble, Parington, 221
Wammock. See also Wamack, Wo-
   mack
Wammock, K. T., 255

Wammock, Richard, 255
Ward, Aaron, 64
Ward, Alexander, 599
Ward, Alfred, 411
Ward, Assadana, 221
Ward, Augustus, 64
Ward, B. F., 107
Ward, Benjamin S., 420
Ward, Franklin J., 91
Ward, George, 360
Ward, George W., 502
Ward, Henry, 258, 420
Ward, James, 318, 354, 588
Ward, James H., 588
Ward, John, 91, 221, 370, 500
Ward, Joshua, 430
Ward, Richard, 500
Ward, Rufus, 460
Ward, Spirious, 501
Wardell. See also Waddell
Wardell, Theo R., 35
Wardrep. See Waldrup
Warlick. See also Warwick
Warlick, J. L., 40
Warlick, Portland A., 40
Warlick, Rufus M., 57
Warner. See also Warren
Warner, Lewis, 510
Warner, Swain, 478
Warner, W. C., 577
Warren. See also Warner
Warren, C. W., 153
Warren, G. H., 154
Warren, G. K., 139, 263, 378, 486
Warren, John A., 577
Warren, John Benjamin, 577
Warren, John Thomas, 430
Warren, Lewellyn P., 62
Warren, Miles C., 588
Warren, Roberson R., 91
Warren, Sam H., 309
Warren, Thomas H., 154, 588
Warren, Thomas K., 210
Warrenton, North Carolina, 136,
   143, 155, 167, 179, 191, 201, 211,
   222, 233, 245
Warrenton, Virginia, 138, 261, 376,
   484
Warters. See also Walters, Waters
Warters, Asa T., 107
Warters, Edward H., 449
Warters, Tobias, 107
Warters, William H., 449
Warters, William M., 449
Warwick. See also Warlick
Warwick, James M., 14
Warwick, Wiley, 364
Wasdon, G., 501
Washington, James A., 451
Washington, Walker, 488
Washington, District of Columbia,
   140, 263, 289, 293, 301, 378, 486
Washington, North Carolina, 259,
   578
Waterberry, William M., 45

Wilson, James, 112, 328
Wilson, Jesse, 318
Wilson, John, 543
Wilson, John A., 554
Wilson, John J., 179
Wilson, John W., 29, 400
Wilson, Joseph, 112
Wilson, Joseph E., 411
Wilson, Joseph H., 83
Wilson, Mc., 127
Wilson, Noel, 364
Wilson, Reuben E., 68, 70
Wilson, Richard, 154
Wilson, Robert W., 112
Wilson, Simon B., 135
Wilson, T. M., 166
Wilson, Thomas H., 29, 210
Wilson, William, 120, 127
Wilson, William G., 565
Wilson, William L., 340
Wilson, North Carolina, 389, 420
Winbery. See Wenberry
Winborn, Stephen, 400
Winchester, Virginia, 66, 68, 137-138, 140, 259-260, 263, 373, 375, 378, 482-484, 486
Windcuff, M., 258
Winder, John H., 141
Winders, Charles A., 411
Winders, Edward, 411
Winders, Henry J., 411
Winders, Samuel R., 412
Windfield. See Winfield
Windfrey. See Winfree
Windham, John A., 132
Windle, M. F., 14
Windley. See also Windly
Windley, Horace A., 588
Windley, William Barrow, 588
Windley, Wyriott A., 588
Windly. See also Windley
Windly, William E., 120
Windsor, North Carolina, 57
Winfield, Benjamin P., 132
Winfield, Samuel T., 588
Winfield, William D., 588
Winfree, W. H. T., 588
Wingate, Angus, 57
Wingate, C. C., 20
Wingate, Henry, 112
Wingate, Murchison, 57
Winkler, Charles A., 357
Winkler, Crist, 69, 83
Winn. See also Wynn
Winn, Starkey, 97
Winslow, Hilkiah, 310
Winslow, Reuben, 64
Winstead, J. W., 450
Winstead, Jordan Cofield, 400
Winstead, S. S., 589
Winston, William A., 24
Winstone. See Winstead, Winston
Winters, Alfred, 40
Winters, John, 255
Winters, Moulton, 40

Winters, Robert W., 256
Winton. See Winborn
Wise, Henry A., 259, 266, 289, 293, 328
Wise, John M., 381, 479
Wise, Merritt P., 461
Wise, Smith J., 97
Wise, William F., 190
Wistman, C. D., 179
Witherington. See also Wetherington
Witherington, Willis, 92
Withers, A., 244
Withers, James D., 244
Witherspoon, Lucius LeRoy, 166
Witherspoon, Sidney L., 166
Witherspoon, William H., 166
Witmore. See Whitmore
Wittich, Earnest L., 24
Wittie, August, 470
Wittington. See Wetherington
Witty. See Wittie
Wofford. See also Wafford
Wofford, George, 300
Woldrope. See Waldrup
Wolfe, Joshua E., 30
Wolfe, T. D., 20
Wolfe, T. J., 20
Wolfenden, John J., 97, 135
Wolffe, George, 20
Wollen. See Wallen
Wolston. See Walston
Womack. See also Wamack, Wammock
Womack, Romalus M., 354
Womble. See also Wamble
Womble, Benjamin F., 8
Womble, James R., 347
Womble, John G., 400
Wommack. See Wamack, Wammock, Womack
Wood. See also Woods
Wood, Alfred J., 179
Wood, Basil M., 565
Wood, Benjamin Franklin, 288
Wood, Britton, 256
Wood, Caleb, 191
Wood, Casper W., 92
Wood, David W., 532
Wood, H. R., 76
Wood, Henry, Jr., 289
Wood, John A., 479
Wood, John L., 532
Wood, Jonathan D., 470
Wood, Lee A., 288
Wood, Lemuel S., 479
Wood, Luke, 301
Wood, Milton, 431
Wood, Murdock, 600
Wood, Thomas F., 488
Wood, William H., 288
Wood, Willis F., 565
Woodall. See also Waddell, Woodell, Woodle
Woodall, W. W., 565

Woodard. See also Woodward
Woodard, B. T., 107
Woodard, John H. W., 589
Woodard, John P., 244
Woodard, Stephen M., 154
Woodard, Tilman F., 92
Woodard, W. G., 107
Woodburn, Lucius L., 61
Woodburn, Theodore B., 318
Woodell. See also Waddell, Woodall, Woodle
Woodell, Allen J., 319
Woodell, Benjamin F., 319
Woodell, Enoch, 319
Woodell, Thomas, 319
Wooden. See Wooten, Wootten
Woodey. See Woody
Woodhouse, M. S., 76
Woodle. See also Waddell, Woodall, Woodell
Woodle, Darius B., 364
Woodle, James, 364
Woodly. See Woody
Woodman, Arthur, 61
Woodruff, Aaron C., 289
Woodruff, David C., 166
Woodruff, Joshua, 470
Woodruff, Richard W., 69-70
Woodruff, Vincent, 76
Woods. See also Wood
Woods, Elbert A., 210
Woods, J. Meredith, 30
Woods, James C., 360
Woods, John H., 278
Woods, John S., 420
Woods, Richard H., 441
Woods, William F., 441
Woodson, Francis M., 340
Woodstock, Virginia, 68
Woodward. See also Woodard
Woodward, George O., 244
Woodward, George W., 364
Woodward, James F., 358
Woodward, William J., 45, 357
Woody, James, 167, 341
Woody, Joseph, 341
Woody, Malan, 167
Woody, William N., 167
Woolard, Wilson B., 589
Wooldridge, C. W., 233
Woosley, Frank, 328
Wooster, John L., 191
Wooten. See also Wootten
Wooten, F. N., 76
Wooten, James G., 101
Wooten, James M., 501
Wooten, Jo G., 76
Wooten, John Barcliff, 121
Wooten, John W., 45
Wooten, Thomas, 532
Wootten. See also Wooten
Wootten, Amos, 600
Work, Henry A., 431
Workman, Elbert G., 191
Worley, Amos P., 341

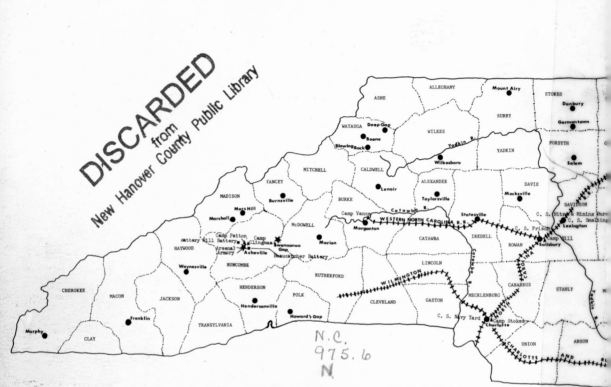

N.C.
975.6
N

Map of North Carolina, 1861–1865

Drawn by James R. Vogt

This map locates the principal camps, forts,
towns, railroads, and engagements fought in
the State during the Civil War.

LEGEND

● – Towns
■ – Forts and batteries
▲ – Camps of instructions
★ – Engagements
✕ – Railroads

V.3